KT-230-122

S H O W C A S E
P R E S E N T S

LAST CHANCE 19/01/24

Wakefield Libraries
& Information Services

WP   ⬛7 MAY 2012   WP

◨ 4 JUL 2012

1 4 MAR 2013   ◧ 9 MAR 2018

2 3 APR 2013   ◧1 APR 2018

0 2 SEP 2015   ◧ 0 MAY 2022

9 MAR 2012   0 9 NOV 2015

1 4 JUN 2012

6 MAR 2012

THE LIBRARY
HMP WAKEFIELD
5 LOVE LANE
WAKEFIELD
WF2 9AG

This book should be returned by the last date stamped
above. You may renew the loan personally, by post or
telephone for a further period if the book is not required by
another reader.

SHOWCASE PRESENTS: ALL-STAR COMICS VOLUME ONE
Published by DC Comics. Cover and compilation Copyright © 2011 DC Comics.
All Rights Reserved. Originally published in single magazine form in ALL-STAR COMICS
58-74, DC COMICS SPECIAL 29 and ADVENTURE COMICS 461-466 Copyright © 1976,
1977, 1978, 1979 DC Comics. All Rights Reserved. All characters, their distinctive
likenesses and related elements featured in this publication are trademarks of DC Comics.
The stories, characters and incidents featured in this publication are entirely fictional.
DC Comics does not read or accept unsolicited submissions of ideas, stories or artwork.

DC Comics, 1700 Broadway, New York, NY 10019
A Warner Bros. Entertainment Company

Printed by RR Donnell

ROLL CALL

HAWKMAN

WILDCAT

POWER GIRL

SUPERMAN

FLASH

WAKEFIELD LIBRARIES

30000010179068

SUSTAINABLE
FORESTRY
INITIATIVE

Certified Fiber Sourcing
www.sfiprogram.org
Fiber used in this product line meets the
sourcing requirements of the SFI program.
www.sfiprogram.org SGS-SFI/COC-US10/81072

TABLE OF CONTENTS

ALL STORIES BY WRITER **PAUL LEVITZ** AND ARTIST **JOE STATON** UNLESS OTHERWISE NOTED.

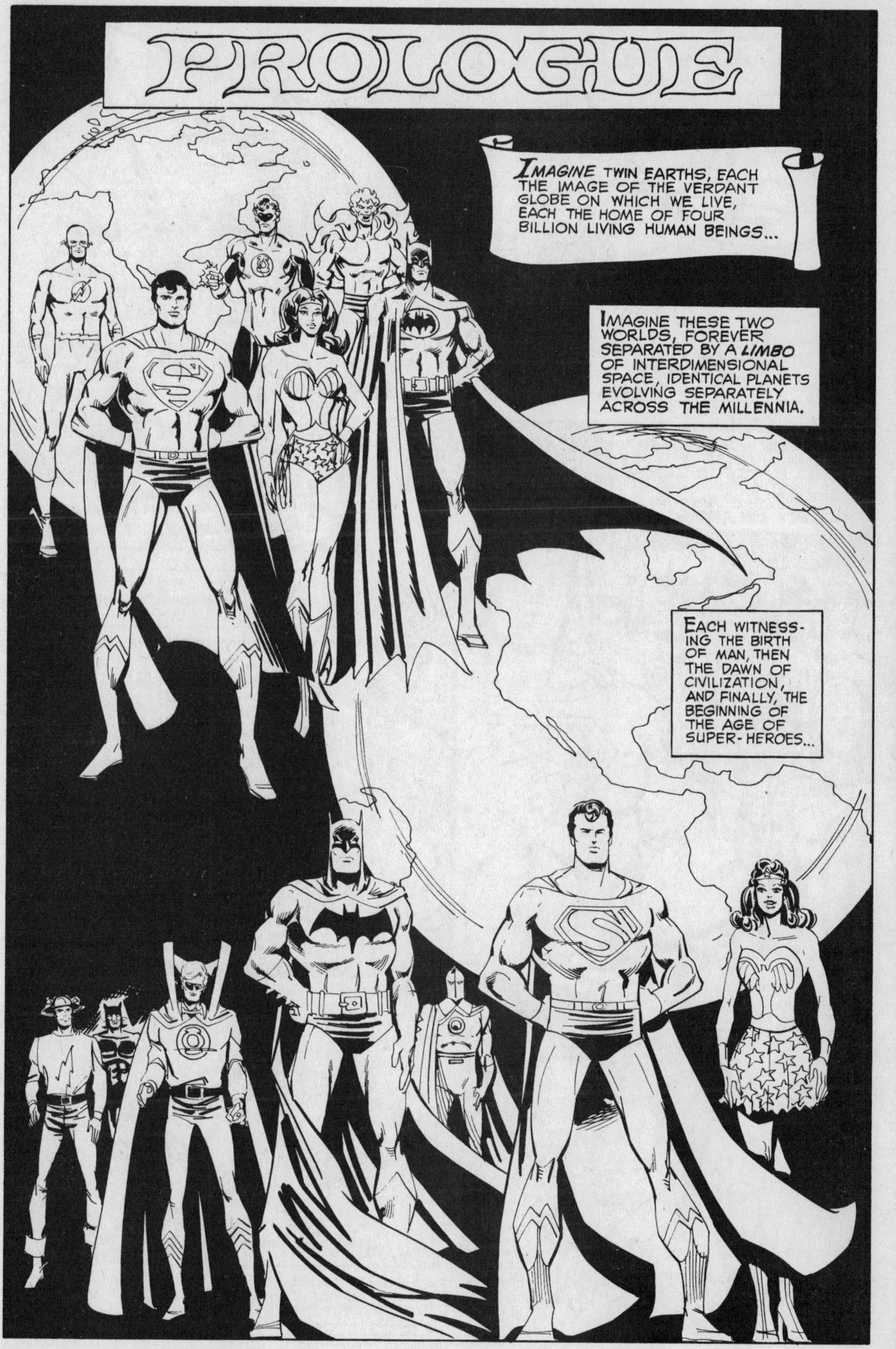
PROLOGUE
IMAGINE TWIN EARTHS, EACH THE IMAGE OF THE VERDANT GLOBE ON WHICH WE LIVE, EACH THE HOME OF FOUR BILLION LIVING HUMAN BEINGS...
IMAGINE THESE TWO WORLDS, FOREVER SEPARATED BY A LIMBO OF INTERDIMENSIONAL SPACE, IDENTICAL PLANETS EVOLVING SEPARATELY ACROSS THE MILLENNIA.
EACH WITNESSING THE BIRTH OF MAN, THEN THE DAWN OF CIVILIZATION, AND FINALLY, THE BEGINNING OF THE AGE OF SUPER-HEROES...

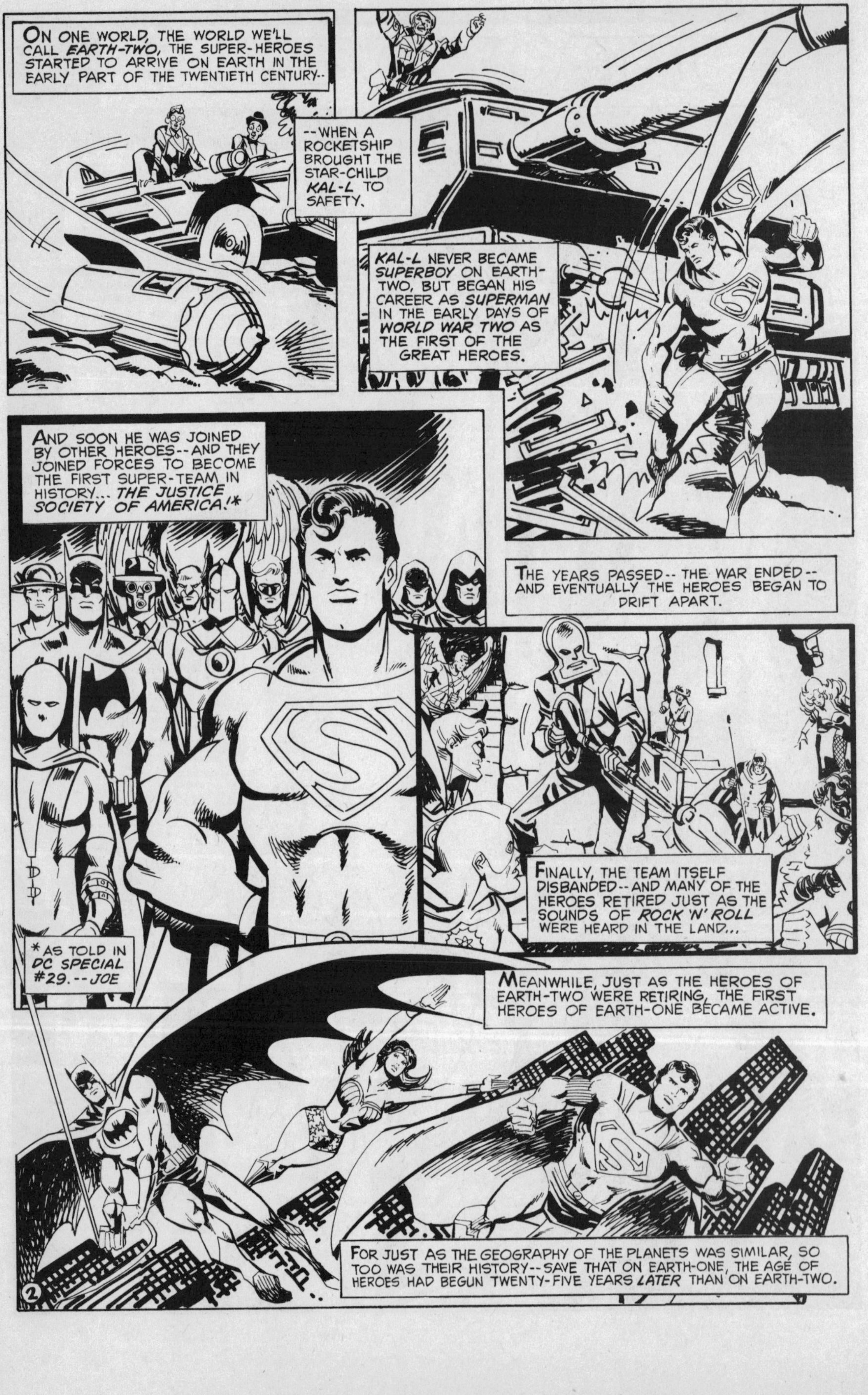
ON ONE WORLD, THE WORLD WE'LL CALL EARTH-TWO, THE SUPER-HEROES STARTED TO ARRIVE ON EARTH IN THE EARLY PART OF THE TWENTIETH CENTURY--
--WHEN A ROCKETSHIP BROUGHT THE STAR-CHILD KAL-L TO SAFETY.
KAL-L NEVER BECAME SUPERBOY ON EARTH-TWO, BUT BEGAN HIS CAREER AS SUPERMAN IN THE EARLY DAYS OF WORLD WAR TWO AS THE FIRST OF THE GREAT HEROES.
AND SOON HE WAS JOINED BY OTHER HEROES--AND THEY JOINED FORCES TO BECOME THE FIRST SUPER-TEAM IN HISTORY... THE JUSTICE SOCIETY OF AMERICA!*
*AS TOLD IN DC SPECIAL #29.--JOE
THE YEARS PASSED--THE WAR ENDED--AND EVENTUALLY THE HEROES BEGAN TO DRIFT APART.
FINALLY, THE TEAM ITSELF DISBANDED--AND MANY OF THE HEROES RETIRED JUST AS THE SOUNDS OF ROCK 'N' ROLL WERE HEARD IN THE LAND...
MEANWHILE, JUST AS THE HEROES OF EARTH-TWO WERE RETIRING, THE FIRST HEROES OF EARTH-ONE BECAME ACTIVE.
FOR JUST AS THE GEOGRAPHY OF THE PLANETS WAS SIMILAR, SO TOO WAS THEIR HISTORY--SAVE THAT ON EARTH-ONE, THE AGE OF HEROES HAD BEGUN TWENTY-FIVE YEARS LATER THAN ON EARTH-TWO.
2

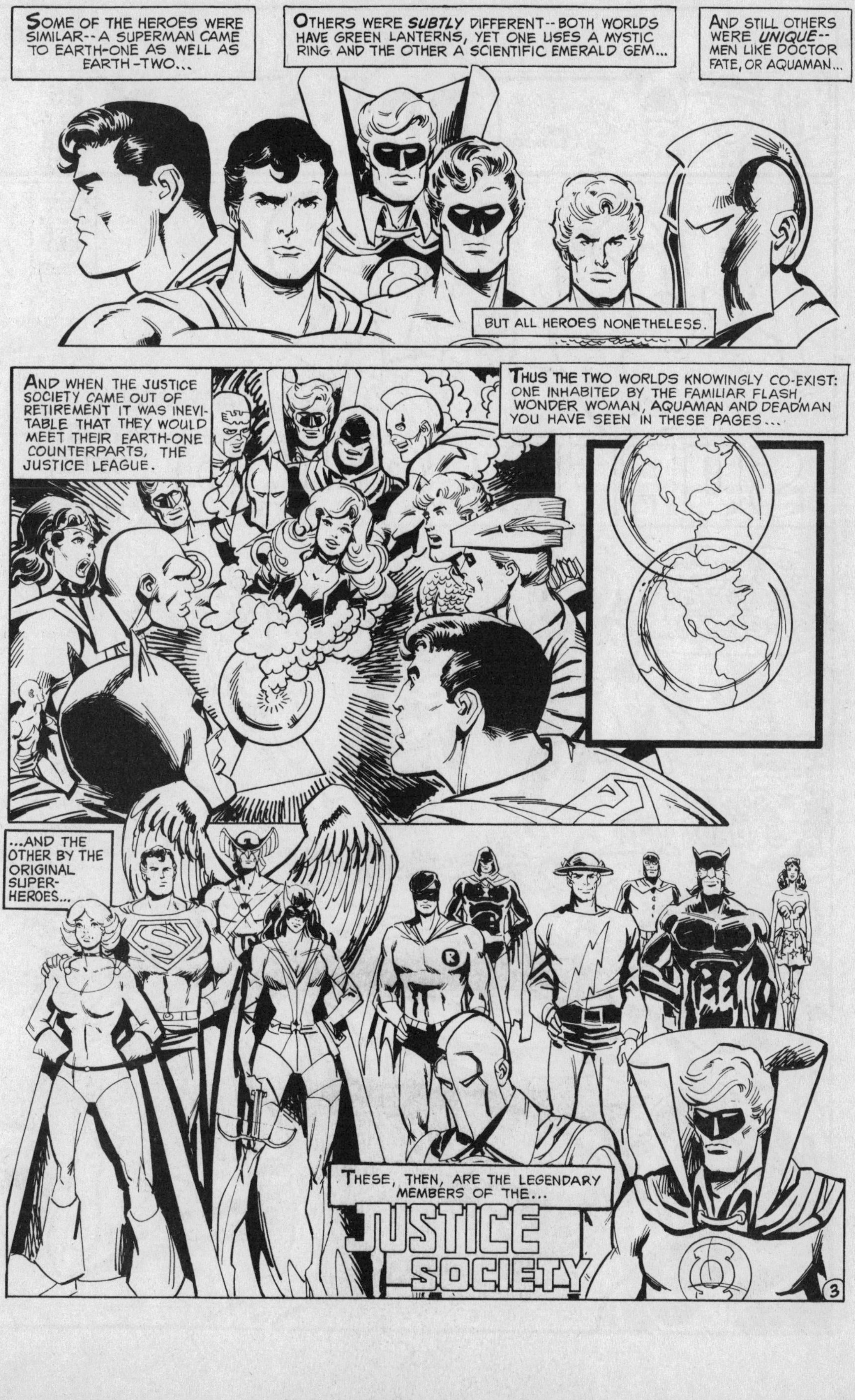
SOME OF THE HEROES WERE SIMILAR-- A SUPERMAN CAME TO EARTH-ONE AS WELL AS EARTH-TWO...
OTHERS WERE SUBTLY DIFFERENT-- BOTH WORLDS HAVE GREEN LANTERNS, YET ONE USES A MYSTIC RING AND THE OTHER A SCIENTIFIC EMERALD GEM...
AND STILL OTHERS WERE UNIQUE-- MEN LIKE DOCTOR FATE, OR AQUAMAN...
BUT ALL HEROES NONETHELESS.
AND WHEN THE JUSTICE SOCIETY CAME OUT OF RETIREMENT IT WAS INEVITABLE THAT THEY WOULD MEET THEIR EARTH-ONE COUNTERPARTS, THE JUSTICE LEAGUE.
THUS THE TWO WORLDS KNOWINGLY CO-EXIST: ONE INHABITED BY THE FAMILIAR FLASH, WONDER WOMAN, AQUAMAN AND DEADMAN YOU HAVE SEEN IN THESE PAGES...
...AND THE OTHER BY THE ORIGINAL SUPER-HEROES...
THESE, THEN, ARE THE LEGENDARY MEMBERS OF THE...
JUSTICE SOCIETY
3

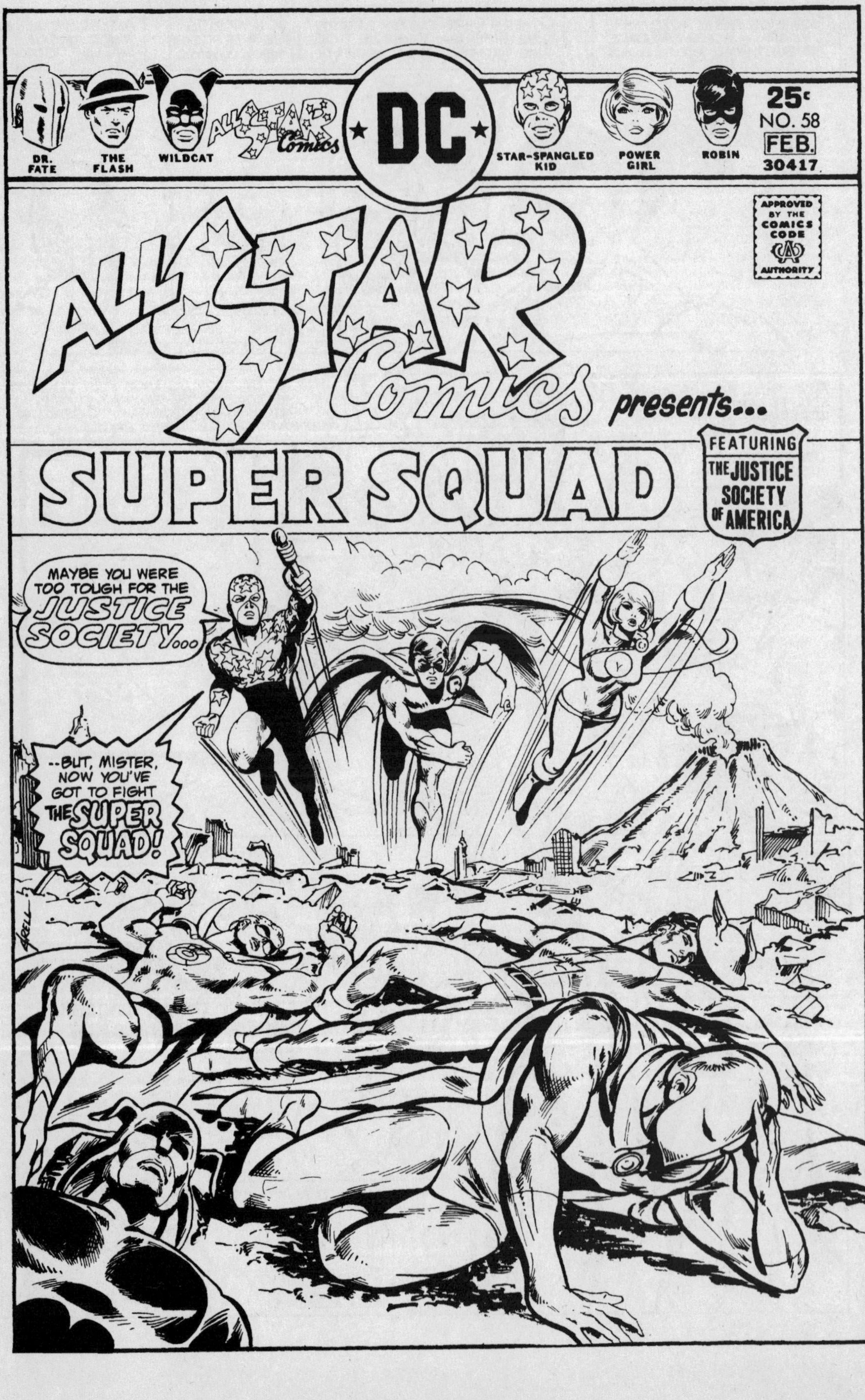
DR. FATE
THE FLASH
WILDCAT
ALL STAR Comics
DC
STAR-SPANGLED KID
POWER GIRL
ROBIN
25¢
NO. 58
FEB.
30417
APPROVED BY THE COMICS CODE AUTHORITY
ALL STAR Comics presents...
SUPER SQUAD
FEATURING THE JUSTICE SOCIETY OF AMERICA
MAYBE YOU WERE TOO TOUGH FOR THE JUSTICE SOCIETY...
--BUT, MISTER, NOW YOU'VE GOT TO FIGHT THE SUPER SQUAD!

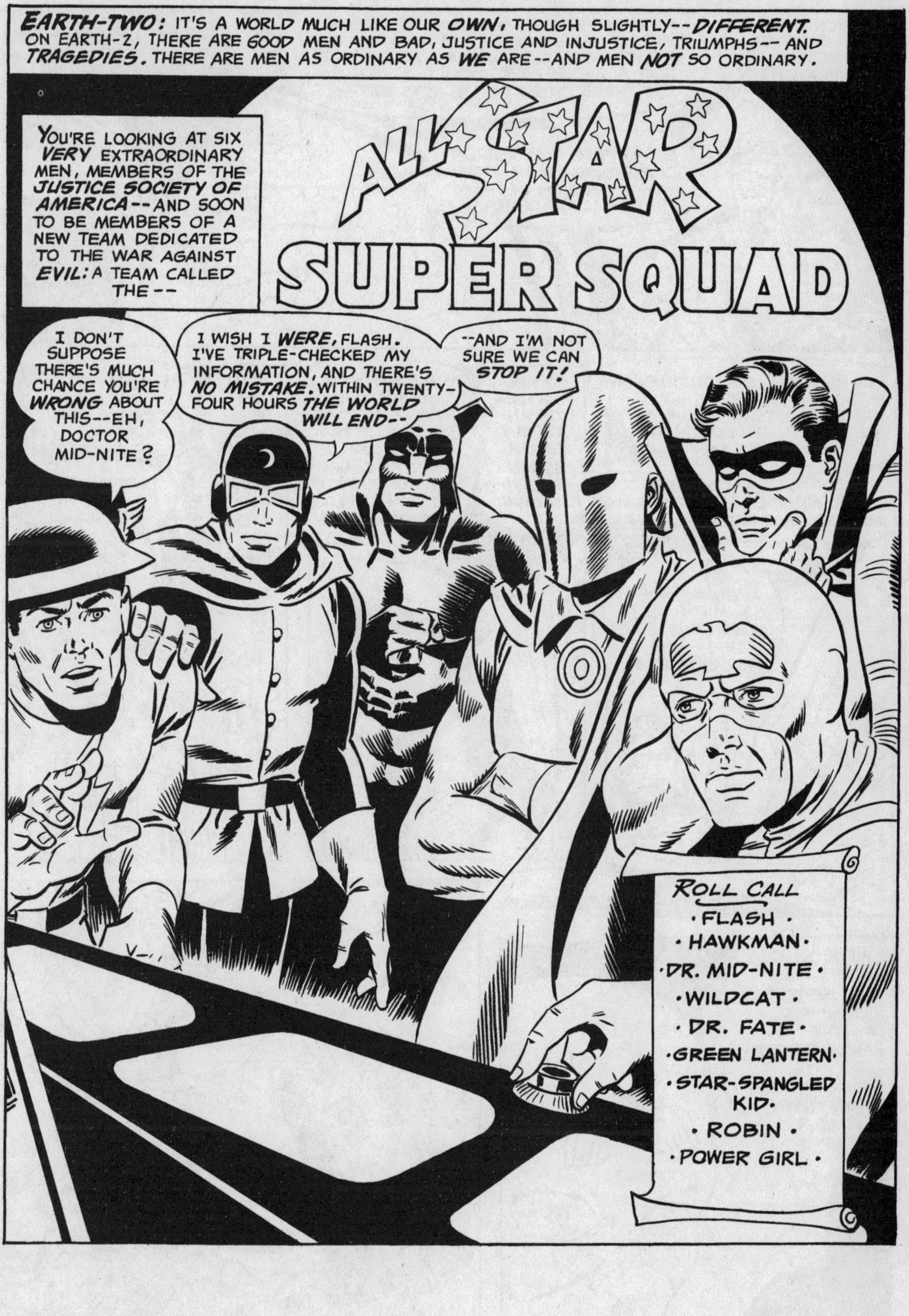
EARTH-TWO: IT'S A WORLD MUCH LIKE OUR OWN, THOUGH SLIGHTLY--DIFFERENT. ON EARTH-2, THERE ARE GOOD MEN AND BAD, JUSTICE AND INJUSTICE, TRIUMPHS-- AND TRAGEDIES. THERE ARE MEN AS ORDINARY AS WE ARE--AND MEN NOT SO ORDINARY.
YOU'RE LOOKING AT SIX VERY EXTRAORDINARY MEN, MEMBERS OF THE JUSTICE SOCIETY OF AMERICA--AND SOON TO BE MEMBERS OF A NEW TEAM DEDICATED TO THE WAR AGAINST EVIL: A TEAM CALLED THE--
ALL STAR SUPER SQUAD
I DON'T SUPPOSE THERE'S MUCH CHANCE YOU'RE WRONG ABOUT THIS--EH, DOCTOR MID-NITE?
I WISH I WERE, FLASH. I'VE TRIPLE-CHECKED MY INFORMATION, AND THERE'S NO MISTAKE. WITHIN TWENTY-FOUR HOURS THE WORLD WILL END--
--AND I'M NOT SURE WE CAN STOP IT!
ROLL CALL
·FLASH·
·HAWKMAN·
·DR. MID-NITE·
·WILDCAT·
·DR. FATE·
·GREEN LANTERN·
·STAR-SPANGLED KID·
·ROBIN·
·POWER GIRL·

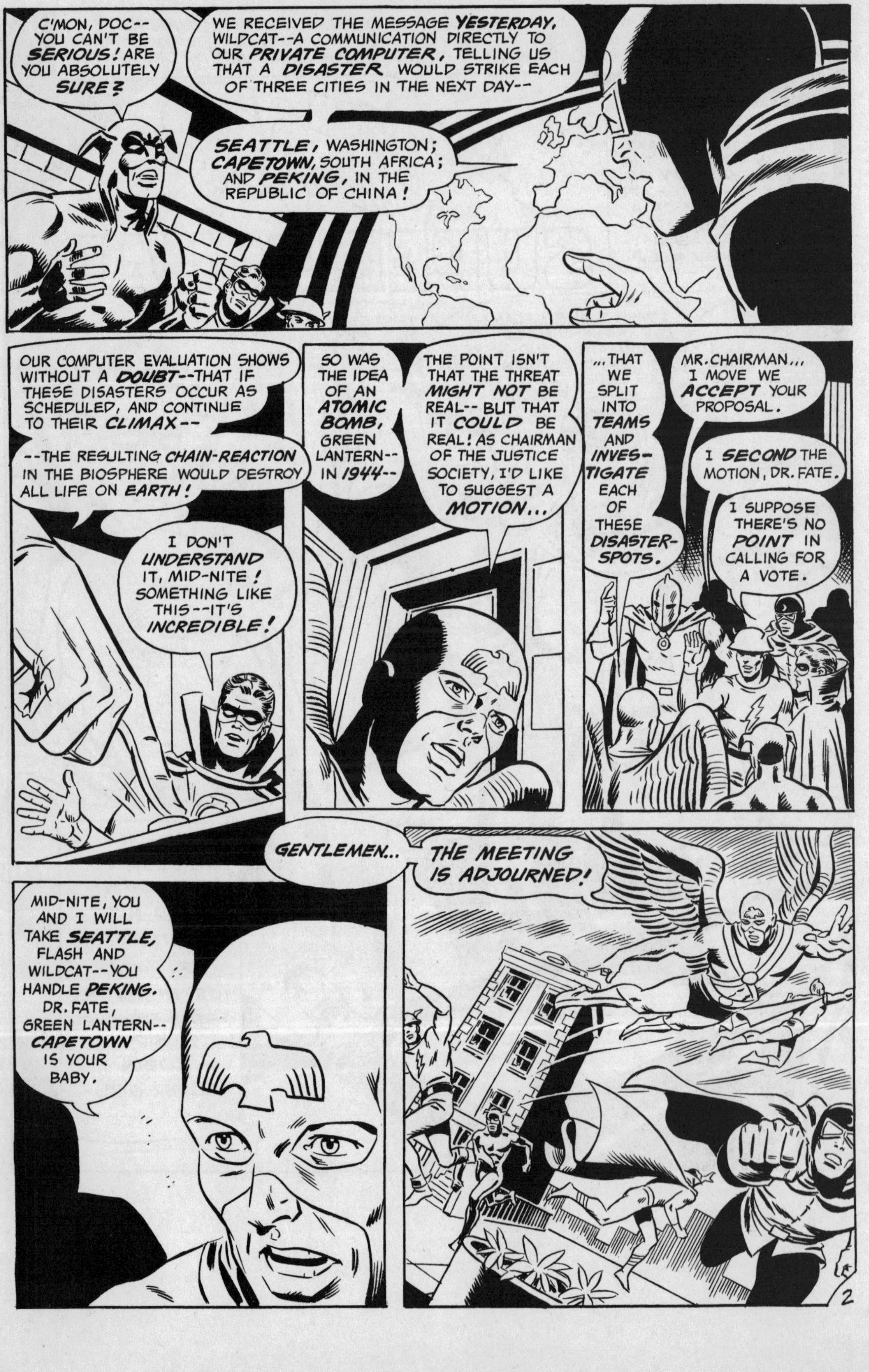
C'MON, DOC-- YOU CAN'T BE SERIOUS! ARE YOU ABSOLUTELY SURE?
WE RECEIVED THE MESSAGE YESTERDAY, WILDCAT--A COMMUNICATION DIRECTLY TO OUR PRIVATE COMPUTER, TELLING US THAT A DISASTER WOULD STRIKE EACH OF THREE CITIES IN THE NEXT DAY--
SEATTLE, WASHINGTON; CAPETOWN, SOUTH AFRICA; AND PEKING, IN THE REPUBLIC OF CHINA!
OUR COMPUTER EVALUATION SHOWS WITHOUT A DOUBT--THAT IF THESE DISASTERS OCCUR AS SCHEDULED, AND CONTINUE TO THEIR CLIMAX--
--THE RESULTING CHAIN-REACTION IN THE BIOSPHERE WOULD DESTROY ALL LIFE ON EARTH!
I DON'T UNDERSTAND IT, MID-NITE! SOMETHING LIKE THIS--IT'S INCREDIBLE!
SO WAS THE IDEA OF AN ATOMIC BOMB, GREEN LANTERN-- IN 1944--
THE POINT ISN'T THAT THE THREAT MIGHT NOT BE REAL-- BUT THAT IT COULD BE REAL! AS CHAIRMAN OF THE JUSTICE SOCIETY, I'D LIKE TO SUGGEST A MOTION...
...THAT WE SPLIT INTO TEAMS AND INVES-TIGATE EACH OF THESE DISASTER-SPOTS.
MR. CHAIRMAN... I MOVE WE ACCEPT YOUR PROPOSAL.
I SECOND THE MOTION, DR. FATE.
I SUPPOSE THERE'S NO POINT IN CALLING FOR A VOTE.
MID-NITE, YOU AND I WILL TAKE SEATTLE, FLASH AND WILDCAT--YOU HANDLE PEKING. DR. FATE, GREEN LANTERN-- CAPETOWN IS YOUR BABY.
GENTLEMEN...
THE MEETING IS ADJOURNED!
2

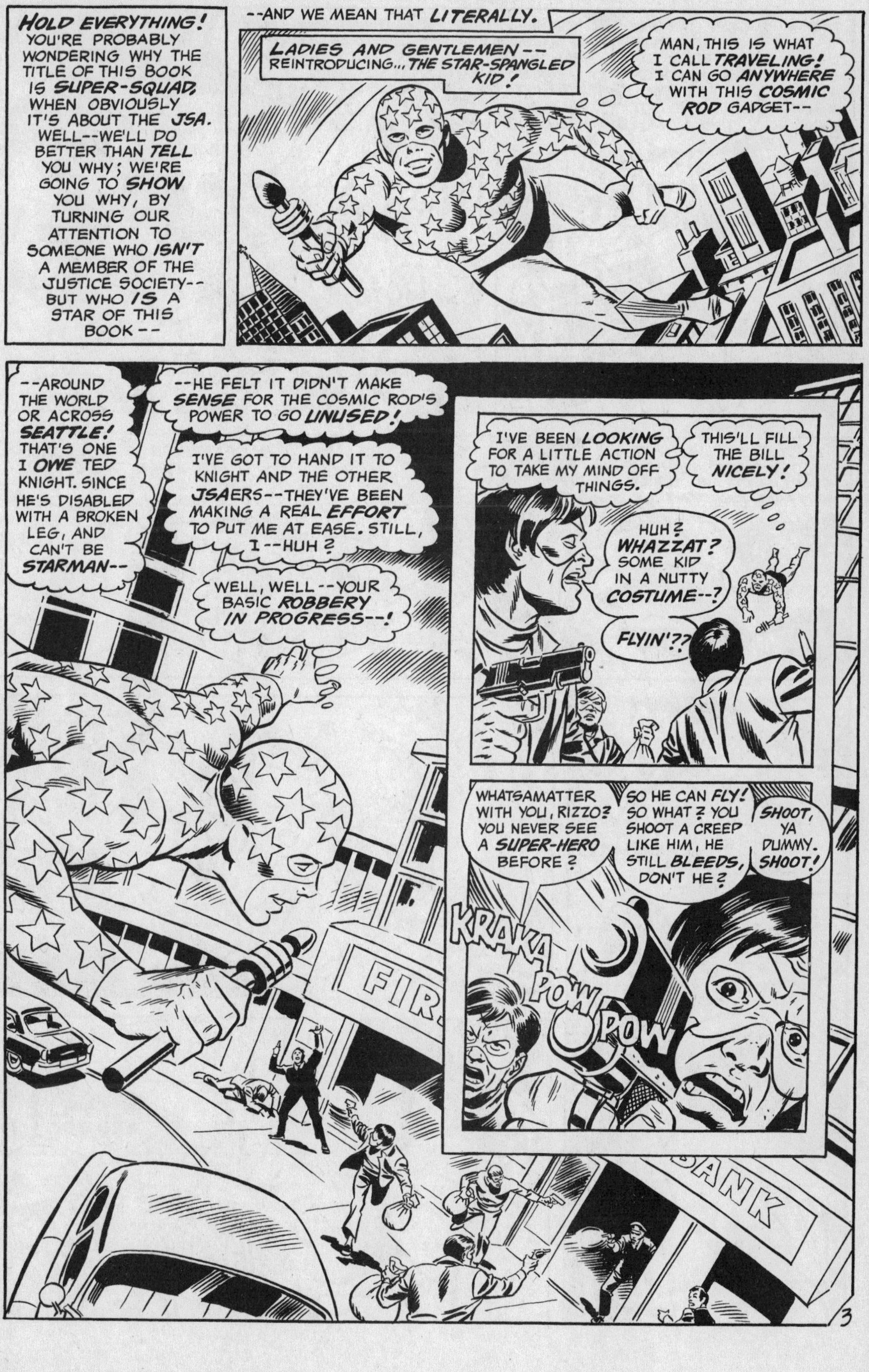
HOLD EVERYTHING! YOU'RE PROBABLY WONDERING WHY THE TITLE OF THIS BOOK IS SUPER-SQUAD, WHEN OBVIOUSLY IT'S ABOUT THE JSA. WELL--WE'LL DO BETTER THAN TELL YOU WHY; WE'RE GOING TO SHOW YOU WHY, BY TURNING OUR ATTENTION TO SOMEONE WHO ISN'T A MEMBER OF THE JUSTICE SOCIETY-- BUT WHO IS A STAR OF THIS BOOK--
--AND WE MEAN THAT LITERALLY.
LADIES AND GENTLEMEN-- REINTRODUCING... THE STAR-SPANGLED KID!
MAN, THIS IS WHAT I CALL TRAVELING! I CAN GO ANYWHERE WITH THIS COSMIC ROD GADGET--
--AROUND THE WORLD OR ACROSS SEATTLE! THAT'S ONE I OWE TED KNIGHT. SINCE HE'S DISABLED WITH A BROKEN LEG, AND CAN'T BE STARMAN--
--HE FELT IT DIDN'T MAKE SENSE FOR THE COSMIC ROD'S POWER TO GO UNUSED!
I'VE GOT TO HAND IT TO KNIGHT AND THE OTHER JSAERS--THEY'VE BEEN MAKING A REAL EFFORT TO PUT ME AT EASE. STILL, I--HUH?
WELL, WELL--YOUR BASIC ROBBERY IN PROGRESS--!
FIR
BANK
I'VE BEEN LOOKING FOR A LITTLE ACTION TO TAKE MY MIND OFF THINGS.
THIS'LL FILL THE BILL NICELY!
HUH? WHAZZAT? SOME KID IN A NUTTY COSTUME--?
FLYIN'??
WHATSAMATTER WITH YOU, RIZZO? YOU NEVER SEE A SUPER-HERO BEFORE?
SO HE CAN FLY! SO WHAT? YOU SHOOT A CREEP LIKE HIM, HE STILL BLEEDS, DON'T HE?
SHOOT, YA DUMMY. SHOOT!
KRAKA
POW
POW
3

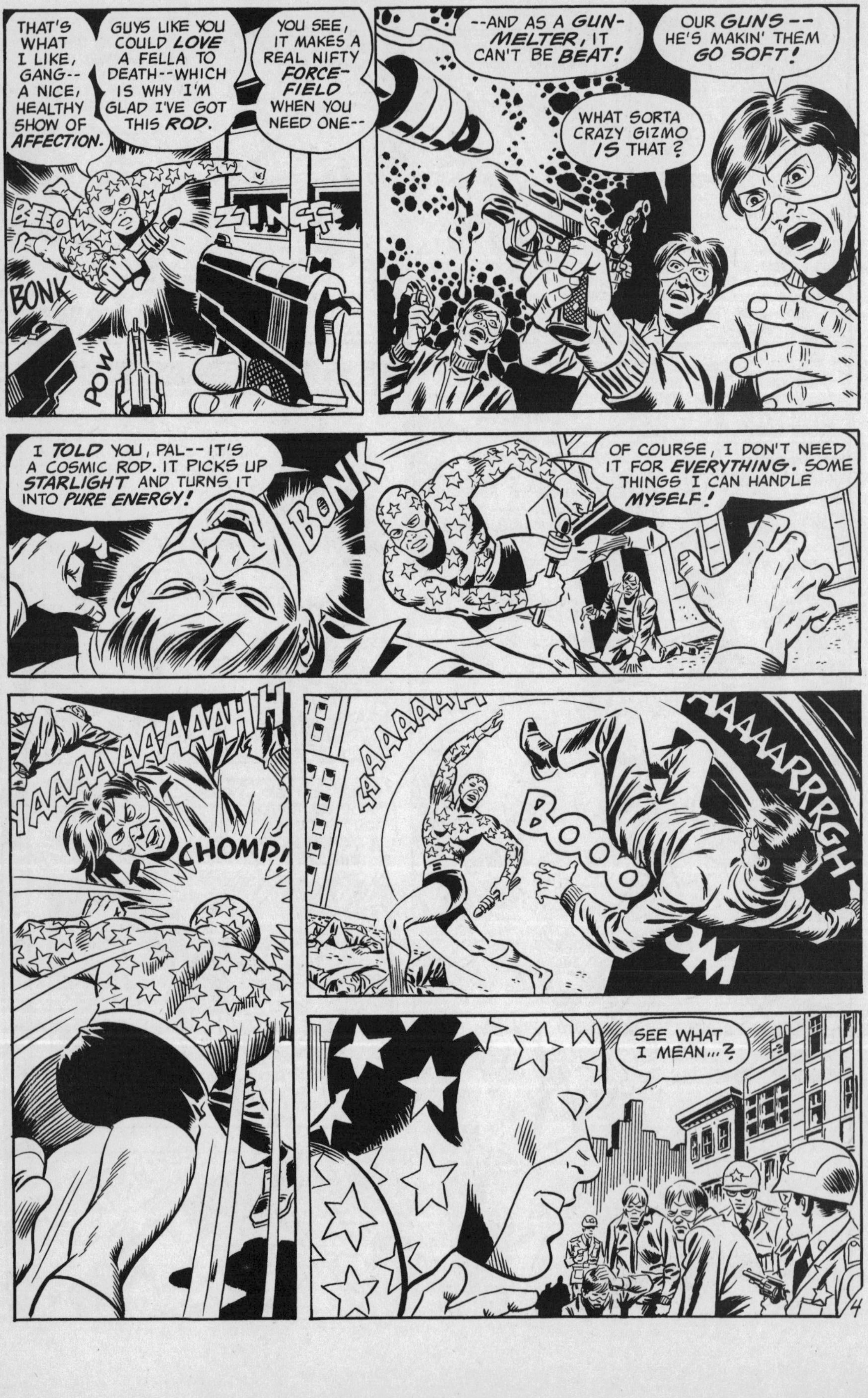
THAT'S WHAT I LIKE, GANG-- A NICE, HEALTHY SHOW OF AFFECTION.
GUYS LIKE YOU COULD LOVE A FELLA TO DEATH--WHICH IS WHY I'M GLAD I'VE GOT THIS ROD.
YOU SEE, IT MAKES A REAL NIFTY FORCE-FIELD WHEN YOU NEED ONE--
BEEOW
ZINGG
BONK
POW
--AND AS A GUN-MELTER, IT CAN'T BE BEAT!
OUR GUNS-- HE'S MAKIN' THEM GO SOFT!
WHAT SORTA CRAZY GIZMO IS THAT?
I TOLD YOU, PAL-- IT'S A COSMIC ROD. IT PICKS UP STARLIGHT AND TURNS IT INTO PURE ENERGY!
BONK
OF COURSE, I DON'T NEED IT FOR EVERYTHING. SOME THINGS I CAN HANDLE MYSELF!
HAAAAAAAAAAAH
CHOMP!
AAAAAAH
BOOOOM
HAAAAARRRGH
SEE WHAT I MEAN...?
4

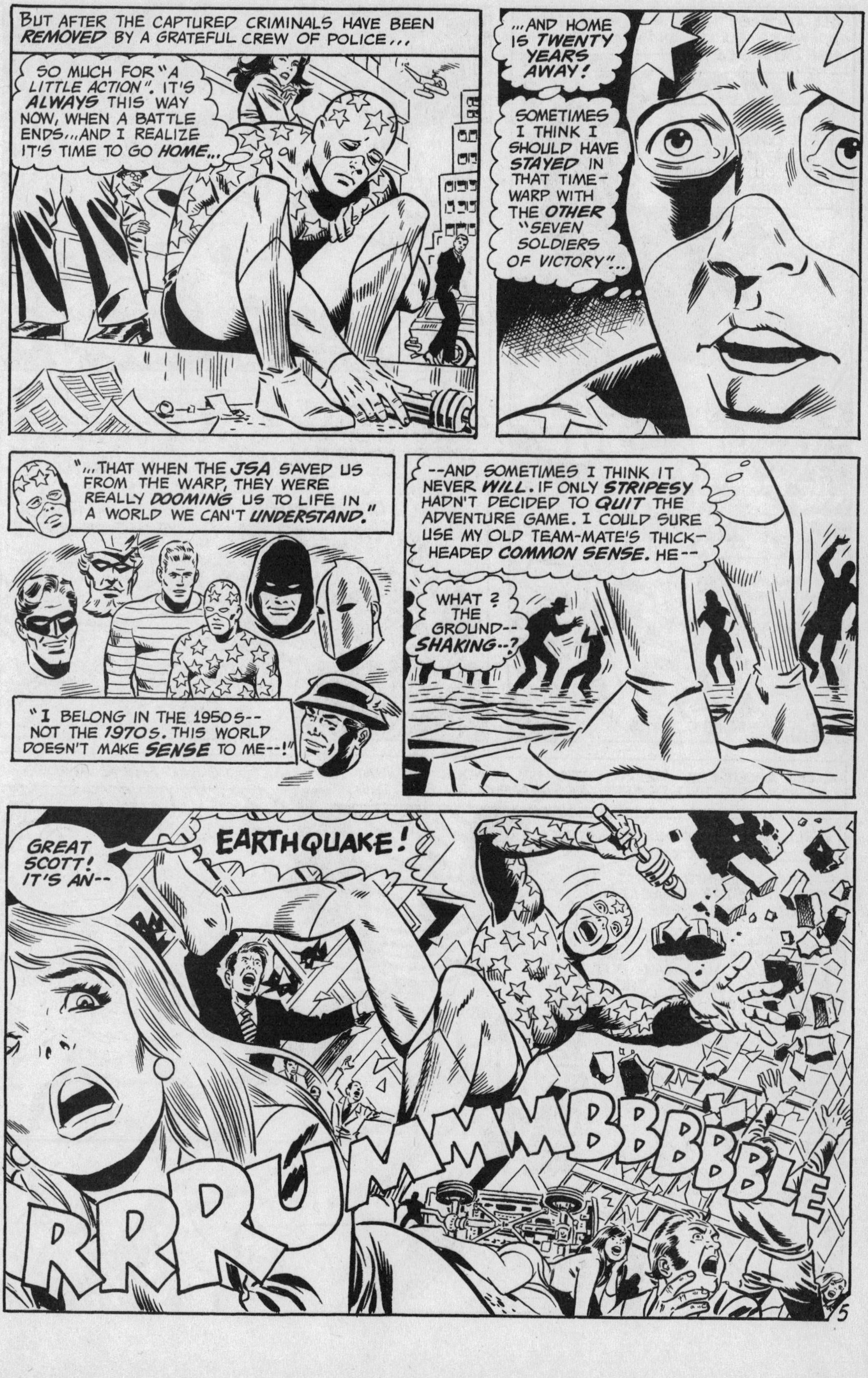
BUT AFTER THE CAPTURED CRIMINALS HAVE BEEN REMOVED BY A GRATEFUL CREW OF POLICE...
SO MUCH FOR "A LITTLE ACTION". IT'S ALWAYS THIS WAY NOW, WHEN A BATTLE ENDS...AND I REALIZE IT'S TIME TO GO HOME...
...AND HOME IS TWENTY YEARS AWAY!
SOMETIMES I THINK I SHOULD HAVE STAYED IN THAT TIME-WARP WITH THE OTHER "SEVEN SOLDIERS OF VICTORY"...
"...THAT WHEN THE JSA SAVED US FROM THE WARP, THEY WERE REALLY DOOMING US TO LIFE IN A WORLD WE CAN'T UNDERSTAND."
"I BELONG IN THE 1950S-- NOT THE 1970S. THIS WORLD DOESN'T MAKE SENSE TO ME--!"
--AND SOMETIMES I THINK IT NEVER WILL. IF ONLY STRIPESY HADN'T DECIDED TO QUIT THE ADVENTURE GAME. I COULD SURE USE MY OLD TEAM-MATE'S THICK-HEADED COMMON SENSE. HE--
WHAT? THE GROUND-- SHAKING--?
GREAT SCOTT! IT'S AN--
EARTHQUAKE!
RRRUMMMMBBBBBBLE
5

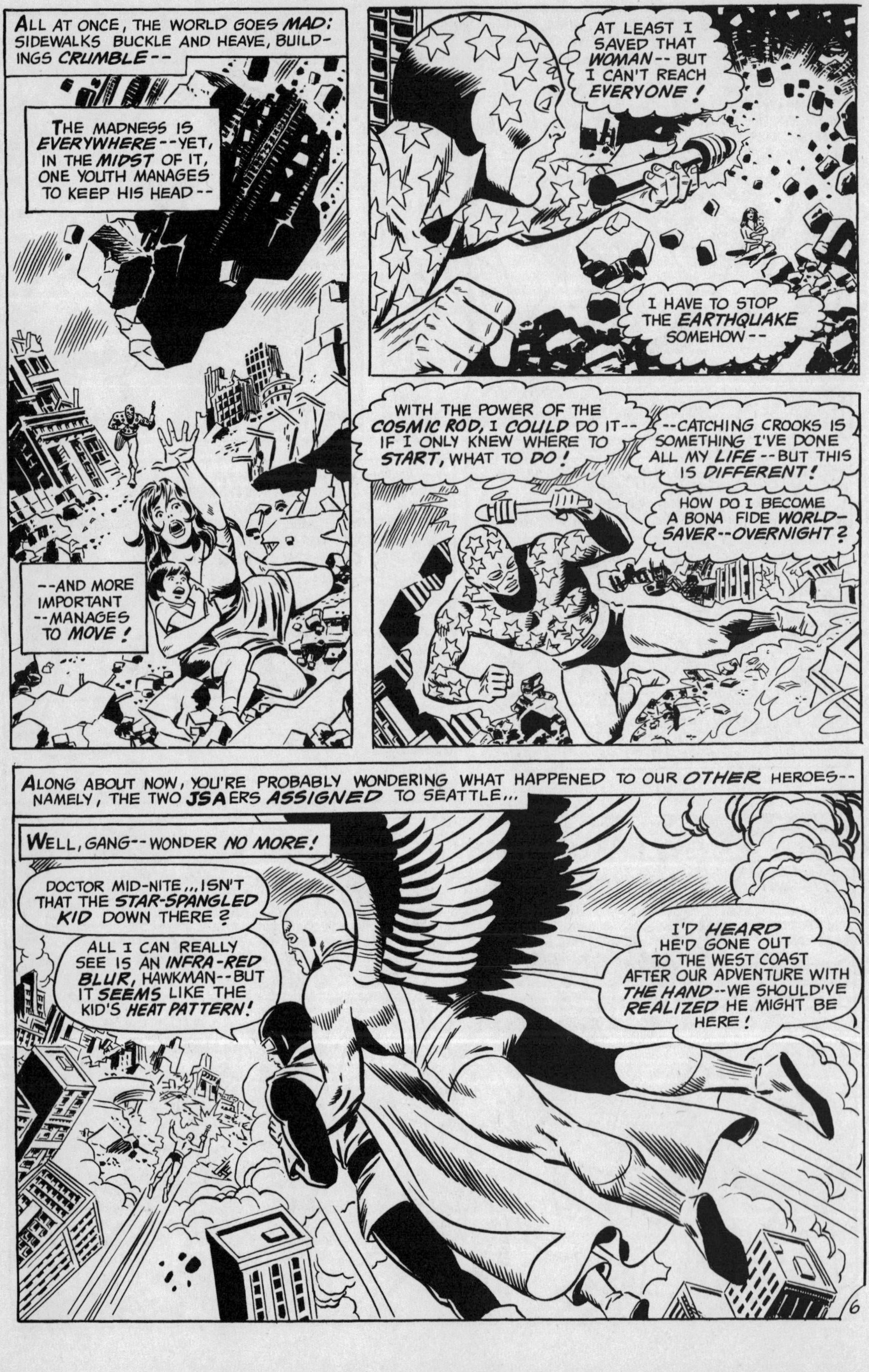
ALL AT ONCE, THE WORLD GOES MAD: SIDEWALKS BUCKLE AND HEAVE, BUILDINGS CRUMBLE--
THE MADNESS IS EVERYWHERE--YET, IN THE MIDST OF IT, ONE YOUTH MANAGES TO KEEP HIS HEAD--
--AND MORE IMPORTANT --MANAGES TO MOVE!
AT LEAST I SAVED THAT WOMAN-- BUT I CAN'T REACH EVERYONE!
I HAVE TO STOP THE EARTHQUAKE SOMEHOW--
WITH THE POWER OF THE COSMIC ROD, I COULD DO IT-- IF I ONLY KNEW WHERE TO START, WHAT TO DO!
--CATCHING CROOKS IS SOMETHING I'VE DONE ALL MY LIFE--BUT THIS IS DIFFERENT!
HOW DO I BECOME A BONA FIDE WORLD-SAVER--OVERNIGHT?
ALONG ABOUT NOW, YOU'RE PROBABLY WONDERING WHAT HAPPENED TO OUR OTHER HEROES-- NAMELY, THE TWO JSAERS ASSIGNED TO SEATTLE...
WELL, GANG--WONDER NO MORE!
DOCTOR MID-NITE...ISN'T THAT THE STAR-SPANGLED KID DOWN THERE?
ALL I CAN REALLY SEE IS AN INFRA-RED BLUR, HAWKMAN--BUT IT SEEMS LIKE THE KID'S HEAT PATTERN!
I'D HEARD HE'D GONE OUT TO THE WEST COAST AFTER OUR ADVENTURE WITH THE HAND--WE SHOULD'VE REALIZED HE MIGHT BE HERE!
6

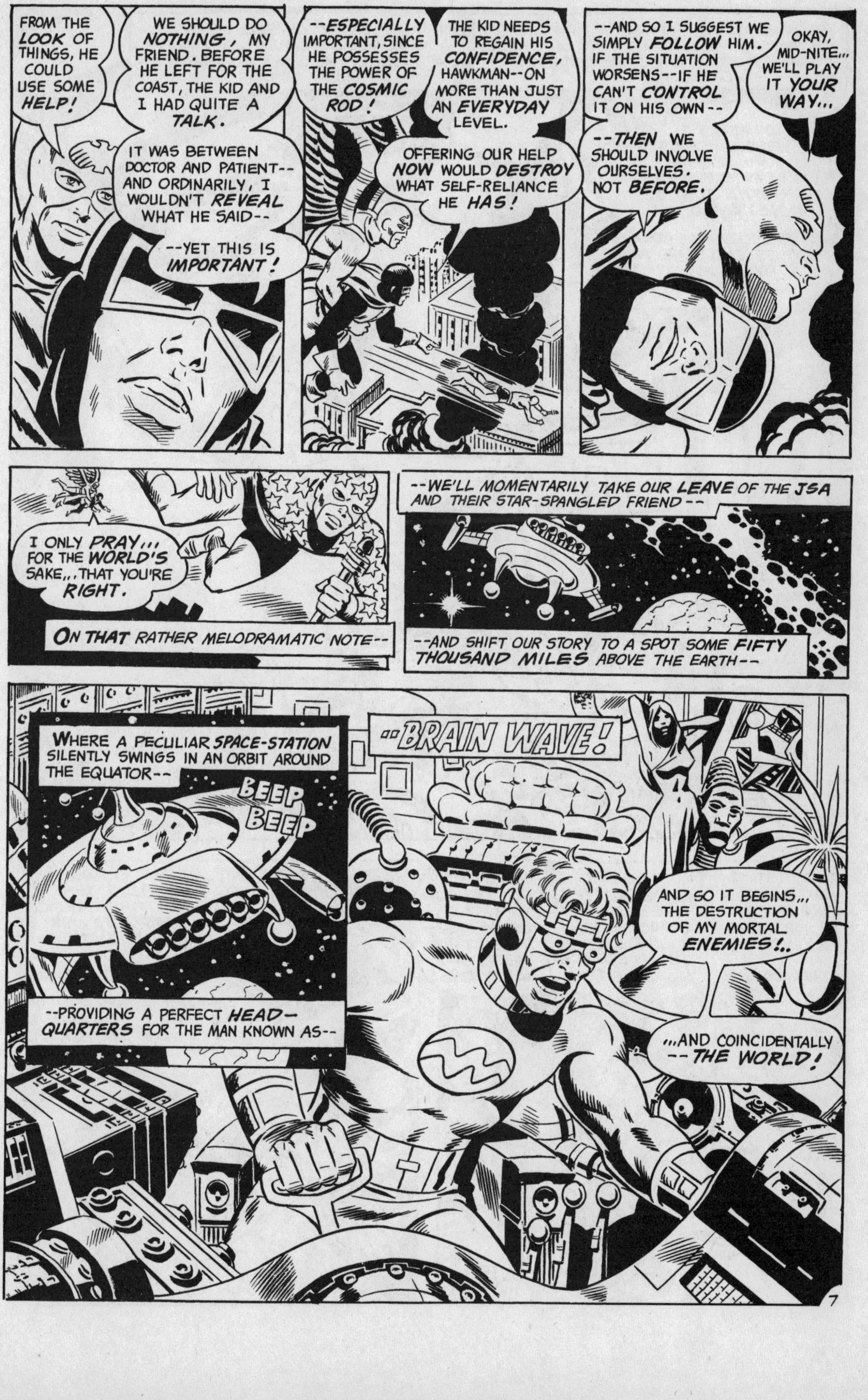
FROM THE LOOK OF THINGS, HE COULD USE SOME HELP!
WE SHOULD DO NOTHING, MY FRIEND. BEFORE HE LEFT FOR THE COAST, THE KID AND I HAD QUITE A TALK.
IT WAS BETWEEN DOCTOR AND PATIENT--AND ORDINARILY, I WOULDN'T REVEAL WHAT HE SAID--
--YET THIS IS IMPORTANT!
--ESPECIALLY IMPORTANT, SINCE HE POSSESSES THE POWER OF THE COSMIC ROD!
THE KID NEEDS TO REGAIN HIS CONFIDENCE, HAWKMAN--ON MORE THAN JUST AN EVERYDAY LEVEL.
OFFERING OUR HELP NOW WOULD DESTROY WHAT SELF-RELIANCE HE HAS!
--AND SO I SUGGEST WE SIMPLY FOLLOW HIM. IF THE SITUATION WORSENS--IF HE CAN'T CONTROL IT ON HIS OWN--
--THEN WE SHOULD INVOLVE OURSELVES. NOT BEFORE.
OKAY, MID-NITE... WE'LL PLAY IT YOUR WAY...
I ONLY PRAY... FOR THE WORLD'S SAKE... THAT YOU'RE RIGHT.
ON THAT RATHER MELODRAMATIC NOTE--
--WE'LL MOMENTARILY TAKE OUR LEAVE OF THE JSA AND THEIR STAR-SPANGLED FRIEND--
--AND SHIFT OUR STORY TO A SPOT SOME FIFTY THOUSAND MILES ABOVE THE EARTH--
WHERE A PECULIAR SPACE-STATION SILENTLY SWINGS IN AN ORBIT AROUND THE EQUATOR--
BEEP BEEP
--PROVIDING A PERFECT HEAD-QUARTERS FOR THE MAN KNOWN AS--
--BRAIN WAVE!
AND SO IT BEGINS... THE DESTRUCTION OF MY MORTAL ENEMIES!..
...AND COINCIDENTALLY --THE WORLD!
7

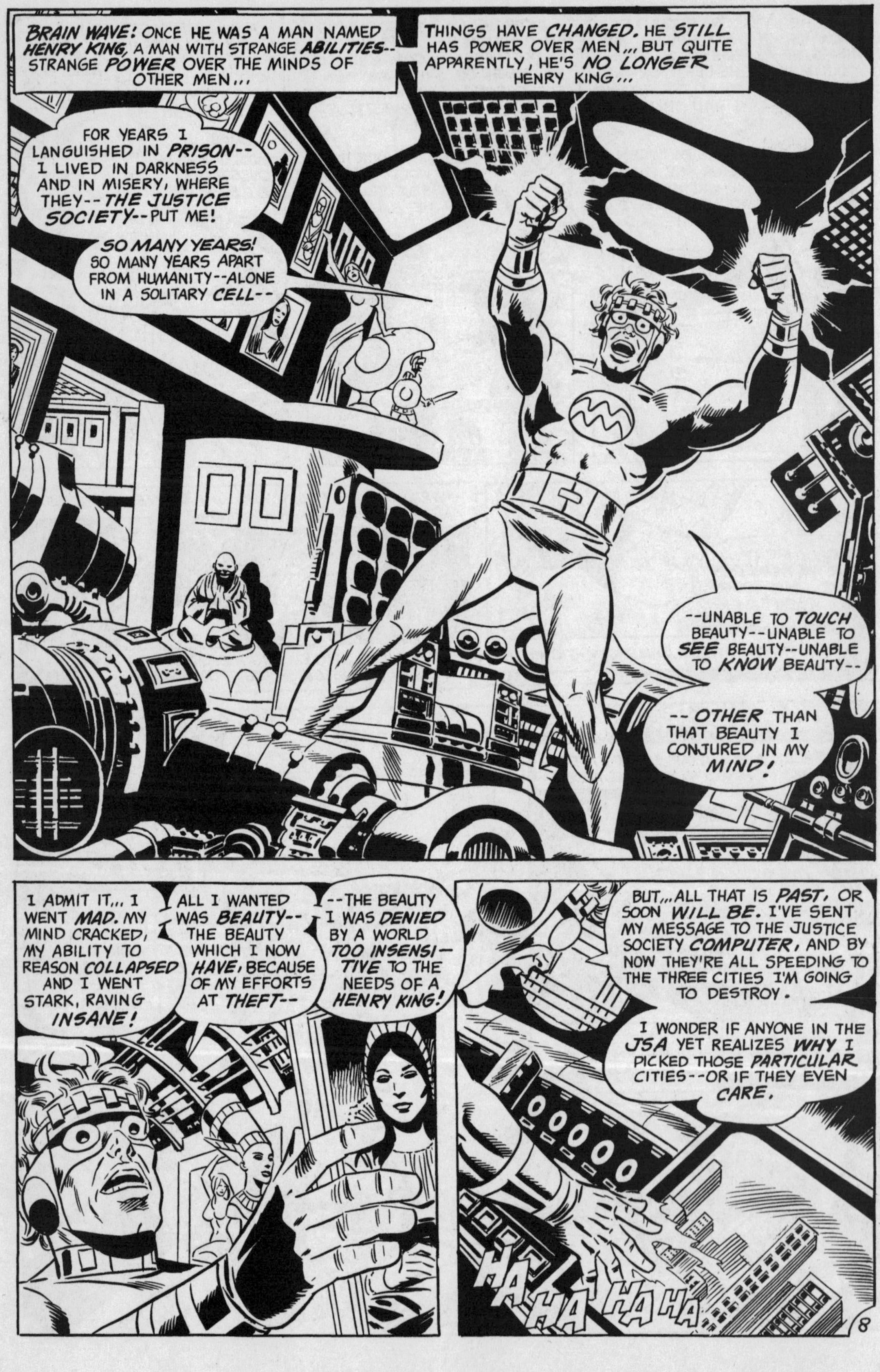
BRAIN WAVE: ONCE HE WAS A MAN NAMED HENRY KING, A MAN WITH STRANGE ABILITIES-- STRANGE POWER OVER THE MINDS OF OTHER MEN...
THINGS HAVE CHANGED. HE STILL HAS POWER OVER MEN... BUT QUITE APPARENTLY, HE'S NO LONGER HENRY KING...
FOR YEARS I LANGUISHED IN PRISON-- I LIVED IN DARKNESS AND IN MISERY, WHERE THEY--THE JUSTICE SOCIETY--PUT ME!
SO MANY YEARS! SO MANY YEARS APART FROM HUMANITY--ALONE IN A SOLITARY CELL--
--UNABLE TO TOUCH BEAUTY--UNABLE TO SEE BEAUTY--UNABLE TO KNOW BEAUTY--
--OTHER THAN THAT BEAUTY I CONJURED IN MY MIND!
I ADMIT IT... I WENT MAD. MY MIND CRACKED, MY ABILITY TO REASON COLLAPSED AND I WENT STARK, RAVING INSANE!
ALL I WANTED WAS BEAUTY-- THE BEAUTY WHICH I NOW HAVE, BECAUSE OF MY EFFORTS AT THEFT--
--THE BEAUTY I WAS DENIED BY A WORLD TOO INSENSITIVE TO THE NEEDS OF A HENRY KING!
BUT... ALL THAT IS PAST, OR SOON WILL BE. I'VE SENT MY MESSAGE TO THE JUSTICE SOCIETY COMPUTER, AND BY NOW THEY'RE ALL SPEEDING TO THE THREE CITIES I'M GOING TO DESTROY.
I WONDER IF ANYONE IN THE JSA YET REALIZES WHY I PICKED THOSE PARTICULAR CITIES--OR IF THEY EVEN CARE.
HA HA HA HA HA
8

READERS FAMILIAR WITH BRAINWAVE ARE DOUBTLESSLY *WONDERING* ABOUT HIS APPARENT *PHYSICAL* CHANGE... AND IF YOU'RE *ONE* OF THOSE READERS, REST ASSURED... EVERYTHING WILL BE *EXPLAINED*...!

WE'VE BEEN QUITE *IMPRESSED* BY YOUR IMPARTIALITY, MR. GRAYSON. EVER SINCE YOU *ARRIVED* LAST WEEK, YOU'VE BEEN MOST *FAIR*...

MEANWHILE (AS THEY SAY), ON THE TERRACE OF A PENTHOUSE OVERLOOKING THE CITY OF *CAPETOWN*...

...IN KEEPING WITH THE *POLICY* OF YOUR *MISSION.* WE HAVE HIGH HOPES FOR YOUR REPORT TO THE *U.N.*

SO HAVE I, MR. KATOBI.

I INTEND TO RECOMMEND A *STUDY* ON THE *U.N.* ATTITUDE TOWARD POLICIES OF *APARTHEID*-- AND I HOPE WE CAN--

WHAT THE--?

AN *EXPLOSION*--!

THRABOOM

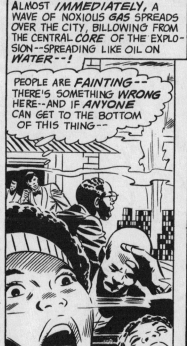

ALMOST *IMMEDIATELY,* A WAVE OF NOXIOUS *GAS* SPREADS OVER THE CITY, BILLOWING FROM THE CENTRAL *CORE* OF THE EXPLOSION--SPREADING LIKE OIL ON *WATER*--!

PEOPLE ARE *FAINTING*-- THERE'S SOMETHING *WRONG* HERE--AND IF *ANYONE* CAN GET TO THE BOTTOM OF THIS THING--

--IT'S *ROBIN*-- THE *EX-BOY WONDER!*

9

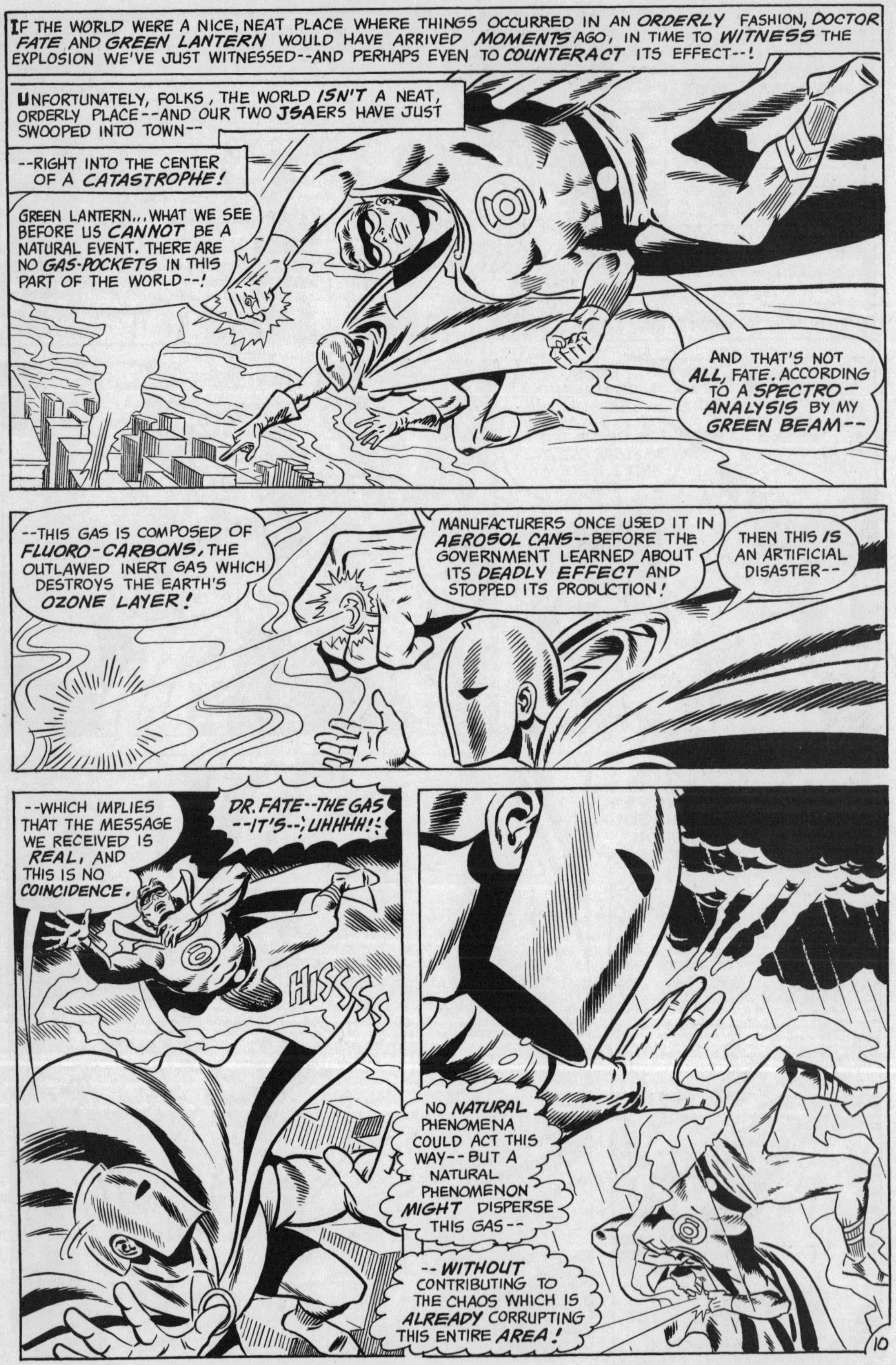
IF THE WORLD WERE A NICE, NEAT PLACE WHERE THINGS OCCURRED IN AN ORDERLY FASHION, DOCTOR FATE AND GREEN LANTERN WOULD HAVE ARRIVED MOMENTS AGO, IN TIME TO WITNESS THE EXPLOSION WE'VE JUST WITNESSED--AND PERHAPS EVEN TO COUNTERACT ITS EFFECT--!
UNFORTUNATELY, FOLKS, THE WORLD ISN'T A NEAT, ORDERLY PLACE--AND OUR TWO JSAERS HAVE JUST SWOOPED INTO TOWN--
--RIGHT INTO THE CENTER OF A CATASTROPHE!
GREEN LANTERN... WHAT WE SEE BEFORE US CANNOT BE A NATURAL EVENT. THERE ARE NO GAS-POCKETS IN THIS PART OF THE WORLD--!
AND THAT'S NOT ALL, FATE. ACCORDING TO A SPECTRO-ANALYSIS BY MY GREEN BEAM--
--THIS GAS IS COMPOSED OF FLUORO-CARBONS, THE OUTLAWED INERT GAS WHICH DESTROYS THE EARTH'S OZONE LAYER!
MANUFACTURERS ONCE USED IT IN AEROSOL CANS--BEFORE THE GOVERNMENT LEARNED ABOUT ITS DEADLY EFFECT AND STOPPED ITS PRODUCTION!
THEN THIS IS AN ARTIFICIAL DISASTER--
--WHICH IMPLIES THAT THE MESSAGE WE RECEIVED IS REAL, AND THIS IS NO COINCIDENCE.
DR. FATE--THE GAS--IT'S--; UHHHH!
HISSSS
NO NATURAL PHENOMENA COULD ACT THIS WAY--BUT A NATURAL PHENOMENON MIGHT DISPERSE THIS GAS--
--WITHOUT CONTRIBUTING TO THE CHAOS WHICH IS ALREADY CORRUPTING THIS ENTIRE AREA!
10

WITHIN SECONDS FATE'S SPELL PRODUCES *STARTLING RESULTS...*

BETWEEN MY *POWER-RING BEAM* AND YOUR *MAGIC,* DR. FATE--WE SEEM TO BE DISPOSING OF THIS DEATH-GAS IN NO TIME *FLAT!*

APPEARANCES ARE OFTEN *DECEIVING,* GREEN LANTERN. WE MUSTN'T ALLOW OURSELVES TO *FORGET--*

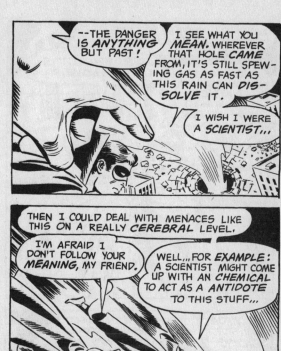

--THE *DANGER* IS *ANYTHING* BUT PAST!

I SEE WHAT YOU *MEAN.* WHEREVER THAT HOLE *CAME* FROM, IT'S STILL SPEW-ING GAS AS FAST AS THIS RAIN CAN *DIS-SOLVE* IT.

I WISH I WERE A *SCIENTIST...*

THEN I COULD DEAL WITH MENACES LIKE THIS ON A REALLY *CEREBRAL* LEVEL.

I'M AFRAID I DON'T FOLLOW YOUR *MEANING,* MY FRIEND.

WELL,,, FOR *EXAMPLE:* A SCIENTIST MIGHT COME UP WITH AN *CHEMICAL* TO ACT AS A *ANTIDOTE* TO THIS STUFF...

...BUT SINCE I'M *NOT* A SCIENTIST, I THINK OF MORE *DIRECT* SOLUTIONS...

...*LIKE THIS!*

WHOMP!

TRUE,,, IT'S NOT A CEREBRAL SOLUTION, GREEN LANTERN. BUT FOR THE PRESENT, IT WILL *DO.*

THANKS, FATE. FROM A THINKER LIKE YOU, THAT'S A COMPLI--EH ?

SAY...IT LOOKS LIKE WE'VE SOME *COMPANY,* FATE,,,!

ROBIN!

11

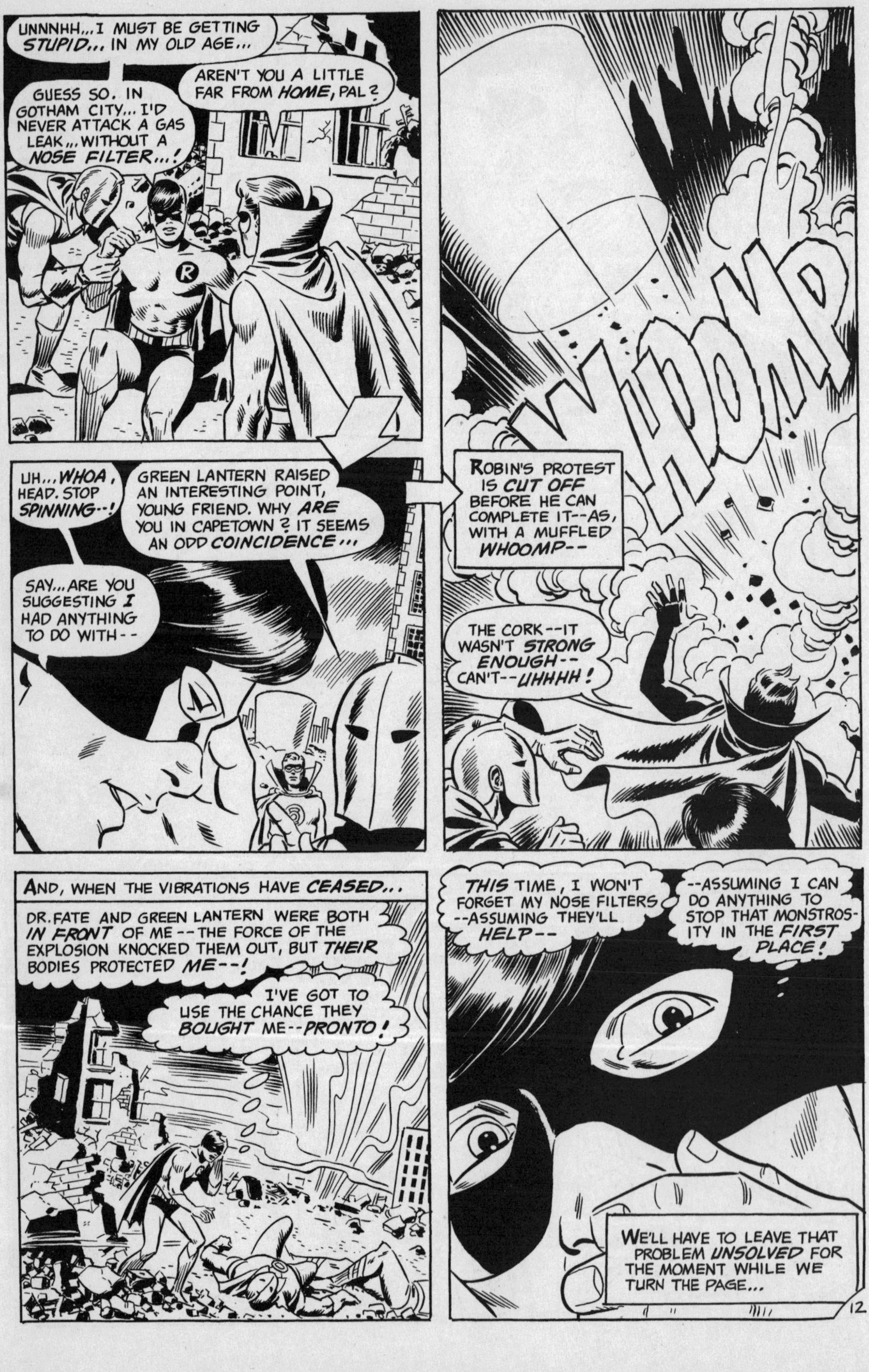
UNNNHH... I MUST BE GETTING STUPID... IN MY OLD AGE...
AREN'T YOU A LITTLE FAR FROM HOME, PAL?
GUESS SO. IN GOTHAM CITY... I'D NEVER ATTACK A GAS LEAK... WITHOUT A NOSE FILTER...!
UH... WHOA, HEAD. STOP SPINNING--!
GREEN LANTERN RAISED AN INTERESTING POINT, YOUNG FRIEND. WHY ARE YOU IN CAPETOWN? IT SEEMS AN ODD COINCIDENCE...
SAY... ARE YOU SUGGESTING I HAD ANYTHING TO DO WITH--
WHOOMP
ROBIN'S PROTEST IS CUT OFF BEFORE HE CAN COMPLETE IT--AS, WITH A MUFFLED WHOOMP--
THE CORK--IT WASN'T STRONG ENOUGH--CAN'T--UHHHH!
AND, WHEN THE VIBRATIONS HAVE CEASED...
DR. FATE AND GREEN LANTERN WERE BOTH IN FRONT OF ME--THE FORCE OF THE EXPLOSION KNOCKED THEM OUT, BUT THEIR BODIES PROTECTED ME--!
I'VE GOT TO USE THE CHANCE THEY BOUGHT ME--PRONTO!
THIS TIME, I WON'T FORGET MY NOSE FILTERS --ASSUMING THEY'LL HELP--
--ASSUMING I CAN DO ANYTHING TO STOP THAT MONSTROSITY IN THE FIRST PLACE!
WE'LL HAVE TO LEAVE THAT PROBLEM UNSOLVED FOR THE MOMENT WHILE WE TURN THE PAGE...
12

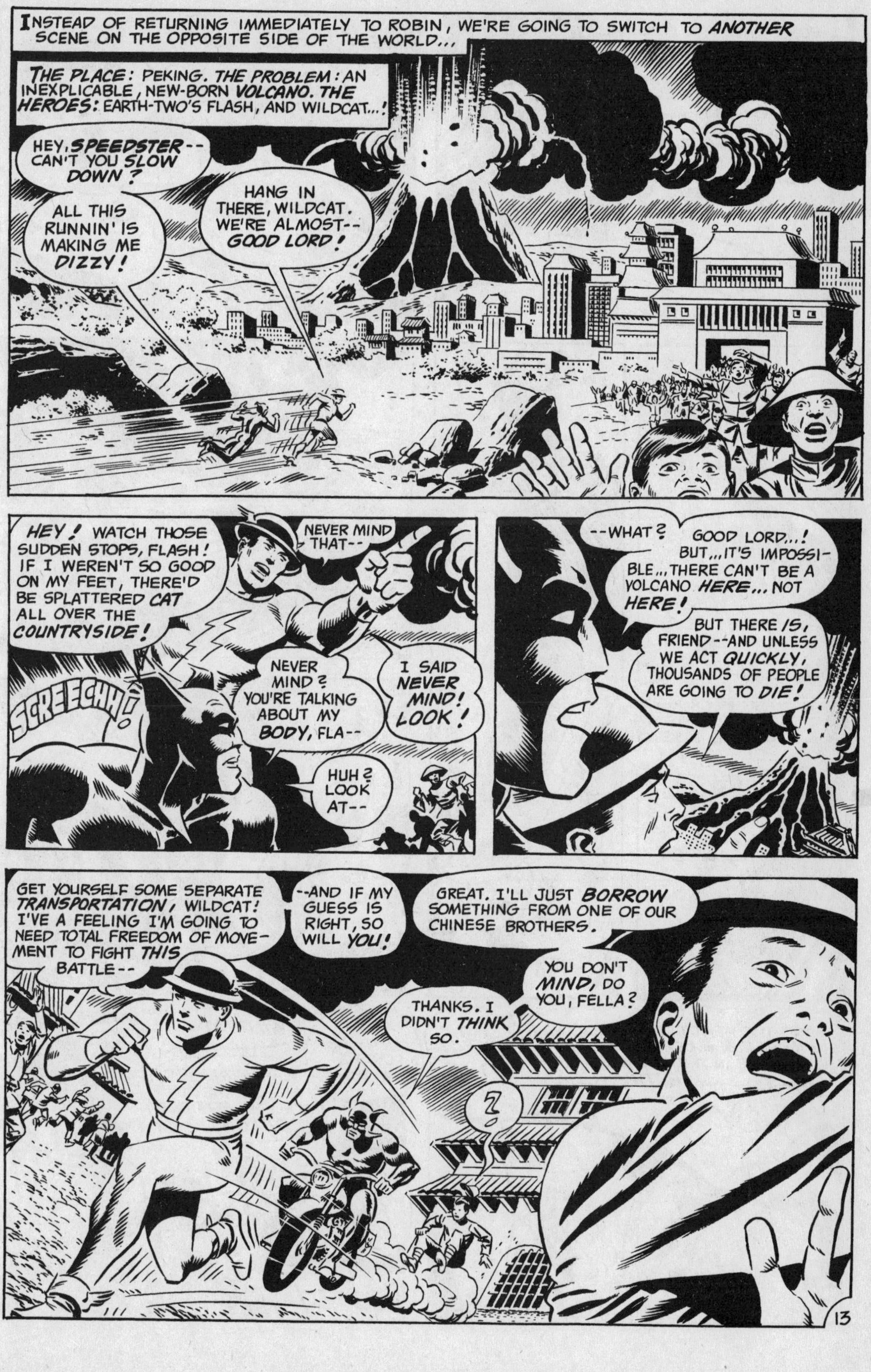
INSTEAD OF RETURNING IMMEDIATELY TO ROBIN, WE'RE GOING TO SWITCH TO ANOTHER SCENE ON THE OPPOSITE SIDE OF THE WORLD...
THE PLACE: PEKING. THE PROBLEM: AN INEXPLICABLE, NEW-BORN VOLCANO. THE HEROES: EARTH-TWO'S FLASH, AND WILDCAT...!
HEY, SPEEDSTER--CAN'T YOU SLOW DOWN?
ALL THIS RUNNIN' IS MAKING ME DIZZY!
HANG IN THERE, WILDCAT. WE'RE ALMOST--GOOD LORD!
HEY! WATCH THOSE SUDDEN STOPS, FLASH! IF I WEREN'T SO GOOD ON MY FEET, THERE'D BE SPLATTERED CAT ALL OVER THE COUNTRYSIDE!
NEVER MIND THAT--
SCREECHH!
NEVER MIND? YOU'RE TALKING ABOUT MY BODY, FLA--
I SAID NEVER MIND! LOOK!
HUH? LOOK AT--
--WHAT?
GOOD LORD...! BUT...IT'S IMPOSSIBLE...THERE CAN'T BE A VOLCANO HERE... NOT HERE!
BUT THERE IS, FRIEND--AND UNLESS WE ACT QUICKLY, THOUSANDS OF PEOPLE ARE GOING TO DIE!
GET YOURSELF SOME SEPARATE TRANSPORTATION, WILDCAT! I'VE A FEELING I'M GOING TO NEED TOTAL FREEDOM OF MOVEMENT TO FIGHT THIS BATTLE--
--AND IF MY GUESS IS RIGHT, SO WILL YOU!
GREAT. I'LL JUST BORROW SOMETHING FROM ONE OF OUR CHINESE BROTHERS.
YOU DON'T MIND, DO YOU, FELLA?
THANKS. I DIDN'T THINK SO.
?
13

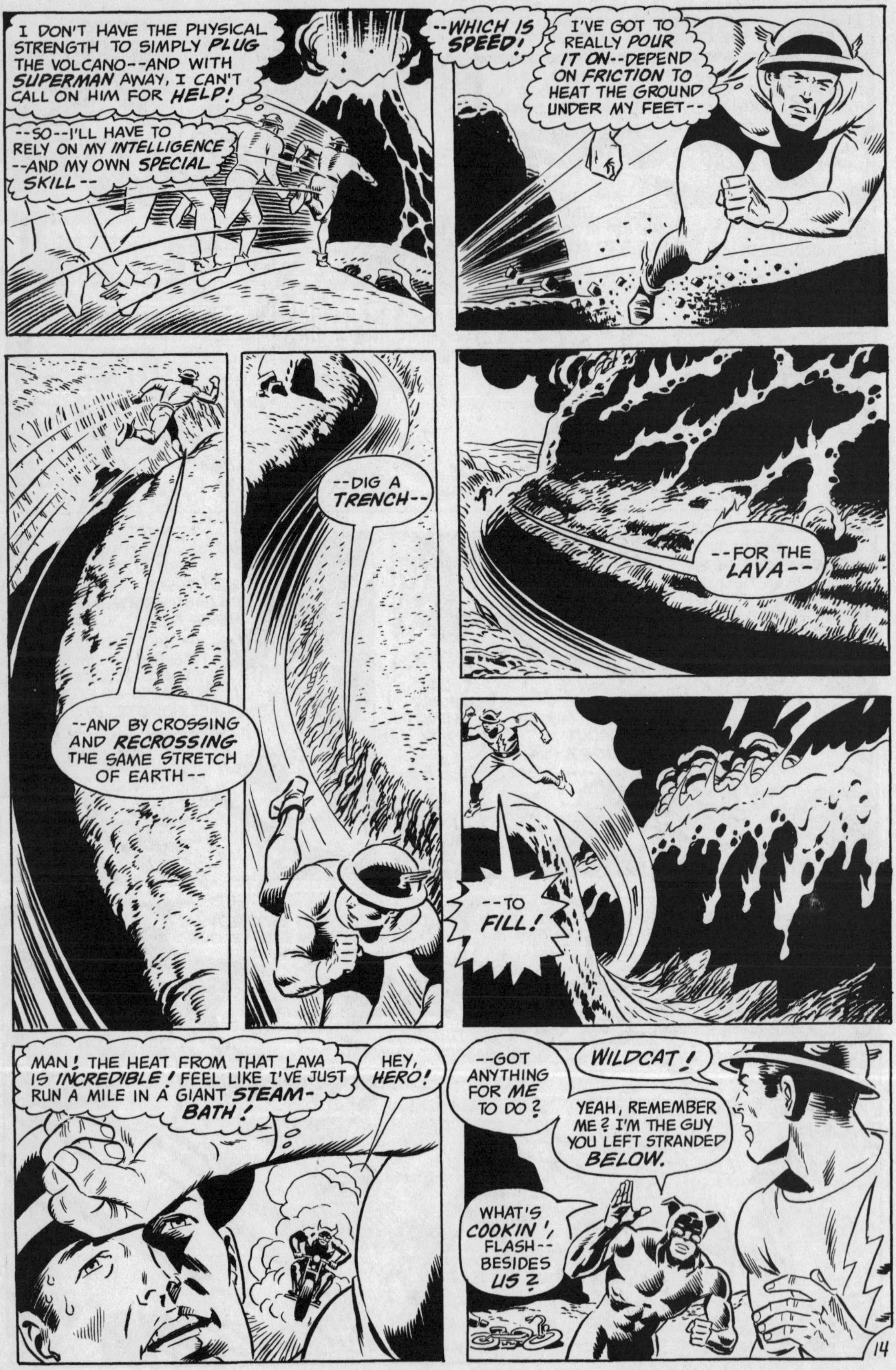
I DON'T HAVE THE PHYSICAL STRENGTH TO SIMPLY PLUG THE VOLCANO--AND WITH SUPERMAN AWAY, I CAN'T CALL ON HIM FOR HELP!
--SO--I'LL HAVE TO RELY ON MY INTELLIGENCE --AND MY OWN SPECIAL SKILL--
--WHICH IS SPEED!
I'VE GOT TO REALLY POUR IT ON--DEPEND ON FRICTION TO HEAT THE GROUND UNDER MY FEET--
--AND BY CROSSING AND RECROSSING THE SAME STRETCH OF EARTH--
--DIG A TRENCH--
--FOR THE LAVA--
--TO FILL!
MAN! THE HEAT FROM THAT LAVA IS INCREDIBLE! FEEL LIKE I'VE JUST RUN A MILE IN A GIANT STEAM-BATH!
HEY, HERO!
--GOT ANYTHING FOR ME TO DO?
WILDCAT!
YEAH, REMEMBER ME? I'M THE GUY YOU LEFT STRANDED BELOW.
WHAT'S COOKIN', FLASH--BESIDES US?
14

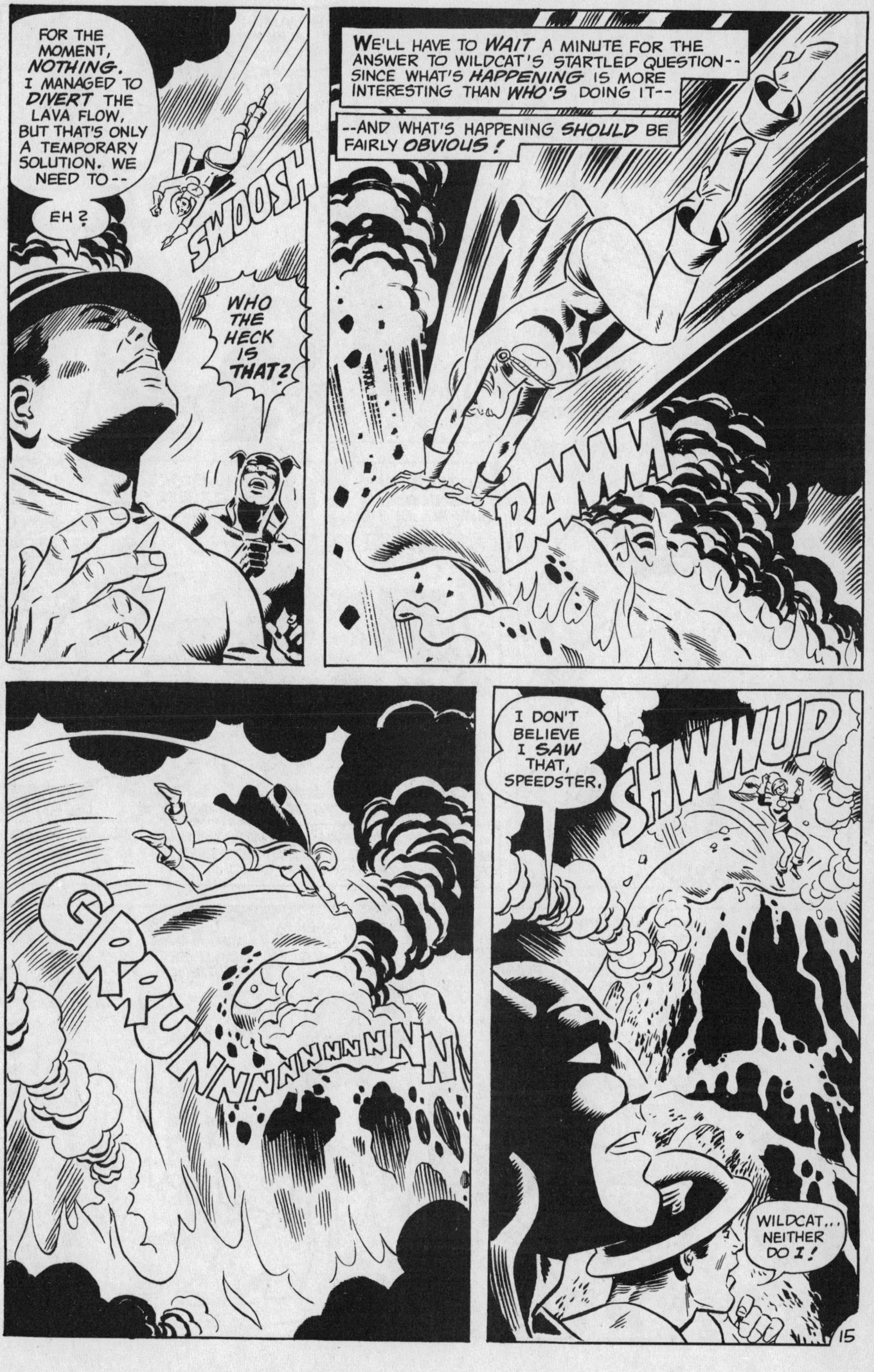
FOR THE MOMENT, NOTHING. I MANAGED TO DIVERT THE LAVA FLOW, BUT THAT'S ONLY A TEMPORARY SOLUTION. WE NEED TO--
EH?
SWOOSH
WHO THE HECK IS THAT?
WE'LL HAVE TO WAIT A MINUTE FOR THE ANSWER TO WILDCAT'S STARTLED QUESTION-- SINCE WHAT'S HAPPENING IS MORE INTERESTING THAN WHO'S DOING IT--
--AND WHAT'S HAPPENING SHOULD BE FAIRLY OBVIOUS!
BAMM
GRRUNNNNNNNNNNN
I DON'T BELIEVE I SAW THAT, SPEEDSTER.
SHWWUP
WILDCAT... NEITHER DO I!
15

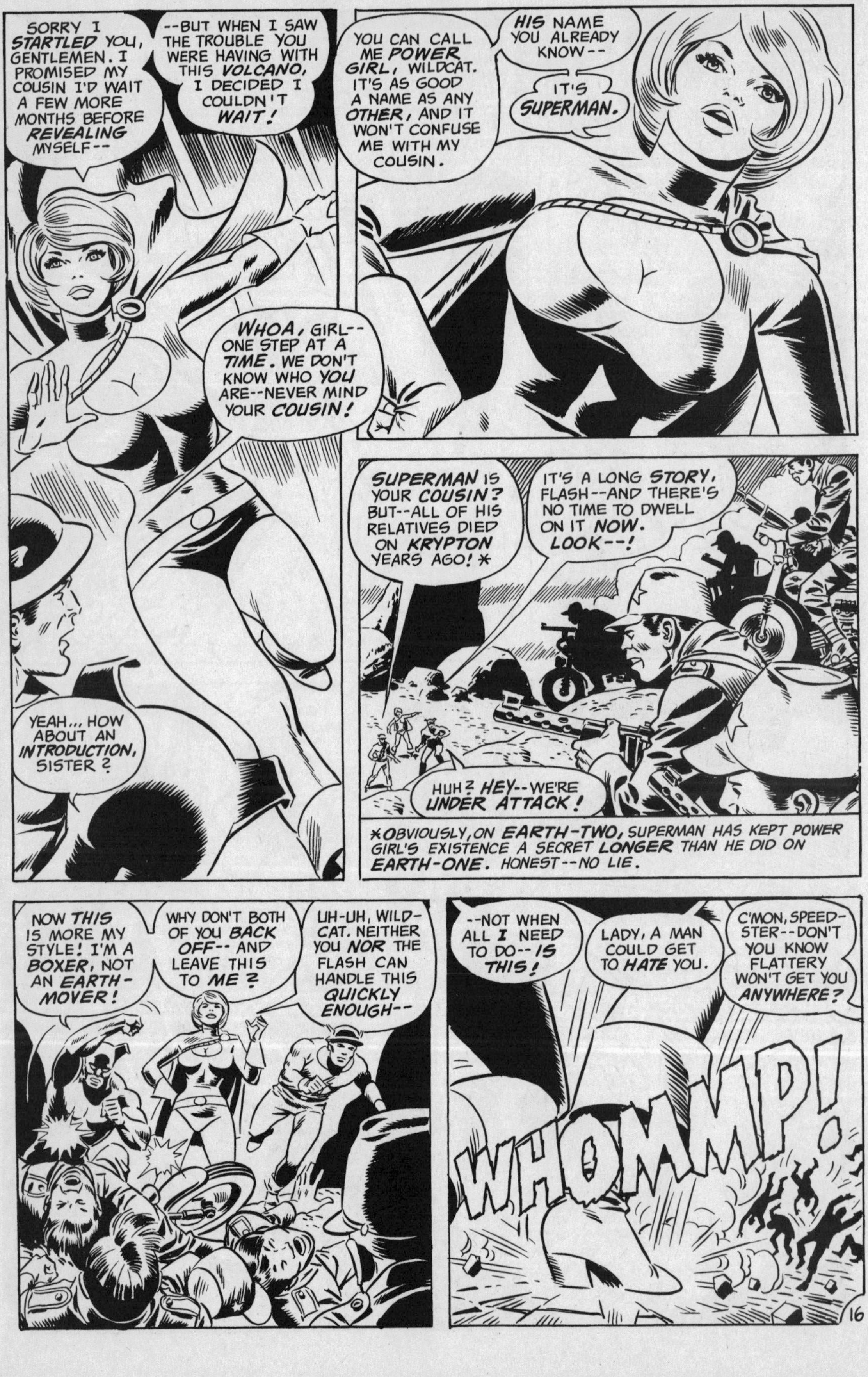
SORRY I STARTLED YOU, GENTLEMEN. I PROMISED MY COUSIN I'D WAIT A FEW MORE MONTHS BEFORE REVEALING MYSELF--
--BUT WHEN I SAW THE TROUBLE YOU WERE HAVING WITH THIS VOLCANO, I DECIDED I COULDN'T WAIT!
WHOA, GIRL-- ONE STEP AT A TIME. WE DON'T KNOW WHO YOU ARE--NEVER MIND YOUR COUSIN!
YEAH... HOW ABOUT AN INTRODUCTION, SISTER?
YOU CAN CALL ME POWER GIRL, WILDCAT. IT'S AS GOOD A NAME AS ANY OTHER, AND IT WON'T CONFUSE ME WITH MY COUSIN.
HIS NAME YOU ALREADY KNOW--
IT'S SUPERMAN.
SUPERMAN IS YOUR COUSIN? BUT--ALL OF HIS RELATIVES DIED ON KRYPTON YEARS AGO! *
IT'S A LONG STORY, FLASH--AND THERE'S NO TIME TO DWELL ON IT NOW. LOOK--!
HUH? HEY--WE'RE UNDER ATTACK!
*OBVIOUSLY, ON EARTH-TWO, SUPERMAN HAS KEPT POWER GIRL'S EXISTENCE A SECRET LONGER THAN HE DID ON EARTH-ONE. HONEST--NO LIE.
NOW THIS IS MORE MY STYLE! I'M A BOXER, NOT AN EARTH-MOVER!
WHY DON'T BOTH OF YOU BACK OFF-- AND LEAVE THIS TO ME?
UH-UH, WILDCAT. NEITHER YOU NOR THE FLASH CAN HANDLE THIS QUICKLY ENOUGH--
--NOT WHEN ALL I NEED TO DO-- IS THIS!
LADY, A MAN COULD GET TO HATE YOU.
C'MON, SPEEDSTER--DON'T YOU KNOW FLATTERY WON'T GET YOU ANYWHERE?
WHOMMP!
16

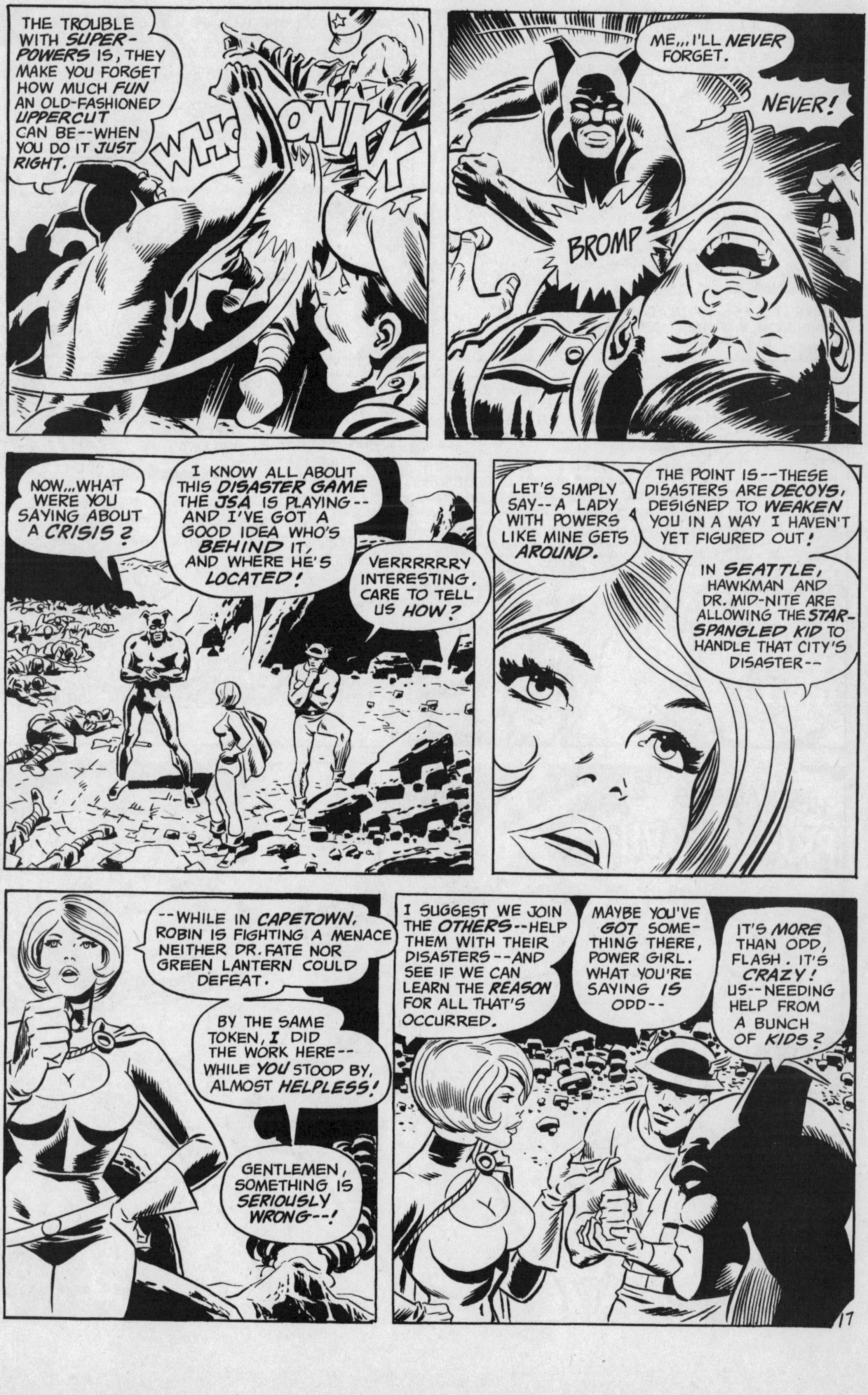
THE TROUBLE WITH SUPER-POWERS IS, THEY MAKE YOU FORGET HOW MUCH FUN AN OLD-FASHIONED UPPERCUT CAN BE--WHEN YOU DO IT JUST RIGHT.
WHONK
ME,,, I'LL NEVER FORGET.
NEVER!
BROMP
NOW... WHAT WERE YOU SAYING ABOUT A CRISIS?
I KNOW ALL ABOUT THIS DISASTER GAME THE JSA IS PLAYING--AND I'VE GOT A GOOD IDEA WHO'S BEHIND IT, AND WHERE HE'S LOCATED!
VERRRRRRY INTERESTING. CARE TO TELL US HOW?
LET'S SIMPLY SAY--A LADY WITH POWERS LIKE MINE GETS AROUND.
THE POINT IS--THESE DISASTERS ARE DECOYS, DESIGNED TO WEAKEN YOU IN A WAY I HAVEN'T YET FIGURED OUT!
IN SEATTLE, HAWKMAN AND DR. MID-NITE ARE ALLOWING THE STAR-SPANGLED KID TO HANDLE THAT CITY'S DISASTER--
--WHILE IN CAPETOWN, ROBIN IS FIGHTING A MENACE NEITHER DR. FATE NOR GREEN LANTERN COULD DEFEAT.
BY THE SAME TOKEN, I DID THE WORK HERE--WHILE YOU STOOD BY, ALMOST HELPLESS!
GENTLEMEN, SOMETHING IS SERIOUSLY WRONG--!
I SUGGEST WE JOIN THE OTHERS--HELP THEM WITH THEIR DISASTERS--AND SEE IF WE CAN LEARN THE REASON FOR ALL THAT'S OCCURRED.
MAYBE YOU'VE GOT SOMETHING THERE, POWER GIRL. WHAT YOU'RE SAYING IS ODD--
IT'S MORE THAN ODD, FLASH. IT'S CRAZY! US--NEEDING HELP FROM A BUNCH OF KIDS?
17

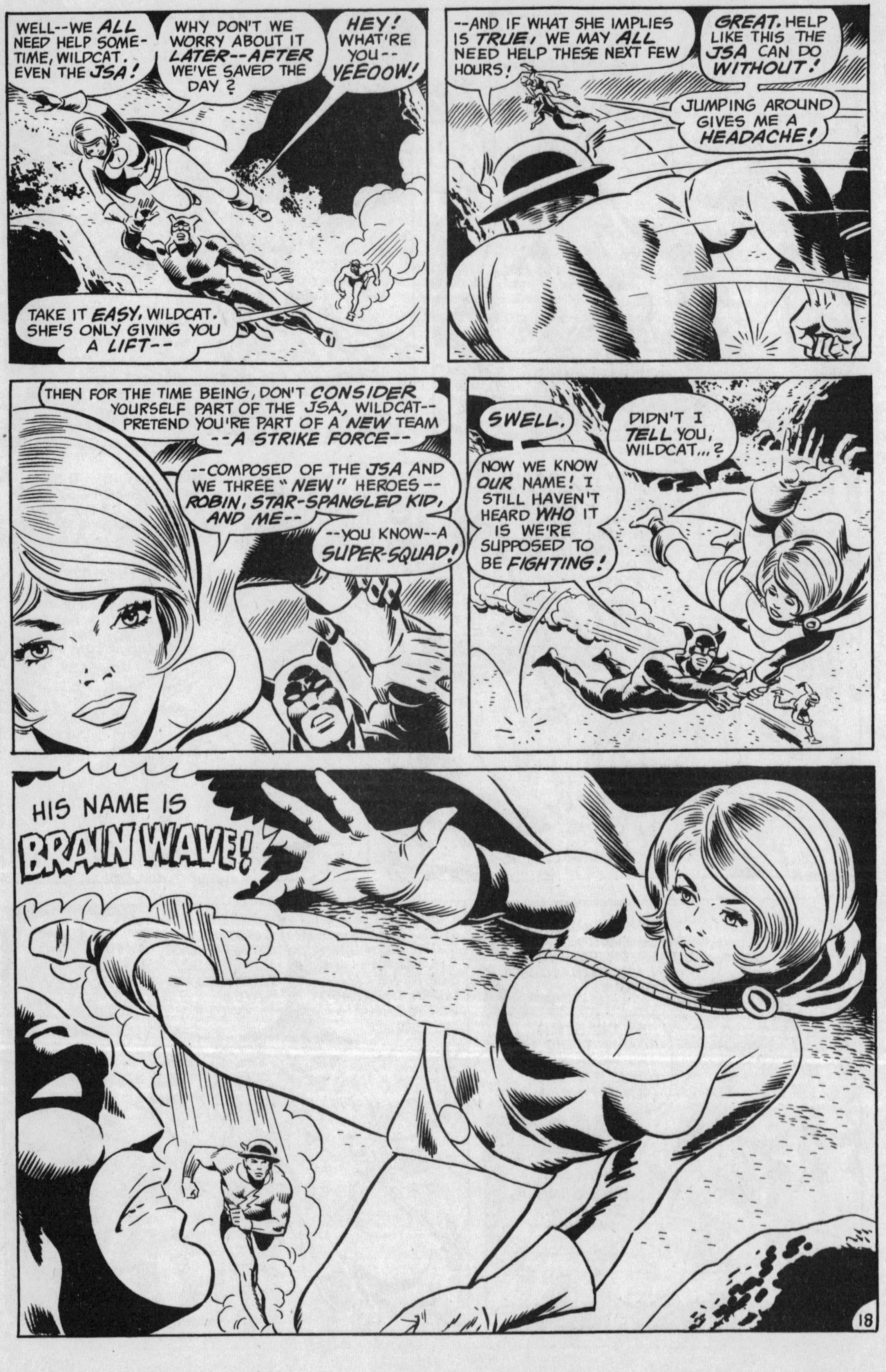
WELL--WE ALL NEED HELP SOME-TIME, WILDCAT. EVEN THE JSA!
WHY DON'T WE WORRY ABOUT IT LATER--AFTER WE'VE SAVED THE DAY?
HEY! WHAT'RE YOU--YEEOOW!
TAKE IT EASY, WILDCAT. SHE'S ONLY GIVING YOU A LIFT--
--AND IF WHAT SHE IMPLIES IS TRUE, WE MAY ALL NEED HELP THESE NEXT FEW HOURS!
GREAT. HELP LIKE THIS THE JSA CAN DO WITHOUT!
JUMPING AROUND GIVES ME A HEADACHE!
THEN FOR THE TIME BEING, DON'T CONSIDER YOURSELF PART OF THE JSA, WILDCAT--PRETEND YOU'RE PART OF A NEW TEAM --A STRIKE FORCE--
--COMPOSED OF THE JSA AND WE THREE "NEW" HEROES--ROBIN, STAR-SPANGLED KID, AND ME--
--YOU KNOW--A SUPER-SQUAD!
SWELL.
NOW WE KNOW OUR NAME! I STILL HAVEN'T HEARD WHO IT IS WE'RE SUPPOSED TO BE FIGHTING!
DIDN'T I TELL YOU, WILDCAT...?
HIS NAME IS BRAIN WAVE!
18

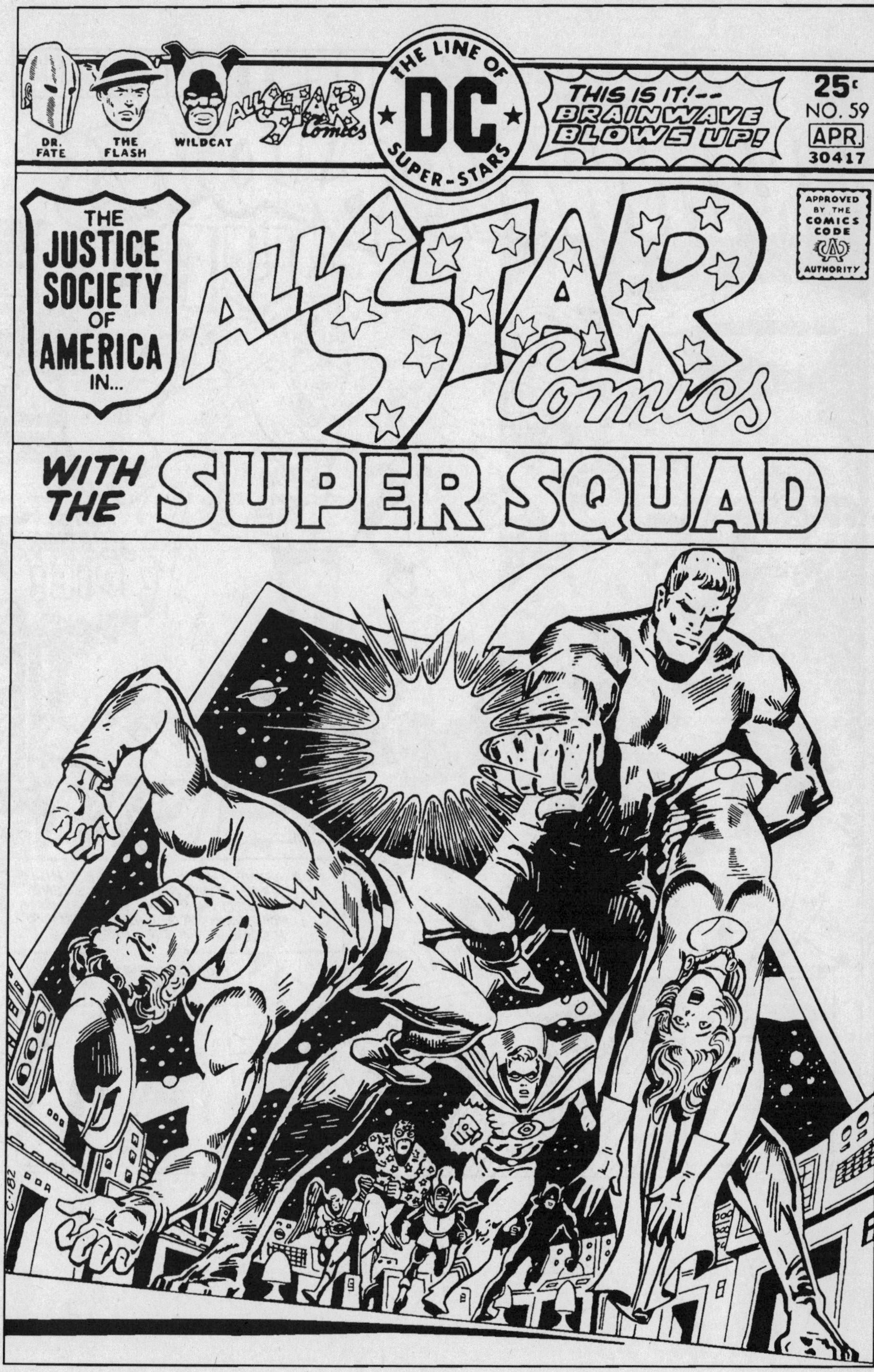
DR. FATE
THE FLASH
WILDCAT
ALL STAR Comics
THE LINE OF DC SUPER-STARS
THIS IS IT!-- BRAINWAVE BLOWS UP!
25¢
NO. 59
APR.
30417
APPROVED BY THE COMICS CODE AUTHORITY
THE JUSTICE SOCIETY OF AMERICA IN...
ALL STAR Comics
WITH THE SUPER SQUAD

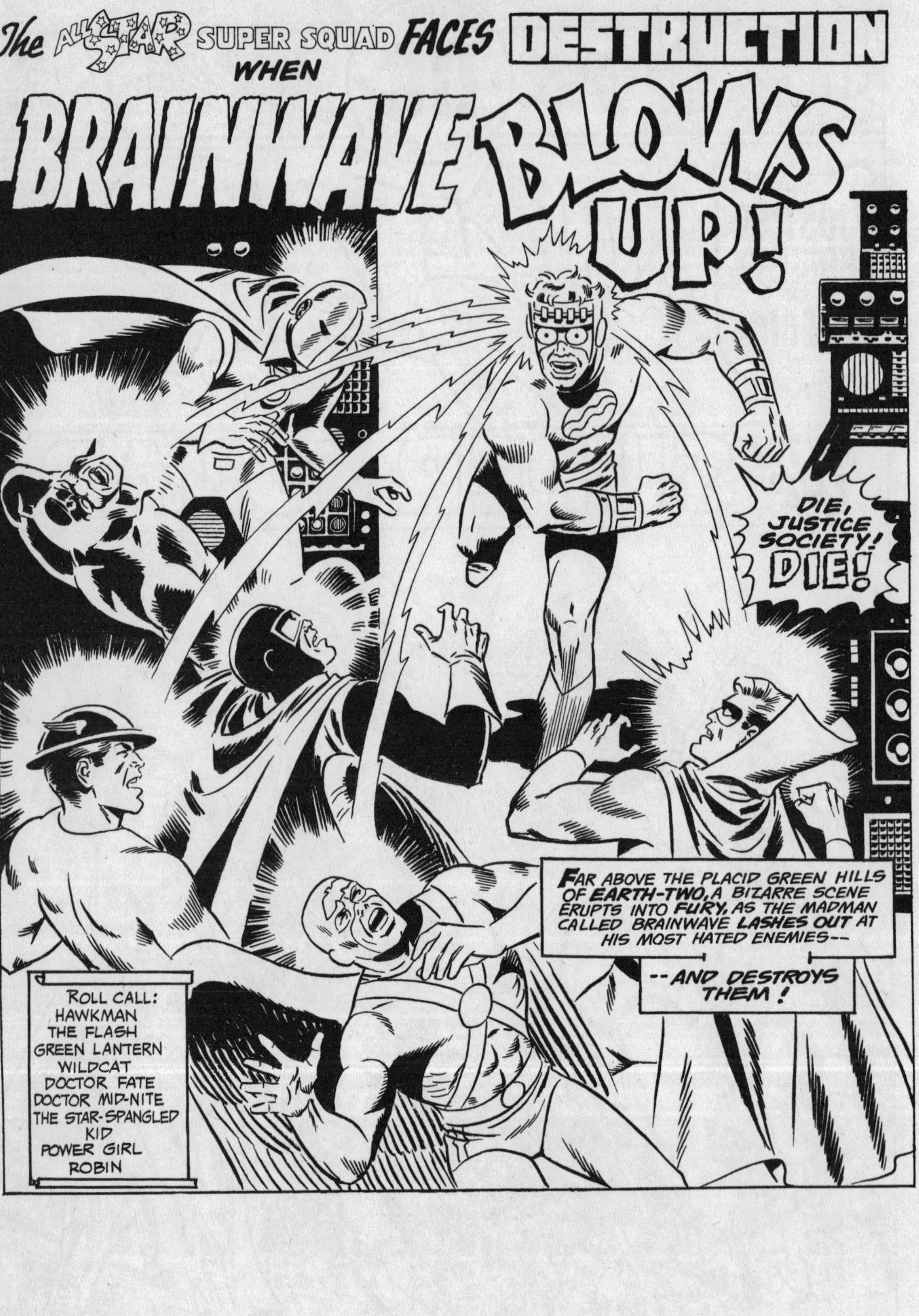

The ALL-STAR SUPER SQUAD FACES DESTRUCTION WHEN
BRAINWAVE BLOWS UP!
DIE, JUSTICE SOCIETY! DIE!
FAR ABOVE THE PLACID GREEN HILLS OF EARTH-TWO, A BIZARRE SCENE ERUPTS INTO FURY, AS THE MADMAN CALLED BRAINWAVE LASHES OUT AT HIS MOST HATED ENEMIES--
--AND DESTROYS THEM!
ROLL CALL:
HAWKMAN
THE FLASH
GREEN LANTERN
WILDCAT
DOCTOR FATE
DOCTOR MID-NITE
THE STAR-SPANGLED KID
POWER GIRL
ROBIN

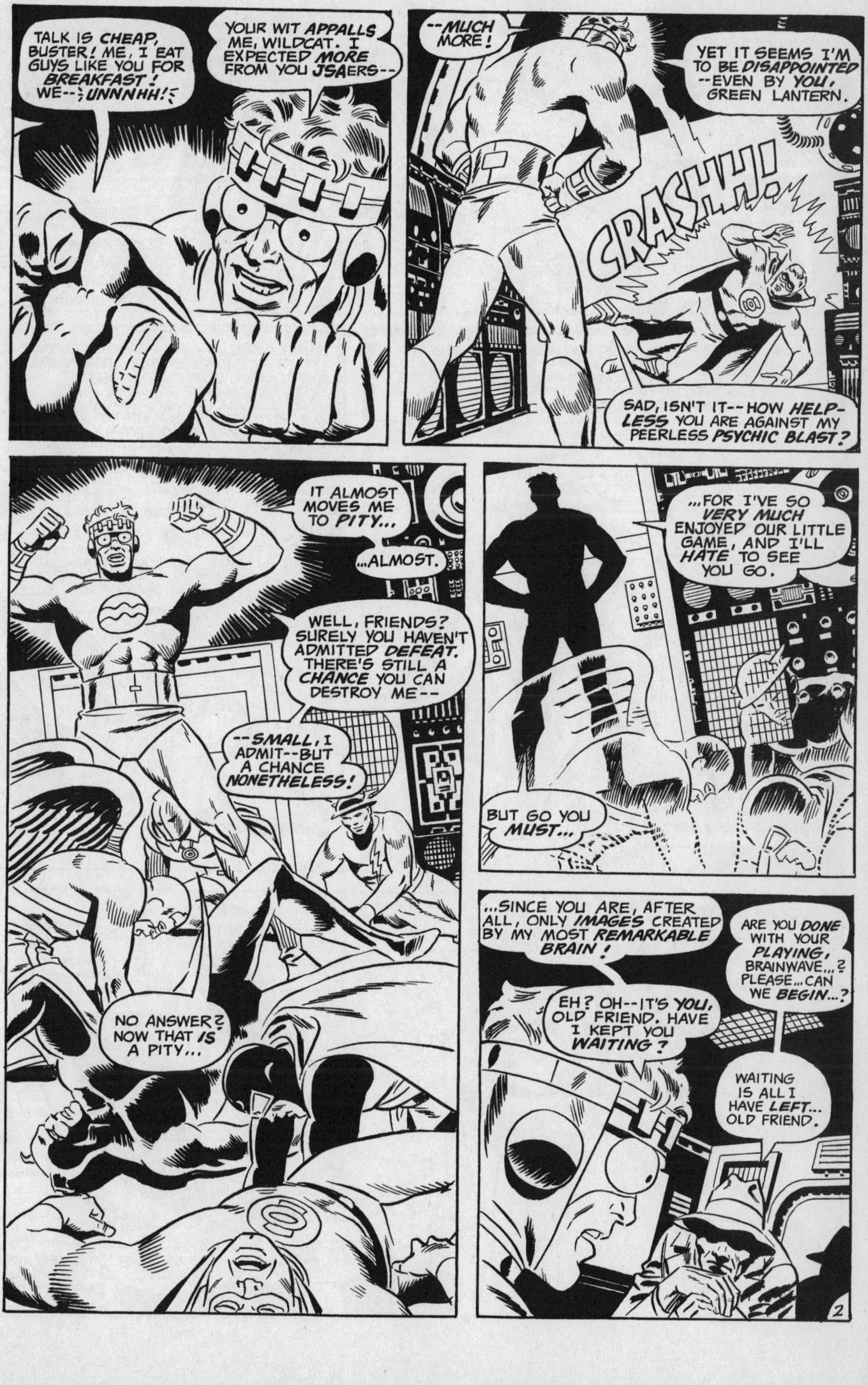
TALK IS CHEAP, BUSTER! ME, I EAT GUYS LIKE YOU FOR BREAKFAST! WE--; UNNNHH!;
YOUR WIT APPALLS ME, WILDCAT. I EXPECTED MORE FROM YOU JSAERS--
--MUCH MORE!
YET IT SEEMS I'M TO BE DISAPPOINTED --EVEN BY YOU, GREEN LANTERN.
CRASHH!
SAD, ISN'T IT--HOW HELP-LESS YOU ARE AGAINST MY PEERLESS PSYCHIC BLAST?
IT ALMOST MOVES ME TO PITY...
...ALMOST.
WELL, FRIENDS? SURELY YOU HAVEN'T ADMITTED DEFEAT. THERE'S STILL A CHANCE YOU CAN DESTROY ME--
--SMALL, I ADMIT--BUT A CHANCE NONETHELESS!
NO ANSWER? NOW THAT IS A PITY...
...FOR I'VE SO VERY MUCH ENJOYED OUR LITTLE GAME, AND I'LL HATE TO SEE YOU GO.
BUT GO YOU MUST...
...SINCE YOU ARE, AFTER ALL, ONLY IMAGES CREATED BY MY MOST REMARKABLE BRAIN!
ARE YOU DONE WITH YOUR PLAYING, BRAINWAVE...? PLEASE...CAN WE BEGIN...?
EH? OH--IT'S YOU, OLD FRIEND. HAVE I KEPT YOU WAITING?
WAITING IS ALL I HAVE LEFT... OLD FRIEND.
2

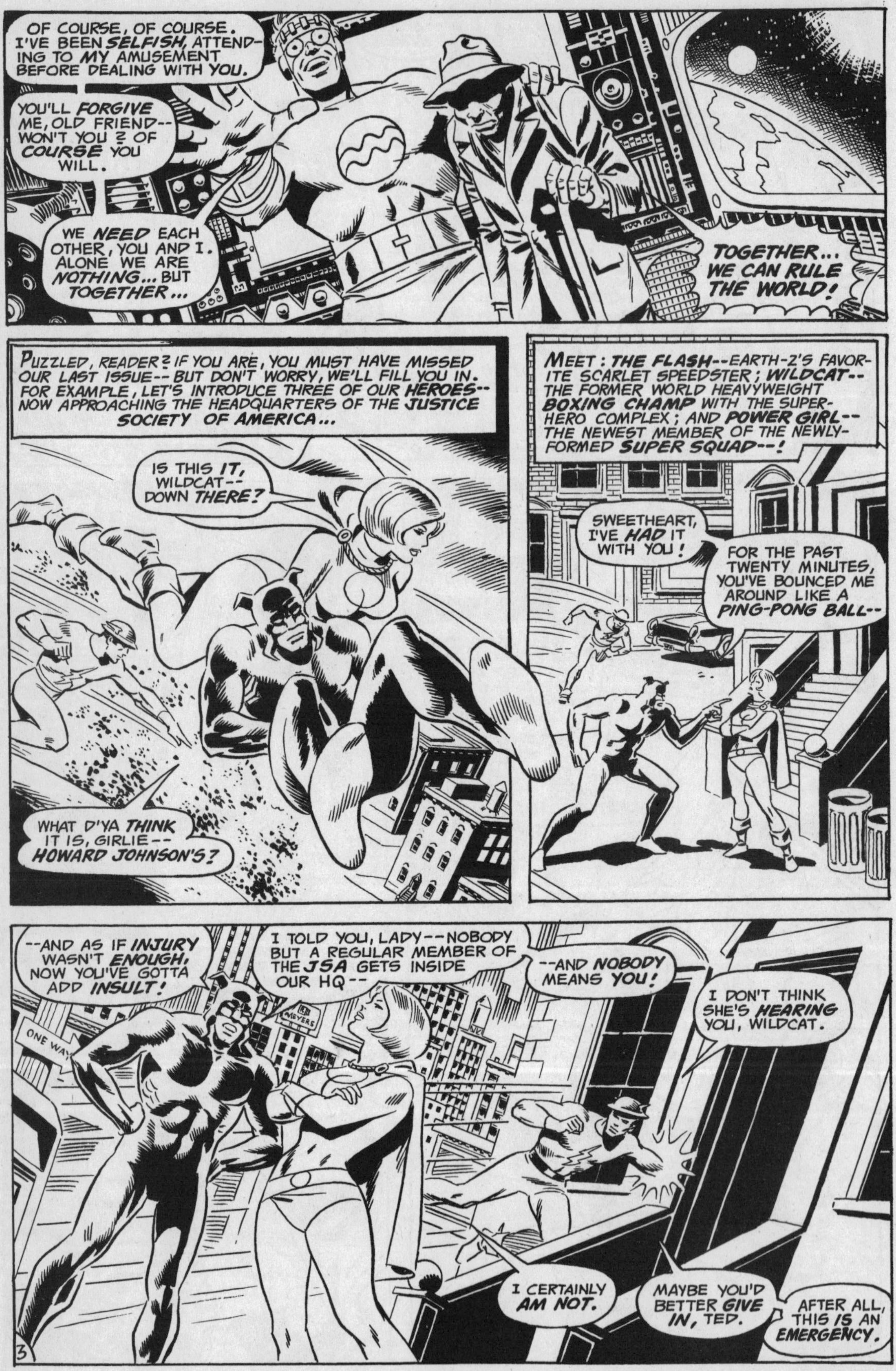
OF COURSE, OF COURSE. I'VE BEEN SELFISH, ATTENDING TO MY AMUSEMENT BEFORE DEALING WITH YOU.
YOU'LL FORGIVE ME, OLD FRIEND-- WON'T YOU ? OF COURSE YOU WILL.
WE NEED EACH OTHER, YOU AND I. ALONE WE ARE NOTHING... BUT TOGETHER...
TOGETHER... WE CAN RULE THE WORLD!
PUZZLED, READER? IF YOU ARE, YOU MUST HAVE MISSED OUR LAST ISSUE-- BUT DON'T WORRY, WE'LL FILL YOU IN. FOR EXAMPLE, LET'S INTRODUCE THREE OF OUR HEROES-- NOW APPROACHING THE HEADQUARTERS OF THE JUSTICE SOCIETY OF AMERICA...
IS THIS IT, WILDCAT-- DOWN THERE?
WHAT D'YA THINK IT IS, GIRLIE-- HOWARD JOHNSON'S?
MEET: THE FLASH--EARTH-2'S FAVORITE SCARLET SPEEDSTER; WILDCAT-- THE FORMER WORLD HEAVYWEIGHT BOXING CHAMP WITH THE SUPER-HERO COMPLEX; AND POWER GIRL-- THE NEWEST MEMBER OF THE NEWLY-FORMED SUPER SQUAD--!
SWEETHEART, I'VE HAD IT WITH YOU!
FOR THE PAST TWENTY MINUTES, YOU'VE BOUNCED ME AROUND LIKE A PING-PONG BALL--
--AND AS IF INJURY WASN'T ENOUGH, NOW YOU'VE GOTTA ADD INSULT!
I TOLD YOU, LADY--NOBODY BUT A REGULAR MEMBER OF THE JSA GETS INSIDE OUR HQ--
--AND NOBODY MEANS YOU!
I DON'T THINK SHE'S HEARING YOU, WILDCAT.
ONE WAY
MEYERS
I CERTAINLY AM NOT.
MAYBE YOU'D BETTER GIVE IN, TED.
AFTER ALL, THIS IS AN EMERGENCY.
3

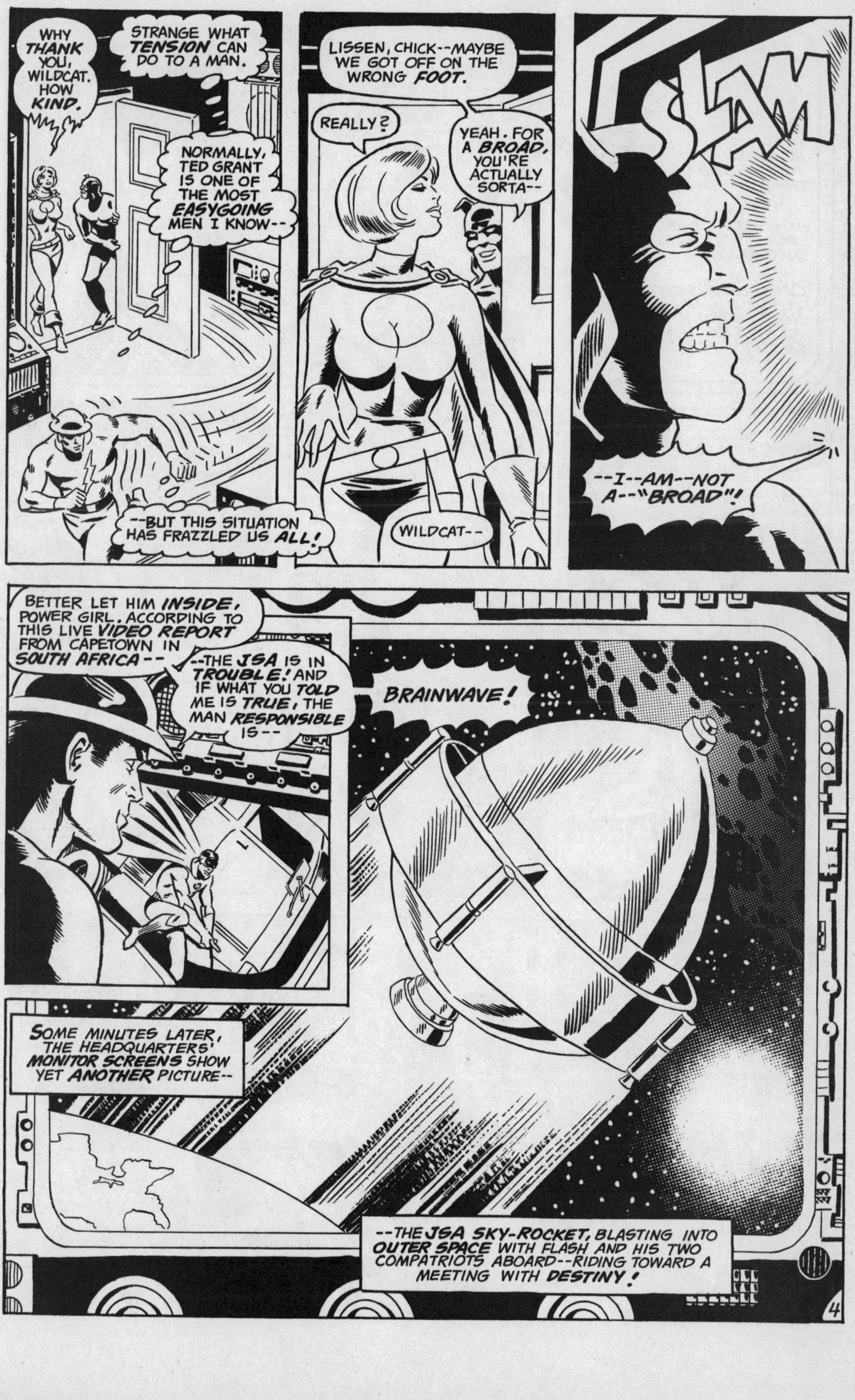
WHY THANK YOU, WILDCAT. HOW KIND.
STRANGE WHAT TENSION CAN DO TO A MAN.
NORMALLY, TED GRANT IS ONE OF THE MOST EASYGOING MEN I KNOW--
--BUT THIS SITUATION HAS FRAZZLED US ALL!
LISSEN, CHICK--MAYBE WE GOT OFF ON THE WRONG FOOT.
REALLY?
YEAH. FOR A BROAD, YOU'RE ACTUALLY SORTA--
WILDCAT--
SLAM
--I--AM--NOT A--"BROAD"!
BETTER LET HIM INSIDE, POWER GIRL. ACCORDING TO THIS LIVE VIDEO REPORT FROM CAPETOWN IN SOUTH AFRICA--
--THE JSA IS IN TROUBLE! AND IF WHAT YOU TOLD ME IS TRUE, THE MAN RESPONSIBLE IS--
BRAINWAVE!
SOME MINUTES LATER, THE HEADQUARTERS' MONITOR SCREENS SHOW YET ANOTHER PICTURE--
--THE JSA SKY-ROCKET, BLASTING INTO OUTER SPACE WITH FLASH AND HIS TWO COMPATRIOTS ABOARD--RIDING TOWARD A MEETING WITH DESTINY!
4

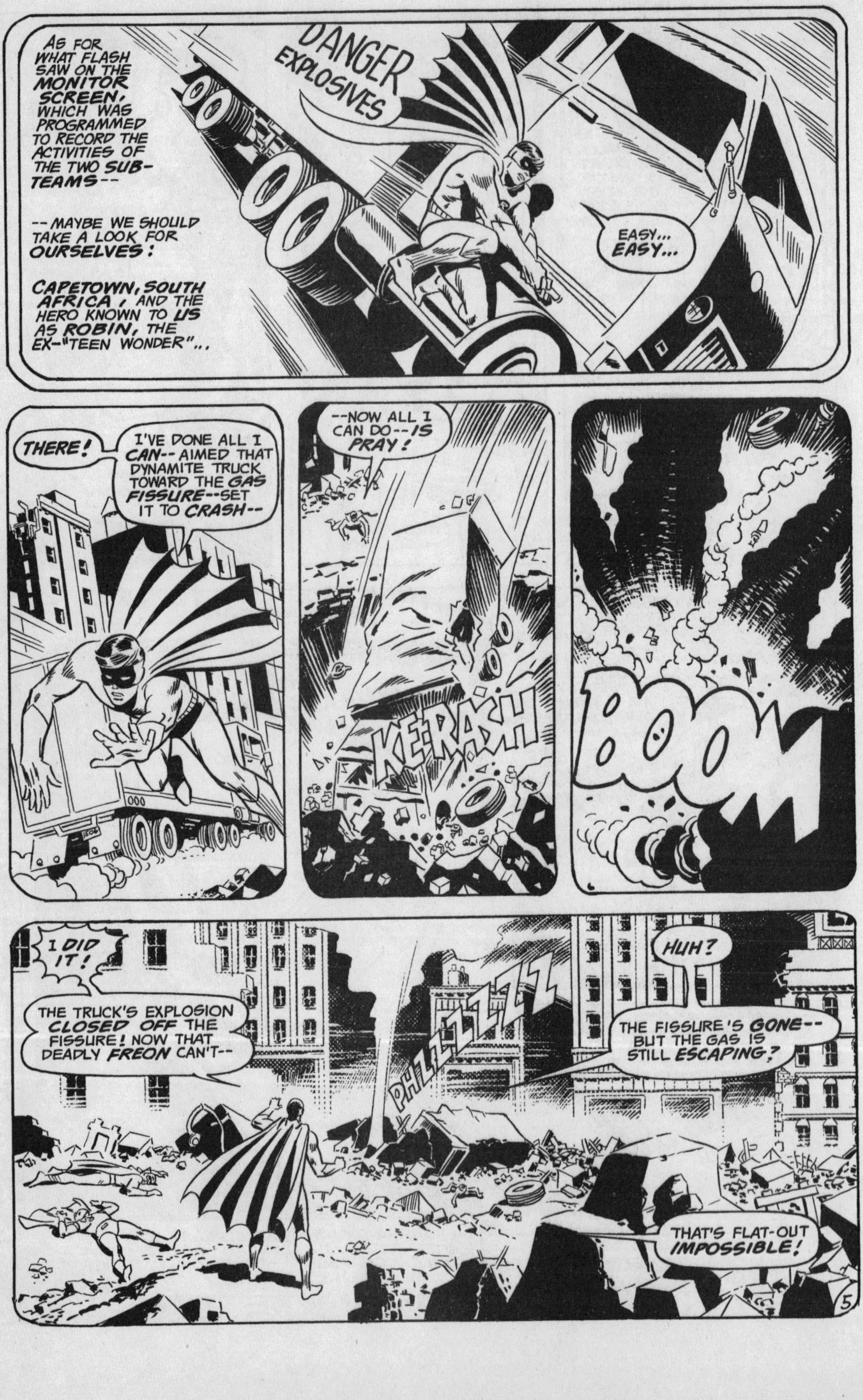
AS FOR WHAT FLASH SAW ON THE MONITOR SCREEN, WHICH WAS PROGRAMMED TO RECORD THE ACTIVITIES OF THE TWO SUB-TEAMS--
-- MAYBE WE SHOULD TAKE A LOOK FOR OURSELVES:
CAPETOWN, SOUTH AFRICA, AND THE HERO KNOWN TO US AS ROBIN, THE EX-"TEEN WONDER"...
DANGER EXPLOSIVES
EASY... EASY...
THERE!
I'VE DONE ALL I CAN-- AIMED THAT DYNAMITE TRUCK TOWARD THE GAS FISSURE--SET IT TO CRASH--
--NOW ALL I CAN DO--IS PRAY!
KE-RASH
BOOM
I DID IT!
THE TRUCK'S EXPLOSION CLOSED OFF THE FISSURE! NOW THAT DEADLY FREON CAN'T--
PHZZZZZZZ
HUH?
THE FISSURE'S GONE-- BUT THE GAS IS STILL ESCAPING?
THAT'S FLAT-OUT IMPOSSIBLE!
5

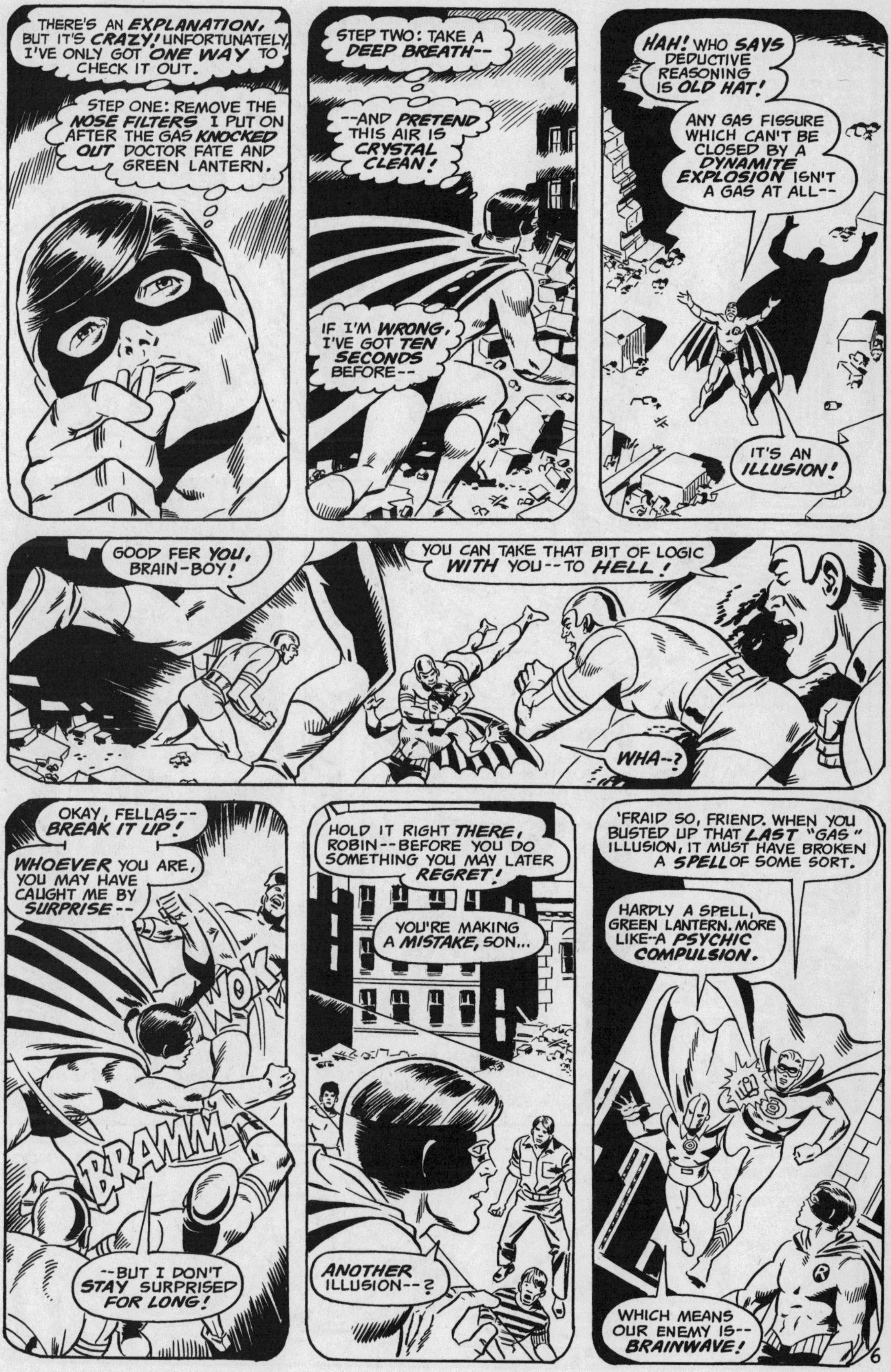
THERE'S AN EXPLANATION, BUT IT'S CRAZY! UNFORTUNATELY, I'VE ONLY GOT ONE WAY TO CHECK IT OUT.
STEP ONE: REMOVE THE NOSE FILTERS I PUT ON AFTER THE GAS KNOCKED OUT DOCTOR FATE AND GREEN LANTERN.
STEP TWO: TAKE A DEEP BREATH--
--AND PRETEND THIS AIR IS CRYSTAL CLEAN!
IF I'M WRONG, I'VE GOT TEN SECONDS BEFORE--
HAH! WHO SAYS DEDUCTIVE REASONING IS OLD HAT!
ANY GAS FISSURE WHICH CAN'T BE CLOSED BY A DYNAMITE EXPLOSION ISN'T A GAS AT ALL--
IT'S AN ILLUSION!
GOOD FER YOU, BRAIN-BOY!
YOU CAN TAKE THAT BIT OF LOGIC WITH YOU--TO HELL!
WHA--?
OKAY, FELLAS-- BREAK IT UP!
WHOEVER YOU ARE, YOU MAY HAVE CAUGHT ME BY SURPRISE--
WOK
BRAMM
--BUT I DON'T STAY SURPRISED FOR LONG!
HOLD IT RIGHT THERE, ROBIN--BEFORE YOU DO SOMETHING YOU MAY LATER REGRET!
YOU'RE MAKING A MISTAKE, SON...
ANOTHER ILLUSION--?
'FRAID SO, FRIEND. WHEN YOU BUSTED UP THAT LAST "GAS" ILLUSION, IT MUST HAVE BROKEN A SPELL OF SOME SORT.
HARDLY A SPELL, GREEN LANTERN. MORE LIKE--A PSYCHIC COMPULSION.
WHICH MEANS OUR ENEMY IS-- BRAINWAVE!
6

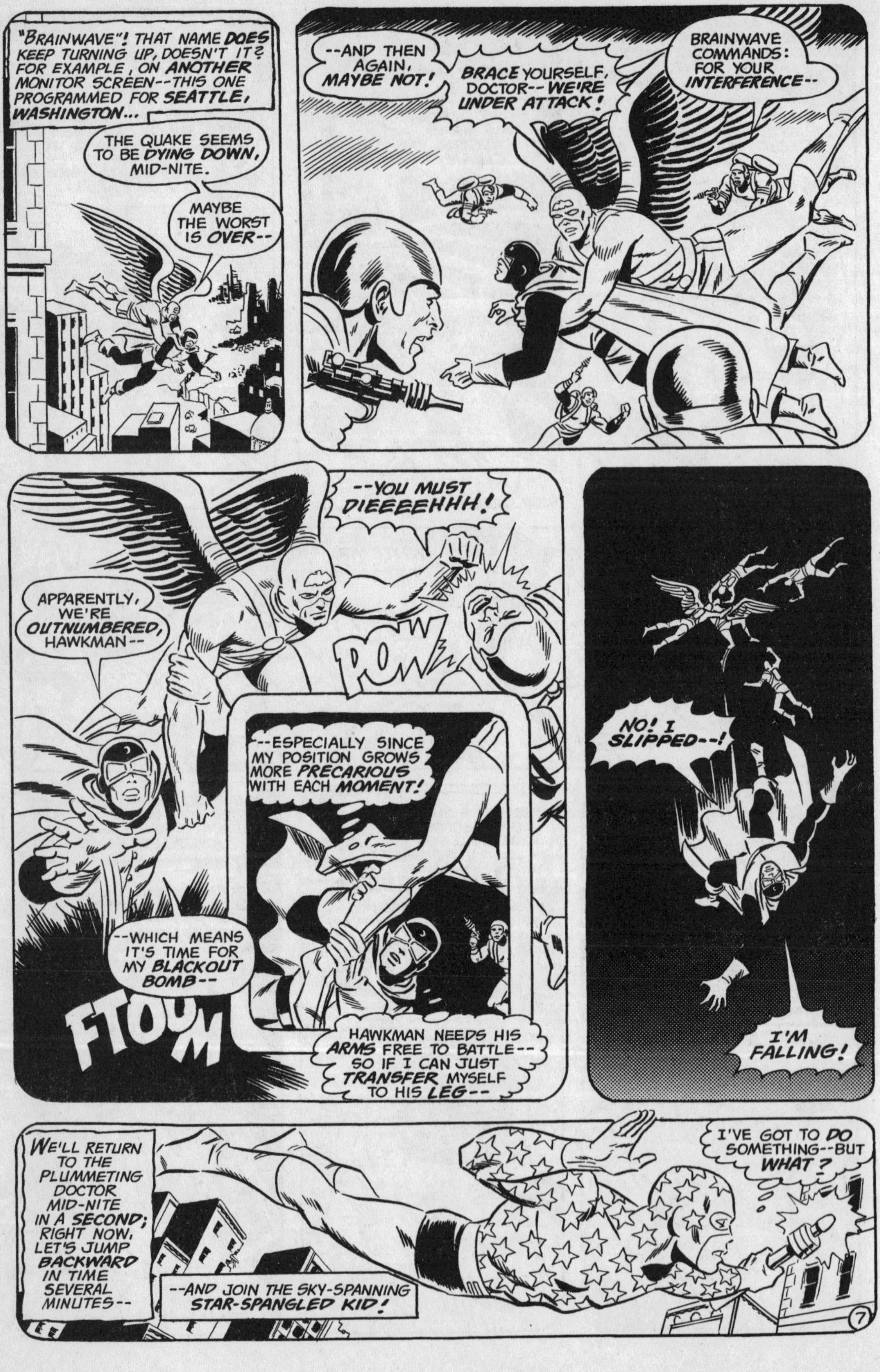
"BRAINWAVE"! THAT NAME DOES KEEP TURNING UP, DOESN'T IT? FOR EXAMPLE, ON ANOTHER MONITOR SCREEN--THIS ONE PROGRAMMED FOR SEATTLE, WASHINGTON...
THE QUAKE SEEMS TO BE DYING DOWN, MID-NITE.
MAYBE THE WORST IS OVER--
--AND THEN AGAIN, MAYBE NOT!
BRACE YOURSELF, DOCTOR--WE'RE UNDER ATTACK!
BRAINWAVE COMMANDS: FOR YOUR INTERFERENCE--
--YOU MUST DIEEEEEHHH!
POW
APPARENTLY, WE'RE OUTNUMBERED, HAWKMAN--
--ESPECIALLY SINCE MY POSITION GROWS MORE PRECARIOUS WITH EACH MOMENT!
--WHICH MEANS IT'S TIME FOR MY BLACKOUT BOMB--
FTOOM
HAWKMAN NEEDS HIS ARMS FREE TO BATTLE--SO IF I CAN JUST TRANSFER MYSELF TO HIS LEG--
NO! I SLIPPED--!
I'M FALLING!
WE'LL RETURN TO THE PLUMMETING DOCTOR MID-NITE IN A SECOND; RIGHT NOW, LET'S JUMP BACKWARD IN TIME SEVERAL MINUTES--
--AND JOIN THE SKY-SPANNING STAR-SPANGLED KID!
I'VE GOT TO DO SOMETHING--BUT WHAT?
7

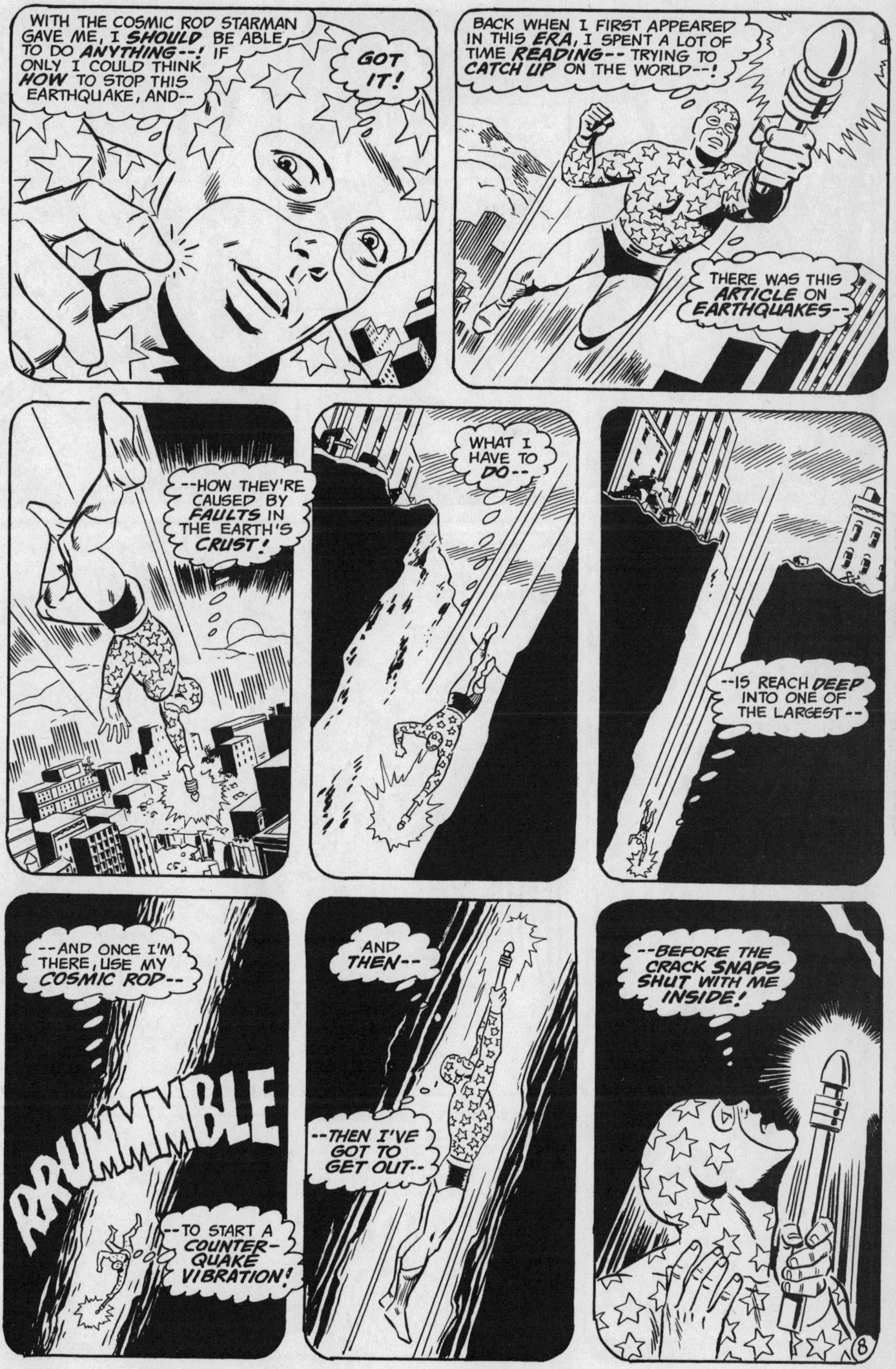
WITH THE COSMIC ROD STARMAN GAVE ME, I SHOULD BE ABLE TO DO ANYTHING--! IF ONLY I COULD THINK HOW TO STOP THIS EARTHQUAKE, AND--
GOT IT!
BACK WHEN I FIRST APPEARED IN THIS ERA, I SPENT A LOT OF TIME READING-- TRYING TO CATCH UP ON THE WORLD--!
THERE WAS THIS ARTICLE ON EARTHQUAKES--
--HOW THEY'RE CAUSED BY FAULTS IN THE EARTH'S CRUST!
WHAT I HAVE TO DO--
--IS REACH DEEP INTO ONE OF THE LARGEST--
--AND ONCE I'M THERE, USE MY COSMIC ROD--
RRUMMMBLE
--TO START A COUNTER-QUAKE VIBRATION!
AND THEN--
--THEN I'VE GOT TO GET OUT--
--BEFORE THE CRACK SNAPS SHUT WITH ME INSIDE!
8

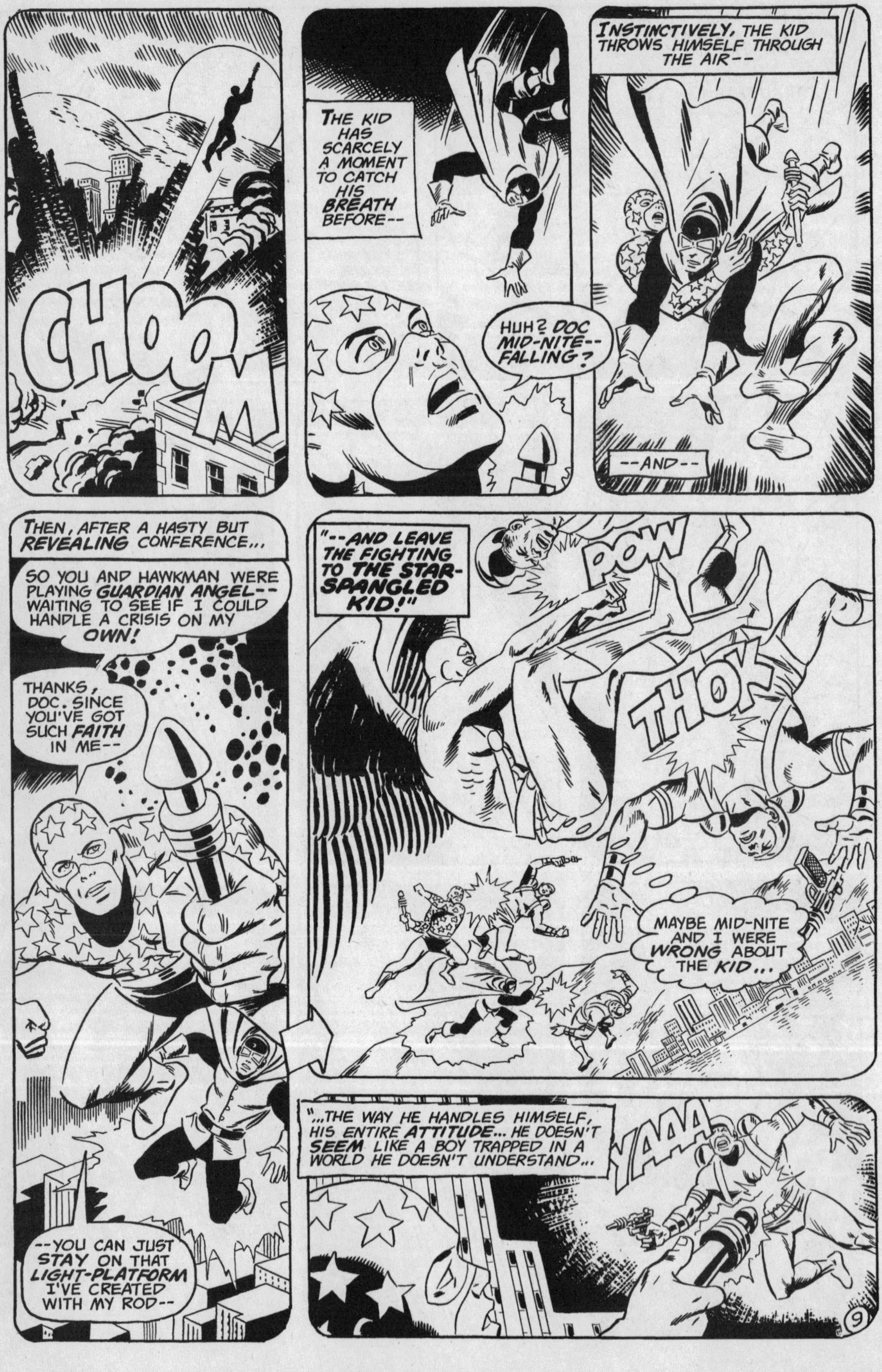
CHOOM
THE KID HAS SCARCELY A MOMENT TO CATCH HIS BREATH BEFORE--
HUH? DOC MID-NITE--FALLING?
INSTINCTIVELY, THE KID THROWS HIMSELF THROUGH THE AIR--
--AND--
THEN, AFTER A HASTY BUT REVEALING CONFERENCE...
SO YOU AND HAWKMAN WERE PLAYING GUARDIAN ANGEL--WAITING TO SEE IF I COULD HANDLE A CRISIS ON MY OWN!
THANKS, DOC. SINCE YOU'VE GOT SUCH FAITH IN ME--
--YOU CAN JUST STAY ON THAT LIGHT-PLATFORM I'VE CREATED WITH MY ROD--
"--AND LEAVE THE FIGHTING TO THE STAR-SPANGLED KID!"
POW
THOK
MAYBE MID-NITE AND I WERE WRONG ABOUT THE KID...
"...THE WAY HE HANDLES HIMSELF, HIS ENTIRE ATTITUDE... HE DOESN'T SEEM LIKE A BOY TRAPPED IN A WORLD HE DOESN'T UNDERSTAND..."
YAAA
9

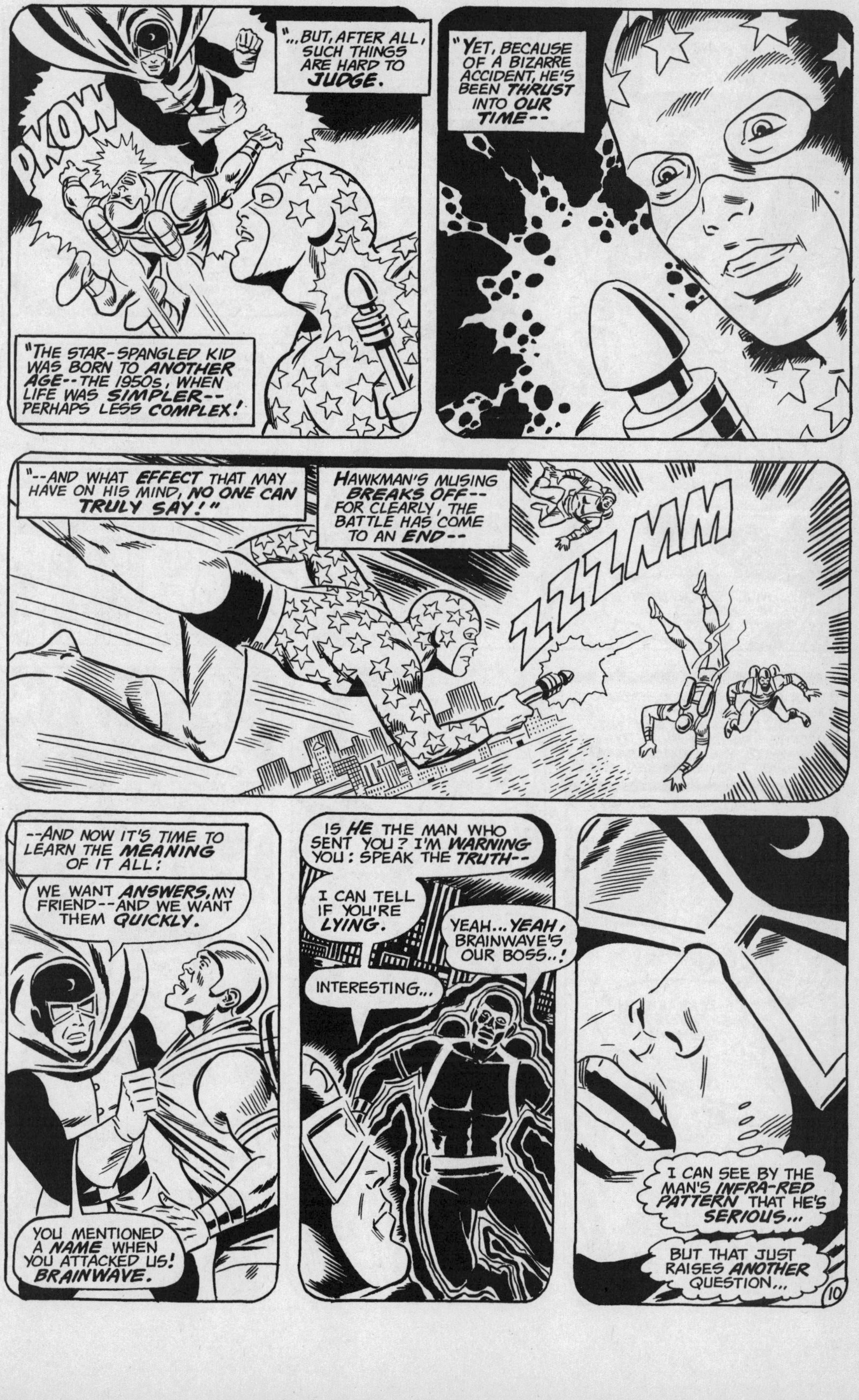
PKOW
"...BUT, AFTER ALL, SUCH THINGS ARE HARD TO JUDGE.
"THE STAR-SPANGLED KID WAS BORN TO ANOTHER AGE--THE 1950s, WHEN LIFE WAS SIMPLER--PERHAPS LESS COMPLEX!
"YET, BECAUSE OF A BIZARRE ACCIDENT, HE'S BEEN THRUST INTO OUR TIME--
"--AND WHAT EFFECT THAT MAY HAVE ON HIS MIND, NO ONE CAN TRULY SAY!"
HAWKMAN'S MUSING BREAKS OFF--FOR CLEARLY, THE BATTLE HAS COME TO AN END--
ZZZMM
--AND NOW IT'S TIME TO LEARN THE MEANING OF IT ALL:
WE WANT ANSWERS, MY FRIEND--AND WE WANT THEM QUICKLY.
YOU MENTIONED A NAME WHEN YOU ATTACKED US! BRAINWAVE.
IS HE THE MAN WHO SENT YOU? I'M WARNING YOU: SPEAK THE TRUTH--
I CAN TELL IF YOU'RE LYING.
YEAH...YEAH, BRAINWAVE'S OUR BOSS..!
INTERESTING...
I CAN SEE BY THE MAN'S INFRA-RED PATTERN THAT HE'S SERIOUS...
BUT THAT JUST RAISES ANOTHER QUESTION...
10

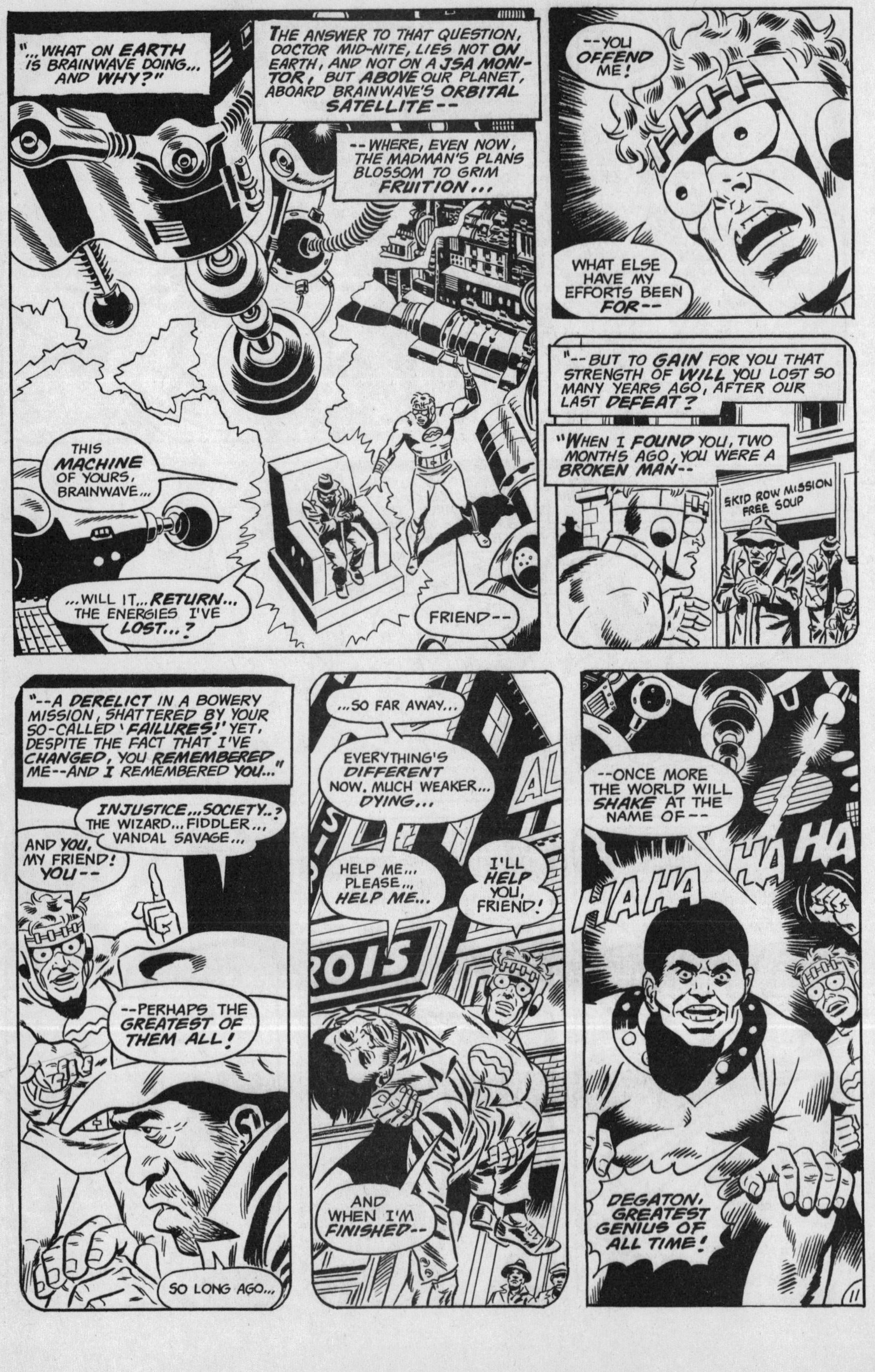
"...WHAT ON EARTH IS BRAINWAVE DOING... AND WHY?"
THE ANSWER TO THAT QUESTION, DOCTOR MID-NITE, LIES NOT ON EARTH, AND NOT ON A JSA MONITOR, BUT ABOVE OUR PLANET, ABOARD BRAINWAVE'S ORBITAL SATELLITE --
-- WHERE, EVEN NOW, THE MADMAN'S PLANS BLOSSOM TO GRIM FRUITION...
THIS MACHINE OF YOURS, BRAINWAVE...
...WILL IT... RETURN... THE ENERGIES I'VE LOST...?
FRIEND--
--YOU OFFEND ME!
WHAT ELSE HAVE MY EFFORTS BEEN FOR--
"--BUT TO GAIN FOR YOU THAT STRENGTH OF WILL YOU LOST SO MANY YEARS AGO, AFTER OUR LAST DEFEAT?
"WHEN I FOUND YOU, TWO MONTHS AGO, YOU WERE A BROKEN MAN--
SKID ROW MISSION
FREE SOUP
"--A DERELICT IN A BOWERY MISSION, SHATTERED BY YOUR SO-CALLED 'FAILURES!' YET, DESPITE THE FACT THAT I'VE CHANGED, YOU REMEMBERED ME--AND I REMEMBERED YOU..."
INJUSTICE... SOCIETY..? THE WIZARD... FIDDLER..., VANDAL SAVAGE...
AND YOU, MY FRIEND! YOU--
--PERHAPS THE GREATEST OF THEM ALL!
SO LONG AGO...
...SO FAR AWAY...
EVERYTHING'S DIFFERENT NOW. MUCH WEAKER... DYING...
HELP ME... PLEASE..., HELP ME...
I'LL HELP YOU, FRIEND!
AND WHEN I'M FINISHED--
--ONCE MORE THE WORLD WILL SHAKE AT THE NAME OF--
HA HA HA HA
DEGATON, GREATEST GENIUS OF ALL TIME!
11

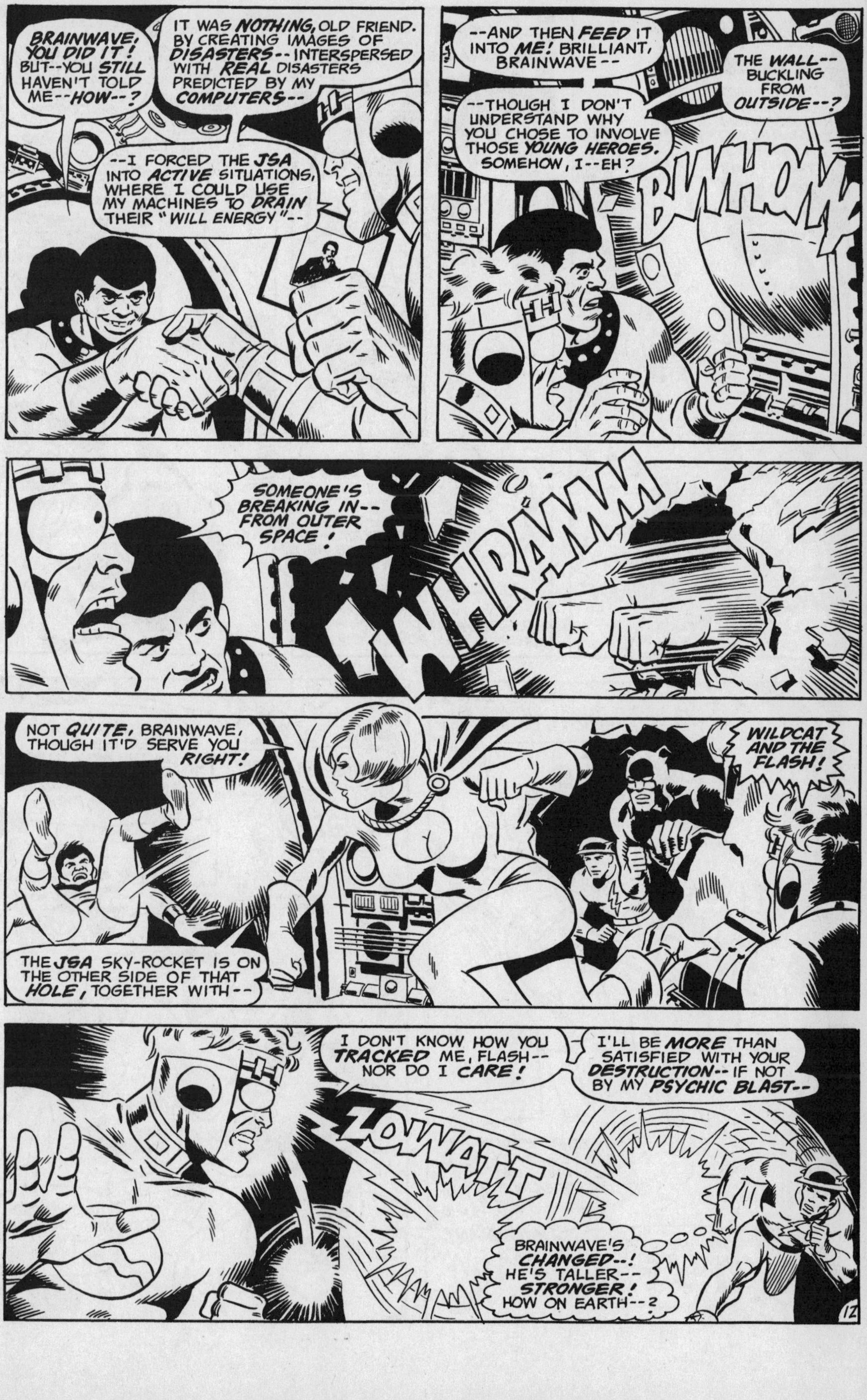
BRAINWAVE, YOU DID IT! BUT--YOU STILL HAVEN'T TOLD ME--HOW--?
IT WAS NOTHING, OLD FRIEND. BY CREATING IMAGES OF DISASTERS--INTERSPERSED WITH REAL DISASTERS PREDICTED BY MY COMPUTERS--
--I FORCED THE JSA INTO ACTIVE SITUATIONS, WHERE I COULD USE MY MACHINES TO DRAIN THEIR "WILL ENERGY"--
--AND THEN FEED IT INTO ME! BRILLIANT, BRAINWAVE--
--THOUGH I DON'T UNDERSTAND WHY YOU CHOSE TO INVOLVE THOSE YOUNG HEROES. SOMEHOW, I--EH?
THE WALL--BUCKLING FROM OUTSIDE--?
SOMEONE'S BREAKING IN--FROM OUTER SPACE!
WHRAMM
NOT QUITE, BRAINWAVE, THOUGH IT'D SERVE YOU RIGHT!
WILDCAT AND THE FLASH!
THE JSA SKY-ROCKET IS ON THE OTHER SIDE OF THAT HOLE, TOGETHER WITH--
I DON'T KNOW HOW YOU TRACKED ME, FLASH--NOR DO I CARE!
I'LL BE MORE THAN SATISFIED WITH YOUR DESTRUCTION--IF NOT BY MY PSYCHIC BLAST--
ZOWATT
BRAINWAVE'S CHANGED--! HE'S TALLER--STRONGER! HOW ON EARTH--?

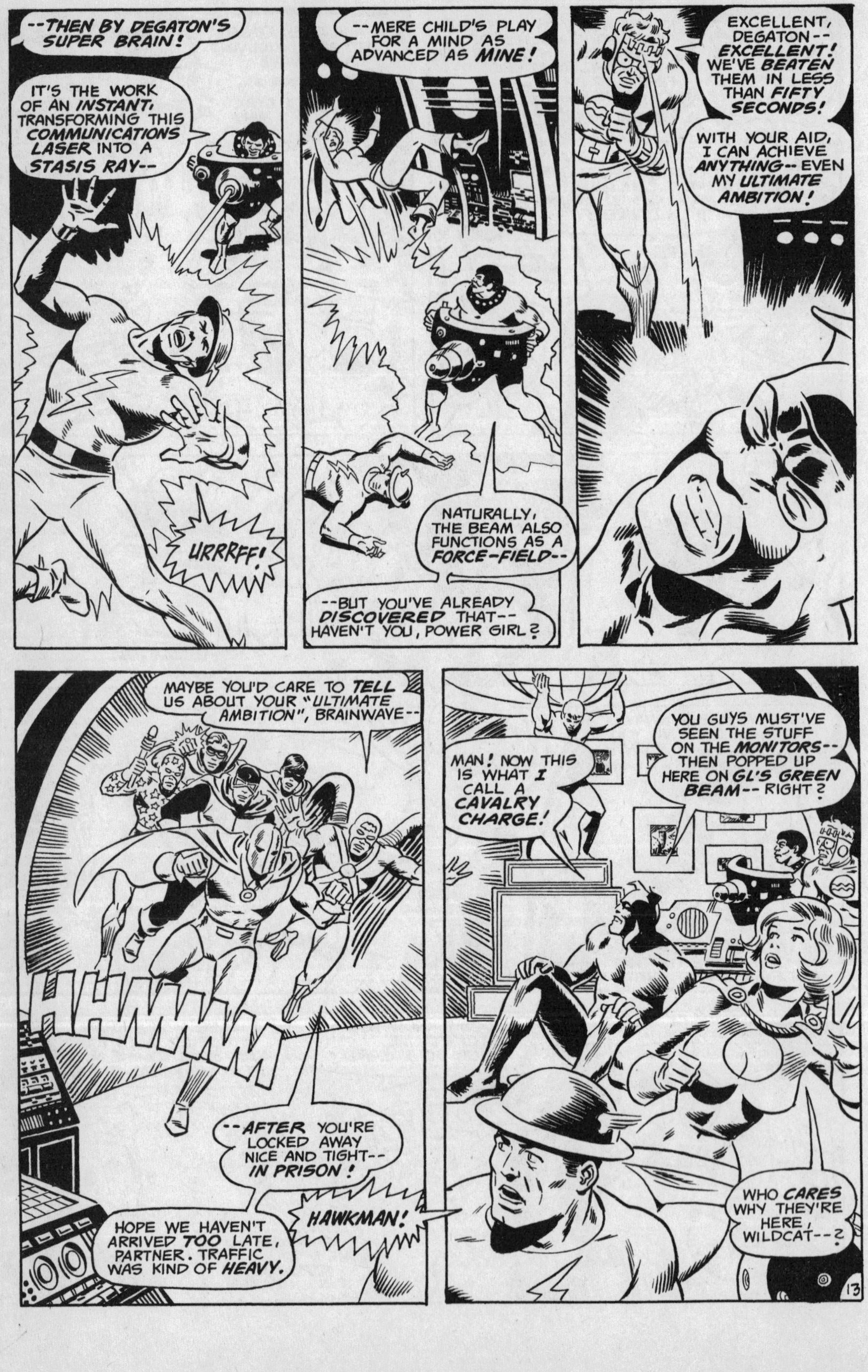
--THEN BY DEGATON'S SUPER BRAIN!
IT'S THE WORK OF AN INSTANT, TRANSFORMING THIS COMMUNICATIONS LASER INTO A STASIS RAY--
URRRFF!
--MERE CHILD'S PLAY FOR A MIND AS ADVANCED AS MINE!
NATURALLY, THE BEAM ALSO FUNCTIONS AS A FORCE-FIELD--
--BUT YOU'VE ALREADY DISCOVERED THAT--HAVEN'T YOU, POWER GIRL?
EXCELLENT, DEGATON--EXCELLENT! WE'VE BEATEN THEM IN LESS THAN FIFTY SECONDS!
WITH YOUR AID, I CAN ACHIEVE ANYTHING--EVEN MY ULTIMATE AMBITION!
MAYBE YOU'D CARE TO TELL US ABOUT YOUR "ULTIMATE AMBITION", BRAINWAVE--
HHMMM
--AFTER YOU'RE LOCKED AWAY NICE AND TIGHT--IN PRISON!
HOPE WE HAVEN'T ARRIVED TOO LATE, PARTNER. TRAFFIC WAS KIND OF HEAVY.
HAWKMAN!
MAN! NOW THIS IS WHAT I CALL A CAVALRY CHARGE!
YOU GUYS MUST'VE SEEN THE STUFF ON THE MONITORS--THEN POPPED UP HERE ON GL'S GREEN BEAM--RIGHT?
WHO CARES WHY THEY'RE HERE, WILDCAT--?
13

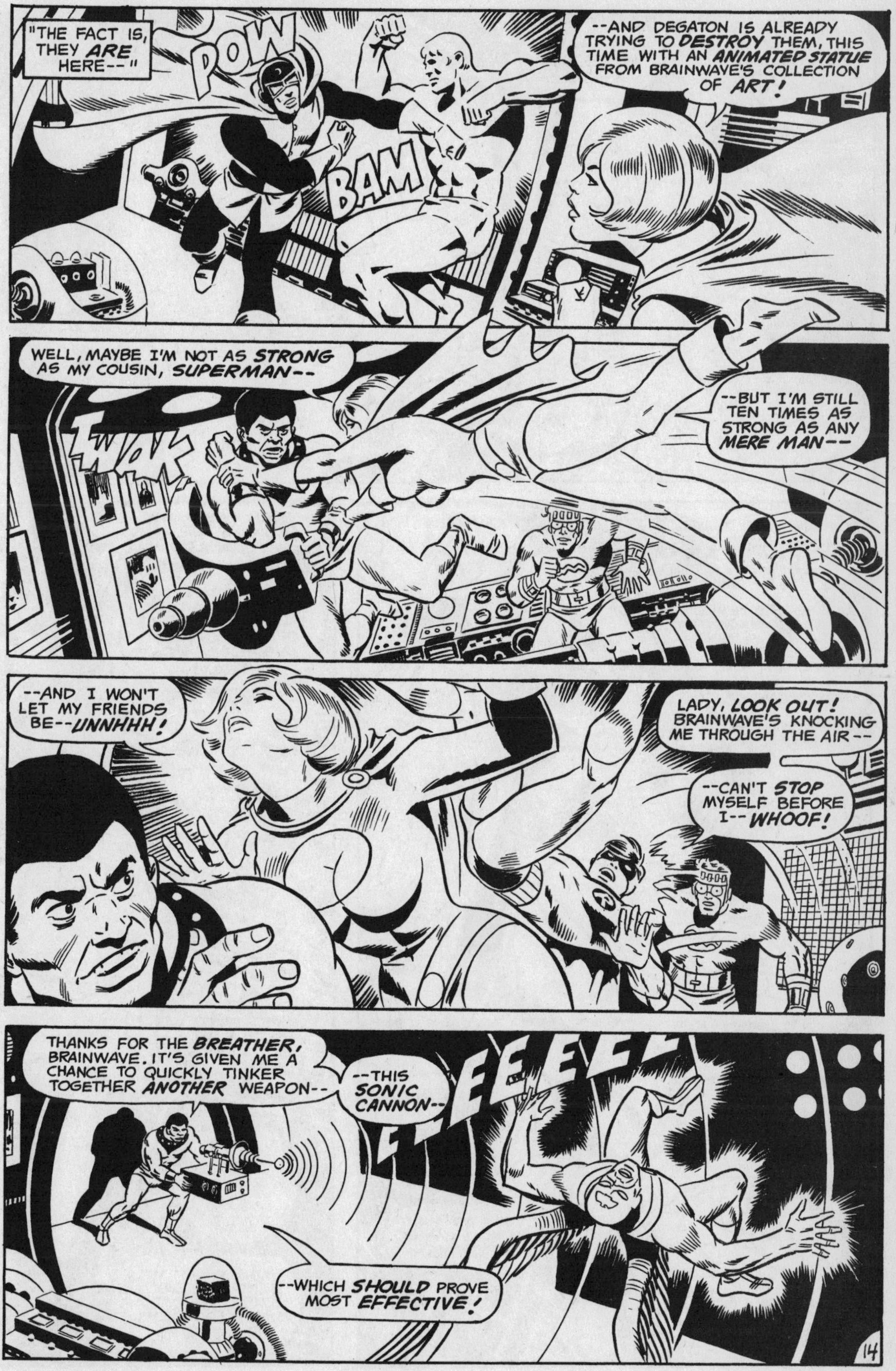
"THE FACT IS, THEY *ARE* HERE--"
POW
BAM
--AND DEGATON IS ALREADY TRYING TO *DESTROY* THEM, THIS TIME WITH AN *ANIMATED STATUE* FROM BRAINWAVE'S COLLECTION OF *ART!*
WELL, MAYBE I'M NOT AS *STRONG* AS MY COUSIN, *SUPERMAN*--
--BUT I'M STILL TEN TIMES AS STRONG AS ANY *MERE MAN*--
--AND I WON'T LET MY FRIENDS BE--*UNNHHH!*
LADY, *LOOK OUT!* BRAINWAVE'S KNOCKING ME THROUGH THE AIR--
--CAN'T *STOP* MYSELF BEFORE I--*WHOOF!*
THANKS FOR THE *BREATHER*, BRAINWAVE. IT'S GIVEN ME A CHANCE TO QUICKLY TINKER TOGETHER *ANOTHER* WEAPON--
--THIS *SONIC CANNON*--
--WHICH *SHOULD* PROVE MOST *EFFECTIVE!*
14

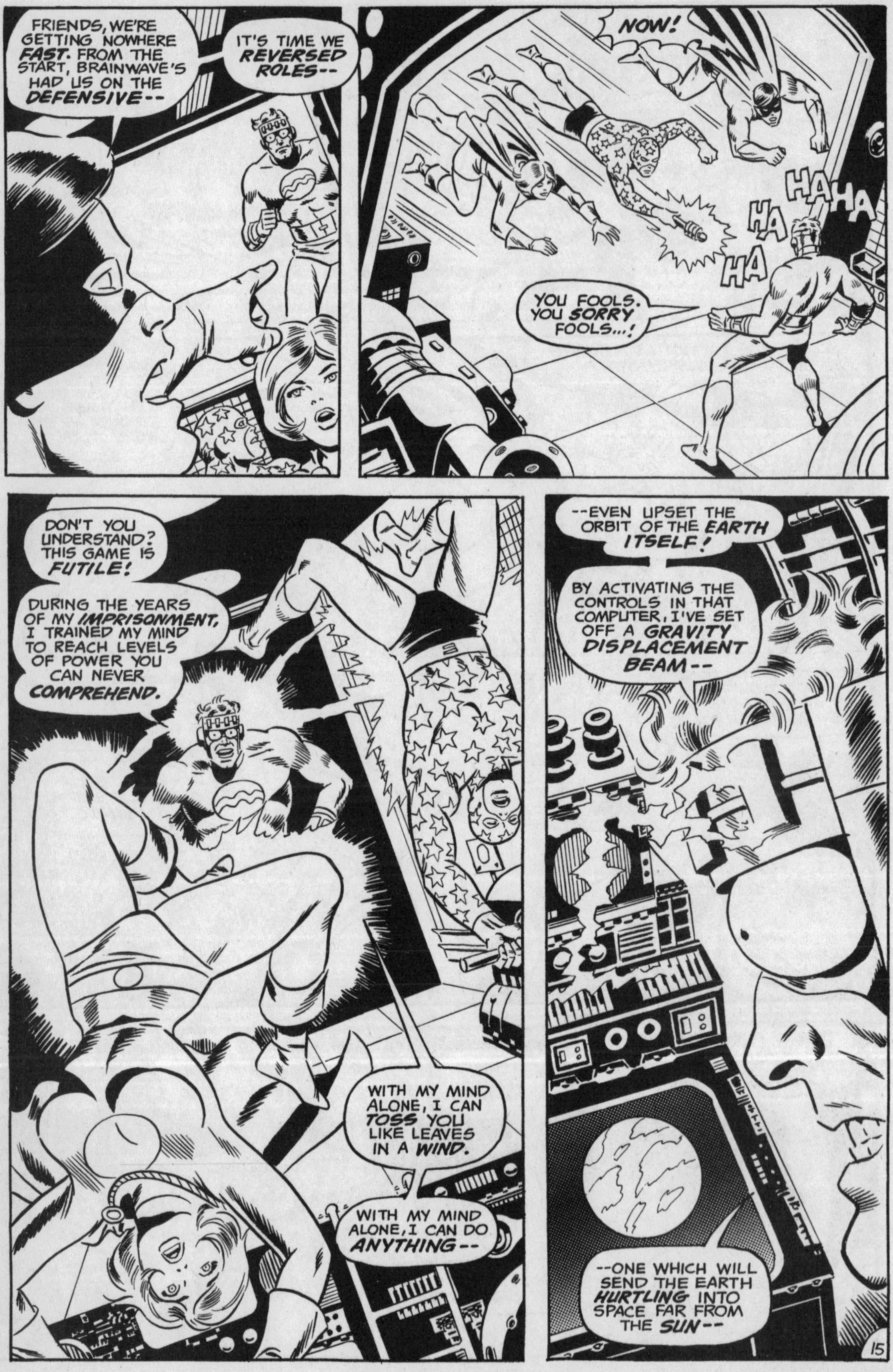
FRIENDS, WE'RE GETTING NOWHERE FAST. FROM THE START, BRAINWAVE'S HAD US ON THE DEFENSIVE--
IT'S TIME WE REVERSED ROLES--
NOW!
HAHAHA HA HA
YOU FOOLS. YOU SORRY FOOLS...!
DON'T YOU UNDERSTAND? THIS GAME IS FUTILE!
DURING THE YEARS OF MY IMPRISONMENT, I TRAINED MY MIND TO REACH LEVELS OF POWER YOU CAN NEVER COMPREHEND.
WITH MY MIND ALONE, I CAN TOSS YOU LIKE LEAVES IN A WIND.
WITH MY MIND ALONE, I CAN DO ANYTHING--
--EVEN UPSET THE ORBIT OF THE EARTH ITSELF!
BY ACTIVATING THE CONTROLS IN THAT COMPUTER, I'VE SET OFF A GRAVITY DISPLACEMENT BEAM--
--ONE WHICH WILL SEND THE EARTH HURTLING INTO SPACE FAR FROM THE SUN--
15

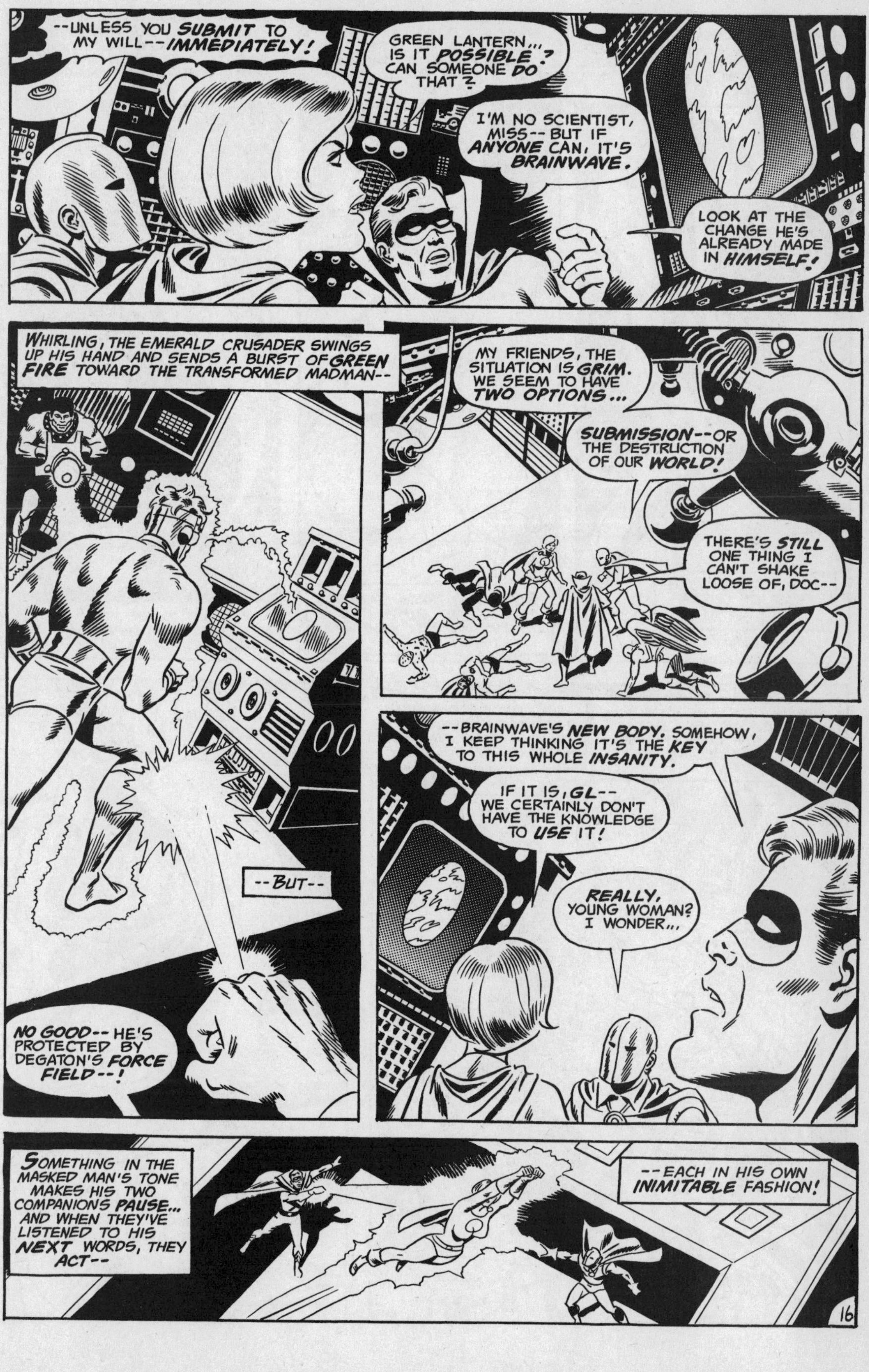
--UNLESS YOU SUBMIT TO MY WILL--IMMEDIATELY!
GREEN LANTERN... IS IT POSSIBLE? CAN SOMEONE DO THAT?
I'M NO SCIENTIST, MISS-- BUT IF ANYONE CAN, IT'S BRAINWAVE.
LOOK AT THE CHANGE HE'S ALREADY MADE IN HIMSELF!
WHIRLING, THE EMERALD CRUSADER SWINGS UP HIS HAND AND SENDS A BURST OF GREEN FIRE TOWARD THE TRANSFORMED MADMAN--
--BUT--
NO GOOD--HE'S PROTECTED BY DEGATON'S FORCE FIELD--!
MY FRIENDS, THE SITUATION IS GRIM. WE SEEM TO HAVE TWO OPTIONS...
SUBMISSION--OR THE DESTRUCTION OF OUR WORLD!
THERE'S STILL ONE THING I CAN'T SHAKE LOOSE OF, DOC--
--BRAINWAVE'S NEW BODY. SOMEHOW, I KEEP THINKING IT'S THE KEY TO THIS WHOLE INSANITY.
IF IT IS, GL-- WE CERTAINLY DON'T HAVE THE KNOWLEDGE TO USE IT!
REALLY, YOUNG WOMAN? I WONDER...
SOMETHING IN THE MASKED MAN'S TONE MAKES HIS TWO COMPANIONS PAUSE... AND WHEN THEY'VE LISTENED TO HIS NEXT WORDS, THEY ACT--
--EACH IN HIS OWN INIMITABLE FASHION!
16

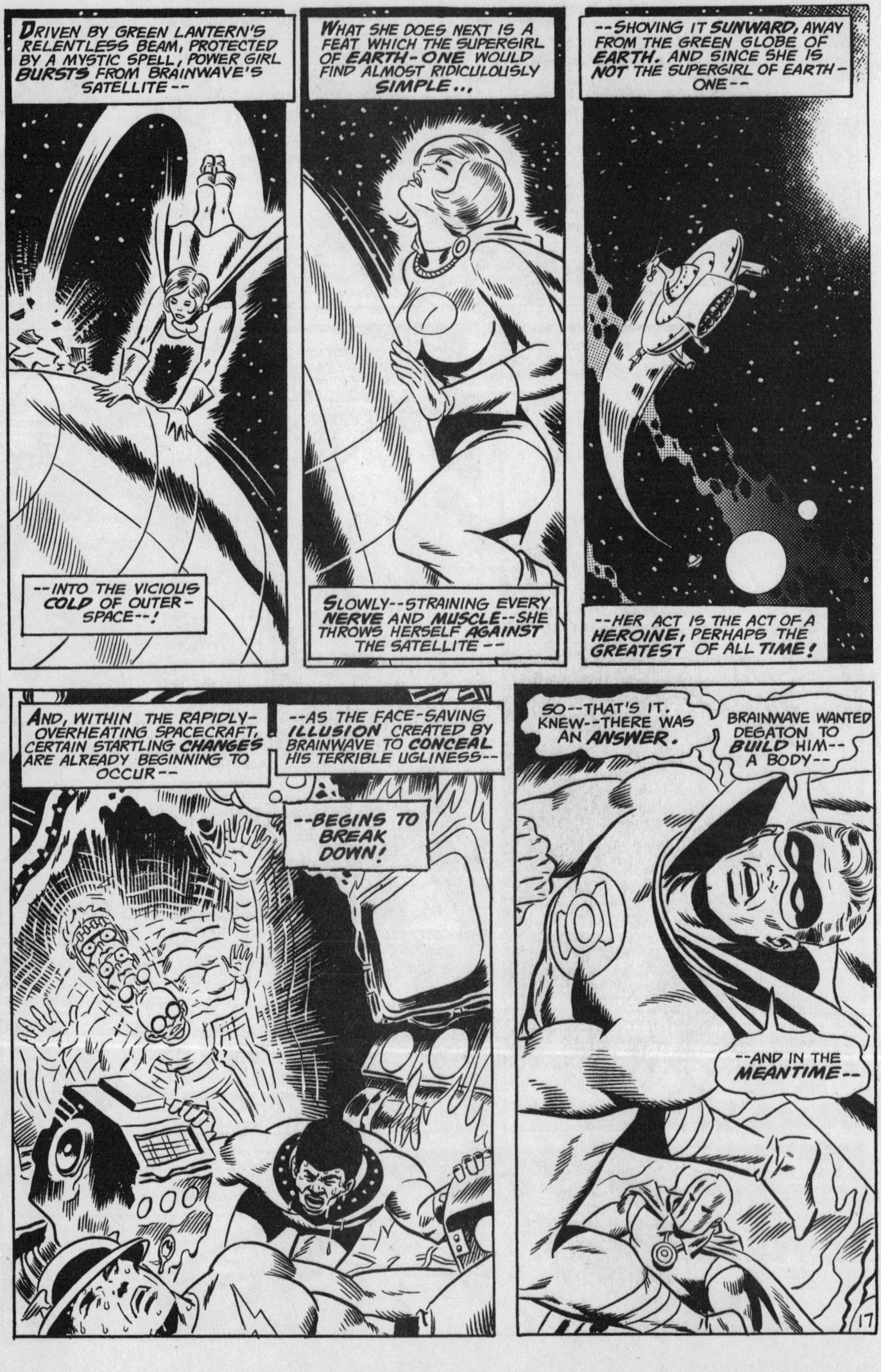
DRIVEN BY GREEN LANTERN'S RELENTLESS BEAM, PROTECTED BY A MYSTIC SPELL, POWER GIRL BURSTS FROM BRAINWAVE'S SATELLITE--
--INTO THE VICIOUS COLD OF OUTER-SPACE--!
WHAT SHE DOES NEXT IS A FEAT WHICH THE SUPERGIRL OF EARTH-ONE WOULD FIND ALMOST RIDICULOUSLY SIMPLE...
SLOWLY--STRAINING EVERY NERVE AND MUSCLE--SHE THROWS HERSELF AGAINST THE SATELLITE--
--SHOVING IT SUNWARD, AWAY FROM THE GREEN GLOBE OF EARTH. AND SINCE SHE IS NOT THE SUPERGIRL OF EARTH-ONE--
--HER ACT IS THE ACT OF A HEROINE, PERHAPS THE GREATEST OF ALL TIME!
AND, WITHIN THE RAPIDLY-OVERHEATING SPACECRAFT, CERTAIN STARTLING CHANGES ARE ALREADY BEGINNING TO OCCUR--
--AS THE FACE-SAVING ILLUSION CREATED BY BRAINWAVE TO CONCEAL HIS TERRIBLE UGLINESS--
--BEGINS TO BREAK DOWN!
SO--THAT'S IT. KNEW--THERE WAS AN ANSWER.
BRAINWAVE WANTED DEGATON TO BUILD HIM--A BODY--
--AND IN THE MEANTIME--
17

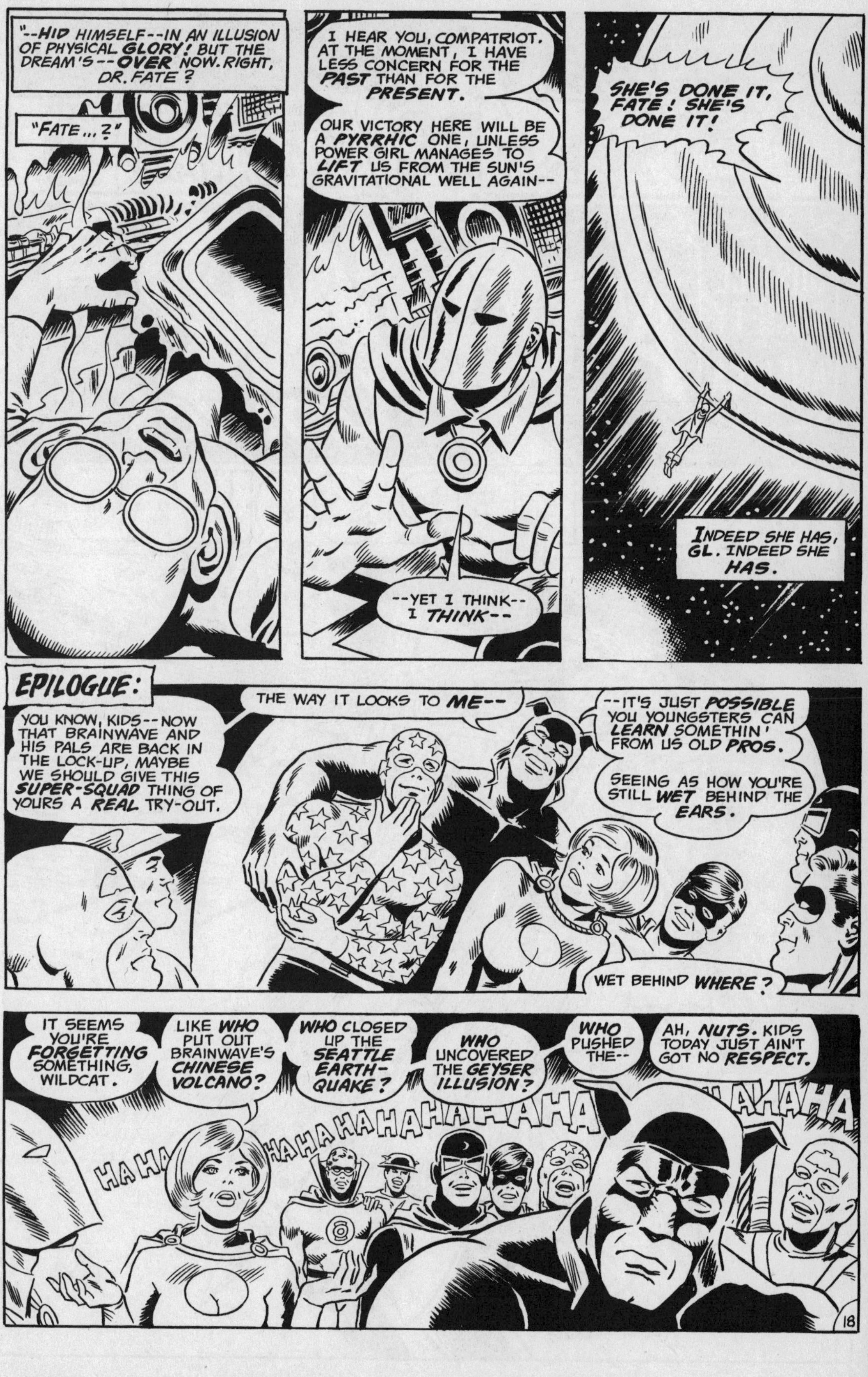
"--HID HIMSELF--IN AN ILLUSION OF PHYSICAL GLORY! BUT THE DREAM'S--OVER NOW. RIGHT, DR. FATE?
"FATE...?"
I HEAR YOU, COMPATRIOT. AT THE MOMENT, I HAVE LESS CONCERN FOR THE PAST THAN FOR THE PRESENT.
OUR VICTORY HERE WILL BE A PYRRHIC ONE, UNLESS POWER GIRL MANAGES TO LIFT US FROM THE SUN'S GRAVITATIONAL WELL AGAIN--
--YET I THINK-- I THINK--
SHE'S DONE IT, FATE! SHE'S DONE IT!
INDEED SHE HAS, GL. INDEED SHE HAS.
EPILOGUE:
YOU KNOW, KIDS--NOW THAT BRAINWAVE AND HIS PALS ARE BACK IN THE LOCK-UP, MAYBE WE SHOULD GIVE THIS SUPER-SQUAD THING OF YOURS A REAL TRY-OUT.
THE WAY IT LOOKS TO ME--
--IT'S JUST POSSIBLE YOU YOUNGSTERS CAN LEARN SOMETHIN' FROM US OLD PROS.
SEEING AS HOW YOU'RE STILL WET BEHIND THE EARS.
WET BEHIND WHERE?
IT SEEMS YOU'RE FORGETTING SOMETHING, WILDCAT.
LIKE WHO PUT OUT BRAINWAVE'S CHINESE VOLCANO?
WHO CLOSED UP THE SEATTLE EARTH-QUAKE?
WHO UNCOVERED THE GEYSER ILLUSION?
WHO PUSHED THE--
AH, NUTS. KIDS TODAY JUST AIN'T GOT NO RESPECT.
HA HA HA HA HA HA HA HA HA HA HA HA
HA HA HA HA
18

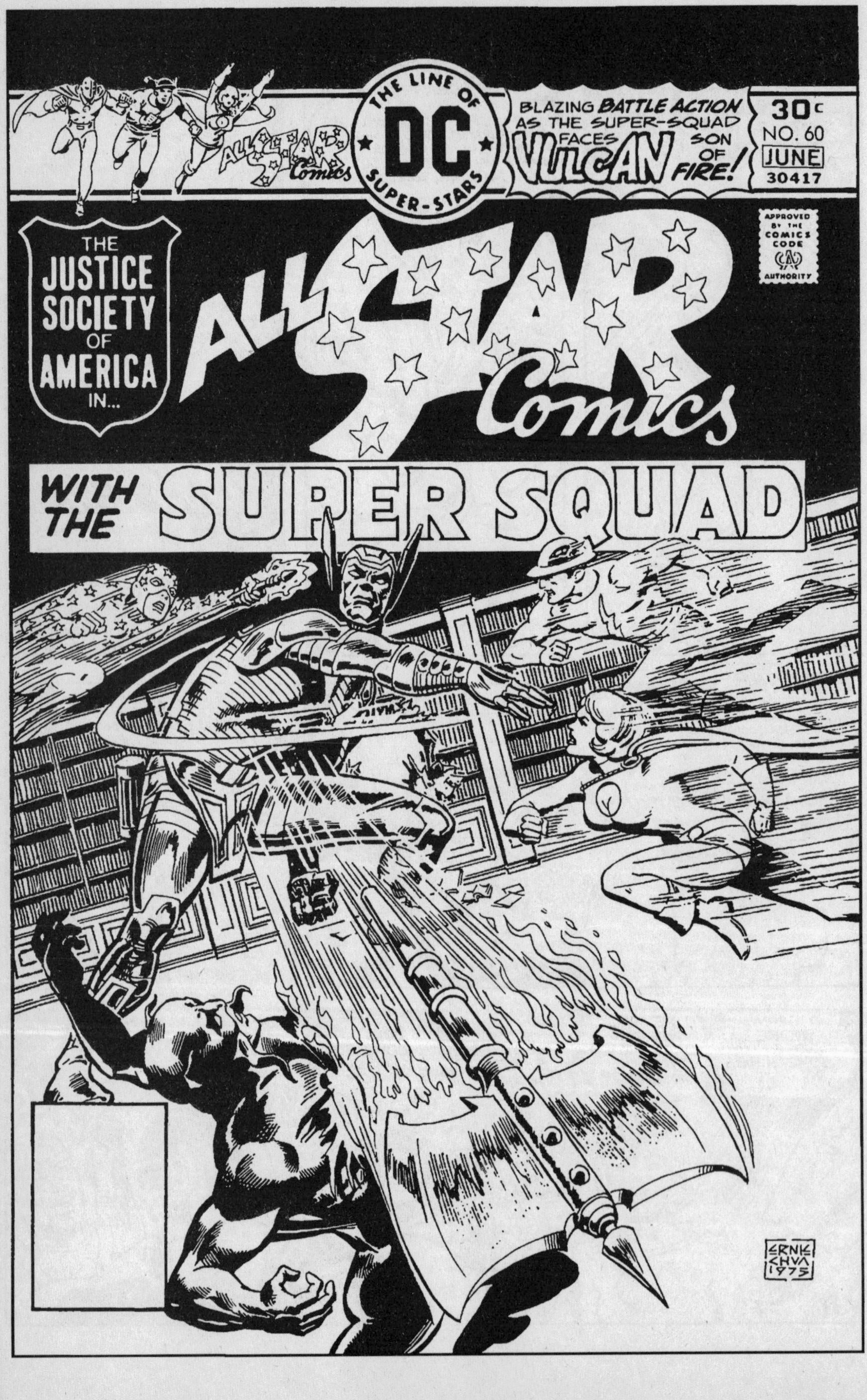
THE LINE OF DC SUPER-STARS
BLAZING BATTLE ACTION AS THE SUPER-SQUAD FACES VULCAN SON OF FIRE!
30¢
NO. 60
JUNE
30417
APPROVED BY THE COMICS CODE AUTHORITY
THE JUSTICE SOCIETY OF AMERICA IN...
ALL STAR Comics
WITH THE SUPER SQUAD
ERNIE CHUA 1975

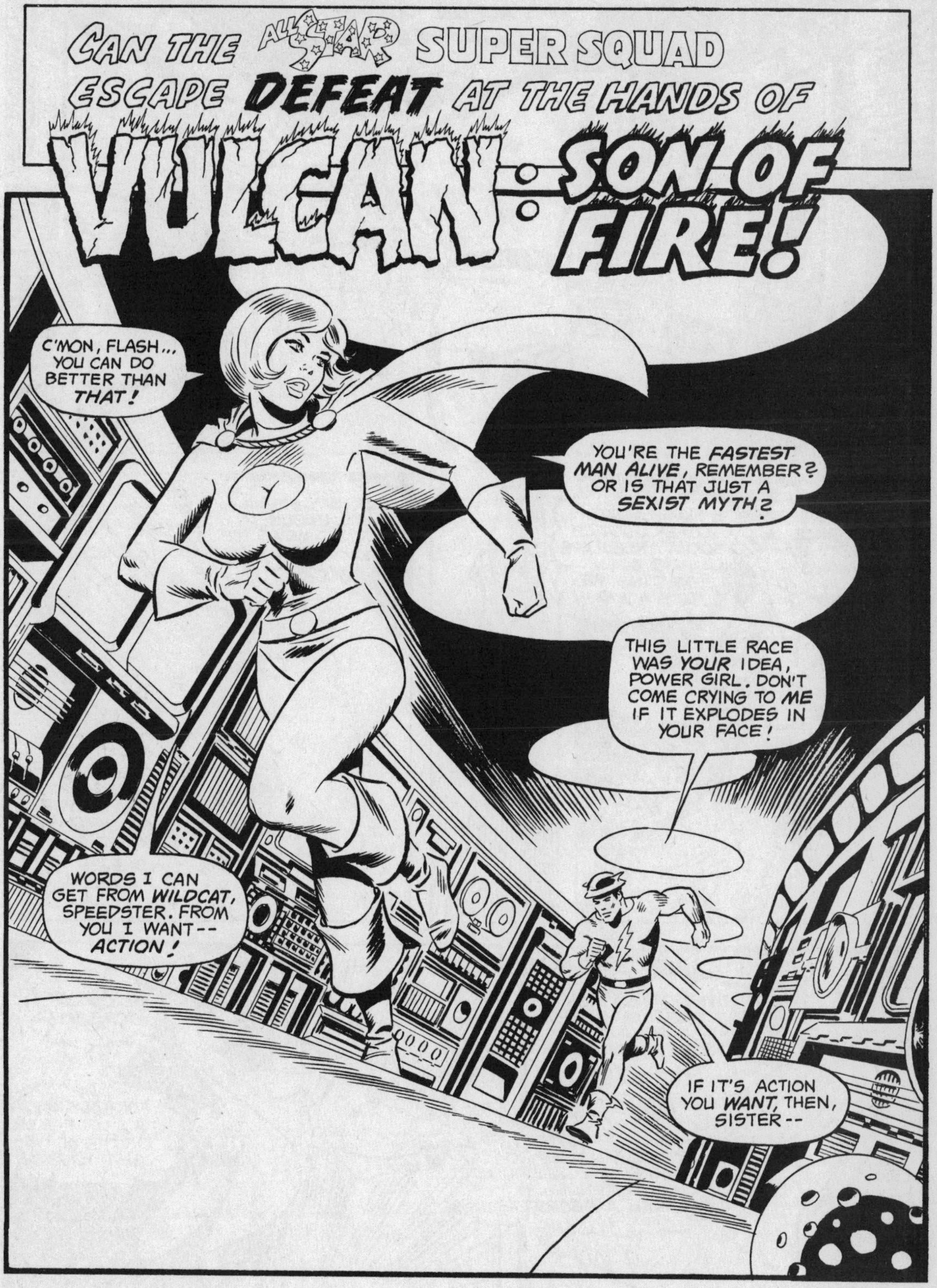
CAN THE ALL-STAR SUPER SQUAD ESCAPE DEFEAT AT THE HANDS OF
VULCAN: SON OF FIRE!
C'MON, FLASH... YOU CAN DO BETTER THAN THAT!
YOU'RE THE FASTEST MAN ALIVE, REMEMBER? OR IS THAT JUST A SEXIST MYTH?
THIS LITTLE RACE WAS YOUR IDEA, POWER GIRL. DON'T COME CRYING TO ME IF IT EXPLODES IN YOUR FACE!
WORDS I CAN GET FROM WILDCAT, SPEEDSTER. FROM YOU I WANT-- ACTION!
IF IT'S ACTION YOU WANT, THEN, SISTER--

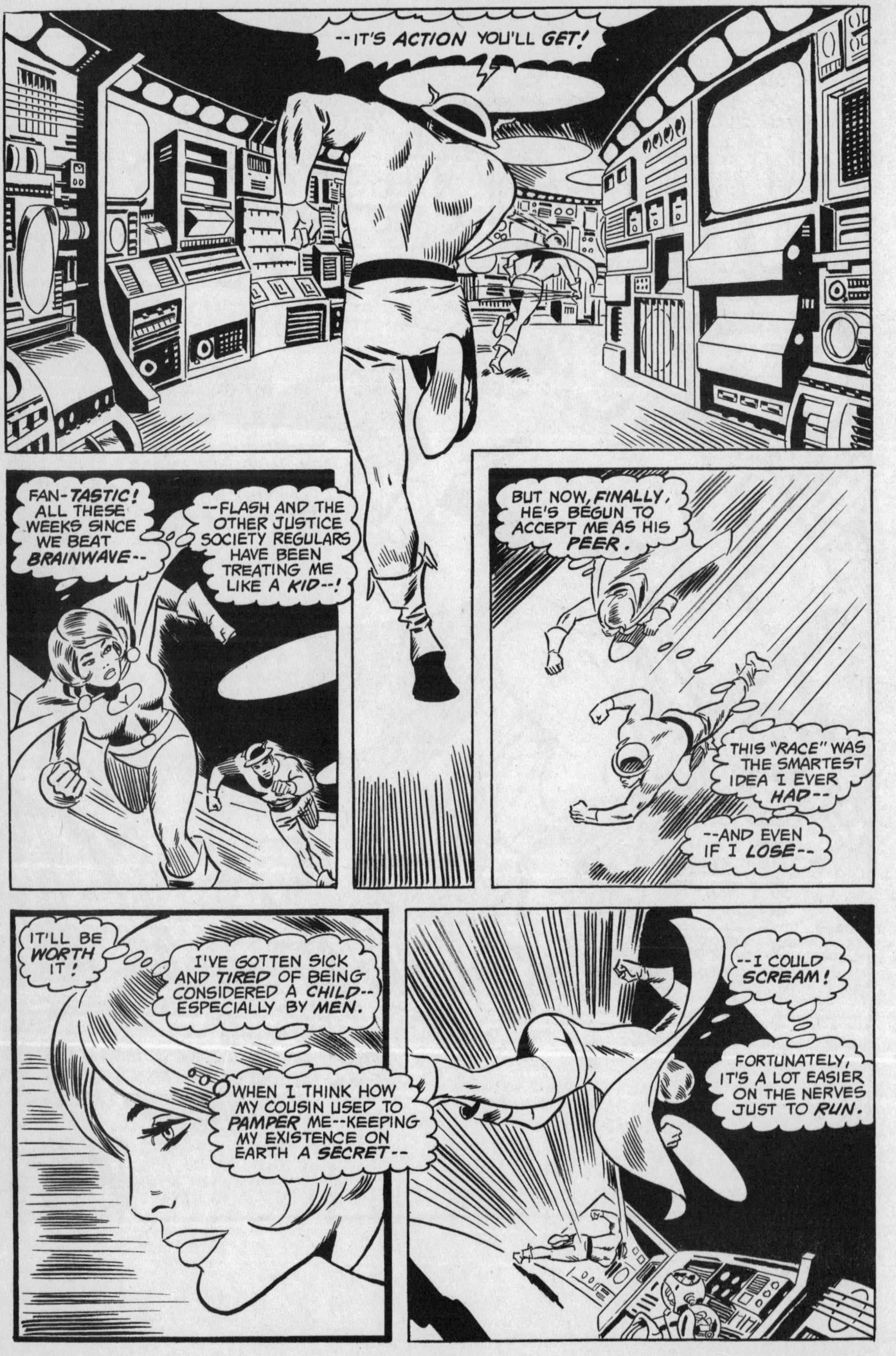
--IT'S ACTION YOU'LL GET!
FAN-TASTIC! ALL THESE WEEKS SINCE WE BEAT BRAINWAVE--
--FLASH AND THE OTHER JUSTICE SOCIETY REGULARS HAVE BEEN TREATING ME LIKE A KID--!
BUT NOW, FINALLY, HE'S BEGUN TO ACCEPT ME AS HIS PEER.
THIS "RACE" WAS THE SMARTEST IDEA I EVER HAD--
--AND EVEN IF I LOSE--
IT'LL BE WORTH IT!
I'VE GOTTEN SICK AND TIRED OF BEING CONSIDERED A CHILD-- ESPECIALLY BY MEN.
WHEN I THINK HOW MY COUSIN USED TO PAMPER ME--KEEPING MY EXISTENCE ON EARTH A SECRET--
--I COULD SCREAM!
FORTUNATELY, IT'S A LOT EASIER ON THE NERVES JUST TO RUN.

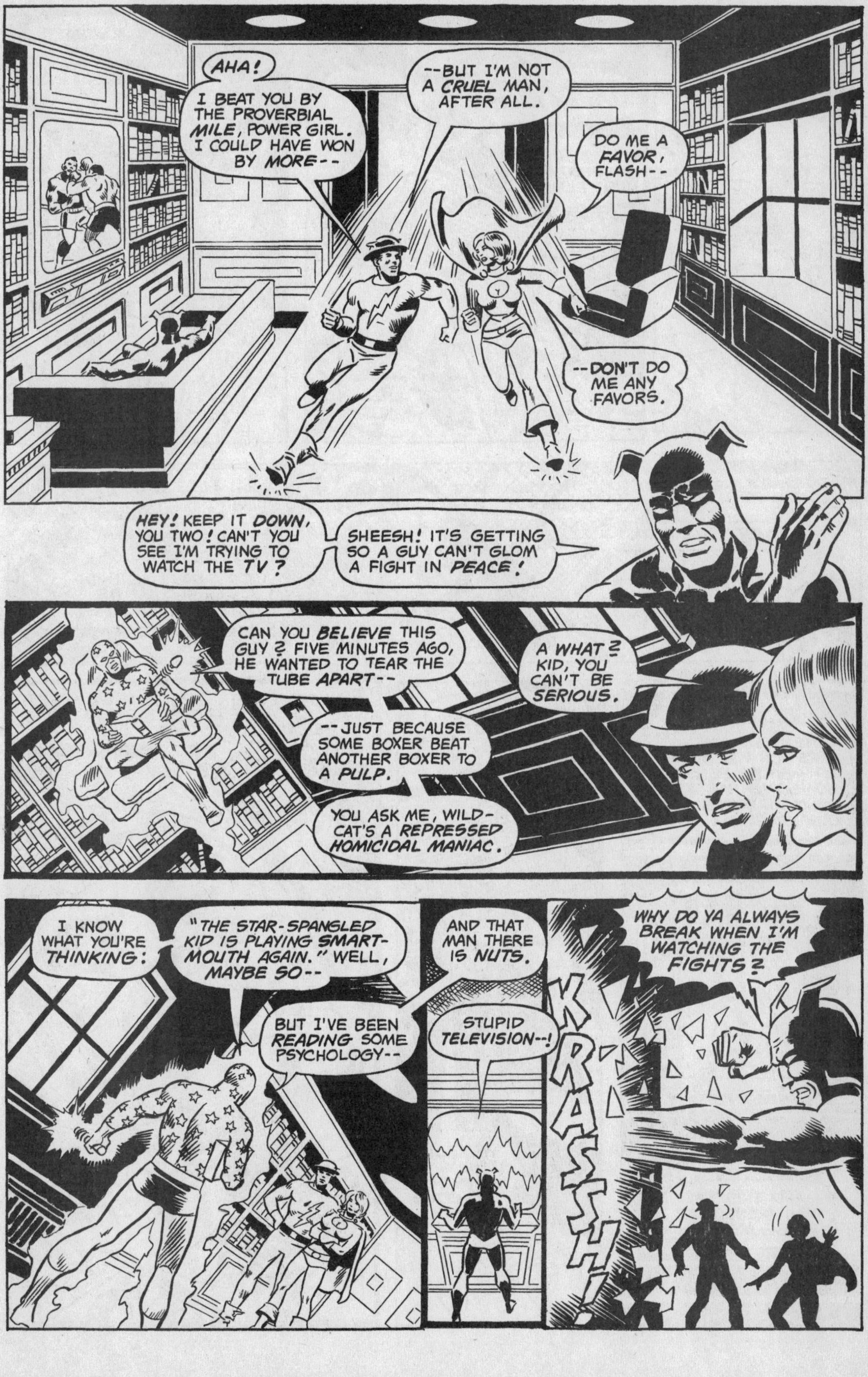
AHA!
I BEAT YOU BY THE PROVERBIAL MILE, POWER GIRL. I COULD HAVE WON BY MORE--
--BUT I'M NOT A CRUEL MAN, AFTER ALL.
DO ME A FAVOR, FLASH--
--DON'T DO ME ANY FAVORS.
HEY! KEEP IT DOWN, YOU TWO! CAN'T YOU SEE I'M TRYING TO WATCH THE TV?
SHEESH! IT'S GETTING SO A GUY CAN'T GLOM A FIGHT IN PEACE!
CAN YOU BELIEVE THIS GUY? FIVE MINUTES AGO, HE WANTED TO TEAR THE TUBE APART--
--JUST BECAUSE SOME BOXER BEAT ANOTHER BOXER TO A PULP.
YOU ASK ME, WILD-CAT'S A REPRESSED HOMICIDAL MANIAC.
A WHAT? KID, YOU CAN'T BE SERIOUS.
I KNOW WHAT YOU'RE THINKING:
"THE STAR-SPANGLED KID IS PLAYING SMART-MOUTH AGAIN." WELL, MAYBE SO--
BUT I'VE BEEN READING SOME PSYCHOLOGY--
AND THAT MAN THERE IS NUTS.
STUPID TELEVISION--!
WHY DO YA ALWAYS BREAK WHEN I'M WATCHING THE FIGHTS?
KRASH!

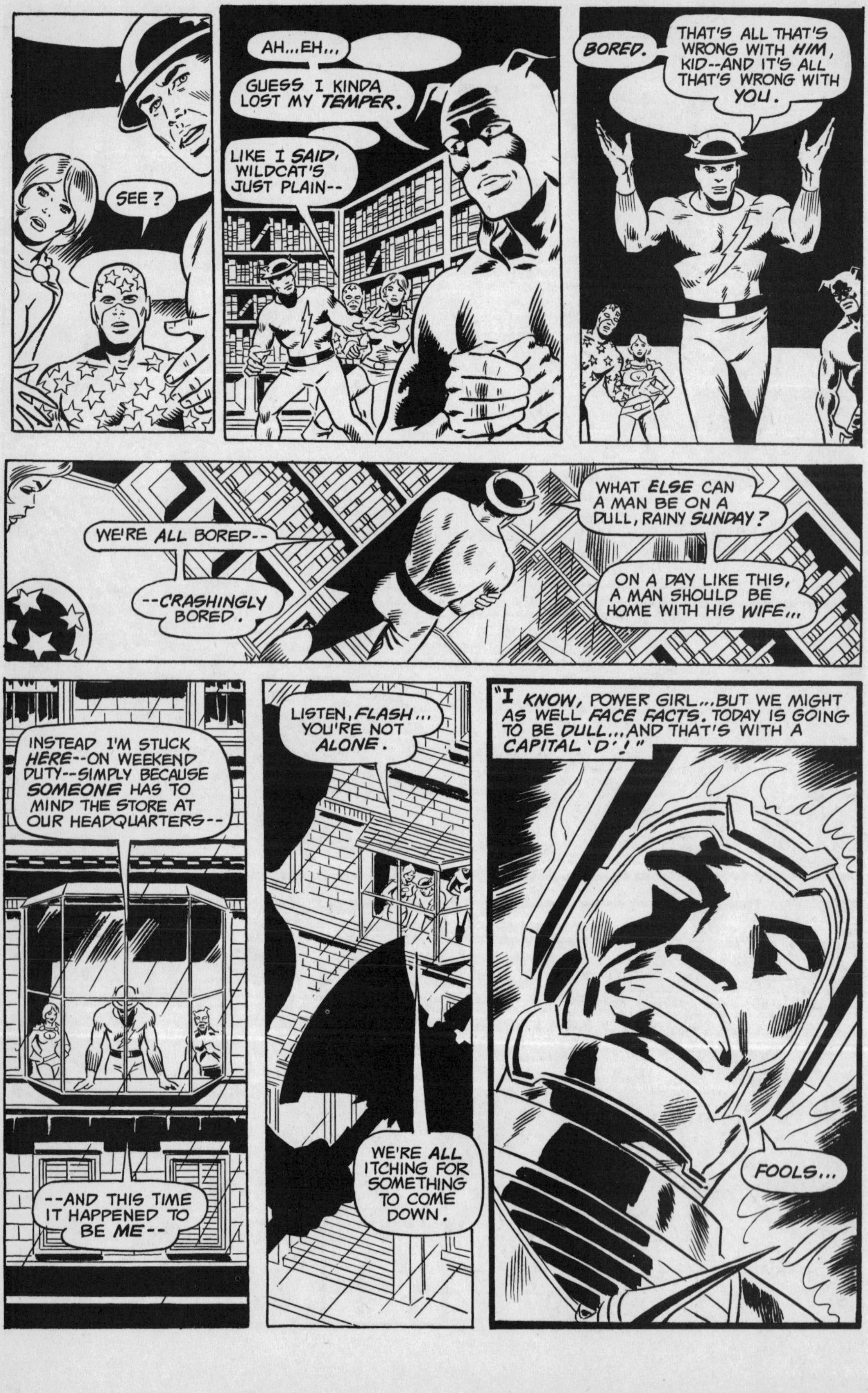
SEE?
AH...EH...
GUESS I KINDA LOST MY TEMPER.
LIKE I SAID, WILDCAT'S JUST PLAIN--
BORED.
THAT'S ALL THAT'S WRONG WITH HIM, KID--AND IT'S ALL THAT'S WRONG WITH YOU.
WE'RE ALL BORED--
--CRASHINGLY BORED.
WHAT ELSE CAN A MAN BE ON A DULL, RAINY SUNDAY?
ON A DAY LIKE THIS, A MAN SHOULD BE HOME WITH HIS WIFE...
INSTEAD I'M STUCK HERE--ON WEEKEND DUTY--SIMPLY BECAUSE SOMEONE HAS TO MIND THE STORE AT OUR HEADQUARTERS--
--AND THIS TIME IT HAPPENED TO BE ME--
LISTEN, FLASH... YOU'RE NOT ALONE.
WE'RE ALL ITCHING FOR SOMETHING TO COME DOWN.
"I KNOW, POWER GIRL...BUT WE MIGHT AS WELL FACE FACTS. TODAY IS GOING TO BE DULL...AND THAT'S WITH A CAPITAL 'D'!"
FOOLS...

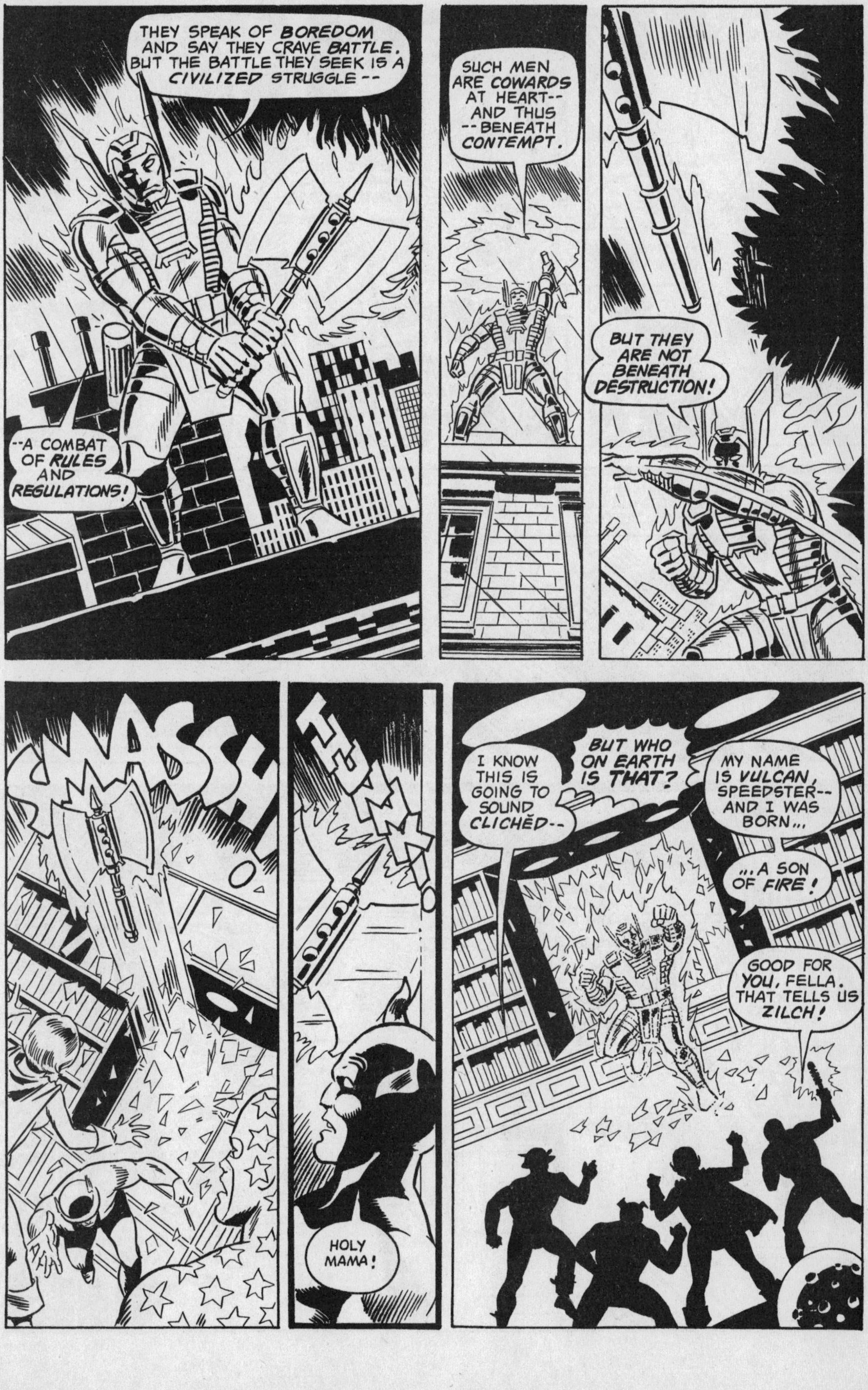
THEY SPEAK OF BOREDOM AND SAY THEY CRAVE BATTLE. BUT THE BATTLE THEY SEEK IS A CIVILIZED STRUGGLE --
--A COMBAT OF RULES AND REGULATIONS!
SUCH MEN ARE COWARDS AT HEART-- AND THUS --BENEATH CONTEMPT.
BUT THEY ARE NOT BENEATH DESTRUCTION!
SMASSH
HOLY MAMA!
I KNOW THIS IS GOING TO SOUND CLICHÉD--
BUT WHO ON EARTH IS THAT?
MY NAME IS VULCAN, SPEEDSTER-- AND I WAS BORN...
...A SON OF FIRE!
GOOD FOR YOU, FELLA. THAT TELLS US ZILCH!

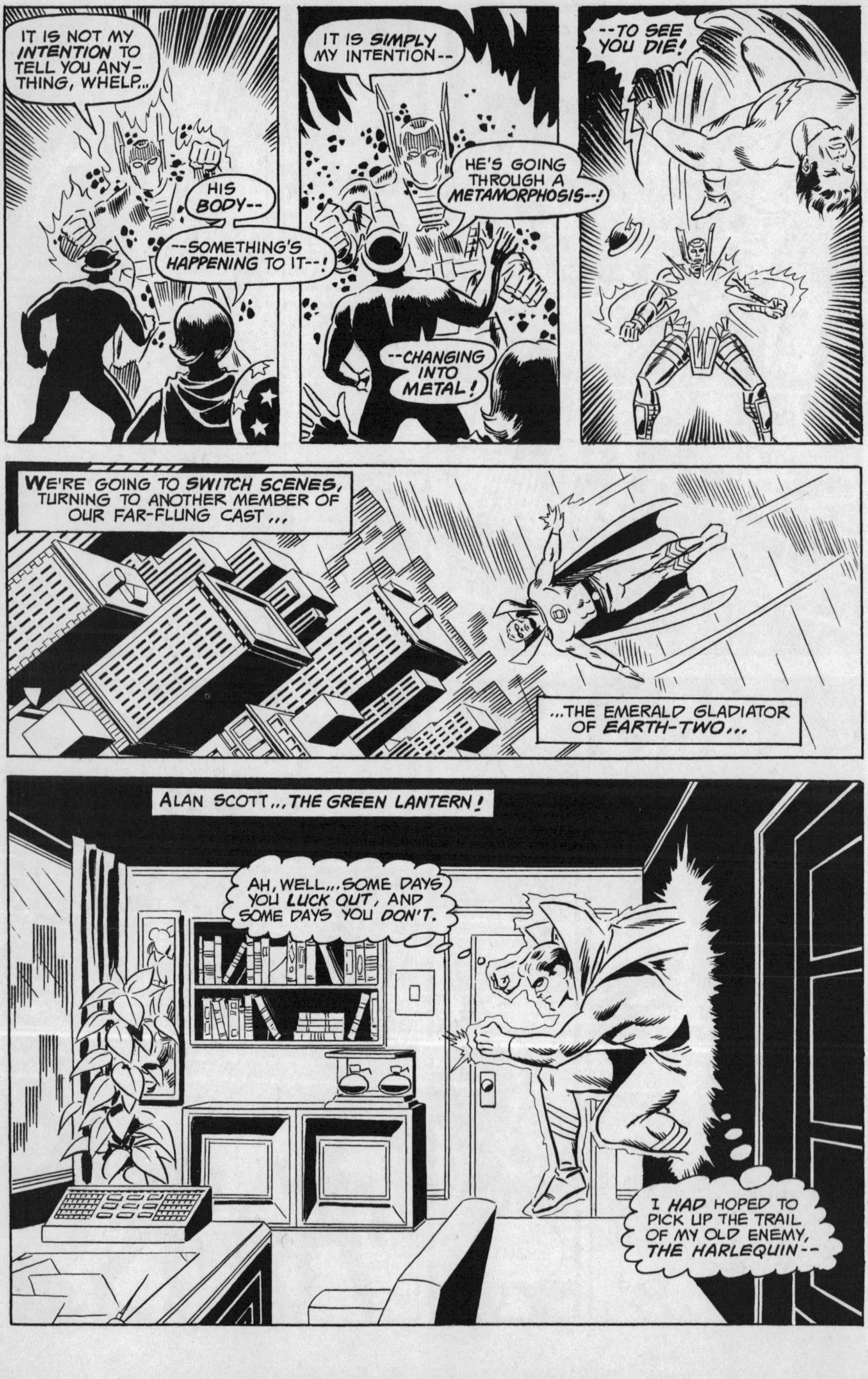
IT IS NOT MY INTENTION TO TELL YOU ANY-THING, WHELP...
HIS BODY--
--SOMETHING'S HAPPENING TO IT--!
IT IS SIMPLY MY INTENTION--
HE'S GOING THROUGH A METAMORPHOSIS--!
--CHANGING INTO METAL!
--TO SEE YOU DIE!
WE'RE GOING TO SWITCH SCENES, TURNING TO ANOTHER MEMBER OF OUR FAR-FLUNG CAST...
...THE EMERALD GLADIATOR OF EARTH-TWO...
ALAN SCOTT... THE GREEN LANTERN!
AH, WELL... SOME DAYS YOU LUCK OUT, AND SOME DAYS YOU DON'T.
I HAD HOPED TO PICK UP THE TRAIL OF MY OLD ENEMY, THE HARLEQUIN--

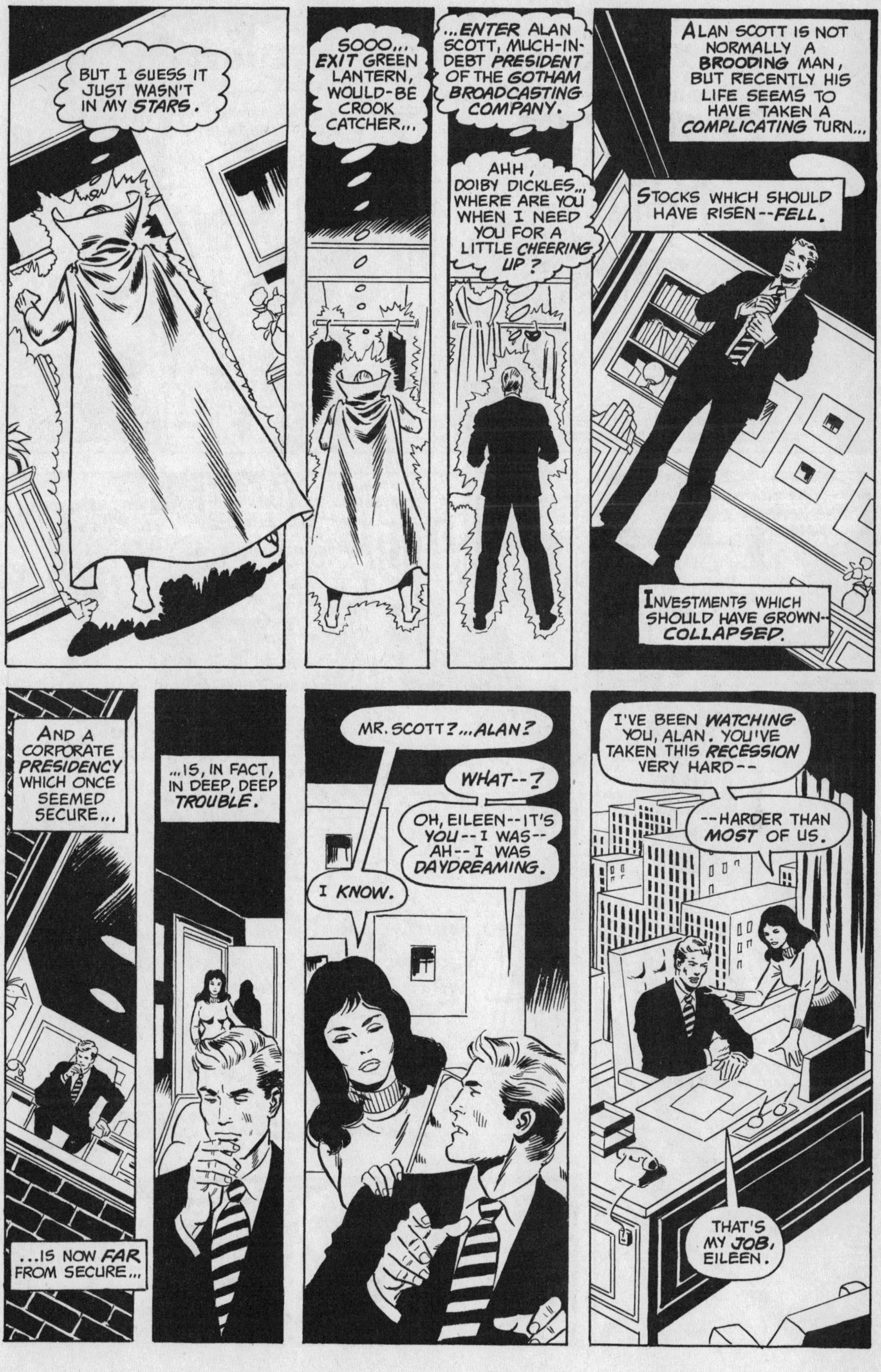
BUT I GUESS IT JUST WASN'T IN MY STARS.
SOOO... EXIT GREEN LANTERN, WOULD-BE CROOK CATCHER...
...ENTER ALAN SCOTT, MUCH-IN-DEBT PRESIDENT OF THE GOTHAM BROADCASTING COMPANY.
AHH, DOIBY DICKLES... WHERE ARE YOU WHEN I NEED YOU FOR A LITTLE CHEERING UP?
ALAN SCOTT IS NOT NORMALLY A BROODING MAN, BUT RECENTLY HIS LIFE SEEMS TO HAVE TAKEN A COMPLICATING TURN...
STOCKS WHICH SHOULD HAVE RISEN--FELL.
INVESTMENTS WHICH SHOULD HAVE GROWN--COLLAPSED.
AND A CORPORATE PRESIDENCY WHICH ONCE SEEMED SECURE...
...IS NOW FAR FROM SECURE...
...IS, IN FACT, IN DEEP, DEEP TROUBLE.
MR. SCOTT?...ALAN?
WHAT--?
OH, EILEEN--IT'S YOU--I WAS--AH--I WAS DAYDREAMING.
I KNOW.
I'VE BEEN WATCHING YOU, ALAN. YOU'VE TAKEN THIS RECESSION VERY HARD--
--HARDER THAN MOST OF US.
THAT'S MY JOB, EILEEN.

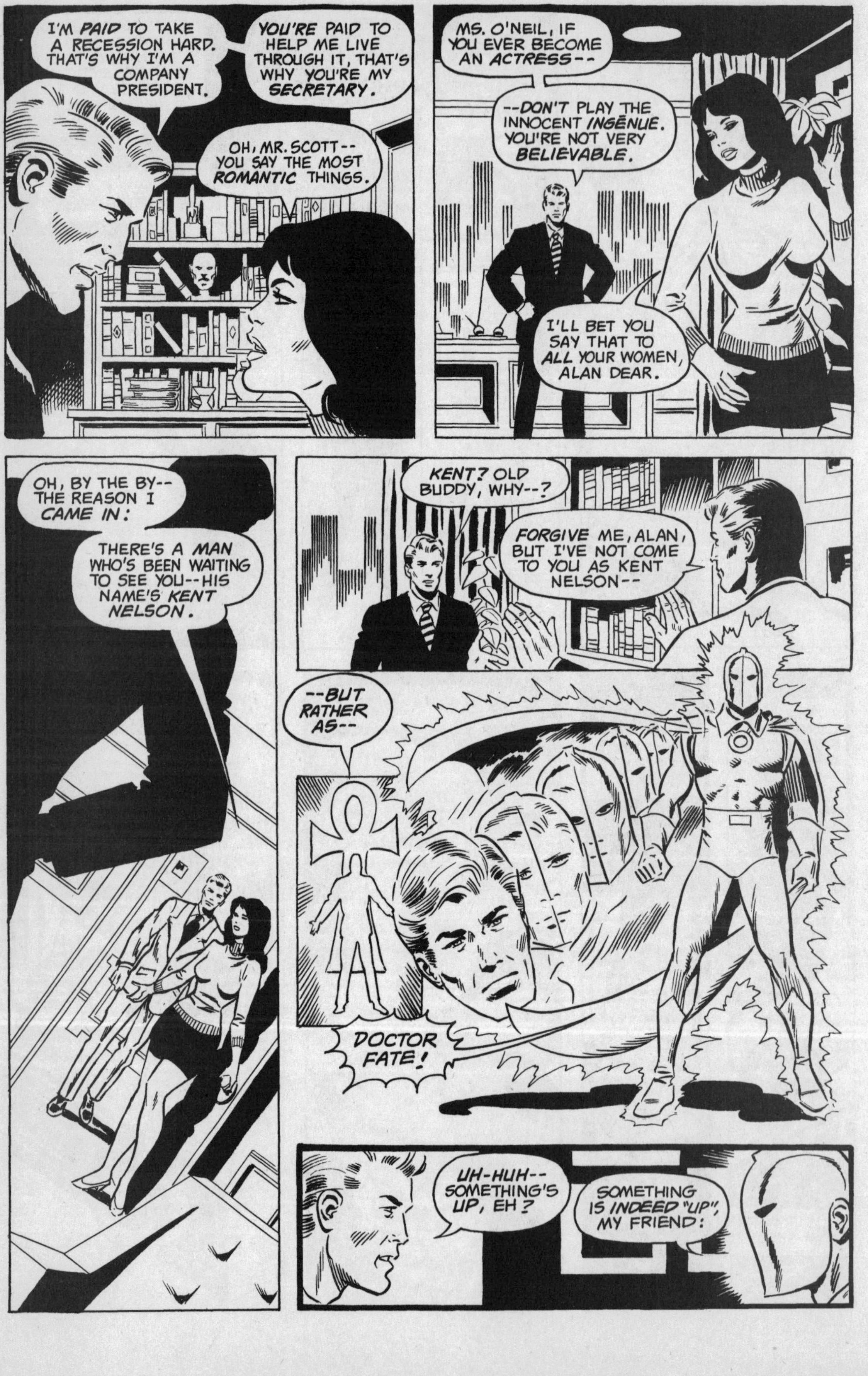
I'M PAID TO TAKE A RECESSION HARD. THAT'S WHY I'M A COMPANY PRESIDENT.
YOU'RE PAID TO HELP ME LIVE THROUGH IT, THAT'S WHY YOU'RE MY SECRETARY.
OH, MR. SCOTT-- YOU SAY THE MOST ROMANTIC THINGS.
MS. O'NEIL, IF YOU EVER BECOME AN ACTRESS--
--DON'T PLAY THE INNOCENT INGÉNUE. YOU'RE NOT VERY BELIEVABLE.
I'LL BET YOU SAY THAT TO ALL YOUR WOMEN, ALAN DEAR.
OH, BY THE BY-- THE REASON I CAME IN:
THERE'S A MAN WHO'S BEEN WAITING TO SEE YOU--HIS NAME'S KENT NELSON.
KENT? OLD BUDDY, WHY--?
FORGIVE ME, ALAN, BUT I'VE NOT COME TO YOU AS KENT NELSON--
--BUT RATHER AS--
DOCTOR FATE!
UH-HUH-- SOMETHING'S UP, EH?
SOMETHING IS INDEED "UP", MY FRIEND:

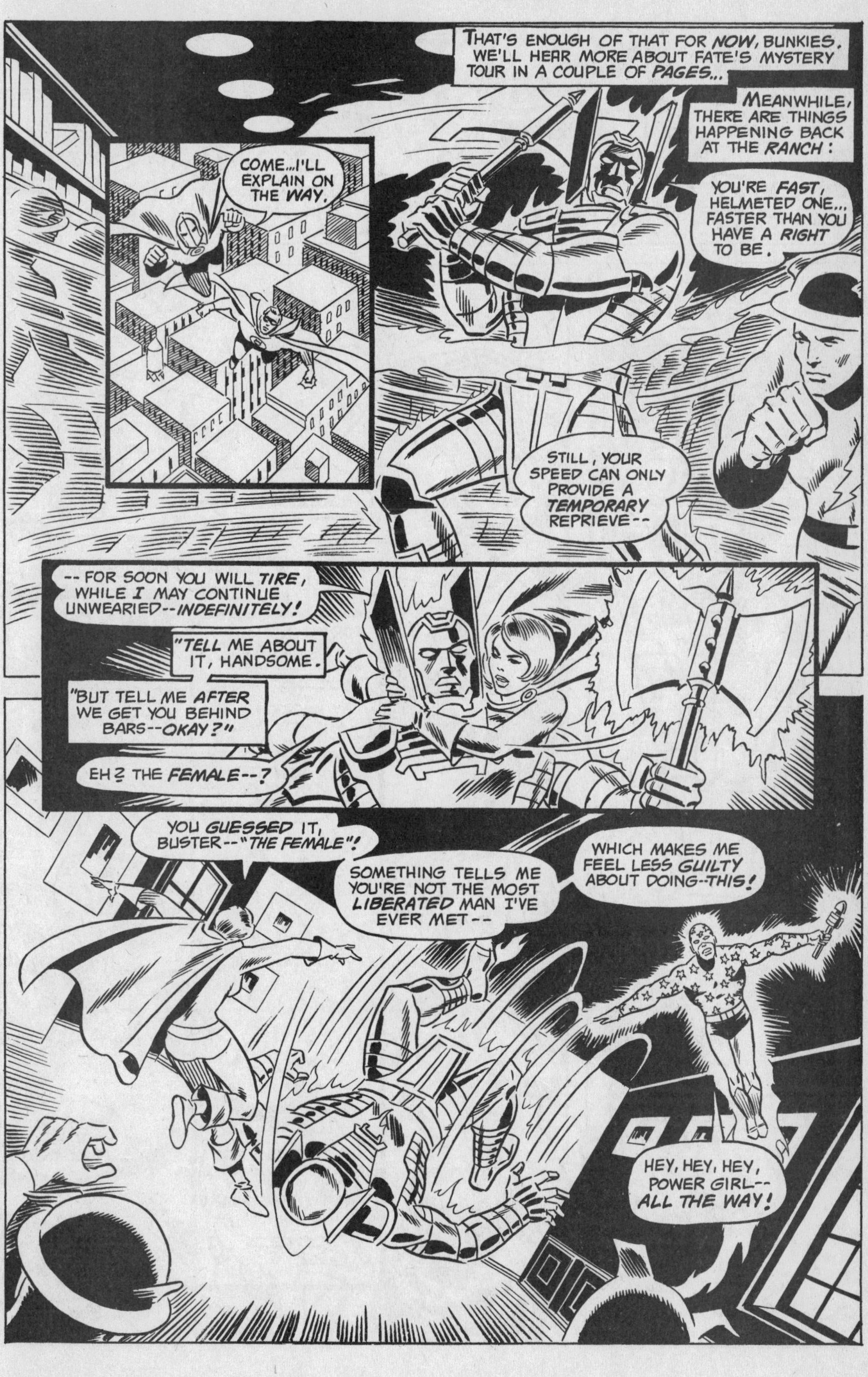
THAT'S ENOUGH OF THAT FOR NOW, BUNKIES. WE'LL HEAR MORE ABOUT FATE'S MYSTERY TOUR IN A COUPLE OF PAGES...
COME...I'LL EXPLAIN ON THE WAY.
MEANWHILE, THERE ARE THINGS HAPPENING BACK AT THE RANCH:
YOU'RE FAST, HELMETED ONE... FASTER THAN YOU HAVE A RIGHT TO BE.
STILL, YOUR SPEED CAN ONLY PROVIDE A TEMPORARY REPRIEVE--
--FOR SOON YOU WILL TIRE, WHILE I MAY CONTINUE UNWEARIED--INDEFINITELY!
"TELL ME ABOUT IT, HANDSOME.
"BUT TELL ME AFTER WE GET YOU BEHIND BARS--OKAY?"
EH? THE FEMALE--?
YOU GUESSED IT, BUSTER--"THE FEMALE"!
SOMETHING TELLS ME YOU'RE NOT THE MOST LIBERATED MAN I'VE EVER MET--
WHICH MAKES ME FEEL LESS GUILTY ABOUT DOING--THIS!
HEY, HEY, HEY, POWER GIRL-- ALL THE WAY!

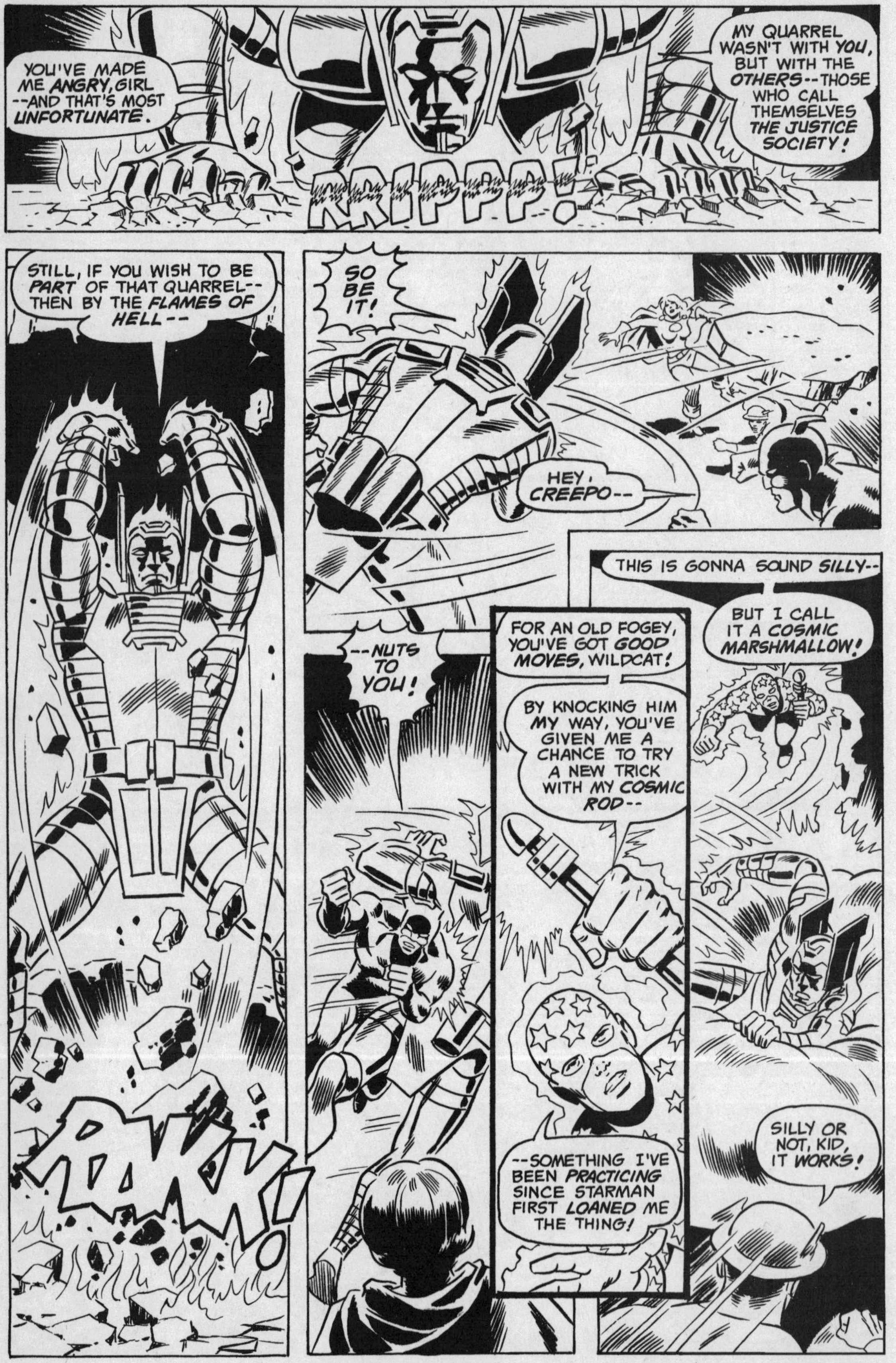
YOU'VE MADE ME ANGRY, GIRL --AND THAT'S MOST UNFORTUNATE.
MY QUARREL WASN'T WITH YOU, BUT WITH THE OTHERS--THOSE WHO CALL THEMSELVES THE JUSTICE SOCIETY!
KRIPPPP!
STILL, IF YOU WISH TO BE PART OF THAT QUARREL-- THEN BY THE FLAMES OF HELL--
SO BE IT!
HEY, CREEPO--
--NUTS TO YOU!
FOR AN OLD FOGEY, YOU'VE GOT GOOD MOVES, WILDCAT!
BY KNOCKING HIM MY WAY, YOU'VE GIVEN ME A CHANCE TO TRY A NEW TRICK WITH MY COSMIC ROD--
--SOMETHING I'VE BEEN PRACTICING SINCE STARMAN FIRST LOANED ME THE THING!
THIS IS GONNA SOUND SILLY--
BUT I CALL IT A COSMIC MARSHMALLOW!
SILLY OR NOT, KID, IT WORKS!

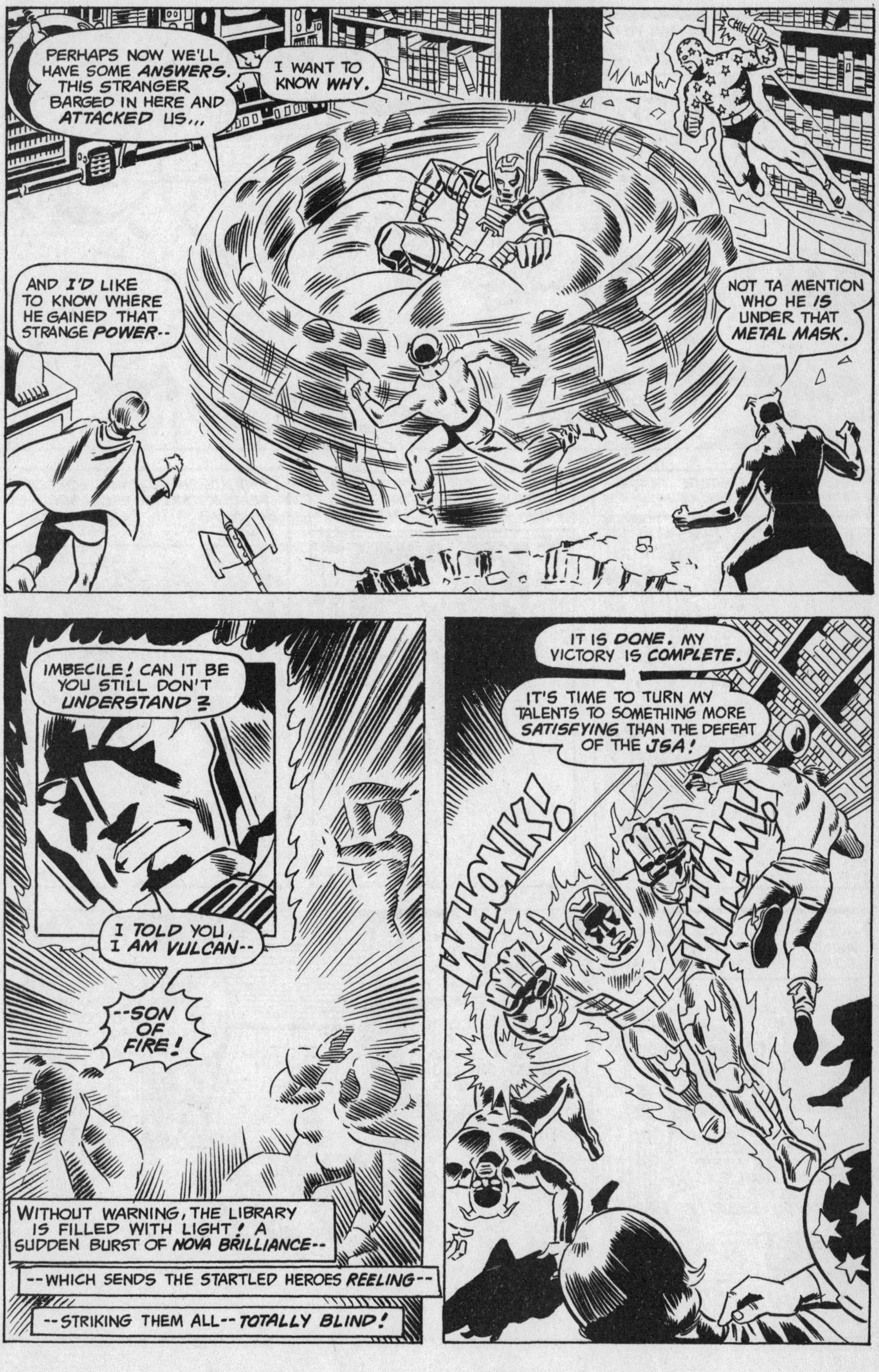
PERHAPS NOW WE'LL HAVE SOME ANSWERS. THIS STRANGER BARGED IN HERE AND ATTACKED US...
I WANT TO KNOW WHY.
AND I'D LIKE TO KNOW WHERE HE GAINED THAT STRANGE POWER--
NOT TA MENTION WHO HE IS UNDER THAT METAL MASK.
IMBECILE! CAN IT BE YOU STILL DON'T UNDERSTAND?
I TOLD YOU, I AM VULCAN--
--SON OF FIRE!
WITHOUT WARNING, THE LIBRARY IS FILLED WITH LIGHT! A SUDDEN BURST OF NOVA BRILLIANCE--
--WHICH SENDS THE STARTLED HEROES REELING--
--STRIKING THEM ALL--TOTALLY BLIND!
IT IS DONE. MY VICTORY IS COMPLETE.
IT'S TIME TO TURN MY TALENTS TO SOMETHING MORE SATISFYING THAN THE DEFEAT OF THE JSA!
WHONK!
WHAM!

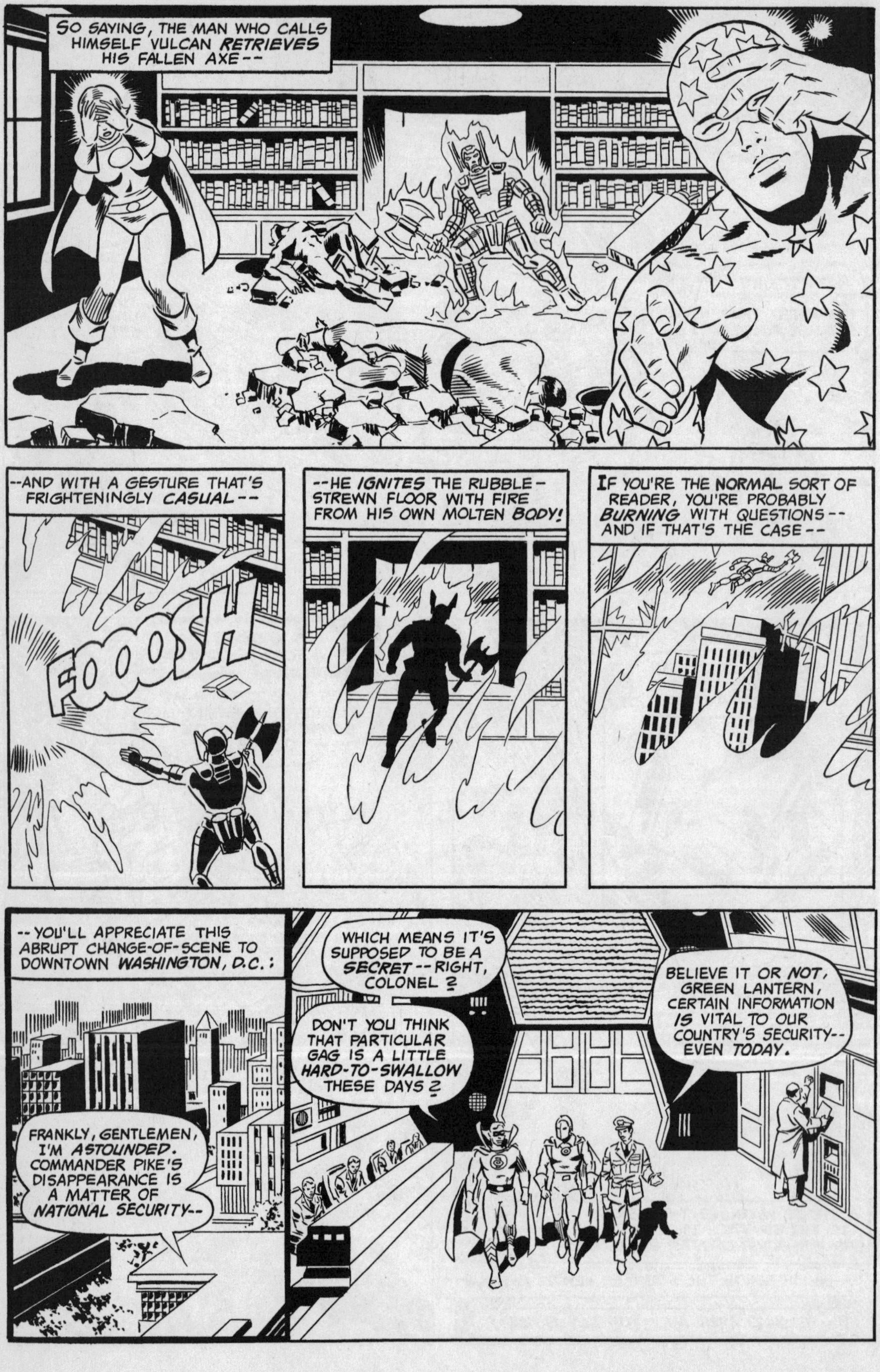
SO SAYING, THE MAN WHO CALLS HIMSELF VULCAN RETRIEVES HIS FALLEN AXE--
--AND WITH A GESTURE THAT'S FRIGHTENINGLY CASUAL--
FOOOSH
--HE IGNITES THE RUBBLE-STREWN FLOOR WITH FIRE FROM HIS OWN MOLTEN BODY!
IF YOU'RE THE NORMAL SORT OF READER, YOU'RE PROBABLY BURNING WITH QUESTIONS--AND IF THAT'S THE CASE--
--YOU'LL APPRECIATE THIS ABRUPT CHANGE-OF-SCENE TO DOWNTOWN WASHINGTON, D.C.:
FRANKLY, GENTLEMEN, I'M ASTOUNDED. COMMANDER PIKE'S DISAPPEARANCE IS A MATTER OF NATIONAL SECURITY--
WHICH MEANS IT'S SUPPOSED TO BE A SECRET--RIGHT, COLONEL?
DON'T YOU THINK THAT PARTICULAR GAG IS A LITTLE HARD-TO-SWALLOW THESE DAYS?
BELIEVE IT OR NOT, GREEN LANTERN, CERTAIN INFORMATION IS VITAL TO OUR COUNTRY'S SECURITY--EVEN TODAY.

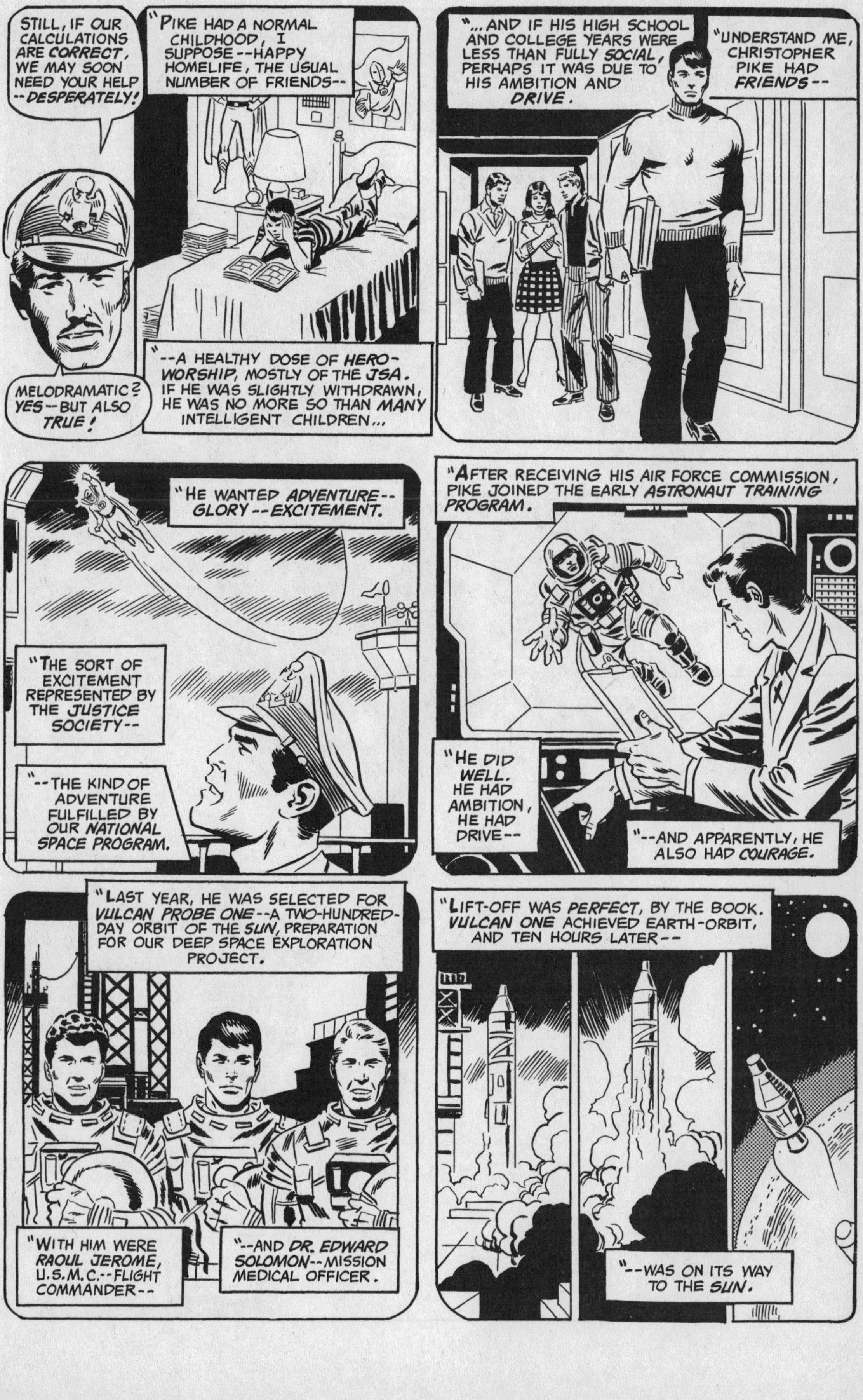
STILL, IF OUR CALCULATIONS ARE CORRECT, WE MAY SOON NEED YOUR HELP --DESPERATELY!
MELODRAMATIC? YES--BUT ALSO TRUE!
"PIKE HAD A NORMAL CHILDHOOD, I SUPPOSE--HAPPY HOMELIFE, THE USUAL NUMBER OF FRIENDS--
"--A HEALTHY DOSE OF HERO-WORSHIP, MOSTLY OF THE JSA. IF HE WAS SLIGHTLY WITHDRAWN, HE WAS NO MORE SO THAN MANY INTELLIGENT CHILDREN...
"...AND IF HIS HIGH SCHOOL AND COLLEGE YEARS WERE LESS THAN FULLY SOCIAL, PERHAPS IT WAS DUE TO HIS AMBITION AND DRIVE.
"UNDERSTAND ME, CHRISTOPHER PIKE HAD FRIENDS--
"HE WANTED ADVENTURE--GLORY--EXCITEMENT.
"THE SORT OF EXCITEMENT REPRESENTED BY THE JUSTICE SOCIETY--
"--THE KIND OF ADVENTURE FULFILLED BY OUR NATIONAL SPACE PROGRAM.
"AFTER RECEIVING HIS AIR FORCE COMMISSION, PIKE JOINED THE EARLY ASTRONAUT TRAINING PROGRAM.
"HE DID WELL. HE HAD AMBITION, HE HAD DRIVE--
"--AND APPARENTLY, HE ALSO HAD COURAGE.
"LAST YEAR, HE WAS SELECTED FOR VULCAN PROBE ONE--A TWO-HUNDRED-DAY ORBIT OF THE SUN, PREPARATION FOR OUR DEEP SPACE EXPLORATION PROJECT.
"WITH HIM WERE RAOUL JEROME, U.S.M.C.--FLIGHT COMMANDER--
"--AND DR. EDWARD SOLOMON--MISSION MEDICAL OFFICER.
"LIFT-OFF WAS PERFECT, BY THE BOOK. VULCAN ONE ACHIEVED EARTH-ORBIT, AND TEN HOURS LATER--
"--WAS ON ITS WAY TO THE SUN.

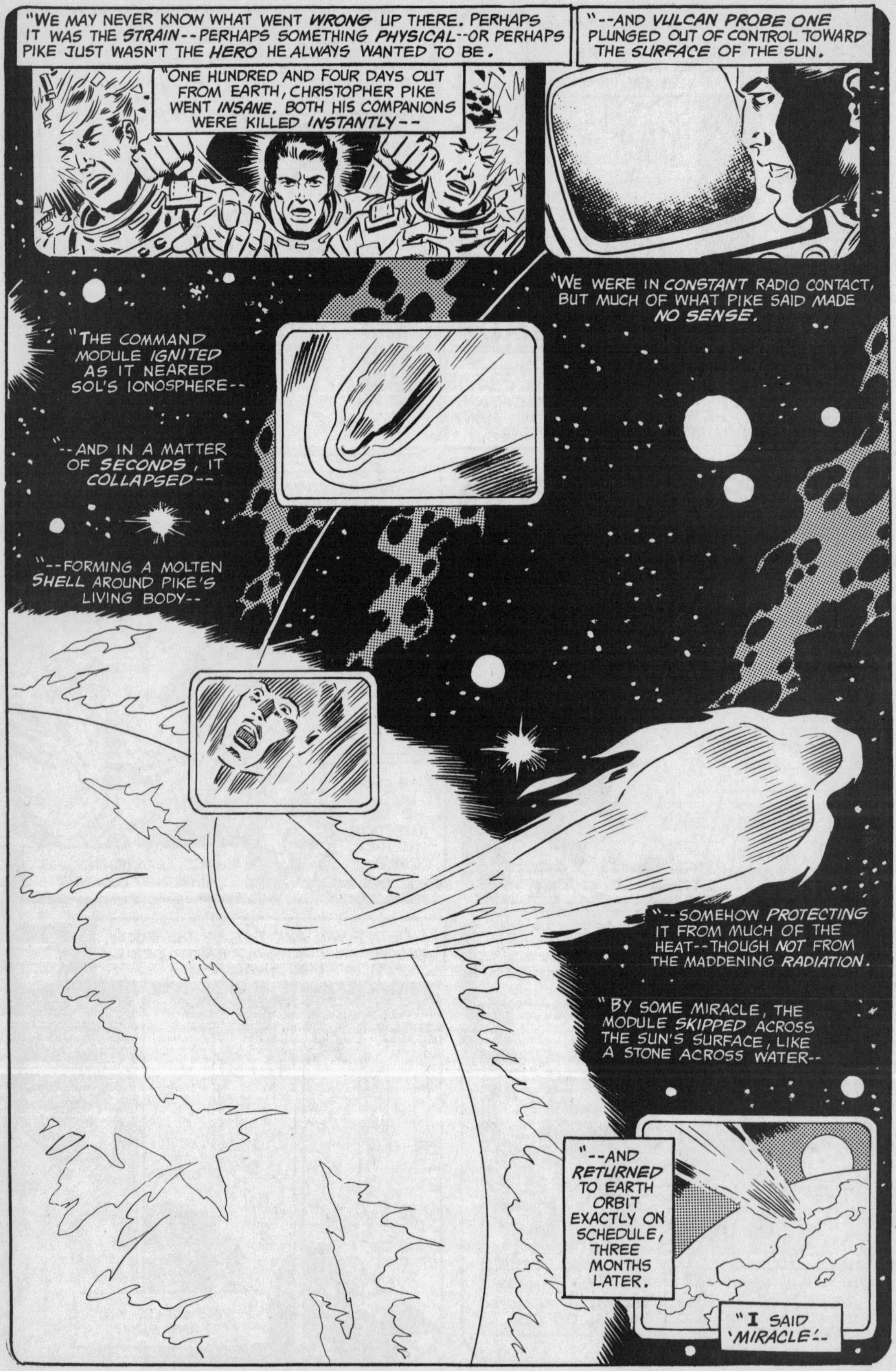
"WE MAY NEVER KNOW WHAT WENT WRONG UP THERE. PERHAPS IT WAS THE STRAIN--PERHAPS SOMETHING PHYSICAL--OR PERHAPS PIKE JUST WASN'T THE HERO HE ALWAYS WANTED TO BE.
"ONE HUNDRED AND FOUR DAYS OUT FROM EARTH, CHRISTOPHER PIKE WENT INSANE. BOTH HIS COMPANIONS WERE KILLED INSTANTLY--
"--AND VULCAN PROBE ONE PLUNGED OUT OF CONTROL TOWARD THE SURFACE OF THE SUN.
"WE WERE IN CONSTANT RADIO CONTACT, BUT MUCH OF WHAT PIKE SAID MADE NO SENSE.
"THE COMMAND MODULE IGNITED AS IT NEARED SOL'S IONOSPHERE--
"--AND IN A MATTER OF SECONDS, IT COLLAPSED--
"--FORMING A MOLTEN SHELL AROUND PIKE'S LIVING BODY--
"--SOMEHOW PROTECTING IT FROM MUCH OF THE HEAT--THOUGH NOT FROM THE MADDENING RADIATION.
"BY SOME MIRACLE, THE MODULE SKIPPED ACROSS THE SUN'S SURFACE, LIKE A STONE ACROSS WATER--
"--AND RETURNED TO EARTH ORBIT EXACTLY ON SCHEDULE, THREE MONTHS LATER.
"I SAID 'MIRACLE'--

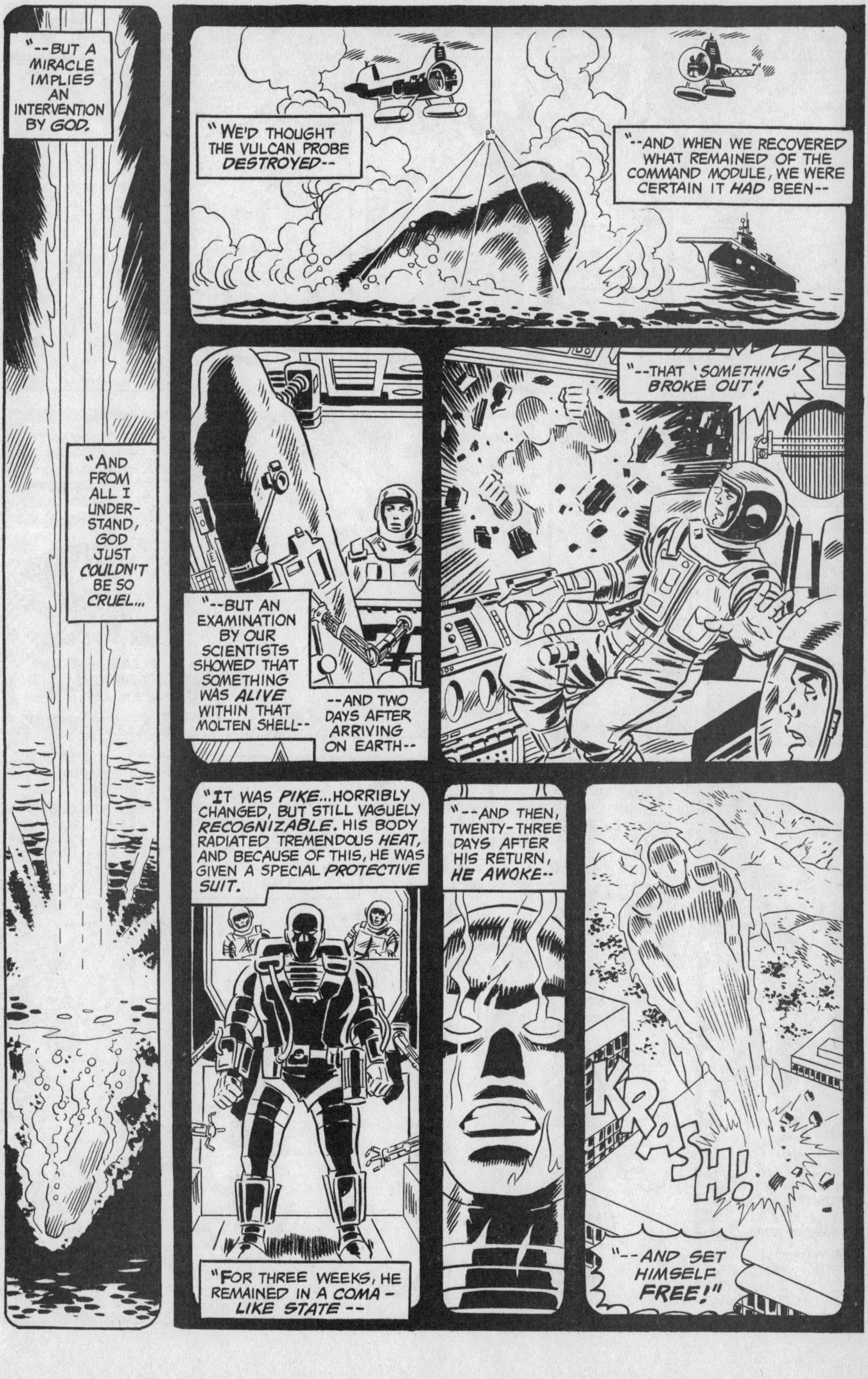
"--BUT A MIRACLE IMPLIES AN INTERVENTION BY GOD.
"AND FROM ALL I UNDER-STAND, GOD JUST COULDN'T BE SO CRUEL...
"WE'D THOUGHT THE VULCAN PROBE DESTROYED--
"--AND WHEN WE RECOVERED WHAT REMAINED OF THE COMMAND MODULE, WE WERE CERTAIN IT HAD BEEN--
"--BUT AN EXAMINATION BY OUR SCIENTISTS SHOWED THAT SOMETHING WAS ALIVE WITHIN THAT MOLTEN SHELL--
--AND TWO DAYS AFTER ARRIVING ON EARTH--
"--THAT 'SOMETHING' BROKE OUT!
"IT WAS PIKE...HORRIBLY CHANGED, BUT STILL VAGUELY RECOGNIZABLE. HIS BODY RADIATED TREMENDOUS HEAT, AND BECAUSE OF THIS, HE WAS GIVEN A SPECIAL PROTECTIVE SUIT.
"FOR THREE WEEKS, HE REMAINED IN A COMA-LIKE STATE --
"--AND THEN, TWENTY-THREE DAYS AFTER HIS RETURN, HE AWOKE--
KRASH!
"--AND SET HIMSELF FREE!"

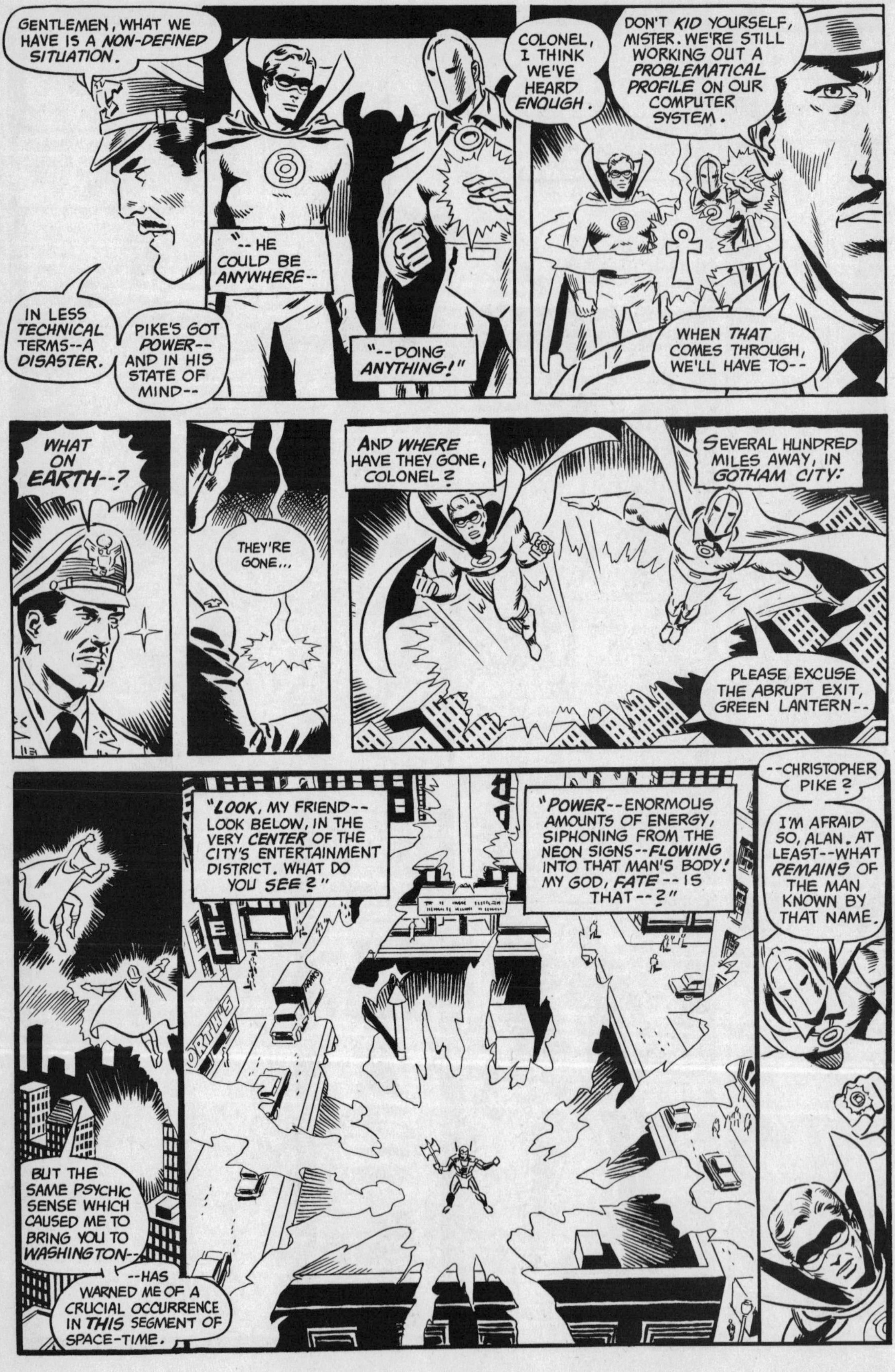
GENTLEMEN, WHAT WE HAVE IS A NON-DEFINED SITUATION.
IN LESS TECHNICAL TERMS--A DISASTER.
PIKE'S GOT POWER--AND IN HIS STATE OF MIND--
"--HE COULD BE ANYWHERE--
"--DOING ANYTHING!"
COLONEL, I THINK WE'VE HEARD ENOUGH.
DON'T KID YOURSELF, MISTER. WE'RE STILL WORKING OUT A PROBLEMATICAL PROFILE ON OUR COMPUTER SYSTEM.
WHEN THAT COMES THROUGH, WE'LL HAVE TO--
WHAT ON EARTH--?
THEY'RE GONE...
AND WHERE HAVE THEY GONE, COLONEL?
SEVERAL HUNDRED MILES AWAY, IN GOTHAM CITY:
PLEASE EXCUSE THE ABRUPT EXIT, GREEN LANTERN--
BUT THE SAME PSYCHIC SENSE WHICH CAUSED ME TO BRING YOU TO WASHINGTON--
--HAS WARNED ME OF A CRUCIAL OCCURRENCE IN THIS SEGMENT OF SPACE-TIME.
"LOOK, MY FRIEND--LOOK BELOW, IN THE VERY CENTER OF THE CITY'S ENTERTAINMENT DISTRICT. WHAT DO YOU SEE?"
"POWER--ENORMOUS AMOUNTS OF ENERGY, SIPHONING FROM THE NEON SIGNS--FLOWING INTO THAT MAN'S BODY! MY GOD, FATE--IS THAT--?"
--CHRISTOPHER PIKE?
I'M AFRAID SO, ALAN. AT LEAST--WHAT REMAINS OF THE MAN KNOWN BY THAT NAME.

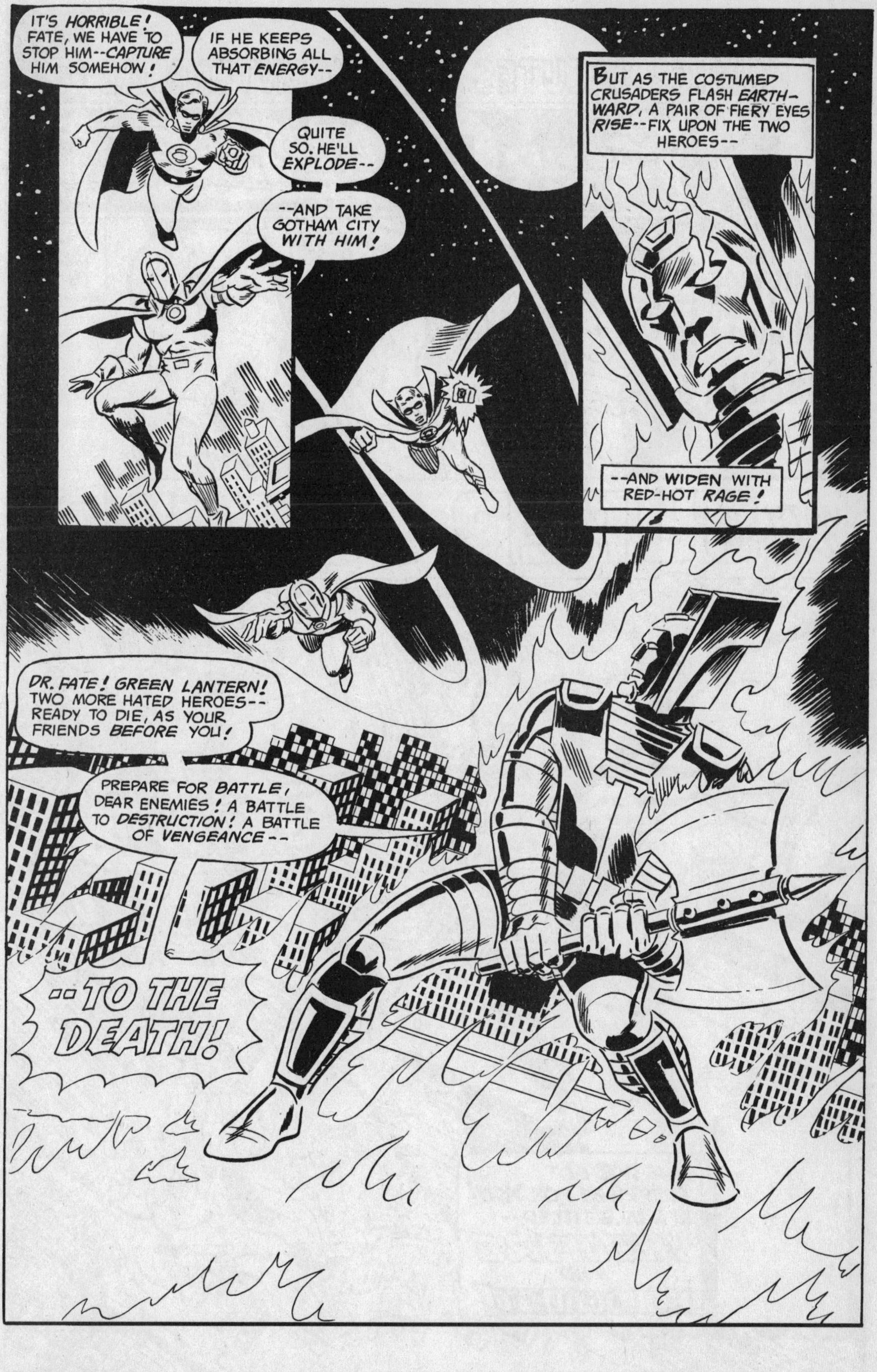
IT'S HORRIBLE! FATE, WE HAVE TO STOP HIM--CAPTURE HIM SOMEHOW!
IF HE KEEPS ABSORBING ALL THAT ENERGY--
QUITE SO. HE'LL EXPLODE--
--AND TAKE GOTHAM CITY WITH HIM!
BUT AS THE COSTUMED CRUSADERS FLASH EARTHWARD, A PAIR OF FIERY EYES RISE--FIX UPON THE TWO HEROES--
--AND WIDEN WITH RED-HOT RAGE!
DR. FATE! GREEN LANTERN! TWO MORE HATED HEROES--READY TO DIE, AS YOUR FRIENDS BEFORE YOU!
PREPARE FOR BATTLE, DEAR ENEMIES! A BATTLE TO DESTRUCTION! A BATTLE OF VENGEANCE--
--TO THE DEATH!

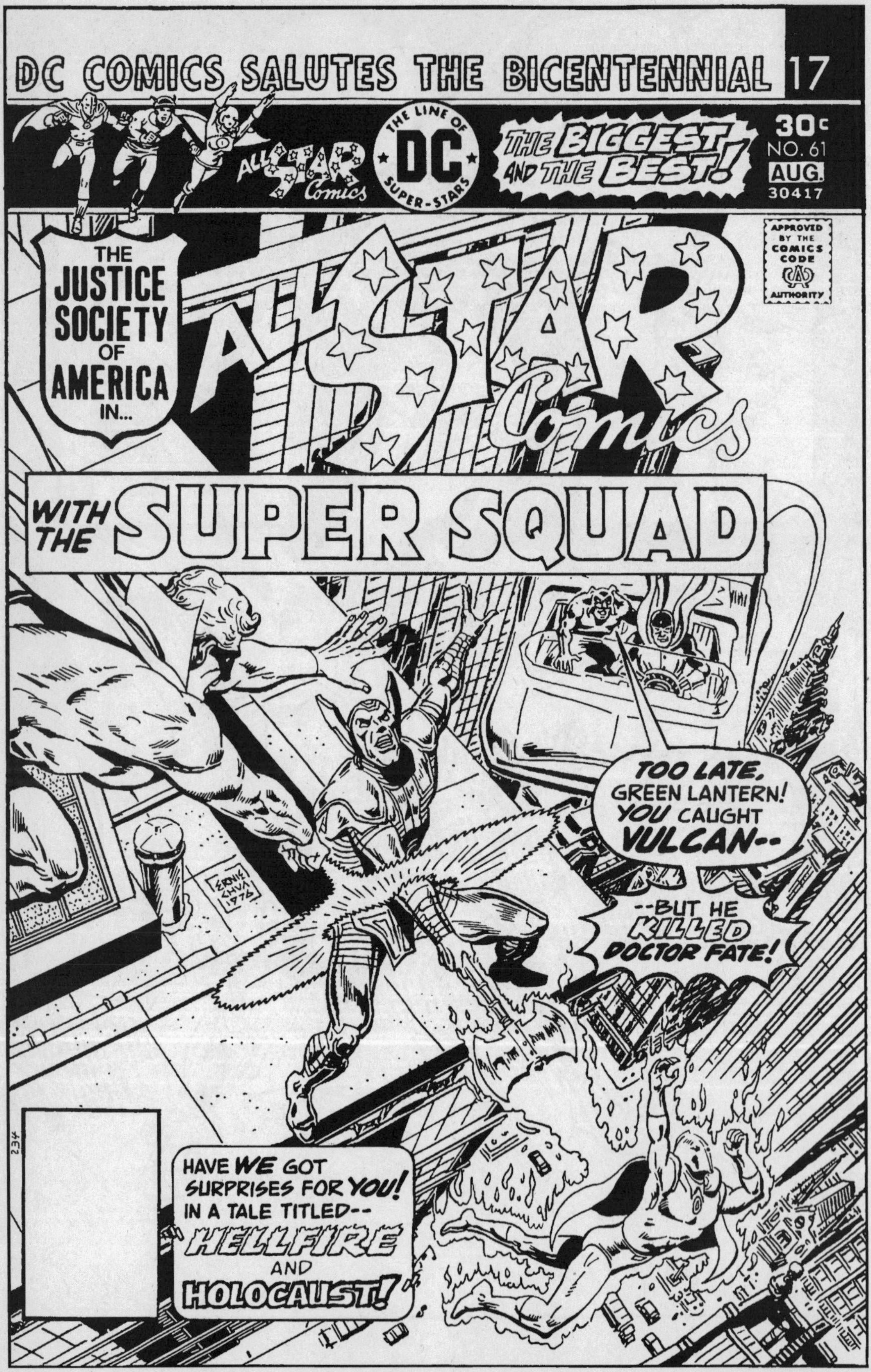
DC COMICS SALUTES THE BICENTENNIAL 17
ALL STAR Comics
THE LINE OF DC SUPER-STARS
THE BIGGEST AND THE BEST!
30¢
NO. 61
AUG.
30417
APPROVED BY THE COMICS CODE AUTHORITY
THE JUSTICE SOCIETY OF AMERICA IN...
ALL STAR Comics
WITH THE SUPER SQUAD
TOO LATE, GREEN LANTERN! YOU CAUGHT VULCAN--
--BUT HE KILLED DOCTOR FATE!
HAVE WE GOT SURPRISES FOR YOU! IN A TALE TITLED-- HELLFIRE AND HOLOCAUST!
ERNIE CHUA 1976

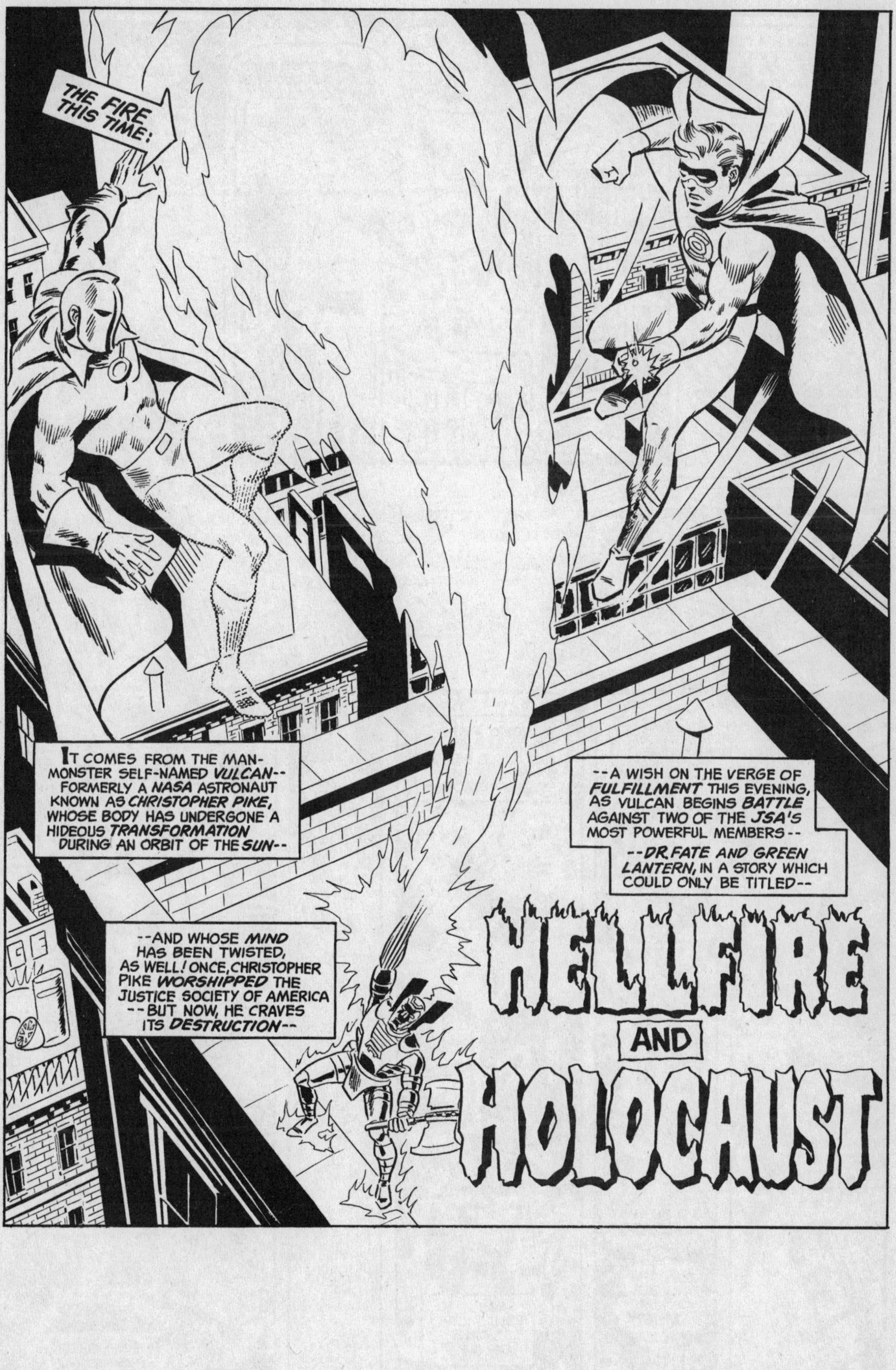
THE FIRE THIS TIME:
IT COMES FROM THE MAN-MONSTER SELF-NAMED VULCAN--FORMERLY A NASA ASTRONAUT KNOWN AS CHRISTOPHER PIKE, WHOSE BODY HAS UNDERGONE A HIDEOUS TRANSFORMATION DURING AN ORBIT OF THE SUN--
--AND WHOSE MIND HAS BEEN TWISTED, AS WELL! ONCE, CHRISTOPHER PIKE WORSHIPPED THE JUSTICE SOCIETY OF AMERICA --BUT NOW, HE CRAVES ITS DESTRUCTION--
--A WISH ON THE VERGE OF FULFILLMENT THIS EVENING, AS VULCAN BEGINS BATTLE AGAINST TWO OF THE JSA'S MOST POWERFUL MEMBERS--
--DR. FATE AND GREEN LANTERN, IN A STORY WHICH COULD ONLY BE TITLED--
HELLFIRE AND HOLOCAUST

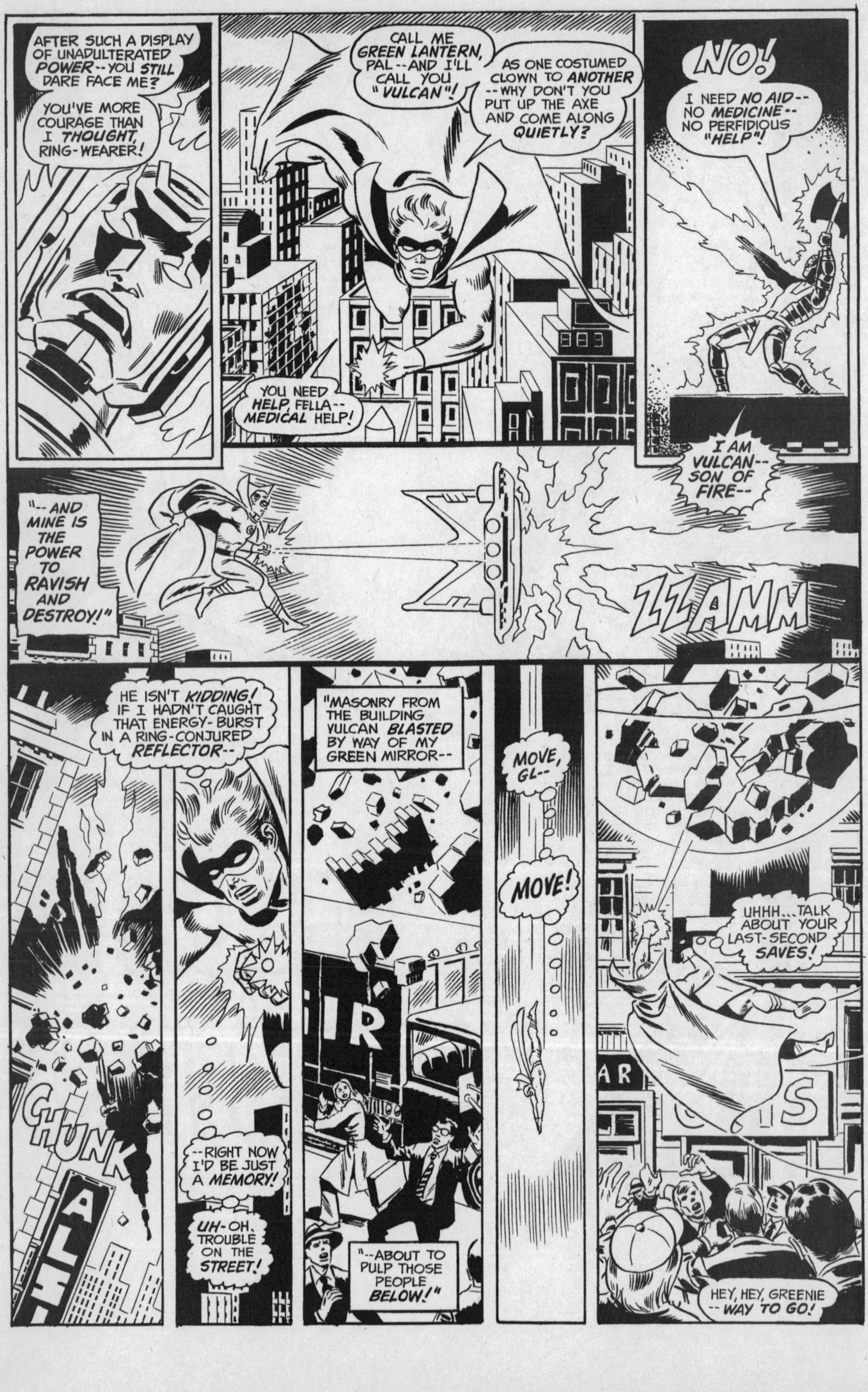
AFTER SUCH A DISPLAY OF UNADULTERATED POWER--YOU STILL DARE FACE ME?
YOU'VE MORE COURAGE THAN I THOUGHT, RING-WEARER!
CALL ME GREEN LANTERN, PAL--AND I'LL CALL YOU "VULCAN"!
AS ONE COSTUMED CLOWN TO ANOTHER--WHY DON'T YOU PUT UP THE AXE AND COME ALONG QUIETLY?
YOU NEED HELP, FELLA--MEDICAL HELP!
NO!
I NEED NO AID--NO MEDICINE--NO PERFIDIOUS "HELP"!
I AM VULCAN--SON OF FIRE--
"--AND MINE IS THE POWER TO RAVISH AND DESTROY!"
ZZAMM
HE ISN'T KIDDING! IF I HADN'T CAUGHT THAT ENERGY-BURST IN A RING-CONJURED REFLECTOR--
CHUNK
--RIGHT NOW I'D BE JUST A MEMORY!
UH-OH. TROUBLE ON THE STREET!
"MASONRY FROM THE BUILDING VULCAN BLASTED BY WAY OF MY GREEN MIRROR--
"--ABOUT TO PULP THOSE PEOPLE BELOW!"
MOVE, GL--
MOVE!
UHHH...TALK ABOUT YOUR LAST-SECOND SAVES!
HEY, HEY, GREENIE--WAY TO GO!

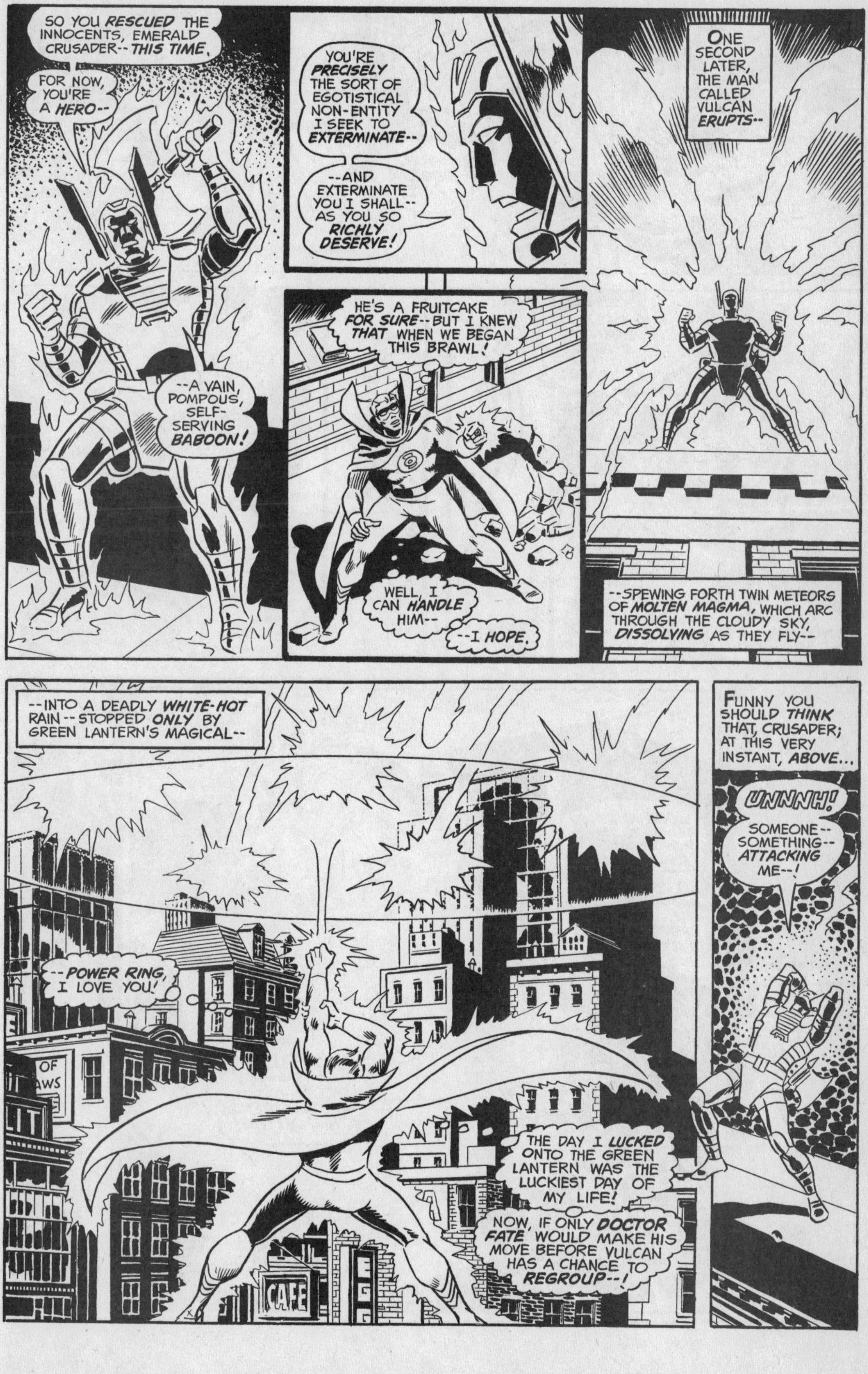
SO YOU RESCUED THE INNOCENTS, EMERALD CRUSADER--THIS TIME.
FOR NOW, YOU'RE A HERO--
YOU'RE PRECISELY THE SORT OF EGOTISTICAL NON-ENTITY I SEEK TO EXTERMINATE--
--AND EXTERMINATE YOU I SHALL--AS YOU SO RICHLY DESERVE!
--A VAIN, POMPOUS, SELF-SERVING BABOON!
ONE SECOND LATER, THE MAN CALLED VULCAN ERUPTS--
HE'S A FRUITCAKE FOR SURE--BUT I KNEW THAT WHEN WE BEGAN THIS BRAWL!
WELL, I CAN HANDLE HIM--
--I HOPE.
--SPEWING FORTH TWIN METEORS OF MOLTEN MAGMA, WHICH ARC THROUGH THE CLOUDY SKY, DISSOLVING AS THEY FLY--
--INTO A DEADLY WHITE-HOT RAIN--STOPPED ONLY BY GREEN LANTERN'S MAGICAL--
--POWER RING, I LOVE YOU!
THE DAY I LUCKED ONTO THE GREEN LANTERN WAS THE LUCKIEST DAY OF MY LIFE!
NOW, IF ONLY DOCTOR FATE WOULD MAKE HIS MOVE BEFORE VULCAN HAS A CHANCE TO REGROUP--!
CAFE
FUNNY YOU SHOULD THINK THAT, CRUSADER; AT THIS VERY INSTANT, ABOVE...
UNNNH!
SOMEONE--SOMETHING--ATTACKING ME--!

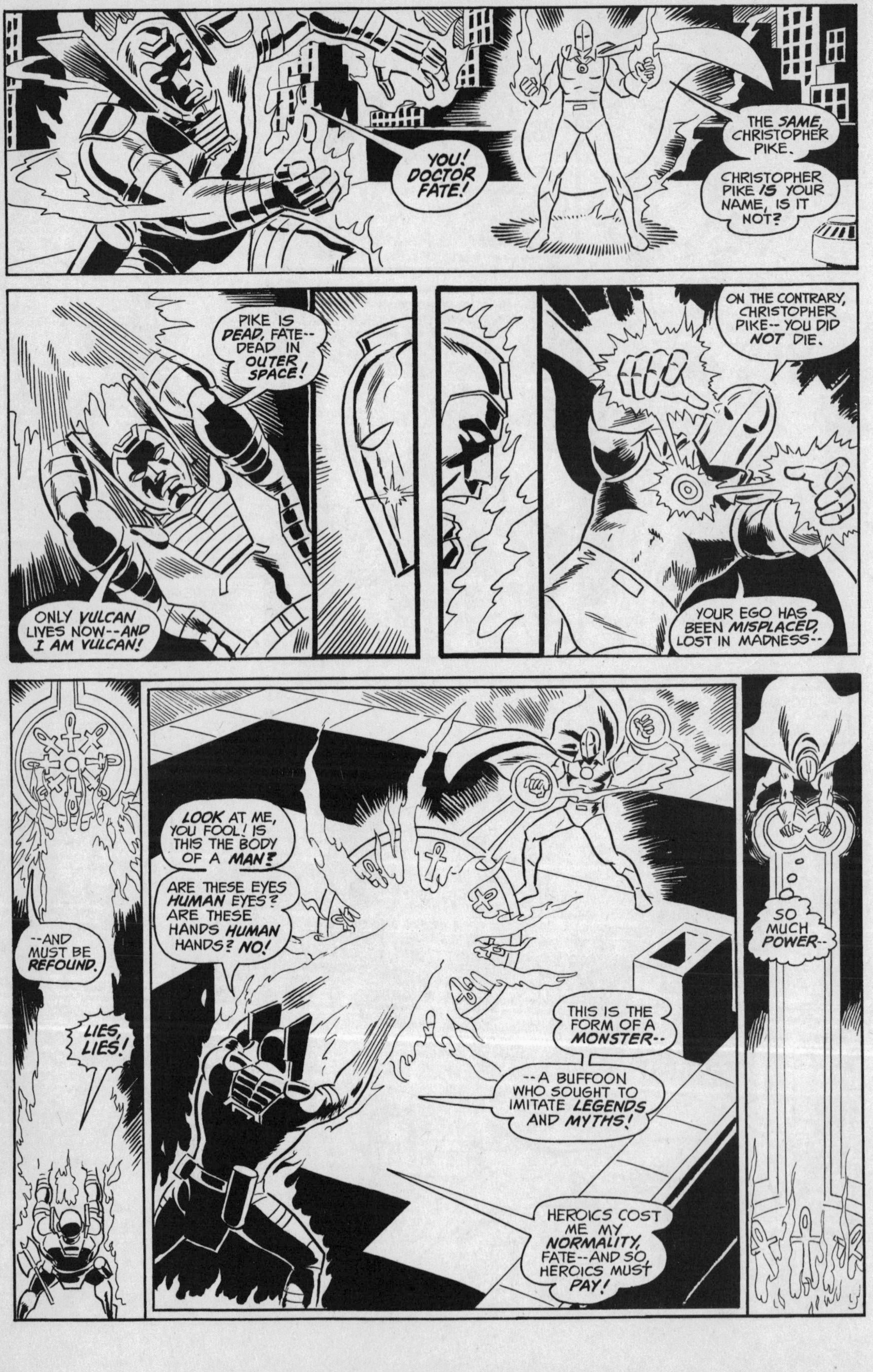
YOU! DOCTOR FATE!
THE SAME, CHRISTOPHER PIKE.
CHRISTOPHER PIKE IS YOUR NAME, IS IT NOT?
PIKE IS DEAD, FATE-- DEAD IN OUTER SPACE!
ONLY VULCAN LIVES NOW--AND I AM VULCAN!
ON THE CONTRARY, CHRISTOPHER PIKE-- YOU DID NOT DIE.
YOUR EGO HAS BEEN MISPLACED, LOST IN MADNESS--
--AND MUST BE REFOUND.
LIES, LIES!
LOOK AT ME, YOU FOOL! IS THIS THE BODY OF A MAN?
ARE THESE EYES HUMAN EYES? ARE THESE HANDS HUMAN HANDS? NO!
THIS IS THE FORM OF A MONSTER--
--A BUFFOON WHO SOUGHT TO IMITATE LEGENDS AND MYTHS!
HEROICS COST ME MY NORMALITY, FATE--AND SO, HEROICS MUST PAY!
SO MUCH POWER--

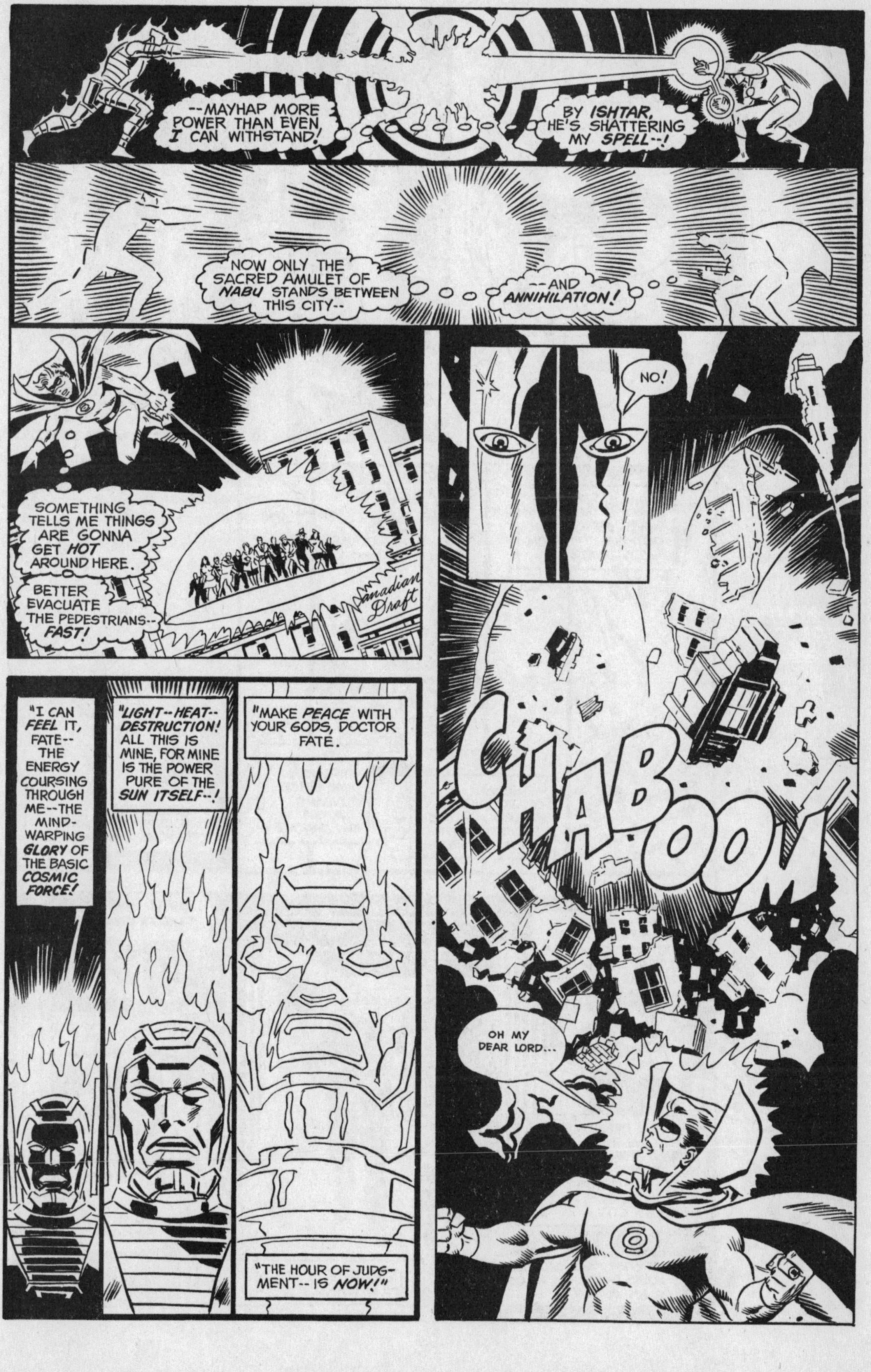
--MAYHAP MORE POWER THAN EVEN, I CAN WITHSTAND!
BY ISHTAR, HE'S SHATTERING MY SPELL--!
NOW ONLY THE SACRED AMULET OF NABU STANDS BETWEEN THIS CITY--
--AND ANNIHILATION!
SOMETHING TELLS ME THINGS ARE GONNA GET HOT AROUND HERE.
BETTER EVACUATE THE PEDESTRIANS--FAST!
Canadian Draft
NO!
"I CAN FEEL IT, FATE--THE ENERGY COURSING THROUGH ME--THE MIND-WARPING GLORY OF THE BASIC COSMIC FORCE!
"LIGHT--HEAT--DESTRUCTION! ALL THIS IS MINE, FOR MINE IS THE POWER PURE OF THE SUN ITSELF--!
"MAKE PEACE WITH YOUR GODS, DOCTOR FATE.
"THE HOUR OF JUDGMENT--IS NOW!"
CHABOOM
OH MY DEAR LORD...

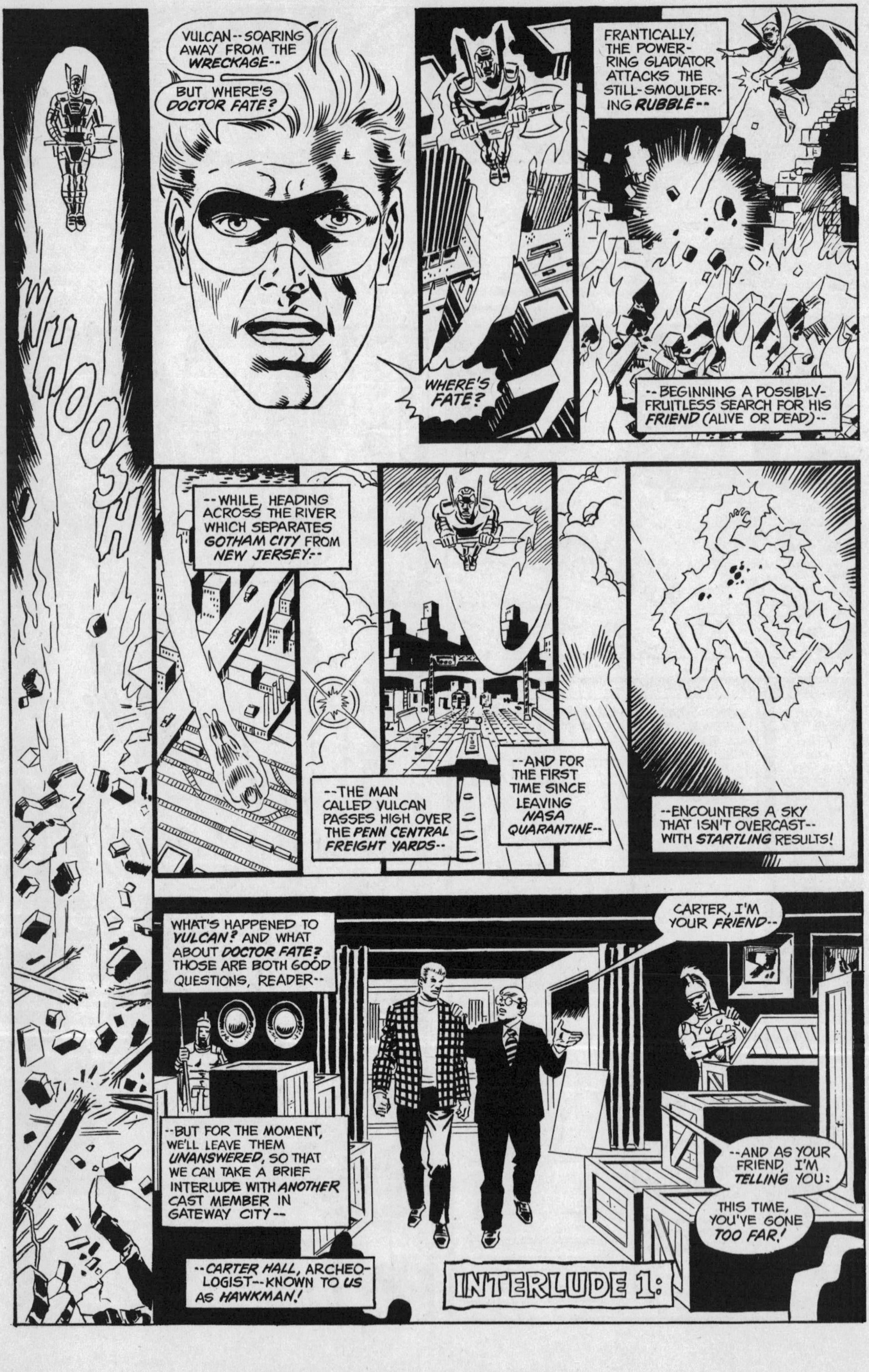
VULCAN--SOARING AWAY FROM THE WRECKAGE--
BUT WHERE'S DOCTOR FATE?
WHOOSH
WHERE'S FATE?
FRANTICALLY, THE POWER-RING GLADIATOR ATTACKS THE STILL-SMOULDERING RUBBLE--
--BEGINNING A POSSIBLY-FRUITLESS SEARCH FOR HIS FRIEND (ALIVE OR DEAD)--
--WHILE, HEADING ACROSS THE RIVER WHICH SEPARATES GOTHAM CITY FROM NEW JERSEY--
--THE MAN CALLED VULCAN PASSES HIGH OVER THE PENN CENTRAL FREIGHT YARDS--
--AND FOR THE FIRST TIME SINCE LEAVING NASA QUARANTINE--
--ENCOUNTERS A SKY THAT ISN'T OVERCAST--WITH STARTLING RESULTS!
WHAT'S HAPPENED TO VULCAN? AND WHAT ABOUT DOCTOR FATE? THOSE ARE BOTH GOOD QUESTIONS, READER--
--BUT FOR THE MOMENT, WE'LL LEAVE THEM UNANSWERED, SO THAT WE CAN TAKE A BRIEF INTERLUDE WITH ANOTHER CAST MEMBER IN GATEWAY CITY--
--CARTER HALL, ARCHEOLOGIST--KNOWN TO US AS HAWKMAN!
INTERLUDE 1:
CARTER, I'M YOUR FRIEND--
--AND AS YOUR FRIEND, I'M TELLING YOU:
THIS TIME, YOU'VE GONE TOO FAR!

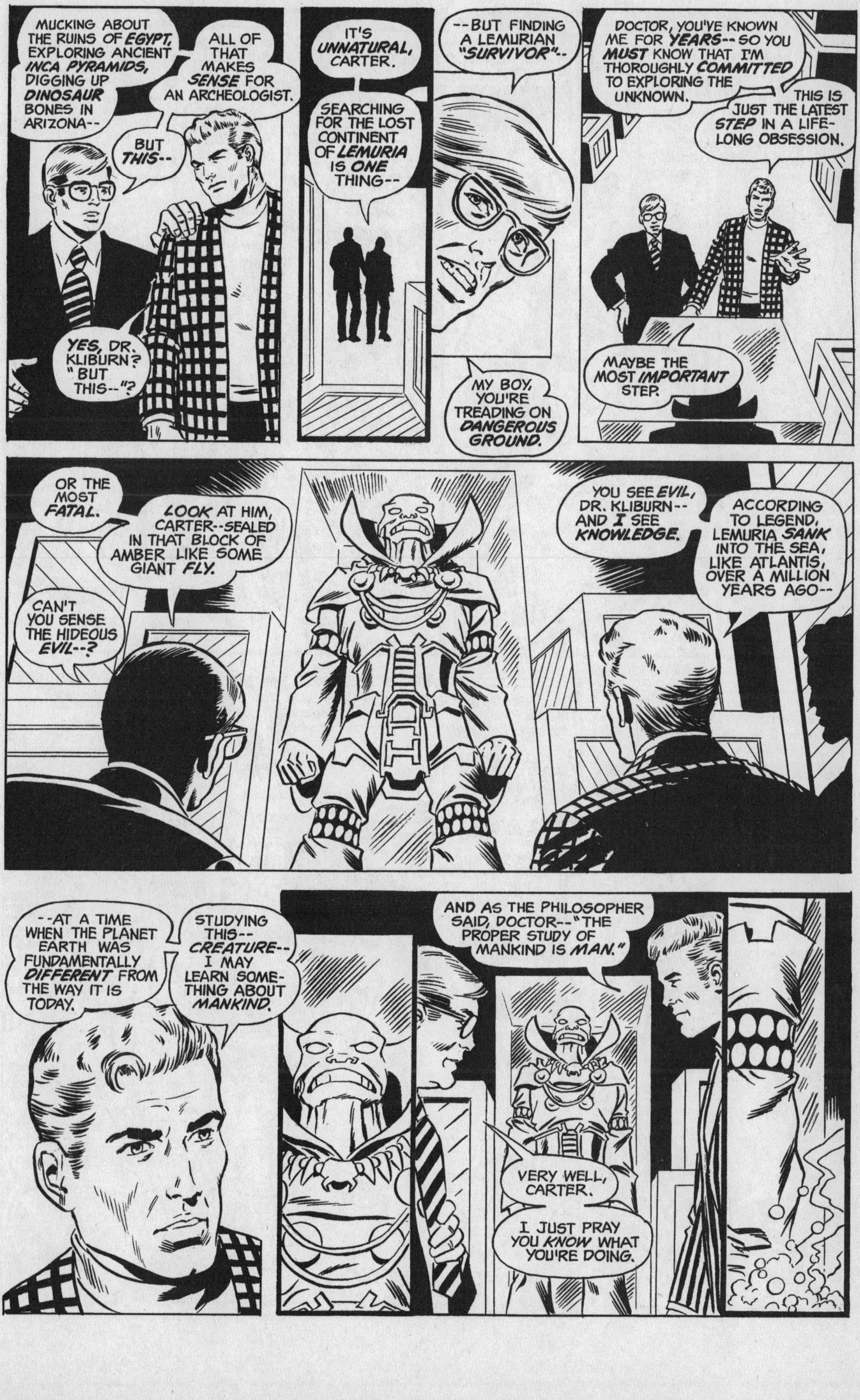
MUCKING ABOUT THE RUINS OF EGYPT, EXPLORING ANCIENT INCA PYRAMIDS, DIGGING UP DINOSAUR BONES IN ARIZONA--
ALL OF THAT MAKES SENSE FOR AN ARCHEOLOGIST.
BUT THIS--
YES, DR. KLIBURN? "BUT THIS--"?
IT'S UNNATURAL, CARTER.
SEARCHING FOR THE LOST CONTINENT OF LEMURIA IS ONE THING--
--BUT FINDING A LEMURIAN "SURVIVOR"--
MY BOY, YOU'RE TREADING ON DANGEROUS GROUND.
DOCTOR, YOU'VE KNOWN ME FOR YEARS-- SO YOU MUST KNOW THAT I'M THOROUGHLY COMMITTED TO EXPLORING THE UNKNOWN.
THIS IS JUST THE LATEST STEP IN A LIFE-LONG OBSESSION.
MAYBE THE MOST IMPORTANT STEP.
OR THE MOST FATAL.
LOOK AT HIM, CARTER--SEALED IN THAT BLOCK OF AMBER LIKE SOME GIANT FLY.
CAN'T YOU SENSE THE HIDEOUS EVIL--?
YOU SEE EVIL, DR. KLIBURN-- AND I SEE KNOWLEDGE.
ACCORDING TO LEGEND, LEMURIA SANK INTO THE SEA, LIKE ATLANTIS, OVER A MILLION YEARS AGO--
--AT A TIME WHEN THE PLANET EARTH WAS FUNDAMENTALLY DIFFERENT FROM THE WAY IT IS TODAY.
STUDYING THIS-- CREATURE-- I MAY LEARN SOME-THING ABOUT MANKIND.
AND AS THE PHILOSOPHER SAID, DOCTOR-- "THE PROPER STUDY OF MANKIND IS MAN."
VERY WELL, CARTER.
I JUST PRAY YOU KNOW WHAT YOU'RE DOING.

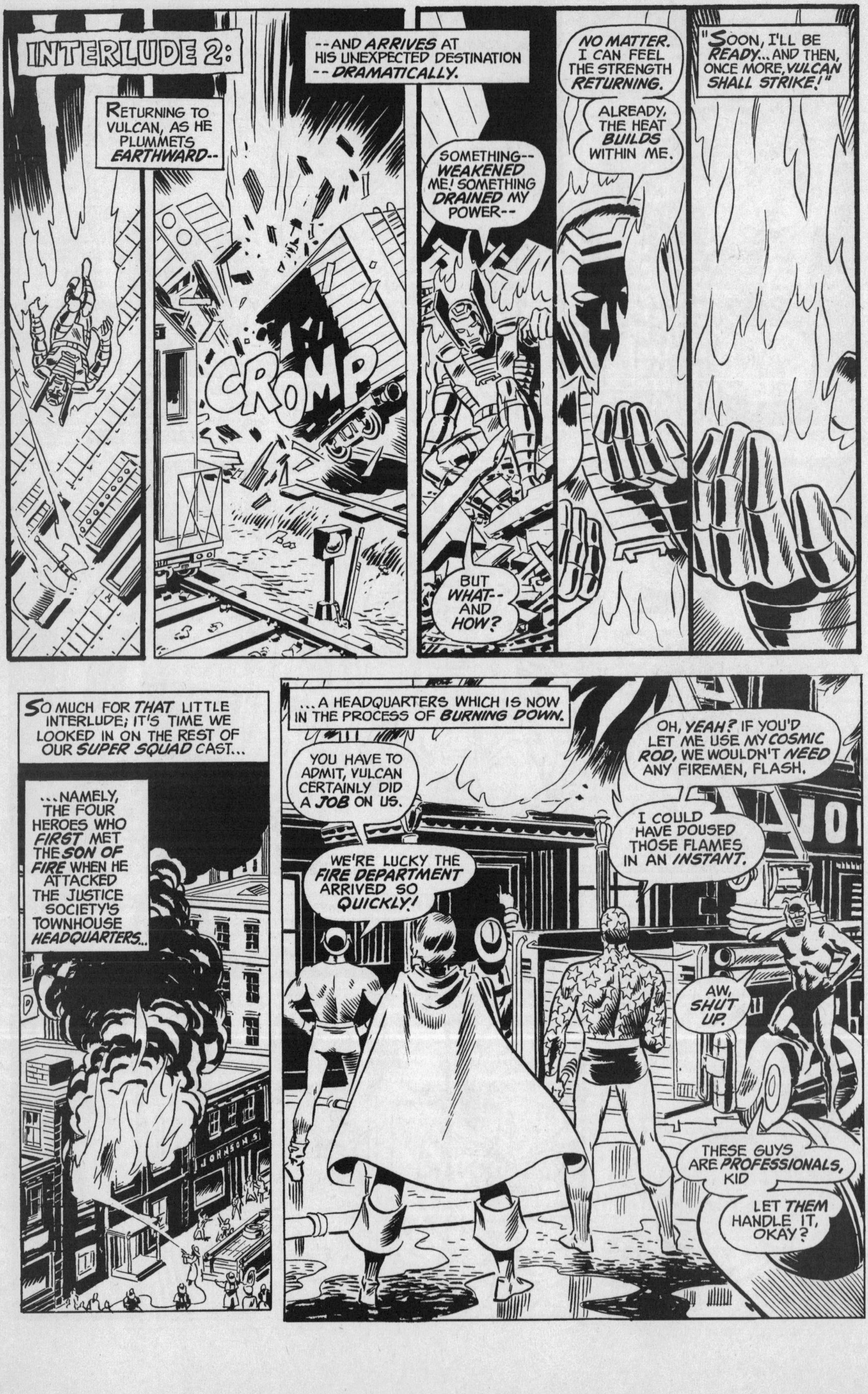
INTERLUDE 2:
RETURNING TO VULCAN, AS HE PLUMMETS EARTHWARD--
--AND ARRIVES AT HIS UNEXPECTED DESTINATION --DRAMATICALLY.
CROMP
SOMETHING--WEAKENED ME! SOMETHING DRAINED MY POWER--
BUT WHAT--AND HOW?
NO MATTER. I CAN FEEL THE STRENGTH RETURNING.
ALREADY, THE HEAT BUILDS WITHIN ME.
"SOON, I'LL BE READY...AND THEN, ONCE MORE, VULCAN SHALL STRIKE!"
SO MUCH FOR THAT LITTLE INTERLUDE; IT'S TIME WE LOOKED IN ON THE REST OF OUR SUPER SQUAD CAST...
...NAMELY, THE FOUR HEROES WHO FIRST MET THE SON OF FIRE WHEN HE ATTACKED THE JUSTICE SOCIETY'S TOWNHOUSE HEADQUARTERS...
JOHNSON'S
...A HEADQUARTERS WHICH IS NOW IN THE PROCESS OF BURNING DOWN.
YOU HAVE TO ADMIT, VULCAN CERTAINLY DID A JOB ON US.
WE'RE LUCKY THE FIRE DEPARTMENT ARRIVED SO QUICKLY!
OH, YEAH? IF YOU'D LET ME USE MY COSMIC ROD, WE WOULDN'T NEED ANY FIREMEN, FLASH.
I COULD HAVE DOUSED THOSE FLAMES IN AN INSTANT.
AW, SHUT UP.
THESE GUYS ARE PROFESSIONALS, KID
LET THEM HANDLE IT, OKAY?

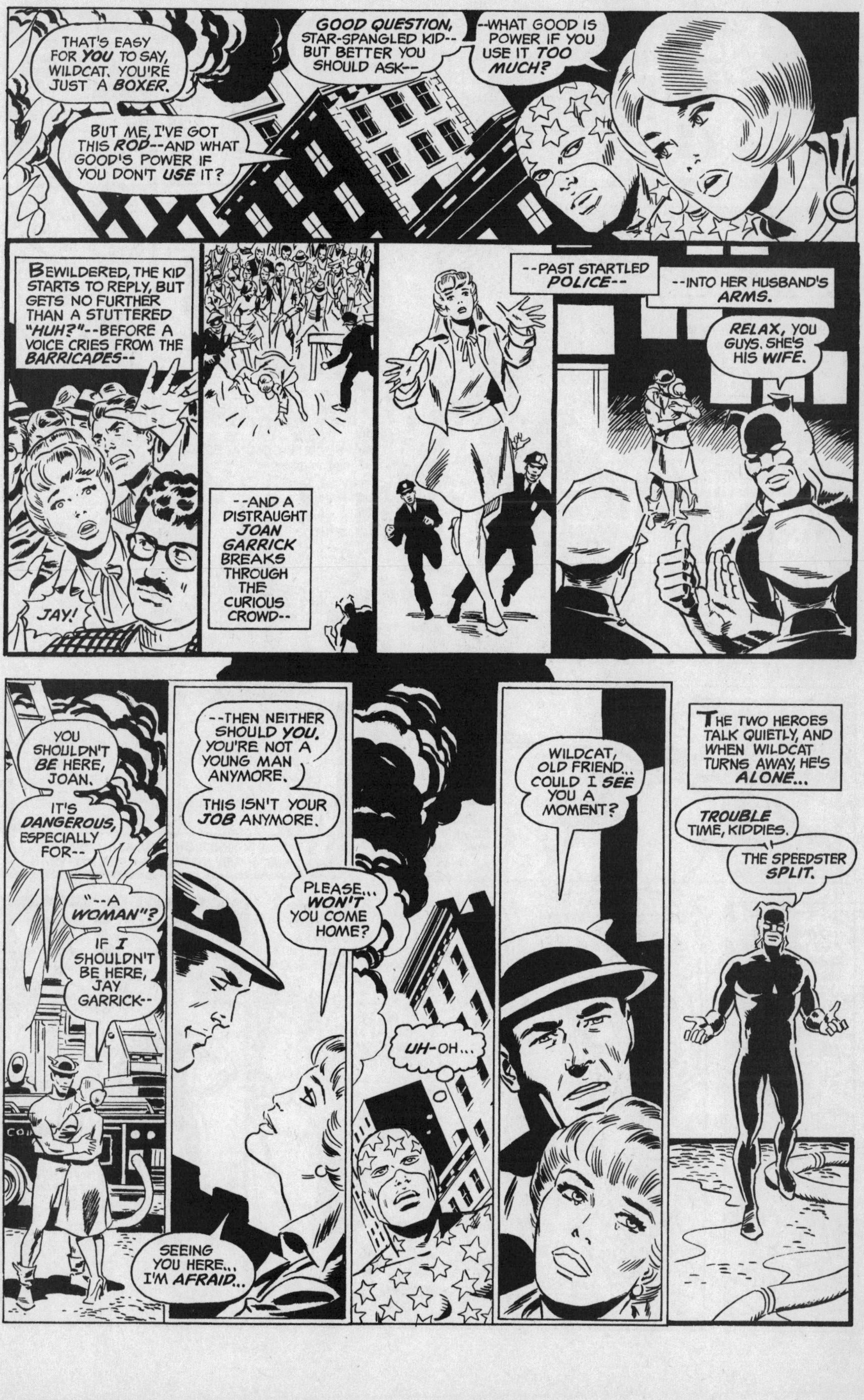
THAT'S EASY FOR YOU TO SAY, WILDCAT. YOU'RE JUST A BOXER.
BUT ME, I'VE GOT THIS ROD--AND WHAT GOOD'S POWER IF YOU DON'T USE IT?
GOOD QUESTION, STAR-SPANGLED KID--BUT BETTER YOU SHOULD ASK--
--WHAT GOOD IS POWER IF YOU USE IT TOO MUCH?
BEWILDERED, THE KID STARTS TO REPLY, BUT GETS NO FURTHER THAN A STUTTERED "HUH?"--BEFORE A VOICE CRIES FROM THE BARRICADES--
JAY!
--AND A DISTRAUGHT JOAN GARRICK BREAKS THROUGH THE CURIOUS CROWD--
--PAST STARTLED POLICE--
--INTO HER HUSBAND'S ARMS.
RELAX, YOU GUYS. SHE'S HIS WIFE.
YOU SHOULDN'T BE HERE, JOAN.
IT'S DANGEROUS, ESPECIALLY FOR--
"--A WOMAN"?
IF I SHOULDN'T BE HERE, JAY GARRICK--
--THEN NEITHER SHOULD YOU. YOU'RE NOT A YOUNG MAN ANYMORE.
THIS ISN'T YOUR JOB ANYMORE.
PLEASE... WON'T YOU COME HOME?
SEEING YOU HERE... I'M AFRAID...
UH-OH...
WILDCAT, OLD FRIEND... COULD I SEE YOU A MOMENT?
THE TWO HEROES TALK QUIETLY, AND WHEN WILDCAT TURNS AWAY, HE'S ALONE...
TROUBLE TIME, KIDDIES.
THE SPEEDSTER SPLIT.

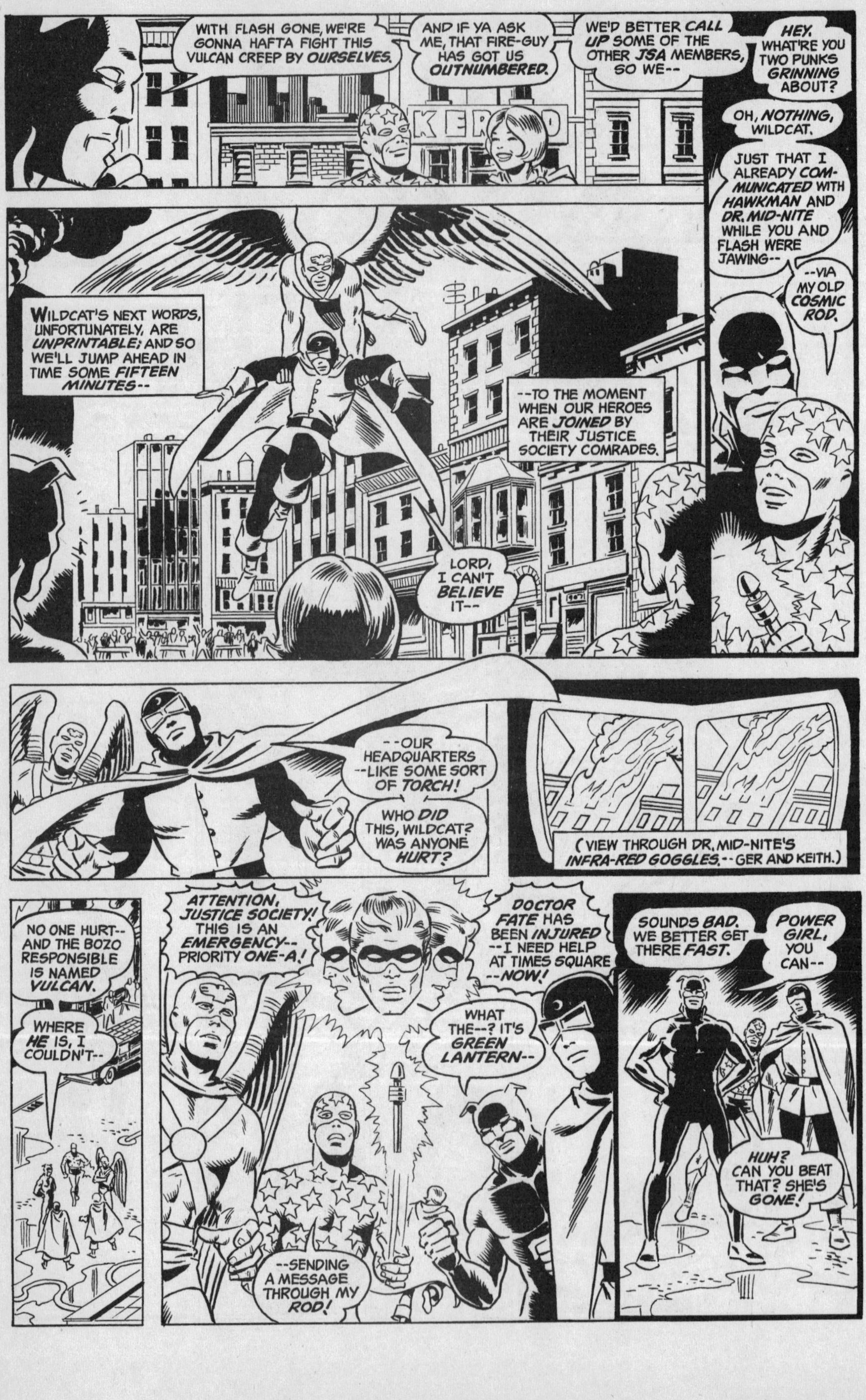
WITH FLASH GONE, WE'RE GONNA HAFTA FIGHT THIS VULCAN CREEP BY OURSELVES.
AND IF YA ASK ME, THAT FIRE-GUY HAS GOT US OUTNUMBERED.
WE'D BETTER CALL UP SOME OF THE OTHER JSA MEMBERS, SO WE--
HEY. WHAT'RE YOU TWO PUNKS GRINNING ABOUT?
OH, NOTHING, WILDCAT.
JUST THAT I ALREADY COMMUNICATED WITH HAWKMAN AND DR. MID-NITE WHILE YOU AND FLASH WERE JAWING--
--VIA MY OLD COSMIC ROD.
WILDCAT'S NEXT WORDS, UNFORTUNATELY, ARE UNPRINTABLE; AND SO WE'LL JUMP AHEAD IN TIME SOME FIFTEEN MINUTES--
--TO THE MOMENT WHEN OUR HEROES ARE JOINED BY THEIR JUSTICE SOCIETY COMRADES.
LORD, I CAN'T BELIEVE IT--
--OUR HEADQUARTERS --LIKE SOME SORT OF TORCH!
WHO DID THIS, WILDCAT? WAS ANYONE HURT?
(VIEW THROUGH DR. MID-NITE'S INFRA-RED GOGGLES.--GER AND KEITH.)
NO ONE HURT-- AND THE BOZO RESPONSIBLE IS NAMED VULCAN.
WHERE HE IS, I COULDN'T--
ATTENTION, JUSTICE SOCIETY! THIS IS AN EMERGENCY-- PRIORITY ONE-A!
DOCTOR FATE HAS BEEN INJURED --I NEED HELP AT TIMES SQUARE --NOW!
WHAT THE--? IT'S GREEN LANTERN--
--SENDING A MESSAGE THROUGH MY ROD!
SOUNDS BAD. WE BETTER GET THERE FAST.
POWER GIRL, YOU CAN--
HUH? CAN YOU BEAT THAT? SHE'S GONE!

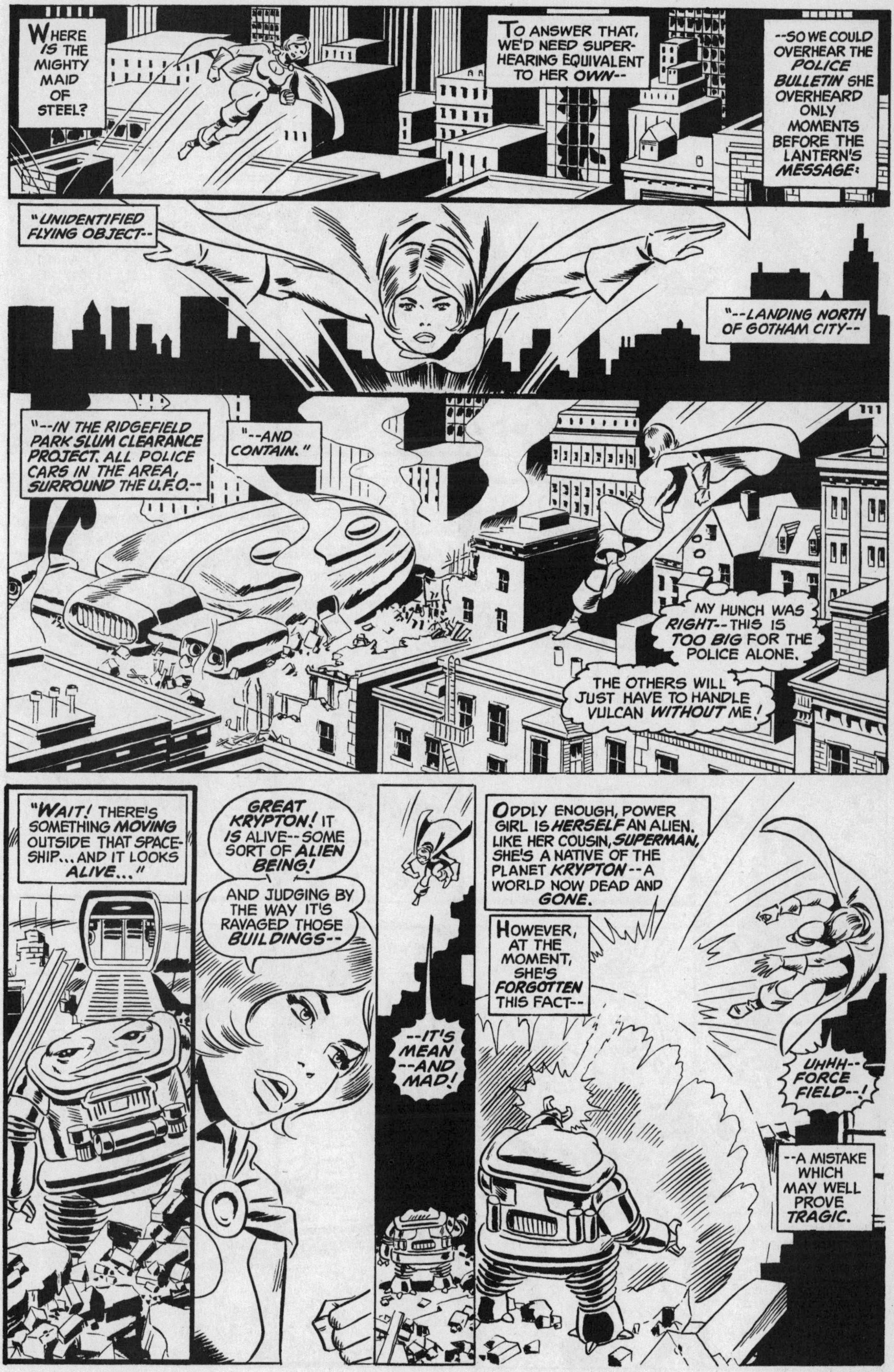
WHERE IS THE MIGHTY MAID OF STEEL?
TO ANSWER THAT, WE'D NEED SUPER-HEARING EQUIVALENT TO HER OWN--
--SO WE COULD OVERHEAR THE POLICE BULLETIN SHE OVERHEARD ONLY MOMENTS BEFORE THE LANTERN'S MESSAGE:
"UNIDENTIFIED FLYING OBJECT--
"--LANDING NORTH OF GOTHAM CITY--
"--IN THE RIDGEFIELD PARK SLUM CLEARANCE PROJECT. ALL POLICE CARS IN THE AREA, SURROUND THE U.F.O.--
"--AND CONTAIN."
MY HUNCH WAS RIGHT--THIS IS TOO BIG FOR THE POLICE ALONE.
THE OTHERS WILL JUST HAVE TO HANDLE VULCAN WITHOUT ME!
"WAIT! THERE'S SOMETHING MOVING OUTSIDE THAT SPACE-SHIP...AND IT LOOKS ALIVE..."
GREAT KRYPTON! IT IS ALIVE--SOME SORT OF ALIEN BEING!
AND JUDGING BY THE WAY IT'S RAVAGED THOSE BUILDINGS--
--IT'S MEAN --AND MAD!
ODDLY ENOUGH, POWER GIRL IS HERSELF AN ALIEN. LIKE HER COUSIN, SUPERMAN, SHE'S A NATIVE OF THE PLANET KRYPTON--A WORLD NOW DEAD AND GONE.
HOWEVER, AT THE MOMENT, SHE'S FORGOTTEN THIS FACT--
UHHH--FORCE FIELD--!
--A MISTAKE WHICH MAY WELL PROVE TRAGIC.

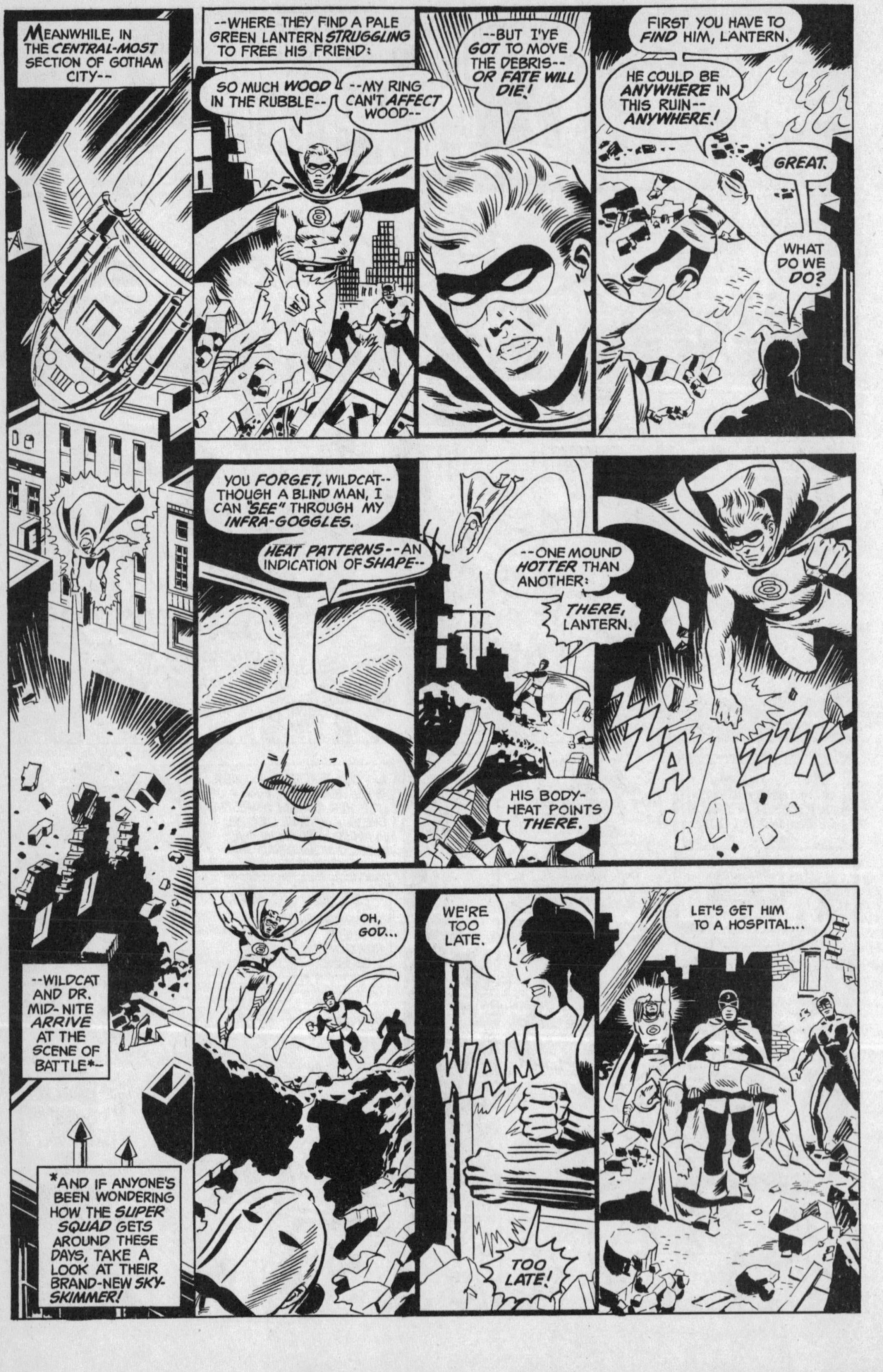
MEANWHILE, IN THE CENTRAL-MOST SECTION OF GOTHAM CITY--
--WHERE THEY FIND A PALE GREEN LANTERN STRUGGLING TO FREE HIS FRIEND:
SO MUCH WOOD IN THE RUBBLE--
--MY RING CAN'T AFFECT WOOD--
--BUT I'VE GOT TO MOVE THE DEBRIS-- OR FATE WILL DIE!
FIRST YOU HAVE TO FIND HIM, LANTERN.
HE COULD BE ANYWHERE IN THIS RUIN-- ANYWHERE!
GREAT.
WHAT DO WE DO?
--WILDCAT AND DR. MID-NITE ARRIVE AT THE SCENE OF BATTLE*--
*AND IF ANYONE'S BEEN WONDERING HOW THE SUPER SQUAD GETS AROUND THESE DAYS, TAKE A LOOK AT THEIR BRAND-NEW SKY-SKIMMER!
YOU FORGET, WILDCAT-- THOUGH A BLIND MAN, I CAN "SEE" THROUGH MY INFRA-GOGGLES.
HEAT PATTERNS--AN INDICATION OF SHAPE--
--ONE MOUND HOTTER THAN ANOTHER:
THERE, LANTERN.
HIS BODY-HEAT POINTS THERE.
ZZAZZK
OH, GOD...
WE'RE TOO LATE.
WAM
TOO LATE!
LET'S GET HIM TO A HOSPITAL...

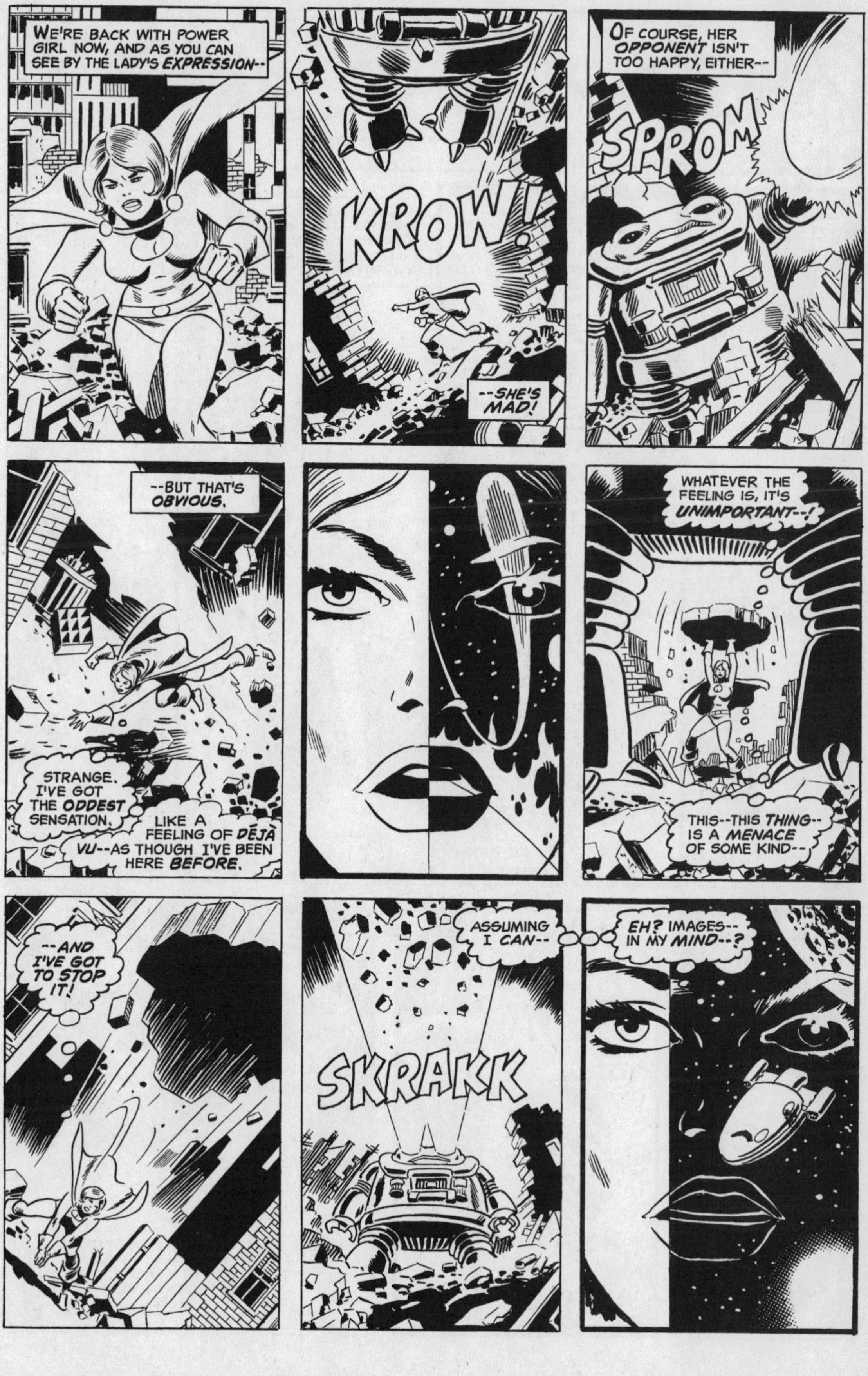
WE'RE BACK WITH POWER GIRL NOW, AND AS YOU CAN SEE BY THE LADY'S EXPRESSION--
KROW!
--SHE'S MAD!
OF COURSE, HER OPPONENT ISN'T TOO HAPPY, EITHER--
SPROM
--BUT THAT'S OBVIOUS.
STRANGE. I'VE GOT THE ODDEST SENSATION.
LIKE A FEELING OF DÉJÀ VU--AS THOUGH I'VE BEEN HERE BEFORE.
WHATEVER THE FEELING IS, IT'S UNIMPORTANT--!
THIS--THIS THING-- IS A MENACE OF SOME KIND--
--AND I'VE GOT TO STOP IT!
ASSUMING I CAN--
SKRAKK
EH? IMAGES-- IN MY MIND--?

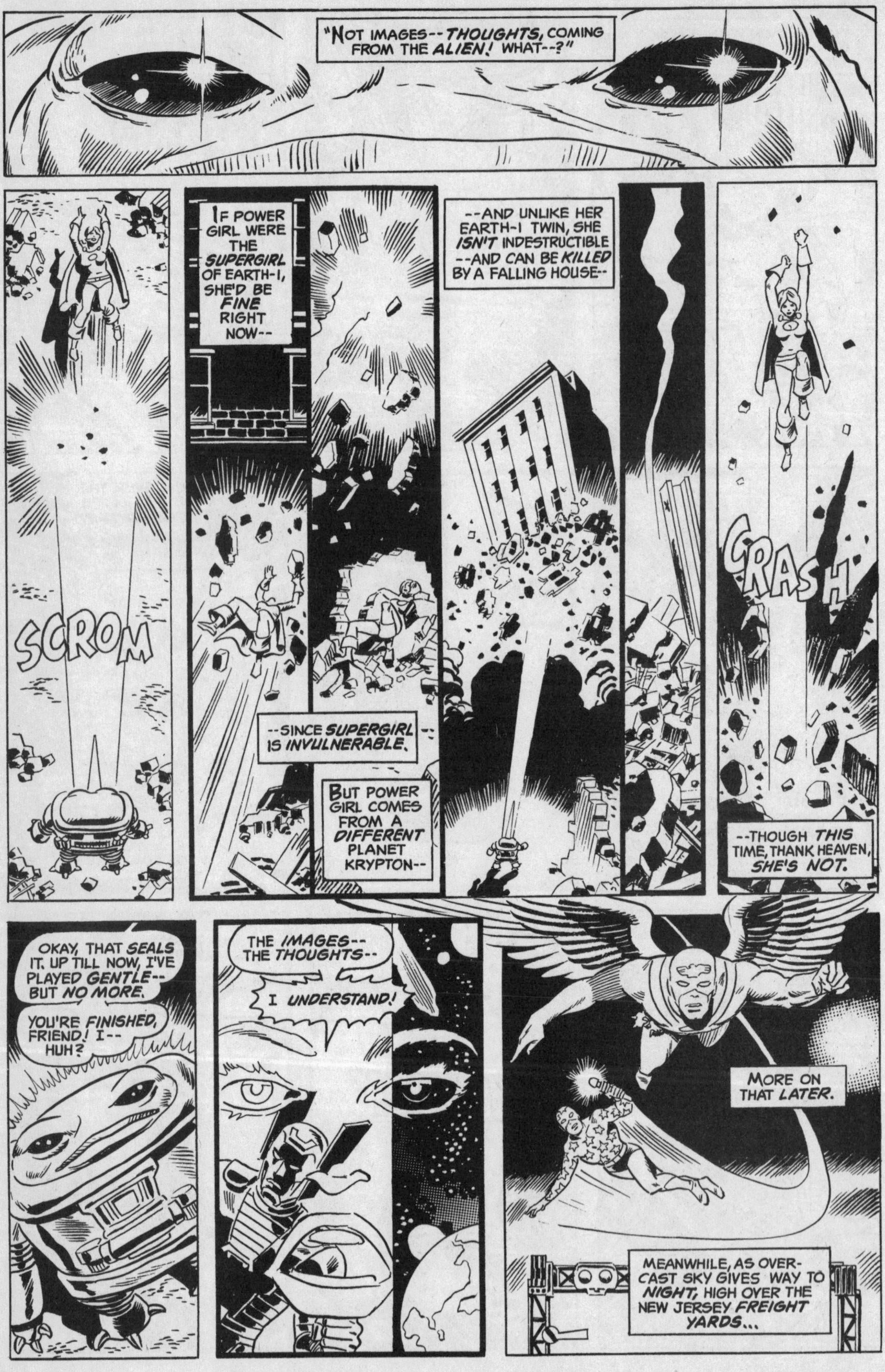
"NOT IMAGES--THOUGHTS, COMING FROM THE ALIEN! WHAT--?"
SCROM
IF POWER GIRL WERE THE SUPERGIRL OF EARTH-1, SHE'D BE FINE RIGHT NOW--
--SINCE SUPERGIRL IS INVULNERABLE.
BUT POWER GIRL COMES FROM A DIFFERENT PLANET KRYPTON--
--AND UNLIKE HER EARTH-1 TWIN, SHE ISN'T INDESTRUCTIBLE --AND CAN BE KILLED BY A FALLING HOUSE--
CRASH
--THOUGH THIS TIME, THANK HEAVEN, SHE'S NOT.
OKAY, THAT SEALS IT. UP TILL NOW, I'VE PLAYED GENTLE-- BUT NO MORE.
YOU'RE FINISHED, FRIEND! I-- HUH?
THE IMAGES-- THE THOUGHTS--
I UNDERSTAND!
MORE ON THAT LATER.
MEANWHILE, AS OVER-CAST SKY GIVES WAY TO NIGHT, HIGH OVER THE NEW JERSEY FREIGHT YARDS...

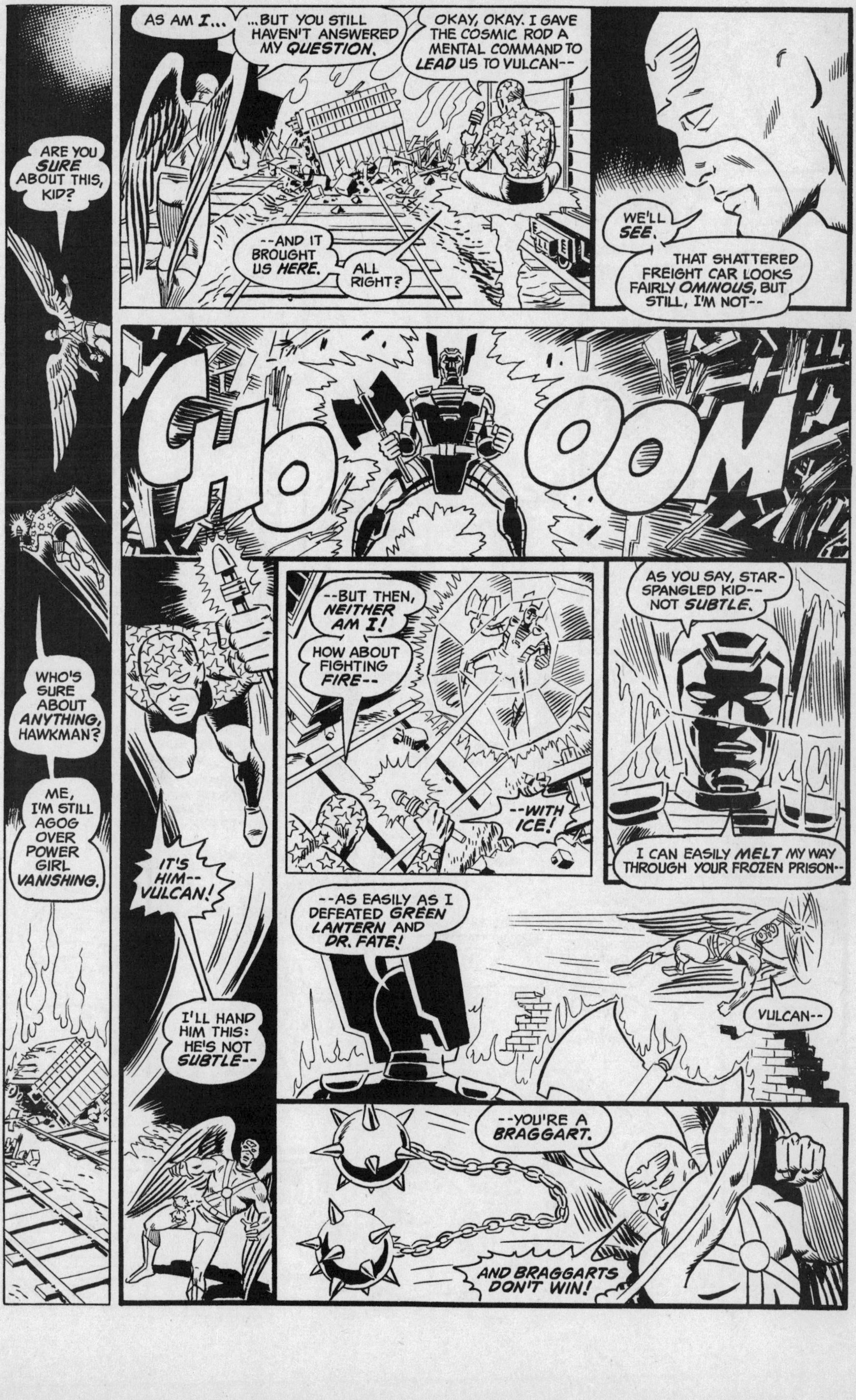
ARE YOU SURE ABOUT THIS, KID?
AS AM I...
...BUT YOU STILL HAVEN'T ANSWERED MY QUESTION.
OKAY, OKAY. I GAVE THE COSMIC ROD A MENTAL COMMAND TO LEAD US TO VULCAN--
--AND IT BROUGHT US HERE.
ALL RIGHT?
WE'LL SEE.
THAT SHATTERED FREIGHT CAR LOOKS FAIRLY OMINOUS, BUT STILL, I'M NOT--
CHOOOM
WHO'S SURE ABOUT ANYTHING, HAWKMAN?
ME, I'M STILL AGOG OVER POWER GIRL VANISHING.
IT'S HIM-- VULCAN!
I'LL HAND HIM THIS: HE'S NOT SUBTLE--
--BUT THEN, NEITHER AM I!
HOW ABOUT FIGHTING FIRE--
--WITH ICE!
AS YOU SAY, STAR-SPANGLED KID-- NOT SUBTLE.
I CAN EASILY MELT MY WAY THROUGH YOUR FROZEN PRISON--
--AS EASILY AS I DEFEATED GREEN LANTERN AND DR. FATE!
VULCAN--
--YOU'RE A BRAGGART.
AND BRAGGARTS DON'T WIN!

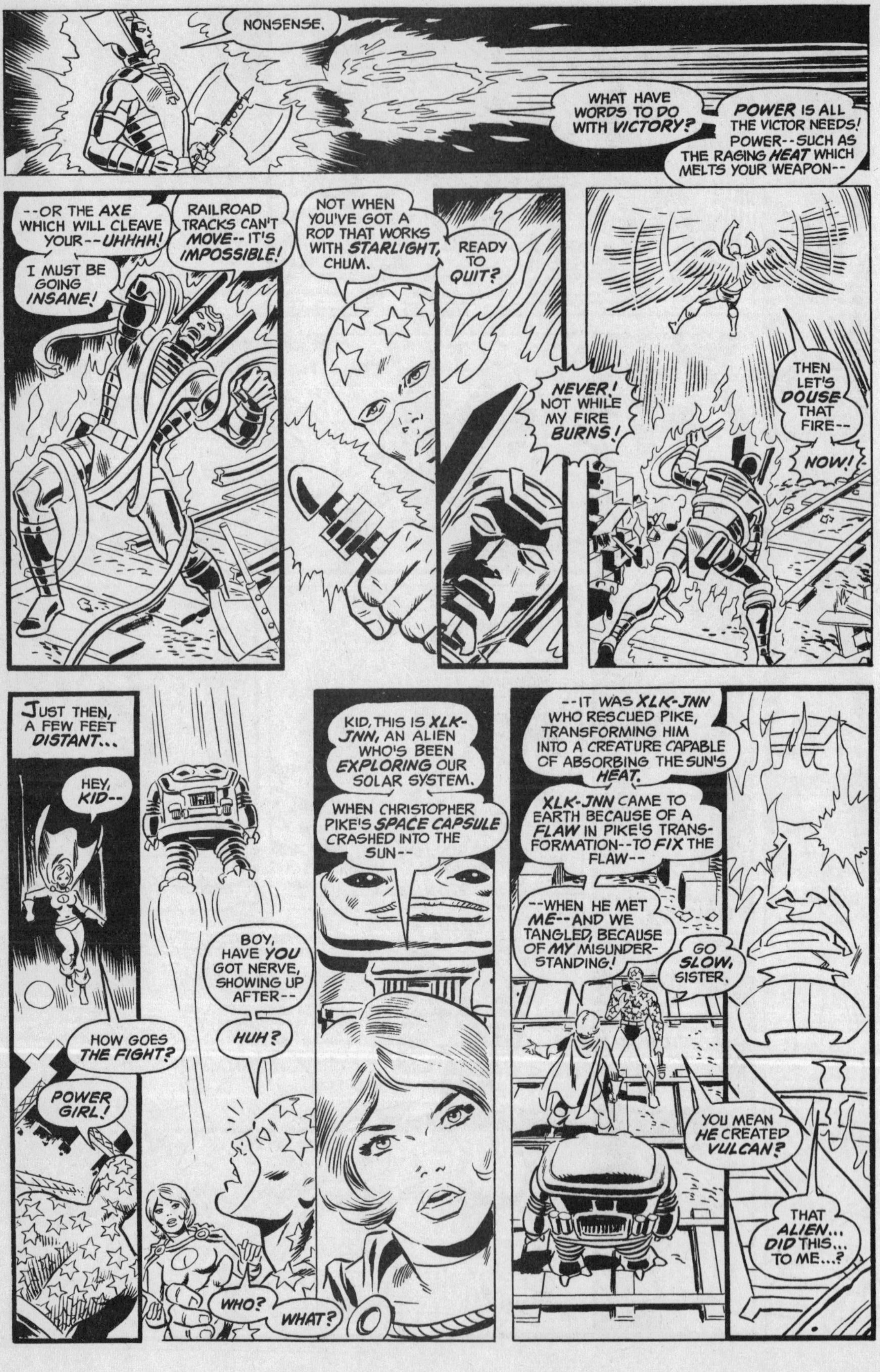
NONSENSE.
WHAT HAVE WORDS TO DO WITH VICTORY?
POWER IS ALL THE VICTOR NEEDS! POWER--SUCH AS THE RAGING HEAT WHICH MELTS YOUR WEAPON--
--OR THE AXE WHICH WILL CLEAVE YOUR--UHHHH!
I MUST BE GOING INSANE!
RAILROAD TRACKS CAN'T MOVE--IT'S IMPOSSIBLE!
NOT WHEN YOU'VE GOT A ROD THAT WORKS WITH STARLIGHT, CHUM.
READY TO QUIT?
NEVER! NOT WHILE MY FIRE BURNS!
THEN LET'S DOUSE THAT FIRE--
NOW!
JUST THEN, A FEW FEET DISTANT...
HEY, KID--
HOW GOES THE FIGHT?
POWER GIRL!
BOY, HAVE YOU GOT NERVE, SHOWING UP AFTER--
HUH?
WHO?
WHAT?
KID, THIS IS XLK-JNN, AN ALIEN WHO'S BEEN EXPLORING OUR SOLAR SYSTEM.
WHEN CHRISTOPHER PIKE'S SPACE CAPSULE CRASHED INTO THE SUN--
--IT WAS XLK-JNN WHO RESCUED PIKE, TRANSFORMING HIM INTO A CREATURE CAPABLE OF ABSORBING THE SUN'S HEAT.
XLK-JNN CAME TO EARTH BECAUSE OF A FLAW IN PIKE'S TRANSFORMATION--TO FIX THE FLAW--
--WHEN HE MET ME--AND WE TANGLED, BECAUSE OF MY MISUNDERSTANDING!
GO SLOW, SISTER.
YOU MEAN HE CREATED VULCAN?
THAT ALIEN... DID THIS... TO ME...?

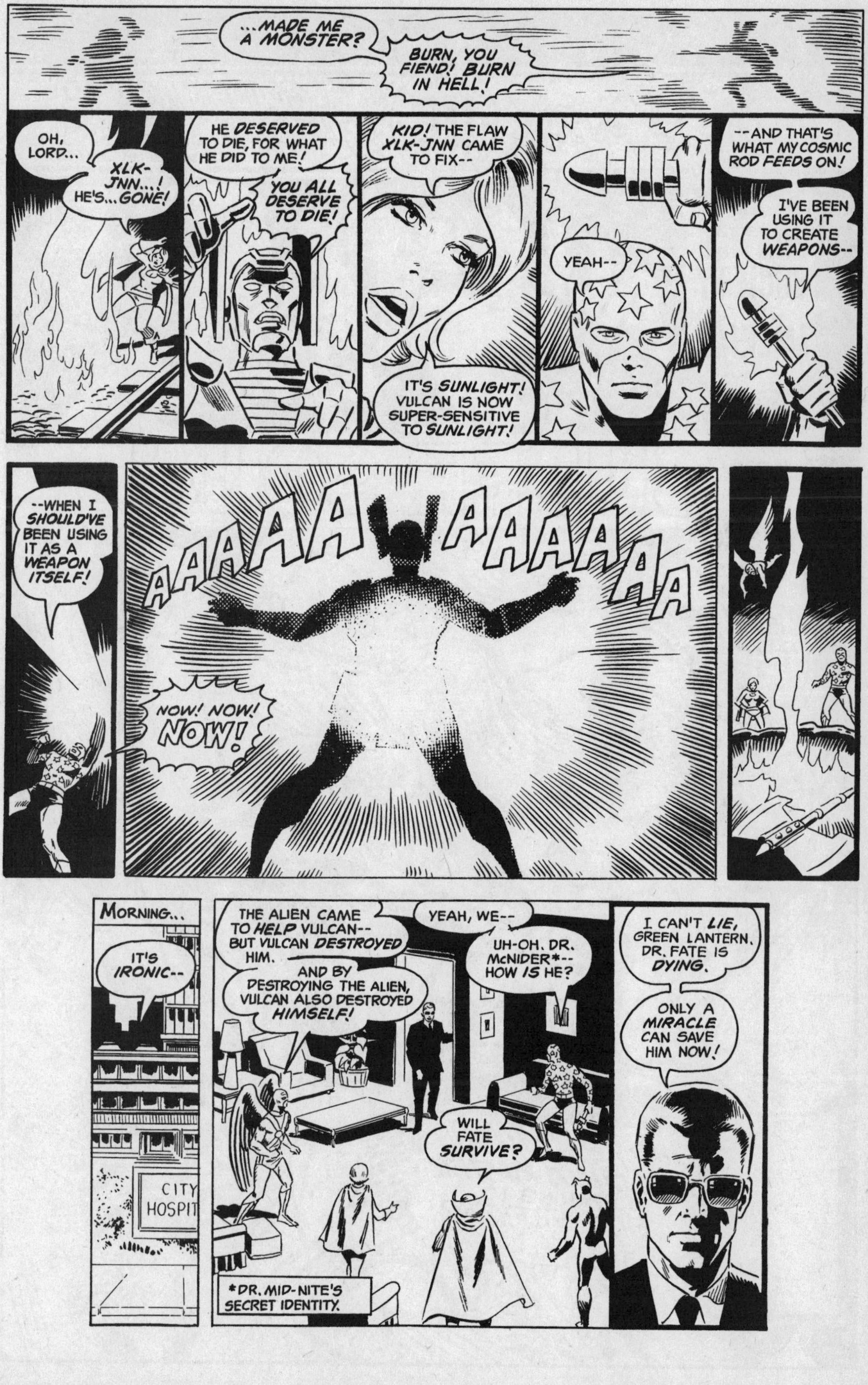
...MADE ME A MONSTER?
BURN, YOU FIEND! BURN IN HELL!
OH, LORD...
XLK-JNN...! HE'S...GONE!
HE DESERVED TO DIE, FOR WHAT HE DID TO ME!
YOU ALL DESERVE TO DIE!
KID! THE FLAW XLK-JNN CAME TO FIX--
IT'S SUNLIGHT! VULCAN IS NOW SUPER-SENSITIVE TO SUNLIGHT!
YEAH--
--AND THAT'S WHAT MY COSMIC ROD FEEDS ON!
I'VE BEEN USING IT TO CREATE WEAPONS--
--WHEN I SHOULD'VE BEEN USING IT AS A WEAPON ITSELF!
AAAAAAAAAAAA
NOW! NOW! NOW!
MORNING...
IT'S IRONIC--
CITY HOSPIT
THE ALIEN CAME TO HELP VULCAN-- BUT VULCAN DESTROYED HIM.
AND BY DESTROYING THE ALIEN, VULCAN ALSO DESTROYED HIMSELF!
YEAH, WE--
UH-OH. DR. McNIDER*-- HOW IS HE?
WILL FATE SURVIVE?
*DR. MID-NITE'S SECRET IDENTITY.
I CAN'T LIE, GREEN LANTERN. DR. FATE IS DYING.
ONLY A MIRACLE CAN SAVE HIM NOW!

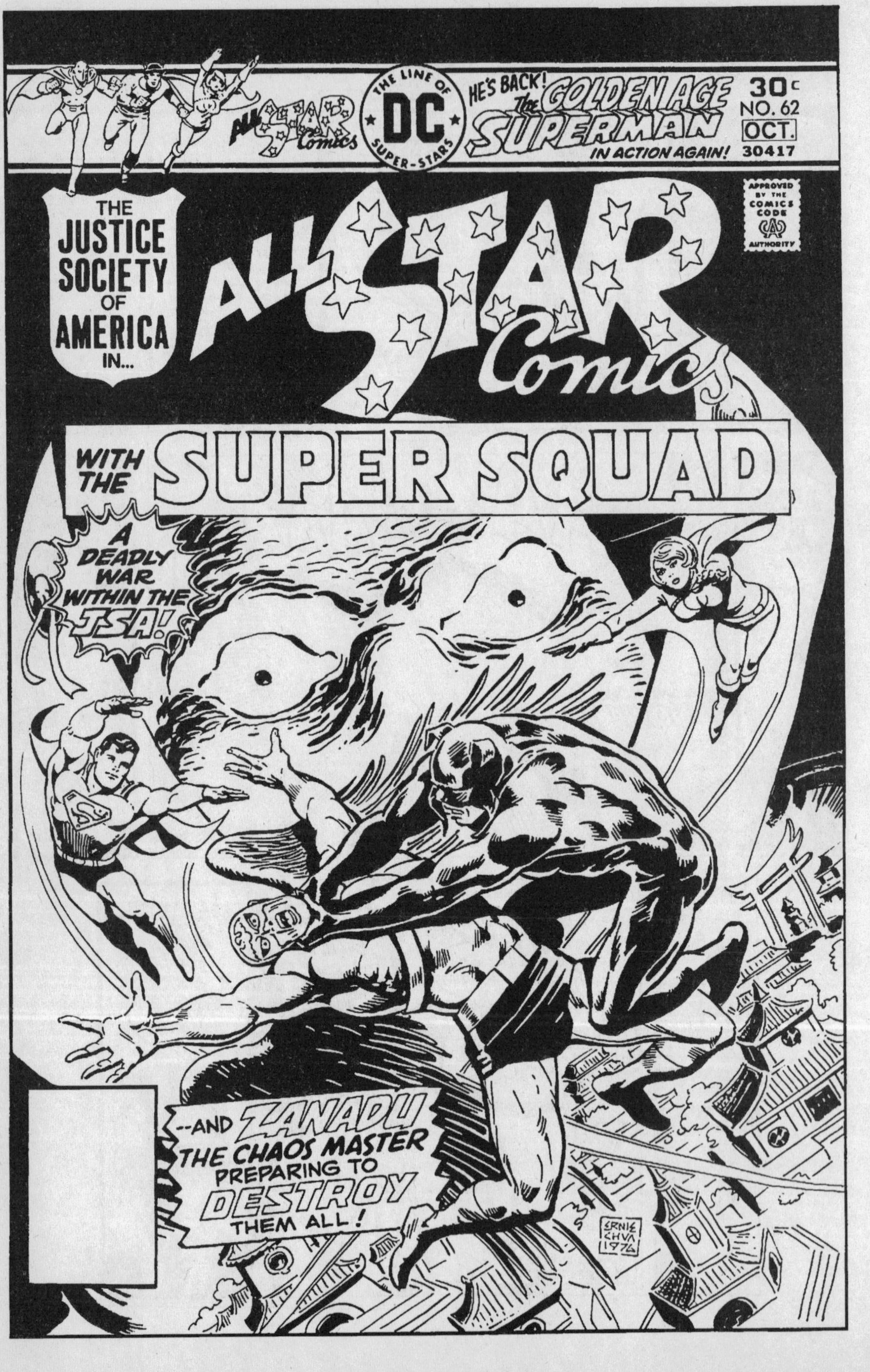
All Star Comics
THE LINE OF DC SUPER-STARS
HE'S BACK! The GOLDEN AGE SUPERMAN IN ACTION AGAIN!
30¢
NO. 62
OCT.
30417
APPROVED BY THE COMICS CODE AUTHORITY
THE JUSTICE SOCIETY OF AMERICA IN...
ALL STAR Comics
WITH THE SUPER SQUAD
A DEADLY WAR WITHIN THE JSA!
--AND ZANADU THE CHAOS MASTER PREPARING TO DESTROY THEM ALL!
ERNIE CHUA 1976

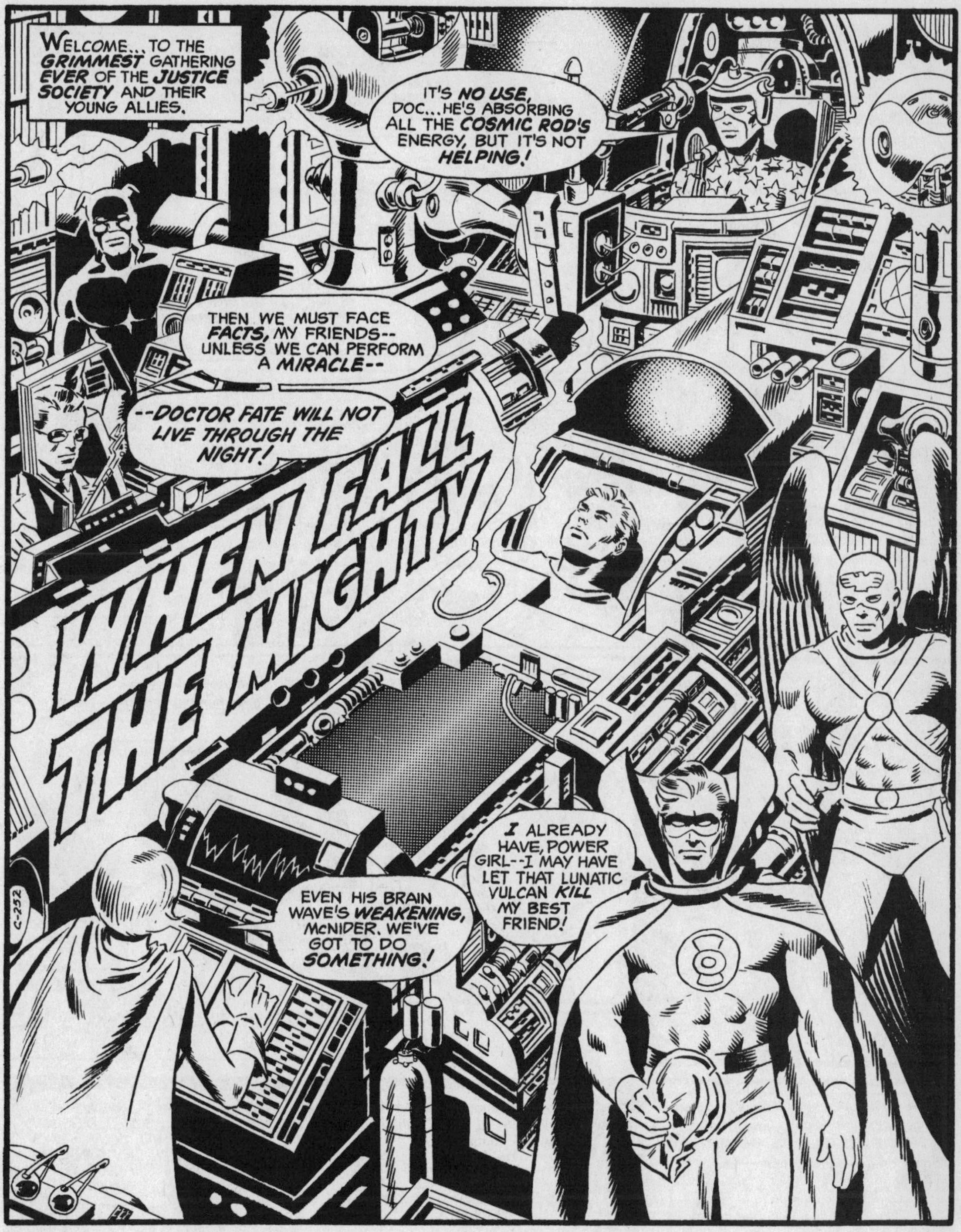
WELCOME... TO THE GRIMMEST GATHERING EVER OF THE JUSTICE SOCIETY AND THEIR YOUNG ALLIES.
IT'S NO USE, DOC... HE'S ABSORBING ALL THE COSMIC ROD'S ENERGY, BUT IT'S NOT HELPING!
THEN WE MUST FACE FACTS, MY FRIENDS-- UNLESS WE CAN PERFORM A MIRACLE--
--DOCTOR FATE WILL NOT LIVE THROUGH THE NIGHT!
WHEN FALL THE MIGHTY
EVEN HIS BRAIN WAVE'S WEAKENING, McNIDER. WE'VE GOT TO DO SOMETHING!
I ALREADY HAVE, POWER GIRL--I MAY HAVE LET THAT LUNATIC VULCAN KILL MY BEST FRIEND!
C-252

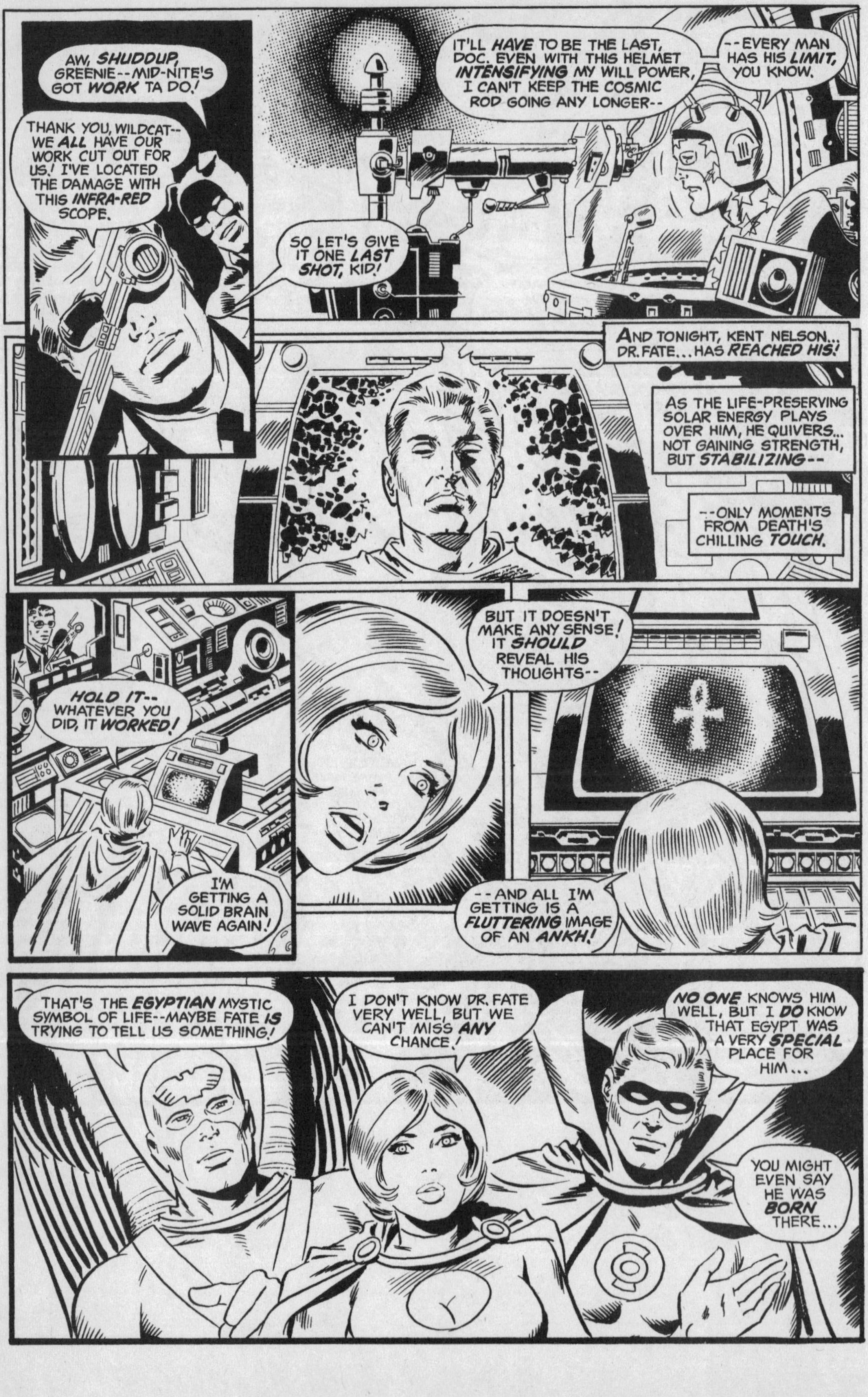
AW, SHUDDUP, GREENIE--MID-NITE'S GOT WORK TA DO!
THANK YOU, WILDCAT-- WE ALL HAVE OUR WORK CUT OUT FOR US! I'VE LOCATED THE DAMAGE WITH THIS INFRA-RED SCOPE.
SO LET'S GIVE IT ONE LAST SHOT, KID!
IT'LL HAVE TO BE THE LAST, DOC. EVEN WITH THIS HELMET INTENSIFYING MY WILL POWER, I CAN'T KEEP THE COSMIC ROD GOING ANY LONGER--
--EVERY MAN HAS HIS LIMIT, YOU KNOW.
AND TONIGHT, KENT NELSON... DR. FATE... HAS REACHED HIS!
AS THE LIFE-PRESERVING SOLAR ENERGY PLAYS OVER HIM, HE QUIVERS... NOT GAINING STRENGTH, BUT STABILIZING--
--ONLY MOMENTS FROM DEATH'S CHILLING TOUCH.
HOLD IT-- WHATEVER YOU DID, IT WORKED!
I'M GETTING A SOLID BRAIN WAVE AGAIN!
BUT IT DOESN'T MAKE ANY SENSE! IT SHOULD REVEAL HIS THOUGHTS--
--AND ALL I'M GETTING IS A FLUTTERING IMAGE OF AN ANKH!
THAT'S THE EGYPTIAN MYSTIC SYMBOL OF LIFE--MAYBE FATE IS TRYING TO TELL US SOMETHING!
I DON'T KNOW DR. FATE VERY WELL, BUT WE CAN'T MISS ANY CHANCE!
NO ONE KNOWS HIM WELL, BUT I DO KNOW THAT EGYPT WAS A VERY SPECIAL PLACE FOR HIM...
YOU MIGHT EVEN SAY HE WAS BORN THERE...

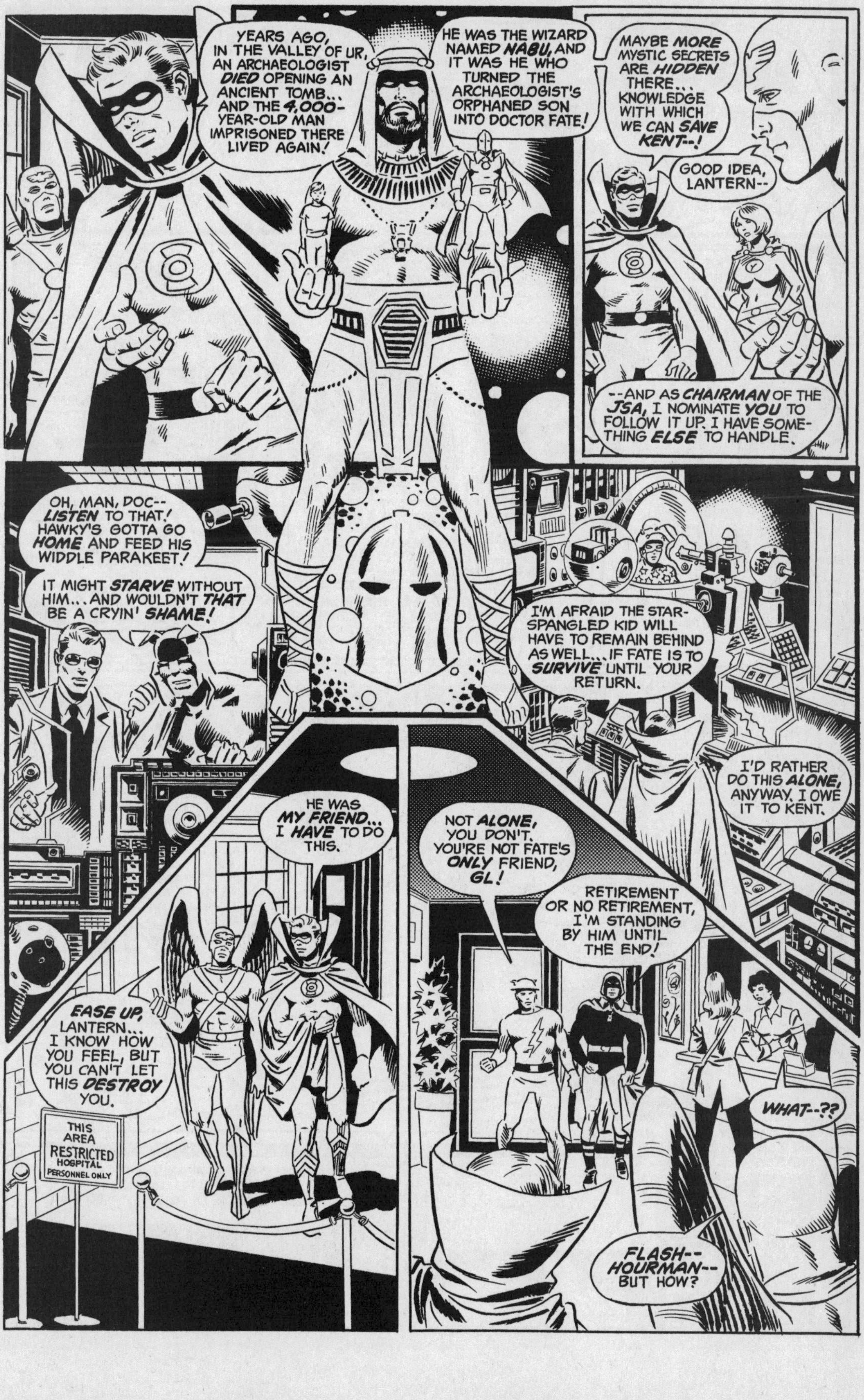
YEARS AGO, IN THE VALLEY OF UR, AN ARCHAEOLOGIST DIED OPENING AN ANCIENT TOMB... AND THE 4,000-YEAR-OLD MAN IMPRISONED THERE LIVED AGAIN!
HE WAS THE WIZARD NAMED NABU, AND IT WAS HE WHO TURNED THE ARCHAEOLOGIST'S ORPHANED SON INTO DOCTOR FATE!
MAYBE MORE MYSTIC SECRETS ARE HIDDEN THERE... KNOWLEDGE WITH WHICH WE CAN SAVE KENT--!
GOOD IDEA, LANTERN--
--AND AS CHAIRMAN OF THE JSA, I NOMINATE YOU TO FOLLOW IT UP. I HAVE SOMETHING ELSE TO HANDLE.
OH, MAN, DOC-- LISTEN TO THAT! HAWKY'S GOTTA GO HOME AND FEED HIS WIDDLE PARAKEET!
IT MIGHT STARVE WITHOUT HIM... AND WOULDN'T THAT BE A CRYIN' SHAME!
I'M AFRAID THE STAR-SPANGLED KID WILL HAVE TO REMAIN BEHIND AS WELL... IF FATE IS TO SURVIVE UNTIL YOUR RETURN.
I'D RATHER DO THIS ALONE, ANYWAY. I OWE IT TO KENT.
HE WAS MY FRIEND... I HAVE TO DO THIS.
EASE UP, LANTERN... I KNOW HOW YOU FEEL, BUT YOU CAN'T LET THIS DESTROY YOU.
THIS AREA RESTRICTED HOSPITAL PERSONNEL ONLY
NOT ALONE, YOU DON'T. YOU'RE NOT FATE'S ONLY FRIEND, GL!
RETIREMENT OR NO RETIREMENT, I'M STANDING BY HIM UNTIL THE END!
WHAT--??
FLASH-- HOURMAN-- BUT HOW?

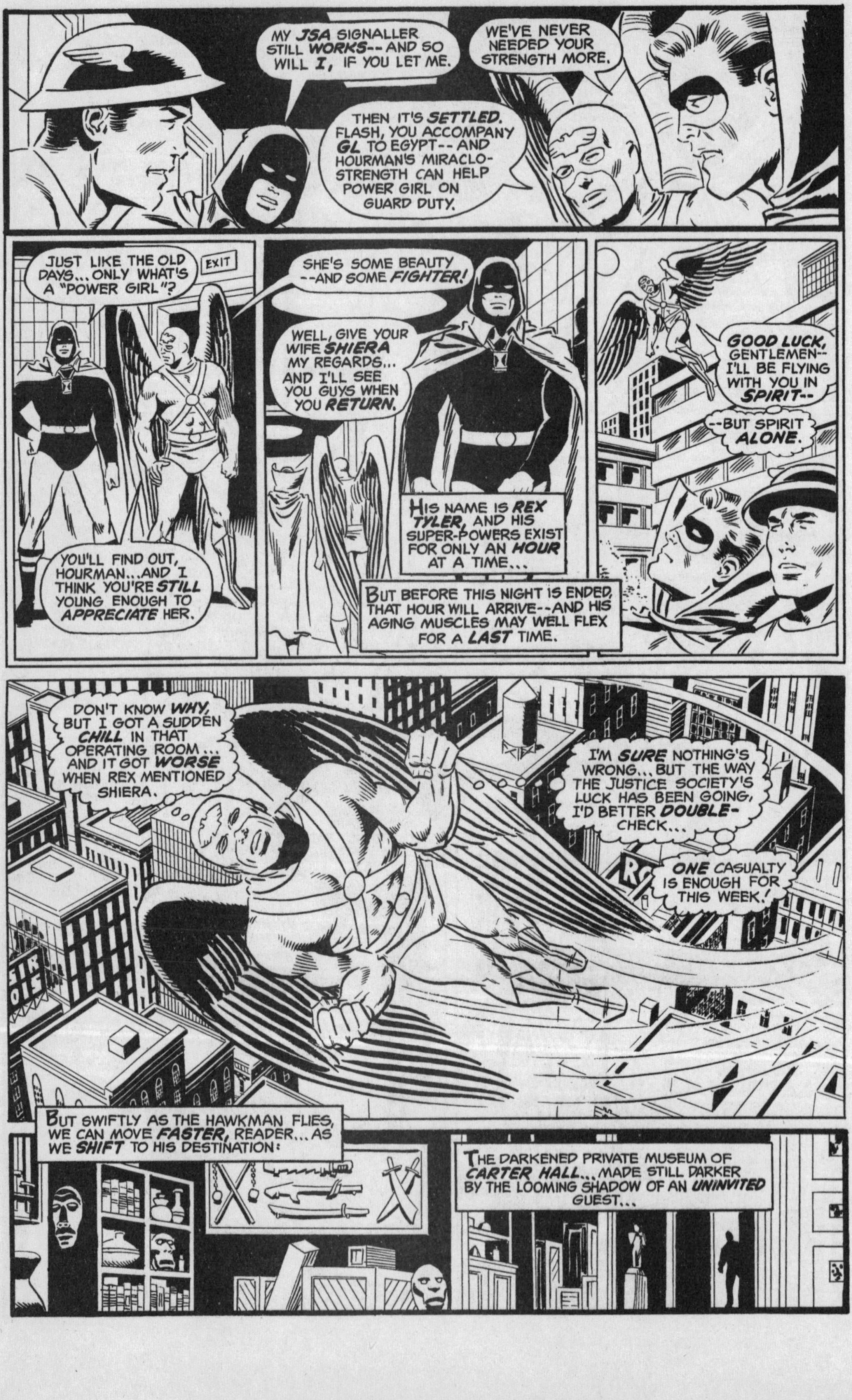

MY JSA SIGNALLER STILL WORKS-- AND SO WILL I, IF YOU LET ME.
WE'VE NEVER NEEDED YOUR STRENGTH MORE.
THEN IT'S SETTLED. FLASH, YOU ACCOMPANY GL TO EGYPT-- AND HOURMAN'S MIRACLO-STRENGTH CAN HELP POWER GIRL ON GUARD DUTY.
JUST LIKE THE OLD DAYS... ONLY WHAT'S A "POWER GIRL"?
EXIT
YOU'LL FIND OUT, HOURMAN... AND I THINK YOU'RE STILL YOUNG ENOUGH TO APPRECIATE HER.
SHE'S SOME BEAUTY --AND SOME FIGHTER!
WELL, GIVE YOUR WIFE SHIERA MY REGARDS... AND I'LL SEE YOU GUYS WHEN YOU RETURN.
HIS NAME IS REX TYLER, AND HIS SUPER-POWERS EXIST FOR ONLY AN HOUR AT A TIME...
BUT BEFORE THIS NIGHT IS ENDED, THAT HOUR WILL ARRIVE--AND HIS AGING MUSCLES MAY WELL FLEX FOR A LAST TIME.
GOOD LUCK, GENTLEMEN-- I'LL BE FLYING WITH YOU IN SPIRIT--
--BUT SPIRIT ALONE.
DON'T KNOW WHY, BUT I GOT A SUDDEN CHILL IN THAT OPERATING ROOM... AND IT GOT WORSE WHEN REX MENTIONED SHIERA.
I'M SURE NOTHING'S WRONG... BUT THE WAY THE JUSTICE SOCIETY'S LUCK HAS BEEN GOING, I'D BETTER DOUBLE-CHECK...
ONE CASUALTY IS ENOUGH FOR THIS WEEK!
BUT SWIFTLY AS THE HAWKMAN FLIES, WE CAN MOVE FASTER, READER... AS WE SHIFT TO HIS DESTINATION:
THE DARKENED PRIVATE MUSEUM OF CARTER HALL... MADE STILL DARKER BY THE LOOMING SHADOW OF AN UNINVITED GUEST...

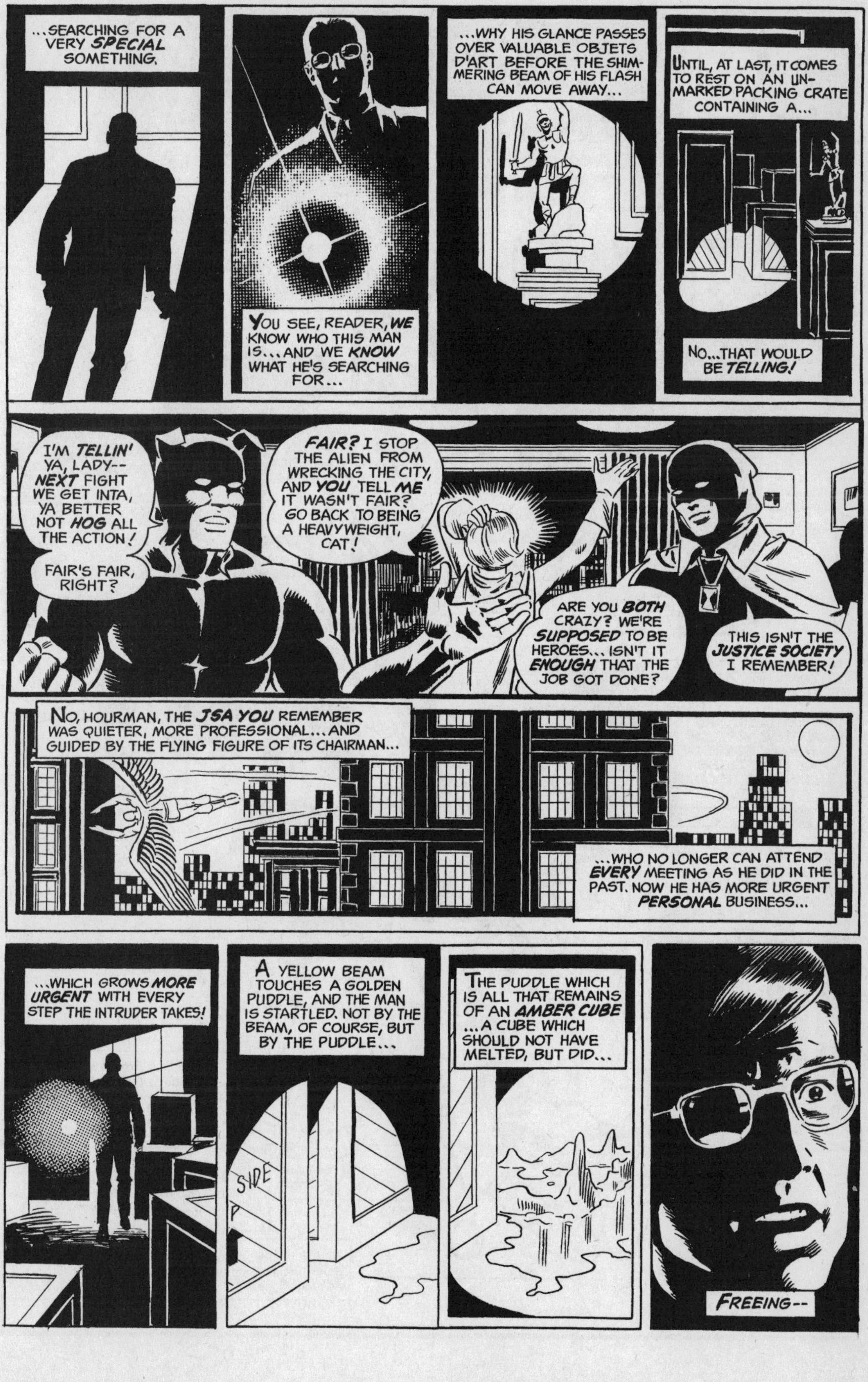
...SEARCHING FOR A VERY SPECIAL SOMETHING.
YOU SEE, READER, WE KNOW WHO THIS MAN IS... AND WE KNOW WHAT HE'S SEARCHING FOR...
...WHY HIS GLANCE PASSES OVER VALUABLE OBJETS D'ART BEFORE THE SHIMMERING BEAM OF HIS FLASH CAN MOVE AWAY...
UNTIL, AT LAST, IT COMES TO REST ON AN UNMARKED PACKING CRATE CONTAINING A...
NO...THAT WOULD BE TELLING!
I'M TELLIN' YA, LADY-- NEXT FIGHT WE GET INTA, YA BETTER NOT HOG ALL THE ACTION!
FAIR'S FAIR, RIGHT?
FAIR? I STOP THE ALIEN FROM WRECKING THE CITY, AND YOU TELL ME IT WASN'T FAIR? GO BACK TO BEING A HEAVYWEIGHT, CAT!
ARE YOU BOTH CRAZY? WE'RE SUPPOSED TO BE HEROES... ISN'T IT ENOUGH THAT THE JOB GOT DONE?
THIS ISN'T THE JUSTICE SOCIETY I REMEMBER!
NO, HOURMAN, THE JSA YOU REMEMBER WAS QUIETER, MORE PROFESSIONAL... AND GUIDED BY THE FLYING FIGURE OF ITS CHAIRMAN...
...WHO NO LONGER CAN ATTEND EVERY MEETING AS HE DID IN THE PAST. NOW HE HAS MORE URGENT PERSONAL BUSINESS...
...WHICH GROWS MORE URGENT WITH EVERY STEP THE INTRUDER TAKES!
A YELLOW BEAM TOUCHES A GOLDEN PUDDLE, AND THE MAN IS STARTLED. NOT BY THE BEAM, OF COURSE, BUT BY THE PUDDLE...
SIDE
THE PUDDLE WHICH IS ALL THAT REMAINS OF AN AMBER CUBE ...A CUBE WHICH SHOULD NOT HAVE MELTED, BUT DID...
FREEING--

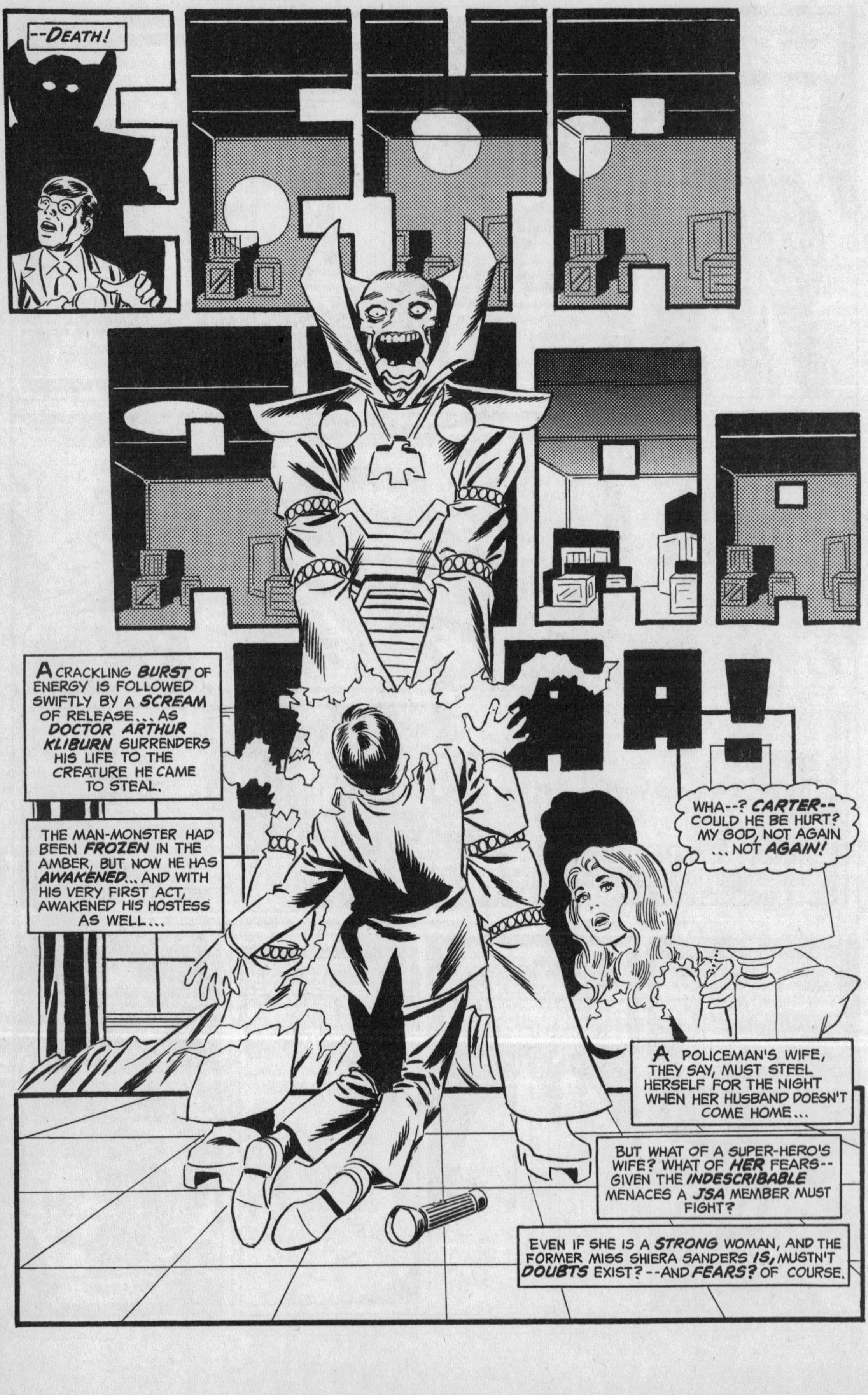
--DEATH!
A CRACKLING BURST OF ENERGY IS FOLLOWED SWIFTLY BY A SCREAM OF RELEASE... AS DOCTOR ARTHUR KLIBURN SURRENDERS HIS LIFE TO THE CREATURE HE CAME TO STEAL.
THE MAN-MONSTER HAD BEEN FROZEN IN THE AMBER, BUT NOW HE HAS AWAKENED... AND WITH HIS VERY FIRST ACT, AWAKENED HIS HOSTESS AS WELL...
WHA--? CARTER-- COULD HE BE HURT? MY GOD, NOT AGAIN ... NOT AGAIN!
A POLICEMAN'S WIFE, THEY SAY, MUST STEEL HERSELF FOR THE NIGHT WHEN HER HUSBAND DOESN'T COME HOME...
BUT WHAT OF A SUPER-HERO'S WIFE? WHAT OF HER FEARS-- GIVEN THE INDESCRIBABLE MENACES A JSA MEMBER MUST FIGHT?
EVEN IF SHE IS A STRONG WOMAN, AND THE FORMER MISS SHIERA SANDERS IS, MUSTN'T DOUBTS EXIST? --AND FEARS? OF COURSE.

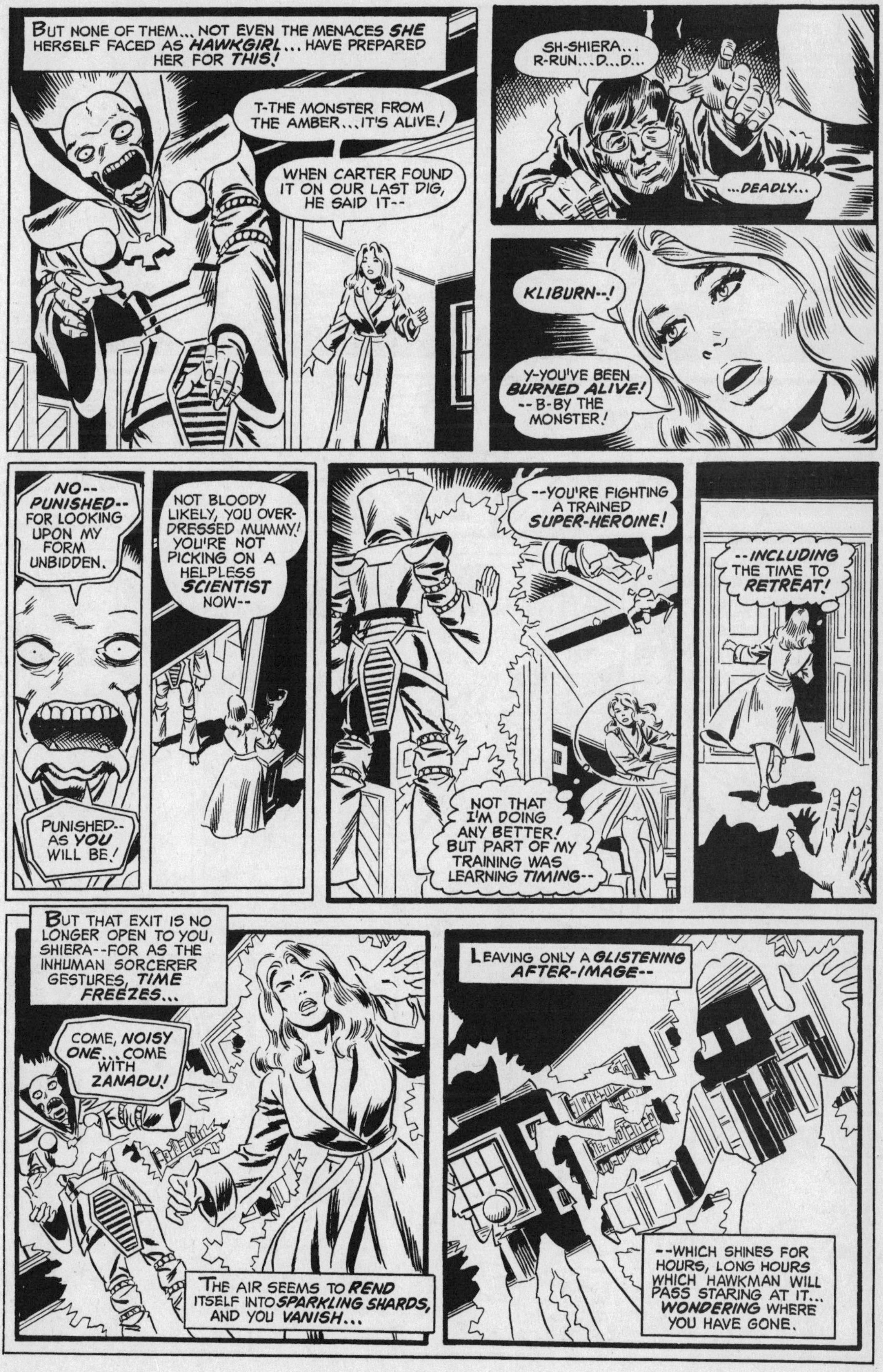
BUT NONE OF THEM... NOT EVEN THE MENACES SHE HERSELF FACED AS HAWKGIRL... HAVE PREPARED HER FOR THIS!
T-THE MONSTER FROM THE AMBER...IT'S ALIVE!
WHEN CARTER FOUND IT ON OUR LAST DIG, HE SAID IT--
SH-SHIERA... R-RUN...D...D...
...DEADLY...
KLIBURN--!
Y-YOU'VE BEEN BURNED ALIVE! --B-BY THE MONSTER!
NO--PUNISHED--FOR LOOKING UPON MY FORM UNBIDDEN.
PUNISHED--AS YOU WILL BE!
NOT BLOODY LIKELY, YOU OVER-DRESSED MUMMY! YOU'RE NOT PICKING ON A HELPLESS SCIENTIST NOW--
--YOU'RE FIGHTING A TRAINED SUPER-HEROINE!
NOT THAT I'M DOING ANY BETTER! BUT PART OF MY TRAINING WAS LEARNING TIMING--
--INCLUDING THE TIME TO RETREAT!
BUT THAT EXIT IS NO LONGER OPEN TO YOU, SHIERA--FOR AS THE INHUMAN SORCERER GESTURES, TIME FREEZES...
COME, NOISY ONE...COME WITH ZANADU!
THE AIR SEEMS TO REND ITSELF INTO SPARKLING SHARDS, AND YOU VANISH...
LEAVING ONLY A GLISTENING AFTER-IMAGE--
--WHICH SHINES FOR HOURS, LONG HOURS WHICH HAWKMAN WILL PASS STARING AT IT... WONDERING WHERE YOU HAVE GONE.

MEANWHILE, HALF A WORLD AWAY, A FIGURE RACES SO QUICKLY THE WATER BELOW CANNOT PART UNDER HIS FEET...WHILE EVEN GREEN LANTERN CAN ONLY KEEP PACE BY BEING DRAGGED ALONG!

DO YOU *REALLY* THINK WE'LL FIND SOMETHING IN EGYPT TO CURE FATE, GL?

I HOPE SO, *FLASH*... AND I HOPE IT *DOESN'T* WANT TO COME ALONG QUIETLY.

I *NEED* SOMETHING TO FIGHT...

SOMETHING TO *KILL!*

HE'S FOUGHT MANY BATTLES BEFORE, THIS EMERALD WARRIOR... AND *SOMETIMES* COMRADES HAVE FALLEN...

BUT NEVER ONE *SO CLOSE*...

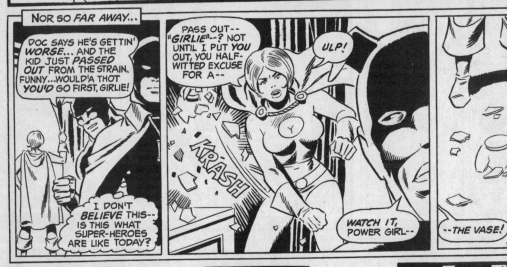

NOR SO *FAR AWAY*...

DOC SAYS HE'S GETTIN' *WORSE*... AND THE KID JUST *PASSED OUT* FROM THE STRAIN. FUNNY...WOULD'A THOT *YOU'D* GO FIRST, GIRLIE!

I DON'T *BELIEVE* THIS-- IS THIS WHAT SUPER-HEROES ARE LIKE TODAY?

PASS OUT-- "GIRLIE"--? NOT UNTIL I PUT *YOU* OUT, YOU HALF-WITTED EXCUSE FOR A--

ULP!

WATCH IT, POWER GIRL--

KRASH

--THE VASE!

STATUARY...

AMBER MELTED...

AND ARTHUR KLIBURN'S *DEATH!*

IRREPLACEABLE ARTIFACTS THAT WE EXCAVATED OURSELVES. WHY WOULD SHIERA SHATTER THEM?

AND THAT BURNING AFTER-IMAGE OF SHIERA AND THE CREATURE. IT'S ALL TIED INTO *LEMURIA*...THE CREATURE ...SHIERA'S DISAPPEARANCE...

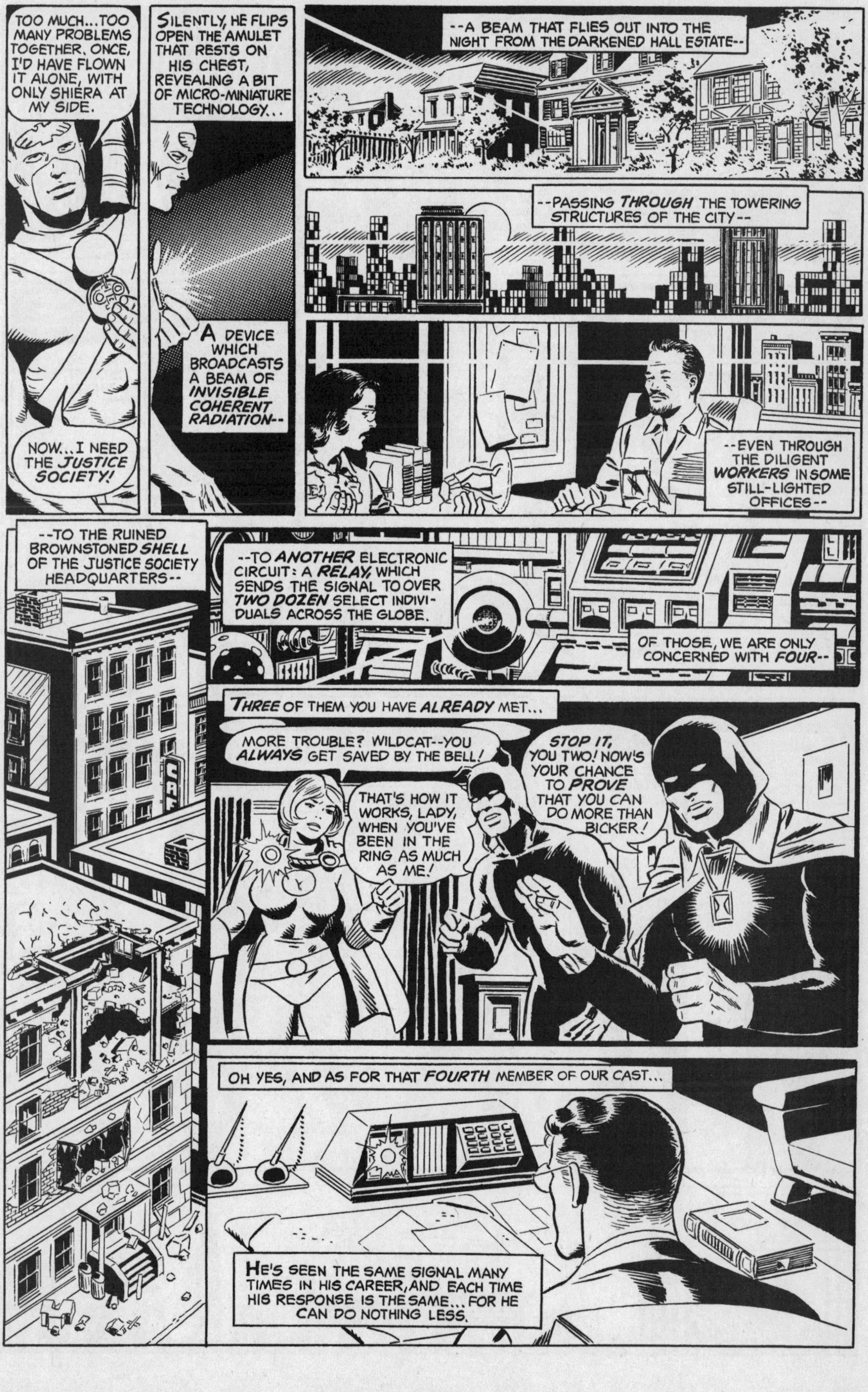
TOO MUCH...TOO MANY PROBLEMS TOGETHER. ONCE, I'D HAVE FLOWN IT ALONE, WITH ONLY SHIERA AT MY SIDE.
NOW...I NEED THE JUSTICE SOCIETY!
SILENTLY, HE FLIPS OPEN THE AMULET THAT RESTS ON HIS CHEST, REVEALING A BIT OF MICRO-MINIATURE TECHNOLOGY...
A DEVICE WHICH BROADCASTS A BEAM OF INVISIBLE COHERENT RADIATION--
--A BEAM THAT FLIES OUT INTO THE NIGHT FROM THE DARKENED HALL ESTATE--
--PASSING THROUGH THE TOWERING STRUCTURES OF THE CITY--
--EVEN THROUGH THE DILIGENT WORKERS IN SOME STILL-LIGHTED OFFICES--
--TO THE RUINED BROWNSTONED SHELL OF THE JUSTICE SOCIETY HEADQUARTERS--
--TO ANOTHER ELECTRONIC CIRCUIT: A RELAY, WHICH SENDS THE SIGNAL TO OVER TWO DOZEN SELECT INDIVIDUALS ACROSS THE GLOBE.
OF THOSE, WE ARE ONLY CONCERNED WITH FOUR--
THREE OF THEM YOU HAVE ALREADY MET...
MORE TROUBLE? WILDCAT--YOU ALWAYS GET SAVED BY THE BELL!
THAT'S HOW IT WORKS, LADY, WHEN YOU'VE BEEN IN THE RING AS MUCH AS ME!
STOP IT, YOU TWO! NOW'S YOUR CHANCE TO PROVE THAT YOU CAN DO MORE THAN BICKER!
OH YES, AND AS FOR THAT FOURTH MEMBER OF OUR CAST...
HE'S SEEN THE SAME SIGNAL MANY TIMES IN HIS CAREER, AND EACH TIME HIS RESPONSE IS THE SAME... FOR HE CAN DO NOTHING LESS.

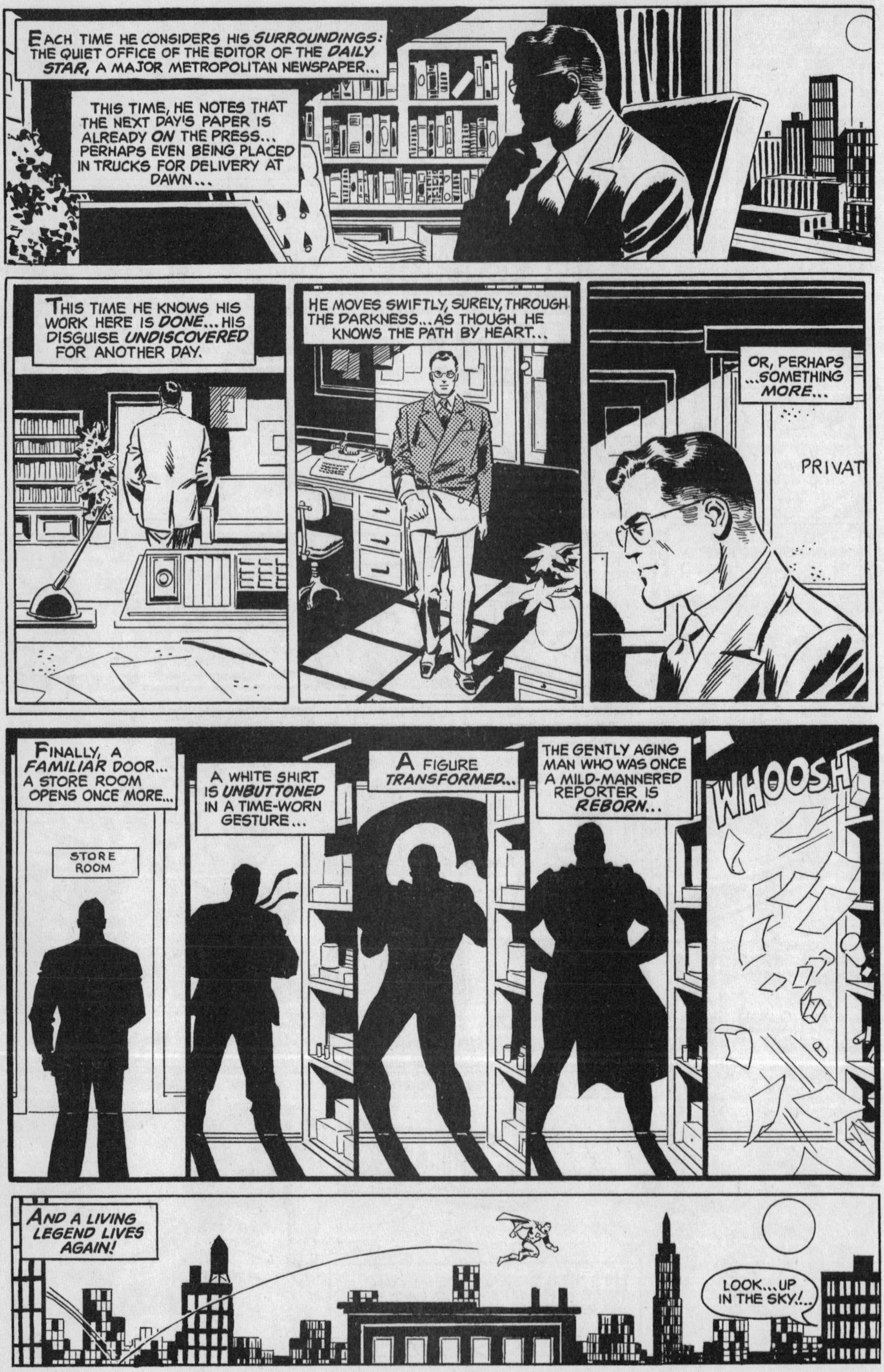
EACH TIME HE CONSIDERS HIS SURROUNDINGS: THE QUIET OFFICE OF THE EDITOR OF THE DAILY STAR, A MAJOR METROPOLITAN NEWSPAPER...
THIS TIME, HE NOTES THAT THE NEXT DAY'S PAPER IS ALREADY ON THE PRESS... PERHAPS EVEN BEING PLACED IN TRUCKS FOR DELIVERY AT DAWN...
THIS TIME HE KNOWS HIS WORK HERE IS DONE... HIS DISGUISE UNDISCOVERED FOR ANOTHER DAY.
HE MOVES SWIFTLY, SURELY, THROUGH THE DARKNESS... AS THOUGH HE KNOWS THE PATH BY HEART...
OR, PERHAPS ...SOMETHING MORE...
PRIVAT
FINALLY, A FAMILIAR DOOR... A STORE ROOM OPENS ONCE MORE...
STORE ROOM
A WHITE SHIRT IS UNBUTTONED IN A TIME-WORN GESTURE...
A FIGURE TRANSFORMED...
THE GENTLY AGING MAN WHO WAS ONCE A MILD-MANNERED REPORTER IS REBORN...
WHOOSH
AND A LIVING LEGEND LIVES AGAIN!
LOOK... UP IN THE SKY!...

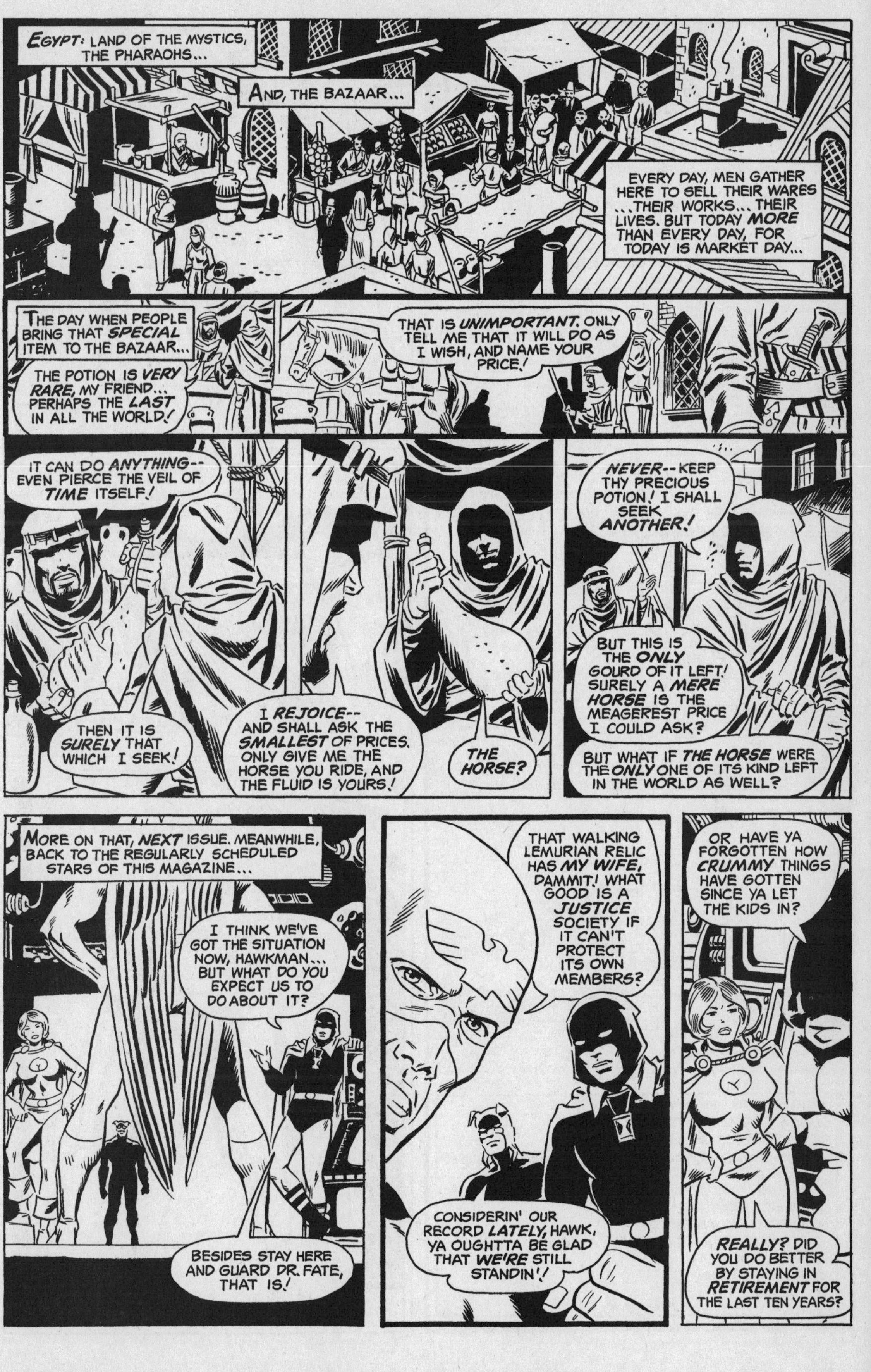
EGYPT: LAND OF THE MYSTICS, THE PHARAOHS...
AND, THE BAZAAR...
EVERY DAY, MEN GATHER HERE TO SELL THEIR WARES ...THEIR WORKS... THEIR LIVES. BUT TODAY MORE THAN EVERY DAY, FOR TODAY IS MARKET DAY...
THE DAY WHEN PEOPLE BRING THAT SPECIAL ITEM TO THE BAZAAR...
THE POTION IS VERY RARE, MY FRIEND... PERHAPS THE LAST IN ALL THE WORLD!
THAT IS UNIMPORTANT. ONLY TELL ME THAT IT WILL DO AS I WISH, AND NAME YOUR PRICE!
IT CAN DO ANYTHING-- EVEN PIERCE THE VEIL OF TIME ITSELF!
THEN IT IS SURELY THAT WHICH I SEEK!
I REJOICE-- AND SHALL ASK THE SMALLEST OF PRICES. ONLY GIVE ME THE HORSE YOU RIDE, AND THE FLUID IS YOURS!
THE HORSE?
NEVER-- KEEP THY PRECIOUS POTION! I SHALL SEEK ANOTHER!
BUT THIS IS THE ONLY GOURD OF IT LEFT! SURELY A MERE HORSE IS THE MEAGEREST PRICE I COULD ASK?
BUT WHAT IF THE HORSE WERE THE ONLY ONE OF ITS KIND LEFT IN THE WORLD AS WELL?
MORE ON THAT, NEXT ISSUE. MEANWHILE, BACK TO THE REGULARLY SCHEDULED STARS OF THIS MAGAZINE...
I THINK WE'VE GOT THE SITUATION NOW, HAWKMAN... BUT WHAT DO YOU EXPECT US TO DO ABOUT IT?
BESIDES STAY HERE AND GUARD DR. FATE, THAT IS!
THAT WALKING LEMURIAN RELIC HAS MY WIFE, DAMMIT! WHAT GOOD IS A JUSTICE SOCIETY IF IT CAN'T PROTECT ITS OWN MEMBERS?
CONSIDERIN' OUR RECORD LATELY, HAWK, YA OUGHTTA BE GLAD THAT WE'RE STILL STANDIN'!
OR HAVE YA FORGOTTEN HOW CRUMMY THINGS HAVE GOTTEN SINCE YA LET THE KIDS IN?
REALLY? DID YOU DO BETTER BY STAYING IN RETIREMENT FOR THE LAST TEN YEARS?

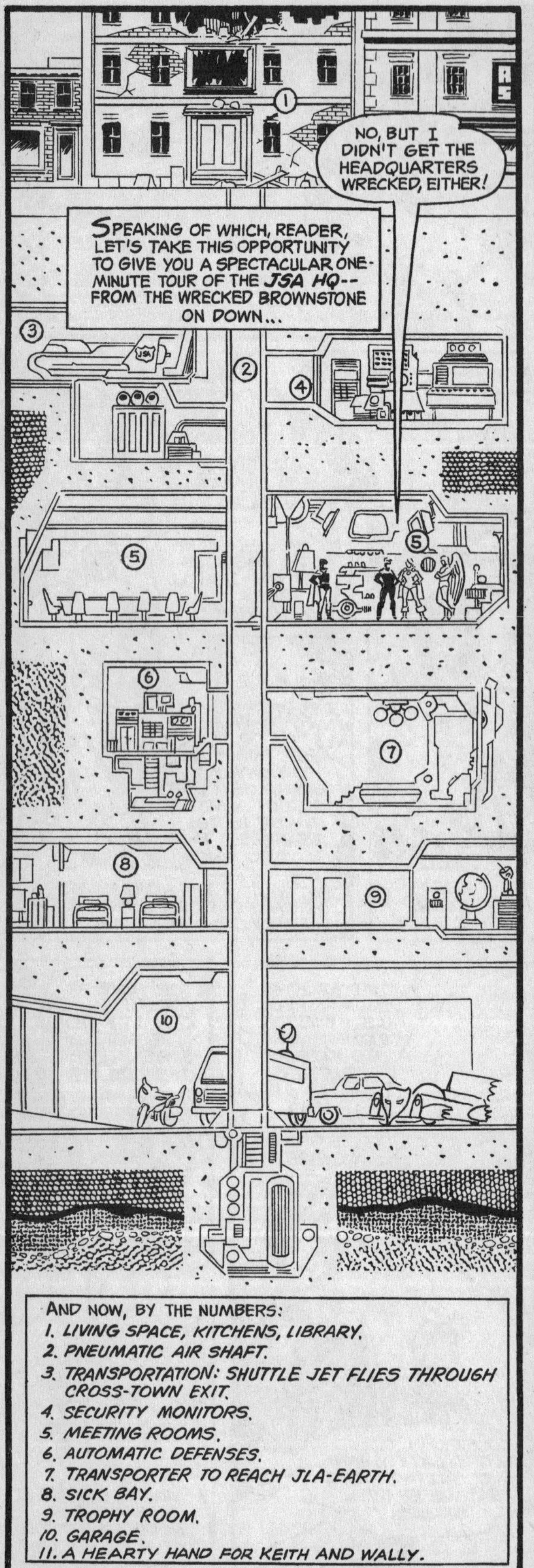
NO, BUT I DIDN'T GET THE HEADQUARTERS WRECKED, EITHER!
SPEAKING OF WHICH, READER, LET'S TAKE THIS OPPORTUNITY TO GIVE YOU A SPECTACULAR ONE-MINUTE TOUR OF THE JSA HQ-- FROM THE WRECKED BROWNSTONE ON DOWN...
AND NOW, BY THE NUMBERS:
1. LIVING SPACE, KITCHENS, LIBRARY.
2. PNEUMATIC AIR SHAFT.
3. TRANSPORTATION: SHUTTLE JET FLIES THROUGH CROSS-TOWN EXIT.
4. SECURITY MONITORS.
5. MEETING ROOMS.
6. AUTOMATIC DEFENSES.
7. TRANSPORTER TO REACH JLA-EARTH.
8. SICK BAY.
9. TROPHY ROOM.
10. GARAGE.
11. A HEARTY HAND FOR KEITH AND WALLY.

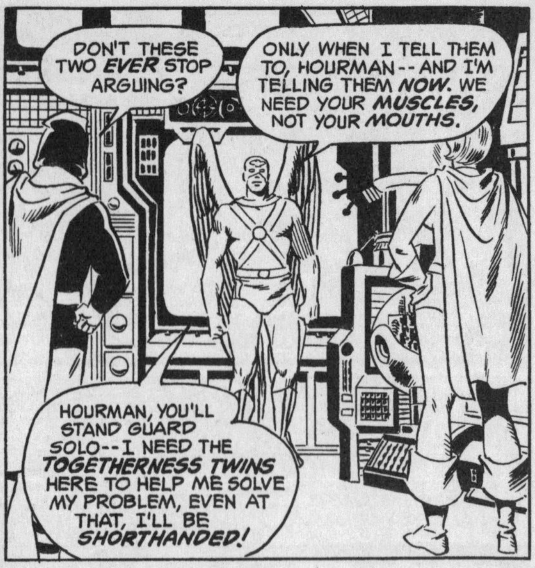
DON'T THESE TWO EVER STOP ARGUING?
ONLY WHEN I TELL THEM TO, HOURMAN-- AND I'M TELLING THEM NOW. WE NEED YOUR MUSCLES, NOT YOUR MOUTHS.
HOURMAN, YOU'LL STAND GUARD SOLO--I NEED THE TOGETHERNESS TWINS HERE TO HELP ME SOLVE MY PROBLEM, EVEN AT THAT, I'LL BE SHORTHANDED!

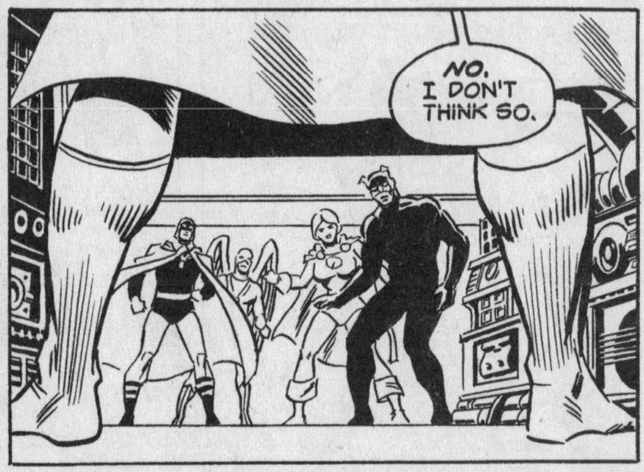
NO. I DON'T THINK SO.

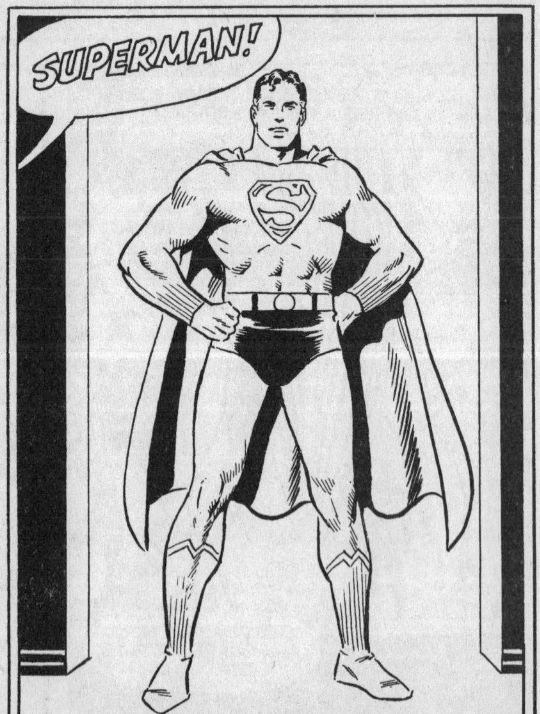
SUPERMAN!

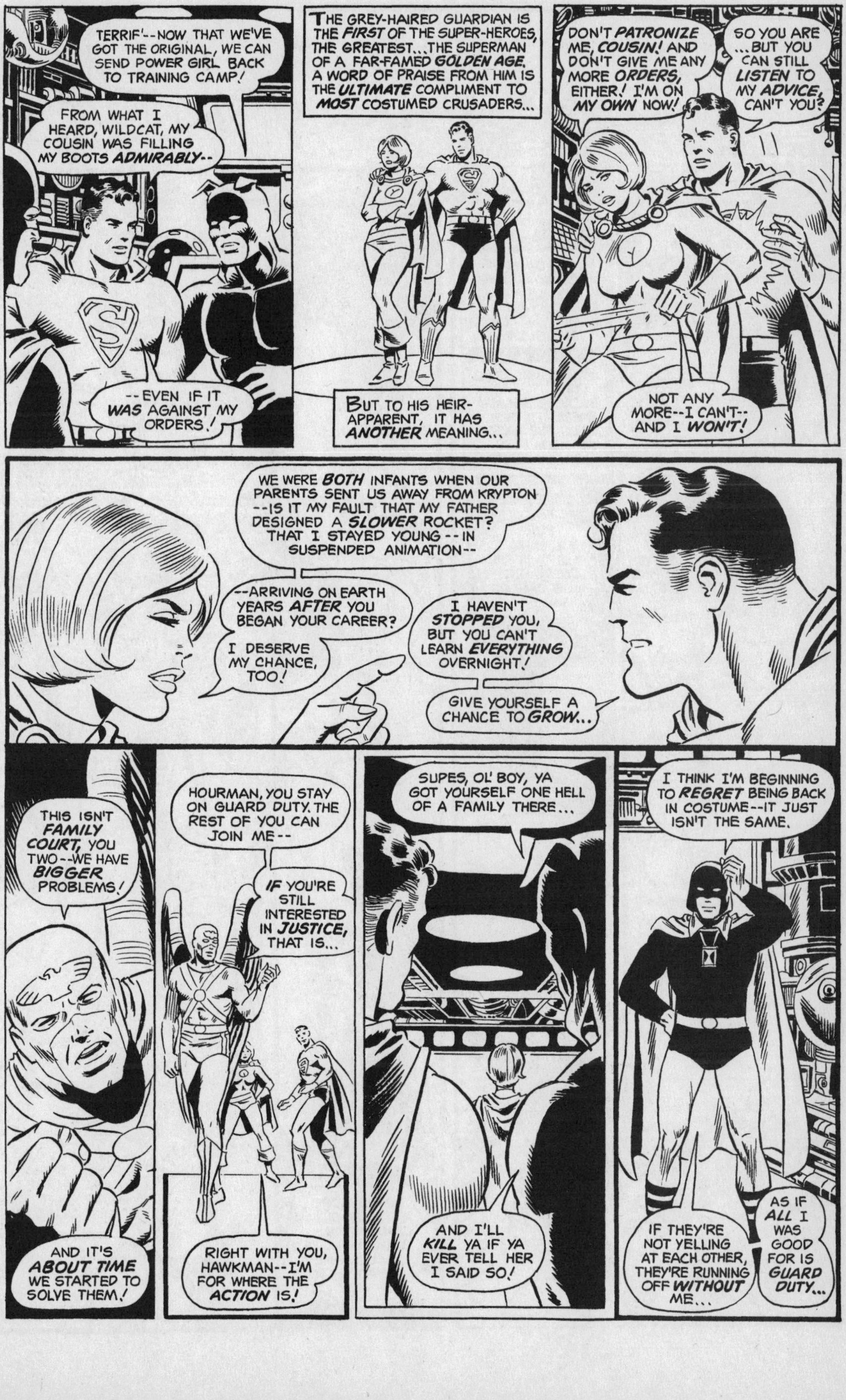
TERRIF'--NOW THAT WE'VE GOT THE ORIGINAL, WE CAN SEND POWER GIRL BACK TO TRAINING CAMP!
FROM WHAT I HEARD, WILDCAT, MY COUSIN WAS FILLING MY BOOTS ADMIRABLY--
--EVEN IF IT WAS AGAINST MY ORDERS!
THE GREY-HAIRED GUARDIAN IS THE FIRST OF THE SUPER-HEROES, THE GREATEST...THE SUPERMAN OF A FAR-FAMED GOLDEN AGE. A WORD OF PRAISE FROM HIM IS THE ULTIMATE COMPLIMENT TO MOST COSTUMED CRUSADERS...
BUT TO HIS HEIR-APPARENT, IT HAS ANOTHER MEANING...
DON'T PATRONIZE ME, COUSIN! AND DON'T GIVE ME ANY MORE ORDERS, EITHER! I'M ON MY OWN NOW!
SO YOU ARE ...BUT YOU CAN STILL LISTEN TO MY ADVICE, CAN'T YOU?
NOT ANY MORE--I CAN'T--AND I WON'T!
WE WERE BOTH INFANTS WHEN OUR PARENTS SENT US AWAY FROM KRYPTON --IS IT MY FAULT THAT MY FATHER DESIGNED A SLOWER ROCKET? THAT I STAYED YOUNG--IN SUSPENDED ANIMATION--
--ARRIVING ON EARTH YEARS AFTER YOU BEGAN YOUR CAREER?
I DESERVE MY CHANCE, TOO!
I HAVEN'T STOPPED YOU, BUT YOU CAN'T LEARN EVERYTHING OVERNIGHT!
GIVE YOURSELF A CHANCE TO GROW...
THIS ISN'T FAMILY COURT, YOU TWO--WE HAVE BIGGER PROBLEMS!
AND IT'S ABOUT TIME WE STARTED TO SOLVE THEM!
HOURMAN, YOU STAY ON GUARD DUTY. THE REST OF YOU CAN JOIN ME--
IF YOU'RE STILL INTERESTED IN JUSTICE, THAT IS...
RIGHT WITH YOU, HAWKMAN--I'M FOR WHERE THE ACTION IS!
SUPES, OL' BOY, YA GOT YOURSELF ONE HELL OF A FAMILY THERE...
AND I'LL KILL YA IF YA EVER TELL HER I SAID SO!
I THINK I'M BEGINNING TO REGRET BEING BACK IN COSTUME--IT JUST ISN'T THE SAME.
IF THEY'RE NOT YELLING AT EACH OTHER, THEY'RE RUNNING OFF WITHOUT ME...
AS IF ALL I WAS GOOD FOR IS GUARD DUTY...

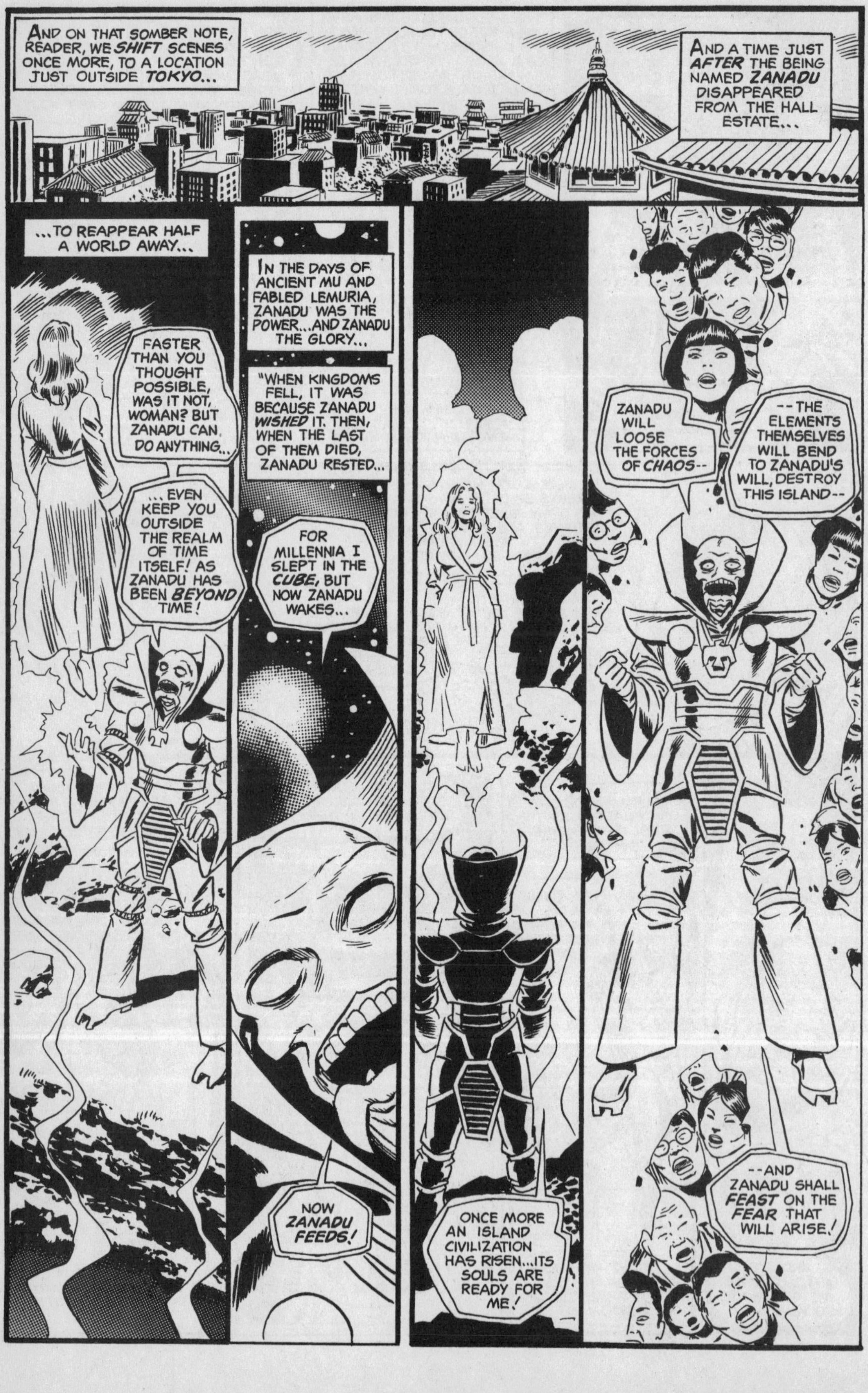
AND ON THAT SOMBER NOTE, READER, WE SHIFT SCENES ONCE MORE, TO A LOCATION JUST OUTSIDE TOKYO...
AND A TIME JUST AFTER THE BEING NAMED ZANADU DISAPPEARED FROM THE HALL ESTATE...
...TO REAPPEAR HALF A WORLD AWAY...
FASTER THAN YOU THOUGHT POSSIBLE, WAS IT NOT, WOMAN? BUT ZANADU CAN DO ANYTHING...
...EVEN KEEP YOU OUTSIDE THE REALM OF TIME ITSELF! AS ZANADU HAS BEEN BEYOND TIME!
IN THE DAYS OF ANCIENT MU AND FABLED LEMURIA, ZANADU WAS THE POWER...AND ZANADU THE GLORY...
"WHEN KINGDOMS FELL, IT WAS BECAUSE ZANADU WISHED IT. THEN, WHEN THE LAST OF THEM DIED, ZANADU RESTED...
FOR MILLENNIA I SLEPT IN THE CUBE, BUT NOW ZANADU WAKES...
NOW ZANADU FEEDS!
ONCE MORE AN ISLAND CIVILIZATION HAS RISEN...ITS SOULS ARE READY FOR ME!
ZANADU WILL LOOSE THE FORCES OF CHAOS--
--THE ELEMENTS THEMSELVES WILL BEND TO ZANADU'S WILL, DESTROY THIS ISLAND--
--AND ZANADU SHALL FEAST ON THE FEAR THAT WILL ARISE!

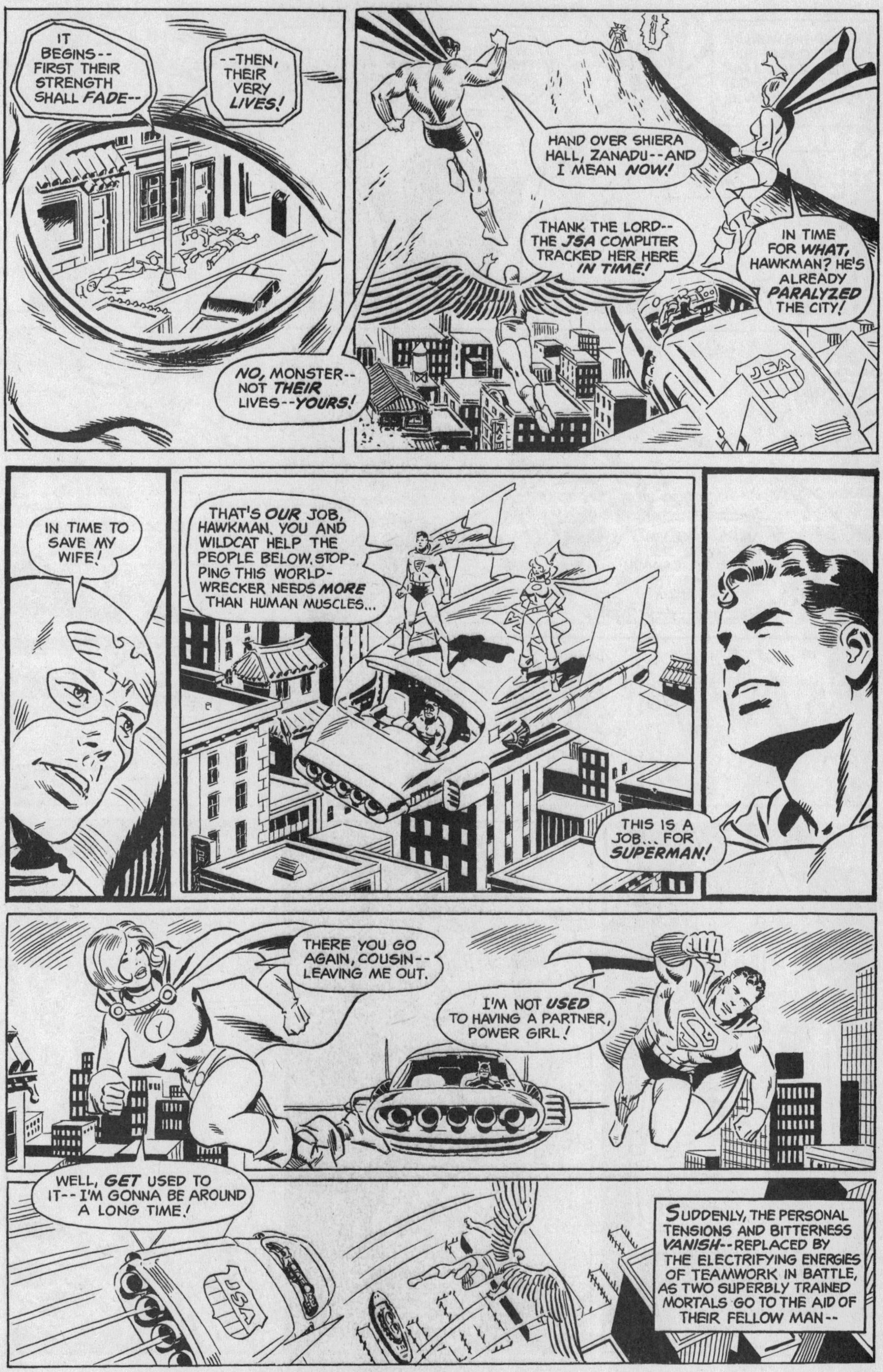
IT BEGINS-- FIRST THEIR STRENGTH SHALL FADE--
--THEN, THEIR VERY LIVES!
NO, MONSTER-- NOT THEIR LIVES--YOURS!
HAND OVER SHIERA HALL, ZANADU--AND I MEAN NOW!
THANK THE LORD-- THE JSA COMPUTER TRACKED HER HERE IN TIME!
IN TIME FOR WHAT, HAWKMAN? HE'S ALREADY PARALYZED THE CITY!
JSA
IN TIME TO SAVE MY WIFE!
THAT'S OUR JOB, HAWKMAN. YOU AND WILDCAT HELP THE PEOPLE BELOW. STOPPING THIS WORLD-WRECKER NEEDS MORE THAN HUMAN MUSCLES...
THIS IS A JOB... FOR SUPERMAN!
THERE YOU GO AGAIN, COUSIN-- LEAVING ME OUT.
I'M NOT USED TO HAVING A PARTNER, POWER GIRL!
WELL, GET USED TO IT-- I'M GONNA BE AROUND A LONG TIME!
SUDDENLY, THE PERSONAL TENSIONS AND BITTERNESS VANISH--REPLACED BY THE ELECTRIFYING ENERGIES OF TEAMWORK IN BATTLE, AS TWO SUPERBLY TRAINED MORTALS GO TO THE AID OF THEIR FELLOW MAN--
JSA

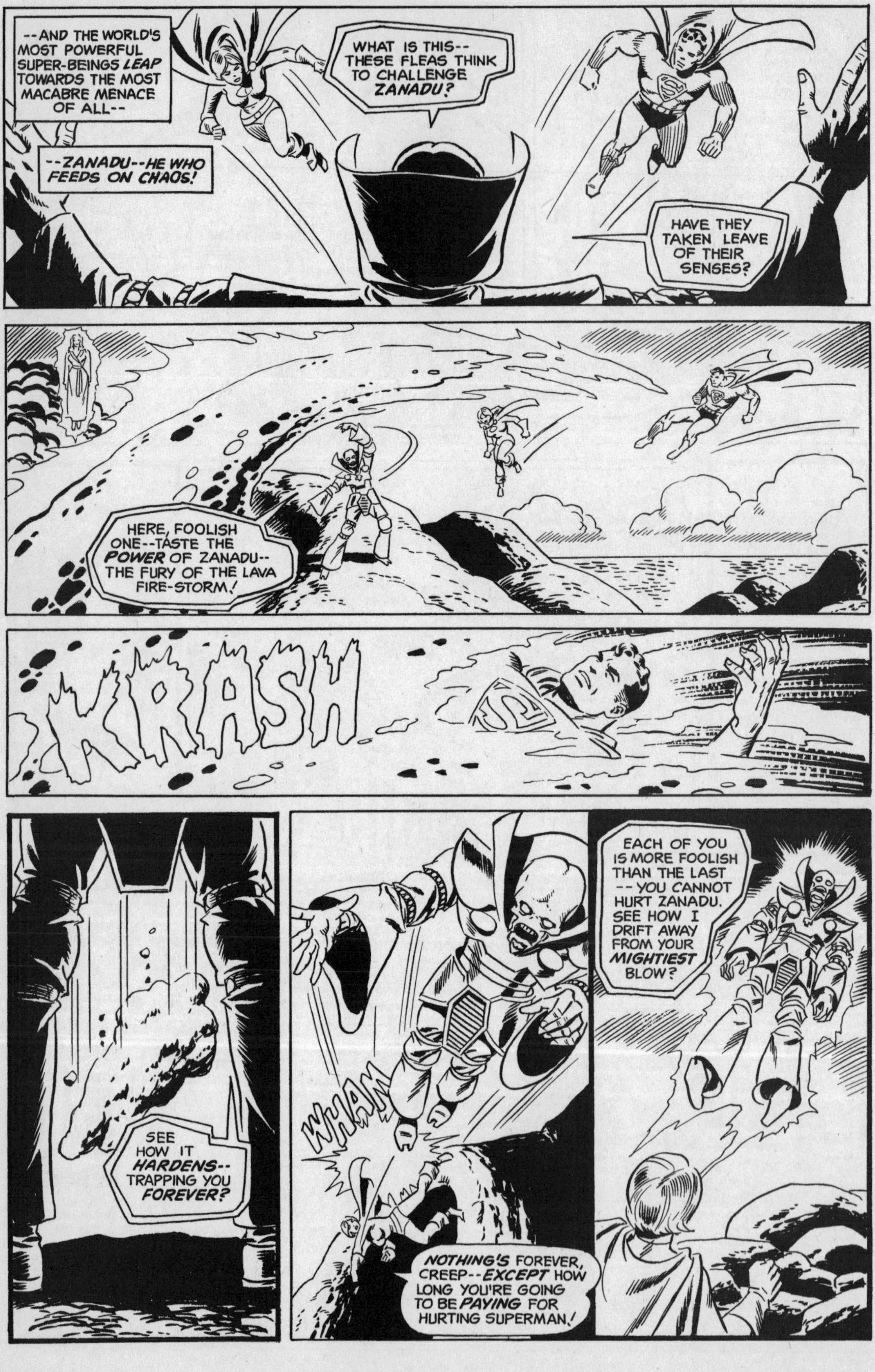
--AND THE WORLD'S MOST POWERFUL SUPER-BEINGS LEAP TOWARDS THE MOST MACABRE MENACE OF ALL--
WHAT IS THIS-- THESE FLEAS THINK TO CHALLENGE ZANADU?
--ZANADU--HE WHO FEEDS ON CHAOS!
HAVE THEY TAKEN LEAVE OF THEIR SENSES?
HERE, FOOLISH ONE--TASTE THE POWER OF ZANADU-- THE FURY OF THE LAVA FIRE-STORM!
KRASH
SEE HOW IT HARDENS-- TRAPPING YOU FOREVER?
WHAM
EACH OF YOU IS MORE FOOLISH THAN THE LAST --YOU CANNOT HURT ZANADU. SEE HOW I DRIFT AWAY FROM YOUR MIGHTIEST BLOW?
NOTHING'S FOREVER, CREEP--EXCEPT HOW LONG YOU'RE GOING TO BE PAYING FOR HURTING SUPERMAN!

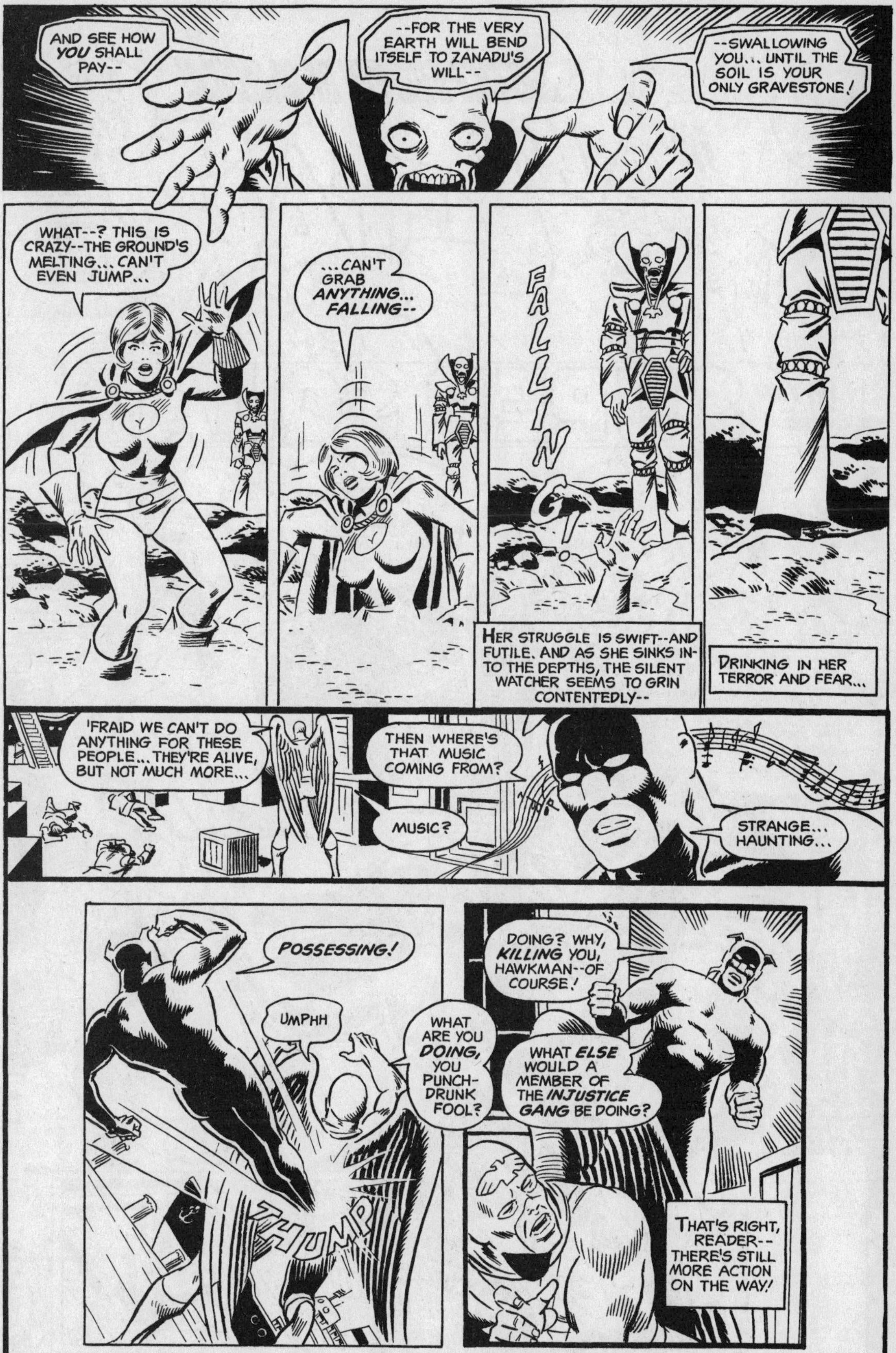
AND SEE HOW YOU SHALL PAY--
--FOR THE VERY EARTH WILL BEND ITSELF TO ZANADU'S WILL--
--SWALLOWING YOU... UNTIL THE SOIL IS YOUR ONLY GRAVESTONE!
WHAT--? THIS IS CRAZY--THE GROUND'S MELTING... CAN'T EVEN JUMP...
...CAN'T GRAB ANYTHING... FALLING--
FALLING!
HER STRUGGLE IS SWIFT--AND FUTILE. AND AS SHE SINKS INTO THE DEPTHS, THE SILENT WATCHER SEEMS TO GRIN CONTENTEDLY--
DRINKING IN HER TERROR AND FEAR...
'FRAID WE CAN'T DO ANYTHING FOR THESE PEOPLE... THEY'RE ALIVE, BUT NOT MUCH MORE...
THEN WHERE'S THAT MUSIC COMING FROM?
MUSIC?
STRANGE... HAUNTING...
POSSESSING!
UMPHH
WHAT ARE YOU DOING, YOU PUNCH-DRUNK FOOL?
THUMP
DOING? WHY, KILLING YOU, HAWKMAN--OF COURSE!
WHAT ELSE WOULD A MEMBER OF THE INJUSTICE GANG BE DOING?
THAT'S RIGHT, READER--THERE'S STILL MORE ACTION ON THE WAY!

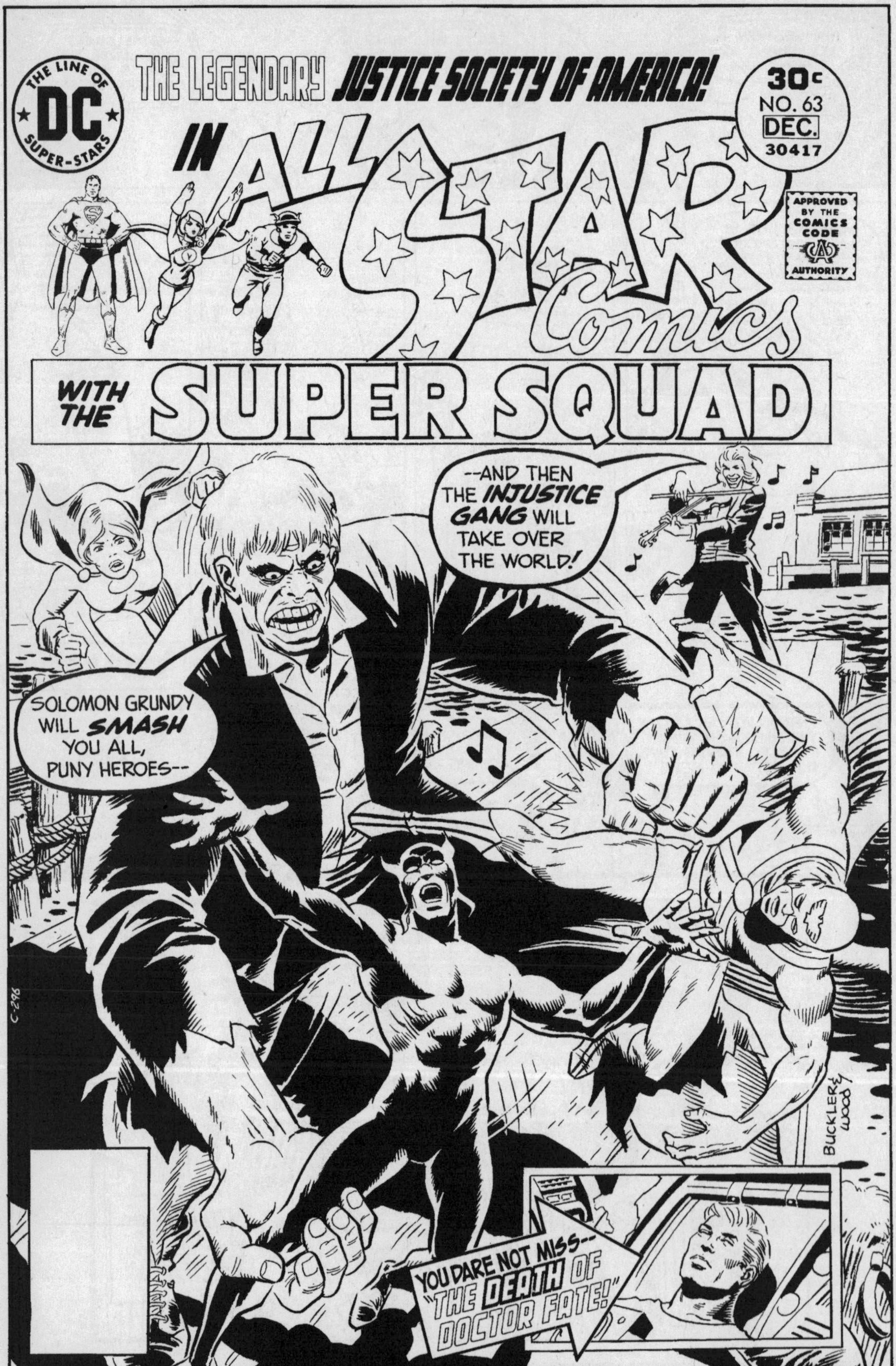
THE LINE OF DC SUPER-STARS
THE LEGENDARY JUSTICE SOCIETY OF AMERICA!
IN ALL STAR Comics
30¢ NO. 63 DEC. 30417
APPROVED BY THE COMICS CODE AUTHORITY
WITH THE SUPER SQUAD
--AND THEN THE INJUSTICE GANG WILL TAKE OVER THE WORLD!
SOLOMON GRUNDY WILL SMASH YOU ALL, PUNY HEROES--
C-296
BUCKLER & WOOD
YOU DARE NOT MISS-- "THE DEATH OF DOCTOR FATE!"

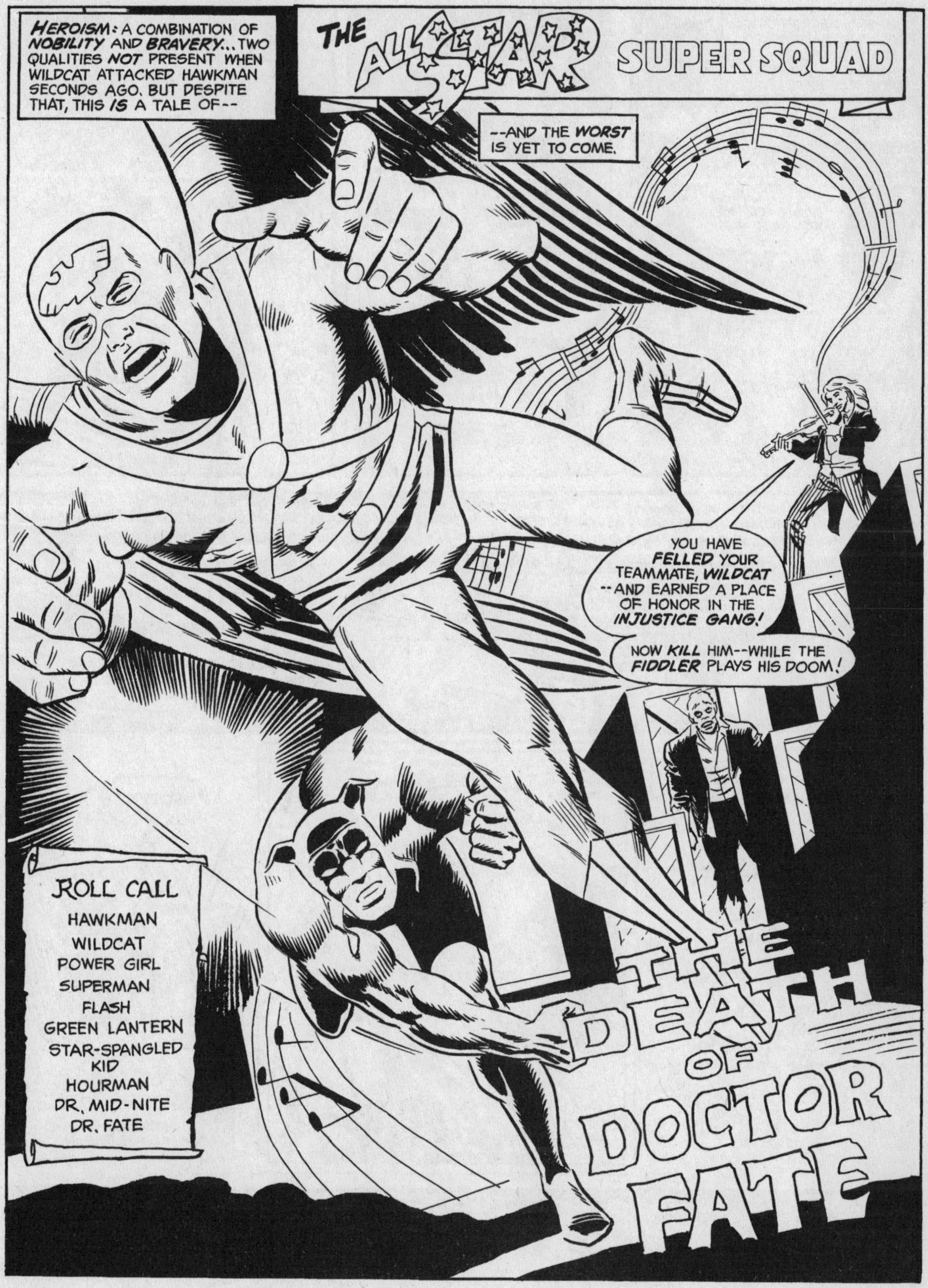
HEROISM: A COMBINATION OF NOBILITY AND BRAVERY... TWO QUALITIES NOT PRESENT WHEN WILDCAT ATTACKED HAWKMAN SECONDS AGO. BUT DESPITE THAT, THIS IS A TALE OF--
THE ALL-STAR SUPER SQUAD
--AND THE WORST IS YET TO COME.
YOU HAVE FELLED YOUR TEAMMATE, WILDCAT --AND EARNED A PLACE OF HONOR IN THE INJUSTICE GANG!
NOW KILL HIM--WHILE THE FIDDLER PLAYS HIS DOOM!
ROLL CALL
HAWKMAN
WILDCAT
POWER GIRL
SUPERMAN
FLASH
GREEN LANTERN
STAR-SPANGLED KID
HOURMAN
DR. MID-NITE
DR. FATE
THE DEATH OF DOCTOR FATE

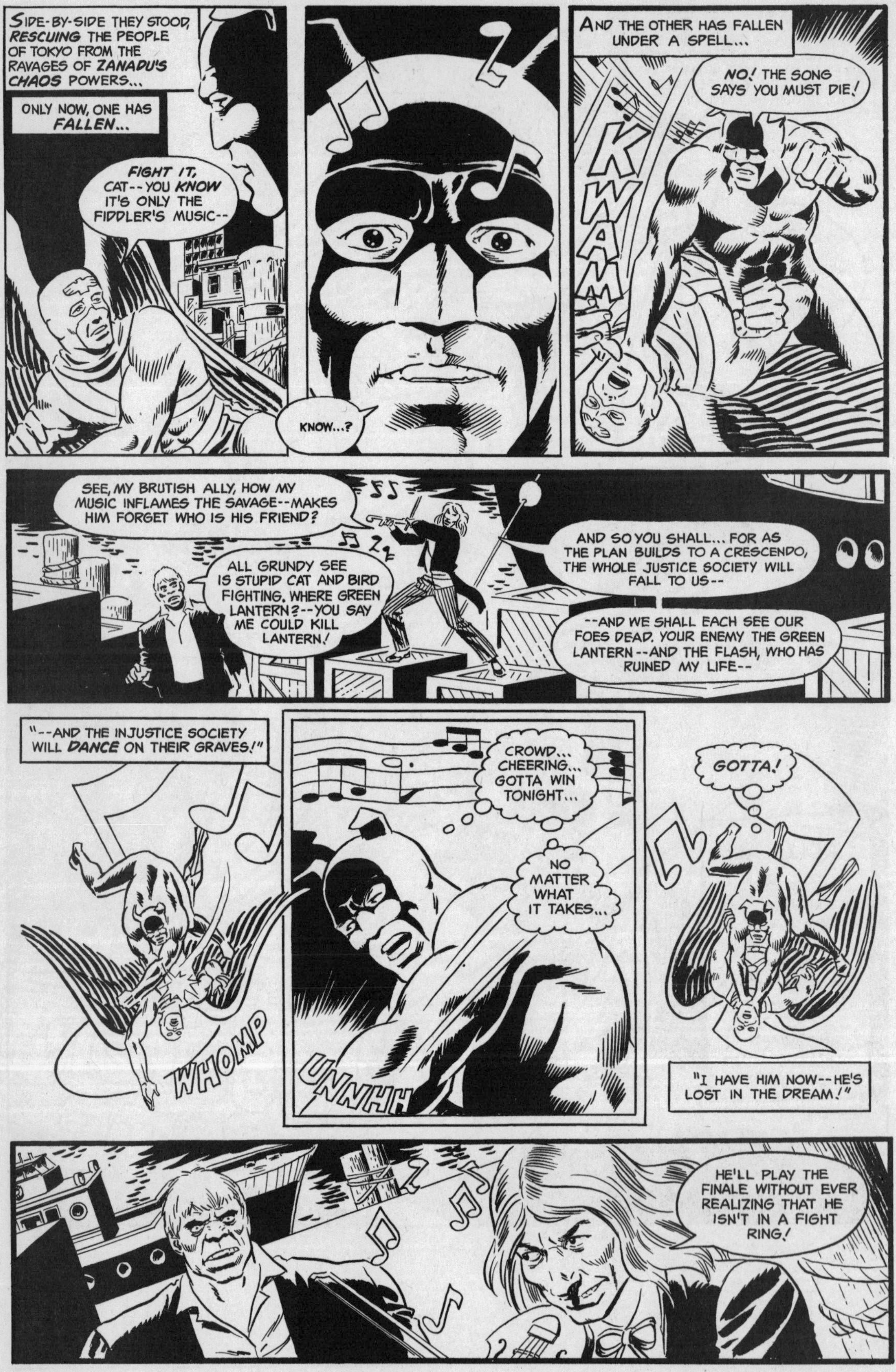
SIDE-BY-SIDE THEY STOOD, RESCUING THE PEOPLE OF TOKYO FROM THE RAVAGES OF ZANADU'S CHAOS POWERS...
ONLY NOW, ONE HAS FALLEN...
FIGHT IT, CAT--YOU KNOW IT'S ONLY THE FIDDLER'S MUSIC--
KNOW...?
AND THE OTHER HAS FALLEN UNDER A SPELL...
NO! THE SONG SAYS YOU MUST DIE!
KWAM
SEE, MY BRUTISH ALLY, HOW MY MUSIC INFLAMES THE SAVAGE--MAKES HIM FORGET WHO IS HIS FRIEND?
ALL GRUNDY SEE IS STUPID CAT AND BIRD FIGHTING. WHERE GREEN LANTERN?--YOU SAY ME COULD KILL LANTERN!
AND SO YOU SHALL... FOR AS THE PLAN BUILDS TO A CRESCENDO, THE WHOLE JUSTICE SOCIETY WILL FALL TO US--
--AND WE SHALL EACH SEE OUR FOES DEAD. YOUR ENEMY THE GREEN LANTERN--AND THE FLASH, WHO HAS RUINED MY LIFE--
"--AND THE INJUSTICE SOCIETY WILL DANCE ON THEIR GRAVES!"
WHOMP
CROWD... CHEERING... GOTTA WIN TONIGHT...
NO MATTER WHAT IT TAKES...
UNNHH
GOTTA!
"I HAVE HIM NOW--HE'S LOST IN THE DREAM!"
HE'LL PLAY THE FINALE WITHOUT EVER REALIZING THAT HE ISN'T IN A FIGHT RING!

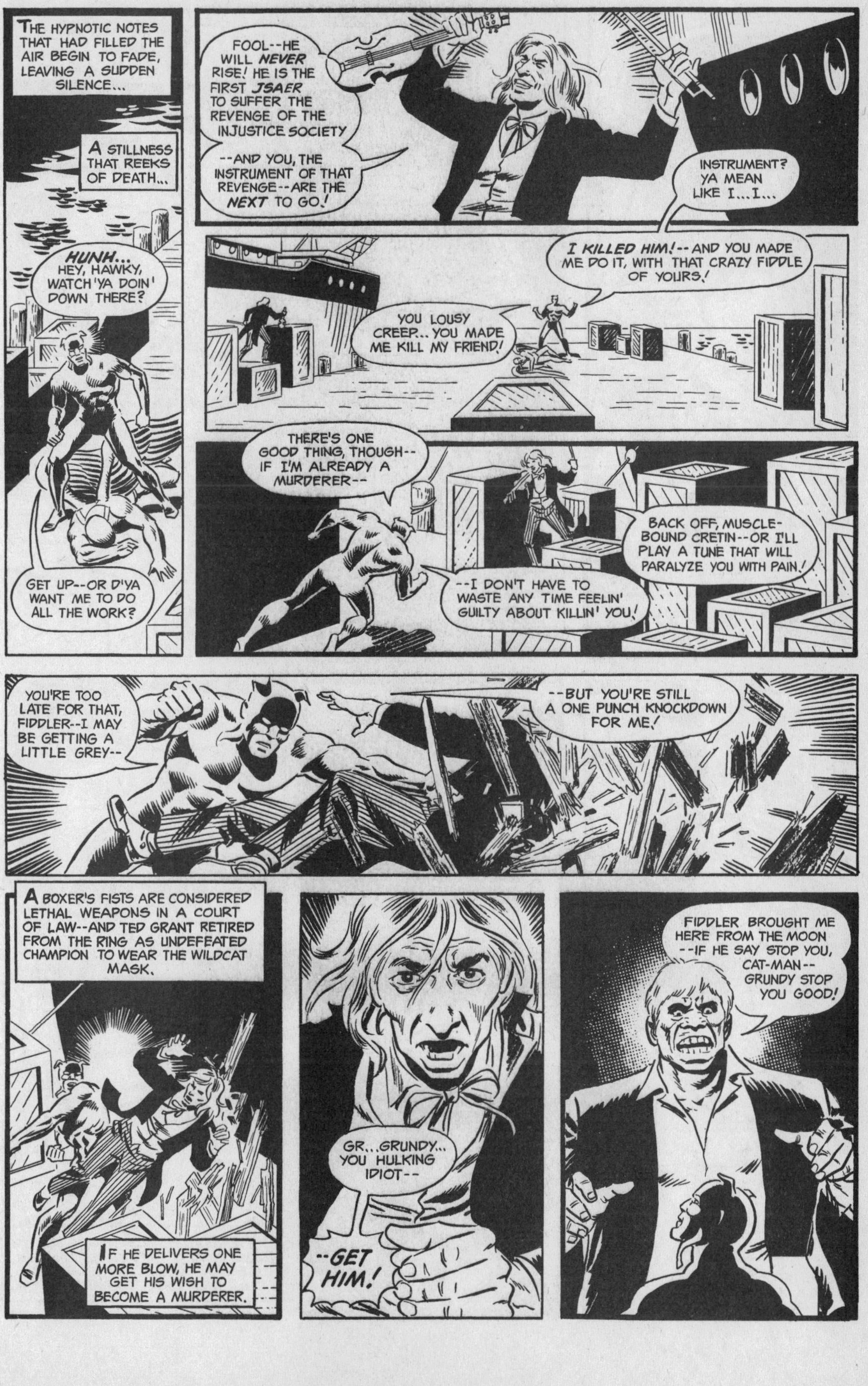
THE HYPNOTIC NOTES THAT HAD FILLED THE AIR BEGIN TO FADE, LEAVING A SUDDEN SILENCE...
A STILLNESS THAT REEKS OF DEATH...
HUNH... HEY, HAWKY, WATCH'YA DOIN' DOWN THERE?
GET UP--OR D'YA WANT ME TO DO ALL THE WORK?
FOOL--HE WILL NEVER RISE! HE IS THE FIRST JSAER TO SUFFER THE REVENGE OF THE INJUSTICE SOCIETY
--AND YOU, THE INSTRUMENT OF THAT REVENGE--ARE THE NEXT TO GO!
INSTRUMENT? YA MEAN LIKE I...I...
I KILLED HIM!--AND YOU MADE ME DO IT, WITH THAT CRAZY FIDDLE OF YOURS!
YOU LOUSY CREEP...YOU MADE ME KILL MY FRIEND!
THERE'S ONE GOOD THING, THOUGH--IF I'M ALREADY A MURDERER--
--I DON'T HAVE TO WASTE ANY TIME FEELIN' GUILTY ABOUT KILLIN' YOU!
BACK OFF, MUSCLE-BOUND CRETIN--OR I'LL PLAY A TUNE THAT WILL PARALYZE YOU WITH PAIN!
YOU'RE TOO LATE FOR THAT, FIDDLER--I MAY BE GETTING A LITTLE GREY--
--BUT YOU'RE STILL A ONE PUNCH KNOCKDOWN FOR ME!
A BOXER'S FISTS ARE CONSIDERED LETHAL WEAPONS IN A COURT OF LAW--AND TED GRANT RETIRED FROM THE RING AS UNDEFEATED CHAMPION TO WEAR THE WILDCAT MASK.
IF HE DELIVERS ONE MORE BLOW, HE MAY GET HIS WISH TO BECOME A MURDERER.
GR...GRUNDY... YOU HULKING IDIOT--
--GET HIM!
FIDDLER BROUGHT ME HERE FROM THE MOON --IF HE SAY STOP YOU, CAT-MAN--GRUNDY STOP YOU GOOD!

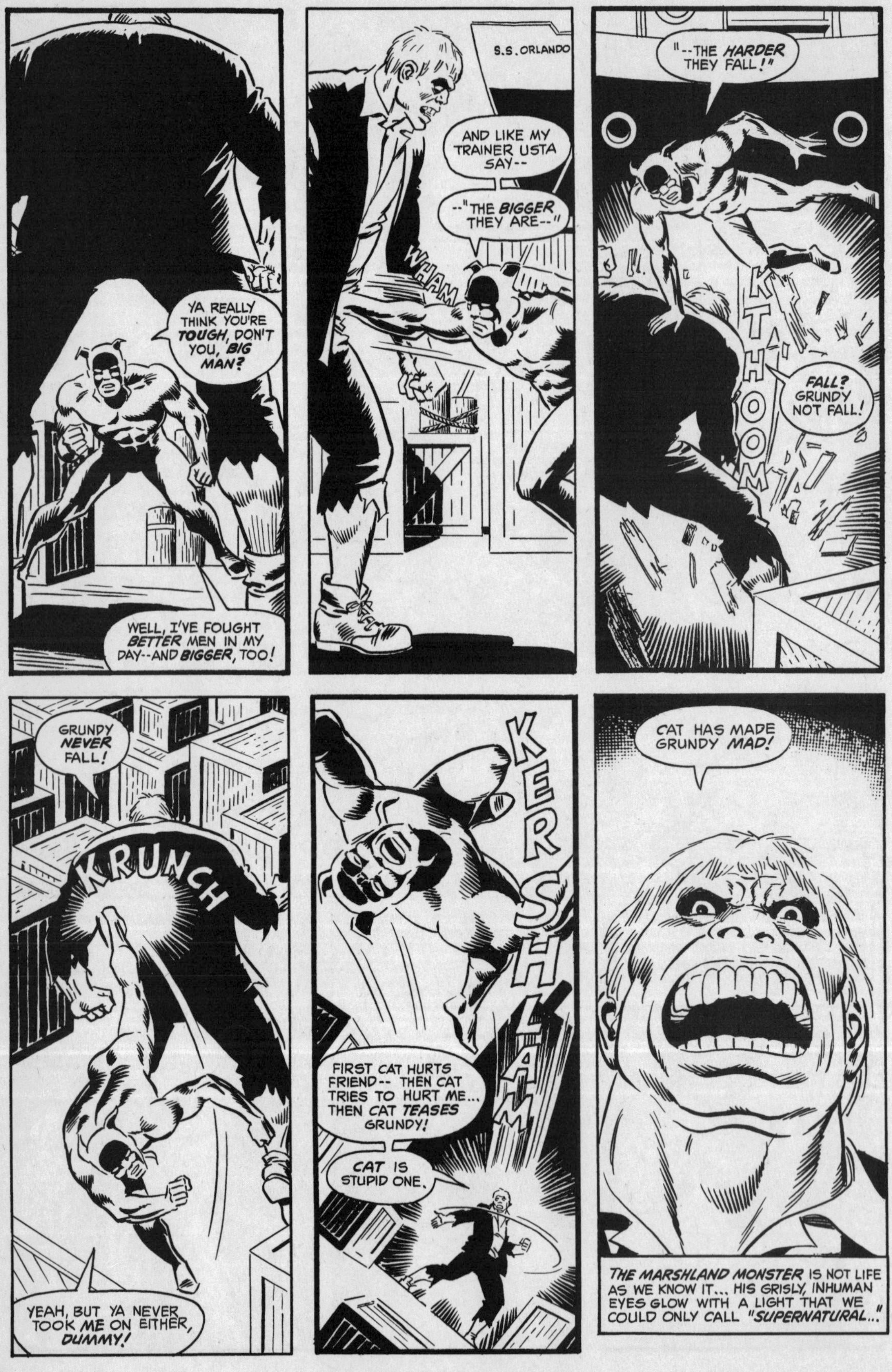
YA REALLY THINK YOU'RE TOUGH, DON'T YOU, BIG MAN?
WELL, I'VE FOUGHT BETTER MEN IN MY DAY--AND BIGGER, TOO!
S.S. ORLANDO
AND LIKE MY TRAINER USTA SAY--
--"THE BIGGER THEY ARE--"
WHAM
"--THE HARDER THEY FALL!"
KTTHOOM
FALL? GRUNDY NOT FALL!
GRUNDY NEVER FALL!
KRUNCH
YEAH, BUT YA NEVER TOOK ME ON EITHER, DUMMY!
KERSHLAM
FIRST CAT HURTS FRIEND-- THEN CAT TRIES TO HURT ME... THEN CAT TEASES GRUNDY!
CAT IS STUPID ONE.
CAT HAS MADE GRUNDY MAD!
THE MARSHLAND MONSTER IS NOT LIFE AS WE KNOW IT... HIS GRISLY, INHUMAN EYES GLOW WITH A LIGHT THAT WE COULD ONLY CALL "SUPERNATURAL..."

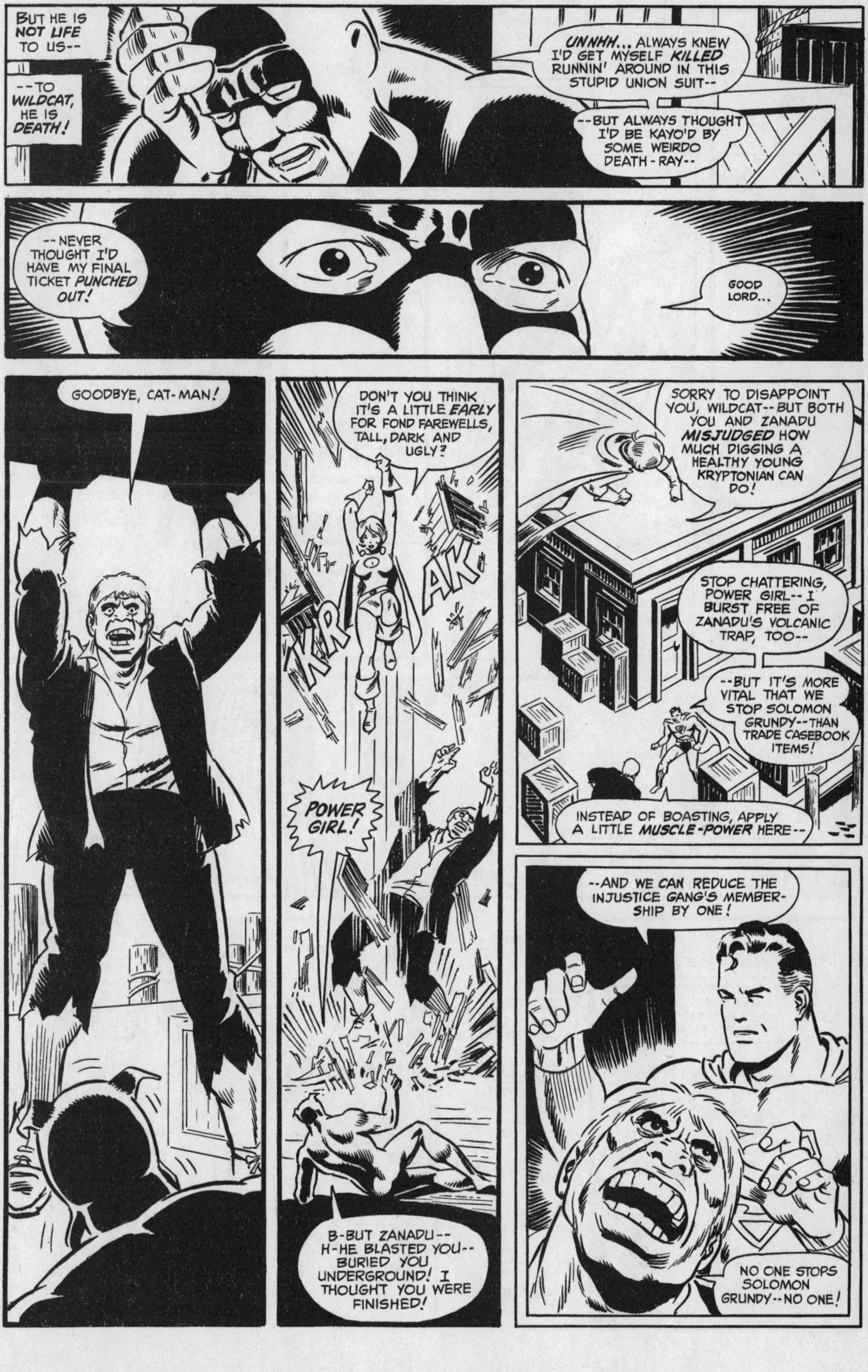
BUT HE IS NOT LIFE TO US--
--TO WILDCAT, HE IS DEATH!
UNNHH... ALWAYS KNEW I'D GET MYSELF KILLED RUNNIN' AROUND IN THIS STUPID UNION SUIT--
--BUT ALWAYS THOUGHT I'D BE KAYO'D BY SOME WEIRDO DEATH-RAY--
--NEVER THOUGHT I'D HAVE MY FINAL TICKET PUNCHED OUT!
GOOD LORD...
GOODBYE, CAT-MAN!
DON'T YOU THINK IT'S A LITTLE EARLY FOR FOND FAREWELLS, TALL, DARK AND UGLY?
KRAK
POWER GIRL!
B-BUT ZANADU-- H-HE BLASTED YOU-- BURIED YOU UNDERGROUND! I THOUGHT YOU WERE FINISHED!
SORRY TO DISAPPOINT YOU, WILDCAT-- BUT BOTH YOU AND ZANADU MISJUDGED HOW MUCH DIGGING A HEALTHY YOUNG KRYPTONIAN CAN DO!
STOP CHATTERING, POWER GIRL-- I BURST FREE OF ZANADU'S VOLCANIC TRAP, TOO--
--BUT IT'S MORE VITAL THAT WE STOP SOLOMON GRUNDY--THAN TRADE CASEBOOK ITEMS!
INSTEAD OF BOASTING, APPLY A LITTLE MUSCLE-POWER HERE--
--AND WE CAN REDUCE THE INJUSTICE GANG'S MEMBERSHIP BY ONE!
NO ONE STOPS SOLOMON GRUNDY--NO ONE!

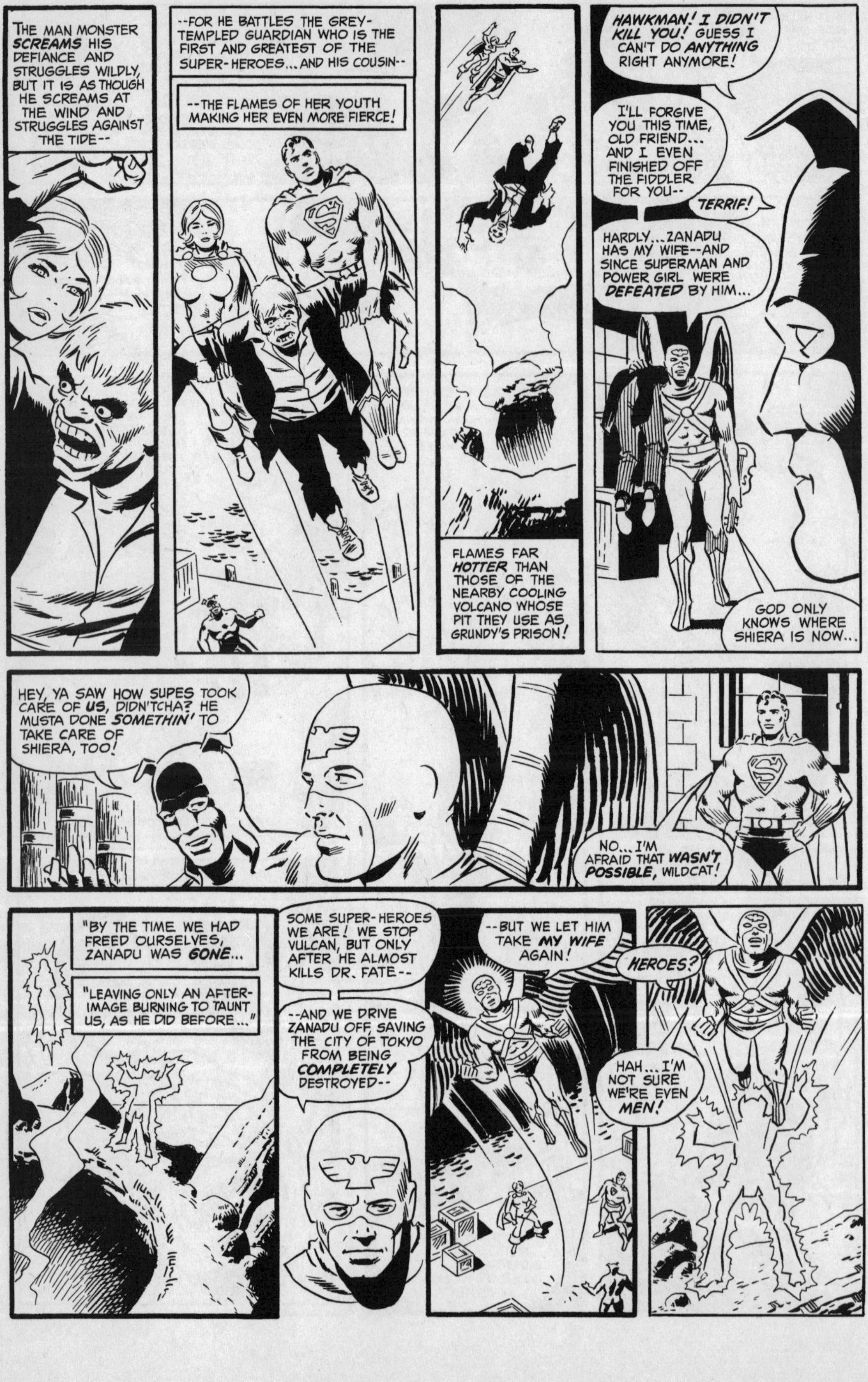

THE MAN MONSTER **SCREAMS** HIS DEFIANCE AND STRUGGLES WILDLY, BUT IT IS AS THOUGH HE SCREAMS AT THE WIND AND STRUGGLES AGAINST THE TIDE--
--FOR HE BATTLES THE GREY-TEMPLED GUARDIAN WHO IS THE FIRST AND GREATEST OF THE SUPER-HEROES... AND HIS COUSIN--
--THE FLAMES OF HER YOUTH MAKING HER EVEN MORE FIERCE!
FLAMES FAR **HOTTER** THAN THOSE OF THE NEARBY COOLING VOLCANO WHOSE PIT THEY USE AS GRUNDY'S PRISON!
HAWKMAN! I DIDN'T KILL YOU! GUESS I CAN'T DO **ANYTHING** RIGHT ANYMORE!
I'LL FORGIVE YOU THIS TIME, OLD FRIEND... AND I EVEN FINISHED OFF THE FIDDLER FOR YOU--
TERRIF!
HARDLY... ZANADU HAS MY WIFE--AND SINCE SUPERMAN AND POWER GIRL WERE **DEFEATED** BY HIM...
GOD ONLY KNOWS WHERE SHIERA IS NOW...
HEY, YA SAW HOW SUPES TOOK CARE OF **US**, DIDN'TCHA? HE MUSTA DONE **SOMETHIN'** TO TAKE CARE OF SHIERA, TOO!
NO... I'M AFRAID THAT **WASN'T POSSIBLE**, WILDCAT!
"BY THE TIME WE HAD FREED OURSELVES, ZANADU WAS **GONE**...
"LEAVING ONLY AN AFTER-IMAGE BURNING TO TAUNT US, AS HE DID BEFORE..."
SOME SUPER-HEROES WE ARE! WE STOP VULCAN, BUT ONLY AFTER HE ALMOST KILLS DR. FATE--
--AND WE DRIVE ZANADU OFF, SAVING THE CITY OF TOKYO FROM BEING **COMPLETELY** DESTROYED--
--BUT WE LET HIM TAKE **MY WIFE** AGAIN!
HEROES?
HAH... I'M NOT SURE WE'RE EVEN **MEN!**

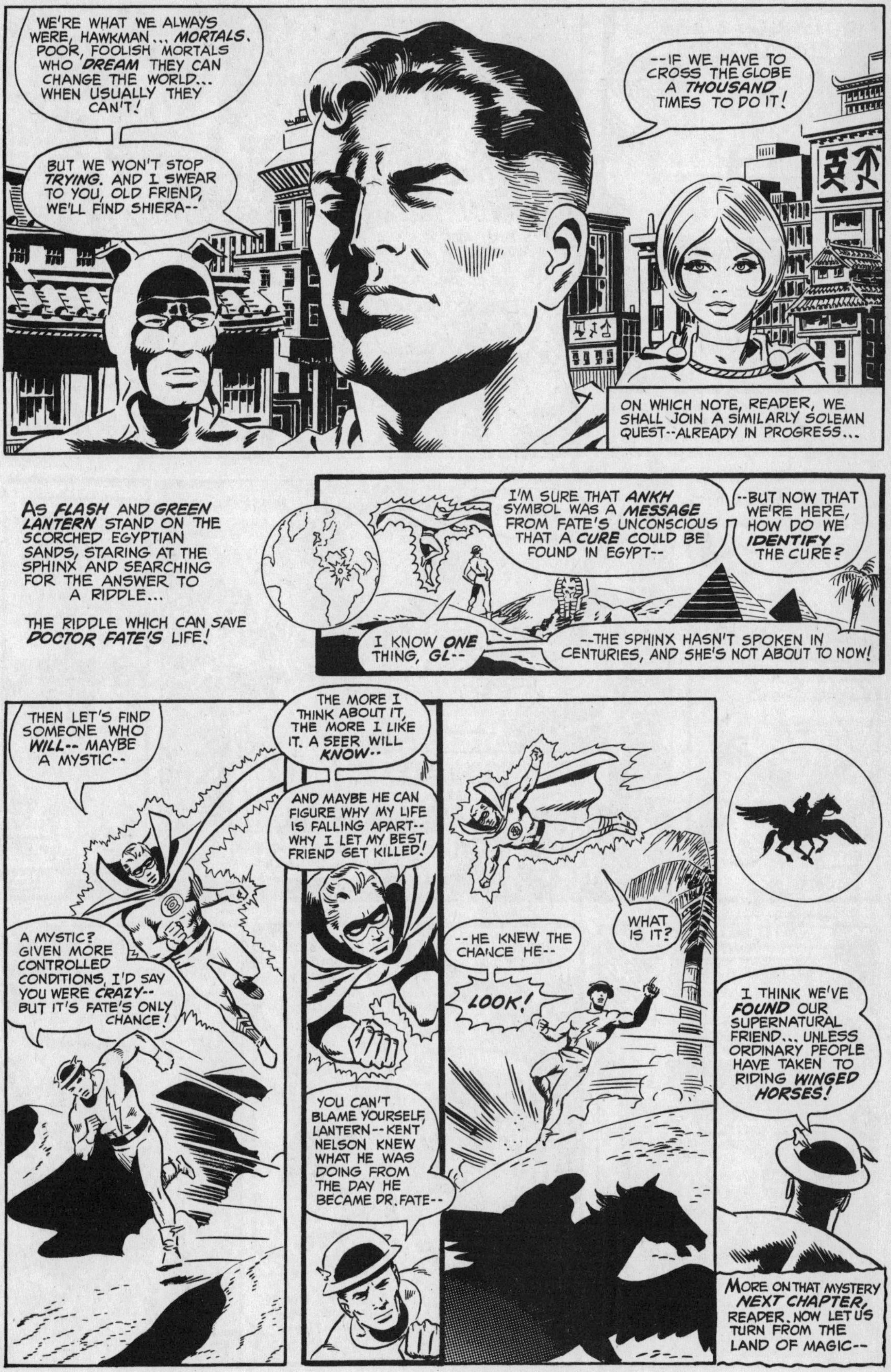
WE'RE WHAT WE ALWAYS WERE, HAWKMAN... MORTALS. POOR, FOOLISH MORTALS WHO DREAM THEY CAN CHANGE THE WORLD... WHEN USUALLY THEY CAN'T!
BUT WE WON'T STOP TRYING. AND I SWEAR TO YOU, OLD FRIEND, WE'LL FIND SHIERA--
--IF WE HAVE TO CROSS THE GLOBE A THOUSAND TIMES TO DO IT!
ON WHICH NOTE, READER, WE SHALL JOIN A SIMILARLY SOLEMN QUEST--ALREADY IN PROGRESS...
AS FLASH AND GREEN LANTERN STAND ON THE SCORCHED EGYPTIAN SANDS, STARING AT THE SPHINX AND SEARCHING FOR THE ANSWER TO A RIDDLE...
THE RIDDLE WHICH CAN SAVE DOCTOR FATE'S LIFE!
I'M SURE THAT ANKH SYMBOL WAS A MESSAGE FROM FATE'S UNCONSCIOUS THAT A CURE COULD BE FOUND IN EGYPT--
--BUT NOW THAT WE'RE HERE, HOW DO WE IDENTIFY THE CURE?
I KNOW ONE THING, GL--
--THE SPHINX HASN'T SPOKEN IN CENTURIES, AND SHE'S NOT ABOUT TO NOW!
THEN LET'S FIND SOMEONE WHO WILL-- MAYBE A MYSTIC--
A MYSTIC? GIVEN MORE CONTROLLED CONDITIONS, I'D SAY YOU WERE CRAZY-- BUT IT'S FATE'S ONLY CHANCE!
THE MORE I THINK ABOUT IT, THE MORE I LIKE IT. A SEER WILL KNOW--
AND MAYBE HE CAN FIGURE WHY MY LIFE IS FALLING APART-- WHY I LET MY BEST FRIEND GET KILLED!
YOU CAN'T BLAME YOURSELF, LANTERN--KENT NELSON KNEW WHAT HE WAS DOING FROM THE DAY HE BECAME DR. FATE--
--HE KNEW THE CHANCE HE--
LOOK!
WHAT IS IT?
I THINK WE'VE FOUND OUR SUPERNATURAL FRIEND... UNLESS ORDINARY PEOPLE HAVE TAKEN TO RIDING WINGED HORSES!
MORE ON THAT MYSTERY NEXT CHAPTER, READER. NOW LET US TURN FROM THE LAND OF MAGIC--

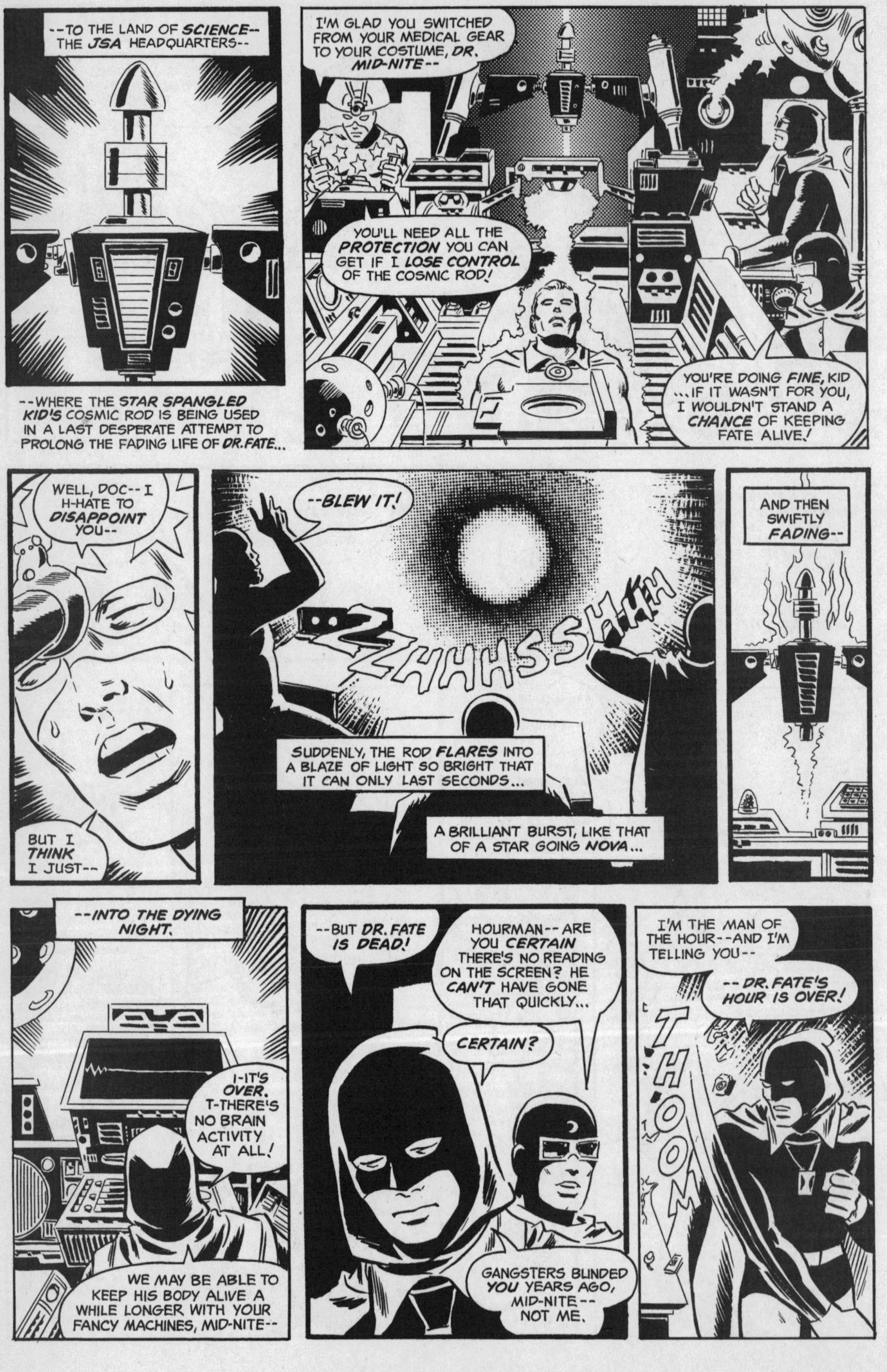
--TO THE LAND OF SCIENCE-- THE JSA HEADQUARTERS--
--WHERE THE STAR SPANGLED KID'S COSMIC ROD IS BEING USED IN A LAST DESPERATE ATTEMPT TO PROLONG THE FADING LIFE OF DR. FATE...
I'M GLAD YOU SWITCHED FROM YOUR MEDICAL GEAR TO YOUR COSTUME, DR. MID-NITE--
YOU'LL NEED ALL THE PROTECTION YOU CAN GET IF I LOSE CONTROL OF THE COSMIC ROD!
YOU'RE DOING FINE, KID ...IF IT WASN'T FOR YOU, I WOULDN'T STAND A CHANCE OF KEEPING FATE ALIVE!
WELL, DOC-- I H-HATE TO DISAPPOINT YOU--
BUT I THINK I JUST--
--BLEW IT!
ZHHHSSSHHH
SUDDENLY, THE ROD FLARES INTO A BLAZE OF LIGHT SO BRIGHT THAT IT CAN ONLY LAST SECONDS...
A BRILLIANT BURST, LIKE THAT OF A STAR GOING NOVA...
AND THEN SWIFTLY FADING--
--INTO THE DYING NIGHT.
I-IT'S OVER. T-THERE'S NO BRAIN ACTIVITY AT ALL!
WE MAY BE ABLE TO KEEP HIS BODY ALIVE A WHILE LONGER WITH YOUR FANCY MACHINES, MID-NITE--
--BUT DR. FATE IS DEAD!
HOURMAN-- ARE YOU CERTAIN THERE'S NO READING ON THE SCREEN? HE CAN'T HAVE GONE THAT QUICKLY...
CERTAIN?
GANGSTERS BLINDED YOU YEARS AGO, MID-NITE-- NOT ME.
I'M THE MAN OF THE HOUR--AND I'M TELLING YOU--
--DR. FATE'S HOUR IS OVER!
THOOM

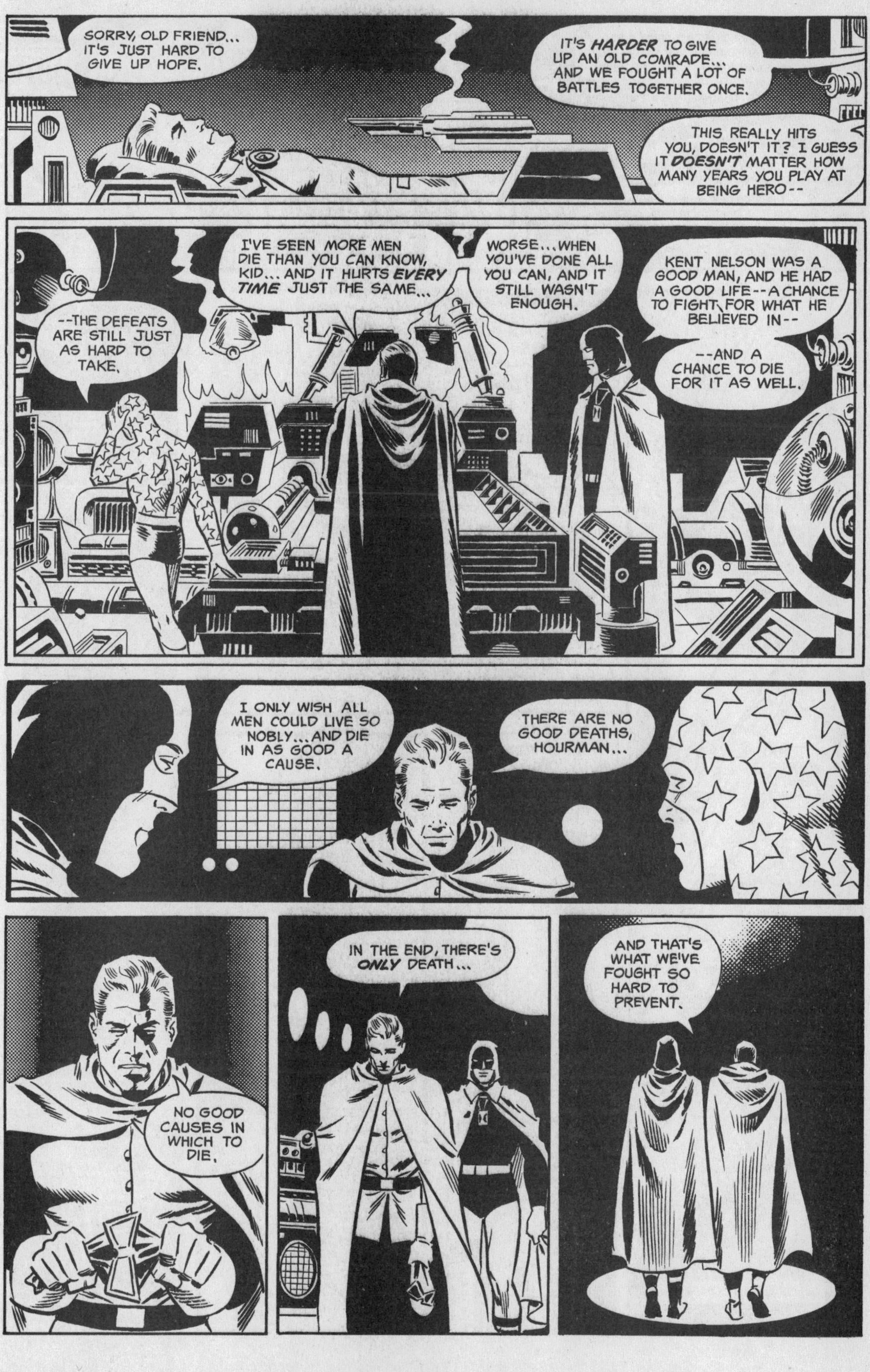
SORRY, OLD FRIEND... IT'S JUST HARD TO GIVE UP HOPE.
IT'S HARDER TO GIVE UP AN OLD COMRADE... AND WE FOUGHT A LOT OF BATTLES TOGETHER ONCE.
THIS REALLY HITS YOU, DOESN'T IT? I GUESS IT DOESN'T MATTER HOW MANY YEARS YOU PLAY AT BEING HERO--
--THE DEFEATS ARE STILL JUST AS HARD TO TAKE.
I'VE SEEN MORE MEN DIE THAN YOU CAN KNOW, KID... AND IT HURTS EVERY TIME JUST THE SAME...
WORSE...WHEN YOU'VE DONE ALL YOU CAN, AND IT STILL WASN'T ENOUGH.
KENT NELSON WAS A GOOD MAN, AND HE HAD A GOOD LIFE--A CHANCE TO FIGHT FOR WHAT HE BELIEVED IN--
--AND A CHANCE TO DIE FOR IT AS WELL.
I ONLY WISH ALL MEN COULD LIVE SO NOBLY...AND DIE IN AS GOOD A CAUSE.
THERE ARE NO GOOD DEATHS, HOURMAN...
NO GOOD CAUSES IN WHICH TO DIE.
IN THE END, THERE'S ONLY DEATH...
AND THAT'S WHAT WE'VE FOUGHT SO HARD TO PREVENT.

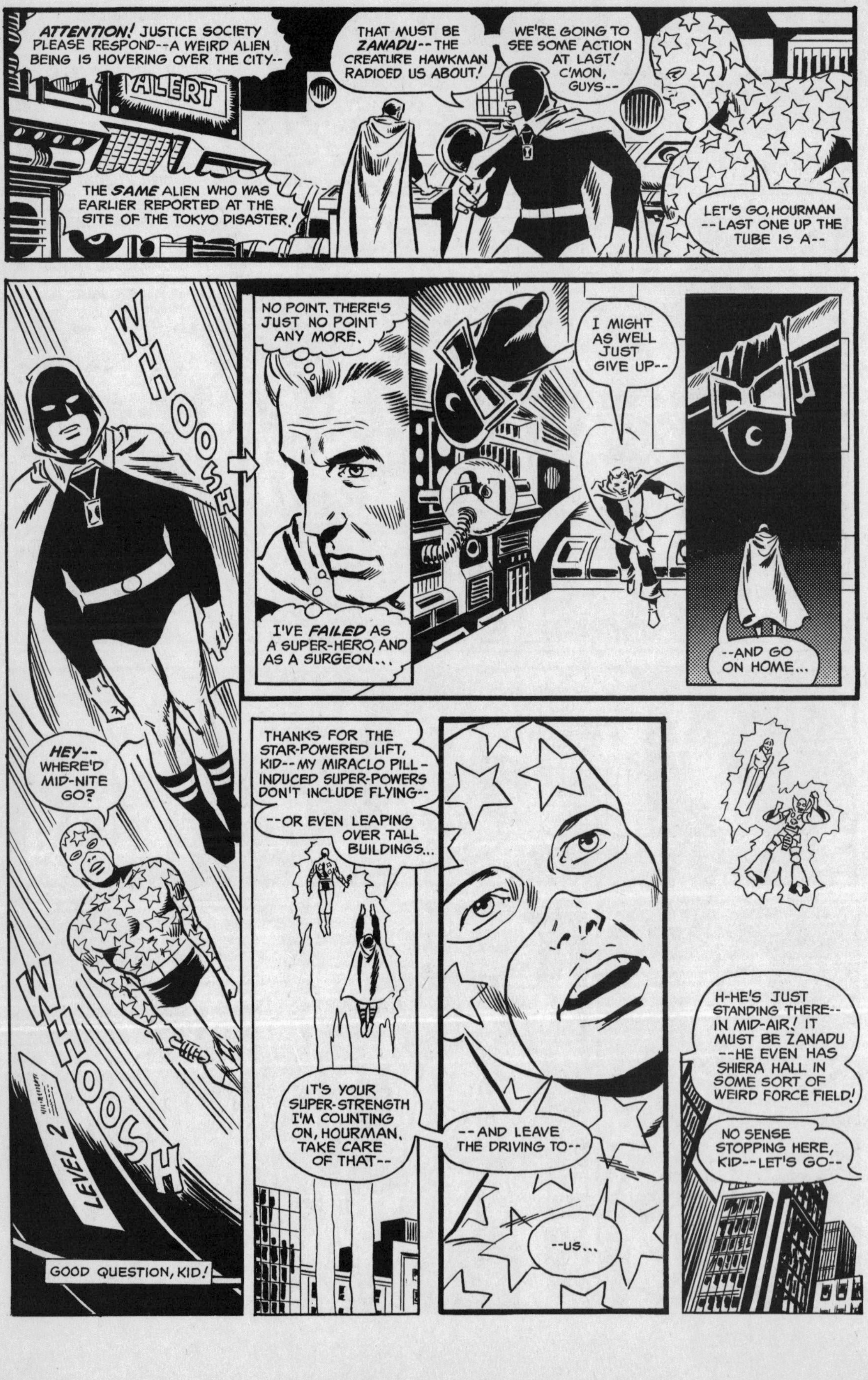
ATTENTION! JUSTICE SOCIETY PLEASE RESPOND--A WEIRD ALIEN BEING IS HOVERING OVER THE CITY--
ALERT
THE SAME ALIEN WHO WAS EARLIER REPORTED AT THE SITE OF THE TOKYO DISASTER!
THAT MUST BE ZANADU--THE CREATURE HAWKMAN RADIOED US ABOUT!
WE'RE GOING TO SEE SOME ACTION AT LAST! C'MON, GUYS--
LET'S GO, HOURMAN--LAST ONE UP THE TUBE IS A--
WHOOSH
NO POINT. THERE'S JUST NO POINT ANY MORE.
I'VE FAILED AS A SUPER-HERO, AND AS A SURGEON...
I MIGHT AS WELL JUST GIVE UP--
--AND GO ON HOME...
HEY--WHERE'D MID-NITE GO?
WHOOSH
LEVEL 2
GOOD QUESTION, KID!
THANKS FOR THE STAR-POWERED LIFT, KID--MY MIRACLO PILL-INDUCED SUPER-POWERS DON'T INCLUDE FLYING--
--OR EVEN LEAPING OVER TALL BUILDINGS...
IT'S YOUR SUPER-STRENGTH I'M COUNTING ON, HOURMAN. TAKE CARE OF THAT--
--AND LEAVE THE DRIVING TO--
--US...
H-HE'S JUST STANDING THERE--IN MID-AIR! IT MUST BE ZANADU--HE EVEN HAS SHIERA HALL IN SOME SORT OF WEIRD FORCE FIELD!
NO SENSE STOPPING HERE, KID--LET'S GO--

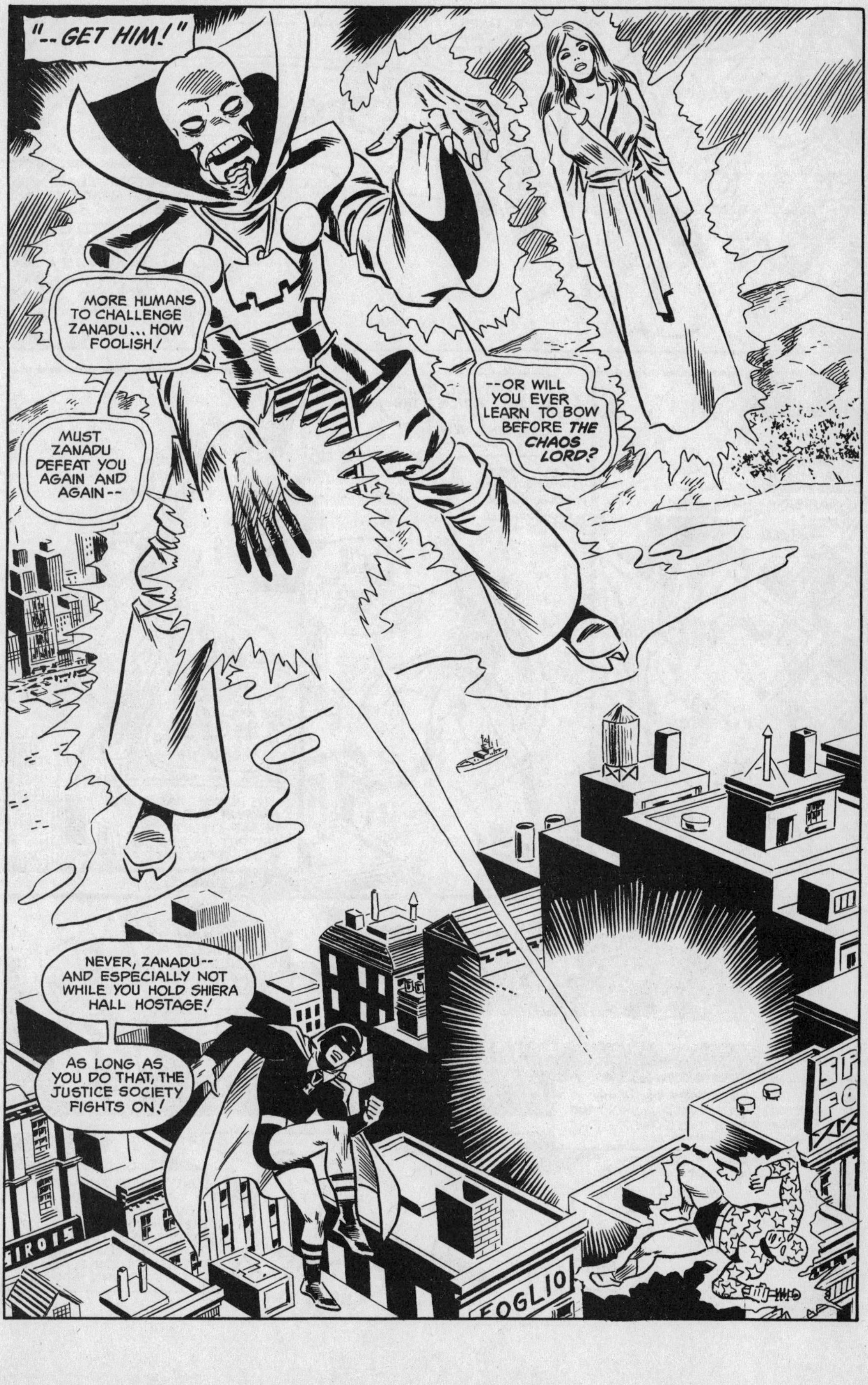
"--GET HIM!"
MORE HUMANS TO CHALLENGE ZANADU... HOW FOOLISH!
MUST ZANADU DEFEAT YOU AGAIN AND AGAIN--
--OR WILL YOU EVER LEARN TO BOW BEFORE THE CHAOS LORD?
NEVER, ZANADU-- AND ESPECIALLY NOT WHILE YOU HOLD SHIERA HALL HOSTAGE!
AS LONG AS YOU DO THAT, THE JUSTICE SOCIETY FIGHTS ON!
FOGLIO
GIROIS

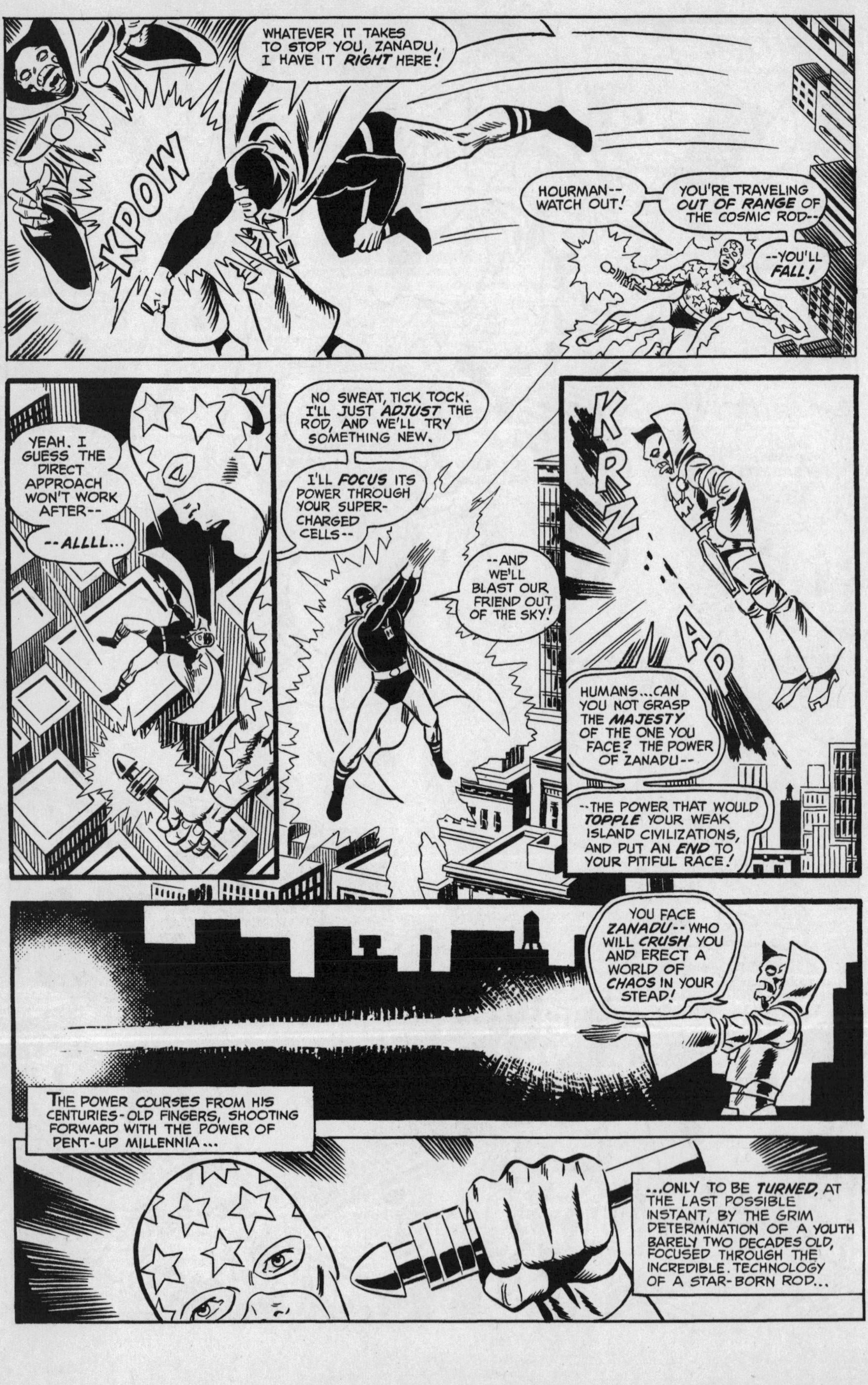
WHATEVER IT TAKES TO STOP YOU, ZANADU, I HAVE IT RIGHT HERE!
KPOW
HOURMAN-- WATCH OUT!
YOU'RE TRAVELING OUT OF RANGE OF THE COSMIC ROD--
--YOU'LL FALL!
YEAH. I GUESS THE DIRECT APPROACH WON'T WORK AFTER--
--ALLLL...
NO SWEAT, TICK TOCK. I'LL JUST ADJUST THE ROD, AND WE'LL TRY SOMETHING NEW.
I'LL FOCUS ITS POWER THROUGH YOUR SUPER-CHARGED CELLS--
--AND WE'LL BLAST OUR FRIEND OUT OF THE SKY!
KRZAAP
HUMANS...CAN YOU NOT GRASP THE MAJESTY OF THE ONE YOU FACE? THE POWER OF ZANADU--
--THE POWER THAT WOULD TOPPLE YOUR WEAK ISLAND CIVILIZATIONS, AND PUT AN END TO YOUR PITIFUL RACE!
YOU FACE ZANADU-- WHO WILL CRUSH YOU AND ERECT A WORLD OF CHAOS IN YOUR STEAD!
THE POWER COURSES FROM HIS CENTURIES-OLD FINGERS, SHOOTING FORWARD WITH THE POWER OF PENT-UP MILLENNIA...
...ONLY TO BE TURNED, AT THE LAST POSSIBLE INSTANT, BY THE GRIM DETERMINATION OF A YOUTH BARELY TWO DECADES OLD, FOCUSED THROUGH THE INCREDIBLE. TECHNOLOGY OF A STAR-BORN ROD...

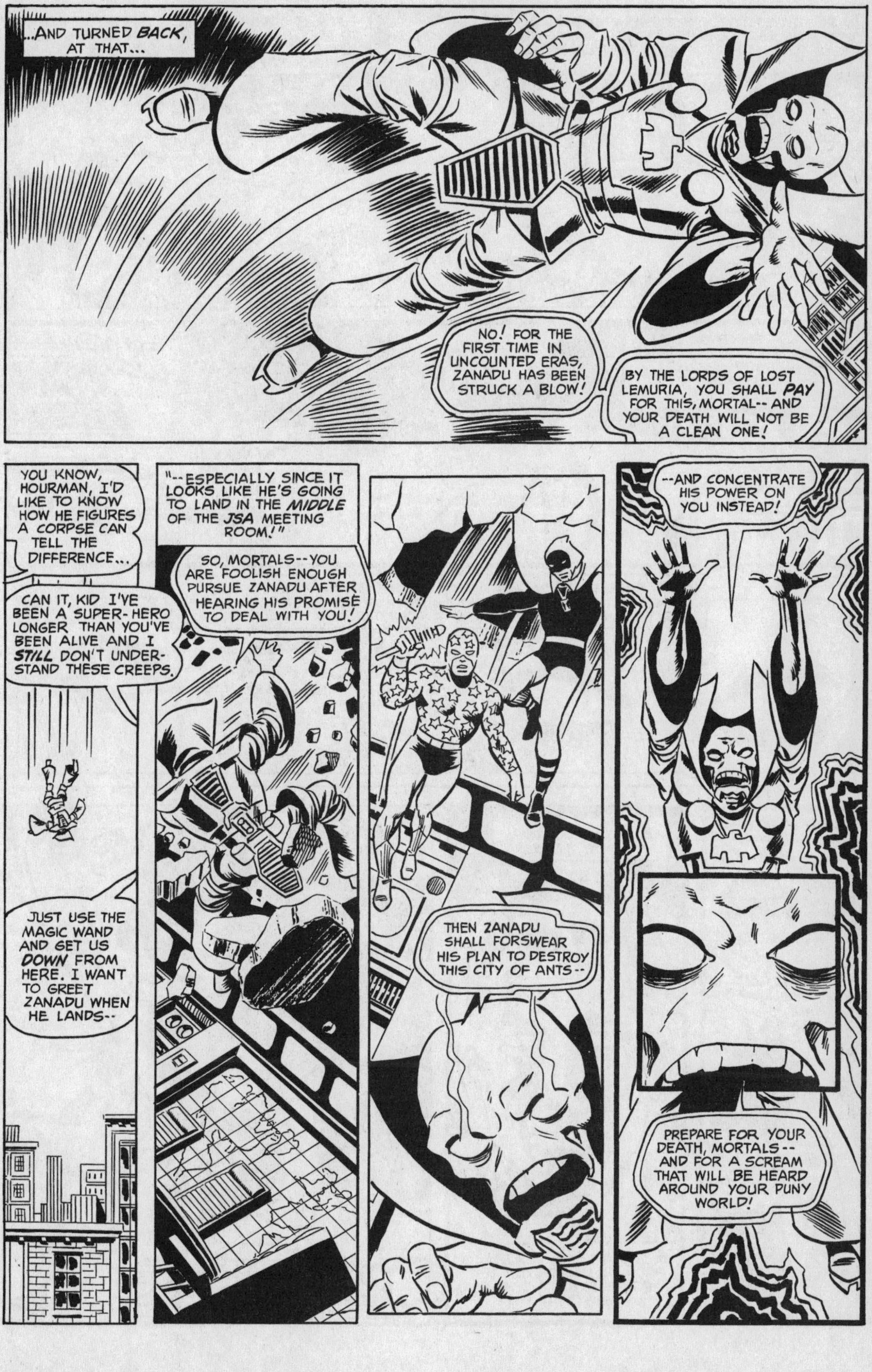
...AND TURNED BACK, AT THAT...
NO! FOR THE FIRST TIME IN UNCOUNTED ERAS, ZANADU HAS BEEN STRUCK A BLOW!
BY THE LORDS OF LOST LEMURIA, YOU SHALL PAY FOR THIS, MORTAL-- AND YOUR DEATH WILL NOT BE A CLEAN ONE!
YOU KNOW, HOURMAN, I'D LIKE TO KNOW HOW HE FIGURES A CORPSE CAN TELL THE DIFFERENCE...
CAN IT, KID I'VE BEEN A SUPER-HERO LONGER THAN YOU'VE BEEN ALIVE AND I STILL DON'T UNDERSTAND THESE CREEPS.
JUST USE THE MAGIC WAND AND GET US DOWN FROM HERE. I WANT TO GREET ZANADU WHEN HE LANDS--
"--ESPECIALLY SINCE IT LOOKS LIKE HE'S GOING TO LAND IN THE MIDDLE OF THE JSA MEETING ROOM!"
SO, MORTALS--YOU ARE FOOLISH ENOUGH PURSUE ZANADU AFTER HEARING HIS PROMISE TO DEAL WITH YOU!
THEN ZANADU SHALL FORSWEAR HIS PLAN TO DESTROY THIS CITY OF ANTS--
--AND CONCENTRATE HIS POWER ON YOU INSTEAD!
PREPARE FOR YOUR DEATH, MORTALS-- AND FOR A SCREAM THAT WILL BE HEARD AROUND YOUR PUNY WORLD!

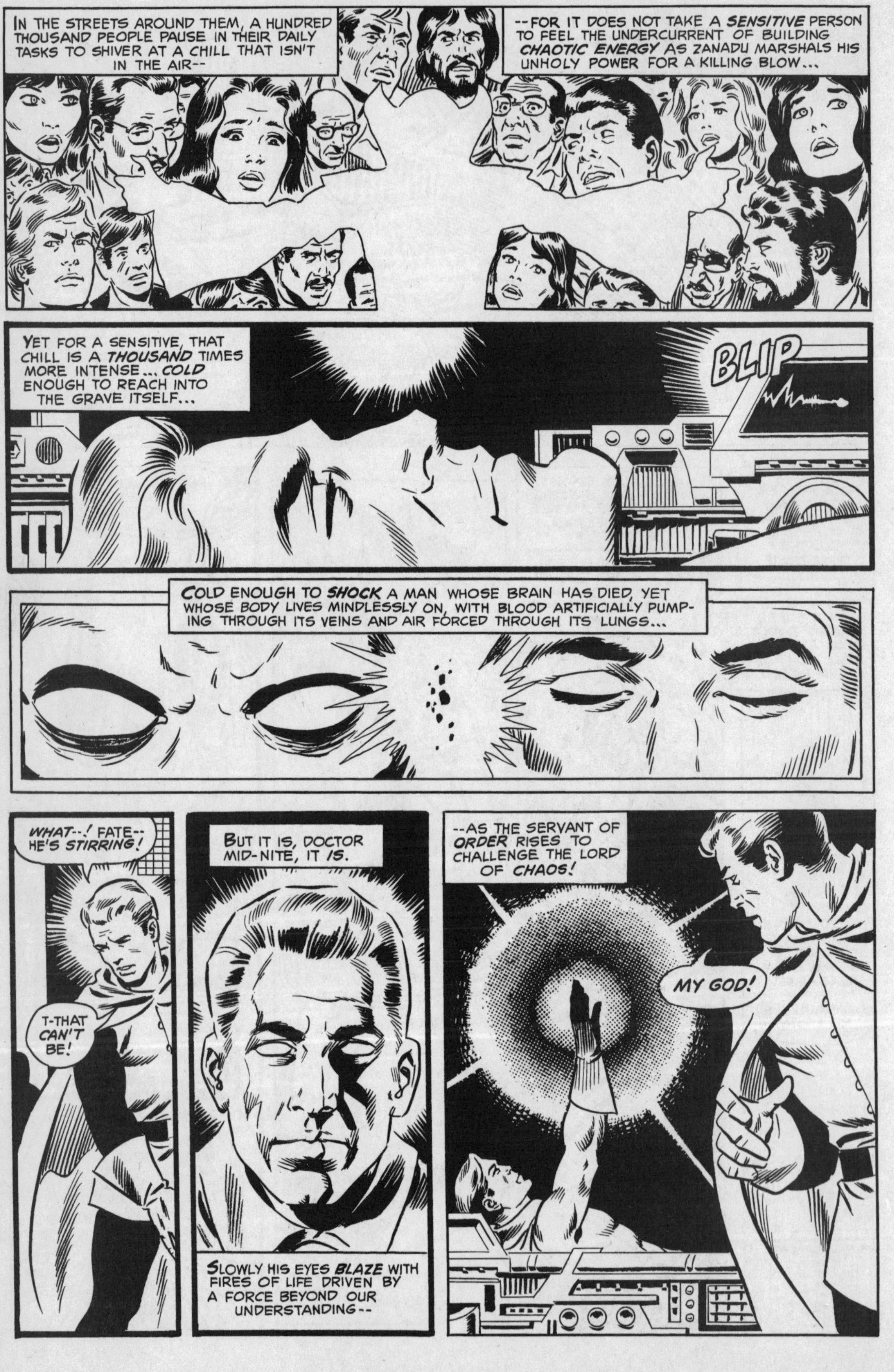
IN THE STREETS AROUND THEM, A HUNDRED THOUSAND PEOPLE PAUSE IN THEIR DAILY TASKS TO SHIVER AT A CHILL THAT ISN'T IN THE AIR--
--FOR IT DOES NOT TAKE A SENSITIVE PERSON TO FEEL THE UNDERCURRENT OF BUILDING CHAOTIC ENERGY AS ZANADU MARSHALS HIS UNHOLY POWER FOR A KILLING BLOW...
YET FOR A SENSITIVE, THAT CHILL IS A THOUSAND TIMES MORE INTENSE... COLD ENOUGH TO REACH INTO THE GRAVE ITSELF...
BLIP
COLD ENOUGH TO SHOCK A MAN WHOSE BRAIN HAS DIED, YET WHOSE BODY LIVES MINDLESSLY ON, WITH BLOOD ARTIFICIALLY PUMPING THROUGH ITS VEINS AND AIR FORCED THROUGH ITS LUNGS...
WHAT--! FATE-- HE'S STIRRING!
T-THAT CAN'T BE!
BUT IT IS, DOCTOR MID-NITE, IT IS.
SLOWLY HIS EYES BLAZE WITH FIRES OF LIFE DRIVEN BY A FORCE BEYOND OUR UNDERSTANDING--
--AS THE SERVANT OF ORDER RISES TO CHALLENGE THE LORD OF CHAOS!
MY GOD!

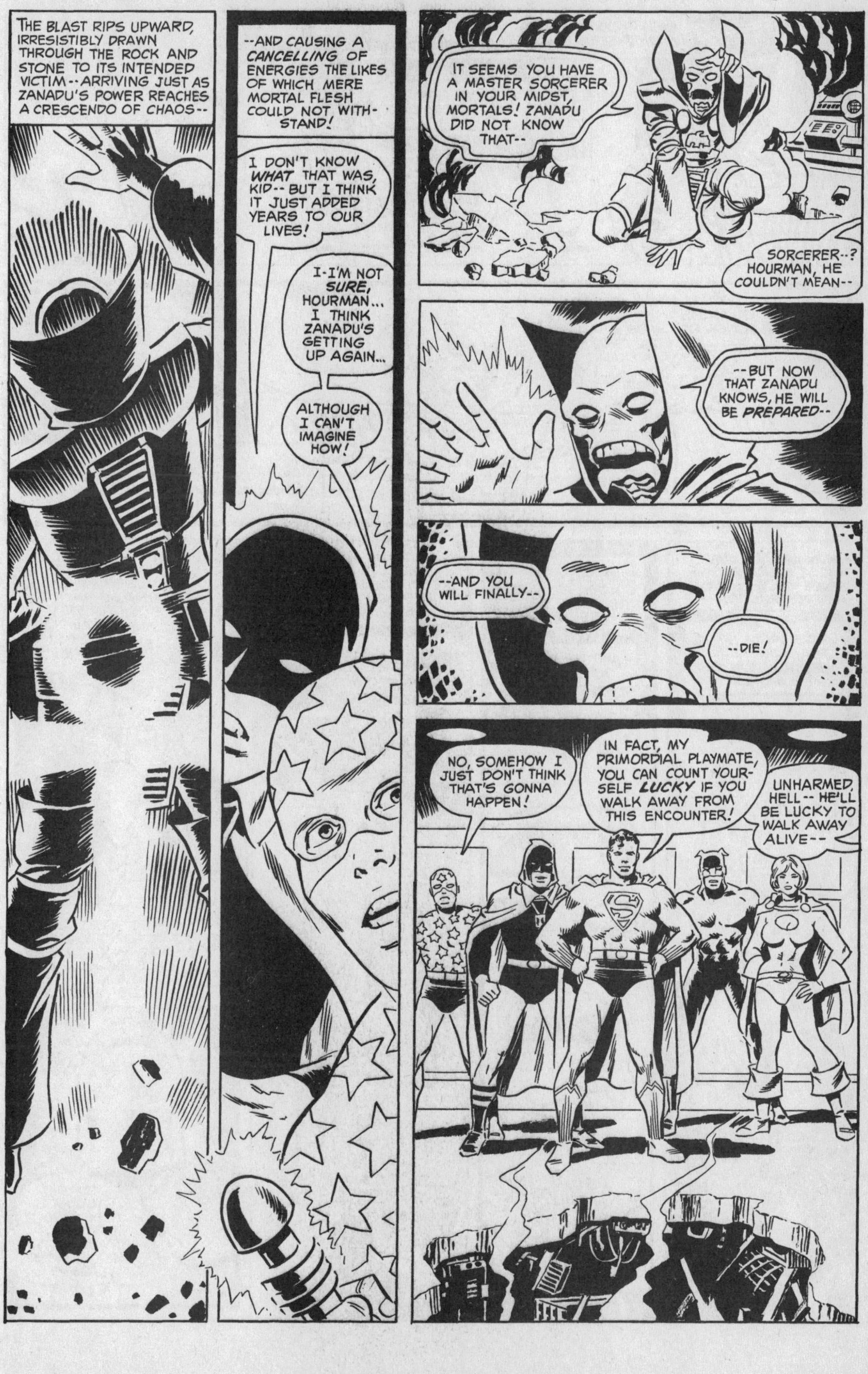
THE BLAST RIPS UPWARD, IRRESISTIBLY DRAWN THROUGH THE ROCK AND STONE TO ITS INTENDED VICTIM--ARRIVING JUST AS ZANADU'S POWER REACHES A CRESCENDO OF CHAOS--
--AND CAUSING A CANCELLING OF ENERGIES THE LIKES OF WHICH MERE MORTAL FLESH COULD NOT WITHSTAND!
I DON'T KNOW WHAT THAT WAS, KID--BUT I THINK IT JUST ADDED YEARS TO OUR LIVES!
I-I'M NOT SURE, HOURMAN... I THINK ZANADU'S GETTING UP AGAIN...
ALTHOUGH I CAN'T IMAGINE HOW!
IT SEEMS YOU HAVE A MASTER SORCERER IN YOUR MIDST, MORTALS! ZANADU DID NOT KNOW THAT--
SORCERER--? HOURMAN, HE COULDN'T MEAN--
--BUT NOW THAT ZANADU KNOWS, HE WILL BE PREPARED--
--AND YOU WILL FINALLY--
--DIE!
NO, SOMEHOW I JUST DON'T THINK THAT'S GONNA HAPPEN!
IN FACT, MY PRIMORDIAL PLAYMATE, YOU CAN COUNT YOURSELF LUCKY IF YOU WALK AWAY FROM THIS ENCOUNTER!
UNHARMED, HELL--HE'LL BE LUCKY TO WALK AWAY ALIVE--

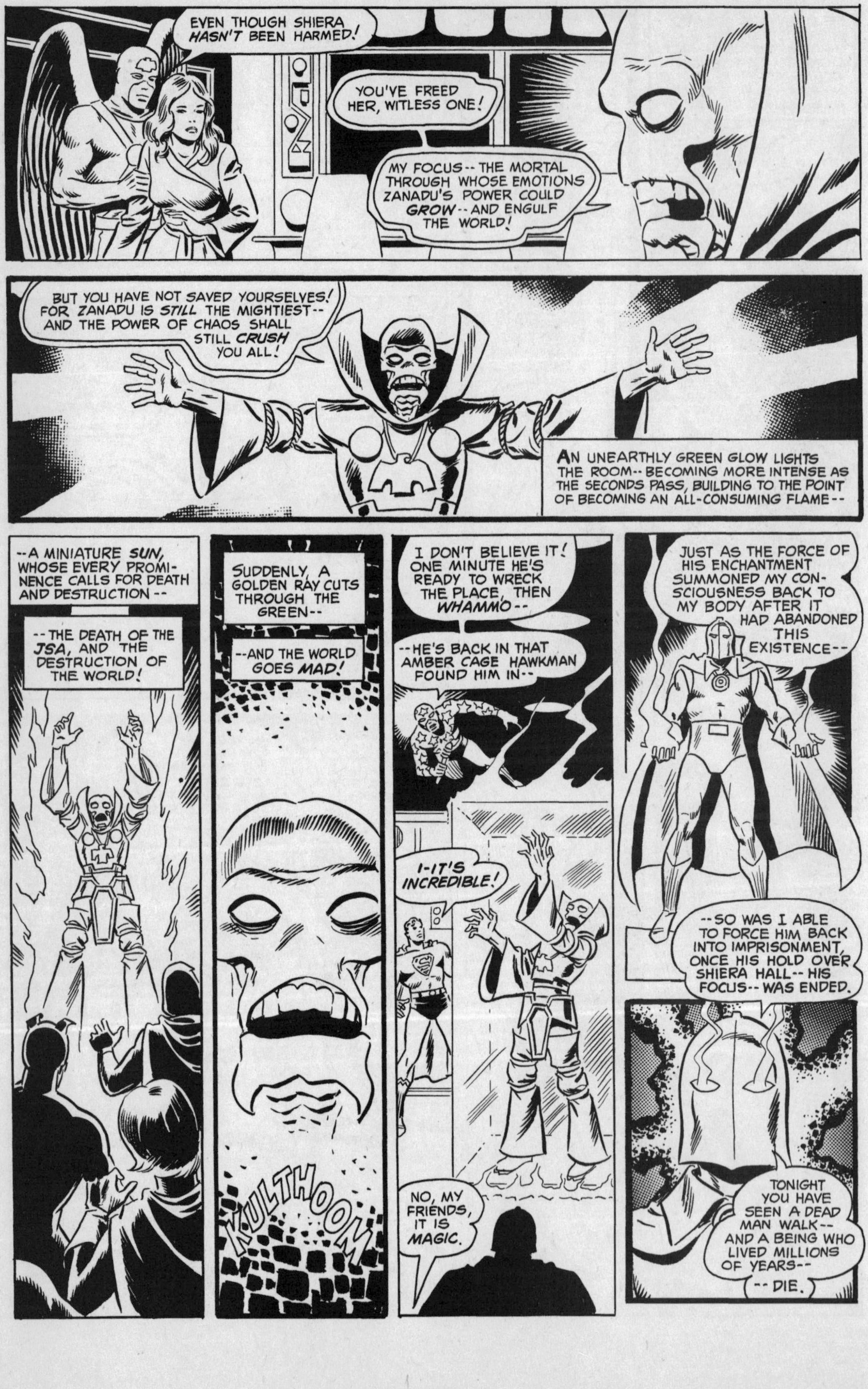
EVEN THOUGH SHIERA HASN'T BEEN HARMED!
YOU'VE FREED HER, WITLESS ONE!
MY FOCUS-- THE MORTAL THROUGH WHOSE EMOTIONS ZANADU'S POWER COULD GROW-- AND ENGULF THE WORLD!
BUT YOU HAVE NOT SAVED YOURSELVES! FOR ZANADU IS STILL THE MIGHTIEST-- AND THE POWER OF CHAOS SHALL STILL CRUSH YOU ALL!
AN UNEARTHLY GREEN GLOW LIGHTS THE ROOM-- BECOMING MORE INTENSE AS THE SECONDS PASS, BUILDING TO THE POINT OF BECOMING AN ALL-CONSUMING FLAME--
--A MINIATURE SUN, WHOSE EVERY PROMINENCE CALLS FOR DEATH AND DESTRUCTION--
--THE DEATH OF THE JSA, AND THE DESTRUCTION OF THE WORLD!
SUDDENLY, A GOLDEN RAY CUTS THROUGH THE GREEN--
--AND THE WORLD GOES MAD!
KULTHOOM
I DON'T BELIEVE IT! ONE MINUTE HE'S READY TO WRECK THE PLACE, THEN WHAMMO--
--HE'S BACK IN THAT AMBER CAGE HAWKMAN FOUND HIM IN--
I-IT'S INCREDIBLE!
NO, MY FRIENDS, IT IS MAGIC.
JUST AS THE FORCE OF HIS ENCHANTMENT SUMMONED MY CONSCIOUSNESS BACK TO MY BODY AFTER IT HAD ABANDONED THIS EXISTENCE--
--SO WAS I ABLE TO FORCE HIM BACK INTO IMPRISONMENT, ONCE HIS HOLD OVER SHIERA HALL-- HIS FOCUS-- WAS ENDED.
TONIGHT YOU HAVE SEEN A DEAD MAN WALK-- AND A BEING WHO LIVED MILLIONS OF YEARS--
-- DIE.

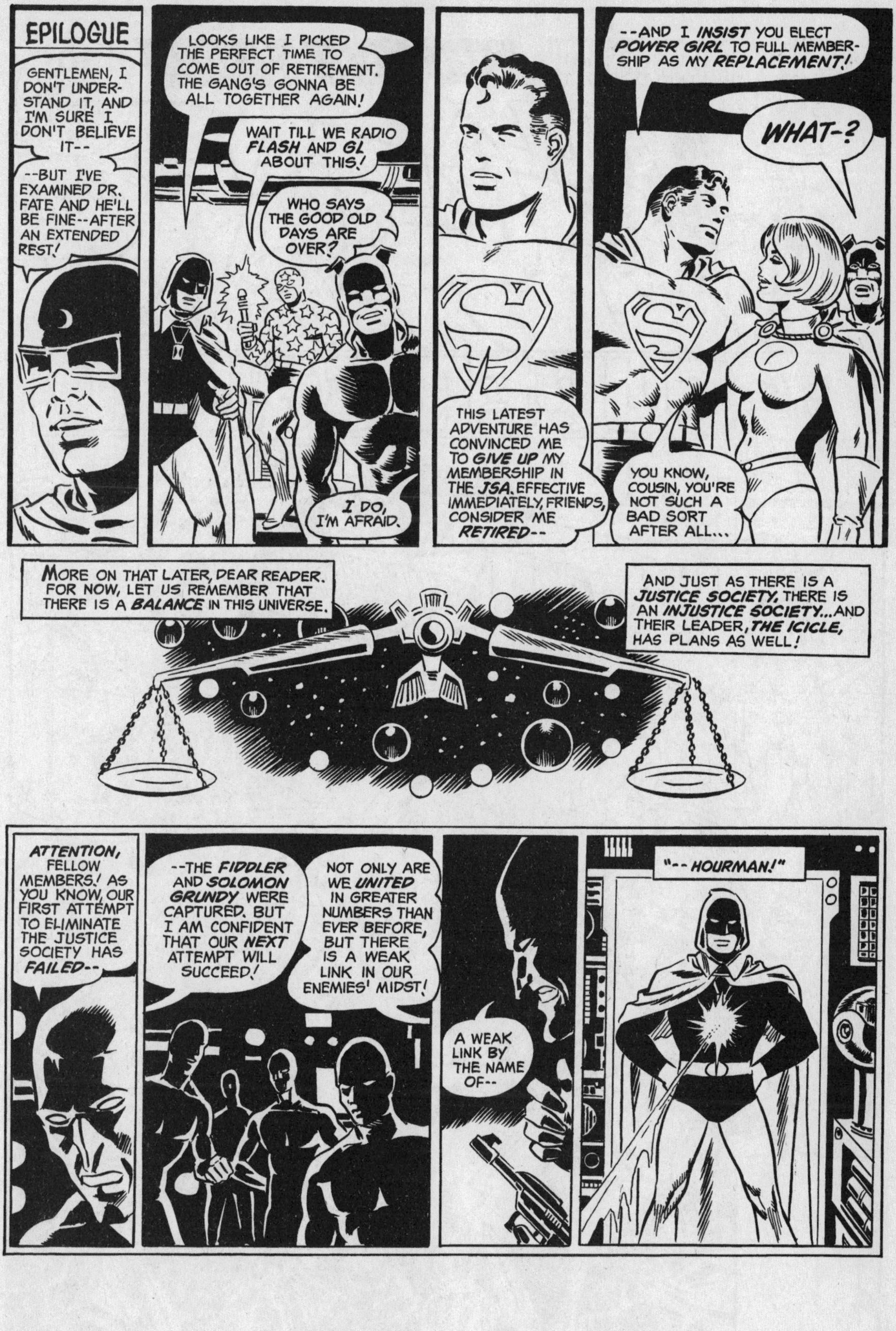
EPILOGUE
GENTLEMEN, I DON'T UNDERSTAND IT, AND I'M SURE I DON'T BELIEVE IT--
--BUT I'VE EXAMINED DR. FATE AND HE'LL BE FINE--AFTER AN EXTENDED REST!
LOOKS LIKE I PICKED THE PERFECT TIME TO COME OUT OF RETIREMENT. THE GANG'S GONNA BE ALL TOGETHER AGAIN!
WAIT TILL WE RADIO FLASH AND GL ABOUT THIS!
WHO SAYS THE GOOD OLD DAYS ARE OVER?
I DO, I'M AFRAID.
THIS LATEST ADVENTURE HAS CONVINCED ME TO GIVE UP MY MEMBERSHIP IN THE JSA. EFFECTIVE IMMEDIATELY, FRIENDS, CONSIDER ME RETIRED--
--AND I INSIST YOU ELECT POWER GIRL TO FULL MEMBERSHIP AS MY REPLACEMENT!
WHAT-?
YOU KNOW, COUSIN, YOU'RE NOT SUCH A BAD SORT AFTER ALL...
MORE ON THAT LATER, DEAR READER. FOR NOW, LET US REMEMBER THAT THERE IS A BALANCE IN THIS UNIVERSE.
AND JUST AS THERE IS A JUSTICE SOCIETY, THERE IS AN INJUSTICE SOCIETY...AND THEIR LEADER, THE ICICLE, HAS PLANS AS WELL!
ATTENTION, FELLOW MEMBERS! AS YOU KNOW, OUR FIRST ATTEMPT TO ELIMINATE THE JUSTICE SOCIETY HAS FAILED--
--THE FIDDLER AND SOLOMON GRUNDY WERE CAPTURED. BUT I AM CONFIDENT THAT OUR NEXT ATTEMPT WILL SUCCEED!
NOT ONLY ARE WE UNITED IN GREATER NUMBERS THAN EVER BEFORE, BUT THERE IS A WEAK LINK IN OUR ENEMIES' MIDST!
A WEAK LINK BY THE NAME OF--
"--HOURMAN!"

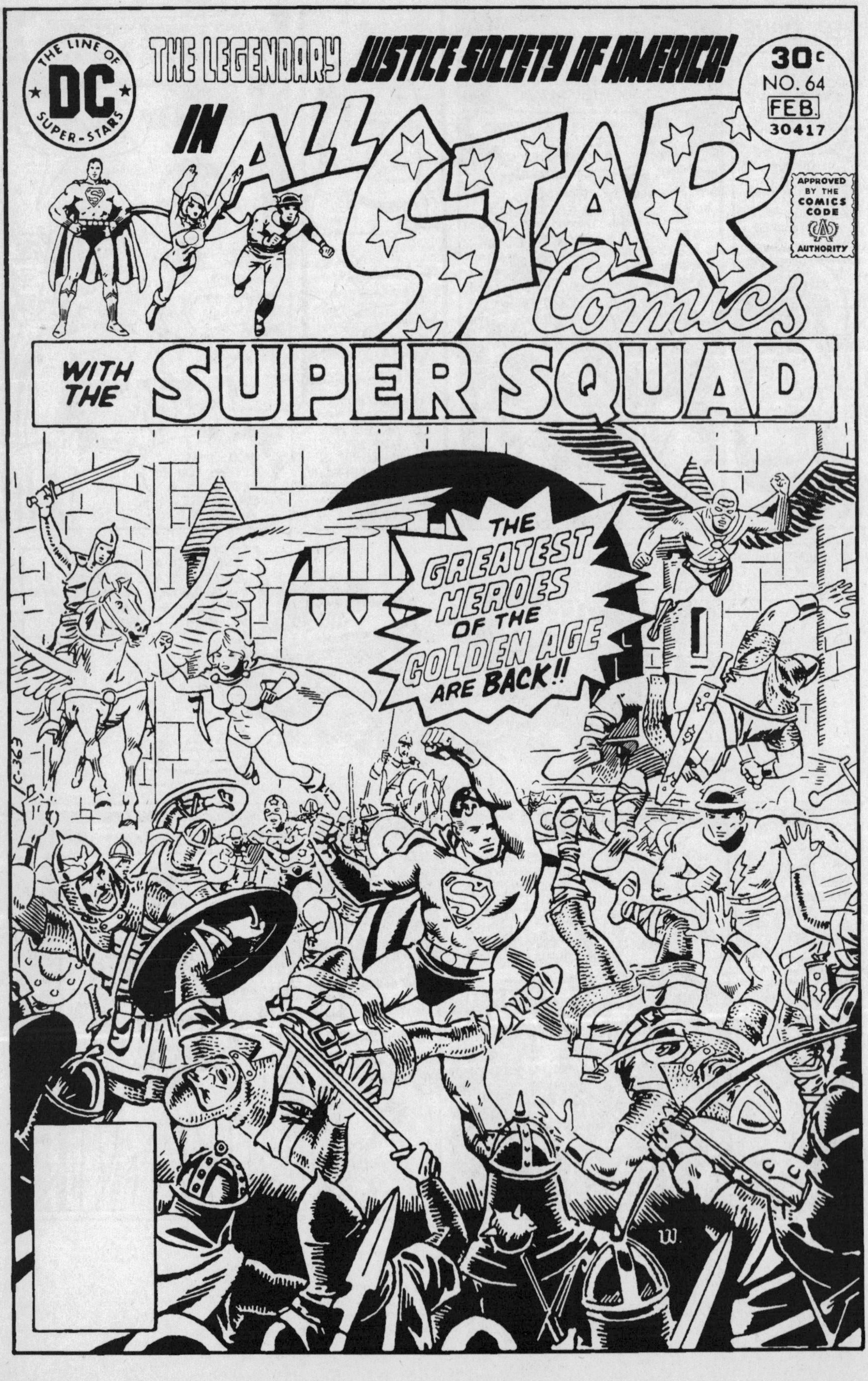
THE LINE OF DC SUPER-STARS
THE LEGENDARY JUSTICE SOCIETY OF AMERICA!
30¢
NO. 64
FEB.
30417
IN ALL STAR Comics
APPROVED BY THE COMICS CODE AUTHORITY
WITH THE SUPER SQUAD
THE GREATEST HEROES OF THE GOLDEN AGE ARE BACK!!
C-363

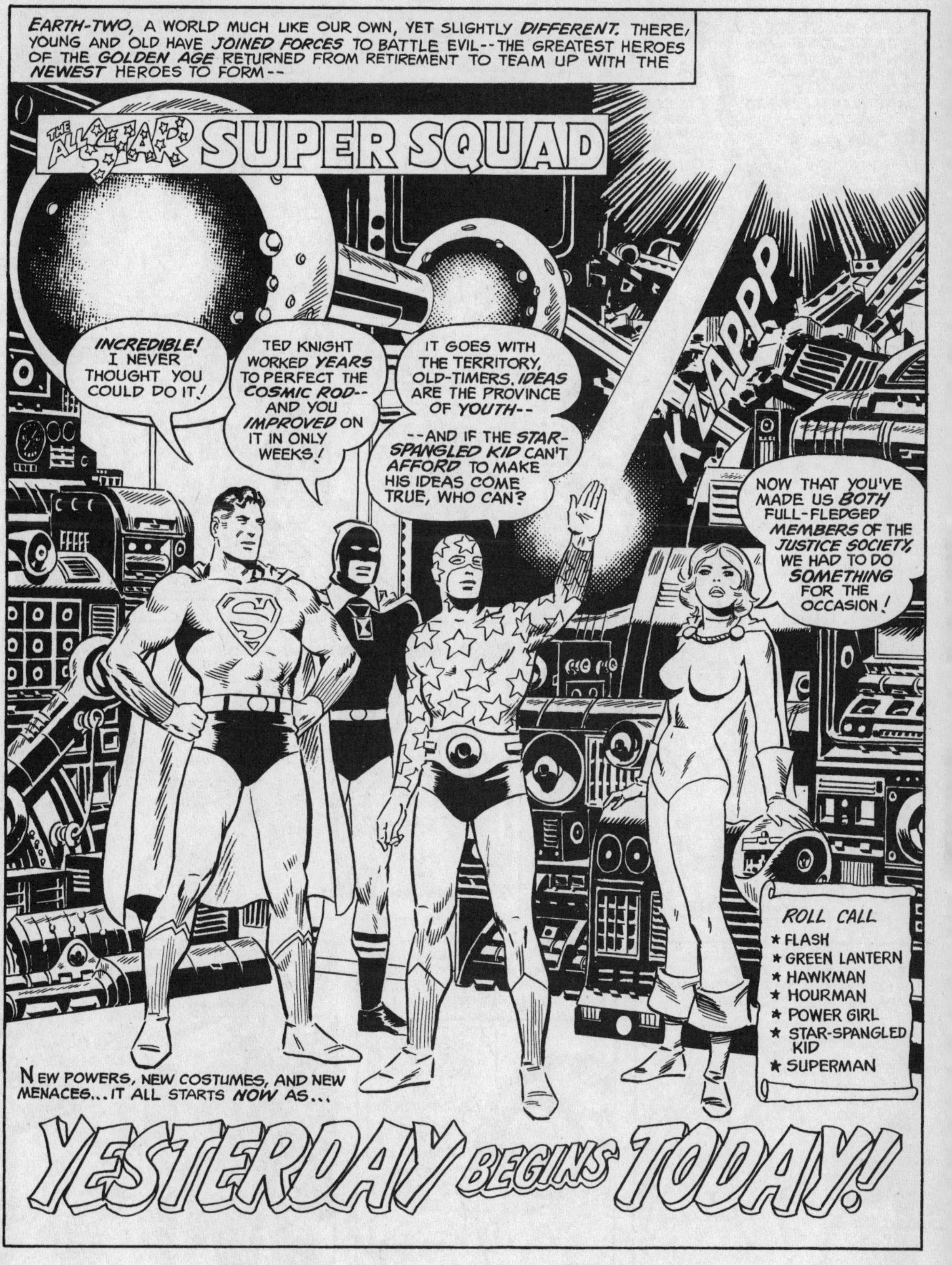
EARTH-TWO, A WORLD MUCH LIKE OUR OWN, YET SLIGHTLY DIFFERENT. THERE, YOUNG AND OLD HAVE JOINED FORCES TO BATTLE EVIL--THE GREATEST HEROES OF THE GOLDEN AGE RETURNED FROM RETIREMENT TO TEAM UP WITH THE NEWEST HEROES TO FORM--
THE ALL-STAR SUPER SQUAD
INCREDIBLE! I NEVER THOUGHT YOU COULD DO IT!
TED KNIGHT WORKED YEARS TO PERFECT THE COSMIC ROD--AND YOU IMPROVED ON IT IN ONLY WEEKS!
IT GOES WITH THE TERRITORY, OLD-TIMERS. IDEAS ARE THE PROVINCE OF YOUTH--
--AND IF THE STAR-SPANGLED KID CAN'T AFFORD TO MAKE HIS IDEAS COME TRUE, WHO CAN?
KZAPPP
NOW THAT YOU'VE MADE US BOTH FULL-FLEDGED MEMBERS OF THE JUSTICE SOCIETY, WE HAD TO DO SOMETHING FOR THE OCCASION!
ROLL CALL
★ FLASH
★ GREEN LANTERN
★ HAWKMAN
★ HOURMAN
★ POWER GIRL
★ STAR-SPANGLED KID
★ SUPERMAN
NEW POWERS, NEW COSTUMES, AND NEW MENACES... IT ALL STARTS NOW AS...
YESTERDAY BEGINS TODAY!

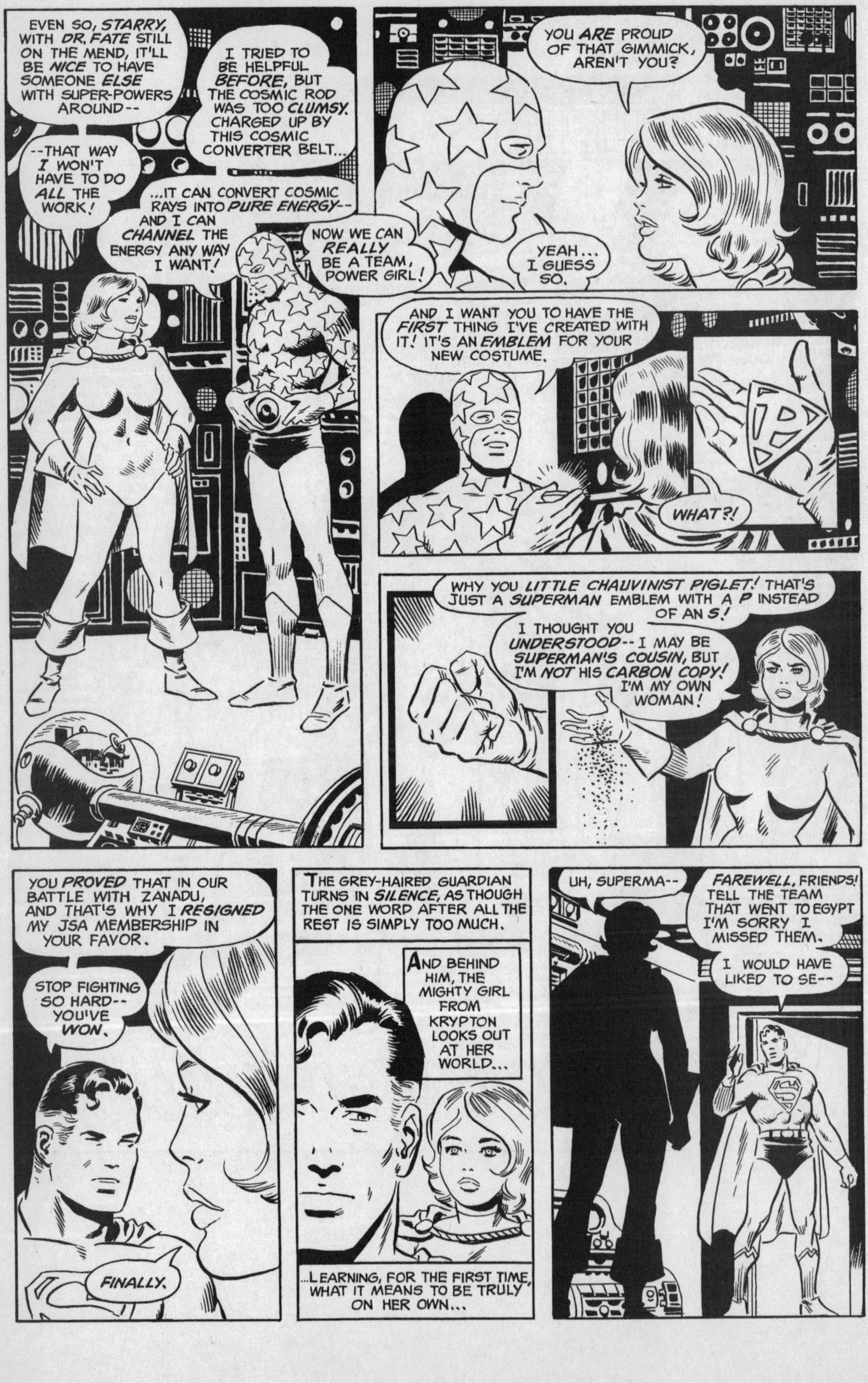
EVEN SO, STARRY, WITH DR. FATE STILL ON THE MEND, IT'LL BE NICE TO HAVE SOMEONE ELSE WITH SUPER-POWERS AROUND--
--THAT WAY I WON'T HAVE TO DO ALL THE WORK!
I TRIED TO BE HELPFUL BEFORE, BUT THE COSMIC ROD WAS TOO CLUMSY. CHARGED UP BY THIS COSMIC CONVERTER BELT...
...IT CAN CONVERT COSMIC RAYS INTO PURE ENERGY-- AND I CAN CHANNEL THE ENERGY ANY WAY I WANT!
NOW WE CAN REALLY BE A TEAM, POWER GIRL!
YOU ARE PROUD OF THAT GIMMICK, AREN'T YOU?
YEAH... I GUESS SO.
AND I WANT YOU TO HAVE THE FIRST THING I'VE CREATED WITH IT! IT'S AN EMBLEM FOR YOUR NEW COSTUME.
WHAT?!
WHY YOU LITTLE CHAUVINIST PIGLET! THAT'S JUST A SUPERMAN EMBLEM WITH A P INSTEAD OF AN S!
I THOUGHT YOU UNDERSTOOD-- I MAY BE SUPERMAN'S COUSIN, BUT I'M NOT HIS CARBON COPY! I'M MY OWN WOMAN!
YOU PROVED THAT IN OUR BATTLE WITH ZANADU, AND THAT'S WHY I RESIGNED MY JSA MEMBERSHIP IN YOUR FAVOR.
STOP FIGHTING SO HARD-- YOU'VE WON.
FINALLY.
THE GREY-HAIRED GUARDIAN TURNS IN SILENCE, AS THOUGH THE ONE WORD AFTER ALL THE REST IS SIMPLY TOO MUCH.
AND BEHIND HIM, THE MIGHTY GIRL FROM KRYPTON LOOKS OUT AT HER WORLD...
...LEARNING, FOR THE FIRST TIME, WHAT IT MEANS TO BE TRULY ON HER OWN...
UH, SUPERMA--
FAREWELL, FRIENDS! TELL THE TEAM THAT WENT TO EGYPT I'M SORRY I MISSED THEM.
I WOULD HAVE LIKED TO SE--

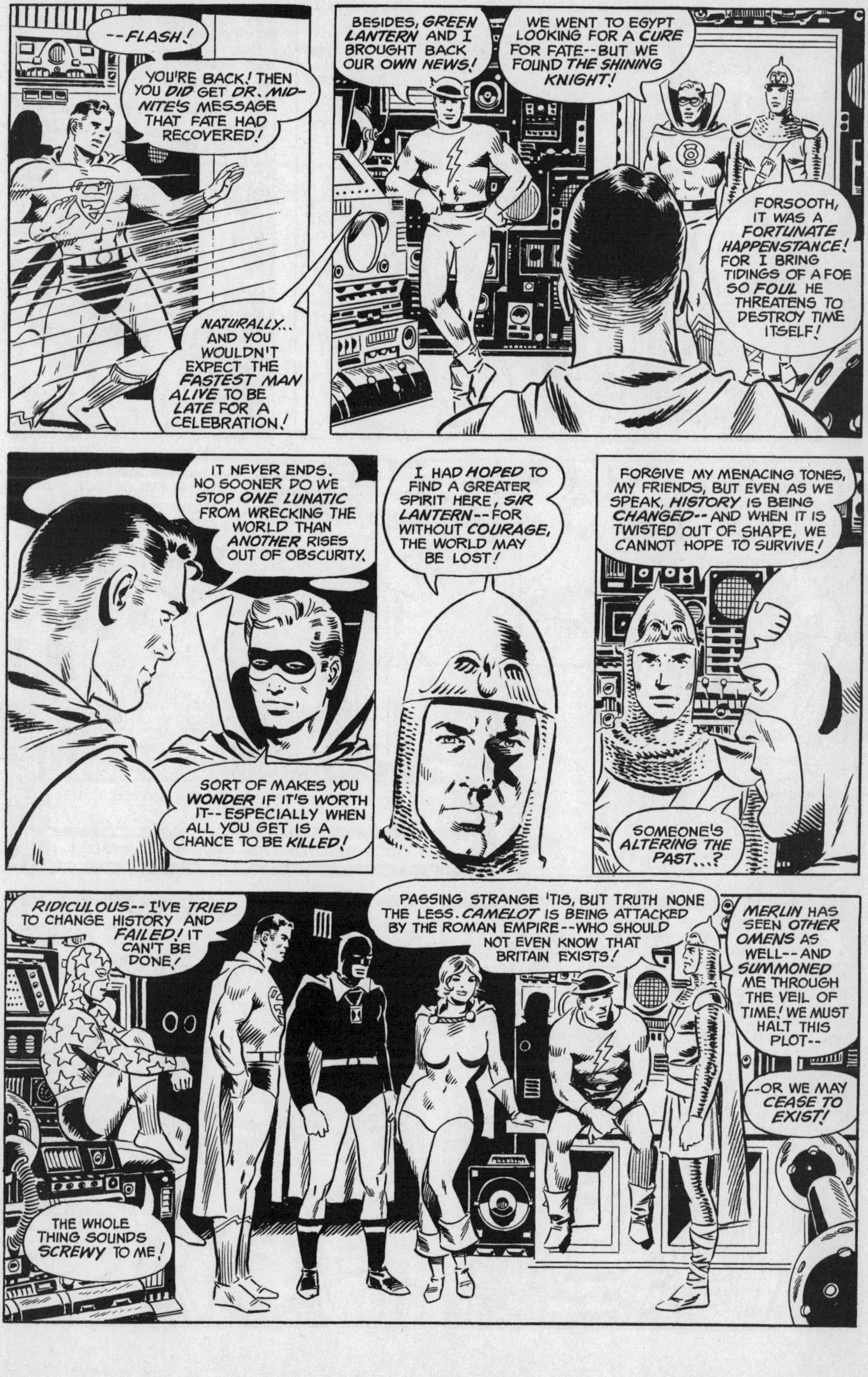
--FLASH!
YOU'RE BACK! THEN YOU DID GET DR. MID-NITE'S MESSAGE THAT FATE HAD RECOVERED!
NATURALLY... AND YOU WOULDN'T EXPECT THE FASTEST MAN ALIVE TO BE LATE FOR A CELEBRATION!
BESIDES, GREEN LANTERN AND I BROUGHT BACK OUR OWN NEWS!
WE WENT TO EGYPT LOOKING FOR A CURE FOR FATE--BUT WE FOUND THE SHINING KNIGHT!
FORSOOTH, IT WAS A FORTUNATE HAPPENSTANCE! FOR I BRING TIDINGS OF A FOE SO FOUL HE THREATENS TO DESTROY TIME ITSELF!
IT NEVER ENDS. NO SOONER DO WE STOP ONE LUNATIC FROM WRECKING THE WORLD THAN ANOTHER RISES OUT OF OBSCURITY.
SORT OF MAKES YOU WONDER IF IT'S WORTH IT--ESPECIALLY WHEN ALL YOU GET IS A CHANCE TO BE KILLED!
I HAD HOPED TO FIND A GREATER SPIRIT HERE, SIR LANTERN--FOR WITHOUT COURAGE, THE WORLD MAY BE LOST!
FORGIVE MY MENACING TONES, MY FRIENDS, BUT EVEN AS WE SPEAK, HISTORY IS BEING CHANGED--AND WHEN IT IS TWISTED OUT OF SHAPE, WE CANNOT HOPE TO SURVIVE!
SOMEONE'S ALTERING THE PAST...?
RIDICULOUS--I'VE TRIED TO CHANGE HISTORY AND FAILED! IT CAN'T BE DONE!
THE WHOLE THING SOUNDS SCREWY TO ME!
PASSING STRANGE 'TIS, BUT TRUTH NONE THE LESS. CAMELOT IS BEING ATTACKED BY THE ROMAN EMPIRE--WHO SHOULD NOT EVEN KNOW THAT BRITAIN EXISTS!
MERLIN HAS SEEN OTHER OMENS AS WELL--AND SUMMONED ME THROUGH THE VEIL OF TIME! WE MUST HALT THIS PLOT--
--OR WE MAY CEASE TO EXIST!

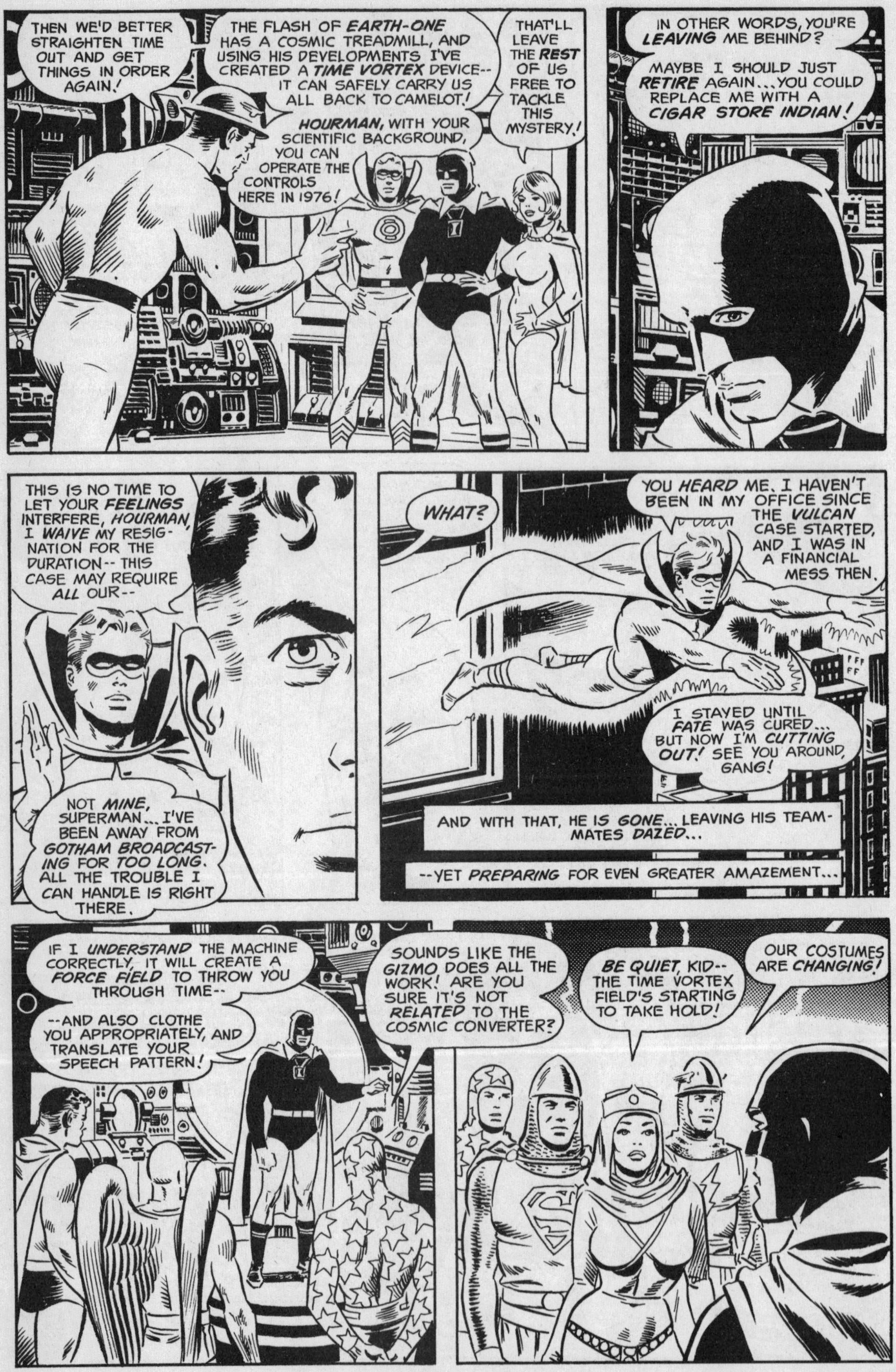
THEN WE'D BETTER STRAIGHTEN TIME OUT AND GET THINGS IN ORDER AGAIN!
THE FLASH OF EARTH-ONE HAS A COSMIC TREADMILL, AND USING HIS DEVELOPMENTS I'VE CREATED A TIME VORTEX DEVICE-- IT CAN SAFELY CARRY US ALL BACK TO CAMELOT!
HOURMAN, WITH YOUR SCIENTIFIC BACKGROUND, YOU CAN OPERATE THE CONTROLS HERE IN 1976!
THAT'LL LEAVE THE REST OF US FREE TO TACKLE THIS MYSTERY!
IN OTHER WORDS, YOU'RE LEAVING ME BEHIND?
MAYBE I SHOULD JUST RETIRE AGAIN... YOU COULD REPLACE ME WITH A CIGAR STORE INDIAN!
THIS IS NO TIME TO LET YOUR FEELINGS INTERFERE, HOURMAN, I WAIVE MY RESIGNATION FOR THE DURATION-- THIS CASE MAY REQUIRE ALL OUR--
NOT MINE, SUPERMAN... I'VE BEEN AWAY FROM GOTHAM BROADCASTING FOR TOO LONG. ALL THE TROUBLE I CAN HANDLE IS RIGHT THERE.
WHAT?
YOU HEARD ME. I HAVEN'T BEEN IN MY OFFICE SINCE THE VULCAN CASE STARTED, AND I WAS IN A FINANCIAL MESS THEN.
I STAYED UNTIL FATE WAS CURED... BUT NOW I'M CUTTING OUT! SEE YOU AROUND, GANG!
AND WITH THAT, HE IS GONE... LEAVING HIS TEAM-MATES DAZED...
--YET PREPARING FOR EVEN GREATER AMAZEMENT...
IF I UNDERSTAND THE MACHINE CORRECTLY, IT WILL CREATE A FORCE FIELD TO THROW YOU THROUGH TIME--
--AND ALSO CLOTHE YOU APPROPRIATELY, AND TRANSLATE YOUR SPEECH PATTERN!
SOUNDS LIKE THE GIZMO DOES ALL THE WORK! ARE YOU SURE IT'S NOT RELATED TO THE COSMIC CONVERTER?
BE QUIET, KID-- THE TIME VORTEX FIELD'S STARTING TO TAKE HOLD!
OUR COSTUMES ARE CHANGING!

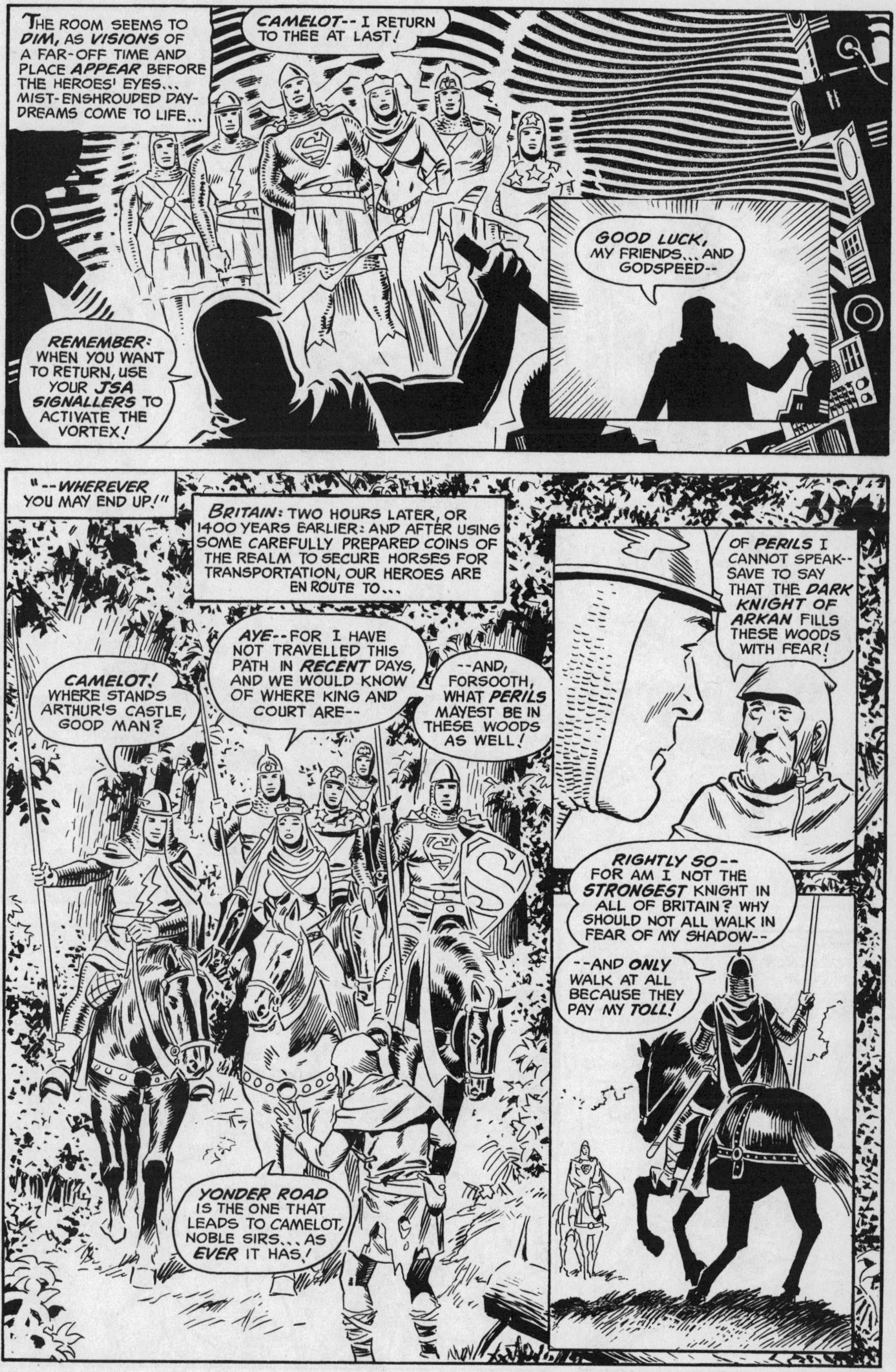
THE ROOM SEEMS TO DIM, AS VISIONS OF A FAR-OFF TIME AND PLACE APPEAR BEFORE THE HEROES' EYES... MIST-ENSHROUDED DAY-DREAMS COME TO LIFE...
CAMELOT-- I RETURN TO THEE AT LAST!
REMEMBER: WHEN YOU WANT TO RETURN, USE YOUR JSA SIGNALLERS TO ACTIVATE THE VORTEX!
GOOD LUCK, MY FRIENDS... AND GODSPEED--
"--WHEREVER YOU MAY END UP!"
BRITAIN: TWO HOURS LATER, OR 1400 YEARS EARLIER: AND AFTER USING SOME CAREFULLY PREPARED COINS OF THE REALM TO SECURE HORSES FOR TRANSPORTATION, OUR HEROES ARE EN ROUTE TO...
CAMELOT! WHERE STANDS ARTHUR'S CASTLE, GOOD MAN?
AYE--FOR I HAVE NOT TRAVELLED THIS PATH IN RECENT DAYS, AND WE WOULD KNOW OF WHERE KING AND COURT ARE--
--AND, FORSOOTH, WHAT PERILS MAYEST BE IN THESE WOODS AS WELL!
YONDER ROAD IS THE ONE THAT LEADS TO CAMELOT, NOBLE SIRS... AS EVER IT HAS!
OF PERILS I CANNOT SPEAK-- SAVE TO SAY THAT THE DARK KNIGHT OF ARKAN FILLS THESE WOODS WITH FEAR!
RIGHTLY SO-- FOR AM I NOT THE STRONGEST KNIGHT IN ALL OF BRITAIN? WHY SHOULD NOT ALL WALK IN FEAR OF MY SHADOW--
--AND ONLY WALK AT ALL BECAUSE THEY PAY MY TOLL!

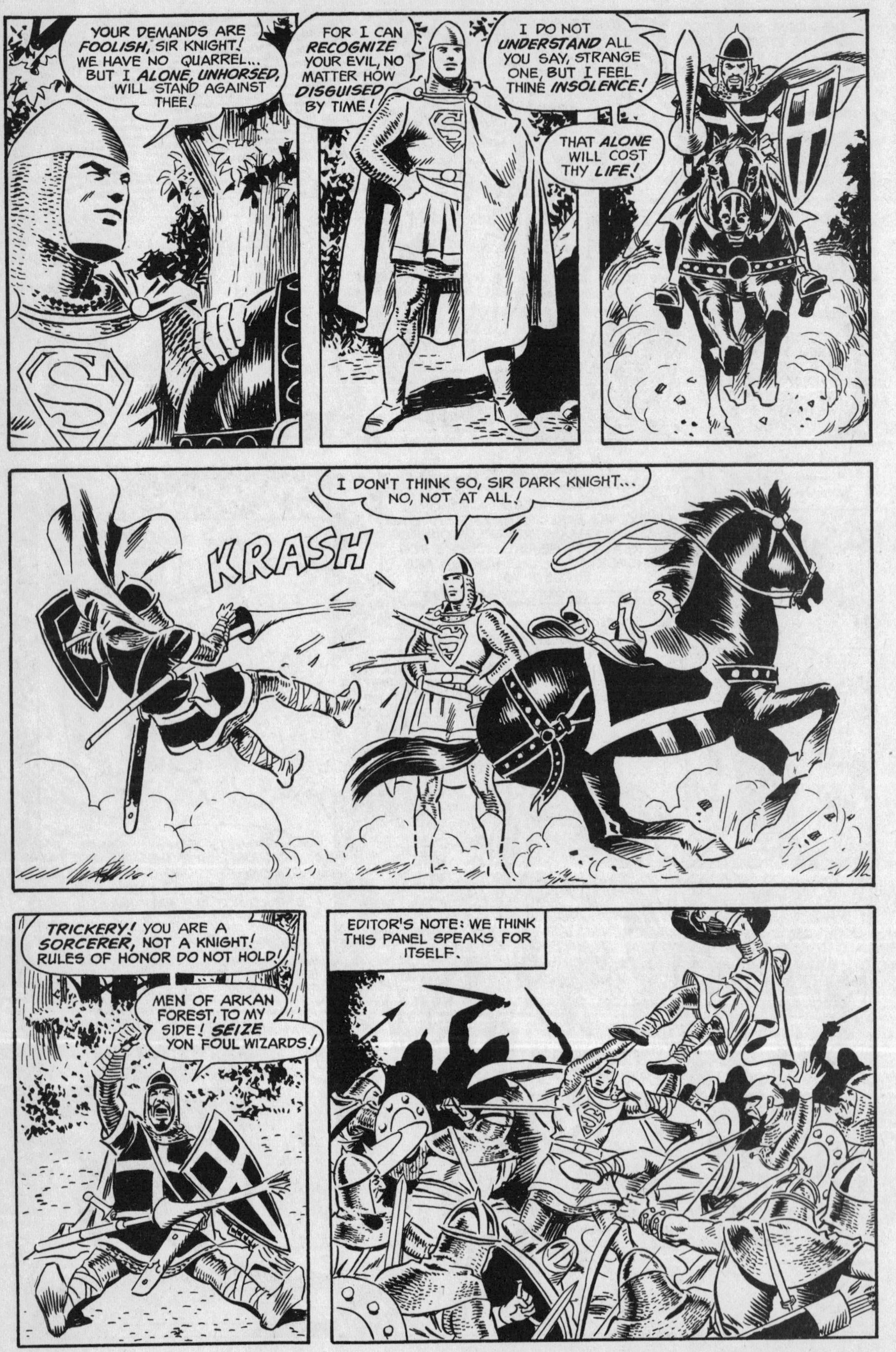
YOUR DEMANDS ARE FOOLISH, SIR KNIGHT! WE HAVE NO QUARREL... BUT I ALONE, UNHORSED, WILL STAND AGAINST THEE!
FOR I CAN RECOGNIZE YOUR EVIL, NO MATTER HOW DISGUISED BY TIME!
I DO NOT UNDERSTAND ALL YOU SAY, STRANGE ONE, BUT I FEEL THINE INSOLENCE!
THAT ALONE WILL COST THY LIFE!
I DON'T THINK SO, SIR DARK KNIGHT... NO, NOT AT ALL!
KRASH
TRICKERY! YOU ARE A SORCERER, NOT A KNIGHT! RULES OF HONOR DO NOT HOLD!
MEN OF ARKAN FOREST, TO MY SIDE! SEIZE YON FOUL WIZARDS!
EDITOR'S NOTE: WE THINK THIS PANEL SPEAKS FOR ITSELF.

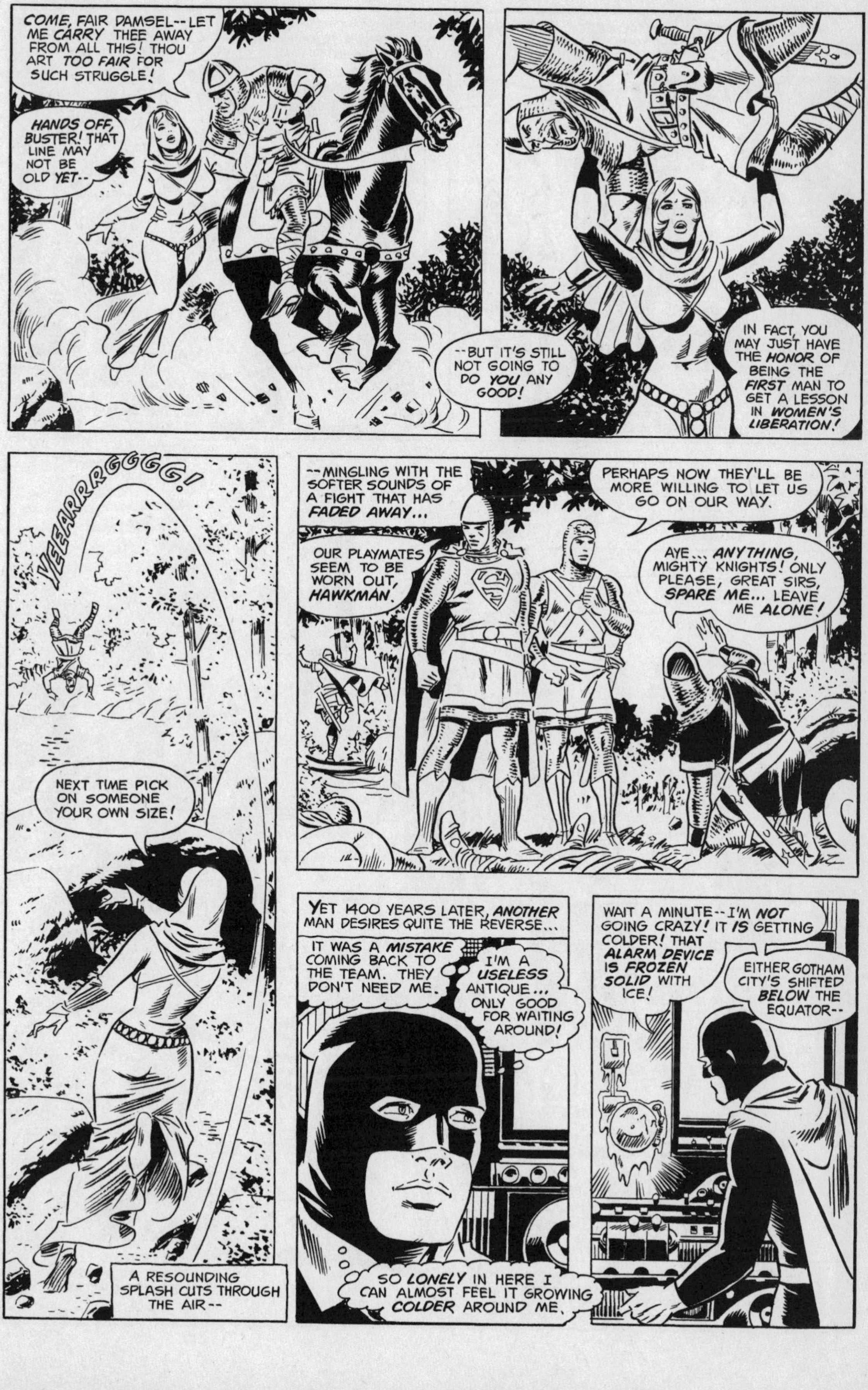
COME, FAIR DAMSEL--LET ME CARRY THEE AWAY FROM ALL THIS! THOU ART TOO FAIR FOR SUCH STRUGGLE!
HANDS OFF, BUSTER! THAT LINE MAY NOT BE OLD YET--
--BUT IT'S STILL NOT GOING TO DO YOU ANY GOOD!
IN FACT, YOU MAY JUST HAVE THE HONOR OF BEING THE FIRST MAN TO GET A LESSON IN WOMEN'S LIBERATION!
YEEARRRGGGG!
NEXT TIME PICK ON SOMEONE YOUR OWN SIZE!
A RESOUNDING SPLASH CUTS THROUGH THE AIR--
--MINGLING WITH THE SOFTER SOUNDS OF A FIGHT THAT HAS FADED AWAY...
PERHAPS NOW THEY'LL BE MORE WILLING TO LET US GO ON OUR WAY.
OUR PLAYMATES SEEM TO BE WORN OUT, HAWKMAN.
AYE... ANYTHING, MIGHTY KNIGHTS! ONLY PLEASE, GREAT SIRS, SPARE ME... LEAVE ME ALONE!
YET 1400 YEARS LATER, ANOTHER MAN DESIRES QUITE THE REVERSE...
IT WAS A MISTAKE COMING BACK TO THE TEAM. THEY DON'T NEED ME.
I'M A USELESS ANTIQUE... ONLY GOOD FOR WAITING AROUND!
SO LONELY IN HERE I CAN ALMOST FEEL IT GROWING COLDER AROUND ME.
WAIT A MINUTE--I'M NOT GOING CRAZY! IT IS GETTING COLDER! THAT ALARM DEVICE IS FROZEN SOLID WITH ICE!
EITHER GOTHAM CITY'S SHIFTED BELOW THE EQUATOR--

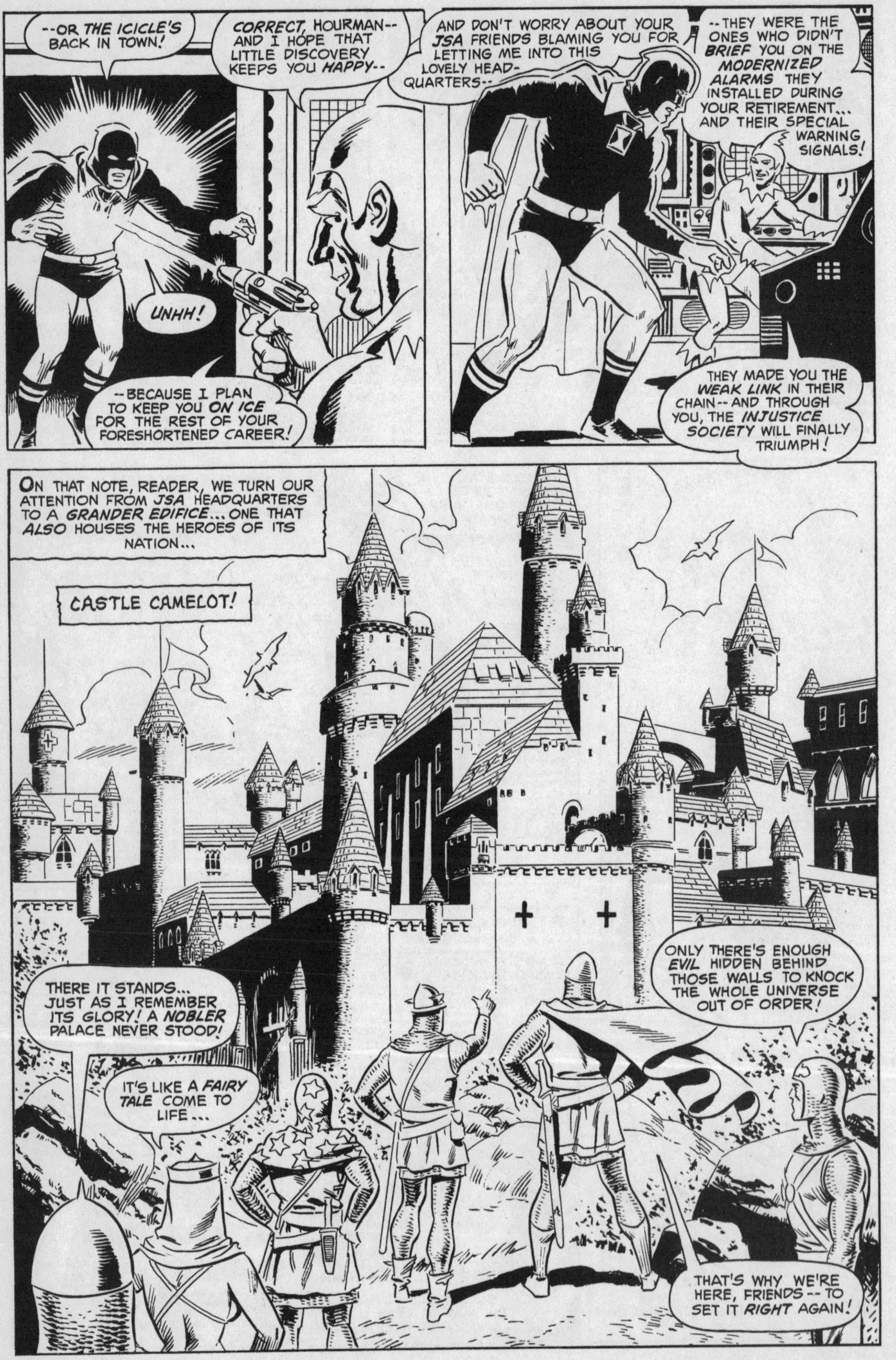
--OR THE ICICLE'S BACK IN TOWN!
CORRECT, HOURMAN-- AND I HOPE THAT LITTLE DISCOVERY KEEPS YOU HAPPY--
UNHH!
--BECAUSE I PLAN TO KEEP YOU ON ICE FOR THE REST OF YOUR FORESHORTENED CAREER!
AND DON'T WORRY ABOUT YOUR JSA FRIENDS BLAMING YOU FOR LETTING ME INTO THIS LOVELY HEAD-QUARTERS--
--THEY WERE THE ONES WHO DIDN'T BRIEF YOU ON THE MODERNIZED ALARMS THEY INSTALLED DURING YOUR RETIREMENT... AND THEIR SPECIAL WARNING SIGNALS!
THEY MADE YOU THE WEAK LINK IN THEIR CHAIN-- AND THROUGH YOU, THE INJUSTICE SOCIETY WILL FINALLY TRIUMPH!
ON THAT NOTE, READER, WE TURN OUR ATTENTION FROM JSA HEADQUARTERS TO A GRANDER EDIFICE... ONE THAT ALSO HOUSES THE HEROES OF ITS NATION...
CASTLE CAMELOT!
THERE IT STANDS... JUST AS I REMEMBER ITS GLORY! A NOBLER PALACE NEVER STOOD!
IT'S LIKE A FAIRY TALE COME TO LIFE...
ONLY THERE'S ENOUGH EVIL HIDDEN BEHIND THOSE WALLS TO KNOCK THE WHOLE UNIVERSE OUT OF ORDER!
THAT'S WHY WE'RE HERE, FRIENDS -- TO SET IT RIGHT AGAIN!

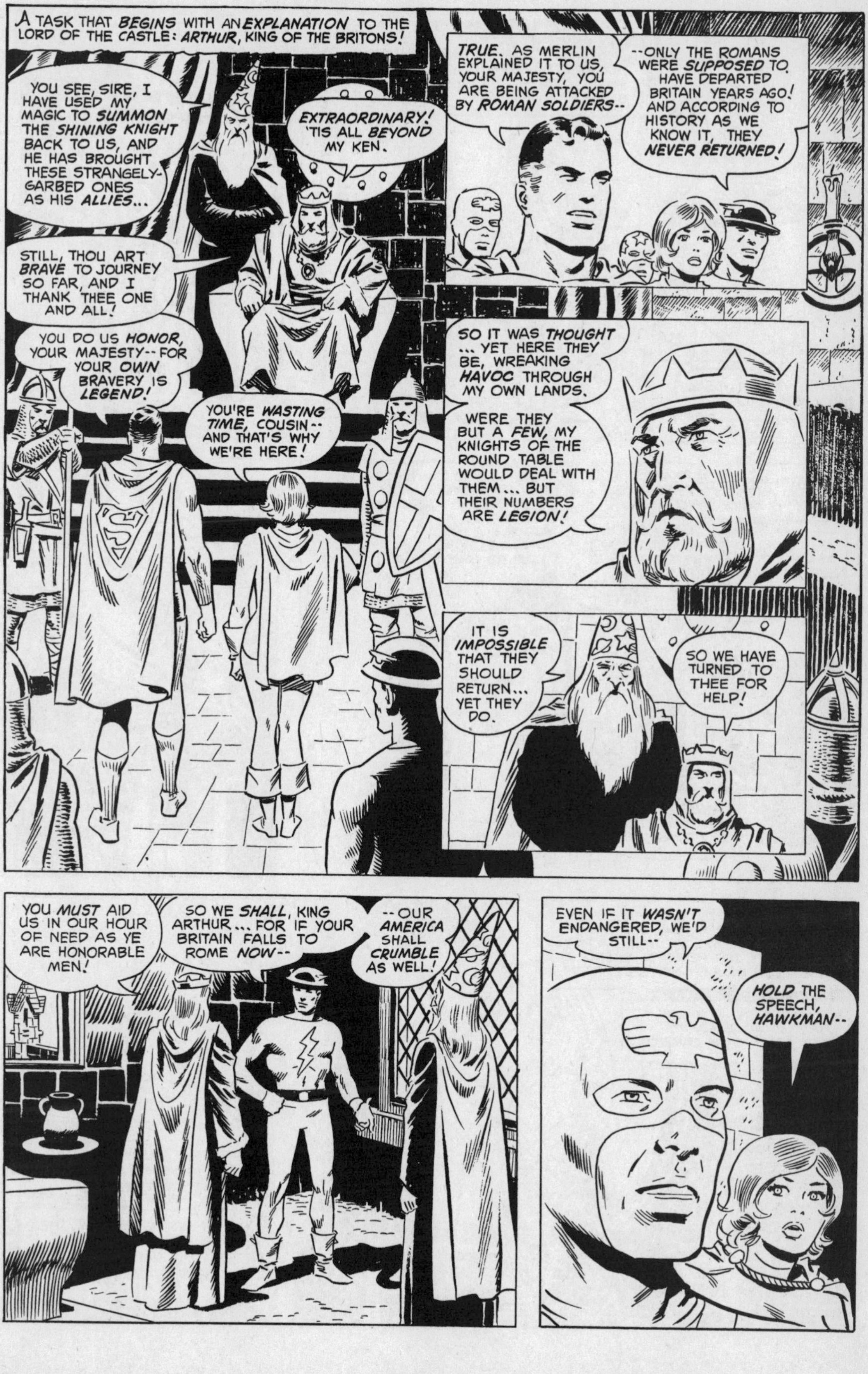
A TASK THAT BEGINS WITH AN EXPLANATION TO THE LORD OF THE CASTLE: ARTHUR, KING OF THE BRITONS!
YOU SEE, SIRE, I HAVE USED MY MAGIC TO SUMMON THE SHINING KNIGHT BACK TO US, AND HE HAS BROUGHT THESE STRANGELY-GARBED ONES AS HIS ALLIES...
EXTRAORDINARY! 'TIS ALL BEYOND MY KEN.
STILL, THOU ART BRAVE TO JOURNEY SO FAR, AND I THANK THEE ONE AND ALL!
YOU DO US HONOR, YOUR MAJESTY-- FOR YOUR OWN BRAVERY IS LEGEND!
YOU'RE WASTING TIME, COUSIN-- AND THAT'S WHY WE'RE HERE!
TRUE. AS MERLIN EXPLAINED IT TO US, YOUR MAJESTY, YOU ARE BEING ATTACKED BY ROMAN SOLDIERS--
--ONLY THE ROMANS WERE SUPPOSED TO HAVE DEPARTED BRITAIN YEARS AGO! AND ACCORDING TO HISTORY AS WE KNOW IT, THEY NEVER RETURNED!
SO IT WAS THOUGHT ... YET HERE THEY BE, WREAKING HAVOC THROUGH MY OWN LANDS.
WERE THEY BUT A FEW, MY KNIGHTS OF THE ROUND TABLE WOULD DEAL WITH THEM... BUT THEIR NUMBERS ARE LEGION!
IT IS IMPOSSIBLE THAT THEY SHOULD RETURN... YET THEY DO.
SO WE HAVE TURNED TO THEE FOR HELP!
YOU MUST AID US IN OUR HOUR OF NEED AS YE ARE HONORABLE MEN!
SO WE SHALL, KING ARTHUR... FOR IF YOUR BRITAIN FALLS TO ROME NOW--
--OUR AMERICA SHALL CRUMBLE AS WELL!
EVEN IF IT WASN'T ENDANGERED, WE'D STILL--
HOLD THE SPEECH, HAWKMAN--

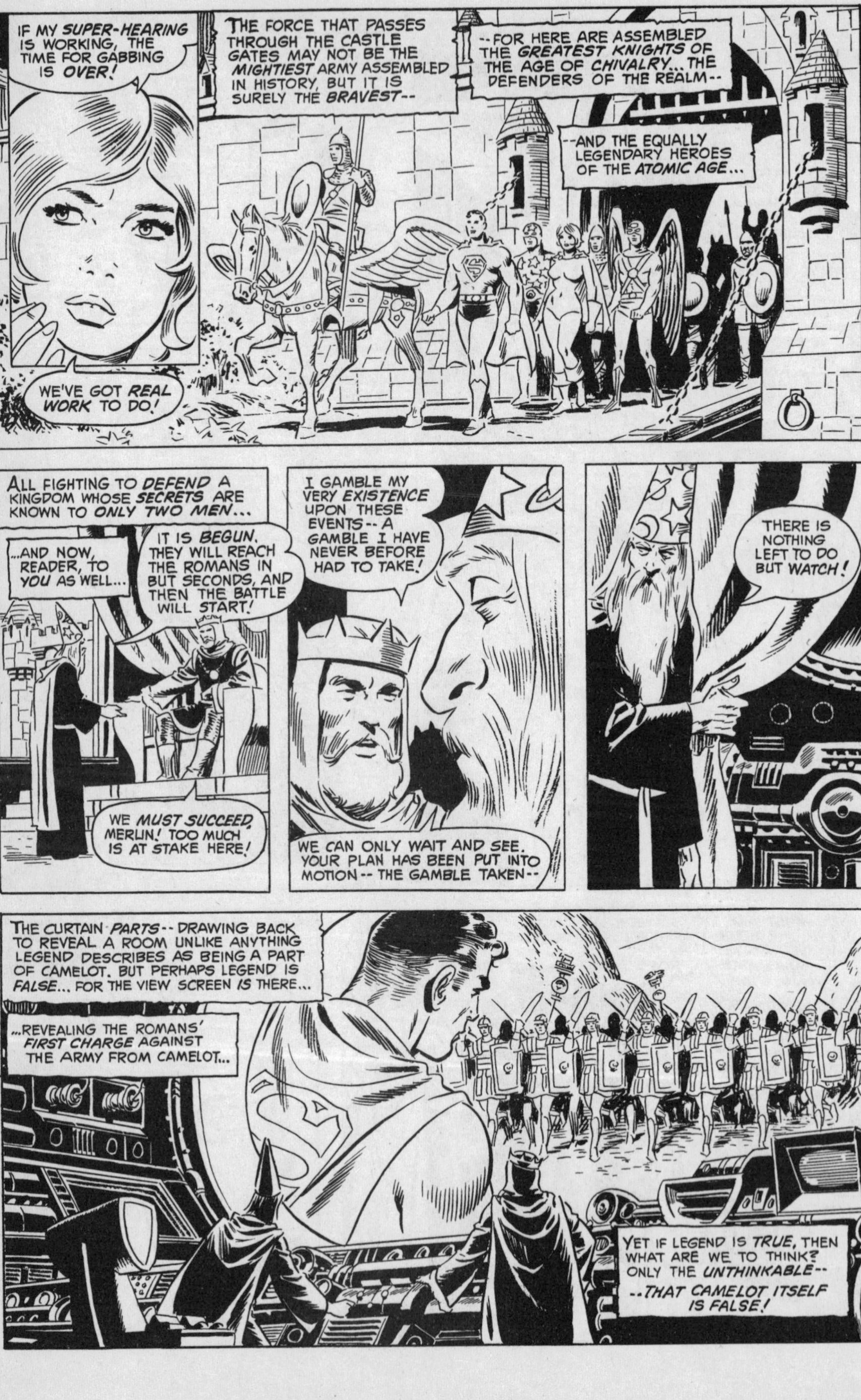
IF MY SUPER-HEARING IS WORKING, THE TIME FOR GABBING IS OVER!
WE'VE GOT REAL WORK TO DO!
THE FORCE THAT PASSES THROUGH THE CASTLE GATES MAY NOT BE THE MIGHTIEST ARMY ASSEMBLED IN HISTORY, BUT IT IS SURELY THE BRAVEST--
--FOR HERE ARE ASSEMBLED THE GREATEST KNIGHTS OF THE AGE OF CHIVALRY... THE DEFENDERS OF THE REALM--
--AND THE EQUALLY LEGENDARY HEROES OF THE ATOMIC AGE...
ALL FIGHTING TO DEFEND A KINGDOM WHOSE SECRETS ARE KNOWN TO ONLY TWO MEN...
...AND NOW, READER, TO YOU AS WELL...
IT IS BEGUN. THEY WILL REACH THE ROMANS IN BUT SECONDS, AND THEN THE BATTLE WILL START!
WE MUST SUCCEED, MERLIN! TOO MUCH IS AT STAKE HERE!
I GAMBLE MY VERY EXISTENCE UPON THESE EVENTS-- A GAMBLE I HAVE NEVER BEFORE HAD TO TAKE!
WE CAN ONLY WAIT AND SEE. YOUR PLAN HAS BEEN PUT INTO MOTION-- THE GAMBLE TAKEN--
THERE IS NOTHING LEFT TO DO BUT WATCH!
THE CURTAIN PARTS-- DRAWING BACK TO REVEAL A ROOM UNLIKE ANYTHING LEGEND DESCRIBES AS BEING A PART OF CAMELOT. BUT PERHAPS LEGEND IS FALSE... FOR THE VIEW SCREEN IS THERE...
...REVEALING THE ROMANS' FIRST CHARGE AGAINST THE ARMY FROM CAMELOT...
YET IF LEGEND IS TRUE, THEN WHAT ARE WE TO THINK? ONLY THE UNTHINKABLE--
--THAT CAMELOT ITSELF IS FALSE!

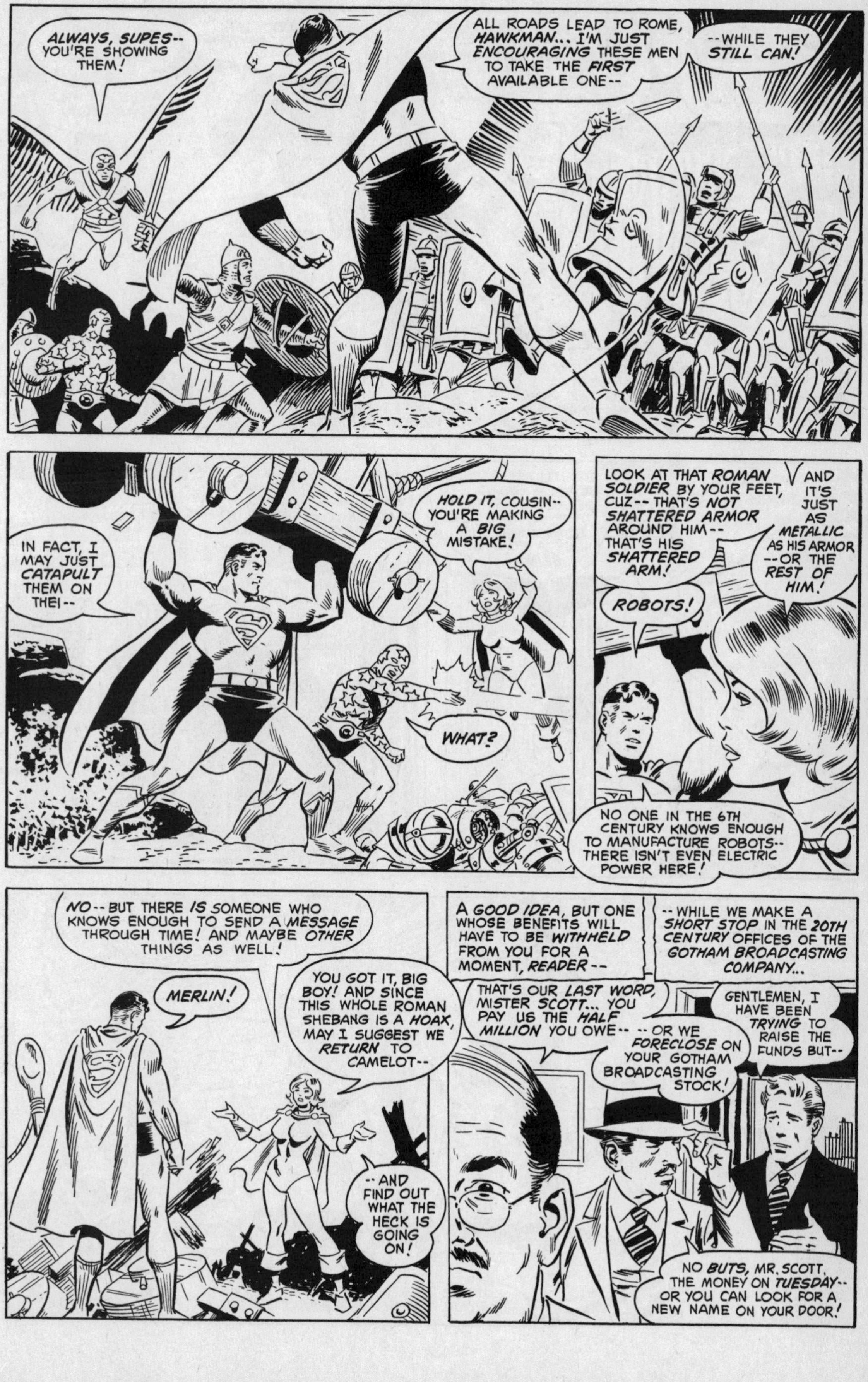
ALWAYS, SUPES-- YOU'RE SHOWING THEM!
ALL ROADS LEAD TO ROME, HAWKMAN... I'M JUST ENCOURAGING THESE MEN TO TAKE THE FIRST AVAILABLE ONE--
--WHILE THEY STILL CAN!
IN FACT, I MAY JUST CATAPULT THEM ON THEI--
HOLD IT, COUSIN-- YOU'RE MAKING A BIG MISTAKE!
WHAT?
LOOK AT THAT ROMAN SOLDIER BY YOUR FEET, CUZ-- THAT'S NOT SHATTERED ARMOR AROUND HIM-- THAT'S HIS SHATTERED ARM!
AND IT'S JUST AS METALLIC AS HIS ARMOR --OR THE REST OF HIM!
ROBOTS!
NO ONE IN THE 6TH CENTURY KNOWS ENOUGH TO MANUFACTURE ROBOTS-- THERE ISN'T EVEN ELECTRIC POWER HERE!
NO-- BUT THERE IS SOMEONE WHO KNOWS ENOUGH TO SEND A MESSAGE THROUGH TIME! AND MAYBE OTHER THINGS AS WELL!
MERLIN!
YOU GOT IT, BIG BOY! AND SINCE THIS WHOLE ROMAN SHEBANG IS A HOAX, MAY I SUGGEST WE RETURN TO CAMELOT--
--AND FIND OUT WHAT THE HECK IS GOING ON!
A GOOD IDEA, BUT ONE WHOSE BENEFITS WILL HAVE TO BE WITHHELD FROM YOU FOR A MOMENT, READER--
--WHILE WE MAKE A SHORT STOP IN THE 20TH CENTURY OFFICES OF THE GOTHAM BROADCASTING COMPANY...
THAT'S OUR LAST WORD, MISTER SCOTT... YOU PAY US THE HALF MILLION YOU OWE--
--OR WE FORECLOSE ON YOUR GOTHAM BROADCASTING STOCK!
GENTLEMEN, I HAVE BEEN TRYING TO RAISE THE FUNDS BUT--
NO BUTS, MR. SCOTT, THE MONEY ON TUESDAY-- OR YOU CAN LOOK FOR A NEW NAME ON YOUR DOOR!

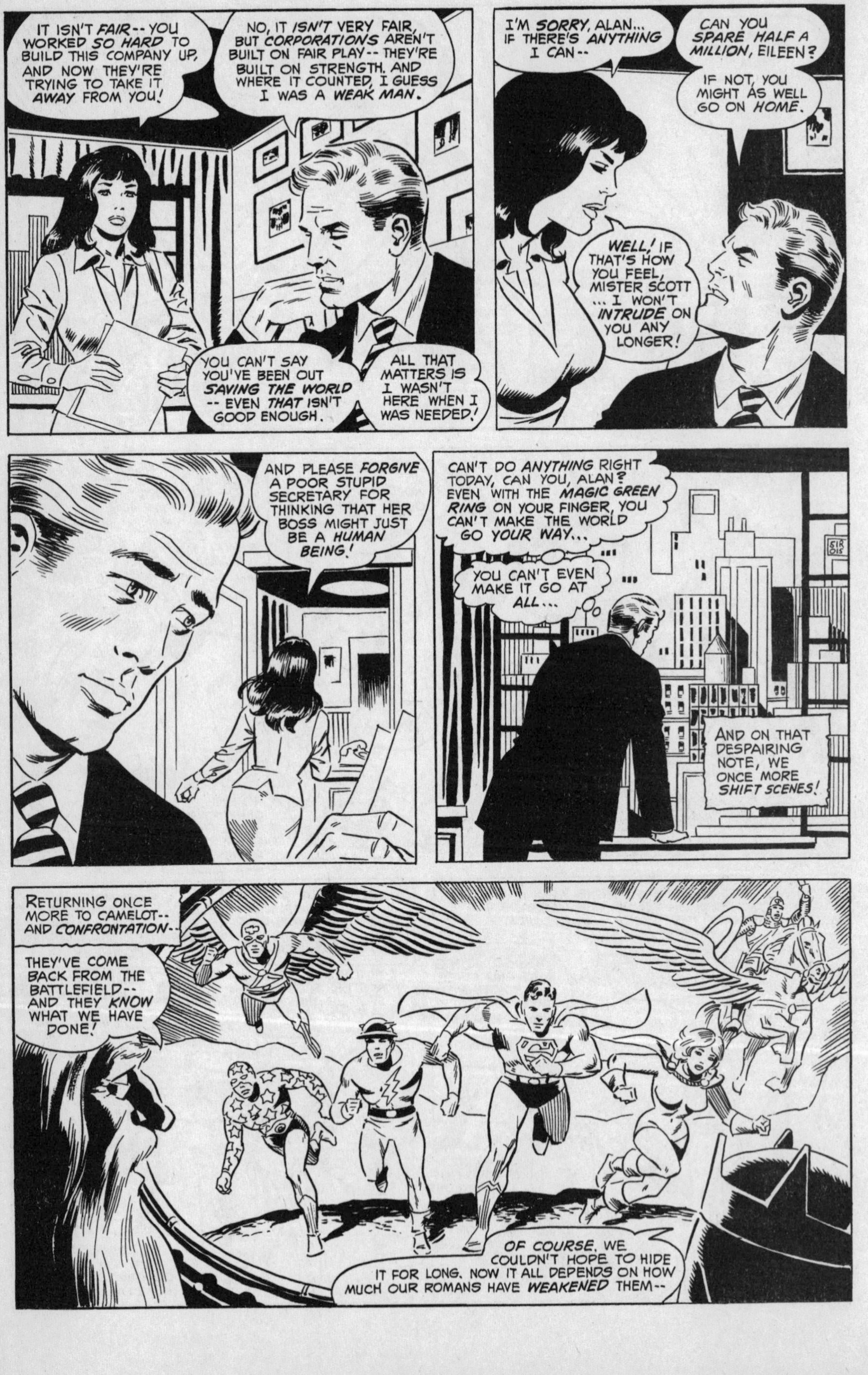
IT ISN'T FAIR -- YOU WORKED SO HARD TO BUILD THIS COMPANY UP, AND NOW THEY'RE TRYING TO TAKE IT AWAY FROM YOU!
NO, IT ISN'T VERY FAIR, BUT CORPORATIONS AREN'T BUILT ON FAIR PLAY -- THEY'RE BUILT ON STRENGTH. AND WHERE IT COUNTED, I GUESS I WAS A WEAK MAN.
YOU CAN'T SAY YOU'VE BEEN OUT SAVING THE WORLD -- EVEN THAT ISN'T GOOD ENOUGH.
ALL THAT MATTERS IS I WASN'T HERE WHEN I WAS NEEDED!
I'M SORRY, ALAN... IF THERE'S ANYTHING I CAN --
CAN YOU SPARE HALF A MILLION, EILEEN?
IF NOT, YOU MIGHT AS WELL GO ON HOME.
WELL! IF THAT'S HOW YOU FEEL, MISTER SCOTT ... I WON'T INTRUDE ON YOU ANY LONGER!
AND PLEASE FORGIVE A POOR STUPID SECRETARY FOR THINKING THAT HER BOSS MIGHT JUST BE A HUMAN BEING!
CAN'T DO ANYTHING RIGHT TODAY, CAN YOU, ALAN? EVEN WITH THE MAGIC GREEN RING ON YOUR FINGER, YOU CAN'T MAKE THE WORLD GO YOUR WAY...
YOU CAN'T EVEN MAKE IT GO AT ALL...
AND ON THAT DESPAIRING NOTE, WE ONCE MORE SHIFT SCENES!
RETURNING ONCE MORE TO CAMELOT -- AND CONFRONTATION --
THEY'VE COME BACK FROM THE BATTLEFIELD -- AND THEY KNOW WHAT WE HAVE DONE!
OF COURSE. WE COULDN'T HOPE TO HIDE IT FOR LONG. NOW IT ALL DEPENDS ON HOW MUCH OUR ROMANS HAVE WEAKENED THEM --

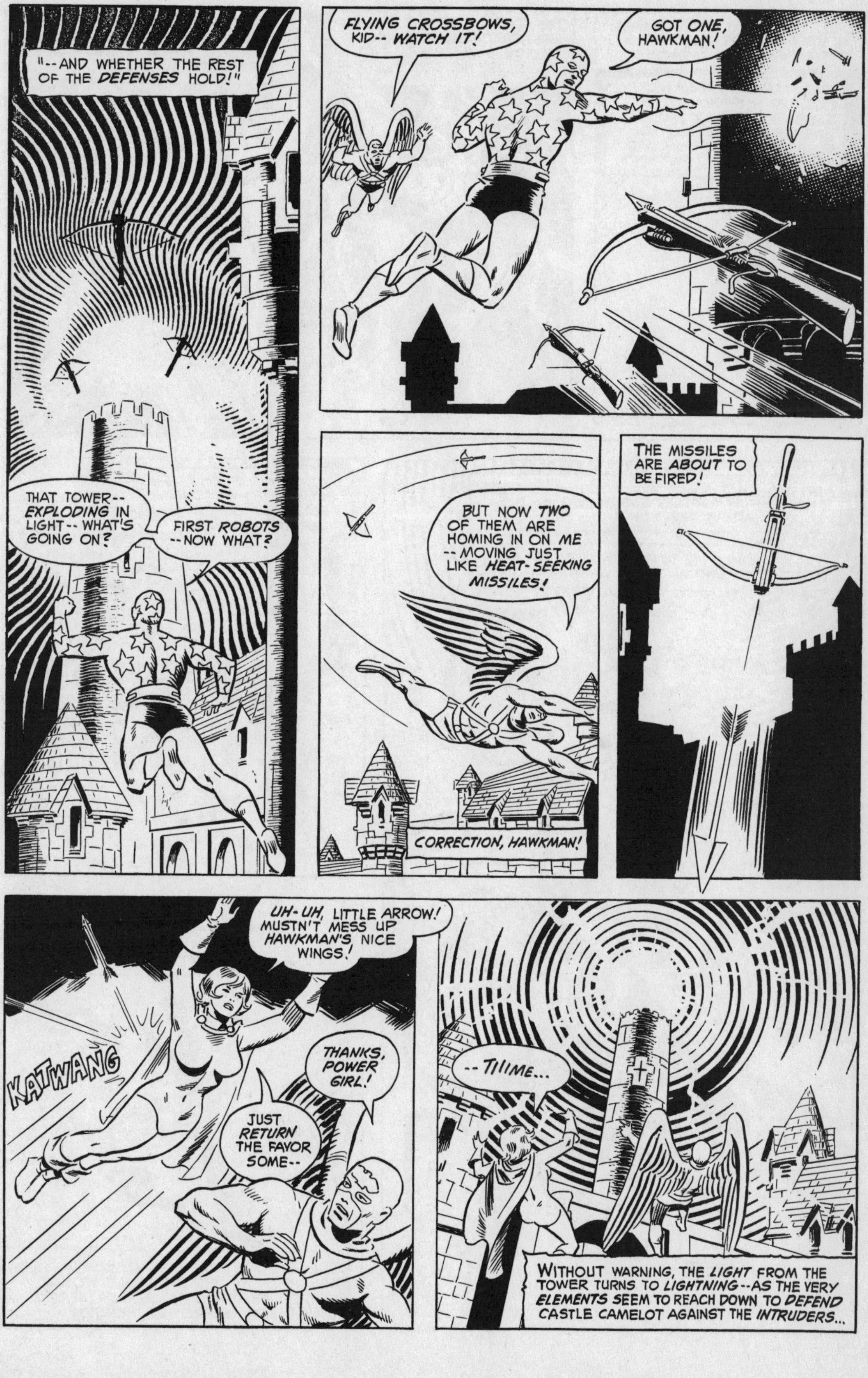
"--AND WHETHER THE REST OF THE DEFENSES HOLD!"
THAT TOWER-- EXPLODING IN LIGHT-- WHAT'S GOING ON?
FIRST ROBOTS --NOW WHAT?
FLYING CROSSBOWS, KID-- WATCH IT!
GOT ONE, HAWKMAN!
BUT NOW TWO OF THEM ARE HOMING IN ON ME --MOVING JUST LIKE HEAT-SEEKING MISSILES!
CORRECTION, HAWKMAN!
THE MISSILES ARE ABOUT TO BE FIRED!
UH-UH, LITTLE ARROW! MUSTN'T MESS UP HAWKMAN'S NICE WINGS!
KATWANG
THANKS, POWER GIRL!
JUST RETURN THE FAVOR SOME--
--TIIIME...
WITHOUT WARNING, THE LIGHT FROM THE TOWER TURNS TO LIGHTNING--AS THE VERY ELEMENTS SEEM TO REACH DOWN TO DEFEND CASTLE CAMELOT AGAINST THE INTRUDERS...

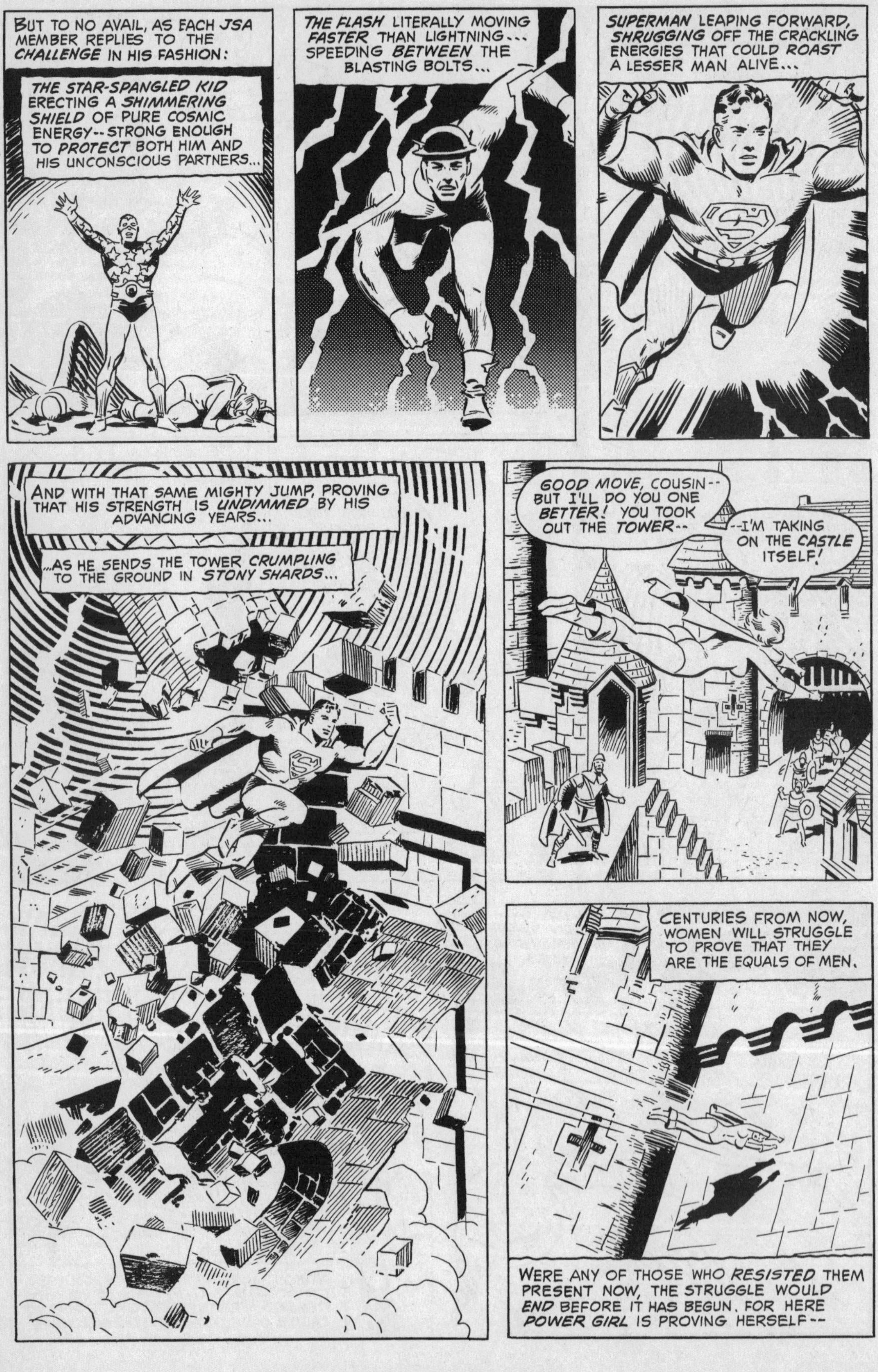
BUT TO NO AVAIL, AS EACH JSA MEMBER REPLIES TO THE CHALLENGE IN HIS FASHION:
THE STAR-SPANGLED KID ERECTING A SHIMMERING SHIELD OF PURE COSMIC ENERGY--STRONG ENOUGH TO PROTECT BOTH HIM AND HIS UNCONSCIOUS PARTNERS...
THE FLASH LITERALLY MOVING FASTER THAN LIGHTNING... SPEEDING BETWEEN THE BLASTING BOLTS...
SUPERMAN LEAPING FORWARD, SHRUGGING OFF THE CRACKLING ENERGIES THAT COULD ROAST A LESSER MAN ALIVE...
AND WITH THAT SAME MIGHTY JUMP, PROVING THAT HIS STRENGTH IS UNDIMMED BY HIS ADVANCING YEARS...
...AS HE SENDS THE TOWER CRUMPLING TO THE GROUND IN STONY SHARDS...
GOOD MOVE, COUSIN-- BUT I'LL DO YOU ONE BETTER! YOU TOOK OUT THE TOWER--
--I'M TAKING ON THE CASTLE ITSELF!
CENTURIES FROM NOW, WOMEN WILL STRUGGLE TO PROVE THAT THEY ARE THE EQUALS OF MEN.
WERE ANY OF THOSE WHO RESISTED THEM PRESENT NOW, THE STRUGGLE WOULD END BEFORE IT HAS BEGUN, FOR HERE POWER GIRL IS PROVING HERSELF--

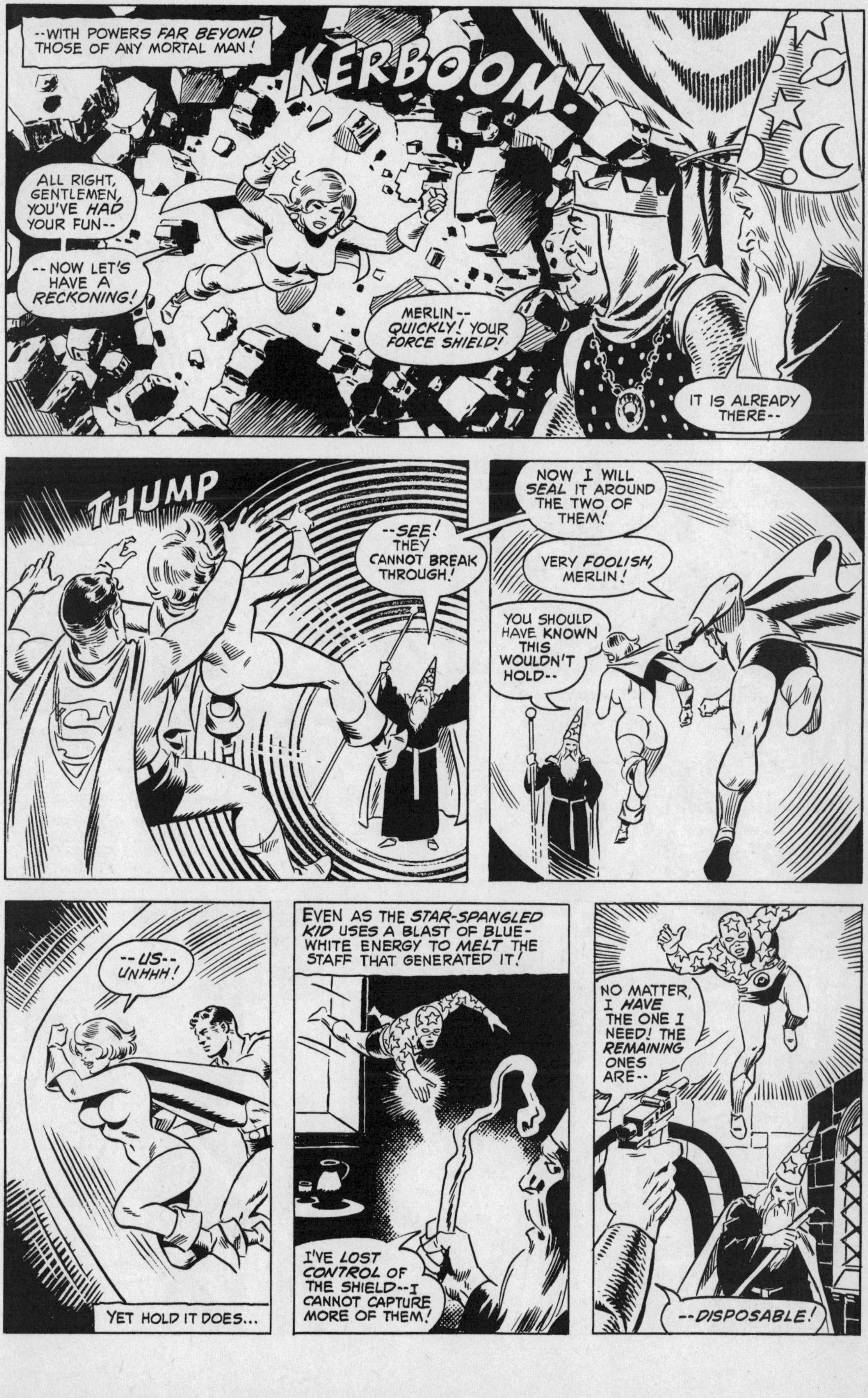
--WITH POWERS FAR BEYOND THOSE OF ANY MORTAL MAN!
KERBOOM!
ALL RIGHT, GENTLEMEN, YOU'VE HAD YOUR FUN--
--NOW LET'S HAVE A RECKONING!
MERLIN--QUICKLY! YOUR FORCE SHIELD!
IT IS ALREADY THERE--
THUMP
--SEE! THEY CANNOT BREAK THROUGH!
NOW I WILL SEAL IT AROUND THE TWO OF THEM!
VERY FOOLISH, MERLIN!
YOU SHOULD HAVE KNOWN THIS WOULDN'T HOLD--
--US--UNHHH!
YET HOLD IT DOES...
EVEN AS THE STAR-SPANGLED KID USES A BLAST OF BLUE-WHITE ENERGY TO MELT THE STAFF THAT GENERATED IT!
I'VE LOST CONTROL OF THE SHIELD--I CANNOT CAPTURE MORE OF THEM!
NO MATTER, I HAVE THE ONE I NEED! THE REMAINING ONES ARE--
--DISPOSABLE!

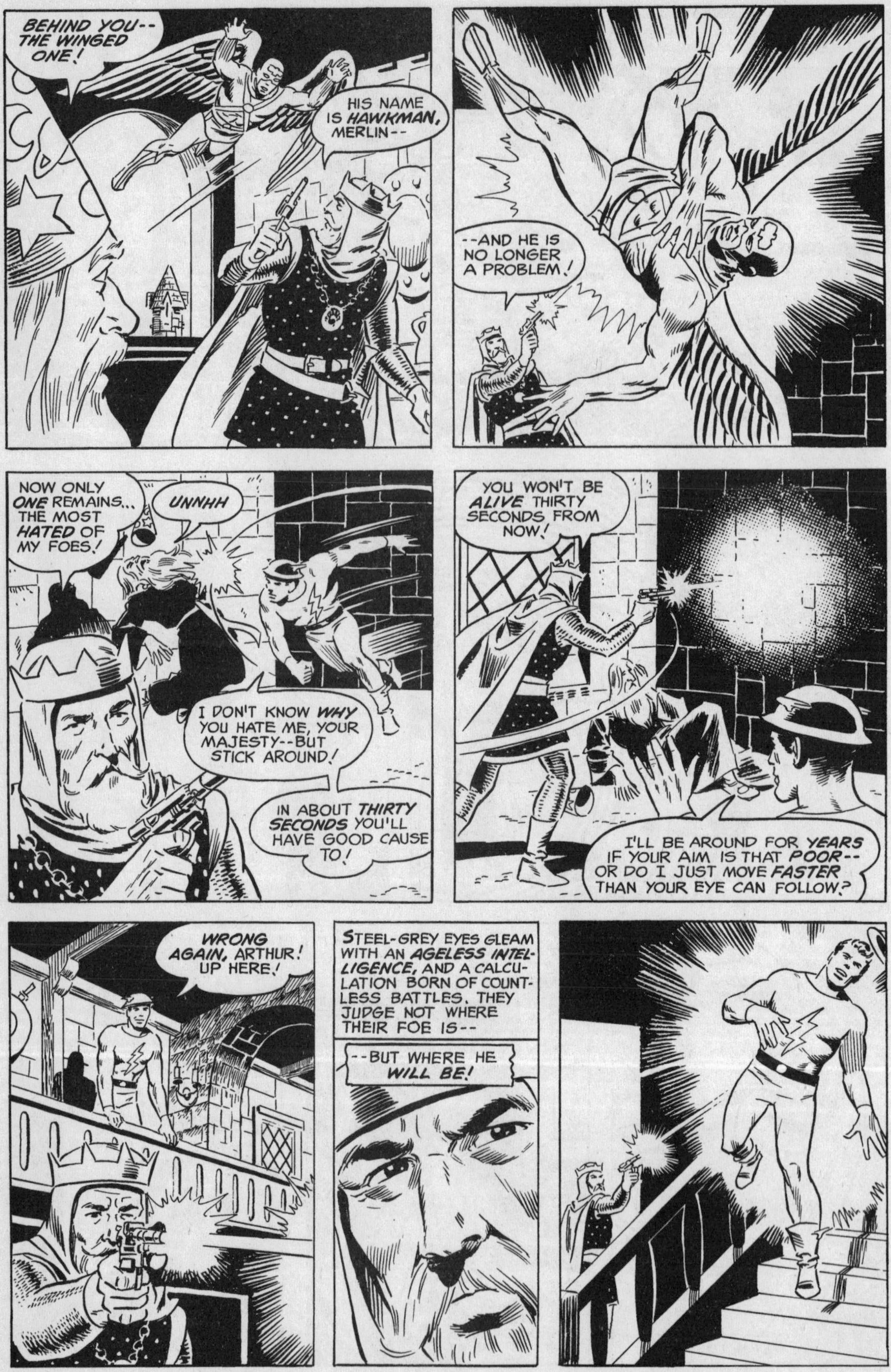
BEHIND YOU-- THE WINGED ONE!
HIS NAME IS HAWKMAN, MERLIN--
--AND HE IS NO LONGER A PROBLEM!
NOW ONLY ONE REMAINS... THE MOST HATED OF MY FOES!
UNNHH
I DON'T KNOW WHY YOU HATE ME, YOUR MAJESTY--BUT STICK AROUND!
IN ABOUT THIRTY SECONDS YOU'LL HAVE GOOD CAUSE TO!
YOU WON'T BE ALIVE THIRTY SECONDS FROM NOW!
I'LL BE AROUND FOR YEARS IF YOUR AIM IS THAT POOR-- OR DO I JUST MOVE FASTER THAN YOUR EYE CAN FOLLOW?
WRONG AGAIN, ARTHUR! UP HERE!
STEEL-GREY EYES GLEAM WITH AN AGELESS INTELLIGENCE, AND A CALCULATION BORN OF COUNTLESS BATTLES. THEY JUDGE NOT WHERE THEIR FOE IS--
--BUT WHERE HE WILL BE!

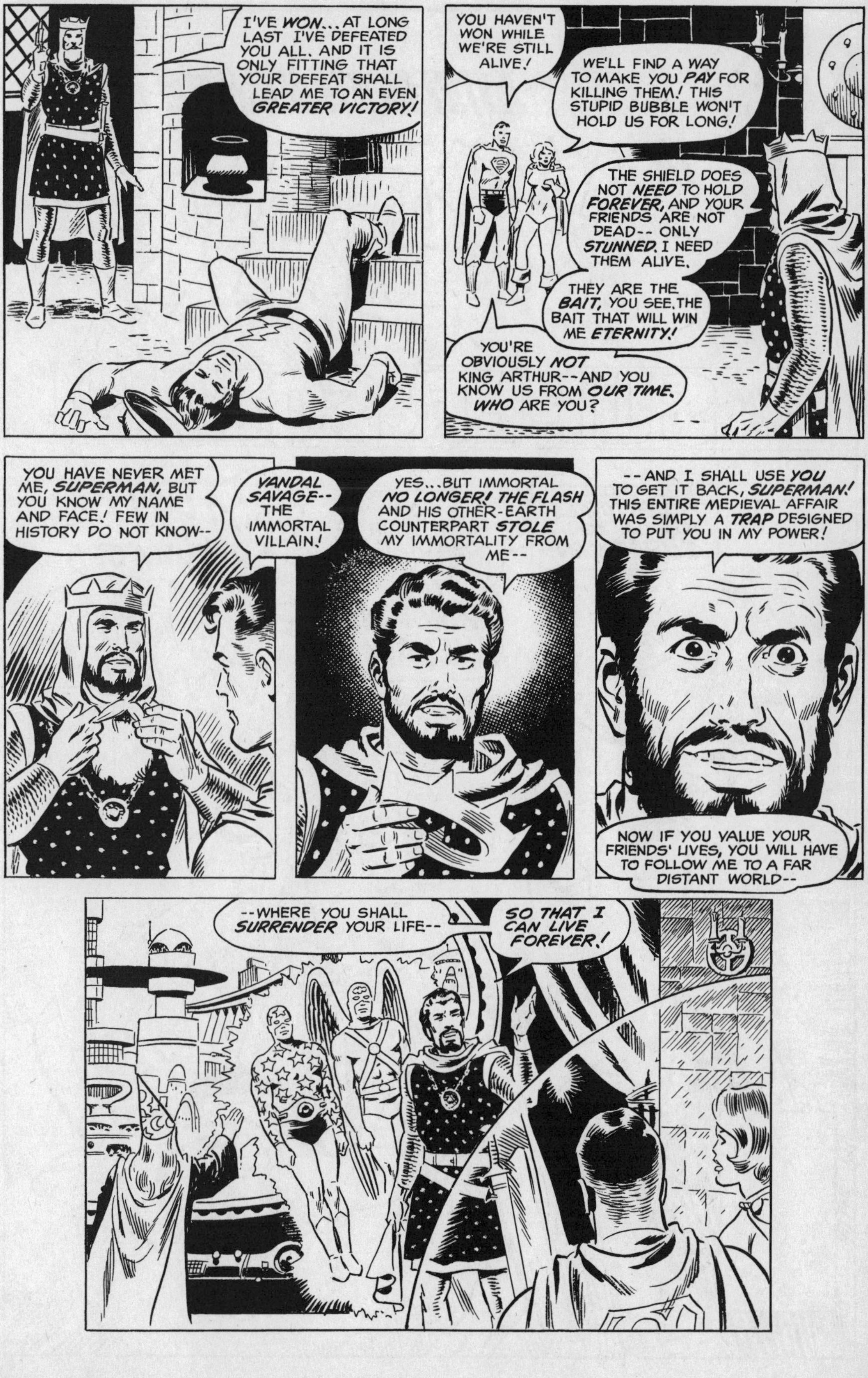
I'VE WON... AT LONG LAST I'VE DEFEATED YOU ALL. AND IT IS ONLY FITTING THAT YOUR DEFEAT SHALL LEAD ME TO AN EVEN GREATER VICTORY!
YOU HAVEN'T WON WHILE WE'RE STILL ALIVE!
WE'LL FIND A WAY TO MAKE YOU PAY FOR KILLING THEM! THIS STUPID BUBBLE WON'T HOLD US FOR LONG!
THE SHIELD DOES NOT NEED TO HOLD FOREVER, AND YOUR FRIENDS ARE NOT DEAD-- ONLY STUNNED. I NEED THEM ALIVE.
THEY ARE THE BAIT, YOU SEE. THE BAIT THAT WILL WIN ME ETERNITY!
YOU'RE OBVIOUSLY NOT KING ARTHUR--AND YOU KNOW US FROM OUR TIME. WHO ARE YOU?
YOU HAVE NEVER MET ME, SUPERMAN, BUT YOU KNOW MY NAME AND FACE! FEW IN HISTORY DO NOT KNOW--
VANDAL SAVAGE-- THE IMMORTAL VILLAIN!
YES... BUT IMMORTAL NO LONGER! THE FLASH AND HIS OTHER-EARTH COUNTERPART STOLE MY IMMORTALITY FROM ME--
--AND I SHALL USE YOU TO GET IT BACK, SUPERMAN! THIS ENTIRE MEDIEVAL AFFAIR WAS SIMPLY A TRAP DESIGNED TO PUT YOU IN MY POWER!
NOW IF YOU VALUE YOUR FRIENDS' LIVES, YOU WILL HAVE TO FOLLOW ME TO A FAR DISTANT WORLD--
--WHERE YOU SHALL SURRENDER YOUR LIFE--
SO THAT I CAN LIVE FOREVER!

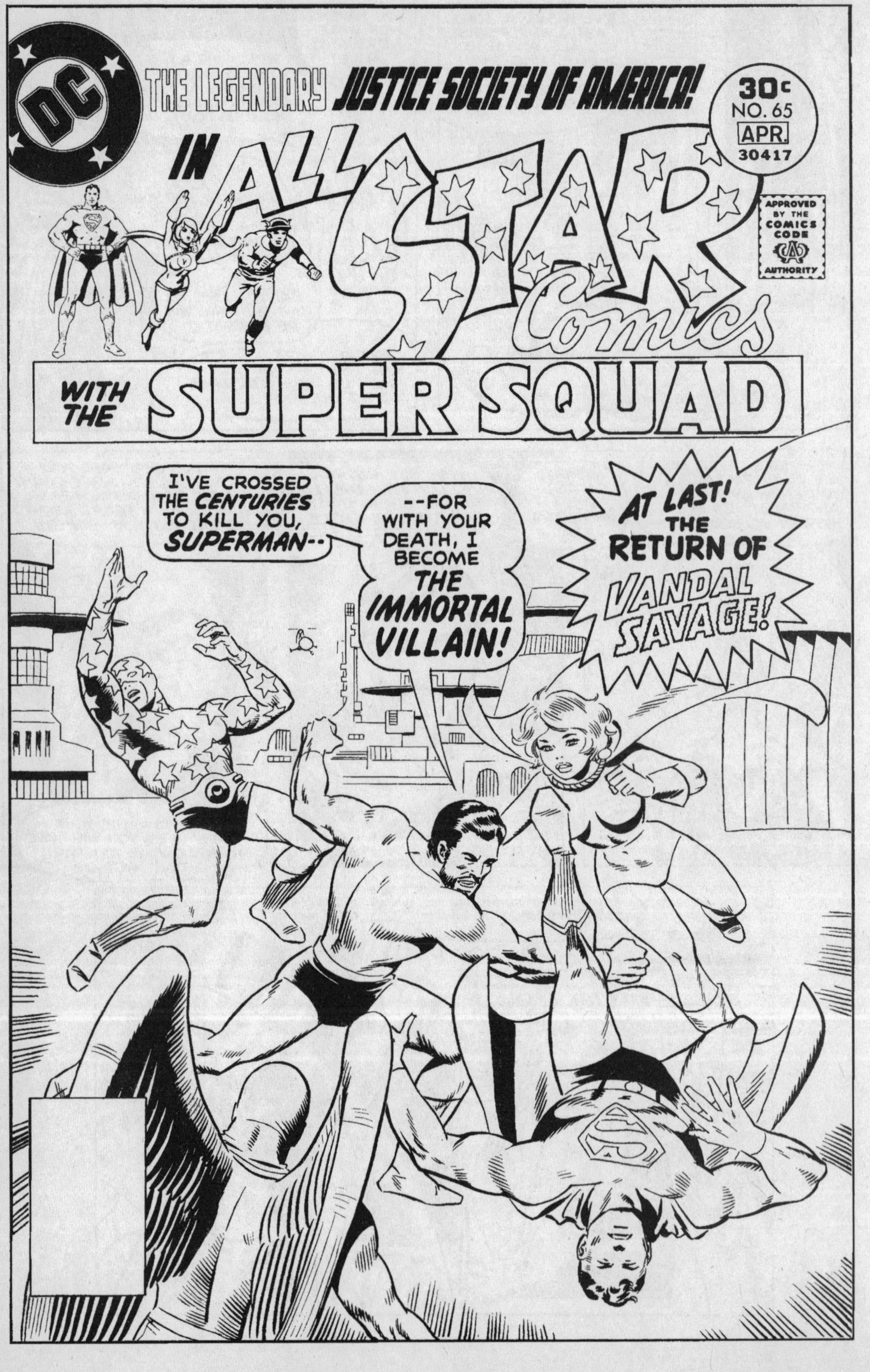

THE LEGENDARY JUSTICE SOCIETY OF AMERICA!
30¢
NO. 65
APR.
30417
IN ALL STAR Comics
APPROVED BY THE COMICS CODE AUTHORITY
WITH THE SUPER SQUAD
I'VE CROSSED THE CENTURIES TO KILL YOU, SUPERMAN--
--FOR WITH YOUR DEATH, I BECOME THE IMMORTAL VILLAIN!
AT LAST! THE RETURN OF VANDAL SAVAGE!

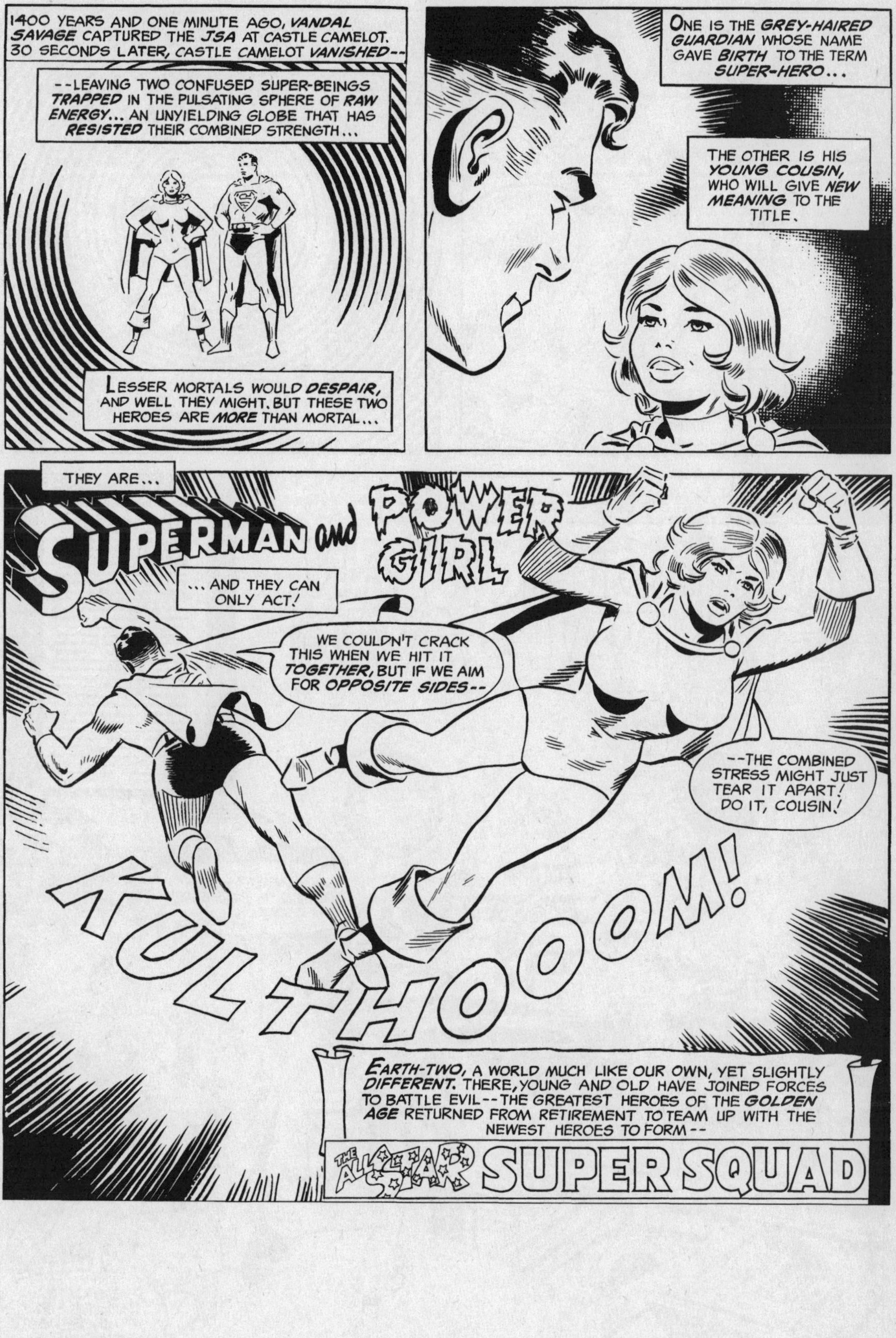
1400 YEARS AND ONE MINUTE AGO, VANDAL SAVAGE CAPTURED THE JSA AT CASTLE CAMELOT. 30 SECONDS LATER, CASTLE CAMELOT VANISHED--
--LEAVING TWO CONFUSED SUPER-BEINGS TRAPPED IN THE PULSATING SPHERE OF RAW ENERGY... AN UNYIELDING GLOBE THAT HAS RESISTED THEIR COMBINED STRENGTH...
LESSER MORTALS WOULD DESPAIR, AND WELL THEY MIGHT. BUT THESE TWO HEROES ARE MORE THAN MORTAL...
ONE IS THE GREY-HAIRED GUARDIAN WHOSE NAME GAVE BIRTH TO THE TERM SUPER-HERO...
THE OTHER IS HIS YOUNG COUSIN, WHO WILL GIVE NEW MEANING TO THE TITLE.
THEY ARE...
SUPERMAN and POWER GIRL
...AND THEY CAN ONLY ACT!
WE COULDN'T CRACK THIS WHEN WE HIT IT TOGETHER, BUT IF WE AIM FOR OPPOSITE SIDES--
--THE COMBINED STRESS MIGHT JUST TEAR IT APART! DO IT, COUSIN!
KULTHOOOM!
EARTH-TWO, A WORLD MUCH LIKE OUR OWN, YET SLIGHTLY DIFFERENT. THERE, YOUNG AND OLD HAVE JOINED FORCES TO BATTLE EVIL--THE GREATEST HEROES OF THE GOLDEN AGE RETURNED FROM RETIREMENT TO TEAM UP WITH THE NEWEST HEROES TO FORM--
THE ALL-STAR SUPER SQUAD

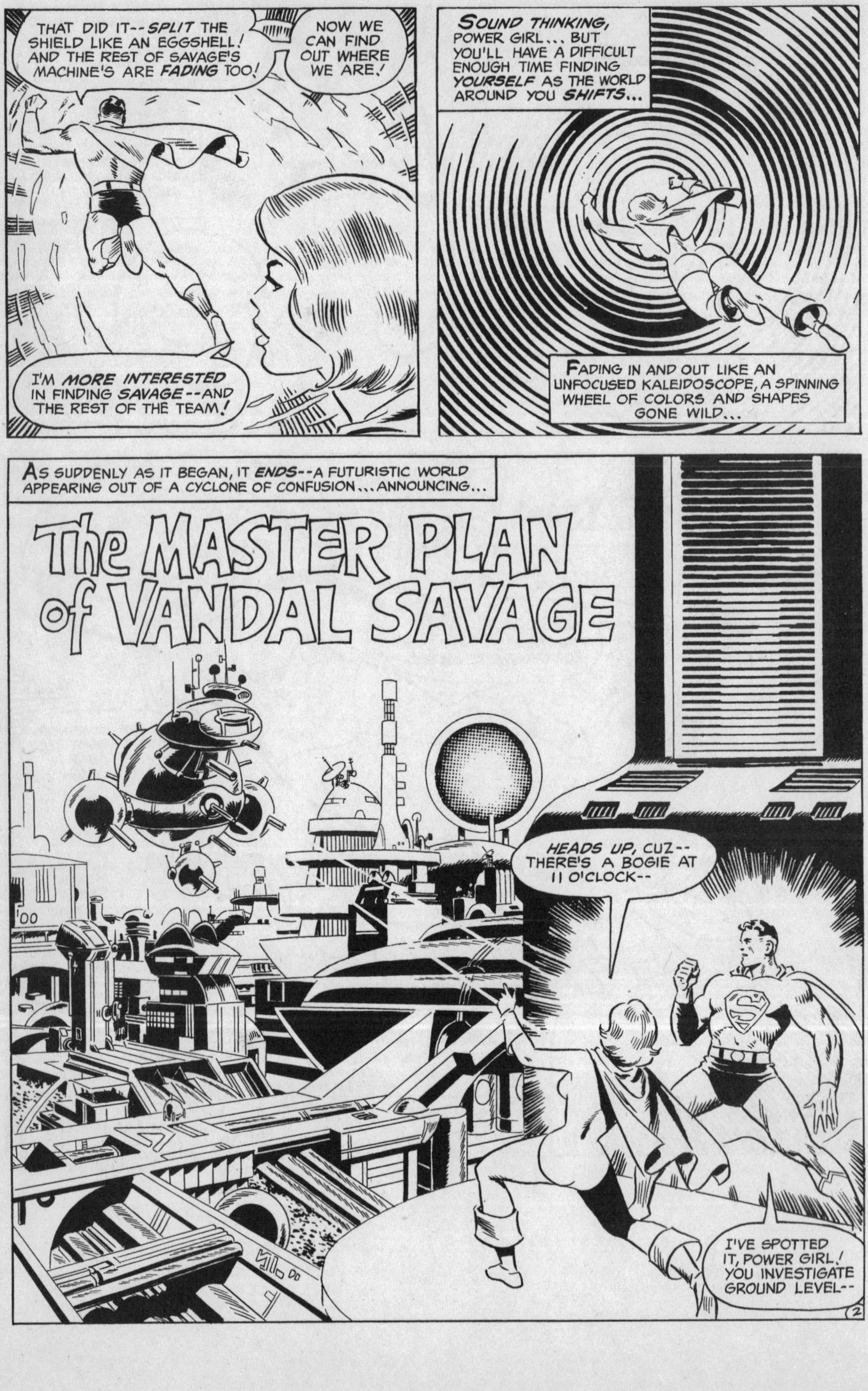
THAT DID IT--SPLIT THE SHIELD LIKE AN EGGSHELL! AND THE REST OF SAVAGE'S MACHINE'S ARE FADING TOO!
NOW WE CAN FIND OUT WHERE WE ARE!
I'M MORE INTERESTED IN FINDING SAVAGE--AND THE REST OF THE TEAM!
SOUND THINKING, POWER GIRL... BUT YOU'LL HAVE A DIFFICULT ENOUGH TIME FINDING YOURSELF AS THE WORLD AROUND YOU SHIFTS...
FADING IN AND OUT LIKE AN UNFOCUSED KALEIDOSCOPE, A SPINNING WHEEL OF COLORS AND SHAPES GONE WILD...
AS SUDDENLY AS IT BEGAN, IT ENDS--A FUTURISTIC WORLD APPEARING OUT OF A CYCLONE OF CONFUSION... ANNOUNCING...
The MASTER PLAN of VANDAL SAVAGE
HEADS UP, CUZ-- THERE'S A BOGIE AT 11 O'CLOCK--
I'VE SPOTTED IT, POWER GIRL! YOU INVESTIGATE GROUND LEVEL--
2

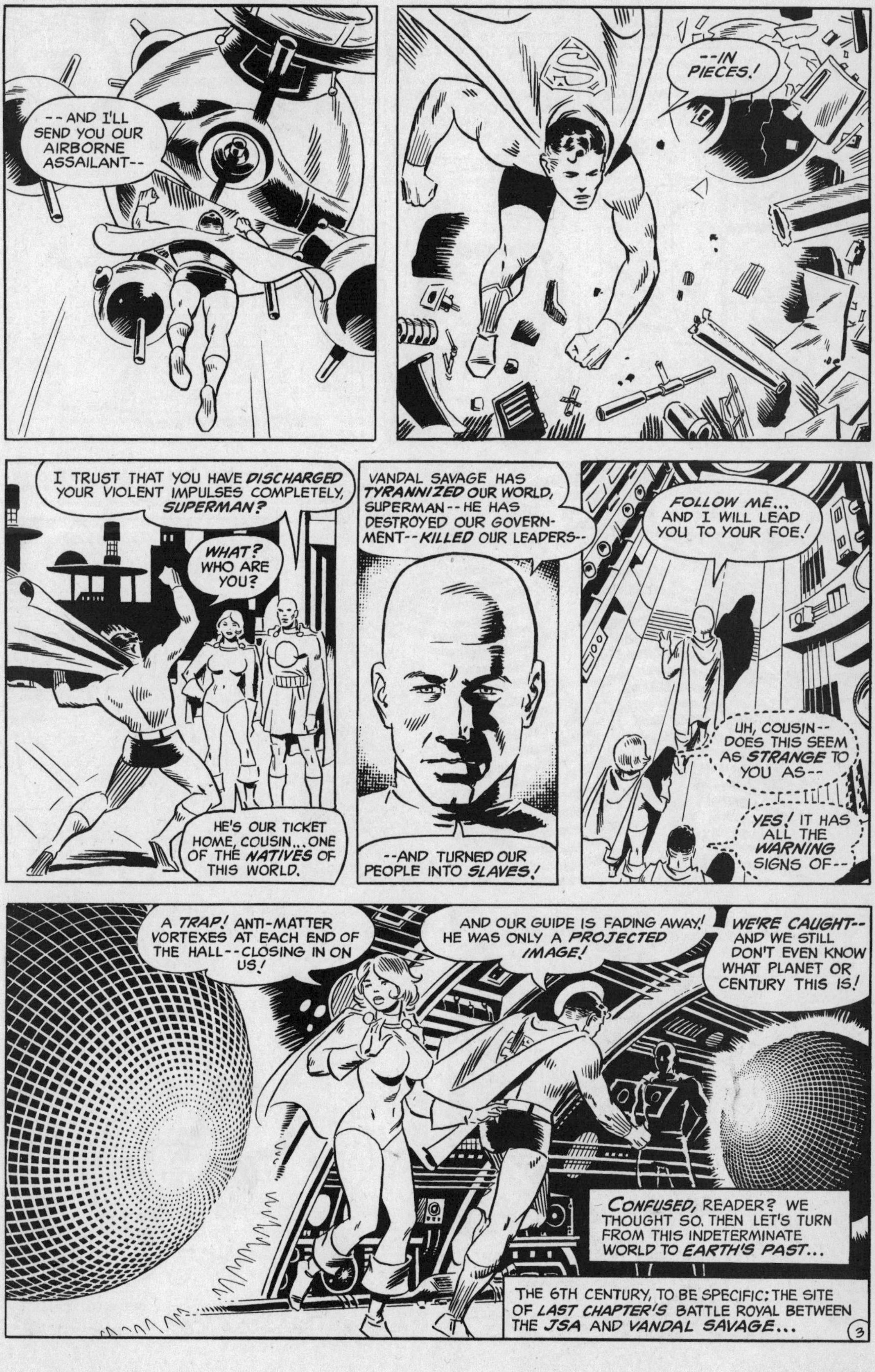
--AND I'LL SEND YOU OUR AIRBORNE ASSAILANT--
--IN PIECES!
I TRUST THAT YOU HAVE DISCHARGED YOUR VIOLENT IMPULSES COMPLETELY, SUPERMAN?
WHAT? WHO ARE YOU?
HE'S OUR TICKET HOME, COUSIN... ONE OF THE NATIVES OF THIS WORLD.
VANDAL SAVAGE HAS TYRANNIZED OUR WORLD, SUPERMAN--HE HAS DESTROYED OUR GOVERNMENT--KILLED OUR LEADERS--
--AND TURNED OUR PEOPLE INTO SLAVES!
FOLLOW ME... AND I WILL LEAD YOU TO YOUR FOE!
UH, COUSIN--DOES THIS SEEM AS STRANGE TO YOU AS--
YES! IT HAS ALL THE WARNING SIGNS OF--
A TRAP! ANTI-MATTER VORTEXES AT EACH END OF THE HALL--CLOSING IN ON US!
AND OUR GUIDE IS FADING AWAY! HE WAS ONLY A PROJECTED IMAGE!
WE'RE CAUGHT--AND WE STILL DON'T EVEN KNOW WHAT PLANET OR CENTURY THIS IS!
CONFUSED, READER? WE THOUGHT SO. THEN LET'S TURN FROM THIS INDETERMINATE WORLD TO EARTH'S PAST...
THE 6TH CENTURY, TO BE SPECIFIC: THE SITE OF LAST CHAPTER'S BATTLE ROYAL BETWEEN THE JSA AND VANDAL SAVAGE...
3

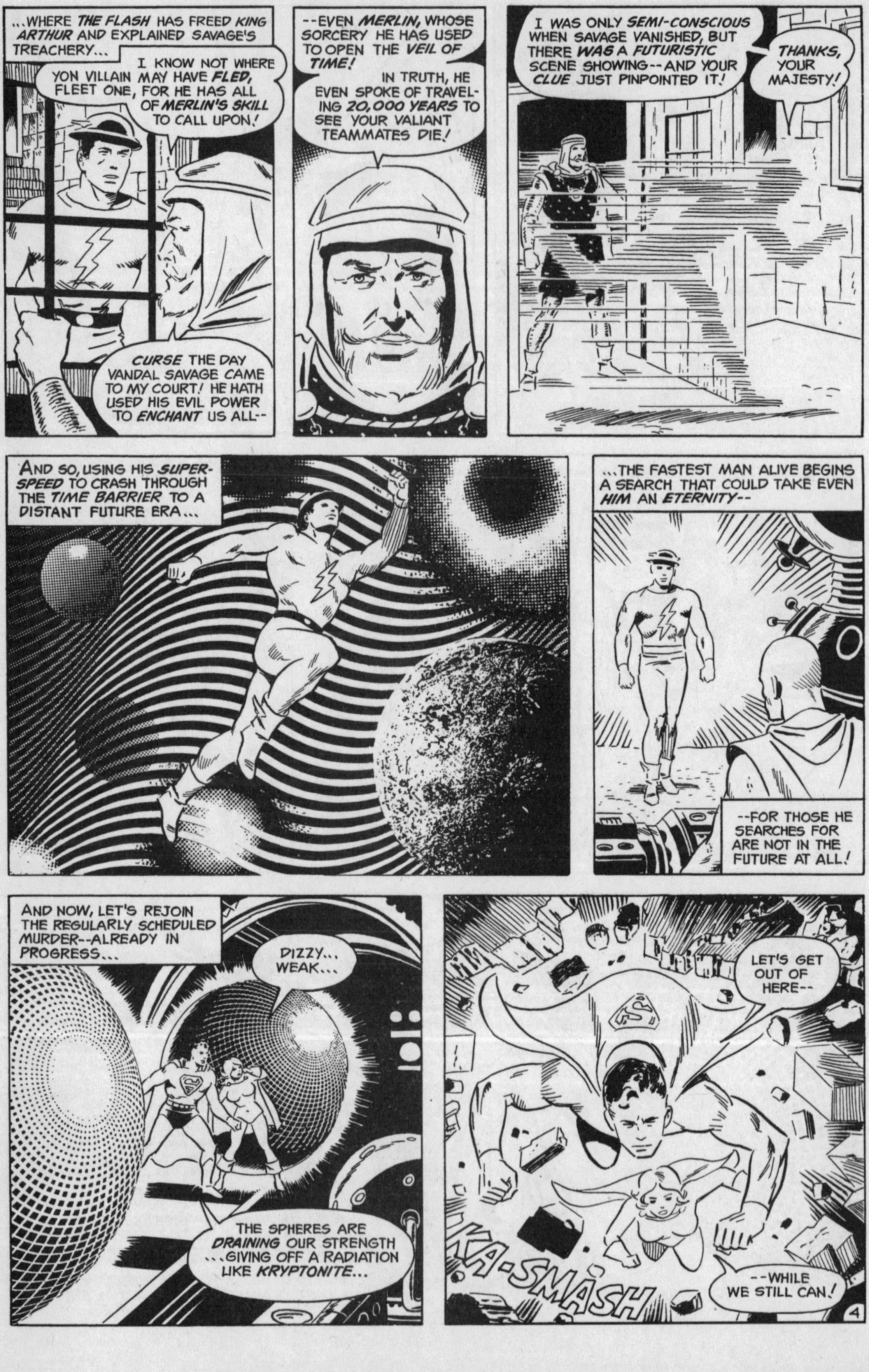
...WHERE THE FLASH HAS FREED KING ARTHUR AND EXPLAINED SAVAGE'S TREACHERY...
I KNOW NOT WHERE YON VILLAIN MAY HAVE FLED, FLEET ONE, FOR HE HAS ALL OF MERLIN'S SKILL TO CALL UPON!
CURSE THE DAY VANDAL SAVAGE CAME TO MY COURT! HE HATH USED HIS EVIL POWER TO ENCHANT US ALL--
--EVEN MERLIN, WHOSE SORCERY HE HAS USED TO OPEN THE VEIL OF TIME!
IN TRUTH, HE EVEN SPOKE OF TRAVELING 20,000 YEARS TO SEE YOUR VALIANT TEAMMATES DIE!
I WAS ONLY SEMI-CONSCIOUS WHEN SAVAGE VANISHED, BUT THERE WAS A FUTURISTIC SCENE SHOWING--AND YOUR CLUE JUST PINPOINTED IT!
THANKS, YOUR MAJESTY!
AND SO, USING HIS SUPER-SPEED TO CRASH THROUGH THE TIME BARRIER TO A DISTANT FUTURE ERA...
...THE FASTEST MAN ALIVE BEGINS A SEARCH THAT COULD TAKE EVEN HIM AN ETERNITY--
--FOR THOSE HE SEARCHES FOR ARE NOT IN THE FUTURE AT ALL!
AND NOW, LET'S REJOIN THE REGULARLY SCHEDULED MURDER--ALREADY IN PROGRESS...
DIZZY... WEAK...
THE SPHERES ARE DRAINING OUR STRENGTH ...GIVING OFF A RADIATION LIKE KRYPTONITE...
LET'S GET OUT OF HERE--
KA-SMASH
--WHILE WE STILL CAN!
4

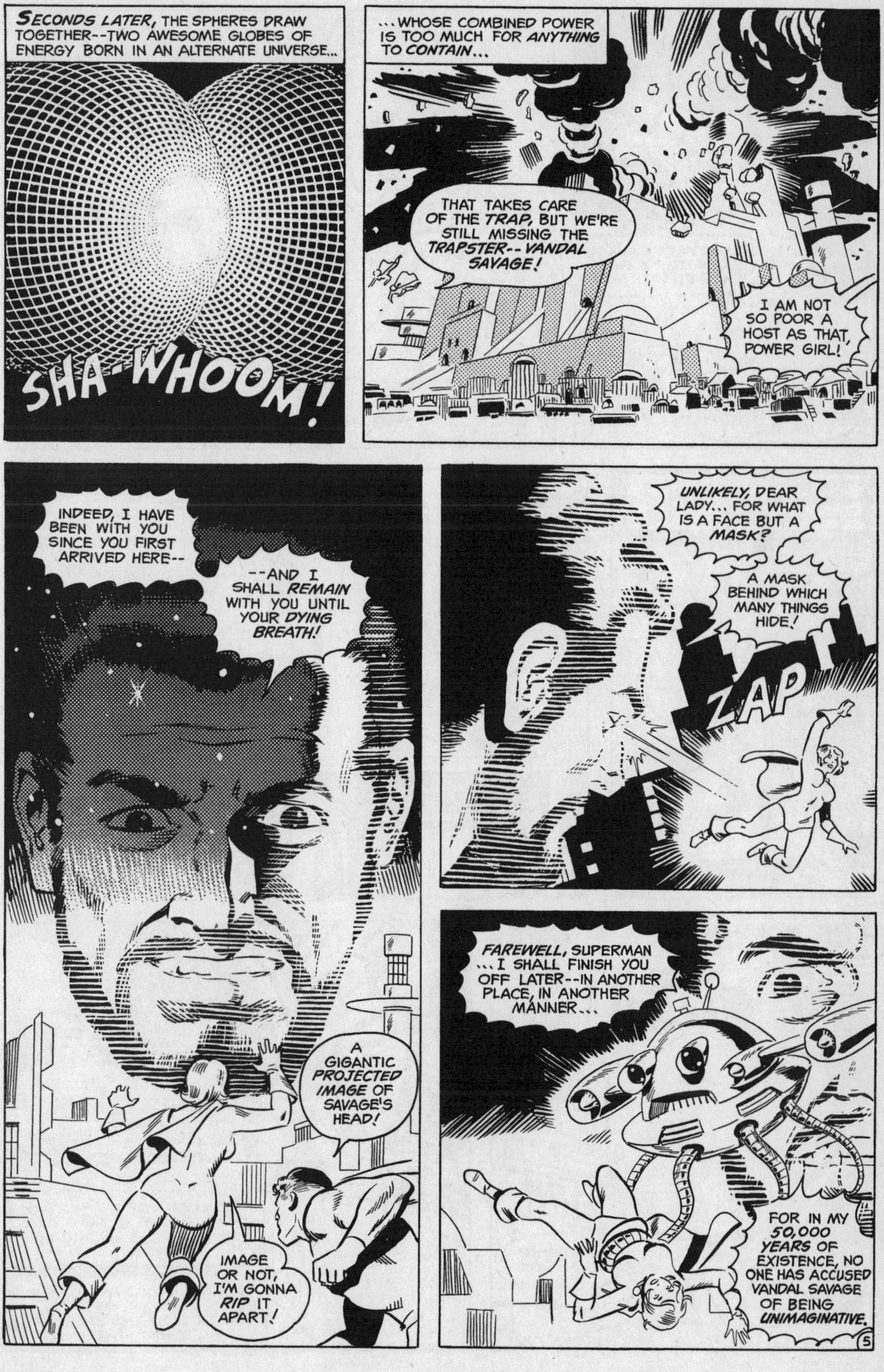
SECONDS LATER, THE SPHERES DRAW TOGETHER--TWO AWESOME GLOBES OF ENERGY BORN IN AN ALTERNATE UNIVERSE...
SHA-WHOOM!
...WHOSE COMBINED POWER IS TOO MUCH FOR ANYTHING TO CONTAIN...
THAT TAKES CARE OF THE TRAP, BUT WE'RE STILL MISSING THE TRAPSTER--VANDAL SAVAGE!
I AM NOT SO POOR A HOST AS THAT, POWER GIRL!
INDEED, I HAVE BEEN WITH YOU SINCE YOU FIRST ARRIVED HERE--
--AND I SHALL REMAIN WITH YOU UNTIL YOUR DYING BREATH!
A GIGANTIC PROJECTED IMAGE OF SAVAGE'S HEAD!
IMAGE OR NOT, I'M GONNA RIP IT APART!
UNLIKELY, DEAR LADY... FOR WHAT IS A FACE BUT A MASK?
A MASK BEHIND WHICH MANY THINGS HIDE!
ZAP
FAREWELL, SUPERMAN ...I SHALL FINISH YOU OFF LATER--IN ANOTHER PLACE, IN ANOTHER MANNER...
FOR IN MY 50,000 YEARS OF EXISTENCE, NO ONE HAS ACCUSED VANDAL SAVAGE OF BEING UNIMAGINATIVE.
5

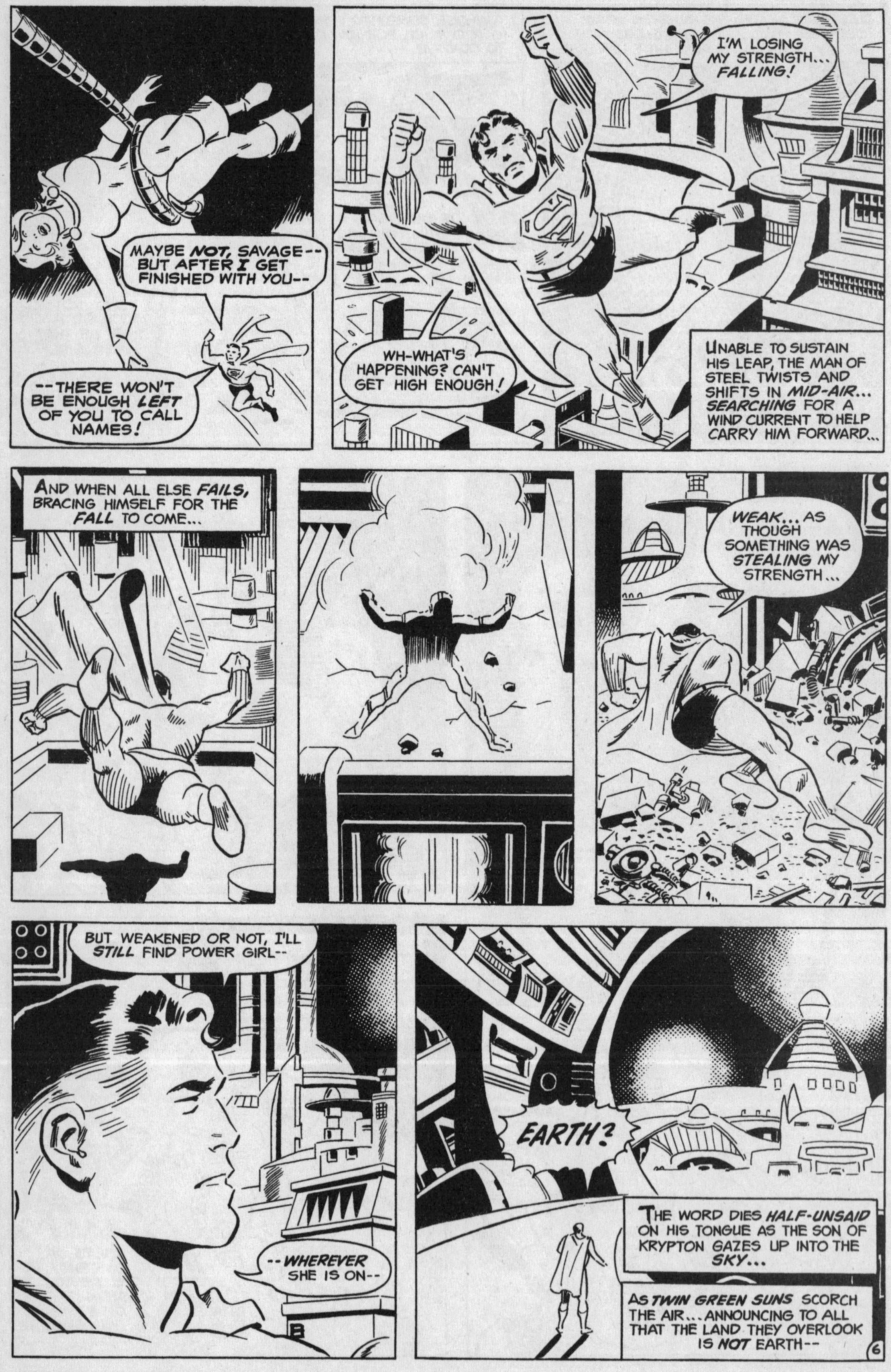
MAYBE NOT, SAVAGE-- BUT AFTER I GET FINISHED WITH YOU--
--THERE WON'T BE ENOUGH LEFT OF YOU TO CALL NAMES!
I'M LOSING MY STRENGTH... FALLING!
WH-WHAT'S HAPPENING? CAN'T GET HIGH ENOUGH!
UNABLE TO SUSTAIN HIS LEAP, THE MAN OF STEEL TWISTS AND SHIFTS IN MID-AIR... SEARCHING FOR A WIND CURRENT TO HELP CARRY HIM FORWARD...
AND WHEN ALL ELSE FAILS, BRACING HIMSELF FOR THE FALL TO COME...
WEAK... AS THOUGH SOMETHING WAS STEALING MY STRENGTH...
BUT WEAKENED OR NOT, I'LL STILL FIND POWER GIRL--
--WHEREVER SHE IS ON--
EARTH?
THE WORD DIES HALF-UNSAID ON HIS TONGUE AS THE SON OF KRYPTON GAZES UP INTO THE SKY...
AS TWIN GREEN SUNS SCORCH THE AIR... ANNOUNCING TO ALL THAT THE LAND THEY OVERLOOK IS NOT EARTH--
6

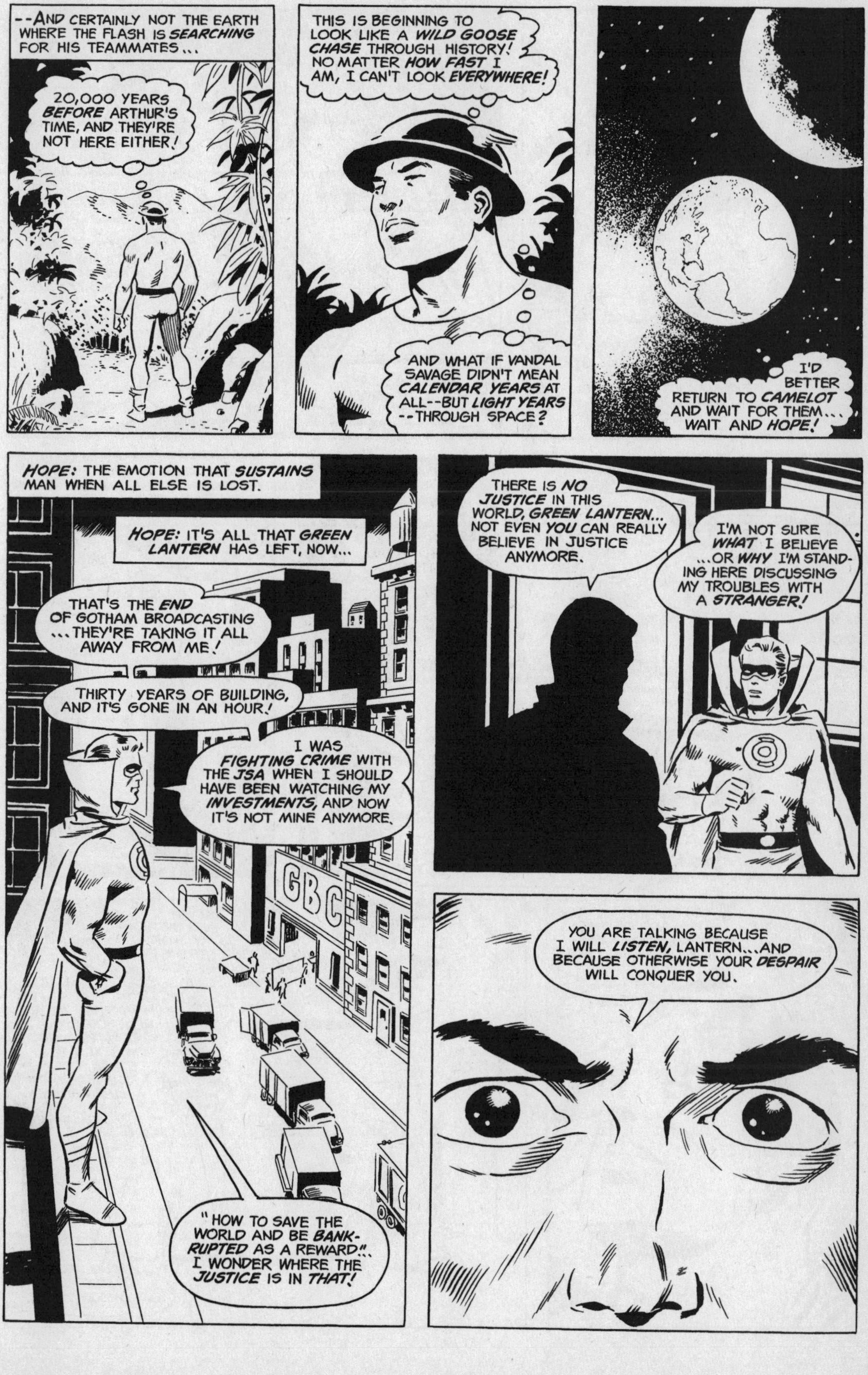
--AND CERTAINLY NOT THE EARTH WHERE THE FLASH IS SEARCHING FOR HIS TEAMMATES...
20,000 YEARS BEFORE ARTHUR'S TIME, AND THEY'RE NOT HERE EITHER!
THIS IS BEGINNING TO LOOK LIKE A WILD GOOSE CHASE THROUGH HISTORY! NO MATTER HOW FAST I AM, I CAN'T LOOK EVERYWHERE!
AND WHAT IF VANDAL SAVAGE DIDN'T MEAN CALENDAR YEARS AT ALL--BUT LIGHT YEARS --THROUGH SPACE?
I'D BETTER RETURN TO CAMELOT AND WAIT FOR THEM... WAIT AND HOPE!
HOPE: THE EMOTION THAT SUSTAINS MAN WHEN ALL ELSE IS LOST.
HOPE: IT'S ALL THAT GREEN LANTERN HAS LEFT, NOW...
THAT'S THE END OF GOTHAM BROADCASTING ...THEY'RE TAKING IT ALL AWAY FROM ME!
THIRTY YEARS OF BUILDING, AND IT'S GONE IN AN HOUR!
I WAS FIGHTING CRIME WITH THE JSA WHEN I SHOULD HAVE BEEN WATCHING MY INVESTMENTS, AND NOW IT'S NOT MINE ANYMORE.
GBC
"HOW TO SAVE THE WORLD AND BE BANKRUPTED AS A REWARD"... I WONDER WHERE THE JUSTICE IS IN THAT!
THERE IS NO JUSTICE IN THIS WORLD, GREEN LANTERN... NOT EVEN YOU CAN REALLY BELIEVE IN JUSTICE ANYMORE.
I'M NOT SURE WHAT I BELIEVE ...OR WHY I'M STANDING HERE DISCUSSING MY TROUBLES WITH A STRANGER!
YOU ARE TALKING BECAUSE I WILL LISTEN, LANTERN...AND BECAUSE OTHERWISE YOUR DESPAIR WILL CONQUER YOU.

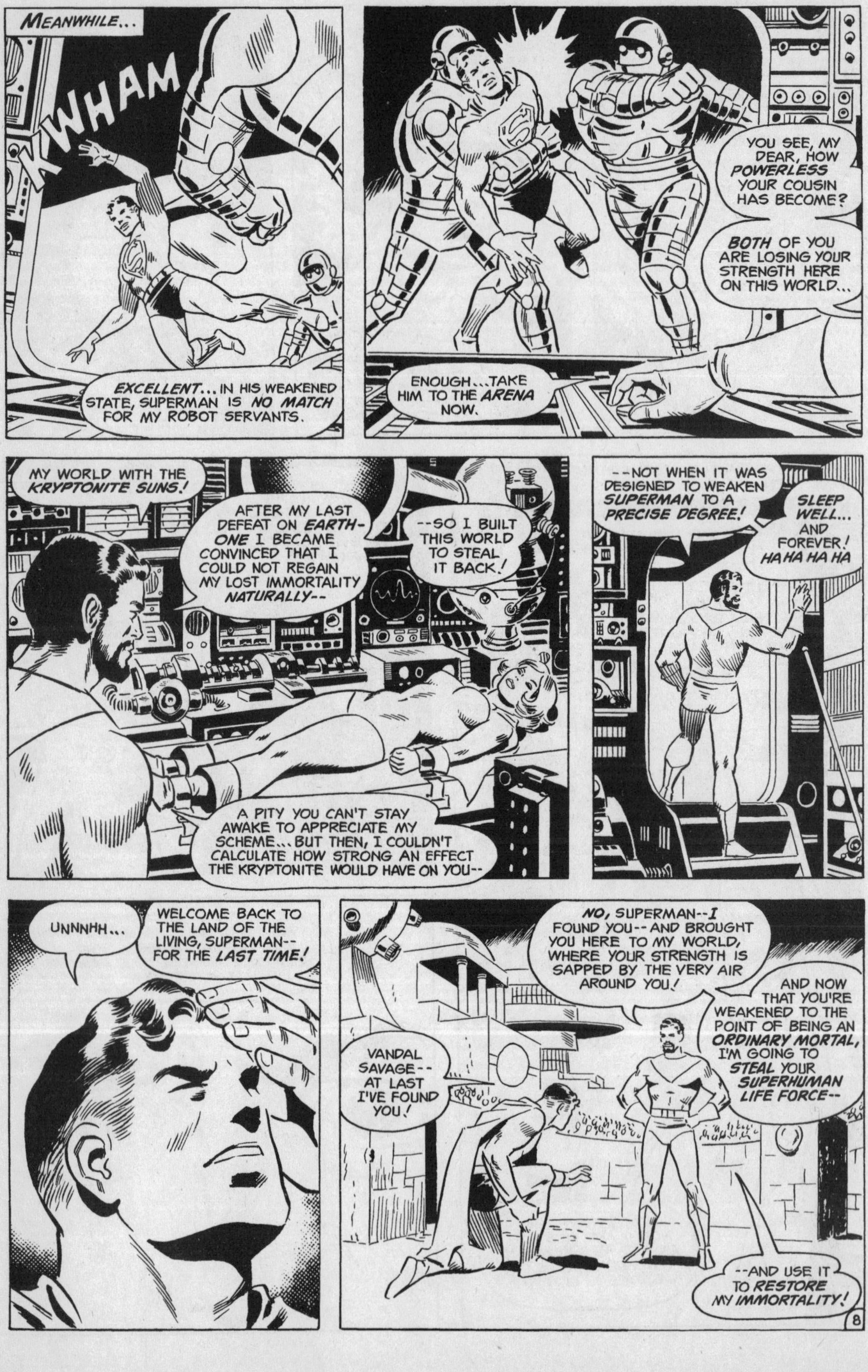
MEANWHILE...
KWHAM
EXCELLENT... IN HIS WEAKENED STATE, SUPERMAN IS NO MATCH FOR MY ROBOT SERVANTS.
YOU SEE, MY DEAR, HOW POWERLESS YOUR COUSIN HAS BECOME?
BOTH OF YOU ARE LOSING YOUR STRENGTH HERE ON THIS WORLD...
ENOUGH... TAKE HIM TO THE ARENA NOW.
MY WORLD WITH THE KRYPTONITE SUNS!
AFTER MY LAST DEFEAT ON EARTH-ONE I BECAME CONVINCED THAT I COULD NOT REGAIN MY LOST IMMORTALITY NATURALLY--
--SO I BUILT THIS WORLD TO STEAL IT BACK!
A PITY YOU CAN'T STAY AWAKE TO APPRECIATE MY SCHEME... BUT THEN, I COULDN'T CALCULATE HOW STRONG AN EFFECT THE KRYPTONITE WOULD HAVE ON YOU--
--NOT WHEN IT WAS DESIGNED TO WEAKEN SUPERMAN TO A PRECISE DEGREE!
SLEEP WELL... AND FOREVER! HA HA HA HA
UNNNHH...
WELCOME BACK TO THE LAND OF THE LIVING, SUPERMAN-- FOR THE LAST TIME!
VANDAL SAVAGE-- AT LAST I'VE FOUND YOU!
NO, SUPERMAN--I FOUND YOU--AND BROUGHT YOU HERE TO MY WORLD, WHERE YOUR STRENGTH IS SAPPED BY THE VERY AIR AROUND YOU!
AND NOW THAT YOU'RE WEAKENED TO THE POINT OF BEING AN ORDINARY MORTAL, I'M GOING TO STEAL YOUR SUPERHUMAN LIFE FORCE--
--AND USE IT TO RESTORE MY IMMORTALITY!
8

BUT FIRST, I'M GOING TO *KILL* YOU--

KCHUNK!

--"*SUPERMAN*"! HA HA HA!

THE ARENA IS STILL, SAVE FOR THE *HEARTBEATS* OF THE *TWO COMBATANTS*-- FOR THEY ARE THE ONLY *LIVING* CREATURES PRESENT.

THE VAST STANDS ARE *FILLED*-- BUT WITH THE *ROBOT CREATIONS* OF VANDAL SAVAGE: METALLIC MONSTERS THAT CANNOT FEEL *PAIN*...

...OR *HOPE*...

...OR THE *COURAGE* OF THE RED-AND-BLUE-GARBED FIGURE WHO FIGHTS ON *DESPERATELY*... WITHOUT THE INCREDIBLE POWER THAT IS HIS *BIRTHRIGHT*!

BUT THERE IS *ONE* WATCHER WHO *CAN* FEEL THESE THINGS... *MERLIN*, THE CAPTIVE WIZARD WHO IS CAPTIVE NO MORE!

WITH VANDAL SAVAGE *CONCENTRATING* ALL HIS STRENGTH ON BATTLING SUPERMAN, HIS HOLD OVER ME HAS BEEN *BROKEN*!

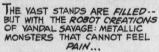

I DO NOT KNOW HOW *LONG* I WILL BE FREE, BUT I MUST ACT WHILE I CAN!

AND SO...

THIS HAND WEAPON IS ALL I COULD FIND FOR YOU, SIR *HAWK-KNIGHT*--

WHAT ABOUT MY *WINGS*, MERLIN?--THEY'D SERVE ME *BETTER* THAN ANY WEAPON!

I FEAR THE WINGS WERE *DESTROYED*--

WATCH OUT, MERLIN--!

PRISONER BEING *FREED*-- UNAUTHORIZED ACTION!

MASTERCOMP ORDERS WIZARD RETURNED TO EARTH'S PAST! --ORDER EXECUTED!

AYEEII!

PRISONER WILL RETURN TO CE--

NOT LIKELY, YOU OVERGROWN TINKERTOY!

9

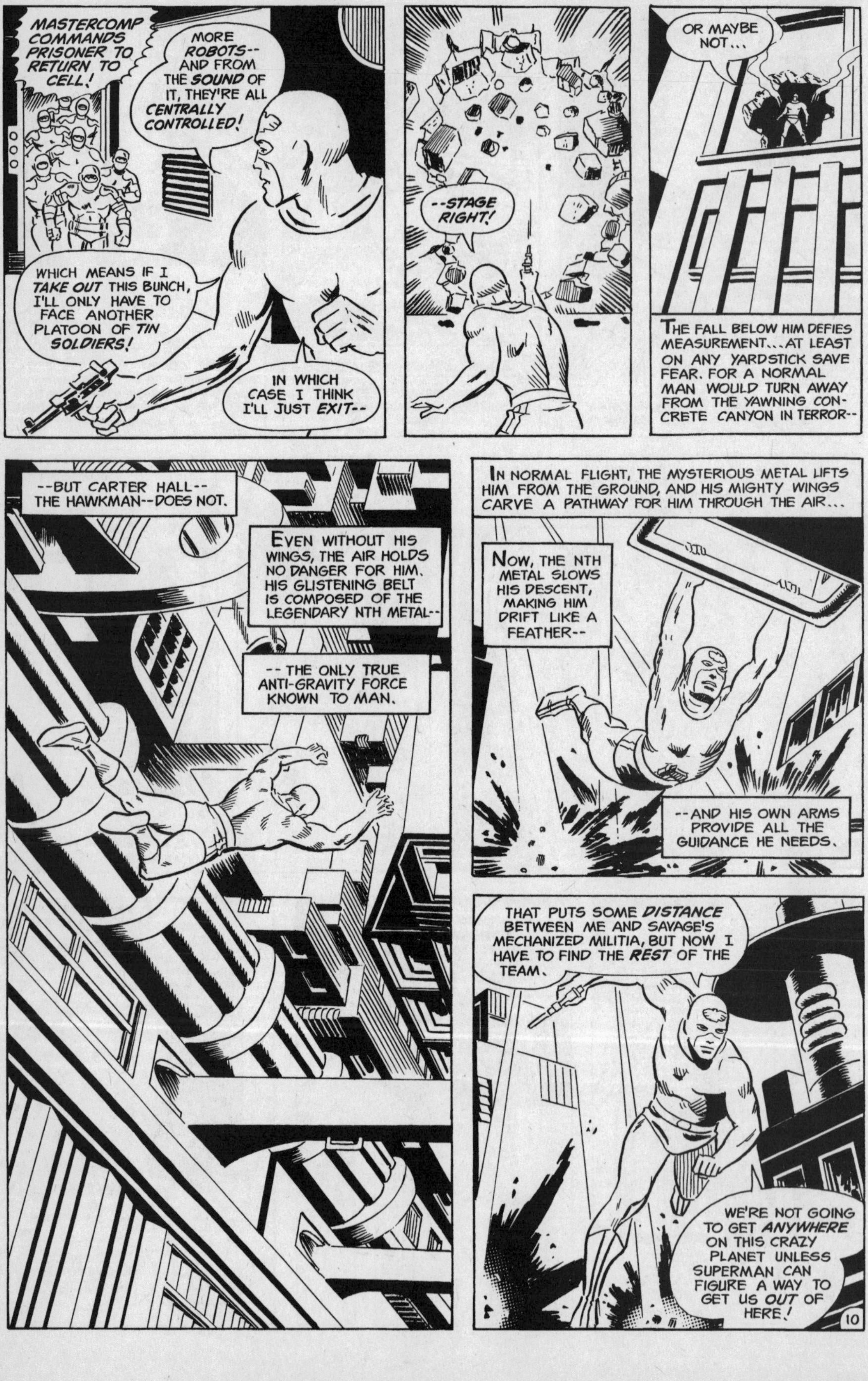
MASTERCOMP COMMANDS PRISONER TO RETURN TO CELL!
MORE ROBOTS-- AND FROM THE SOUND OF IT, THEY'RE ALL CENTRALLY CONTROLLED!
WHICH MEANS IF I TAKE OUT THIS BUNCH, I'LL ONLY HAVE TO FACE ANOTHER PLATOON OF TIN SOLDIERS!
IN WHICH CASE I THINK I'LL JUST EXIT--
--STAGE RIGHT!
OR MAYBE NOT...
THE FALL BELOW HIM DEFIES MEASUREMENT... AT LEAST ON ANY YARDSTICK SAVE FEAR. FOR A NORMAL MAN WOULD TURN AWAY FROM THE YAWNING CONCRETE CANYON IN TERROR--
--BUT CARTER HALL-- THE HAWKMAN--DOES NOT.
EVEN WITHOUT HIS WINGS, THE AIR HOLDS NO DANGER FOR HIM. HIS GLISTENING BELT IS COMPOSED OF THE LEGENDARY NTH METAL--
-- THE ONLY TRUE ANTI-GRAVITY FORCE KNOWN TO MAN.
IN NORMAL FLIGHT, THE MYSTERIOUS METAL LIFTS HIM FROM THE GROUND, AND HIS MIGHTY WINGS CARVE A PATHWAY FOR HIM THROUGH THE AIR...
NOW, THE NTH METAL SLOWS HIS DESCENT, MAKING HIM DRIFT LIKE A FEATHER--
--AND HIS OWN ARMS PROVIDE ALL THE GUIDANCE HE NEEDS.
THAT PUTS SOME DISTANCE BETWEEN ME AND SAVAGE'S MECHANIZED MILITIA, BUT NOW I HAVE TO FIND THE REST OF THE TEAM.
WE'RE NOT GOING TO GET ANYWHERE ON THIS CRAZY PLANET UNLESS SUPERMAN CAN FIGURE A WAY TO GET US OUT OF HERE!
10

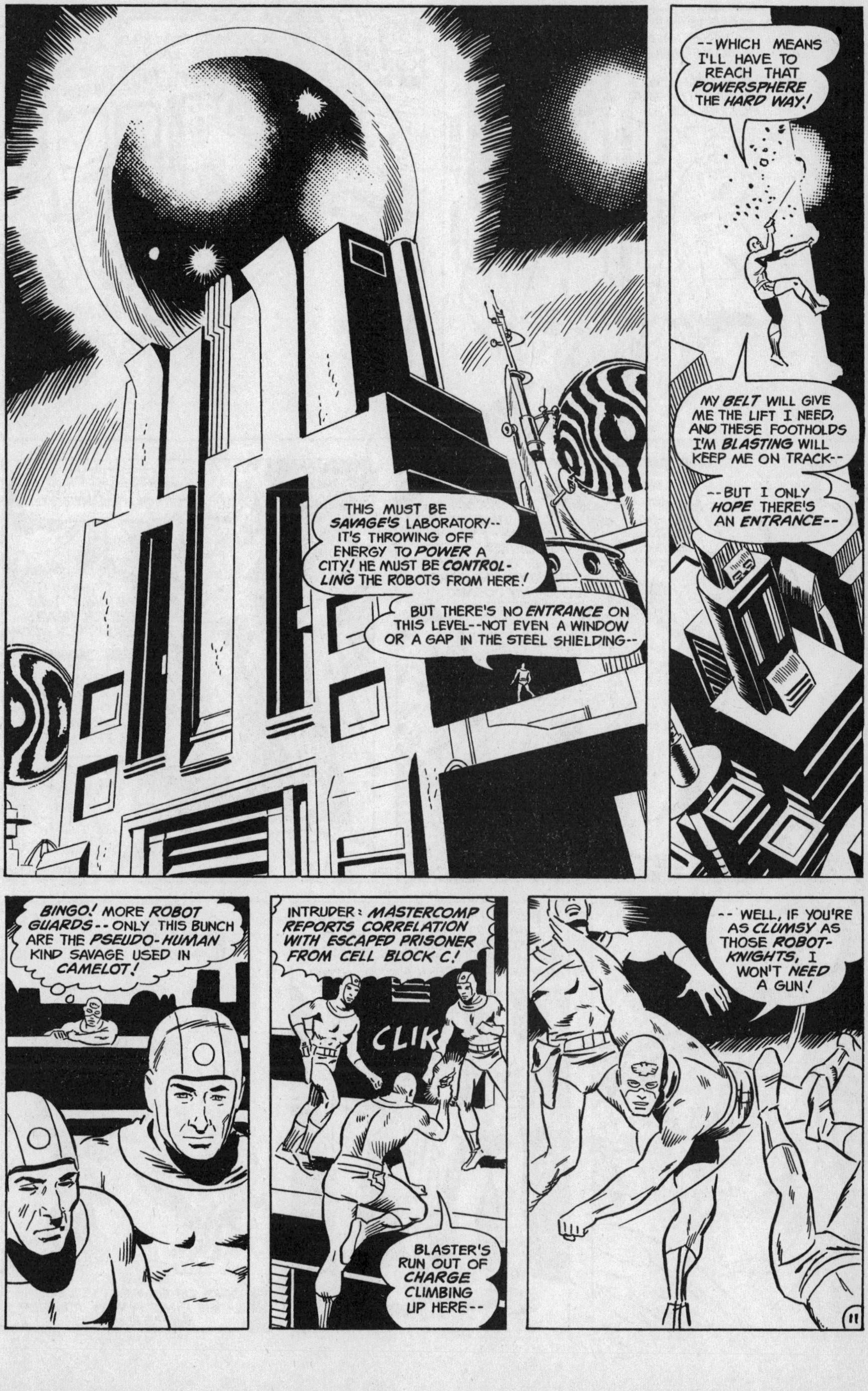
THIS MUST BE SAVAGE'S LABORATORY-- IT'S THROWING OFF ENERGY TO POWER A CITY! HE MUST BE CONTROL-LING THE ROBOTS FROM HERE!
BUT THERE'S NO ENTRANCE ON THIS LEVEL--NOT EVEN A WINDOW OR A GAP IN THE STEEL SHIELDING--
--WHICH MEANS I'LL HAVE TO REACH THAT POWERSPHERE THE HARD WAY!
MY BELT WILL GIVE ME THE LIFT I NEED, AND THESE FOOTHOLDS I'M BLASTING WILL KEEP ME ON TRACK--
--BUT I ONLY HOPE THERE'S AN ENTRANCE--
BINGO! MORE ROBOT GUARDS--ONLY THIS BUNCH ARE THE PSEUDO-HUMAN KIND SAVAGE USED IN CAMELOT!
INTRUDER: MASTERCOMP REPORTS CORRELATION WITH ESCAPED PRISONER FROM CELL BLOCK C!
CLIK
BLASTER'S RUN OUT OF CHARGE CLIMBING UP HERE--
--WELL, IF YOU'RE AS CLUMSY AS THOSE ROBOT-KNIGHTS, I WON'T NEED A GUN!
11

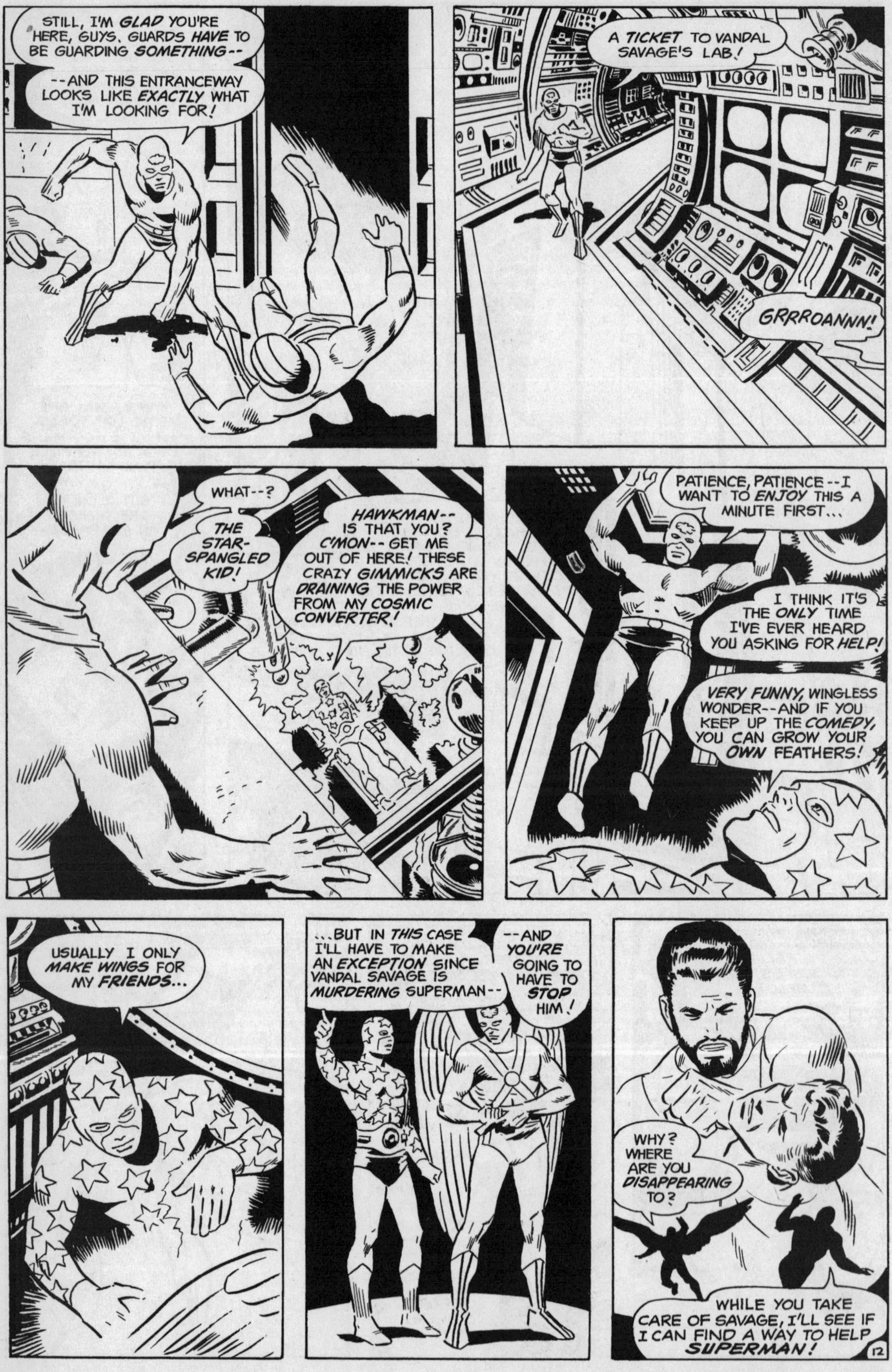
STILL, I'M GLAD YOU'RE HERE, GUYS. GUARDS HAVE TO BE GUARDING SOMETHING--
--AND THIS ENTRANCEWAY LOOKS LIKE EXACTLY WHAT I'M LOOKING FOR!
A TICKET TO VANDAL SAVAGE'S LAB!
GRRROANNN!
WHAT--?
THE STAR-SPANGLED KID!
HAWKMAN--IS THAT YOU? C'MON--GET ME OUT OF HERE! THESE CRAZY GIMMICKS ARE DRAINING THE POWER FROM MY COSMIC CONVERTER!
PATIENCE, PATIENCE--I WANT TO ENJOY THIS A MINUTE FIRST...
I THINK IT'S THE ONLY TIME I'VE EVER HEARD YOU ASKING FOR HELP!
VERY FUNNY, WINGLESS WONDER--AND IF YOU KEEP UP THE COMEDY, YOU CAN GROW YOUR OWN FEATHERS!
USUALLY I ONLY MAKE WINGS FOR MY FRIENDS...
...BUT IN THIS CASE I'LL HAVE TO MAKE AN EXCEPTION SINCE VANDAL SAVAGE IS MURDERING SUPERMAN--
--AND YOU'RE GOING TO HAVE TO STOP HIM!
WHY? WHERE ARE YOU DISAPPEARING TO?
WHILE YOU TAKE CARE OF SAVAGE, I'LL SEE IF I CAN FIND A WAY TO HELP SUPERMAN!
12

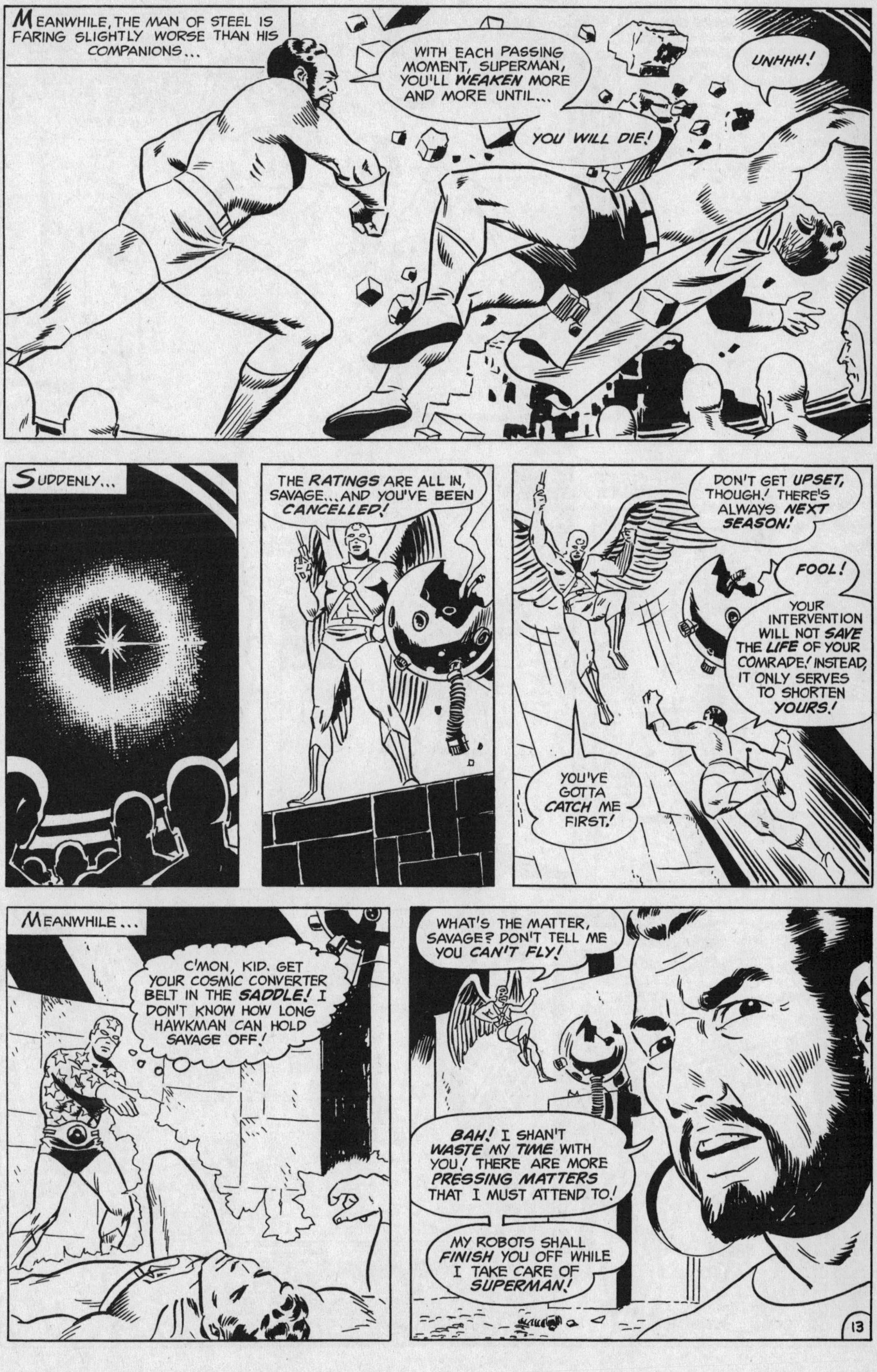
MEANWHILE, THE MAN OF STEEL IS FARING SLIGHTLY WORSE THAN HIS COMPANIONS...
WITH EACH PASSING MOMENT, SUPERMAN, YOU'LL WEAKEN MORE AND MORE UNTIL...
YOU WILL DIE!
UNHHH!
SUDDENLY...
THE RATINGS ARE ALL IN, SAVAGE...AND YOU'VE BEEN CANCELLED!
DON'T GET UPSET, THOUGH! THERE'S ALWAYS NEXT SEASON!
FOOL!
YOUR INTERVENTION WILL NOT SAVE THE LIFE OF YOUR COMRADE! INSTEAD, IT ONLY SERVES TO SHORTEN YOURS!
YOU'VE GOTTA CATCH ME FIRST!
MEANWHILE...
C'MON, KID. GET YOUR COSMIC CONVERTER BELT IN THE SADDLE! I DON'T KNOW HOW LONG HAWKMAN CAN HOLD SAVAGE OFF!
WHAT'S THE MATTER, SAVAGE? DON'T TELL ME YOU CAN'T FLY!
BAH! I SHAN'T WASTE MY TIME WITH YOU! THERE ARE MORE PRESSING MATTERS THAT I MUST ATTEND TO!
MY ROBOTS SHALL FINISH YOU OFF WHILE I TAKE CARE OF SUPERMAN!
13

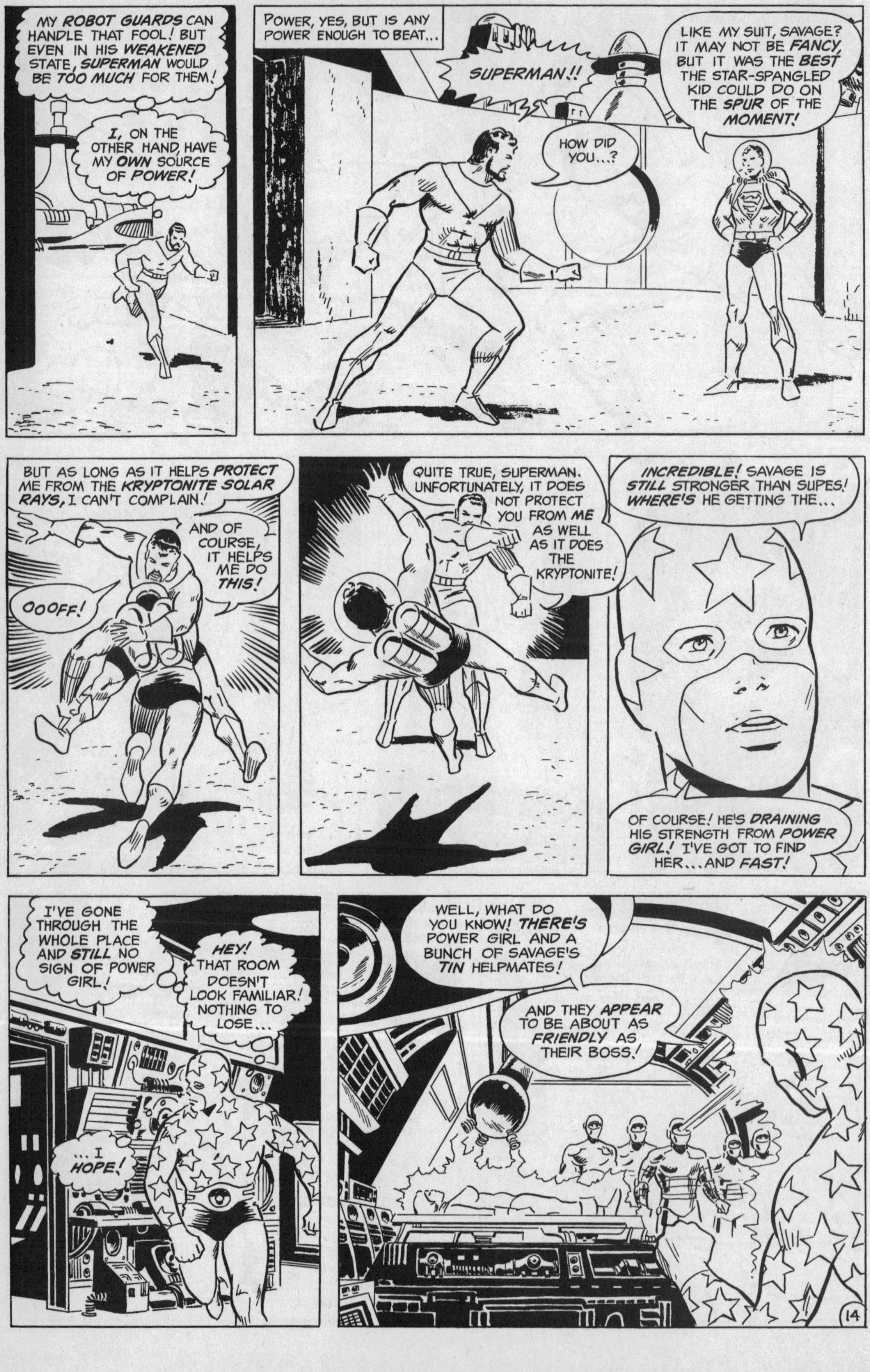
MY ROBOT GUARDS CAN HANDLE THAT FOOL! BUT EVEN IN HIS WEAKENED STATE, SUPERMAN WOULD BE TOO MUCH FOR THEM!
I, ON THE OTHER HAND, HAVE MY OWN SOURCE OF POWER!
POWER, YES, BUT IS ANY POWER ENOUGH TO BEAT...
SUPERMAN!!
LIKE MY SUIT, SAVAGE? IT MAY NOT BE FANCY, BUT IT WAS THE BEST THE STAR-SPANGLED KID COULD DO ON THE SPUR OF THE MOMENT!
HOW DID YOU...?
BUT AS LONG AS IT HELPS PROTECT ME FROM THE KRYPTONITE SOLAR RAYS, I CAN'T COMPLAIN!
AND OF COURSE, IT HELPS ME DO THIS!
OOOFF!
QUITE TRUE, SUPERMAN. UNFORTUNATELY, IT DOES NOT PROTECT YOU FROM ME AS WELL AS IT DOES THE KRYPTONITE!
INCREDIBLE! SAVAGE IS STILL STRONGER THAN SUPES! WHERE'S HE GETTING THE...
OF COURSE! HE'S DRAINING HIS STRENGTH FROM POWER GIRL! I'VE GOT TO FIND HER...AND FAST!
I'VE GONE THROUGH THE WHOLE PLACE AND STILL NO SIGN OF POWER GIRL!
HEY! THAT ROOM DOESN'T LOOK FAMILIAR! NOTHING TO LOSE...
...I HOPE!
WELL, WHAT DO YOU KNOW! THERE'S POWER GIRL AND A BUNCH OF SAVAGE'S TIN HELPMATES!
AND THEY APPEAR TO BE ABOUT AS FRIENDLY AS THEIR BOSS!
14

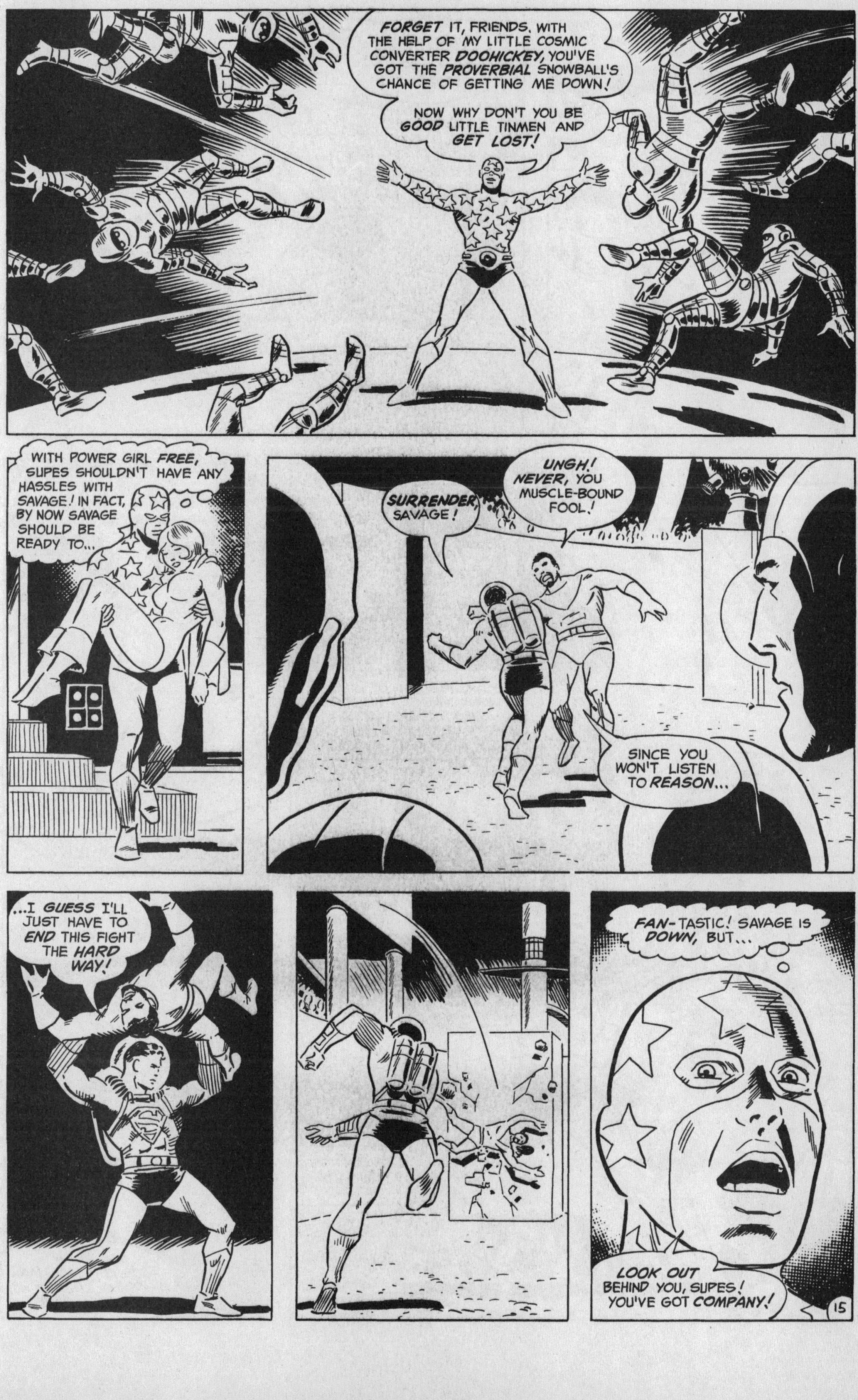
FORGET IT, FRIENDS, WITH THE HELP OF MY LITTLE COSMIC CONVERTER DOOHICKEY, YOU'VE GOT THE PROVERBIAL SNOWBALL'S CHANCE OF GETTING ME DOWN!
NOW WHY DON'T YOU BE GOOD LITTLE TINMEN AND GET LOST!
WITH POWER GIRL FREE, SUPES SHOULDN'T HAVE ANY HASSLES WITH SAVAGE! IN FACT, BY NOW SAVAGE SHOULD BE READY TO...
SURRENDER, SAVAGE!
UNGH! NEVER, YOU MUSCLE-BOUND FOOL!
SINCE YOU WON'T LISTEN TO REASON...
...I GUESS I'LL JUST HAVE TO END THIS FIGHT THE HARD WAY!
FAN-TASTIC! SAVAGE IS DOWN, BUT...
LOOK OUT BEHIND YOU, SUPES! YOU'VE GOT COMPANY!
15

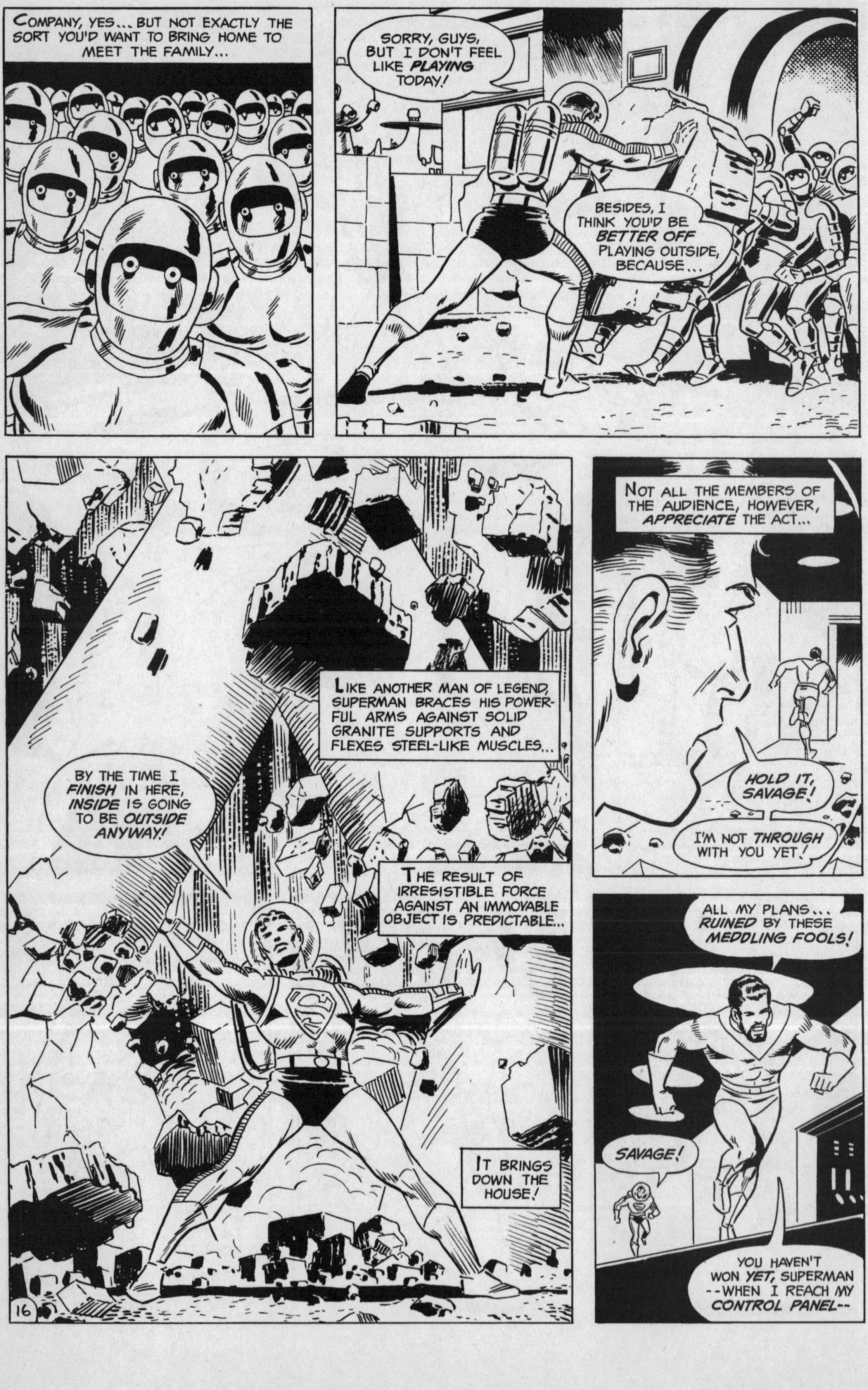
COMPANY, YES... BUT NOT EXACTLY THE SORT YOU'D WANT TO BRING HOME TO MEET THE FAMILY...
SORRY, GUYS, BUT I DON'T FEEL LIKE PLAYING TODAY!
BESIDES, I THINK YOU'D BE BETTER OFF PLAYING OUTSIDE, BECAUSE...
LIKE ANOTHER MAN OF LEGEND, SUPERMAN BRACES HIS POWERFUL ARMS AGAINST SOLID GRANITE SUPPORTS AND FLEXES STEEL-LIKE MUSCLES...
BY THE TIME I FINISH IN HERE, INSIDE IS GOING TO BE OUTSIDE ANYWAY!
THE RESULT OF IRRESISTIBLE FORCE AGAINST AN IMMOVABLE OBJECT IS PREDICTABLE...
IT BRINGS DOWN THE HOUSE!
16
NOT ALL THE MEMBERS OF THE AUDIENCE, HOWEVER, APPRECIATE THE ACT...
HOLD IT, SAVAGE!
I'M NOT THROUGH WITH YOU YET!
ALL MY PLANS... RUINED BY THESE MEDDLING FOOLS!
SAVAGE!
YOU HAVEN'T WON YET, SUPERMAN --WHEN I REACH MY CONTROL PANEL--

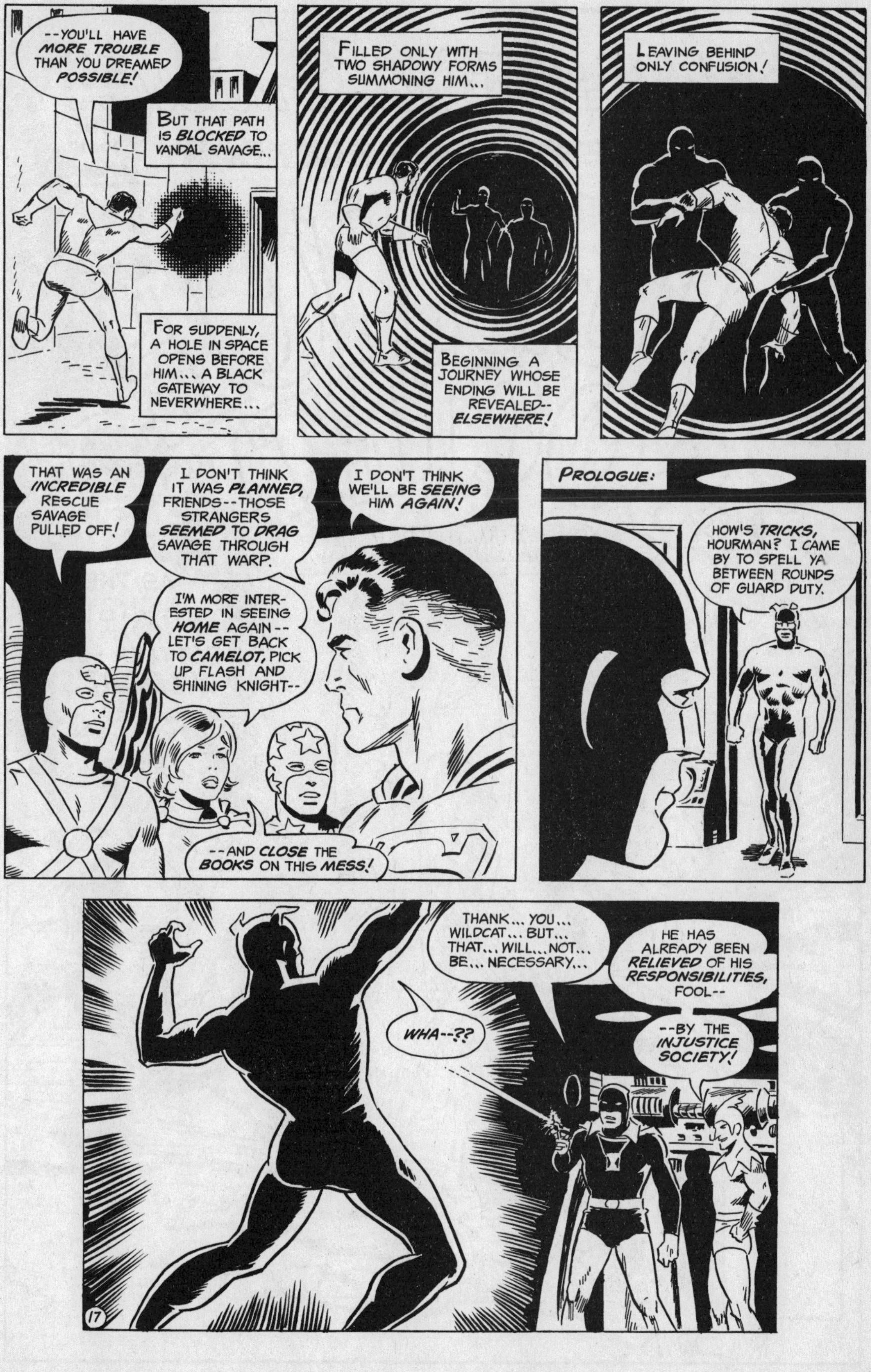
--YOU'LL HAVE MORE TROUBLE THAN YOU DREAMED POSSIBLE!
BUT THAT PATH IS BLOCKED TO VANDAL SAVAGE...
FOR SUDDENLY, A HOLE IN SPACE OPENS BEFORE HIM... A BLACK GATEWAY TO NEVERWHERE...
FILLED ONLY WITH TWO SHADOWY FORMS SUMMONING HIM...
BEGINNING A JOURNEY WHOSE ENDING WILL BE REVEALED--ELSEWHERE!
LEAVING BEHIND ONLY CONFUSION!
THAT WAS AN INCREDIBLE RESCUE SAVAGE PULLED OFF!
I DON'T THINK IT WAS PLANNED, FRIENDS--THOSE STRANGERS SEEMED TO DRAG SAVAGE THROUGH THAT WARP.
I DON'T THINK WE'LL BE SEEING HIM AGAIN!
I'M MORE INTERESTED IN SEEING HOME AGAIN--LET'S GET BACK TO CAMELOT, PICK UP FLASH AND SHINING KNIGHT--
--AND CLOSE THE BOOKS ON THIS MESS!
PROLOGUE:
HOW'S TRICKS, HOURMAN? I CAME BY TO SPELL YA BETWEEN ROUNDS OF GUARD DUTY.
THANK... YOU... WILDCAT... BUT... THAT... WILL... NOT... BE... NECESSARY...
HE HAS ALREADY BEEN RELIEVED OF HIS RESPONSIBILITIES, FOOL--
WHA--??
--BY THE INJUSTICE SOCIETY!
17

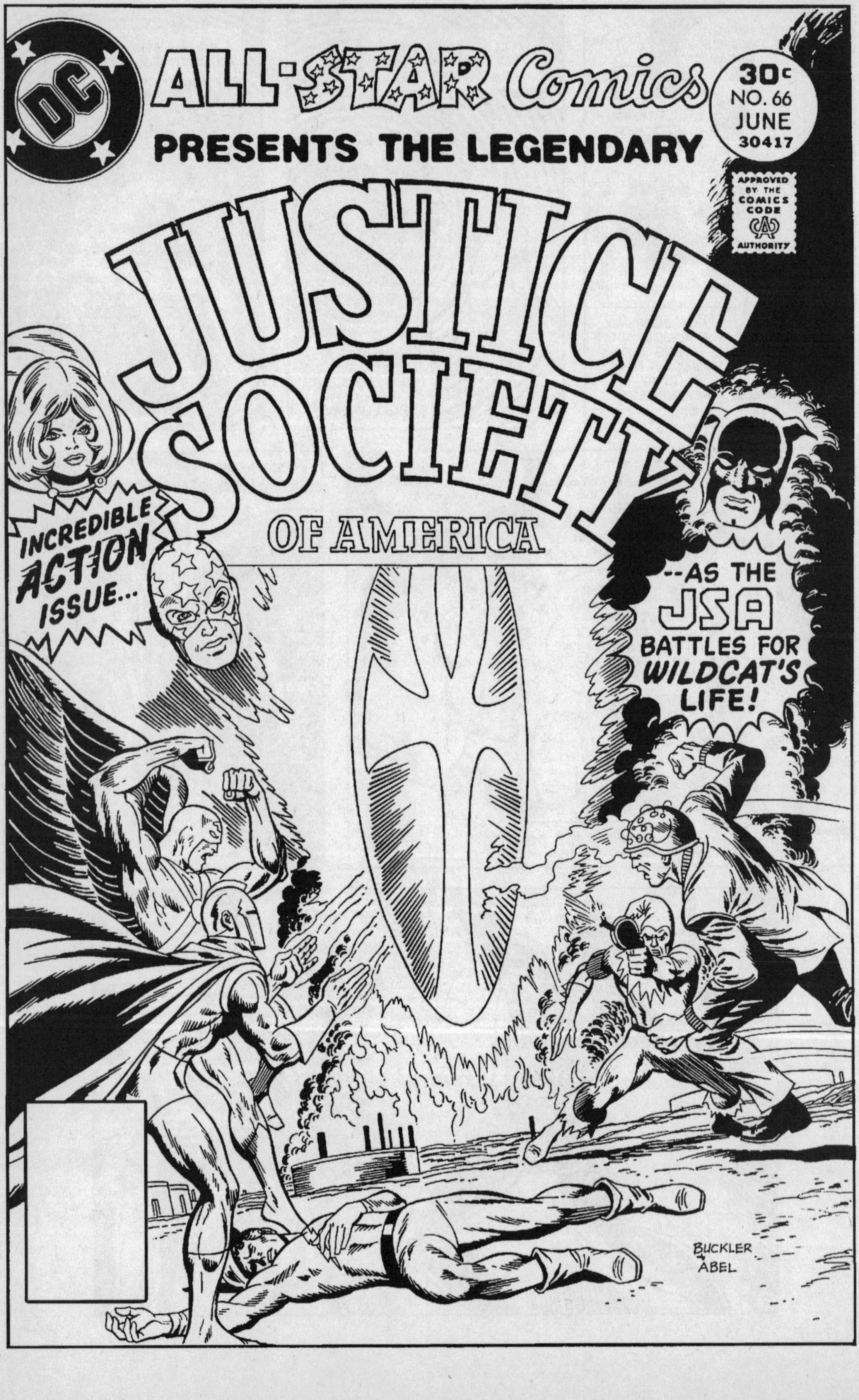
ALL-STAR Comics
PRESENTS THE LEGENDARY
30¢
NO. 66
JUNE
30417
APPROVED BY THE COMICS CODE AUTHORITY
JUSTICE SOCIETY
OF AMERICA
INCREDIBLE ACTION ISSUE...
--AS THE JSA BATTLES FOR WILDCAT'S LIFE!
BUCKLER + ABEL

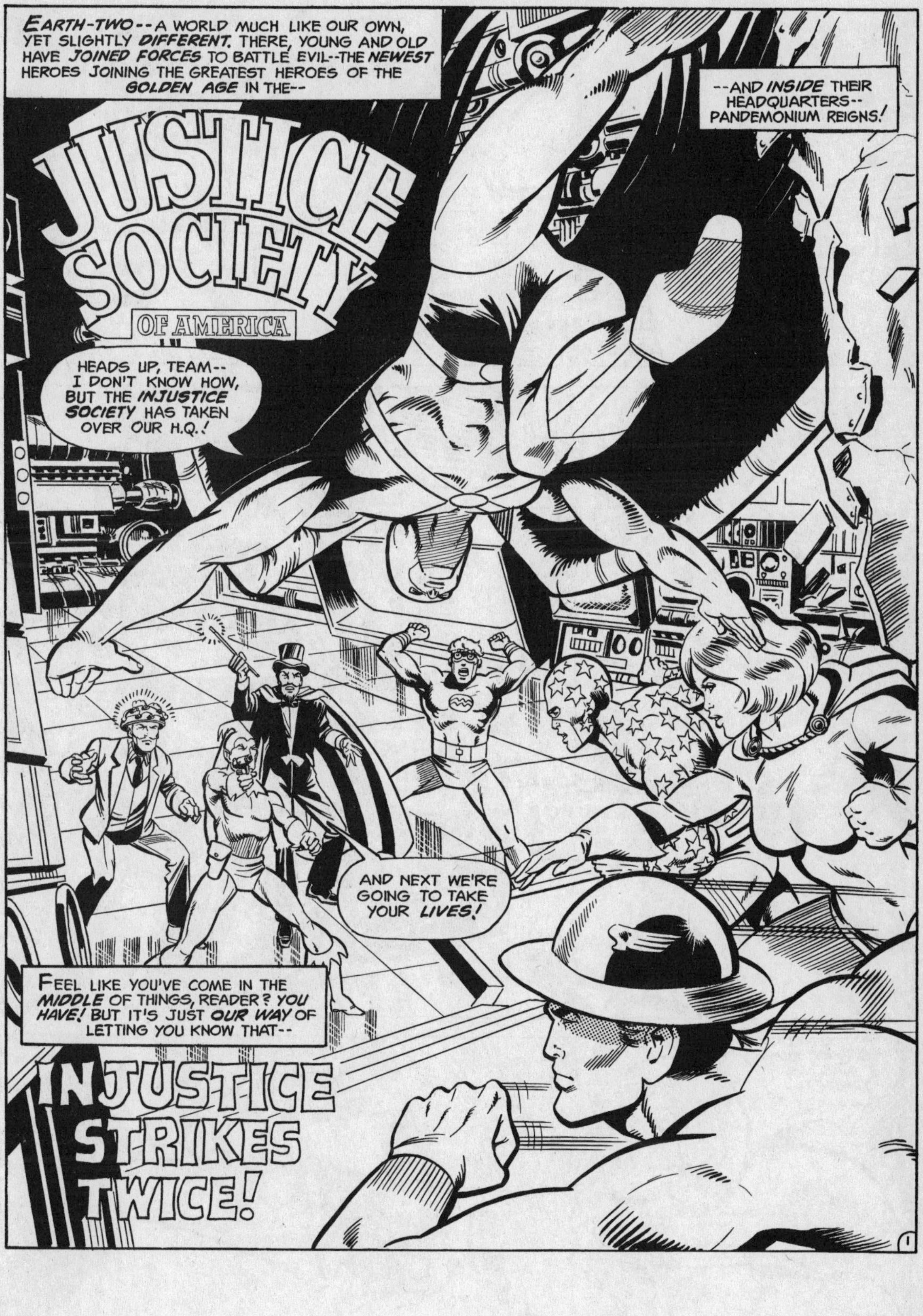
EARTH-TWO--A WORLD MUCH LIKE OUR OWN, YET SLIGHTLY DIFFERENT. THERE, YOUNG AND OLD HAVE JOINED FORCES TO BATTLE EVIL--THE NEWEST HEROES JOINING THE GREATEST HEROES OF THE GOLDEN AGE IN THE--
--AND INSIDE THEIR HEADQUARTERS--PANDEMONIUM REIGNS!
JUSTICE SOCIETY OF AMERICA
HEADS UP, TEAM-- I DON'T KNOW HOW, BUT THE INJUSTICE SOCIETY HAS TAKEN OVER OUR H.Q.!
AND NEXT WE'RE GOING TO TAKE YOUR LIVES!
FEEL LIKE YOU'VE COME IN THE MIDDLE OF THINGS, READER? YOU HAVE! BUT IT'S JUST OUR WAY OF LETTING YOU KNOW THAT--
INJUSTICE STRIKES TWICE!
1

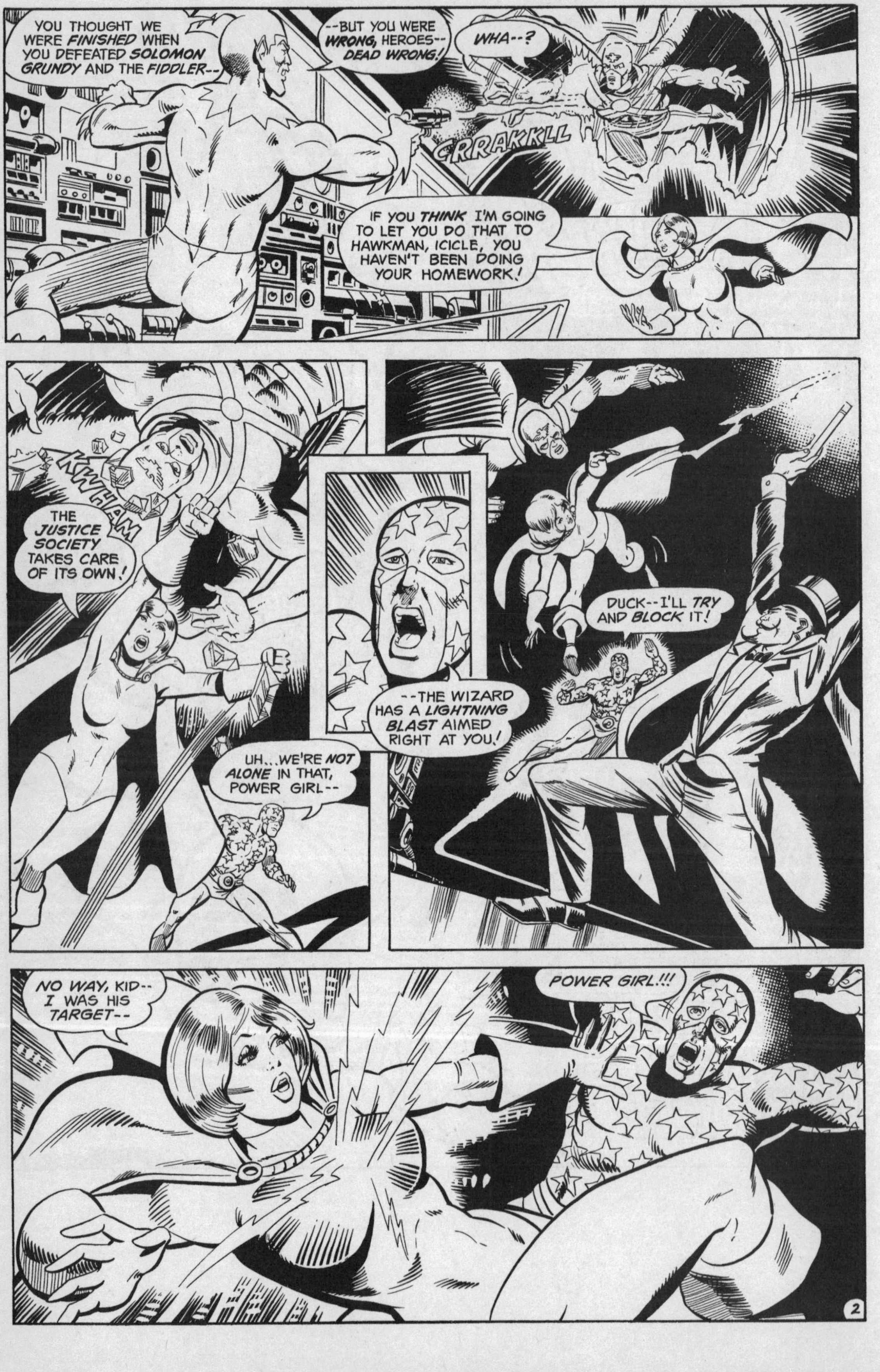
YOU THOUGHT WE WERE *FINISHED* WHEN YOU DEFEATED *SOLOMON GRUNDY* AND THE *FIDDLER*--
--BUT YOU WERE *WRONG,* HEROES-- *DEAD WRONG!*
WHA--?
CRRAKKLL
IF YOU *THINK* I'M GOING TO LET YOU DO THAT TO HAWKMAN, ICICLE, YOU HAVEN'T BEEN DOING YOUR HOMEWORK!
KWHAM
THE *JUSTICE SOCIETY* TAKES CARE OF ITS OWN!
UH...WE'RE *NOT ALONE* IN THAT, POWER GIRL--
--THE WIZARD HAS A *LIGHTNING BLAST* AIMED RIGHT AT YOU!
DUCK--I'LL *TRY* AND *BLOCK* IT!
NO WAY, KID-- I WAS HIS TARGET--
POWER GIRL!!!
2

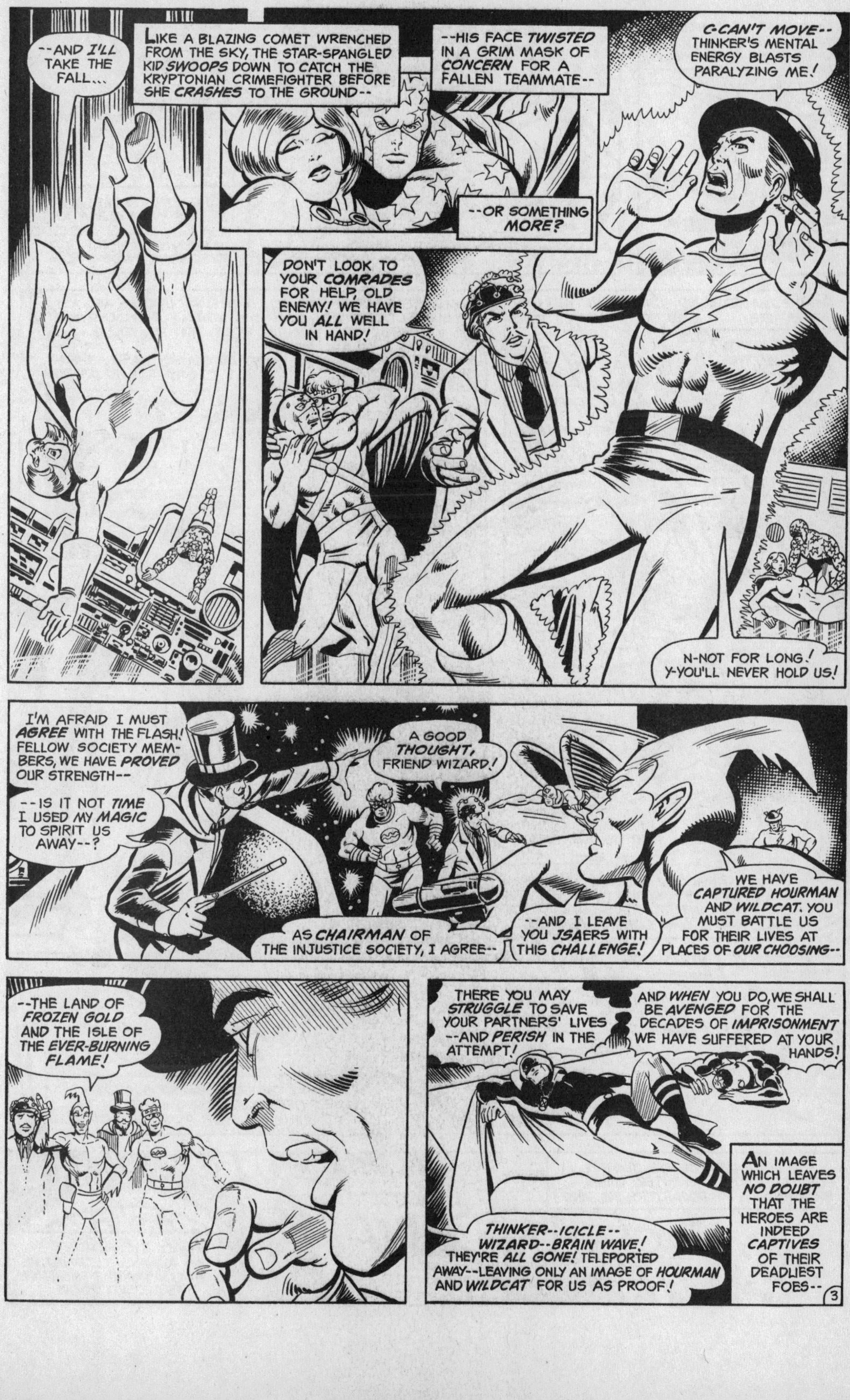
--AND I'LL TAKE THE FALL...
LIKE A BLAZING COMET WRENCHED FROM THE SKY, THE STAR-SPANGLED KID SWOOPS DOWN TO CATCH THE KRYPTONIAN CRIMEFIGHTER BEFORE SHE CRASHES TO THE GROUND--
--HIS FACE TWISTED IN A GRIM MASK OF CONCERN FOR A FALLEN TEAMMATE--
--OR SOMETHING MORE?
C-CAN'T MOVE-- THINKER'S MENTAL ENERGY BLASTS PARALYZING ME!
DON'T LOOK TO YOUR COMRADES FOR HELP, OLD ENEMY! WE HAVE YOU ALL WELL IN HAND!
N-NOT FOR LONG! Y-YOU'LL NEVER HOLD US!
I'M AFRAID I MUST AGREE WITH THE FLASH! FELLOW SOCIETY MEMBERS, WE HAVE PROVED OUR STRENGTH--
--IS IT NOT TIME I USED MY MAGIC TO SPIRIT US AWAY--?
A GOOD THOUGHT, FRIEND WIZARD!
AS CHAIRMAN OF THE INJUSTICE SOCIETY, I AGREE--
--AND I LEAVE YOU JSAERS WITH THIS CHALLENGE!
WE HAVE CAPTURED HOURMAN AND WILDCAT. YOU MUST BATTLE US FOR THEIR LIVES AT PLACES OF OUR CHOOSING--
--THE LAND OF FROZEN GOLD AND THE ISLE OF THE EVER-BURNING FLAME!
THERE YOU MAY STRUGGLE TO SAVE YOUR PARTNERS' LIVES --AND PERISH IN THE ATTEMPT!
AND WHEN YOU DO, WE SHALL BE AVENGED FOR THE DECADES OF IMPRISONMENT WE HAVE SUFFERED AT YOUR HANDS!
THINKER--ICICLE--WIZARD--BRAIN WAVE! THEY'RE ALL GONE! TELEPORTED AWAY--LEAVING ONLY AN IMAGE OF HOURMAN AND WILDCAT FOR US AS PROOF!
AN IMAGE WHICH LEAVES NO DOUBT THAT THE HEROES ARE INDEED CAPTIVES OF THEIR DEADLIEST FOES--
3

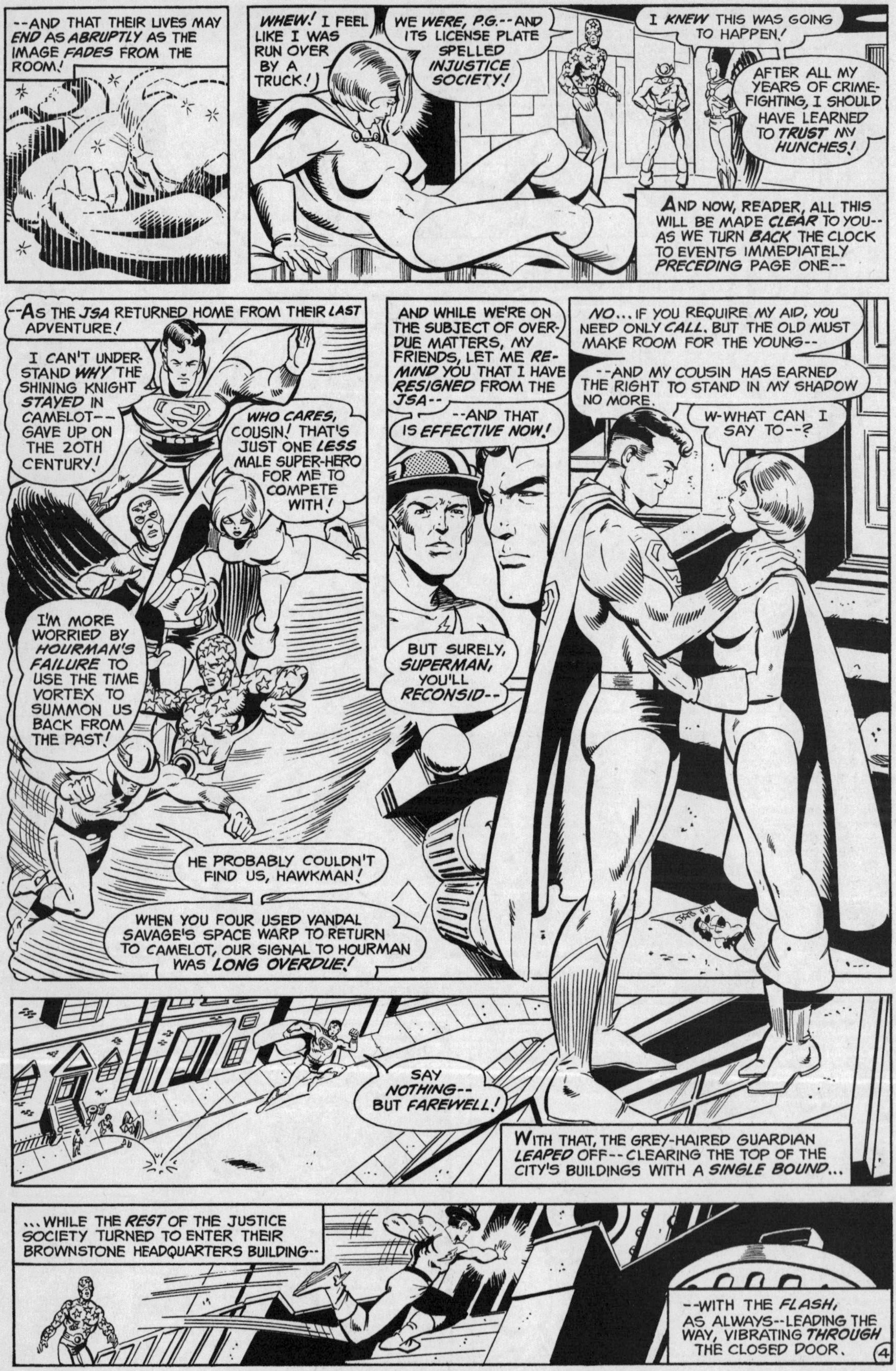
--AND THAT THEIR LIVES MAY END AS ABRUPTLY AS THE IMAGE FADES FROM THE ROOM!
WHEW! I FEEL LIKE I WAS RUN OVER BY A TRUCK!
WE WERE, P.G.--AND ITS LICENSE PLATE SPELLED INJUSTICE SOCIETY!
I KNEW THIS WAS GOING TO HAPPEN!
AFTER ALL MY YEARS OF CRIME-FIGHTING, I SHOULD HAVE LEARNED TO TRUST MY HUNCHES!
AND NOW, READER, ALL THIS WILL BE MADE CLEAR TO YOU--AS WE TURN BACK THE CLOCK TO EVENTS IMMEDIATELY PRECEDING PAGE ONE--
--AS THE JSA RETURNED HOME FROM THEIR LAST ADVENTURE!
I CAN'T UNDERSTAND WHY THE SHINING KNIGHT STAYED IN CAMELOT--GAVE UP ON THE 20TH CENTURY!
WHO CARES, COUSIN! THAT'S JUST ONE LESS MALE SUPER-HERO FOR ME TO COMPETE WITH!
I'M MORE WORRIED BY HOURMAN'S FAILURE TO USE THE TIME VORTEX TO SUMMON US BACK FROM THE PAST!
HE PROBABLY COULDN'T FIND US, HAWKMAN!
WHEN YOU FOUR USED VANDAL SAVAGE'S SPACE WARP TO RETURN TO CAMELOT, OUR SIGNAL TO HOURMAN WAS LONG OVERDUE!
AND WHILE WE'RE ON THE SUBJECT OF OVERDUE MATTERS, MY FRIENDS, LET ME REMIND YOU THAT I HAVE RESIGNED FROM THE JSA--
--AND THAT IS EFFECTIVE NOW!
BUT SURELY, SUPERMAN, YOU'LL RECONSID--
NO... IF YOU REQUIRE MY AID, YOU NEED ONLY CALL. BUT THE OLD MUST MAKE ROOM FOR THE YOUNG--
--AND MY COUSIN HAS EARNED THE RIGHT TO STAND IN MY SHADOW NO MORE.
W-WHAT CAN I SAY TO--?
SAY NOTHING--BUT FAREWELL!
WITH THAT, THE GREY-HAIRED GUARDIAN LEAPED OFF--CLEARING THE TOP OF THE CITY'S BUILDINGS WITH A SINGLE BOUND...
...WHILE THE REST OF THE JUSTICE SOCIETY TURNED TO ENTER THEIR BROWNSTONE HEADQUARTERS BUILDING--
--WITH THE FLASH, AS ALWAYS--LEADING THE WAY, VIBRATING THROUGH THE CLOSED DOOR.
4

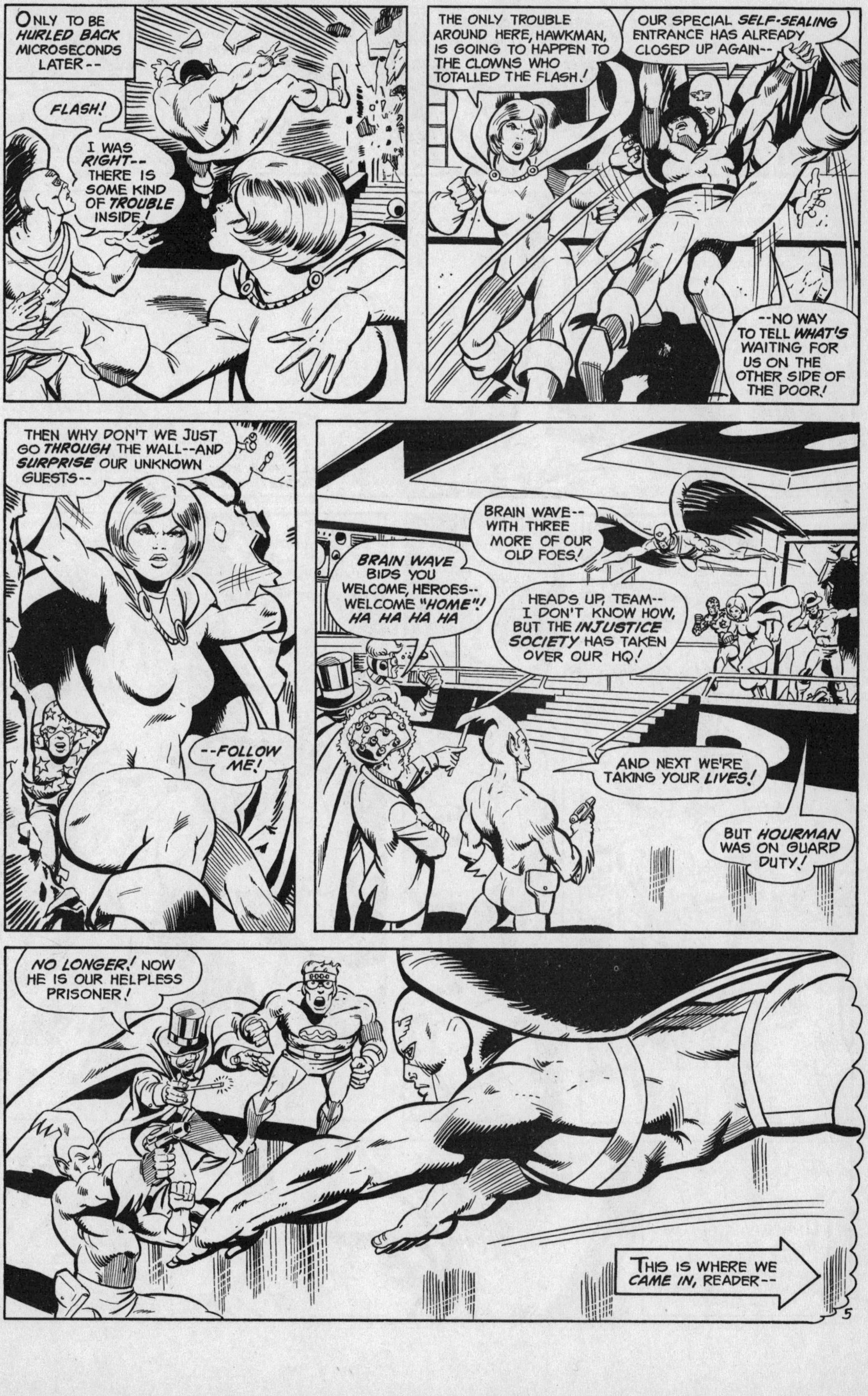
ONLY TO BE HURLED BACK MICROSECONDS LATER--
FLASH!
I WAS RIGHT--THERE IS SOME KIND OF TROUBLE INSIDE!
THE ONLY TROUBLE AROUND HERE, HAWKMAN, IS GOING TO HAPPEN TO THE CLOWNS WHO TOTALLED THE FLASH!
OUR SPECIAL SELF-SEALING ENTRANCE HAS ALREADY CLOSED UP AGAIN--
--NO WAY TO TELL WHAT'S WAITING FOR US ON THE OTHER SIDE OF THE DOOR!
THEN WHY DON'T WE JUST GO THROUGH THE WALL--AND SURPRISE OUR UNKNOWN GUESTS--
--FOLLOW ME!
BRAIN WAVE--WITH THREE MORE OF OUR OLD FOES!
BRAIN WAVE BIDS YOU WELCOME, HEROES--WELCOME "HOME"! HA HA HA HA
HEADS UP, TEAM--I DON'T KNOW HOW, BUT THE INJUSTICE SOCIETY HAS TAKEN OVER OUR HQ!
AND NEXT WE'RE TAKING YOUR LIVES!
BUT HOURMAN WAS ON GUARD DUTY!
NO LONGER! NOW HE IS OUR HELPLESS PRISONER!
THIS IS WHERE WE CAME IN, READER--
5

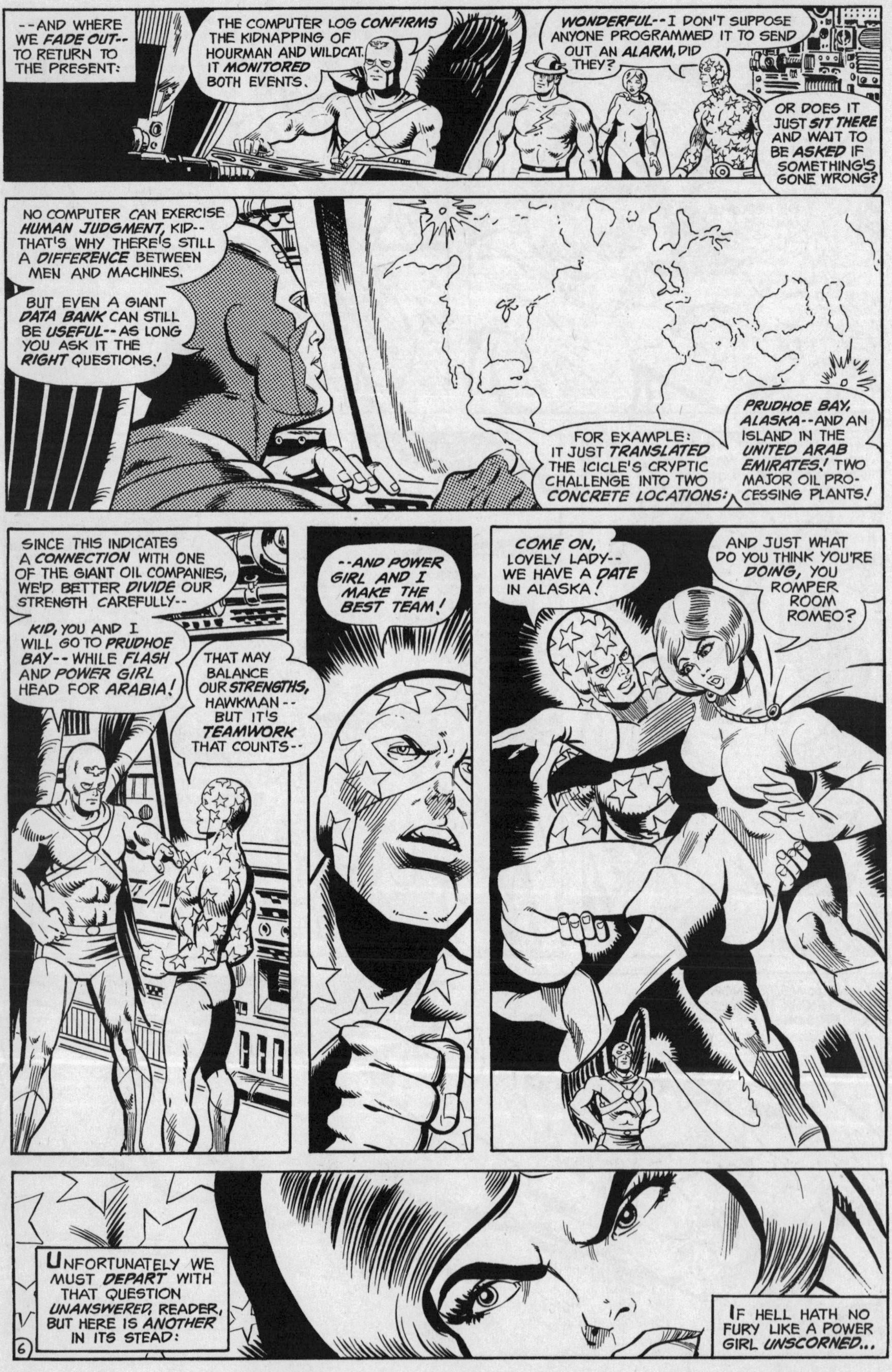
--AND WHERE WE FADE OUT-- TO RETURN TO THE PRESENT:
THE COMPUTER LOG CONFIRMS THE KIDNAPPING OF HOURMAN AND WILDCAT. IT MONITORED BOTH EVENTS.
WONDERFUL--I DON'T SUPPOSE ANYONE PROGRAMMED IT TO SEND OUT AN ALARM, DID THEY?
OR DOES IT JUST SIT THERE AND WAIT TO BE ASKED IF SOMETHING'S GONE WRONG?
NO COMPUTER CAN EXERCISE HUMAN JUDGMENT, KID-- THAT'S WHY THERE'S STILL A DIFFERENCE BETWEEN MEN AND MACHINES.
BUT EVEN A GIANT DATA BANK CAN STILL BE USEFUL--AS LONG YOU ASK IT THE RIGHT QUESTIONS!
FOR EXAMPLE: IT JUST TRANSLATED THE ICICLE'S CRYPTIC CHALLENGE INTO TWO CONCRETE LOCATIONS:
PRUDHOE BAY, ALASKA--AND AN ISLAND IN THE UNITED ARAB EMIRATES! TWO MAJOR OIL PROCESSING PLANTS!
SINCE THIS INDICATES A CONNECTION WITH ONE OF THE GIANT OIL COMPANIES, WE'D BETTER DIVIDE OUR STRENGTH CAREFULLY--
KID, YOU AND I WILL GO TO PRUDHOE BAY--WHILE FLASH AND POWER GIRL HEAD FOR ARABIA!
THAT MAY BALANCE OUR STRENGTHS, HAWKMAN-- BUT IT'S TEAMWORK THAT COUNTS--
--AND POWER GIRL AND I MAKE THE BEST TEAM!
COME ON, LOVELY LADY-- WE HAVE A DATE IN ALASKA!
AND JUST WHAT DO YOU THINK YOU'RE DOING, YOU ROMPER ROOM ROMEO?
UNFORTUNATELY WE MUST DEPART WITH THAT QUESTION UNANSWERED, READER, BUT HERE IS ANOTHER IN ITS STEAD:
IF HELL HATH NO FURY LIKE A POWER GIRL UNSCORNED...
6

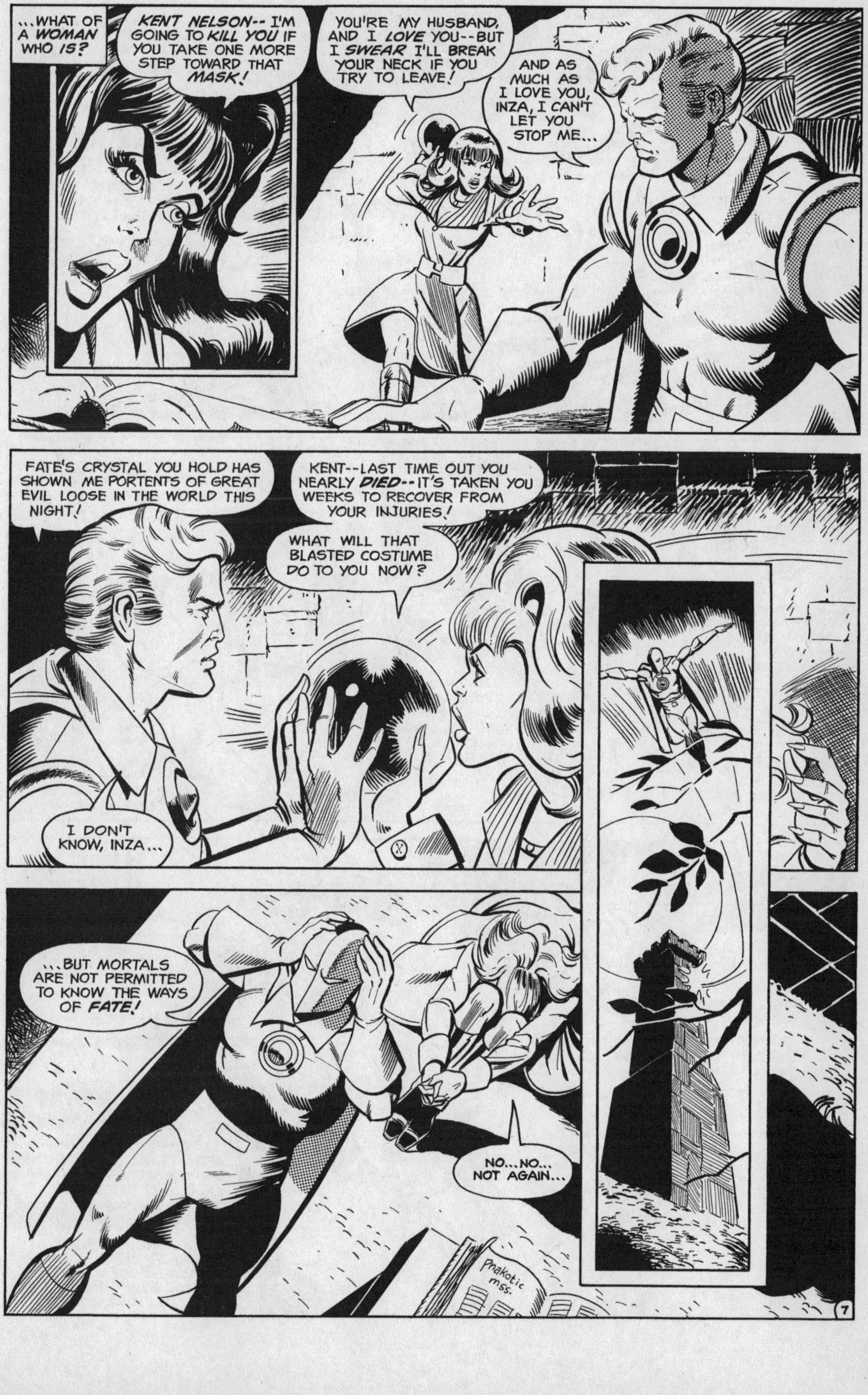
...WHAT OF A WOMAN WHO IS?
KENT NELSON-- I'M GOING TO KILL YOU IF YOU TAKE ONE MORE STEP TOWARD THAT MASK!
YOU'RE MY HUSBAND, AND I LOVE YOU--BUT I SWEAR I'LL BREAK YOUR NECK IF YOU TRY TO LEAVE!
AND AS MUCH AS I LOVE YOU, INZA, I CAN'T LET YOU STOP ME...
FATE'S CRYSTAL YOU HOLD HAS SHOWN ME PORTENTS OF GREAT EVIL LOOSE IN THE WORLD THIS NIGHT!
KENT--LAST TIME OUT YOU NEARLY DIED--IT'S TAKEN YOU WEEKS TO RECOVER FROM YOUR INJURIES!
WHAT WILL THAT BLASTED COSTUME DO TO YOU NOW?
I DON'T KNOW, INZA...
...BUT MORTALS ARE NOT PERMITTED TO KNOW THE WAYS OF FATE!
NO...NO... NOT AGAIN...
Phakotic mss.
7

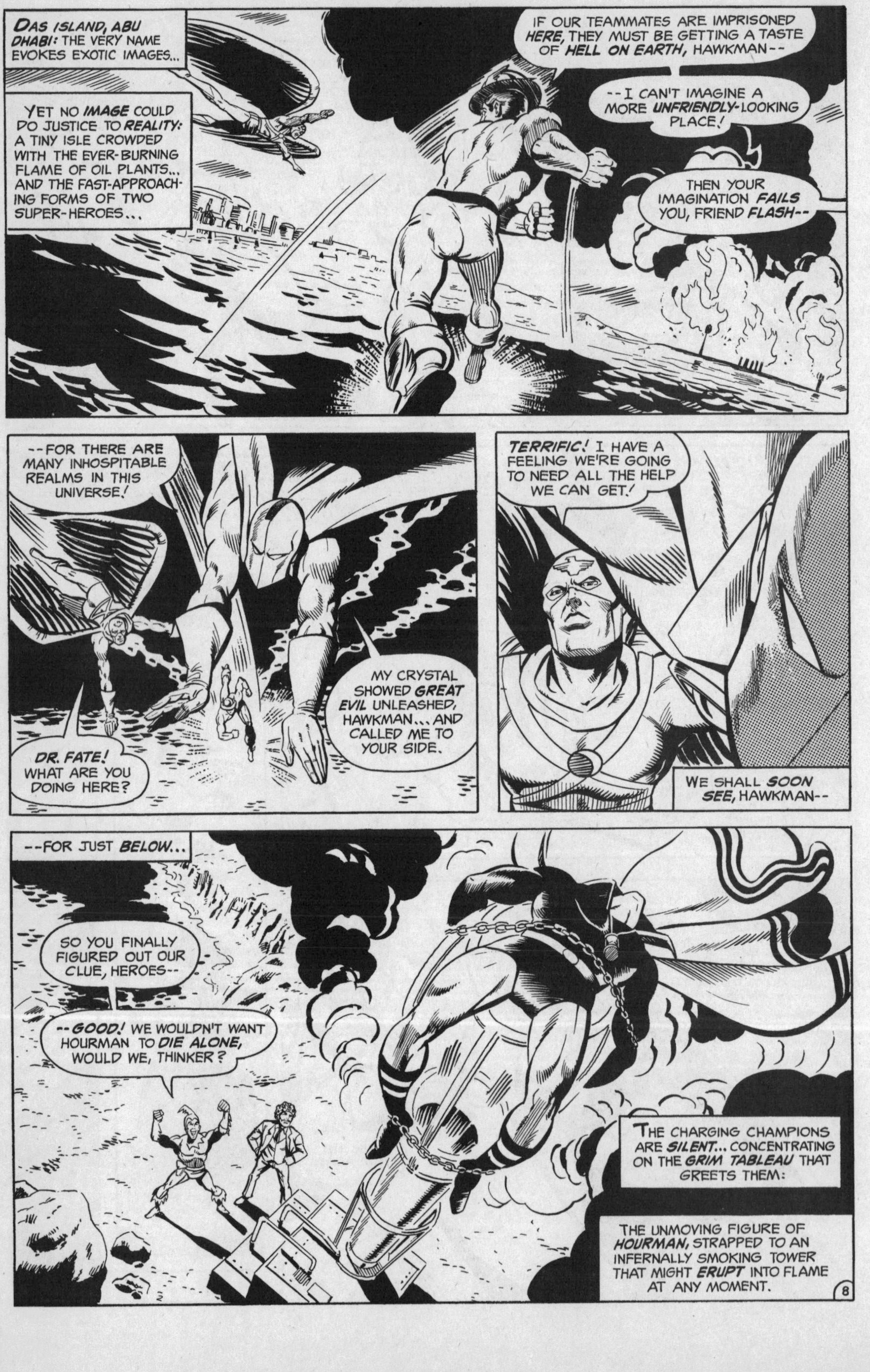
DAS ISLAND, ABU DHABI: THE VERY NAME EVOKES EXOTIC IMAGES...
YET NO IMAGE COULD DO JUSTICE TO REALITY: A TINY ISLE CROWDED WITH THE EVER-BURNING FLAME OF OIL PLANTS... AND THE FAST-APPROACHING FORMS OF TWO SUPER-HEROES...
IF OUR TEAMMATES ARE IMPRISONED HERE, THEY MUST BE GETTING A TASTE OF HELL ON EARTH, HAWKMAN--
--I CAN'T IMAGINE A MORE UNFRIENDLY-LOOKING PLACE!
THEN YOUR IMAGINATION FAILS YOU, FRIEND FLASH--
--FOR THERE ARE MANY INHOSPITABLE REALMS IN THIS UNIVERSE!
DR. FATE! WHAT ARE YOU DOING HERE?
MY CRYSTAL SHOWED GREAT EVIL UNLEASHED, HAWKMAN... AND CALLED ME TO YOUR SIDE.
TERRIFIC! I HAVE A FEELING WE'RE GOING TO NEED ALL THE HELP WE CAN GET!
WE SHALL SOON SEE, HAWKMAN--
--FOR JUST BELOW...
SO YOU FINALLY FIGURED OUT OUR CLUE, HEROES--
--GOOD! WE WOULDN'T WANT HOURMAN TO DIE ALONE, WOULD WE, THINKER?
THE CHARGING CHAMPIONS ARE SILENT... CONCENTRATING ON THE GRIM TABLEAU THAT GREETS THEM:
THE UNMOVING FIGURE OF HOURMAN, STRAPPED TO AN INFERNALLY SMOKING TOWER THAT MIGHT ERUPT INTO FLAME AT ANY MOMENT.
8

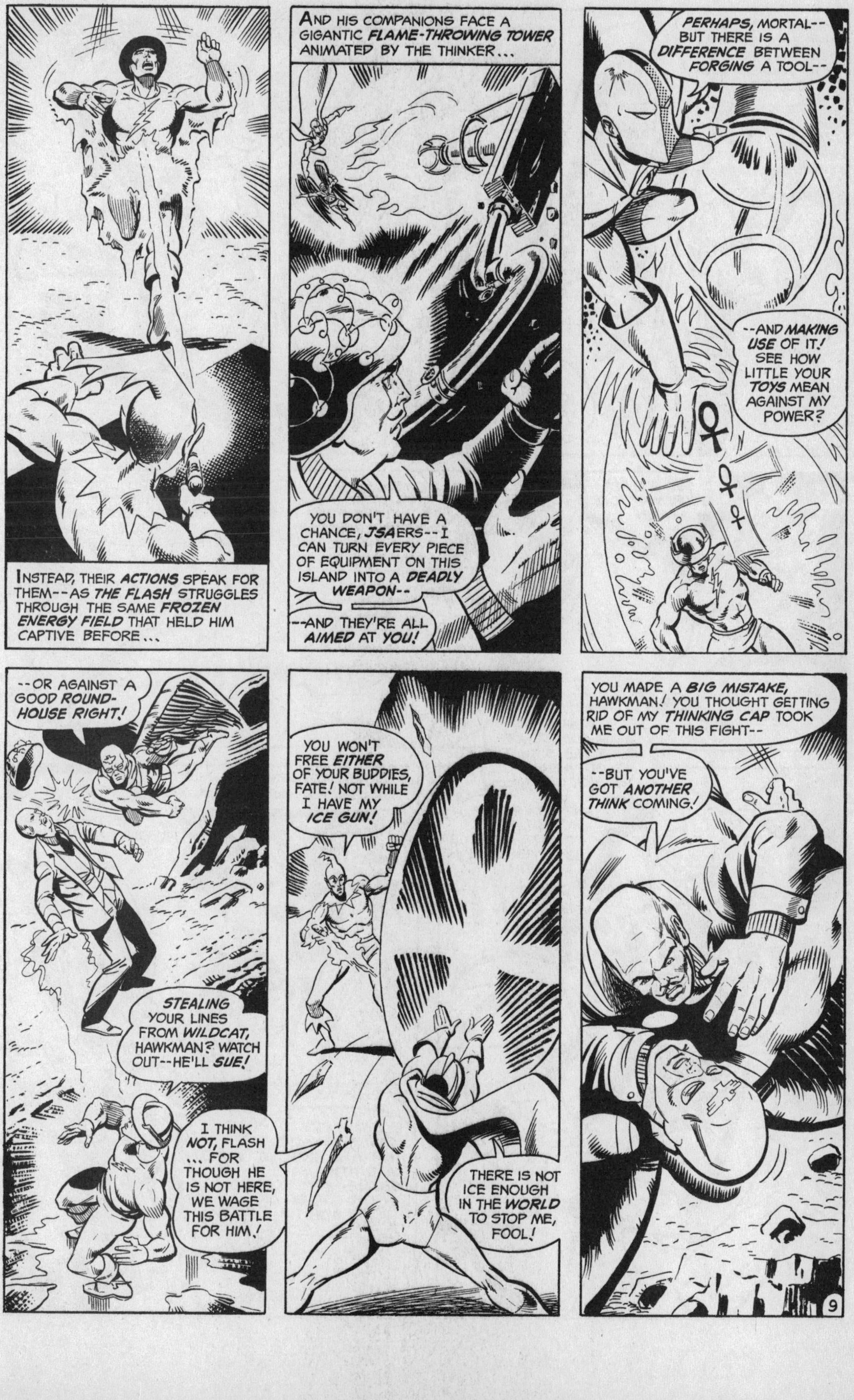

INSTEAD, THEIR ACTIONS SPEAK FOR THEM--AS THE FLASH STRUGGLES THROUGH THE SAME FROZEN ENERGY FIELD THAT HELD HIM CAPTIVE BEFORE...
AND HIS COMPANIONS FACE A GIGANTIC FLAME-THROWING TOWER ANIMATED BY THE THINKER...
YOU DON'T HAVE A CHANCE, JSAERS--I CAN TURN EVERY PIECE OF EQUIPMENT ON THIS ISLAND INTO A DEADLY WEAPON--
--AND THEY'RE ALL AIMED AT YOU!
PERHAPS, MORTAL--BUT THERE IS A DIFFERENCE BETWEEN FORGING A TOOL--
--AND MAKING USE OF IT! SEE HOW LITTLE YOUR TOYS MEAN AGAINST MY POWER?
--OR AGAINST A GOOD ROUND-HOUSE RIGHT!
STEALING YOUR LINES FROM WILDCAT, HAWKMAN? WATCH OUT--HE'LL SUE!
I THINK NOT, FLASH ...FOR THOUGH HE IS NOT HERE, WE WAGE THIS BATTLE FOR HIM!
YOU WON'T FREE EITHER OF YOUR BUDDIES, FATE! NOT WHILE I HAVE MY ICE GUN!
THERE IS NOT ICE ENOUGH IN THE WORLD TO STOP ME, FOOL!
YOU MADE A BIG MISTAKE, HAWKMAN! YOU THOUGHT GETTING RID OF MY THINKING CAP TOOK ME OUT OF THIS FIGHT--
--BUT YOU'VE GOT ANOTHER THINK COMING!
9

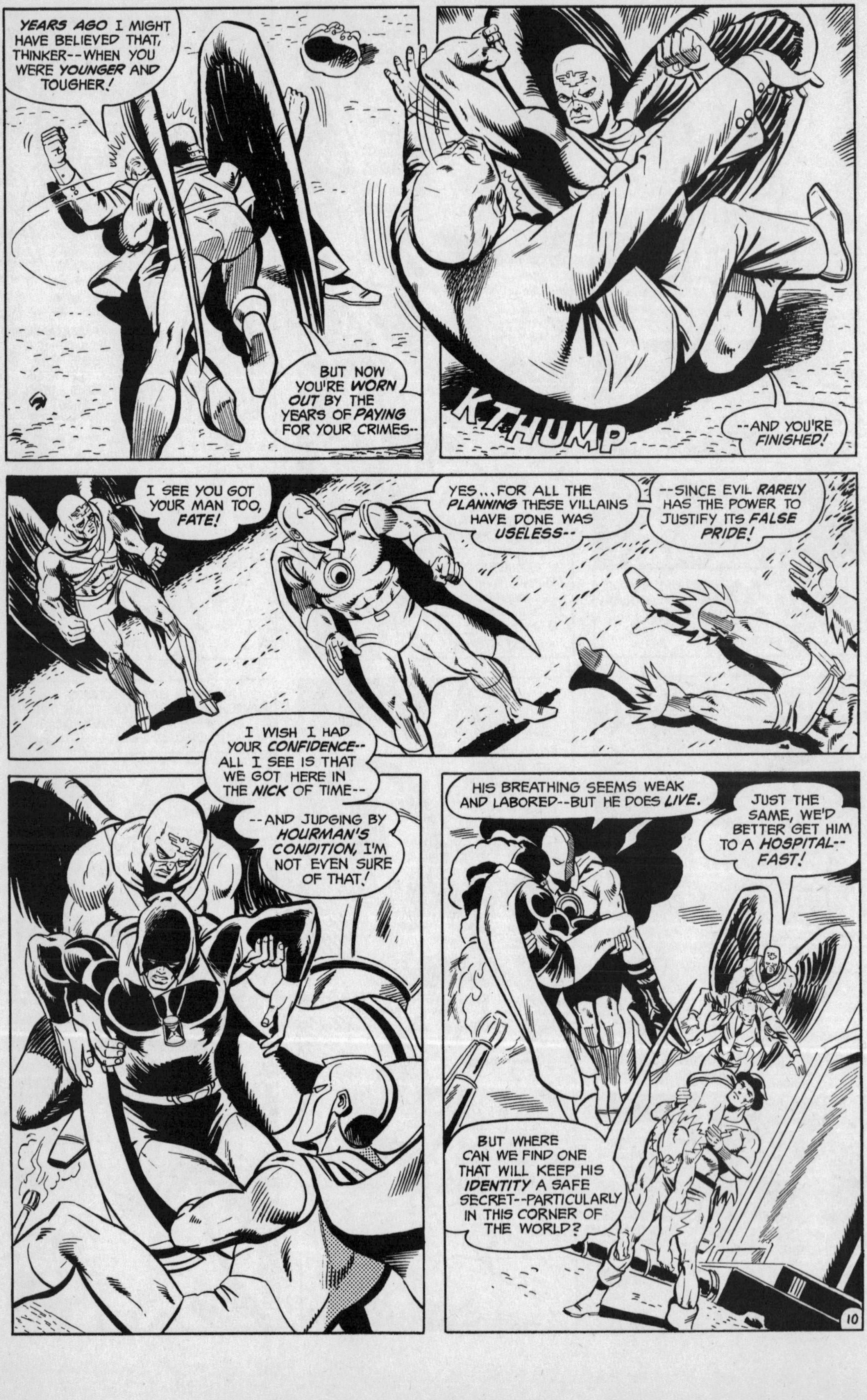
YEARS AGO I MIGHT HAVE BELIEVED THAT, THINKER--WHEN YOU WERE YOUNGER AND TOUGHER!
BUT NOW YOU'RE WORN OUT BY THE YEARS OF PAYING FOR YOUR CRIMES--
KTHUMP
--AND YOU'RE FINISHED!
I SEE YOU GOT YOUR MAN TOO, FATE!
YES...FOR ALL THE PLANNING THESE VILLAINS HAVE DONE WAS USELESS--
--SINCE EVIL RARELY HAS THE POWER TO JUSTIFY ITS FALSE PRIDE!
I WISH I HAD YOUR CONFIDENCE--ALL I SEE IS THAT WE GOT HERE IN THE NICK OF TIME--
--AND JUDGING BY HOURMAN'S CONDITION, I'M NOT EVEN SURE OF THAT!
HIS BREATHING SEEMS WEAK AND LABORED--BUT HE DOES LIVE.
JUST THE SAME, WE'D BETTER GET HIM TO A HOSPITAL--FAST!
BUT WHERE CAN WE FIND ONE THAT WILL KEEP HIS IDENTITY A SAFE SECRET--PARTICULARLY IN THIS CORNER OF THE WORLD?
10

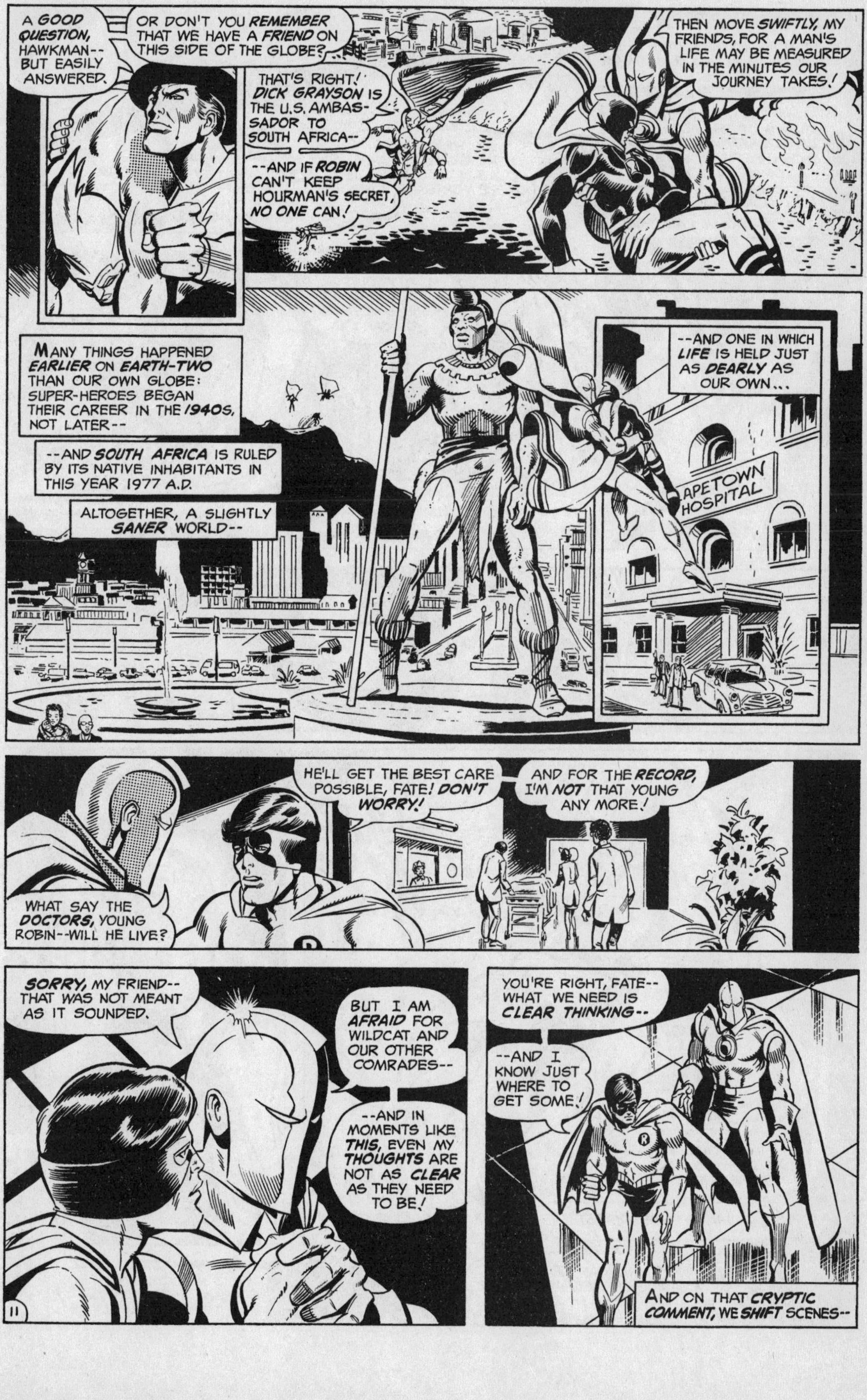
A GOOD QUESTION, HAWKMAN-- BUT EASILY ANSWERED.
OR DON'T YOU REMEMBER THAT WE HAVE A FRIEND ON THIS SIDE OF THE GLOBE?
THAT'S RIGHT! DICK GRAYSON IS THE U.S. AMBASSADOR TO SOUTH AFRICA--
--AND IF ROBIN CAN'T KEEP HOURMAN'S SECRET, NO ONE CAN!
THEN MOVE SWIFTLY, MY FRIENDS, FOR A MAN'S LIFE MAY BE MEASURED IN THE MINUTES OUR JOURNEY TAKES!
MANY THINGS HAPPENED EARLIER ON EARTH-TWO THAN OUR OWN GLOBE: SUPER-HEROES BEGAN THEIR CAREER IN THE 1940S, NOT LATER--
--AND SOUTH AFRICA IS RULED BY ITS NATIVE INHABITANTS IN THIS YEAR 1977 A.D.
ALTOGETHER, A SLIGHTLY SANER WORLD--
--AND ONE IN WHICH LIFE IS HELD JUST AS DEARLY AS OUR OWN...
CAPETOWN HOSPITAL
WHAT SAY THE DOCTORS, YOUNG ROBIN--WILL HE LIVE?
HE'LL GET THE BEST CARE POSSIBLE, FATE! DON'T WORRY!
AND FOR THE RECORD, I'M NOT THAT YOUNG ANY MORE!
SORRY, MY FRIEND-- THAT WAS NOT MEANT AS IT SOUNDED.
BUT I AM AFRAID FOR WILDCAT AND OUR OTHER COMRADES--
--AND IN MOMENTS LIKE THIS, EVEN MY THOUGHTS ARE NOT AS CLEAR AS THEY NEED TO BE!
11
YOU'RE RIGHT, FATE-- WHAT WE NEED IS CLEAR THINKING--
--AND I KNOW JUST WHERE TO GET SOME!
AND ON THAT CRYPTIC COMMENT, WE SHIFT SCENES--

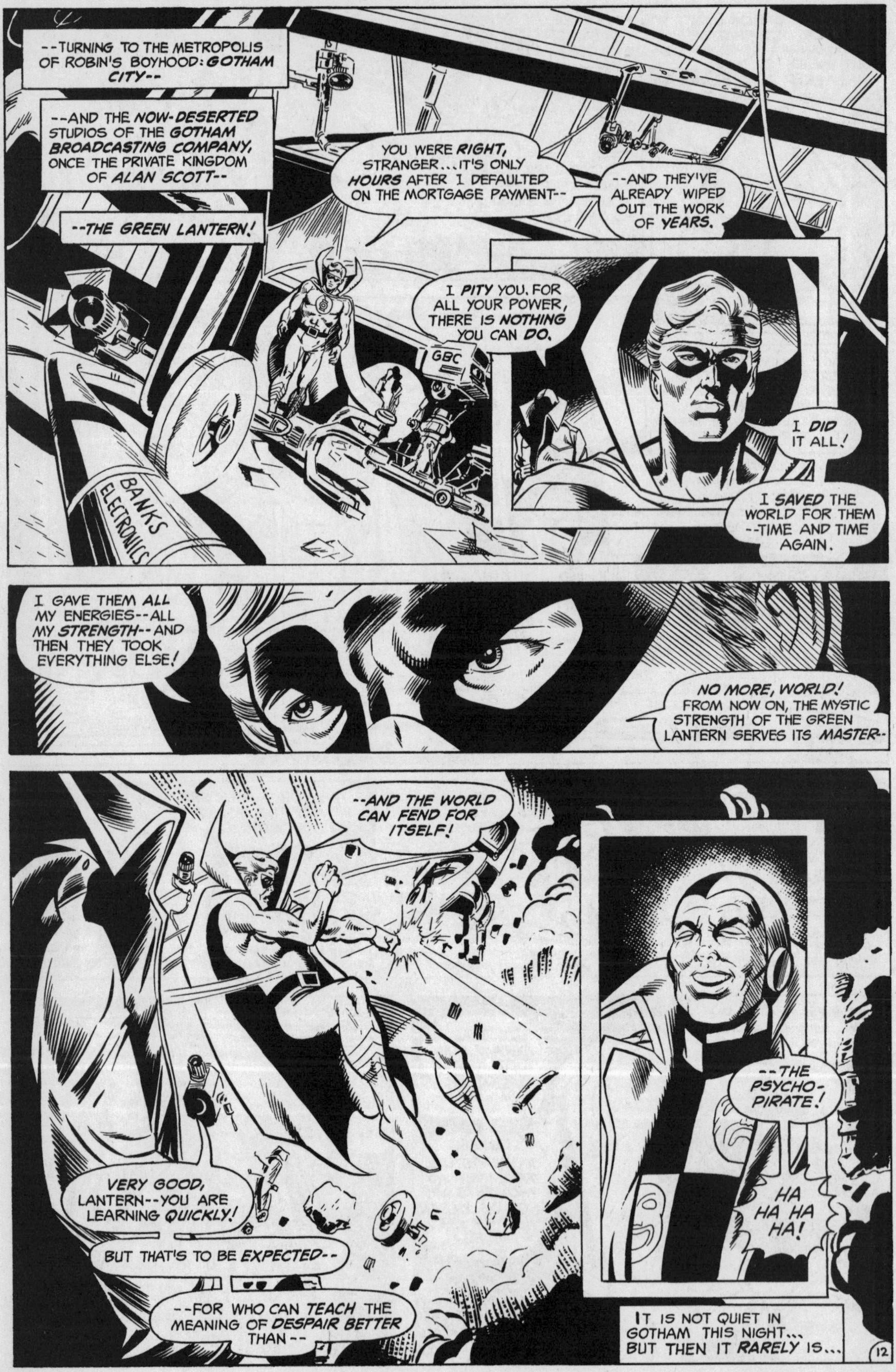

--TURNING TO THE METROPOLIS OF ROBIN'S BOYHOOD: GOTHAM CITY--
--AND THE NOW-DESERTED STUDIOS OF THE GOTHAM BROADCASTING COMPANY, ONCE THE PRIVATE KINGDOM OF ALAN SCOTT--
--THE GREEN LANTERN!
YOU WERE RIGHT, STRANGER...IT'S ONLY HOURS AFTER I DEFAULTED ON THE MORTGAGE PAYMENT--
--AND THEY'VE ALREADY WIPED OUT THE WORK OF YEARS.
I PITY YOU. FOR ALL YOUR POWER, THERE IS NOTHING YOU CAN DO.
GBC
BANKS ELECTRONICS
I DID IT ALL!
I SAVED THE WORLD FOR THEM --TIME AND TIME AGAIN.
I GAVE THEM ALL MY ENERGIES--ALL MY STRENGTH--AND THEN THEY TOOK EVERYTHING ELSE!
NO MORE, WORLD! FROM NOW ON, THE MYSTIC STRENGTH OF THE GREEN LANTERN SERVES ITS MASTER--
--AND THE WORLD CAN FEND FOR ITSELF!
VERY GOOD, LANTERN--YOU ARE LEARNING QUICKLY!
BUT THAT'S TO BE EXPECTED--
--FOR WHO CAN TEACH THE MEANING OF DESPAIR BETTER THAN--
--THE PSYCHO-PIRATE!
HA HA HA HA!
IT IS NOT QUIET IN GOTHAM THIS NIGHT... BUT THEN IT RARELY IS...
12

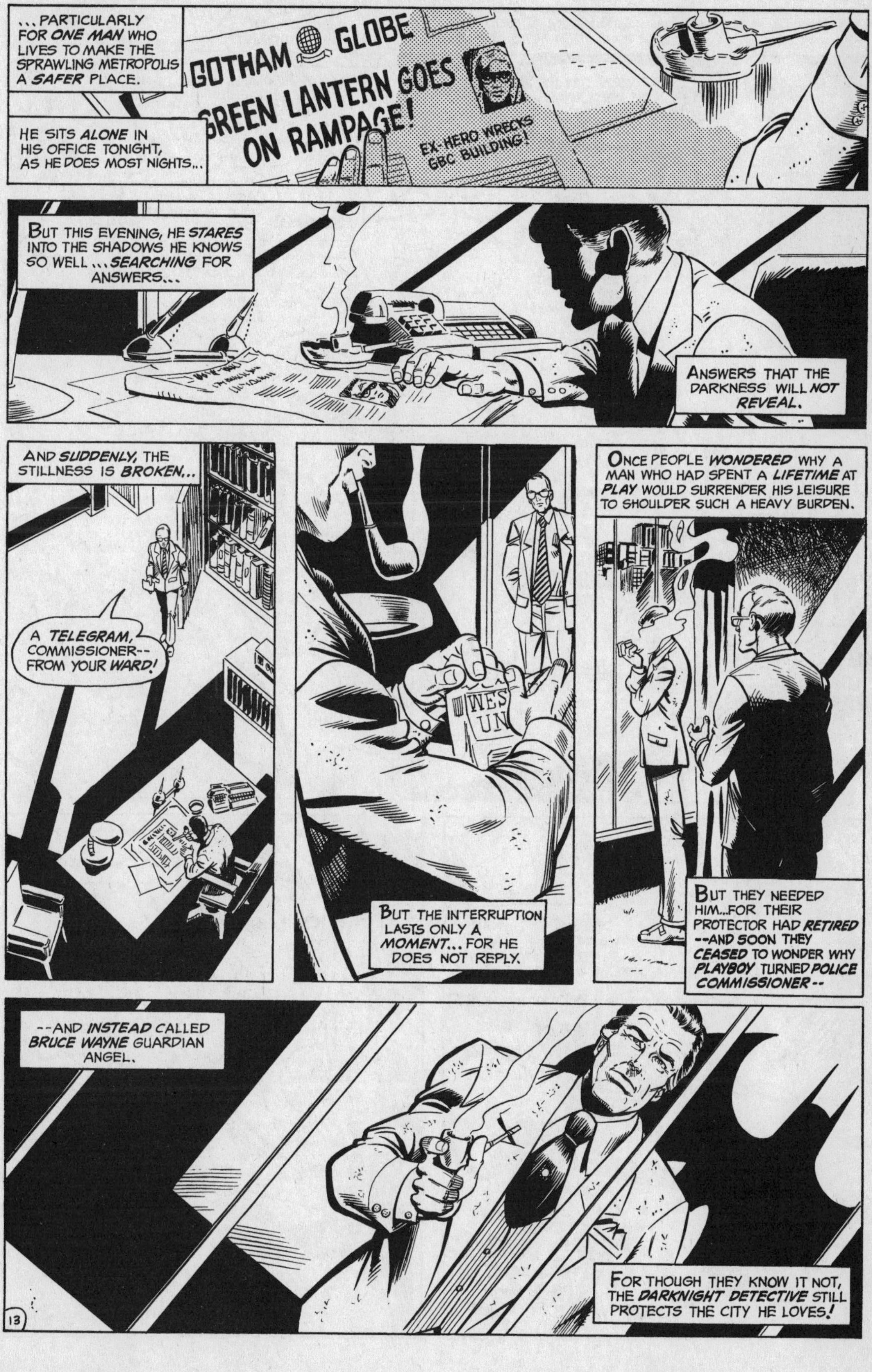
...PARTICULARLY FOR ONE MAN WHO LIVES TO MAKE THE SPRAWLING METROPOLIS A SAFER PLACE.
GOTHAM GLOBE
GREEN LANTERN GOES ON RAMPAGE!
EX-HERO WRECKS GBC BUILDING!
HE SITS ALONE IN HIS OFFICE TONIGHT, AS HE DOES MOST NIGHTS...
BUT THIS EVENING, HE STARES INTO THE SHADOWS HE KNOWS SO WELL ...SEARCHING FOR ANSWERS...
ANSWERS THAT THE DARKNESS WILL NOT REVEAL.
AND SUDDENLY, THE STILLNESS IS BROKEN...
A TELEGRAM, COMMISSIONER-- FROM YOUR WARD!
BUT THE INTERRUPTION LASTS ONLY A MOMENT... FOR HE DOES NOT REPLY.
ONCE PEOPLE WONDERED WHY A MAN WHO HAD SPENT A LIFETIME AT PLAY WOULD SURRENDER HIS LEISURE TO SHOULDER SUCH A HEAVY BURDEN.
BUT THEY NEEDED HIM...FOR THEIR PROTECTOR HAD RETIRED --AND SOON THEY CEASED TO WONDER WHY PLAYBOY TURNED POLICE COMMISSIONER--
--AND INSTEAD CALLED BRUCE WAYNE GUARDIAN ANGEL.
FOR THOUGH THEY KNOW IT NOT, THE DARKNIGHT DETECTIVE STILL PROTECTS THE CITY HE LOVES!
13

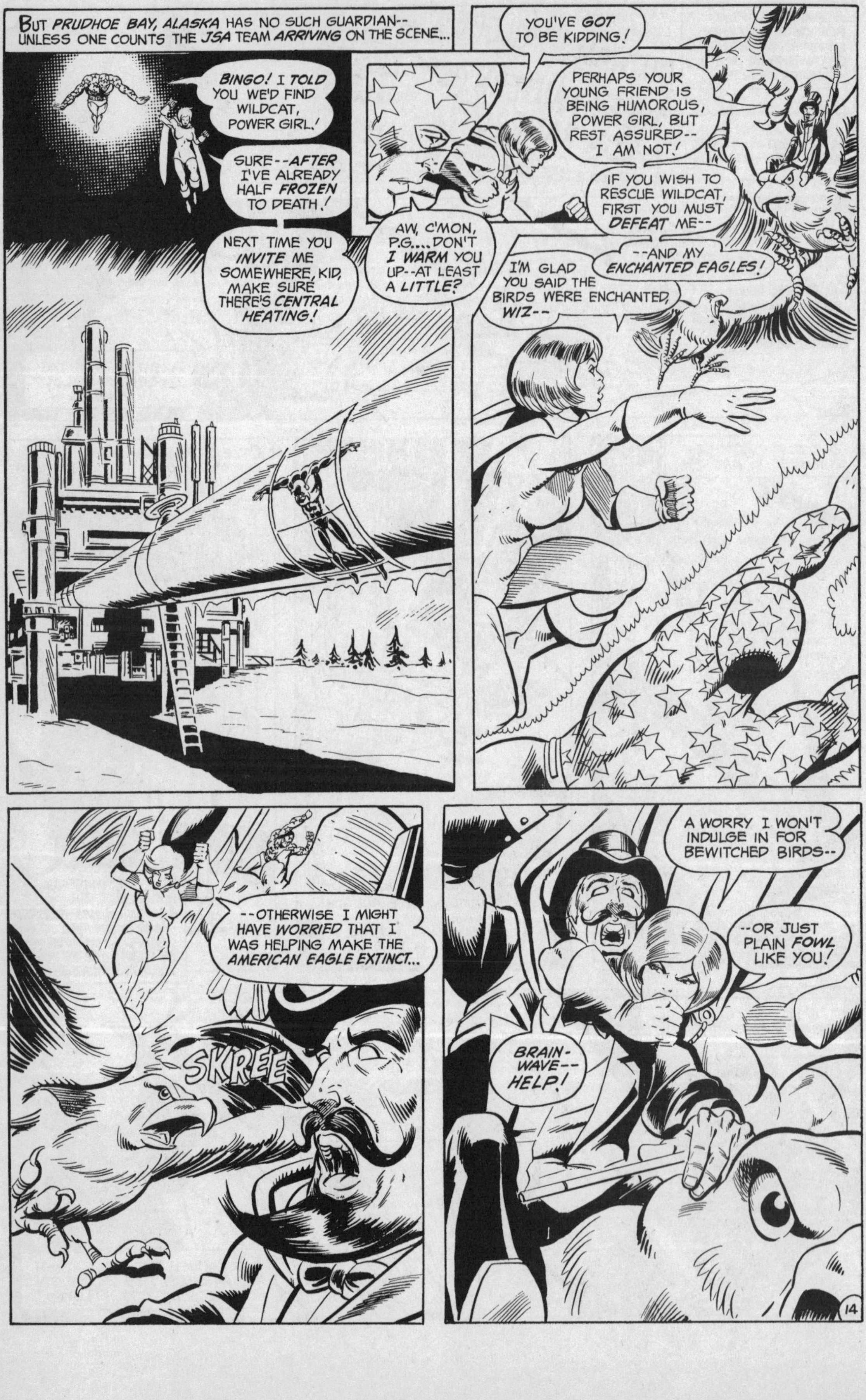

BUT PRUDHOE BAY, ALASKA HAS NO SUCH GUARDIAN-- UNLESS ONE COUNTS THE JSA TEAM ARRIVING ON THE SCENE...
BINGO! I TOLD YOU WE'D FIND WILDCAT, POWER GIRL!
SURE--AFTER I'VE ALREADY HALF FROZEN TO DEATH!
NEXT TIME YOU INVITE ME SOMEWHERE, KID, MAKE SURE THERE'S CENTRAL HEATING!
AW, C'MON, P.G.... DON'T I WARM YOU UP--AT LEAST A LITTLE?
YOU'VE GOT TO BE KIDDING!
PERHAPS YOUR YOUNG FRIEND IS BEING HUMOROUS, POWER GIRL, BUT REST ASSURED-- I AM NOT!
IF YOU WISH TO RESCUE WILDCAT, FIRST YOU MUST DEFEAT ME--
--AND MY ENCHANTED EAGLES!
I'M GLAD YOU SAID THE BIRDS WERE ENCHANTED, WIZ--
--OTHERWISE I MIGHT HAVE WORRIED THAT I WAS HELPING MAKE THE AMERICAN EAGLE EXTINCT...
SKREEE
A WORRY I WON'T INDULGE IN FOR BEWITCHED BIRDS--
--OR JUST PLAIN FOWL LIKE YOU!
BRAIN-WAVE--HELP!
14

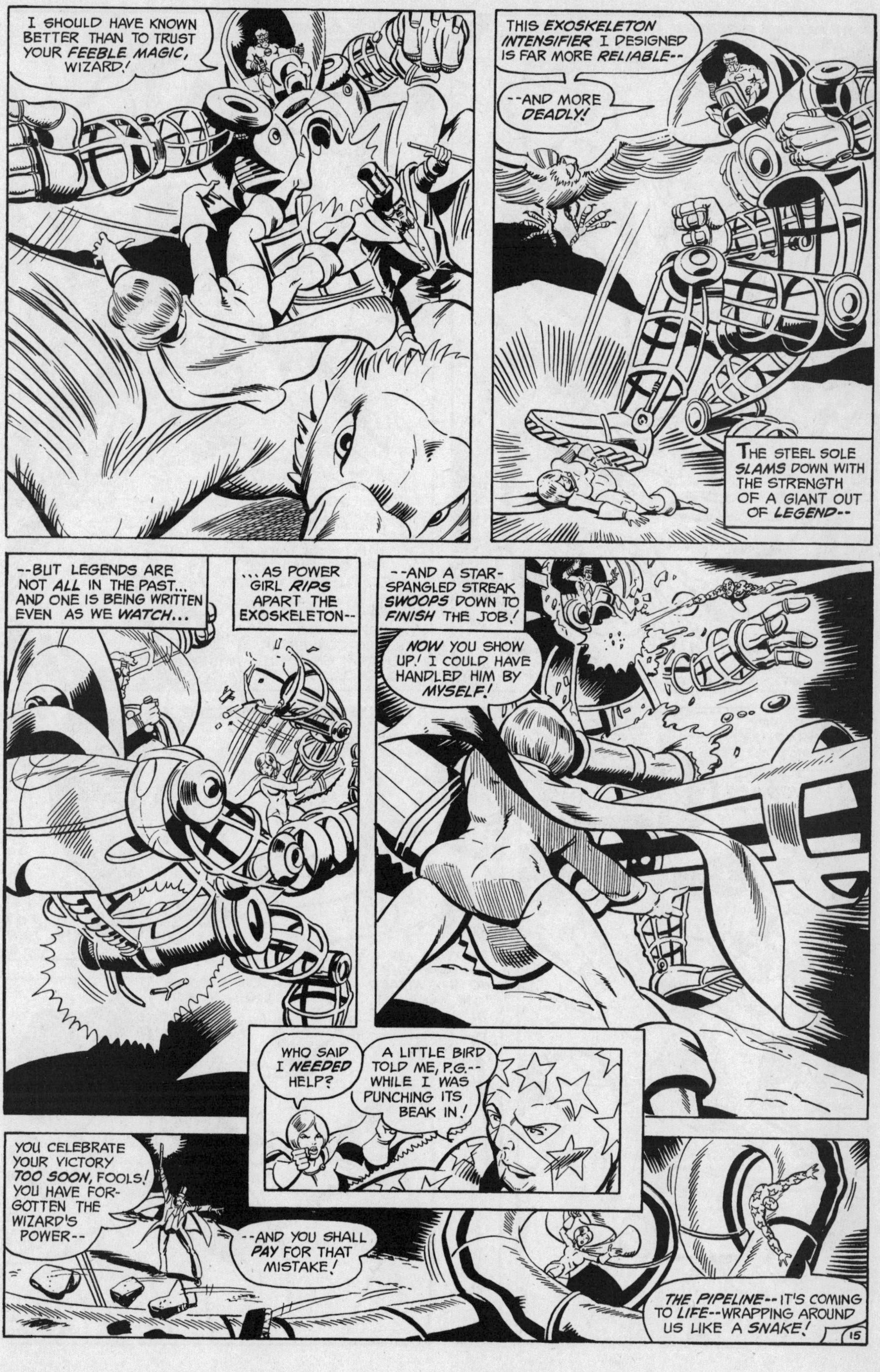
I SHOULD HAVE KNOWN BETTER THAN TO TRUST YOUR FEEBLE MAGIC, WIZARD!
THIS EXOSKELETON INTENSIFIER I DESIGNED IS FAR MORE RELIABLE--
--AND MORE DEADLY!
THE STEEL SOLE SLAMS DOWN WITH THE STRENGTH OF A GIANT OUT OF LEGEND--
--BUT LEGENDS ARE NOT ALL IN THE PAST... AND ONE IS BEING WRITTEN EVEN AS WE WATCH...
...AS POWER GIRL RIPS APART THE EXOSKELETON--
--AND A STAR-SPANGLED STREAK SWOOPS DOWN TO FINISH THE JOB!
NOW YOU SHOW UP! I COULD HAVE HANDLED HIM BY MYSELF!
WHO SAID I NEEDED HELP?
A LITTLE BIRD TOLD ME, P.G.--WHILE I WAS PUNCHING ITS BEAK IN!
YOU CELEBRATE YOUR VICTORY TOO SOON, FOOLS! YOU HAVE FORGOTTEN THE WIZARD'S POWER--
--AND YOU SHALL PAY FOR THAT MISTAKE!
THE PIPELINE--IT'S COMING TO LIFE--WRAPPING AROUND US LIKE A SNAKE!
15

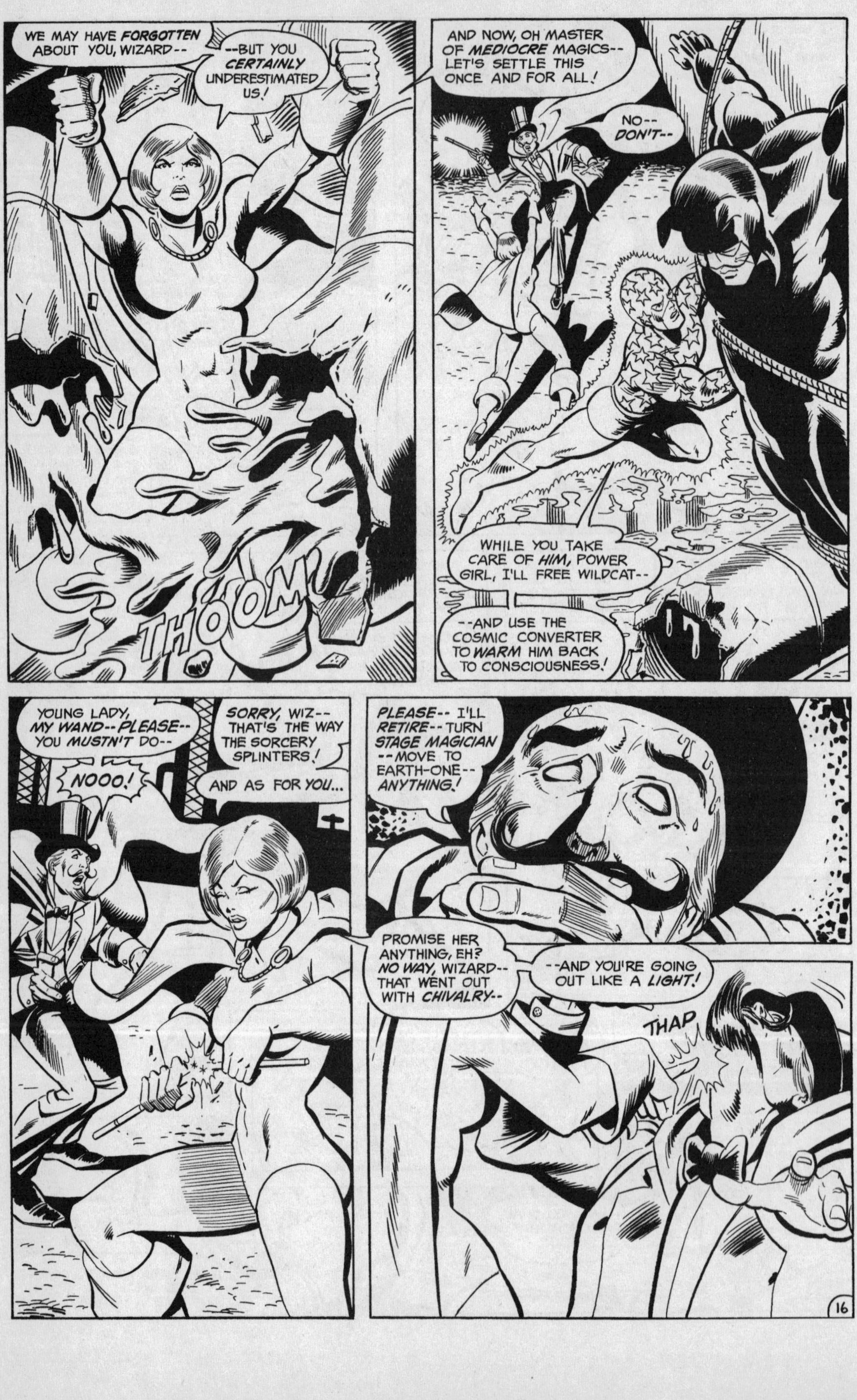

WE MAY HAVE FORGOTTEN ABOUT YOU, WIZARD--
--BUT YOU CERTAINLY UNDERESTIMATED US!
THOOOM
AND NOW, OH MASTER OF MEDIOCRE MAGICS--LET'S SETTLE THIS ONCE AND FOR ALL!
NO--DON'T--
WHILE YOU TAKE CARE OF HIM, POWER GIRL, I'LL FREE WILDCAT--
--AND USE THE COSMIC CONVERTER TO WARM HIM BACK TO CONSCIOUSNESS!
YOUNG LADY, MY WAND--PLEASE--YOU MUSTN'T DO--
NOOO!
SORRY, WIZ--THAT'S THE WAY THE SORCERY SPLINTERS!
AND AS FOR YOU...
PLEASE-- I'LL RETIRE--TURN STAGE MAGICIAN--MOVE TO EARTH-ONE--ANYTHING!
PROMISE HER ANYTHING, EH? NO WAY, WIZARD--THAT WENT OUT WITH CHIVALRY--
--AND YOU'RE GOING OUT LIKE A LIGHT!
THAP
16

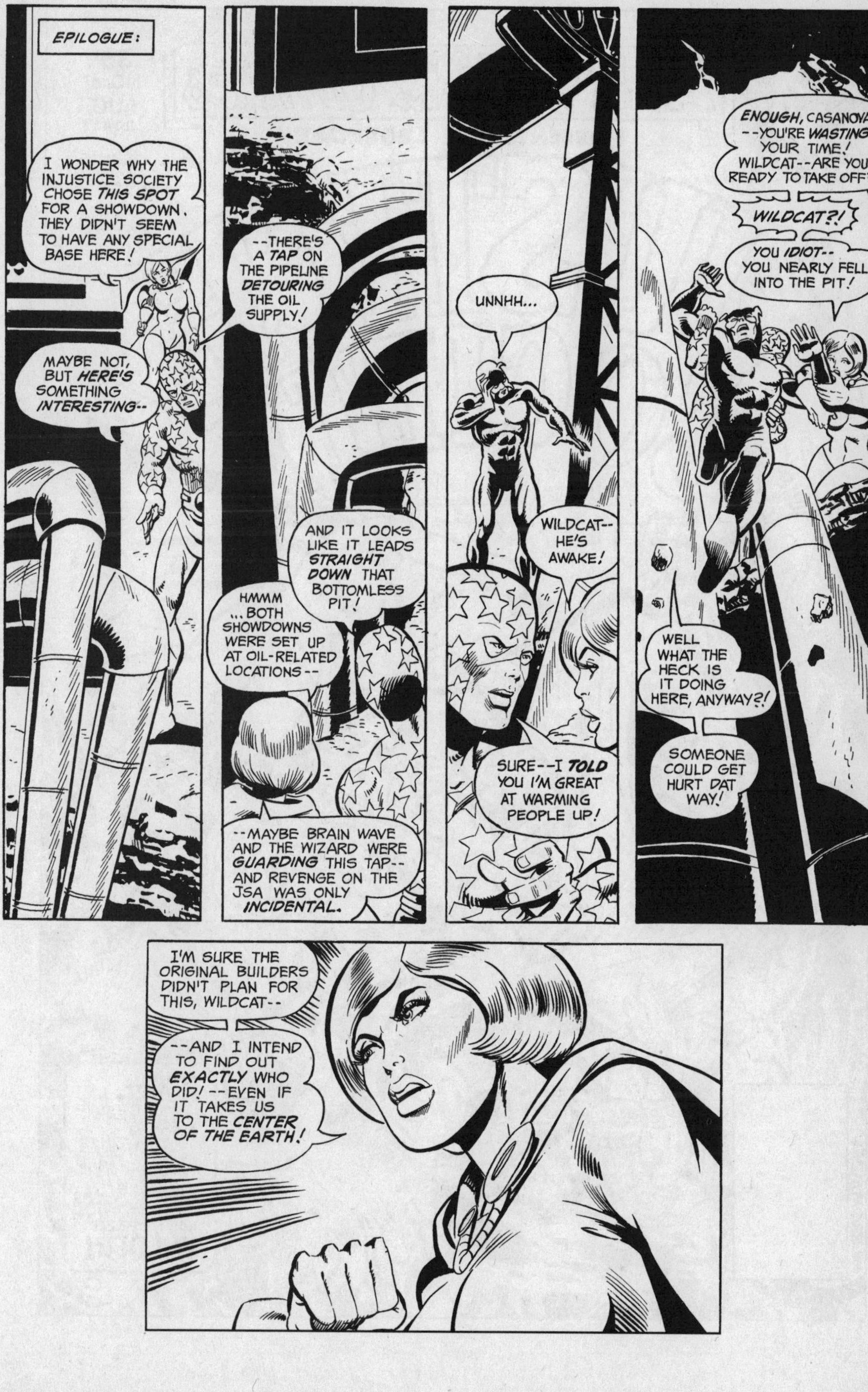
EPILOGUE:
I WONDER WHY THE INJUSTICE SOCIETY CHOSE THIS SPOT FOR A SHOWDOWN. THEY DIDN'T SEEM TO HAVE ANY SPECIAL BASE HERE!
MAYBE NOT, BUT HERE'S SOMETHING INTERESTING--
--THERE'S A TAP ON THE PIPELINE DETOURING THE OIL SUPPLY!
AND IT LOOKS LIKE IT LEADS STRAIGHT DOWN THAT BOTTOMLESS PIT!
HMMM ...BOTH SHOWDOWNS WERE SET UP AT OIL-RELATED LOCATIONS--
--MAYBE BRAIN WAVE AND THE WIZARD WERE GUARDING THIS TAP--AND REVENGE ON THE JSA WAS ONLY INCIDENTAL.
UNNHH...
WILDCAT--HE'S AWAKE!
SURE--I TOLD YOU I'M GREAT AT WARMING PEOPLE UP!
ENOUGH, CASANOVA --YOU'RE WASTING YOUR TIME! WILDCAT--ARE YOU READY TO TAKE OFF?
WILDCAT?!
YOU IDIOT--YOU NEARLY FELL INTO THE PIT!
WELL WHAT THE HECK IS IT DOING HERE, ANYWAY?!
SOMEONE COULD GET HURT DAT WAY!
I'M SURE THE ORIGINAL BUILDERS DIDN'T PLAN FOR THIS, WILDCAT--
--AND I INTEND TO FIND OUT EXACTLY WHO DID! --EVEN IF IT TAKES US TO THE CENTER OF THE EARTH!

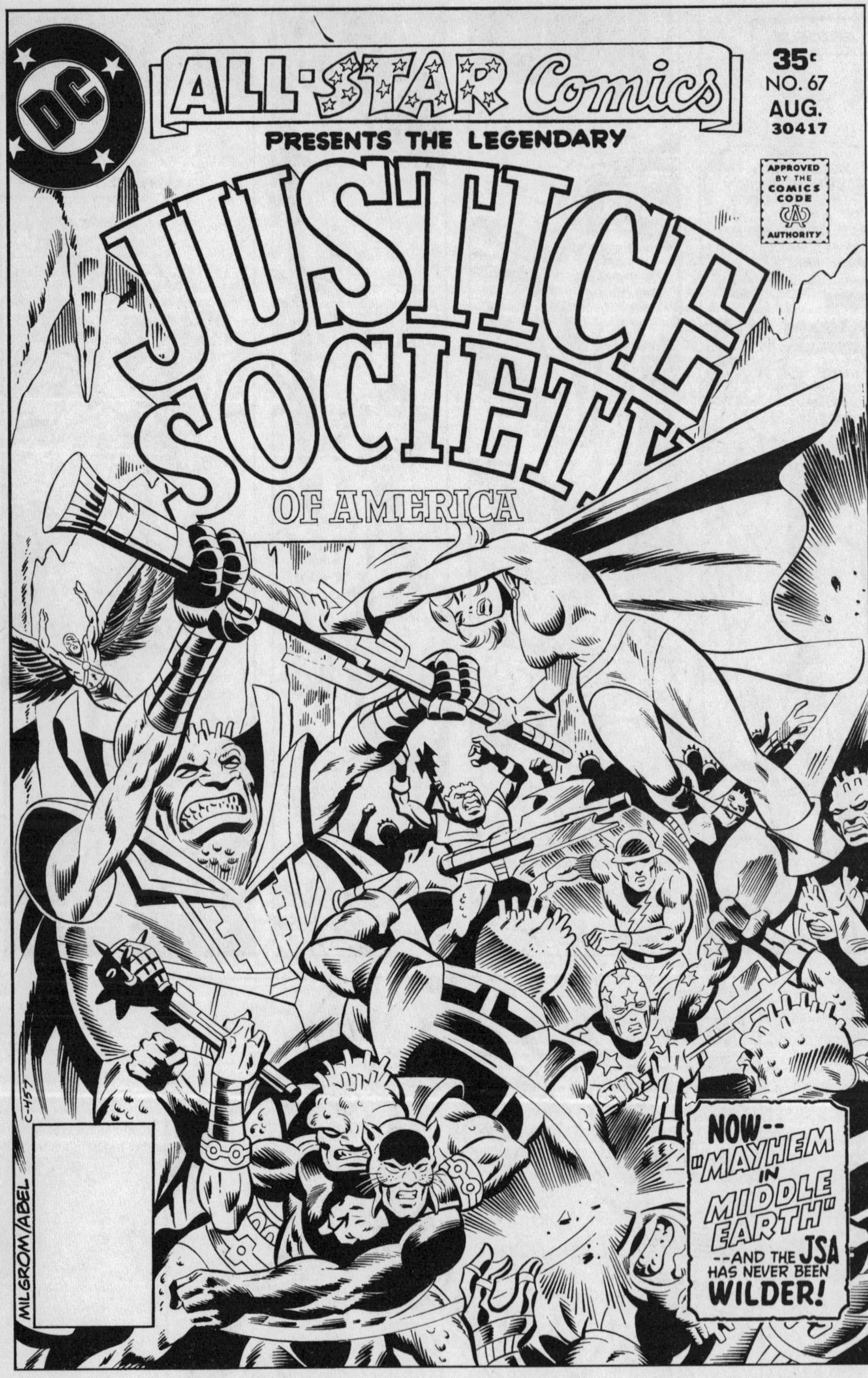
ALL-STAR Comics
PRESENTS THE LEGENDARY
JUSTICE SOCIETY OF AMERICA
35¢
NO. 67
AUG.
30417
APPROVED BY THE COMICS CODE AUTHORITY
NOW-- "MAYHEM IN MIDDLE EARTH" --AND THE JSA HAS NEVER BEEN WILDER!
MILGROM/ABEL
C-457

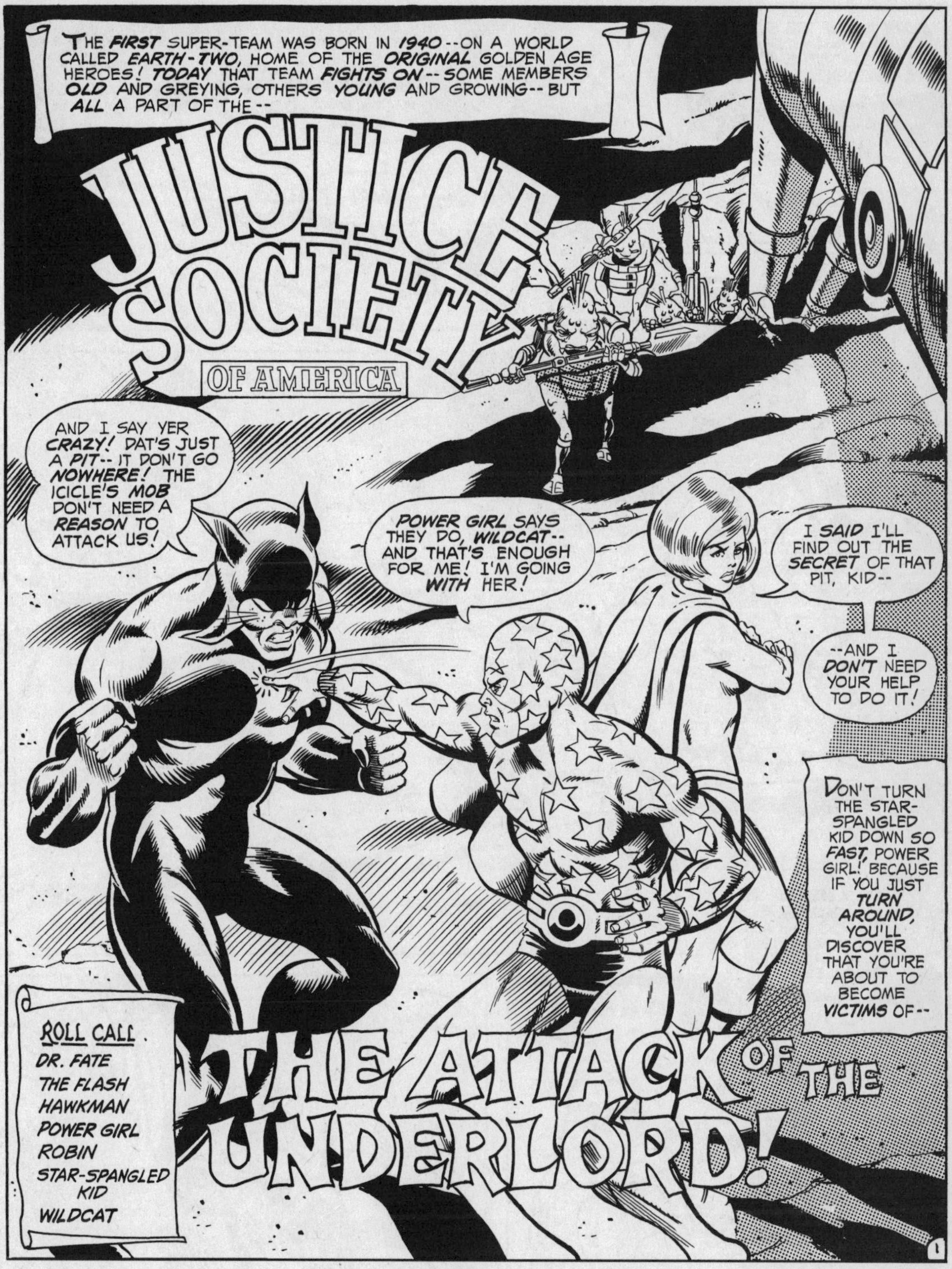
THE FIRST SUPER-TEAM WAS BORN IN 1940--ON A WORLD CALLED EARTH-TWO, HOME OF THE ORIGINAL GOLDEN AGE HEROES! TODAY THAT TEAM FIGHTS ON--SOME MEMBERS OLD AND GREYING, OTHERS YOUNG AND GROWING--BUT ALL A PART OF THE--
JUSTICE SOCIETY OF AMERICA
AND I SAY YER CRAZY! DAT'S JUST A PIT--IT DON'T GO NOWHERE! THE ICICLE'S MOB DON'T NEED A REASON TO ATTACK US!
POWER GIRL SAYS THEY DO, WILDCAT--AND THAT'S ENOUGH FOR ME! I'M GOING WITH HER!
I SAID I'LL FIND OUT THE SECRET OF THAT PIT, KID--
--AND I DON'T NEED YOUR HELP TO DO IT!
DON'T TURN THE STAR-SPANGLED KID DOWN SO FAST, POWER GIRL! BECAUSE IF YOU JUST TURN AROUND, YOU'LL DISCOVER THAT YOU'RE ABOUT TO BECOME VICTIMS OF--
THE ATTACK OF THE UNDERLORD!
ROLL CALL
DR. FATE
THE FLASH
HAWKMAN
POWER GIRL
ROBIN
STAR-SPANGLED KID
WILDCAT
1

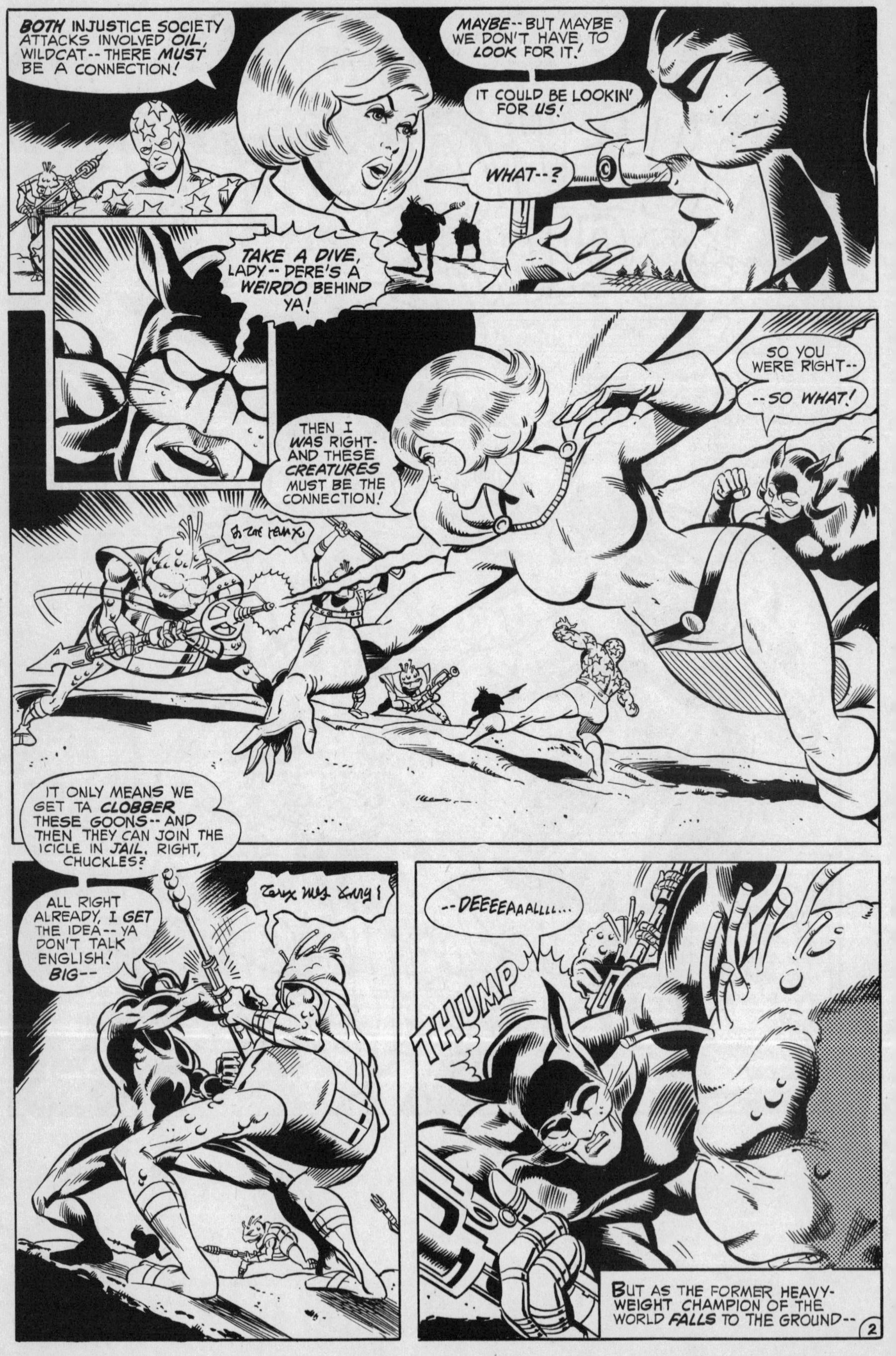
BOTH INJUSTICE SOCIETY ATTACKS INVOLVED OIL, WILDCAT-- THERE MUST BE A CONNECTION!
MAYBE-- BUT MAYBE WE DON'T HAVE, TO LOOK FOR IT!
IT COULD BE LOOKIN' FOR US!
WHAT--?
TAKE A DIVE, LADY-- DERE'S A WEIRDO BEHIND YA!
THEN I WAS RIGHT- AND THESE CREATURES MUST BE THE CONNECTION!
SO YOU WERE RIGHT--
--SO WHAT!
IT ONLY MEANS WE GET TA CLOBBER THESE GOONS-- AND THEN THEY CAN JOIN THE ICICLE IN JAIL, RIGHT, CHUCKLES?
ALL RIGHT ALREADY, I GET THE IDEA-- YA DON'T TALK ENGLISH! BIG--
--DEEEEAAALLLL...
THUMP
BUT AS THE FORMER HEAVY-WEIGHT CHAMPION OF THE WORLD FALLS TO THE GROUND--
2

--THE CURRENT COSMIC-ENERGY-POWERED CRUSADER RUSHES TO HIS AID...

WILDCAT, WHEN WILL YOU LEARN THAT WE'RE NOT FIGHTING IN A PRIZE RING! YOU HAVE TO WATCH MORE THAN ONE OPPONENT!

BLASTING FORWARD WITH THE FORCE OF THE STARS, THE BEAMS PUSH THE AWKWARD CREATURES BACK--

--INTO THE DARKNESS OF THE PIT!

BUT THIS TIME, CARRYING AN UNWILLING-- AND UNCONSCIOUS-- PASSENGER!

OKAY, UGLIES-- OFF YOU GO! JUST DROP WILDCAT AND--

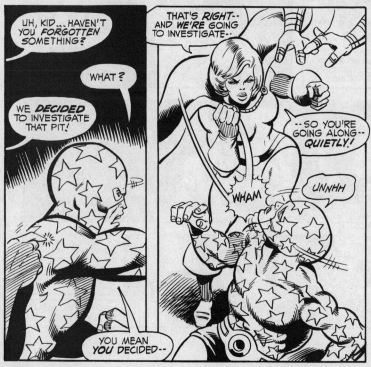

UH, KID...HAVEN'T YOU FORGOTTEN SOMETHING?

WHAT?

WE DECIDED TO INVESTIGATE THAT PIT!

THAT'S RIGHT-- AND WE'RE GOING TO INVESTIGATE--

--SO YOU'RE GOING ALONG-- QUIETLY!

WHAM

UNNHH

YOU MEAN YOU DECIDED--

WITH THAT, THE YOUNG KRYPTONIAN SURRENDERS TO HER MISSHAPEN CAPTORS--BUT NOT BEFORE ACTIVATING HER JSA SIGNAL DEVICE...

THE ALARM WHICH WILL SUMMON HELP FROM ACROSS THE GLOBE--

3

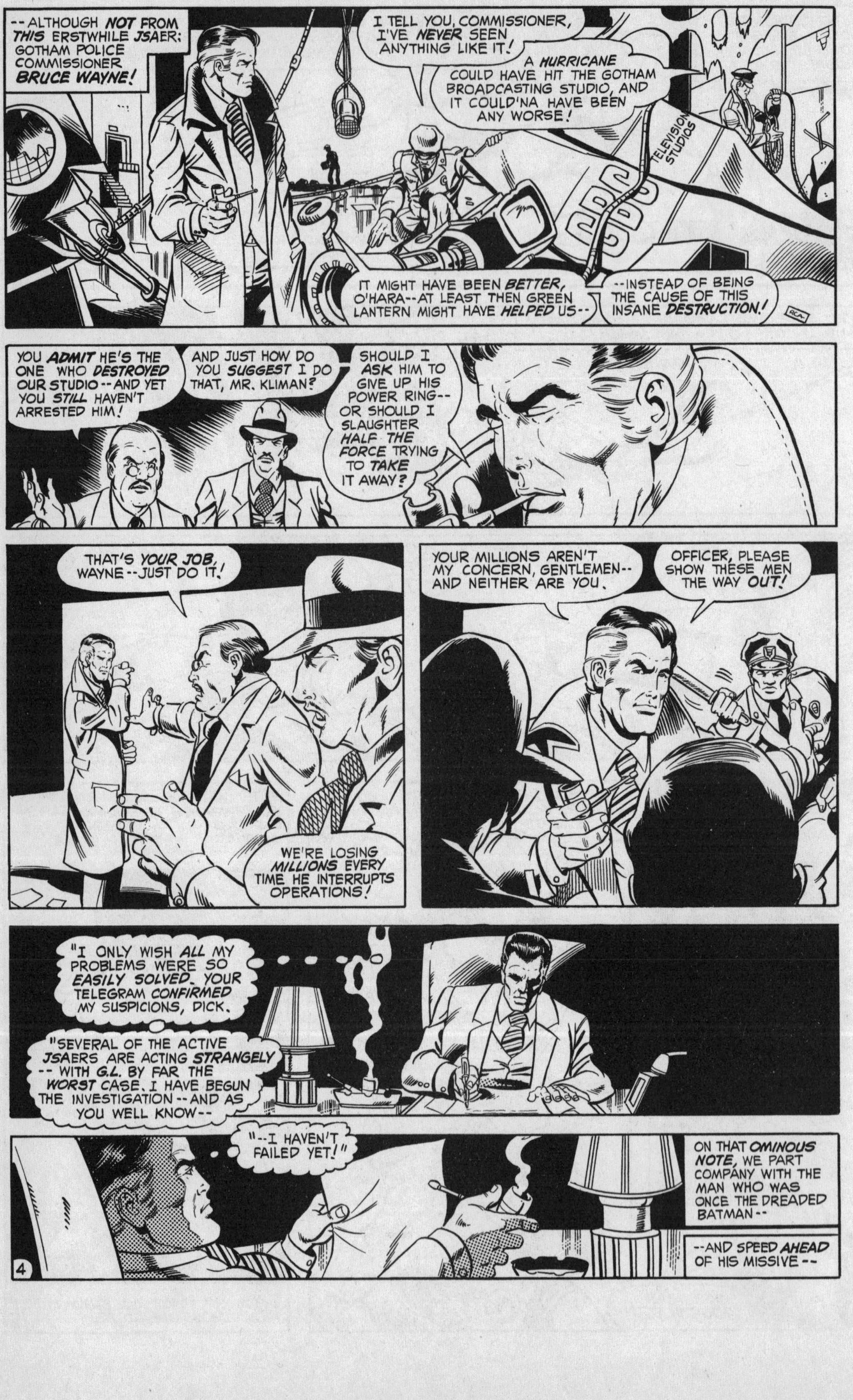
--ALTHOUGH NOT FROM THIS ERSTWHILE JSAER: GOTHAM POLICE COMMISSIONER BRUCE WAYNE!
I TELL YOU, COMMISSIONER, I'VE NEVER SEEN ANYTHING LIKE IT!
A HURRICANE COULD HAVE HIT THE GOTHAM BROADCASTING STUDIO, AND IT COULD'NA HAVE BEEN ANY WORSE!
TELEVISION STUDIOS
GBC
IT MIGHT HAVE BEEN BETTER, O'HARA--AT LEAST THEN GREEN LANTERN MIGHT HAVE HELPED US--
--INSTEAD OF BEING THE CAUSE OF THIS INSANE DESTRUCTION!
YOU ADMIT HE'S THE ONE WHO DESTROYED OUR STUDIO--AND YET YOU STILL HAVEN'T ARRESTED HIM!
AND JUST HOW DO YOU SUGGEST I DO THAT, MR. KLIMAN?
SHOULD I ASK HIM TO GIVE UP HIS POWER RING--OR SHOULD I SLAUGHTER HALF THE FORCE TRYING TO TAKE IT AWAY?
THAT'S YOUR JOB, WAYNE--JUST DO IT!
WE'RE LOSING MILLIONS EVERY TIME HE INTERRUPTS OPERATIONS!
YOUR MILLIONS AREN'T MY CONCERN, GENTLEMEN--AND NEITHER ARE YOU.
OFFICER, PLEASE SHOW THESE MEN THE WAY OUT!
"I ONLY WISH ALL MY PROBLEMS WERE SO EASILY SOLVED. YOUR TELEGRAM CONFIRMED MY SUSPICIONS, DICK.
"SEVERAL OF THE ACTIVE JSAERS ARE ACTING STRANGELY--WITH G.L. BY FAR THE WORST CASE. I HAVE BEGUN THE INVESTIGATION--AND AS YOU WELL KNOW--
"--I HAVEN'T FAILED YET!"
ON THAT OMINOUS NOTE, WE PART COMPANY WITH THE MAN WHO WAS ONCE THE DREADED BATMAN--
--AND SPEED AHEAD OF HIS MISSIVE--
4

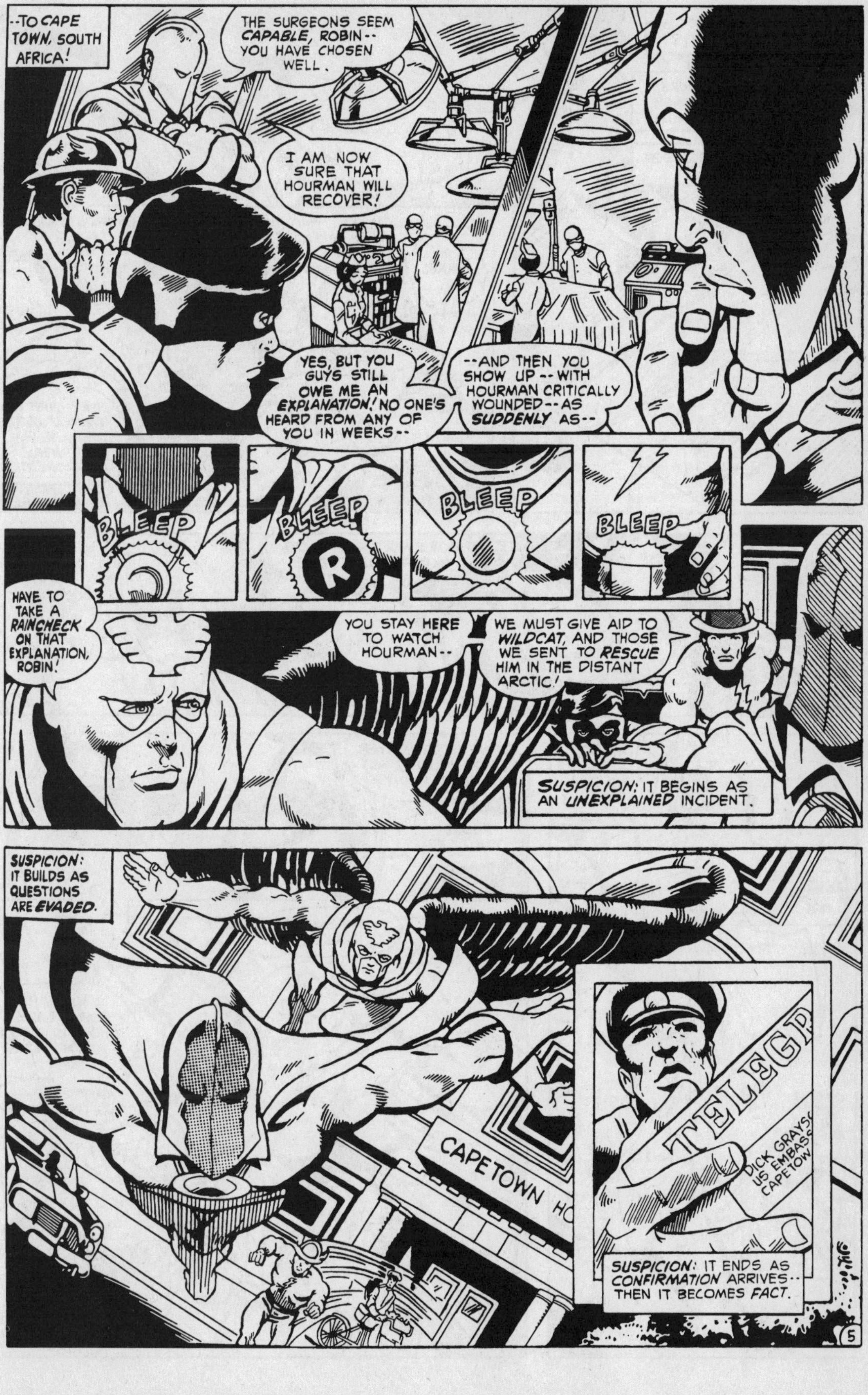
--TO CAPE TOWN, SOUTH AFRICA!
THE SURGEONS SEEM CAPABLE, ROBIN-- YOU HAVE CHOSEN WELL.
I AM NOW SURE THAT HOURMAN WILL RECOVER!
YES, BUT YOU GUYS STILL OWE ME AN EXPLANATION! NO ONE'S HEARD FROM ANY OF YOU IN WEEKS--
--AND THEN YOU SHOW UP--WITH HOURMAN CRITICALLY WOUNDED--AS SUDDENLY AS--
BLEEP
BLEEP
R
BLEEP
BLEEP
HAVE TO TAKE A RAINCHECK ON THAT EXPLANATION, ROBIN!
YOU STAY HERE TO WATCH HOURMAN--
WE MUST GIVE AID TO WILDCAT, AND THOSE WE SENT TO RESCUE HIM IN THE DISTANT ARCTIC!
SUSPICION: IT BEGINS AS AN UNEXPLAINED INCIDENT.
SUSPICION: IT BUILDS AS QUESTIONS ARE EVADED.
CAPETOWN HO
TELEGR
DICK GRAYS
US EMBASS
CAPETOW
SUSPICION: IT ENDS AS CONFIRMATION ARRIVES-- THEN IT BECOMES FACT.
5

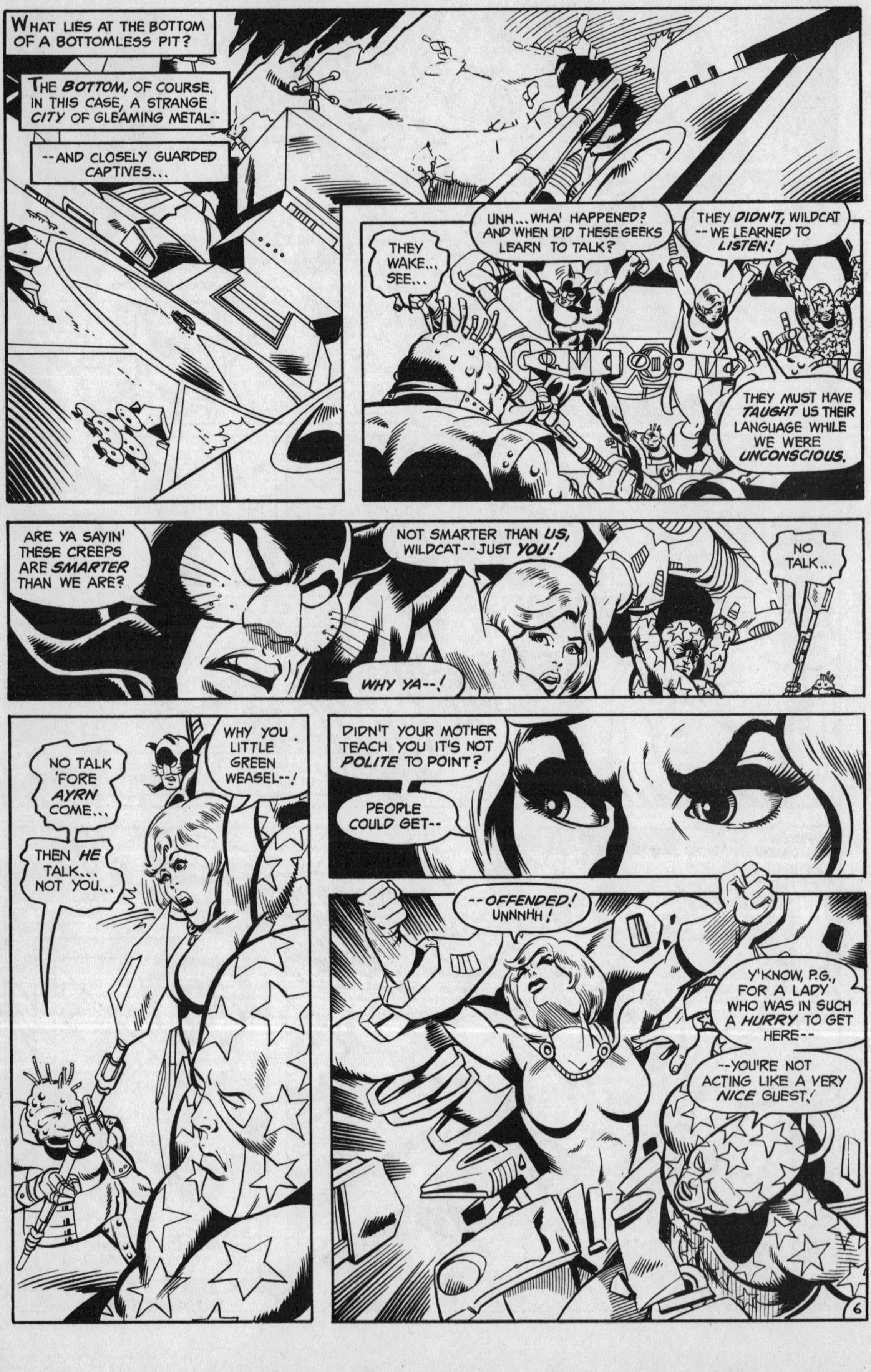
WHAT LIES AT THE BOTTOM OF A BOTTOMLESS PIT?
THE BOTTOM, OF COURSE. IN THIS CASE, A STRANGE CITY OF GLEAMING METAL--
--AND CLOSELY GUARDED CAPTIVES...
THEY WAKE... SEE...
UNH... WHA' HAPPENED? AND WHEN DID THESE GEEKS LEARN TO TALK?
THEY DIDN'T, WILDCAT -- WE LEARNED TO LISTEN!
THEY MUST HAVE TAUGHT US THEIR LANGUAGE WHILE WE WERE UNCONSCIOUS.
ARE YA SAYIN' THESE CREEPS ARE SMARTER THAN WE ARE?
NOT SMARTER THAN US, WILDCAT--JUST YOU!
NO TALK...
WHY YA--!
NO TALK 'FORE AYRN COME...
THEN HE TALK... NOT YOU...
WHY YOU LITTLE GREEN WEASEL--!
DIDN'T YOUR MOTHER TEACH YOU IT'S NOT POLITE TO POINT?
PEOPLE COULD GET--
--OFFENDED! UNNNHH!
Y'KNOW, P.G., FOR A LADY WHO WAS IN SUCH A HURRY TO GET HERE--
--YOU'RE NOT ACTING LIKE A VERY NICE GUEST!
6

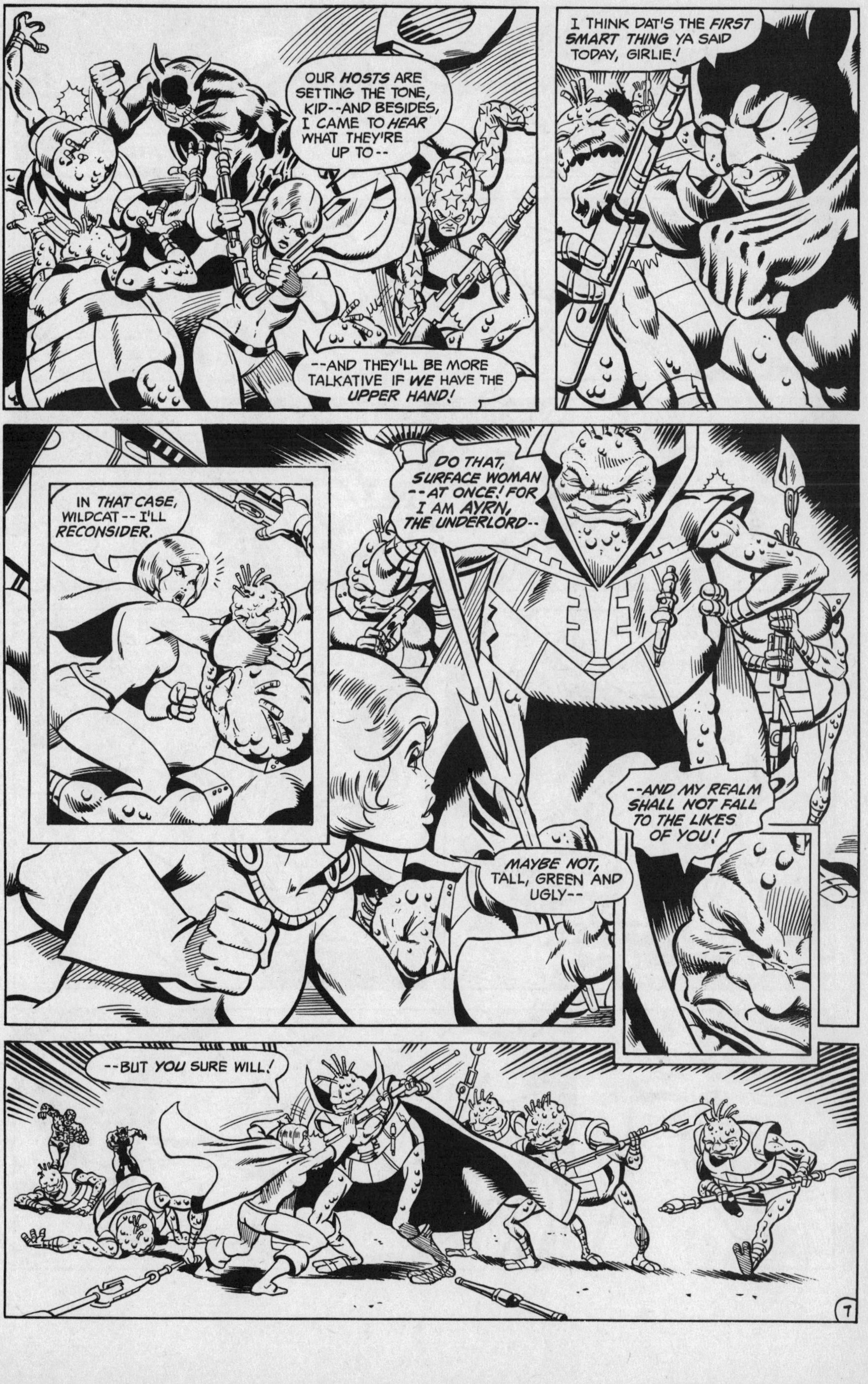
OUR HOSTS ARE SETTING THE TONE, KID--AND BESIDES, I CAME TO HEAR WHAT THEY'RE UP TO--
--AND THEY'LL BE MORE TALKATIVE IF WE HAVE THE UPPER HAND!
I THINK DAT'S THE FIRST SMART THING YA SAID TODAY, GIRLIE!
IN THAT CASE, WILDCAT -- I'LL RECONSIDER.
DO THAT, SURFACE WOMAN --AT ONCE! FOR I AM AYRN, THE UNDERLORD--
--AND MY REALM SHALL NOT FALL TO THE LIKES OF YOU!
MAYBE NOT, TALL, GREEN AND UGLY--
--BUT YOU SURE WILL!
7

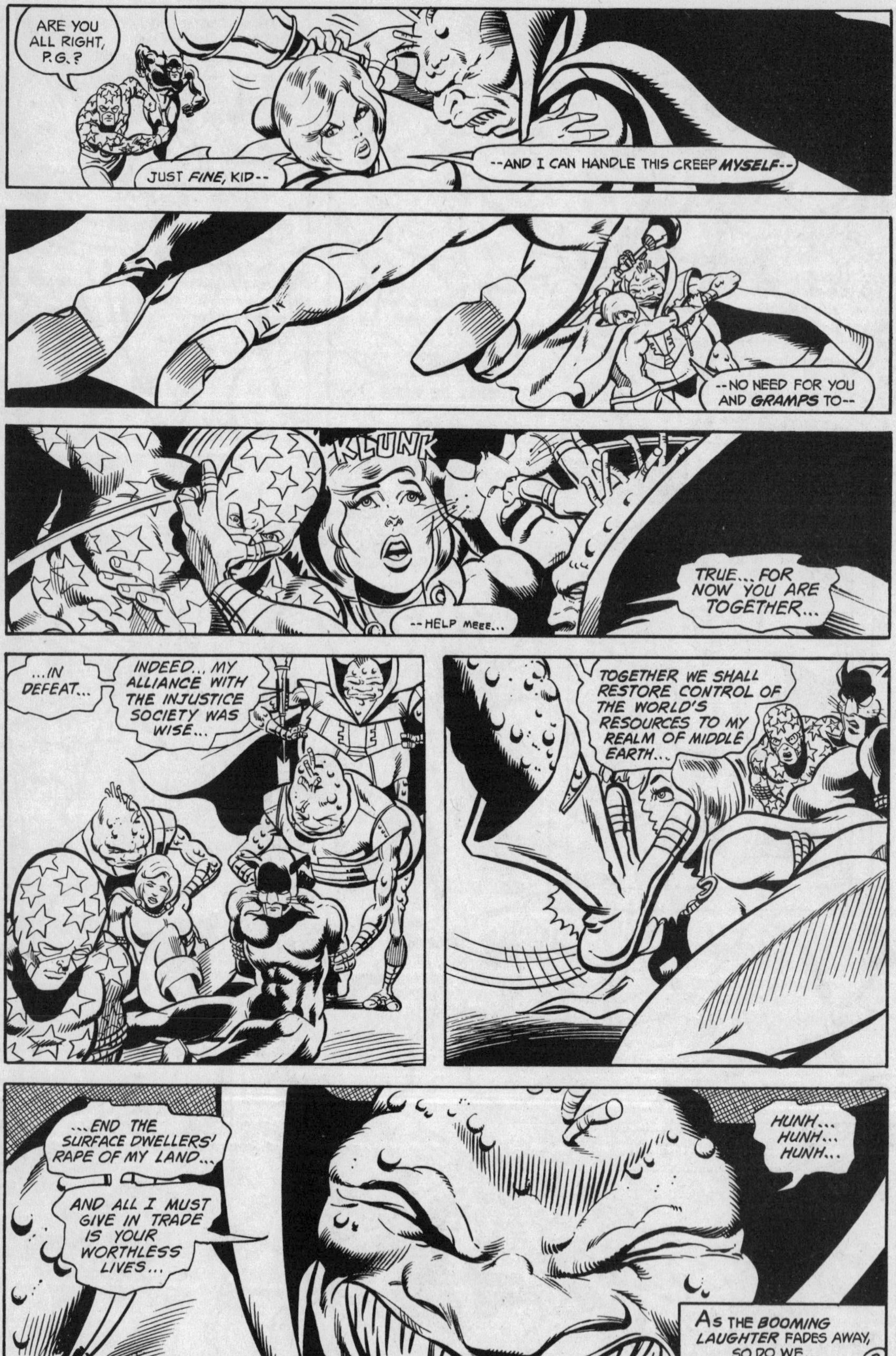
ARE YOU ALL RIGHT, P.G.?
JUST FINE, KID--
--AND I CAN HANDLE THIS CREEP MYSELF--
--NO NEED FOR YOU AND GRAMPS TO--
KLUNK
--HELP MEEE...
TRUE... FOR NOW YOU ARE TOGETHER...
...IN DEFEAT...
INDEED... MY ALLIANCE WITH THE INJUSTICE SOCIETY WAS WISE...
TOGETHER WE SHALL RESTORE CONTROL OF THE WORLD'S RESOURCES TO MY REALM OF MIDDLE EARTH...
...END THE SURFACE DWELLERS' RAPE OF MY LAND...
AND ALL I MUST GIVE IN TRADE IS YOUR WORTHLESS LIVES...
HUNH... HUNH... HUNH...
AS THE BOOMING LAUGHTER FADES AWAY, SO DO WE...
8

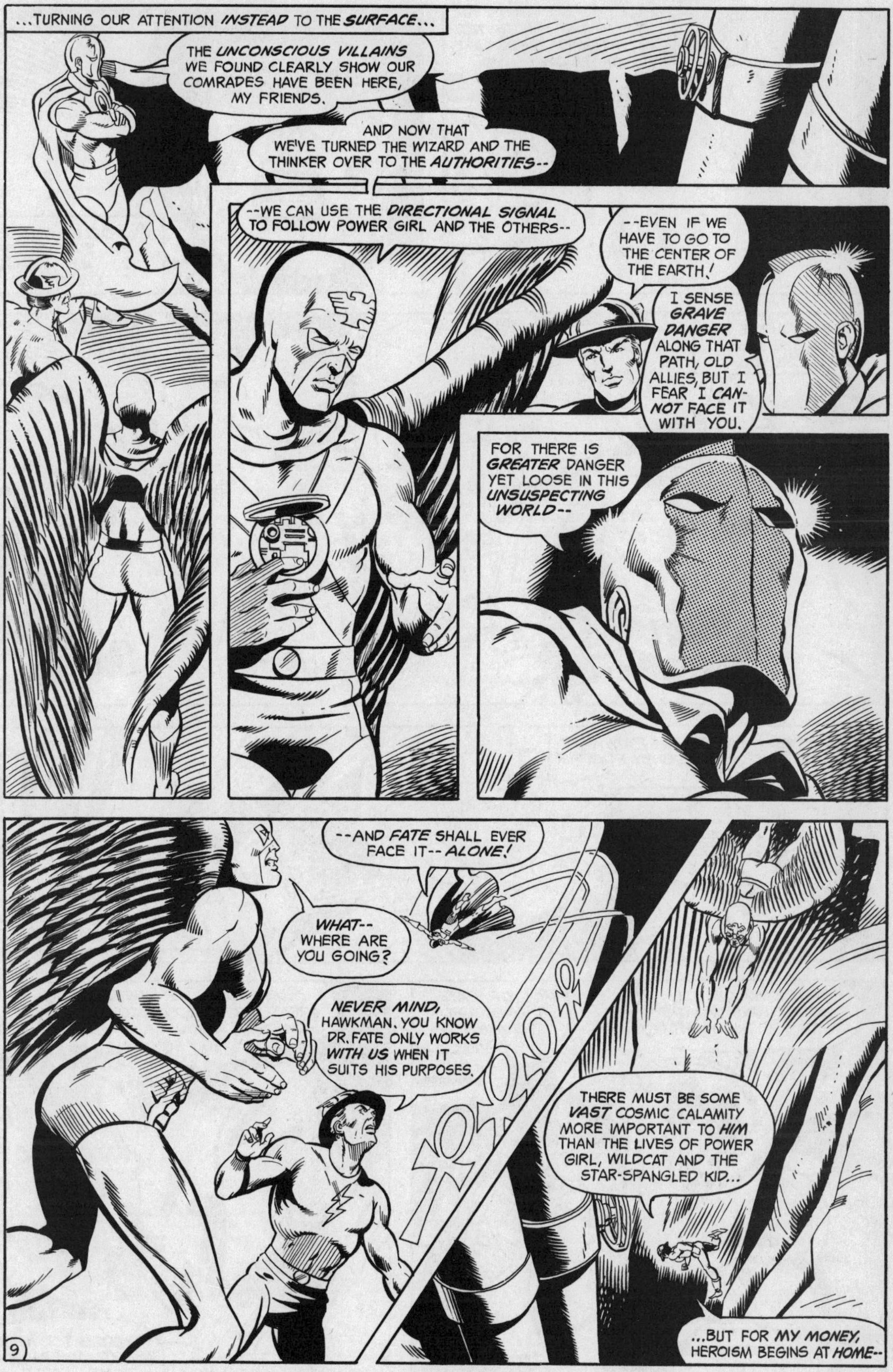
...TURNING OUR ATTENTION INSTEAD TO THE SURFACE...
THE UNCONSCIOUS VILLAINS WE FOUND CLEARLY SHOW OUR COMRADES HAVE BEEN HERE, MY FRIENDS.
AND NOW THAT WE'VE TURNED THE WIZARD AND THE THINKER OVER TO THE AUTHORITIES--
--WE CAN USE THE DIRECTIONAL SIGNAL TO FOLLOW POWER GIRL AND THE OTHERS--
--EVEN IF WE HAVE TO GO TO THE CENTER OF THE EARTH!
I SENSE GRAVE DANGER ALONG THAT PATH, OLD ALLIES, BUT I FEAR I CAN-NOT FACE IT WITH YOU.
FOR THERE IS GREATER DANGER YET LOOSE IN THIS UNSUSPECTING WORLD--
--AND FATE SHALL EVER FACE IT--ALONE!
WHAT-- WHERE ARE YOU GOING?
NEVER MIND, HAWKMAN. YOU KNOW DR. FATE ONLY WORKS WITH US WHEN IT SUITS HIS PURPOSES.
THERE MUST BE SOME VAST COSMIC CALAMITY MORE IMPORTANT TO HIM THAN THE LIVES OF POWER GIRL, WILDCAT AND THE STAR-SPANGLED KID...
...BUT FOR MY MONEY, HEROISM BEGINS AT HOME--
9

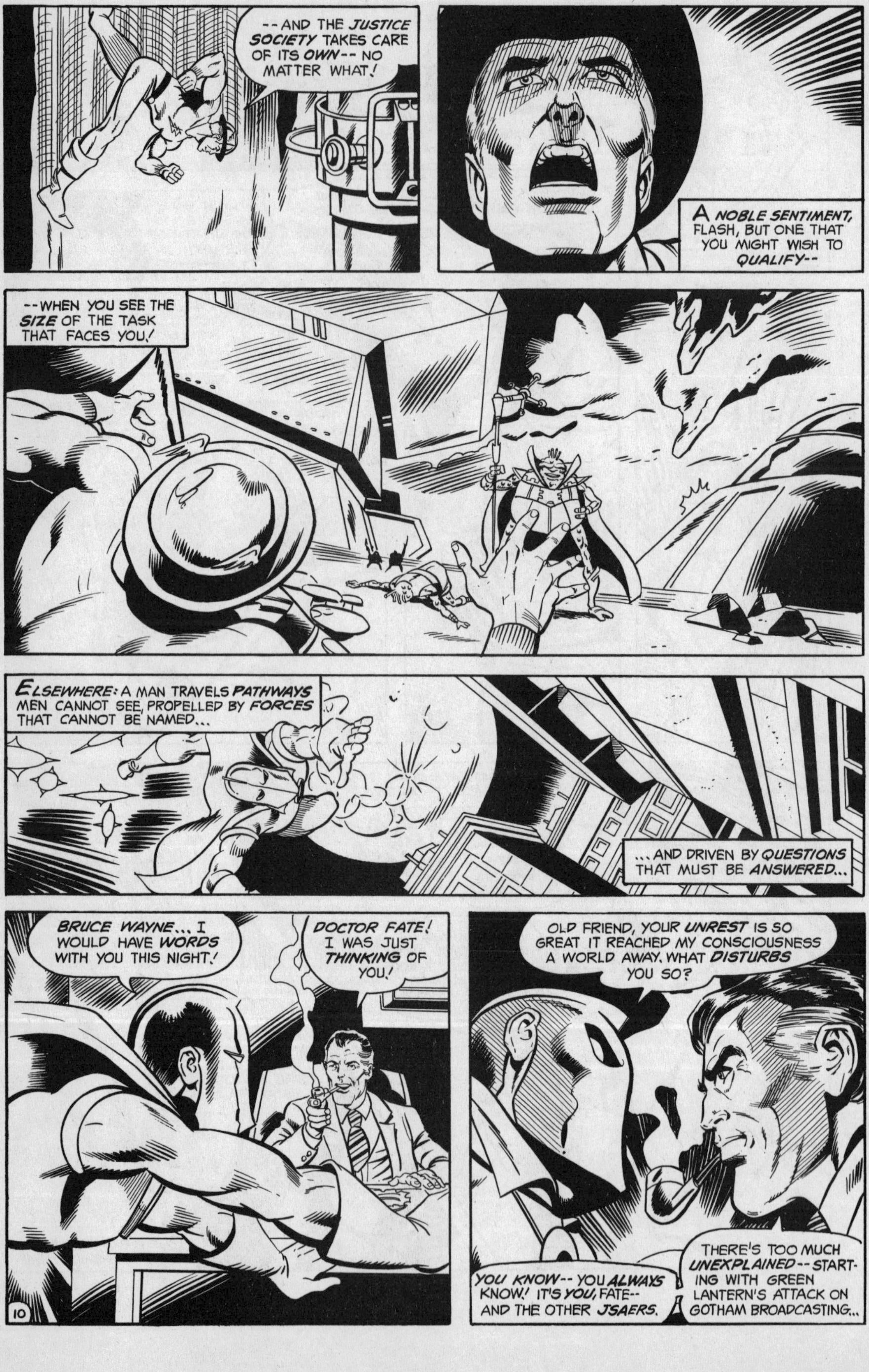
--AND THE JUSTICE SOCIETY TAKES CARE OF ITS OWN-- NO MATTER WHAT!
A NOBLE SENTIMENT, FLASH, BUT ONE THAT YOU MIGHT WISH TO QUALIFY--
--WHEN YOU SEE THE SIZE OF THE TASK THAT FACES YOU!
ELSEWHERE: A MAN TRAVELS PATHWAYS MEN CANNOT SEE, PROPELLED BY FORCES THAT CANNOT BE NAMED...
...AND DRIVEN BY QUESTIONS THAT MUST BE ANSWERED...
BRUCE WAYNE... I WOULD HAVE WORDS WITH YOU THIS NIGHT!
DOCTOR FATE! I WAS JUST THINKING OF YOU!
10
OLD FRIEND, YOUR UNREST IS SO GREAT IT REACHED MY CONSCIOUSNESS A WORLD AWAY. WHAT DISTURBS YOU SO?
YOU KNOW-- YOU ALWAYS KNOW! IT'S YOU, FATE-- AND THE OTHER JSAERS.
THERE'S TOO MUCH UNEXPLAINED-- STARTING WITH GREEN LANTERN'S ATTACK ON GOTHAM BROADCASTING...

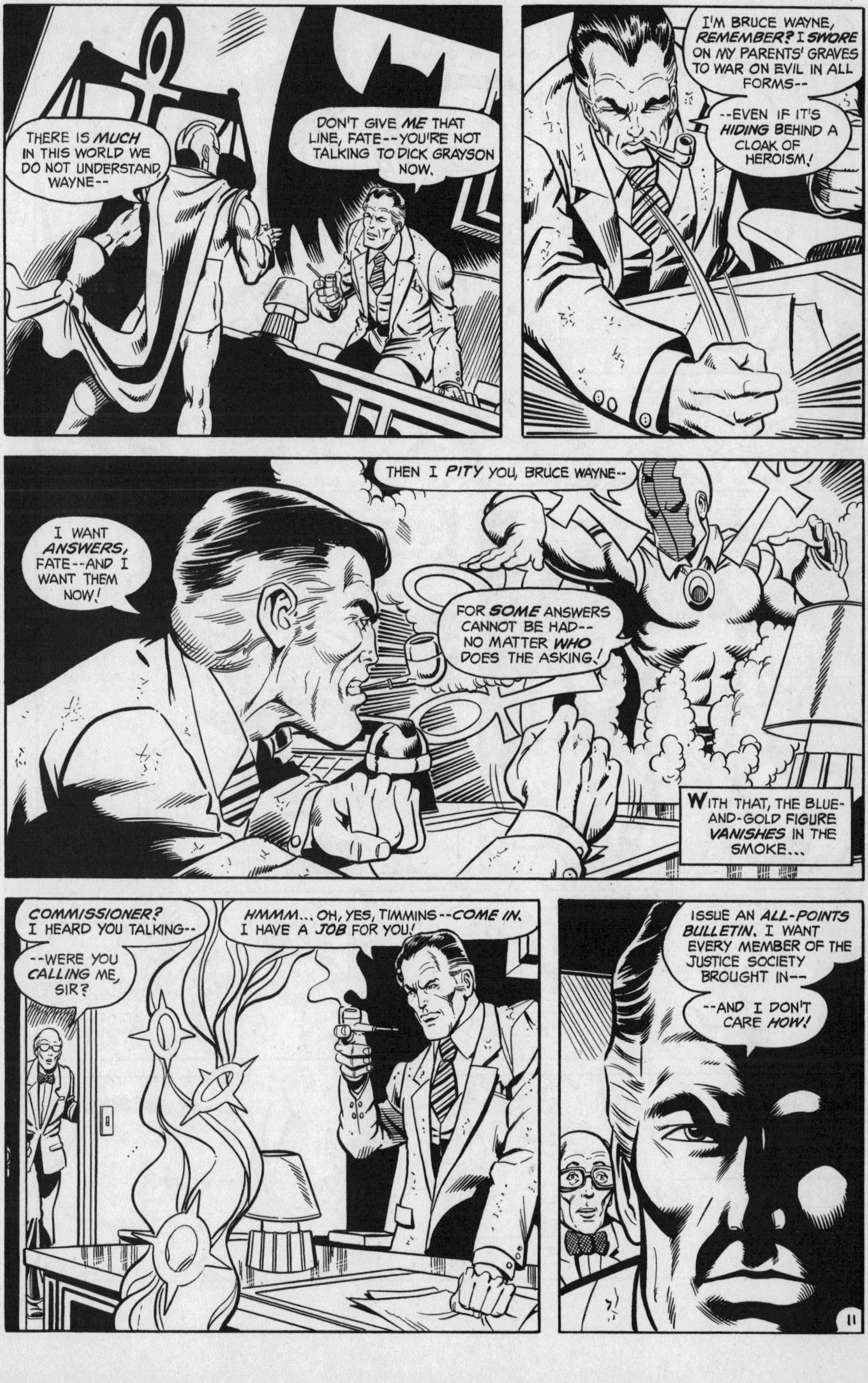
THERE IS *MUCH* IN THIS WORLD WE DO NOT UNDERSTAND, WAYNE--
DON'T GIVE *ME* THAT LINE, FATE--YOU'RE NOT TALKING TO DICK GRAYSON NOW.
I'M BRUCE WAYNE, *REMEMBER?* I *SWORE* ON MY PARENTS' GRAVES TO WAR ON EVIL IN ALL FORMS--
--EVEN IF IT'S *HIDING* BEHIND A CLOAK OF HEROISM!
I WANT *ANSWERS,* FATE--AND I WANT THEM NOW!
THEN I *PITY* YOU, BRUCE WAYNE--
FOR *SOME* ANSWERS CANNOT BE HAD-- NO MATTER *WHO* DOES THE ASKING!
WITH THAT, THE BLUE-AND-GOLD FIGURE *VANISHES* IN THE SMOKE...
COMMISSIONER? I HEARD YOU TALKING--
--WERE YOU *CALLING* ME, SIR?
HMMM... OH, YES, TIMMINS--*COME IN.* I HAVE A *JOB* FOR YOU!
ISSUE AN *ALL-POINTS BULLETIN.* I WANT EVERY MEMBER OF THE JUSTICE SOCIETY BROUGHT IN--
--AND I DON'T CARE *HOW!*
11

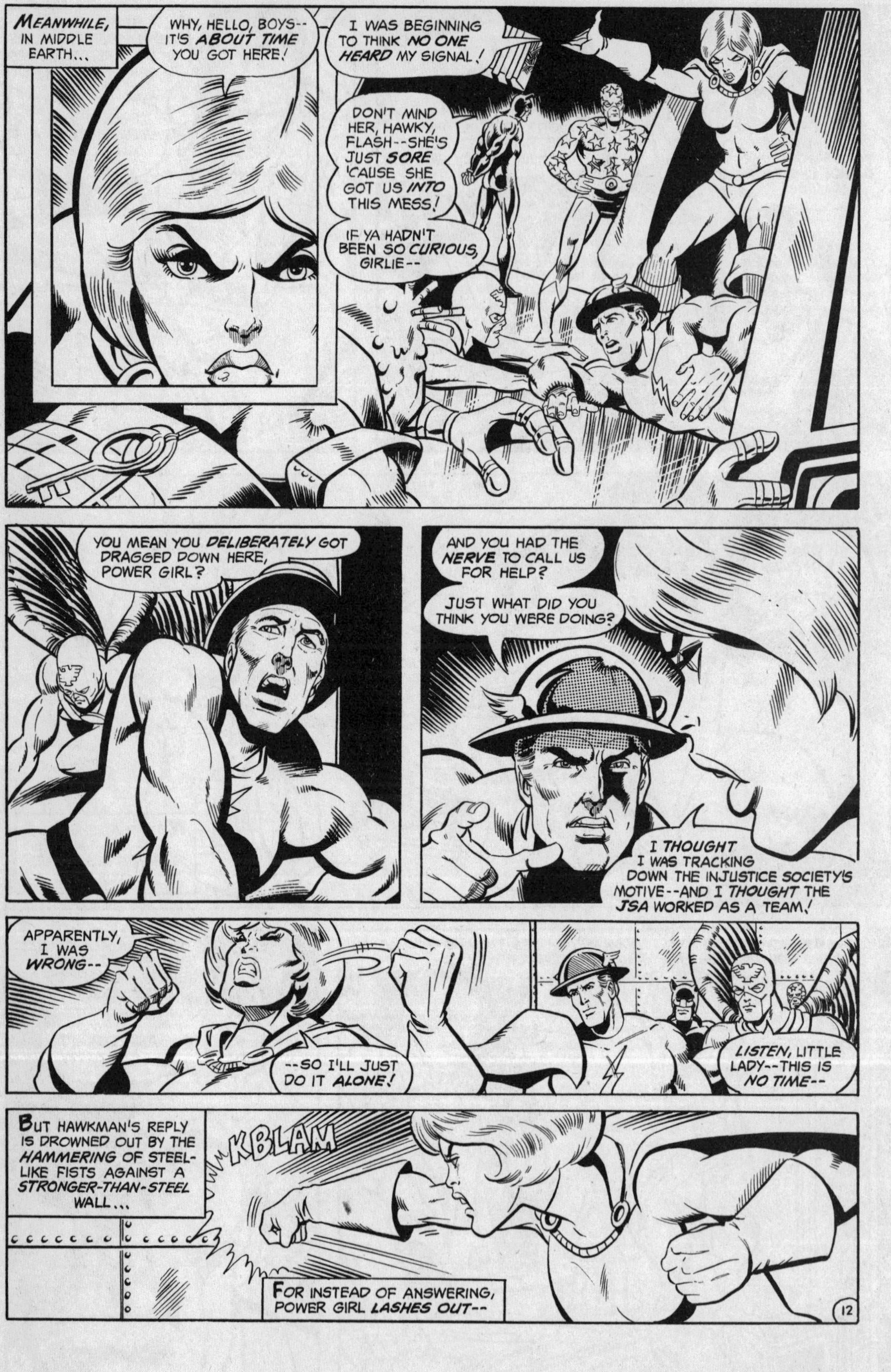
MEANWHILE, IN MIDDLE EARTH...
WHY, HELLO, BOYS-- IT'S ABOUT TIME YOU GOT HERE!
I WAS BEGINNING TO THINK NO ONE HEARD MY SIGNAL!
DON'T MIND HER, HAWKY, FLASH--SHE'S JUST SORE 'CAUSE SHE GOT US INTO THIS MESS!
IF YA HADN'T BEEN SO CURIOUS, GIRLIE--
YOU MEAN YOU DELIBERATELY GOT DRAGGED DOWN HERE, POWER GIRL?
AND YOU HAD THE NERVE TO CALL US FOR HELP?
JUST WHAT DID YOU THINK YOU WERE DOING?
I THOUGHT I WAS TRACKING DOWN THE INJUSTICE SOCIETY'S MOTIVE--AND I THOUGHT THE JSA WORKED AS A TEAM!
APPARENTLY, I WAS WRONG--
--SO I'LL JUST DO IT ALONE!
LISTEN, LITTLE LADY--THIS IS NO TIME--
BUT HAWKMAN'S REPLY IS DROWNED OUT BY THE HAMMERING OF STEEL-LIKE FISTS AGAINST A STRONGER-THAN-STEEL WALL...
KBLAM
FOR INSTEAD OF ANSWERING, POWER GIRL LASHES OUT--
12

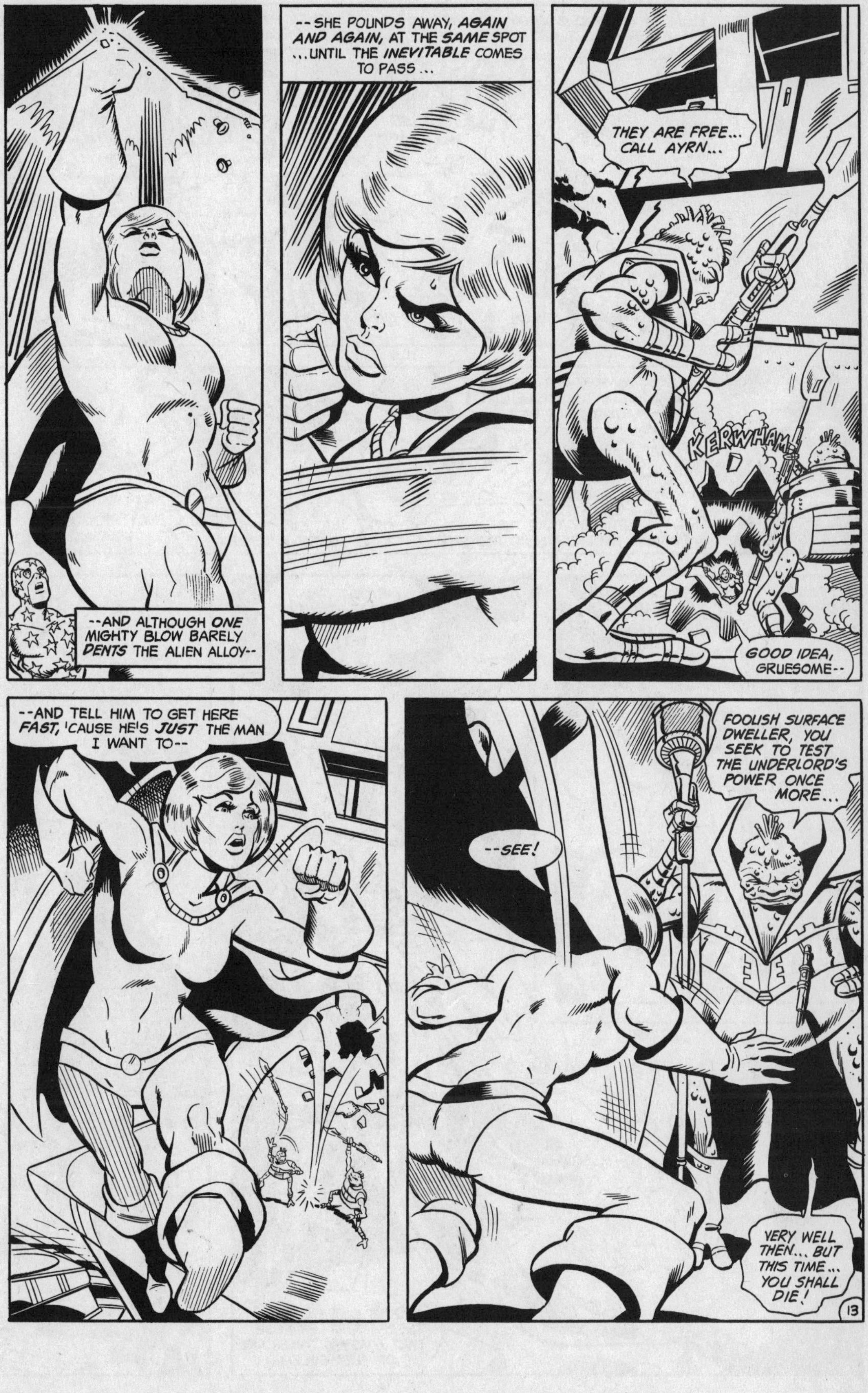
--AND ALTHOUGH ONE MIGHTY BLOW BARELY DENTS THE ALIEN ALLOY--
--SHE POUNDS AWAY, AGAIN AND AGAIN, AT THE SAME SPOT ...UNTIL THE INEVITABLE COMES TO PASS...
THEY ARE FREE... CALL AYRN...
KERWHAM
GOOD IDEA, GRUESOME--
--AND TELL HIM TO GET HERE FAST, 'CAUSE HE'S JUST THE MAN I WANT TO--
--SEE!
FOOLISH SURFACE DWELLER, YOU SEEK TO TEST THE UNDERLORD'S POWER ONCE MORE...
VERY WELL THEN... BUT THIS TIME... YOU SHALL DIE!
13

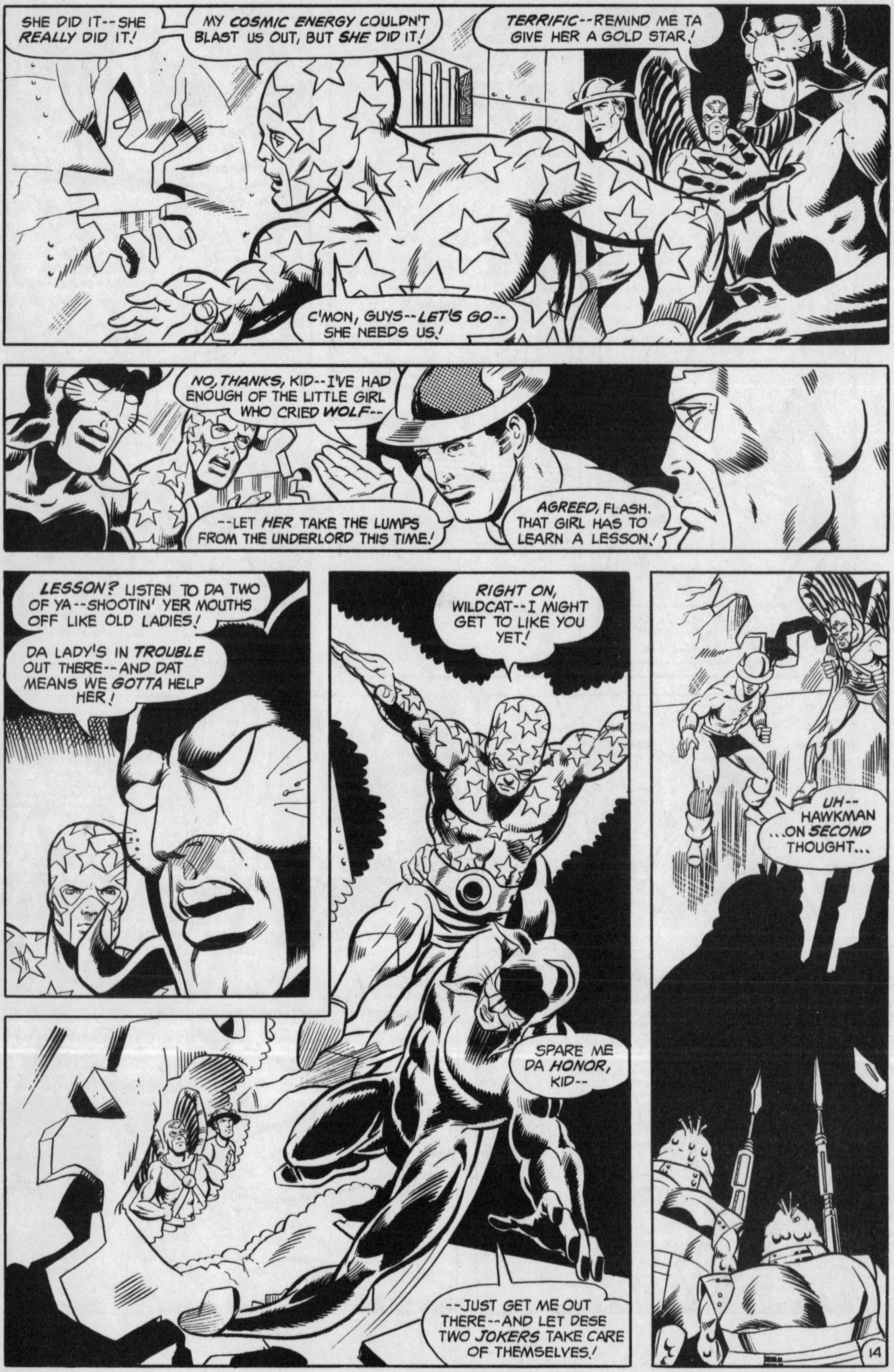
SHE DID IT--SHE REALLY DID IT!
MY COSMIC ENERGY COULDN'T BLAST US OUT, BUT SHE DID IT!
TERRIFIC--REMIND ME TA GIVE HER A GOLD STAR!
C'MON, GUYS--LET'S GO--SHE NEEDS US!
NO, THANKS, KID--I'VE HAD ENOUGH OF THE LITTLE GIRL WHO CRIED WOLF--
--LET HER TAKE THE LUMPS FROM THE UNDERLORD THIS TIME!
AGREED, FLASH. THAT GIRL HAS TO LEARN A LESSON!
LESSON? LISTEN TO DA TWO OF YA--SHOOTIN' YER MOUTHS OFF LIKE OLD LADIES!
DA LADY'S IN TROUBLE OUT THERE--AND DAT MEANS WE GOTTA HELP HER!
RIGHT ON, WILDCAT--I MIGHT GET TO LIKE YOU YET!
SPARE ME DA HONOR, KID--
--JUST GET ME OUT THERE--AND LET DESE TWO JOKERS TAKE CARE OF THEMSELVES!
UH--HAWKMAN ...ON SECOND THOUGHT...
14

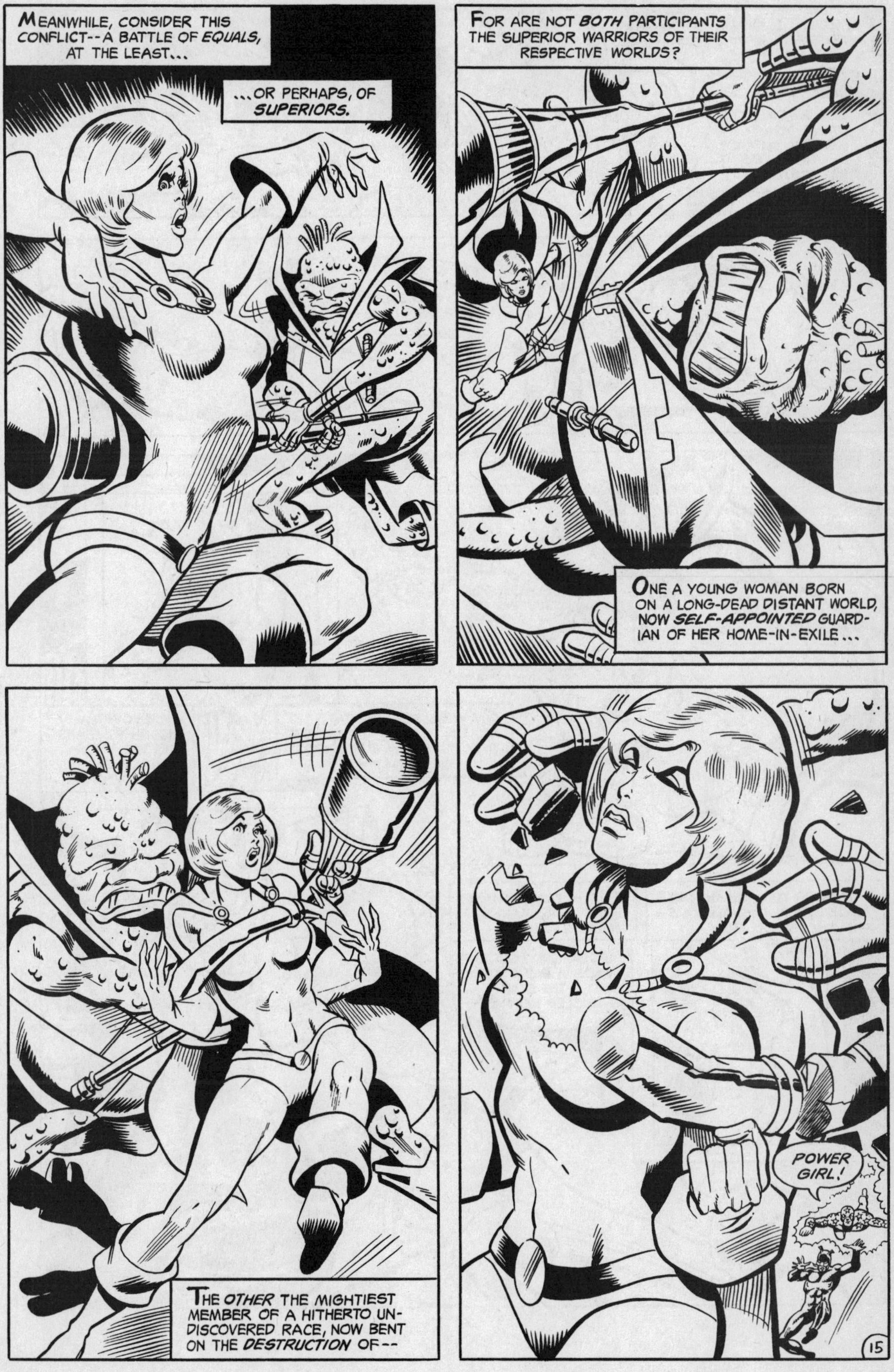
MEANWHILE, CONSIDER THIS CONFLICT--A BATTLE OF EQUALS, AT THE LEAST...
...OR PERHAPS, OF SUPERIORS.
FOR ARE NOT BOTH PARTICIPANTS THE SUPERIOR WARRIORS OF THEIR RESPECTIVE WORLDS?
ONE A YOUNG WOMAN BORN ON A LONG-DEAD DISTANT WORLD, NOW SELF-APPOINTED GUARDIAN OF HER HOME-IN-EXILE...
THE OTHER THE MIGHTIEST MEMBER OF A HITHERTO UNDISCOVERED RACE, NOW BENT ON THE DESTRUCTION OF--
POWER GIRL!
15

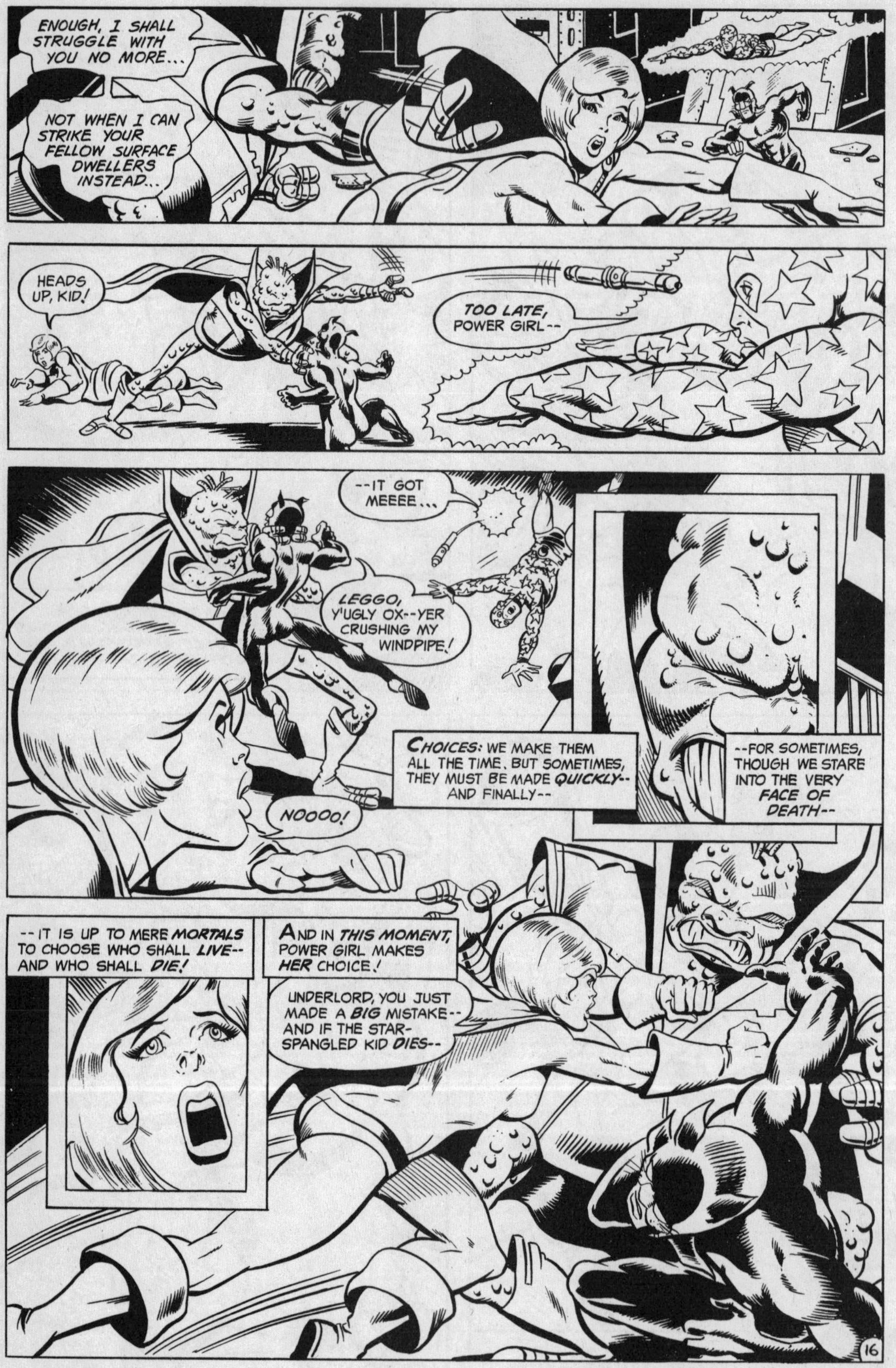
ENOUGH, I SHALL STRUGGLE WITH YOU NO MORE...
NOT WHEN I CAN STRIKE YOUR FELLOW SURFACE DWELLERS INSTEAD...
HEADS UP, KID!
TOO LATE, POWER GIRL--
--IT GOT MEEEE...
LEGGO, Y'UGLY OX--YER CRUSHING MY WINDPIPE!
NOOOO!
CHOICES: WE MAKE THEM ALL THE TIME. BUT SOMETIMES, THEY MUST BE MADE QUICKLY--AND FINALLY--
--FOR SOMETIMES, THOUGH WE STARE INTO THE VERY FACE OF DEATH--
--IT IS UP TO MERE MORTALS TO CHOOSE WHO SHALL LIVE--AND WHO SHALL DIE!
AND IN THIS MOMENT, POWER GIRL MAKES HER CHOICE!
UNDERLORD, YOU JUST MADE A BIG MISTAKE--AND IF THE STAR-SPANGLED KID DIES--
16

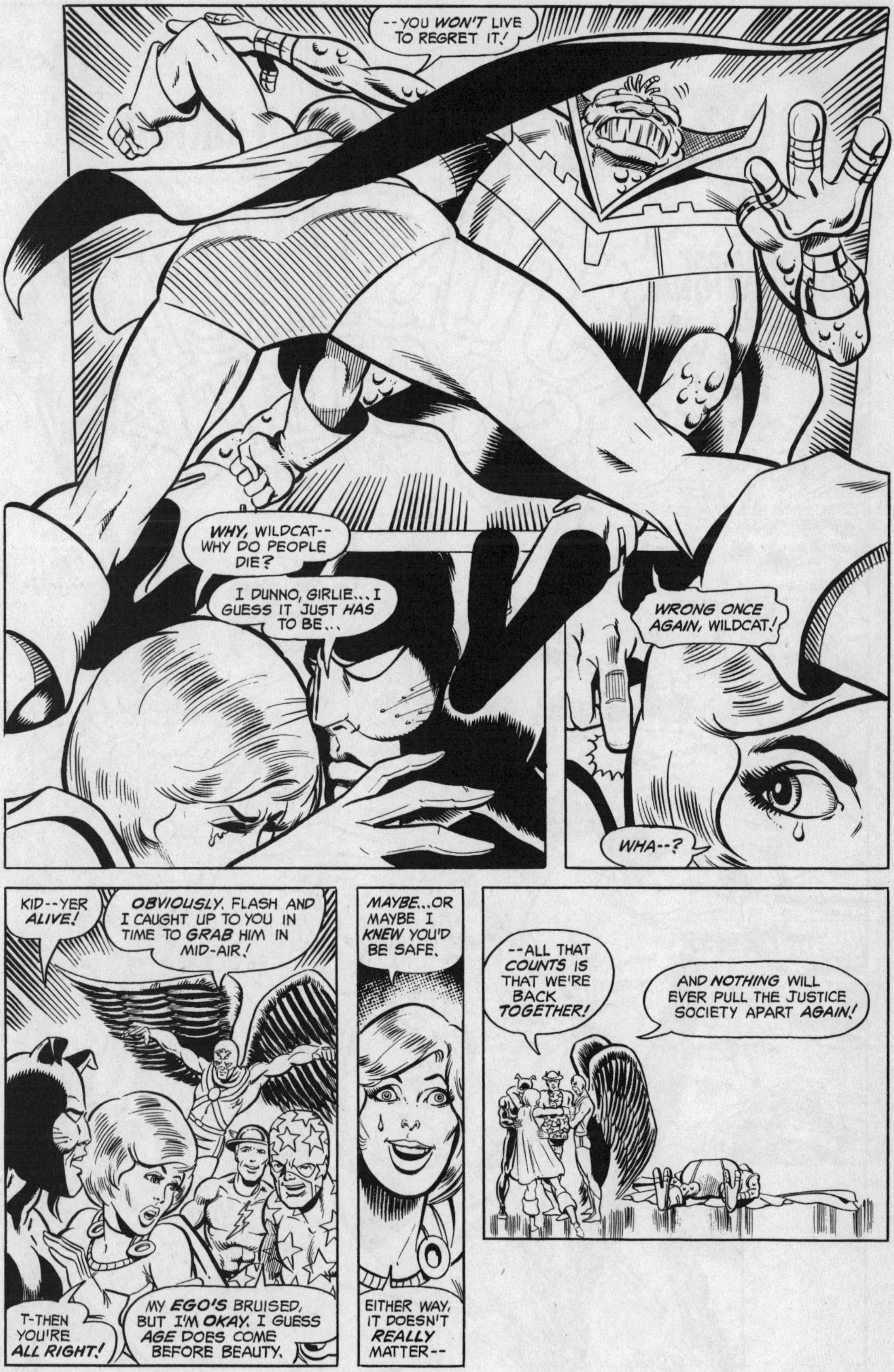
--YOU WON'T LIVE TO REGRET IT!
WHY, WILDCAT-- WHY DO PEOPLE DIE?
I DUNNO, GIRLIE... I GUESS IT JUST HAS TO BE...
WRONG ONCE AGAIN, WILDCAT!
WHA--?
KID--YER ALIVE!
OBVIOUSLY. FLASH AND I CAUGHT UP TO YOU IN TIME TO GRAB HIM IN MID-AIR!
T-THEN YOU'RE ALL RIGHT!
MY EGO'S BRUISED, BUT I'M OKAY. I GUESS AGE DOES COME BEFORE BEAUTY.
MAYBE...OR MAYBE I KNEW YOU'D BE SAFE.
EITHER WAY, IT DOESN'T REALLY MATTER--
--ALL THAT COUNTS IS THAT WE'RE BACK TOGETHER!
AND NOTHING WILL EVER PULL THE JUSTICE SOCIETY APART AGAIN!

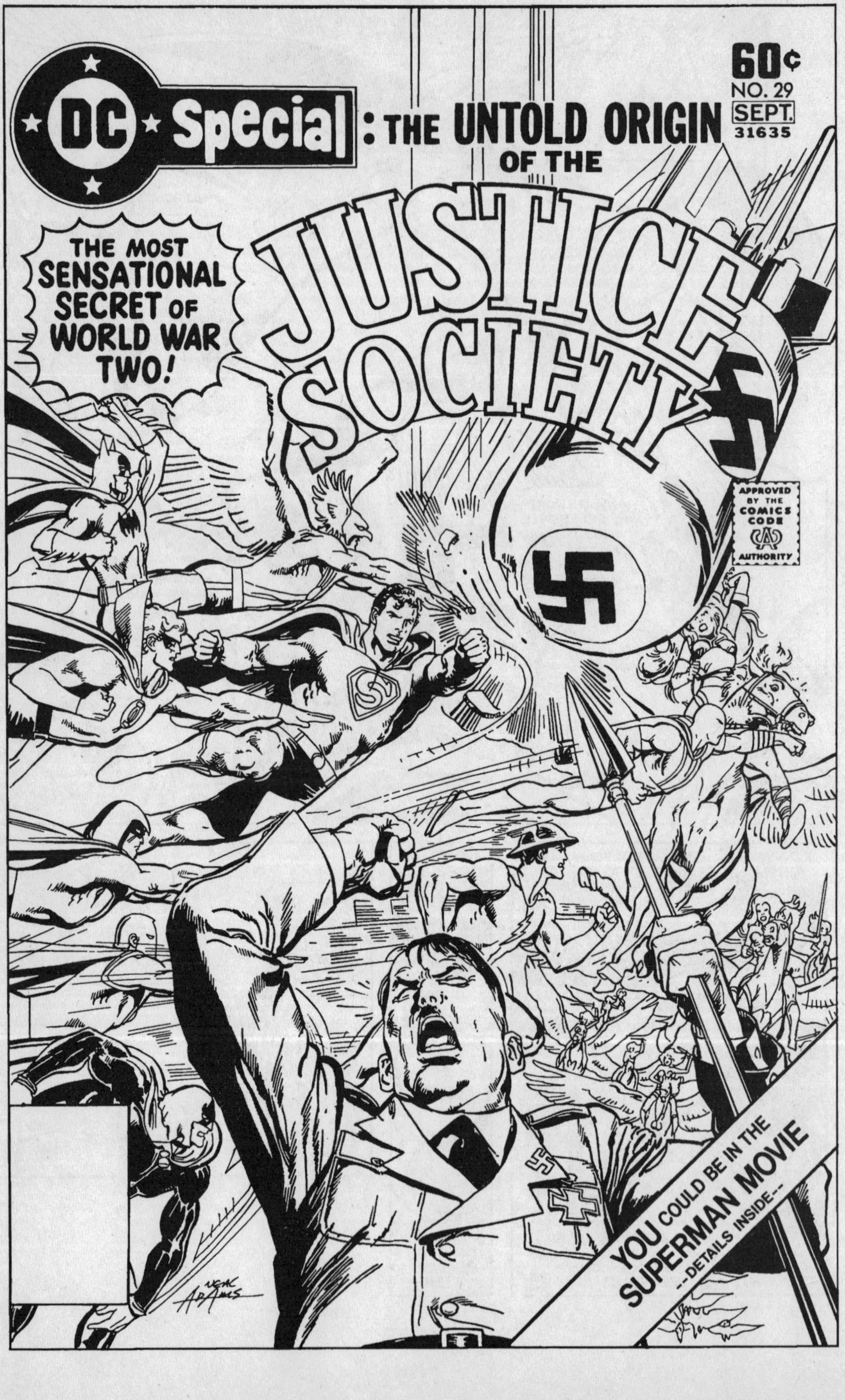
60¢
NO. 29
SEPT.
31635
DC Special: THE UNTOLD ORIGIN OF THE
JUSTICE SOCIETY
THE MOST SENSATIONAL SECRET OF WORLD WAR TWO!
APPROVED BY THE COMICS CODE AUTHORITY
YOU COULD BE IN THE SUPERMAN MOVIE
--DETAILS INSIDE--

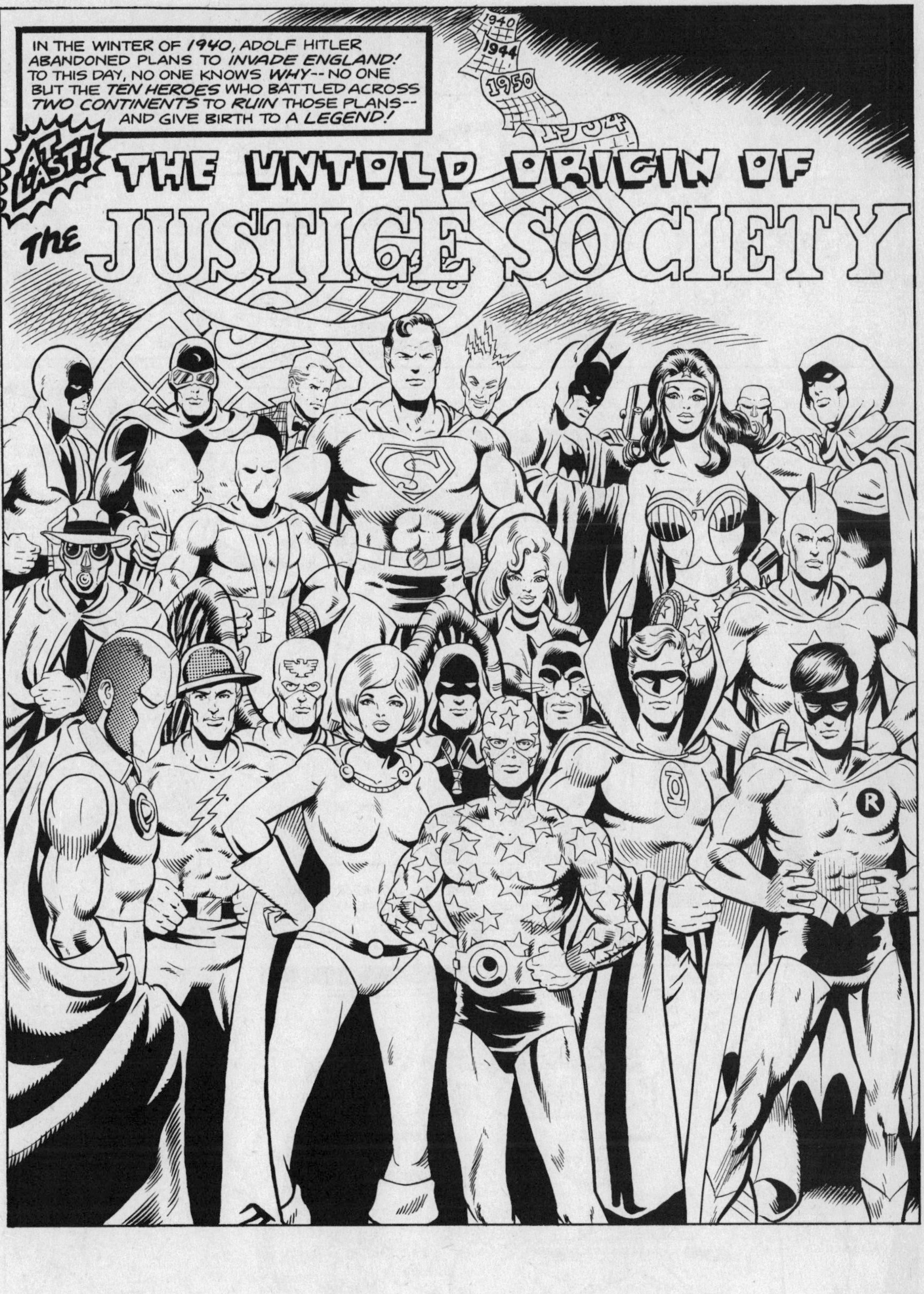
IN THE WINTER OF 1940, ADOLF HITLER ABANDONED PLANS TO INVADE ENGLAND! TO THIS DAY, NO ONE KNOWS WHY-- NO ONE BUT THE TEN HEROES WHO BATTLED ACROSS TWO CONTINENTS TO RUIN THOSE PLANS-- AND GIVE BIRTH TO A LEGEND!
1940
1944
1950
AT LAST!
THE UNTOLD ORIGIN OF
THE JUSTICE SOCIETY
R

PROLOGUE

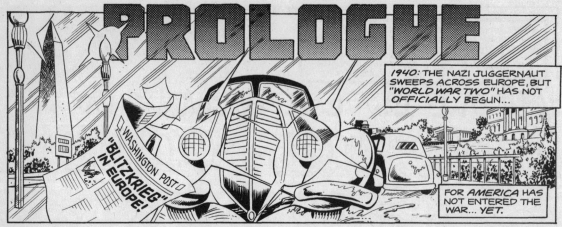

1940: THE NAZI JUGGERNAUT SWEEPS ACROSS EUROPE, BUT "WORLD WAR TWO" HAS NOT OFFICIALLY BEGUN...

WASHINGTON POST "BLITZKRIEG" IN EUROPE!

FOR AMERICA HAS NOT ENTERED THE WAR... YET.

FRANKLIN DELANO ROOSEVELT HAS JUST BEEN RE-ELECTED FOR AN UNPRECEDENTED THIRD TERM AS PRESIDENT, AND HE HAS PROMISED AMERICA PEACE...

A PROMISE HE IS HARD-PRESSED TO KEEP.

FOR THE STORM THAT DRENCHES WASHINGTON IS MINOR--

--WHEN COMPARED TO THE MAELSTROM THAT WILL RAGE WHEN THIS MESSENGER DELIVERS HIS THUNDEROUS NEWS...

A BULLETIN FROM "INTREPID" FOR THE PRESIDENT!

IT IS IMPERATIVE THAT I SEE HIM-- AT ONCE!

YES, SIR!

AND SO...

GOOD TO SEE YOU AGAIN, SMYTHE. I TRUST "INTREPID" IS WELL--

--WE CAN'T HAVE THE CHIEF OF BRITISH SECURITY COORDINATION OUT OF COMMISSION.

MR. STEPHENSON IS FINE, SIR. IT IS THE HEALTH OF THE REST OF THE WORLD THAT WORRIES HIM.

2

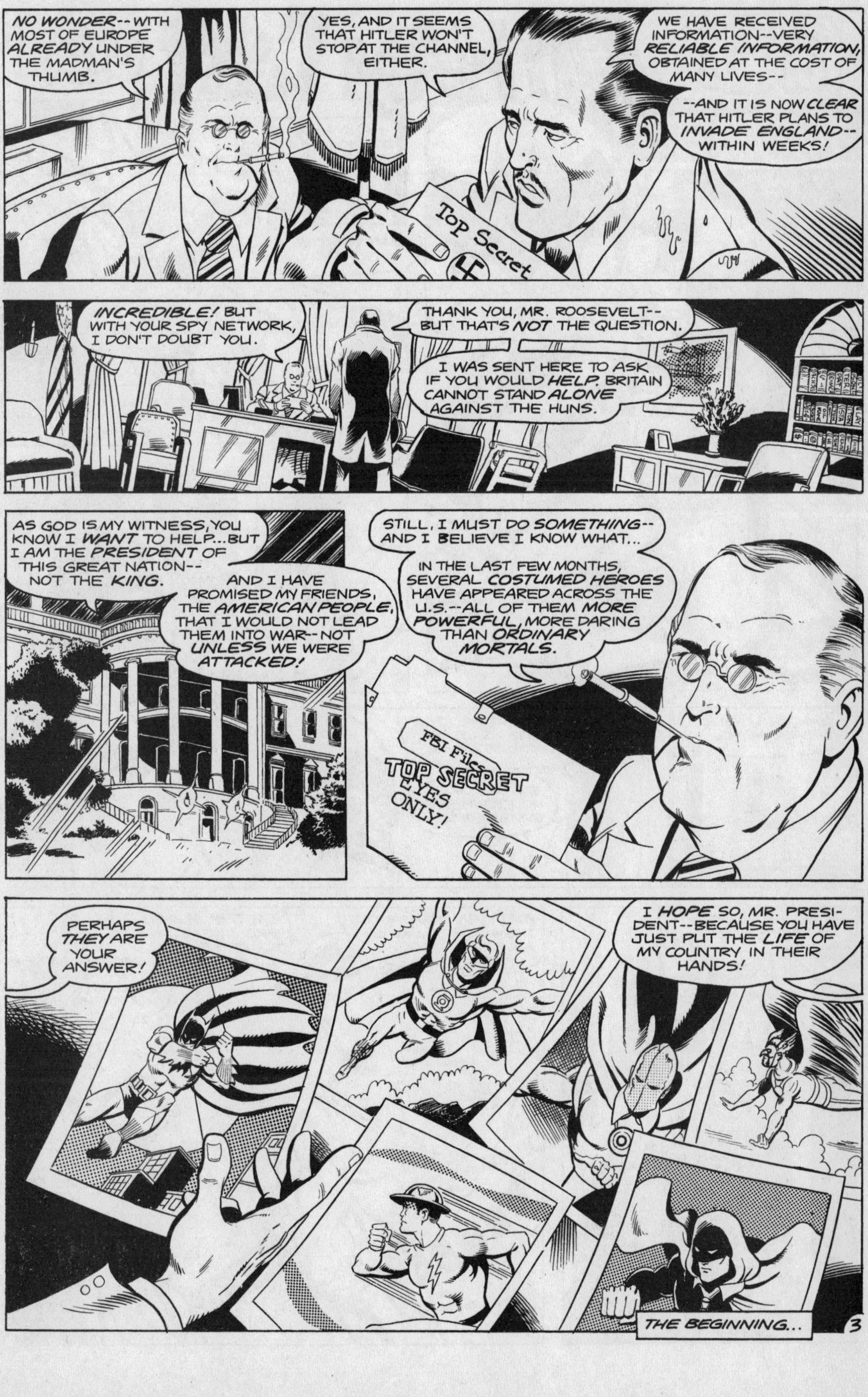
NO WONDER--WITH MOST OF EUROPE ALREADY UNDER THE MADMAN'S THUMB.
YES, AND IT SEEMS THAT HITLER WON'T STOP AT THE CHANNEL, EITHER.
WE HAVE RECEIVED INFORMATION--VERY RELIABLE INFORMATION, OBTAINED AT THE COST OF MANY LIVES--
--AND IT IS NOW CLEAR THAT HITLER PLANS TO INVADE ENGLAND--WITHIN WEEKS!
Top Secret
INCREDIBLE! BUT WITH YOUR SPY NETWORK, I DON'T DOUBT YOU.
THANK YOU, MR. ROOSEVELT--BUT THAT'S NOT THE QUESTION.
I WAS SENT HERE TO ASK IF YOU WOULD HELP. BRITAIN CANNOT STAND ALONE AGAINST THE HUNS.
AS GOD IS MY WITNESS, YOU KNOW I WANT TO HELP...BUT I AM THE PRESIDENT OF THIS GREAT NATION--NOT THE KING.
AND I HAVE PROMISED MY FRIENDS, THE AMERICAN PEOPLE, THAT I WOULD NOT LEAD THEM INTO WAR--NOT UNLESS WE WERE ATTACKED!
STILL, I MUST DO SOMETHING--AND I BELIEVE I KNOW WHAT...
IN THE LAST FEW MONTHS, SEVERAL COSTUMED HEROES HAVE APPEARED ACROSS THE U.S.--ALL OF THEM MORE POWERFUL, MORE DARING THAN ORDINARY MORTALS.
FBI Files
TOP SECRET EYES ONLY!
PERHAPS THEY ARE YOUR ANSWER!
I HOPE SO, MR. PRESIDENT--BECAUSE YOU HAVE JUST PUT THE LIFE OF MY COUNTRY IN THEIR HANDS!
THE BEGINNING...
3

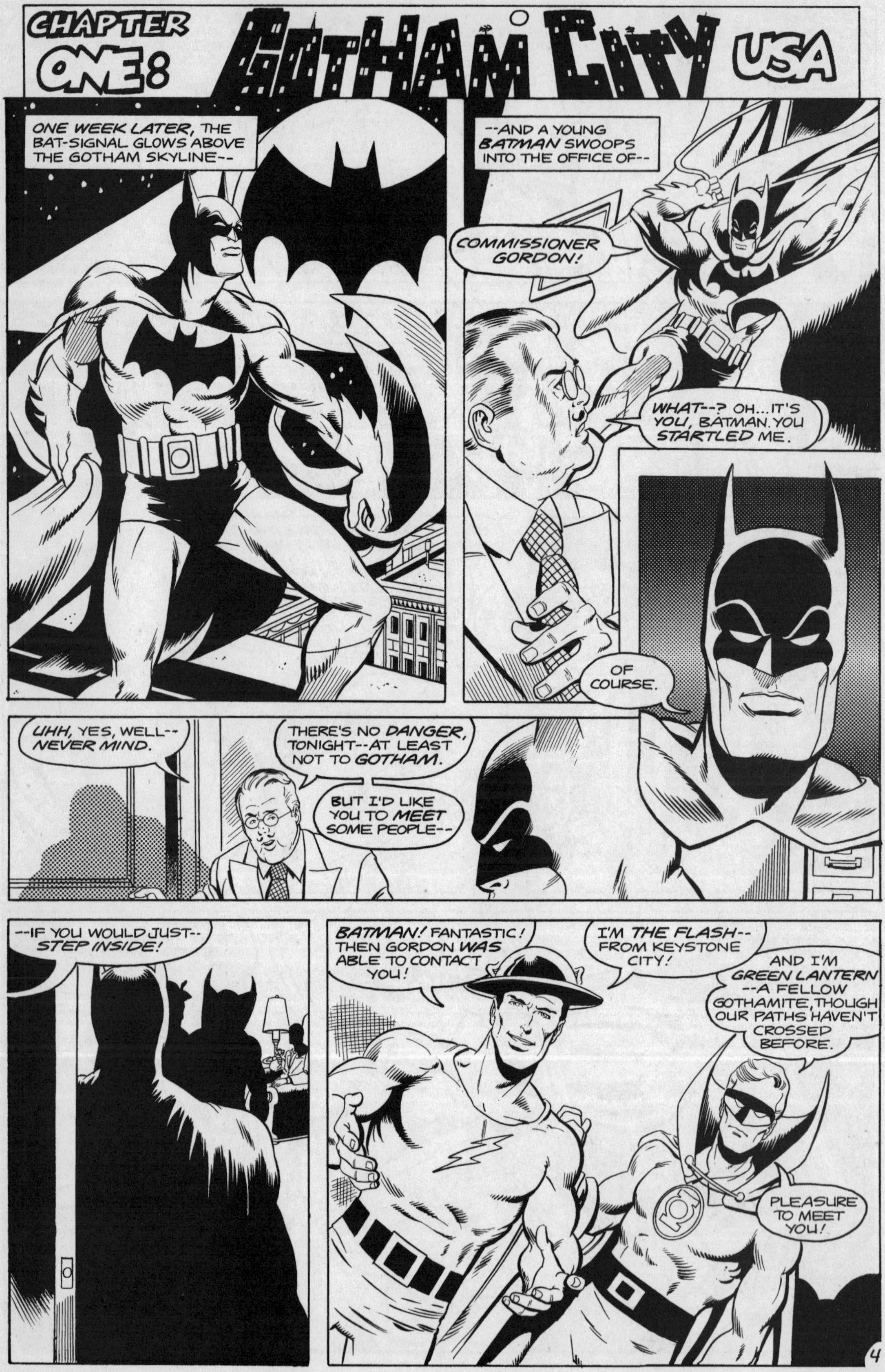
CHAPTER ONE 8
GOTHAM CITY USA
ONE WEEK LATER, THE BAT-SIGNAL GLOWS ABOVE THE GOTHAM SKYLINE--
--AND A YOUNG BATMAN SWOOPS INTO THE OFFICE OF--
COMMISSIONER GORDON!
WHAT--? OH... IT'S YOU, BATMAN. YOU STARTLED ME.
OF COURSE.
UHH, YES, WELL-- NEVER MIND.
THERE'S NO DANGER, TONIGHT--AT LEAST NOT TO GOTHAM.
BUT I'D LIKE YOU TO MEET SOME PEOPLE--
--IF YOU WOULD JUST-- STEP INSIDE!
BATMAN! FANTASTIC! THEN GORDON WAS ABLE TO CONTACT YOU!
I'M THE FLASH-- FROM KEYSTONE CITY!
AND I'M GREEN LANTERN --A FELLOW GOTHAMITE, THOUGH OUR PATHS HAVEN'T CROSSED BEFORE.
PLEASURE TO MEET YOU!
4

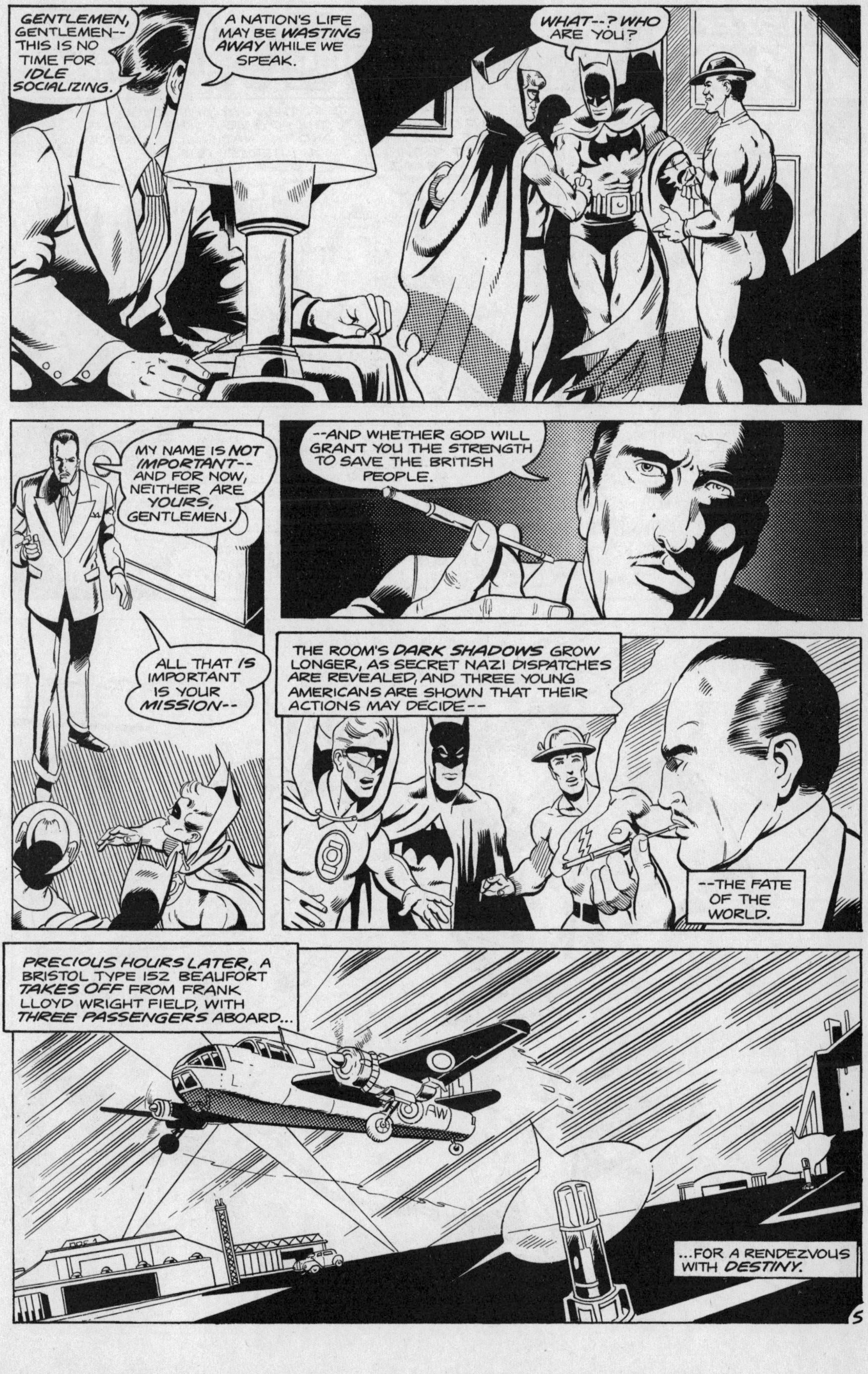
GENTLEMEN, GENTLEMEN-- THIS IS NO TIME FOR IDLE SOCIALIZING.
A NATION'S LIFE MAY BE WASTING AWAY WHILE WE SPEAK.
WHAT--? WHO ARE YOU?
MY NAME IS NOT IMPORTANT-- AND FOR NOW, NEITHER ARE YOURS, GENTLEMEN.
ALL THAT IS IMPORTANT IS YOUR MISSION--
--AND WHETHER GOD WILL GRANT YOU THE STRENGTH TO SAVE THE BRITISH PEOPLE.
THE ROOM'S DARK SHADOWS GROW LONGER, AS SECRET NAZI DISPATCHES ARE REVEALED, AND THREE YOUNG AMERICANS ARE SHOWN THAT THEIR ACTIONS MAY DECIDE--
--THE FATE OF THE WORLD.
PRECIOUS HOURS LATER, A BRISTOL TYPE 152 BEAUFORT TAKES OFF FROM FRANK LLOYD WRIGHT FIELD, WITH THREE PASSENGERS ABOARD...
...FOR A RENDEZVOUS WITH DESTINY.
5

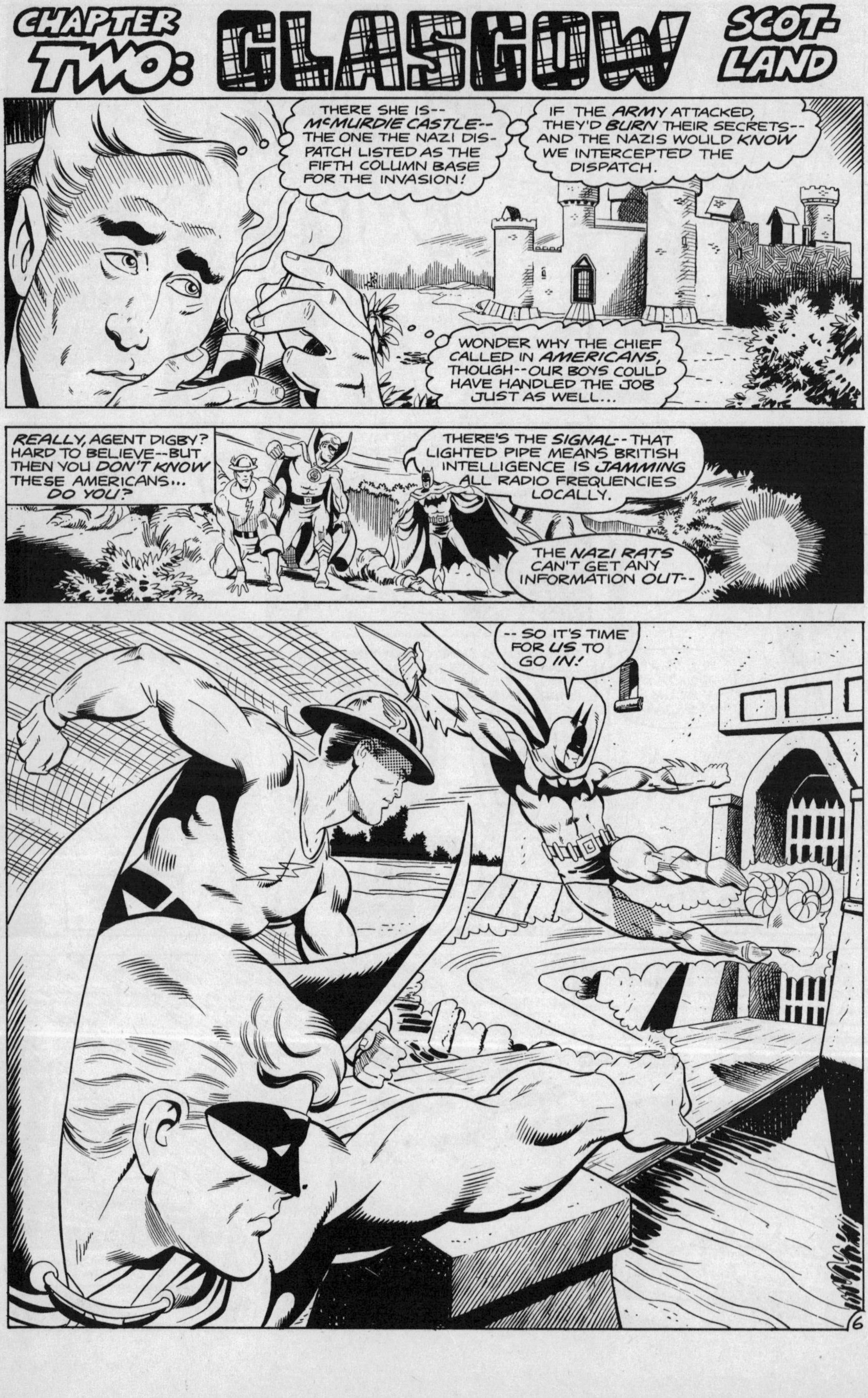
CHAPTER TWO: GLASGOW SCOTLAND
THERE SHE IS-- McMURDIE CASTLE-- THE ONE THE NAZI DISPATCH LISTED AS THE FIFTH COLUMN BASE FOR THE INVASION!
IF THE ARMY ATTACKED, THEY'D BURN THEIR SECRETS-- AND THE NAZIS WOULD KNOW WE INTERCEPTED THE DISPATCH.
WONDER WHY THE CHIEF CALLED IN AMERICANS, THOUGH--OUR BOYS COULD HAVE HANDLED THE JOB JUST AS WELL...
REALLY, AGENT DIGBY? HARD TO BELIEVE--BUT THEN YOU DON'T KNOW THESE AMERICANS... DO YOU?
THERE'S THE SIGNAL-- THAT LIGHTED PIPE MEANS BRITISH INTELLIGENCE IS JAMMING ALL RADIO FREQUENCIES LOCALLY.
THE NAZI RATS CAN'T GET ANY INFORMATION OUT--
--SO IT'S TIME FOR US TO GO IN!
6

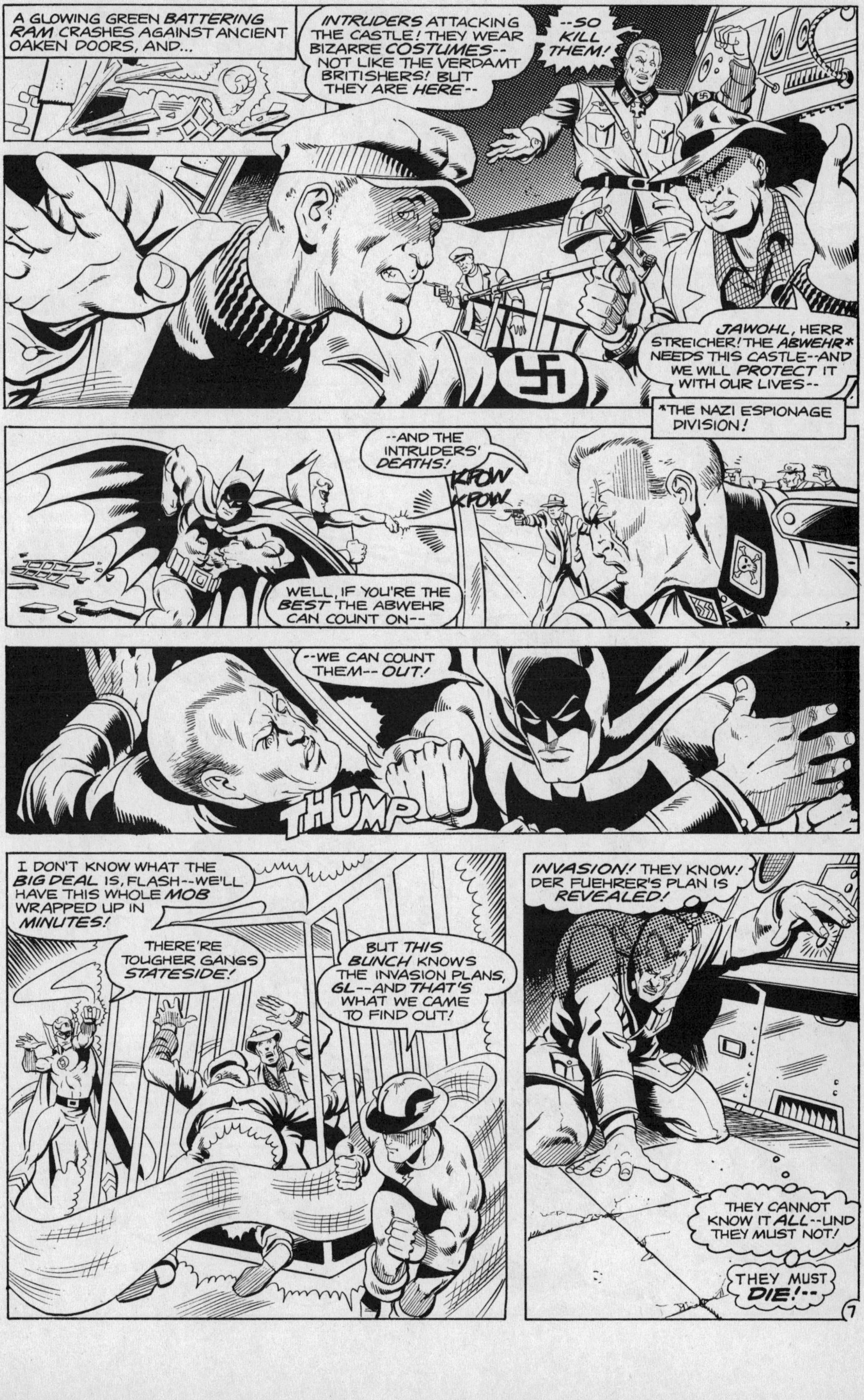
A GLOWING GREEN BATTERING RAM CRASHES AGAINST ANCIENT OAKEN DOORS, AND...
INTRUDERS ATTACKING THE CASTLE! THEY WEAR BIZARRE COSTUMES-- NOT LIKE THE VERDAMT BRITISHERS! BUT THEY ARE HERE--
--SO KILL THEM!
JAWOHL, HERR STREICHER! THE ABWEHR* NEEDS THIS CASTLE--AND WE WILL PROTECT IT WITH OUR LIVES--
*THE NAZI ESPIONAGE DIVISION!
--AND THE INTRUDERS' DEATHS!
KPOW
KPOW
WELL, IF YOU'RE THE BEST THE ABWEHR CAN COUNT ON--
--WE CAN COUNT THEM-- OUT!
THUMP
I DON'T KNOW WHAT THE BIG DEAL IS, FLASH--WE'LL HAVE THIS WHOLE MOB WRAPPED UP IN MINUTES!
THERE'RE TOUGHER GANGS STATESIDE!
BUT THIS BUNCH KNOWS THE INVASION PLANS, GL--AND THAT'S WHAT WE CAME TO FIND OUT!
INVASION! THEY KNOW! DER FUEHRER'S PLAN IS REVEALED!
THEY CANNOT KNOW IT ALL--UND THEY MUST NOT!
THEY MUST DIE!--
7

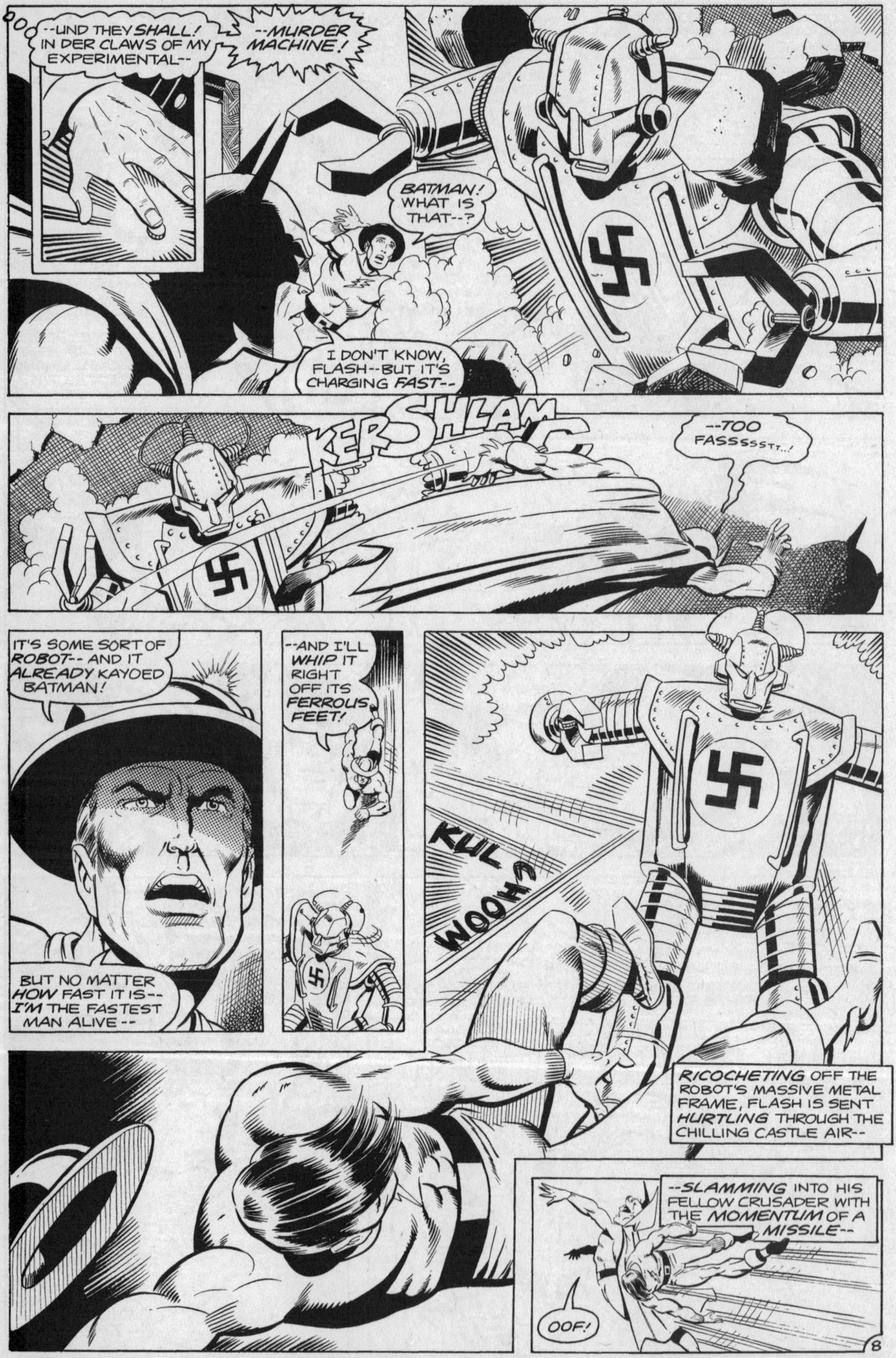
--UND THEY SHALL! IN DER CLAWS OF MY EXPERIMENTAL--
--MURDER MACHINE!
BATMAN! WHAT IS THAT--?
I DON'T KNOW, FLASH--BUT IT'S CHARGING FAST--
KERSHLAM
--TOO FASSSSSTT...!
IT'S SOME SORT OF ROBOT-- AND IT ALREADY KAYOED BATMAN!
BUT NO MATTER HOW FAST IT IS-- I'M THE FASTEST MAN ALIVE--
--AND I'LL WHIP IT RIGHT OFF ITS FERROUS FEET!
KULCHOOM
RICOCHETING OFF THE ROBOT'S MASSIVE METAL FRAME, FLASH IS SENT HURTLING THROUGH THE CHILLING CASTLE AIR--
--SLAMMING INTO HIS FELLOW CRUSADER WITH THE MOMENTUM OF A MISSILE--
OOF!
8

--AND FOR A MOMENT THE ROOM IS VERY *STILL*...

THE CAGE--IT *FADES* AWAY! WE'RE *FREE*!

YES--THE GREEN OBJECTS SEEMED TO LAST ONLY AS LONG AS THE CLOAKED ONE WAS *CONSCIOUS*!

THESE AMERIKANERS ARE *FASCINATING*-- EVEN IF THEY WERE *NO MATCH* FOR SUPERIOR *ARYAN* TECHNOLOGY!

DER FUEHRER *HIMSELF* WILL WANT TO SEE THEM IN *BERLIN*!

INTERLUDE: SALEM, MASSACHUSETTS

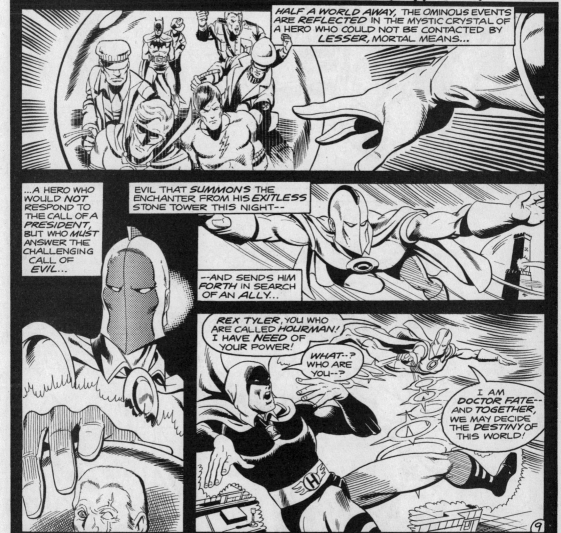

HALF A WORLD AWAY, THE OMINOUS EVENTS ARE *REFLECTED* IN THE MYSTIC CRYSTAL OF A HERO WHO COULD NOT BE CONTACTED BY *LESSER*, MORTAL MEANS...

...A HERO WHO WOULD *NOT* RESPOND TO THE CALL OF A *PRESIDENT*, BUT WHO *MUST* ANSWER THE *CHALLENGING* CALL OF *EVIL*...

EVIL THAT *SUMMONS* THE ENCHANTER FROM HIS *EXITLESS* STONE TOWER THIS NIGHT--

--AND SENDS HIM *FORTH* IN SEARCH OF AN *ALLY*...

REX TYLER, YOU WHO ARE CALLED *HOURMAN*! I HAVE *NEED* OF YOUR POWER!

WHAT--? WHO ARE YOU--?

I AM *DOCTOR FATE*-- AND *TOGETHER*, WE MAY DECIDE THE *DESTINY* OF THIS WORLD!

9

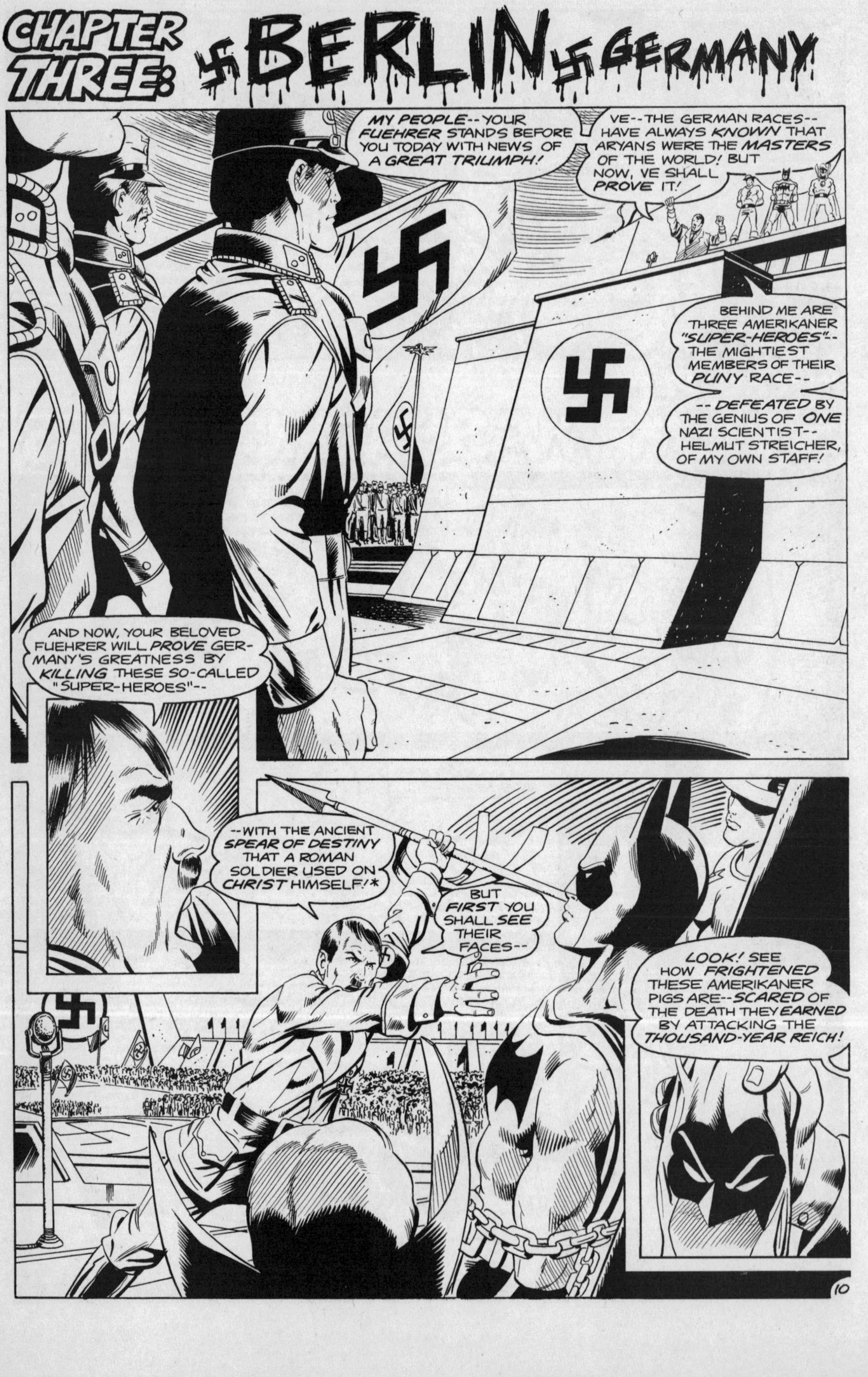
CHAPTER THREE: BERLIN GERMANY
MY PEOPLE--YOUR FUEHRER STANDS BEFORE YOU TODAY WITH NEWS OF A GREAT TRIUMPH!
VE--THE GERMAN RACES--HAVE ALWAYS KNOWN THAT ARYANS WERE THE MASTERS OF THE WORLD! BUT NOW, VE SHALL PROVE IT!
BEHIND ME ARE THREE AMERIKANER "SUPER-HEROES"--THE MIGHTIEST MEMBERS OF THEIR PUNY RACE--
--DEFEATED BY THE GENIUS OF ONE NAZI SCIENTIST--HELMUT STREICHER, OF MY OWN STAFF!
AND NOW, YOUR BELOVED FUEHRER WILL PROVE GERMANY'S GREATNESS BY KILLING THESE SO-CALLED "SUPER-HEROES"--
--WITH THE ANCIENT SPEAR OF DESTINY THAT A ROMAN SOLDIER USED ON CHRIST HIMSELF!*
BUT FIRST YOU SHALL SEE THEIR FACES--
LOOK! SEE HOW FRIGHTENED THESE AMERIKANER PIGS ARE--SCARED OF THE DEATH THEY EARNED BY ATTACKING THE THOUSAND-YEAR REICH!
10

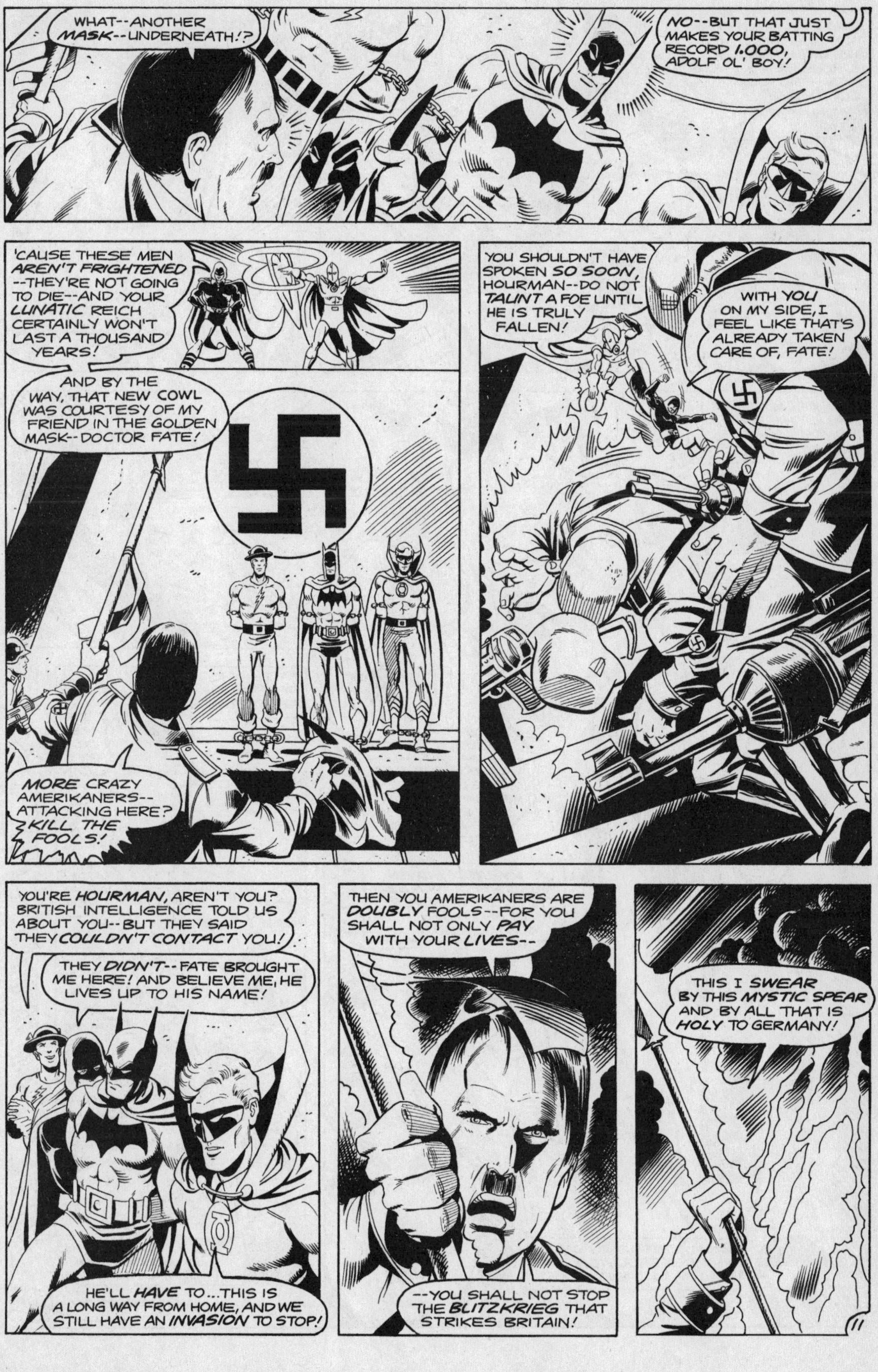
WHAT--ANOTHER MASK--UNDERNEATH!?
NO--BUT THAT JUST MAKES YOUR BATTING RECORD 1.000, ADOLF OL' BOY!
'CAUSE THESE MEN AREN'T FRIGHTENED--THEY'RE NOT GOING TO DIE--AND YOUR LUNATIC REICH CERTAINLY WON'T LAST A THOUSAND YEARS!
AND BY THE WAY, THAT NEW COWL WAS COURTESY OF MY FRIEND IN THE GOLDEN MASK--DOCTOR FATE!
MORE CRAZY AMERIKANERS--ATTACKING HERE? KILL THE FOOLS!
YOU SHOULDN'T HAVE SPOKEN SO SOON, HOURMAN--DO NOT TAUNT A FOE UNTIL HE IS TRULY FALLEN!
WITH YOU ON MY SIDE, I FEEL LIKE THAT'S ALREADY TAKEN CARE OF, FATE!
YOU'RE HOURMAN, AREN'T YOU? BRITISH INTELLIGENCE TOLD US ABOUT YOU--BUT THEY SAID THEY COULDN'T CONTACT YOU!
THEY DIDN'T--FATE BROUGHT ME HERE! AND BELIEVE ME, HE LIVES UP TO HIS NAME!
HE'LL HAVE TO...THIS IS A LONG WAY FROM HOME, AND WE STILL HAVE AN INVASION TO STOP!
THEN YOU AMERIKANERS ARE DOUBLY FOOLS--FOR YOU SHALL NOT ONLY PAY WITH YOUR LIVES--
--YOU SHALL NOT STOP THE BLITZKRIEG THAT STRIKES BRITAIN!
THIS I SWEAR BY THIS MYSTIC SPEAR AND BY ALL THAT IS HOLY TO GERMANY!
11

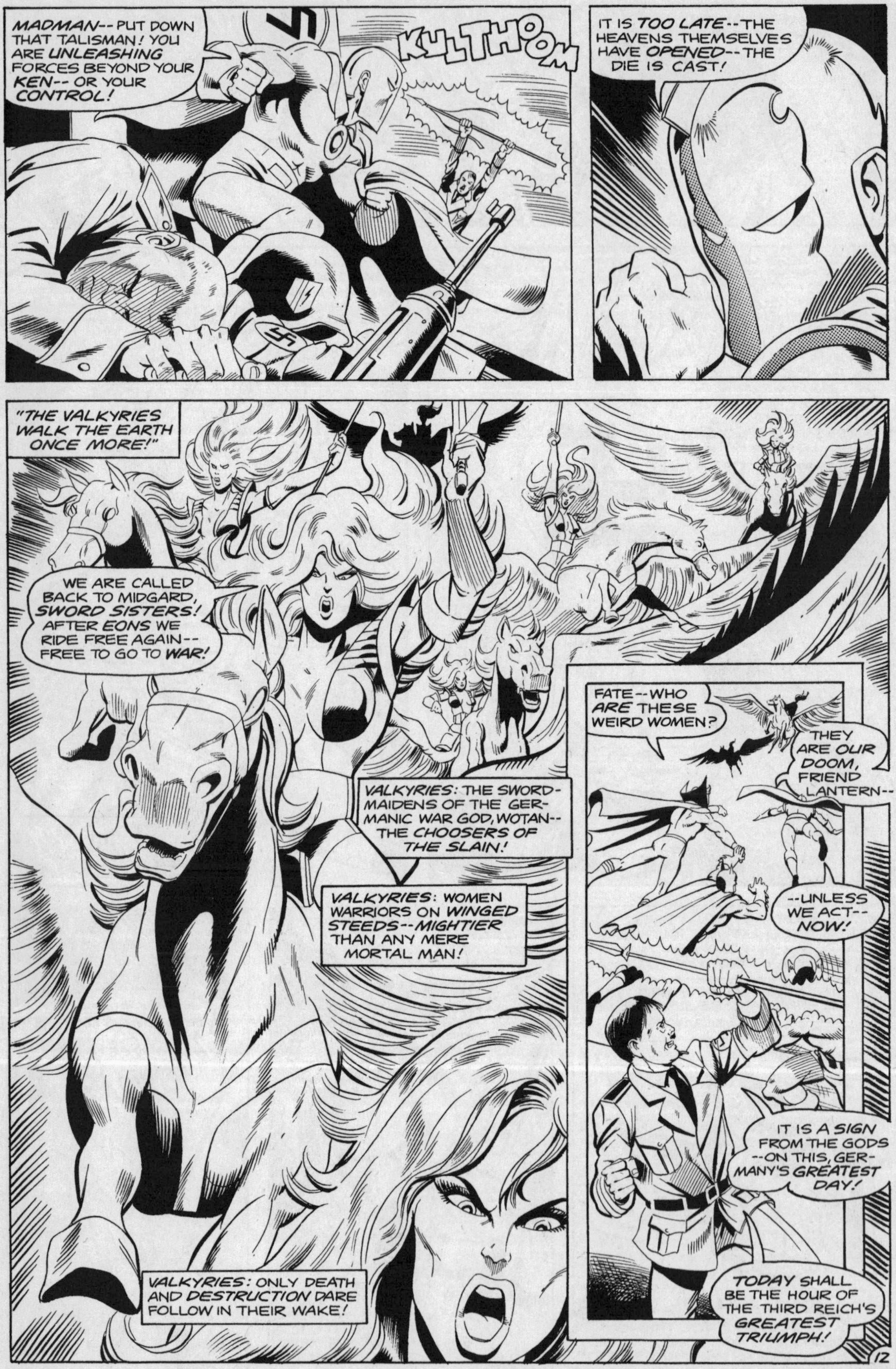
MADMAN--PUT DOWN THAT TALISMAN! YOU ARE UNLEASHING FORCES BEYOND YOUR KEN--OR YOUR CONTROL!
KULTHOOM
IT IS TOO LATE--THE HEAVENS THEMSELVES HAVE OPENED--THE DIE IS CAST!
"THE VALKYRIES WALK THE EARTH ONCE MORE!"
WE ARE CALLED BACK TO MIDGARD, SWORD SISTERS! AFTER EONS WE RIDE FREE AGAIN--FREE TO GO TO WAR!
VALKYRIES: THE SWORD-MAIDENS OF THE GER-MANIC WAR GOD, WOTAN--THE CHOOSERS OF THE SLAIN!
VALKYRIES: WOMEN WARRIORS ON WINGED STEEDS--MIGHTIER THAN ANY MERE MORTAL MAN!
VALKYRIES: ONLY DEATH AND DESTRUCTION DARE FOLLOW IN THEIR WAKE!
FATE--WHO ARE THESE WEIRD WOMEN?
THEY ARE OUR DOOM, FRIEND LANTERN--
--UNLESS WE ACT--NOW!
IT IS A SIGN FROM THE GODS--ON THIS, GER-MANY'S GREATEST DAY!
TODAY SHALL BE THE HOUR OF THE THIRD REICH'S GREATEST TRIUMPH!
12

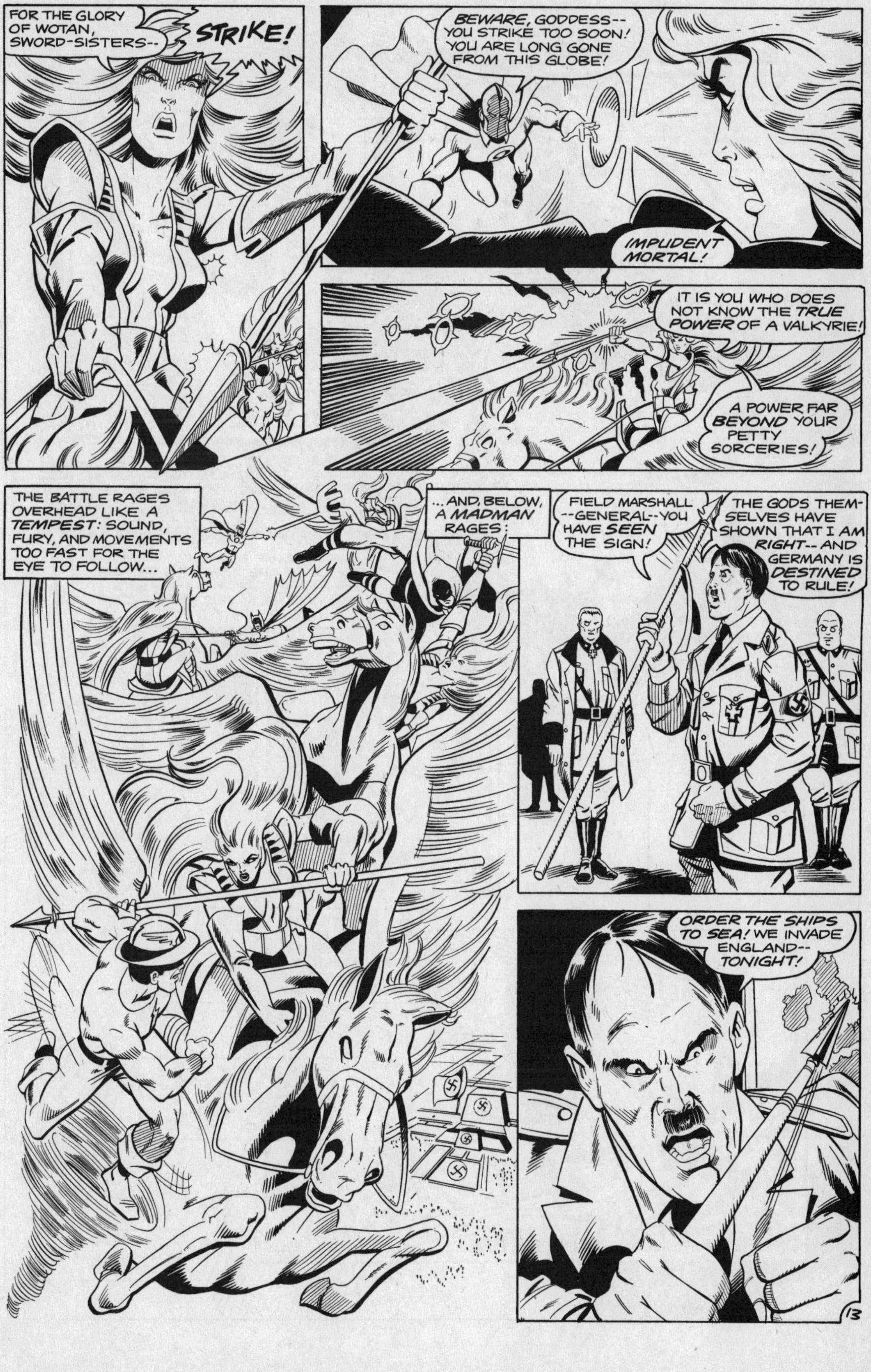
FOR THE GLORY OF WOTAN, SWORD-SISTERS--
STRIKE!
BEWARE, GODDESS-- YOU STRIKE TOO SOON! YOU ARE LONG GONE FROM THIS GLOBE!
IMPUDENT MORTAL!
IT IS YOU WHO DOES NOT KNOW THE TRUE POWER OF A VALKYRIE!
A POWER FAR BEYOND YOUR PETTY SORCERIES!
THE BATTLE RAGES OVERHEAD LIKE A TEMPEST: SOUND, FURY, AND MOVEMENTS TOO FAST FOR THE EYE TO FOLLOW...
...AND, BELOW, A MADMAN RAGES:
FIELD MARSHALL --GENERAL--YOU HAVE SEEN THE SIGN!
THE GODS THEMSELVES HAVE SHOWN THAT I AM RIGHT-- AND GERMANY IS DESTINED TO RULE!
ORDER THE SHIPS TO SEA! WE INVADE ENGLAND-- TONIGHT!
13

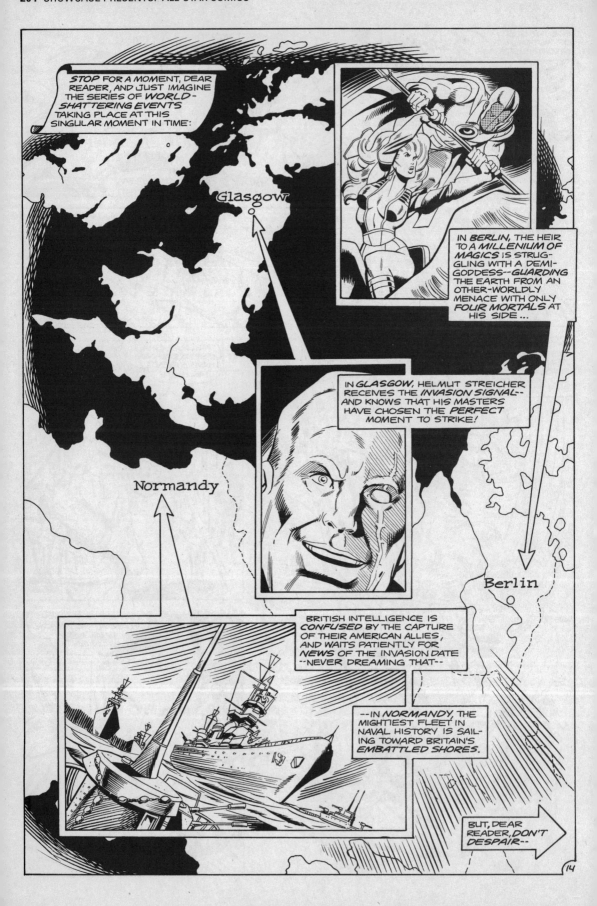

STOP FOR A MOMENT, DEAR READER, AND JUST IMAGINE THE SERIES OF *WORLD-SHATTERING EVENTS* TAKING PLACE AT THIS *SINGULAR MOMENT IN TIME:*

Glasgow

IN *BERLIN*, THE HEIR TO A *MILLENIUM OF MAGICS* IS STRUGGLING WITH A DEMI-GODDESS--*GUARDING* THE EARTH FROM AN OTHER-WORLDLY MENACE WITH ONLY *FOUR MORTALS* AT HIS SIDE ...

IN *GLASGOW*, HELMUT STREICHER RECEIVES THE *INVASION SIGNAL*-- AND KNOWS THAT HIS MASTERS HAVE CHOSEN THE *PERFECT MOMENT* TO STRIKE!

Normandy

Berlin

BRITISH INTELLIGENCE IS *CONFUSED* BY THE CAPTURE OF THEIR AMERICAN ALLIES, AND WAITS PATIENTLY FOR *NEWS* OF THE INVASION DATE --NEVER DREAMING THAT--

--IN *NORMANDY*, THE MIGHTIEST FLEET IN NAVAL HISTORY IS SAIL-ING TOWARD BRITAIN'S *EMBATTLED SHORES.*

BUT, DEAR READER, *DON'T DESPAIR--*

14

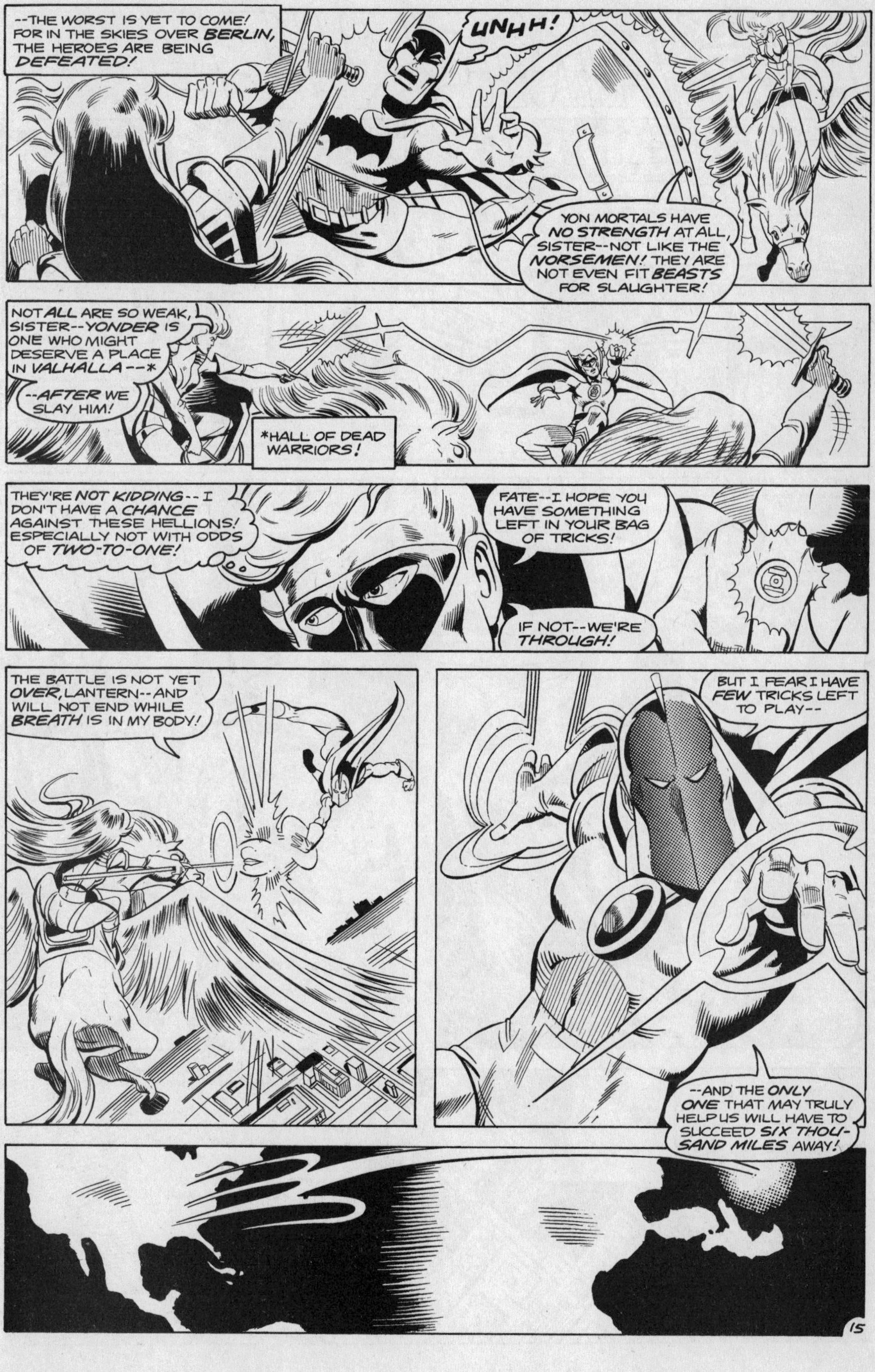
--THE WORST IS YET TO COME! FOR IN THE SKIES OVER BERLIN, THE HEROES ARE BEING DEFEATED!
UNHH!
YON MORTALS HAVE NO STRENGTH AT ALL, SISTER--NOT LIKE THE NORSEMEN! THEY ARE NOT EVEN FIT BEASTS FOR SLAUGHTER!
NOT ALL ARE SO WEAK, SISTER--YONDER IS ONE WHO MIGHT DESERVE A PLACE IN VALHALLA--*
--AFTER WE SLAY HIM!
*HALL OF DEAD WARRIORS!
THEY'RE NOT KIDDING--I DON'T HAVE A CHANCE AGAINST THESE HELLIONS! ESPECIALLY NOT WITH ODDS OF TWO-TO-ONE!
FATE--I HOPE YOU HAVE SOMETHING LEFT IN YOUR BAG OF TRICKS!
IF NOT--WE'RE THROUGH!
THE BATTLE IS NOT YET OVER, LANTERN--AND WILL NOT END WHILE BREATH IS IN MY BODY!
BUT I FEAR I HAVE FEW TRICKS LEFT TO PLAY--
--AND THE ONLY ONE THAT MAY TRULY HELP US WILL HAVE TO SUCCEED SIX THOUSAND MILES AWAY!
15

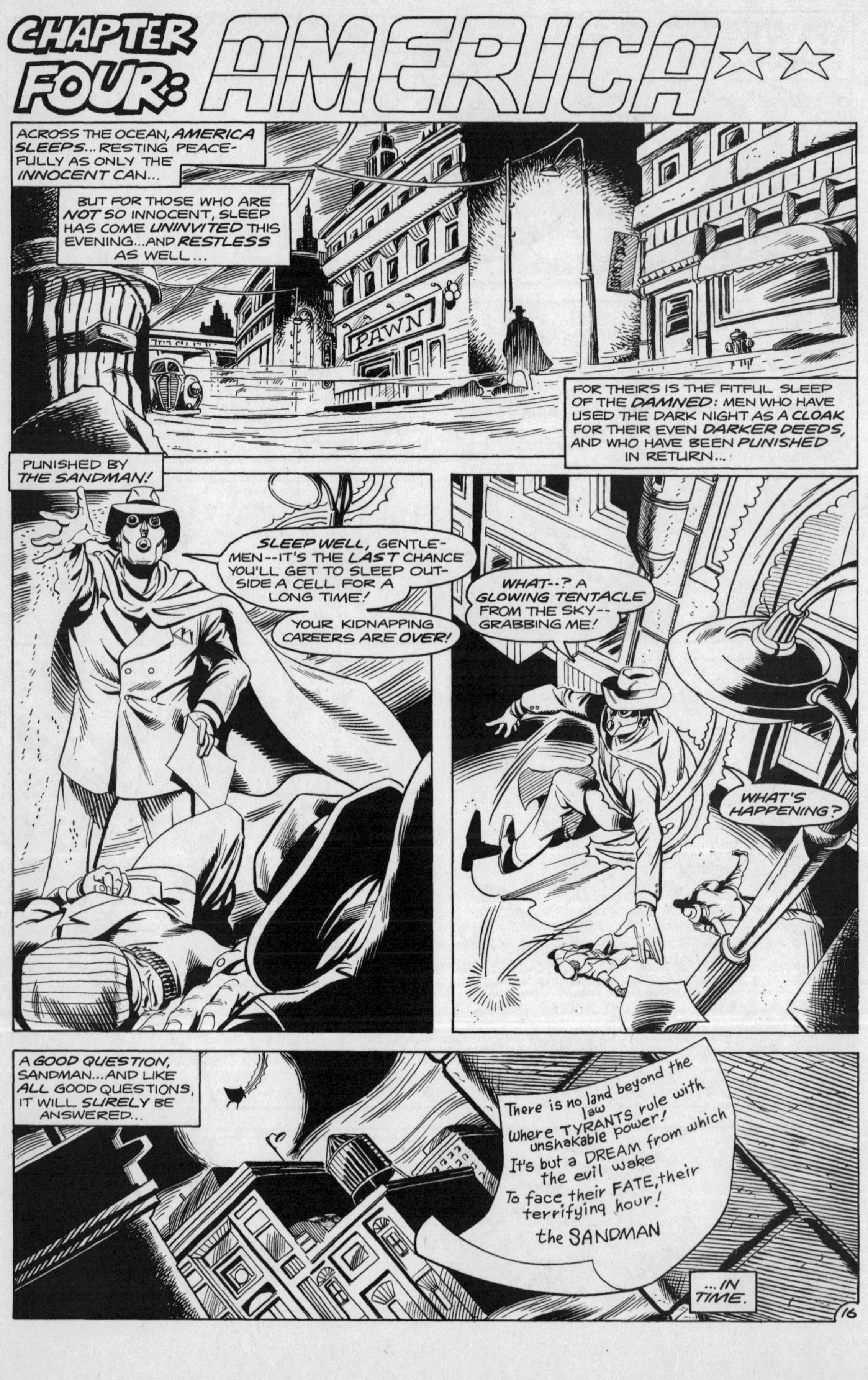
CHAPTER FOUR: AMERICA
ACROSS THE OCEAN, AMERICA SLEEPS... RESTING PEACEFULLY AS ONLY THE INNOCENT CAN...
BUT FOR THOSE WHO ARE NOT SO INNOCENT, SLEEP HAS COME UNINVITED THIS EVENING... AND RESTLESS AS WELL...
PAWN
FOR THEIRS IS THE FITFUL SLEEP OF THE DAMNED: MEN WHO HAVE USED THE DARK NIGHT AS A CLOAK FOR THEIR EVEN DARKER DEEDS, AND WHO HAVE BEEN PUNISHED IN RETURN...
PUNISHED BY THE SANDMAN!
SLEEP WELL, GENTLEMEN--IT'S THE LAST CHANCE YOU'LL GET TO SLEEP OUTSIDE A CELL FOR A LONG TIME!
YOUR KIDNAPPING CAREERS ARE OVER!
WHAT--? A GLOWING TENTACLE FROM THE SKY--GRABBING ME!
WHAT'S HAPPENING?
A GOOD QUESTION, SANDMAN... AND LIKE ALL GOOD QUESTIONS, IT WILL SURELY BE ANSWERED...
There is no land beyond the law
Where TYRANTS rule with unshakable power!
It's but a DREAM from which the evil wake
To face their FATE, their terrifying hour!
the SANDMAN
...IN TIME.
16

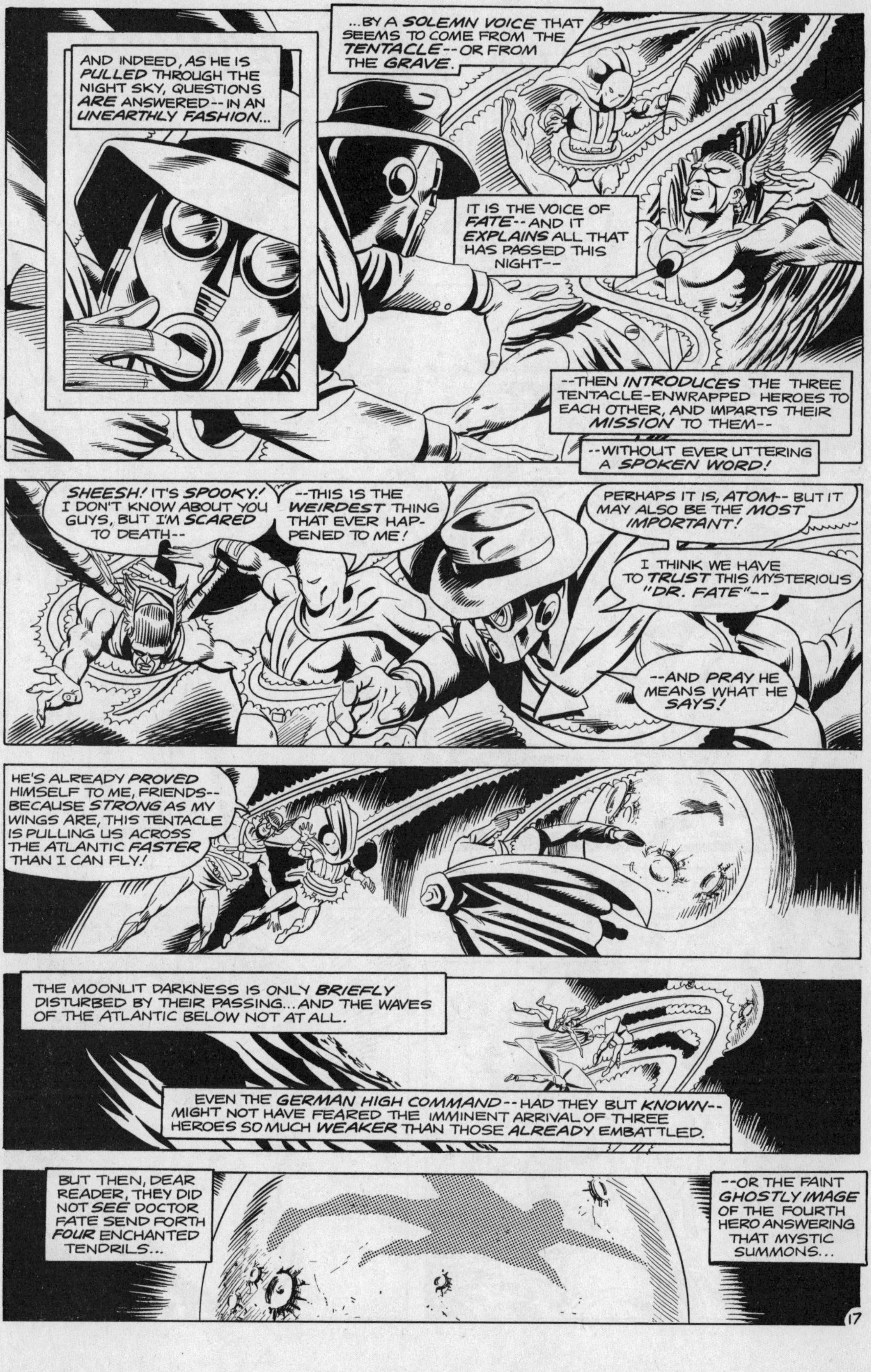
AND INDEED, AS HE IS PULLED THROUGH THE NIGHT SKY, QUESTIONS ARE ANSWERED--IN AN UNEARTHLY FASHION...
...BY A SOLEMN VOICE THAT SEEMS TO COME FROM THE TENTACLE--OR FROM THE GRAVE.
IT IS THE VOICE OF FATE--AND IT EXPLAINS ALL THAT HAS PASSED THIS NIGHT--
--THEN INTRODUCES THE THREE TENTACLE-ENWRAPPED HEROES TO EACH OTHER, AND IMPARTS THEIR MISSION TO THEM--
--WITHOUT EVER UTTERING A SPOKEN WORD!
SHEESH! IT'S SPOOKY! I DON'T KNOW ABOUT YOU GUYS, BUT I'M SCARED TO DEATH--
--THIS IS THE WEIRDEST THING THAT EVER HAPPENED TO ME!
PERHAPS IT IS, ATOM--BUT IT MAY ALSO BE THE MOST IMPORTANT!
I THINK WE HAVE TO TRUST THIS MYSTERIOUS "DR. FATE"--
--AND PRAY HE MEANS WHAT HE SAYS!
HE'S ALREADY PROVED HIMSELF TO ME, FRIENDS--BECAUSE STRONG AS MY WINGS ARE, THIS TENTACLE IS PULLING US ACROSS THE ATLANTIC FASTER THAN I CAN FLY!
THE MOONLIT DARKNESS IS ONLY BRIEFLY DISTURBED BY THEIR PASSING...AND THE WAVES OF THE ATLANTIC BELOW NOT AT ALL.
EVEN THE GERMAN HIGH COMMAND--HAD THEY BUT KNOWN--MIGHT NOT HAVE FEARED THE IMMINENT ARRIVAL OF THREE HEROES SO MUCH WEAKER THAN THOSE ALREADY EMBATTLED.
BUT THEN, DEAR READER, THEY DID NOT SEE DOCTOR FATE SEND FORTH FOUR ENCHANTED TENDRILS...
--OR THE FAINT GHOSTLY IMAGE OF THE FOURTH HERO ANSWERING THAT MYSTIC SUMMONS...
17

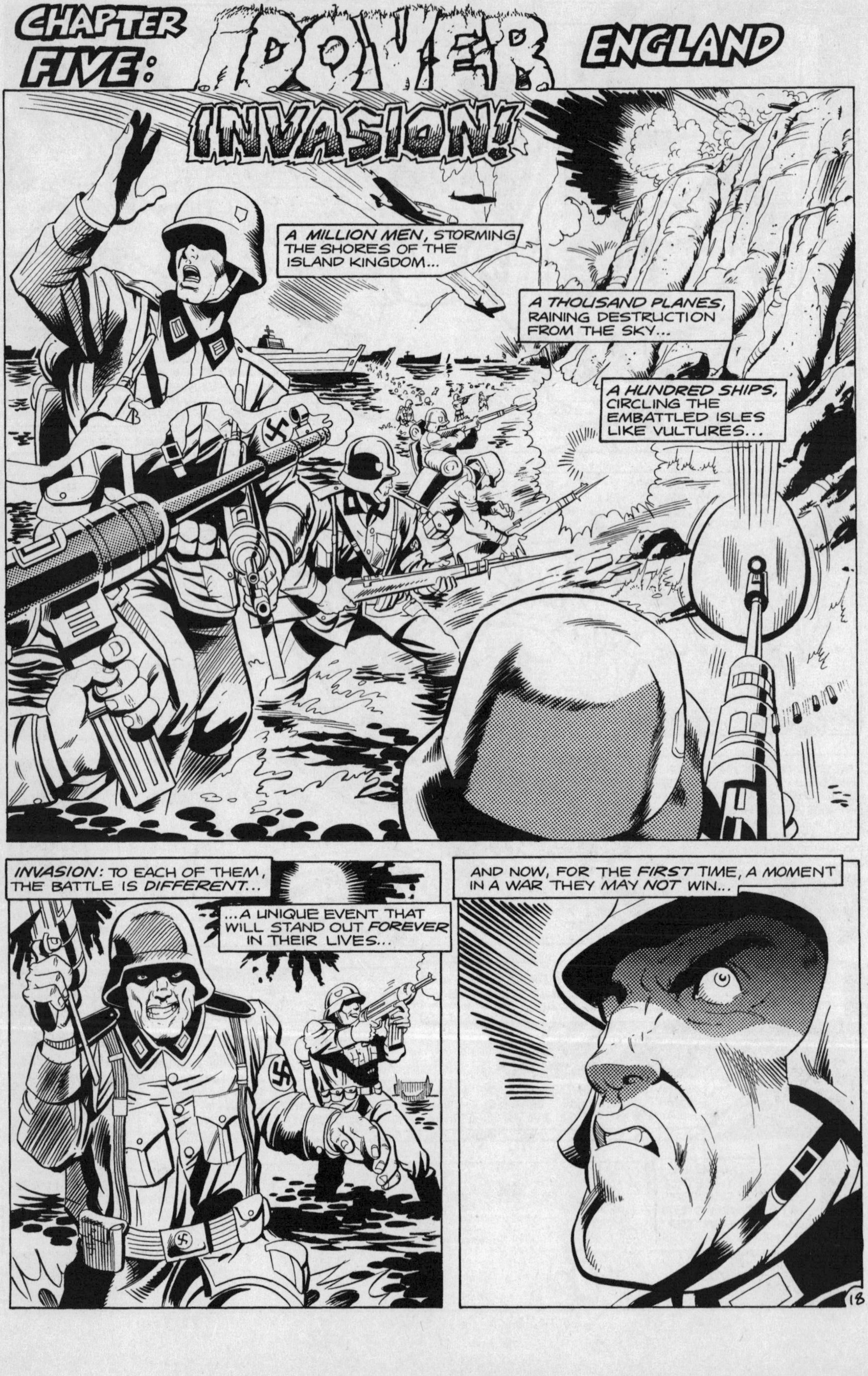
CHAPTER FIVE: DOVER ENGLAND
INVASION!
A MILLION MEN, STORMING THE SHORES OF THE ISLAND KINGDOM...
A THOUSAND PLANES, RAINING DESTRUCTION FROM THE SKY...
A HUNDRED SHIPS, CIRCLING THE EMBATTLED ISLES LIKE VULTURES...
INVASION: TO EACH OF THEM, THE BATTLE IS DIFFERENT...
...A UNIQUE EVENT THAT WILL STAND OUT FOREVER IN THEIR LIVES...
AND NOW, FOR THE FIRST TIME, A MOMENT IN A WAR THEY MAY NOT WIN...
18

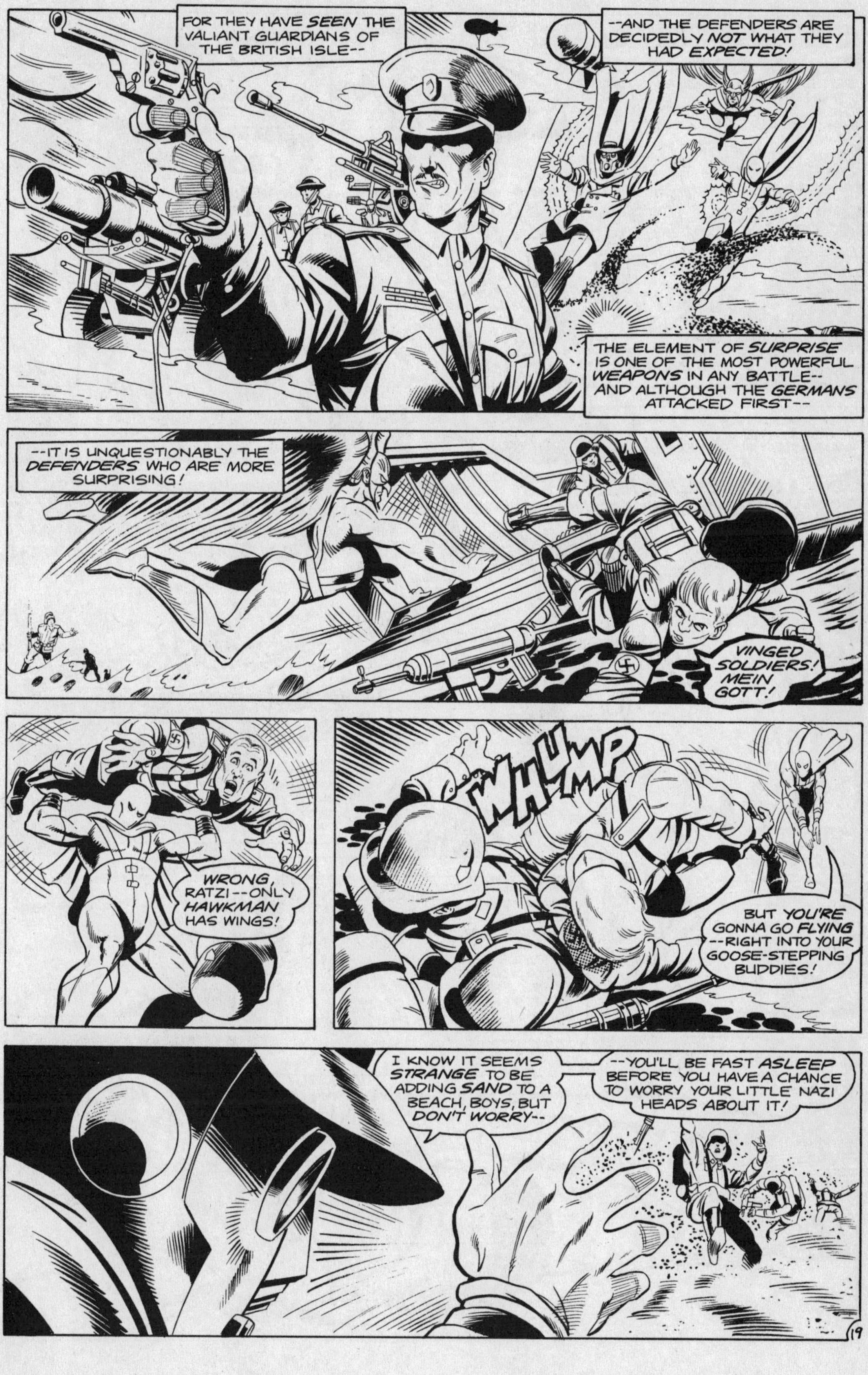
FOR THEY HAVE SEEN THE VALIANT GUARDIANS OF THE BRITISH ISLE--
--AND THE DEFENDERS ARE DECIDEDLY NOT WHAT THEY HAD EXPECTED!
THE ELEMENT OF SURPRISE IS ONE OF THE MOST POWERFUL WEAPONS IN ANY BATTLE-- AND ALTHOUGH THE GERMANS ATTACKED FIRST--
--IT IS UNQUESTIONABLY THE DEFENDERS WHO ARE MORE SURPRISING!
VINGED SOLDIERS! MEIN GOTT!
WRONG, RATZI--ONLY HAWKMAN HAS WINGS!
WHUMP
BUT YOU'RE GONNA GO FLYING --RIGHT INTO YOUR GOOSE-STEPPING BUDDIES!
I KNOW IT SEEMS STRANGE TO BE ADDING SAND TO A BEACH, BOYS, BUT DON'T WORRY--
--YOU'LL BE FAST ASLEEP BEFORE YOU HAVE A CHANCE TO WORRY YOUR LITTLE NAZI HEADS ABOUT IT!
19

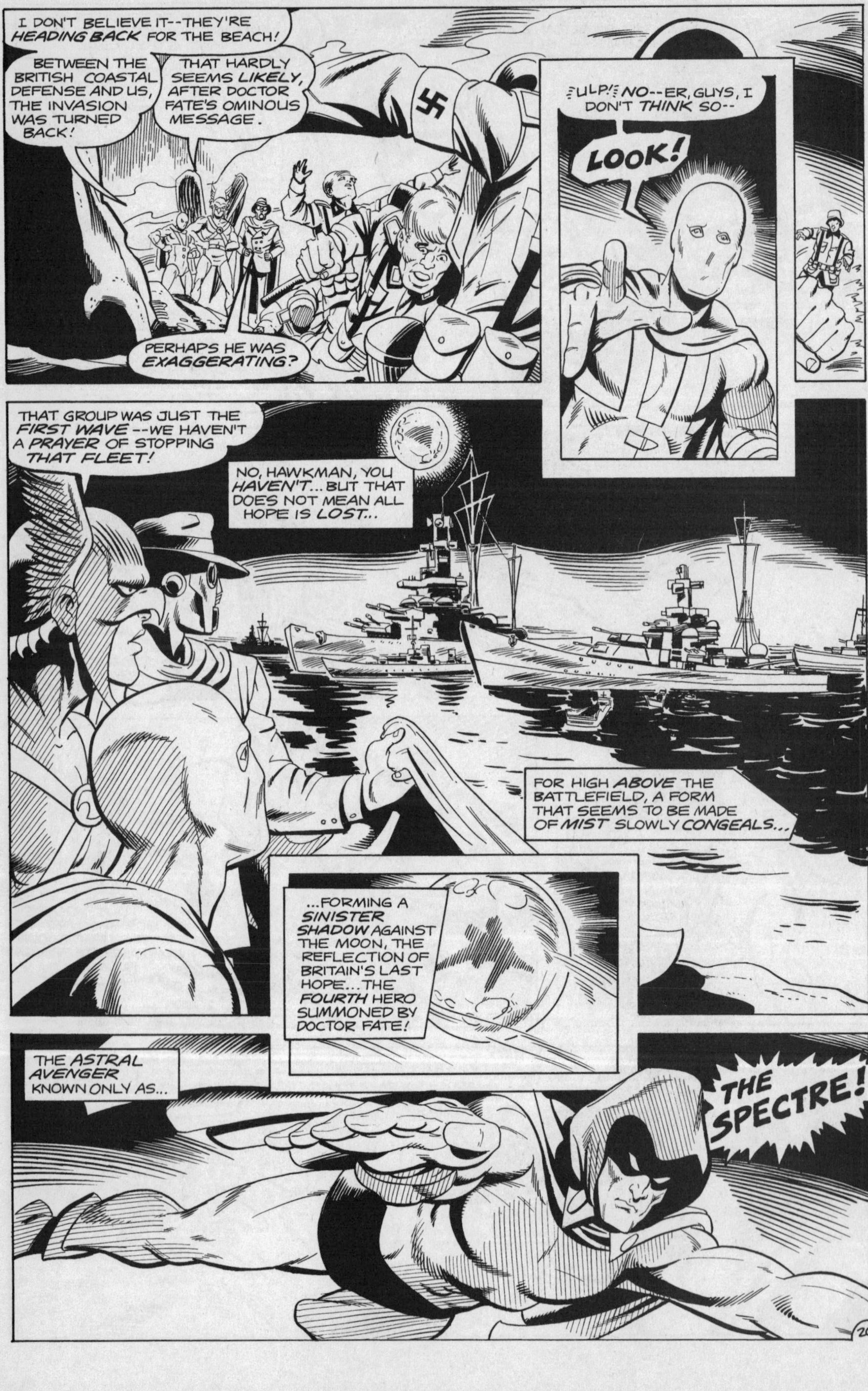
I DON'T BELIEVE IT--THEY'RE HEADING BACK FOR THE BEACH!
BETWEEN THE BRITISH COASTAL DEFENSE AND US, THE INVASION WAS TURNED BACK!
THAT HARDLY SEEMS LIKELY, AFTER DOCTOR FATE'S OMINOUS MESSAGE.
PERHAPS HE WAS EXAGGERATING?
GULP! NO--ER, GUYS, I DON'T THINK SO--
LOOK!
THAT GROUP WAS JUST THE FIRST WAVE--WE HAVEN'T A PRAYER OF STOPPING THAT FLEET!
NO, HAWKMAN, YOU HAVEN'T... BUT THAT DOES NOT MEAN ALL HOPE IS LOST...
FOR HIGH ABOVE THE BATTLEFIELD, A FORM THAT SEEMS TO BE MADE OF MIST SLOWLY CONGEALS...
...FORMING A SINISTER SHADOW AGAINST THE MOON, THE REFLECTION OF BRITAIN'S LAST HOPE... THE FOURTH HERO SUMMONED BY DOCTOR FATE!
THE ASTRAL AVENGER KNOWN ONLY AS...
THE SPECTRE!
20

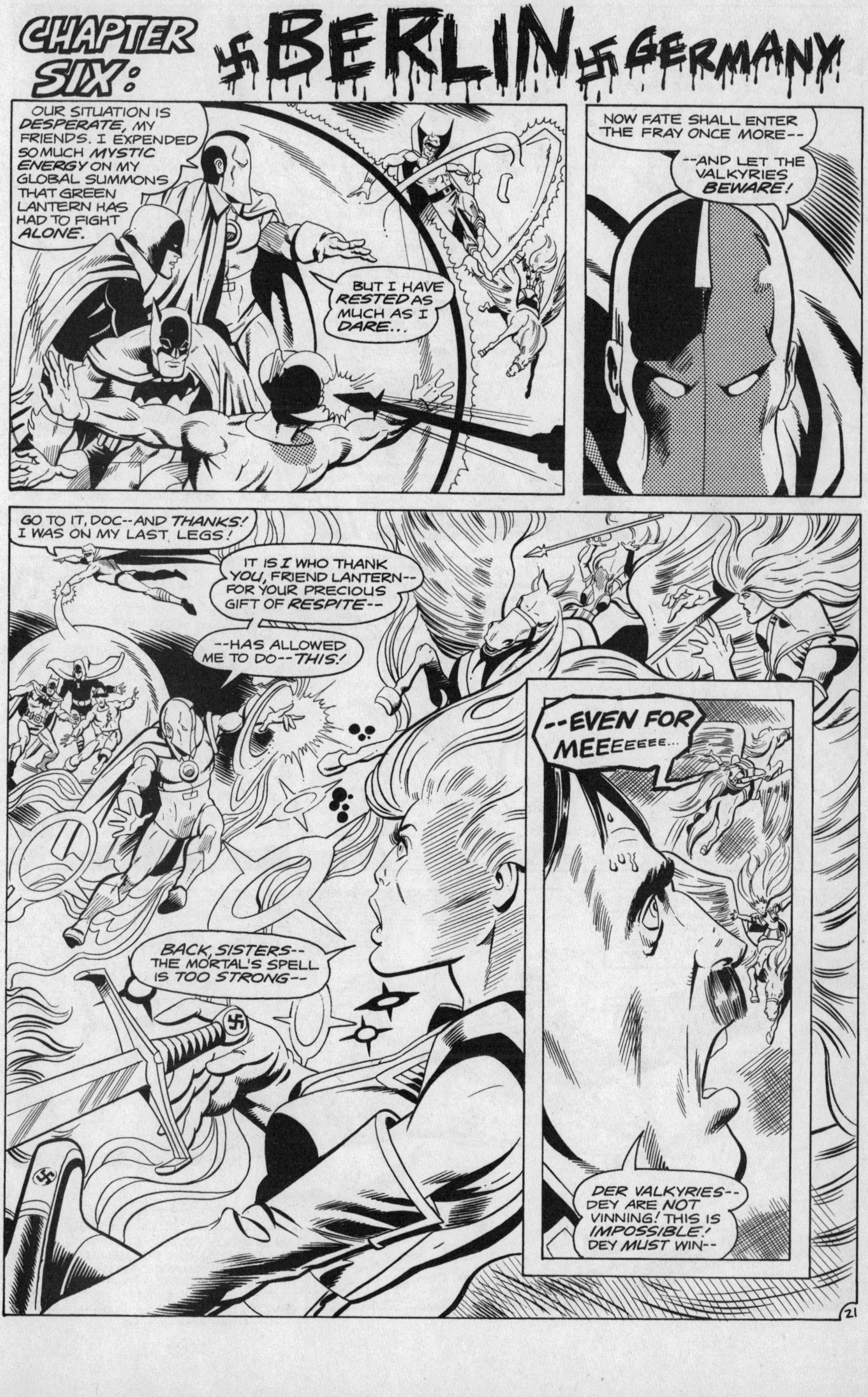
CHAPTER SIX: BERLIN GERMANY
OUR SITUATION IS DESPERATE, MY FRIENDS. I EXPENDED SO MUCH MYSTIC ENERGY ON MY GLOBAL SUMMONS THAT GREEN LANTERN HAS HAD TO FIGHT ALONE.
BUT I HAVE RESTED AS MUCH AS I DARE...
NOW FATE SHALL ENTER THE FRAY ONCE MORE--
--AND LET THE VALKYRIES BEWARE!
GO TO IT, DOC--AND THANKS! I WAS ON MY LAST LEGS!
IT IS I WHO THANK YOU, FRIEND LANTERN-- FOR YOUR PRECIOUS GIFT OF RESPITE--
--HAS ALLOWED ME TO DO--THIS!
BACK, SISTERS-- THE MORTAL'S SPELL IS TOO STRONG--
DER VALKYRIES-- DEY ARE NOT VINNING! THIS IS IMPOSSIBLE! DEY MUST WIN--
--EVEN FOR MEEEEEE...
21

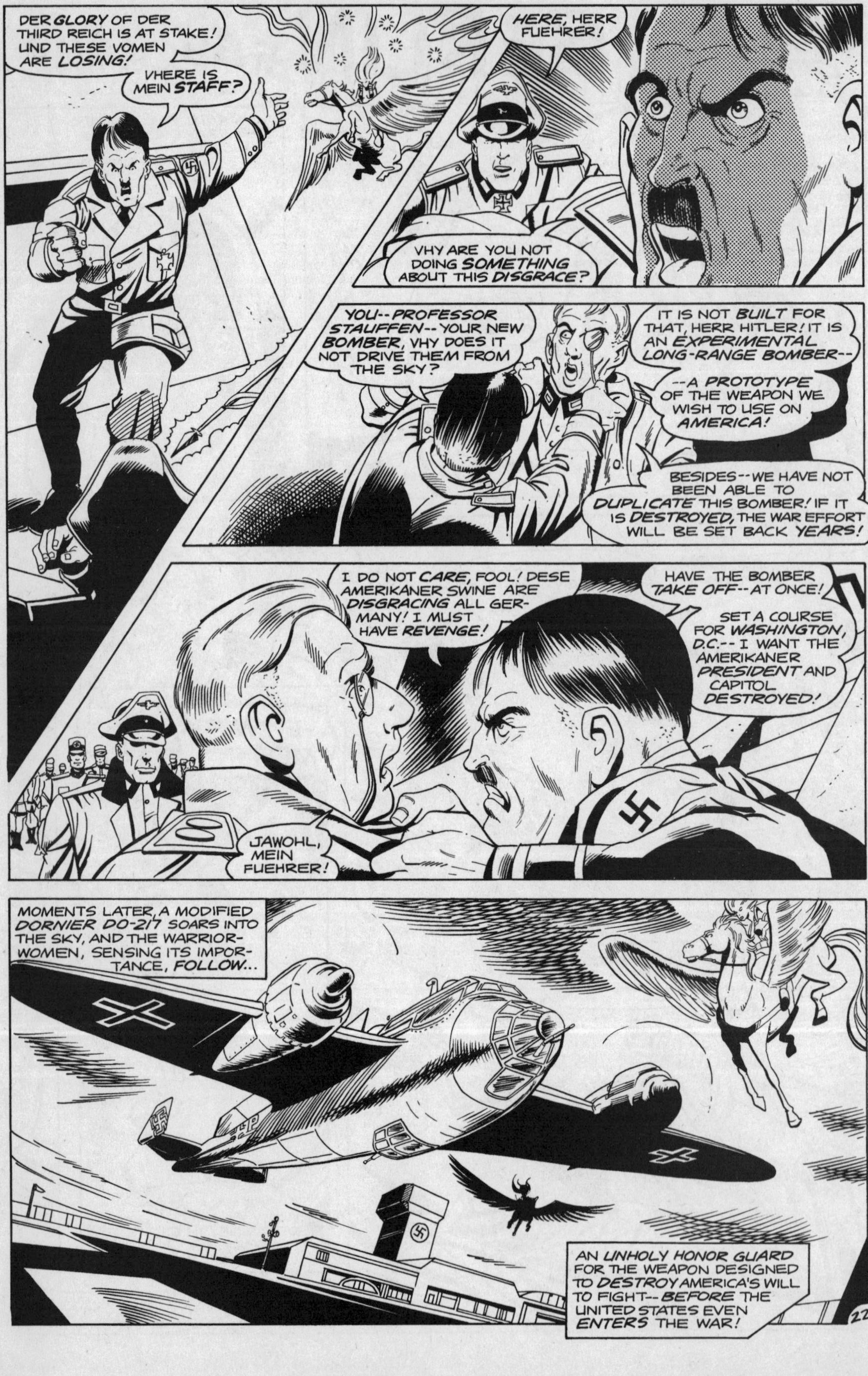
DER GLORY OF DER THIRD REICH IS AT STAKE! UND THESE VOMEN ARE LOSING!
VHERE IS MEIN STAFF?
HERE, HERR FUEHRER!
VHY ARE YOU NOT DOING SOMETHING ABOUT THIS DISGRACE?
YOU--PROFESSOR STAUFFEN--YOUR NEW BOMBER, VHY DOES IT NOT DRIVE THEM FROM THE SKY?
IT IS NOT BUILT FOR THAT, HERR HITLER! IT IS AN EXPERIMENTAL LONG-RANGE BOMBER--
--A PROTOTYPE OF THE WEAPON WE WISH TO USE ON AMERICA!
BESIDES--WE HAVE NOT BEEN ABLE TO DUPLICATE THIS BOMBER! IF IT IS DESTROYED, THE WAR EFFORT WILL BE SET BACK YEARS!
I DO NOT CARE, FOOL! DESE AMERIKANER SWINE ARE DISGRACING ALL GERMANY! I MUST HAVE REVENGE!
HAVE THE BOMBER TAKE OFF--AT ONCE!
SET A COURSE FOR WASHINGTON, D.C.--I WANT THE AMERIKANER PRESIDENT AND CAPITOL DESTROYED!
JAWOHL, MEIN FUEHRER!
MOMENTS LATER, A MODIFIED DORNIER DO-217 SOARS INTO THE SKY, AND THE WARRIOR-WOMEN, SENSING ITS IMPORTANCE, FOLLOW...
AN UNHOLY HONOR GUARD FOR THE WEAPON DESIGNED TO DESTROY AMERICA'S WILL TO FIGHT--BEFORE THE UNITED STATES EVEN ENTERS THE WAR!
22

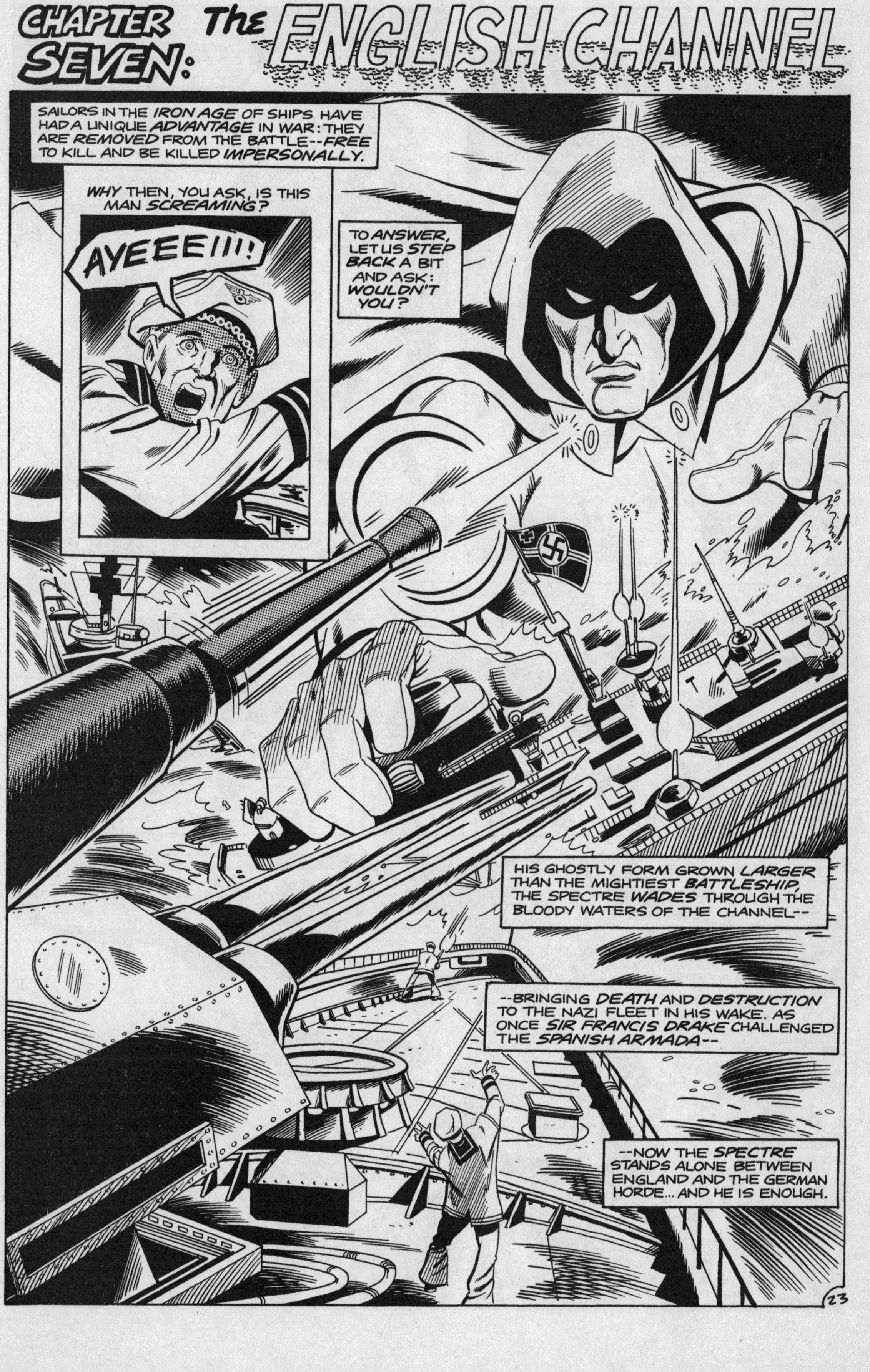
CHAPTER SEVEN: The ENGLISH CHANNEL
SAILORS IN THE IRON AGE OF SHIPS HAVE HAD A UNIQUE ADVANTAGE IN WAR: THEY ARE REMOVED FROM THE BATTLE--FREE TO KILL AND BE KILLED IMPERSONALLY.
WHY THEN, YOU ASK, IS THIS MAN SCREAMING?
AYEEEIIII!
TO ANSWER, LET US STEP BACK A BIT AND ASK: WOULDN'T YOU?
HIS GHOSTLY FORM GROWN LARGER THAN THE MIGHTIEST BATTLESHIP, THE SPECTRE WADES THROUGH THE BLOODY WATERS OF THE CHANNEL--
--BRINGING DEATH AND DESTRUCTION TO THE NAZI FLEET IN HIS WAKE. AS ONCE SIR FRANCIS DRAKE CHALLENGED THE SPANISH ARMADA--
--NOW THE SPECTRE STANDS ALONE BETWEEN ENGLAND AND THE GERMAN HORDE... AND HE IS ENOUGH.
23

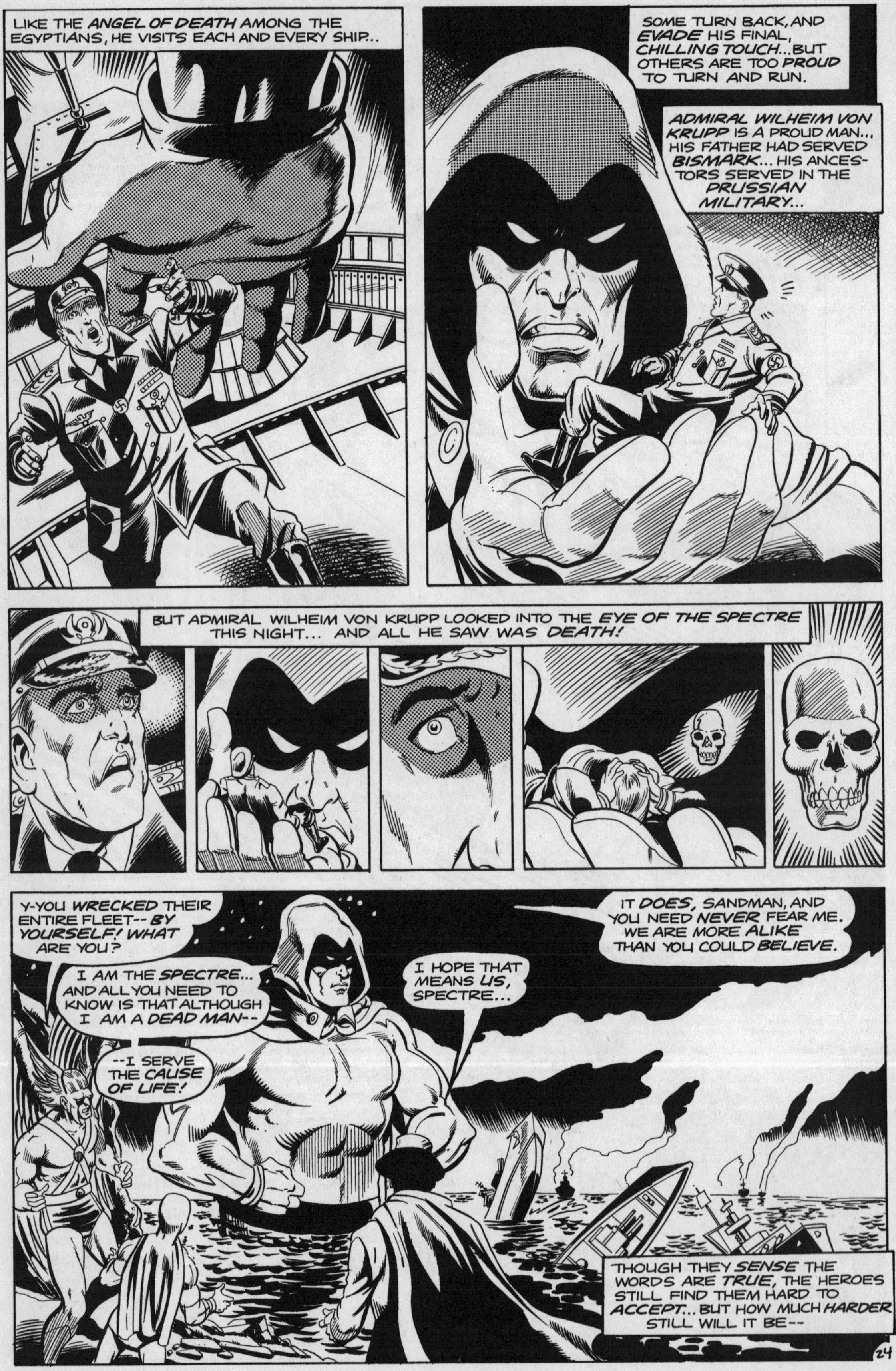
LIKE THE ANGEL OF DEATH AMONG THE EGYPTIANS, HE VISITS EACH AND EVERY SHIP...
SOME TURN BACK, AND EVADE HIS FINAL, CHILLING TOUCH...BUT OTHERS ARE TOO PROUD TO TURN AND RUN.
ADMIRAL WILHEIM VON KRUPP IS A PROUD MAN... HIS FATHER HAD SERVED BISMARK... HIS ANCESTORS SERVED IN THE PRUSSIAN MILITARY...
BUT ADMIRAL WILHEIM VON KRUPP LOOKED INTO THE EYE OF THE SPECTRE THIS NIGHT... AND ALL HE SAW WAS DEATH!
Y-YOU WRECKED THEIR ENTIRE FLEET-- BY YOURSELF! WHAT ARE YOU?
I AM THE SPECTRE... AND ALL YOU NEED TO KNOW IS THAT ALTHOUGH I AM A DEAD MAN--
--I SERVE THE CAUSE OF LIFE!
I HOPE THAT MEANS US, SPECTRE...
IT DOES, SANDMAN, AND YOU NEED NEVER FEAR ME. WE ARE MORE ALIKE THAN YOU COULD BELIEVE.
THOUGH THEY SENSE THE WORDS ARE TRUE, THE HEROES STILL FIND THEM HARD TO ACCEPT... BUT HOW MUCH HARDER STILL WILL IT BE--
24

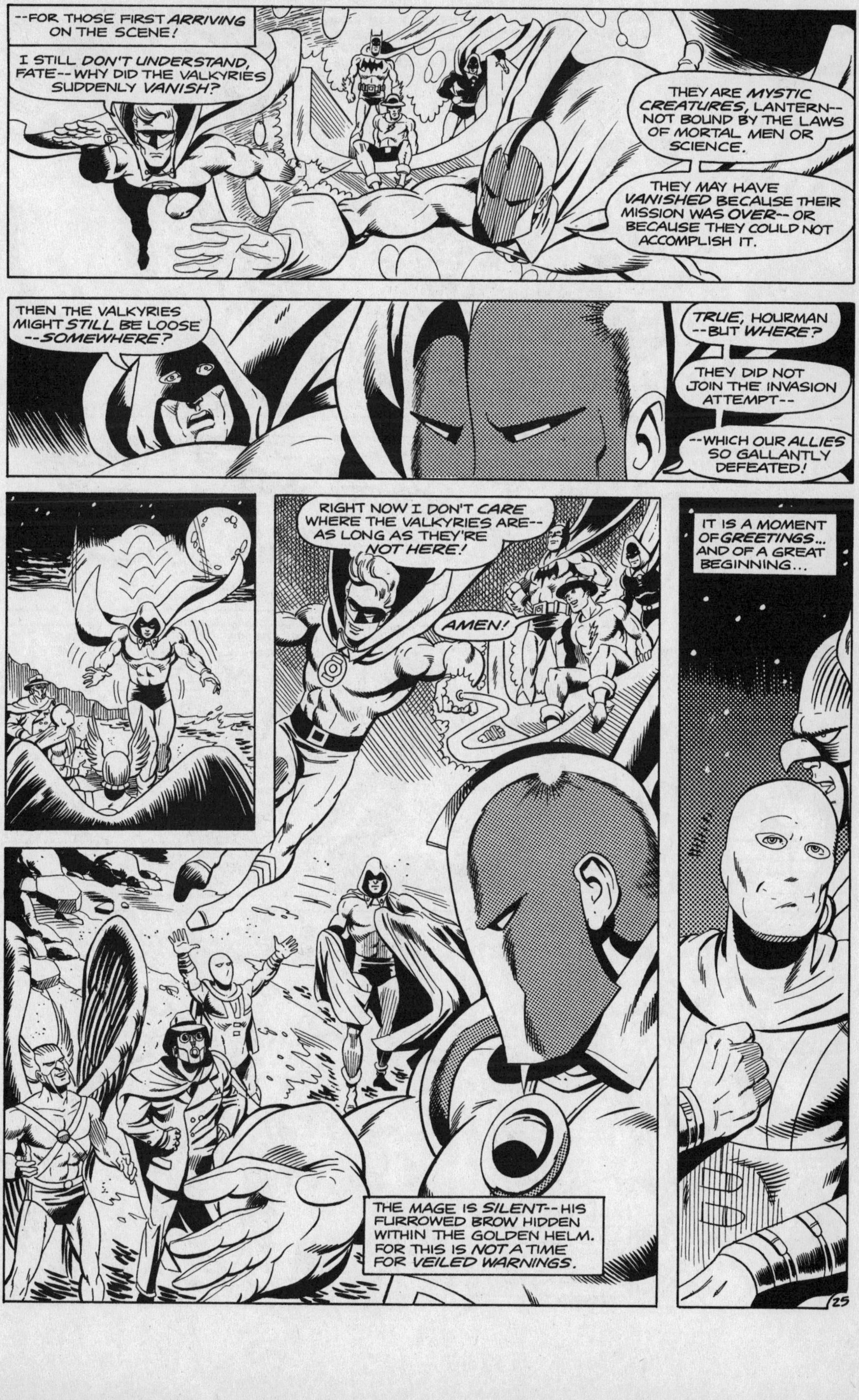
--FOR THOSE FIRST ARRIVING ON THE SCENE!
I STILL DON'T UNDERSTAND, FATE--WHY DID THE VALKYRIES SUDDENLY VANISH?
THEY ARE MYSTIC CREATURES, LANTERN-- NOT BOUND BY THE LAWS OF MORTAL MEN OR SCIENCE.
THEY MAY HAVE VANISHED BECAUSE THEIR MISSION WAS OVER-- OR BECAUSE THEY COULD NOT ACCOMPLISH IT.
THEN THE VALKYRIES MIGHT STILL BE LOOSE --SOMEWHERE?
TRUE, HOURMAN --BUT WHERE?
THEY DID NOT JOIN THE INVASION ATTEMPT--
--WHICH OUR ALLIES SO GALLANTLY DEFEATED!
RIGHT NOW I DON'T CARE WHERE THE VALKYRIES ARE-- AS LONG AS THEY'RE NOT HERE!
AMEN!
IT IS A MOMENT OF GREETINGS... AND OF A GREAT BEGINNING...
THE MAGE IS SILENT--HIS FURROWED BROW HIDDEN WITHIN THE GOLDEN HELM. FOR THIS IS NOT A TIME FOR VEILED WARNINGS.
25

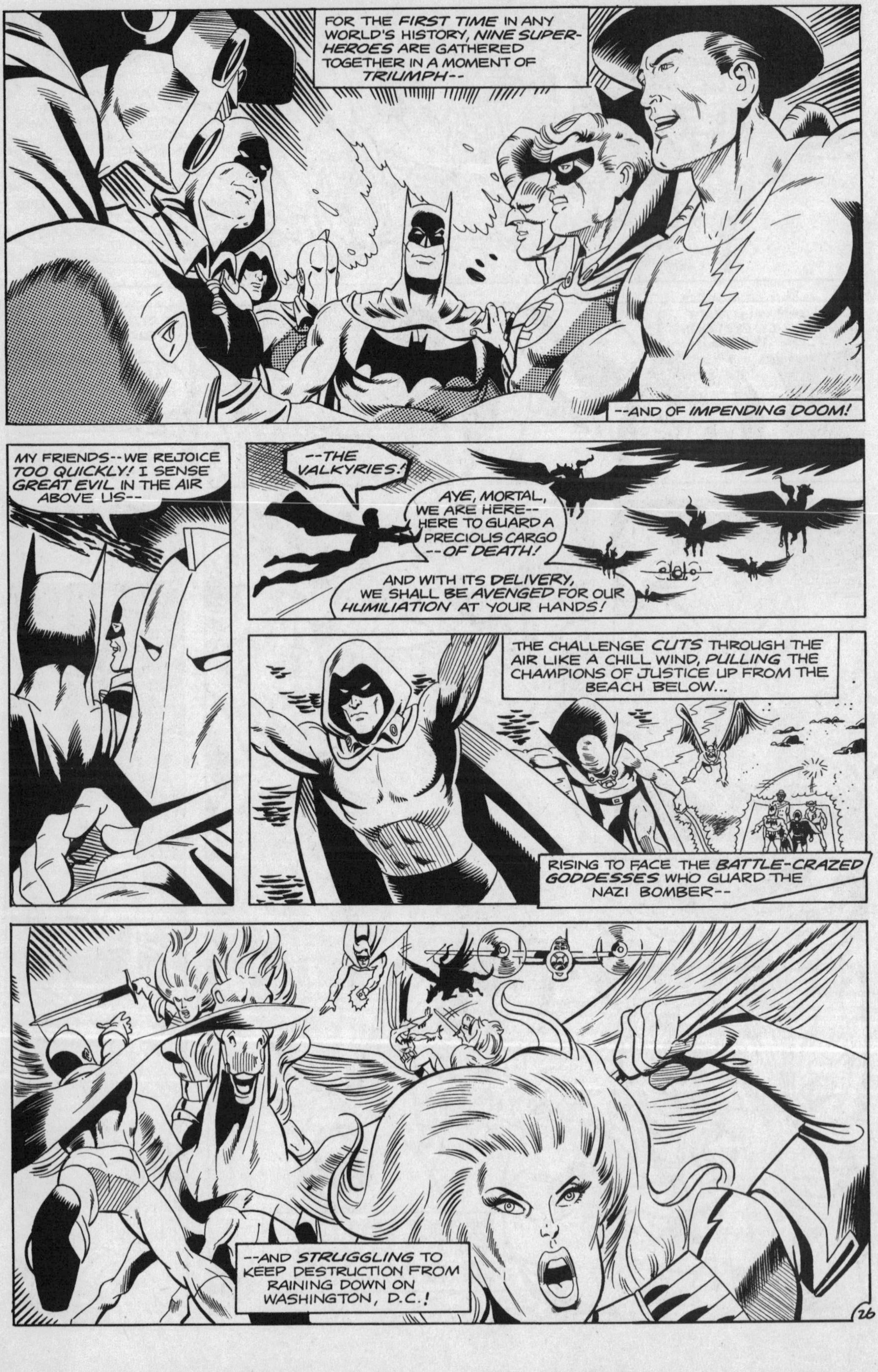
FOR THE FIRST TIME IN ANY WORLD'S HISTORY, NINE SUPER-HEROES ARE GATHERED TOGETHER IN A MOMENT OF TRIUMPH--
--AND OF IMPENDING DOOM!
MY FRIENDS--WE REJOICE TOO QUICKLY! I SENSE GREAT EVIL IN THE AIR ABOVE US--
--THE VALKYRIES!
AYE, MORTAL, WE ARE HERE-- HERE TO GUARD A PRECIOUS CARGO --OF DEATH!
AND WITH ITS DELIVERY, WE SHALL BE AVENGED FOR OUR HUMILIATION AT YOUR HANDS!
THE CHALLENGE CUTS THROUGH THE AIR LIKE A CHILL WIND, PULLING THE CHAMPIONS OF JUSTICE UP FROM THE BEACH BELOW...
RISING TO FACE THE BATTLE-CRAZED GODDESSES WHO GUARD THE NAZI BOMBER--
--AND STRUGGLING TO KEEP DESTRUCTION FROM RAINING DOWN ON WASHINGTON, D.C.!
26

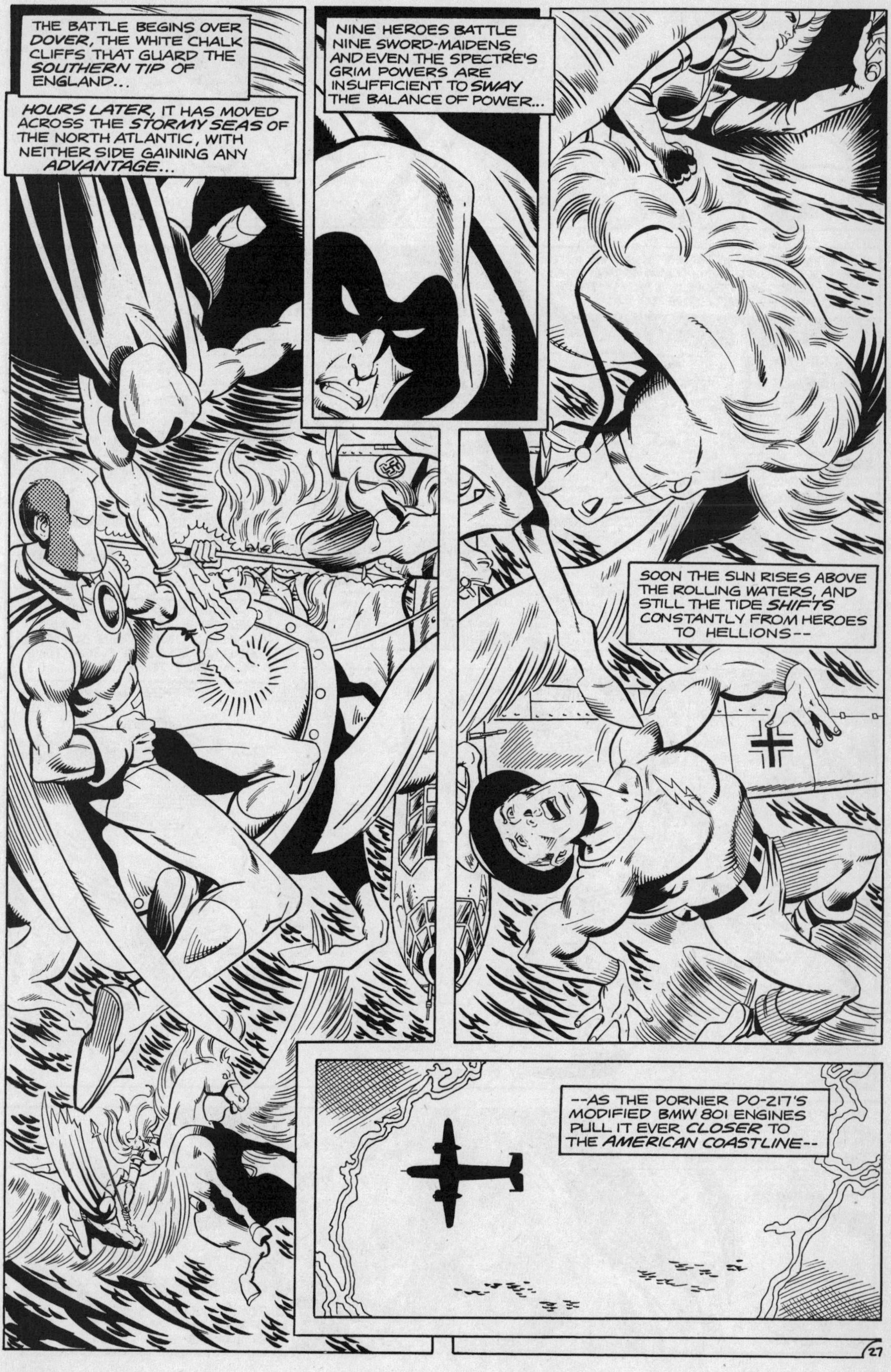
THE BATTLE BEGINS OVER DOVER, THE WHITE CHALK CLIFFS THAT GUARD THE SOUTHERN TIP OF ENGLAND...
HOURS LATER, IT HAS MOVED ACROSS THE STORMY SEAS OF THE NORTH ATLANTIC, WITH NEITHER SIDE GAINING ANY ADVANTAGE...
NINE HEROES BATTLE NINE SWORD-MAIDENS, AND EVEN THE SPECTRE'S GRIM POWERS ARE INSUFFICIENT TO SWAY THE BALANCE OF POWER...
SOON THE SUN RISES ABOVE THE ROLLING WATERS, AND STILL THE TIDE SHIFTS CONSTANTLY FROM HEROES TO HELLIONS--
--AS THE DORNIER DO-217'S MODIFIED BMW 801 ENGINES PULL IT EVER CLOSER TO THE AMERICAN COASTLINE--
27

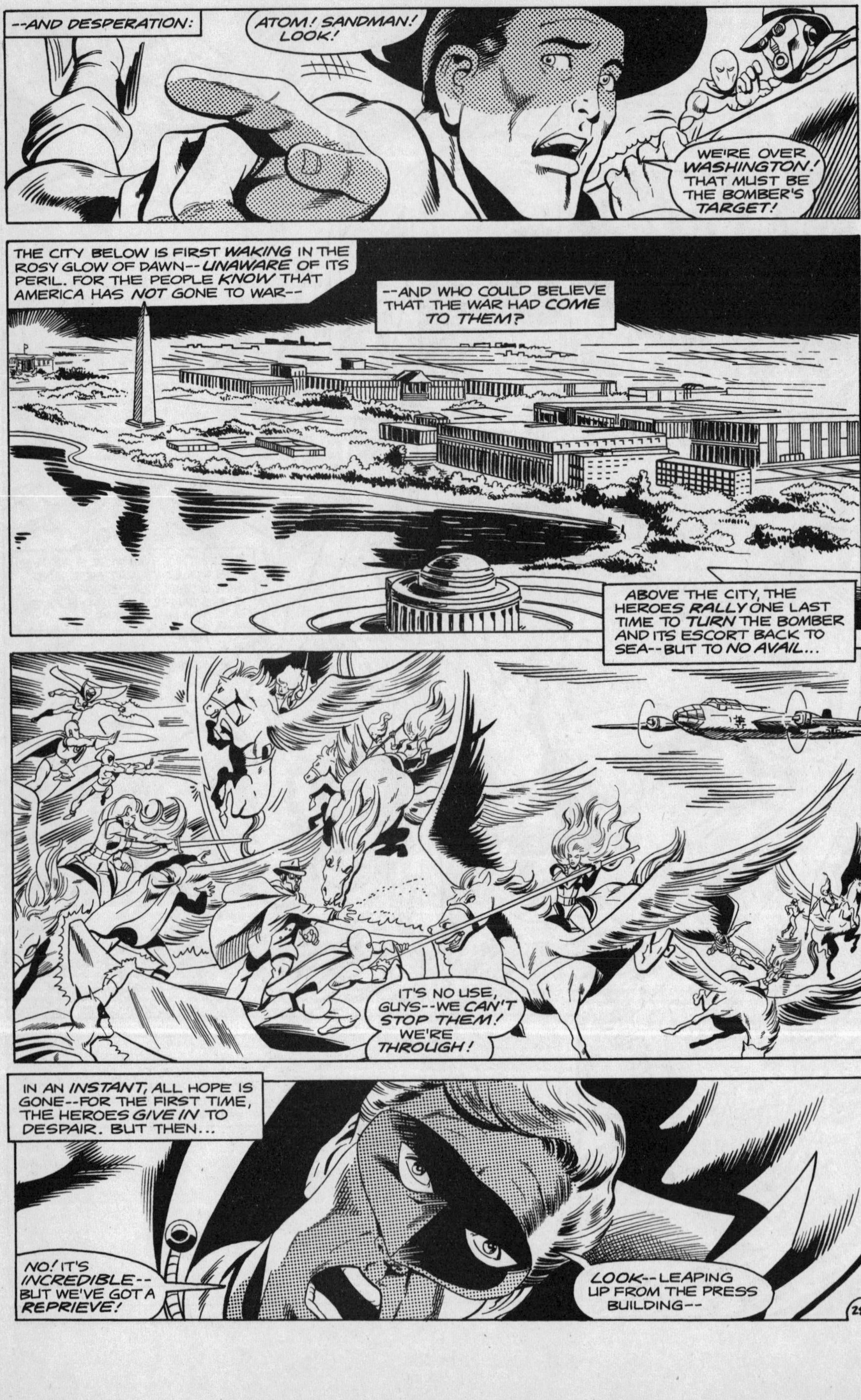
--AND DESPERATION:
ATOM! SANDMAN! LOOK!
WE'RE OVER WASHINGTON! THAT MUST BE THE BOMBER'S TARGET!
THE CITY BELOW IS FIRST WAKING IN THE ROSY GLOW OF DAWN--UNAWARE OF ITS PERIL. FOR THE PEOPLE KNOW THAT AMERICA HAS NOT GONE TO WAR--
--AND WHO COULD BELIEVE THAT THE WAR HAD COME TO THEM?
ABOVE THE CITY, THE HEROES RALLY ONE LAST TIME TO TURN THE BOMBER AND ITS ESCORT BACK TO SEA--BUT TO NO AVAIL...
IT'S NO USE, GUYS--WE CAN'T STOP THEM! WE'RE THROUGH!
IN AN INSTANT, ALL HOPE IS GONE--FOR THE FIRST TIME, THE HEROES GIVE IN TO DESPAIR. BUT THEN...
NO! IT'S INCREDIBLE--BUT WE'VE GOT A REPRIEVE!
LOOK--LEAPING UP FROM THE PRESS BUILDING--
28

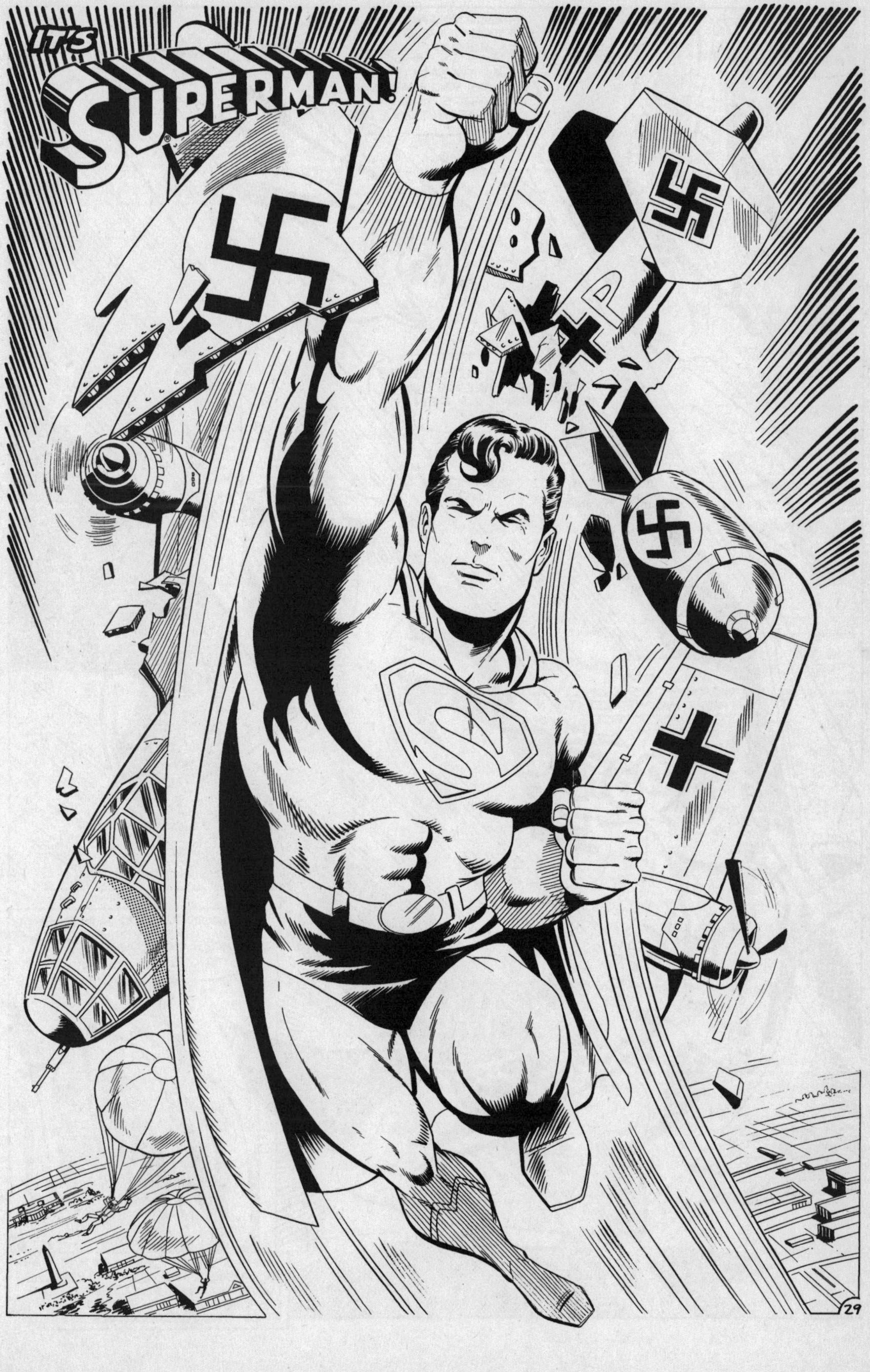
IT'S
SUPERMAN!
29

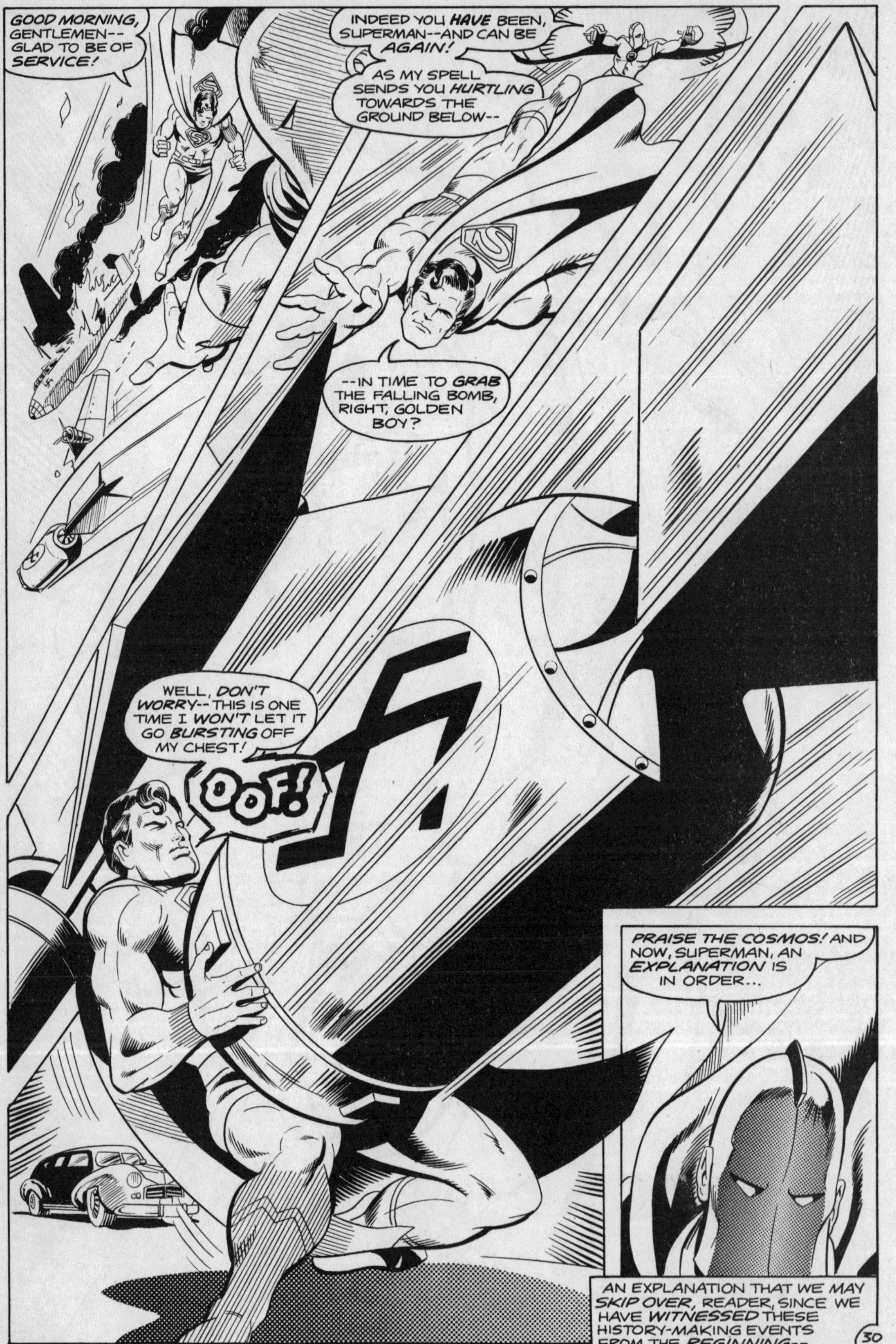
GOOD MORNING, GENTLEMEN-- GLAD TO BE OF SERVICE!
INDEED YOU HAVE BEEN, SUPERMAN--AND CAN BE AGAIN!
AS MY SPELL SENDS YOU HURTLING TOWARDS THE GROUND BELOW--
--IN TIME TO GRAB THE FALLING BOMB, RIGHT, GOLDEN BOY?
WELL, DON'T WORRY--THIS IS ONE TIME I WON'T LET IT GO BURSTING OFF MY CHEST!
OOF!
PRAISE THE COSMOS! AND NOW, SUPERMAN, AN EXPLANATION IS IN ORDER...
AN EXPLANATION THAT WE MAY SKIP OVER, READER, SINCE WE HAVE WITNESSED THESE HISTORY-MAKING EVENTS FROM THE BEGINNING--
30

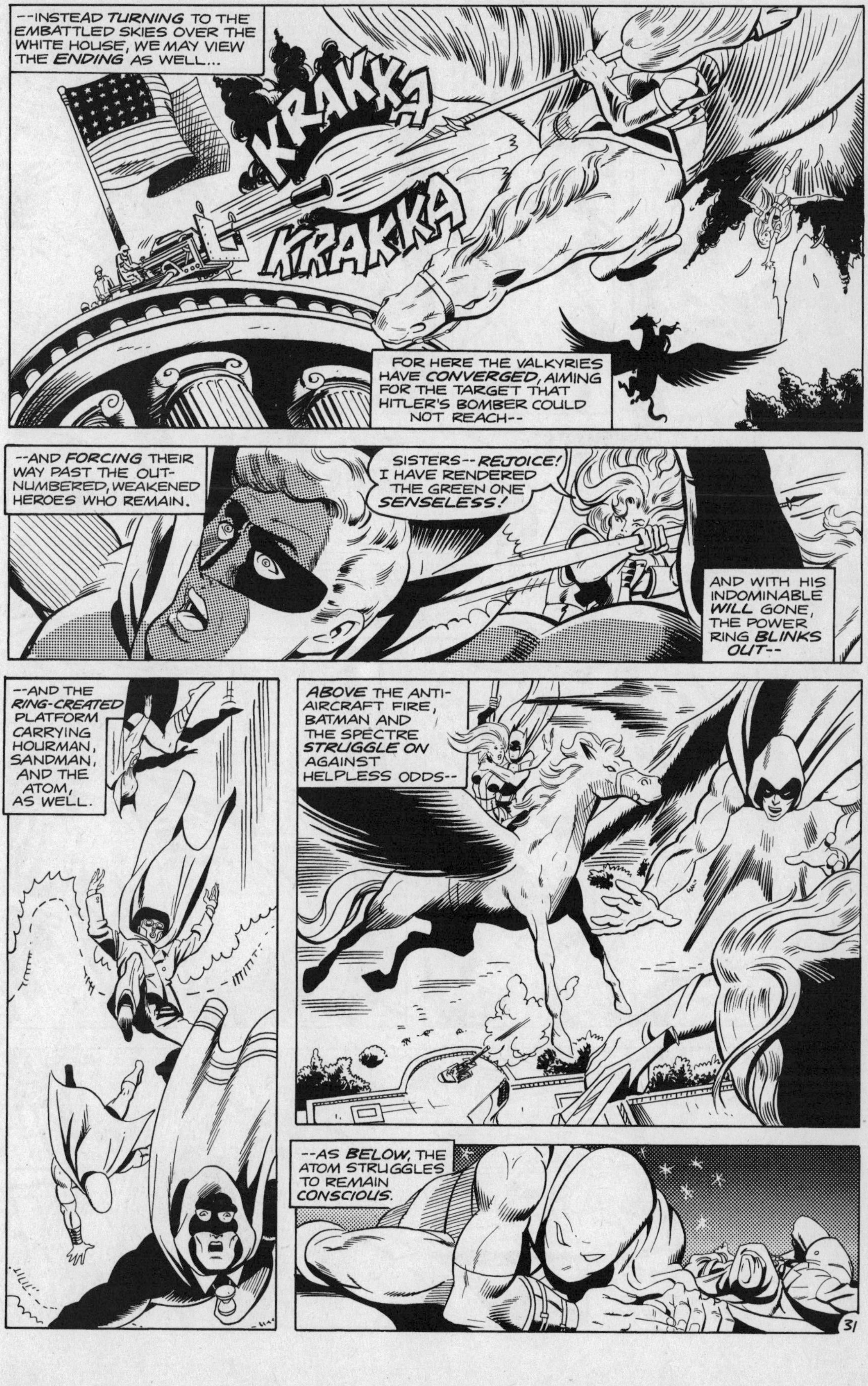
--INSTEAD TURNING TO THE EMBATTLED SKIES OVER THE WHITE HOUSE, WE MAY VIEW THE ENDING AS WELL...
KRAKKA
KRAKKA
FOR HERE THE VALKYRIES HAVE CONVERGED, AIMING FOR THE TARGET THAT HITLER'S BOMBER COULD NOT REACH--
--AND FORCING THEIR WAY PAST THE OUT-NUMBERED, WEAKENED HEROES WHO REMAIN.
SISTERS--REJOICE! I HAVE RENDERED THE GREEN ONE SENSELESS!
AND WITH HIS INDOMINABLE WILL GONE, THE POWER RING BLINKS OUT--
--AND THE RING-CREATED PLATFORM CARRYING HOURMAN, SANDMAN, AND THE ATOM, AS WELL.
ABOVE THE ANTI-AIRCRAFT FIRE, BATMAN AND THE SPECTRE STRUGGLE ON AGAINST HELPLESS ODDS--
--AS BELOW, THE ATOM STRUGGLES TO REMAIN CONSCIOUS.
31

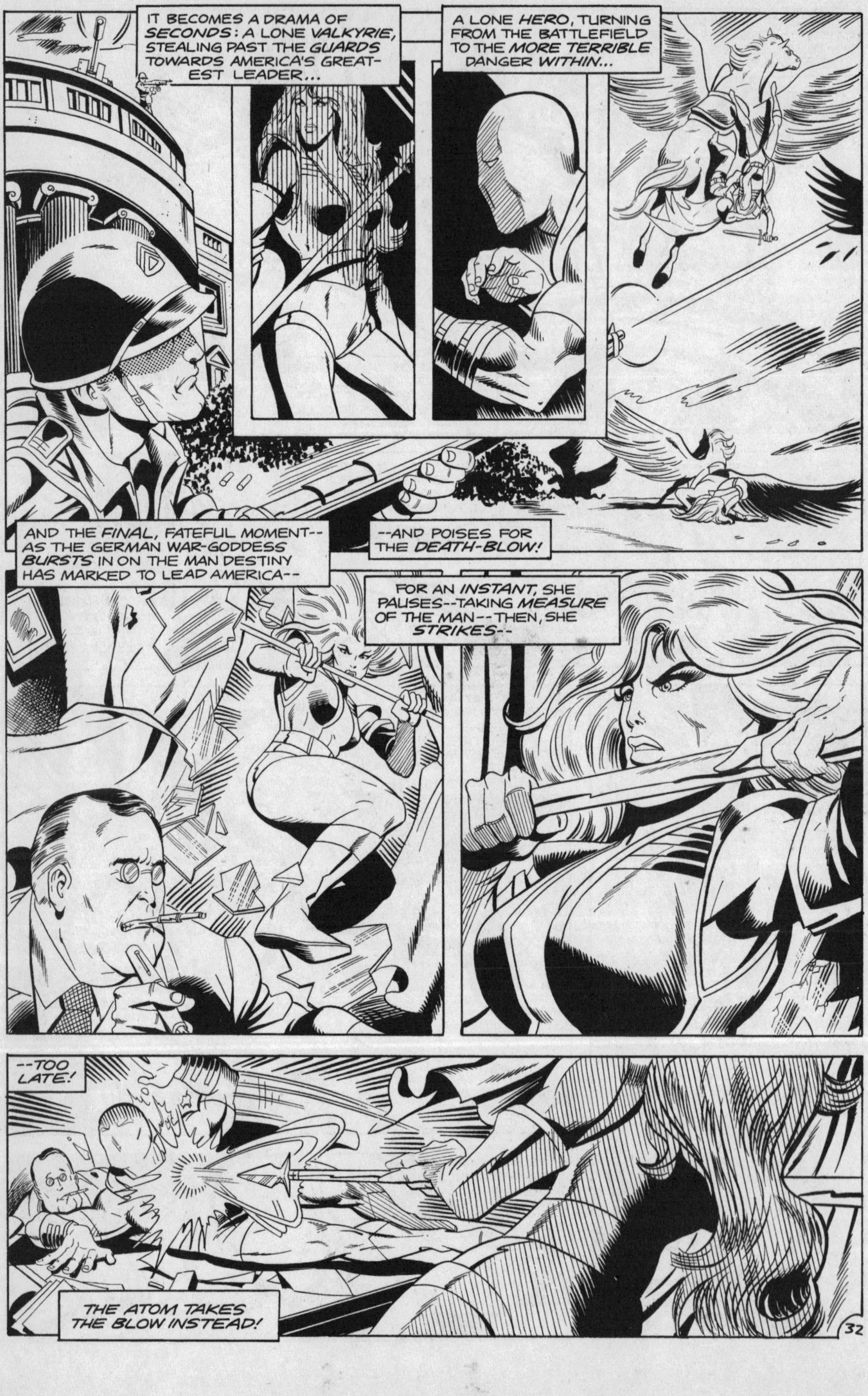
IT BECOMES A DRAMA OF SECONDS: A LONE VALKYRIE, STEALING PAST THE GUARDS TOWARDS AMERICA'S GREAT-EST LEADER...
A LONE HERO, TURNING FROM THE BATTLEFIELD TO THE MORE TERRIBLE DANGER WITHIN...
AND THE FINAL, FATEFUL MOMENT--AS THE GERMAN WAR-GODDESS BURSTS IN ON THE MAN DESTINY HAS MARKED TO LEAD AMERICA--
--AND POISES FOR THE DEATH-BLOW!
FOR AN INSTANT, SHE PAUSES--TAKING MEASURE OF THE MAN--THEN, SHE STRIKES--
--TOO LATE!
THE ATOM TAKES THE BLOW INSTEAD!
32

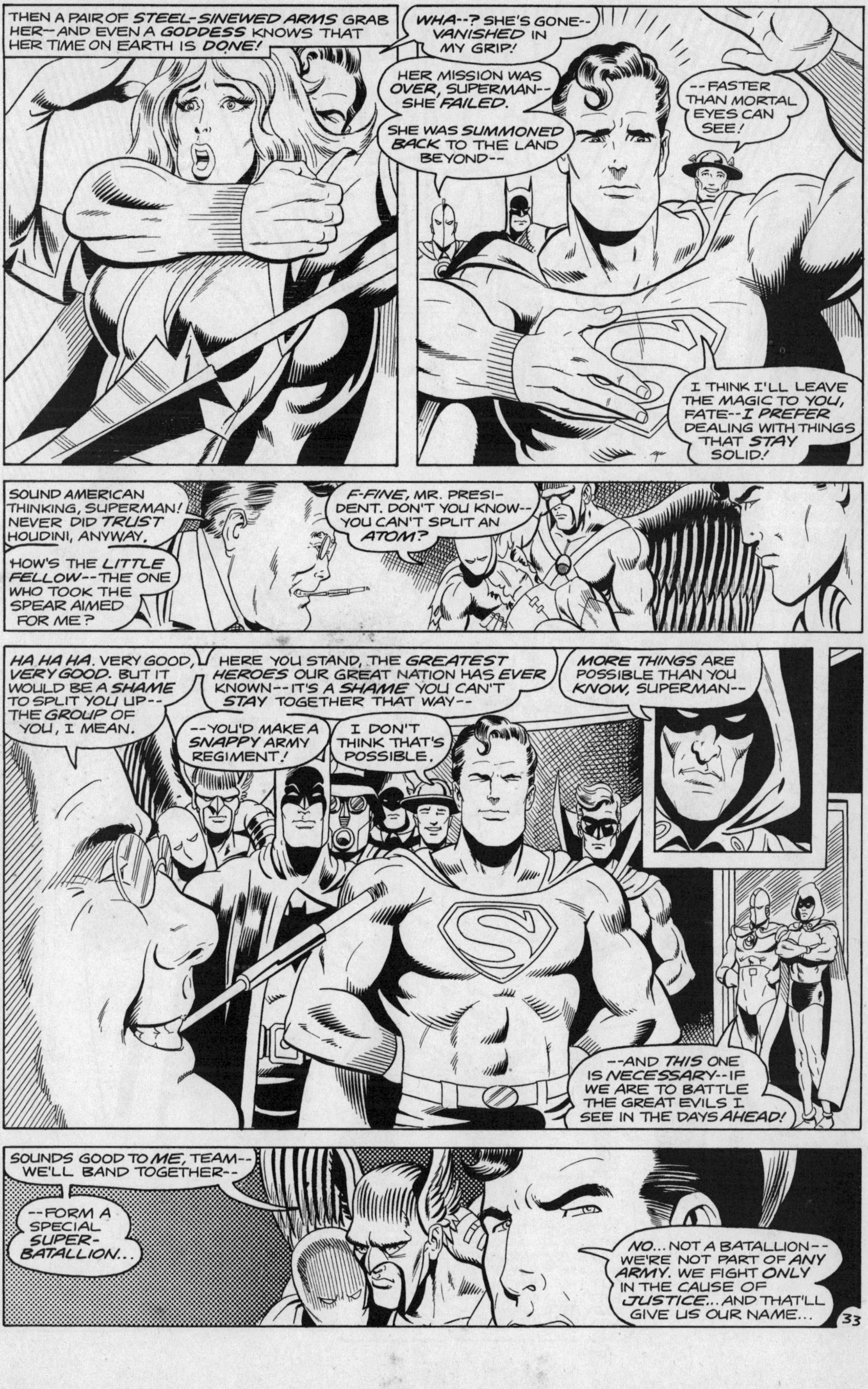
THEN A PAIR OF STEEL-SINEWED ARMS GRAB HER--AND EVEN A GODDESS KNOWS THAT HER TIME ON EARTH IS DONE!
WHA--? SHE'S GONE-- VANISHED IN MY GRIP!
HER MISSION WAS OVER, SUPERMAN-- SHE FAILED.
SHE WAS SUMMONED BACK TO THE LAND BEYOND--
--FASTER THAN MORTAL EYES CAN SEE!
I THINK I'LL LEAVE THE MAGIC TO YOU, FATE--I PREFER DEALING WITH THINGS THAT STAY SOLID!
SOUND AMERICAN THINKING, SUPERMAN! NEVER DID TRUST HOUDINI, ANYWAY.
HOW'S THE LITTLE FELLOW--THE ONE WHO TOOK THE SPEAR AIMED FOR ME?
F-FINE, MR. PRESIDENT. DON'T YOU KNOW-- YOU CAN'T SPLIT AN ATOM?
HA HA HA. VERY GOOD, VERY GOOD. BUT IT WOULD BE A SHAME TO SPLIT YOU UP-- THE GROUP OF YOU, I MEAN.
HERE YOU STAND, THE GREATEST HEROES OUR GREAT NATION HAS EVER KNOWN--IT'S A SHAME YOU CAN'T STAY TOGETHER THAT WAY--
--YOU'D MAKE A SNAPPY ARMY REGIMENT!
I DON'T THINK THAT'S POSSIBLE.
MORE THINGS ARE POSSIBLE THAN YOU KNOW, SUPERMAN--
--AND THIS ONE IS NECESSARY--IF WE ARE TO BATTLE THE GREAT EVILS I SEE IN THE DAYS AHEAD!
SOUNDS GOOD TO ME, TEAM-- WE'LL BAND TOGETHER--
--FORM A SPECIAL SUPER-BATALLION...
NO... NOT A BATALLION-- WE'RE NOT PART OF ANY ARMY. WE FIGHT ONLY IN THE CAUSE OF JUSTICE... AND THAT'LL GIVE US OUR NAME...
33

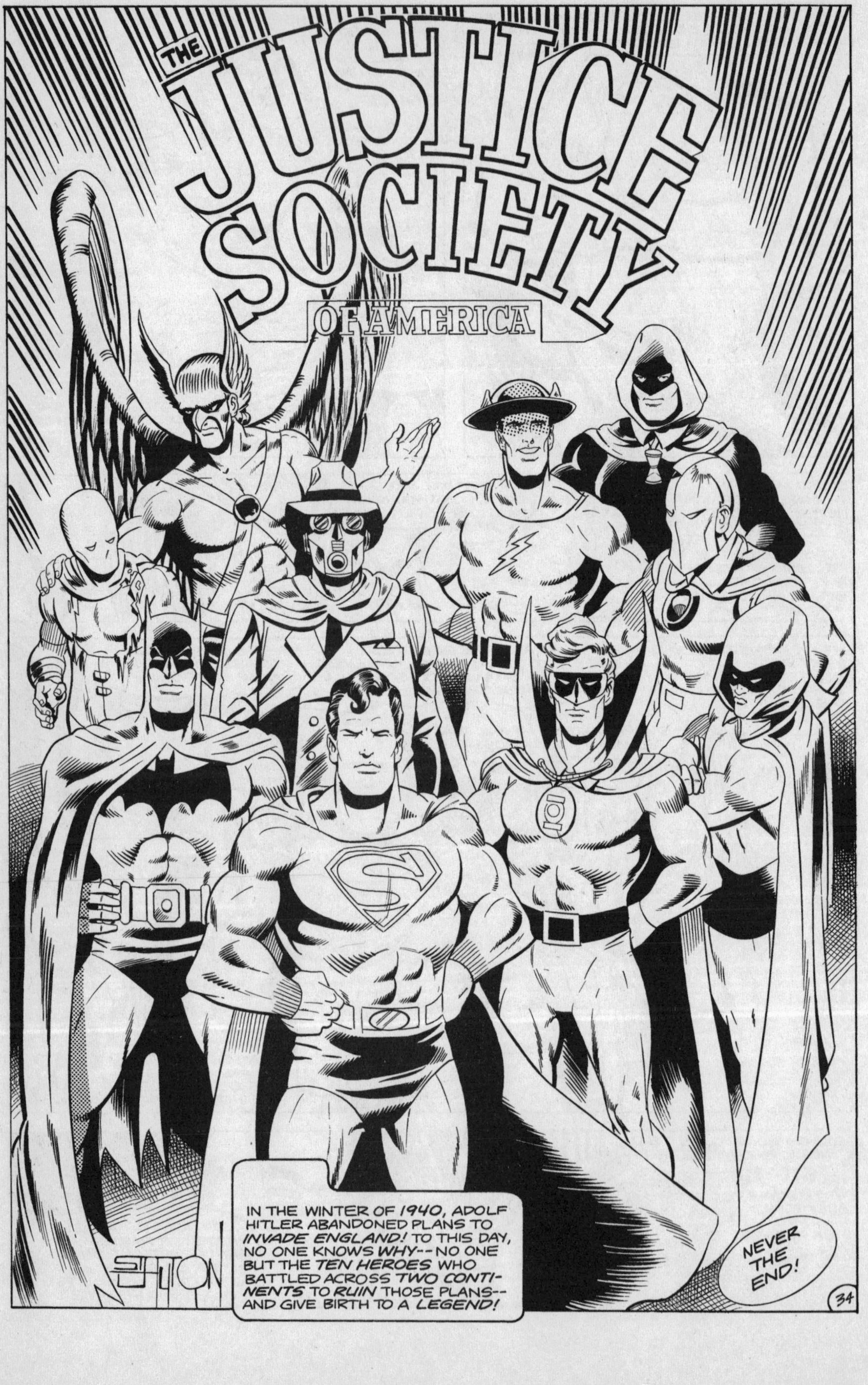
THE JUSTICE SOCIETY OF AMERICA
IN THE WINTER OF 1940, ADOLF HITLER ABANDONED PLANS TO INVADE ENGLAND! TO THIS DAY, NO ONE KNOWS WHY-- NO ONE BUT THE TEN HEROES WHO BATTLED ACROSS TWO CONTINENTS TO RUIN THOSE PLANS-- AND GIVE BIRTH TO A LEGEND!
NEVER THE END!
34

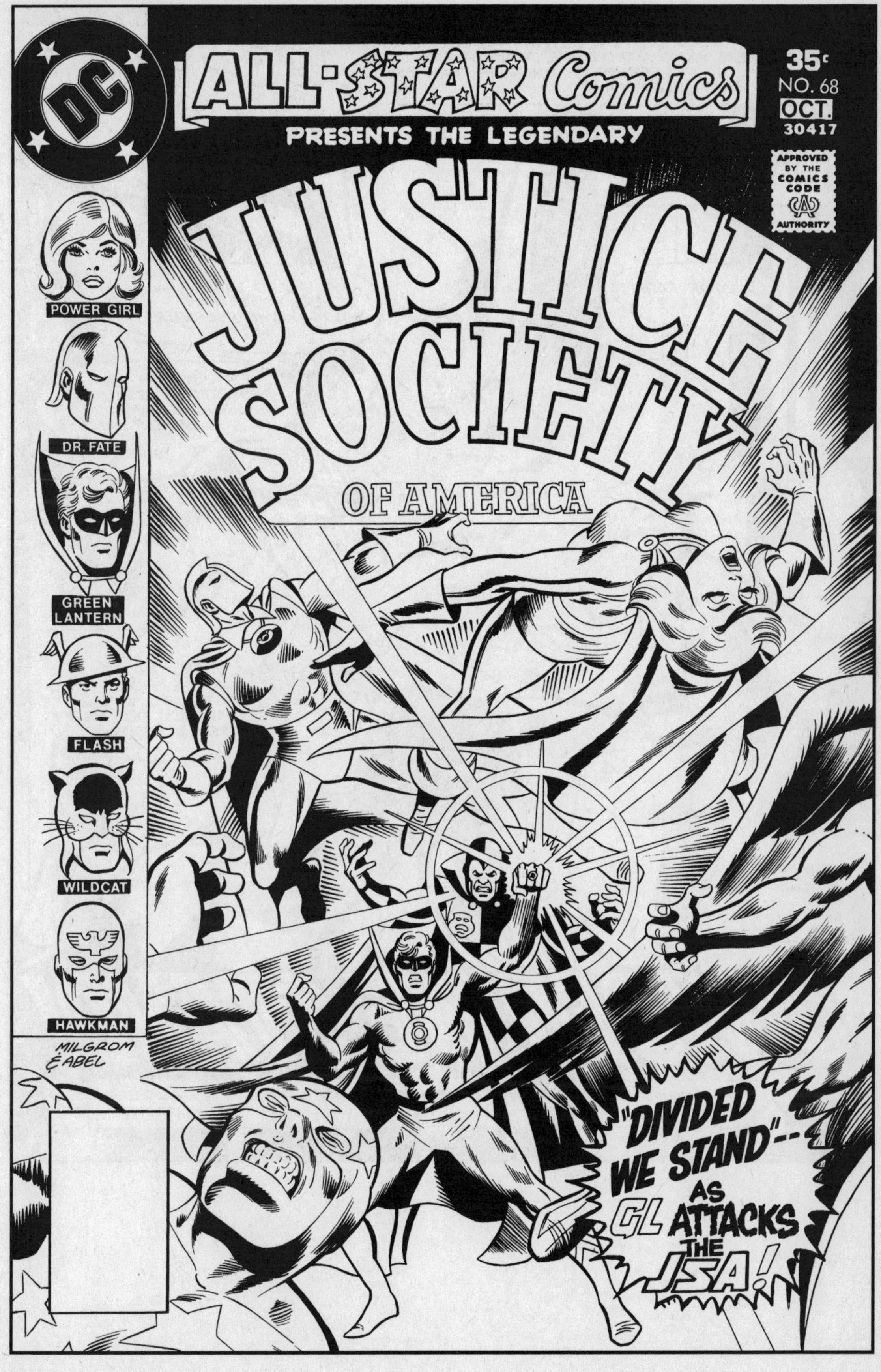
ALL-STAR Comics
PRESENTS THE LEGENDARY
JUSTICE SOCIETY
OF AMERICA
35¢
NO. 68
OCT.
30417
APPROVED BY THE COMICS CODE AUTHORITY
POWER GIRL
DR. FATE
GREEN LANTERN
FLASH
WILDCAT
HAWKMAN
MILGROM & ABEL
"DIVIDED WE STAND"-- AS GL ATTACKS THE JSA!

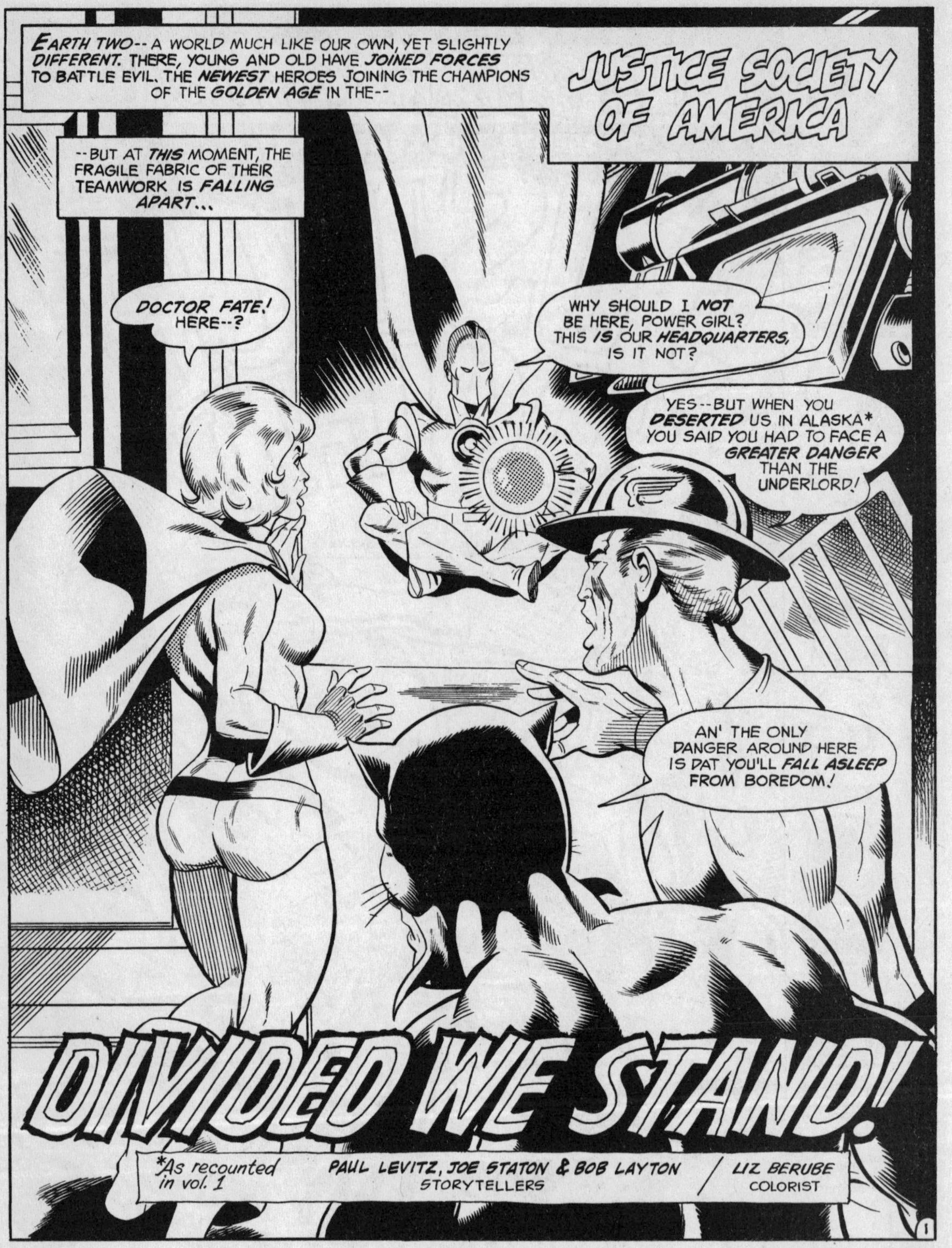
EARTH TWO-- A WORLD MUCH LIKE OUR OWN, YET SLIGHTLY DIFFERENT. THERE, YOUNG AND OLD HAVE JOINED FORCES TO BATTLE EVIL. THE NEWEST HEROES JOINING THE CHAMPIONS OF THE GOLDEN AGE IN THE--
JUSTICE SOCIETY OF AMERICA
--BUT AT THIS MOMENT, THE FRAGILE FABRIC OF THEIR TEAMWORK IS FALLING APART...
DOCTOR FATE! HERE--?
WHY SHOULD I NOT BE HERE, POWER GIRL? THIS IS OUR HEADQUARTERS, IS IT NOT?
YES--BUT WHEN YOU DESERTED US IN ALASKA* YOU SAID YOU HAD TO FACE A GREATER DANGER THAN THE UNDERLORD!
AN' THE ONLY DANGER AROUND HERE IS DAT YOU'LL FALL ASLEEP FROM BOREDOM!
DIVIDED WE STAND!
*As recounted in vol. 1
PAUL LEVITZ, JOE STATON & BOB LAYTON STORYTELLERS
LIZ BERUBE COLORIST
1

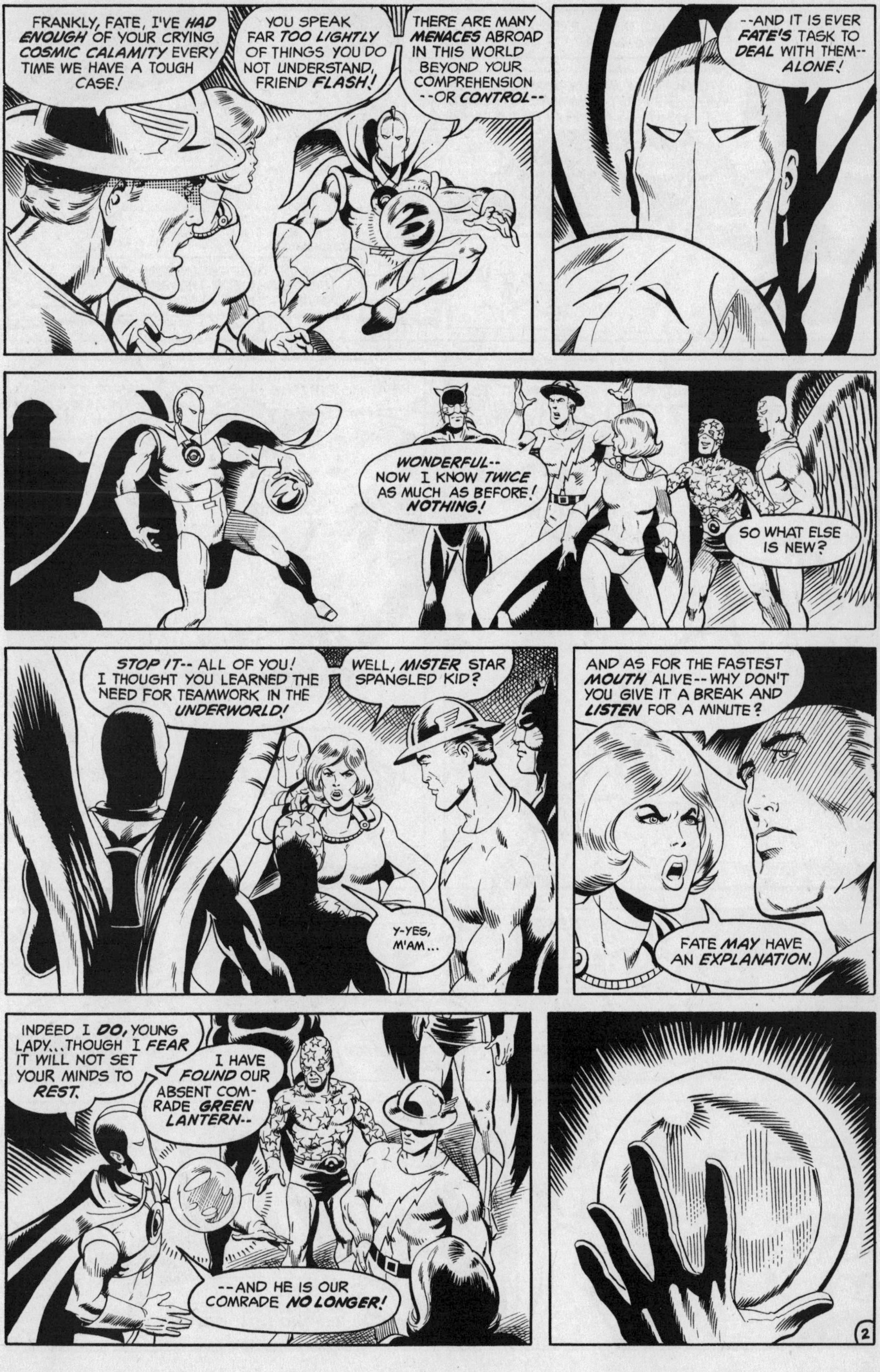
FRANKLY, FATE, I'VE HAD ENOUGH OF YOUR CRYING COSMIC CALAMITY EVERY TIME WE HAVE A TOUGH CASE!
YOU SPEAK FAR TOO LIGHTLY OF THINGS YOU DO NOT UNDERSTAND, FRIEND FLASH!
THERE ARE MANY MENACES ABROAD IN THIS WORLD BEYOND YOUR COMPREHENSION --OR CONTROL--
--AND IT IS EVER FATE'S TASK TO DEAL WITH THEM-- ALONE!
WONDERFUL-- NOW I KNOW TWICE AS MUCH AS BEFORE! NOTHING!
SO WHAT ELSE IS NEW?
STOP IT-- ALL OF YOU! I THOUGHT YOU LEARNED THE NEED FOR TEAMWORK IN THE UNDERWORLD!
WELL, MISTER STAR SPANGLED KID?
Y-YES, M'AM...
AND AS FOR THE FASTEST MOUTH ALIVE-- WHY DON'T YOU GIVE IT A BREAK AND LISTEN FOR A MINUTE?
FATE MAY HAVE AN EXPLANATION.
INDEED I DO, YOUNG LADY...THOUGH I FEAR IT WILL NOT SET YOUR MINDS TO REST.
I HAVE FOUND OUR ABSENT COM-RADE GREEN LANTERN--
--AND HE IS OUR COMRADE NO LONGER!
2

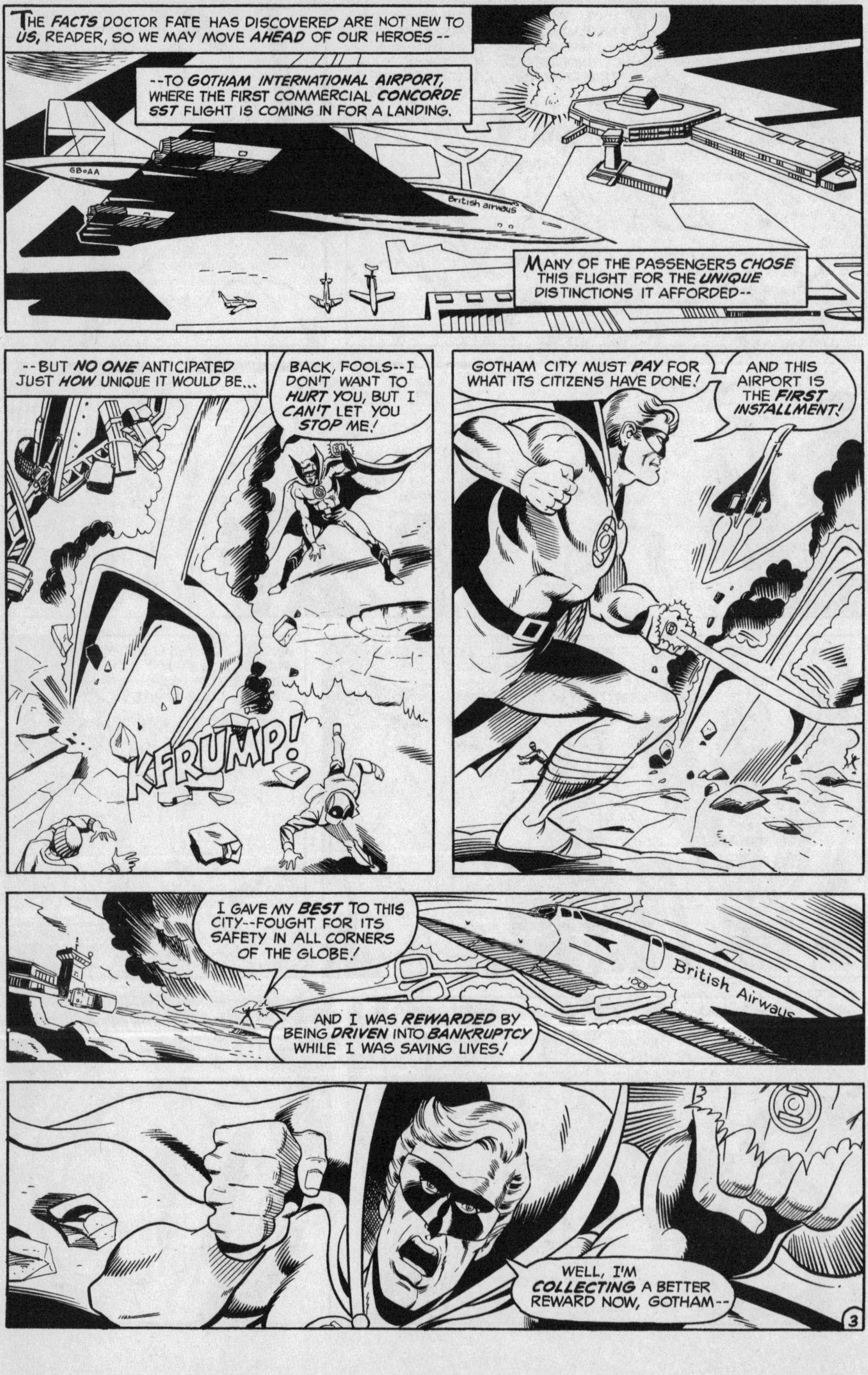
THE FACTS DOCTOR FATE HAS DISCOVERED ARE NOT NEW TO US, READER, SO WE MAY MOVE AHEAD OF OUR HEROES --
--TO GOTHAM INTERNATIONAL AIRPORT, WHERE THE FIRST COMMERCIAL CONCORDE SST FLIGHT IS COMING IN FOR A LANDING.
GBOAA
British airways
MANY OF THE PASSENGERS CHOSE THIS FLIGHT FOR THE UNIQUE DISTINCTIONS IT AFFORDED--
--BUT NO ONE ANTICIPATED JUST HOW UNIQUE IT WOULD BE...
BACK, FOOLS--I DON'T WANT TO HURT YOU, BUT I CAN'T LET YOU STOP ME!
KFRUMP!
GOTHAM CITY MUST PAY FOR WHAT ITS CITIZENS HAVE DONE!
AND THIS AIRPORT IS THE FIRST INSTALLMENT!
I GAVE MY BEST TO THIS CITY--FOUGHT FOR ITS SAFETY IN ALL CORNERS OF THE GLOBE!
British Airways
AND I WAS REWARDED BY BEING DRIVEN INTO BANKRUPTCY WHILE I WAS SAVING LIVES!
WELL, I'M COLLECTING A BETTER REWARD NOW, GOTHAM--
3

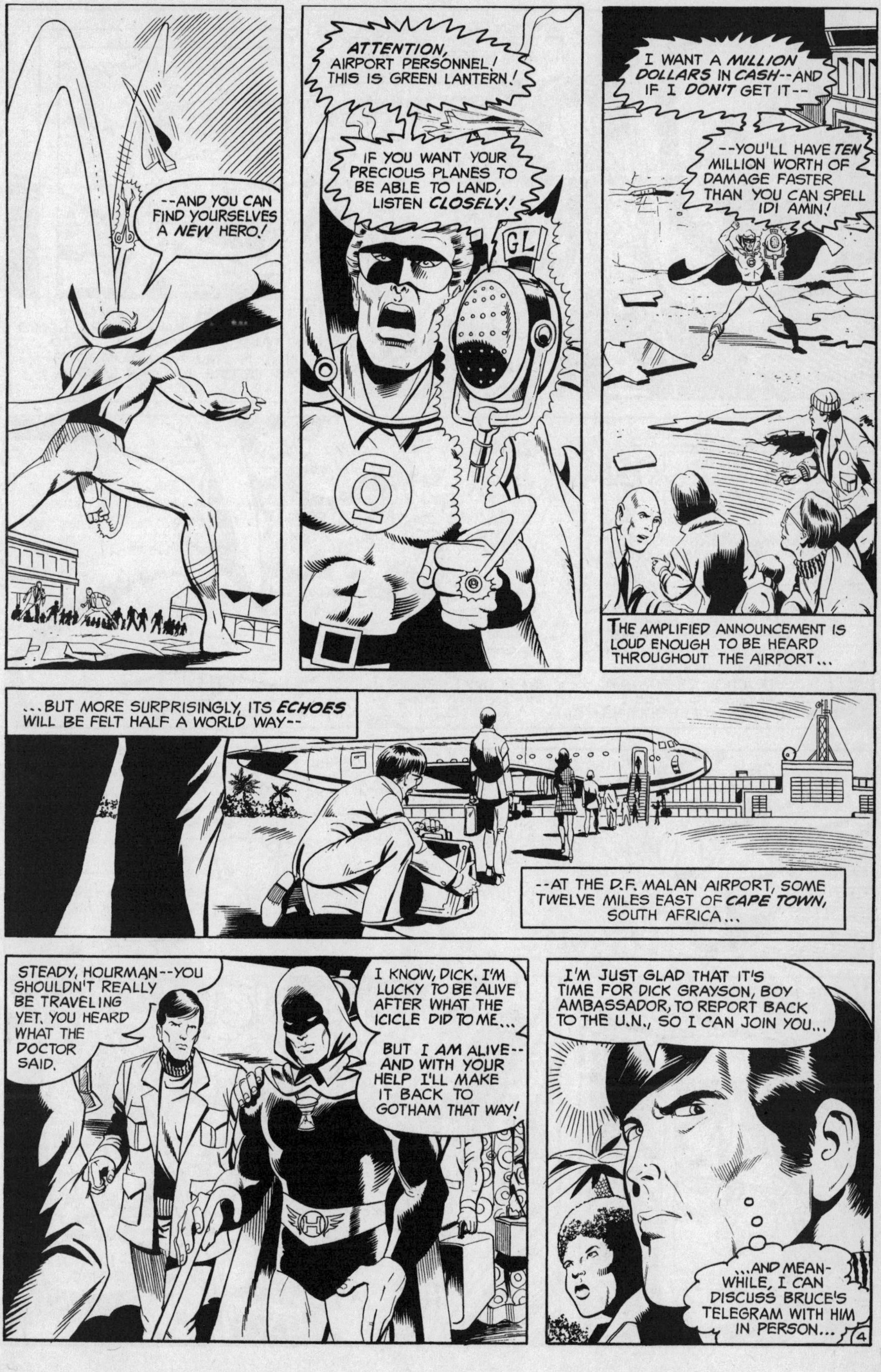
--AND YOU CAN FIND YOURSELVES A NEW HERO!
ATTENTION, AIRPORT PERSONNEL! THIS IS GREEN LANTERN!
IF YOU WANT YOUR PRECIOUS PLANES TO BE ABLE TO LAND, LISTEN CLOSELY!
GL
I WANT A MILLION DOLLARS IN CASH--AND IF I DON'T GET IT--
--YOU'LL HAVE TEN MILLION WORTH OF DAMAGE FASTER THAN YOU CAN SPELL IDI AMIN!
THE AMPLIFIED ANNOUNCEMENT IS LOUD ENOUGH TO BE HEARD THROUGHOUT THE AIRPORT...
...BUT MORE SURPRISINGLY, ITS ECHOES WILL BE FELT HALF A WORLD WAY--
--AT THE D.F. MALAN AIRPORT, SOME TWELVE MILES EAST OF CAPE TOWN, SOUTH AFRICA...
STEADY, HOURMAN--YOU SHOULDN'T REALLY BE TRAVELING YET. YOU HEARD WHAT THE DOCTOR SAID.
I KNOW, DICK. I'M LUCKY TO BE ALIVE AFTER WHAT THE ICICLE DID TO ME...
BUT I AM ALIVE--AND WITH YOUR HELP I'LL MAKE IT BACK TO GOTHAM THAT WAY!
I'M JUST GLAD THAT IT'S TIME FOR DICK GRAYSON, BOY AMBASSADOR, TO REPORT BACK TO THE U.N., SO I CAN JOIN YOU...
...AND MEAN-WHILE, I CAN DISCUSS BRUCE'S TELEGRAM WITH HIM IN PERSON...
4

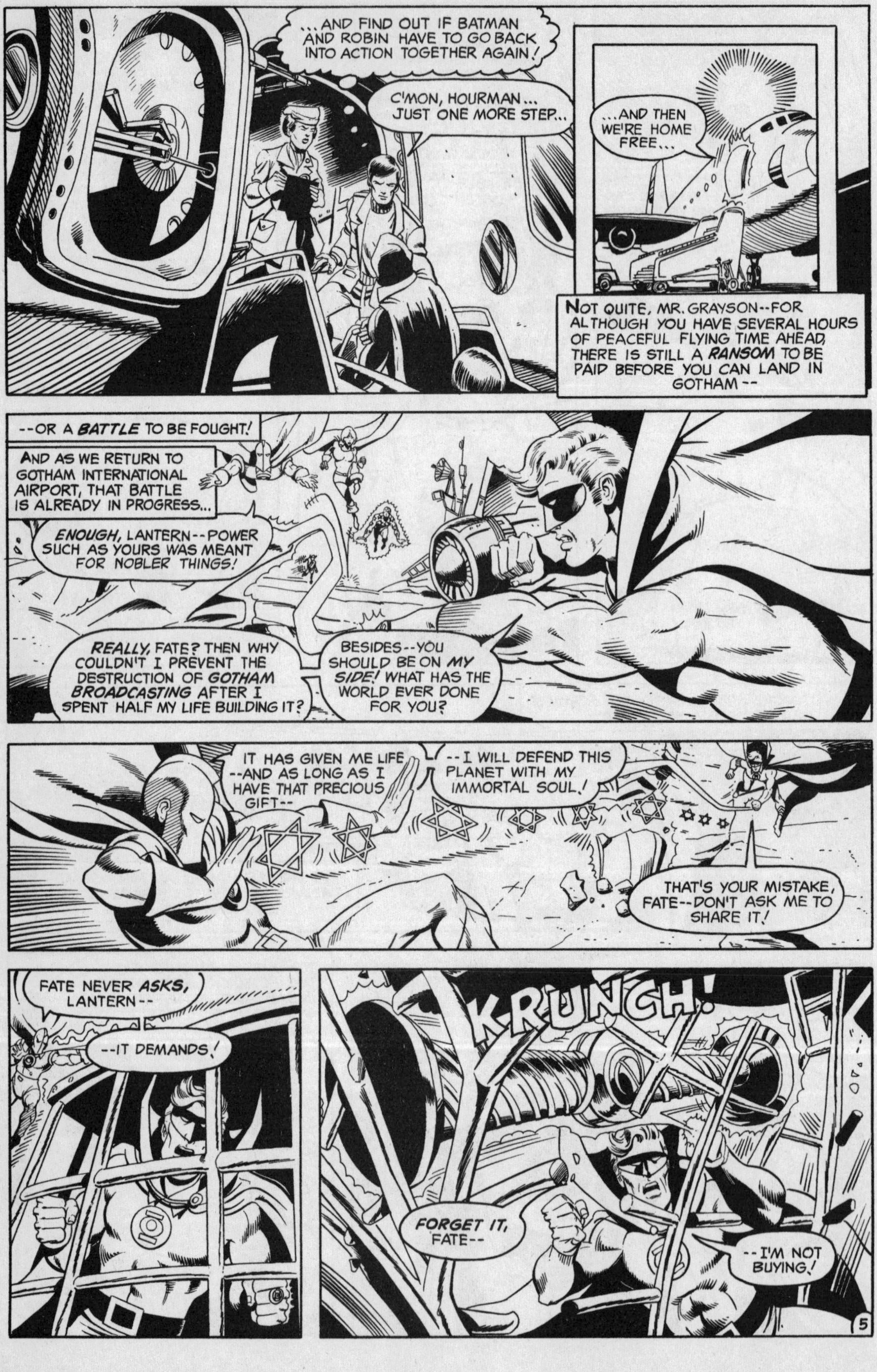
...AND FIND OUT IF BATMAN AND ROBIN HAVE TO GO BACK INTO ACTION TOGETHER AGAIN!
C'MON, HOURMAN... JUST ONE MORE STEP...
...AND THEN WE'RE HOME FREE...
NOT QUITE, MR. GRAYSON--FOR ALTHOUGH YOU HAVE SEVERAL HOURS OF PEACEFUL FLYING TIME AHEAD, THERE IS STILL A RANSOM TO BE PAID BEFORE YOU CAN LAND IN GOTHAM--
--OR A BATTLE TO BE FOUGHT!
AND AS WE RETURN TO GOTHAM INTERNATIONAL AIRPORT, THAT BATTLE IS ALREADY IN PROGRESS...
ENOUGH, LANTERN--POWER SUCH AS YOURS WAS MEANT FOR NOBLER THINGS!
REALLY, FATE? THEN WHY COULDN'T I PREVENT THE DESTRUCTION OF GOTHAM BROADCASTING AFTER I SPENT HALF MY LIFE BUILDING IT?
BESIDES--YOU SHOULD BE ON MY SIDE! WHAT HAS THE WORLD EVER DONE FOR YOU?
IT HAS GIVEN ME LIFE --AND AS LONG AS I HAVE THAT PRECIOUS GIFT--
--I WILL DEFEND THIS PLANET WITH MY IMMORTAL SOUL!
THAT'S YOUR MISTAKE, FATE--DON'T ASK ME TO SHARE IT!
FATE NEVER ASKS, LANTERN--
--IT DEMANDS!
KRUNCH!
FORGET IT, FATE--
--I'M NOT BUYING!
5

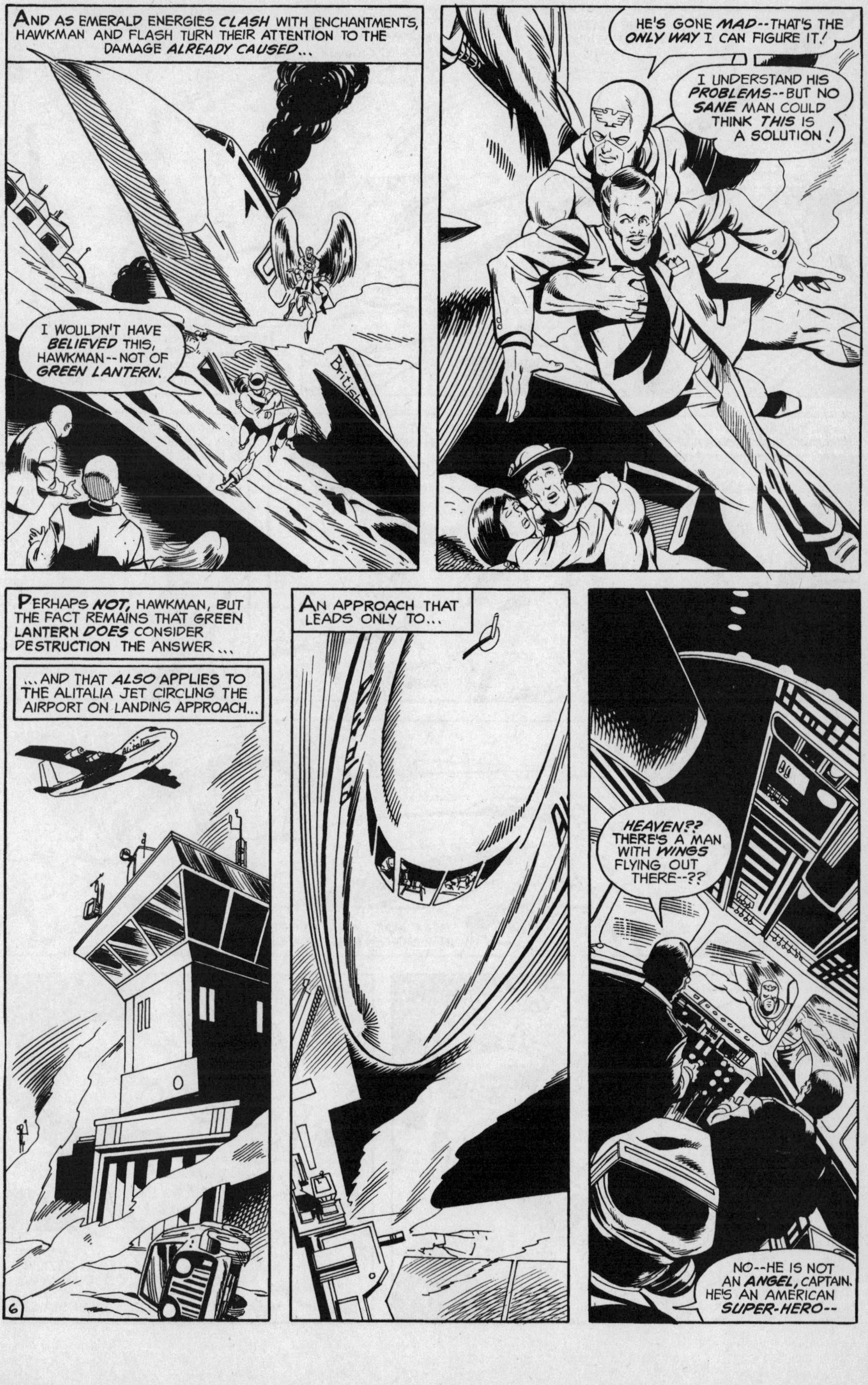
AND AS EMERALD ENERGIES CLASH WITH ENCHANTMENTS, HAWKMAN AND FLASH TURN THEIR ATTENTION TO THE DAMAGE ALREADY CAUSED...
I WOULDN'T HAVE BELIEVED THIS, HAWKMAN--NOT OF GREEN LANTERN.
British
HE'S GONE MAD--THAT'S THE ONLY WAY I CAN FIGURE IT!
I UNDERSTAND HIS PROBLEMS--BUT NO SANE MAN COULD THINK THIS IS A SOLUTION!
PERHAPS NOT, HAWKMAN, BUT THE FACT REMAINS THAT GREEN LANTERN DOES CONSIDER DESTRUCTION THE ANSWER...
...AND THAT ALSO APPLIES TO THE ALITALIA JET CIRCLING THE AIRPORT ON LANDING APPROACH...
Alitalia
6
AN APPROACH THAT LEADS ONLY TO...
HEAVEN?? THERE'S A MAN WITH WINGS FLYING OUT THERE--??
NO--HE IS NOT AN ANGEL, CAPTAIN. HE'S AN AMERICAN SUPER-HERO--

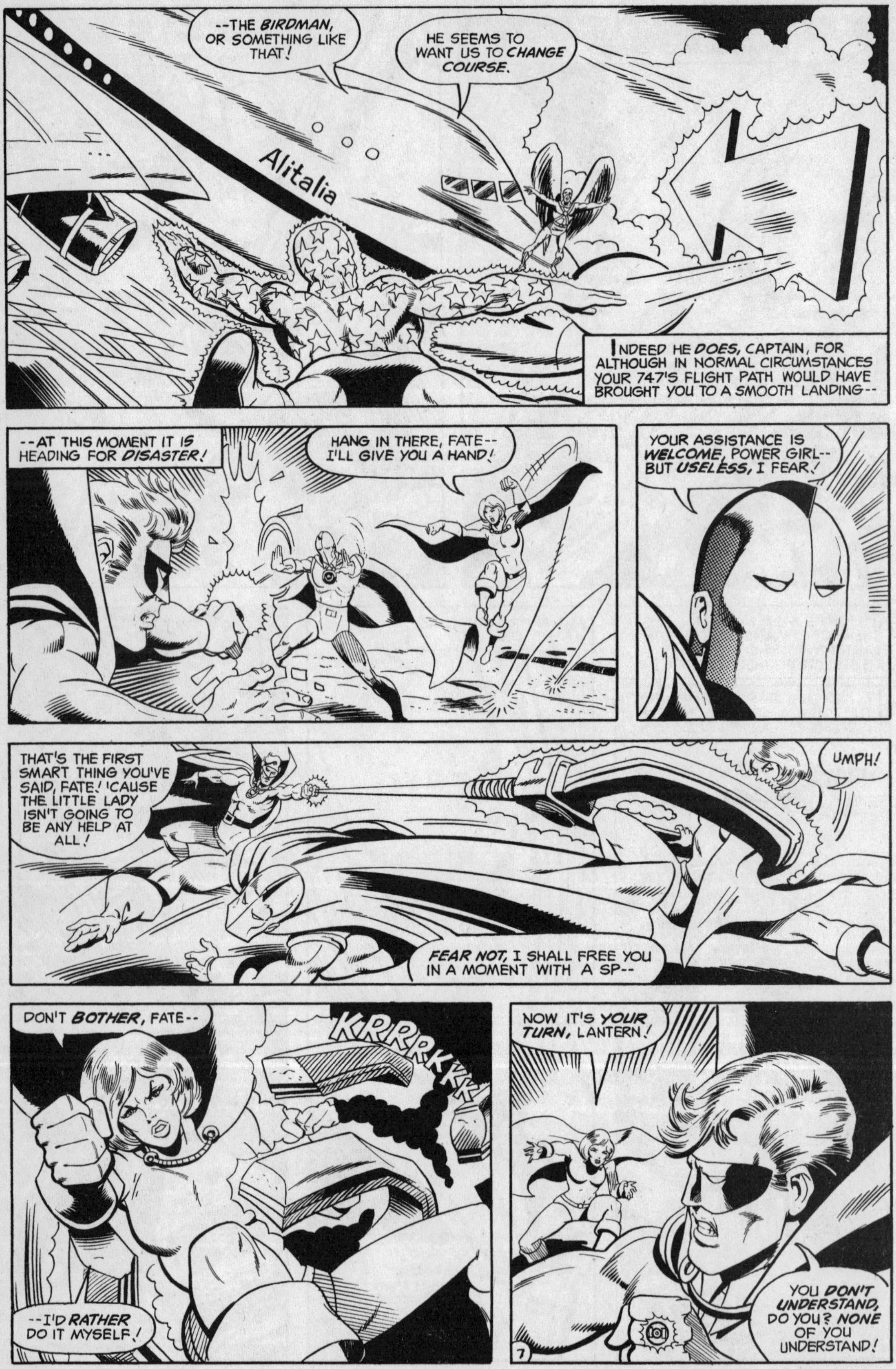
--THE BIRDMAN, OR SOMETHING LIKE THAT!
HE SEEMS TO WANT US TO CHANGE COURSE.
Alitalia
INDEED HE DOES, CAPTAIN, FOR ALTHOUGH IN NORMAL CIRCUMSTANCES YOUR 747'S FLIGHT PATH WOULD HAVE BROUGHT YOU TO A SMOOTH LANDING--
--AT THIS MOMENT IT IS HEADING FOR DISASTER!
HANG IN THERE, FATE-- I'LL GIVE YOU A HAND!
YOUR ASSISTANCE IS WELCOME, POWER GIRL-- BUT USELESS, I FEAR!
THAT'S THE FIRST SMART THING YOU'VE SAID, FATE! 'CAUSE THE LITTLE LADY ISN'T GOING TO BE ANY HELP AT ALL!
UMPH!
FEAR NOT, I SHALL FREE YOU IN A MOMENT WITH A SP--
DON'T BOTHER, FATE--
KRRRRKKK
--I'D RATHER DO IT MYSELF!
NOW IT'S YOUR TURN, LANTERN!
YOU DON'T UNDERSTAND, DO YOU? NONE OF YOU UNDERSTAND!
7

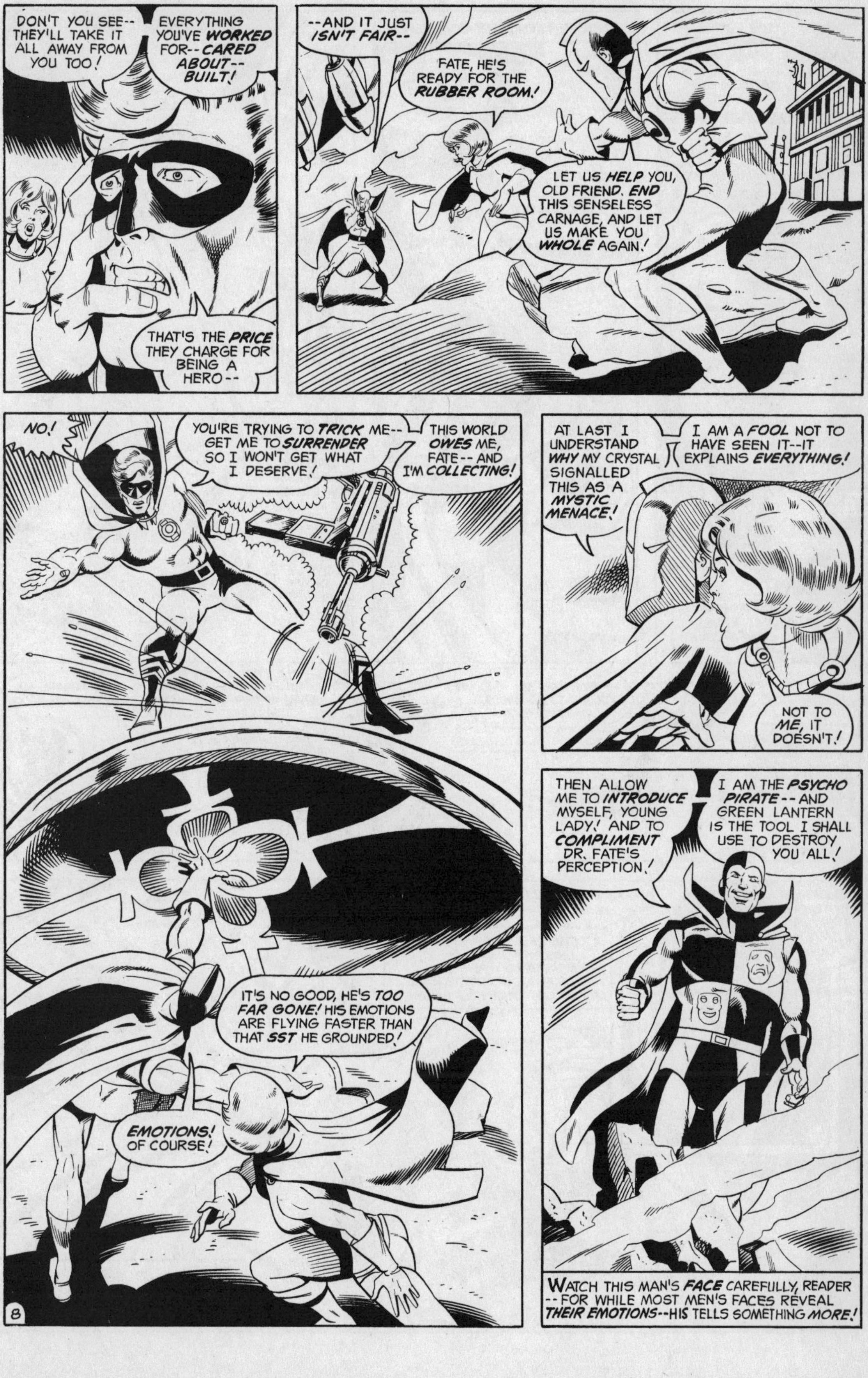
DON'T YOU SEE-- THEY'LL TAKE IT ALL AWAY FROM YOU TOO!
EVERYTHING YOU'VE WORKED FOR--CARED ABOUT--BUILT!
THAT'S THE PRICE THEY CHARGE FOR BEING A HERO--
--AND IT JUST ISN'T FAIR--
FATE, HE'S READY FOR THE RUBBER ROOM!
LET US HELP YOU, OLD FRIEND. END THIS SENSELESS CARNAGE, AND LET US MAKE YOU WHOLE AGAIN!
NO!
YOU'RE TRYING TO TRICK ME-- GET ME TO SURRENDER SO I WON'T GET WHAT I DESERVE!
THIS WORLD OWES ME, FATE-- AND I'M COLLECTING!
IT'S NO GOOD, HE'S TOO FAR GONE! HIS EMOTIONS ARE FLYING FASTER THAN THAT SST HE GROUNDED!
EMOTIONS! OF COURSE!
8
AT LAST I UNDERSTAND WHY MY CRYSTAL SIGNALLED THIS AS A MYSTIC MENACE!
I AM A FOOL NOT TO HAVE SEEN IT--IT EXPLAINS EVERYTHING!
NOT TO ME, IT DOESN'T!
THEN ALLOW ME TO INTRODUCE MYSELF, YOUNG LADY! AND TO COMPLIMENT DR. FATE'S PERCEPTION!
I AM THE PSYCHO PIRATE-- AND GREEN LANTERN IS THE TOOL I SHALL USE TO DESTROY YOU ALL!
WATCH THIS MAN'S FACE CAREFULLY, READER --FOR WHILE MOST MEN'S FACES REVEAL THEIR EMOTIONS--HIS TELLS SOMETHING MORE!

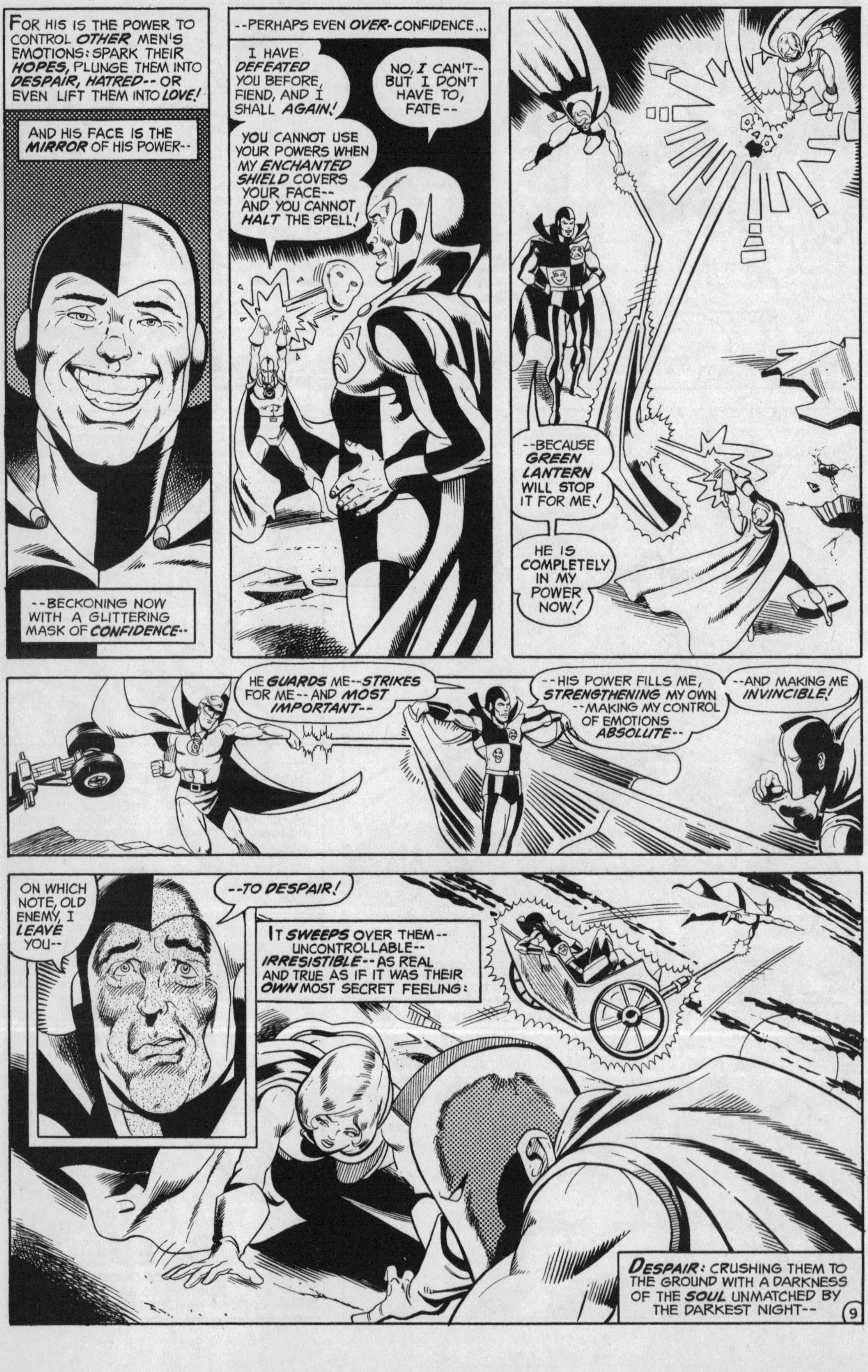
FOR HIS IS THE POWER TO CONTROL OTHER MEN'S EMOTIONS: SPARK THEIR HOPES, PLUNGE THEM INTO DESPAIR, HATRED-- OR EVEN LIFT THEM INTO LOVE!
AND HIS FACE IS THE MIRROR OF HIS POWER--
--BECKONING NOW WITH A GLITTERING MASK OF CONFIDENCE--
--PERHAPS EVEN OVER-CONFIDENCE...
I HAVE DEFEATED YOU BEFORE, FIEND, AND I SHALL AGAIN!
YOU CANNOT USE YOUR POWERS WHEN MY ENCHANTED SHIELD COVERS YOUR FACE-- AND YOU CANNOT HALT THE SPELL!
NO, I CAN'T-- BUT I DON'T HAVE TO, FATE--
--BECAUSE GREEN LANTERN WILL STOP IT FOR ME!
HE IS COMPLETELY IN MY POWER NOW!
HE GUARDS ME--STRIKES FOR ME-- AND MOST IMPORTANT--
--HIS POWER FILLS ME, STRENGTHENING MY OWN --MAKING MY CONTROL OF EMOTIONS ABSOLUTE--
--AND MAKING ME INVINCIBLE!
ON WHICH NOTE, OLD ENEMY, I LEAVE YOU--
--TO DESPAIR!
IT SWEEPS OVER THEM-- UNCONTROLLABLE-- IRRESISTIBLE-- AS REAL AND TRUE AS IF IT WAS THEIR OWN MOST SECRET FEELING:
DESPAIR: CRUSHING THEM TO THE GROUND WITH A DARKNESS OF THE SOUL UNMATCHED BY THE DARKEST NIGHT--
9

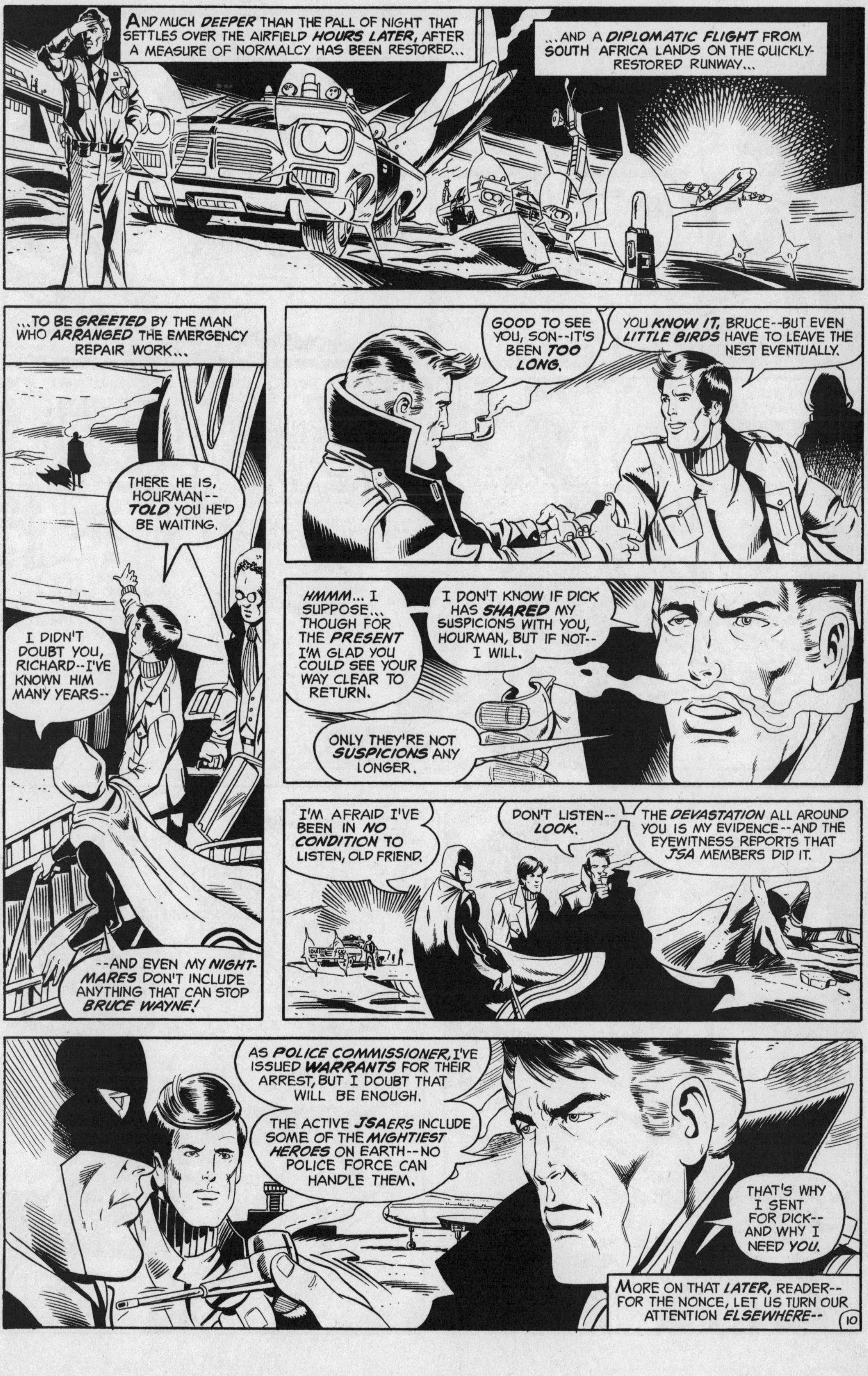
AND MUCH DEEPER THAN THE PALL OF NIGHT THAT SETTLES OVER THE AIRFIELD HOURS LATER, AFTER A MEASURE OF NORMALCY HAS BEEN RESTORED...
...AND A DIPLOMATIC FLIGHT FROM SOUTH AFRICA LANDS ON THE QUICKLY-RESTORED RUNWAY...
...TO BE GREETED BY THE MAN WHO ARRANGED THE EMERGENCY REPAIR WORK...
THERE HE IS, HOURMAN--TOLD YOU HE'D BE WAITING.
I DIDN'T DOUBT YOU, RICHARD--I'VE KNOWN HIM MANY YEARS--
--AND EVEN MY NIGHT-MARES DON'T INCLUDE ANYTHING THAT CAN STOP BRUCE WAYNE!
GOOD TO SEE YOU, SON--IT'S BEEN TOO LONG.
YOU KNOW IT, BRUCE--BUT EVEN LITTLE BIRDS HAVE TO LEAVE THE NEST EVENTUALLY.
HMMM... I SUPPOSE... THOUGH FOR THE PRESENT I'M GLAD YOU COULD SEE YOUR WAY CLEAR TO RETURN.
I DON'T KNOW IF DICK HAS SHARED MY SUSPICIONS WITH YOU, HOURMAN, BUT IF NOT--I WILL.
ONLY THEY'RE NOT SUSPICIONS ANY LONGER.
I'M AFRAID I'VE BEEN IN NO CONDITION TO LISTEN, OLD FRIEND.
DON'T LISTEN--LOOK.
THE DEVASTATION ALL AROUND YOU IS MY EVIDENCE--AND THE EYEWITNESS REPORTS THAT JSA MEMBERS DID IT.
AS POLICE COMMISSIONER, I'VE ISSUED WARRANTS FOR THEIR ARREST, BUT I DOUBT THAT WILL BE ENOUGH.
THE ACTIVE JSAERS INCLUDE SOME OF THE MIGHTIEST HEROES ON EARTH--NO POLICE FORCE CAN HANDLE THEM.
THAT'S WHY I SENT FOR DICK--AND WHY I NEED YOU.
MORE ON THAT LATER, READER--FOR THE NONCE, LET US TURN OUR ATTENTION ELSEWHERE--
10

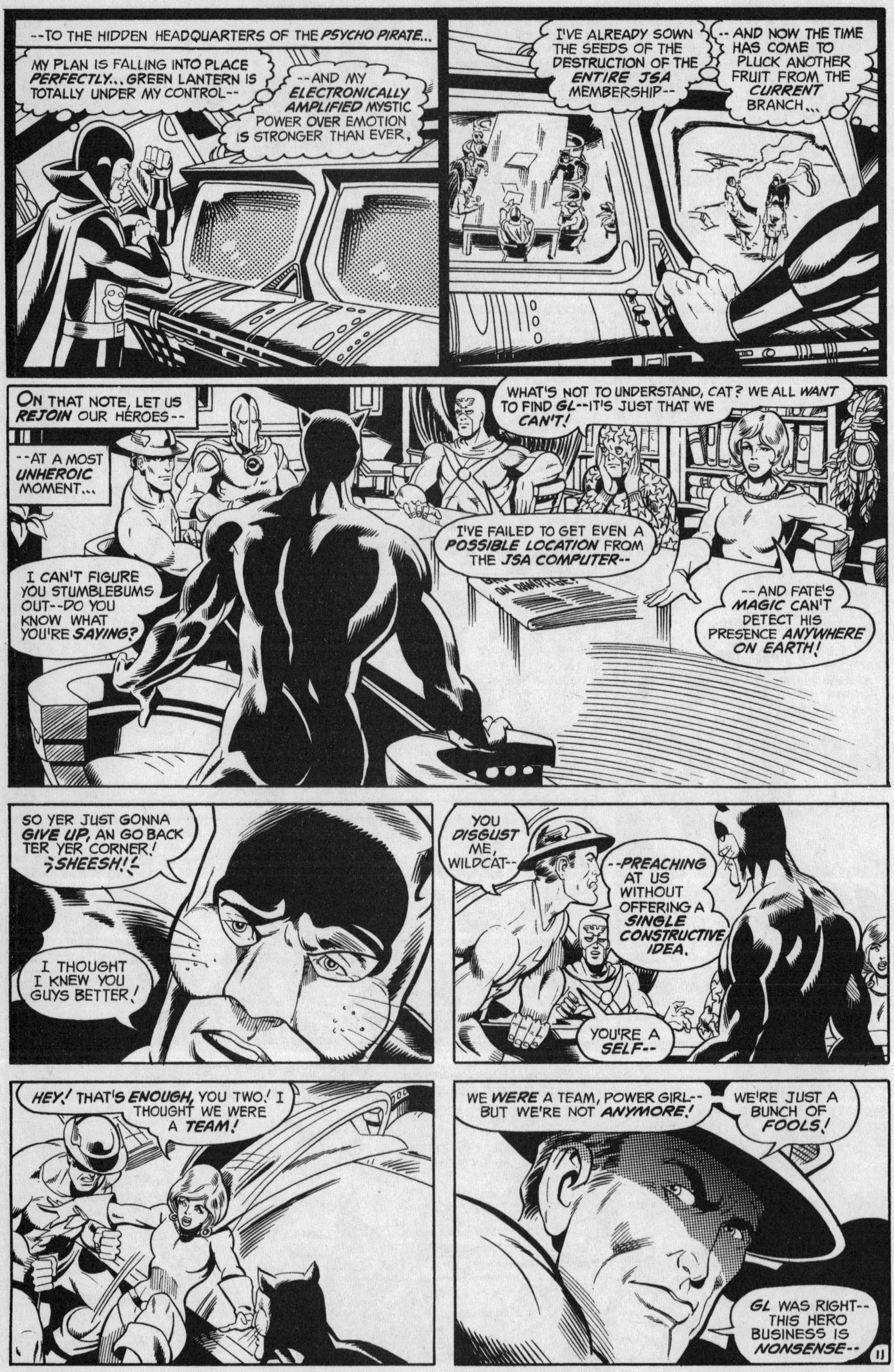
--TO THE HIDDEN HEADQUARTERS OF THE PSYCHO PIRATE...
MY PLAN IS FALLING INTO PLACE PERFECTLY... GREEN LANTERN IS TOTALLY UNDER MY CONTROL--
--AND MY ELECTRONICALLY AMPLIFIED MYSTIC POWER OVER EMOTION IS STRONGER THAN EVER.
I'VE ALREADY SOWN THE SEEDS OF THE DESTRUCTION OF THE ENTIRE JSA MEMBERSHIP--
--AND NOW THE TIME HAS COME TO PLUCK ANOTHER FRUIT FROM THE CURRENT BRANCH...
ON THAT NOTE, LET US REJOIN OUR HEROES--
--AT A MOST UNHEROIC MOMENT...
I CAN'T FIGURE YOU STUMBLEBUMS OUT--DO YOU KNOW WHAT YOU'RE SAYING?
WHAT'S NOT TO UNDERSTAND, CAT? WE ALL WANT TO FIND GL--IT'S JUST THAT WE CAN'T!
I'VE FAILED TO GET EVEN A POSSIBLE LOCATION FROM THE JSA COMPUTER--
--AND FATE'S MAGIC CAN'T DETECT HIS PRESENCE ANYWHERE ON EARTH!
SO YER JUST GONNA GIVE UP, AN GO BACK TER YER CORNER! SHEESH!
I THOUGHT I KNEW YOU GUYS BETTER!
YOU DISGUST ME, WILDCAT--
--PREACHING AT US WITHOUT OFFERING A SINGLE CONSTRUCTIVE IDEA.
YOU'RE A SELF--
HEY! THAT'S ENOUGH, YOU TWO! I THOUGHT WE WERE A TEAM!
WE WERE A TEAM, POWER GIRL--BUT WE'RE NOT ANYMORE!
WE'RE JUST A BUNCH OF FOOLS!
GL WAS RIGHT--THIS HERO BUSINESS IS NONSENSE--
11

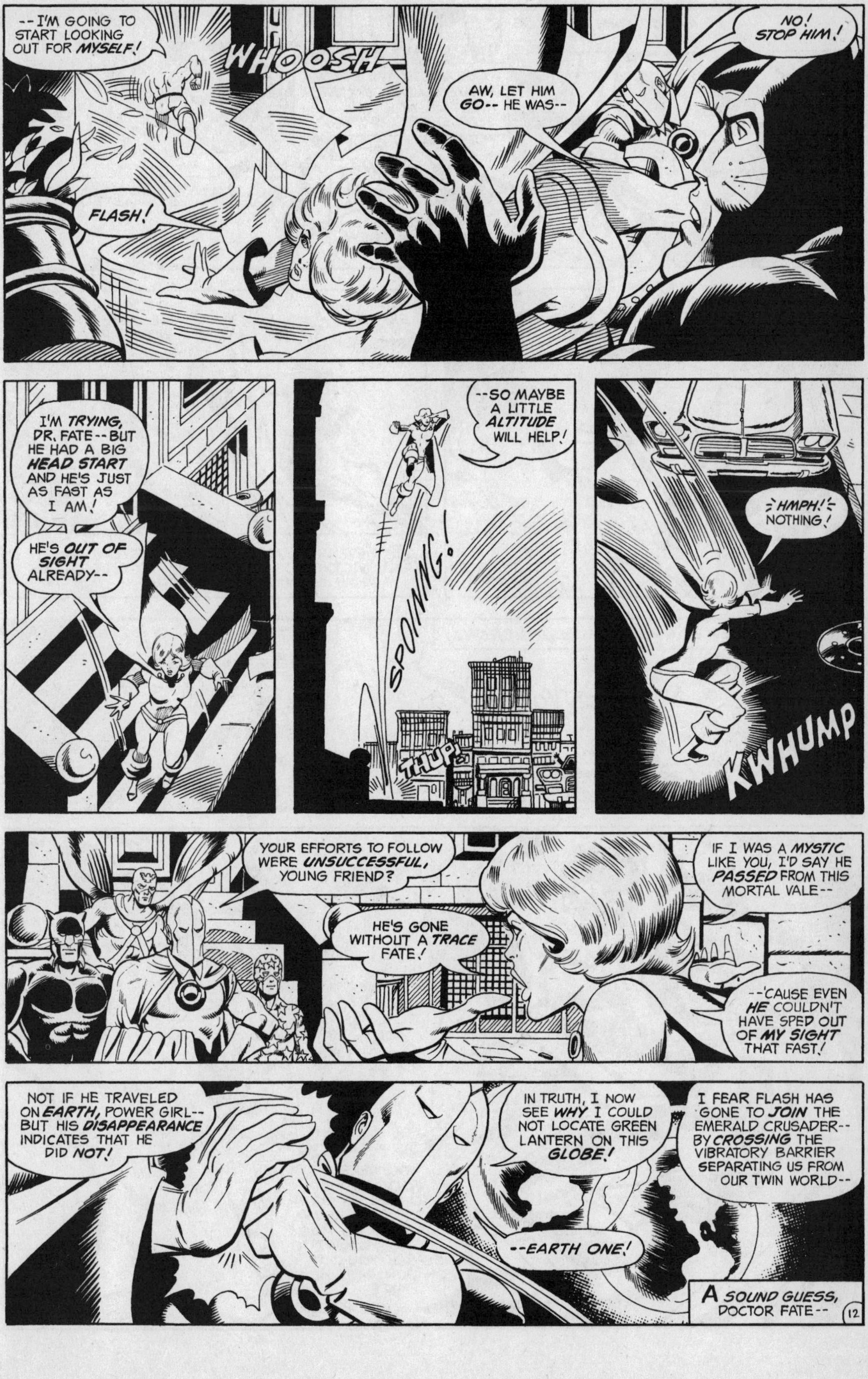
--I'M GOING TO START LOOKING OUT FOR MYSELF!
WHOOSH
FLASH!
AW, LET HIM GO-- HE WAS--
NO! STOP HIM!
I'M TRYING, DR. FATE--BUT HE HAD A BIG HEAD START AND HE'S JUST AS FAST AS I AM!
HE'S OUT OF SIGHT ALREADY--
--SO MAYBE A LITTLE ALTITUDE WILL HELP!
SPOING!
THUP!
HMPH! NOTHING!
KWHUMP
YOUR EFFORTS TO FOLLOW WERE UNSUCCESSFUL, YOUNG FRIEND?
HE'S GONE WITHOUT A TRACE FATE!
IF I WAS A MYSTIC LIKE YOU, I'D SAY HE PASSED FROM THIS MORTAL VALE--
--'CAUSE EVEN HE COULDN'T HAVE SPED OUT OF MY SIGHT THAT FAST!
NOT IF HE TRAVELED ON EARTH, POWER GIRL--BUT HIS DISAPPEARANCE INDICATES THAT HE DID NOT!
IN TRUTH, I NOW SEE WHY I COULD NOT LOCATE GREEN LANTERN ON THIS GLOBE!
I FEAR FLASH HAS GONE TO JOIN THE EMERALD CRUSADER--BY CROSSING THE VIBRATORY BARRIER SEPARATING US FROM OUR TWIN WORLD--
--EARTH ONE!
A SOUND GUESS, DOCTOR FATE--
12

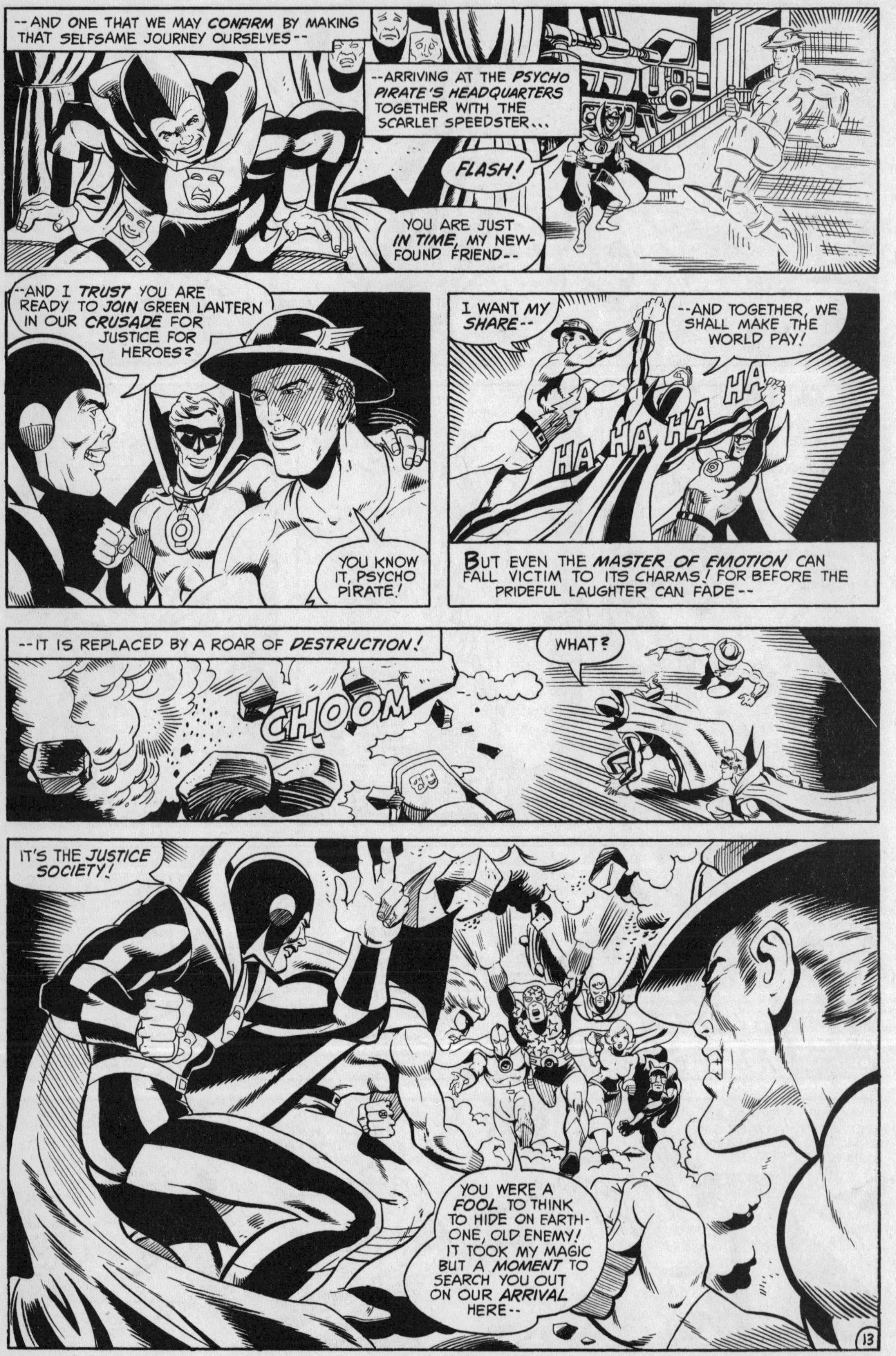
--AND ONE THAT WE MAY CONFIRM BY MAKING THAT SELFSAME JOURNEY OURSELVES--
--ARRIVING AT THE PSYCHO PIRATE'S HEADQUARTERS TOGETHER WITH THE SCARLET SPEEDSTER...
FLASH!
YOU ARE JUST IN TIME, MY NEW-FOUND FRIEND--
--AND I TRUST YOU ARE READY TO JOIN GREEN LANTERN IN OUR CRUSADE FOR JUSTICE FOR HEROES?
YOU KNOW IT, PSYCHO PIRATE!
I WANT MY SHARE--
--AND TOGETHER, WE SHALL MAKE THE WORLD PAY!
HA HA HA HA
BUT EVEN THE MASTER OF EMOTION CAN FALL VICTIM TO ITS CHARMS! FOR BEFORE THE PRIDEFUL LAUGHTER CAN FADE--
--IT IS REPLACED BY A ROAR OF DESTRUCTION!
WHAT?
CHOOM
IT'S THE JUSTICE SOCIETY!
YOU WERE A FOOL TO THINK TO HIDE ON EARTH-ONE, OLD ENEMY! IT TOOK MY MAGIC BUT A MOMENT TO SEARCH YOU OUT ON OUR ARRIVAL HERE--
13

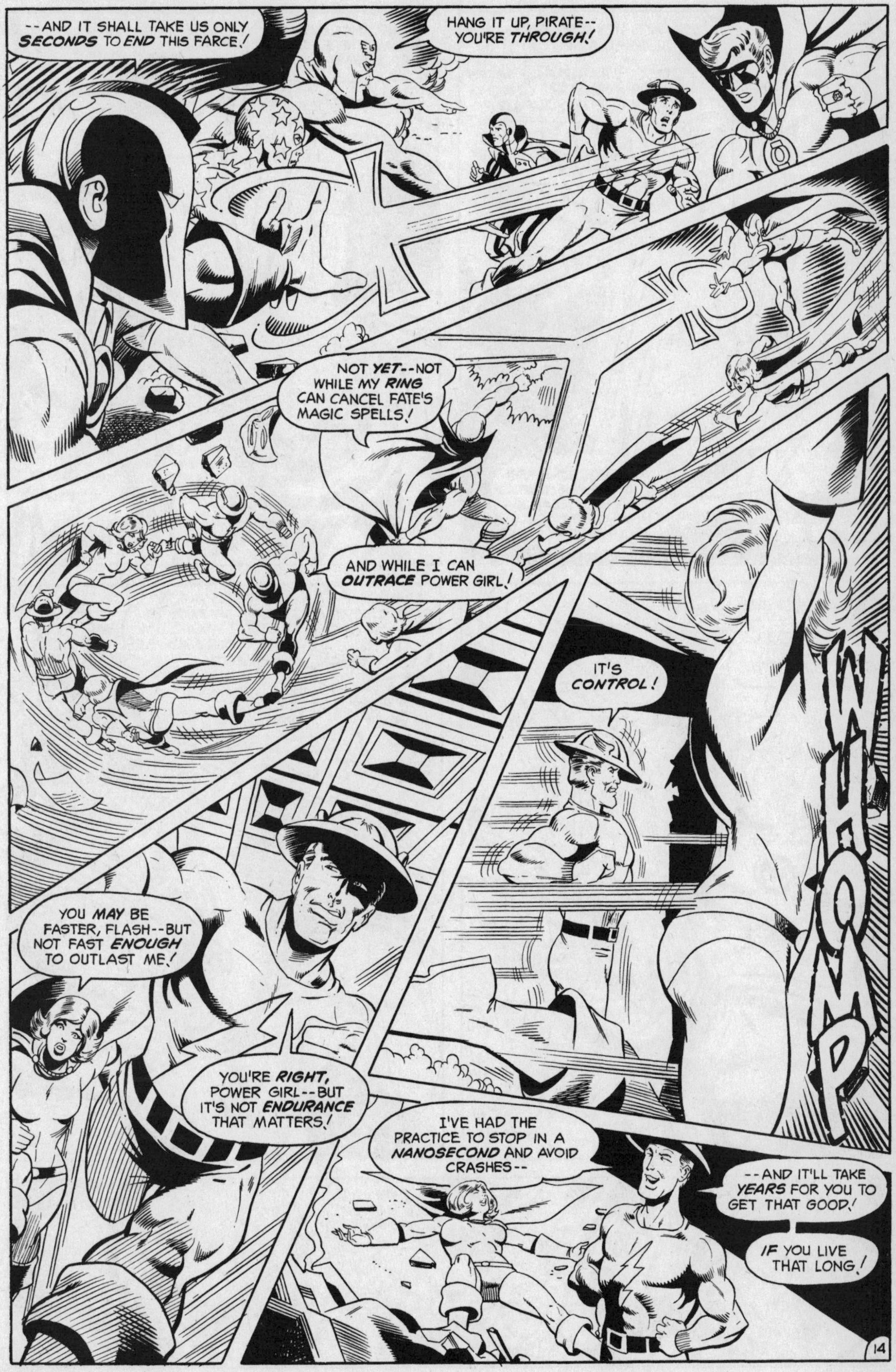
--AND IT SHALL TAKE US ONLY SECONDS TO END THIS FARCE!
HANG IT UP, PIRATE-- YOU'RE THROUGH!
NOT YET--NOT WHILE MY RING CAN CANCEL FATE'S MAGIC SPELLS!
AND WHILE I CAN OUTRACE POWER GIRL!
IT'S CONTROL!
WHOMP
YOU MAY BE FASTER, FLASH--BUT NOT FAST ENOUGH TO OUTLAST ME!
YOU'RE RIGHT, POWER GIRL--BUT IT'S NOT ENDURANCE THAT MATTERS!
I'VE HAD THE PRACTICE TO STOP IN A NANOSECOND AND AVOID CRASHES--
--AND IT'LL TAKE YEARS FOR YOU TO GET THAT GOOD!
IF YOU LIVE THAT LONG!
14

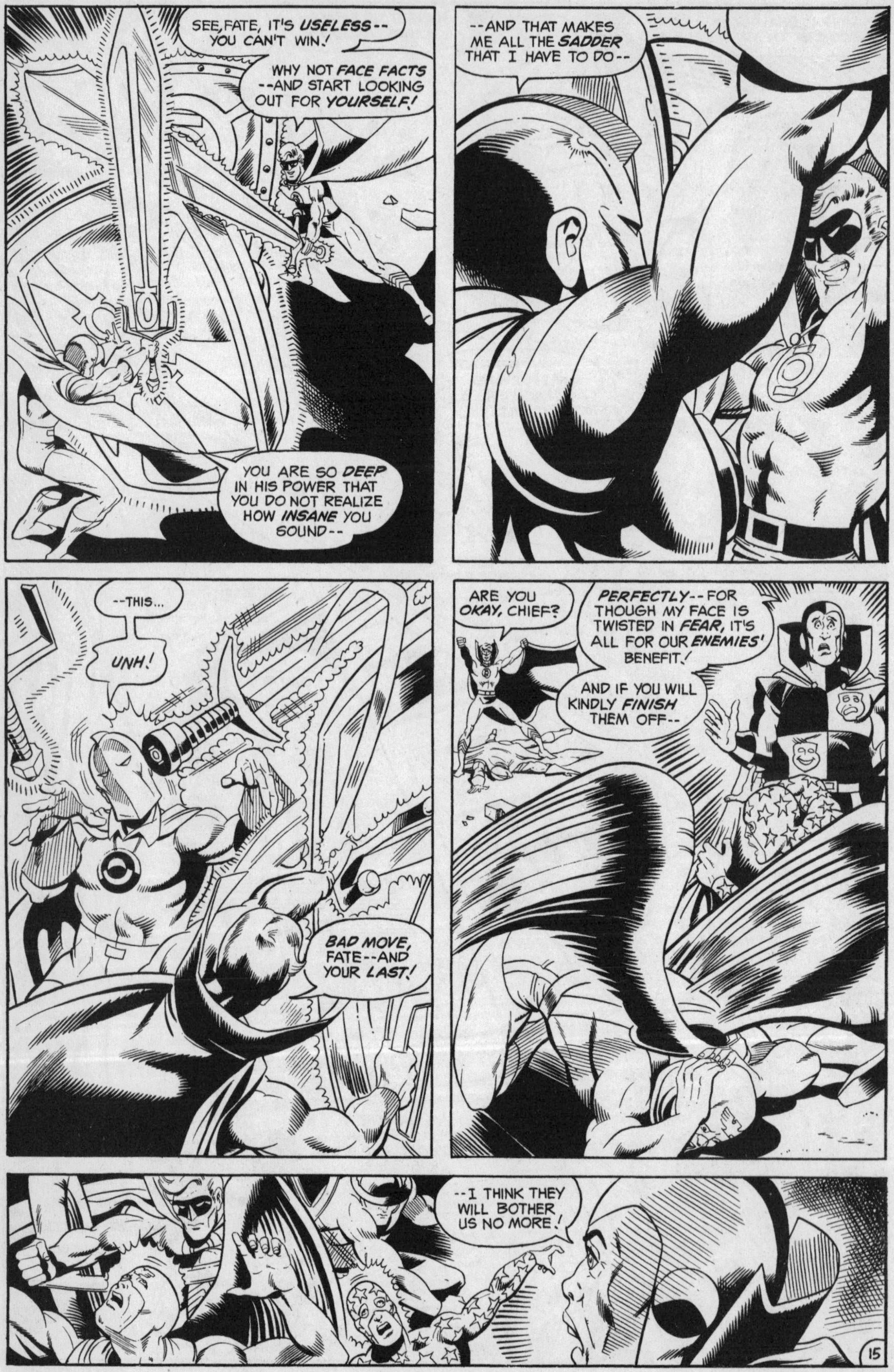
SEE, FATE, IT'S USELESS-- YOU CAN'T WIN!
WHY NOT FACE FACTS --AND START LOOKING OUT FOR YOURSELF!
YOU ARE SO DEEP IN HIS POWER THAT YOU DO NOT REALIZE HOW INSANE YOU SOUND--
--AND THAT MAKES ME ALL THE SADDER THAT I HAVE TO DO--
--THIS...
UNH!
BAD MOVE, FATE--AND YOUR LAST!
ARE YOU OKAY, CHIEF?
PERFECTLY--FOR THOUGH MY FACE IS TWISTED IN FEAR, IT'S ALL FOR OUR ENEMIES' BENEFIT!
AND IF YOU WILL KINDLY FINISH THEM OFF--
--I THINK THEY WILL BOTHER US NO MORE!
15

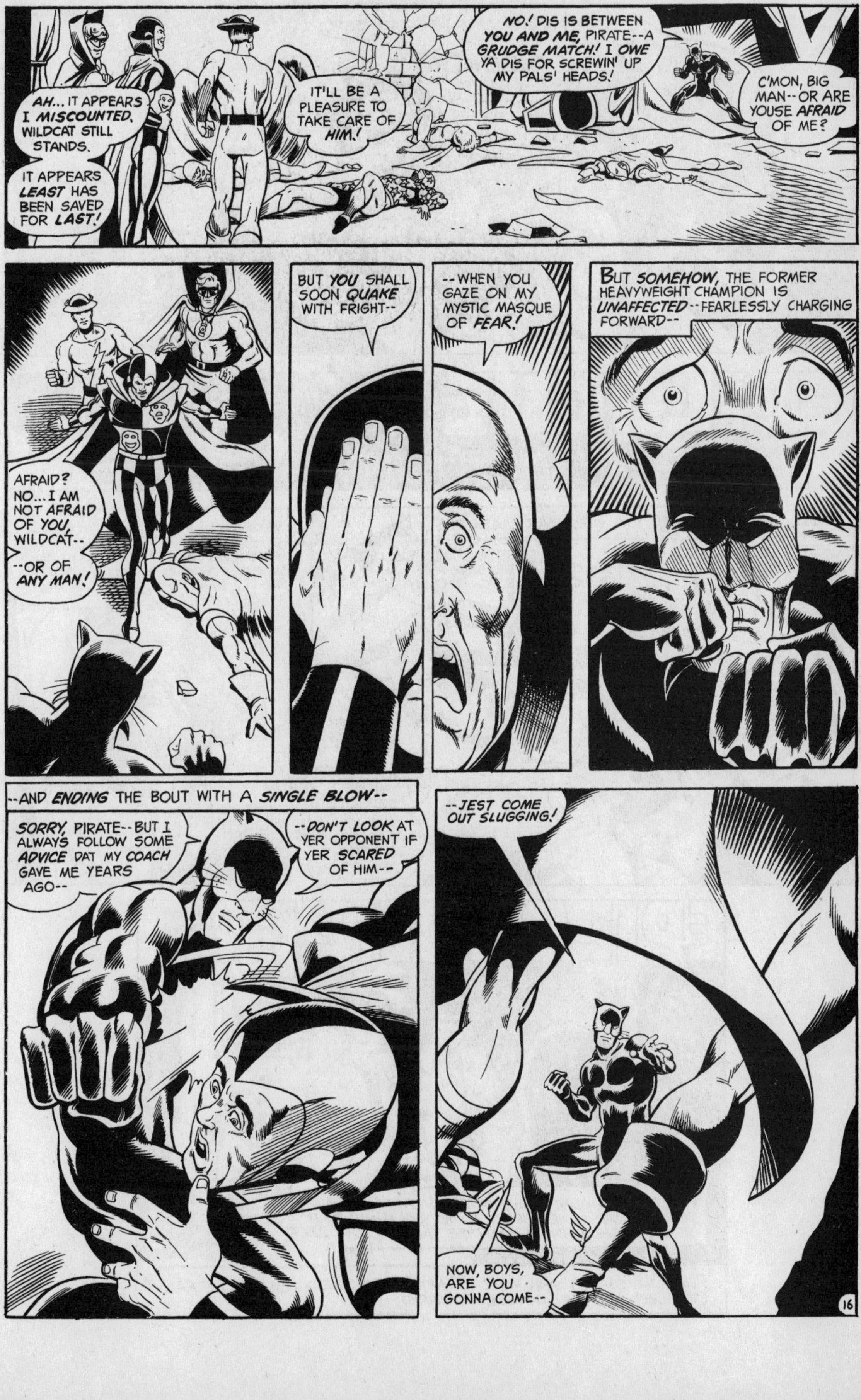
AH... IT APPEARS I MISCOUNTED. WILDCAT STILL STANDS.
IT APPEARS LEAST HAS BEEN SAVED FOR LAST!
IT'LL BE A PLEASURE TO TAKE CARE OF HIM!
NO! DIS IS BETWEEN YOU AND ME, PIRATE--A GRUDGE MATCH! I OWE YA DIS FOR SCREWIN' UP MY PALS' HEADS!
C'MON, BIG MAN--OR ARE YOUSE AFRAID OF ME?
AFRAID? NO...I AM NOT AFRAID OF YOU, WILDCAT--
--OR OF ANY MAN!
BUT YOU SHALL SOON QUAKE WITH FRIGHT--
--WHEN YOU GAZE ON MY MYSTIC MASQUE OF FEAR!
BUT SOMEHOW, THE FORMER HEAVYWEIGHT CHAMPION IS UNAFFECTED--FEARLESSLY CHARGING FORWARD--
--AND ENDING THE BOUT WITH A SINGLE BLOW--
SORRY, PIRATE--BUT I ALWAYS FOLLOW SOME ADVICE DAT MY COACH GAVE ME YEARS AGO--
--DON'T LOOK AT YER OPPONENT IF YER SCARED OF HIM--
--JEST COME OUT SLUGGING!
NOW, BOYS, ARE YOU GONNA COME--
16

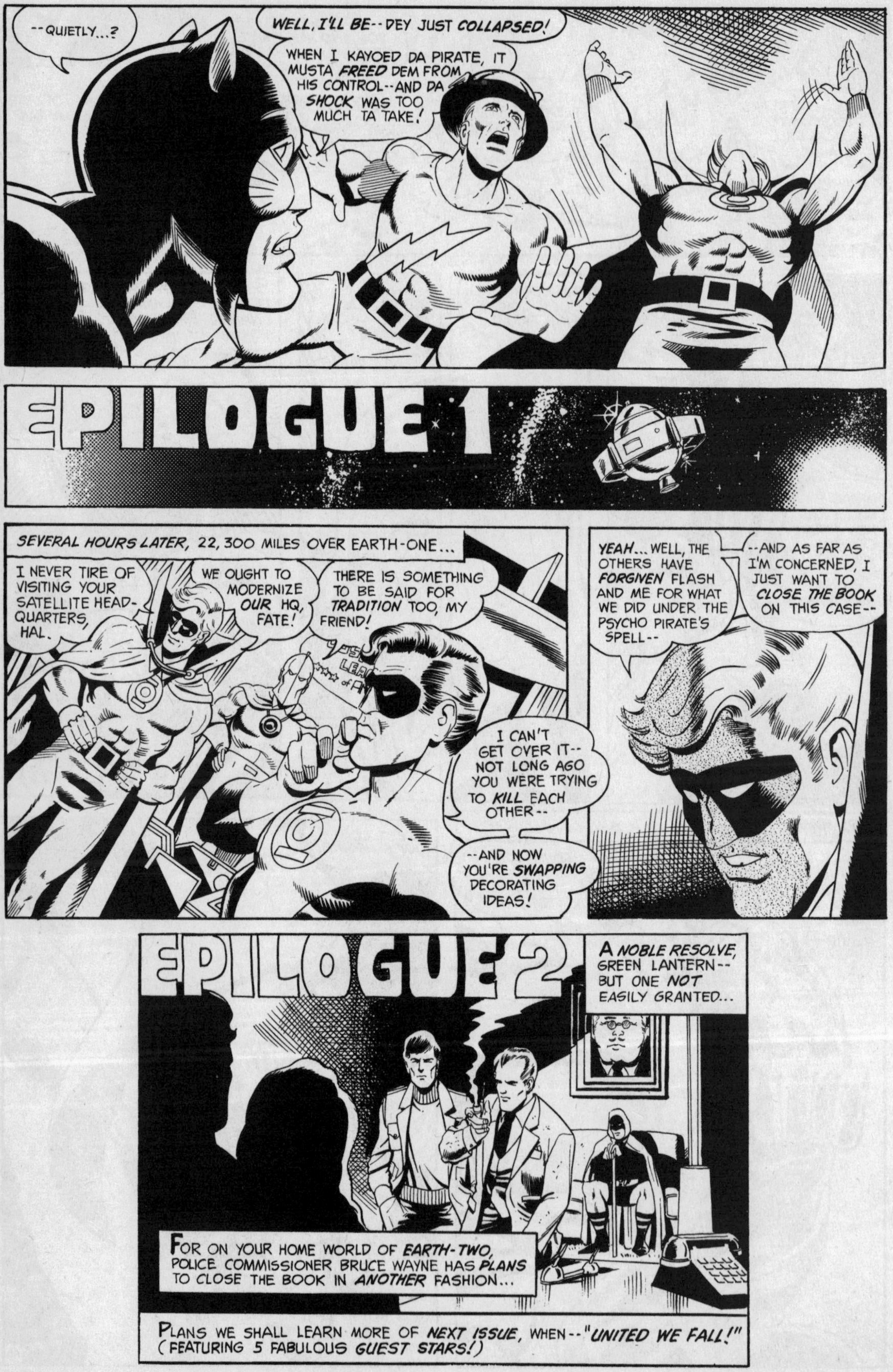
--QUIETLY...?
WELL, I'LL BE--DEY JUST COLLAPSED!
WHEN I KAYOED DA PIRATE, IT MUSTA FREED DEM FROM HIS CONTROL--AND DA SHOCK WAS TOO MUCH TA TAKE!
EPILOGUE 1
SEVERAL HOURS LATER, 22,300 MILES OVER EARTH-ONE...
I NEVER TIRE OF VISITING YOUR SATELLITE HEADQUARTERS, HAL.
WE OUGHT TO MODERNIZE OUR HQ, FATE!
THERE IS SOMETHING TO BE SAID FOR TRADITION TOO, MY FRIEND!
I CAN'T GET OVER IT--NOT LONG AGO YOU WERE TRYING TO KILL EACH OTHER--
--AND NOW YOU'RE SWAPPING DECORATING IDEAS!
YEAH... WELL, THE OTHERS HAVE FORGIVEN FLASH AND ME FOR WHAT WE DID UNDER THE PSYCHO PIRATE'S SPELL--
--AND AS FAR AS I'M CONCERNED, I JUST WANT TO CLOSE THE BOOK ON THIS CASE--
EPILOGUE 2
A NOBLE RESOLVE, GREEN LANTERN--BUT ONE NOT EASILY GRANTED...
FOR ON YOUR HOME WORLD OF EARTH-TWO, POLICE COMMISSIONER BRUCE WAYNE HAS PLANS TO CLOSE THE BOOK IN ANOTHER FASHION...
PLANS WE SHALL LEARN MORE OF NEXT ISSUE, WHEN--"UNITED WE FALL!" (FEATURING 5 FABULOUS GUEST STARS!)

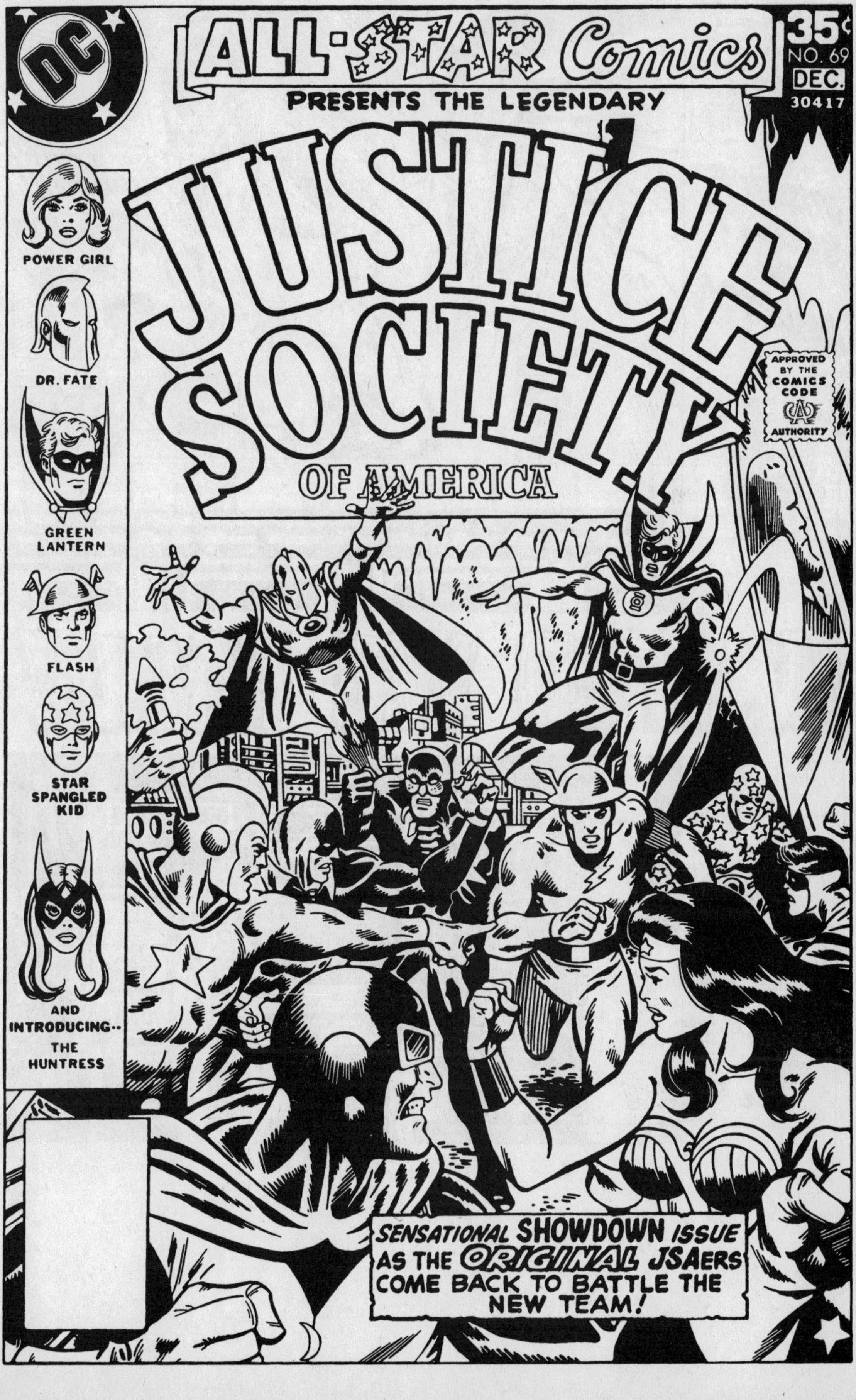

DC
ALL-STAR Comics
35¢
NO. 69
DEC.
30417
PRESENTS THE LEGENDARY
JUSTICE SOCIETY OF AMERICA
POWER GIRL
DR. FATE
GREEN LANTERN
FLASH
STAR SPANGLED KID
AND INTRODUCING.. THE HUNTRESS
APPROVED BY THE COMICS CODE AUTHORITY
SENSATIONAL SHOWDOWN ISSUE AS THE ORIGINAL JSAERS COME BACK TO BATTLE THE NEW TEAM!

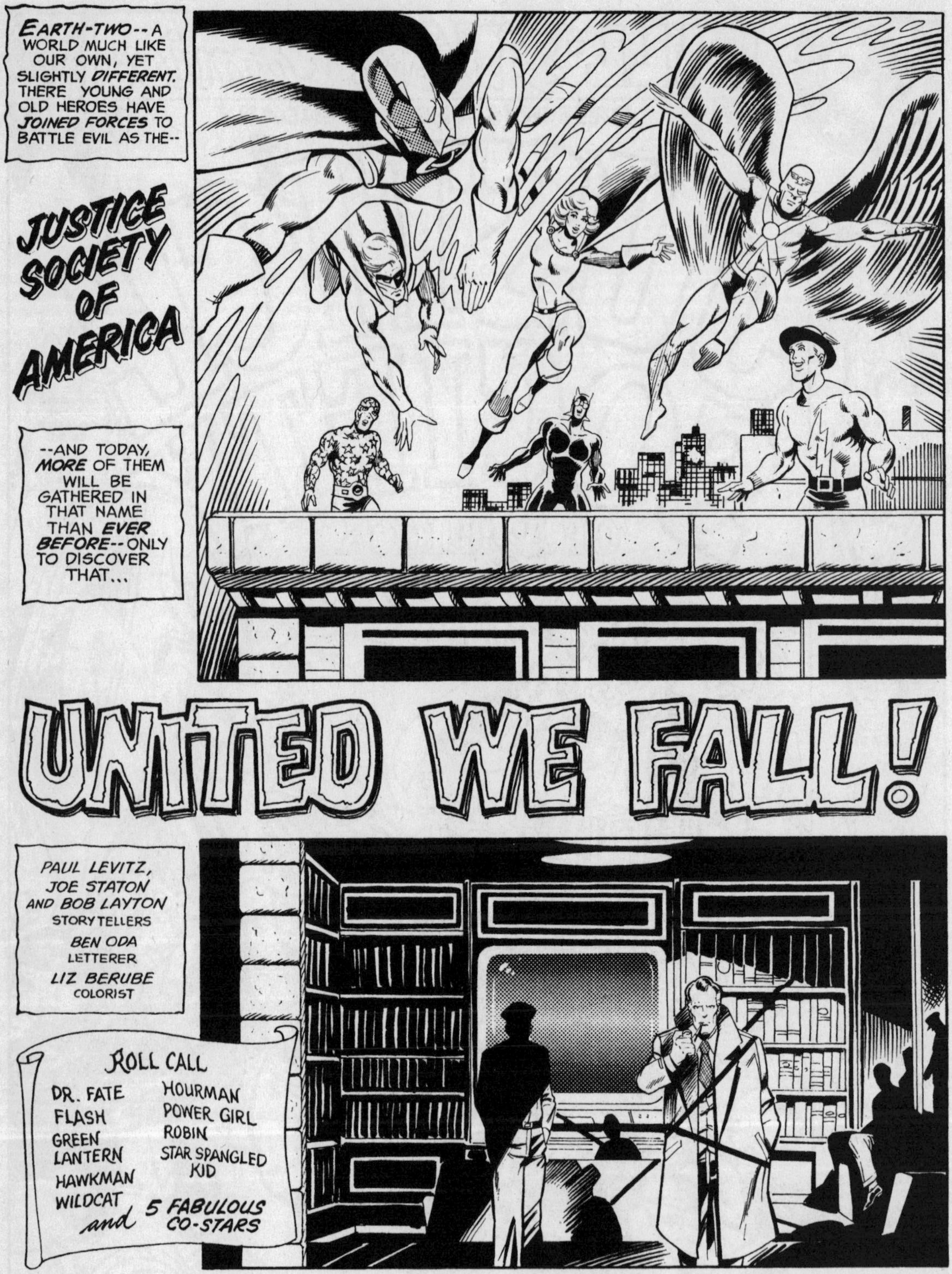
EARTH-TWO--A WORLD MUCH LIKE OUR OWN, YET SLIGHTLY DIFFERENT. THERE YOUNG AND OLD HEROES HAVE JOINED FORCES TO BATTLE EVIL AS THE--
JUSTICE SOCIETY OF AMERICA
--AND TODAY, MORE OF THEM WILL BE GATHERED IN THAT NAME THAN EVER BEFORE--ONLY TO DISCOVER THAT...
UNITED WE FALL!
PAUL LEVITZ, JOE STATON AND BOB LAYTON STORYTELLERS
BEN ODA LETTERER
LIZ BERUBE COLORIST
ROLL CALL
DR. FATE
FLASH
GREEN LANTERN
HAWKMAN
WILDCAT
HOURMAN
POWER GIRL
ROBIN
STAR SPANGLED KID
and 5 FABULOUS CO-STARS

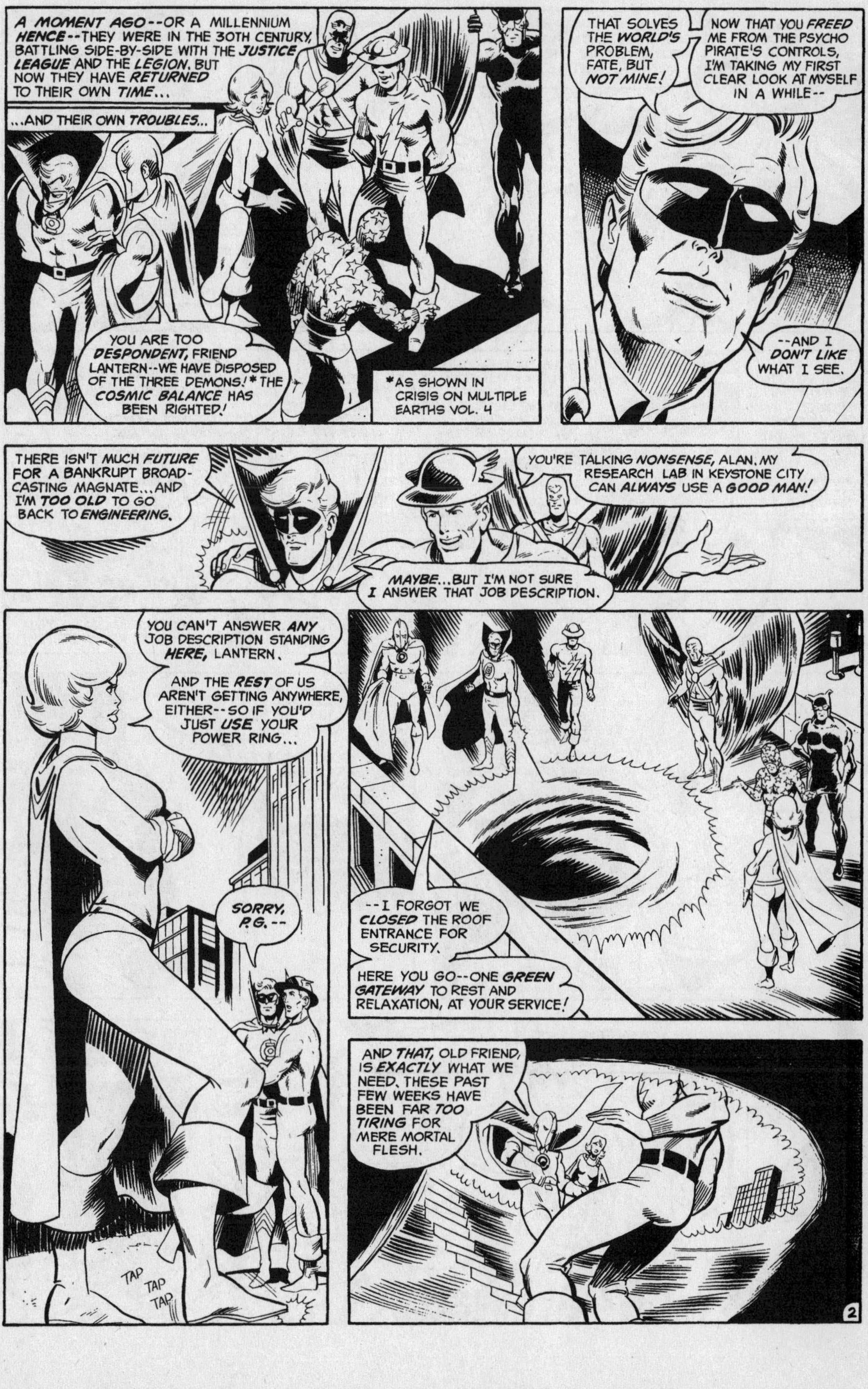
A MOMENT AGO--OR A MILLENNIUM HENCE--THEY WERE IN THE 30TH CENTURY, BATTLING SIDE-BY-SIDE WITH THE JUSTICE LEAGUE AND THE LEGION. BUT NOW THEY HAVE RETURNED TO THEIR OWN TIME...
...AND THEIR OWN TROUBLES...
YOU ARE TOO DESPONDENT, FRIEND LANTERN--WE HAVE DISPOSED OF THE THREE DEMONS!* THE COSMIC BALANCE HAS BEEN RIGHTED!
*AS SHOWN IN CRISIS ON MULTIPLE EARTHS VOL. 4
THAT SOLVES THE WORLD'S PROBLEM, FATE, BUT NOT MINE!
NOW THAT YOU FREED ME FROM THE PSYCHO PIRATE'S CONTROLS, I'M TAKING MY FIRST CLEAR LOOK AT MYSELF IN A WHILE--
--AND I DON'T LIKE WHAT I SEE.
THERE ISN'T MUCH FUTURE FOR A BANKRUPT BROAD-CASTING MAGNATE...AND I'M TOO OLD TO GO BACK TO ENGINEERING.
YOU'RE TALKING NONSENSE, ALAN. MY RESEARCH LAB IN KEYSTONE CITY CAN ALWAYS USE A GOOD MAN!
MAYBE...BUT I'M NOT SURE I ANSWER THAT JOB DESCRIPTION.
YOU CAN'T ANSWER ANY JOB DESCRIPTION STANDING HERE, LANTERN.
AND THE REST OF US AREN'T GETTING ANYWHERE, EITHER--SO IF YOU'D JUST USE YOUR POWER RING...
SORRY, P.G.--
TAP TAP TAP
--I FORGOT WE CLOSED THE ROOF ENTRANCE FOR SECURITY.
HERE YOU GO--ONE GREEN GATEWAY TO REST AND RELAXATION, AT YOUR SERVICE!
AND THAT, OLD FRIEND, IS EXACTLY WHAT WE NEED. THESE PAST FEW WEEKS HAVE BEEN FAR TOO TIRING FOR MERE MORTAL FLESH.
2

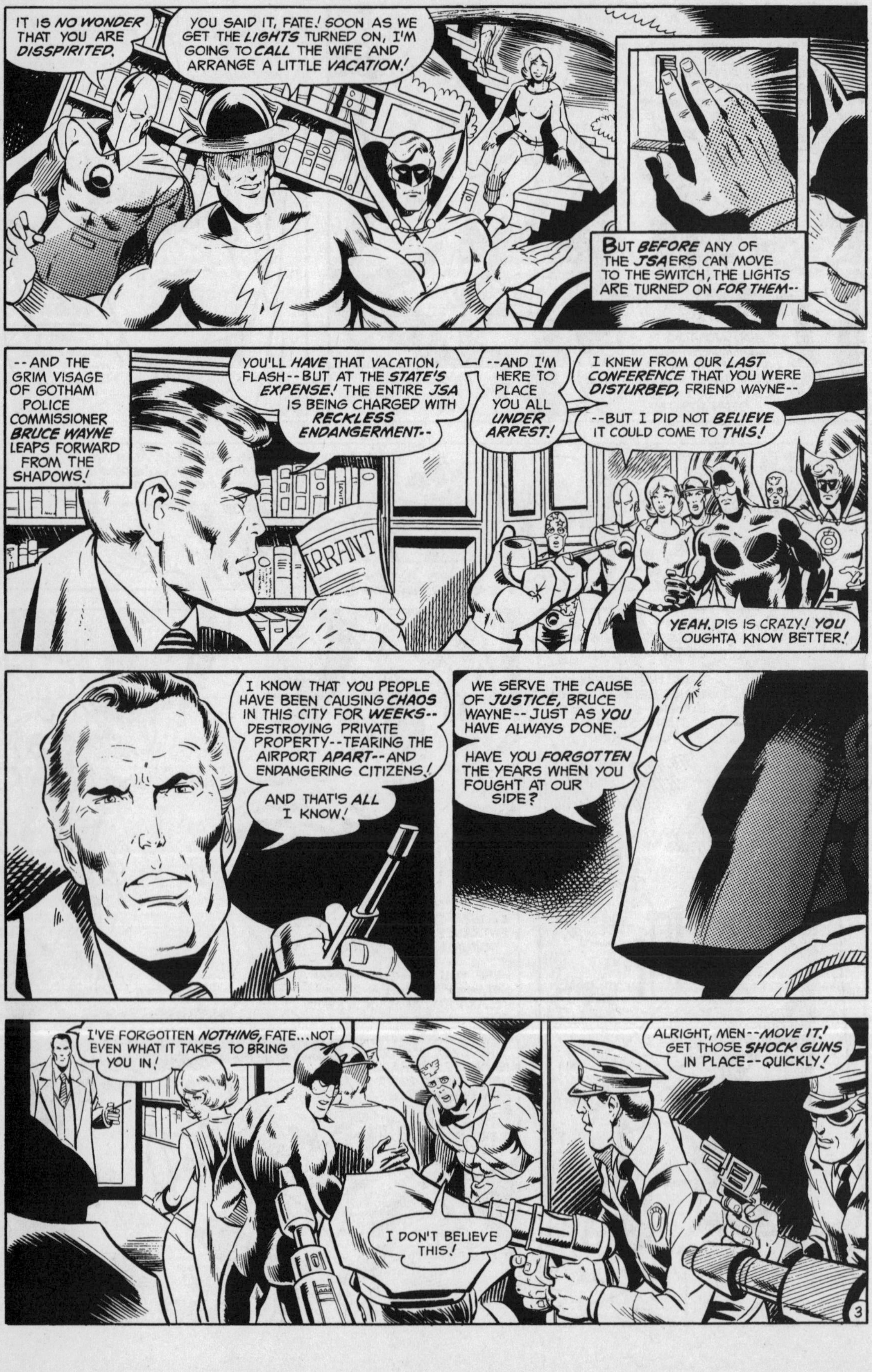
IT IS NO WONDER THAT YOU ARE DISSPIRITED.
YOU SAID IT, FATE! SOON AS WE GET THE LIGHTS TURNED ON, I'M GOING TO CALL THE WIFE AND ARRANGE A LITTLE VACATION!
BUT BEFORE ANY OF THE JSA'ERS CAN MOVE TO THE SWITCH, THE LIGHTS ARE TURNED ON FOR THEM--
--AND THE GRIM VISAGE OF GOTHAM POLICE COMMISSIONER BRUCE WAYNE LEAPS FORWARD FROM THE SHADOWS!
YOU'LL HAVE THAT VACATION, FLASH--BUT AT THE STATE'S EXPENSE! THE ENTIRE JSA IS BEING CHARGED WITH RECKLESS ENDANGERMENT--
--AND I'M HERE TO PLACE YOU ALL UNDER ARREST!
I KNEW FROM OUR LAST CONFERENCE THAT YOU WERE DISTURBED, FRIEND WAYNE--
--BUT I DID NOT BELIEVE IT COULD COME TO THIS!
YEAH. DIS IS CRAZY! YOU OUGHTA KNOW BETTER!
I KNOW THAT YOU PEOPLE HAVE BEEN CAUSING CHAOS IN THIS CITY FOR WEEKS--DESTROYING PRIVATE PROPERTY--TEARING THE AIRPORT APART--AND ENDANGERING CITIZENS!
AND THAT'S ALL I KNOW!
WE SERVE THE CAUSE OF JUSTICE, BRUCE WAYNE--JUST AS YOU HAVE ALWAYS DONE.
HAVE YOU FORGOTTEN THE YEARS WHEN YOU FOUGHT AT OUR SIDE?
I'VE FORGOTTEN NOTHING, FATE...NOT EVEN WHAT IT TAKES TO BRING YOU IN!
I DON'T BELIEVE THIS!
ALRIGHT, MEN--MOVE IT! GET THOSE SHOCK GUNS IN PLACE--QUICKLY!
3

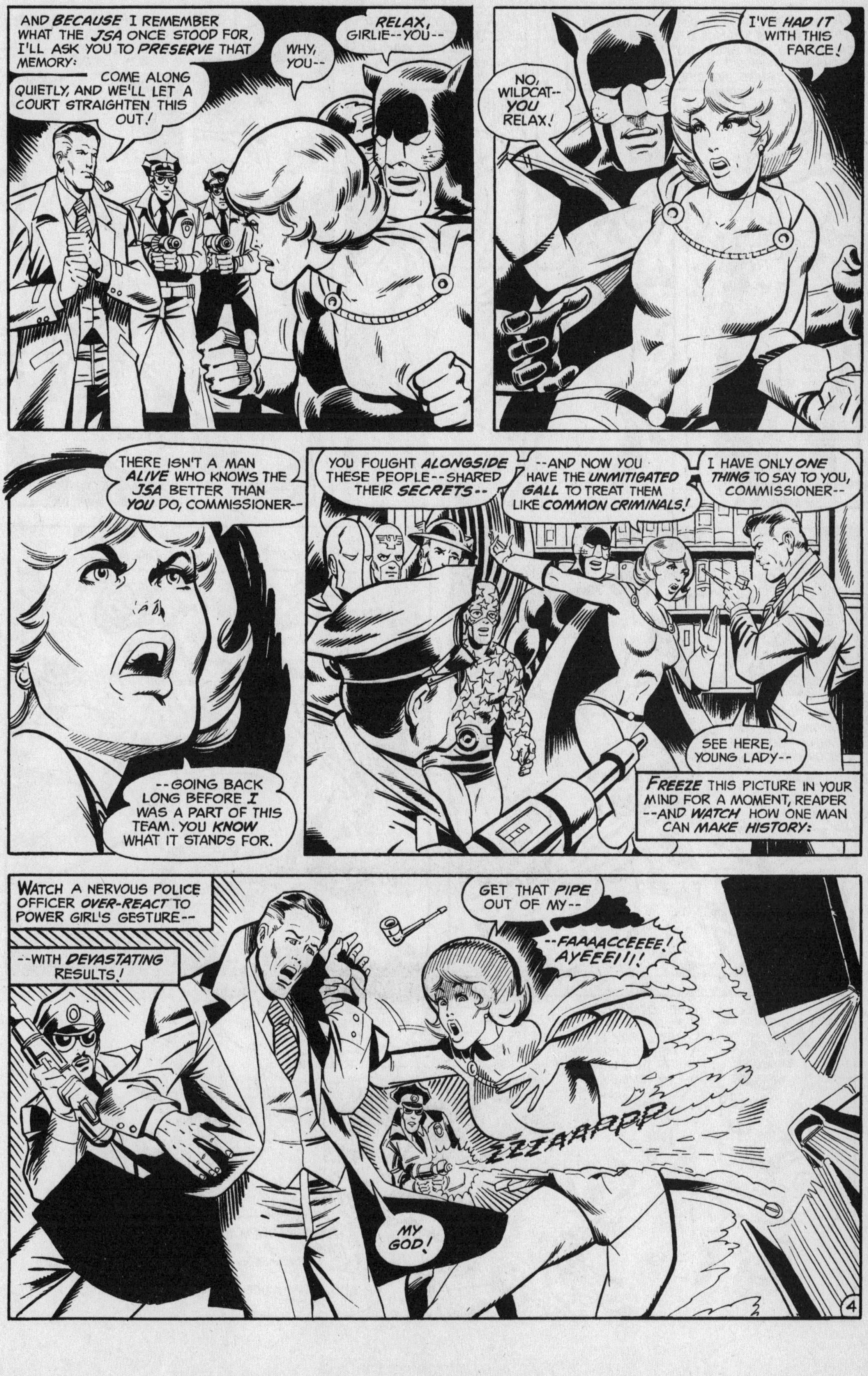
AND BECAUSE I REMEMBER WHAT THE JSA ONCE STOOD FOR, I'LL ASK YOU TO PRESERVE THAT MEMORY:
COME ALONG QUIETLY, AND WE'LL LET A COURT STRAIGHTEN THIS OUT!
WHY, YOU--
RELAX, GIRLIE--YOU--
I'VE HAD IT WITH THIS FARCE!
NO, WILDCAT-- YOU RELAX!
THERE ISN'T A MAN ALIVE WHO KNOWS THE JSA BETTER THAN YOU DO, COMMISSIONER--
--GOING BACK LONG BEFORE I WAS A PART OF THIS TEAM. YOU KNOW WHAT IT STANDS FOR.
YOU FOUGHT ALONGSIDE THESE PEOPLE--SHARED THEIR SECRETS--
--AND NOW YOU HAVE THE UNMITIGATED GALL TO TREAT THEM LIKE COMMON CRIMINALS!
I HAVE ONLY ONE THING TO SAY TO YOU, COMMISSIONER--
SEE HERE, YOUNG LADY--
FREEZE THIS PICTURE IN YOUR MIND FOR A MOMENT, READER --AND WATCH HOW ONE MAN CAN MAKE HISTORY:
WATCH A NERVOUS POLICE OFFICER OVER-REACT TO POWER GIRL'S GESTURE--
--WITH DEVASTATING RESULTS!
GET THAT PIPE OUT OF MY--
--FAAAACCEEEE! AYEEE!!!!
ZZZAAPPP
MY GOD!
4

BORN UNDER KRYPTON'S SCARLET SUN, NOTHING *LESS* THAN A *BURSTING SHELL* CAN PIERCE HER SKIN...BUT *TODAY'S* TECHNOLOGY HAS FAR *SURPASSED* THE BURSTING SHELL.

MAN HAS CONQUERED *ELECTRICITY--* AND THE *ATOM--* AND FOR *EACH*, CONQUEST HAS TAKEN A *HEAVY TOLL*.

IN THIS MOMENT, A *NEW CHARGE* HAS BEEN ADDED TO THAT TOLL ...AND THE PRICE MAY BE *POWER GIRL'S LIFE!*

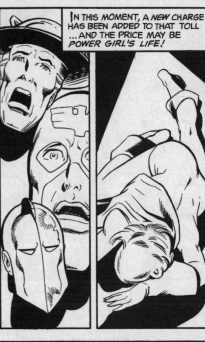

WAYNE... *GET AWAY FROM THAT GIRL!*

DON'T LET THEM *INTIMIDATE* YOU, MEN -- YOU *HAVE* YOUR ORDERS --

--BRING THEM IN!

YER *KIDDIN'!* DESE STUMBLEBUMS STOP *US?*

WAYNE, YER A BIGGER *FOOL* DEN I THOUGHT!

HE IS *INDEED,* WILDCAT! AND HE'LL *PAY* FOR HIS FOOLISHNESS IF THAT GIRL *DIES!*

SHE IS *GRIEVOUSLY INJURED,* FRIEND FLASH -- BUT THE SPARK OF *LIFE* STILL REMAINS!

FOR THAT WE MAY *PRAISE* THE LORDS OF ORDER --

--AND *DAMN* BRUCE WAYNE.

⑤

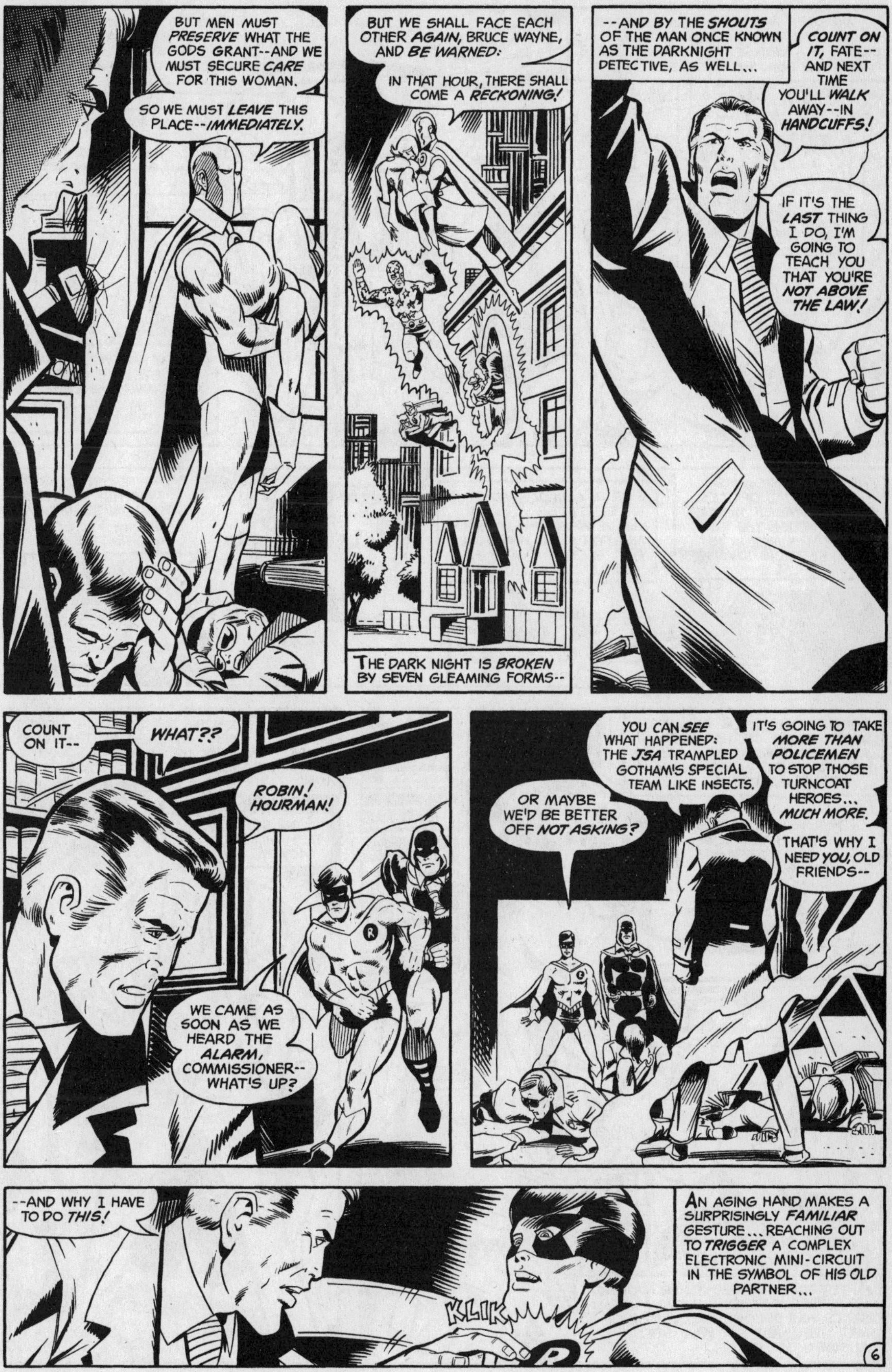
BUT MEN MUST PRESERVE WHAT THE GODS GRANT--AND WE MUST SECURE CARE FOR THIS WOMAN.
SO WE MUST LEAVE THIS PLACE--IMMEDIATELY.
BUT WE SHALL FACE EACH OTHER AGAIN, BRUCE WAYNE, AND BE WARNED:
IN THAT HOUR, THERE SHALL COME A RECKONING!
THE DARK NIGHT IS BROKEN BY SEVEN GLEAMING FORMS--
--AND BY THE SHOUTS OF THE MAN ONCE KNOWN AS THE DARKNIGHT DETECTIVE, AS WELL...
COUNT ON IT, FATE--AND NEXT TIME YOU'LL WALK AWAY--IN HANDCUFFS!
IF IT'S THE LAST THING I DO, I'M GOING TO TEACH YOU THAT YOU'RE NOT ABOVE THE LAW!
COUNT ON IT--
WHAT??
ROBIN! HOURMAN!
WE CAME AS SOON AS WE HEARD THE ALARM, COMMISSIONER--WHAT'S UP?
YOU CAN SEE WHAT HAPPENED: THE JSA TRAMPLED GOTHAM'S SPECIAL TEAM LIKE INSECTS.
OR MAYBE WE'D BE BETTER OFF NOT ASKING?
IT'S GOING TO TAKE MORE THAN POLICEMEN TO STOP THOSE TURNCOAT HEROES... MUCH MORE.
THAT'S WHY I NEED YOU, OLD FRIENDS--
--AND WHY I HAVE TO DO THIS!
AN AGING HAND MAKES A SURPRISINGLY FAMILIAR GESTURE... REACHING OUT TO TRIGGER A COMPLEX ELECTRONIC MINI-CIRCUIT IN THE SYMBOL OF HIS OLD PARTNER...
KLIK
6

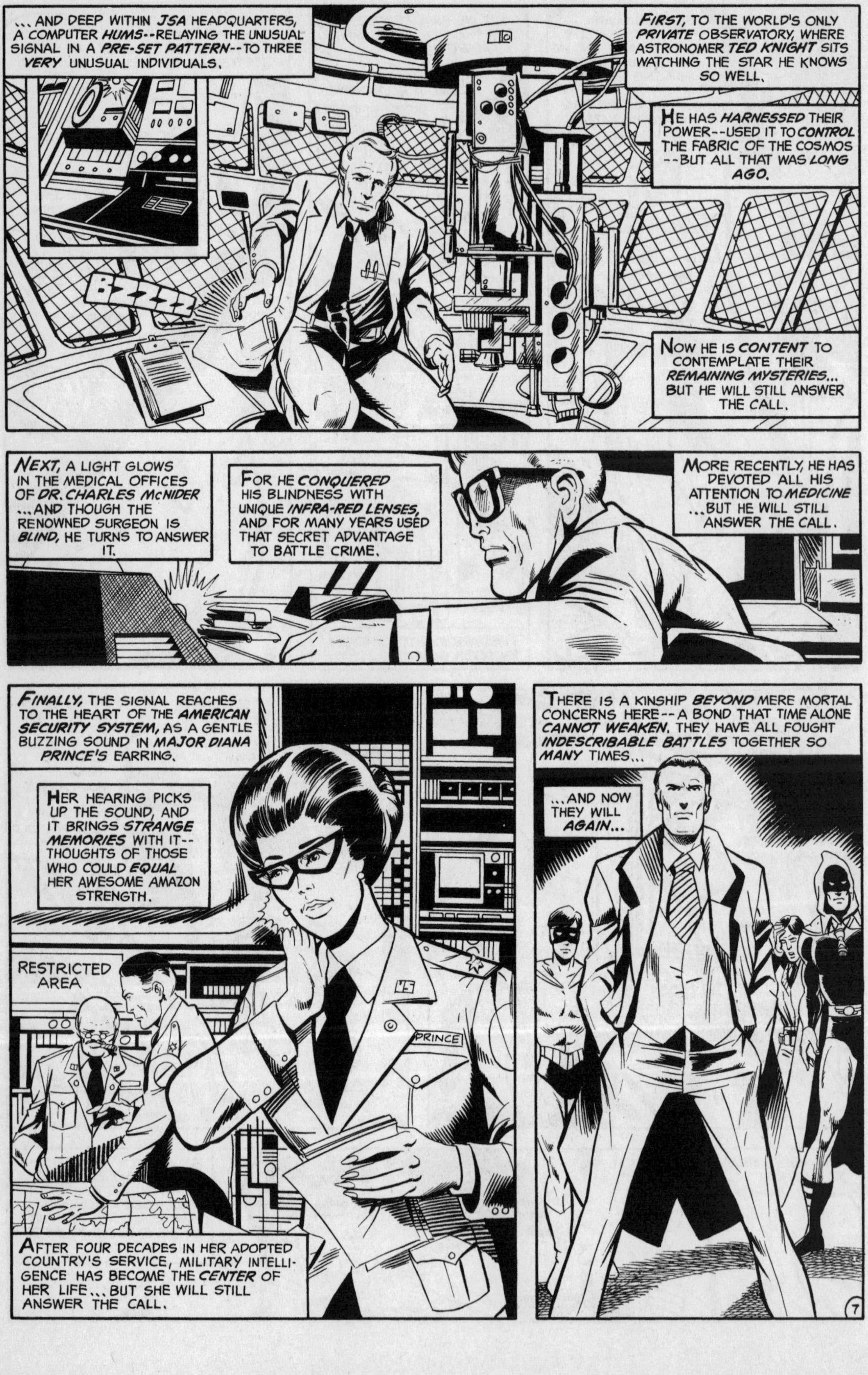
...AND DEEP WITHIN JSA HEADQUARTERS, A COMPUTER HUMS--RELAYING THE UNUSUAL SIGNAL IN A PRE-SET PATTERN--TO THREE VERY UNUSUAL INDIVIDUALS.
FIRST, TO THE WORLD'S ONLY PRIVATE OBSERVATORY, WHERE ASTRONOMER TED KNIGHT SITS WATCHING THE STAR HE KNOWS SO WELL.
HE HAS HARNESSED THEIR POWER--USED IT TO CONTROL THE FABRIC OF THE COSMOS --BUT ALL THAT WAS LONG AGO.
BZZZZ
NOW HE IS CONTENT TO CONTEMPLATE THEIR REMAINING MYSTERIES... BUT HE WILL STILL ANSWER THE CALL.
NEXT, A LIGHT GLOWS IN THE MEDICAL OFFICES OF DR. CHARLES McNIDER ...AND THOUGH THE RENOWNED SURGEON IS BLIND, HE TURNS TO ANSWER IT.
FOR HE CONQUERED HIS BLINDNESS WITH UNIQUE INFRA-RED LENSES, AND FOR MANY YEARS USED THAT SECRET ADVANTAGE TO BATTLE CRIME.
MORE RECENTLY, HE HAS DEVOTED ALL HIS ATTENTION TO MEDICINE ...BUT HE WILL STILL ANSWER THE CALL.
FINALLY, THE SIGNAL REACHES TO THE HEART OF THE AMERICAN SECURITY SYSTEM, AS A GENTLE BUZZING SOUND IN MAJOR DIANA PRINCE'S EARRING.
HER HEARING PICKS UP THE SOUND, AND IT BRINGS STRANGE MEMORIES WITH IT-- THOUGHTS OF THOSE WHO COULD EQUAL HER AWESOME AMAZON STRENGTH.
RESTRICTED AREA
PRINCE
AFTER FOUR DECADES IN HER ADOPTED COUNTRY'S SERVICE, MILITARY INTELLIGENCE HAS BECOME THE CENTER OF HER LIFE... BUT SHE WILL STILL ANSWER THE CALL.
THERE IS A KINSHIP BEYOND MERE MORTAL CONCERNS HERE--A BOND THAT TIME ALONE CANNOT WEAKEN. THEY HAVE ALL FOUGHT INDESCRIBABLE BATTLES TOGETHER SO MANY TIMES...
...AND NOW THEY WILL AGAIN...
7

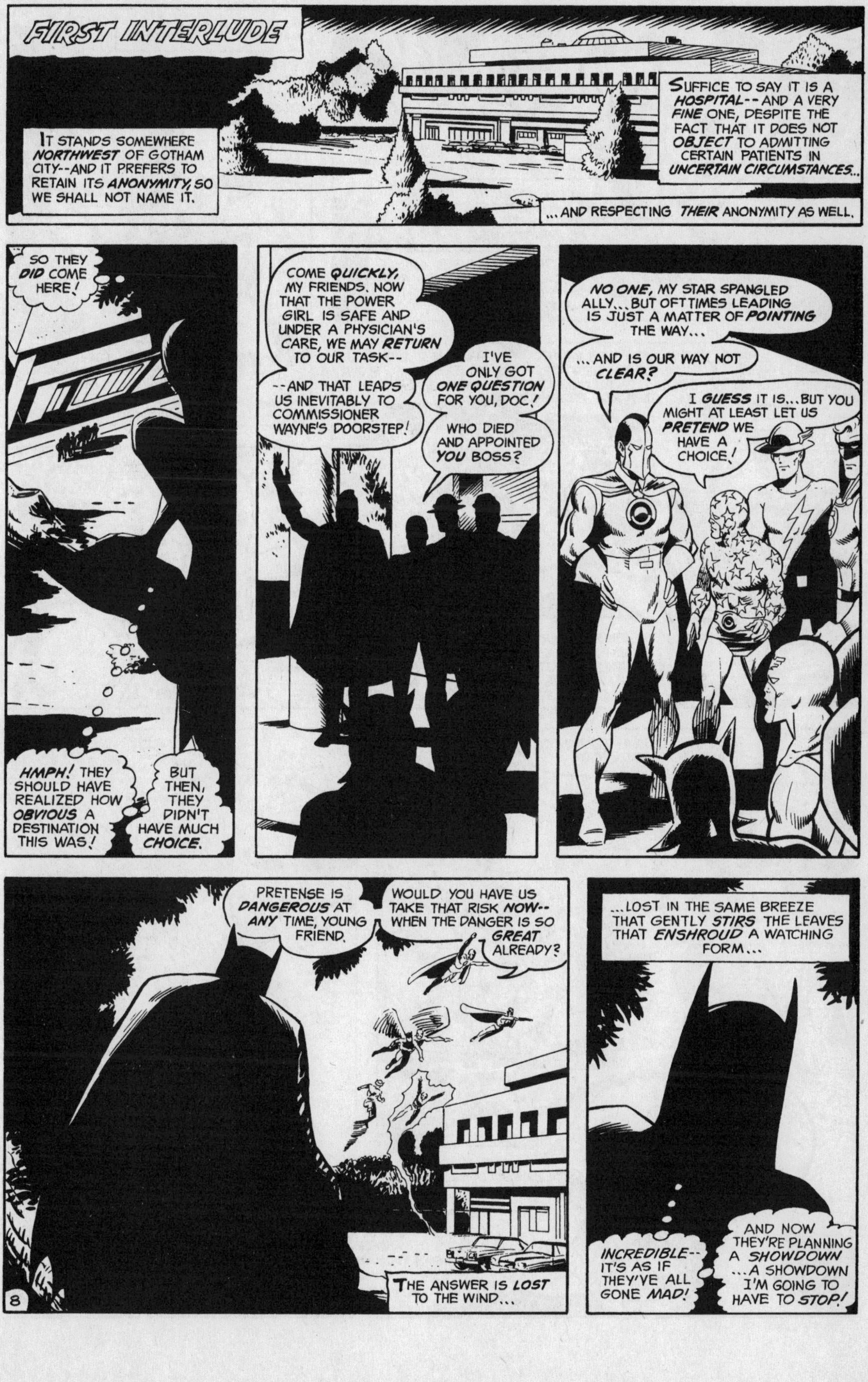
FIRST INTERLUDE
IT STANDS SOMEWHERE NORTHWEST OF GOTHAM CITY--AND IT PREFERS TO RETAIN ITS ANONYMITY, SO WE SHALL NOT NAME IT.
SUFFICE TO SAY IT IS A HOSPITAL--AND A VERY FINE ONE, DESPITE THE FACT THAT IT DOES NOT OBJECT TO ADMITTING CERTAIN PATIENTS IN UNCERTAIN CIRCUMSTANCES...
...AND RESPECTING THEIR ANONYMITY AS WELL.
SO THEY DID COME HERE!
HMPH! THEY SHOULD HAVE REALIZED HOW OBVIOUS A DESTINATION THIS WAS!
BUT THEN, THEY DIDN'T HAVE MUCH CHOICE.
COME QUICKLY, MY FRIENDS. NOW THAT THE POWER GIRL IS SAFE AND UNDER A PHYSICIAN'S CARE, WE MAY RETURN TO OUR TASK--
--AND THAT LEADS US INEVITABLY TO COMMISSIONER WAYNE'S DOORSTEP!
I'VE ONLY GOT ONE QUESTION FOR YOU, DOC!
WHO DIED AND APPOINTED YOU BOSS?
NO ONE, MY STAR SPANGLED ALLY...BUT OFTTIMES LEADING IS JUST A MATTER OF POINTING THE WAY...
...AND IS OUR WAY NOT CLEAR?
I GUESS IT IS...BUT YOU MIGHT AT LEAST LET US PRETEND WE HAVE A CHOICE!
PRETENSE IS DANGEROUS AT ANY TIME, YOUNG FRIEND.
WOULD YOU HAVE US TAKE THAT RISK NOW--WHEN THE DANGER IS SO GREAT ALREADY?
THE ANSWER IS LOST TO THE WIND...
8
...LOST IN THE SAME BREEZE THAT GENTLY STIRS THE LEAVES THAT ENSHROUD A WATCHING FORM...
INCREDIBLE--IT'S AS IF THEY'VE ALL GONE MAD!
AND NOW THEY'RE PLANNING A SHOWDOWN ...A SHOWDOWN I'M GOING TO HAVE TO STOP!

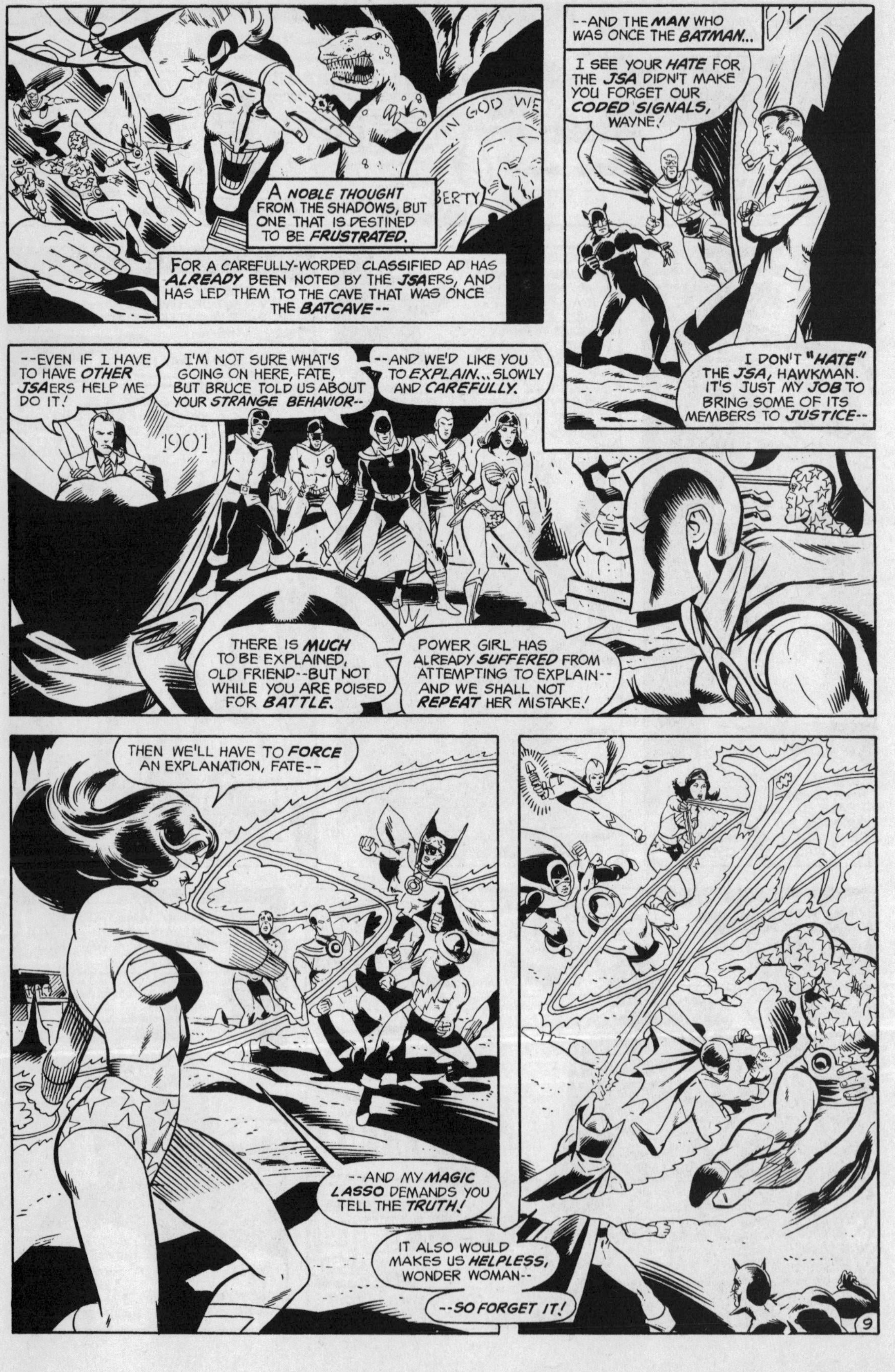
A NOBLE THOUGHT FROM THE SHADOWS, BUT ONE THAT IS DESTINED TO BE FRUSTRATED.
FOR A CAREFULLY-WORDED CLASSIFIED AD HAS ALREADY BEEN NOTED BY THE JSAERS, AND HAS LED THEM TO THE CAVE THAT WAS ONCE THE BATCAVE--
--AND THE MAN WHO WAS ONCE THE BATMAN...
I SEE YOUR HATE FOR THE JSA DIDN'T MAKE YOU FORGET OUR CODED SIGNALS, WAYNE!
I DON'T "HATE" THE JSA, HAWKMAN. IT'S JUST MY JOB TO BRING SOME OF ITS MEMBERS TO JUSTICE--
--EVEN IF I HAVE TO HAVE OTHER JSAERS HELP ME DO IT!
I'M NOT SURE WHAT'S GOING ON HERE, FATE, BUT BRUCE TOLD US ABOUT YOUR STRANGE BEHAVIOR--
--AND WE'D LIKE YOU TO EXPLAIN... SLOWLY AND CAREFULLY.
THERE IS MUCH TO BE EXPLAINED, OLD FRIEND--BUT NOT WHILE YOU ARE POISED FOR BATTLE.
POWER GIRL HAS ALREADY SUFFERED FROM ATTEMPTING TO EXPLAIN--AND WE SHALL NOT REPEAT HER MISTAKE!
THEN WE'LL HAVE TO FORCE AN EXPLANATION, FATE--
--AND MY MAGIC LASSO DEMANDS YOU TELL THE TRUTH!
IT ALSO WOULD MAKES US HELPLESS, WONDER WOMAN--
--SO FORGET IT!
9

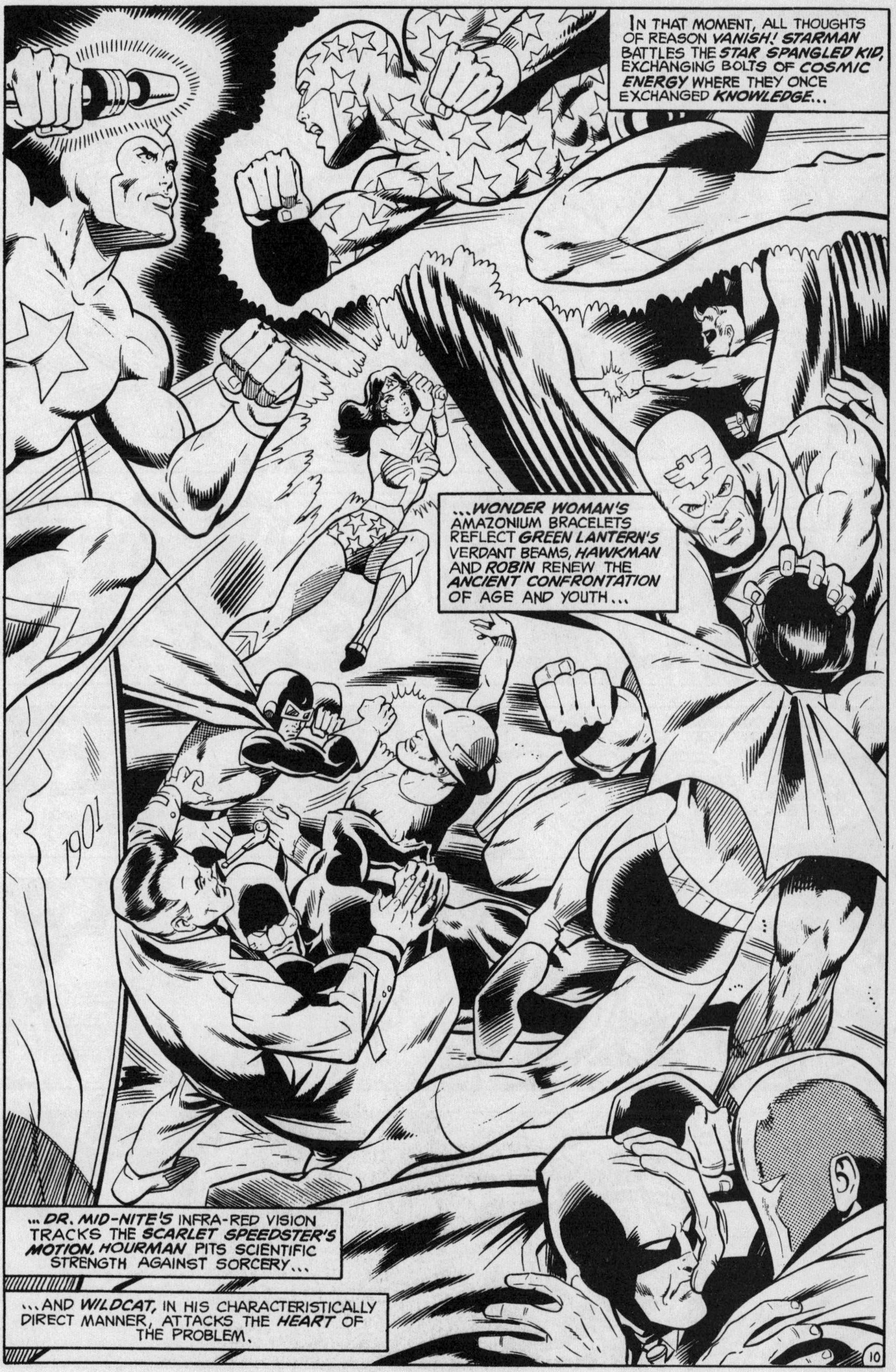
IN THAT MOMENT, ALL THOUGHTS OF REASON VANISH! STARMAN BATTLES THE STAR SPANGLED KID, EXCHANGING BOLTS OF COSMIC ENERGY WHERE THEY ONCE EXCHANGED KNOWLEDGE...
...WONDER WOMAN'S AMAZONIUM BRACELETS REFLECT GREEN LANTERN'S VERDANT BEAMS, HAWKMAN AND ROBIN RENEW THE ANCIENT CONFRONTATION OF AGE AND YOUTH...
1901
...DR. MID-NITE'S INFRA-RED VISION TRACKS THE SCARLET SPEEDSTER'S MOTION. HOURMAN PITS SCIENTIFIC STRENGTH AGAINST SORCERY...
...AND WILDCAT, IN HIS CHARACTERISTICALLY DIRECT MANNER, ATTACKS THE HEART OF THE PROBLEM.
10

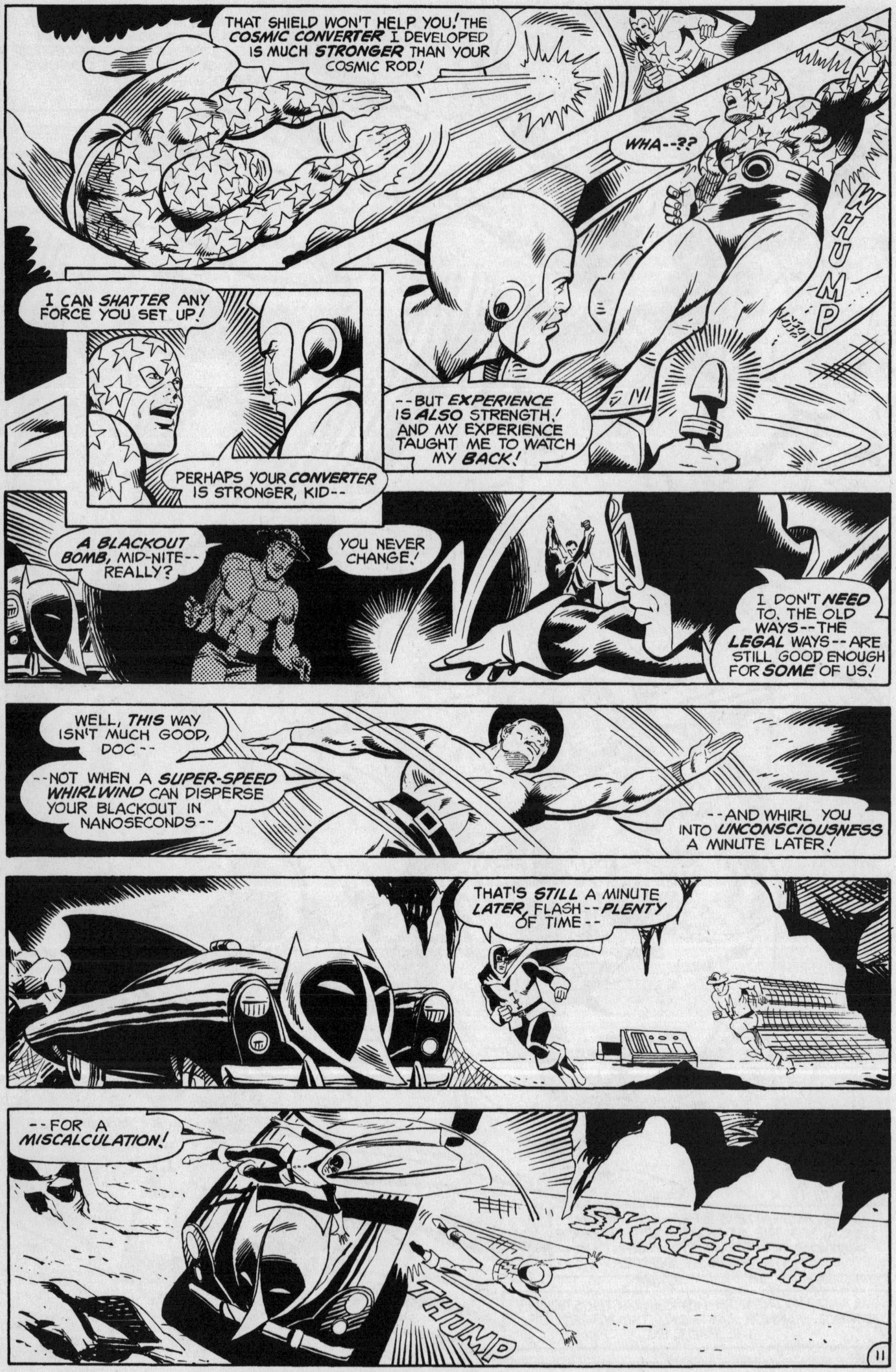
THAT SHIELD WON'T HELP YOU! THE COSMIC CONVERTER I DEVELOPED IS MUCH STRONGER THAN YOUR COSMIC ROD!
WHA--??
WHUMP
I CAN SHATTER ANY FORCE YOU SET UP!
PERHAPS YOUR CONVERTER IS STRONGER, KID--
--BUT EXPERIENCE IS ALSO STRENGTH! AND MY EXPERIENCE TAUGHT ME TO WATCH MY BACK!
A BLACKOUT BOMB, MID-NITE--REALLY?
YOU NEVER CHANGE!
I DON'T NEED TO. THE OLD WAYS--THE LEGAL WAYS--ARE STILL GOOD ENOUGH FOR SOME OF US!
WELL, THIS WAY ISN'T MUCH GOOD, DOC--
--NOT WHEN A SUPER-SPEED WHIRLWIND CAN DISPERSE YOUR BLACKOUT IN NANOSECONDS--
--AND WHIRL YOU INTO UNCONSCIOUSNESS A MINUTE LATER!
THAT'S STILL A MINUTE LATER, FLASH--PLENTY OF TIME--
--FOR A MISCALCULATION!
SKREEECH
THUMP
11

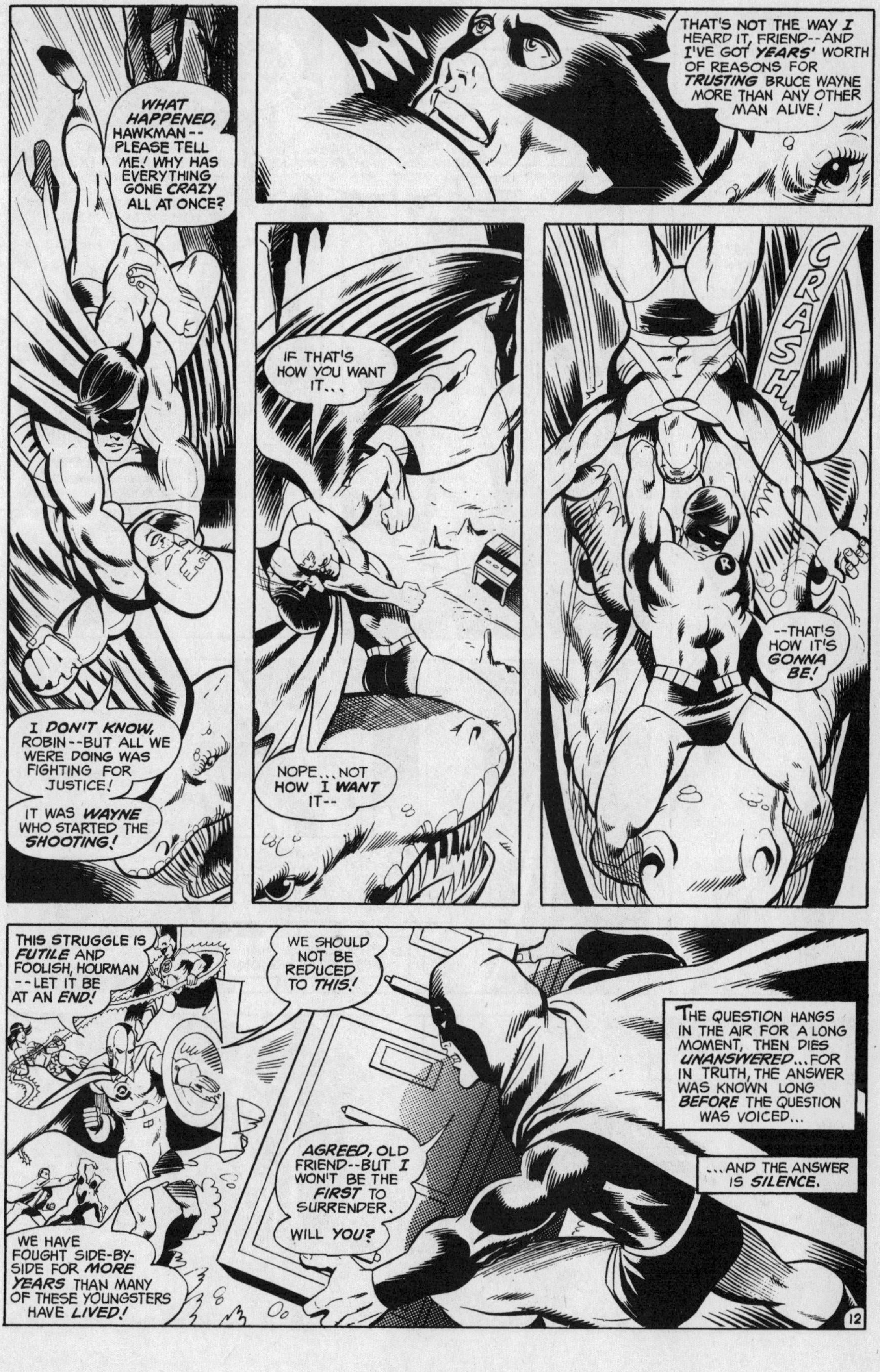
WHAT HAPPENED, HAWKMAN-- PLEASE TELL ME! WHY HAS EVERYTHING GONE CRAZY ALL AT ONCE?
I DON'T KNOW, ROBIN--BUT ALL WE WERE DOING WAS FIGHTING FOR JUSTICE!
IT WAS WAYNE WHO STARTED THE SHOOTING!
THAT'S NOT THE WAY I HEARD IT, FRIEND--AND I'VE GOT YEARS' WORTH OF REASONS FOR TRUSTING BRUCE WAYNE MORE THAN ANY OTHER MAN ALIVE!
IF THAT'S HOW YOU WANT IT...
NOPE...NOT HOW I WANT IT--
CRASH
--THAT'S HOW IT'S GONNA BE!
THIS STRUGGLE IS FUTILE AND FOOLISH, HOURMAN --LET IT BE AT AN END!
WE SHOULD NOT BE REDUCED TO THIS!
WE HAVE FOUGHT SIDE-BY-SIDE FOR MORE YEARS THAN MANY OF THESE YOUNGSTERS HAVE LIVED!
AGREED, OLD FRIEND--BUT I WON'T BE THE FIRST TO SURRENDER.
WILL YOU?
THE QUESTION HANGS IN THE AIR FOR A LONG MOMENT, THEN DIES UNANSWERED...FOR IN TRUTH, THE ANSWER WAS KNOWN LONG BEFORE THE QUESTION WAS VOICED...
...AND THE ANSWER IS SILENCE.
12

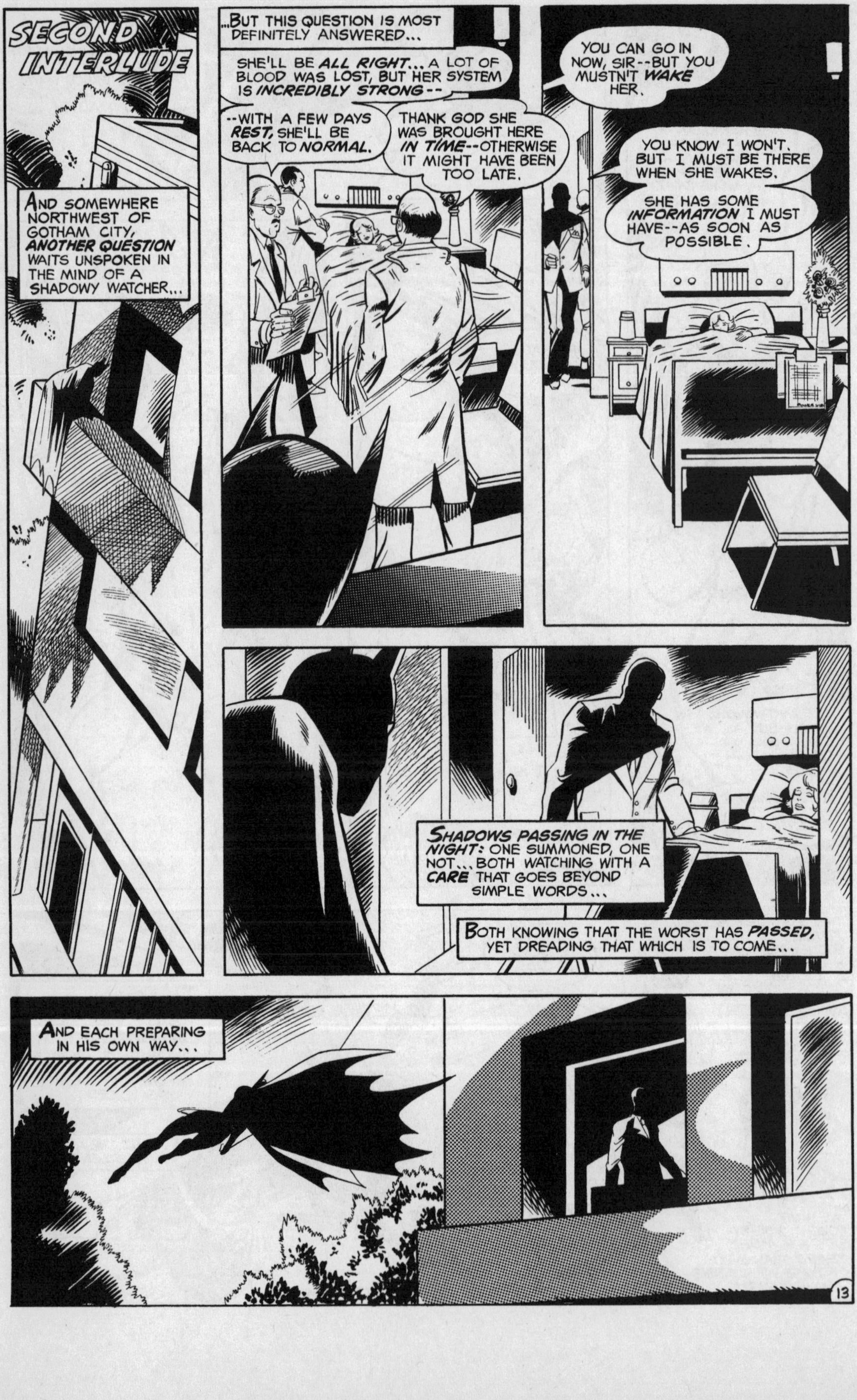
SECOND INTERLUDE
AND SOMEWHERE NORTHWEST OF GOTHAM CITY, ANOTHER QUESTION WAITS UNSPOKEN IN THE MIND OF A SHADOWY WATCHER...
...BUT THIS QUESTION IS MOST DEFINITELY ANSWERED...
SHE'LL BE ALL RIGHT... A LOT OF BLOOD WAS LOST, BUT HER SYSTEM IS INCREDIBLY STRONG--
--WITH A FEW DAYS REST, SHE'LL BE BACK TO NORMAL.
THANK GOD SHE WAS BROUGHT HERE IN TIME--OTHERWISE IT MIGHT HAVE BEEN TOO LATE.
YOU CAN GO IN NOW, SIR--BUT YOU MUSTN'T WAKE HER.
YOU KNOW I WON'T. BUT I MUST BE THERE WHEN SHE WAKES.
SHE HAS SOME INFORMATION I MUST HAVE--AS SOON AS POSSIBLE.
SHADOWS PASSING IN THE NIGHT: ONE SUMMONED, ONE NOT... BOTH WATCHING WITH A CARE THAT GOES BEYOND SIMPLE WORDS...
BOTH KNOWING THAT THE WORST HAS PASSED, YET DREADING THAT WHICH IS TO COME...
AND EACH PREPARING IN HIS OWN WAY...
13

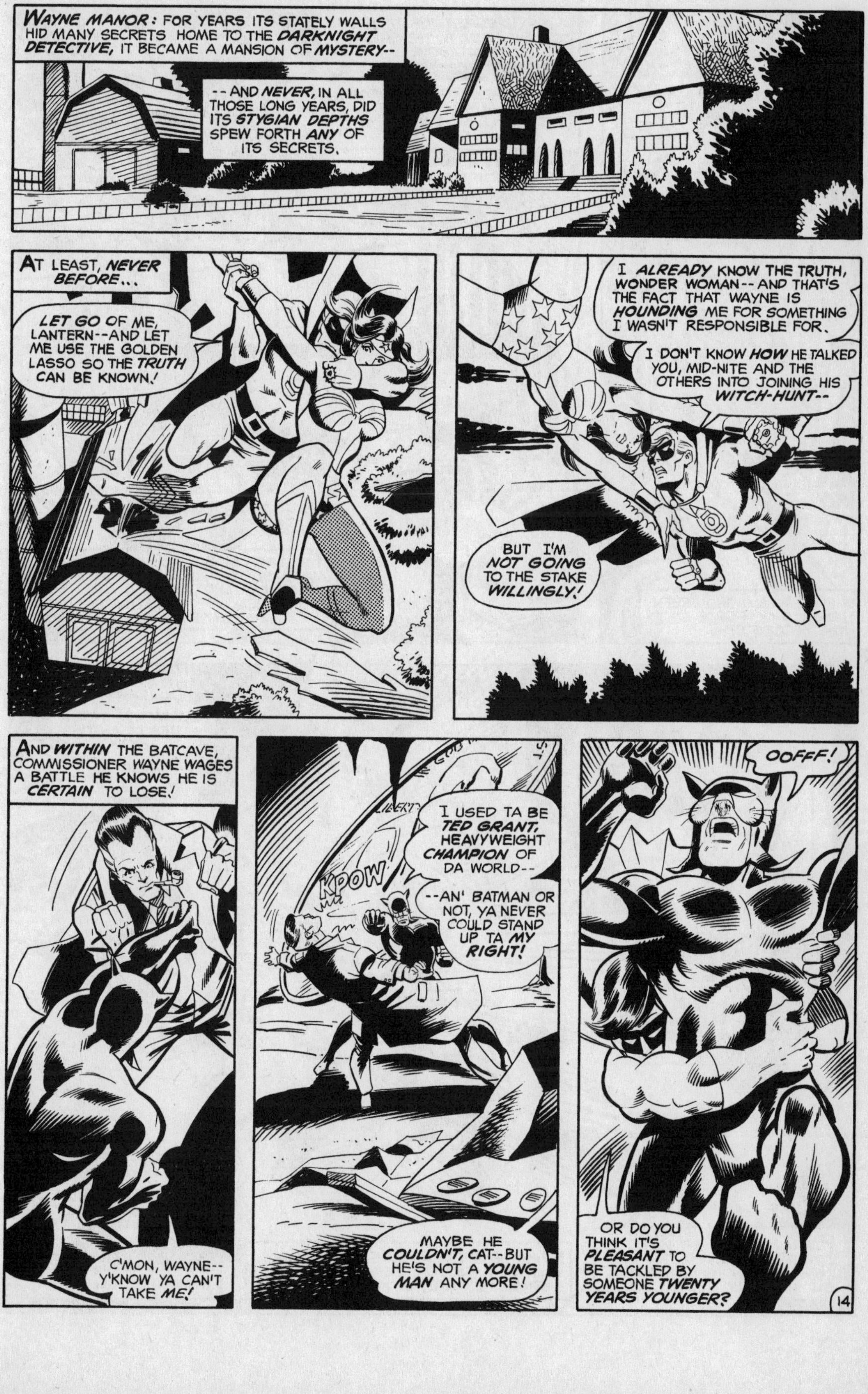
WAYNE MANOR: FOR YEARS ITS STATELY WALLS HID MANY SECRETS HOME TO THE DARKNIGHT DETECTIVE, IT BECAME A MANSION OF MYSTERY--
--AND NEVER, IN ALL THOSE LONG YEARS, DID ITS STYGIAN DEPTHS SPEW FORTH ANY OF ITS SECRETS.
AT LEAST, NEVER BEFORE...
LET GO OF ME, LANTERN--AND LET ME USE THE GOLDEN LASSO SO THE TRUTH CAN BE KNOWN!
I ALREADY KNOW THE TRUTH, WONDER WOMAN--AND THAT'S THE FACT THAT WAYNE IS HOUNDING ME FOR SOMETHING I WASN'T RESPONSIBLE FOR.
I DON'T KNOW HOW HE TALKED YOU, MID-NITE AND THE OTHERS INTO JOINING HIS WITCH-HUNT--
BUT I'M NOT GOING TO THE STAKE WILLINGLY!
AND WITHIN THE BATCAVE, COMMISSIONER WAYNE WAGES A BATTLE HE KNOWS HE IS CERTAIN TO LOSE!
C'MON, WAYNE--Y'KNOW YA CAN'T TAKE ME!
KPOW
I USED TA BE TED GRANT, HEAVYWEIGHT CHAMPION OF DA WORLD--
--AN' BATMAN OR NOT, YA NEVER COULD STAND UP TA MY RIGHT!
MAYBE HE COULDN'T, CAT--BUT HE'S NOT A YOUNG MAN ANY MORE!
OOFFF!
OR DO YOU THINK IT'S PLEASANT TO BE TACKLED BY SOMEONE TWENTY YEARS YOUNGER?
14

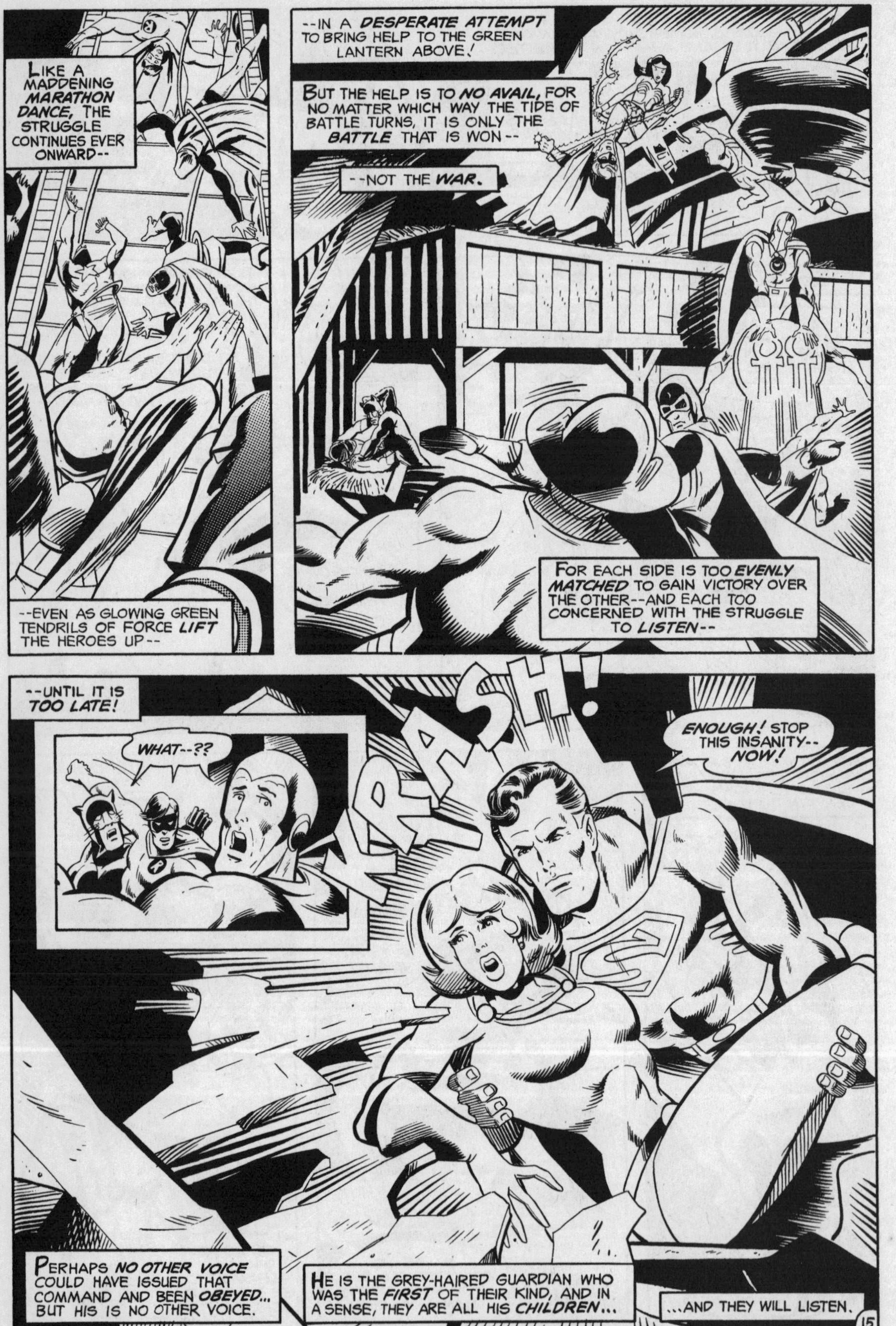
LIKE A MADDENING MARATHON DANCE, THE STRUGGLE CONTINUES EVER ONWARD--
--EVEN AS GLOWING GREEN TENDRILS OF FORCE LIFT THE HEROES UP--
--IN A DESPERATE ATTEMPT TO BRING HELP TO THE GREEN LANTERN ABOVE!
BUT THE HELP IS TO NO AVAIL, FOR NO MATTER WHICH WAY THE TIDE OF BATTLE TURNS, IT IS ONLY THE BATTLE THAT IS WON--
--NOT THE WAR.
FOR EACH SIDE IS TOO EVENLY MATCHED TO GAIN VICTORY OVER THE OTHER--AND EACH TOO CONCERNED WITH THE STRUGGLE TO LISTEN--
--UNTIL IT IS TOO LATE!
KRASH!
WHAT--??
ENOUGH! STOP THIS INSANITY-- NOW!
PERHAPS NO OTHER VOICE COULD HAVE ISSUED THAT COMMAND AND BEEN OBEYED... BUT HIS IS NO OTHER VOICE.
HE IS THE GREY-HAIRED GUARDIAN WHO WAS THE FIRST OF THEIR KIND, AND IN A SENSE, THEY ARE ALL HIS CHILDREN...
...AND THEY WILL LISTEN.
15

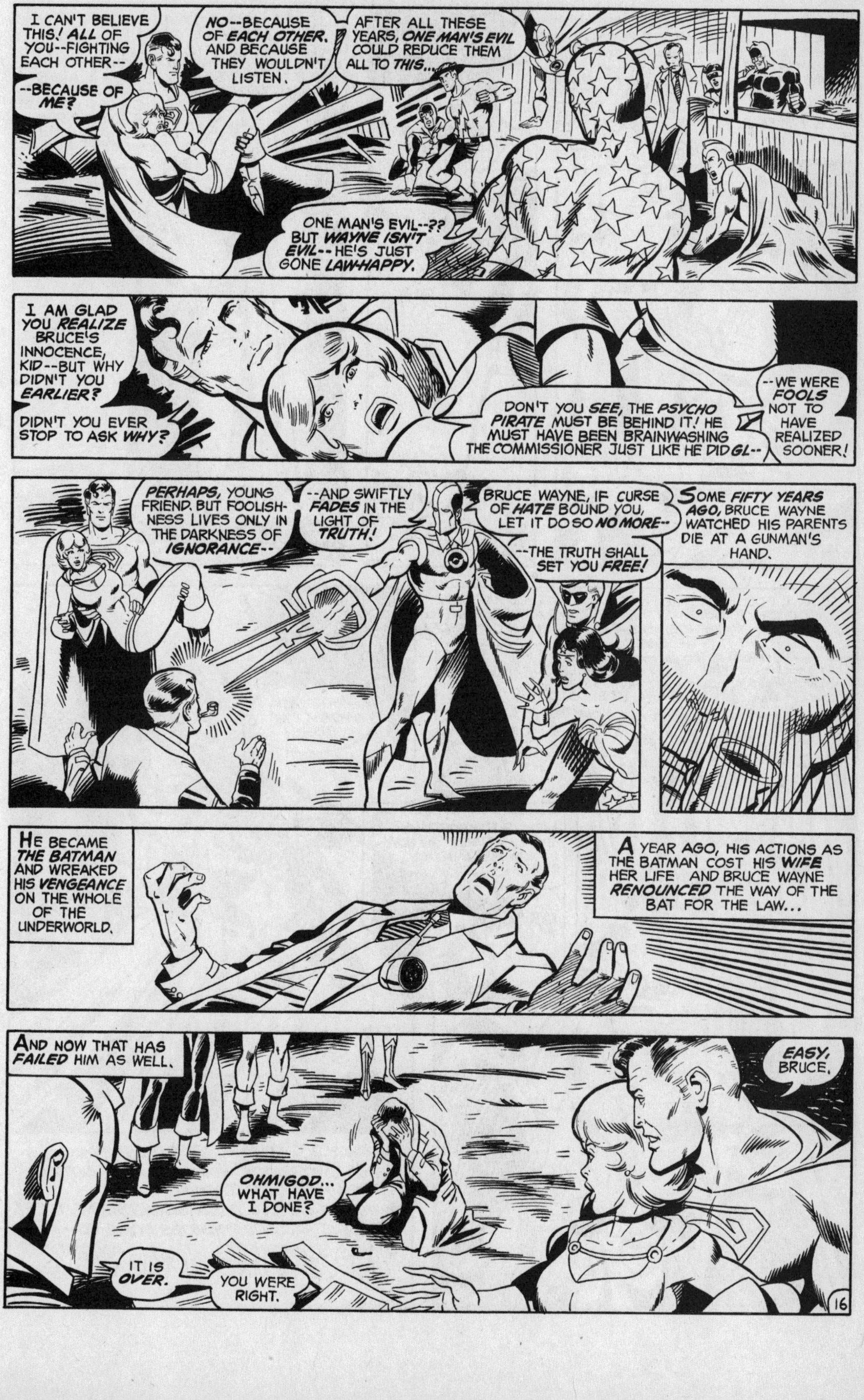

I CAN'T BELIEVE THIS! ALL OF YOU--FIGHTING EACH OTHER--
--BECAUSE OF ME?
NO--BECAUSE OF EACH OTHER. AND BECAUSE THEY WOULDN'T LISTEN.
AFTER ALL THESE YEARS, ONE MAN'S EVIL COULD REDUCE THEM ALL TO THIS...
ONE MAN'S EVIL--?? BUT WAYNE ISN'T EVIL--HE'S JUST GONE LAW-HAPPY.
I AM GLAD YOU REALIZE BRUCE'S INNOCENCE, KID--BUT WHY DIDN'T YOU EARLIER?
DIDN'T YOU EVER STOP TO ASK WHY?
DON'T YOU SEE, THE PSYCHO PIRATE MUST BE BEHIND IT! HE MUST HAVE BEEN BRAINWASHING THE COMMISSIONER JUST LIKE HE DID GL--
--WE WERE FOOLS NOT TO HAVE REALIZED SOONER!
PERHAPS, YOUNG FRIEND. BUT FOOLISHNESS LIVES ONLY IN THE DARKNESS OF IGNORANCE--
--AND SWIFTLY FADES IN THE LIGHT OF TRUTH!
BRUCE WAYNE, IF CURSE OF HATE BOUND YOU, LET IT DO SO NO MORE--
--THE TRUTH SHALL SET YOU FREE!
SOME FIFTY YEARS AGO, BRUCE WAYNE WATCHED HIS PARENTS DIE AT A GUNMAN'S HAND.
HE BECAME THE BATMAN AND WREAKED HIS VENGEANCE ON THE WHOLE OF THE UNDERWORLD.
A YEAR AGO, HIS ACTIONS AS THE BATMAN COST HIS WIFE HER LIFE AND BRUCE WAYNE RENOUNCED THE WAY OF THE BAT FOR THE LAW...
AND NOW THAT HAS FAILED HIM AS WELL.
EASY, BRUCE.
OHMIGOD... WHAT HAVE I DONE?
IT IS OVER.
YOU WERE RIGHT.
16

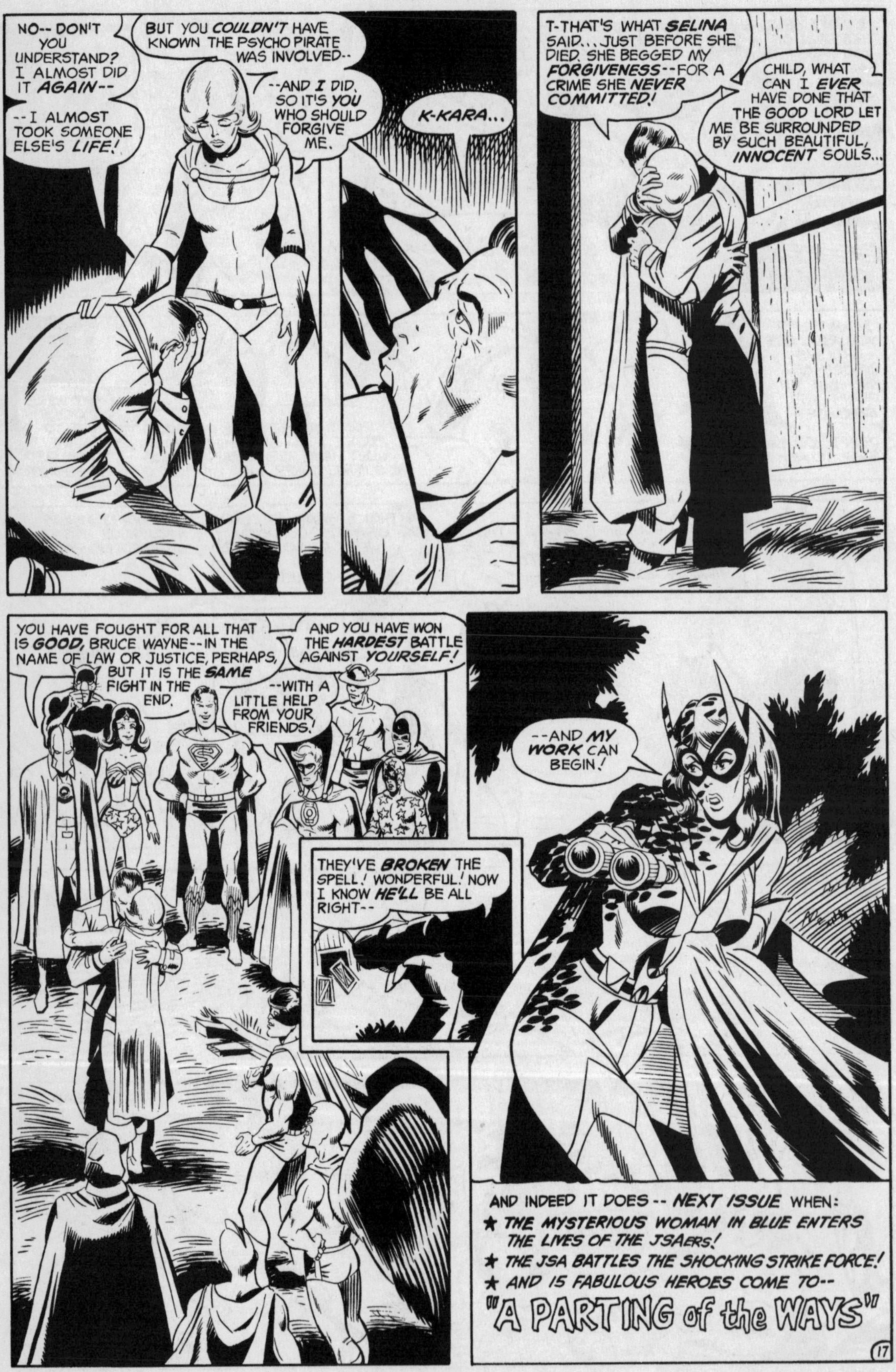
NO-- DON'T YOU UNDERSTAND? I ALMOST DID IT AGAIN--
--I ALMOST TOOK SOMEONE ELSE'S LIFE!
BUT YOU COULDN'T HAVE KNOWN THE PSYCHO PIRATE WAS INVOLVED--
--AND I DID, SO IT'S YOU WHO SHOULD FORGIVE ME.
K-KARA...
T-THAT'S WHAT SELINA SAID... JUST BEFORE SHE DIED. SHE BEGGED MY FORGIVENESS--FOR A CRIME SHE NEVER COMMITTED!
CHILD, WHAT CAN I EVER HAVE DONE THAT THE GOOD LORD LET ME BE SURROUNDED BY SUCH BEAUTIFUL, INNOCENT SOULS...
YOU HAVE FOUGHT FOR ALL THAT IS GOOD, BRUCE WAYNE--IN THE NAME OF LAW OR JUSTICE, PERHAPS, BUT IT IS THE SAME FIGHT IN THE END.
AND YOU HAVE WON THE HARDEST BATTLE AGAINST YOURSELF!
--WITH A LITTLE HELP FROM YOUR FRIENDS!
THEY'VE BROKEN THE SPELL! WONDERFUL! NOW I KNOW HE'LL BE ALL RIGHT--
--AND MY WORK CAN BEGIN!
AND INDEED IT DOES -- NEXT ISSUE WHEN:
★ THE MYSTERIOUS WOMAN IN BLUE ENTERS THE LIVES OF THE JSAERS!
★ THE JSA BATTLES THE SHOCKING STRIKE FORCE!
★ AND 15 FABULOUS HEROES COME TO--
"A PARTING of the WAYS"
17

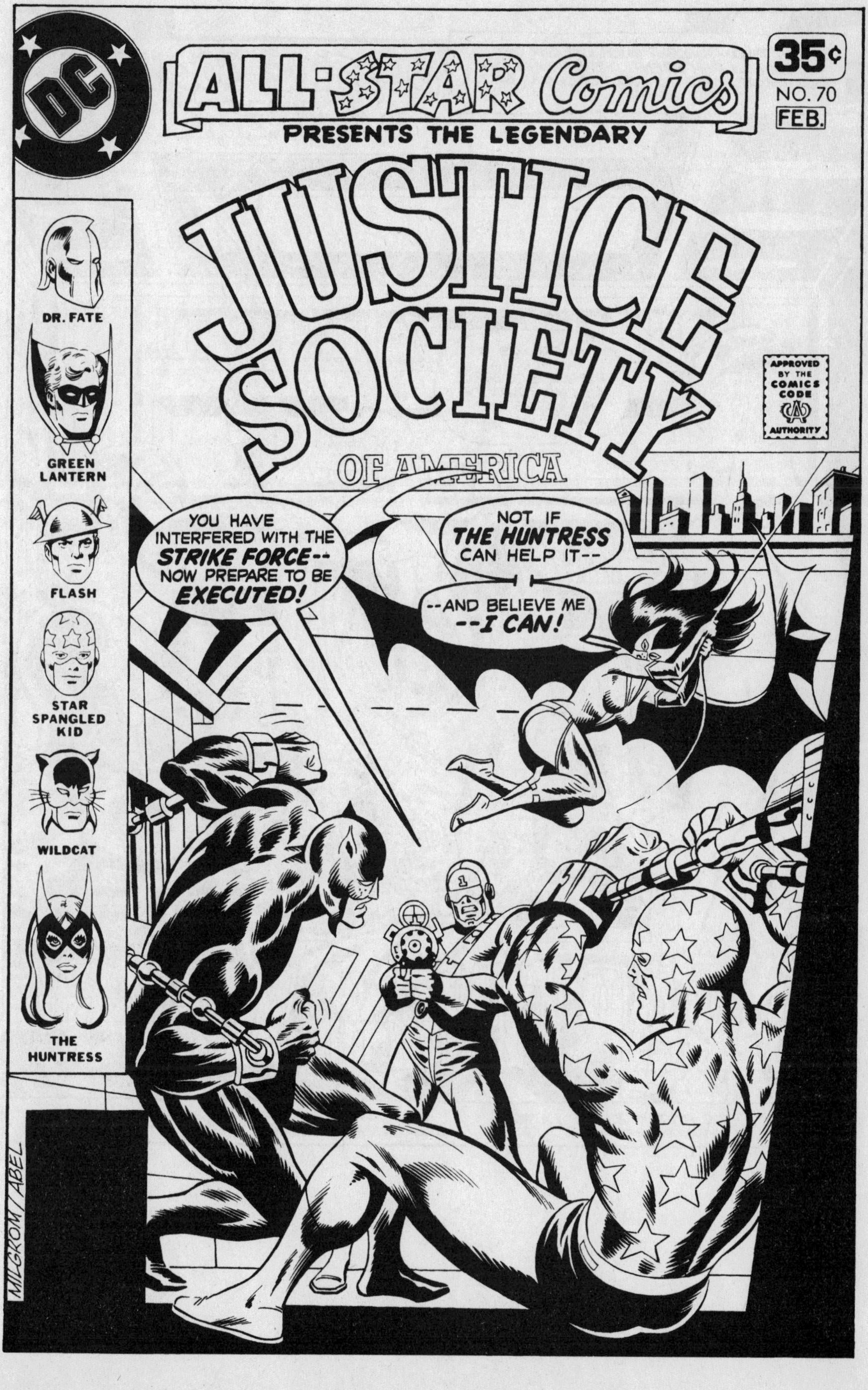
DC
ALL-STAR Comics
35¢
NO. 70
FEB.
PRESENTS THE LEGENDARY
JUSTICE SOCIETY
OF AMERICA
APPROVED BY THE COMICS CODE AUTHORITY
DR. FATE
GREEN LANTERN
FLASH
STAR SPANGLED KID
WILDCAT
THE HUNTRESS
YOU HAVE INTERFERED WITH THE STRIKE FORCE-- NOW PREPARE TO BE EXECUTED!
NOT IF THE HUNTRESS CAN HELP IT--
--AND BELIEVE ME --I CAN!
MILGROM/ABEL

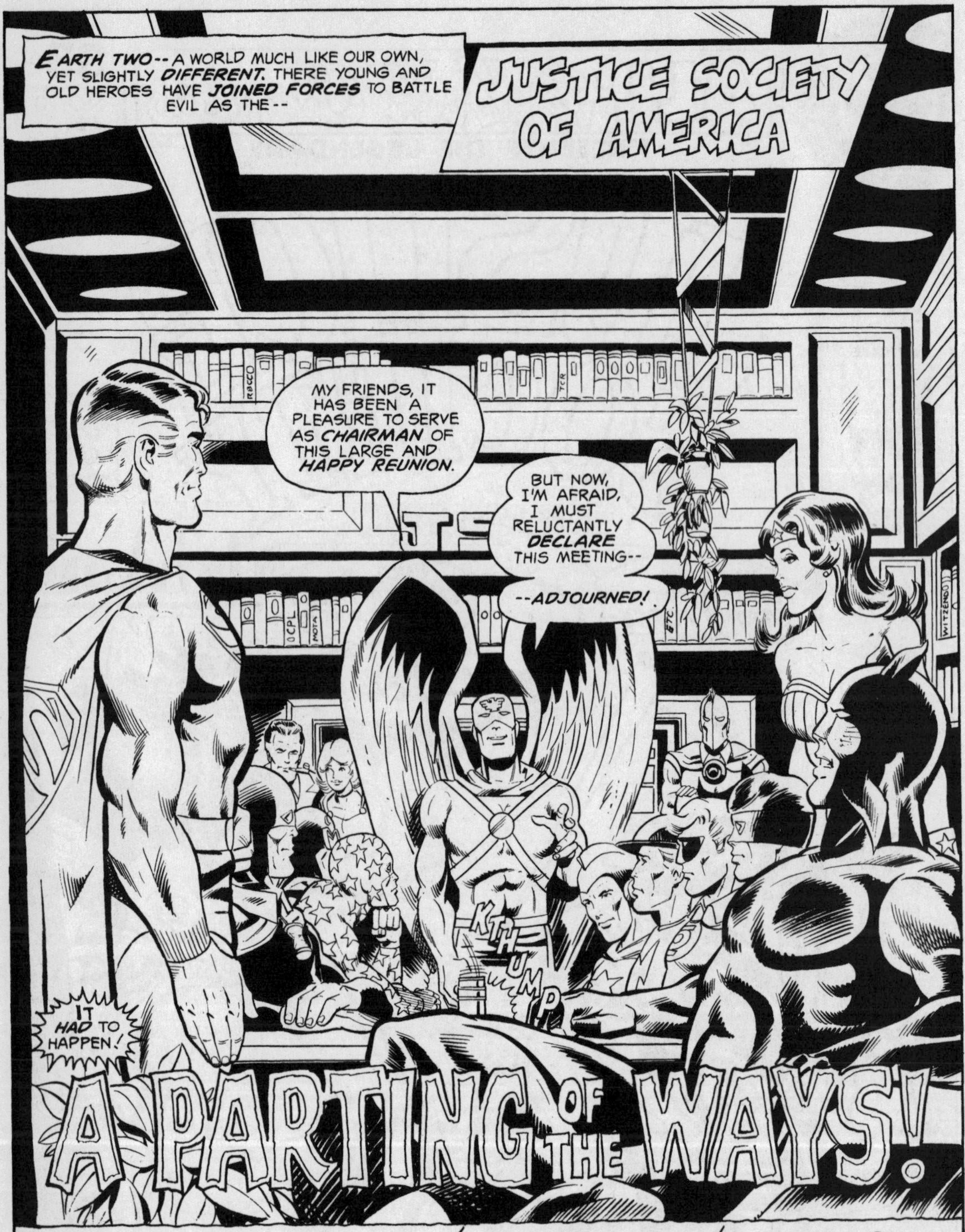
EARTH TWO-- A WORLD MUCH LIKE OUR OWN, YET SLIGHTLY DIFFERENT. THERE YOUNG AND OLD HEROES HAVE JOINED FORCES TO BATTLE EVIL AS THE --
JUSTICE SOCIETY OF AMERICA
MY FRIENDS, IT HAS BEEN A PLEASURE TO SERVE AS CHAIRMAN OF THIS LARGE AND HAPPY REUNION.
BUT NOW, I'M AFRAID, I MUST RELUCTANTLY DECLARE THIS MEETING--
--ADJOURNED!
KTHUMP
IT HAD TO HAPPEN!
A PARTING OF THE WAYS!
PAUL LEVITZ, JOE STATON & BOB LAYTON STORYTELLERS
BEN ODA - LETTERER
JERRY SERPE - COLORIST
JOE ORLANDO EDITOR

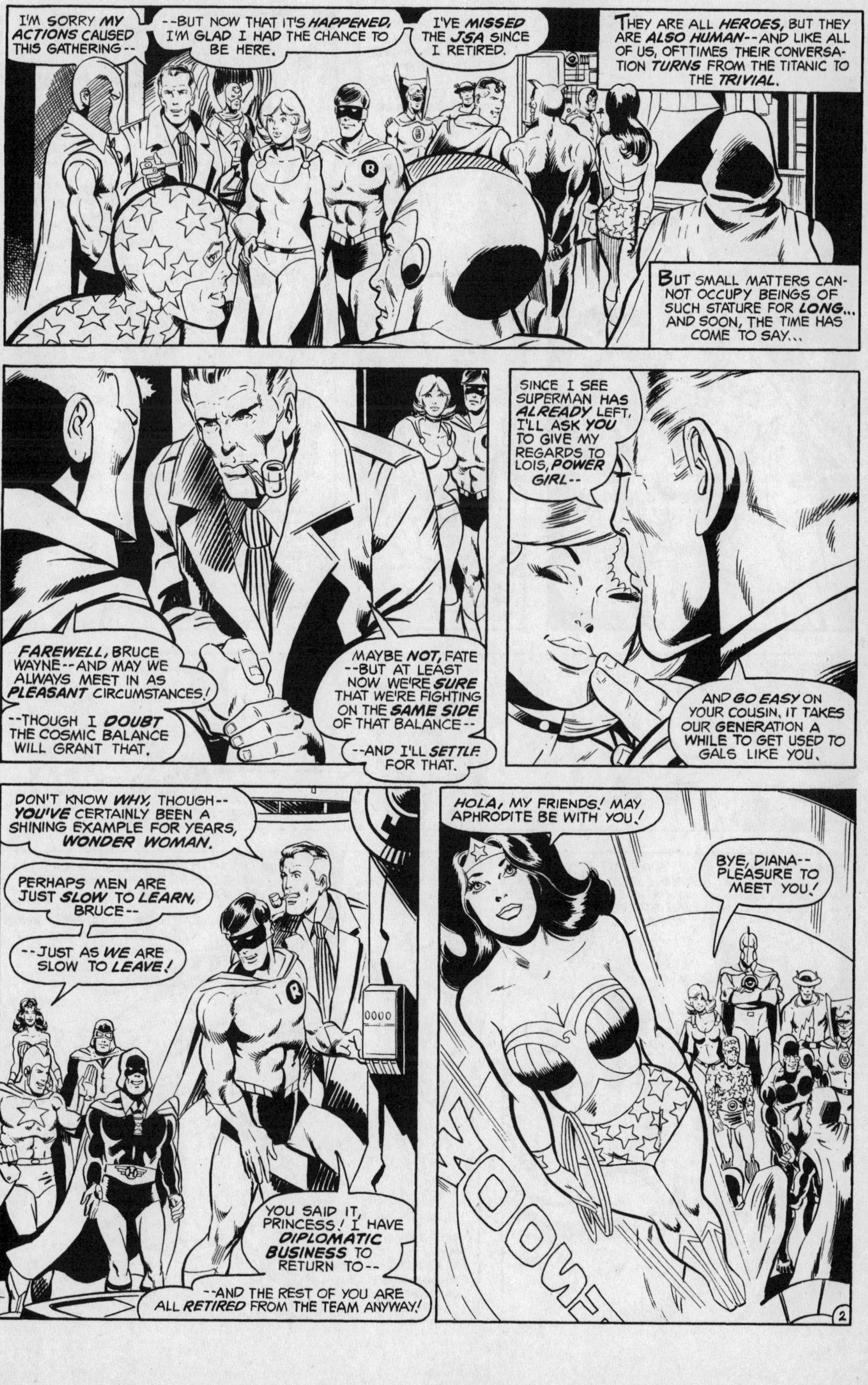
I'M SORRY MY ACTIONS CAUSED THIS GATHERING--
--BUT NOW THAT IT'S HAPPENED, I'M GLAD I HAD THE CHANCE TO BE HERE.
I'VE MISSED THE JSA SINCE I RETIRED.
THEY ARE ALL HEROES, BUT THEY ARE ALSO HUMAN--AND LIKE ALL OF US, OFTTIMES THEIR CONVERSATION TURNS FROM THE TITANIC TO THE TRIVIAL.
BUT SMALL MATTERS CANNOT OCCUPY BEINGS OF SUCH STATURE FOR LONG... AND SOON, THE TIME HAS COME TO SAY...
FAREWELL, BRUCE WAYNE--AND MAY WE ALWAYS MEET IN AS PLEASANT CIRCUMSTANCES!
--THOUGH I DOUBT THE COSMIC BALANCE WILL GRANT THAT.
MAYBE NOT, FATE --BUT AT LEAST NOW WE'RE SURE THAT WE'RE FIGHTING ON THE SAME SIDE OF THAT BALANCE--
--AND I'LL SETTLE FOR THAT.
SINCE I SEE SUPERMAN HAS ALREADY LEFT, I'LL ASK YOU TO GIVE MY REGARDS TO LOIS, POWER GIRL--
AND GO EASY ON YOUR COUSIN. IT TAKES OUR GENERATION A WHILE TO GET USED TO GALS LIKE YOU.
DON'T KNOW WHY, THOUGH--YOU'VE CERTAINLY BEEN A SHINING EXAMPLE FOR YEARS, WONDER WOMAN.
PERHAPS MEN ARE JUST SLOW TO LEARN, BRUCE--
--JUST AS WE ARE SLOW TO LEAVE!
YOU SAID IT, PRINCESS! I HAVE DIPLOMATIC BUSINESS TO RETURN TO--
--AND THE REST OF YOU ARE ALL RETIRED FROM THE TEAM ANYWAY!
HOLA, MY FRIENDS! MAY APHRODITE BE WITH YOU!
BYE, DIANA--PLEASURE TO MEET YOU!
ZOOM!
2

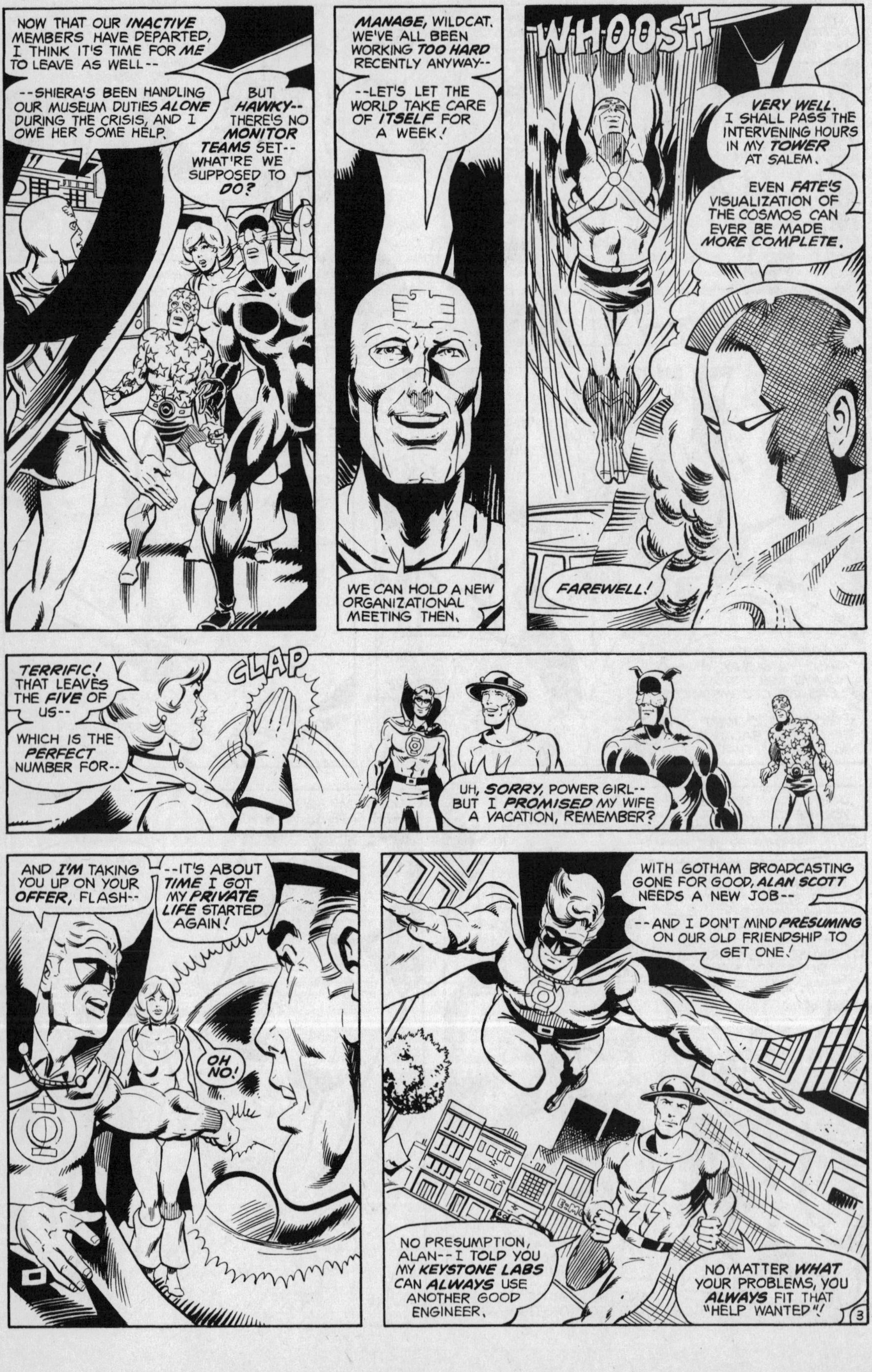
NOW THAT OUR INACTIVE MEMBERS HAVE DEPARTED, I THINK IT'S TIME FOR ME TO LEAVE AS WELL--
--SHIERA'S BEEN HANDLING OUR MUSEUM DUTIES ALONE DURING THE CRISIS, AND I OWE HER SOME HELP.
BUT HAWKY-- THERE'S NO MONITOR TEAMS SET-- WHAT'RE WE SUPPOSED TO DO?
MANAGE, WILDCAT. WE'VE ALL BEEN WORKING TOO HARD RECENTLY ANYWAY--
--LET'S LET THE WORLD TAKE CARE OF ITSELF FOR A WEEK!
WE CAN HOLD A NEW ORGANIZATIONAL MEETING THEN.
WHOOSH
VERY WELL. I SHALL PASS THE INTERVENING HOURS IN MY TOWER AT SALEM.
EVEN FATE'S VISUALIZATION OF THE COSMOS CAN EVER BE MADE MORE COMPLETE.
FAREWELL!
TERRIFIC! THAT LEAVES THE FIVE OF US--
WHICH IS THE PERFECT NUMBER FOR--
CLAP
UH, SORRY, POWER GIRL-- BUT I PROMISED MY WIFE A VACATION, REMEMBER?
AND I'M TAKING YOU UP ON YOUR OFFER, FLASH--
--IT'S ABOUT TIME I GOT MY PRIVATE LIFE STARTED AGAIN!
OH NO!
WITH GOTHAM BROADCASTING GONE FOR GOOD, ALAN SCOTT NEEDS A NEW JOB--
--AND I DON'T MIND PRESUMING ON OUR OLD FRIENDSHIP TO GET ONE!
NO PRESUMPTION, ALAN-- I TOLD YOU MY KEYSTONE LABS CAN ALWAYS USE ANOTHER GOOD ENGINEER.
NO MATTER WHAT YOUR PROBLEMS, YOU ALWAYS FIT THAT "HELP WANTED"!
3

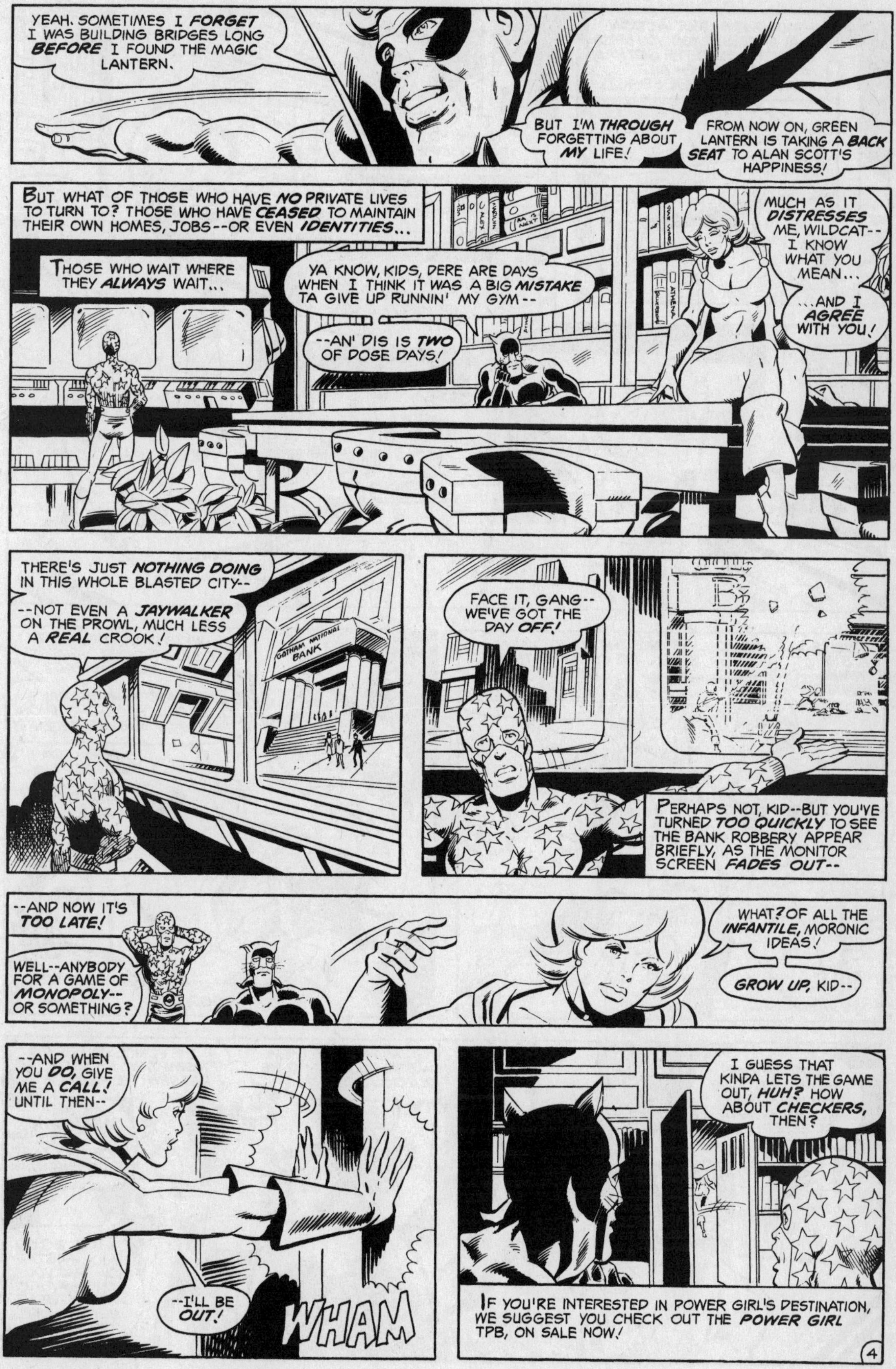
YEAH. SOMETIMES I FORGET I WAS BUILDING BRIDGES LONG BEFORE I FOUND THE MAGIC LANTERN.
BUT I'M THROUGH FORGETTING ABOUT MY LIFE!
FROM NOW ON, GREEN LANTERN IS TAKING A BACK SEAT TO ALAN SCOTT'S HAPPINESS!
BUT WHAT OF THOSE WHO HAVE NO PRIVATE LIVES TO TURN TO? THOSE WHO HAVE CEASED TO MAINTAIN THEIR OWN HOMES, JOBS--OR EVEN IDENTITIES...
THOSE WHO WAIT WHERE THEY ALWAYS WAIT...
YA KNOW, KIDS, DERE ARE DAYS WHEN I THINK IT WAS A BIG MISTAKE TA GIVE UP RUNNIN' MY GYM--
--AN' DIS IS TWO OF DOSE DAYS!
MUCH AS IT DISTRESSES ME, WILDCAT--I KNOW WHAT YOU MEAN...
...AND I AGREE WITH YOU!
THERE'S JUST NOTHING DOING IN THIS WHOLE BLASTED CITY--
--NOT EVEN A JAYWALKER ON THE PROWL, MUCH LESS A REAL CROOK!
GOTHAM NATIONAL BANK
FACE IT, GANG--WE'VE GOT THE DAY OFF!
PERHAPS NOT, KID--BUT YOU'VE TURNED TOO QUICKLY TO SEE THE BANK ROBBERY APPEAR BRIEFLY, AS THE MONITOR SCREEN FADES OUT--
--AND NOW IT'S TOO LATE!
WELL--ANYBODY FOR A GAME OF MONOPOLY--OR SOMETHING?
WHAT? OF ALL THE INFANTILE, MORONIC IDEAS!
GROW UP, KID--
--AND WHEN YOU DO, GIVE ME A CALL! UNTIL THEN--
--I'LL BE OUT!
WHAM
I GUESS THAT KINDA LETS THE GAME OUT, HUH? HOW ABOUT CHECKERS, THEN?
IF YOU'RE INTERESTED IN POWER GIRL'S DESTINATION, WE SUGGEST YOU CHECK OUT THE POWER GIRL TPB, ON SALE NOW!
4

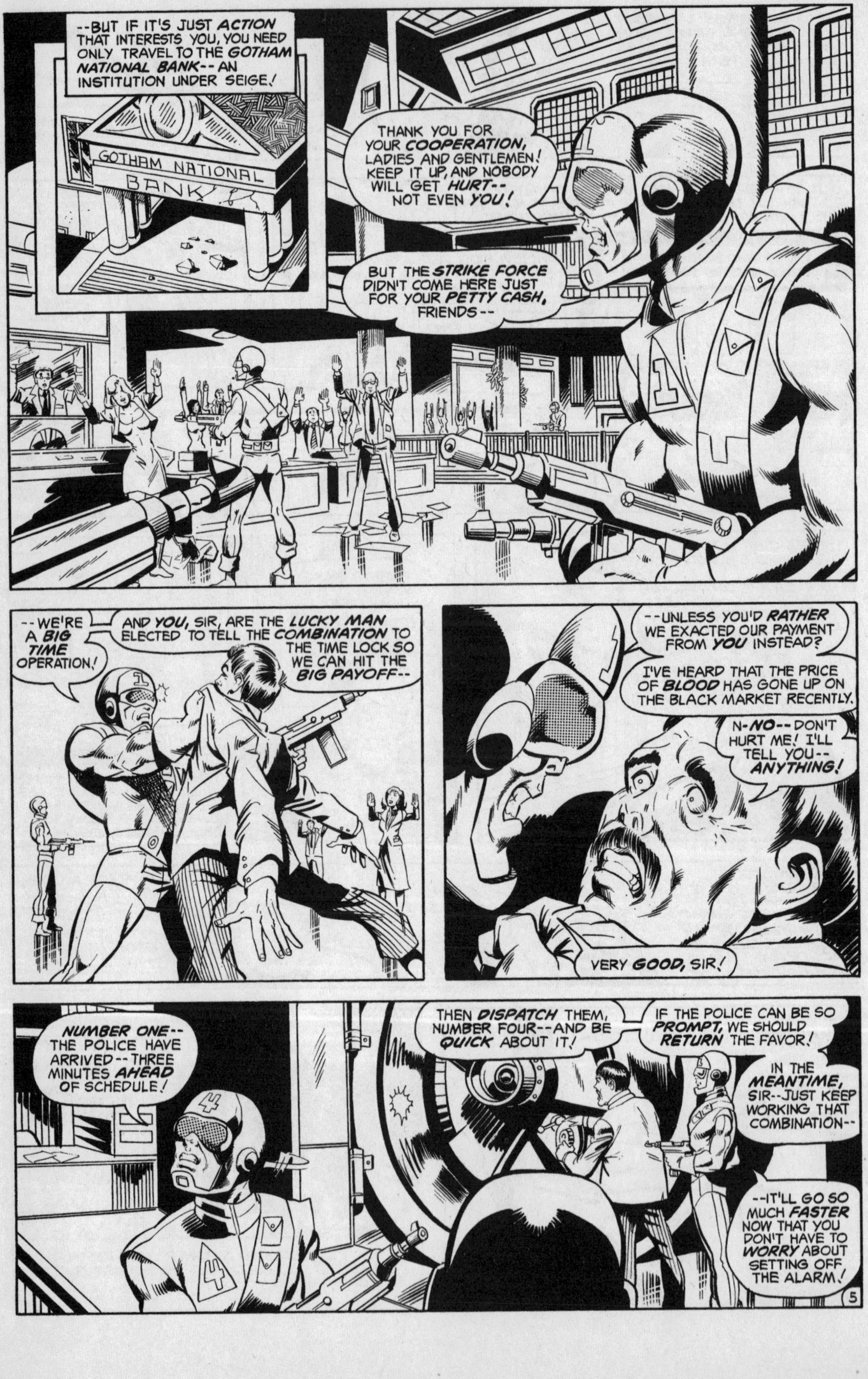
--BUT IF IT'S JUST ACTION THAT INTERESTS YOU, YOU NEED ONLY TRAVEL TO THE GOTHAM NATIONAL BANK--AN INSTITUTION UNDER SEIGE!
GOTHAM NATIONAL BANK
THANK YOU FOR YOUR COOPERATION, LADIES AND GENTLEMEN! KEEP IT UP, AND NOBODY WILL GET HURT--NOT EVEN YOU!
BUT THE STRIKE FORCE DIDN'T COME HERE JUST FOR YOUR PETTY CASH, FRIENDS--
--WE'RE A BIG TIME OPERATION!
AND YOU, SIR, ARE THE LUCKY MAN ELECTED TO TELL THE COMBINATION TO THE TIME LOCK SO WE CAN HIT THE BIG PAYOFF--
--UNLESS YOU'D RATHER WE EXACTED OUR PAYMENT FROM YOU INSTEAD?
I'VE HEARD THAT THE PRICE OF BLOOD HAS GONE UP ON THE BLACK MARKET RECENTLY.
N-NO--DON'T HURT ME! I'LL TELL YOU--ANYTHING!
VERY GOOD, SIR!
NUMBER ONE--THE POLICE HAVE ARRIVED--THREE MINUTES AHEAD OF SCHEDULE!
THEN DISPATCH THEM, NUMBER FOUR--AND BE QUICK ABOUT IT!
IF THE POLICE CAN BE SO PROMPT, WE SHOULD RETURN THE FAVOR!
IN THE MEANTIME, SIR--JUST KEEP WORKING THAT COMBINATION--
--IT'LL GO SO MUCH FASTER NOW THAT YOU DON'T HAVE TO WORRY ABOUT SETTING OFF THE ALARM!
5

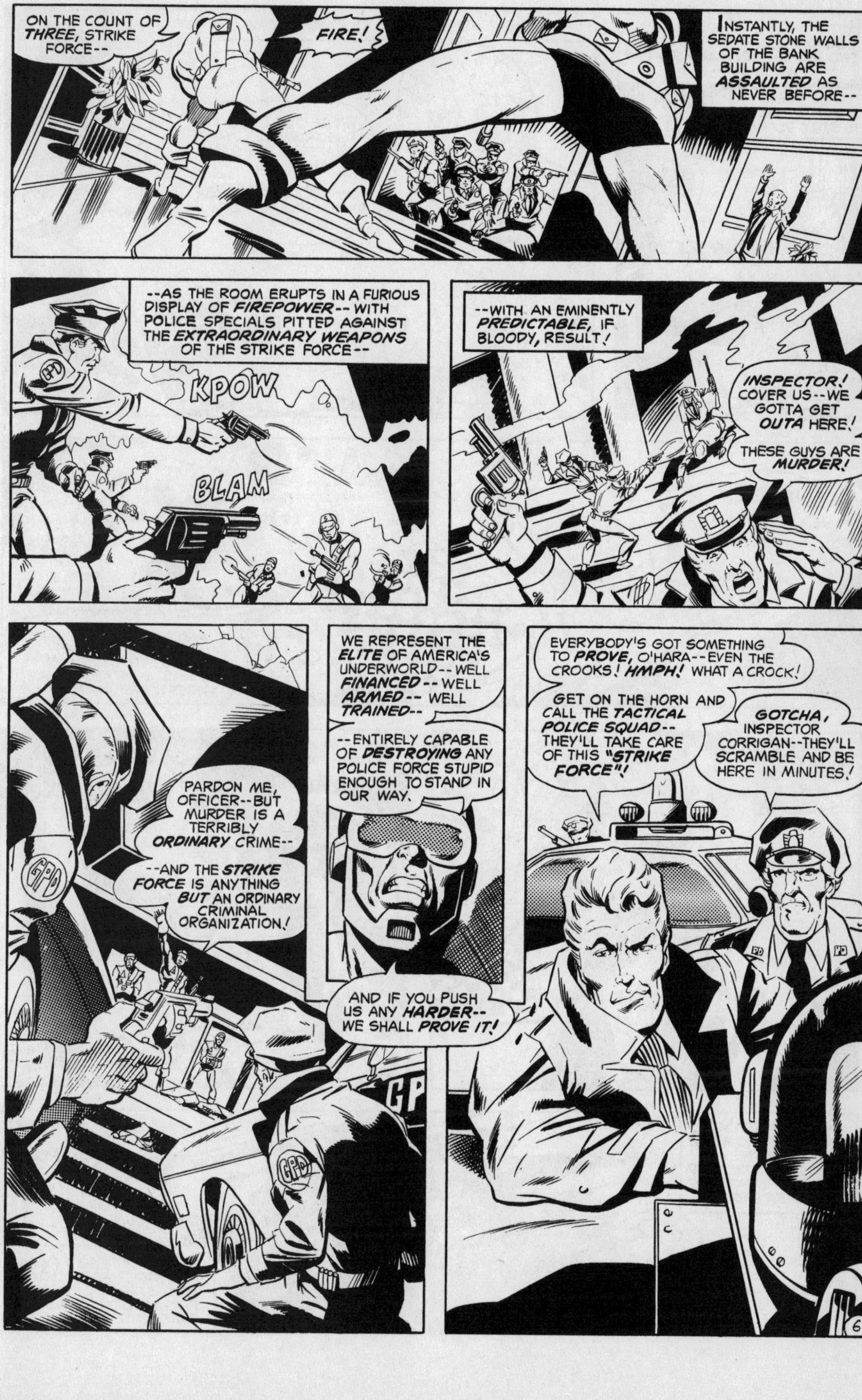
ON THE COUNT OF THREE, STRIKE FORCE--
FIRE!
INSTANTLY, THE SEDATE STONE WALLS OF THE BANK BUILDING ARE ASSAULTED AS NEVER BEFORE--
--AS THE ROOM ERUPTS IN A FURIOUS DISPLAY OF FIREPOWER-- WITH POLICE SPECIALS PITTED AGAINST THE EXTRAORDINARY WEAPONS OF THE STRIKE FORCE--
KPOW
BLAM
--WITH AN EMINENTLY PREDICTABLE, IF BLOODY, RESULT!
INSPECTOR! COVER US--WE GOTTA GET OUTA HERE!
THESE GUYS ARE MURDER!
PARDON ME, OFFICER--BUT MURDER IS A TERRIBLY ORDINARY CRIME--
--AND THE STRIKE FORCE IS ANYTHING BUT AN ORDINARY CRIMINAL ORGANIZATION!
WE REPRESENT THE ELITE OF AMERICA'S UNDERWORLD-- WELL FINANCED -- WELL ARMED -- WELL TRAINED--
--ENTIRELY CAPABLE OF DESTROYING ANY POLICE FORCE STUPID ENOUGH TO STAND IN OUR WAY.
AND IF YOU PUSH US ANY HARDER-- WE SHALL PROVE IT!
EVERYBODY'S GOT SOMETHING TO PROVE, O'HARA--EVEN THE CROOKS! HMPH! WHAT A CROCK!
GET ON THE HORN AND CALL THE TACTICAL POLICE SQUAD-- THEY'LL TAKE CARE OF THIS "STRIKE FORCE"!
GOTCHA, INSPECTOR CORRIGAN--THEY'LL SCRAMBLE AND BE HERE IN MINUTES!
6

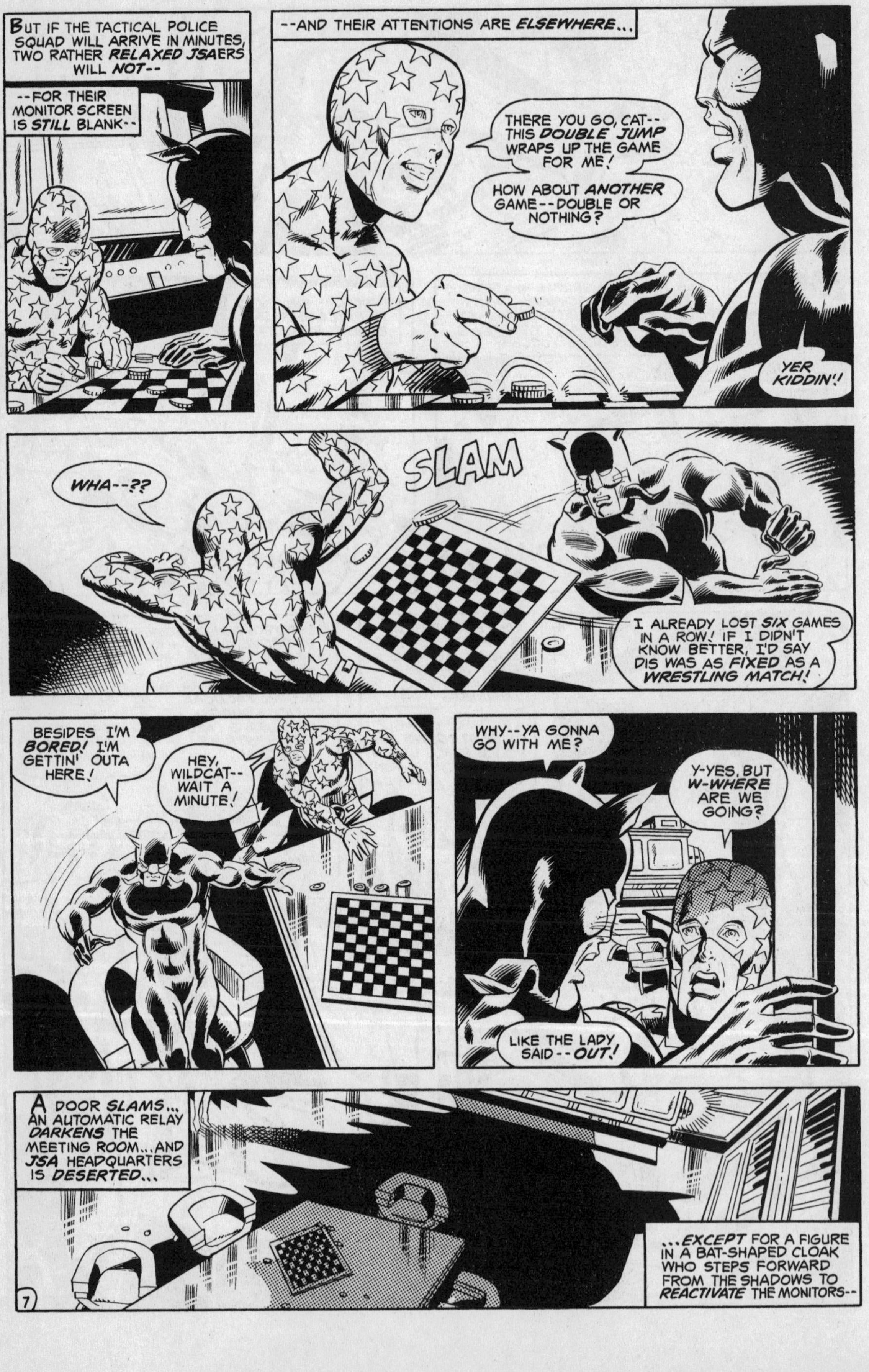
BUT IF THE TACTICAL POLICE SQUAD WILL ARRIVE IN MINUTES, TWO RATHER RELAXED JSAERS WILL NOT--
--FOR THEIR MONITOR SCREEN IS STILL BLANK--
--AND THEIR ATTENTIONS ARE ELSEWHERE...
THERE YOU GO, CAT-- THIS DOUBLE JUMP WRAPS UP THE GAME FOR ME!
HOW ABOUT ANOTHER GAME--DOUBLE OR NOTHING?
YER KIDDIN'!
WHA--??
SLAM
I ALREADY LOST SIX GAMES IN A ROW! IF I DIDN'T KNOW BETTER, I'D SAY DIS WAS AS FIXED AS A WRESTLING MATCH!
BESIDES I'M BORED! I'M GETTIN' OUTA HERE!
HEY, WILDCAT-- WAIT A MINUTE!
WHY--YA GONNA GO WITH ME?
Y-YES, BUT W-WHERE ARE WE GOING?
LIKE THE LADY SAID--OUT!
A DOOR SLAMS... AN AUTOMATIC RELAY DARKENS THE MEETING ROOM... AND JSA HEADQUARTERS IS DESERTED...
...EXCEPT FOR A FIGURE IN A BAT-SHAPED CLOAK WHO STEPS FORWARD FROM THE SHADOWS TO REACTIVATE THE MONITORS--
7

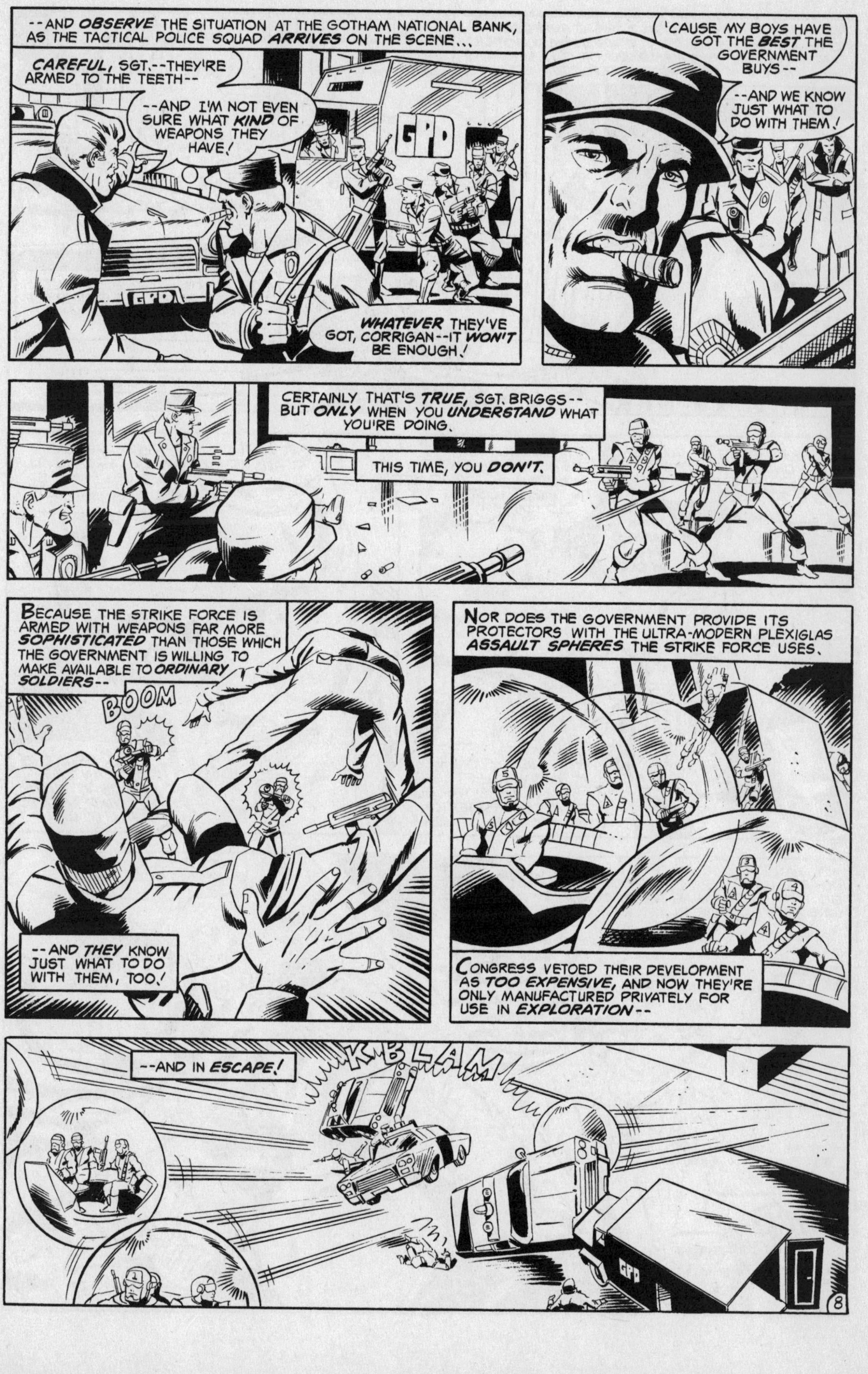
--AND OBSERVE THE SITUATION AT THE GOTHAM NATIONAL BANK, AS THE TACTICAL POLICE SQUAD ARRIVES ON THE SCENE...
CAREFUL, SGT.--THEY'RE ARMED TO THE TEETH--
--AND I'M NOT EVEN SURE WHAT KIND OF WEAPONS THEY HAVE!
GPD
WHATEVER THEY'VE GOT, CORRIGAN--IT WON'T BE ENOUGH!
'CAUSE MY BOYS HAVE GOT THE BEST THE GOVERNMENT BUYS--
--AND WE KNOW JUST WHAT TO DO WITH THEM!
CERTAINLY THAT'S TRUE, SGT. BRIGGS--BUT ONLY WHEN YOU UNDERSTAND WHAT YOU'RE DOING.
THIS TIME, YOU DON'T.
BECAUSE THE STRIKE FORCE IS ARMED WITH WEAPONS FAR MORE SOPHISTICATED THAN THOSE WHICH THE GOVERNMENT IS WILLING TO MAKE AVAILABLE TO ORDINARY SOLDIERS--
BOOM
--AND THEY KNOW JUST WHAT TO DO WITH THEM, TOO!
NOR DOES THE GOVERNMENT PROVIDE ITS PROTECTORS WITH THE ULTRA-MODERN PLEXIGLAS ASSAULT SPHERES THE STRIKE FORCE USES.
CONGRESS VETOED THEIR DEVELOPMENT AS TOO EXPENSIVE, AND NOW THEY'RE ONLY MANUFACTURED PRIVATELY FOR USE IN EXPLORATION--
--AND IN ESCAPE!
KBLAM
GPD
8

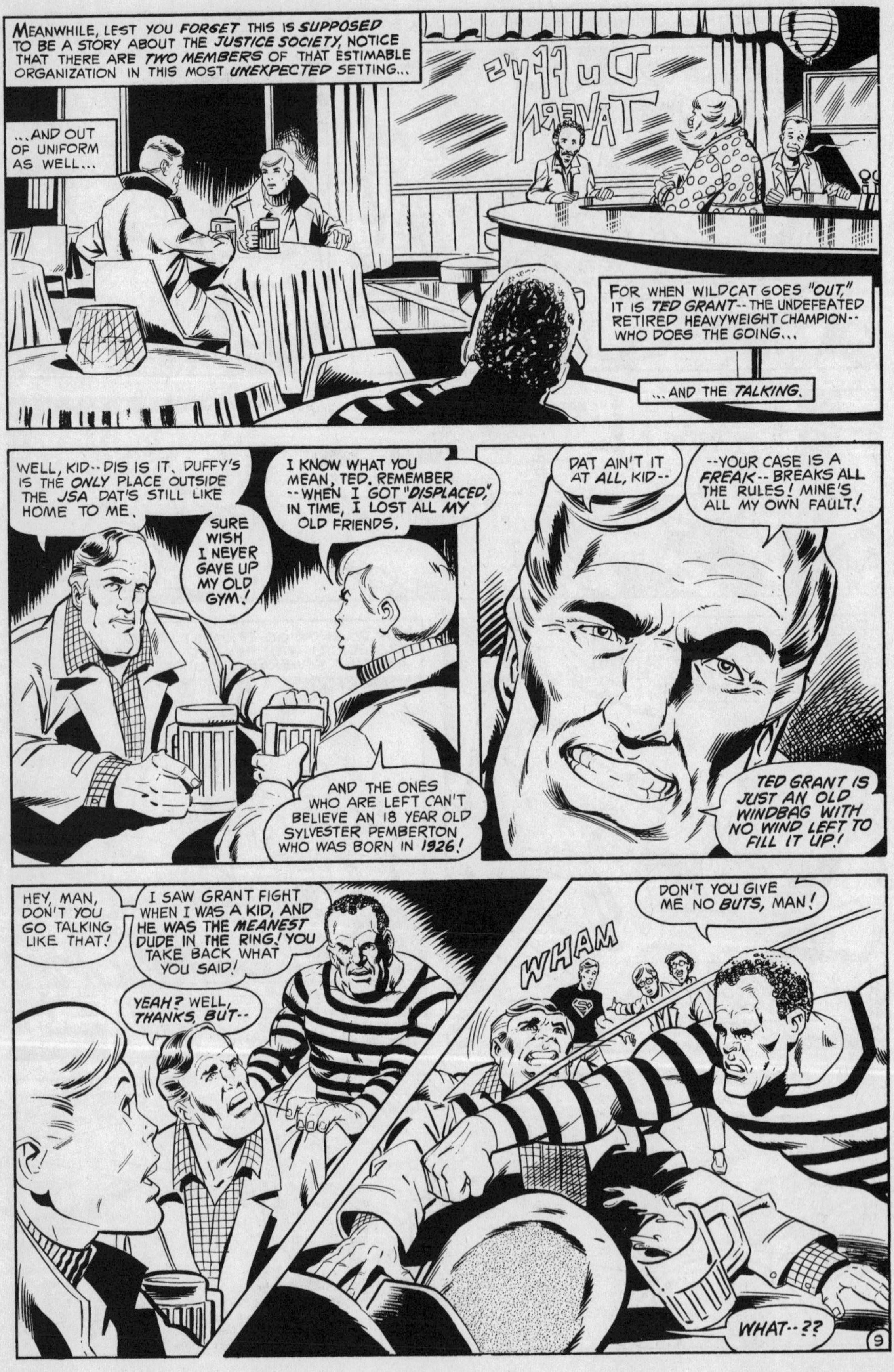
MEANWHILE, LEST YOU FORGET THIS IS SUPPOSED TO BE A STORY ABOUT THE JUSTICE SOCIETY, NOTICE THAT THERE ARE TWO MEMBERS OF THAT ESTIMABLE ORGANIZATION IN THIS MOST UNEXPECTED SETTING...
...AND OUT OF UNIFORM AS WELL...
FOR WHEN WILDCAT GOES "OUT," IT IS TED GRANT-- THE UNDEFEATED RETIRED HEAVYWEIGHT CHAMPION-- WHO DOES THE GOING...
...AND THE TALKING.
WELL, KID-- DIS IS IT. DUFFY'S IS THE ONLY PLACE OUTSIDE THE JSA DAT'S STILL LIKE HOME TO ME.
SURE WISH I NEVER GAVE UP MY OLD GYM!
I KNOW WHAT YOU MEAN, TED. REMEMBER --WHEN I GOT "DISPLACED," IN TIME, I LOST ALL MY OLD FRIENDS.
AND THE ONES WHO ARE LEFT CAN'T BELIEVE AN 18 YEAR OLD SYLVESTER PEMBERTON WHO WAS BORN IN 1926!
DAT AIN'T IT AT ALL, KID--
--YOUR CASE IS A FREAK-- BREAKS ALL THE RULES! MINE'S ALL MY OWN FAULT!
TED GRANT IS JUST AN OLD WINDBAG WITH NO WIND LEFT TO FILL IT UP!
HEY, MAN, DON'T YOU GO TALKING LIKE THAT!
I SAW GRANT FIGHT WHEN I WAS A KID, AND HE WAS THE MEANEST DUDE IN THE RING! YOU TAKE BACK WHAT YOU SAID!
YEAH? WELL, THANKS, BUT--
DON'T YOU GIVE ME NO BUTS, MAN!
WHAM
WHAT--??
9

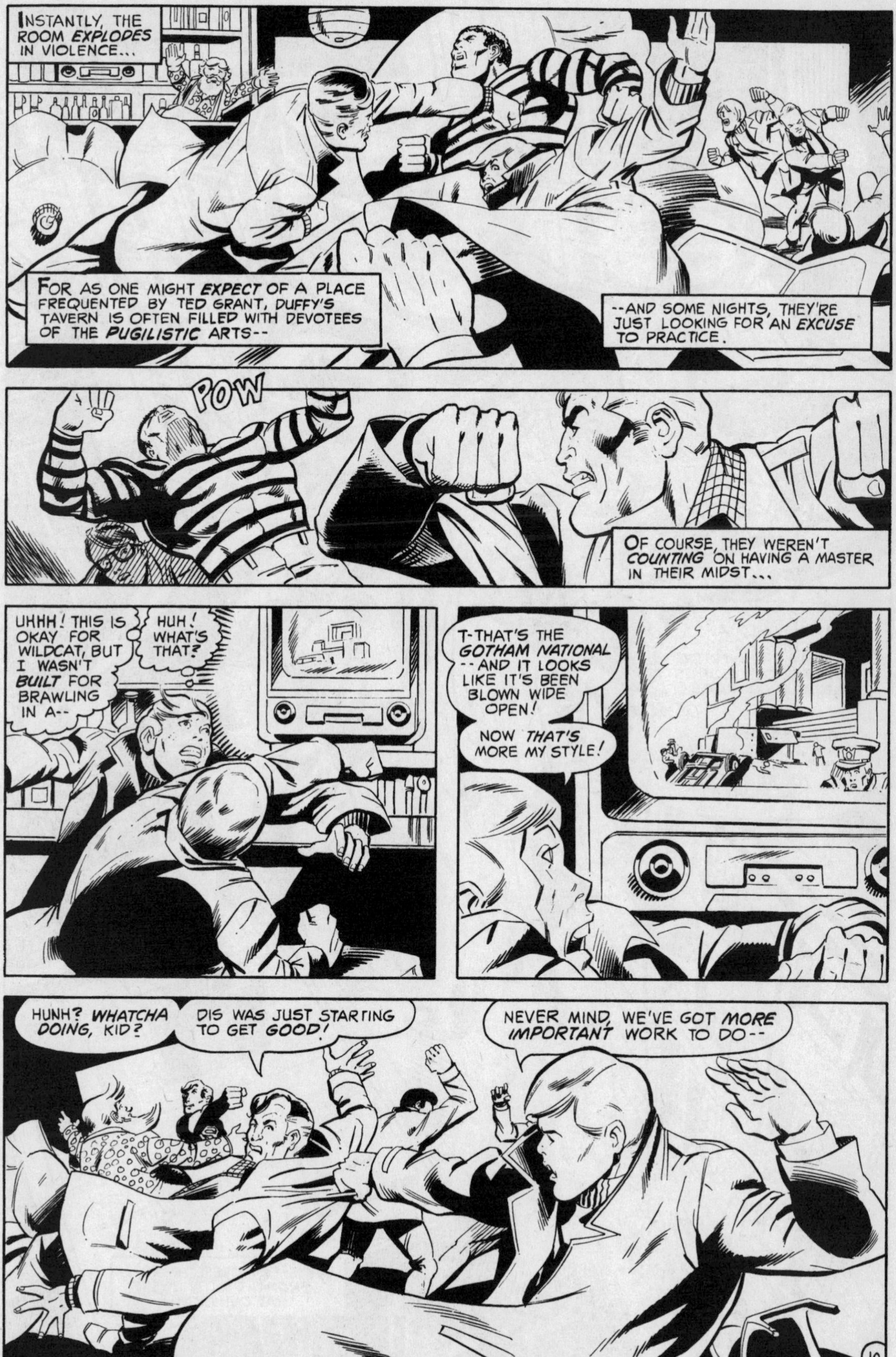
INSTANTLY, THE ROOM EXPLODES IN VIOLENCE...
FOR AS ONE MIGHT EXPECT OF A PLACE FREQUENTED BY TED GRANT, DUFFY'S TAVERN IS OFTEN FILLED WITH DEVOTEES OF THE PUGILISTIC ARTS--
--AND SOME NIGHTS, THEY'RE JUST LOOKING FOR AN EXCUSE TO PRACTICE.
POW
OF COURSE, THEY WEREN'T COUNTING ON HAVING A MASTER IN THEIR MIDST...
UHHH! THIS IS OKAY FOR WILDCAT, BUT I WASN'T BUILT FOR BRAWLING IN A--
HUH! WHAT'S THAT?
T-THAT'S THE GOTHAM NATIONAL --AND IT LOOKS LIKE IT'S BEEN BLOWN WIDE OPEN!
NOW THAT'S MORE MY STYLE!
HUNH? WHATCHA DOING, KID?
DIS WAS JUST STARTING TO GET GOOD!
NEVER MIND, WE'VE GOT MORE IMPORTANT WORK TO DO--
10

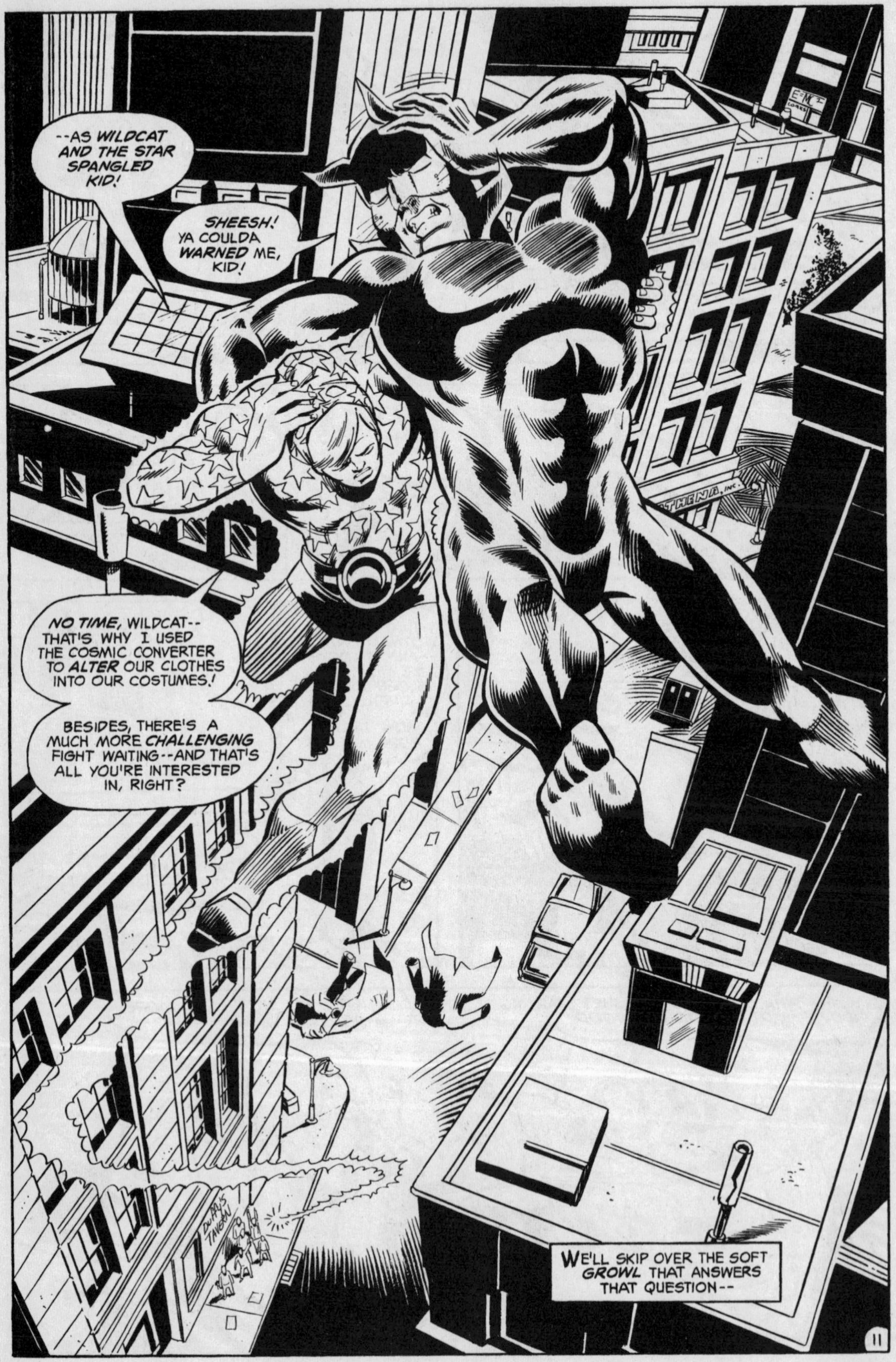
--AS WILDCAT AND THE STAR SPANGLED KID!
SHEESH! YA COULDA WARNED ME, KID!
NO TIME, WILDCAT-- THAT'S WHY I USED THE COSMIC CONVERTER TO ALTER OUR CLOTHES INTO OUR COSTUMES!
BESIDES, THERE'S A MUCH MORE CHALLENGING FIGHT WAITING--AND THAT'S ALL YOU'RE INTERESTED IN, RIGHT?
WE'LL SKIP OVER THE SOFT GROWL THAT ANSWERS THAT QUESTION--
11

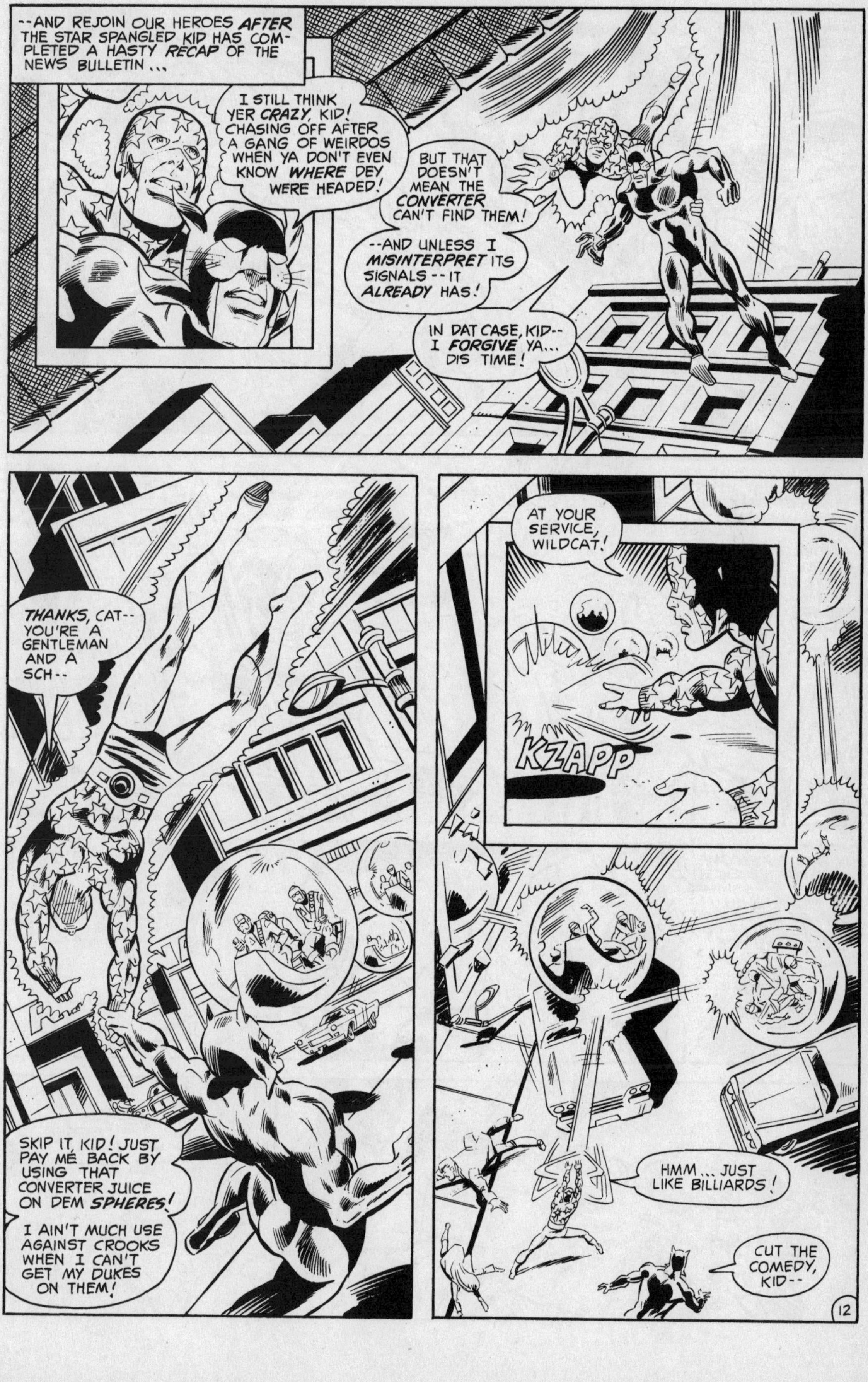
--AND REJOIN OUR HEROES AFTER THE STAR SPANGLED KID HAS COMPLETED A HASTY RECAP OF THE NEWS BULLETIN...
I STILL THINK YER CRAZY, KID! CHASING OFF AFTER A GANG OF WEIRDOS WHEN YA DON'T EVEN KNOW WHERE DEY WERE HEADED!
BUT THAT DOESN'T MEAN THE CONVERTER CAN'T FIND THEM!
--AND UNLESS I MISINTERPRET ITS SIGNALS--IT ALREADY HAS!
IN DAT CASE, KID-- I FORGIVE YA... DIS TIME!
THANKS, CAT-- YOU'RE A GENTLEMAN AND A SCH--
SKIP IT, KID! JUST PAY ME BACK BY USING THAT CONVERTER JUICE ON DEM SPHERES!
I AIN'T MUCH USE AGAINST CROOKS WHEN I CAN'T GET MY DUKES ON THEM!
AT YOUR SERVICE, WILDCAT!
KZAPP
HMM... JUST LIKE BILLIARDS!
CUT THE COMEDY, KID--
12

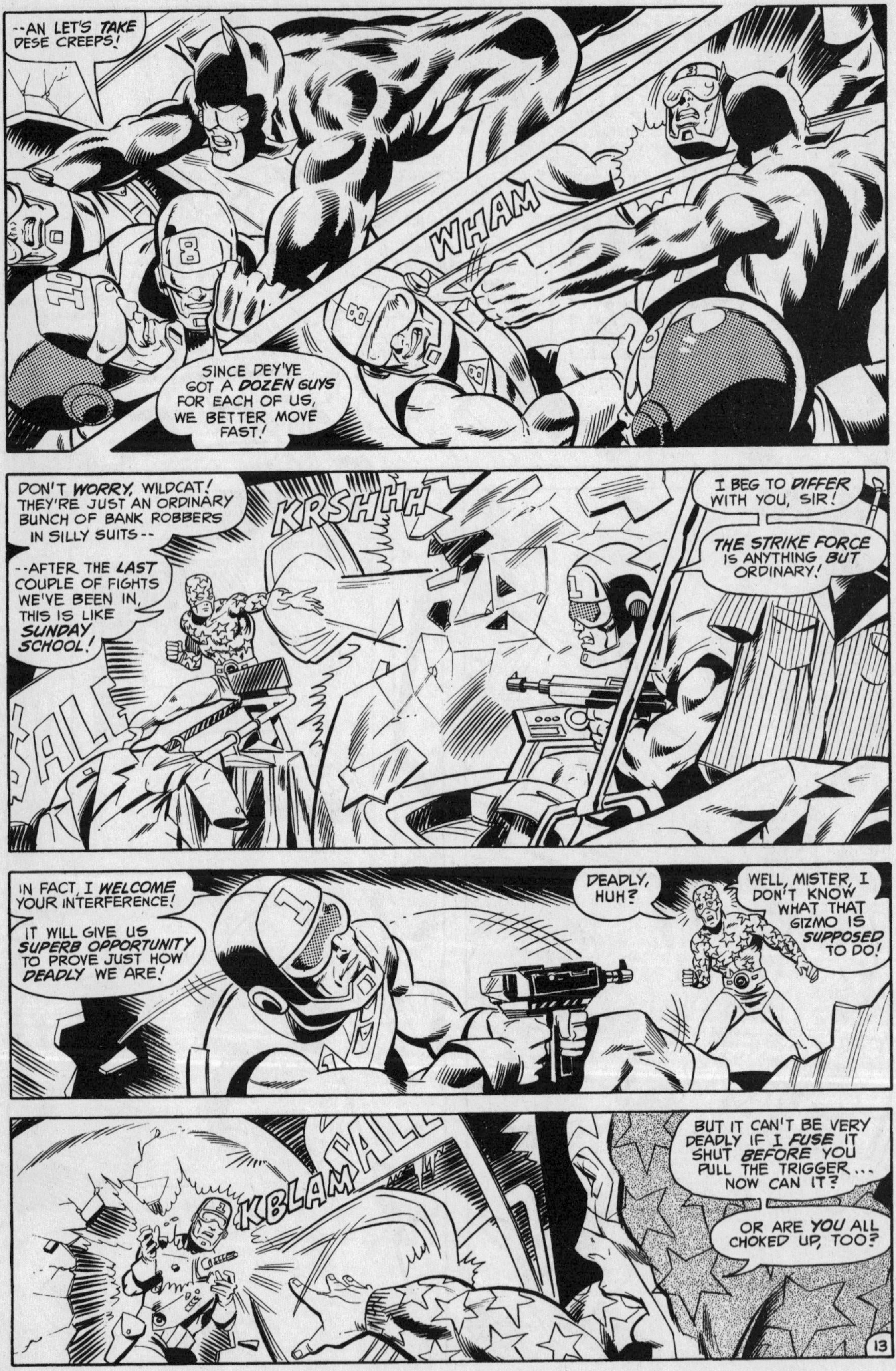
--AN LET'S TAKE DESE CREEPS!
WHAM
SINCE DEY'VE GOT A DOZEN GUYS FOR EACH OF US, WE BETTER MOVE FAST!
DON'T WORRY, WILDCAT! THEY'RE JUST AN ORDINARY BUNCH OF BANK ROBBERS IN SILLY SUITS--
--AFTER THE LAST COUPLE OF FIGHTS WE'VE BEEN IN, THIS IS LIKE SUNDAY SCHOOL!
KRSHHH
I BEG TO DIFFER WITH YOU, SIR!
THE STRIKE FORCE IS ANYTHING BUT ORDINARY!
IN FACT, I WELCOME YOUR INTERFERENCE!
IT WILL GIVE US SUPERB OPPORTUNITY TO PROVE JUST HOW DEADLY WE ARE!
DEADLY, HUH?
WELL, MISTER, I DON'T KNOW WHAT THAT GIZMO IS SUPPOSED TO DO!
BUT IT CAN'T BE VERY DEADLY IF I FUSE IT SHUT BEFORE YOU PULL THE TRIGGER... NOW CAN IT?
KBLAM
OR ARE YOU ALL CHOKED UP, TOO?
13

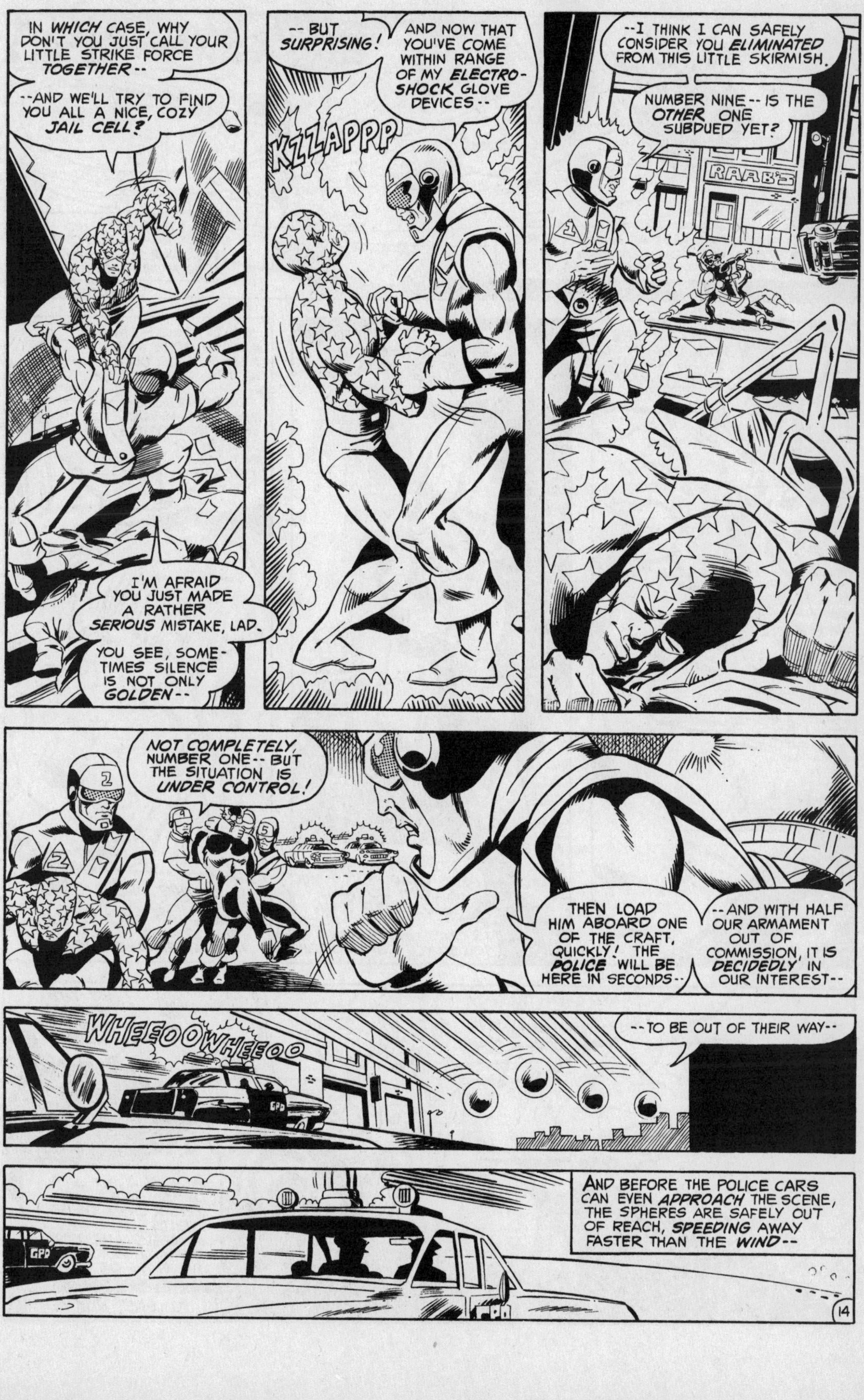
IN WHICH CASE, WHY DON'T YOU JUST CALL YOUR LITTLE STRIKE FORCE TOGETHER--
--AND WE'LL TRY TO FIND YOU ALL A NICE, COZY JAIL CELL?
I'M AFRAID YOU JUST MADE A RATHER SERIOUS MISTAKE, LAD.
YOU SEE, SOMETIMES SILENCE IS NOT ONLY GOLDEN--
-- BUT SURPRISING!
AND NOW THAT YOU'VE COME WITHIN RANGE OF MY ELECTRO-SHOCK GLOVE DEVICES--
KZZAPPP
--I THINK I CAN SAFELY CONSIDER YOU ELIMINATED FROM THIS LITTLE SKIRMISH.
NUMBER NINE-- IS THE OTHER ONE SUBDUED YET?
RAAB'S
NOT COMPLETELY, NUMBER ONE-- BUT THE SITUATION IS UNDER CONTROL!
THEN LOAD HIM ABOARD ONE OF THE CRAFT, QUICKLY! THE POLICE WILL BE HERE IN SECONDS--
--AND WITH HALF OUR ARMAMENT OUT OF COMMISSION, IT IS DECIDEDLY IN OUR INTEREST--
WHEEEOOWHEEOO
--TO BE OUT OF THEIR WAY--
GPD
AND BEFORE THE POLICE CARS CAN EVEN APPROACH THE SCENE, THE SPHERES ARE SAFELY OUT OF REACH, SPEEDING AWAY FASTER THAN THE WIND--
GPD
14

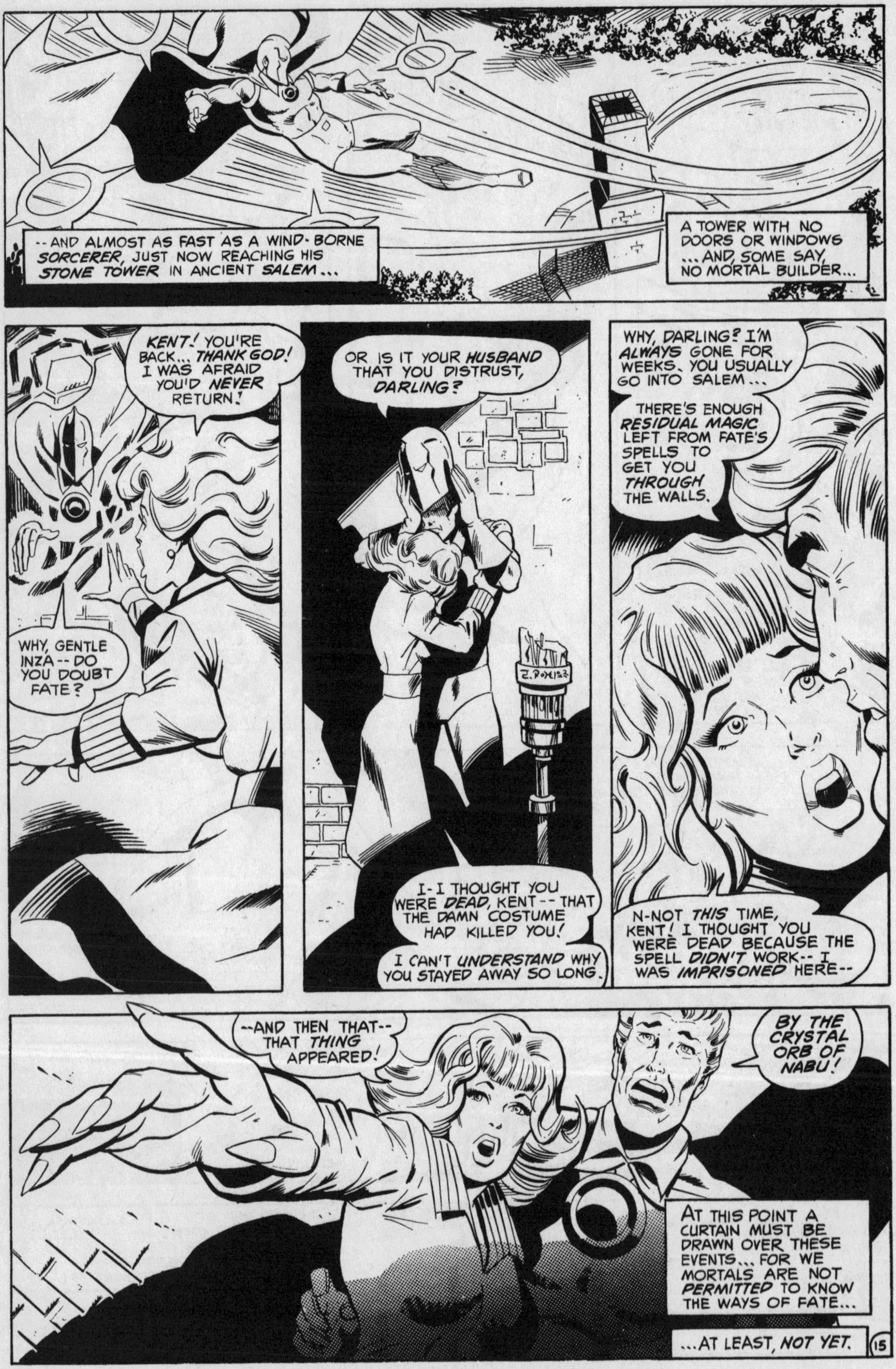
--AND ALMOST AS FAST AS A WIND-BORNE SORCERER, JUST NOW REACHING HIS STONE TOWER IN ANCIENT SALEM...
A TOWER WITH NO DOORS OR WINDOWS ...AND, SOME SAY, NO MORTAL BUILDER...
KENT! YOU'RE BACK... THANK GOD! I WAS AFRAID YOU'D NEVER RETURN!
WHY, GENTLE INZA -- DO YOU DOUBT FATE?
OR IS IT YOUR HUSBAND THAT YOU DISTRUST, DARLING?
I-I THOUGHT YOU WERE DEAD, KENT -- THAT THE DAMN COSTUME HAD KILLED YOU!
I CAN'T UNDERSTAND WHY YOU STAYED AWAY SO LONG.
WHY, DARLING? I'M ALWAYS GONE FOR WEEKS. YOU USUALLY GO INTO SALEM...
THERE'S ENOUGH RESIDUAL MAGIC LEFT FROM FATE'S SPELLS TO GET YOU THROUGH THE WALLS.
N-NOT THIS TIME, KENT! I THOUGHT YOU WERE DEAD BECAUSE THE SPELL DIDN'T WORK-- I WAS IMPRISONED HERE--
--AND THEN THAT-- THAT THING APPEARED!
BY THE CRYSTAL ORB OF NABU!
AT THIS POINT A CURTAIN MUST BE DRAWN OVER THESE EVENTS... FOR WE MORTALS ARE NOT PERMITTED TO KNOW THE WAYS OF FATE...
...AT LEAST, NOT YET.
15

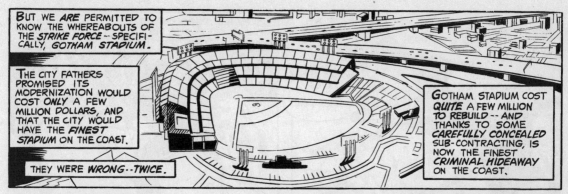

BUT WE *ARE* PERMITTED TO KNOW THE WHEREABOUTS OF THE *STRIKE FORCE* -- SPECIFI- CALLY, *GOTHAM STADIUM*.

THE CITY FATHERS PROMISED ITS MODERNIZATION WOULD COST *ONLY* A FEW MILLION DOLLARS, AND THAT THE CITY WOULD HAVE THE *FINEST STADIUM* ON THE COAST.

THEY WERE *WRONG*--*TWICE.*

GOTHAM STADIUM COST *QUITE* A FEW MILLION TO REBUILD -- AND THANKS TO SOME *CAREFULLY CONCEALED* SUB-CONTRACTING, IS NOW THE FINEST *CRIMINAL HIDEAWAY* ON THE COAST.

THE STRIKE FORCE *ONLY* BUYS THE BEST.

HEY, CAT-- *WAKE UP!*

UNHH.

WE'RE IN *LUCK*, WILDCAT-- THEY FORGOT TO TAKE MY CONVERTER BELT AWAY.

WHOOPIE! GOT ANY *ASPIRIN* IN IT, KID?

I'VE GOT A *BETTER* CURE FOR THAT HEADACHE, WILDCAT--

WHAT--??

--A WAY *OUT* OF HERE!

W-WHO ARE YA, LADY? AND WHAT THE HECK ARE YA *DOING* HERE--

--WHERE- EVER HERE IS!

I *TRACKED* YOU, WILDCAT... THAT'S WHY I CALL MYSELF *THE HUNTRESS!*

AND IF YOU'LL JUST *BE QUIET*, WE CAN GET OUT OF HERE *WITHOUT* THE STRIKE FORCE *NOTICING!*

WHAT'S THE *BIG RUSH*, SISTER?

ARE YA *AFRAID* OF DESE STRIKE FORCE BUMS?

--OR ARE YA JUST *LEADING* US INTO A *TRAP* DAT DEY HAVE SET FOR US?

16

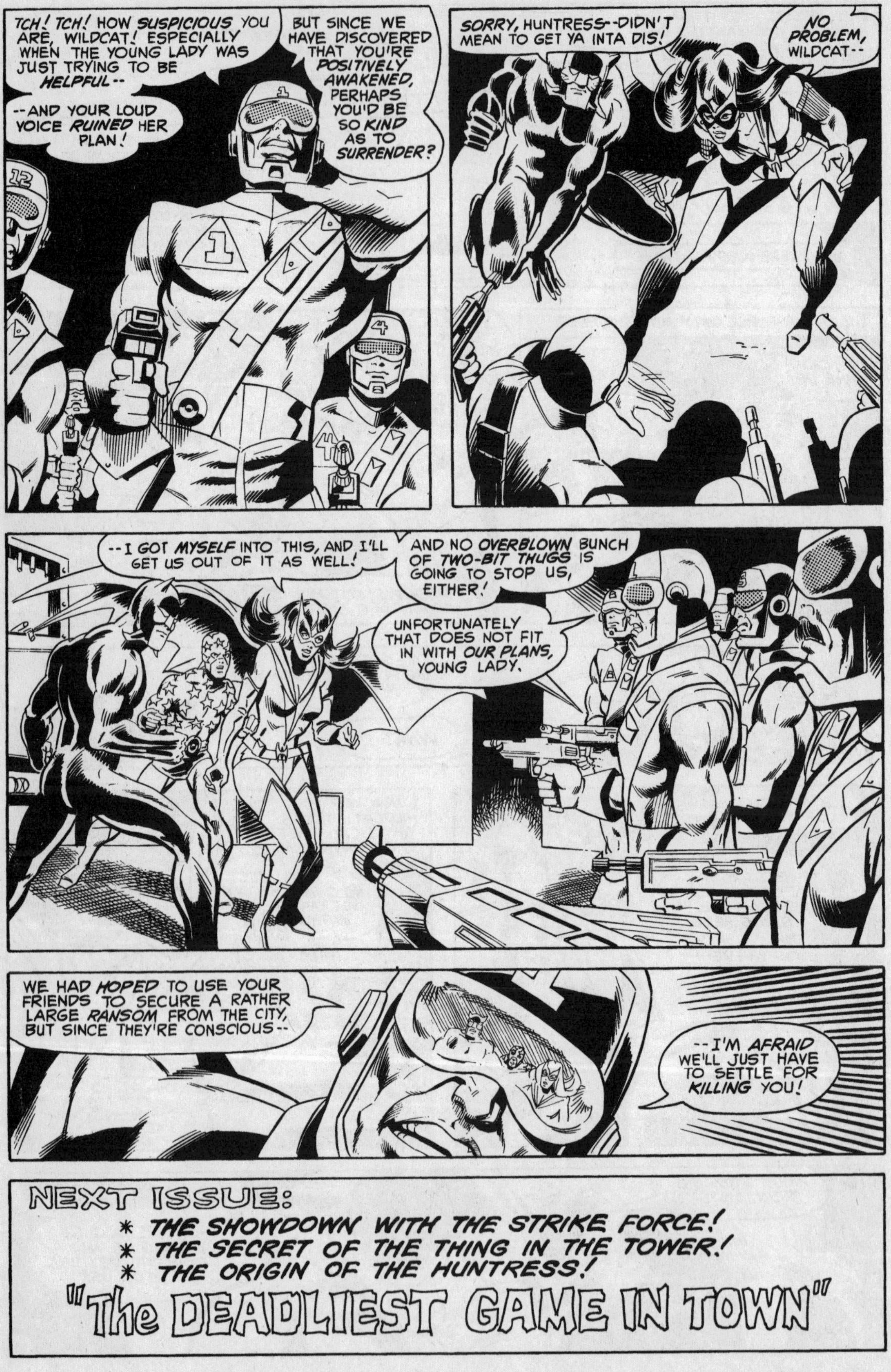
TCH! TCH! HOW SUSPICIOUS YOU ARE, WILDCAT! ESPECIALLY WHEN THE YOUNG LADY WAS JUST TRYING TO BE HELPFUL--
--AND YOUR LOUD VOICE RUINED HER PLAN!
BUT SINCE WE HAVE DISCOVERED THAT YOU'RE POSITIVELY AWAKENED, PERHAPS YOU'D BE SO KIND AS TO SURRENDER?
SORRY, HUNTRESS--DIDN'T MEAN TO GET YA INTA DIS!
NO PROBLEM, WILDCAT--
--I GOT MYSELF INTO THIS, AND I'LL GET US OUT OF IT AS WELL!
AND NO OVERBLOWN BUNCH OF TWO-BIT THUGS IS GOING TO STOP US, EITHER!
UNFORTUNATELY THAT DOES NOT FIT IN WITH OUR PLANS, YOUNG LADY.
WE HAD HOPED TO USE YOUR FRIENDS TO SECURE A RATHER LARGE RANSOM FROM THE CITY, BUT SINCE THEY'RE CONSCIOUS--
--I'M AFRAID WE'LL JUST HAVE TO SETTLE FOR KILLING YOU!

NEXT ISSUE:

* THE SHOWDOWN WITH THE STRIKE FORCE!
* THE SECRET OF THE THING IN THE TOWER!
* THE ORIGIN OF THE HUNTRESS!

"The DEADLIEST GAME IN TOWN"

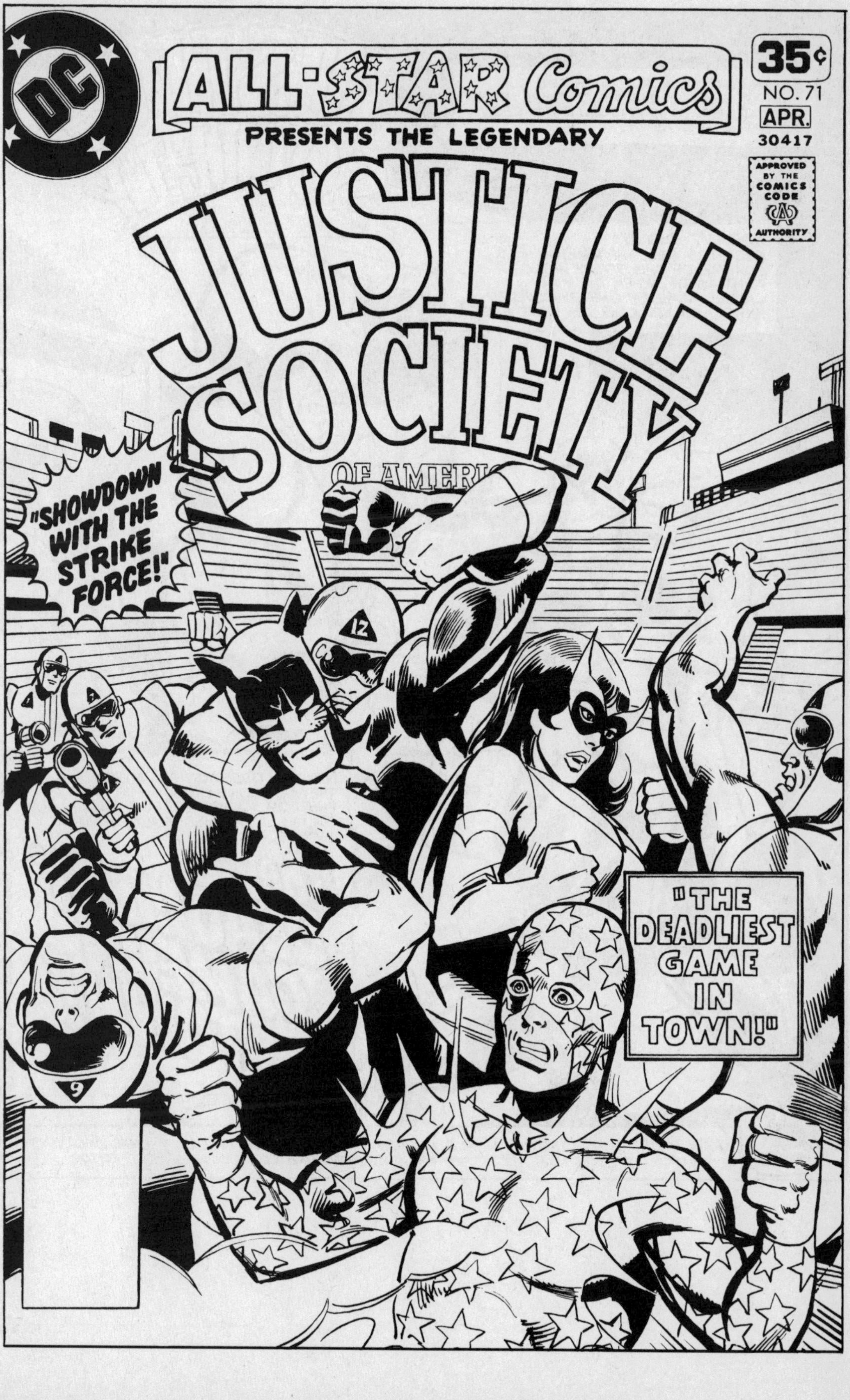
DC
ALL-STAR Comics
PRESENTS THE LEGENDARY
JUSTICE SOCIETY
OF AMERICA
35¢
NO. 71
APR.
30417
APPROVED BY THE COMICS CODE AUTHORITY
"SHOWDOWN WITH THE STRIKE FORCE!"
"THE DEADLIEST GAME IN TOWN!"
12
9

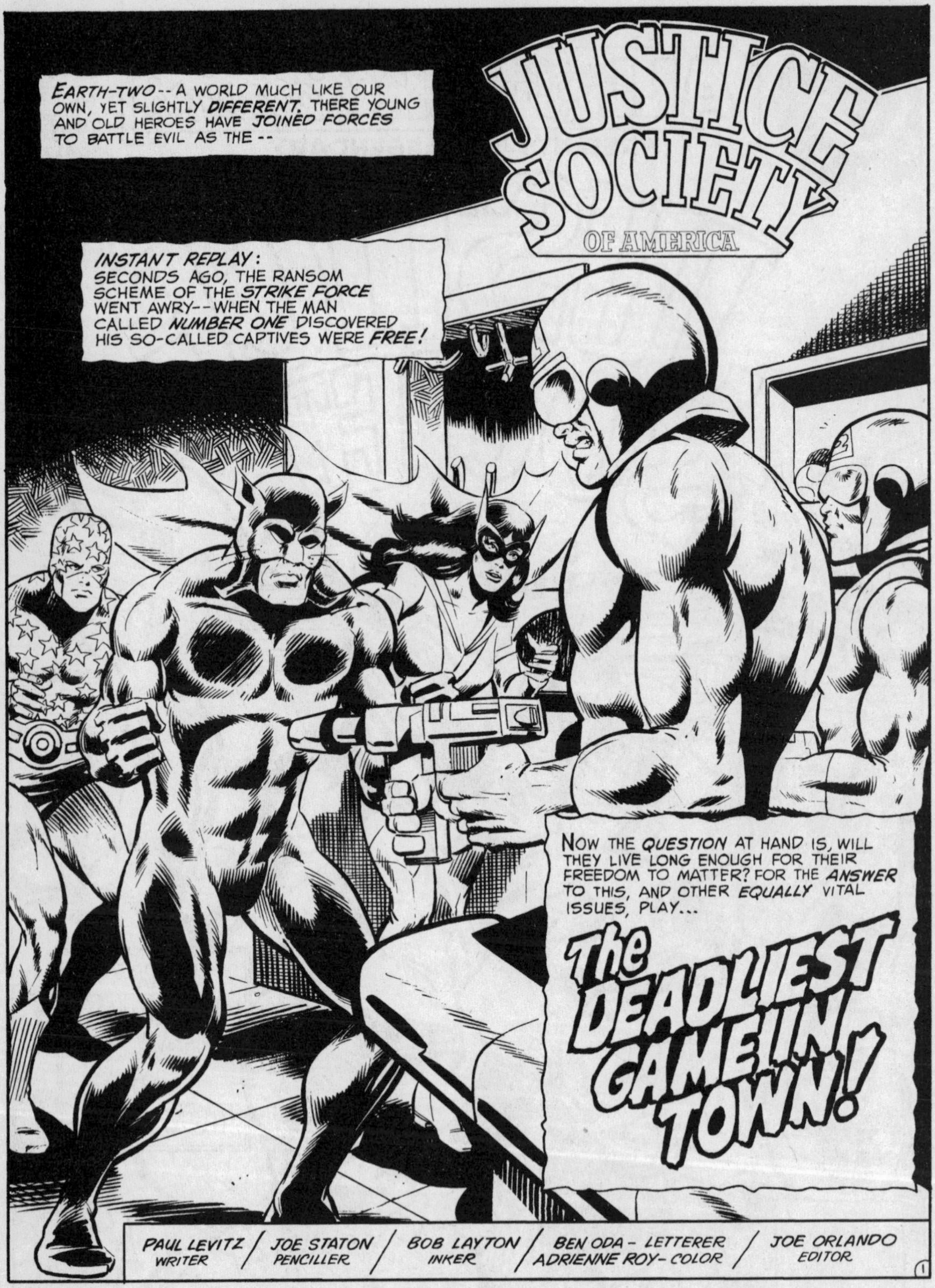
EARTH-TWO-- A WORLD MUCH LIKE OUR OWN, YET SLIGHTLY DIFFERENT. THERE YOUNG AND OLD HEROES HAVE JOINED FORCES TO BATTLE EVIL AS THE --
JUSTICE SOCIETY OF AMERICA
INSTANT REPLAY: SECONDS AGO, THE RANSOM SCHEME OF THE STRIKE FORCE WENT AWRY-- WHEN THE MAN CALLED NUMBER ONE DISCOVERED HIS SO-CALLED CAPTIVES WERE FREE!
NOW THE QUESTION AT HAND IS, WILL THEY LIVE LONG ENOUGH FOR THEIR FREEDOM TO MATTER? FOR THE ANSWER TO THIS, AND OTHER EQUALLY VITAL ISSUES, PLAY...
The DEADLIEST GAME IN TOWN!
PAUL LEVITZ WRITER / JOE STATON PENCILLER / BOB LAYTON INKER / BEN ODA - LETTERER ADRIENNE ROY - COLOR / JOE ORLANDO EDITOR
1

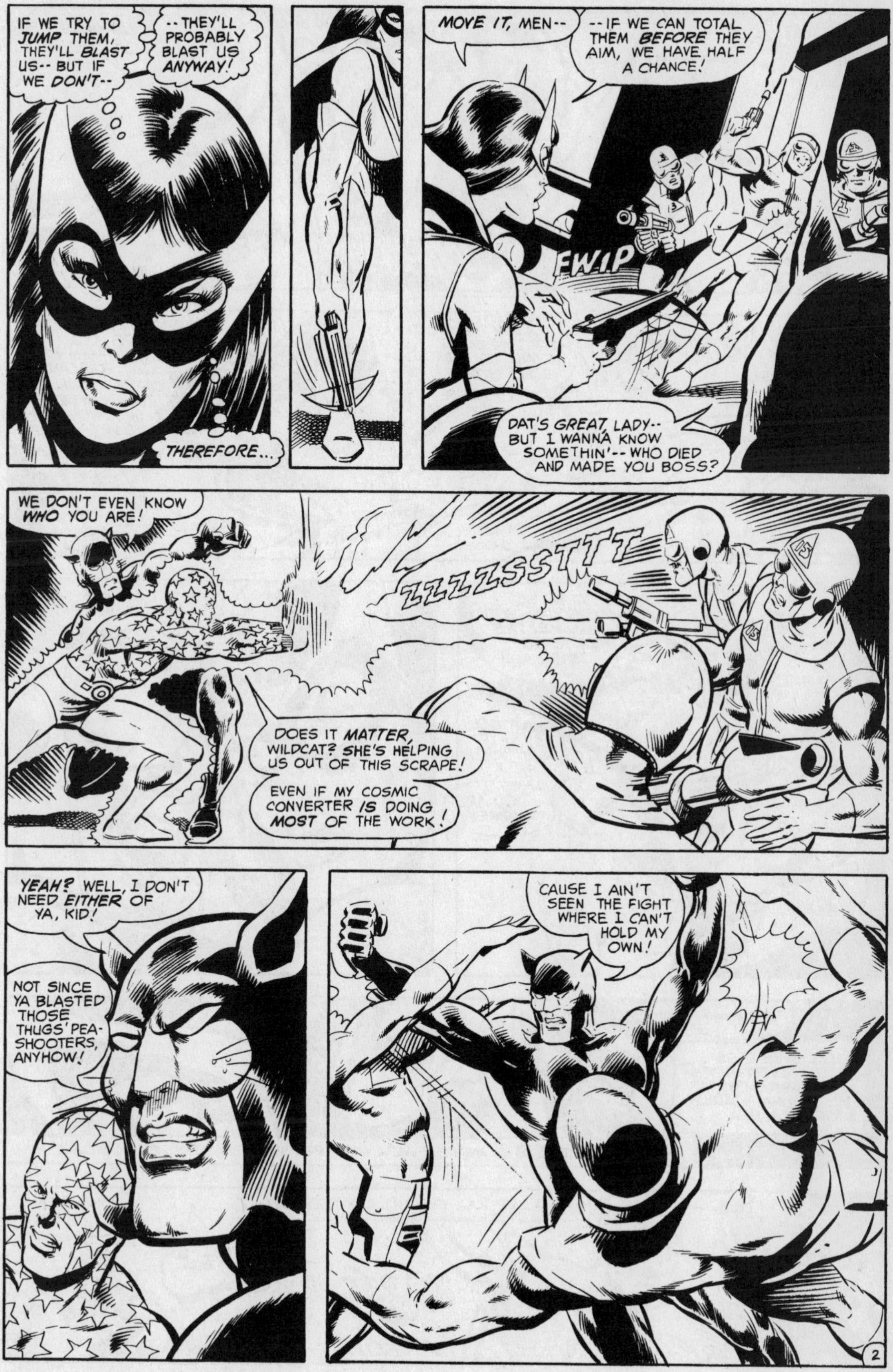
IF WE TRY TO JUMP THEM, THEY'LL BLAST US-- BUT IF WE DON'T--
--THEY'LL PROBABLY BLAST US ANYWAY!
THEREFORE...
MOVE IT, MEN--
--IF WE CAN TOTAL THEM BEFORE THEY AIM, WE HAVE HALF A CHANCE!
FWIP
DAT'S GREAT, LADY-- BUT I WANNA KNOW SOMETHIN'-- WHO DIED AND MADE YOU BOSS?
WE DON'T EVEN KNOW WHO YOU ARE!
ZZZZSSTTT
DOES IT MATTER, WILDCAT? SHE'S HELPING US OUT OF THIS SCRAPE!
EVEN IF MY COSMIC CONVERTER IS DOING MOST OF THE WORK!
YEAH? WELL, I DON'T NEED EITHER OF YA, KID!
NOT SINCE YA BLASTED THOSE THUGS' PEA-SHOOTERS, ANYHOW!
CAUSE I AIN'T SEEN THE FIGHT WHERE I CAN'T HOLD MY OWN!
2

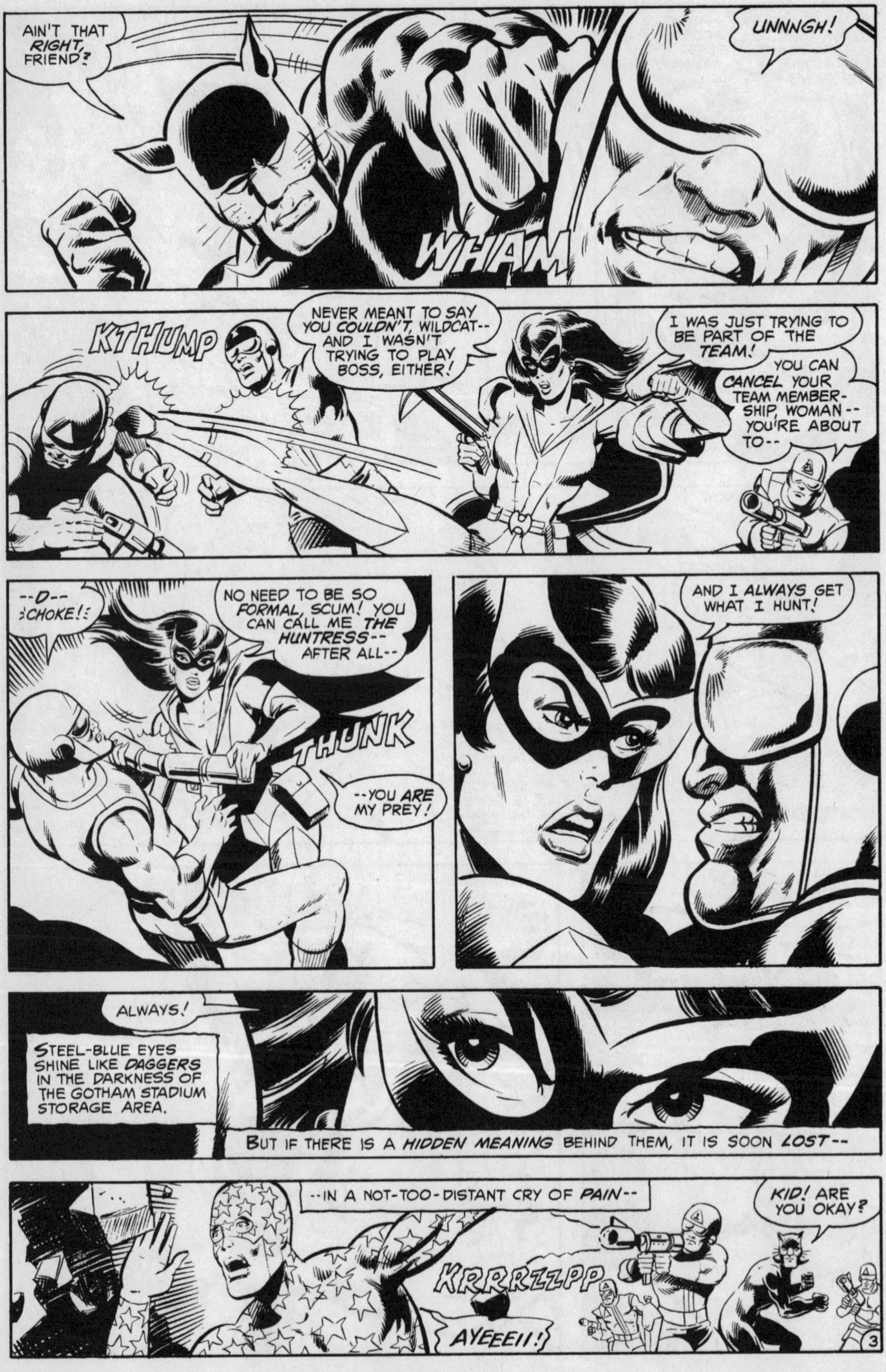
AIN'T THAT RIGHT, FRIEND?
UNNNGH!
WHAM
KTHUMP
NEVER MEANT TO SAY YOU COULDN'T, WILDCAT-- AND I WASN'T TRYING TO PLAY BOSS, EITHER!
I WAS JUST TRYING TO BE PART OF THE TEAM!
YOU CAN CANCEL YOUR TEAM MEMBERSHIP, WOMAN -- YOU'RE ABOUT TO--
--D-- CHOKE!
NO NEED TO BE SO FORMAL, SCUM! YOU CAN CALL ME THE HUNTRESS-- AFTER ALL--
THUNK
--YOU ARE MY PREY!
AND I ALWAYS GET WHAT I HUNT!
ALWAYS!
STEEL-BLUE EYES SHINE LIKE DAGGERS IN THE DARKNESS OF THE GOTHAM STADIUM STORAGE AREA.
BUT IF THERE IS A HIDDEN MEANING BEHIND THEM, IT IS SOON LOST--
--IN A NOT-TOO-DISTANT CRY OF PAIN--
KID! ARE YOU OKAY?
KRRRZZPP
AYEEEII!
3

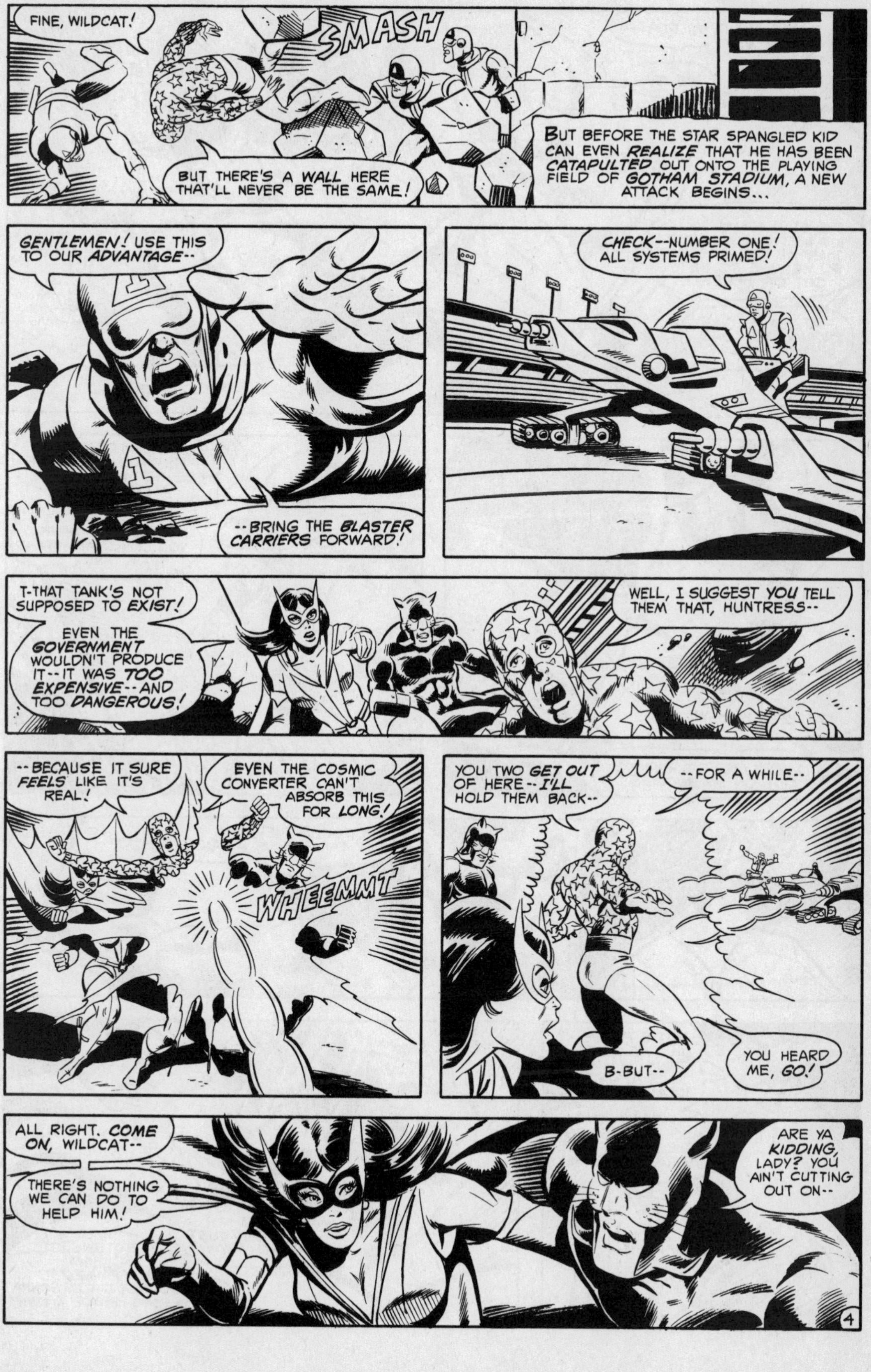
FINE, WILDCAT!
SMASH
BUT THERE'S A WALL HERE THAT'LL NEVER BE THE SAME!
BUT BEFORE THE STAR SPANGLED KID CAN EVEN REALIZE THAT HE HAS BEEN CATAPULTED OUT ONTO THE PLAYING FIELD OF GOTHAM STADIUM, A NEW ATTACK BEGINS...
GENTLEMEN! USE THIS TO OUR ADVANTAGE--
--BRING THE BLASTER CARRIERS FORWARD!
CHECK--NUMBER ONE! ALL SYSTEMS PRIMED!
T-THAT TANK'S NOT SUPPOSED TO EXIST!
EVEN THE GOVERNMENT WOULDN'T PRODUCE IT--IT WAS TOO EXPENSIVE--AND TOO DANGEROUS!
WELL, I SUGGEST YOU TELL THEM THAT, HUNTRESS--
--BECAUSE IT SURE FEELS LIKE IT'S REAL!
EVEN THE COSMIC CONVERTER CAN'T ABSORB THIS FOR LONG!
WHEEMMT
YOU TWO GET OUT OF HERE--I'LL HOLD THEM BACK--
--FOR A WHILE--
B-BUT--
YOU HEARD ME, GO!
ALL RIGHT. COME ON, WILDCAT--
THERE'S NOTHING WE CAN DO TO HELP HIM!
ARE YA KIDDING, LADY? YOU AIN'T CUTTING OUT ON--
4

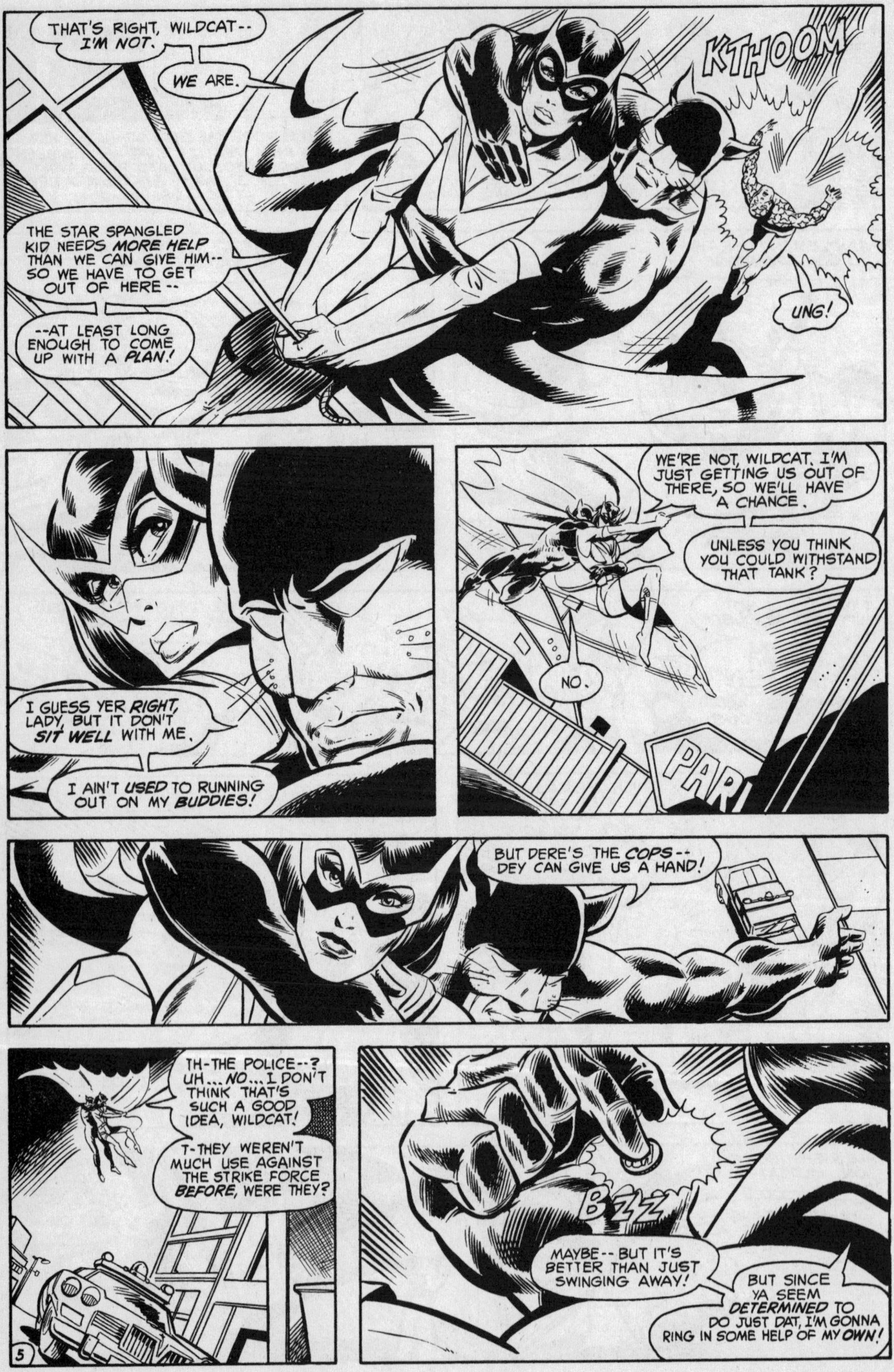
THAT'S RIGHT, WILDCAT-- I'M NOT.
WE ARE.
KTHOOM
THE STAR SPANGLED KID NEEDS MORE HELP THAN WE CAN GIVE HIM-- SO WE HAVE TO GET OUT OF HERE--
--AT LEAST LONG ENOUGH TO COME UP WITH A PLAN!
UNG!
I GUESS YER RIGHT, LADY, BUT IT DON'T SIT WELL WITH ME.
I AIN'T USED TO RUNNING OUT ON MY BUDDIES!
WE'RE NOT, WILDCAT. I'M JUST GETTING US OUT OF THERE, SO WE'LL HAVE A CHANCE.
UNLESS YOU THINK YOU COULD WITHSTAND THAT TANK?
NO.
PAR
BUT DERE'S THE COPS-- DEY CAN GIVE US A HAND!
TH-THE POLICE--? UH... NO... I DON'T THINK THAT'S SUCH A GOOD IDEA, WILDCAT!
T-THEY WEREN'T MUCH USE AGAINST THE STRIKE FORCE BEFORE, WERE THEY?
5
BZZ
MAYBE-- BUT IT'S BETTER THAN JUST SWINGING AWAY!
BUT SINCE YA SEEM DETERMINED TO DO JUST DAT, I'M GONNA RING IN SOME HELP OF MY OWN!

BUT UNFORTUNATELY, HELP IS DESTINED *NOT* TO ARRIVE-- AT LEAST NOT IN RESPONSE TO THAT SIGNAL.

FOR AFTER THE LAST *GENERAL* MEETING, THE SIGNALLERS WERE *RESET*-- AND NOW ONLY THE *ACTIVE* MEMBERS' DEVICES ARE ON AUTOMATIC.

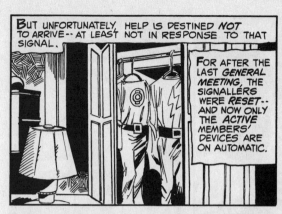

AND BUZZERS SOUNDING IN *EMPTY* CLOSETS RARELY BRING A RESPONSE.

VERY RARELY.

ESPECIALLY WHEN THE MEN WHO THE COSTUMES FIT ARE *ELSEWHERE* -- AT THE KEYSTONE RESEARCH LABS.

SO YOU SEE, ALAN, THIS IS THE *ADVANCED ANALYSIS SECTION* --

--MOSTLY DEVOTED TO *GOVERNMENT CONTRACTS*, YOU UNDERSTAND!

I GUESS I'LL GET THE HANG OF IT *EVENTUALLY*, JAY. RIGHT NOW IT ALL JUST SEEMS TO *BLEND TOGETHER.*

WELL, YOU'LL BE WORKING IN THE *ENGINEERING* LAB ANYWAY, SO THIS ISN'T TOO IMPORTANT.

WORKING, MAN, THAT SOUNDS *NICE!*

YOU KNOW, JAY, I THINK YOU SAVED MY LIFE BY GIVING ME THIS JOB.

FOR THE FIRST TIME IN *MONTHS*, I FEEL LIKE A HUMAN BEING AGAIN -- AND NOT JUST A PART OF THE POWER RING!

AND IN WITCH-HAUNTED *SALEM,* THE ALARM IS HEARD...

...BUT ONLY BY EARS THAT *KNOW* THEY WILL *NOT LISTEN...*

YES... PERHAPS THAT *IS* THE ANSWER ...

KENT, WHAT ARE YOU TALKING ABOUT?

AND WHY AREN'T YOU *DOING* SOMETHING ABOUT THAT-- THAT THING!

6

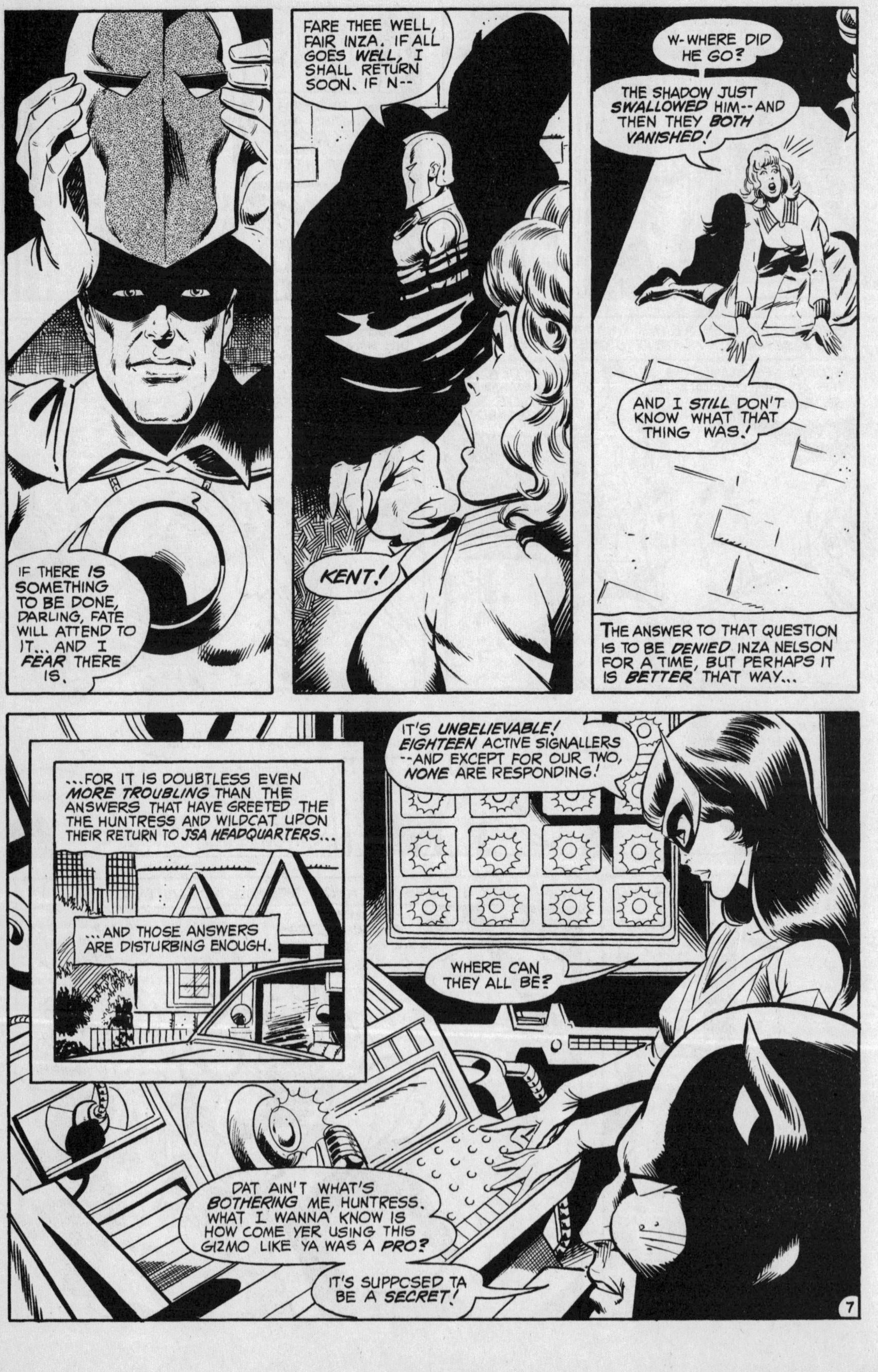
IF THERE IS SOMETHING TO BE DONE, DARLING, FATE WILL ATTEND TO IT... AND I FEAR THERE IS.
FARE THEE WELL, FAIR INZA. IF ALL GOES WELL, I SHALL RETURN SOON. IF N--
KENT!
W-WHERE DID HE GO?
THE SHADOW JUST SWALLOWED HIM--AND THEN THEY BOTH VANISHED!
AND I STILL DON'T KNOW WHAT THAT THING WAS!
THE ANSWER TO THAT QUESTION IS TO BE DENIED INZA NELSON FOR A TIME, BUT PERHAPS IT IS BETTER THAT WAY...
...FOR IT IS DOUBTLESS EVEN MORE TROUBLING THAN THE ANSWERS THAT HAVE GREETED THE THE HUNTRESS AND WILDCAT UPON THEIR RETURN TO JSA HEADQUARTERS...
...AND THOSE ANSWERS ARE DISTURBING ENOUGH.
IT'S UNBELIEVABLE! EIGHTEEN ACTIVE SIGNALLERS --AND EXCEPT FOR OUR TWO, NONE ARE RESPONDING!
WHERE CAN THEY ALL BE?
DAT AIN'T WHAT'S BOTHERING ME, HUNTRESS. WHAT I WANNA KNOW IS HOW COME YER USING THIS GIZMO LIKE YA WAS A PRO?
IT'S SUPPOSED TA BE A SECRET!
7

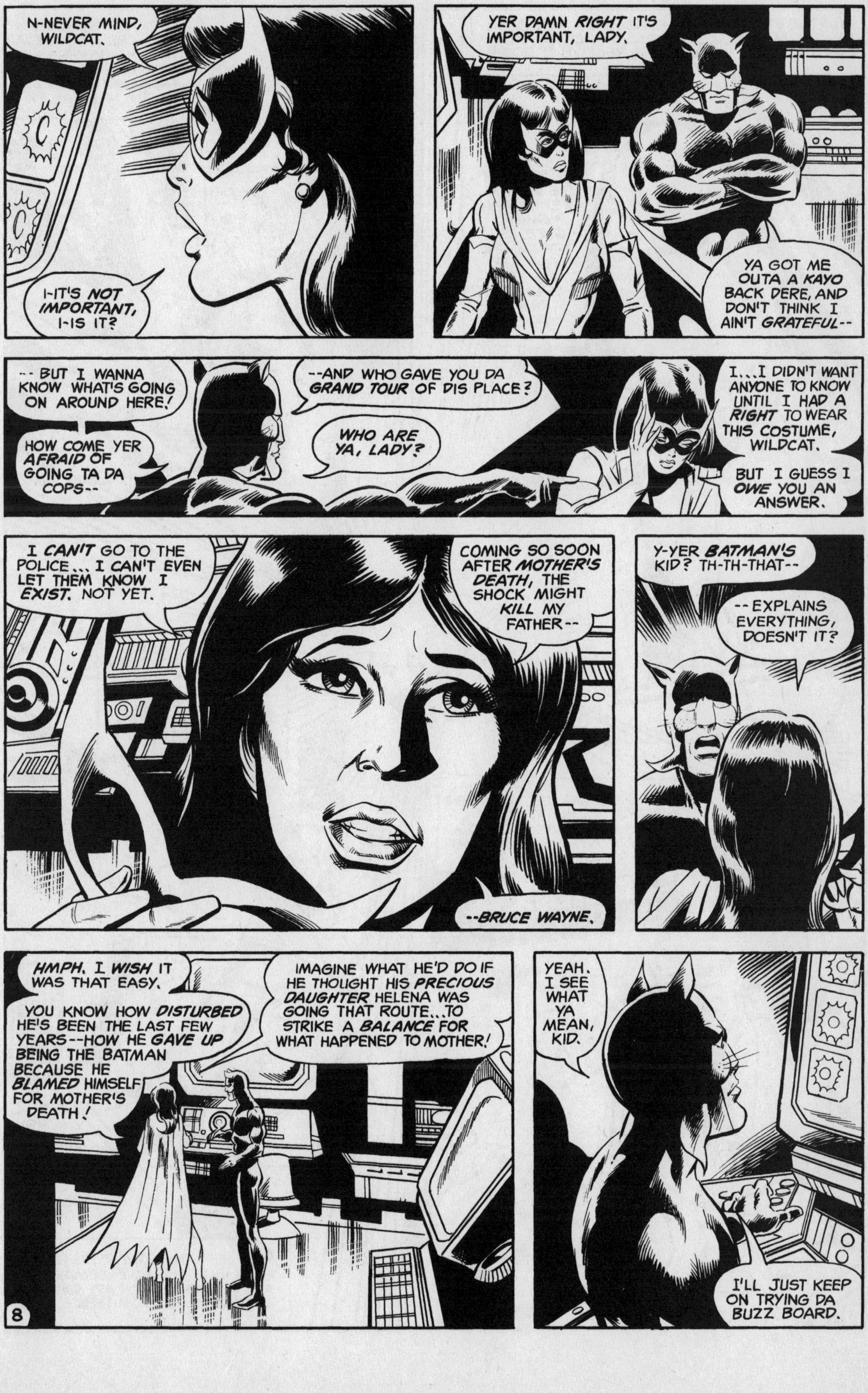
N-NEVER MIND, WILDCAT.
I-IT'S NOT IMPORTANT, I-IS IT?
YER DAMN RIGHT IT'S IMPORTANT, LADY.
YA GOT ME OUTA A KAYO BACK DERE, AND DON'T THINK I AIN'T GRATEFUL--
-- BUT I WANNA KNOW WHAT'S GOING ON AROUND HERE!
HOW COME YER AFRAID OF GOING TA DA COPS--
--AND WHO GAVE YOU DA GRAND TOUR OF DIS PLACE?
WHO ARE YA, LADY?
I...I DIDN'T WANT ANYONE TO KNOW UNTIL I HAD A RIGHT TO WEAR THIS COSTUME, WILDCAT.
BUT I GUESS I OWE YOU AN ANSWER.
I CAN'T GO TO THE POLICE... I CAN'T EVEN LET THEM KNOW I EXIST. NOT YET.
COMING SO SOON AFTER MOTHER'S DEATH, THE SHOCK MIGHT KILL MY FATHER--
--BRUCE WAYNE.
Y-YER BATMAN'S KID? TH-TH-THAT--
--EXPLAINS EVERYTHING, DOESN'T IT?
HMPH. I WISH IT WAS THAT EASY.
YOU KNOW HOW DISTURBED HE'S BEEN THE LAST FEW YEARS--HOW HE GAVE UP BEING THE BATMAN BECAUSE HE BLAMED HIMSELF FOR MOTHER'S DEATH!
IMAGINE WHAT HE'D DO IF HE THOUGHT HIS PRECIOUS DAUGHTER HELENA WAS GOING THAT ROUTE...TO STRIKE A BALANCE FOR WHAT HAPPENED TO MOTHER!
8
YEAH. I SEE WHAT YA MEAN, KID.
I'LL JUST KEEP ON TRYING DA BUZZ BOARD.

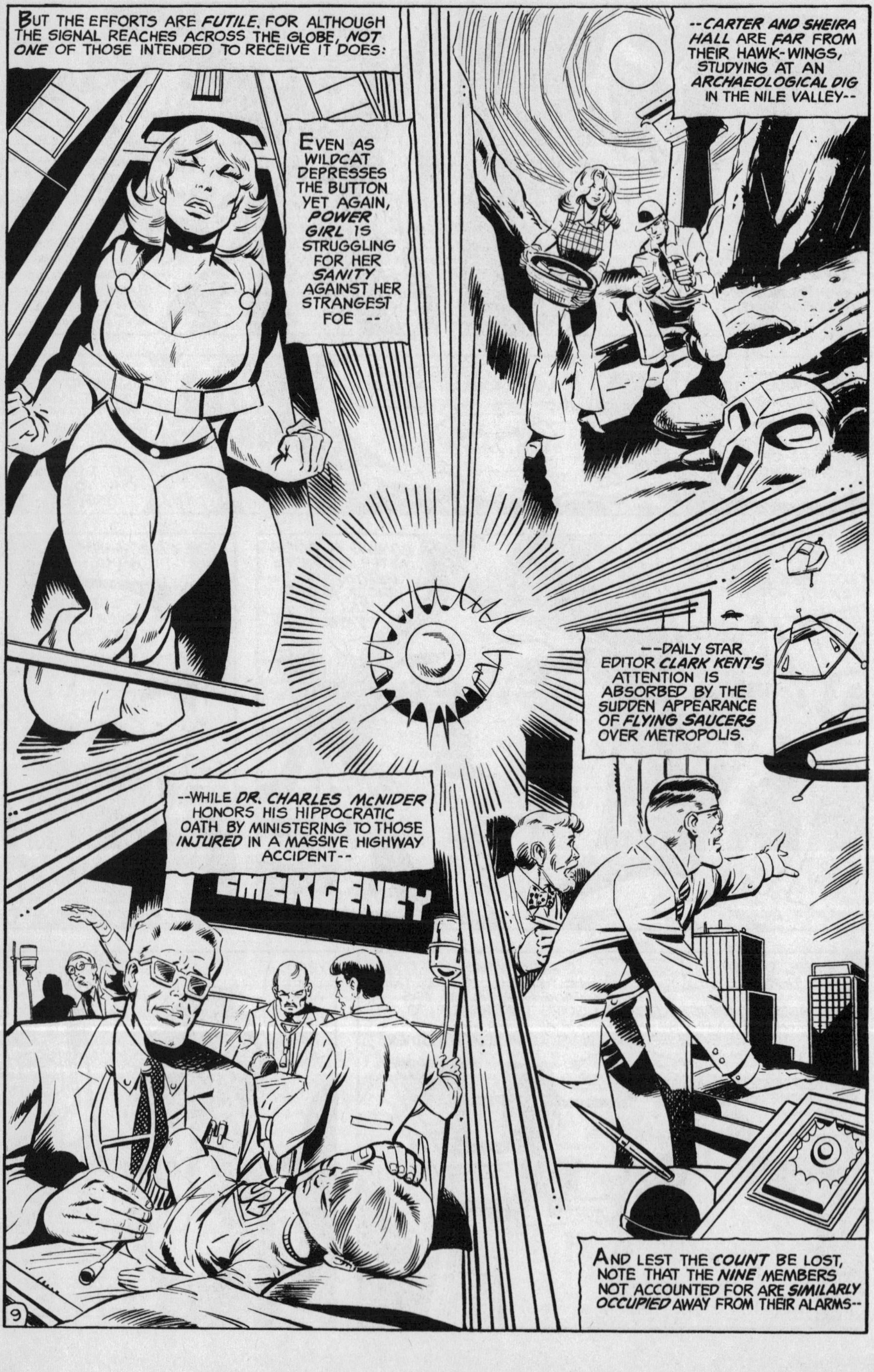
BUT THE EFFORTS ARE FUTILE. FOR ALTHOUGH THE SIGNAL REACHES ACROSS THE GLOBE, NOT ONE OF THOSE INTENDED TO RECEIVE IT DOES:
EVEN AS WILDCAT DEPRESSES THE BUTTON YET AGAIN, POWER GIRL IS STRUGGLING FOR HER SANITY AGAINST HER STRANGEST FOE --
--CARTER AND SHEIRA HALL ARE FAR FROM THEIR HAWK-WINGS, STUDYING AT AN ARCHAEOLOGICAL DIG IN THE NILE VALLEY--
--DAILY STAR EDITOR CLARK KENT'S ATTENTION IS ABSORBED BY THE SUDDEN APPEARANCE OF FLYING SAUCERS OVER METROPOLIS.
--WHILE DR. CHARLES McNIDER HONORS HIS HIPPOCRATIC OATH BY MINISTERING TO THOSE INJURED IN A MASSIVE HIGHWAY ACCIDENT--
EMERGENCY
AND LEST THE COUNT BE LOST, NOTE THAT THE NINE MEMBERS NOT ACCOUNTED FOR ARE SIMILARLY OCCUPIED AWAY FROM THEIR ALARMS--
9

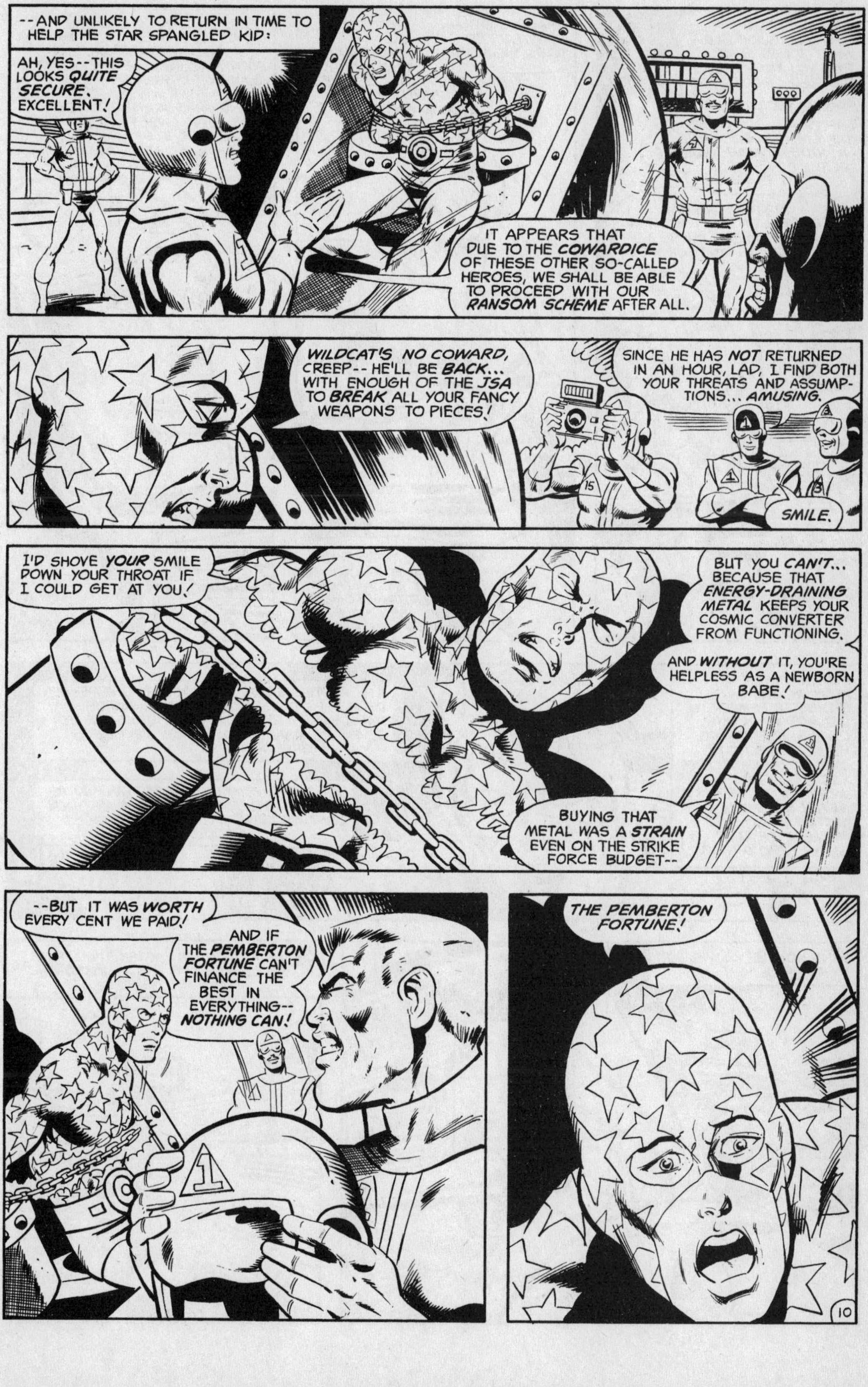
--AND UNLIKELY TO RETURN IN TIME TO HELP THE STAR SPANGLED KID:
AH, YES--THIS LOOKS QUITE SECURE. EXCELLENT!
IT APPEARS THAT DUE TO THE COWARDICE OF THESE OTHER SO-CALLED HEROES, WE SHALL BE ABLE TO PROCEED WITH OUR RANSOM SCHEME AFTER ALL.
WILDCAT'S NO COWARD, CREEP--HE'LL BE BACK... WITH ENOUGH OF THE JSA TO BREAK ALL YOUR FANCY WEAPONS TO PIECES!
SINCE HE HAS NOT RETURNED IN AN HOUR, LAD, I FIND BOTH YOUR THREATS AND ASSUMPTIONS... AMUSING.
SMILE.
I'D SHOVE YOUR SMILE DOWN YOUR THROAT IF I COULD GET AT YOU!
BUT YOU CAN'T... BECAUSE THAT ENERGY-DRAINING METAL KEEPS YOUR COSMIC CONVERTER FROM FUNCTIONING.
AND WITHOUT IT, YOU'RE HELPLESS AS A NEWBORN BABE!
BUYING THAT METAL WAS A STRAIN EVEN ON THE STRIKE FORCE BUDGET--
--BUT IT WAS WORTH EVERY CENT WE PAID!
AND IF THE PEMBERTON FORTUNE CAN'T FINANCE THE BEST IN EVERYTHING--NOTHING CAN!
THE PEMBERTON FORTUNE!
10

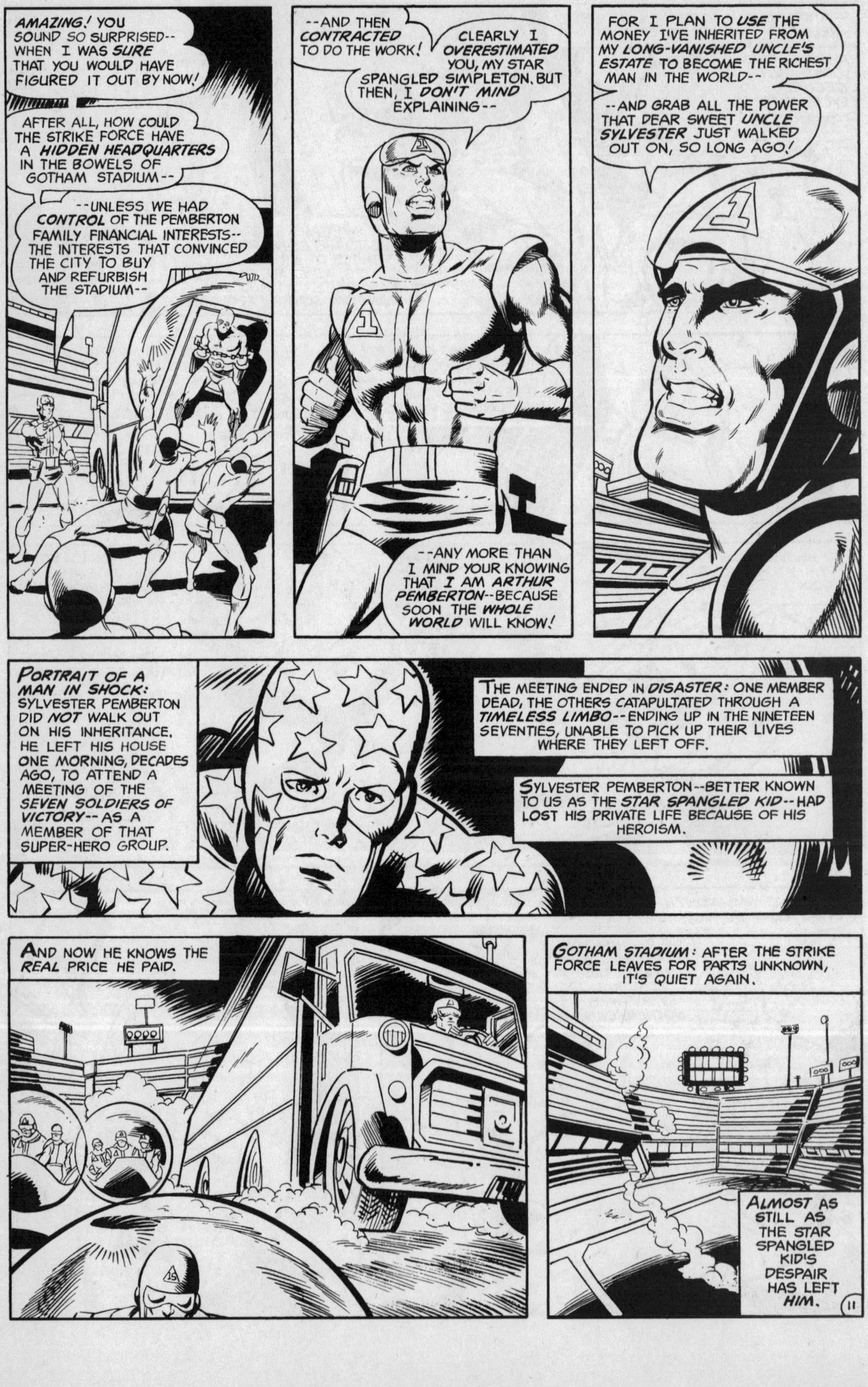
AMAZING! YOU SOUND SO SURPRISED-- WHEN I WAS SURE THAT YOU WOULD HAVE FIGURED IT OUT BY NOW!
AFTER ALL, HOW COULD THE STRIKE FORCE HAVE A HIDDEN HEADQUARTERS IN THE BOWELS OF GOTHAM STADIUM--
--UNLESS WE HAD CONTROL OF THE PEMBERTON FAMILY FINANCIAL INTERESTS-- THE INTERESTS THAT CONVINCED THE CITY TO BUY AND REFURBISH THE STADIUM--
--AND THEN CONTRACTED TO DO THE WORK!
CLEARLY I OVERESTIMATED YOU, MY STAR SPANGLED SIMPLETON. BUT THEN, I DON'T MIND EXPLAINING--
--ANY MORE THAN I MIND YOUR KNOWING THAT I AM ARTHUR PEMBERTON--BECAUSE SOON THE WHOLE WORLD WILL KNOW!
FOR I PLAN TO USE THE MONEY I'VE INHERITED FROM MY LONG-VANISHED UNCLE'S ESTATE TO BECOME THE RICHEST MAN IN THE WORLD--
--AND GRAB ALL THE POWER THAT DEAR SWEET UNCLE SYLVESTER JUST WALKED OUT ON, SO LONG AGO!
PORTRAIT OF A MAN IN SHOCK: SYLVESTER PEMBERTON DID NOT WALK OUT ON HIS INHERITANCE. HE LEFT HIS HOUSE ONE MORNING, DECADES AGO, TO ATTEND A MEETING OF THE SEVEN SOLDIERS OF VICTORY-- AS A MEMBER OF THAT SUPER-HERO GROUP.
THE MEETING ENDED IN DISASTER: ONE MEMBER DEAD, THE OTHERS CATAPULTATED THROUGH A TIMELESS LIMBO--ENDING UP IN THE NINETEEN SEVENTIES, UNABLE TO PICK UP THEIR LIVES WHERE THEY LEFT OFF.
SYLVESTER PEMBERTON--BETTER KNOWN TO US AS THE STAR SPANGLED KID--HAD LOST HIS PRIVATE LIFE BECAUSE OF HIS HEROISM.
AND NOW HE KNOWS THE REAL PRICE HE PAID.
GOTHAM STADIUM: AFTER THE STRIKE FORCE LEAVES FOR PARTS UNKNOWN, IT'S QUIET AGAIN.
ALMOST AS STILL AS THE STAR SPANGLED KID'S DESPAIR HAS LEFT HIM.
11

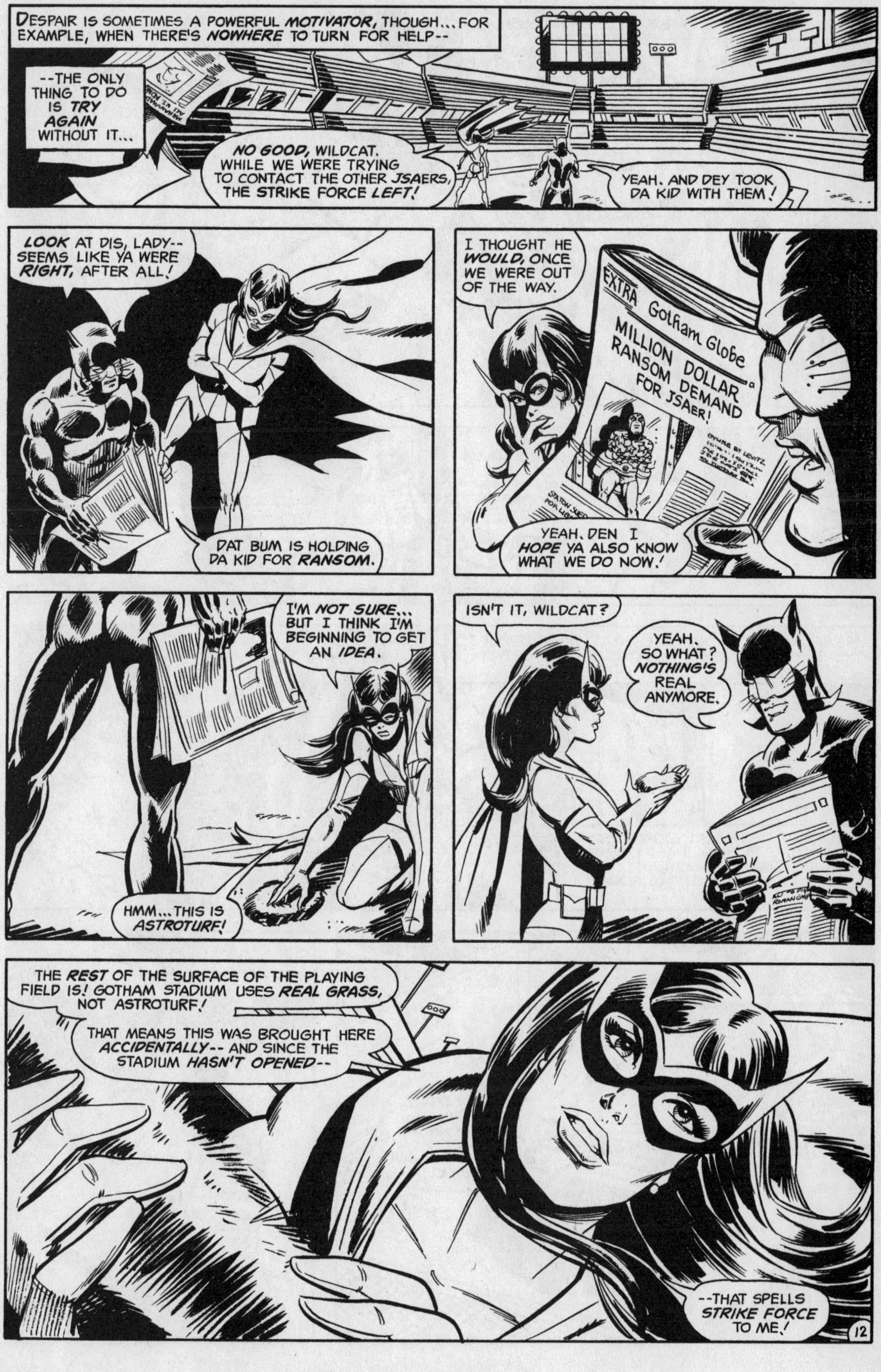
DESPAIR IS SOMETIMES A POWERFUL MOTIVATOR, THOUGH... FOR EXAMPLE, WHEN THERE'S NOWHERE TO TURN FOR HELP--
--THE ONLY THING TO DO IS TRY AGAIN WITHOUT IT...
NO GOOD, WILDCAT. WHILE WE WERE TRYING TO CONTACT THE OTHER JSAERS, THE STRIKE FORCE LEFT!
YEAH. AND DEY TOOK DA KID WITH THEM!
LOOK AT DIS, LADY-- SEEMS LIKE YA WERE RIGHT, AFTER ALL!
DAT BUM IS HOLDING DA KID FOR RANSOM.
I THOUGHT HE WOULD, ONCE WE WERE OUT OF THE WAY.
EXTRA Gotham Globe
MILLION DOLLAR RANSOM DEMAND FOR JSAER!
YEAH. DEN I HOPE YA ALSO KNOW WHAT WE DO NOW!
I'M NOT SURE... BUT I THINK I'M BEGINNING TO GET AN IDEA.
HMM... THIS IS ASTROTURF!
ISN'T IT, WILDCAT?
YEAH. SO WHAT? NOTHING'S REAL ANYMORE.
THE REST OF THE SURFACE OF THE PLAYING FIELD IS! GOTHAM STADIUM USES REAL GRASS, NOT ASTROTURF!
THAT MEANS THIS WAS BROUGHT HERE ACCIDENTALLY-- AND SINCE THE STADIUM HASN'T OPENED--
--THAT SPELLS STRIKE FORCE TO ME!
12

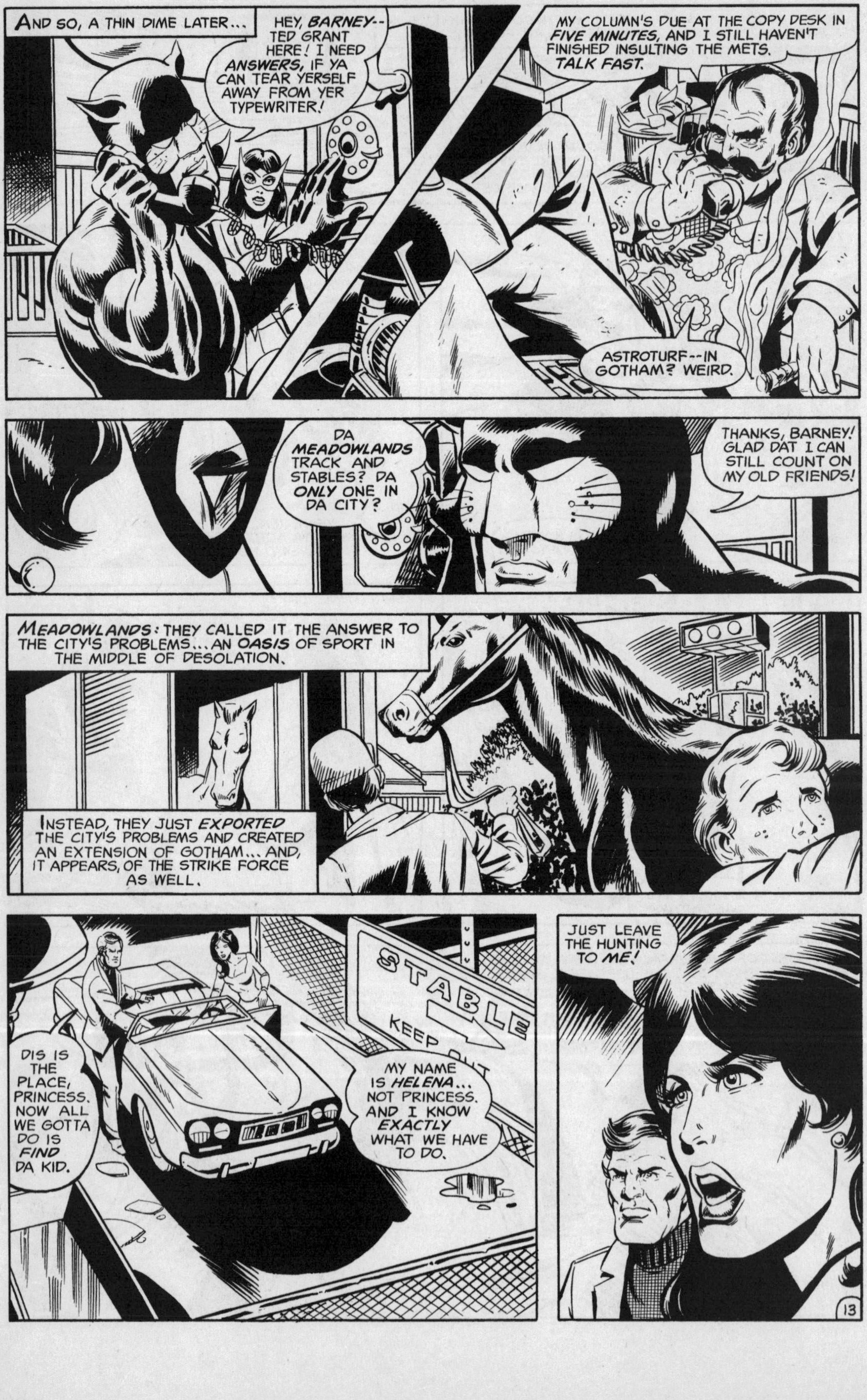
AND SO, A THIN DIME LATER...
HEY, BARNEY-- TED GRANT HERE! I NEED ANSWERS, IF YA CAN TEAR YERSELF AWAY FROM YER TYPEWRITER!
MY COLUMN'S DUE AT THE COPY DESK IN FIVE MINUTES, AND I STILL HAVEN'T FINISHED INSULTING THE METS. TALK FAST.
ASTROTURF--IN GOTHAM? WEIRD.
DA MEADOWLANDS TRACK AND STABLES? DA ONLY ONE IN DA CITY?
THANKS, BARNEY! GLAD DAT I CAN STILL COUNT ON MY OLD FRIENDS!
MEADOWLANDS: THEY CALLED IT THE ANSWER TO THE CITY'S PROBLEMS... AN OASIS OF SPORT IN THE MIDDLE OF DESOLATION.
INSTEAD, THEY JUST EXPORTED THE CITY'S PROBLEMS AND CREATED AN EXTENSION OF GOTHAM... AND, IT APPEARS, OF THE STRIKE FORCE AS WELL.
STABLE
DIS IS THE PLACE, PRINCESS. NOW ALL WE GOTTA DO IS FIND DA KID.
MY NAME IS HELENA... NOT PRINCESS. AND I KNOW EXACTLY WHAT WE HAVE TO DO.
JUST LEAVE THE HUNTING TO ME!
13

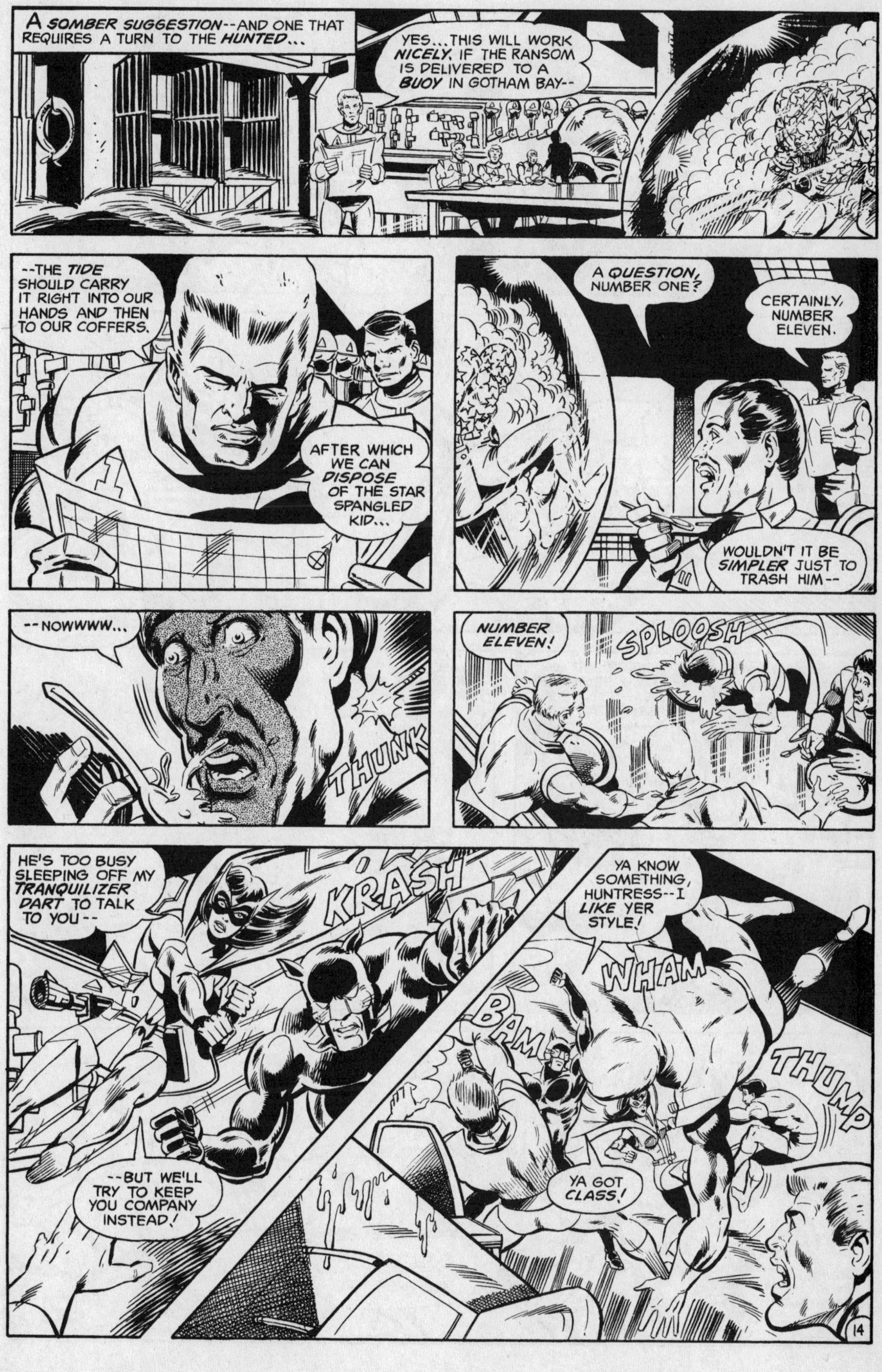
A SOMBER SUGGESTION--AND ONE THAT REQUIRES A TURN TO THE HUNTED...
YES...THIS WILL WORK NICELY. IF THE RANSOM IS DELIVERED TO A BUOY IN GOTHAM BAY--
--THE TIDE SHOULD CARRY IT RIGHT INTO OUR HANDS AND THEN TO OUR COFFERS.
AFTER WHICH WE CAN DISPOSE OF THE STAR SPANGLED KID...
A QUESTION, NUMBER ONE?
CERTAINLY, NUMBER ELEVEN.
WOULDN'T IT BE SIMPLER JUST TO TRASH HIM--
--NOWWWW...
THUNK
NUMBER ELEVEN!
SPLOOSH
HE'S TOO BUSY SLEEPING OFF MY TRANQUILIZER DART TO TALK TO YOU--
KRASH
--BUT WE'LL TRY TO KEEP YOU COMPANY INSTEAD!
YA KNOW SOMETHING, HUNTRESS--I LIKE YER STYLE!
WHAM
BAM
THUMP
YA GOT CLASS!
14

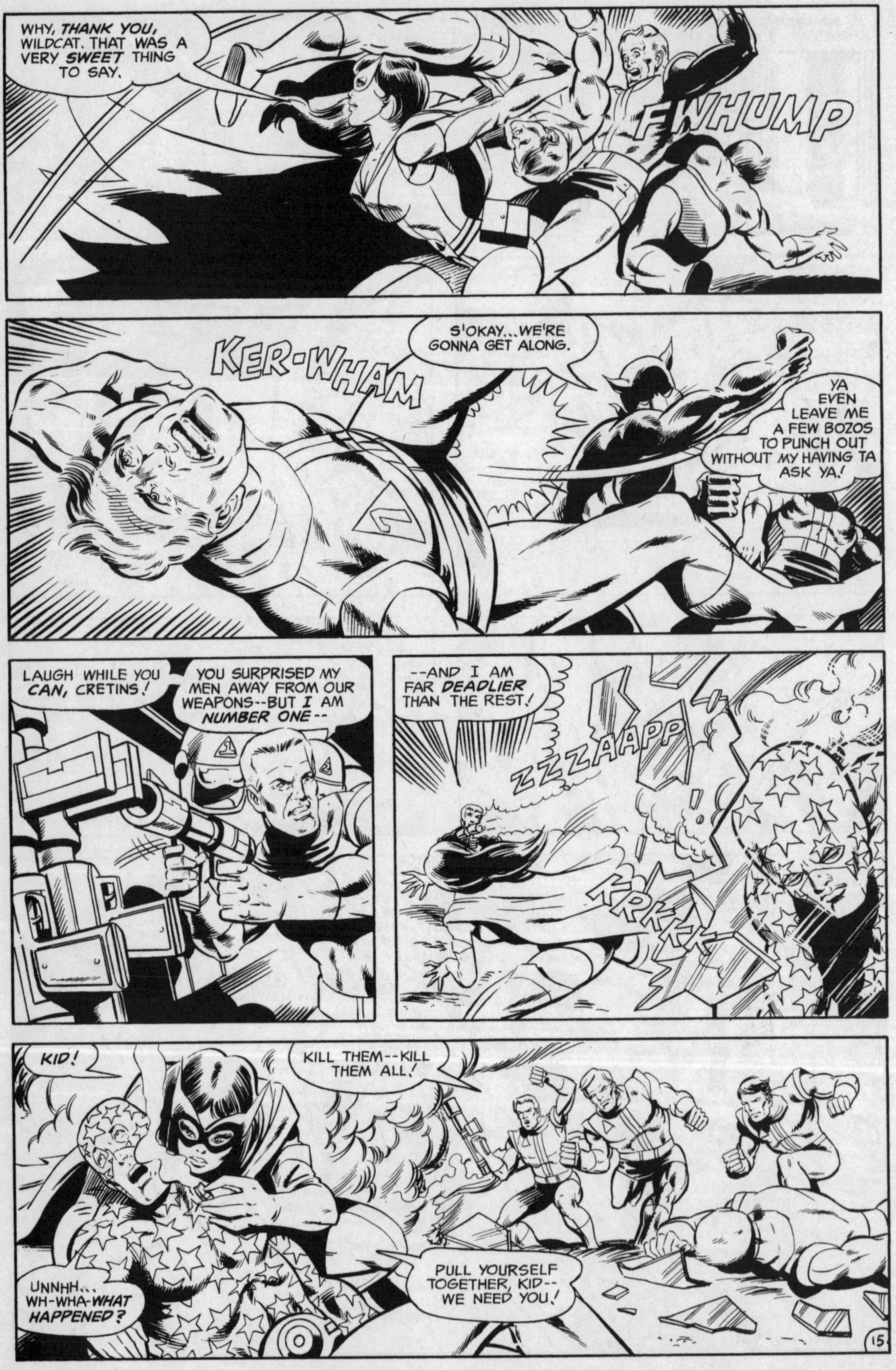
WHY, THANK YOU, WILDCAT. THAT WAS A VERY SWEET THING TO SAY.
FWHUMP
KER-WHAM
S'OKAY...WE'RE GONNA GET ALONG.
YA EVEN LEAVE ME A FEW BOZOS TO PUNCH OUT WITHOUT MY HAVING TA ASK YA!
LAUGH WHILE YOU CAN, CRETINS!
YOU SURPRISED MY MEN AWAY FROM OUR WEAPONS--BUT I AM NUMBER ONE--
--AND I AM FAR DEADLIER THAN THE REST!
ZZZAAAPP
KRKKK
KID!
KILL THEM--KILL THEM ALL!
UNNHH... WH-WHA-WHAT HAPPENED?
PULL YOURSELF TOGETHER, KID--WE NEED YOU!
15

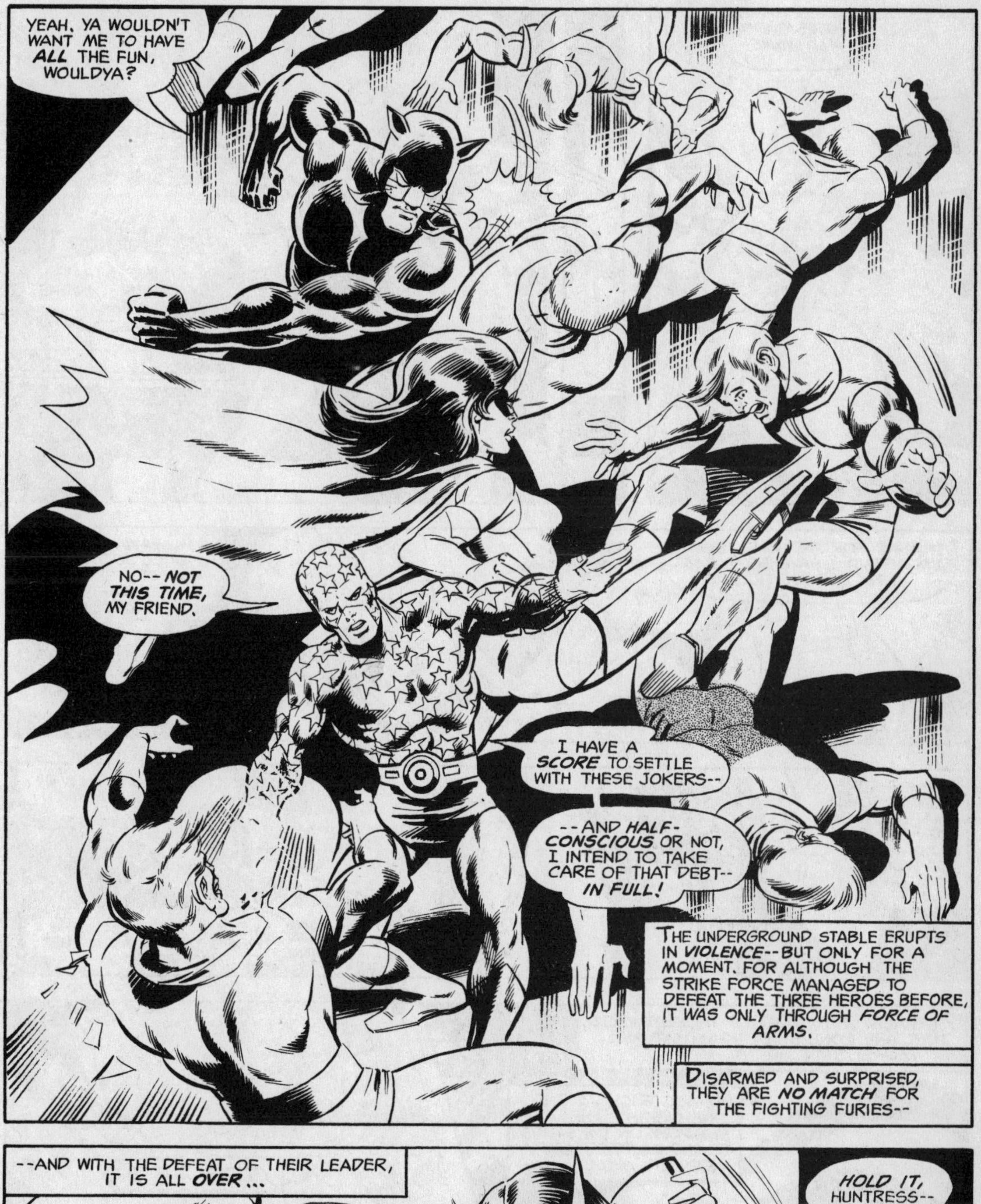
YEAH, YA WOULDN'T WANT ME TO HAVE ALL THE FUN, WOULDYA?
NO-- NOT THIS TIME, MY FRIEND.
I HAVE A SCORE TO SETTLE WITH THESE JOKERS--
--AND HALF-CONSCIOUS OR NOT, I INTEND TO TAKE CARE OF THAT DEBT-- IN FULL!
THE UNDERGROUND STABLE ERUPTS IN VIOLENCE--BUT ONLY FOR A MOMENT. FOR ALTHOUGH THE STRIKE FORCE MANAGED TO DEFEAT THE THREE HEROES BEFORE, IT WAS ONLY THROUGH FORCE OF ARMS.
DISARMED AND SURPRISED, THEY ARE NO MATCH FOR THE FIGHTING FURIES--

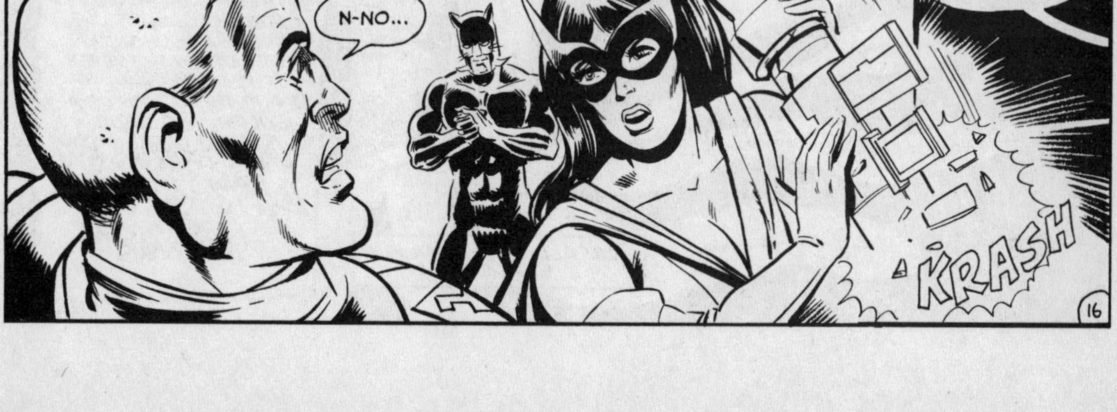
--AND WITH THE DEFEAT OF THEIR LEADER, IT IS ALL OVER...
N-NO...
HOLD IT, HUNTRESS--
KRASH
16

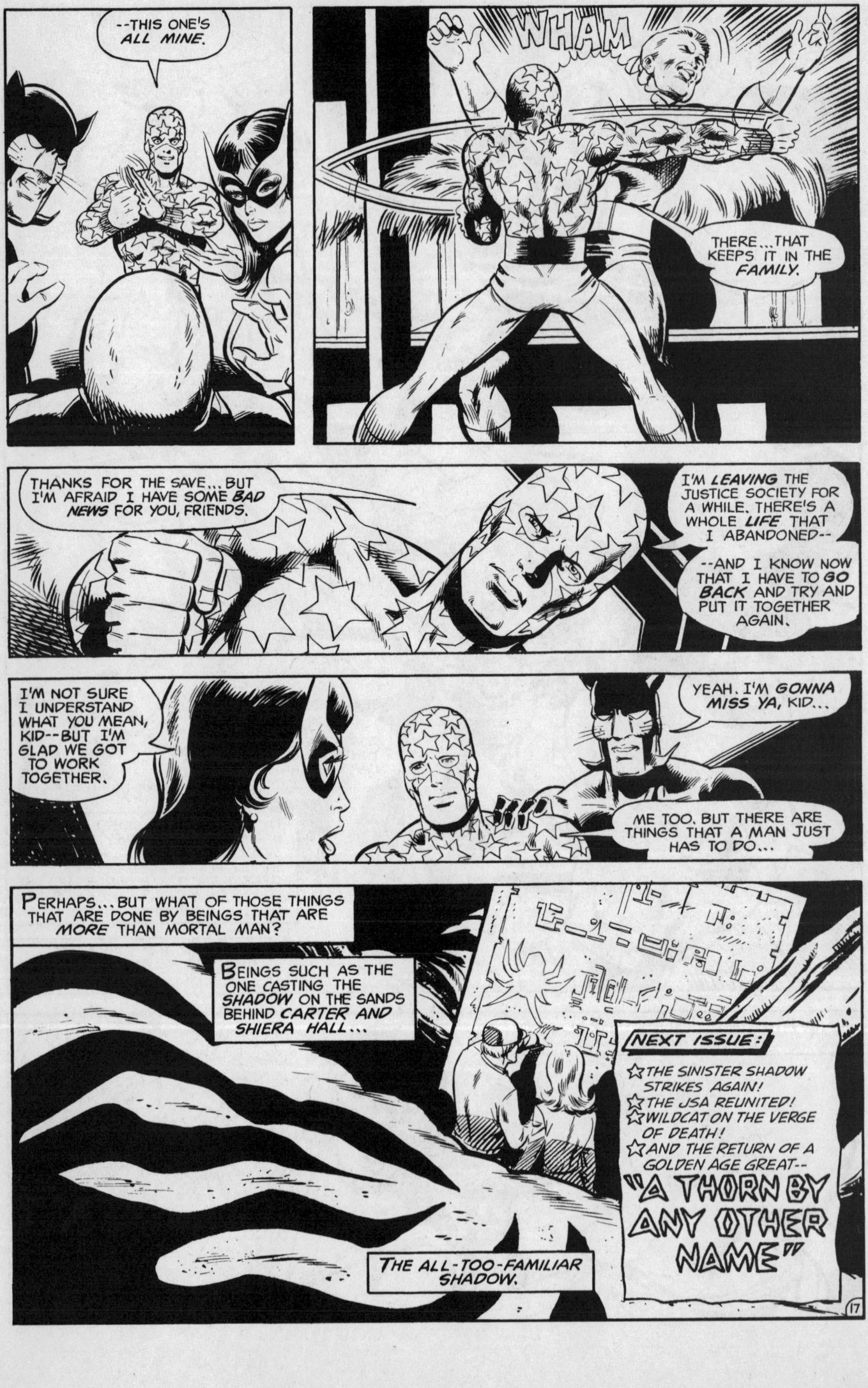
--THIS ONE'S ALL MINE.
WHAM
THERE...THAT KEEPS IT IN THE FAMILY.
THANKS FOR THE SAVE... BUT I'M AFRAID I HAVE SOME BAD NEWS FOR YOU, FRIENDS.
I'M LEAVING THE JUSTICE SOCIETY FOR A WHILE. THERE'S A WHOLE LIFE THAT I ABANDONED--
--AND I KNOW NOW THAT I HAVE TO GO BACK AND TRY AND PUT IT TOGETHER AGAIN.
I'M NOT SURE I UNDERSTAND WHAT YOU MEAN, KID--BUT I'M GLAD WE GOT TO WORK TOGETHER.
YEAH. I'M GONNA MISS YA, KID...
ME TOO. BUT THERE ARE THINGS THAT A MAN JUST HAS TO DO...
PERHAPS... BUT WHAT OF THOSE THINGS THAT ARE DONE BY BEINGS THAT ARE MORE THAN MORTAL MAN?
BEINGS SUCH AS THE ONE CASTING THE SHADOW ON THE SANDS BEHIND CARTER AND SHIERA HALL...
THE ALL-TOO-FAMILIAR SHADOW.
NEXT ISSUE:
THE SINISTER SHADOW STRIKES AGAIN!
THE JSA REUNITED!
WILDCAT ON THE VERGE OF DEATH!
AND THE RETURN OF A GOLDEN AGE GREAT--
"A THORN BY ANY OTHER NAME"
17

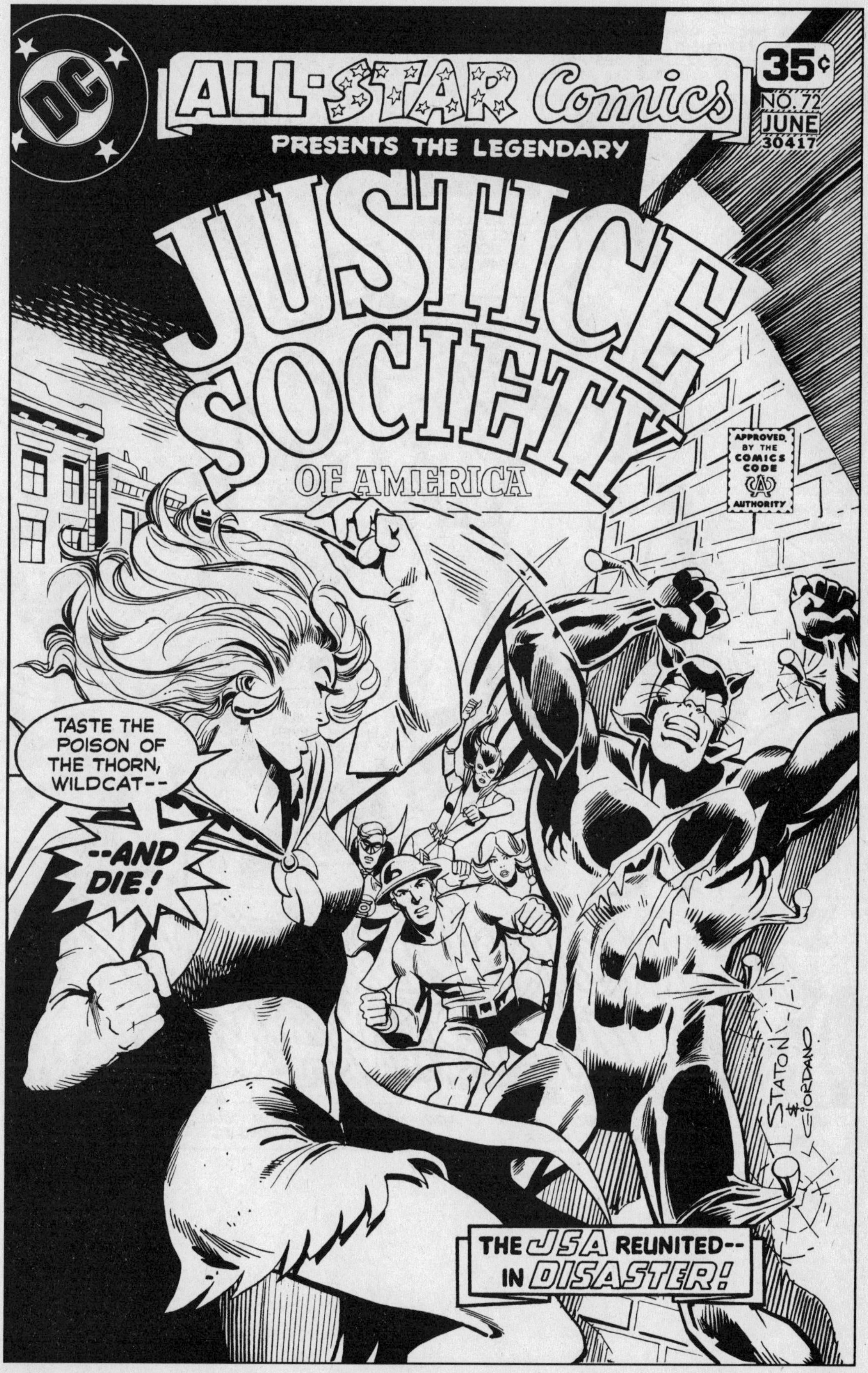
DC
ALL-STAR Comics
35¢
NO. 72
JUNE
30417
PRESENTS THE LEGENDARY
JUSTICE SOCIETY
OF AMERICA
APPROVED BY THE COMICS CODE AUTHORITY
TASTE THE POISON OF THE THORN, WILDCAT--
--AND DIE!
STATON & GIORDANO
THE JSA REUNITED-- IN DISASTER!

EARTH TWO -- A WORLD MUCH LIKE OUR OWN, YET SLIGHTLY *DIFFERENT*. THERE, YOUNG AND OLD HEROES HAVE *JOINED FORCES* TO BATTLE EVIL AS THE --

JUSTICE SOCIETY OF AMERICA

KC PD

THAT'S A *GOOD MAN* LYING THERE, JSAERS... A *VERY GOOD MAN*.

JACK REILLY WAS THE BEST *DETECTIVE* ON MY SQUAD...TILL THE *THORN* GOT HIM!

REILLY WAS HER *SEVENTH* VICTIM, WASN'T HE, CHIEF FARBER?

BUT THE COUNT WILL END AT SEVEN, FRIENDS! IT *MUST!*

KEEP KEYSTONE KLEAN

A THORN BY ANY OTHER NAME

PAUL LEVITZ	JOE STATON	BOB LAYTON	ADRIENNE ROY	BEN ODA	JOE ORLANDO
WRITER	PENCILLER	INKER	COLORIST	LETTERER	EDITOR

1

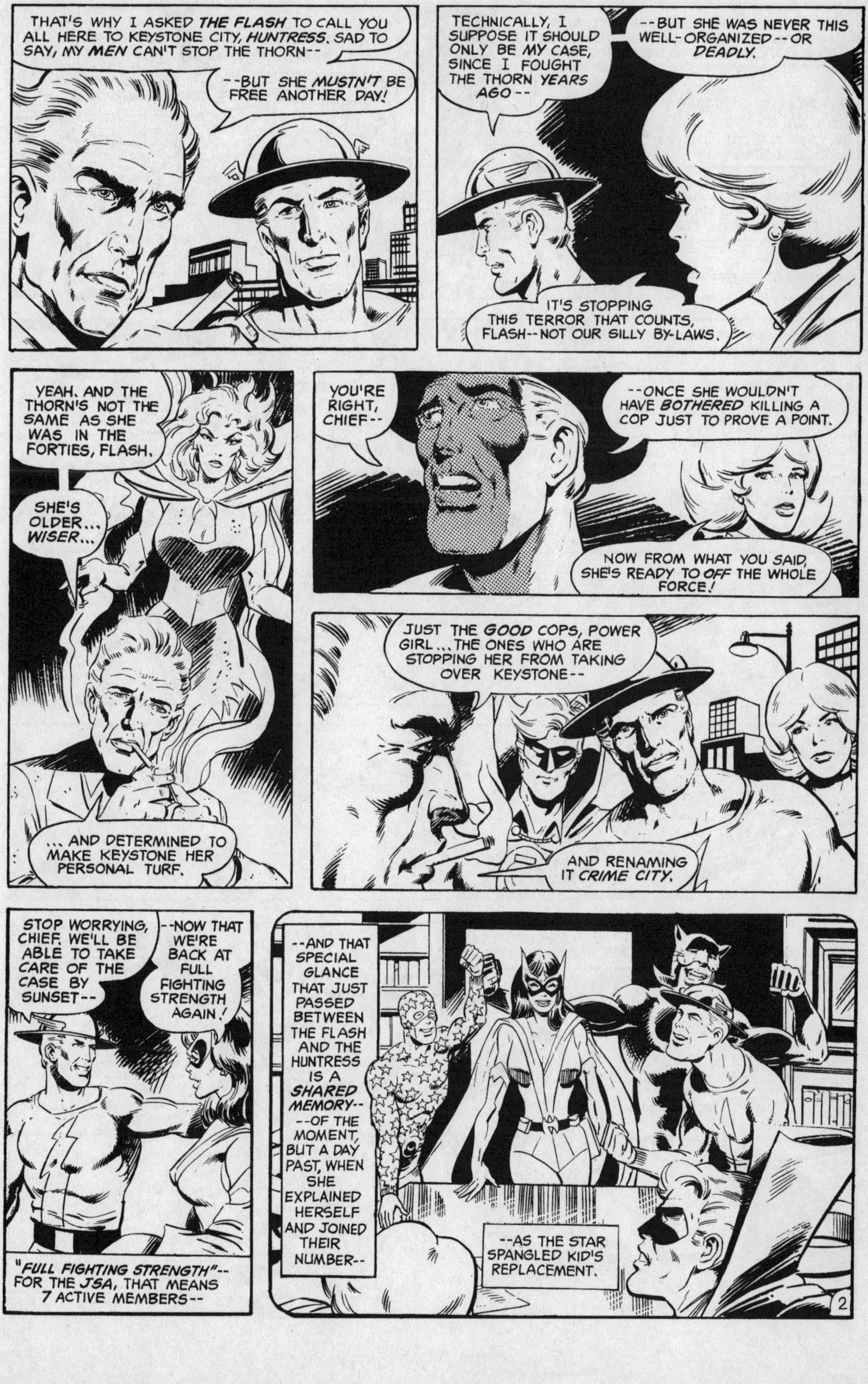
THAT'S WHY I ASKED THE FLASH TO CALL YOU ALL HERE TO KEYSTONE CITY, HUNTRESS. SAD TO SAY, MY MEN CAN'T STOP THE THORN--
--BUT SHE MUSTN'T BE FREE ANOTHER DAY!
TECHNICALLY, I SUPPOSE IT SHOULD ONLY BE MY CASE, SINCE I FOUGHT THE THORN YEARS AGO--
--BUT SHE WAS NEVER THIS WELL-ORGANIZED--OR DEADLY.
IT'S STOPPING THIS TERROR THAT COUNTS, FLASH--NOT OUR SILLY BY-LAWS.
YEAH. AND THE THORN'S NOT THE SAME AS SHE WAS IN THE FORTIES, FLASH.
SHE'S OLDER... WISER...
...AND DETERMINED TO MAKE KEYSTONE HER PERSONAL TURF.
YOU'RE RIGHT, CHIEF--
--ONCE SHE WOULDN'T HAVE BOTHERED KILLING A COP JUST TO PROVE A POINT.
NOW FROM WHAT YOU SAID, SHE'S READY TO OFF THE WHOLE FORCE!
JUST THE GOOD COPS, POWER GIRL... THE ONES WHO ARE STOPPING HER FROM TAKING OVER KEYSTONE--
AND RENAMING IT CRIME CITY.
STOP WORRYING, CHIEF. WE'LL BE ABLE TO TAKE CARE OF THE CASE BY SUNSET--
--NOW THAT WE'RE BACK AT FULL FIGHTING STRENGTH AGAIN!
"FULL FIGHTING STRENGTH"--FOR THE JSA, THAT MEANS 7 ACTIVE MEMBERS--
--AND THAT SPECIAL GLANCE THAT JUST PASSED BETWEEN THE FLASH AND THE HUNTRESS IS A SHARED MEMORY--
--OF THE MOMENT, BUT A DAY PAST, WHEN SHE EXPLAINED HERSELF AND JOINED THEIR NUMBER--
--AS THE STAR SPANGLED KID'S REPLACEMENT.
2

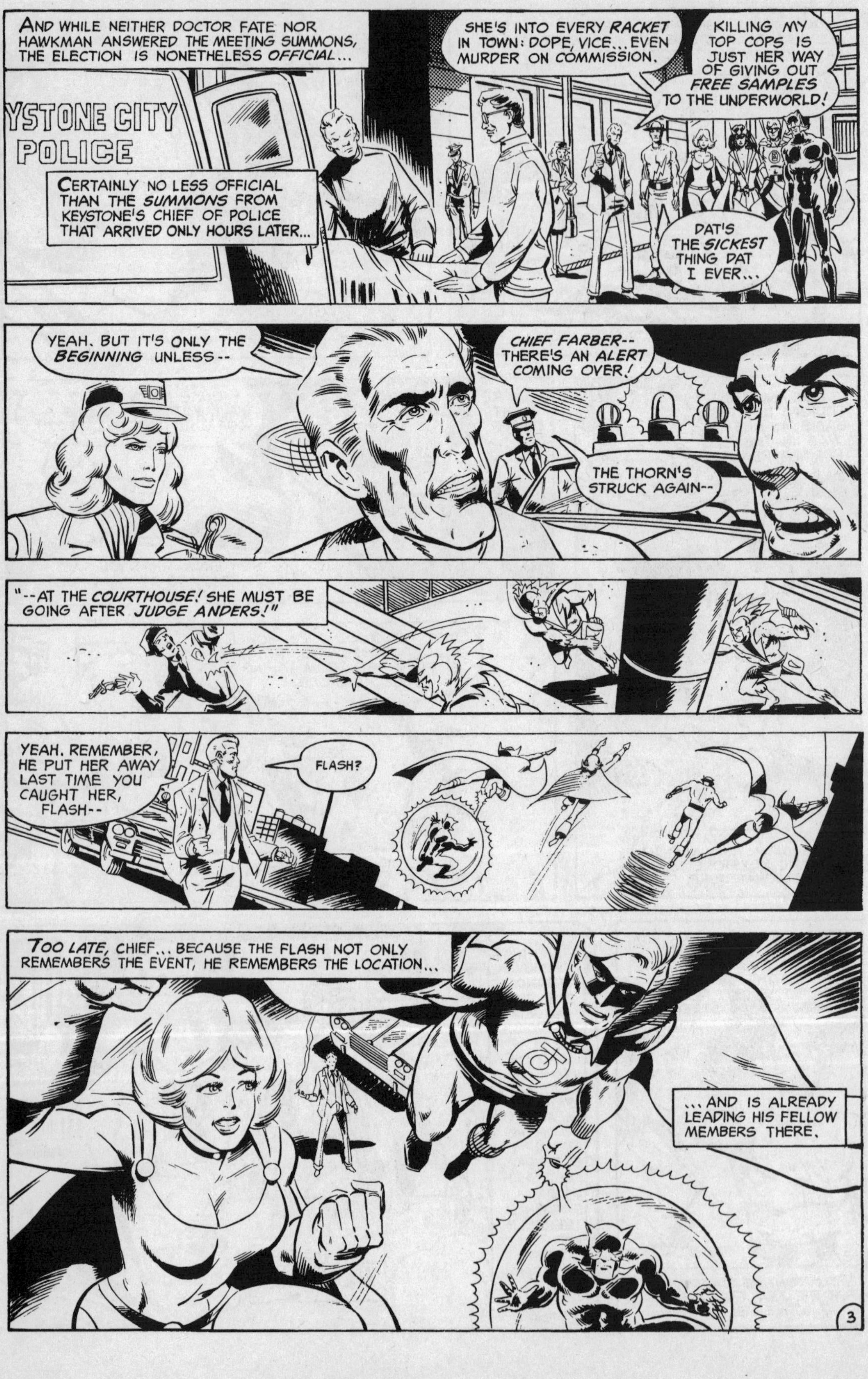
AND WHILE NEITHER DOCTOR FATE NOR HAWKMAN ANSWERED THE MEETING SUMMONS, THE ELECTION IS NONETHELESS OFFICIAL...
YSTONE CITY POLICE
CERTAINLY NO LESS OFFICIAL THAN THE SUMMONS FROM KEYSTONE'S CHIEF OF POLICE THAT ARRIVED ONLY HOURS LATER...
SHE'S INTO EVERY RACKET IN TOWN: DOPE, VICE... EVEN MURDER ON COMMISSION.
KILLING MY TOP COPS IS JUST HER WAY OF GIVING OUT FREE SAMPLES TO THE UNDERWORLD!
DAT'S THE SICKEST THING DAT I EVER...
YEAH. BUT IT'S ONLY THE BEGINNING UNLESS--
CHIEF FARBER-- THERE'S AN ALERT COMING OVER!
THE THORN'S STRUCK AGAIN--
"--AT THE COURTHOUSE! SHE MUST BE GOING AFTER JUDGE ANDERS!"
YEAH. REMEMBER, HE PUT HER AWAY LAST TIME YOU CAUGHT HER, FLASH--
FLASH?
TOO LATE, CHIEF... BECAUSE THE FLASH NOT ONLY REMEMBERS THE EVENT, HE REMEMBERS THE LOCATION...
...AND IS ALREADY LEADING HIS FELLOW MEMBERS THERE.
3

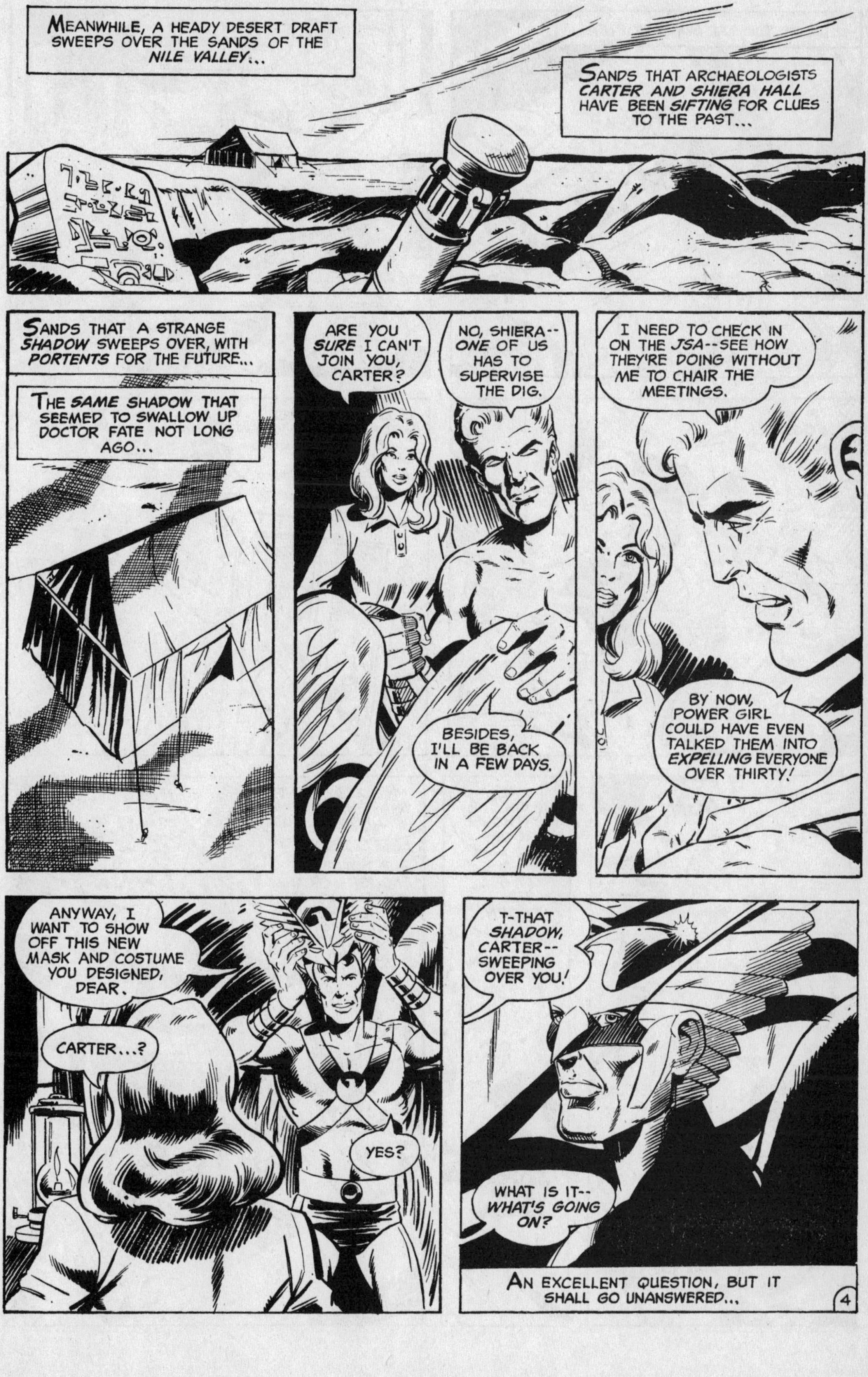
MEANWHILE, A HEADY DESERT DRAFT SWEEPS OVER THE SANDS OF THE NILE VALLEY...
SANDS THAT ARCHAEOLOGISTS CARTER AND SHIERA HALL HAVE BEEN SIFTING FOR CLUES TO THE PAST...
SANDS THAT A STRANGE SHADOW SWEEPS OVER, WITH PORTENTS FOR THE FUTURE...
THE SAME SHADOW THAT SEEMED TO SWALLOW UP DOCTOR FATE NOT LONG AGO...
ARE YOU SURE I CAN'T JOIN YOU, CARTER?
NO, SHIERA--ONE OF US HAS TO SUPERVISE THE DIG.
BESIDES, I'LL BE BACK IN A FEW DAYS.
I NEED TO CHECK IN ON THE JSA--SEE HOW THEY'RE DOING WITHOUT ME TO CHAIR THE MEETINGS.
BY NOW, POWER GIRL COULD HAVE EVEN TALKED THEM INTO EXPELLING EVERYONE OVER THIRTY!
ANYWAY, I WANT TO SHOW OFF THIS NEW MASK AND COSTUME YOU DESIGNED, DEAR.
CARTER...?
YES?
T-THAT SHADOW, CARTER--SWEEPING OVER YOU!
WHAT IS IT--WHAT'S GOING ON?
AN EXCELLENT QUESTION, BUT IT SHALL GO UNANSWERED...
4

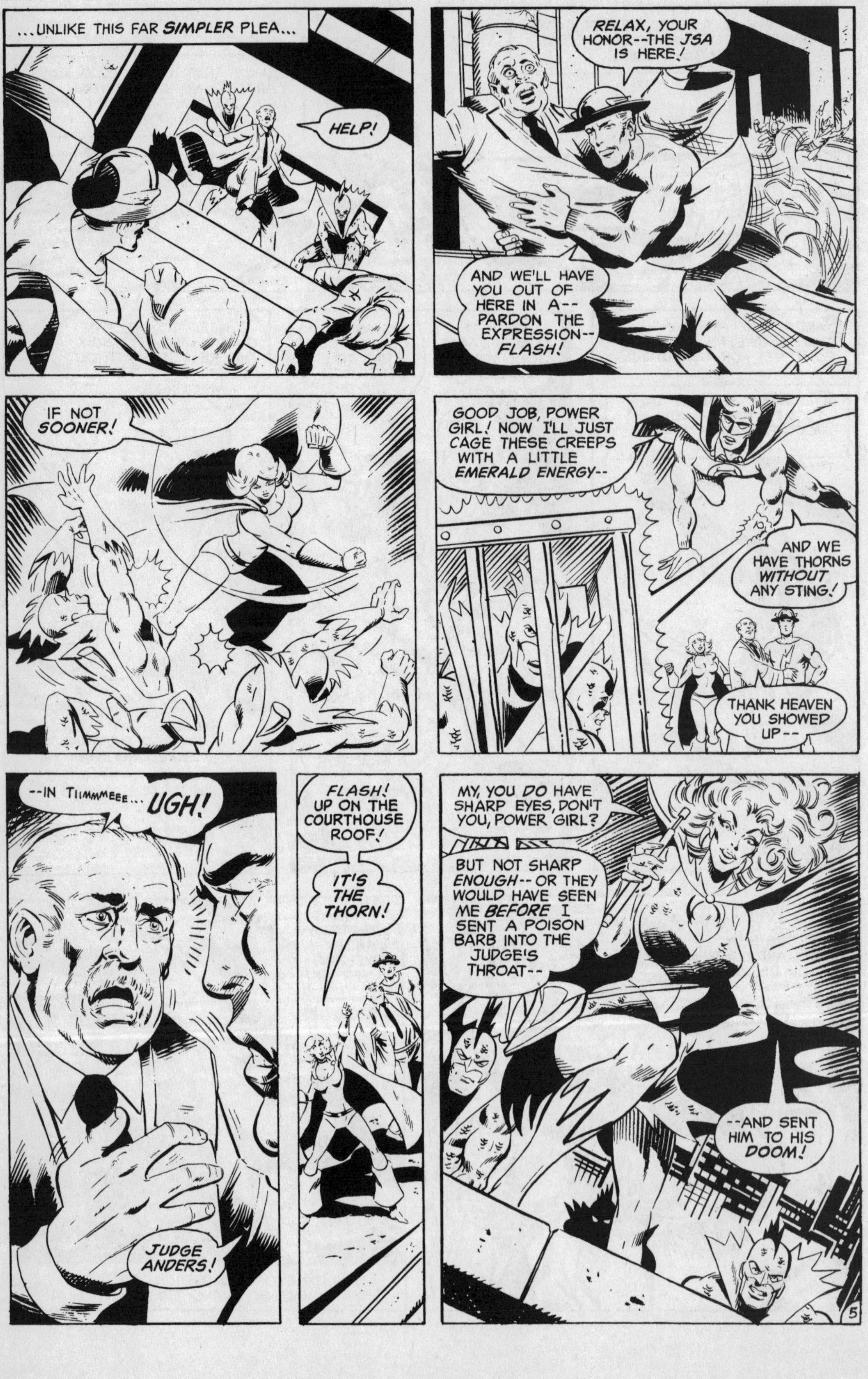
...UNLIKE THIS FAR SIMPLER PLEA...
HELP!
RELAX, YOUR HONOR--THE JSA IS HERE!
AND WE'LL HAVE YOU OUT OF HERE IN A-- PARDON THE EXPRESSION-- FLASH!
IF NOT SOONER!
GOOD JOB, POWER GIRL! NOW I'LL JUST CAGE THESE CREEPS WITH A LITTLE EMERALD ENERGY--
AND WE HAVE THORNS WITHOUT ANY STING!
THANK HEAVEN YOU SHOWED UP--
--IN TIIMMMEEE... UGH!
JUDGE ANDERS!
FLASH! UP ON THE COURTHOUSE ROOF!
IT'S THE THORN!
MY, YOU DO HAVE SHARP EYES, DON'T YOU, POWER GIRL?
BUT NOT SHARP ENOUGH--OR THEY WOULD HAVE SEEN ME BEFORE I SENT A POISON BARB INTO THE JUDGE'S THROAT--
--AND SENT HIM TO HIS DOOM!
5

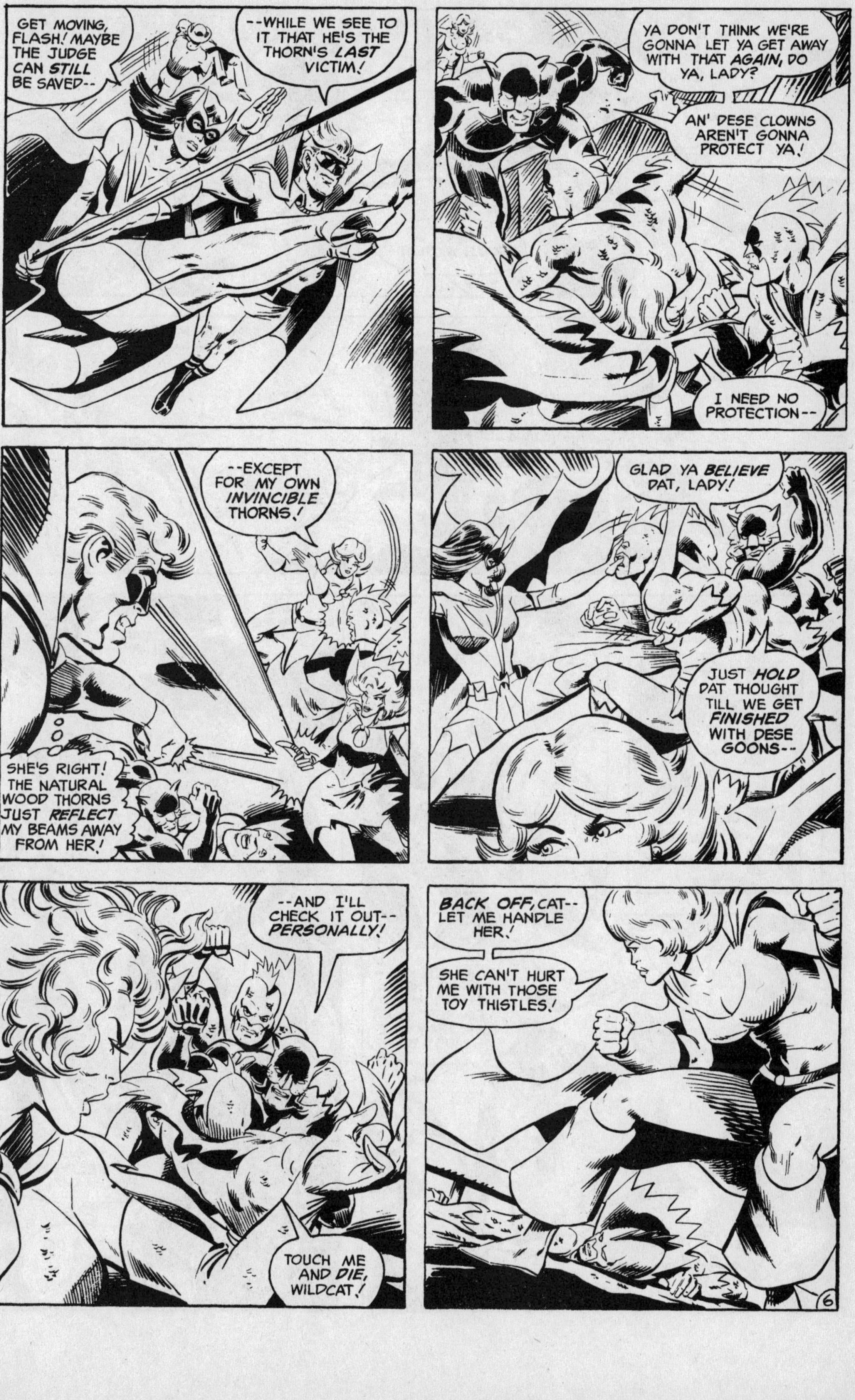
GET MOVING, FLASH! MAYBE THE JUDGE CAN STILL BE SAVED--
--WHILE WE SEE TO IT THAT HE'S THE THORN'S LAST VICTIM!
YA DON'T THINK WE'RE GONNA LET YA GET AWAY WITH THAT AGAIN, DO YA, LADY?
AN' DESE CLOWNS AREN'T GONNA PROTECT YA!
I NEED NO PROTECTION--
--EXCEPT FOR MY OWN INVINCIBLE THORNS!
SHE'S RIGHT! THE NATURAL WOOD THORNS JUST REFLECT MY BEAMS AWAY FROM HER!
GLAD YA BELIEVE DAT, LADY!
JUST HOLD DAT THOUGHT TILL WE GET FINISHED WITH DESE GOONS--
--AND I'LL CHECK IT OUT--PERSONALLY!
TOUCH ME AND DIE, WILDCAT!
BACK OFF, CAT--LET ME HANDLE HER!
SHE CAN'T HURT ME WITH THOSE TOY THISTLES!
6

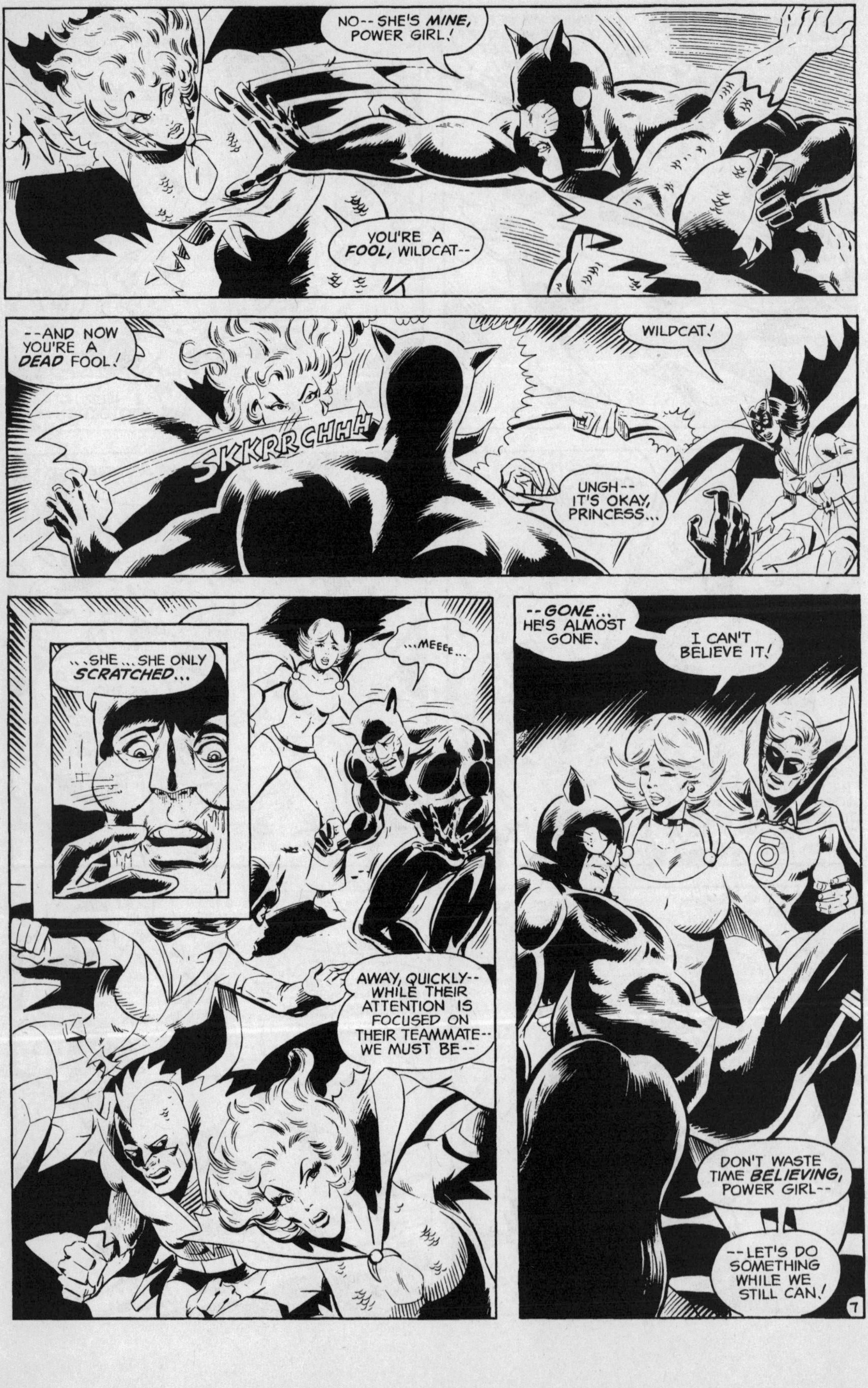
NO-- SHE'S *MINE,* POWER GIRL!
YOU'RE A *FOOL,* WILDCAT--
--AND NOW YOU'RE A *DEAD* FOOL!
WILDCAT!
SKKRRCHHH
UNGH-- IT'S OKAY, PRINCESS...
...SHE ...SHE ONLY *SCRATCHED*...
...MEEEE...
AWAY, QUICKLY-- WHILE THEIR ATTENTION IS FOCUSED ON THEIR TEAMMATE-- WE MUST BE--
--*GONE*... HE'S ALMOST GONE.
I CAN'T BELIEVE IT!
DON'T WASTE TIME *BELIEVING,* POWER GIRL--
--LET'S DO SOMETHING WHILE WE STILL CAN!
7

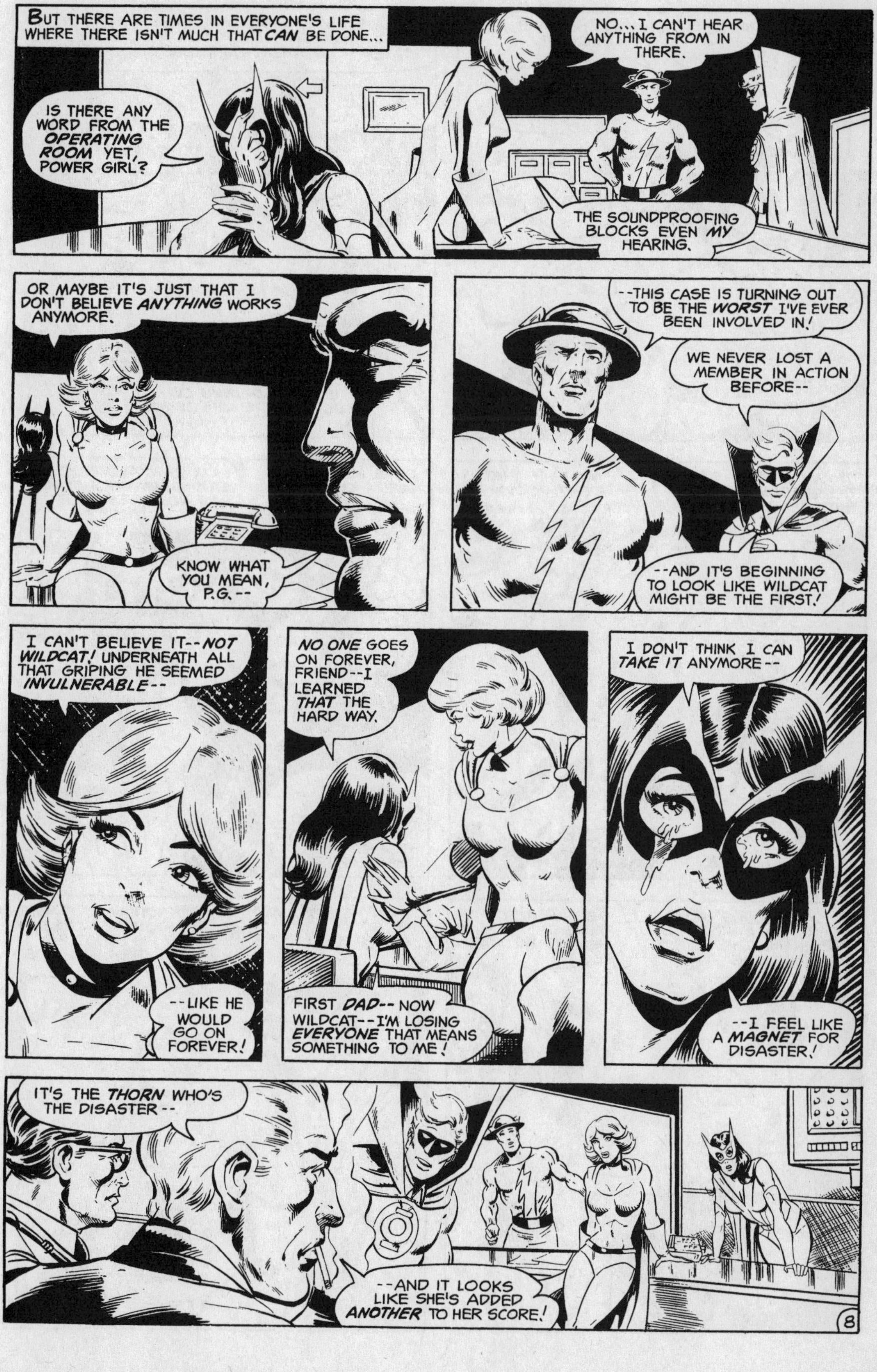
BUT THERE ARE TIMES IN EVERYONE'S LIFE WHERE THERE ISN'T MUCH THAT CAN BE DONE...
IS THERE ANY WORD FROM THE OPERATING ROOM YET, POWER GIRL?
NO... I CAN'T HEAR ANYTHING FROM IN THERE.
THE SOUNDPROOFING BLOCKS EVEN MY HEARING.
OR MAYBE IT'S JUST THAT I DON'T BELIEVE ANYTHING WORKS ANYMORE.
KNOW WHAT YOU MEAN, P.G.--
--THIS CASE IS TURNING OUT TO BE THE WORST I'VE EVER BEEN INVOLVED IN!
WE NEVER LOST A MEMBER IN ACTION BEFORE--
--AND IT'S BEGINNING TO LOOK LIKE WILDCAT MIGHT BE THE FIRST!
I CAN'T BELIEVE IT--NOT WILDCAT! UNDERNEATH ALL THAT GRIPING HE SEEMED INVULNERABLE--
--LIKE HE WOULD GO ON FOREVER!
NO ONE GOES ON FOREVER, FRIEND--I LEARNED THAT THE HARD WAY.
FIRST DAD-- NOW WILDCAT--I'M LOSING EVERYONE THAT MEANS SOMETHING TO ME!
I DON'T THINK I CAN TAKE IT ANYMORE--
--I FEEL LIKE A MAGNET FOR DISASTER!
IT'S THE THORN WHO'S THE DISASTER--
--AND IT LOOKS LIKE SHE'S ADDED ANOTHER TO HER SCORE!
8

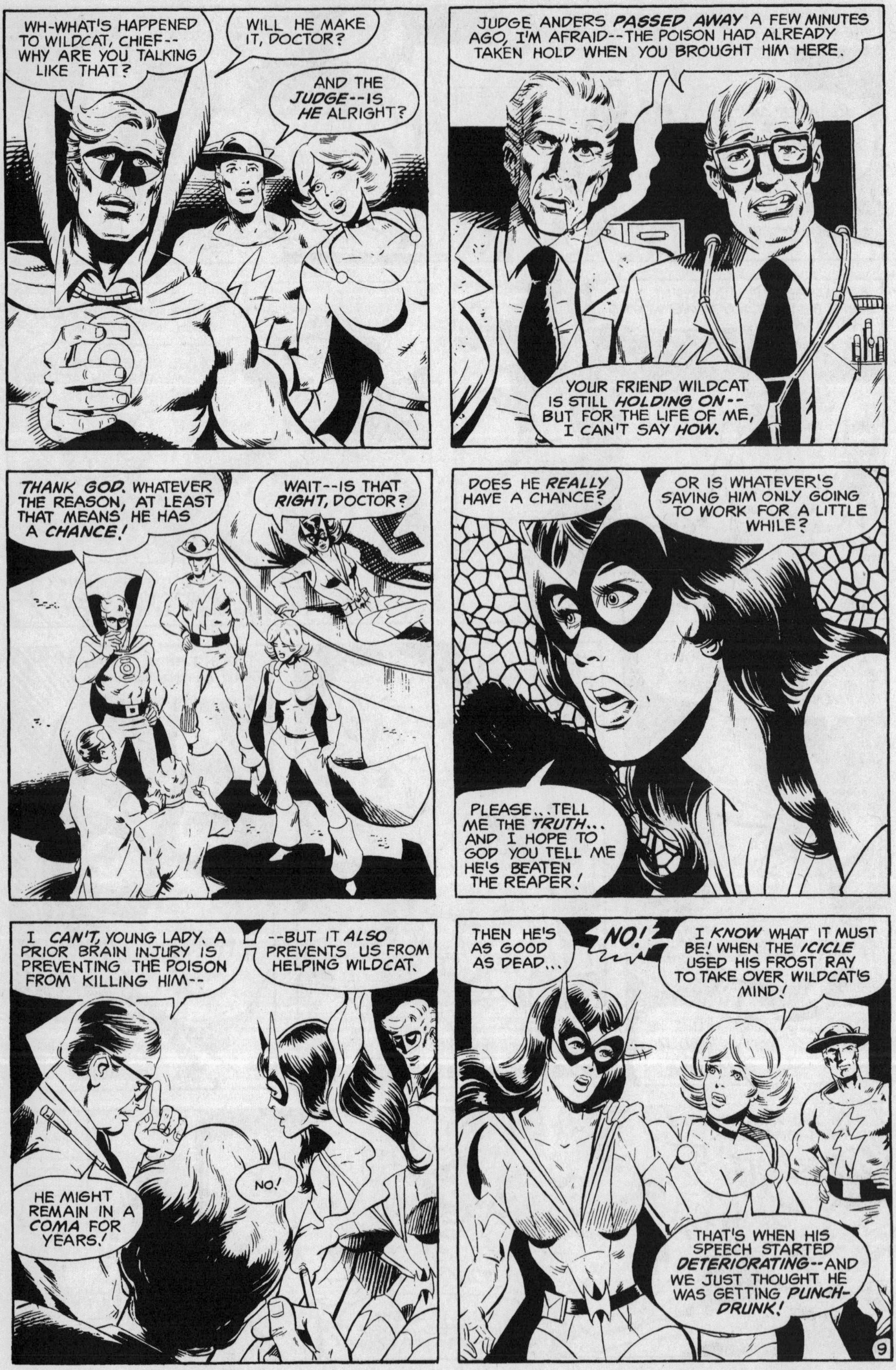
WH-WHAT'S HAPPENED TO WILDCAT, CHIEF-- WHY ARE YOU TALKING LIKE THAT?
WILL HE MAKE IT, DOCTOR?
AND THE JUDGE--IS HE ALRIGHT?
JUDGE ANDERS PASSED AWAY A FEW MINUTES AGO, I'M AFRAID--THE POISON HAD ALREADY TAKEN HOLD WHEN YOU BROUGHT HIM HERE.
YOUR FRIEND WILDCAT IS STILL HOLDING ON-- BUT FOR THE LIFE OF ME, I CAN'T SAY HOW.
THANK GOD. WHATEVER THE REASON, AT LEAST THAT MEANS HE HAS A CHANCE!
WAIT--IS THAT RIGHT, DOCTOR?
DOES HE REALLY HAVE A CHANCE?
OR IS WHATEVER'S SAVING HIM ONLY GOING TO WORK FOR A LITTLE WHILE?
PLEASE... TELL ME THE TRUTH... AND I HOPE TO GOD YOU TELL ME HE'S BEATEN THE REAPER!
I CAN'T, YOUNG LADY. A PRIOR BRAIN INJURY IS PREVENTING THE POISON FROM KILLING HIM--
--BUT IT ALSO PREVENTS US FROM HELPING WILDCAT.
HE MIGHT REMAIN IN A COMA FOR YEARS!
NO!
THEN HE'S AS GOOD AS DEAD...
NO!
I KNOW WHAT IT MUST BE! WHEN THE ICICLE USED HIS FROST RAY TO TAKE OVER WILDCAT'S MIND!
THAT'S WHEN HIS SPEECH STARTED DETERIORATING--AND WE JUST THOUGHT HE WAS GETTING PUNCH-DRUNK!
9

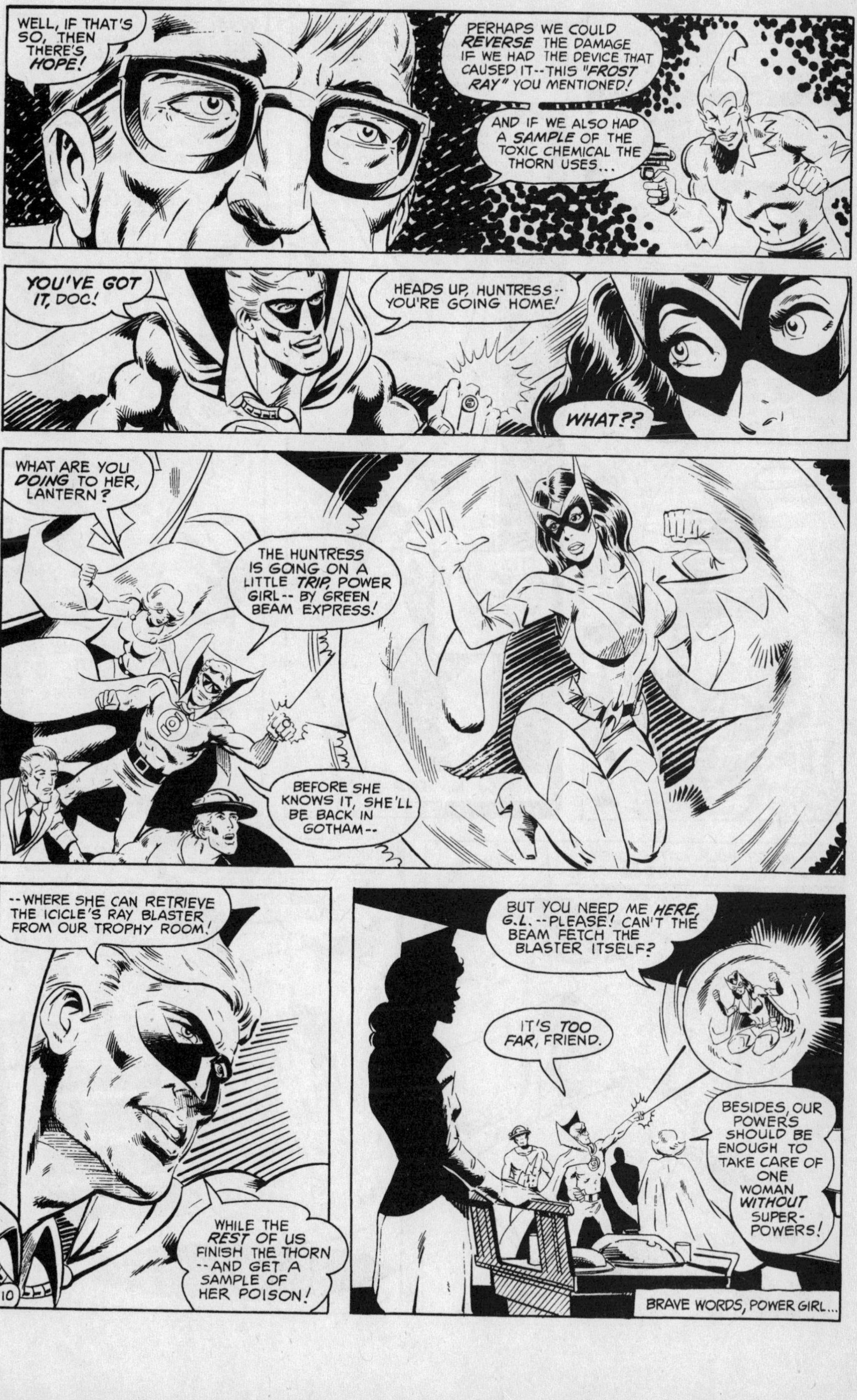
WELL, IF THAT'S SO, THEN THERE'S HOPE!
PERHAPS WE COULD REVERSE THE DAMAGE IF WE HAD THE DEVICE THAT CAUSED IT--THIS "FROST RAY" YOU MENTIONED!
AND IF WE ALSO HAD A SAMPLE OF THE TOXIC CHEMICAL THE THORN USES...
YOU'VE GOT IT, DOC!
HEADS UP, HUNTRESS--YOU'RE GOING HOME!
WHAT??
WHAT ARE YOU DOING TO HER, LANTERN?
THE HUNTRESS IS GOING ON A LITTLE TRIP, POWER GIRL--BY GREEN BEAM EXPRESS!
BEFORE SHE KNOWS IT, SHE'LL BE BACK IN GOTHAM--
--WHERE SHE CAN RETRIEVE THE ICICLE'S RAY BLASTER FROM OUR TROPHY ROOM!
WHILE THE REST OF US FINISH THE THORN --AND GET A SAMPLE OF HER POISON!
10
BUT YOU NEED ME HERE, G.L.--PLEASE! CAN'T THE BEAM FETCH THE BLASTER ITSELF?
IT'S TOO FAR, FRIEND.
BESIDES, OUR POWERS SHOULD BE ENOUGH TO TAKE CARE OF ONE WOMAN WITHOUT SUPER-POWERS!
BRAVE WORDS, POWER GIRL...

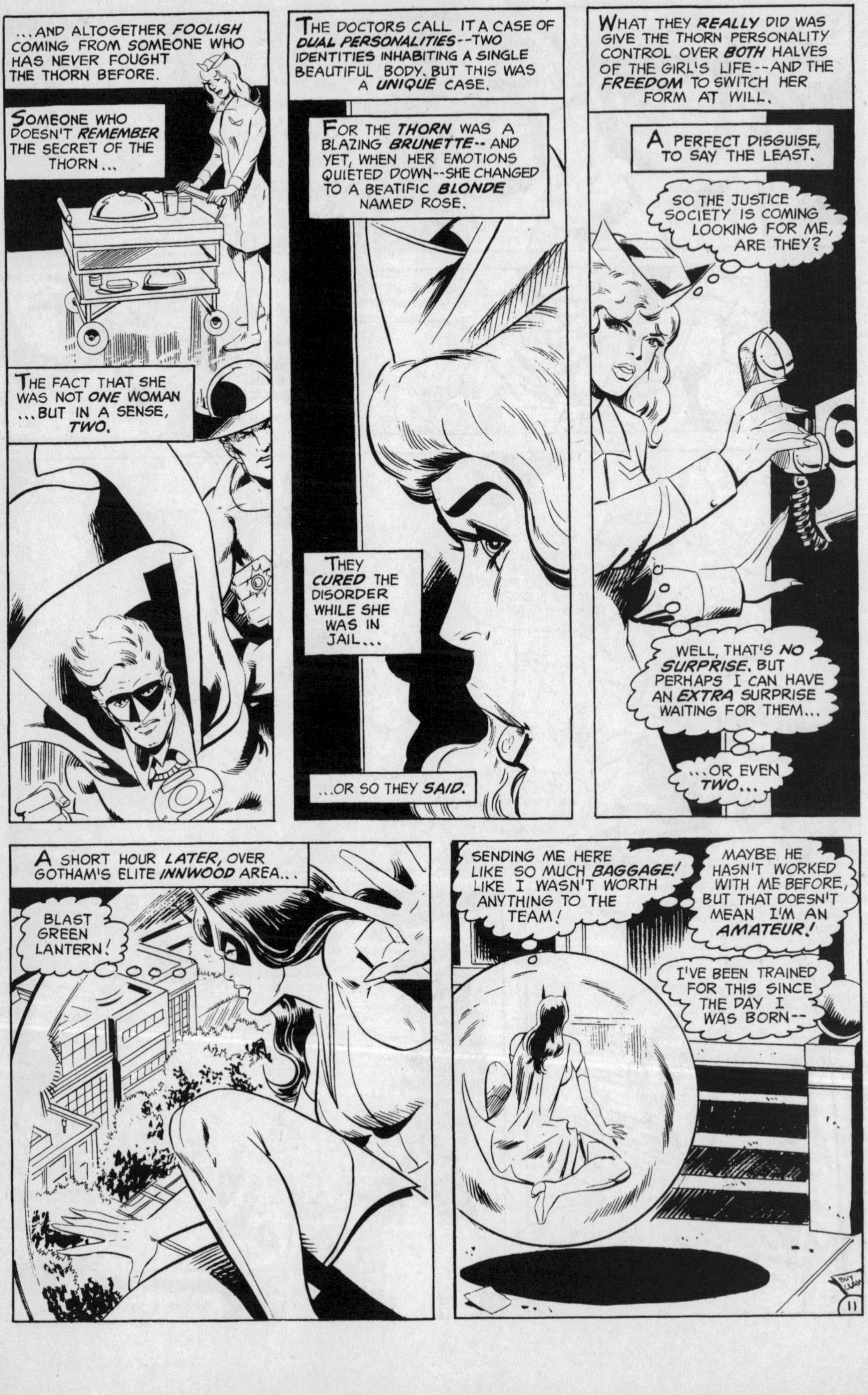
...AND ALTOGETHER FOOLISH COMING FROM SOMEONE WHO HAS NEVER FOUGHT THE THORN BEFORE.
SOMEONE WHO DOESN'T REMEMBER THE SECRET OF THE THORN...
THE FACT THAT SHE WAS NOT ONE WOMAN ...BUT IN A SENSE, TWO.
THE DOCTORS CALL IT A CASE OF DUAL PERSONALITIES--TWO IDENTITIES INHABITING A SINGLE BEAUTIFUL BODY. BUT THIS WAS A UNIQUE CASE.
FOR THE THORN WAS A BLAZING BRUNETTE-- AND YET, WHEN HER EMOTIONS QUIETED DOWN--SHE CHANGED TO A BEATIFIC BLONDE NAMED ROSE.
THEY CURED THE DISORDER WHILE SHE WAS IN JAIL...
...OR SO THEY SAID.
WHAT THEY REALLY DID WAS GIVE THE THORN PERSONALITY CONTROL OVER BOTH HALVES OF THE GIRL'S LIFE--AND THE FREEDOM TO SWITCH HER FORM AT WILL.
A PERFECT DISGUISE, TO SAY THE LEAST.
SO THE JUSTICE SOCIETY IS COMING LOOKING FOR ME, ARE THEY?
WELL, THAT'S NO SURPRISE. BUT PERHAPS I CAN HAVE AN EXTRA SURPRISE WAITING FOR THEM...
...OR EVEN TWO...
A SHORT HOUR LATER, OVER GOTHAM'S ELITE INNWOOD AREA...
BLAST GREEN LANTERN!
SENDING ME HERE LIKE SO MUCH BAGGAGE! LIKE I WASN'T WORTH ANYTHING TO THE TEAM!
MAYBE HE HASN'T WORKED WITH ME BEFORE, BUT THAT DOESN'T MEAN I'M AN AMATEUR!
I'VE BEEN TRAINED FOR THIS SINCE THE DAY I WAS BORN--
11

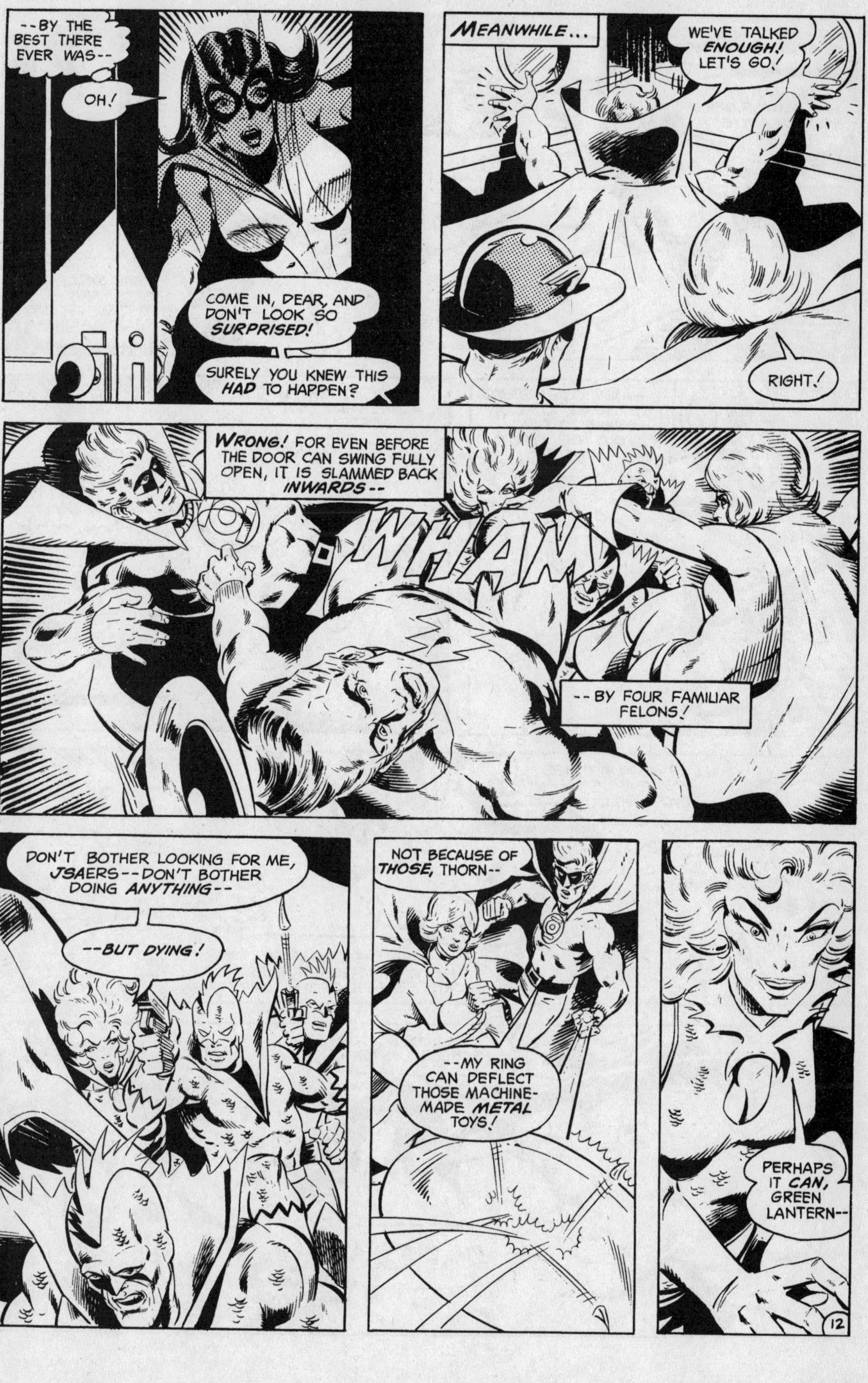
--BY THE BEST THERE EVER WAS--
OH!
COME IN, DEAR, AND DON'T LOOK SO SURPRISED!
SURELY YOU KNEW THIS HAD TO HAPPEN?
MEANWHILE...
WE'VE TALKED ENOUGH! LET'S GO!
RIGHT!
WRONG! FOR EVEN BEFORE THE DOOR CAN SWING FULLY OPEN, IT IS SLAMMED BACK INWARDS--
WHAM
--BY FOUR FAMILIAR FELONS!
DON'T BOTHER LOOKING FOR ME, JSAERS--DON'T BOTHER DOING ANYTHING--
--BUT DYING!
NOT BECAUSE OF THOSE, THORN--
--MY RING CAN DEFLECT THOSE MACHINE-MADE METAL TOYS!
PERHAPS IT CAN, GREEN LANTERN--
12

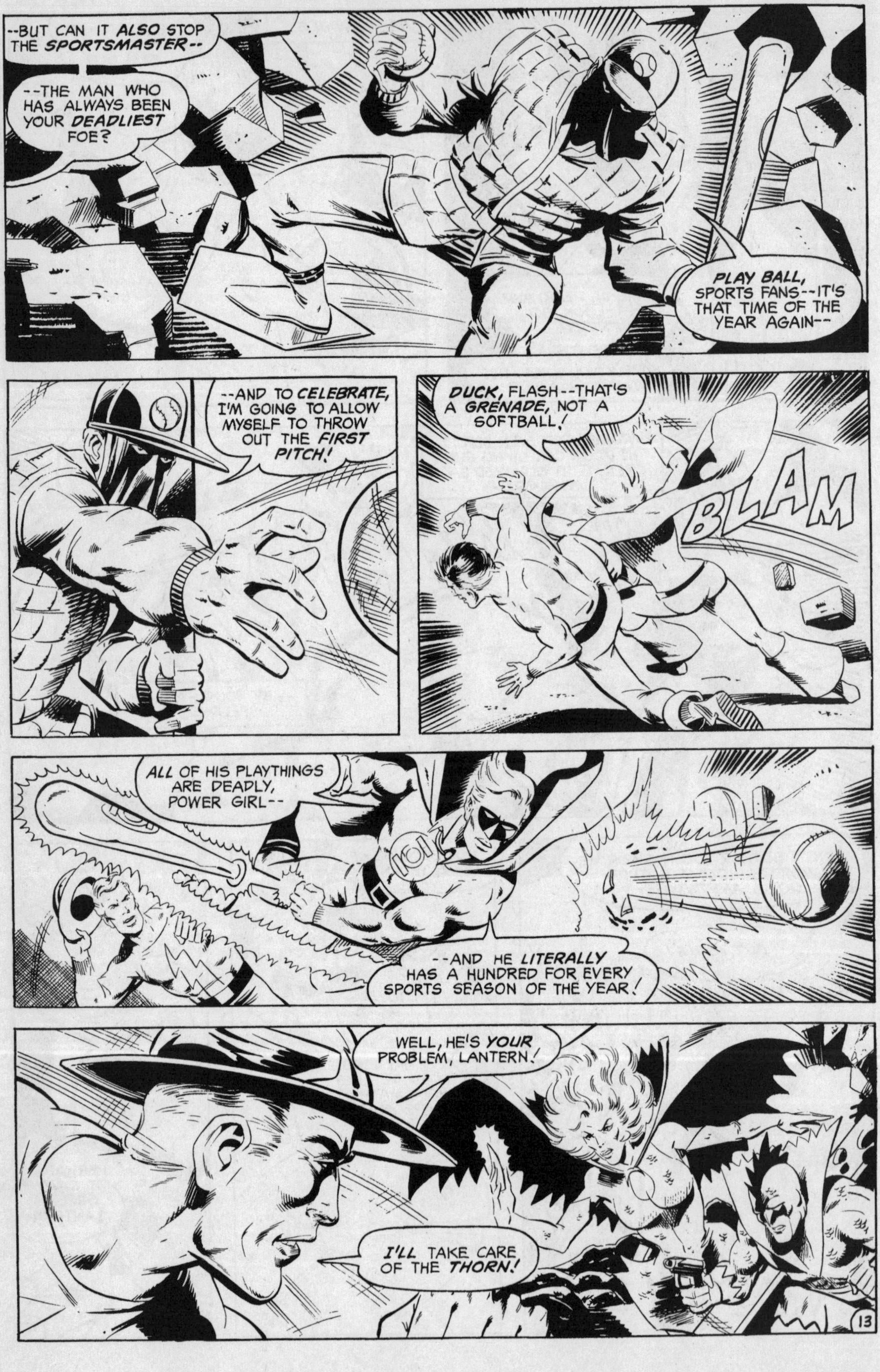
--BUT CAN IT ALSO STOP THE SPORTSMASTER--
--THE MAN WHO HAS ALWAYS BEEN YOUR DEADLIEST FOE?
PLAY BALL, SPORTS FANS--IT'S THAT TIME OF THE YEAR AGAIN--
--AND TO CELEBRATE, I'M GOING TO ALLOW MYSELF TO THROW OUT THE FIRST PITCH!
DUCK, FLASH--THAT'S A GRENADE, NOT A SOFTBALL!
BLAM
ALL OF HIS PLAYTHINGS ARE DEADLY, POWER GIRL--
--AND HE LITERALLY HAS A HUNDRED FOR EVERY SPORTS SEASON OF THE YEAR!
WELL, HE'S YOUR PROBLEM, LANTERN!
I'LL TAKE CARE OF THE THORN!
13

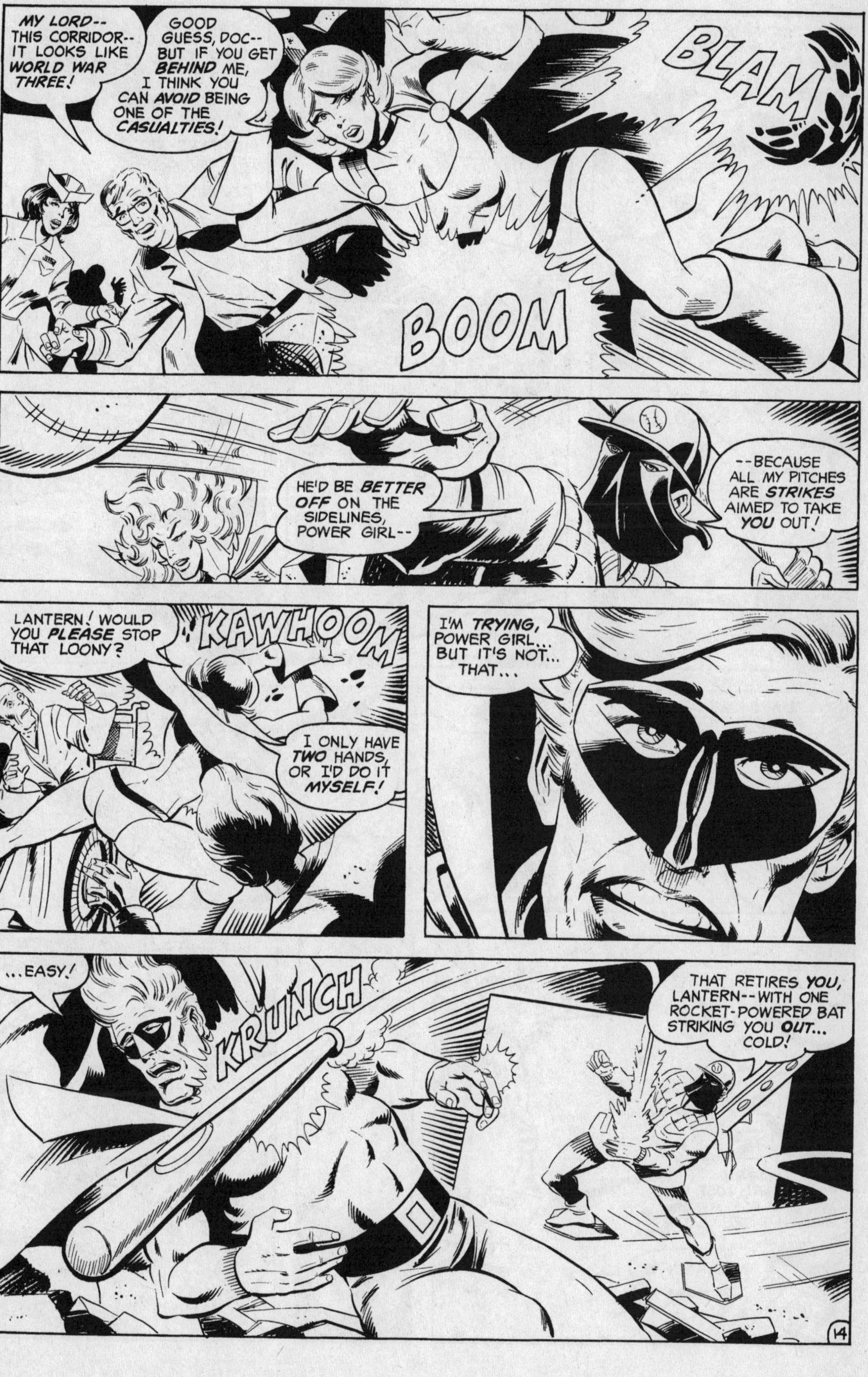
MY LORD-- THIS CORRIDOR-- IT LOOKS LIKE WORLD WAR THREE!
GOOD GUESS, DOC-- BUT IF YOU GET BEHIND ME, I THINK YOU CAN AVOID BEING ONE OF THE CASUALTIES!
BLAM
BOOM
HE'D BE BETTER OFF ON THE SIDELINES, POWER GIRL--
--BECAUSE ALL MY PITCHES ARE STRIKES AIMED TO TAKE YOU OUT!
LANTERN! WOULD YOU PLEASE STOP THAT LOONY?
KAWHOOM
I ONLY HAVE TWO HANDS, OR I'D DO IT MYSELF!
I'M TRYING, POWER GIRL... BUT IT'S NOT... THAT...
...EASY!
KRUNCH
THAT RETIRES YOU, LANTERN--WITH ONE ROCKET-POWERED BAT STRIKING YOU OUT... COLD!
14

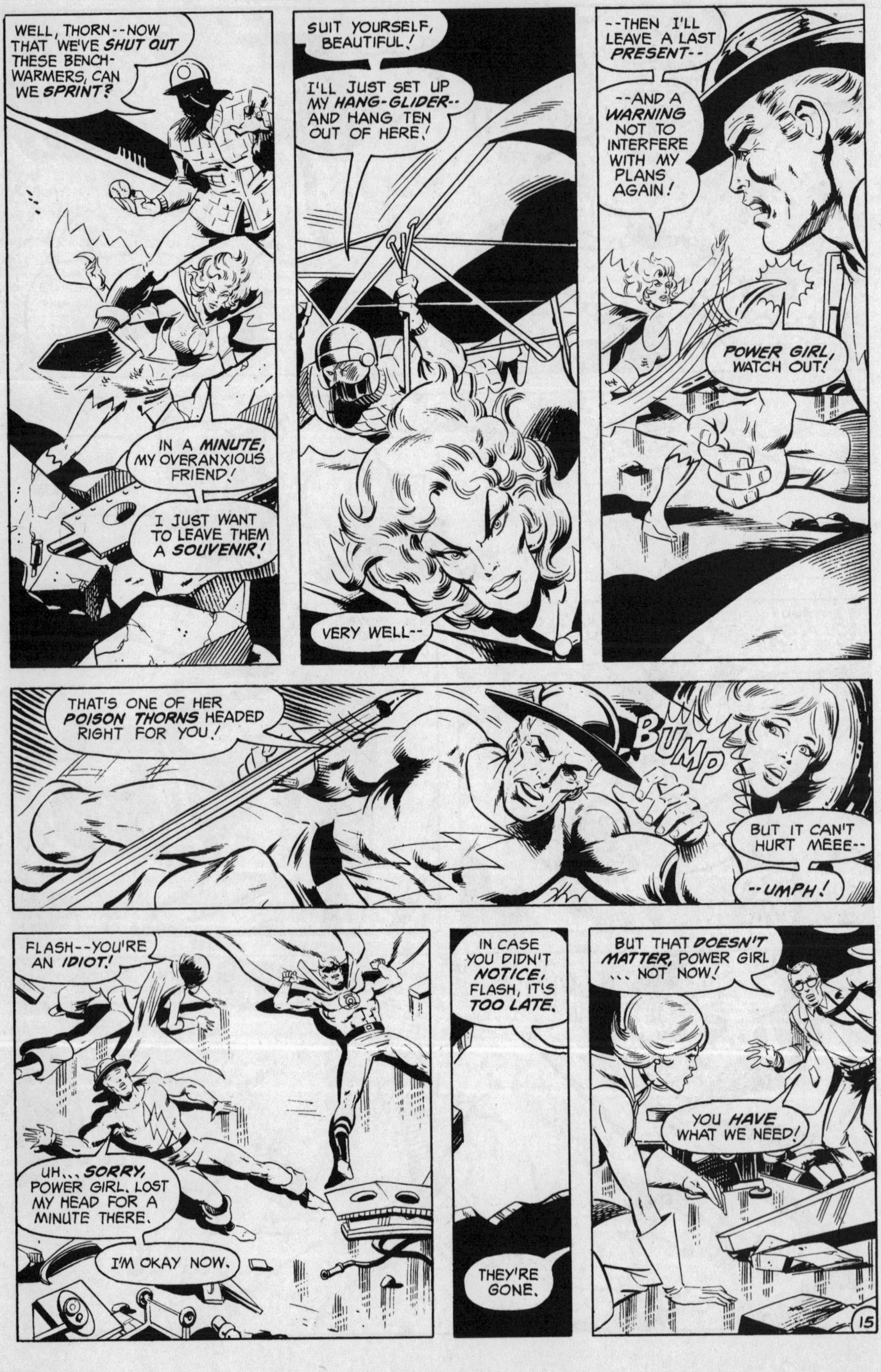
WELL, THORN--NOW THAT WE'VE SHUT OUT THESE BENCH-WARMERS, CAN WE SPRINT?
IN A MINUTE, MY OVERANXIOUS FRIEND!
I JUST WANT TO LEAVE THEM A SOUVENIR!
SUIT YOURSELF, BEAUTIFUL!
I'LL JUST SET UP MY HANG-GLIDER--AND HANG TEN OUT OF HERE!
VERY WELL--
--THEN I'LL LEAVE A LAST PRESENT--
--AND A WARNING NOT TO INTERFERE WITH MY PLANS AGAIN!
POWER GIRL, WATCH OUT!
THAT'S ONE OF HER POISON THORNS HEADED RIGHT FOR YOU!
BUMP
BUT IT CAN'T HURT MEEE--
--UMPH!
FLASH--YOU'RE AN IDIOT!
UH... SORRY, POWER GIRL. LOST MY HEAD FOR A MINUTE THERE.
I'M OKAY NOW.
IN CASE YOU DIDN'T NOTICE, FLASH, IT'S TOO LATE.
THEY'RE GONE.
BUT THAT DOESN'T MATTER, POWER GIRL ... NOT NOW!
YOU HAVE WHAT WE NEED!
15

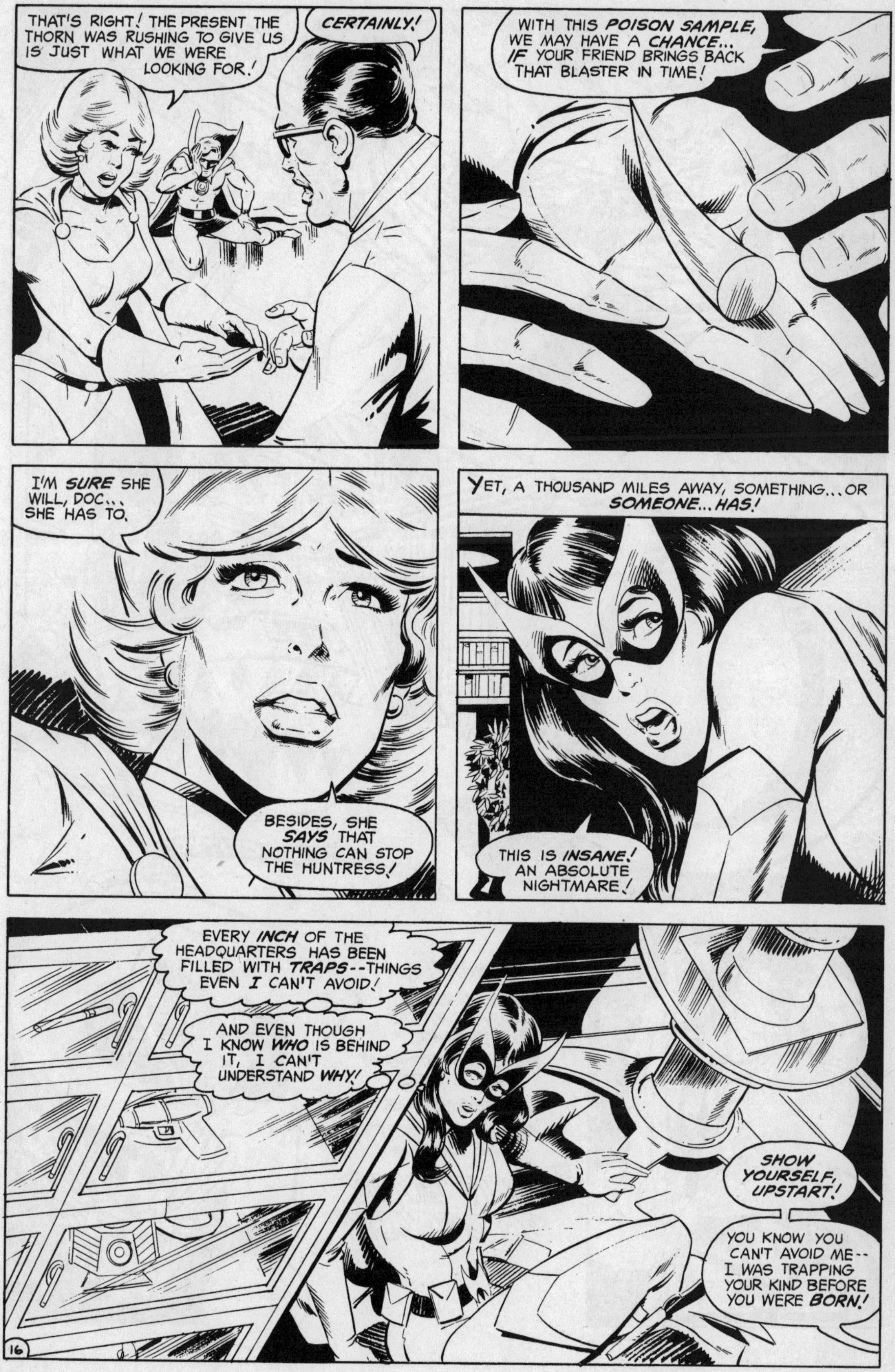
THAT'S RIGHT! THE PRESENT THE THORN WAS RUSHING TO GIVE US IS JUST WHAT WE WERE LOOKING FOR!
CERTAINLY!
WITH THIS POISON SAMPLE, WE MAY HAVE A CHANCE... IF YOUR FRIEND BRINGS BACK THAT BLASTER IN TIME!
I'M SURE SHE WILL, DOC... SHE HAS TO.
BESIDES, SHE SAYS THAT NOTHING CAN STOP THE HUNTRESS!
YET, A THOUSAND MILES AWAY, SOMETHING... OR SOMEONE... HAS!
THIS IS INSANE! AN ABSOLUTE NIGHTMARE!
EVERY INCH OF THE HEADQUARTERS HAS BEEN FILLED WITH TRAPS--THINGS EVEN I CAN'T AVOID!
AND EVEN THOUGH I KNOW WHO IS BEHIND IT, I CAN'T UNDERSTAND WHY!
SHOW YOURSELF, UPSTART!
YOU KNOW YOU CAN'T AVOID ME-- I WAS TRAPPING YOUR KIND BEFORE YOU WERE BORN!
16

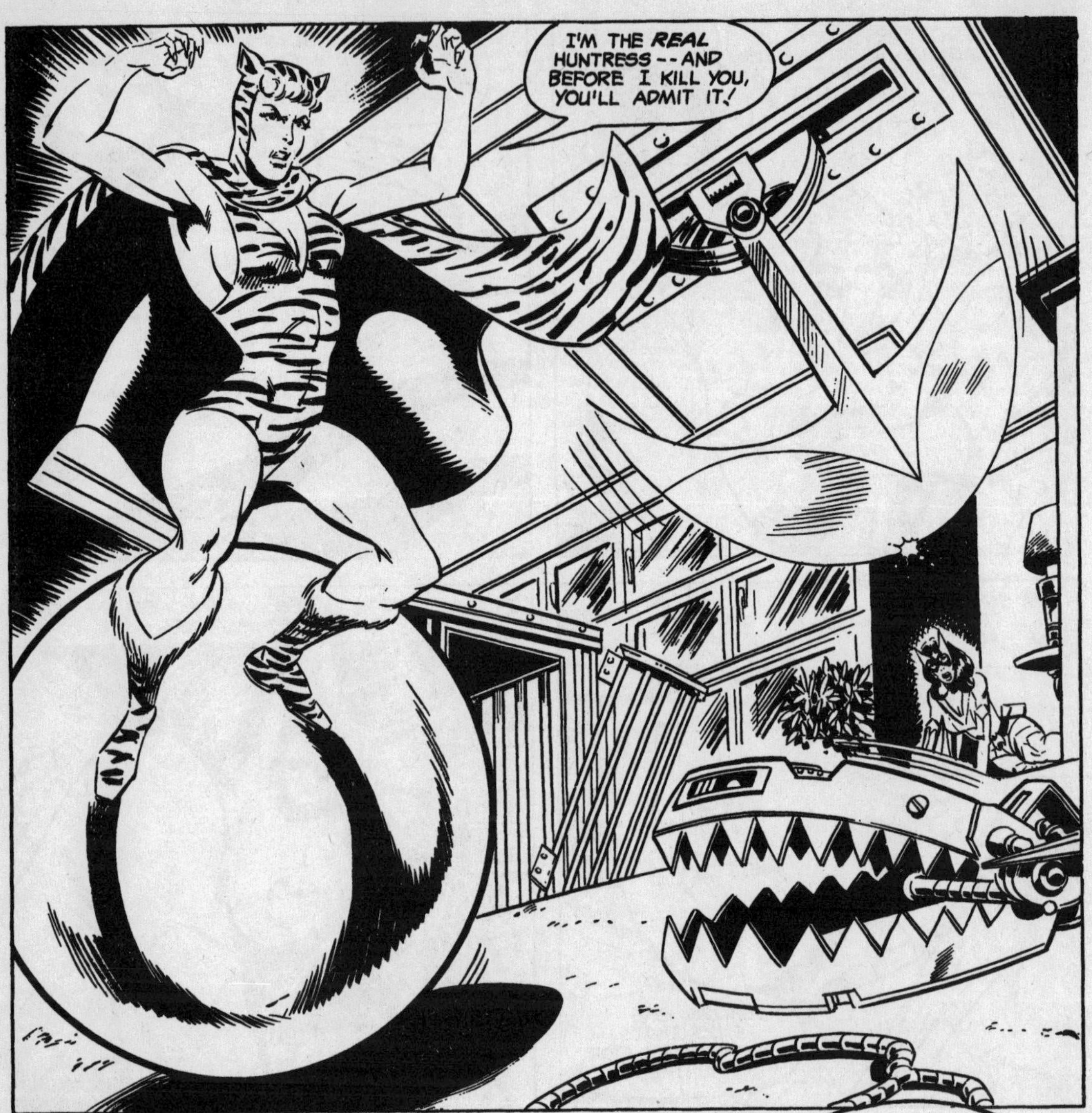
I'M THE REAL HUNTRESS--AND BEFORE I KILL YOU, YOU'LL ADMIT IT!

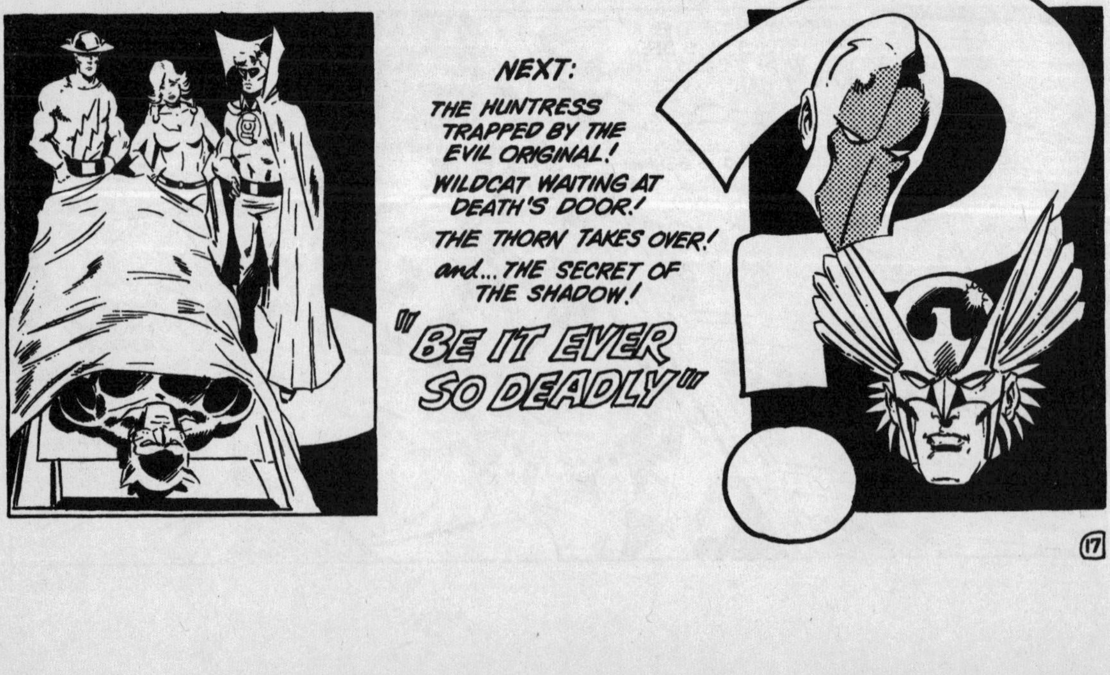
NEXT:
THE HUNTRESS TRAPPED BY THE EVIL ORIGINAL!
WILDCAT WAITING AT DEATH'S DOOR!
THE THORN TAKES OVER!
and... THE SECRET OF THE SHADOW!
"BE IT EVER SO DEADLY"
17

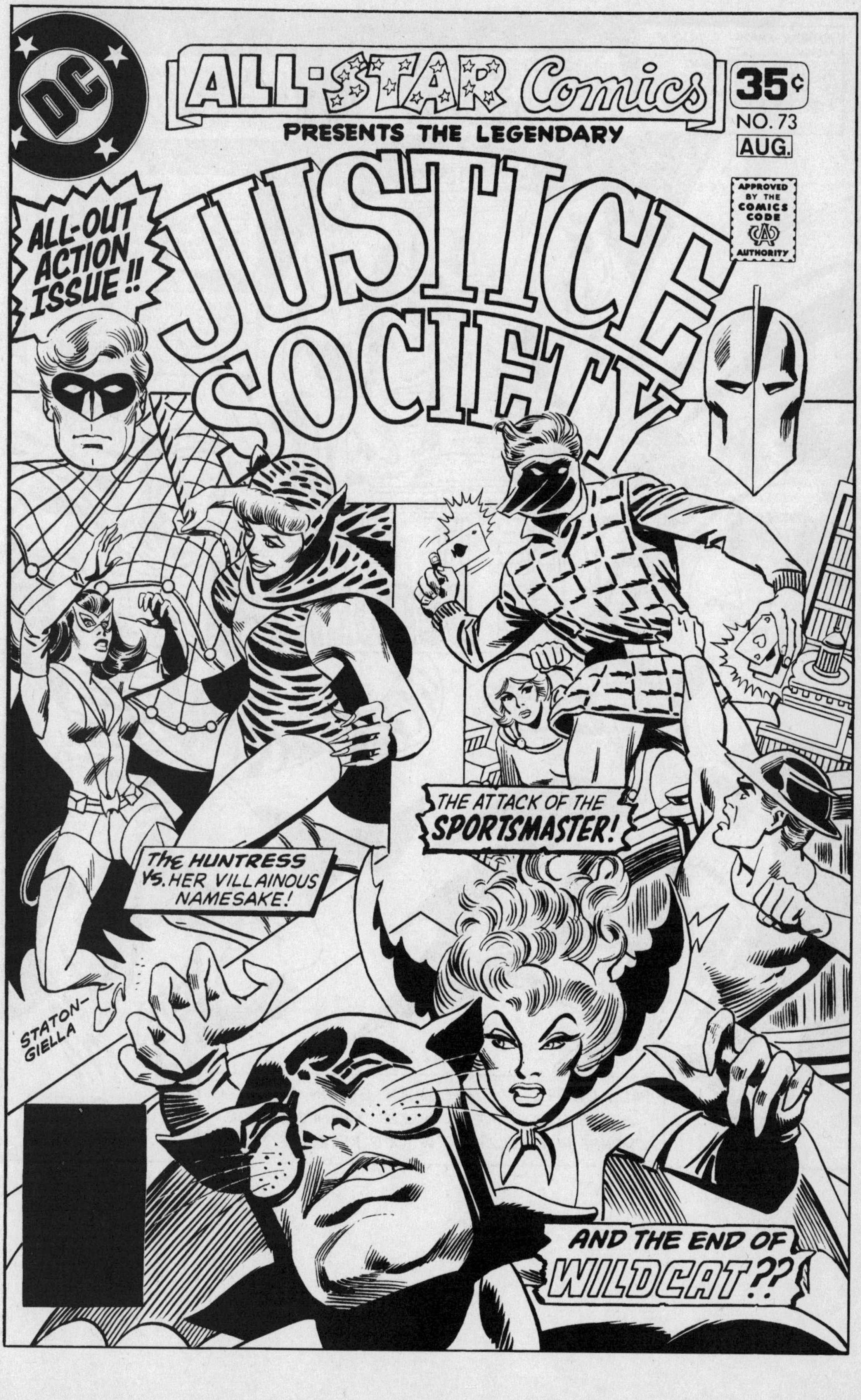
DC
ALL-STAR Comics
35¢
NO. 73
AUG.
PRESENTS THE LEGENDARY
JUSTICE SOCIETY
APPROVED BY THE COMICS CODE AUTHORITY
ALL-OUT ACTION ISSUE !!
THE ATTACK OF THE SPORTSMASTER!
The HUNTRESS VS. HER VILLAINOUS NAMESAKE!
STATON-GIELLA
AND THE END OF WILDCAT??

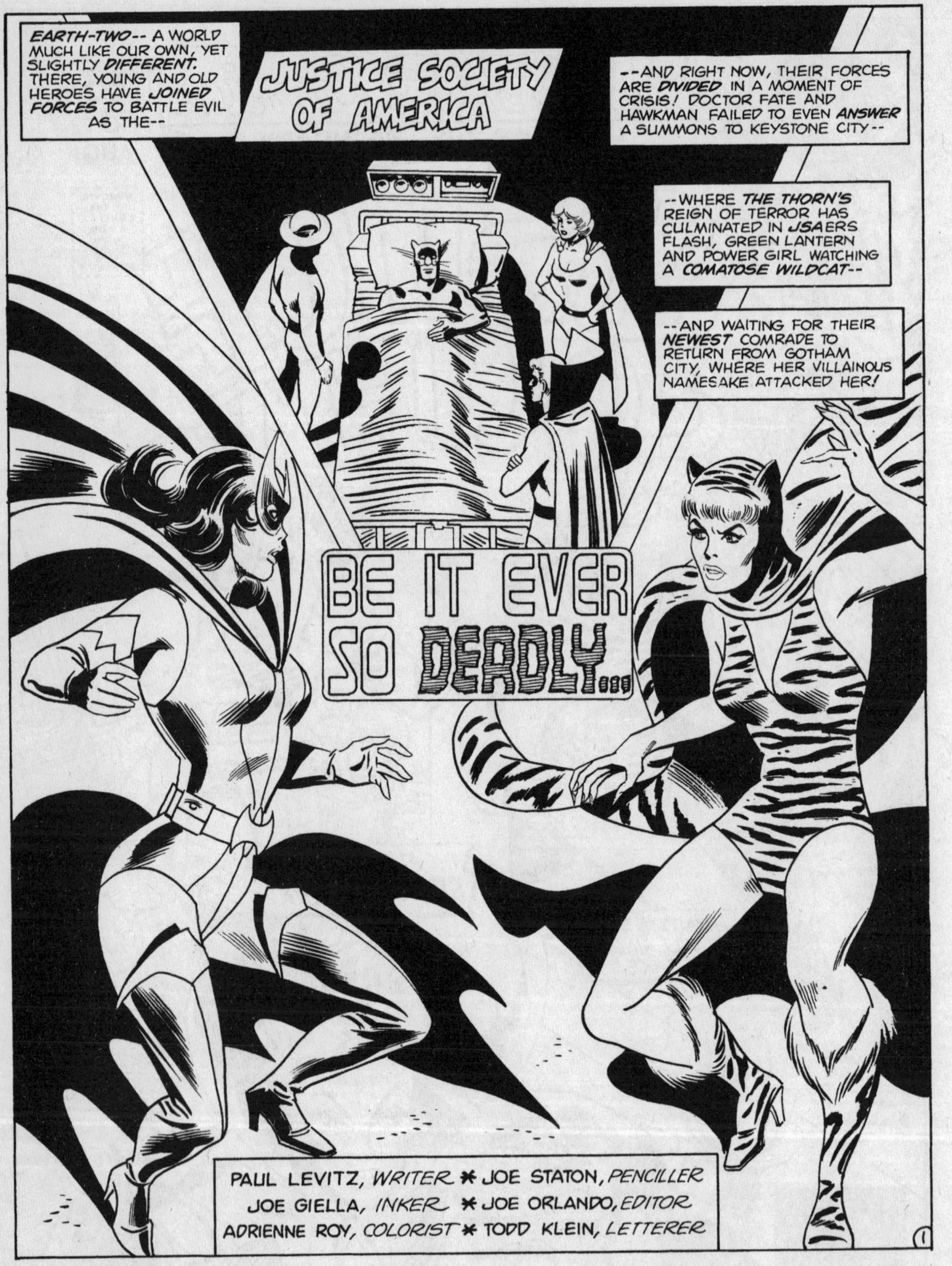
EARTH-TWO-- A WORLD MUCH LIKE OUR OWN, YET SLIGHTLY DIFFERENT. THERE, YOUNG AND OLD HEROES HAVE JOINED FORCES TO BATTLE EVIL AS THE--
JUSTICE SOCIETY OF AMERICA
--AND RIGHT NOW, THEIR FORCES ARE DIVIDED IN A MOMENT OF CRISIS! DOCTOR FATE AND HAWKMAN FAILED TO EVEN ANSWER A SUMMONS TO KEYSTONE CITY--
--WHERE THE THORN'S REIGN OF TERROR HAS CULMINATED IN JSAERS FLASH, GREEN LANTERN AND POWER GIRL WATCHING A COMATOSE WILDCAT--
--AND WAITING FOR THEIR NEWEST COMRADE TO RETURN FROM GOTHAM CITY, WHERE HER VILLAINOUS NAMESAKE ATTACKED HER!
BE IT EVER SO DEADLY...
PAUL LEVITZ, WRITER * JOE STATON, PENCILLER
JOE GIELLA, INKER * JOE ORLANDO, EDITOR
ADRIENNE ROY, COLORIST * TODD KLEIN, LETTERER
1

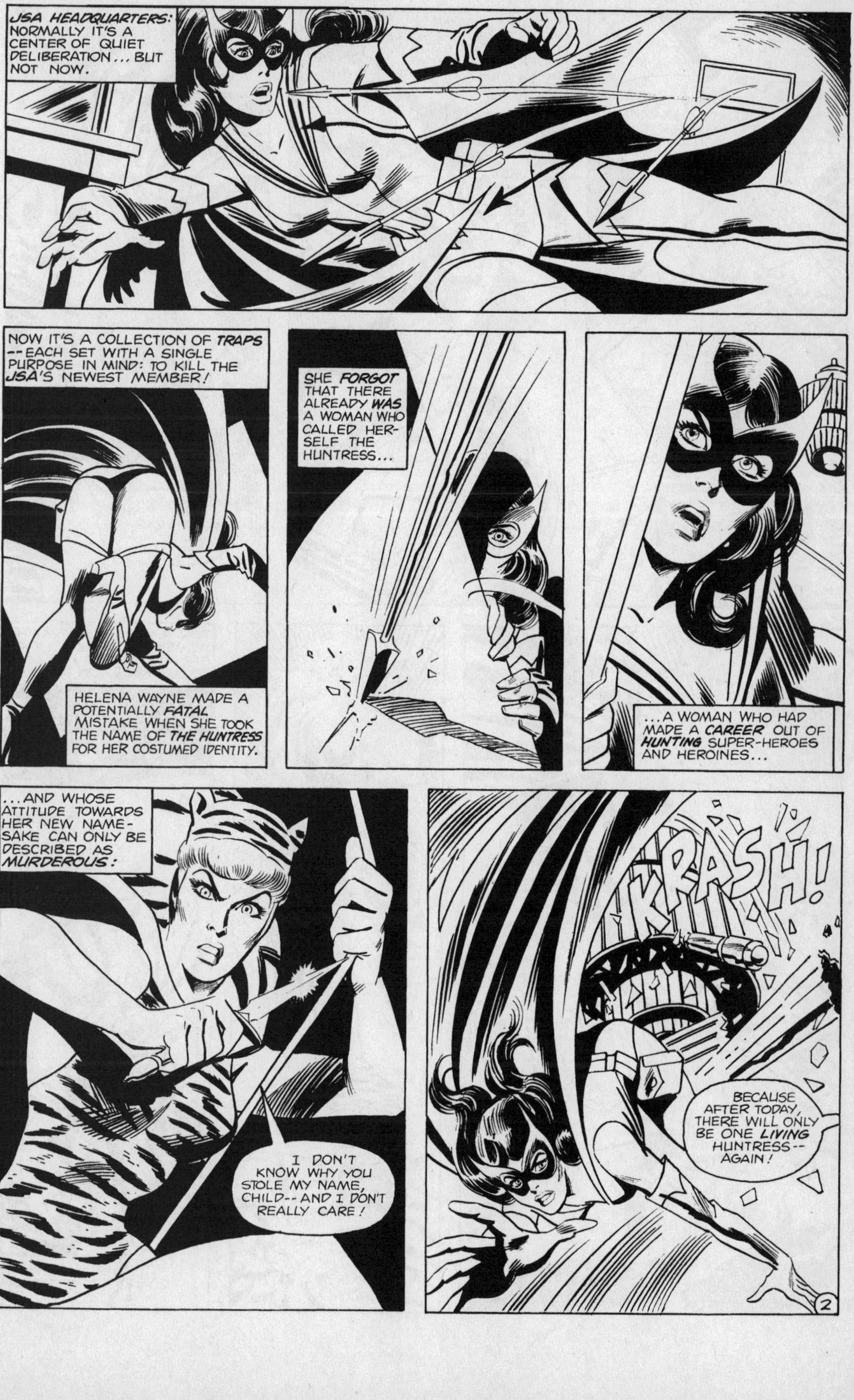

JSA HEADQUARTERS: NORMALLY IT'S A CENTER OF QUIET DELIBERATION... BUT NOT NOW.
NOW IT'S A COLLECTION OF TRAPS -- EACH SET WITH A SINGLE PURPOSE IN MIND: TO KILL THE JSA'S NEWEST MEMBER!
HELENA WAYNE MADE A POTENTIALLY FATAL MISTAKE WHEN SHE TOOK THE NAME OF THE HUNTRESS FOR HER COSTUMED IDENTITY.
SHE FORGOT THAT THERE ALREADY WAS A WOMAN WHO CALLED HER-SELF THE HUNTRESS...
...A WOMAN WHO HAD MADE A CAREER OUT OF HUNTING SUPER-HEROES AND HEROINES...
...AND WHOSE ATTITUDE TOWARDS HER NEW NAME-SAKE CAN ONLY BE DESCRIBED AS MURDEROUS:
I DON'T KNOW WHY YOU STOLE MY NAME, CHILD-- AND I DON'T REALLY CARE!
KRASH!
BECAUSE AFTER TODAY, THERE WILL ONLY BE ONE LIVING HUNTRESS-- AGAIN!
2

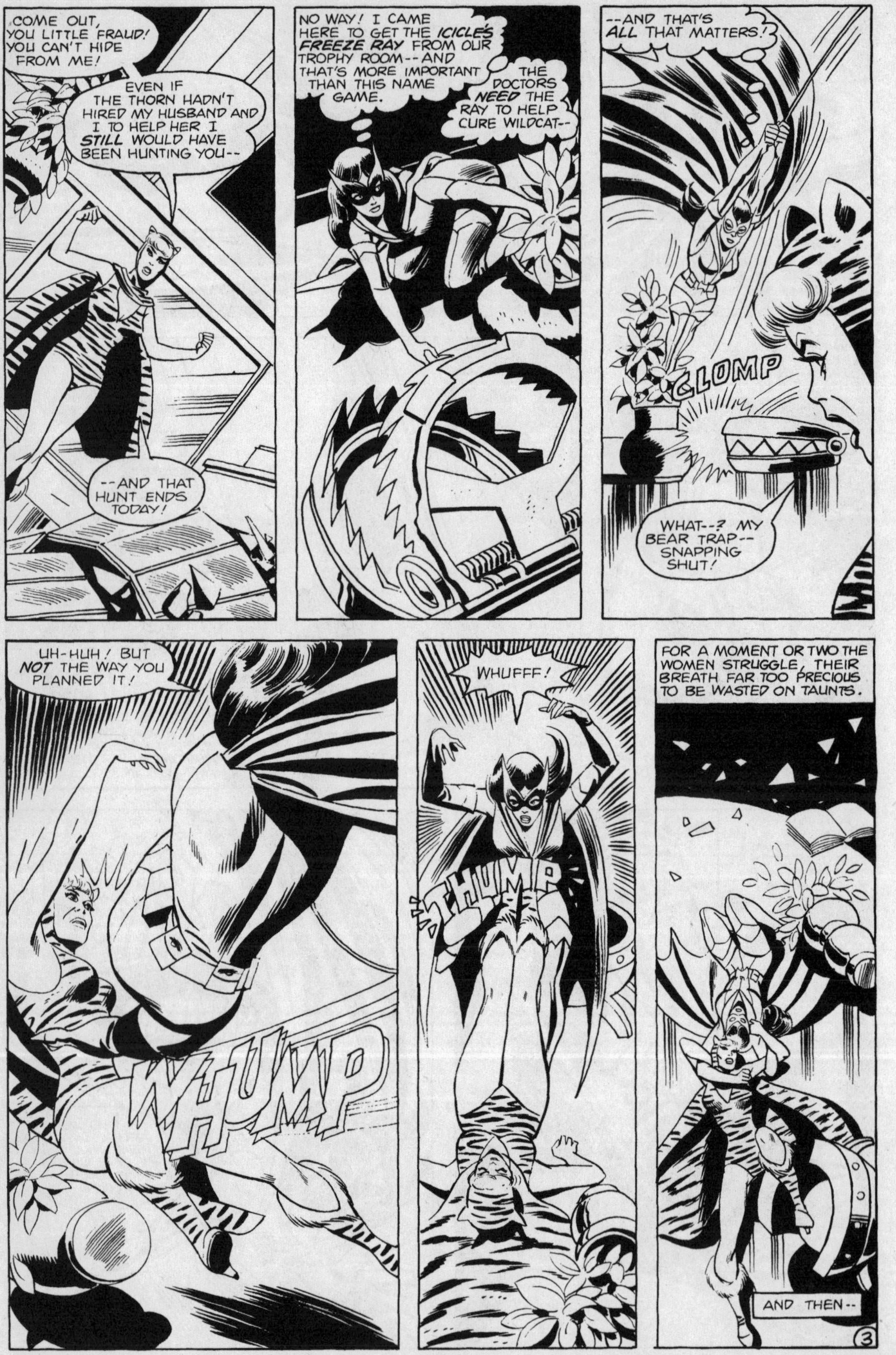
COME OUT, YOU LITTLE FRAUD! YOU CAN'T HIDE FROM ME!
EVEN IF THE THORN HADN'T HIRED MY HUSBAND AND I TO HELP HER I STILL WOULD HAVE BEEN HUNTING YOU--
--AND THAT HUNT ENDS TODAY!
NO WAY! I CAME HERE TO GET THE ICICLE'S FREEZE RAY FROM OUR TROPHY ROOM--AND THAT'S MORE IMPORTANT THAN THIS NAME GAME.
THE DOCTORS NEED THE RAY TO HELP CURE WILDCAT--
--AND THAT'S ALL THAT MATTERS!
CLOMP
WHAT--? MY BEAR TRAP-- SNAPPING SHUT!
UH-HUH! BUT NOT THE WAY YOU PLANNED IT!
WHUMP
WHUFFF!
THUMP
FOR A MOMENT OR TWO THE WOMEN STRUGGLE, THEIR BREATH FAR TOO PRECIOUS TO BE WASTED ON TAUNTS.
AND THEN--
3

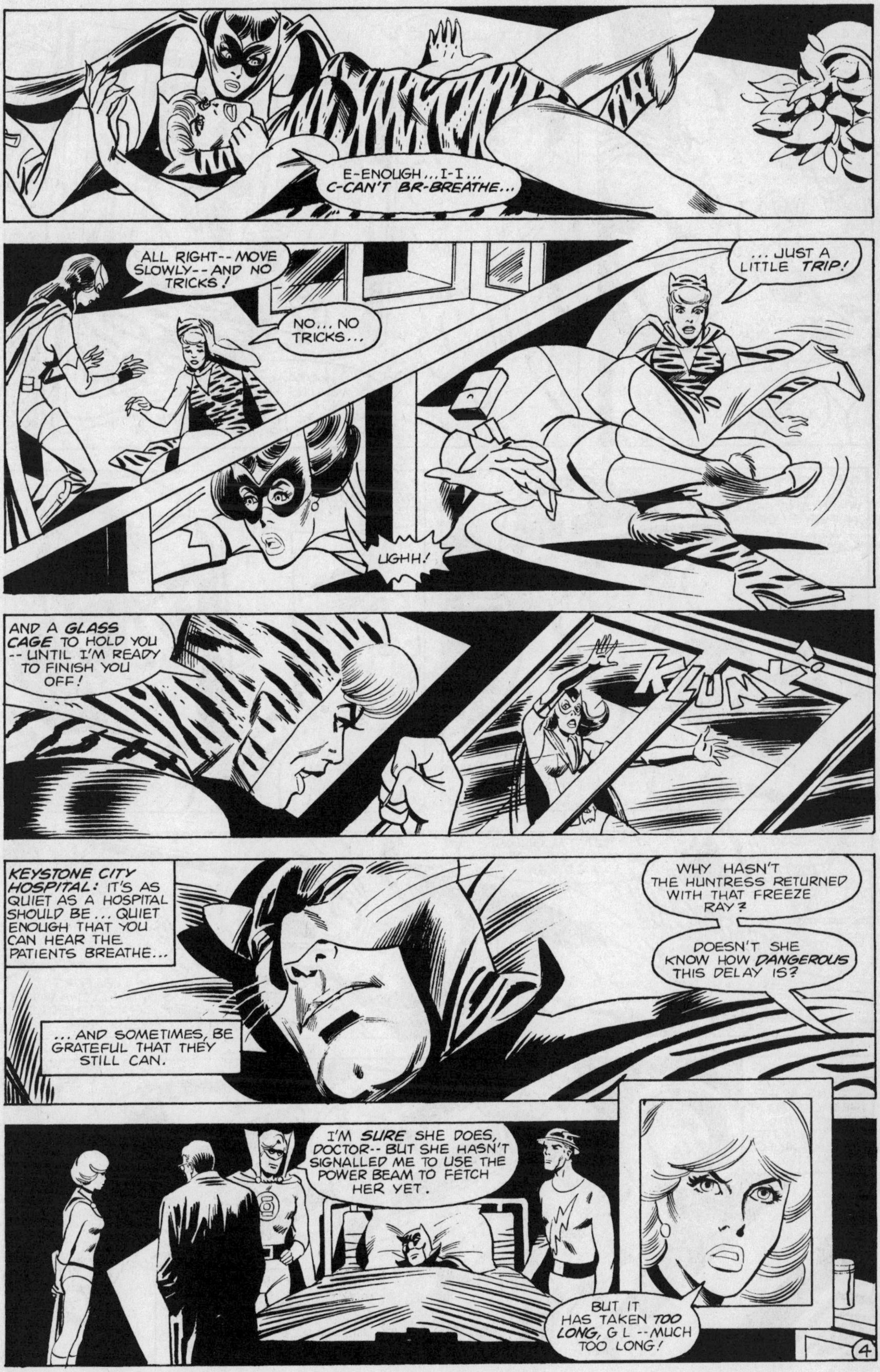
E-ENOUGH... I-I... C-CAN'T BR-BREATHE...
ALL RIGHT-- MOVE SLOWLY-- AND NO TRICKS!
NO... NO TRICKS...
... JUST A LITTLE TRIP!
UGHH!
AND A GLASS CAGE TO HOLD YOU -- UNTIL I'M READY TO FINISH YOU OFF!
KLUNK!
KEYSTONE CITY HOSPITAL: IT'S AS QUIET AS A HOSPITAL SHOULD BE... QUIET ENOUGH THAT YOU CAN HEAR THE PATIENTS BREATHE...
... AND SOMETIMES, BE GRATEFUL THAT THEY STILL CAN.
WHY HASN'T THE HUNTRESS RETURNED WITH THAT FREEZE RAY?
DOESN'T SHE KNOW HOW DANGEROUS THIS DELAY IS?
I'M SURE SHE DOES, DOCTOR-- BUT SHE HASN'T SIGNALLED ME TO USE THE POWER BEAM TO FETCH HER YET.
BUT IT HAS TAKEN TOO LONG, G L --MUCH TOO LONG!
4

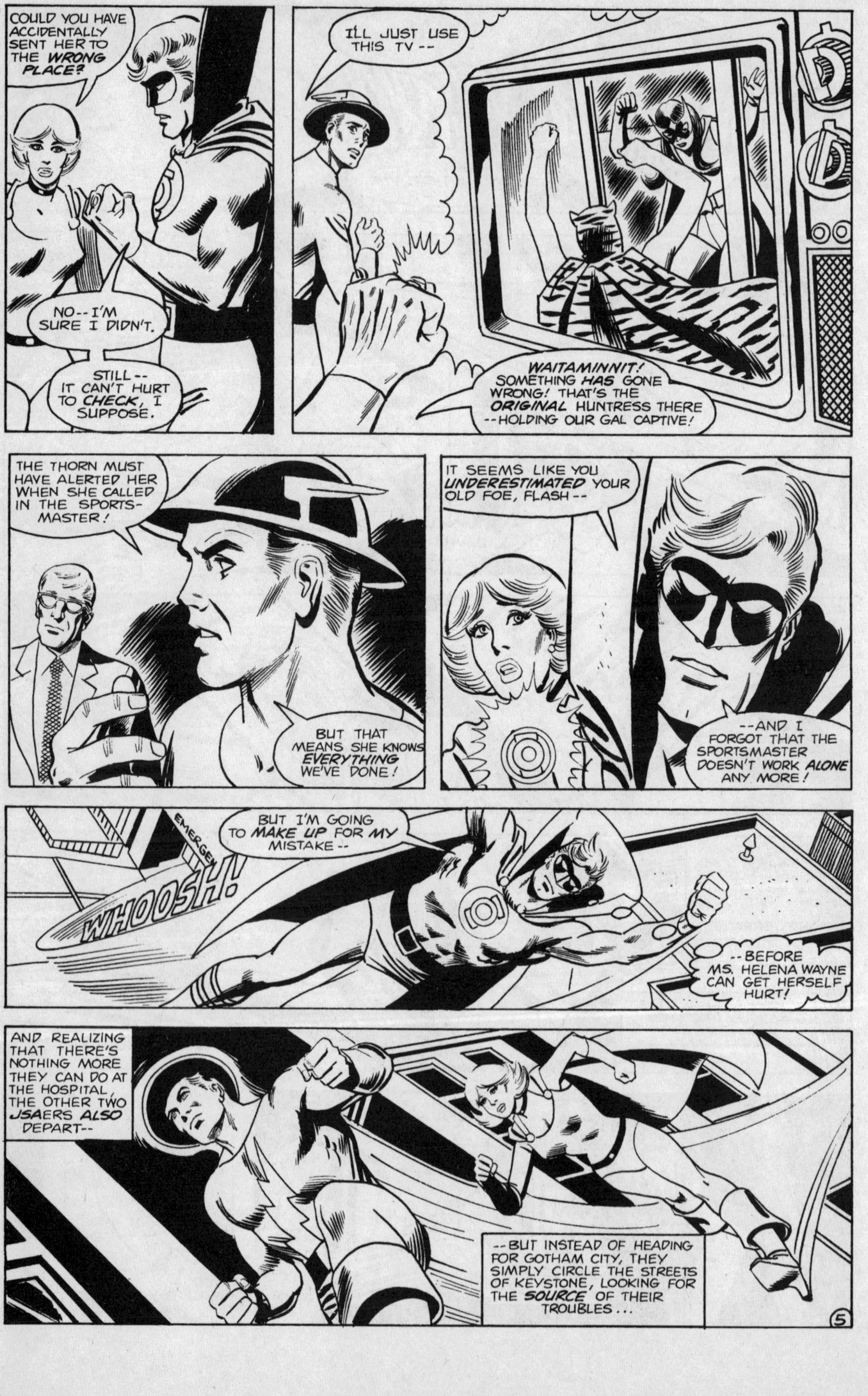
COULD YOU HAVE ACCIDENTALLY SENT HER TO THE WRONG PLACE?
NO-- I'M SURE I DIDN'T.
STILL-- IT CAN'T HURT TO CHECK, I SUPPOSE.
I'LL JUST USE THIS TV --
WAITAMINNIT! SOMETHING HAS GONE WRONG! THAT'S THE ORIGINAL HUNTRESS THERE --HOLDING OUR GAL CAPTIVE!
THE THORN MUST HAVE ALERTED HER WHEN SHE CALLED IN THE SPORTS-MASTER!
BUT THAT MEANS SHE KNOWS EVERYTHING WE'VE DONE!
IT SEEMS LIKE YOU UNDERESTIMATED YOUR OLD FOE, FLASH --
--AND I FORGOT THAT THE SPORTSMASTER DOESN'T WORK ALONE ANY MORE!
BUT I'M GOING TO MAKE UP FOR MY MISTAKE --
WHOOSH!
--BEFORE MS. HELENA WAYNE CAN GET HERSELF HURT!
AND REALIZING THAT THERE'S NOTHING MORE THEY CAN DO AT THE HOSPITAL, THE OTHER TWO JSAERS ALSO DEPART--
--BUT INSTEAD OF HEADING FOR GOTHAM CITY, THEY SIMPLY CIRCLE THE STREETS OF KEYSTONE, LOOKING FOR THE SOURCE OF THEIR TROUBLES...
5

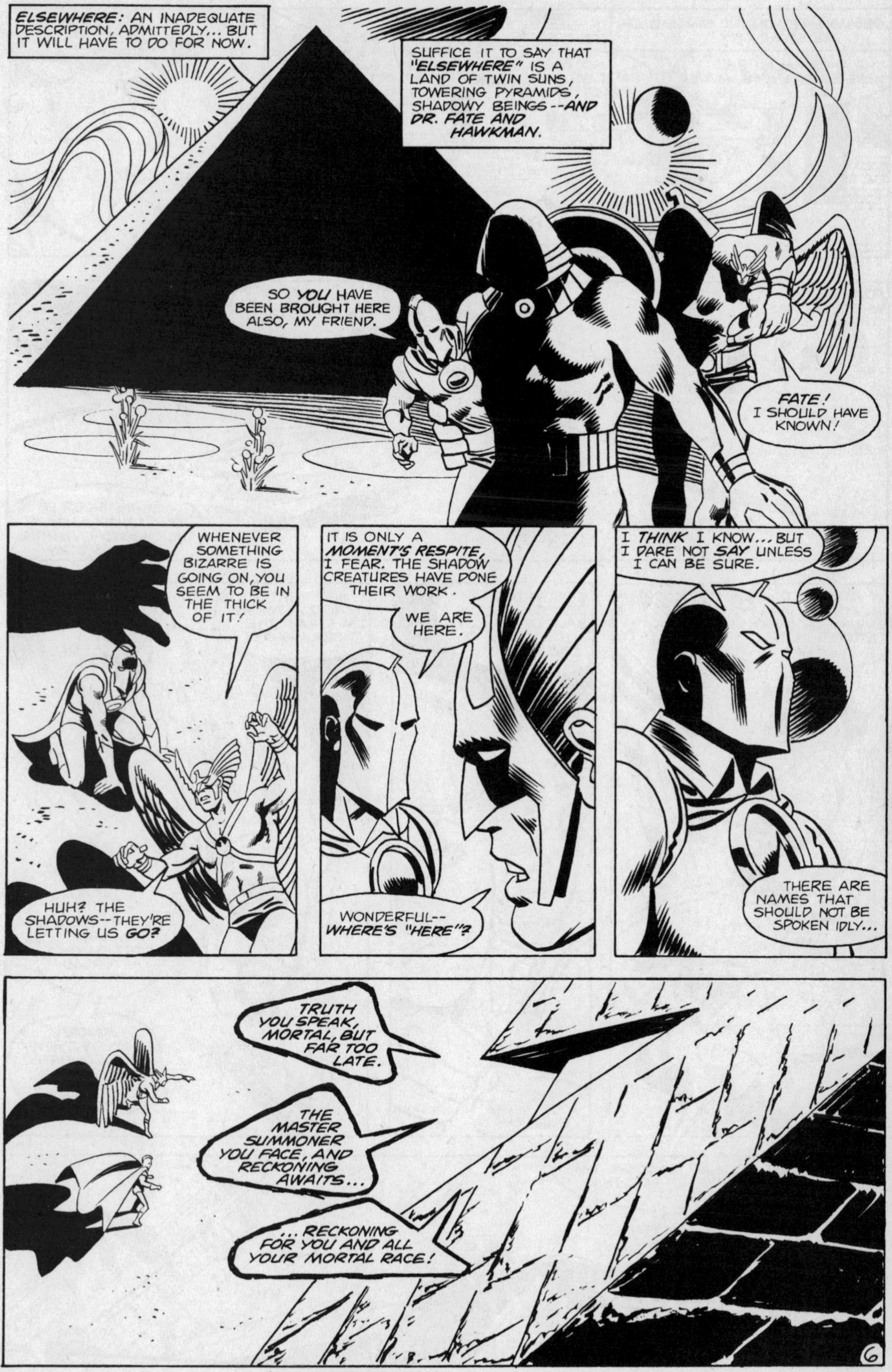
ELSEWHERE: AN INADEQUATE DESCRIPTION, ADMITTEDLY... BUT IT WILL HAVE TO DO FOR NOW.
SUFFICE IT TO SAY THAT "ELSEWHERE" IS A LAND OF TWIN SUNS, TOWERING PYRAMIDS, SHADOWY BEINGS--AND DR. FATE AND HAWKMAN.
SO YOU HAVE BEEN BROUGHT HERE ALSO, MY FRIEND.
FATE! I SHOULD HAVE KNOWN!
WHENEVER SOMETHING BIZARRE IS GOING ON, YOU SEEM TO BE IN THE THICK OF IT!
HUH? THE SHADOWS--THEY'RE LETTING US GO?
IT IS ONLY A MOMENT'S RESPITE, I FEAR. THE SHADOW CREATURES HAVE DONE THEIR WORK.
WE ARE HERE.
WONDERFUL-- WHERE'S "HERE"?
I THINK I KNOW... BUT I DARE NOT SAY UNLESS I CAN BE SURE.
THERE ARE NAMES THAT SHOULD NOT BE SPOKEN IDLY...
TRUTH YOU SPEAK, MORTAL, BUT FAR TOO LATE.
THE MASTER SUMMONER YOU FACE, AND RECKONING AWAITS...
...RECKONING FOR YOU AND ALL YOUR MORTAL RACE!
6

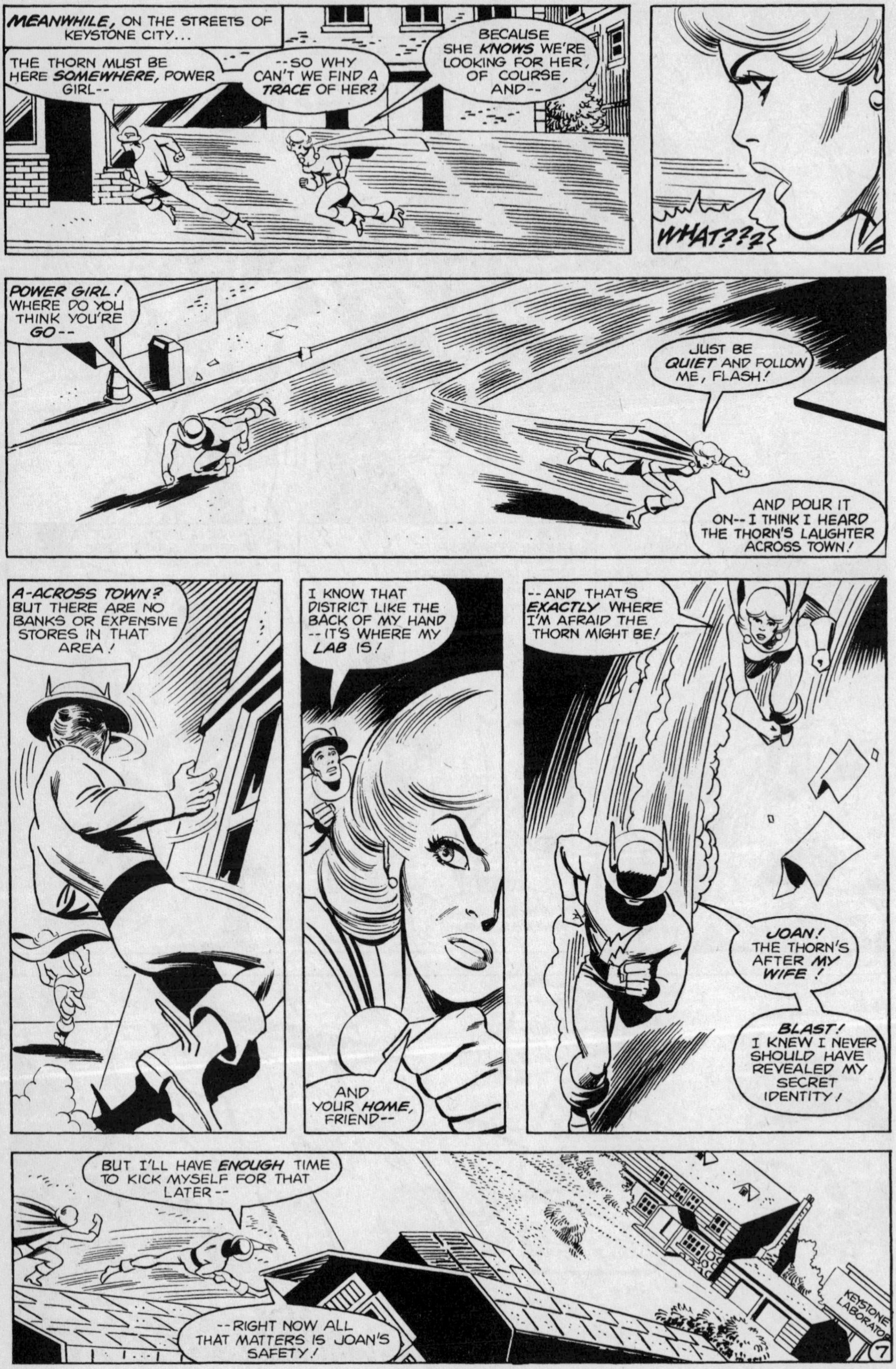
MEANWHILE, ON THE STREETS OF KEYSTONE CITY...
THE THORN MUST BE HERE SOMEWHERE, POWER GIRL--
--SO WHY CAN'T WE FIND A TRACE OF HER?
BECAUSE SHE KNOWS WE'RE LOOKING FOR HER, OF COURSE, AND--
WHAT???
POWER GIRL! WHERE DO YOU THINK YOU'RE GO--
JUST BE QUIET AND FOLLOW ME, FLASH!
AND POUR IT ON--I THINK I HEARD THE THORN'S LAUGHTER ACROSS TOWN!
A-ACROSS TOWN? BUT THERE ARE NO BANKS OR EXPENSIVE STORES IN THAT AREA!
I KNOW THAT DISTRICT LIKE THE BACK OF MY HAND --IT'S WHERE MY LAB IS!
AND YOUR HOME, FRIEND--
--AND THAT'S EXACTLY WHERE I'M AFRAID THE THORN MIGHT BE!
JOAN! THE THORN'S AFTER MY WIFE!
BLAST! I KNEW I NEVER SHOULD HAVE REVEALED MY SECRET IDENTITY!
BUT I'LL HAVE ENOUGH TIME TO KICK MYSELF FOR THAT LATER--
--RIGHT NOW ALL THAT MATTERS IS JOAN'S SAFETY!
KEYSTONE LABORATO
7

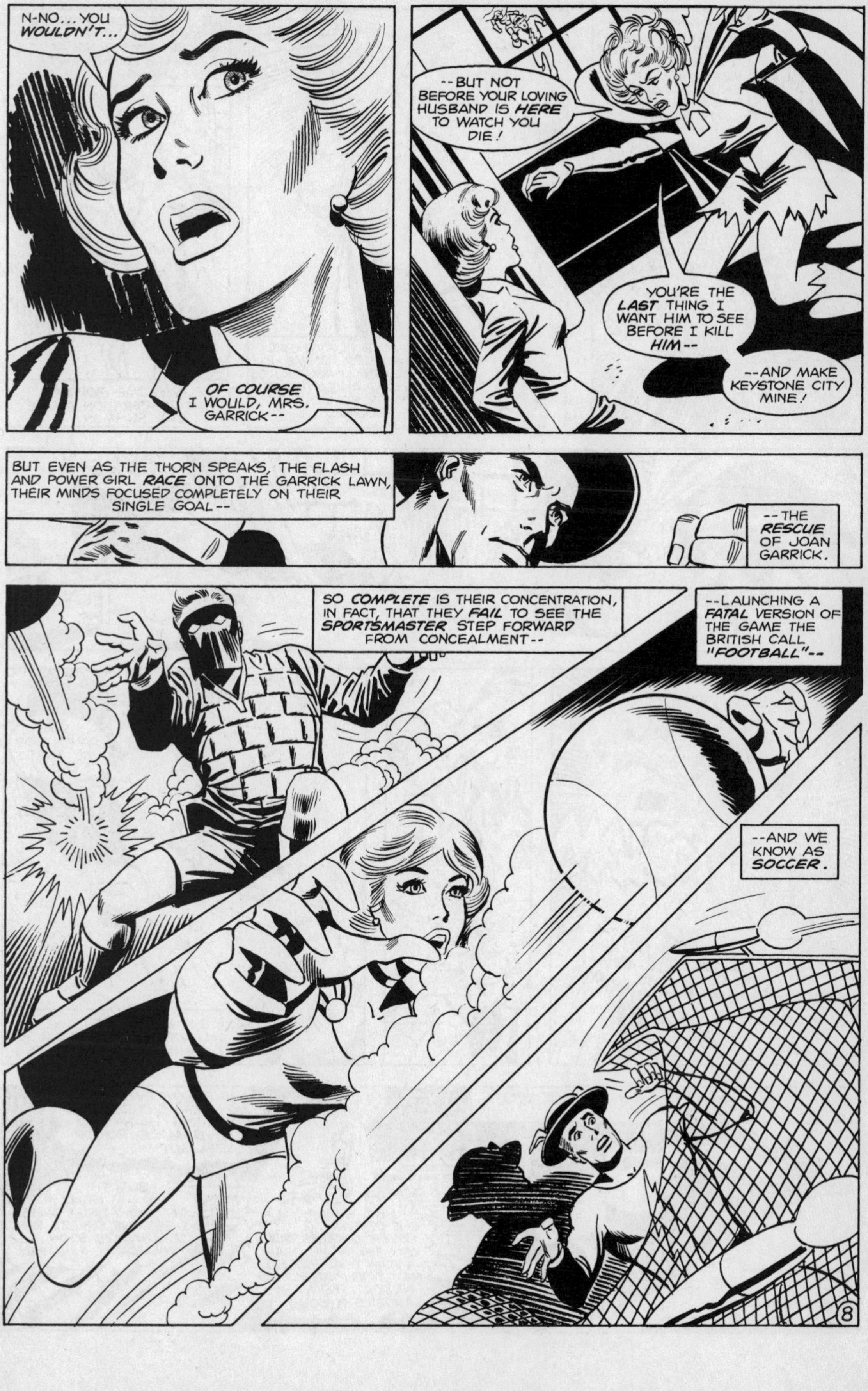
N-NO... YOU WOULDN'T...
OF COURSE I WOULD, MRS. GARRICK--
--BUT NOT BEFORE YOUR LOVING HUSBAND IS HERE TO WATCH YOU DIE!
YOU'RE THE LAST THING I WANT HIM TO SEE BEFORE I KILL HIM--
--AND MAKE KEYSTONE CITY MINE!
BUT EVEN AS THE THORN SPEAKS, THE FLASH AND POWER GIRL RACE ONTO THE GARRICK LAWN, THEIR MINDS FOCUSED COMPLETELY ON THEIR SINGLE GOAL--
--THE RESCUE OF JOAN GARRICK.
SO COMPLETE IS THEIR CONCENTRATION, IN FACT, THAT THEY FAIL TO SEE THE SPORTSMASTER STEP FORWARD FROM CONCEALMENT--
--LAUNCHING A FATAL VERSION OF THE GAME THE BRITISH CALL "FOOTBALL"--
--AND WE KNOW AS SOCCER.
8

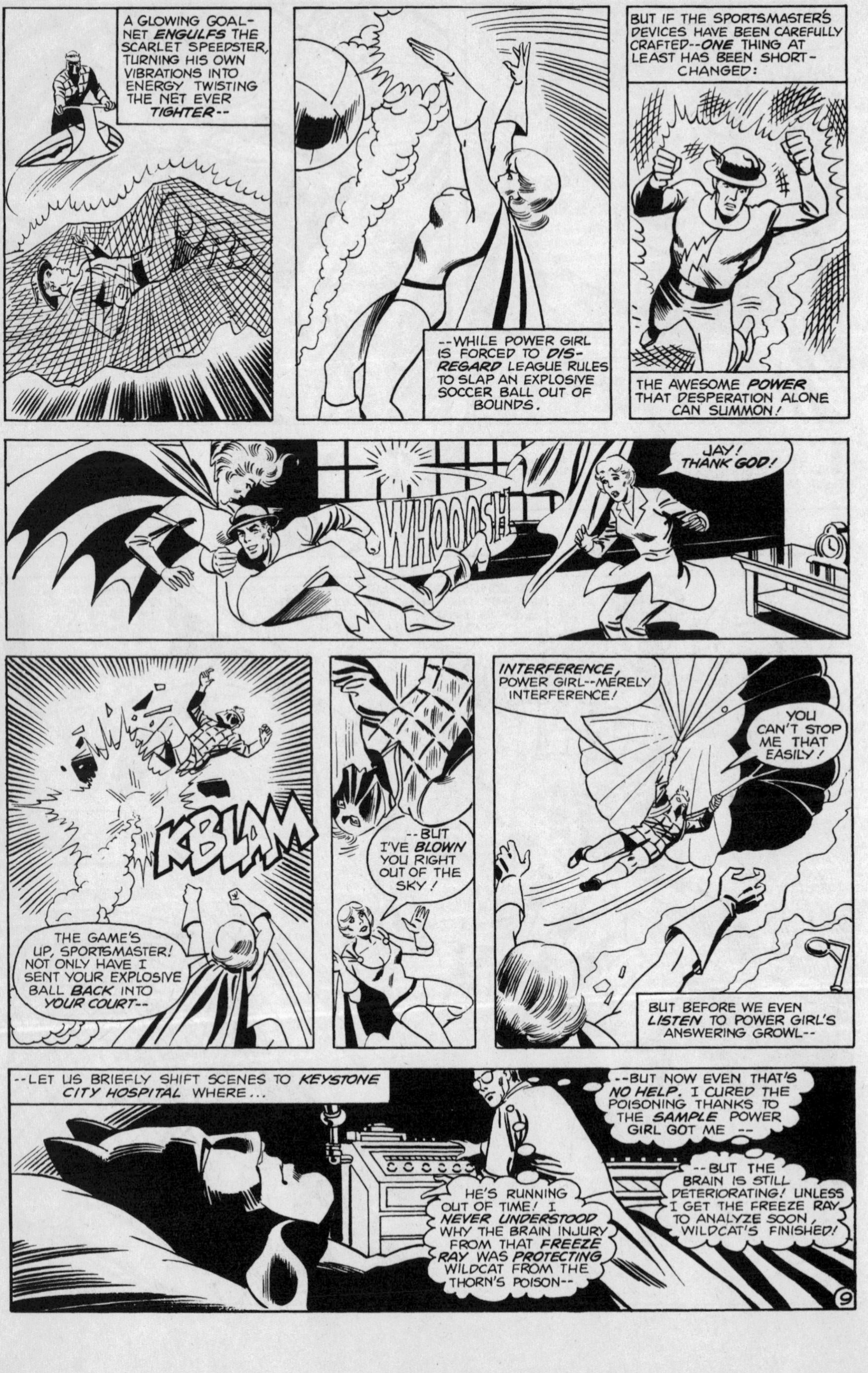
A GLOWING GOAL-NET ENGULFS THE SCARLET SPEEDSTER, TURNING HIS OWN VIBRATIONS INTO ENERGY TWISTING THE NET EVER TIGHTER--
--WHILE POWER GIRL IS FORCED TO DIS-REGARD LEAGUE RULES TO SLAP AN EXPLOSIVE SOCCER BALL OUT OF BOUNDS.
BUT IF THE SPORTSMASTER'S DEVICES HAVE BEEN CAREFULLY CRAFTED--ONE THING AT LEAST HAS BEEN SHORT-CHANGED:
THE AWESOME POWER THAT DESPERATION ALONE CAN SUMMON!
WHOOOSH
JAY! THANK GOD!
KBLAM
THE GAME'S UP, SPORTSMASTER! NOT ONLY HAVE I SENT YOUR EXPLOSIVE BALL BACK INTO YOUR COURT--
--BUT I'VE BLOWN YOU RIGHT OUT OF THE SKY!
INTERFERENCE, POWER GIRL--MERELY INTERFERENCE!
YOU CAN'T STOP ME THAT EASILY!
BUT BEFORE WE EVEN LISTEN TO POWER GIRL'S ANSWERING GROWL--
--LET US BRIEFLY SHIFT SCENES TO KEYSTONE CITY HOSPITAL WHERE...
HE'S RUNNING OUT OF TIME! I NEVER UNDERSTOOD WHY THE BRAIN INJURY FROM THAT FREEZE RAY WAS PROTECTING WILDCAT FROM THE THORN'S POISON--
--BUT NOW EVEN THAT'S NO HELP. I CURED THE POISONING THANKS TO THE SAMPLE POWER GIRL GOT ME --
--BUT THE BRAIN IS STILL DETERIORATING! UNLESS I GET THE FREEZE RAY TO ANALYZE SOON, WILDCAT'S FINISHED!
9

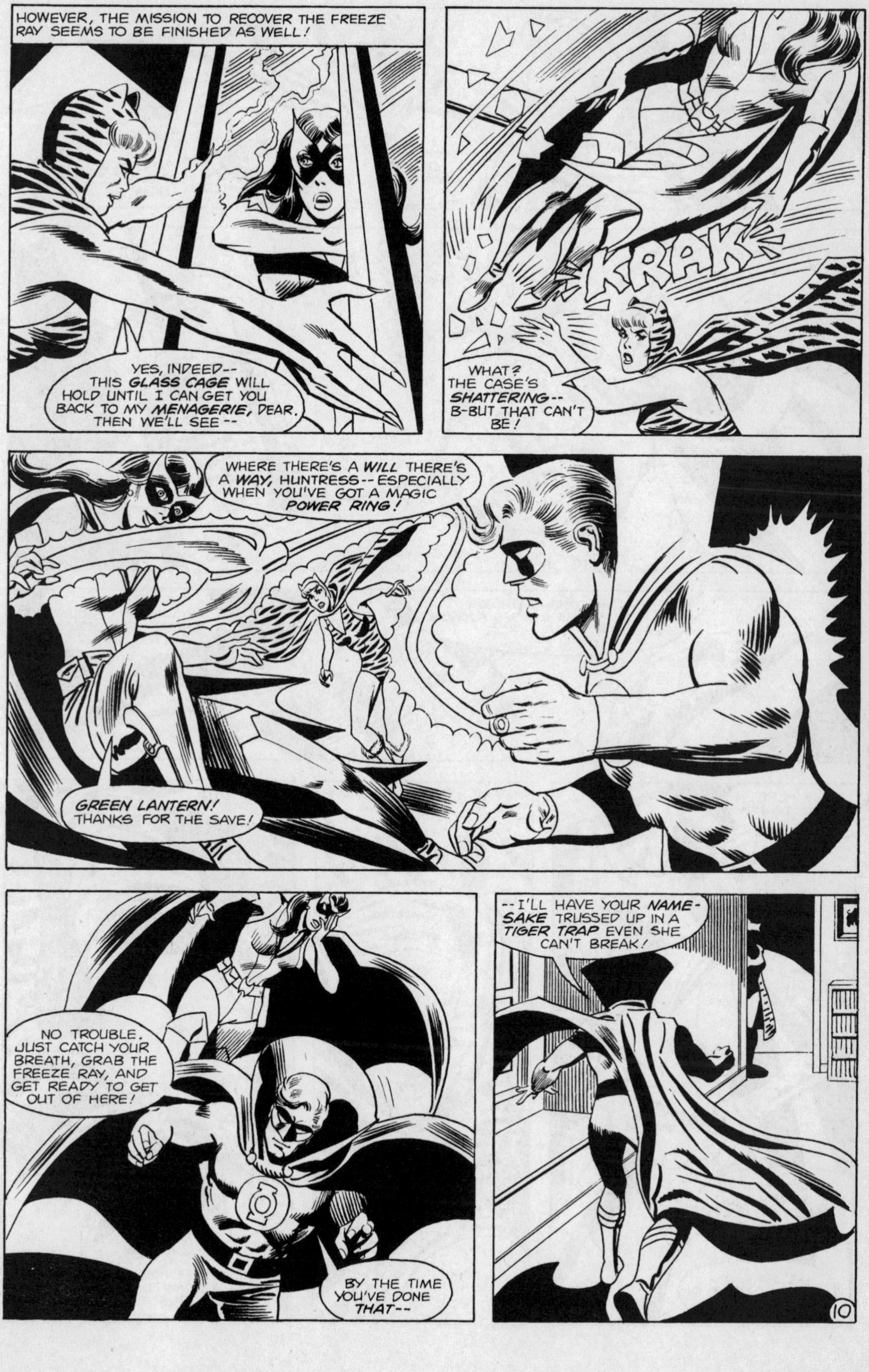
HOWEVER, THE MISSION TO RECOVER THE FREEZE RAY SEEMS TO BE FINISHED AS WELL!
YES, INDEED-- THIS GLASS CAGE WILL HOLD UNTIL I CAN GET YOU BACK TO MY MENAGERIE, DEAR. THEN WE'LL SEE--
KRAK
WHAT? THE CASE'S SHATTERING-- B-BUT THAT CAN'T BE!
WHERE THERE'S A WILL THERE'S A WAY, HUNTRESS-- ESPECIALLY WHEN YOU'VE GOT A MAGIC POWER RING!
GREEN LANTERN! THANKS FOR THE SAVE!
NO TROUBLE. JUST CATCH YOUR BREATH, GRAB THE FREEZE RAY, AND GET READY TO GET OUT OF HERE!
BY THE TIME YOU'VE DONE THAT--
--I'LL HAVE YOUR NAME-SAKE TRUSSED UP IN A TIGER TRAP EVEN SHE CAN'T BREAK!
10

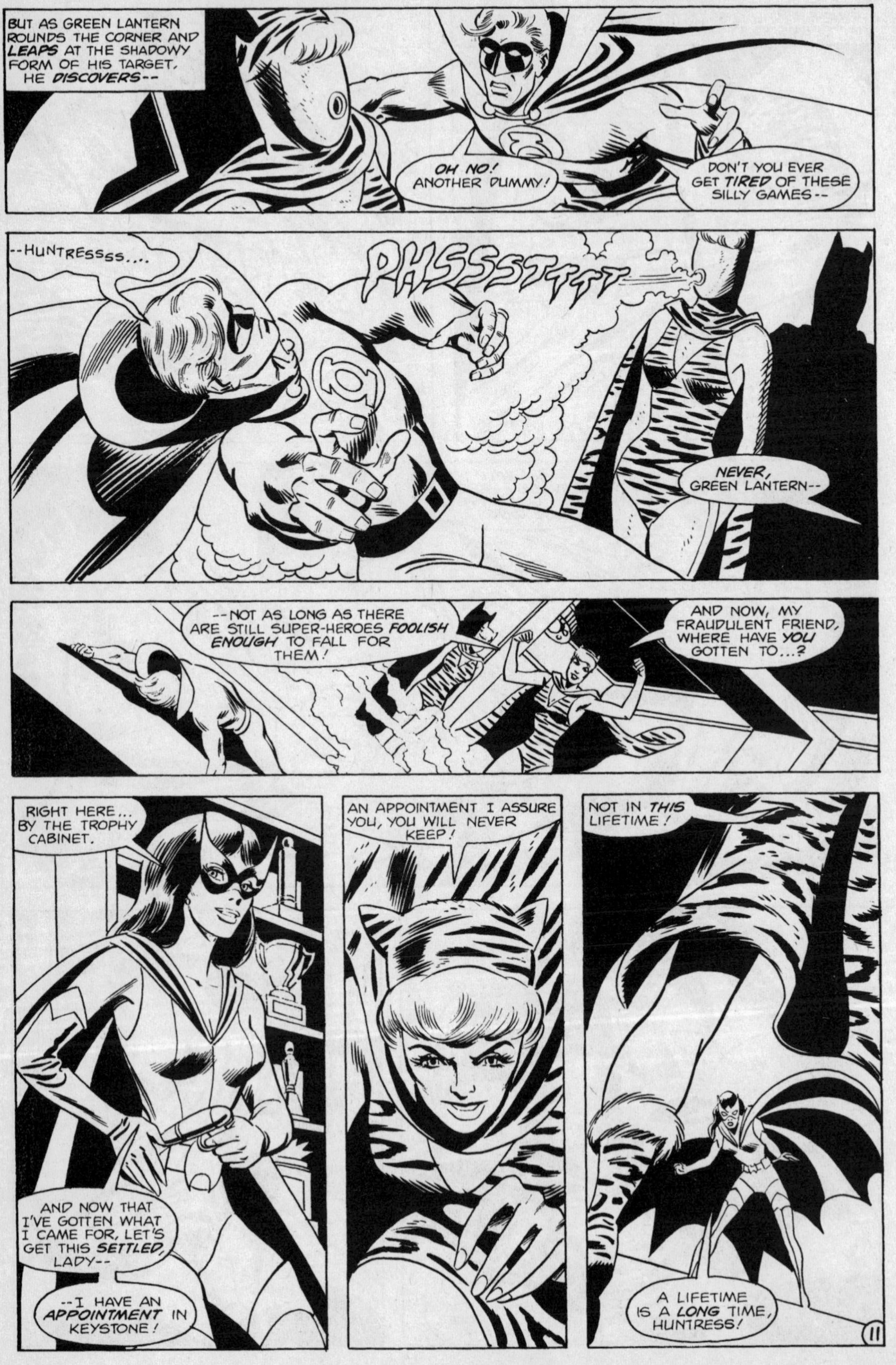
BUT AS GREEN LANTERN ROUNDS THE CORNER AND LEAPS AT THE SHADOWY FORM OF HIS TARGET, HE DISCOVERS--
OH NO! ANOTHER DUMMY!
DON'T YOU EVER GET TIRED OF THESE SILLY GAMES--
--HUNTRESSSS....
PHSSSTTTT
NEVER, GREEN LANTERN--
--NOT AS LONG AS THERE ARE STILL SUPER-HEROES FOOLISH ENOUGH TO FALL FOR THEM!
AND NOW, MY FRAUDULENT FRIEND, WHERE HAVE YOU GOTTEN TO...?
RIGHT HERE... BY THE TROPHY CABINET.
AND NOW THAT I'VE GOTTEN WHAT I CAME FOR, LET'S GET THIS SETTLED, LADY--
--I HAVE AN APPOINTMENT IN KEYSTONE!
AN APPOINTMENT I ASSURE YOU, YOU WILL NEVER KEEP!
NOT IN THIS LIFETIME!
A LIFETIME IS A LONG TIME, HUNTRESS!
11

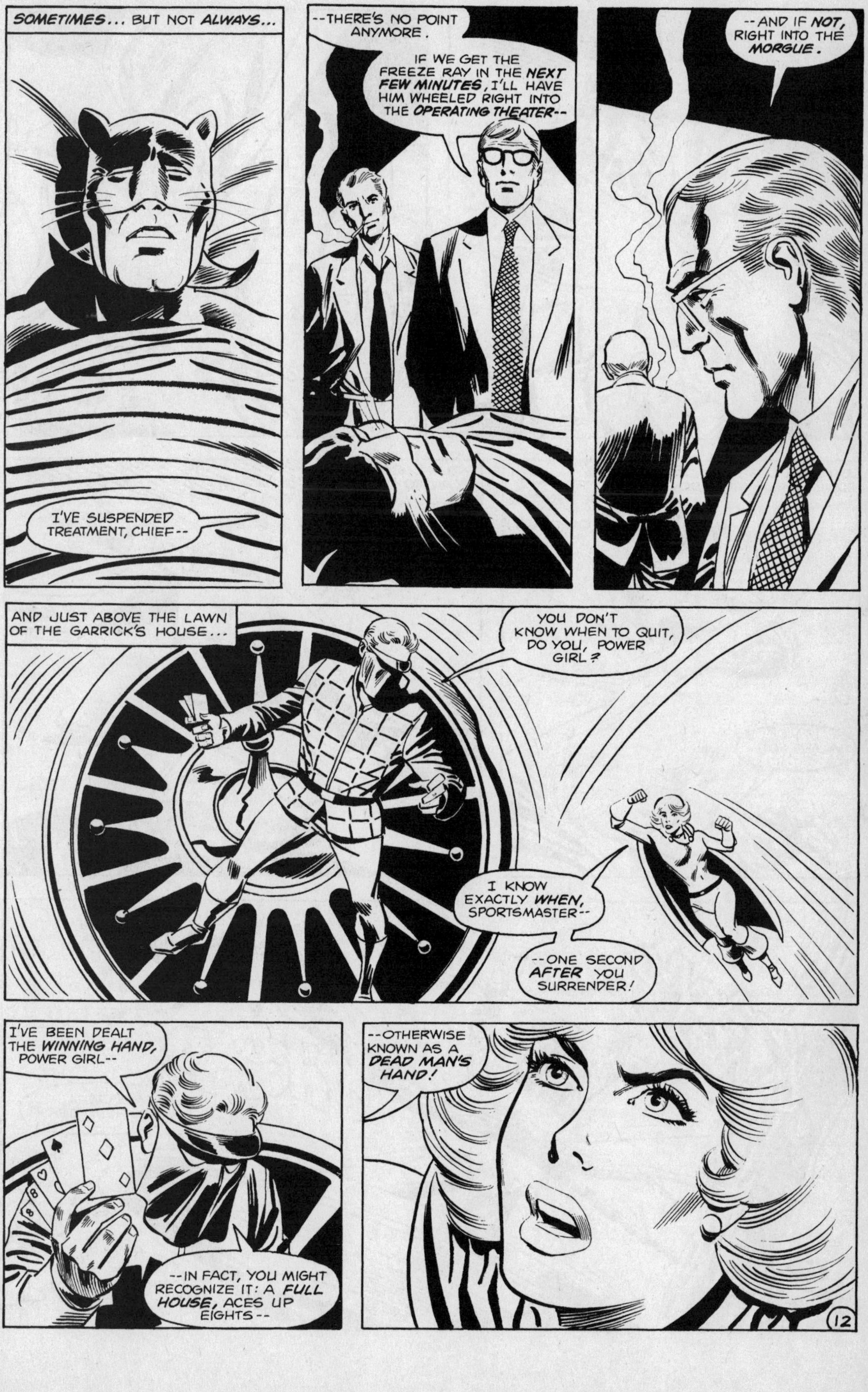
SOMETIMES... BUT NOT ALWAYS...
I'VE SUSPENDED TREATMENT, CHIEF--
--THERE'S NO POINT ANYMORE.
IF WE GET THE FREEZE RAY IN THE NEXT FEW MINUTES, I'LL HAVE HIM WHEELED RIGHT INTO THE OPERATING THEATER--
--AND IF NOT, RIGHT INTO THE MORGUE.
AND JUST ABOVE THE LAWN OF THE GARRICK'S HOUSE...
YOU DON'T KNOW WHEN TO QUIT, DO YOU, POWER GIRL?
I KNOW EXACTLY WHEN, SPORTSMASTER--
--ONE SECOND AFTER YOU SURRENDER!
I'VE BEEN DEALT THE WINNING HAND, POWER GIRL--
--IN FACT, YOU MIGHT RECOGNIZE IT: A FULL HOUSE, ACES UP EIGHTS--
--OTHERWISE KNOWN AS A DEAD MAN'S HAND!
12

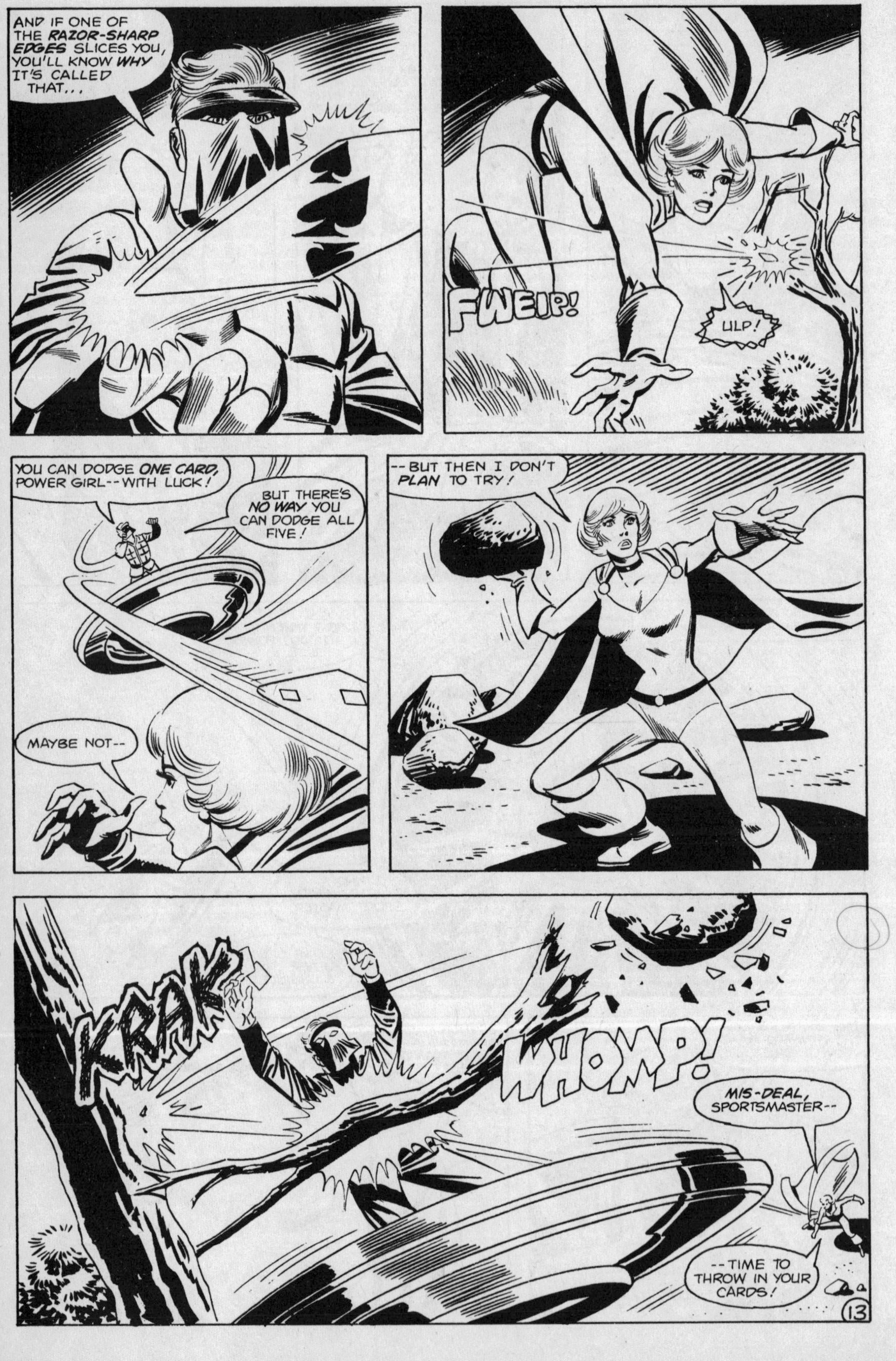
AND IF ONE OF THE RAZOR-SHARP EDGES SLICES YOU, YOU'LL KNOW WHY IT'S CALLED THAT...
FWEIP!
ULP!
YOU CAN DODGE ONE CARD, POWER GIRL--WITH LUCK!
BUT THERE'S NO WAY YOU CAN DODGE ALL FIVE!
MAYBE NOT--
--BUT THEN I DON'T PLAN TO TRY!
KRAK
WHOMP!
MIS-DEAL, SPORTSMASTER--
--TIME TO THROW IN YOUR CARDS!
13

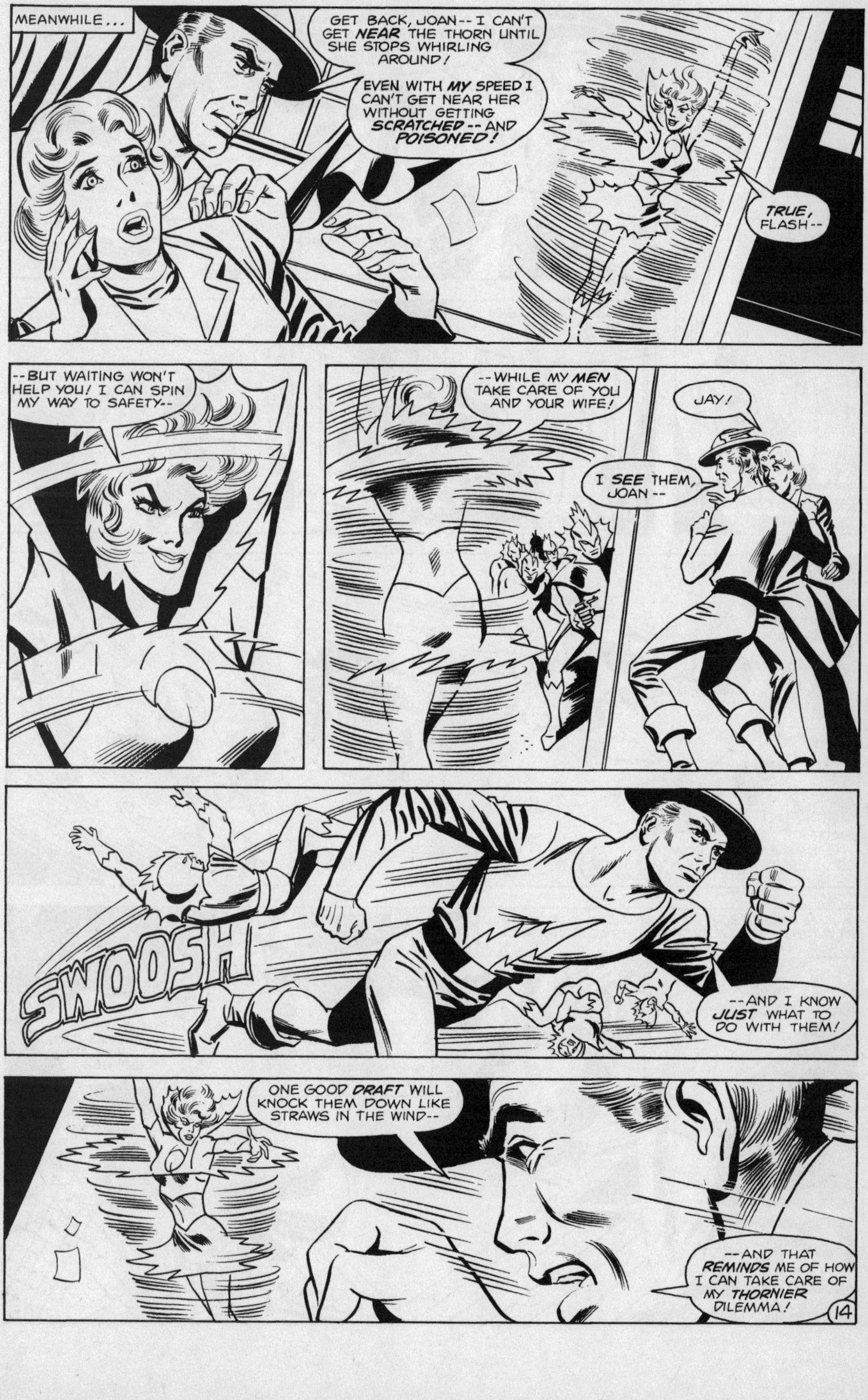
MEANWHILE...
GET BACK, JOAN -- I CAN'T GET NEAR THE THORN UNTIL SHE STOPS WHIRLING AROUND!
EVEN WITH MY SPEED I CAN'T GET NEAR HER WITHOUT GETTING SCRATCHED -- AND POISONED!
TRUE, FLASH --
-- BUT WAITING WON'T HELP YOU! I CAN SPIN MY WAY TO SAFETY--
-- WHILE MY MEN TAKE CARE OF YOU AND YOUR WIFE!
JAY!
I SEE THEM, JOAN --
SWOOSH
-- AND I KNOW JUST WHAT TO DO WITH THEM!
ONE GOOD DRAFT WILL KNOCK THEM DOWN LIKE STRAWS IN THE WIND--
-- AND THAT REMINDS ME OF HOW I CAN TAKE CARE OF MY THORNIER DILEMMA!
14

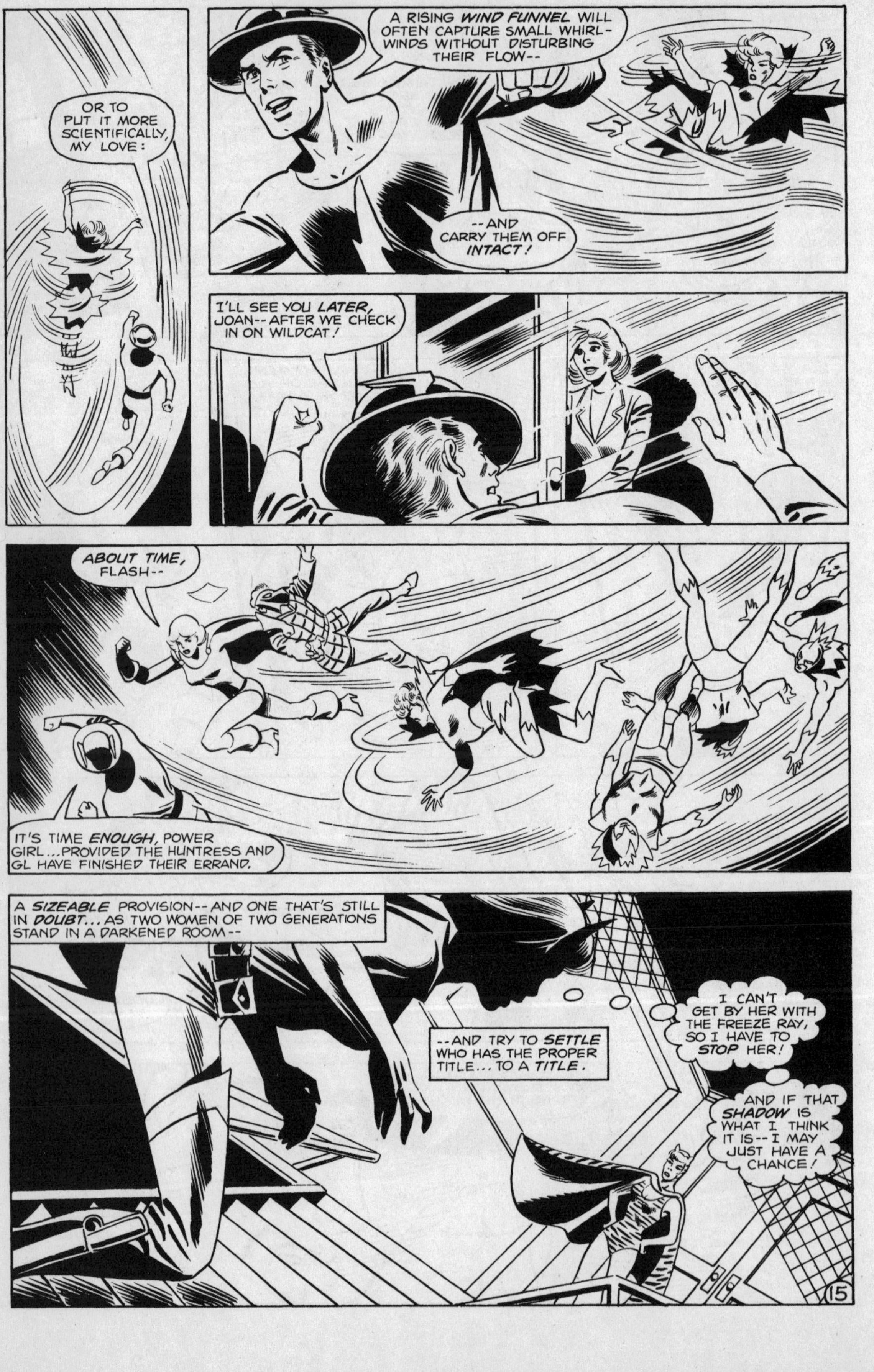
OR TO PUT IT MORE SCIENTIFICALLY, MY LOVE:
A RISING WIND FUNNEL WILL OFTEN CAPTURE SMALL WHIRLWINDS WITHOUT DISTURBING THEIR FLOW--
--AND CARRY THEM OFF INTACT!
I'LL SEE YOU LATER, JOAN--AFTER WE CHECK IN ON WILDCAT!
ABOUT TIME, FLASH--
IT'S TIME ENOUGH, POWER GIRL...PROVIDED THE HUNTRESS AND GL HAVE FINISHED THEIR ERRAND.
A SIZEABLE PROVISION--AND ONE THAT'S STILL IN DOUBT... AS TWO WOMEN OF TWO GENERATIONS STAND IN A DARKENED ROOM--
--AND TRY TO SETTLE WHO HAS THE PROPER TITLE... TO A TITLE.
I CAN'T GET BY HER WITH THE FREEZE RAY, SO I HAVE TO STOP HER!
AND IF THAT SHADOW IS WHAT I THINK IT IS--I MAY JUST HAVE A CHANCE!
15

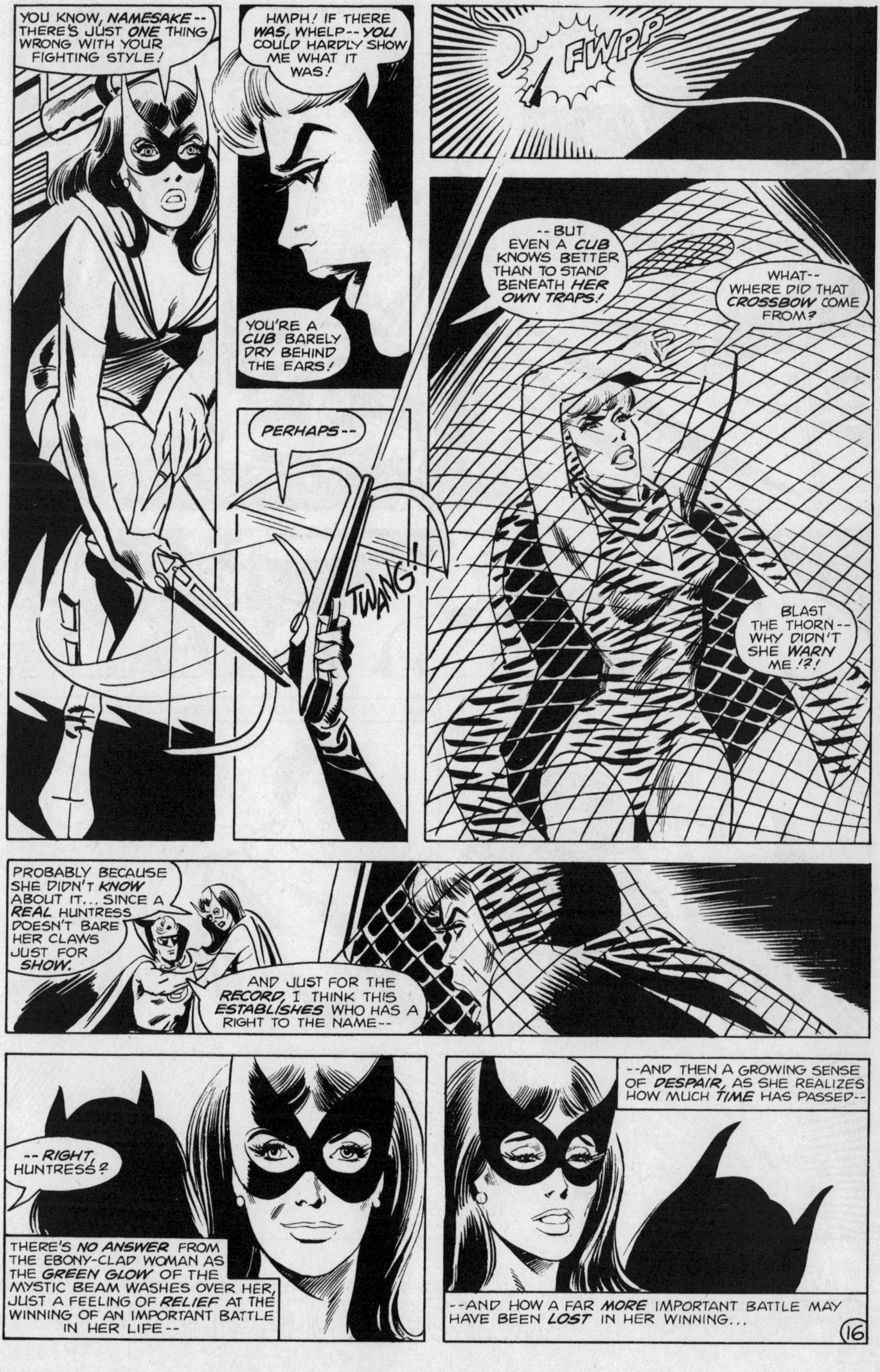
YOU KNOW, NAMESAKE-- THERE'S JUST ONE THING WRONG WITH YOUR FIGHTING STYLE!
HMPH! IF THERE WAS, WHELP-- YOU COULD HARDLY SHOW ME WHAT IT WAS!
YOU'RE A CUB BARELY DRY BEHIND THE EARS!
FWPP
PERHAPS--
TWANG!
--BUT EVEN A CUB KNOWS BETTER THAN TO STAND BENEATH HER OWN TRAPS!
WHAT-- WHERE DID THAT CROSSBOW COME FROM?
BLAST THE THORN-- WHY DIDN'T SHE WARN ME!?!
PROBABLY BECAUSE SHE DIDN'T KNOW ABOUT IT... SINCE A REAL HUNTRESS DOESN'T BARE HER CLAWS JUST FOR SHOW.
AND JUST FOR THE RECORD, I THINK THIS ESTABLISHES WHO HAS A RIGHT TO THE NAME--
--RIGHT, HUNTRESS?
THERE'S NO ANSWER FROM THE EBONY-CLAD WOMAN AS THE GREEN GLOW OF THE MYSTIC BEAM WASHES OVER HER, JUST A FEELING OF RELIEF AT THE WINNING OF AN IMPORTANT BATTLE IN HER LIFE--
--AND THEN A GROWING SENSE OF DESPAIR, AS SHE REALIZES HOW MUCH TIME HAS PASSED--
--AND HOW A FAR MORE IMPORTANT BATTLE MAY HAVE BEEN LOST IN HER WINNING...
16

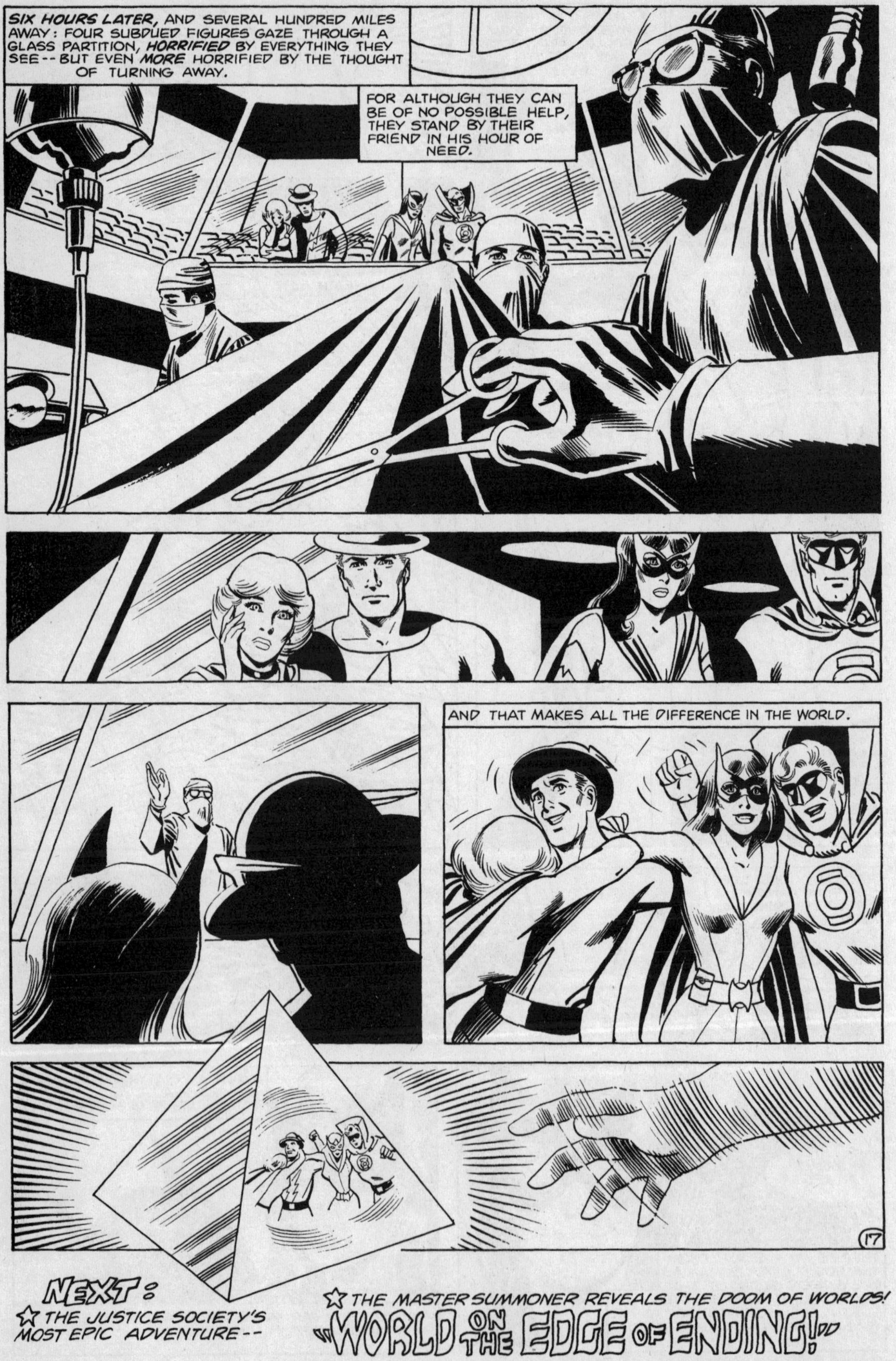
SIX HOURS LATER, AND SEVERAL HUNDRED MILES AWAY: FOUR SUBDUED FIGURES GAZE THROUGH A GLASS PARTITION, HORRIFIED BY EVERYTHING THEY SEE--BUT EVEN MORE HORRIFIED BY THE THOUGHT OF TURNING AWAY.
FOR ALTHOUGH THEY CAN BE OF NO POSSIBLE HELP, THEY STAND BY THEIR FRIEND IN HIS HOUR OF NEED.
AND THAT MAKES ALL THE DIFFERENCE IN THE WORLD.
17
NEXT:
☆ THE JUSTICE SOCIETY'S MOST EPIC ADVENTURE--
☆ THE MASTER SUMMONER REVEALS THE DOOM OF WORLDS!
"WORLD ON THE EDGE OF ENDING!"

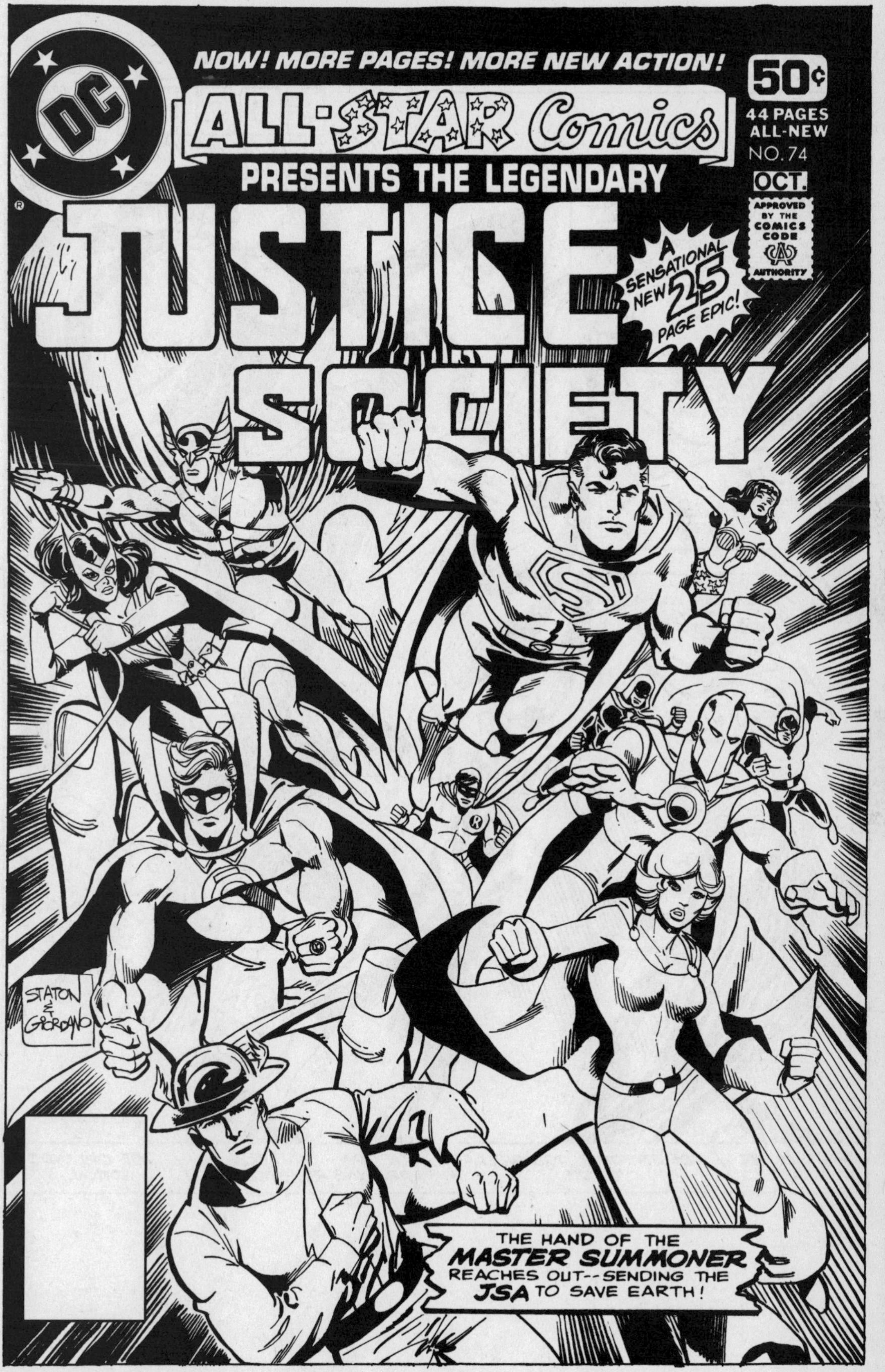
NOW! MORE PAGES! MORE NEW ACTION!
DC
ALL-STAR Comics
50¢
44 PAGES ALL-NEW
NO. 74
OCT.
APPROVED BY THE COMICS CODE AUTHORITY
PRESENTS THE LEGENDARY
JUSTICE SOCIETY
A SENSATIONAL NEW 25 PAGE EPIC!
STATON & GIORDANO
THE HAND OF THE MASTER SUMMONER REACHES OUT--SENDING THE JSA TO SAVE EARTH!

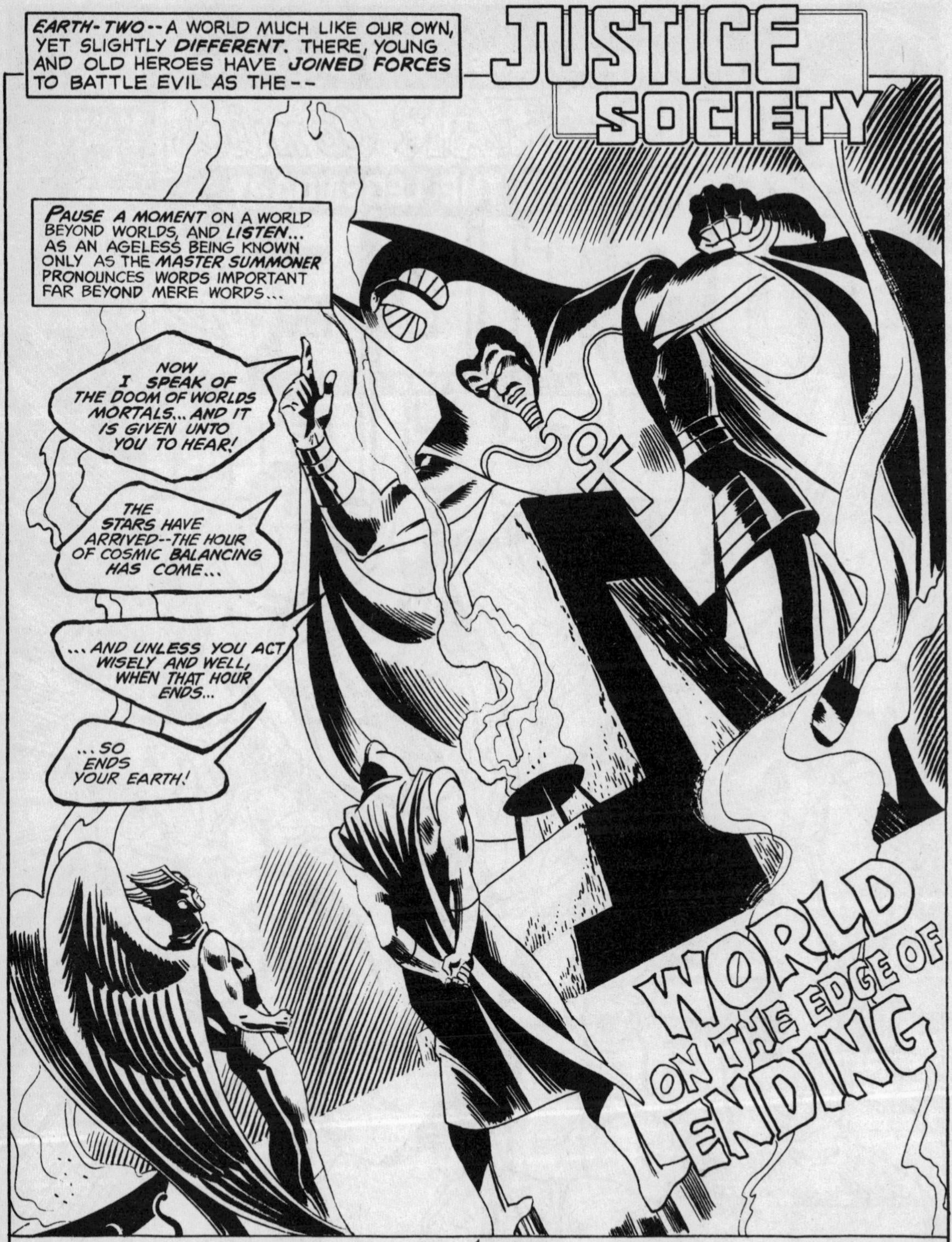
EARTH-TWO--A WORLD MUCH LIKE OUR OWN, YET SLIGHTLY DIFFERENT. THERE, YOUNG AND OLD HEROES HAVE JOINED FORCES TO BATTLE EVIL AS THE--
JUSTICE SOCIETY
PAUSE A MOMENT ON A WORLD BEYOND WORLDS, AND LISTEN... AS AN AGELESS BEING KNOWN ONLY AS THE MASTER SUMMONER PRONOUNCES WORDS IMPORTANT FAR BEYOND MERE WORDS...
NOW I SPEAK OF THE DOOM OF WORLDS MORTALS... AND IT IS GIVEN UNTO YOU TO HEAR!
THE STARS HAVE ARRIVED--THE HOUR OF COSMIC BALANCING HAS COME...
...AND UNLESS YOU ACT WISELY AND WELL, WHEN THAT HOUR ENDS...
...SO ENDS YOUR EARTH!
WORLD ON THE EDGE OF ENDING
PAUL LEVITZ WRITER / JOE STATON & JOE GIELLA ARTISTS / BEN ODA - LETTERER ADRIENNE ROY - COLORIST / JOE ORLANDO EDITOR

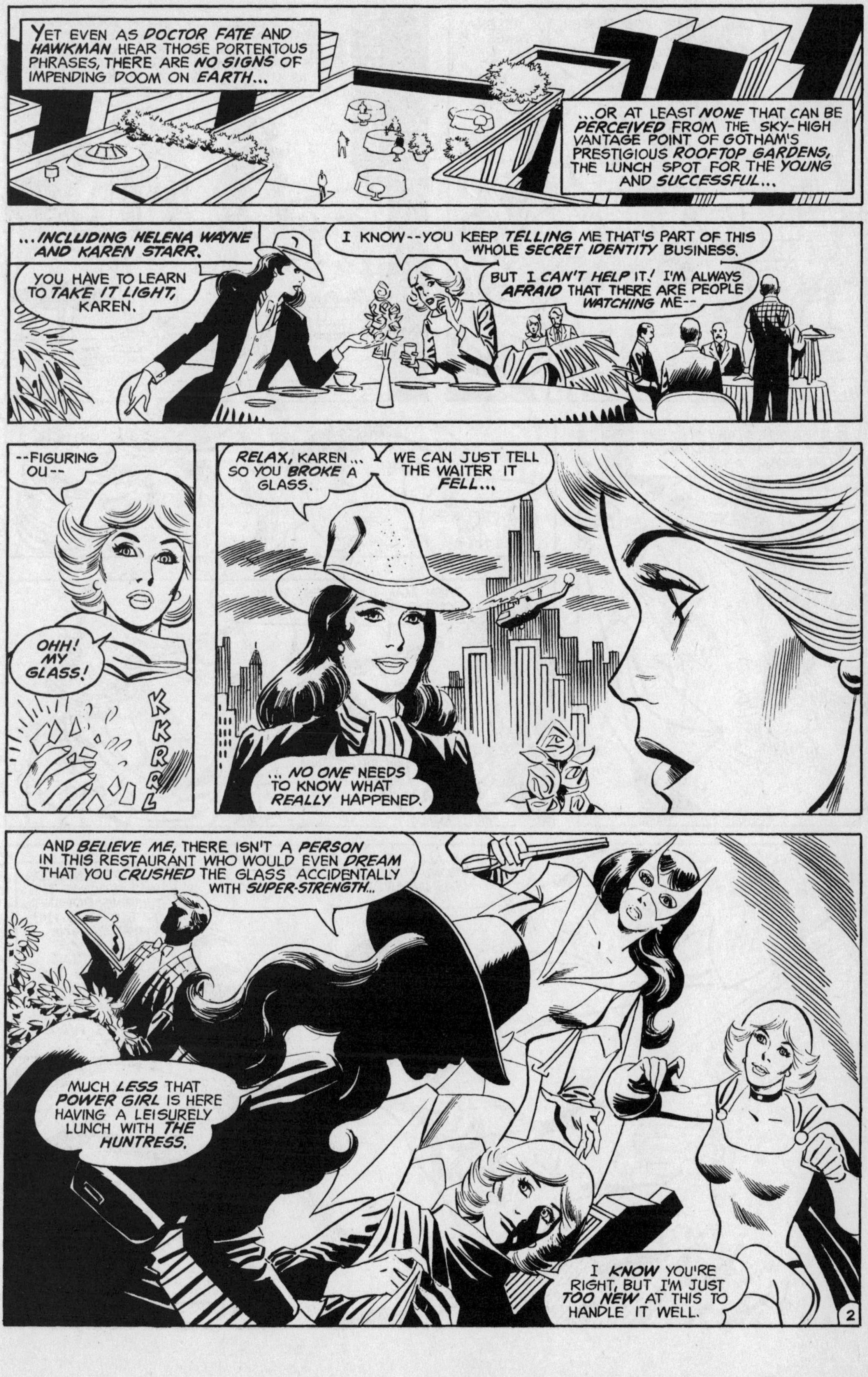
YET EVEN AS DOCTOR FATE AND HAWKMAN HEAR THOSE PORTENTOUS PHRASES, THERE ARE NO SIGNS OF IMPENDING DOOM ON EARTH...
...OR AT LEAST NONE THAT CAN BE PERCEIVED FROM THE SKY-HIGH VANTAGE POINT OF GOTHAM'S PRESTIGIOUS ROOFTOP GARDENS, THE LUNCH SPOT FOR THE YOUNG AND SUCCESSFUL...
...INCLUDING HELENA WAYNE AND KAREN STARR.
YOU HAVE TO LEARN TO TAKE IT LIGHT, KAREN.
I KNOW--YOU KEEP TELLING ME THAT'S PART OF THIS WHOLE SECRET IDENTITY BUSINESS.
BUT I CAN'T HELP IT! I'M ALWAYS AFRAID THAT THERE ARE PEOPLE WATCHING ME--
--FIGURING OU--
OHH! MY GLASS!
KKRRL
RELAX, KAREN... SO YOU BROKE A GLASS.
WE CAN JUST TELL THE WAITER IT FELL...
...NO ONE NEEDS TO KNOW WHAT REALLY HAPPENED.
AND BELIEVE ME, THERE ISN'T A PERSON IN THIS RESTAURANT WHO WOULD EVEN DREAM THAT YOU CRUSHED THE GLASS ACCIDENTALLY WITH SUPER-STRENGTH...
MUCH LESS THAT POWER GIRL IS HERE HAVING A LEISURELY LUNCH WITH THE HUNTRESS.
I KNOW YOU'RE RIGHT, BUT I'M JUST TOO NEW AT THIS TO HANDLE IT WELL.
2

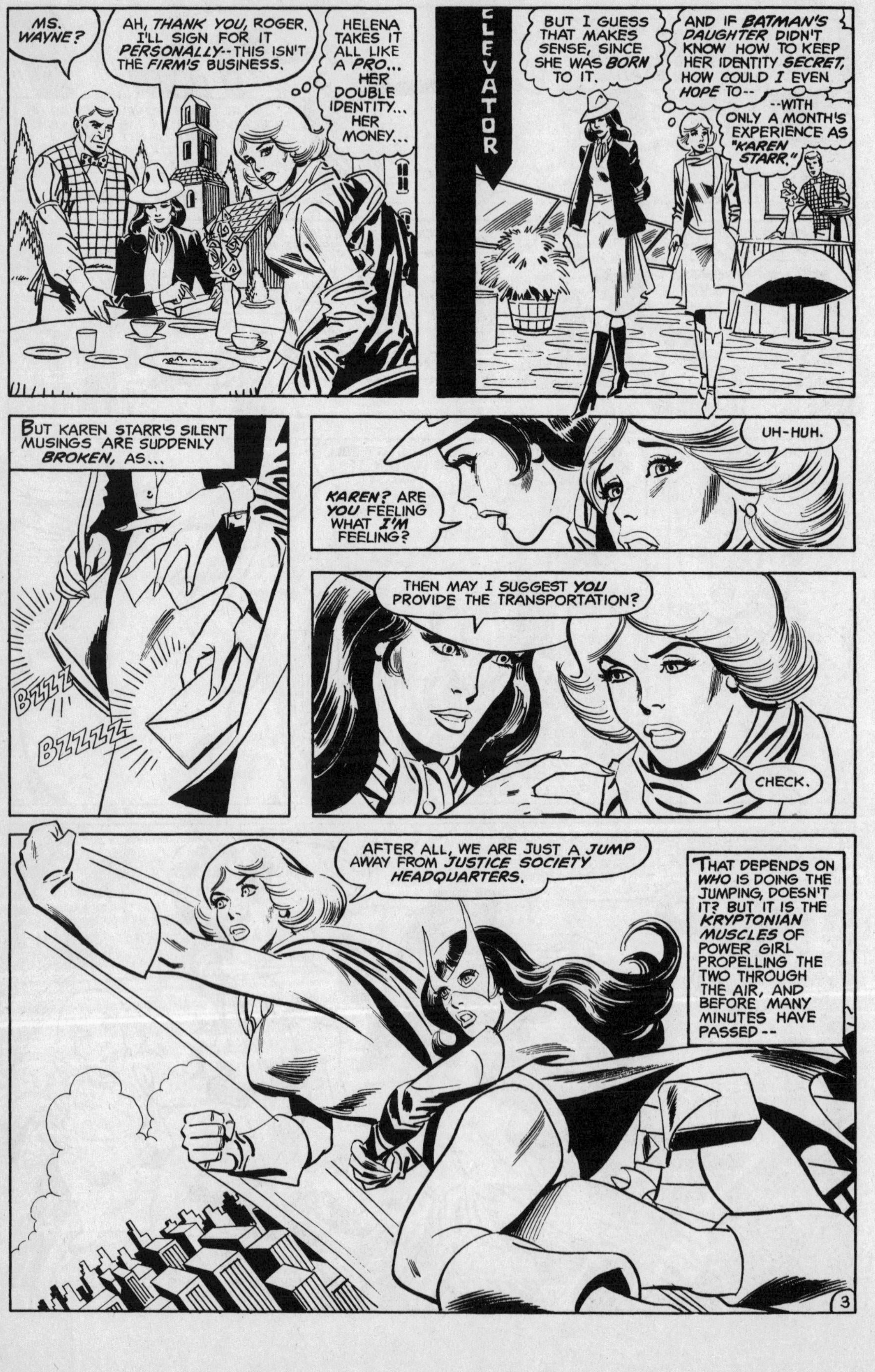
MS. WAYNE?
AH, THANK YOU, ROGER. I'LL SIGN FOR IT PERSONALLY--THIS ISN'T THE FIRM'S BUSINESS.
HELENA TAKES IT ALL LIKE A PRO... HER DOUBLE IDENTITY... HER MONEY...
ELEVATOR
BUT I GUESS THAT MAKES SENSE, SINCE SHE WAS BORN TO IT.
AND IF BATMAN'S DAUGHTER DIDN'T KNOW HOW TO KEEP HER IDENTITY SECRET, HOW COULD I EVEN HOPE TO--
--WITH ONLY A MONTH'S EXPERIENCE AS "KAREN STARR."
BUT KAREN STARR'S SILENT MUSINGS ARE SUDDENLY BROKEN, AS...
BZZZ
BZZZZ
UH-HUH.
KAREN? ARE YOU FEELING WHAT I'M FEELING?
THEN MAY I SUGGEST YOU PROVIDE THE TRANSPORTATION?
CHECK.
AFTER ALL, WE ARE JUST A JUMP AWAY FROM JUSTICE SOCIETY HEADQUARTERS.
THAT DEPENDS ON WHO IS DOING THE JUMPING, DOESN'T IT? BUT IT IS THE KRYPTONIAN MUSCLES OF POWER GIRL PROPELLING THE TWO THROUGH THE AIR, AND BEFORE MANY MINUTES HAVE PASSED --
3

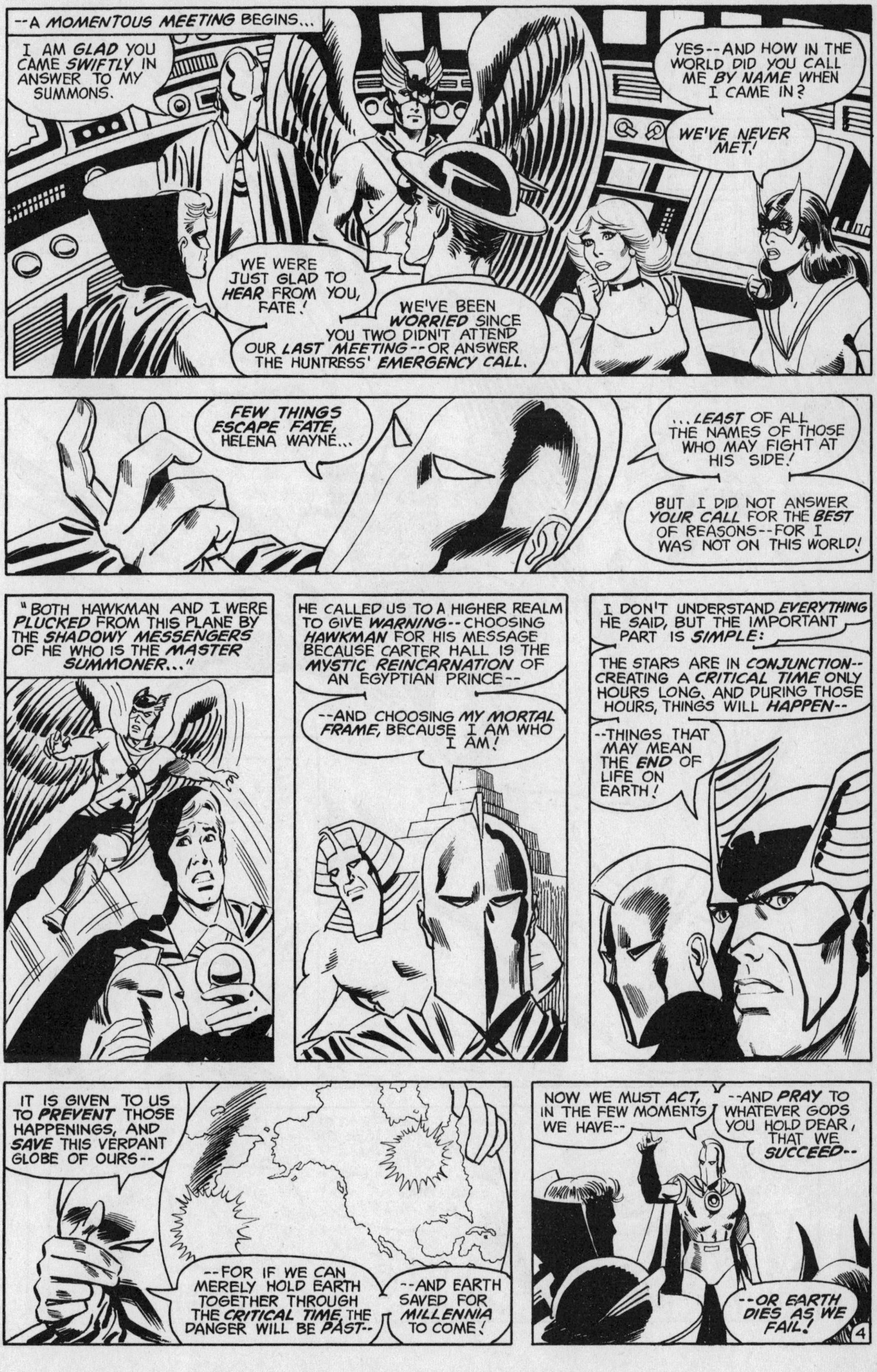
--A MOMENTOUS MEETING BEGINS...
I AM GLAD YOU CAME SWIFTLY IN ANSWER TO MY SUMMONS.
YES--AND HOW IN THE WORLD DID YOU CALL ME BY NAME WHEN I CAME IN?
WE'VE NEVER MET!
WE WERE JUST GLAD TO HEAR FROM YOU, FATE!
WE'VE BEEN WORRIED SINCE YOU TWO DIDN'T ATTEND OUR LAST MEETING--OR ANSWER THE HUNTRESS' EMERGENCY CALL.
FEW THINGS ESCAPE FATE, HELENA WAYNE...
...LEAST OF ALL THE NAMES OF THOSE WHO MAY FIGHT AT HIS SIDE!
BUT I DID NOT ANSWER YOUR CALL FOR THE BEST OF REASONS--FOR I WAS NOT ON THIS WORLD!
"BOTH HAWKMAN AND I WERE PLUCKED FROM THIS PLANE BY THE SHADOWY MESSENGERS OF HE WHO IS THE MASTER SUMMONER..."
HE CALLED US TO A HIGHER REALM TO GIVE WARNING--CHOOSING HAWKMAN FOR HIS MESSAGE BECAUSE CARTER HALL IS THE MYSTIC REINCARNATION OF AN EGYPTIAN PRINCE--
--AND CHOOSING MY MORTAL FRAME, BECAUSE I AM WHO I AM!
I DON'T UNDERSTAND EVERYTHING HE SAID, BUT THE IMPORTANT PART IS SIMPLE:
THE STARS ARE IN CONJUNCTION--CREATING A CRITICAL TIME ONLY HOURS LONG, AND DURING THOSE HOURS, THINGS WILL HAPPEN--
--THINGS THAT MAY MEAN THE END OF LIFE ON EARTH!
IT IS GIVEN TO US TO PREVENT THOSE HAPPENINGS, AND SAVE THIS VERDANT GLOBE OF OURS--
--FOR IF WE CAN MERELY HOLD EARTH TOGETHER THROUGH THE CRITICAL TIME THE DANGER WILL BE PAST--
--AND EARTH SAVED FOR MILLENNIA TO COME!
NOW WE MUST ACT, IN THE FEW MOMENTS WE HAVE--
--AND PRAY TO WHATEVER GODS YOU HOLD DEAR, THAT WE SUCCEED--
--OR EARTH DIES AS WE FAIL!
4

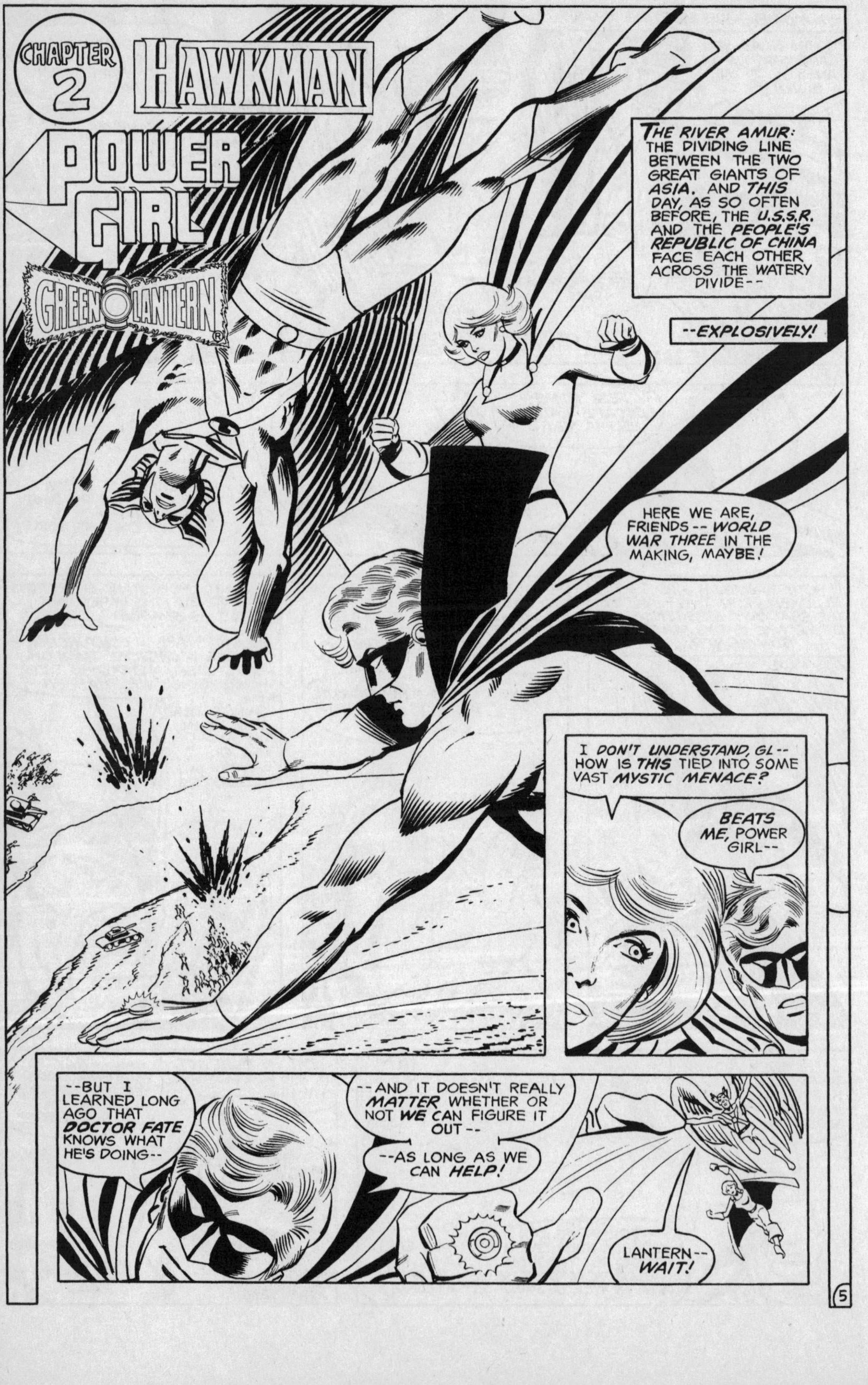
CHAPTER 2
HAWKMAN
POWER GIRL
GREEN LANTERN ®
THE RIVER AMUR: THE DIVIDING LINE BETWEEN THE TWO GREAT GIANTS OF ASIA. AND THIS DAY, AS SO OFTEN BEFORE, THE U.S.S.R. AND THE PEOPLE'S REPUBLIC OF CHINA FACE EACH OTHER ACROSS THE WATERY DIVIDE--
--EXPLOSIVELY!
HERE WE ARE, FRIENDS -- WORLD WAR THREE IN THE MAKING, MAYBE!
I DON'T UNDERSTAND, GL -- HOW IS THIS TIED INTO SOME VAST MYSTIC MENACE?
BEATS ME, POWER GIRL--
--BUT I LEARNED LONG AGO THAT DOCTOR FATE KNOWS WHAT HE'S DOING--
--AND IT DOESN'T REALLY MATTER WHETHER OR NOT WE CAN FIGURE IT OUT --
--AS LONG AS WE CAN HELP!
LANTERN-- WAIT!
5

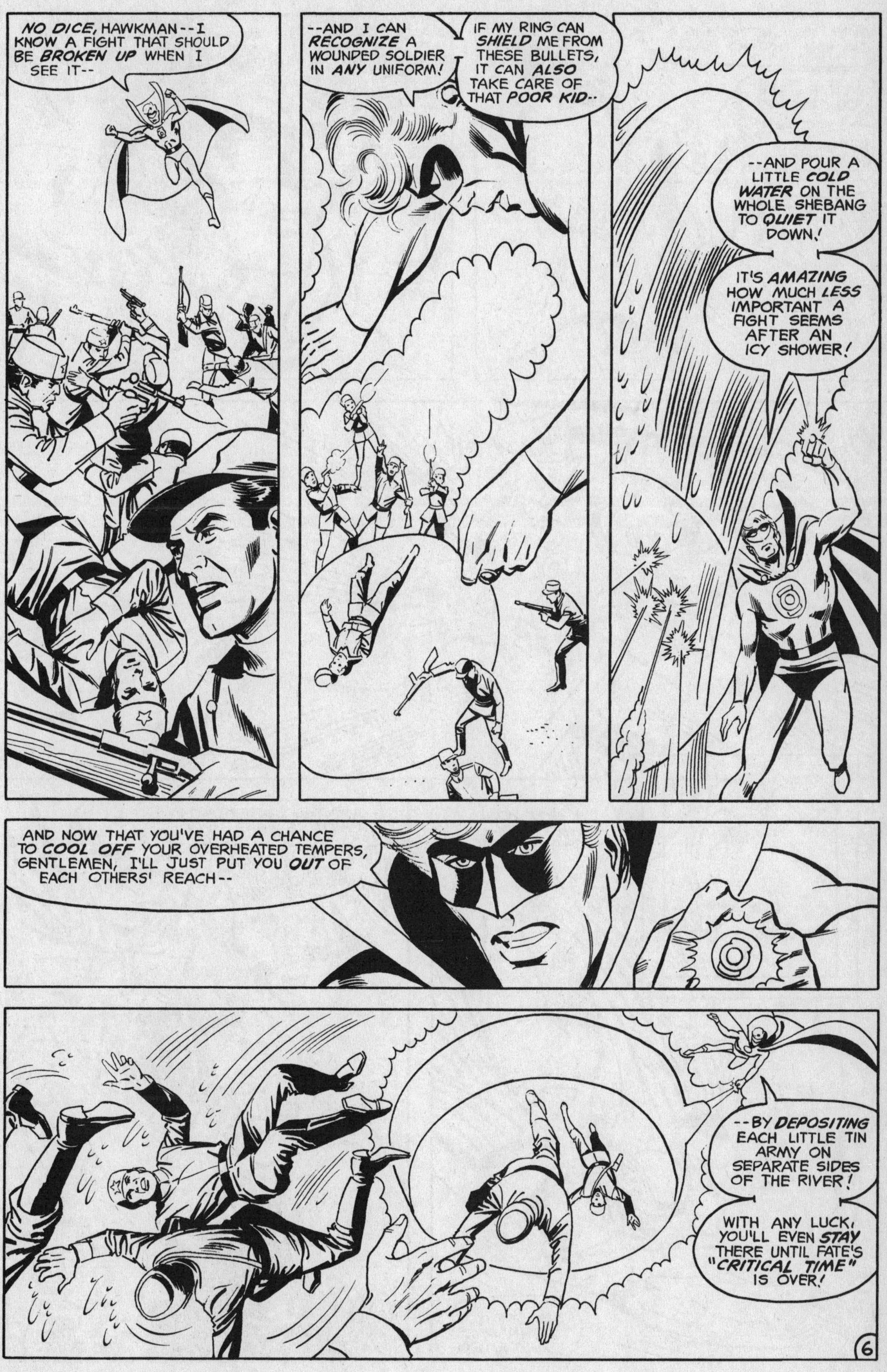
NO DICE, HAWKMAN--I KNOW A FIGHT THAT SHOULD BE BROKEN UP WHEN I SEE IT--
--AND I CAN RECOGNIZE A WOUNDED SOLDIER IN ANY UNIFORM!
IF MY RING CAN SHIELD ME FROM THESE BULLETS, IT CAN ALSO TAKE CARE OF THAT POOR KID--
--AND POUR A LITTLE COLD WATER ON THE WHOLE SHEBANG TO QUIET IT DOWN!
IT'S AMAZING HOW MUCH LESS IMPORTANT A FIGHT SEEMS AFTER AN ICY SHOWER!
AND NOW THAT YOU'VE HAD A CHANCE TO COOL OFF YOUR OVERHEATED TEMPERS, GENTLEMEN, I'LL JUST PUT YOU OUT OF EACH OTHERS' REACH--
--BY DEPOSITING EACH LITTLE TIN ARMY ON SEPARATE SIDES OF THE RIVER!
WITH ANY LUCK, YOU'LL EVEN STAY THERE UNTIL FATE'S "CRITICAL TIME" IS OVER!
6

NOW I'LL JUST *SEE* IF I CAN HELP THAT KID PULL--

LANTERN, ARE YOU *CRAZY?*

THAT'S *NOT* WHAT WE'RE HERE FOR!

MAYBE *YOU'RE* NOT, HAWKMAN. I ALWAYS TRY TO SAVE--

GL-- DUCK!

WHAT--??

OUT OF THE--

KRAKK-WOOM!

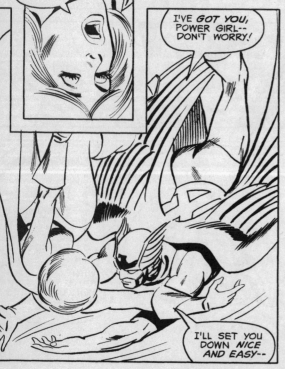

--WAY...

I'VE *GOT YOU,* POWER GIRL-- DON'T WORRY!

I'LL SET YOU DOWN *NICE* AND *EASY*--

--AND THE LANTERN WON'T EVEN *NOTICE* WHAT HAPPENED?

I SAW, HAWKMAN--AND POWER GIRL *KNOWS* I'M GRATEFUL, BUT *THIS* KID NEEDS MY ATTENTION *MORE* THAN *SHE* DOES.

7

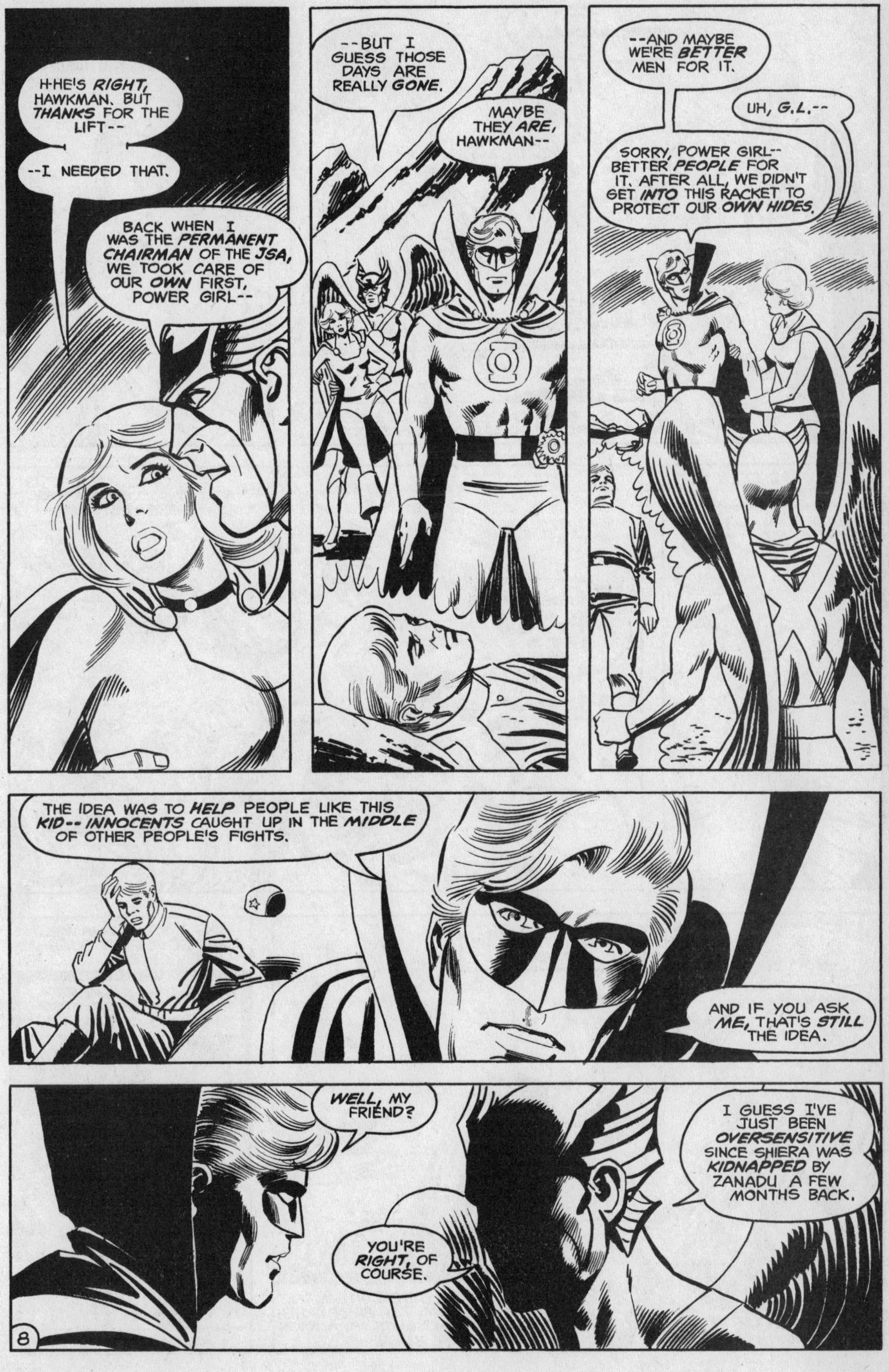
H-HE'S RIGHT, HAWKMAN. BUT THANKS FOR THE LIFT--
--I NEEDED THAT.
BACK WHEN I WAS THE PERMANENT CHAIRMAN OF THE JSA, WE TOOK CARE OF OUR OWN FIRST, POWER GIRL--
--BUT I GUESS THOSE DAYS ARE REALLY GONE.
MAYBE THEY ARE, HAWKMAN--
--AND MAYBE WE'RE BETTER MEN FOR IT.
UH, G.L.--
SORRY, POWER GIRL-- BETTER PEOPLE FOR IT. AFTER ALL, WE DIDN'T GET INTO THIS RACKET TO PROTECT OUR OWN HIDES.
THE IDEA WAS TO HELP PEOPLE LIKE THIS KID-- INNOCENTS CAUGHT UP IN THE MIDDLE OF OTHER PEOPLE'S FIGHTS.
AND IF YOU ASK ME, THAT'S STILL THE IDEA.
WELL, MY FRIEND?
I GUESS I'VE JUST BEEN OVERSENSITIVE SINCE SHIERA WAS KIDNAPPED BY ZANADU A FEW MONTHS BACK.
YOU'RE RIGHT, OF COURSE.
8

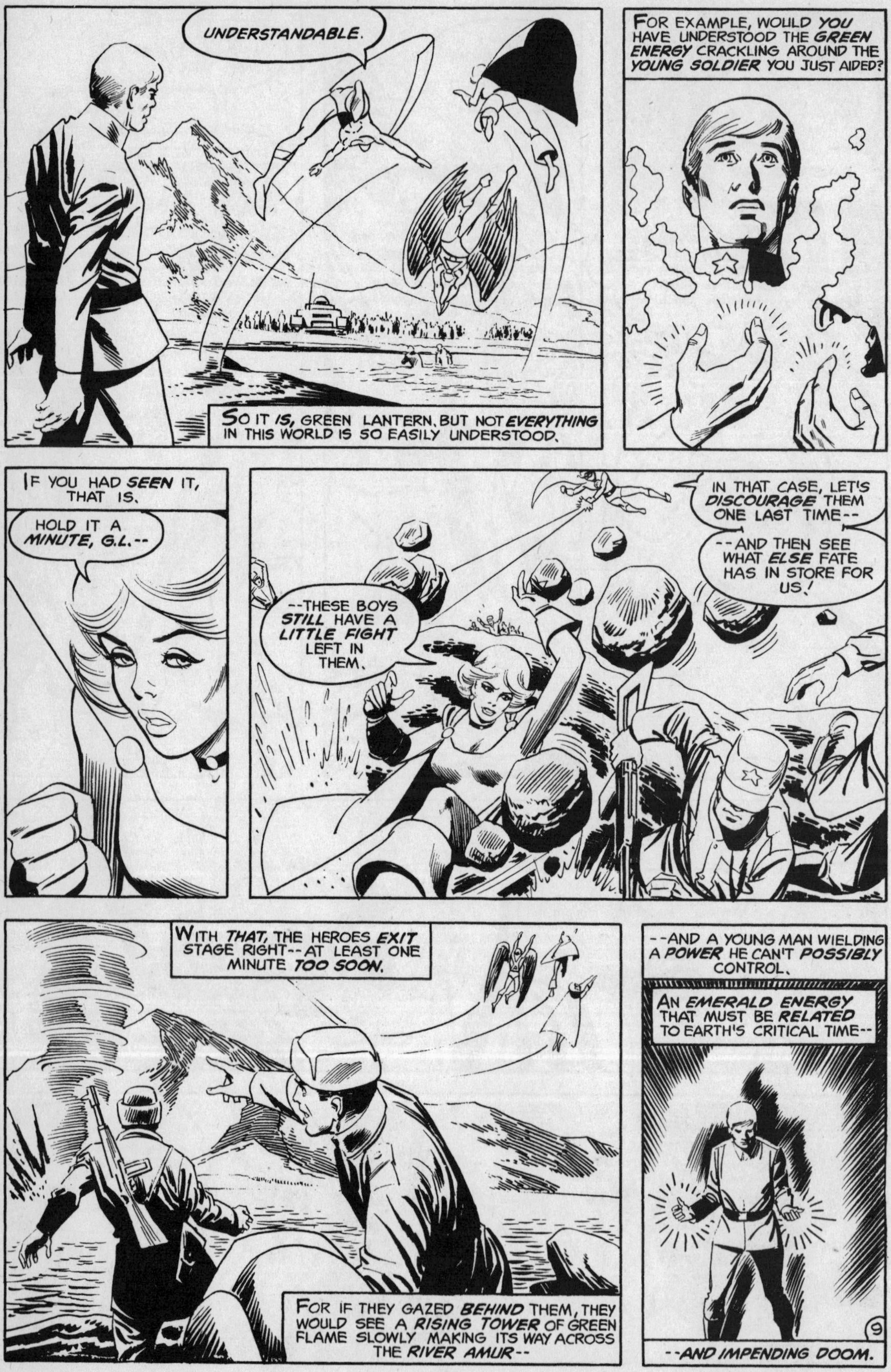
UNDERSTANDABLE.
SO IT IS, GREEN LANTERN, BUT NOT EVERYTHING IN THIS WORLD IS SO EASILY UNDERSTOOD.
FOR EXAMPLE, WOULD YOU HAVE UNDERSTOOD THE GREEN ENERGY CRACKLING AROUND THE YOUNG SOLDIER YOU JUST AIDED?
IF YOU HAD SEEN IT, THAT IS.
HOLD IT A MINUTE, G.L.--
--THESE BOYS STILL HAVE A LITTLE FIGHT LEFT IN THEM.
IN THAT CASE, LET'S DISCOURAGE THEM ONE LAST TIME--
--AND THEN SEE WHAT ELSE FATE HAS IN STORE FOR US!
WITH THAT, THE HEROES EXIT STAGE RIGHT--AT LEAST ONE MINUTE TOO SOON.
FOR IF THEY GAZED BEHIND THEM, THEY WOULD SEE A RISING TOWER OF GREEN FLAME SLOWLY MAKING ITS WAY ACROSS THE RIVER AMUR--
--AND A YOUNG MAN WIELDING A POWER HE CAN'T POSSIBLY CONTROL.
AN EMERALD ENERGY THAT MUST BE RELATED TO EARTH'S CRITICAL TIME--
9
--AND IMPENDING DOOM.

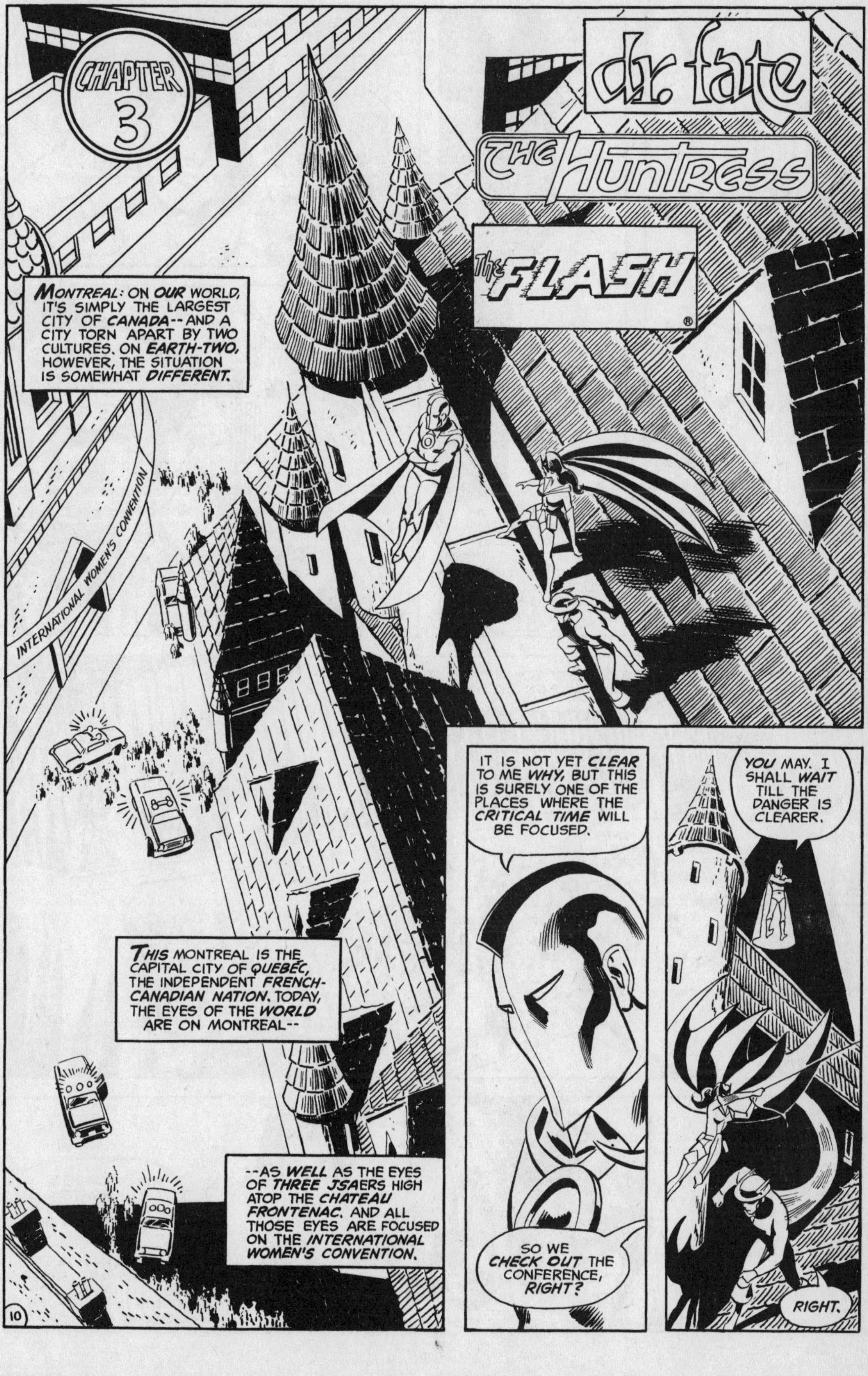
CHAPTER 3
dr. fate
THE HUNTRESS
The FLASH
MONTREAL: ON OUR WORLD, IT'S SIMPLY THE LARGEST CITY OF CANADA--AND A CITY TORN APART BY TWO CULTURES. ON EARTH-TWO, HOWEVER, THE SITUATION IS SOMEWHAT DIFFERENT.
INTERNATIONAL WOMEN'S CONVENTION
THIS MONTREAL IS THE CAPITAL CITY OF QUEBÉC, THE INDEPENDENT FRENCH-CANADIAN NATION. TODAY, THE EYES OF THE WORLD ARE ON MONTREAL--
--AS WELL AS THE EYES OF THREE JSAERS HIGH ATOP THE CHATEAU FRONTENAC. AND ALL THOSE EYES ARE FOCUSED ON THE INTERNATIONAL WOMEN'S CONVENTION.
10
IT IS NOT YET CLEAR TO ME WHY, BUT THIS IS SURELY ONE OF THE PLACES WHERE THE CRITICAL TIME WILL BE FOCUSED.
SO WE CHECK OUT THE CONFERENCE, RIGHT?
YOU MAY. I SHALL WAIT TILL THE DANGER IS CLEARER.
RIGHT.

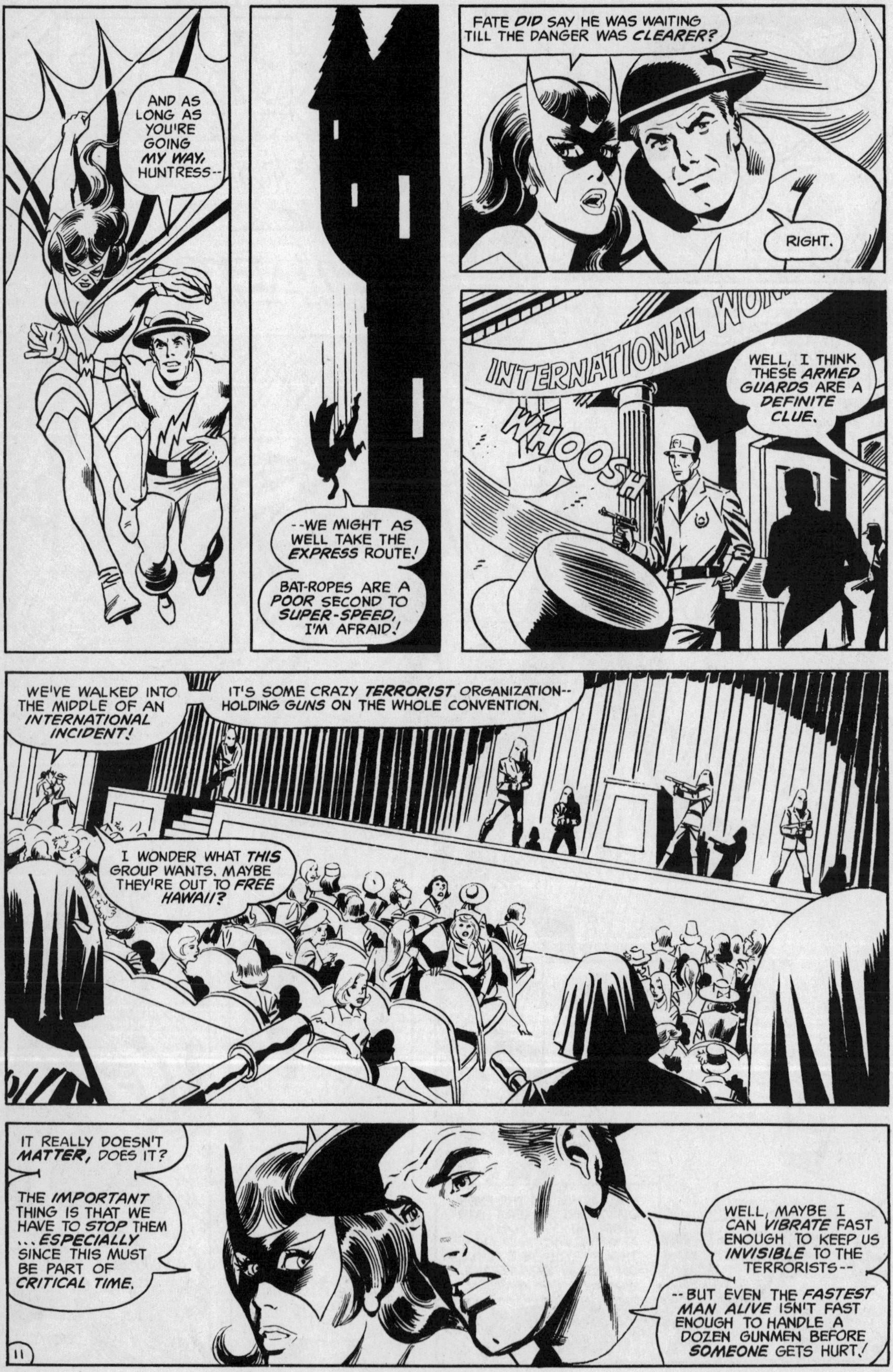
AND AS LONG AS YOU'RE GOING MY WAY, HUNTRESS--
--WE MIGHT AS WELL TAKE THE EXPRESS ROUTE!
BAT-ROPES ARE A POOR SECOND TO SUPER-SPEED, I'M AFRAID!
FATE DID SAY HE WAS WAITING TILL THE DANGER WAS CLEARER?
RIGHT.
INTERNATIONAL WOM
WHOOSH
WELL, I THINK THESE ARMED GUARDS ARE A DEFINITE CLUE.
WE'VE WALKED INTO THE MIDDLE OF AN INTERNATIONAL INCIDENT!
IT'S SOME CRAZY TERRORIST ORGANIZATION-- HOLDING GUNS ON THE WHOLE CONVENTION.
I WONDER WHAT THIS GROUP WANTS. MAYBE THEY'RE OUT TO FREE HAWAII?
IT REALLY DOESN'T MATTER, DOES IT?
THE IMPORTANT THING IS THAT WE HAVE TO STOP THEM ...ESPECIALLY SINCE THIS MUST BE PART OF CRITICAL TIME.
WELL, MAYBE I CAN VIBRATE FAST ENOUGH TO KEEP US INVISIBLE TO THE TERRORISTS--
--BUT EVEN THE FASTEST MAN ALIVE ISN'T FAST ENOUGH TO HANDLE A DOZEN GUNMEN BEFORE SOMEONE GETS HURT!
11

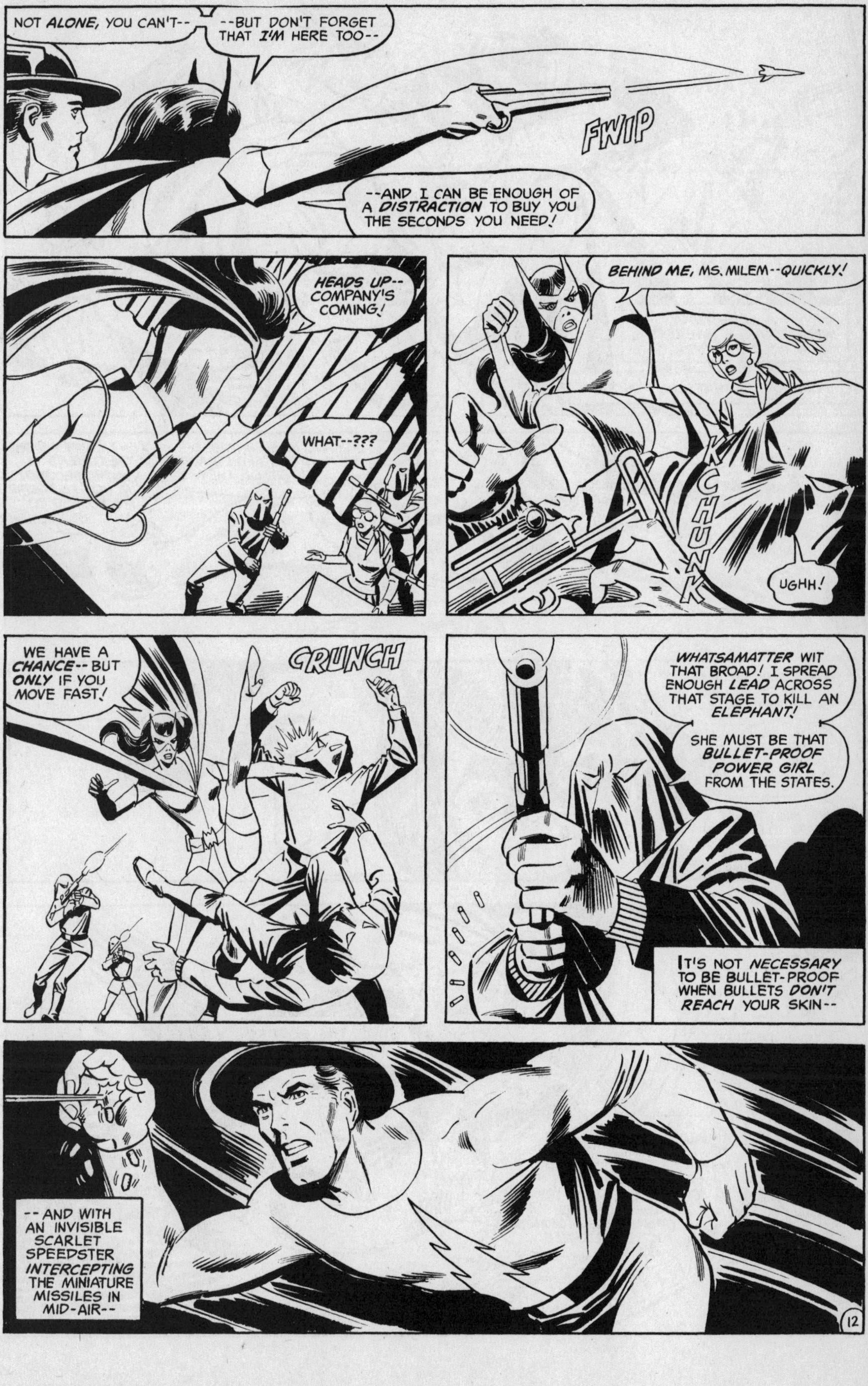
NOT ALONE, YOU CAN'T--
--BUT DON'T FORGET THAT I'M HERE TOO--
FWIP
--AND I CAN BE ENOUGH OF A DISTRACTION TO BUY YOU THE SECONDS YOU NEED!
HEADS UP-- COMPANY'S COMING!
WHAT--???
BEHIND ME, MS. MILEM--QUICKLY!
K-CHUNK
UGHH!
WE HAVE A CHANCE--BUT ONLY IF YOU MOVE FAST!
CRUNCH
WHATSAMATTER WIT THAT BROAD! I SPREAD ENOUGH LEAD ACROSS THAT STAGE TO KILL AN ELEPHANT!
SHE MUST BE THAT BULLET-PROOF POWER GIRL FROM THE STATES.
IT'S NOT NECESSARY TO BE BULLET-PROOF WHEN BULLETS DON'T REACH YOUR SKIN--
--AND WITH AN INVISIBLE SCARLET SPEEDSTER INTERCEPTING THE MINIATURE MISSILES IN MID-AIR--
12

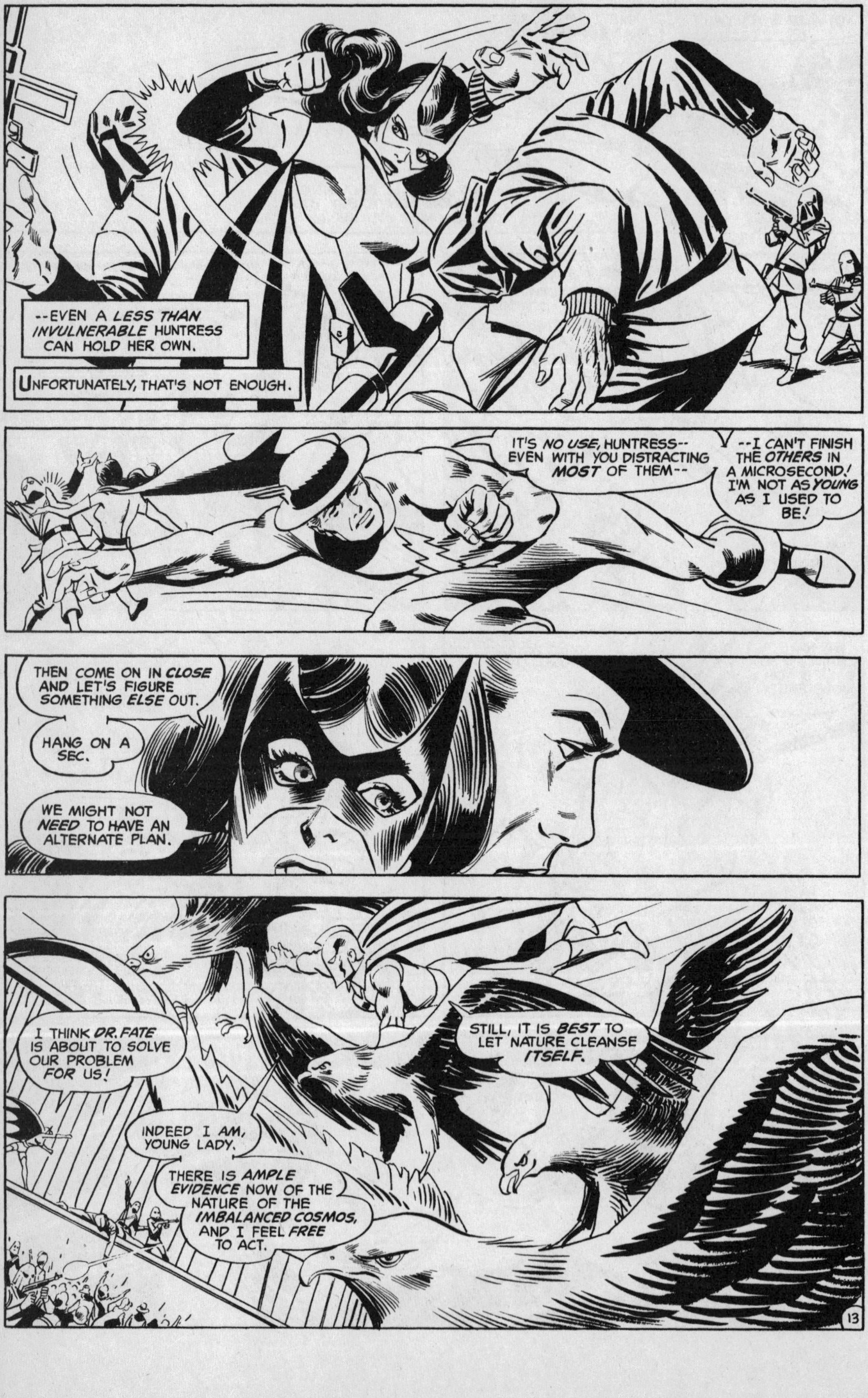
--EVEN A LESS THAN INVULNERABLE HUNTRESS CAN HOLD HER OWN.
UNFORTUNATELY, THAT'S NOT ENOUGH.
IT'S NO USE, HUNTRESS-- EVEN WITH YOU DISTRACTING MOST OF THEM--
--I CAN'T FINISH THE OTHERS IN A MICROSECOND! I'M NOT AS YOUNG AS I USED TO BE!
THEN COME ON IN CLOSE AND LET'S FIGURE SOMETHING ELSE OUT.
HANG ON A SEC.
WE MIGHT NOT NEED TO HAVE AN ALTERNATE PLAN.
I THINK DR. FATE IS ABOUT TO SOLVE OUR PROBLEM FOR US!
STILL, IT IS BEST TO LET NATURE CLEANSE ITSELF.
INDEED I AM, YOUNG LADY.
THERE IS AMPLE EVIDENCE NOW OF THE NATURE OF THE IMBALANCED COSMOS, AND I FEEL FREE TO ACT.
13

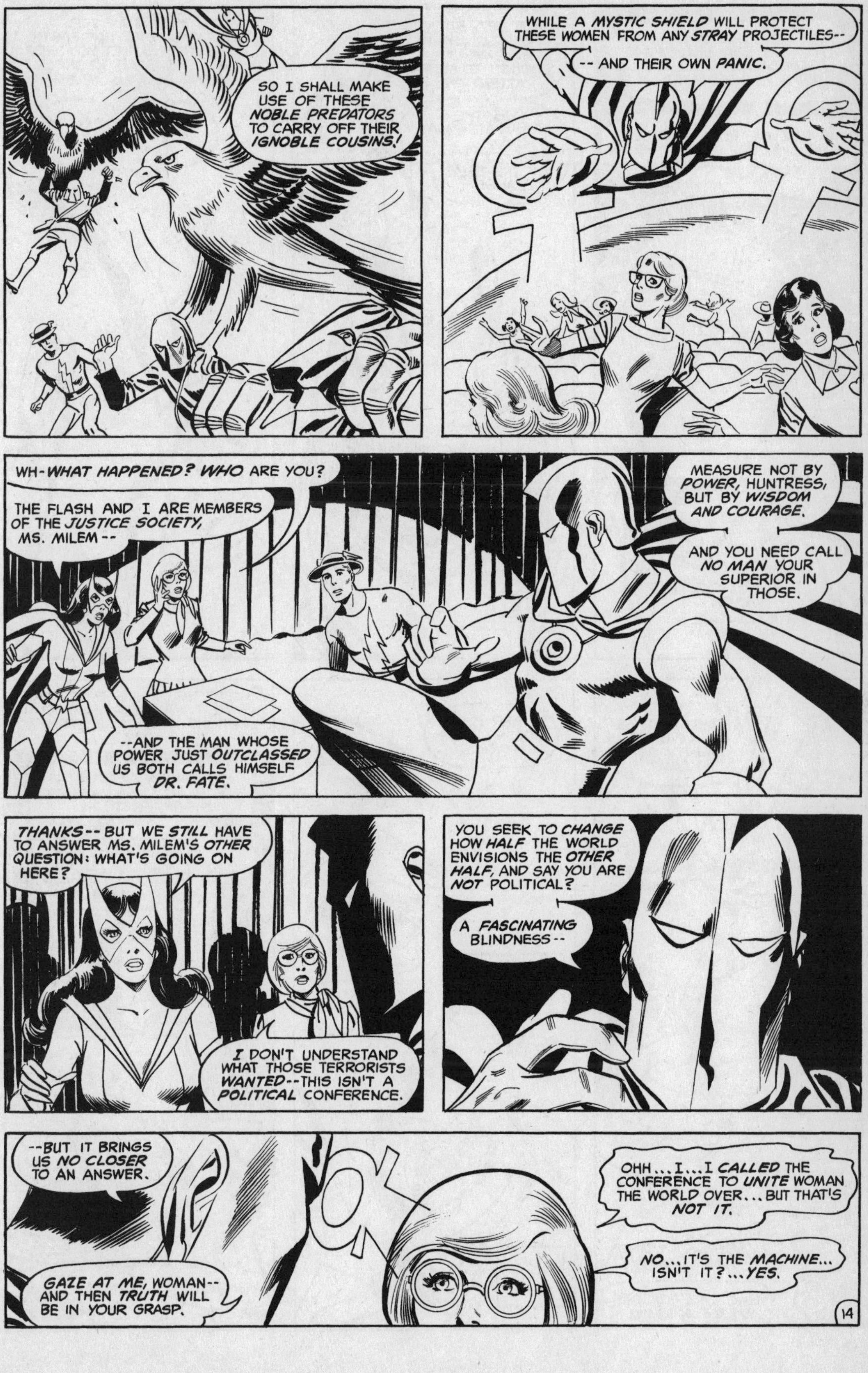
SO I SHALL MAKE USE OF THESE NOBLE PREDATORS TO CARRY OFF THEIR IGNOBLE COUSINS!
WHILE A MYSTIC SHIELD WILL PROTECT THESE WOMEN FROM ANY STRAY PROJECTILES--
-- AND THEIR OWN PANIC.
WH-WHAT HAPPENED? WHO ARE YOU?
THE FLASH AND I ARE MEMBERS OF THE JUSTICE SOCIETY, MS. MILEM --
--AND THE MAN WHOSE POWER JUST OUTCLASSED US BOTH CALLS HIMSELF DR. FATE.
MEASURE NOT BY POWER, HUNTRESS, BUT BY WISDOM AND COURAGE.
AND YOU NEED CALL NO MAN YOUR SUPERIOR IN THOSE.
THANKS-- BUT WE STILL HAVE TO ANSWER MS. MILEM'S OTHER QUESTION: WHAT'S GOING ON HERE?
I DON'T UNDERSTAND WHAT THOSE TERRORISTS WANTED--THIS ISN'T A POLITICAL CONFERENCE.
YOU SEEK TO CHANGE HOW HALF THE WORLD ENVISIONS THE OTHER HALF, AND SAY YOU ARE NOT POLITICAL?
A FASCINATING BLINDNESS --
--BUT IT BRINGS US NO CLOSER TO AN ANSWER.
GAZE AT ME, WOMAN-- AND THEN TRUTH WILL BE IN YOUR GRASP.
OHH...I...I CALLED THE CONFERENCE TO UNITE WOMAN THE WORLD OVER... BUT THAT'S NOT IT.
NO... IT'S THE MACHINE... ISN'T IT?... YES.
14

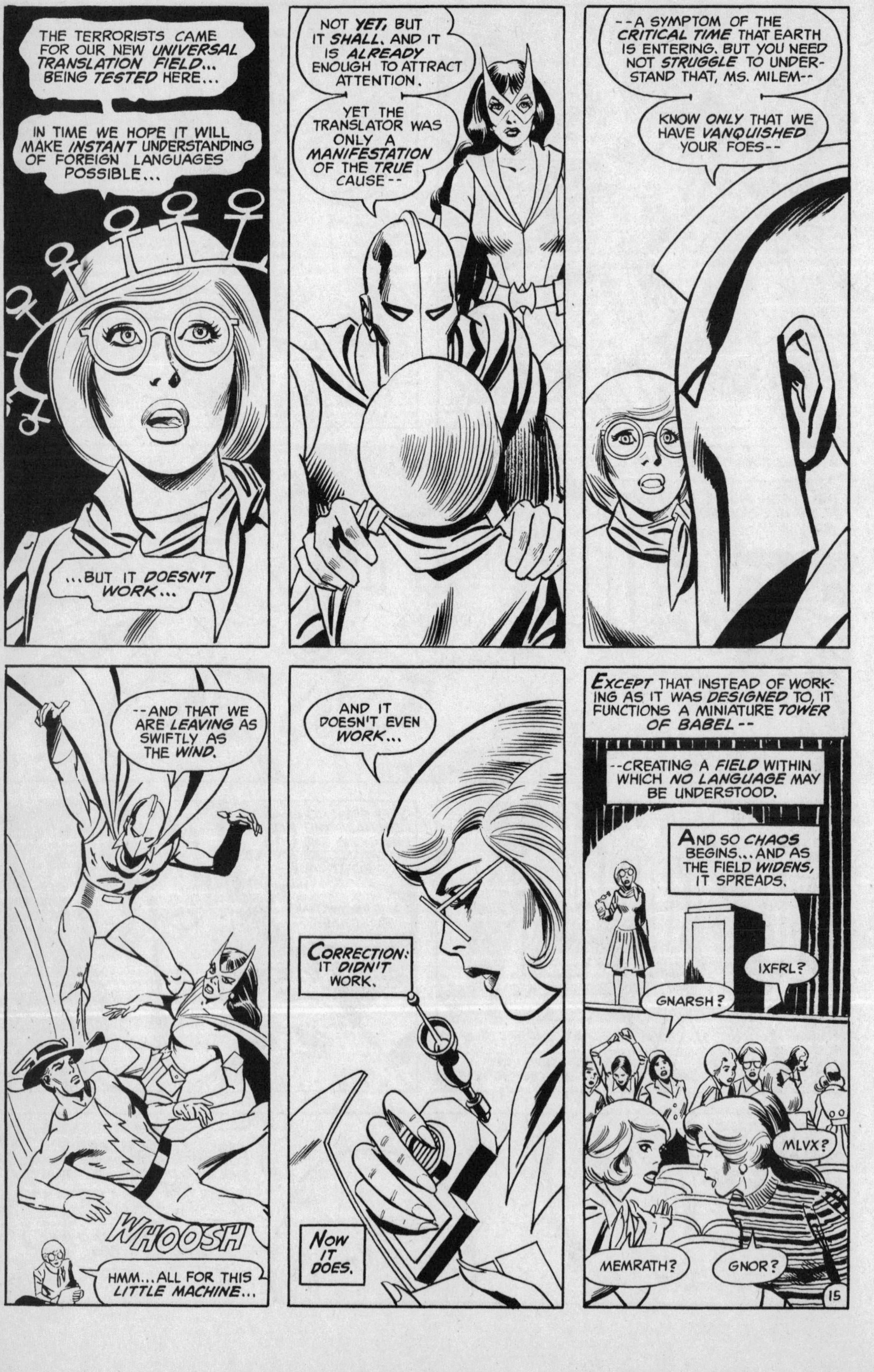
THE TERRORISTS CAME FOR OUR NEW UNIVERSAL TRANSLATION FIELD... BEING TESTED HERE...
IN TIME WE HOPE IT WILL MAKE INSTANT UNDERSTANDING OF FOREIGN LANGUAGES POSSIBLE...
...BUT IT DOESN'T WORK...
NOT YET, BUT IT SHALL. AND IT IS ALREADY ENOUGH TO ATTRACT ATTENTION.
YET THE TRANSLATOR WAS ONLY A MANIFESTATION OF THE TRUE CAUSE--
--A SYMPTOM OF THE CRITICAL TIME THAT EARTH IS ENTERING. BUT YOU NEED NOT STRUGGLE TO UNDERSTAND THAT, MS. MILEM--
KNOW ONLY THAT WE HAVE VANQUISHED YOUR FOES--
--AND THAT WE ARE LEAVING AS SWIFTLY AS THE WIND.
WHOOSH
HMM...ALL FOR THIS LITTLE MACHINE...
AND IT DOESN'T EVEN WORK...
CORRECTION: IT DIDN'T WORK.
NOW IT DOES.
EXCEPT THAT INSTEAD OF WORKING AS IT WAS DESIGNED TO, IT FUNCTIONS A MINIATURE TOWER OF BABEL--
--CREATING A FIELD WITHIN WHICH NO LANGUAGE MAY BE UNDERSTOOD.
AND SO CHAOS BEGINS...AND AS THE FIELD WIDENS, IT SPREADS.
IXFRL?
GNARSH?
MLVX?
MEMRATH?
GNOR?
15

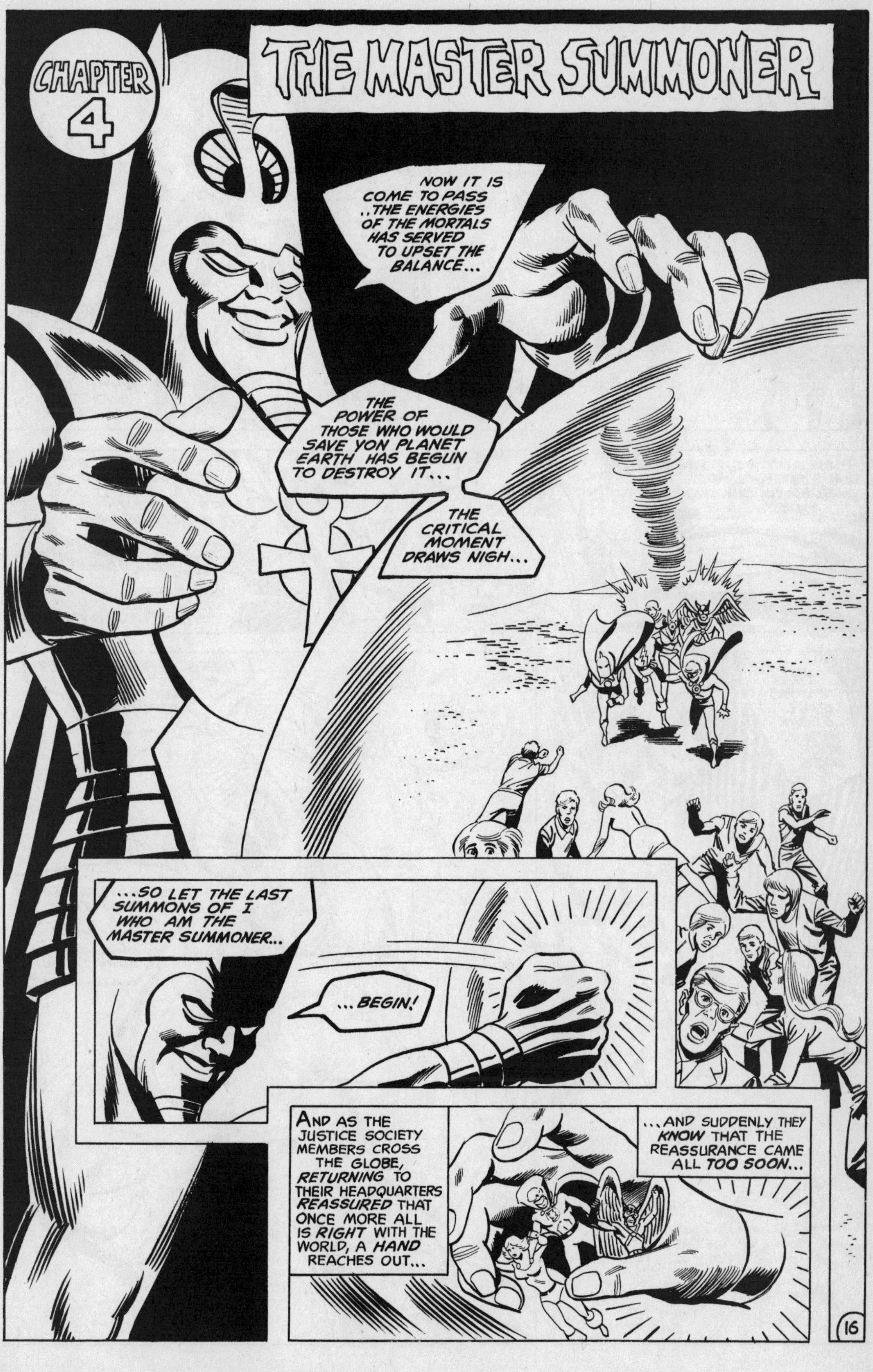
CHAPTER 4
THE MASTER SUMMONER
NOW IT IS COME TO PASS ..THE ENERGIES OF THE MORTALS HAS SERVED TO UPSET THE BALANCE...
THE POWER OF THOSE WHO WOULD SAVE YON PLANET EARTH HAS BEGUN TO DESTROY IT...
THE CRITICAL MOMENT DRAWS NIGH...
...SO LET THE LAST SUMMONS OF I WHO AM THE MASTER SUMMONER...
...BEGIN!
AND AS THE JUSTICE SOCIETY MEMBERS CROSS THE GLOBE, RETURNING TO THEIR HEADQUARTERS REASSURED THAT ONCE MORE ALL IS RIGHT WITH THE WORLD, A HAND REACHES OUT...
...AND SUDDENLY THEY KNOW THAT THE REASSURANCE CAME ALL TOO SOON...
16

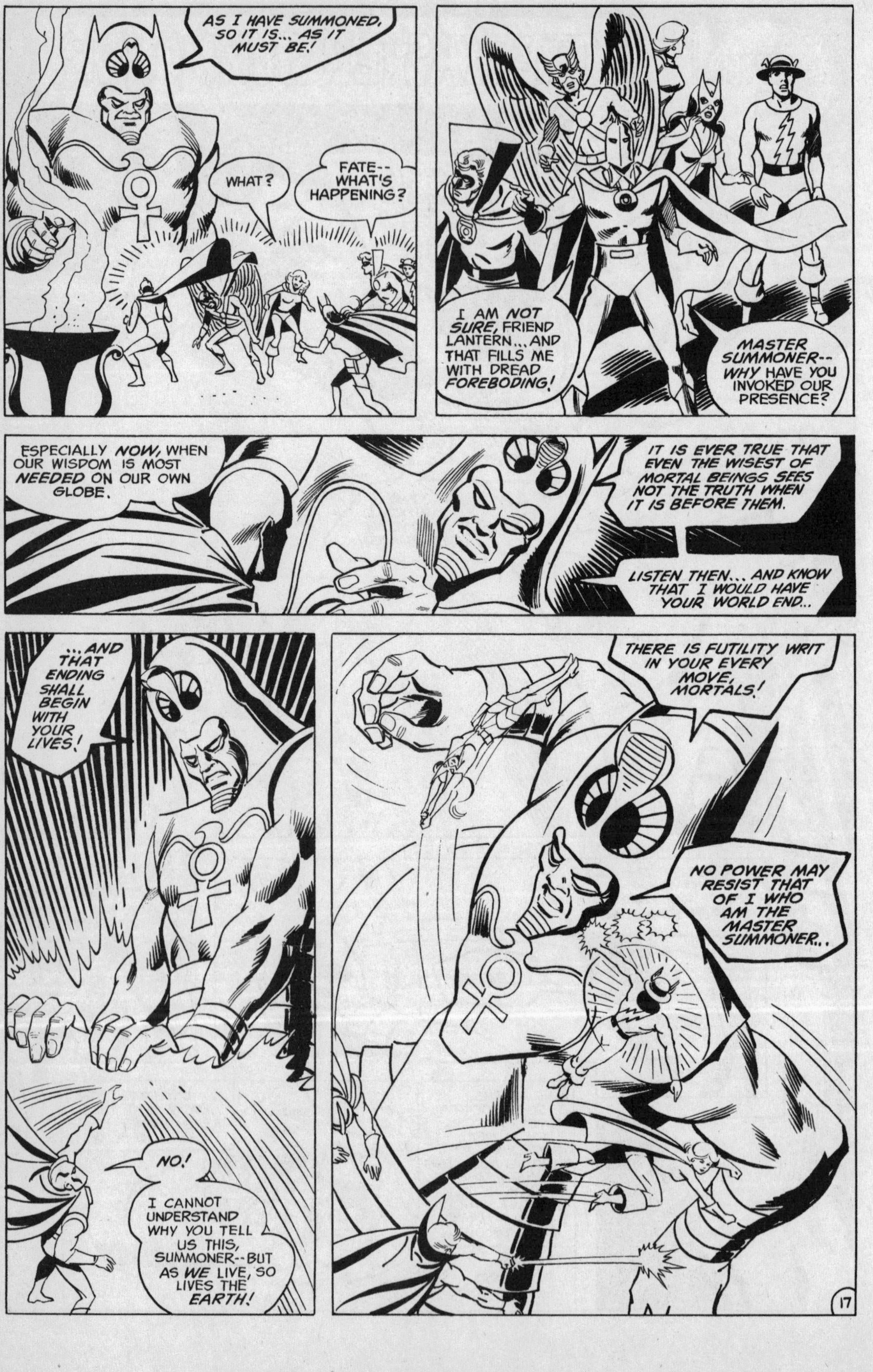
AS I HAVE SUMMONED, SO IT IS... AS IT MUST BE!
WHAT?
FATE-- WHAT'S HAPPENING?
I AM NOT SURE, FRIEND LANTERN... AND THAT FILLS ME WITH DREAD FOREBODING!
MASTER SUMMONER-- WHY HAVE YOU INVOKED OUR PRESENCE?
ESPECIALLY NOW, WHEN OUR WISDOM IS MOST NEEDED ON OUR OWN GLOBE.
IT IS EVER TRUE THAT EVEN THE WISEST OF MORTAL BEINGS SEES NOT THE TRUTH WHEN IT IS BEFORE THEM.
LISTEN THEN... AND KNOW THAT I WOULD HAVE YOUR WORLD END...
...AND THAT ENDING SHALL BEGIN WITH YOUR LIVES!
NO!
I CANNOT UNDERSTAND WHY YOU TELL US THIS, SUMMONER--BUT AS WE LIVE, SO LIVES THE EARTH!
THERE IS FUTILITY WRIT IN YOUR EVERY MOVE, MORTALS!
NO POWER MAY RESIST THAT OF I WHO AM THE MASTER SUMMONER...
17

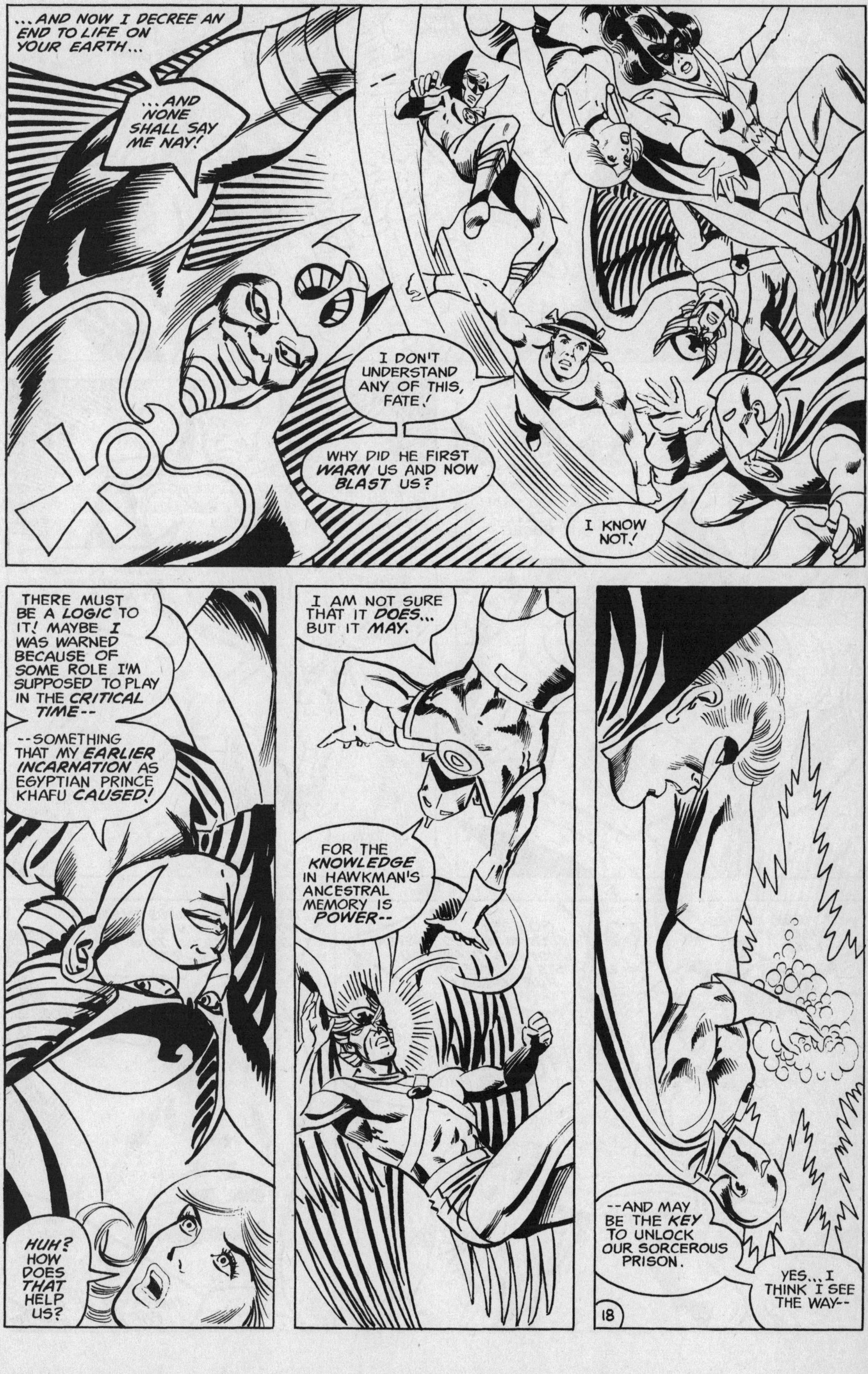
...AND NOW I DECREE AN END TO LIFE ON YOUR EARTH...
...AND NONE SHALL SAY ME NAY!
I DON'T UNDERSTAND ANY OF THIS, FATE!
WHY DID HE FIRST WARN US AND NOW BLAST US?
I KNOW NOT!
THERE MUST BE A LOGIC TO IT! MAYBE I WAS WARNED BECAUSE OF SOME ROLE I'M SUPPOSED TO PLAY IN THE CRITICAL TIME--
--SOMETHING THAT MY EARLIER INCARNATION AS EGYPTIAN PRINCE KHAFU CAUSED!
HUH? HOW DOES THAT HELP US?
I AM NOT SURE THAT IT DOES... BUT IT MAY.
FOR THE KNOWLEDGE IN HAWKMAN'S ANCESTRAL MEMORY IS POWER--
--AND MAY BE THE KEY TO UNLOCK OUR SORCEROUS PRISON.
YES... I THINK I SEE THE WAY--
18

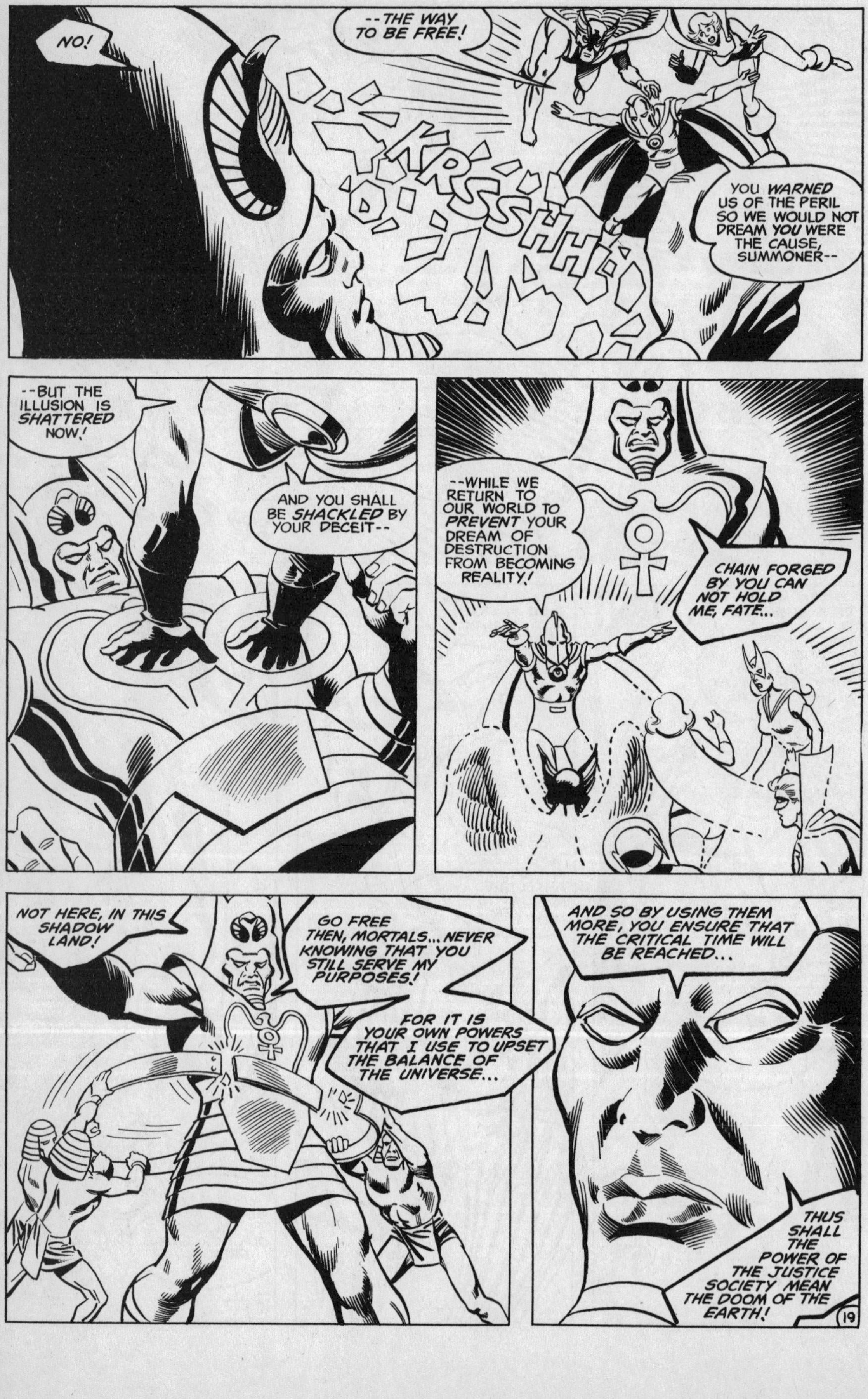
NO!
--THE WAY TO BE FREE!
KRSSHH!
YOU WARNED US OF THE PERIL SO WE WOULD NOT DREAM YOU WERE THE CAUSE, SUMMONER--
--BUT THE ILLUSION IS SHATTERED NOW!
AND YOU SHALL BE SHACKLED BY YOUR DECEIT--
--WHILE WE RETURN TO OUR WORLD TO PREVENT YOUR DREAM OF DESTRUCTION FROM BECOMING REALITY!
CHAIN FORGED BY YOU CAN NOT HOLD ME, FATE...
NOT HERE, IN THIS SHADOW LAND!
GO FREE THEN, MORTALS... NEVER KNOWING THAT YOU STILL SERVE MY PURPOSES!
FOR IT IS YOUR OWN POWERS THAT I USE TO UPSET THE BALANCE OF THE UNIVERSE...
AND SO BY USING THEM MORE, YOU ENSURE THAT THE CRITICAL TIME WILL BE REACHED...
THUS SHALL THE POWER OF THE JUSTICE SOCIETY MEAN THE DOOM OF THE EARTH!
19

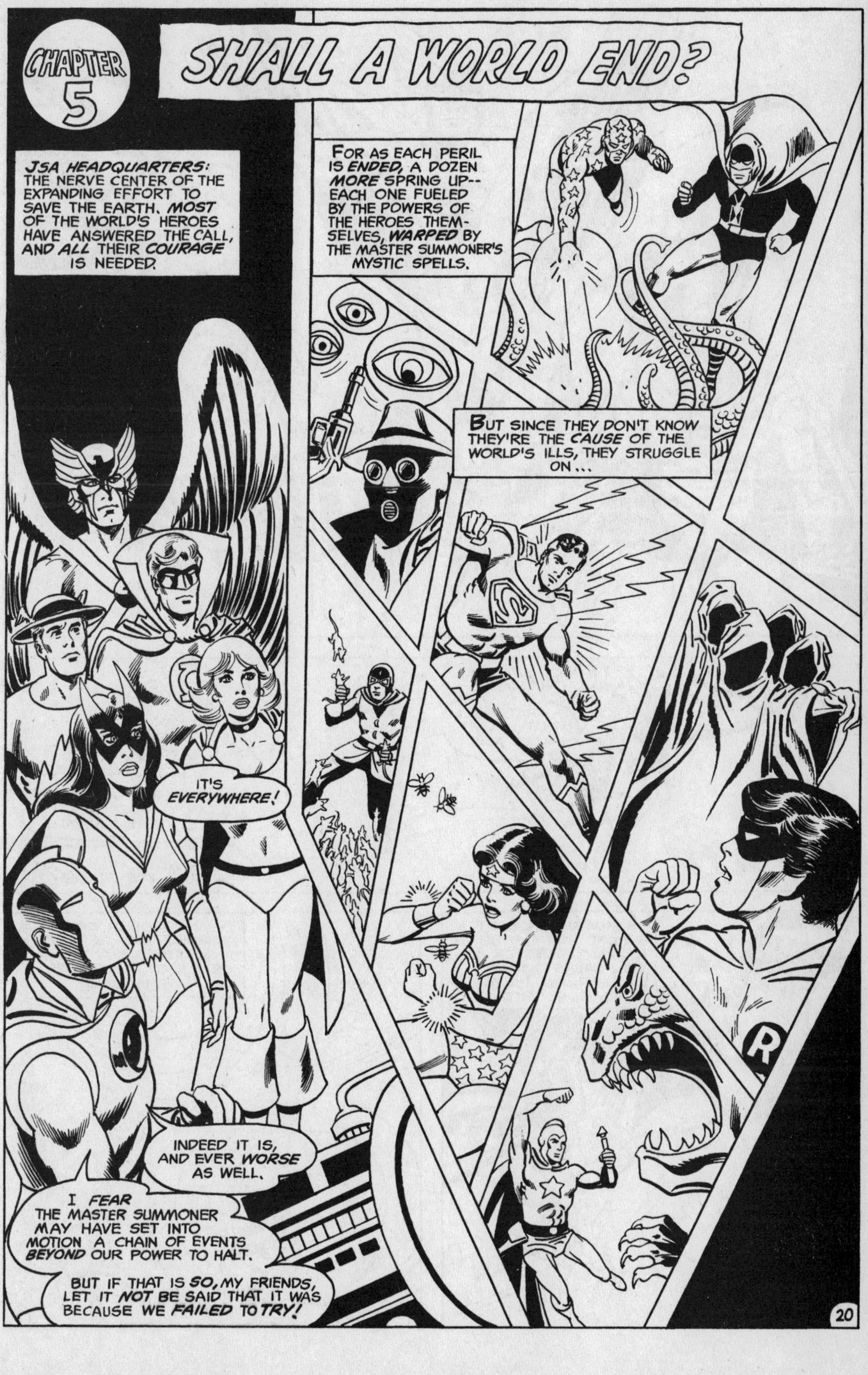
CHAPTER 5
SHALL A WORLD END?
JSA HEADQUARTERS: THE NERVE CENTER OF THE EXPANDING EFFORT TO SAVE THE EARTH. MOST OF THE WORLD'S HEROES HAVE ANSWERED THE CALL, AND ALL THEIR COURAGE IS NEEDED.
IT'S EVERYWHERE!
INDEED IT IS, AND EVER WORSE AS WELL.
I FEAR THE MASTER SUMMONER MAY HAVE SET INTO MOTION A CHAIN OF EVENTS BEYOND OUR POWER TO HALT.
BUT IF THAT IS SO, MY FRIENDS, LET IT NOT BE SAID THAT IT WAS BECAUSE WE FAILED TO TRY!
FOR AS EACH PERIL IS ENDED, A DOZEN MORE SPRING UP-- EACH ONE FUELED BY THE POWERS OF THE HEROES THEMSELVES, WARPED BY THE MASTER SUMMONER'S MYSTIC SPELLS.
BUT SINCE THEY DON'T KNOW THEY'RE THE CAUSE OF THE WORLD'S ILLS, THEY STRUGGLE ON...
20

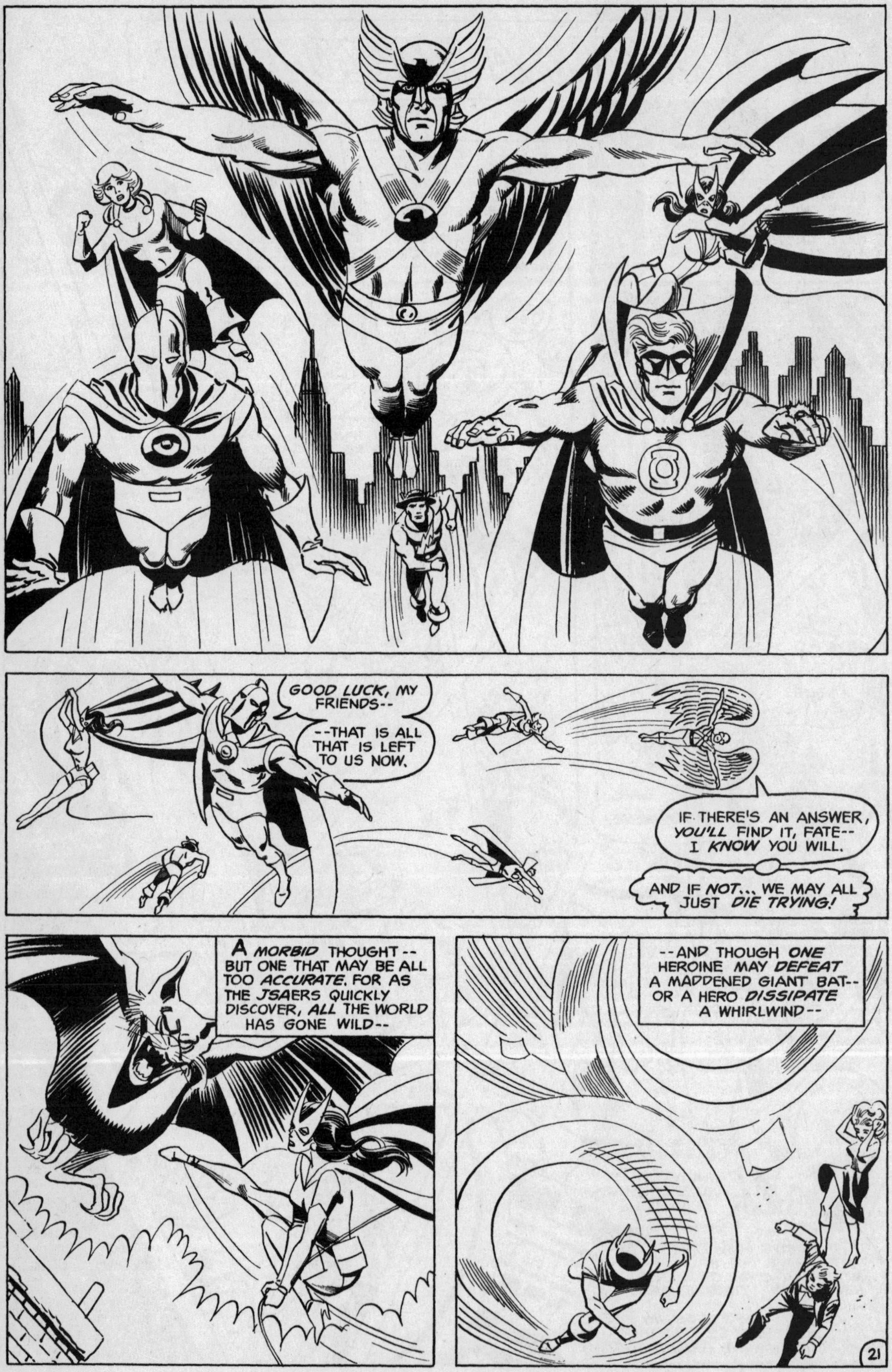
GOOD LUCK, MY FRIENDS--
--THAT IS ALL THAT IS LEFT TO US NOW.
IF THERE'S AN ANSWER, YOU'LL FIND IT, FATE-- I KNOW YOU WILL.
AND IF NOT... WE MAY ALL JUST DIE TRYING!
A MORBID THOUGHT -- BUT ONE THAT MAY BE ALL TOO ACCURATE, FOR AS THE JSAERS QUICKLY DISCOVER, ALL THE WORLD HAS GONE WILD--
--AND THOUGH ONE HEROINE MAY DEFEAT A MADDENED GIANT BAT-- OR A HERO DISSIPATE A WHIRLWIND--
21

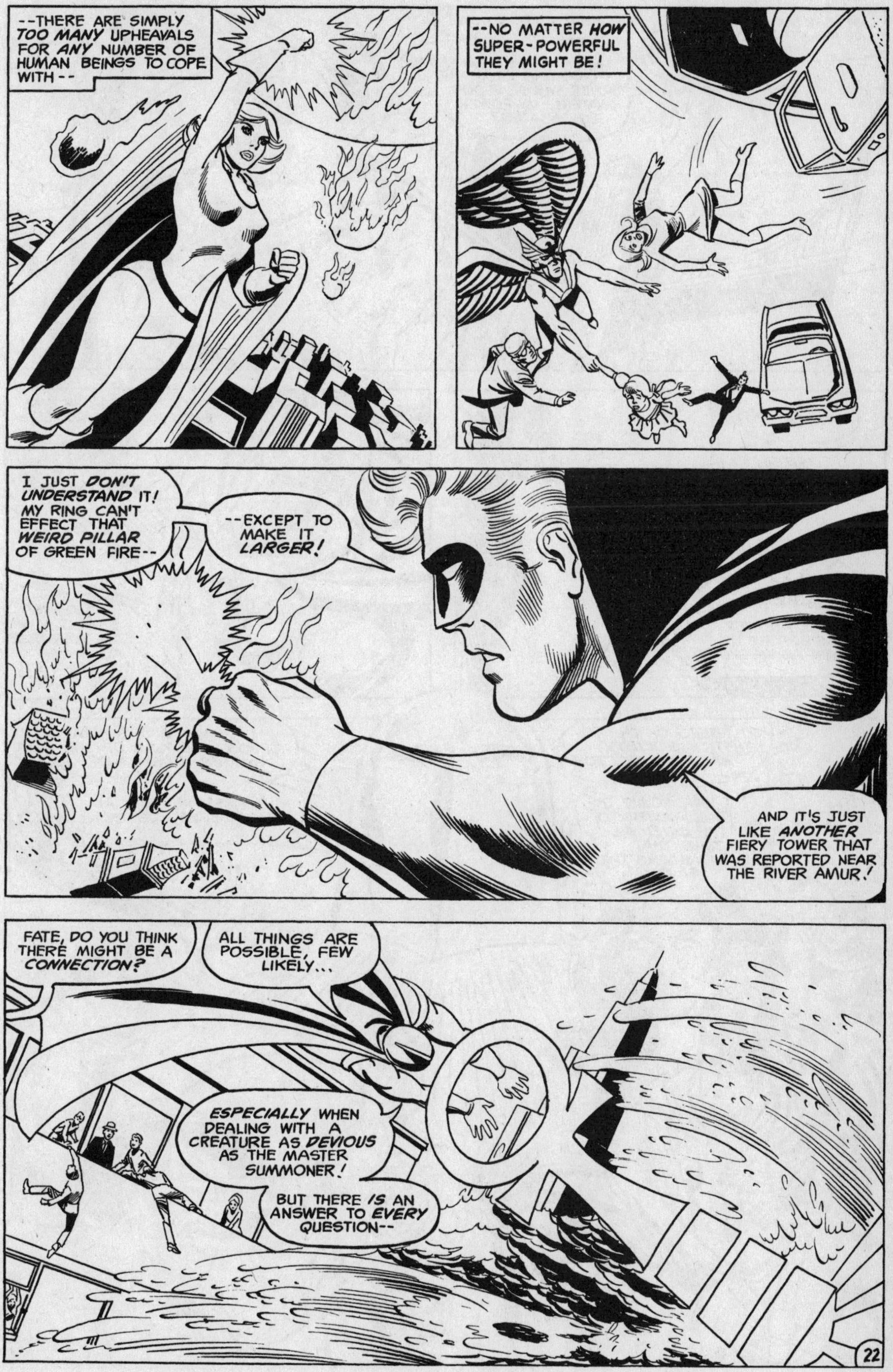
--THERE ARE SIMPLY TOO MANY UPHEAVALS FOR ANY NUMBER OF HUMAN BEINGS TO COPE WITH--
--NO MATTER HOW SUPER-POWERFUL THEY MIGHT BE!
I JUST DON'T UNDERSTAND IT! MY RING CAN'T EFFECT THAT WEIRD PILLAR OF GREEN FIRE--
--EXCEPT TO MAKE IT LARGER!
AND IT'S JUST LIKE ANOTHER FIERY TOWER THAT WAS REPORTED NEAR THE RIVER AMUR!
FATE, DO YOU THINK THERE MIGHT BE A CONNECTION?
ALL THINGS ARE POSSIBLE, FEW LIKELY...
ESPECIALLY WHEN DEALING WITH A CREATURE AS DEVIOUS AS THE MASTER SUMMONER!
BUT THERE IS AN ANSWER TO EVERY QUESTION--
22

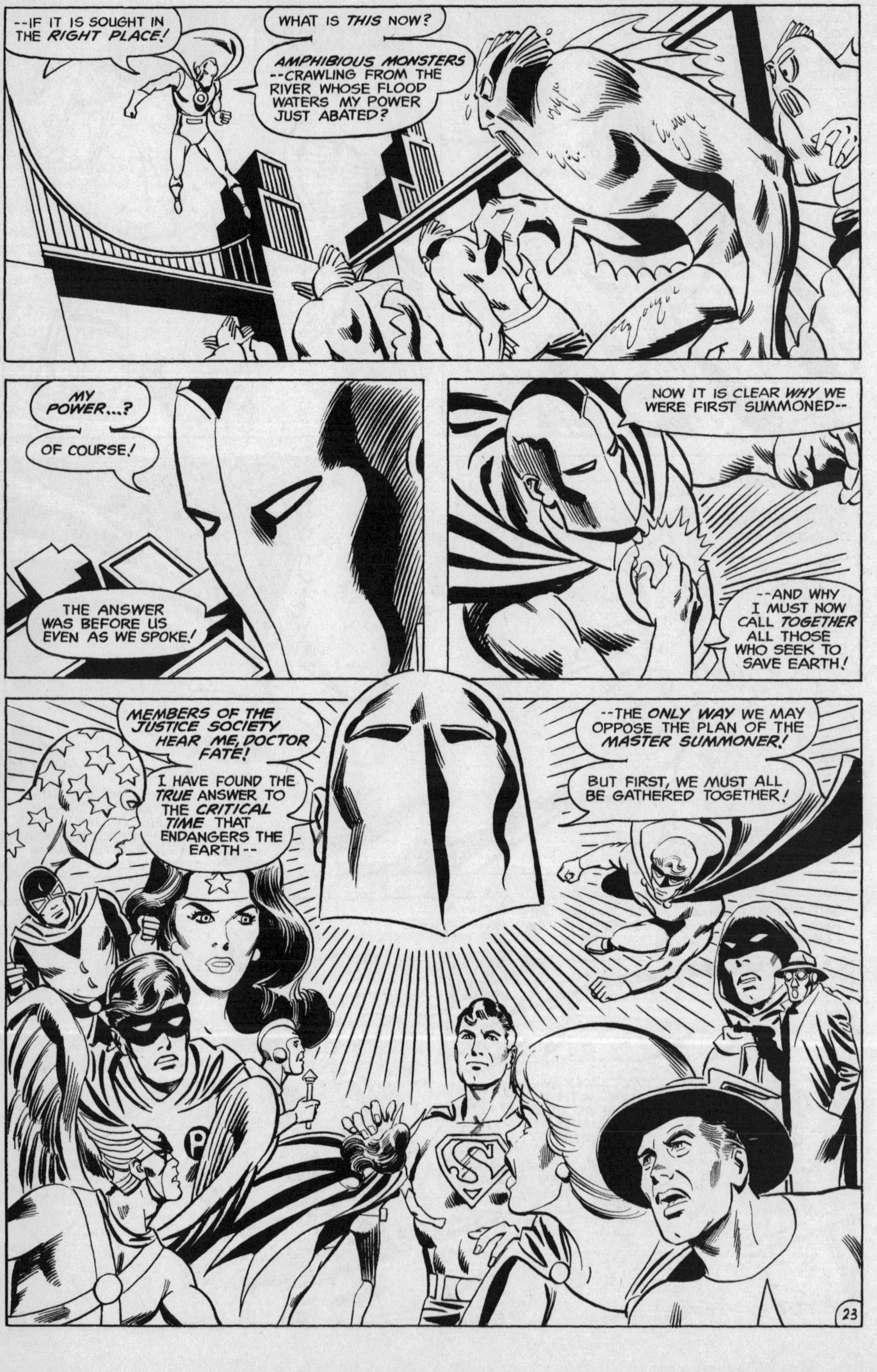
--IF IT IS SOUGHT IN THE *RIGHT PLACE!*
WHAT IS *THIS* NOW?
AMPHIBIOUS MONSTERS --CRAWLING FROM THE RIVER WHOSE FLOOD WATERS MY POWER JUST ABATED?
MY POWER...?
OF COURSE!
THE ANSWER WAS BEFORE US EVEN AS WE SPOKE!
NOW IT IS CLEAR *WHY* WE WERE FIRST SUMMONED--
--AND WHY I MUST NOW CALL *TOGETHER* ALL THOSE WHO SEEK TO SAVE EARTH!
MEMBERS OF THE JUSTICE SOCIETY HEAR ME, DOCTOR FATE!
I HAVE FOUND THE *TRUE* ANSWER TO THE *CRITICAL TIME* THAT ENDANGERS THE EARTH--
--THE *ONLY WAY* WE MAY OPPOSE THE PLAN OF THE *MASTER SUMMONER!*
BUT FIRST, WE MUST ALL BE GATHERED TOGETHER!
23

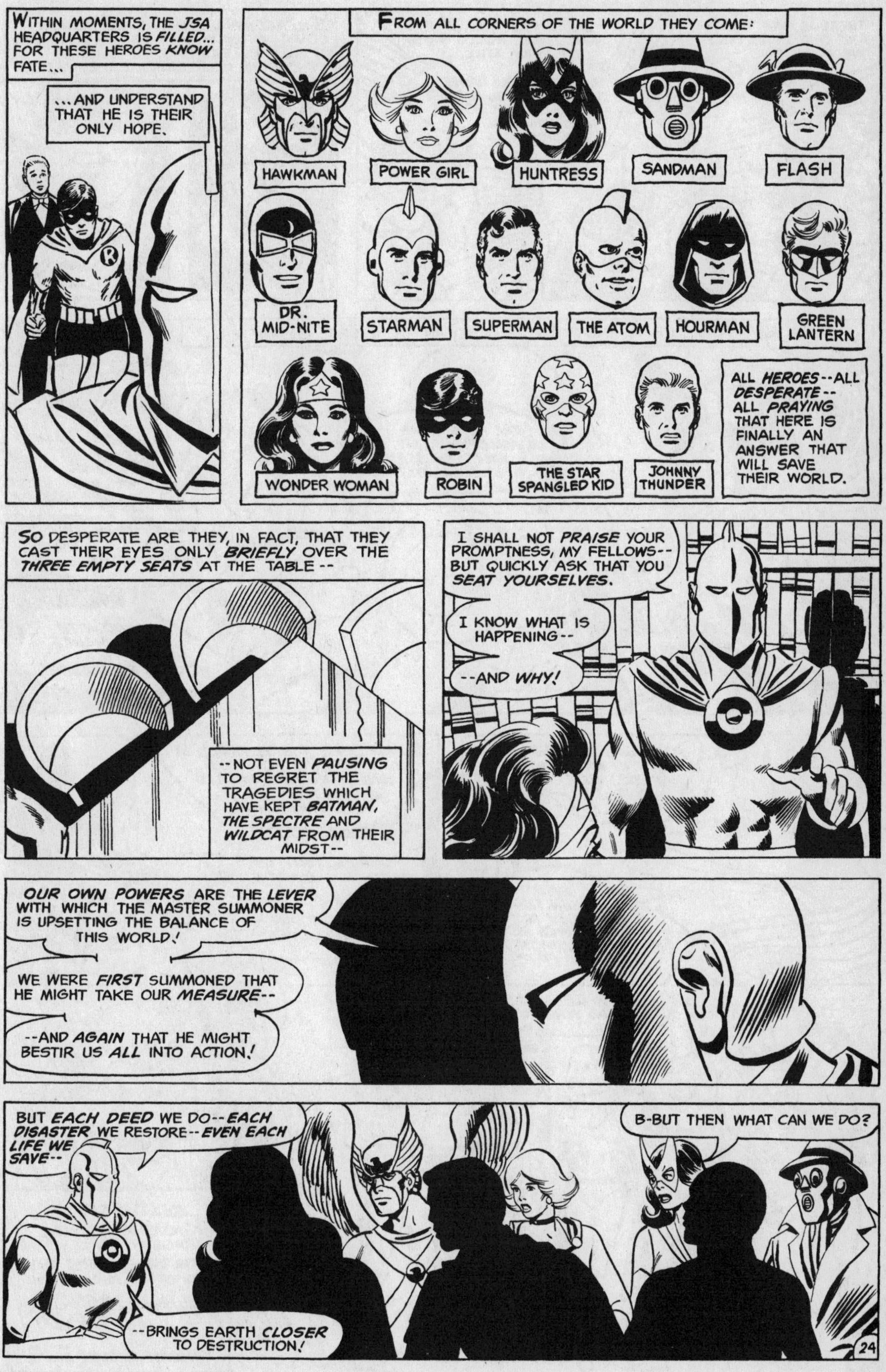
WITHIN MOMENTS, THE JSA HEADQUARTERS IS FILLED... FOR THESE HEROES KNOW FATE...
...AND UNDERSTAND THAT HE IS THEIR ONLY HOPE.
FROM ALL CORNERS OF THE WORLD THEY COME:
HAWKMAN
POWER GIRL
HUNTRESS
SANDMAN
FLASH
DR. MID-NITE
STARMAN
SUPERMAN
THE ATOM
HOURMAN
GREEN LANTERN
WONDER WOMAN
ROBIN
THE STAR SPANGLED KID
JOHNNY THUNDER
ALL HEROES--ALL DESPERATE--ALL PRAYING THAT HERE IS FINALLY AN ANSWER THAT WILL SAVE THEIR WORLD.
SO DESPERATE ARE THEY, IN FACT, THAT THEY CAST THEIR EYES ONLY BRIEFLY OVER THE THREE EMPTY SEATS AT THE TABLE--
--NOT EVEN PAUSING TO REGRET THE TRAGEDIES WHICH HAVE KEPT BATMAN, THE SPECTRE AND WILDCAT FROM THEIR MIDST--
I SHALL NOT PRAISE YOUR PROMPTNESS, MY FELLOWS--BUT QUICKLY ASK THAT YOU SEAT YOURSELVES.
I KNOW WHAT IS HAPPENING--
--AND WHY!
OUR OWN POWERS ARE THE LEVER WITH WHICH THE MASTER SUMMONER IS UPSETTING THE BALANCE OF THIS WORLD!
WE WERE FIRST SUMMONED THAT HE MIGHT TAKE OUR MEASURE--
--AND AGAIN THAT HE MIGHT BESTIR US ALL INTO ACTION!
BUT EACH DEED WE DO--EACH DISASTER WE RESTORE--EVEN EACH LIFE WE SAVE--
--BRINGS EARTH CLOSER TO DESTRUCTION!
B-BUT THEN WHAT CAN WE DO?
24

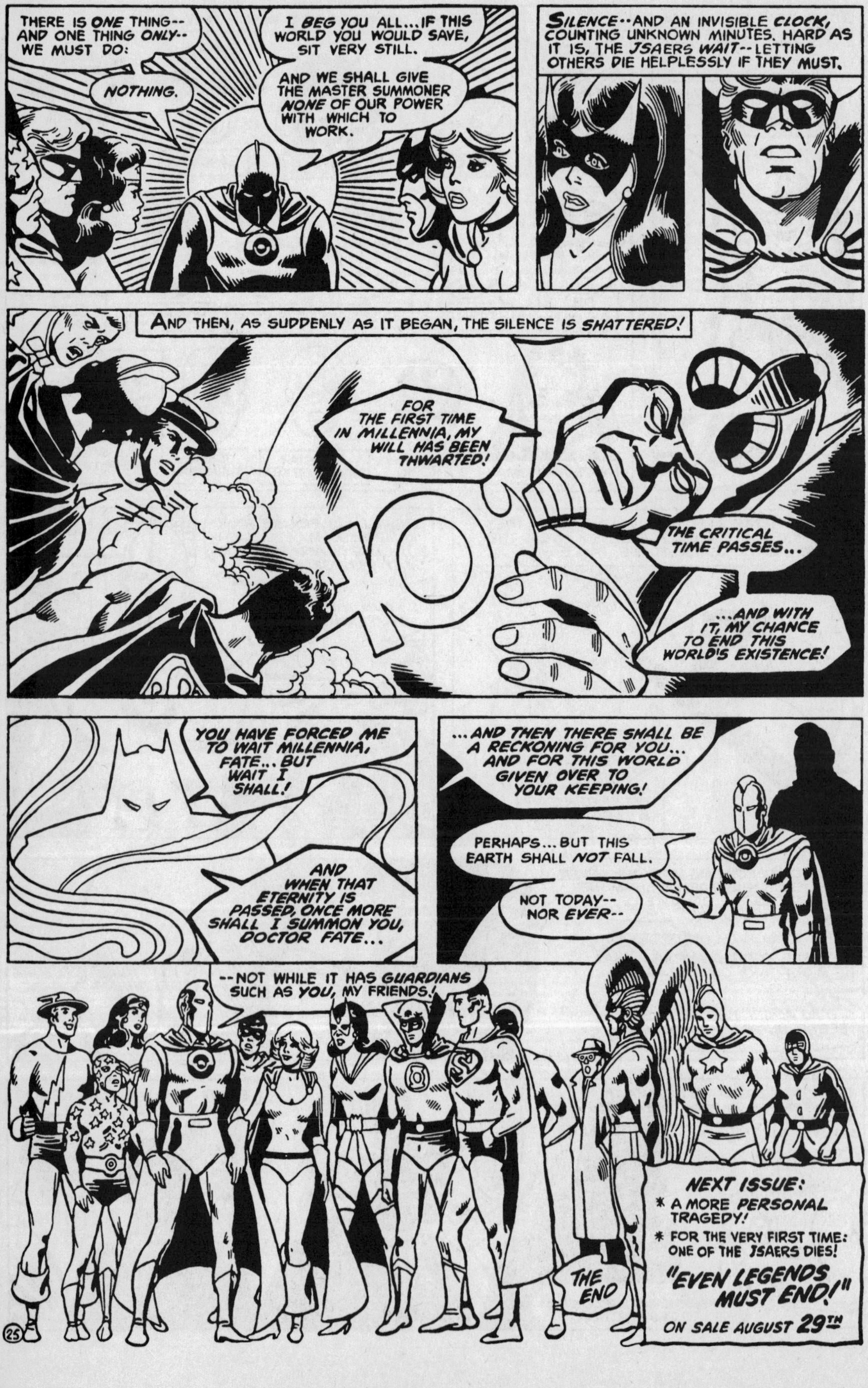
THERE IS ONE THING-- AND ONE THING ONLY-- WE MUST DO:
NOTHING.
I BEG YOU ALL...IF THIS WORLD YOU WOULD SAVE, SIT VERY STILL.
AND WE SHALL GIVE THE MASTER SUMMONER NONE OF OUR POWER WITH WHICH TO WORK.
SILENCE--AND AN INVISIBLE CLOCK, COUNTING UNKNOWN MINUTES. HARD AS IT IS, THE JSAERS WAIT--LETTING OTHERS DIE HELPLESSLY IF THEY MUST.
AND THEN, AS SUDDENLY AS IT BEGAN, THE SILENCE IS SHATTERED!
FOR THE FIRST TIME IN MILLENNIA, MY WILL HAS BEEN THWARTED!
THE CRITICAL TIME PASSES...
...AND WITH IT, MY CHANCE TO END THIS WORLD'S EXISTENCE!
YOU HAVE FORCED ME TO WAIT MILLENNIA, FATE... BUT WAIT I SHALL!
AND WHEN THAT ETERNITY IS PASSED, ONCE MORE SHALL I SUMMON YOU, DOCTOR FATE...
...AND THEN THERE SHALL BE A RECKONING FOR YOU... AND FOR THIS WORLD GIVEN OVER TO YOUR KEEPING!
PERHAPS... BUT THIS EARTH SHALL NOT FALL.
NOT TODAY-- NOR EVER--
--NOT WHILE IT HAS GUARDIANS SUCH AS YOU, MY FRIENDS!
THE END
NEXT ISSUE:
* A MORE PERSONAL TRAGEDY!
* FOR THE VERY FIRST TIME: ONE OF THE JSAERS DIES!
"EVEN LEGENDS MUST END!"
ON SALE AUGUST 29TH
25

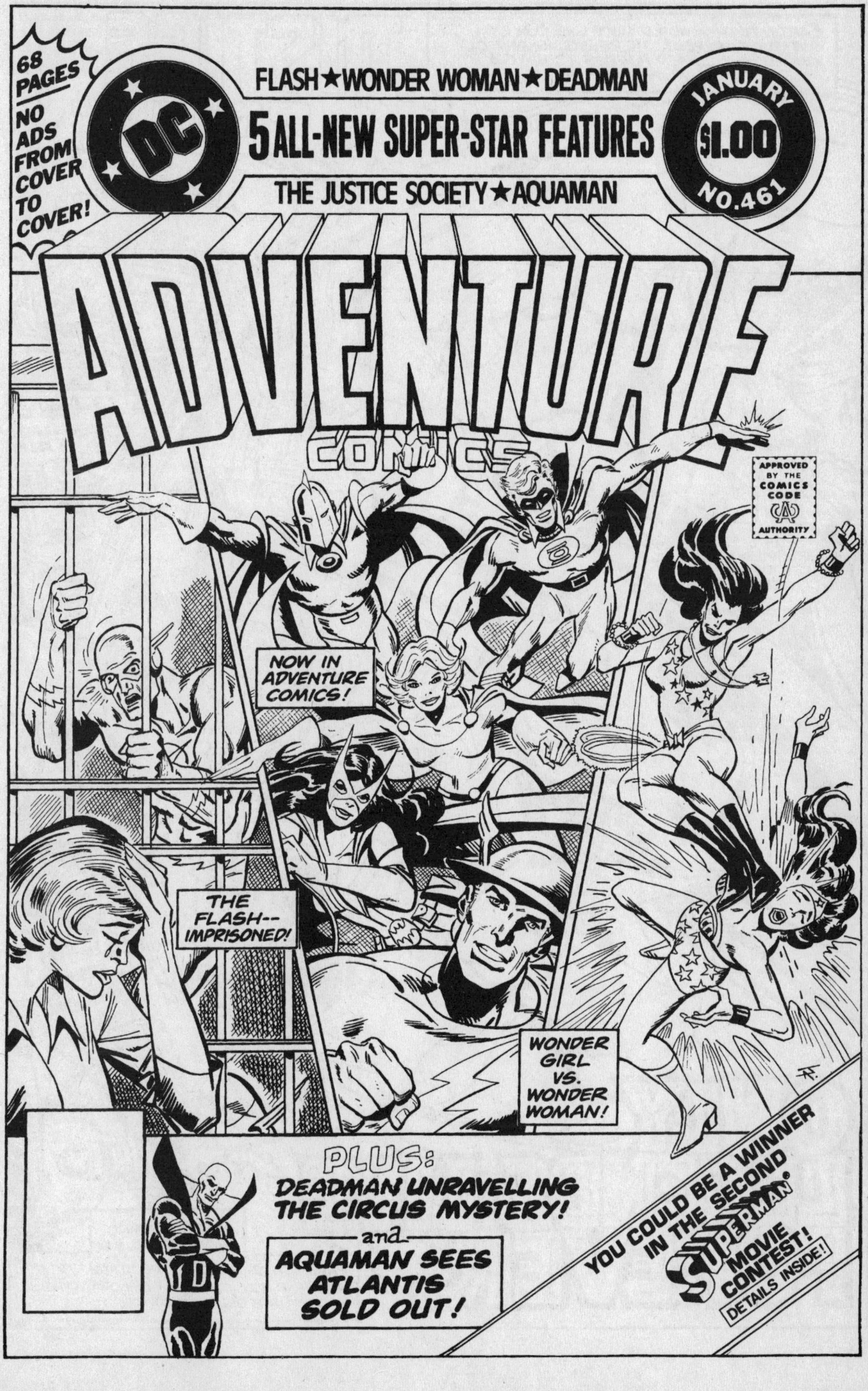
68 PAGES
NO ADS FROM COVER TO COVER!
DC
FLASH ★ WONDER WOMAN ★ DEADMAN
5 ALL-NEW SUPER-STAR FEATURES
THE JUSTICE SOCIETY ★ AQUAMAN
JANUARY
$1.00
NO. 461
ADVENTURE COMICS
APPROVED BY THE COMICS CODE AUTHORITY
NOW IN ADVENTURE COMICS!
THE FLASH-- IMPRISONED!
WONDER GIRL VS. WONDER WOMAN!
PLUS:
DEADMAN UNRAVELLING THE CIRCUS MYSTERY!
and
AQUAMAN SEES ATLANTIS SOLD OUT!
YOU COULD BE A WINNER IN THE SECOND SUPERMAN MOVIE CONTEST!
DETAILS INSIDE!

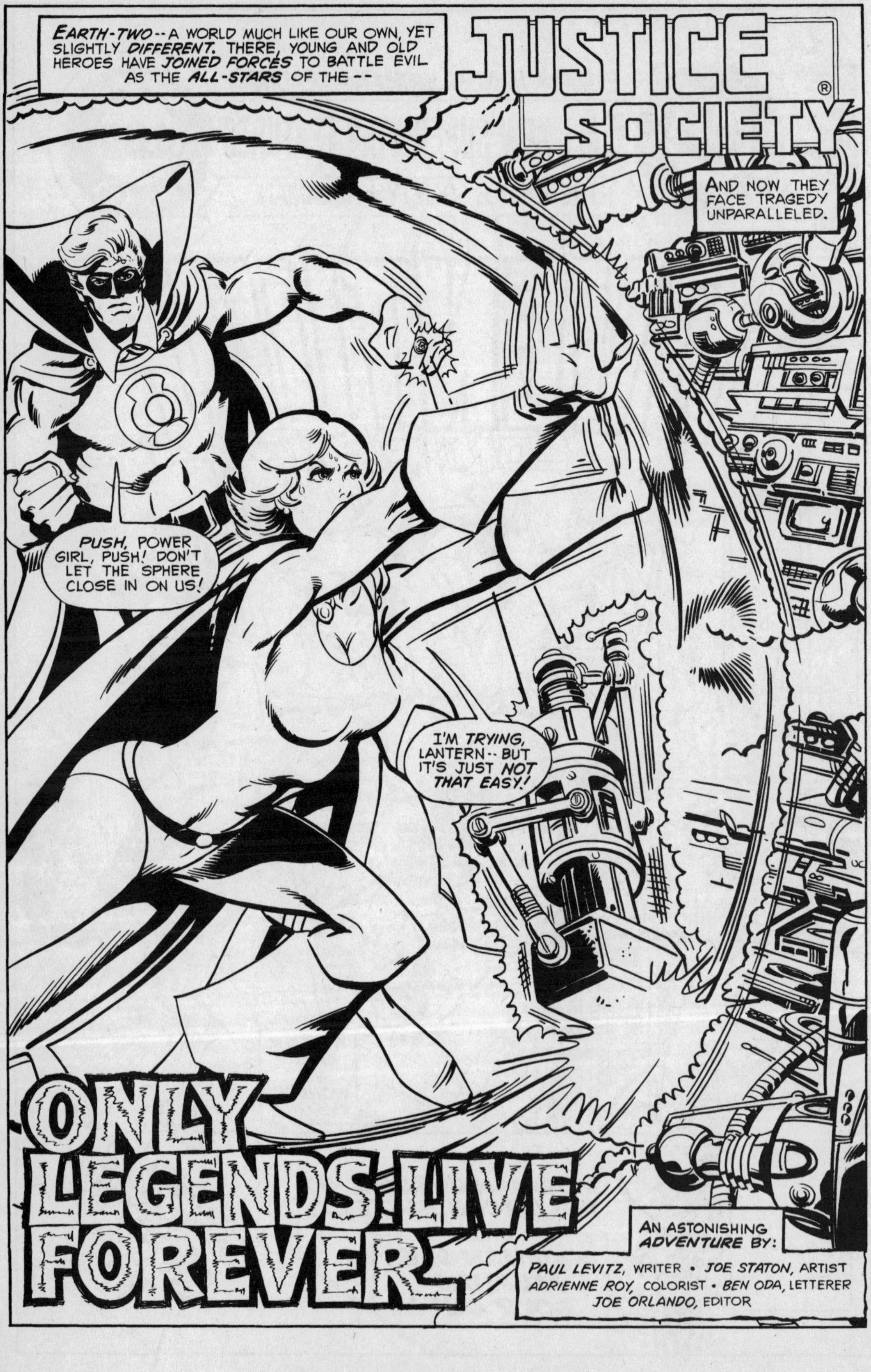
EARTH-TWO -- A WORLD MUCH LIKE OUR OWN, YET SLIGHTLY DIFFERENT. THERE, YOUNG AND OLD HEROES HAVE JOINED FORCES TO BATTLE EVIL AS THE ALL-STARS OF THE --
JUSTICE SOCIETY®
AND NOW THEY FACE TRAGEDY UNPARALLELED.
PUSH, POWER GIRL, PUSH! DON'T LET THE SPHERE CLOSE IN ON US!
I'M TRYING, LANTERN -- BUT IT'S JUST NOT THAT EASY!
ONLY LEGENDS LIVE FOREVER
AN ASTONISHING ADVENTURE BY:
PAUL LEVITZ, WRITER • JOE STATON, ARTIST
ADRIENNE ROY, COLORIST • BEN ODA, LETTERER
JOE ORLANDO, EDITOR

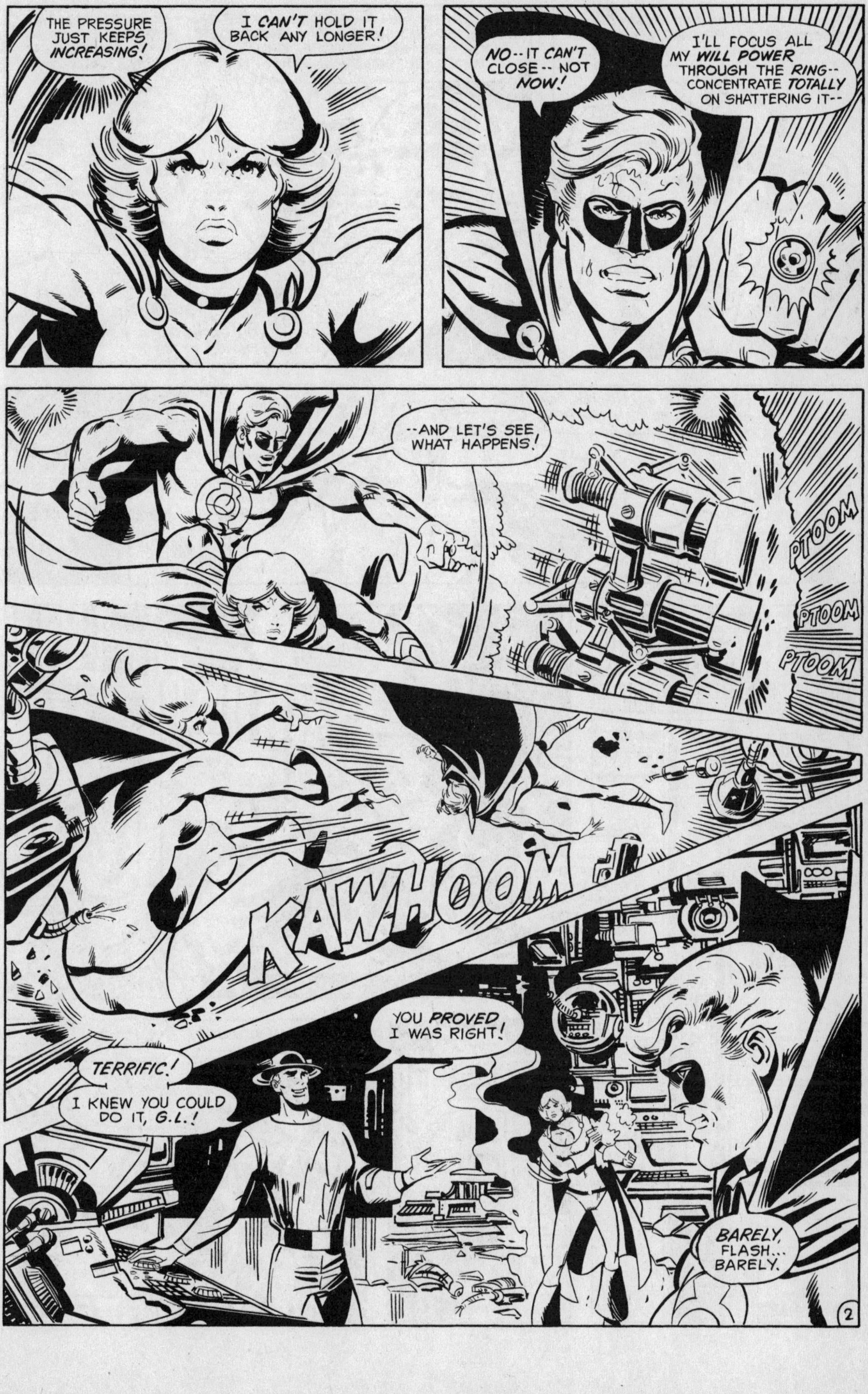
THE PRESSURE JUST KEEPS INCREASING!
I CAN'T HOLD IT BACK ANY LONGER!
NO--IT CAN'T CLOSE--NOT NOW!
I'LL FOCUS ALL MY WILL POWER THROUGH THE RING--CONCENTRATE TOTALLY ON SHATTERING IT--
--AND LET'S SEE WHAT HAPPENS!
PTOOM
PTOOM
PTOOM
KAWHOOM
TERRIFIC! I KNEW YOU COULD DO IT, G.L.!
YOU PROVED I WAS RIGHT!
BARELY, FLASH... BARELY.
2

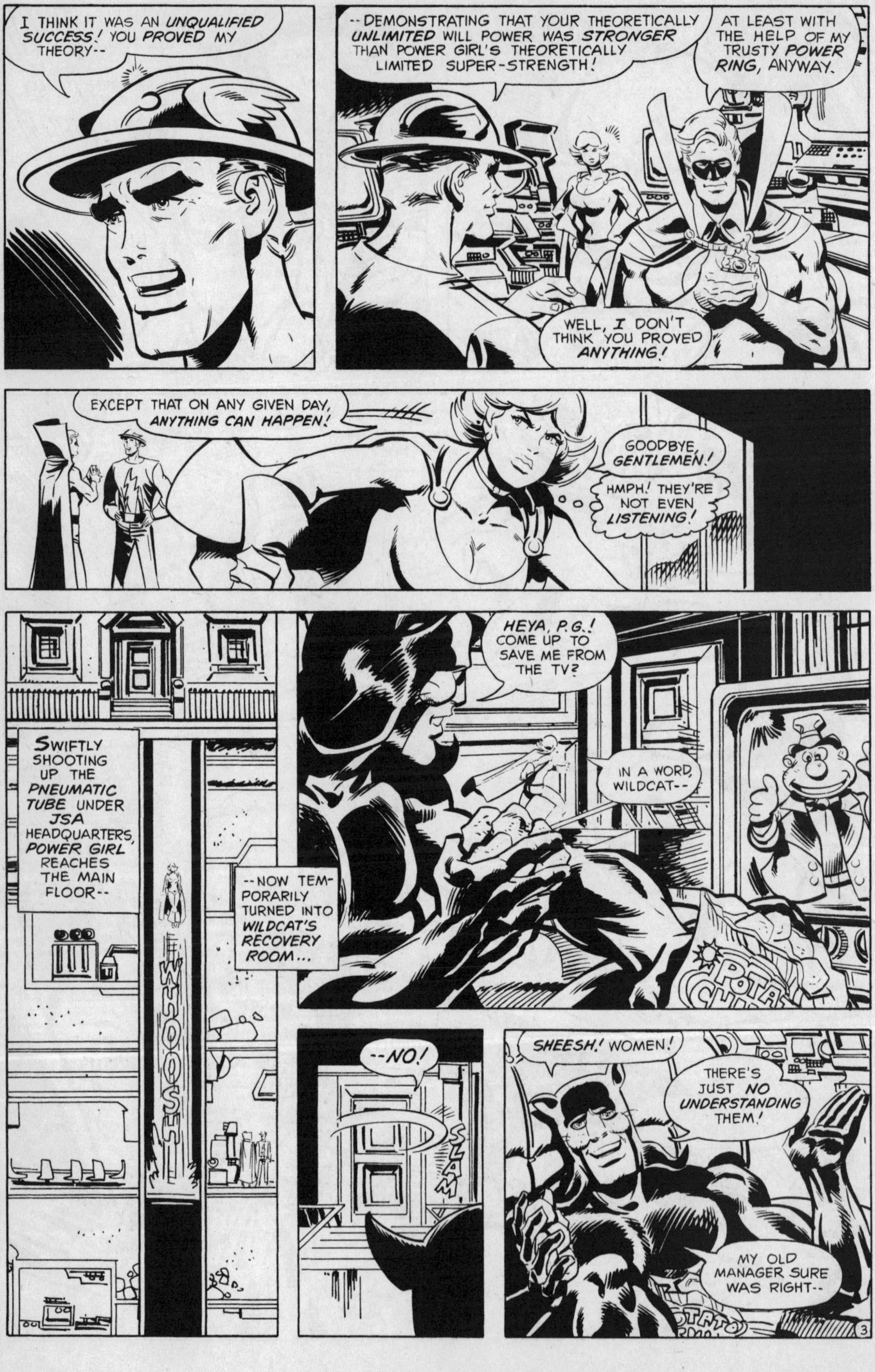
I THINK IT WAS AN UNQUALIFIED SUCCESS! YOU PROVED MY THEORY--
--DEMONSTRATING THAT YOUR THEORETICALLY UNLIMITED WILL POWER WAS STRONGER THAN POWER GIRL'S THEORETICALLY LIMITED SUPER-STRENGTH!
AT LEAST WITH THE HELP OF MY TRUSTY POWER RING, ANYWAY.
WELL, I DON'T THINK YOU PROVED ANYTHING!
EXCEPT THAT ON ANY GIVEN DAY, ANYTHING CAN HAPPEN!
GOODBYE, GENTLEMEN!
HMPH! THEY'RE NOT EVEN LISTENING!
SWIFTLY SHOOTING UP THE PNEUMATIC TUBE UNDER JSA HEADQUARTERS, POWER GIRL REACHES THE MAIN FLOOR--
WHOOSH
--NOW TEMPORARILY TURNED INTO WILDCAT'S RECOVERY ROOM...
HEYA, P.G.! COME UP TO SAVE ME FROM THE TV?
IN A WORD, WILDCAT--
--NO!
SLAM
SHEESH! WOMEN!
THERE'S JUST NO UNDERSTANDING THEM!
MY OLD MANAGER SURE WAS RIGHT--
3

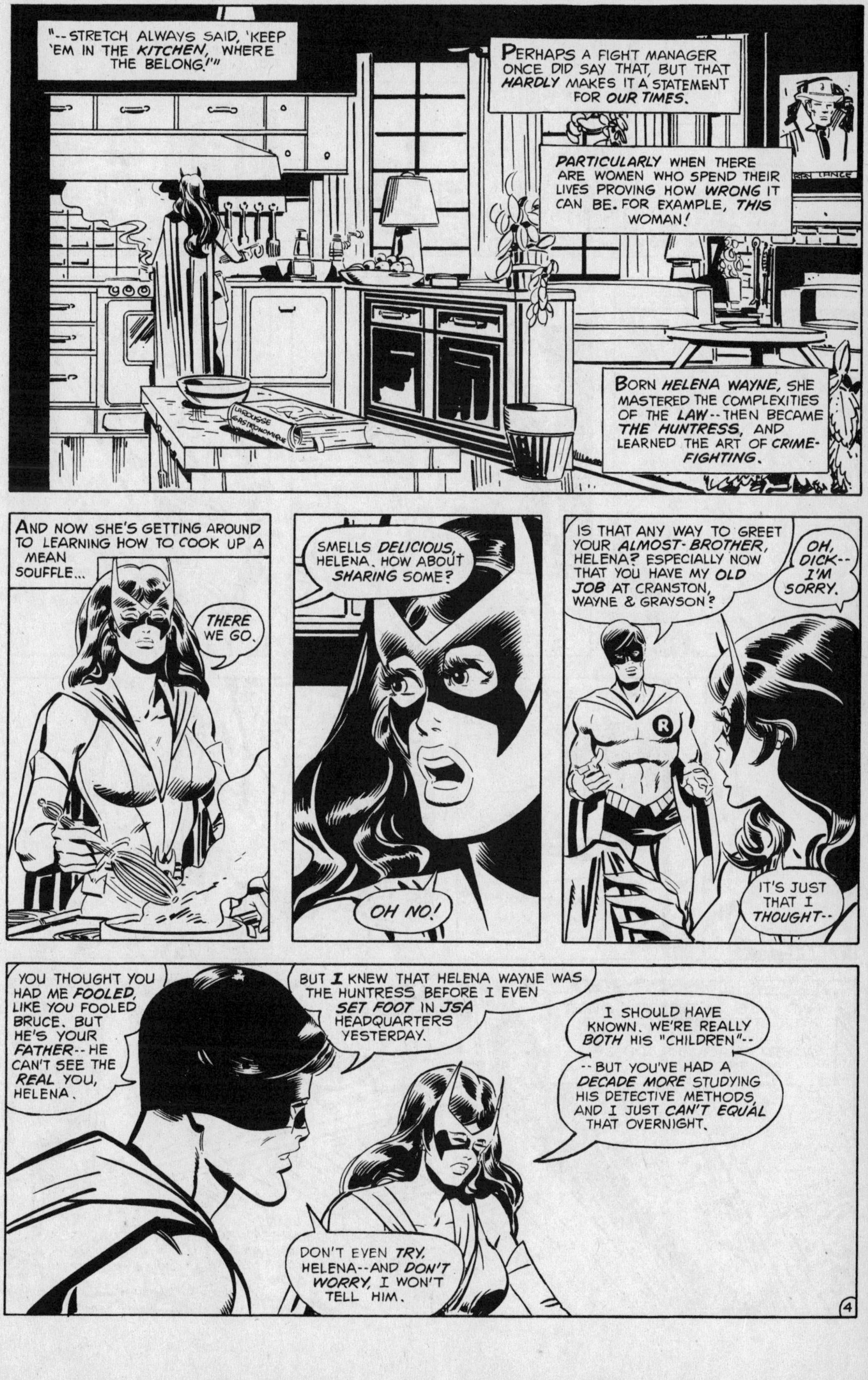
"--STRETCH ALWAYS SAID, 'KEEP 'EM IN THE *KITCHEN,* WHERE THE BELONG!'"
PERHAPS A FIGHT MANAGER ONCE DID SAY THAT, BUT THAT *HARDLY* MAKES IT A STATEMENT FOR *OUR TIMES*.
PARTICULARLY WHEN THERE ARE WOMEN WHO SPEND THEIR LIVES PROVING HOW *WRONG* IT CAN BE. FOR EXAMPLE, *THIS* WOMAN!
LAROUSSE GASTRONOMIQUE
BORN *HELENA WAYNE,* SHE MASTERED THE COMPLEXITIES OF THE *LAW*--THEN BECAME *THE HUNTRESS,* AND LEARNED THE ART OF *CRIME-FIGHTING*.
AND NOW SHE'S GETTING AROUND TO LEARNING HOW TO COOK UP A MEAN SOUFFLE...
THERE WE GO.
SMELLS *DELICIOUS,* HELENA. HOW ABOUT *SHARING* SOME?
OH NO!
IS THAT ANY WAY TO GREET YOUR *ALMOST-BROTHER,* HELENA? ESPECIALLY NOW THAT YOU HAVE MY *OLD JOB* AT CRANSTON, WAYNE & GRAYSON?
OH, DICK-- I'M SORRY.
IT'S JUST THAT I *THOUGHT*--
YOU THOUGHT YOU HAD ME *FOOLED,* LIKE YOU FOOLED BRUCE. BUT HE'S YOUR *FATHER*--HE CAN'T SEE THE *REAL* YOU, HELENA.
BUT *I* KNEW THAT HELENA WAYNE WAS THE HUNTRESS BEFORE I EVEN *SET FOOT* IN *JSA* HEADQUARTERS YESTERDAY.
I SHOULD HAVE KNOWN. WE'RE REALLY *BOTH* HIS "CHILDREN"--
--BUT YOU'VE HAD A *DECADE MORE* STUDYING HIS DETECTIVE METHODS, AND I JUST *CAN'T EQUAL* THAT OVERNIGHT.
DON'T EVEN *TRY,* HELENA--AND *DON'T WORRY,* I WON'T TELL HIM.
4

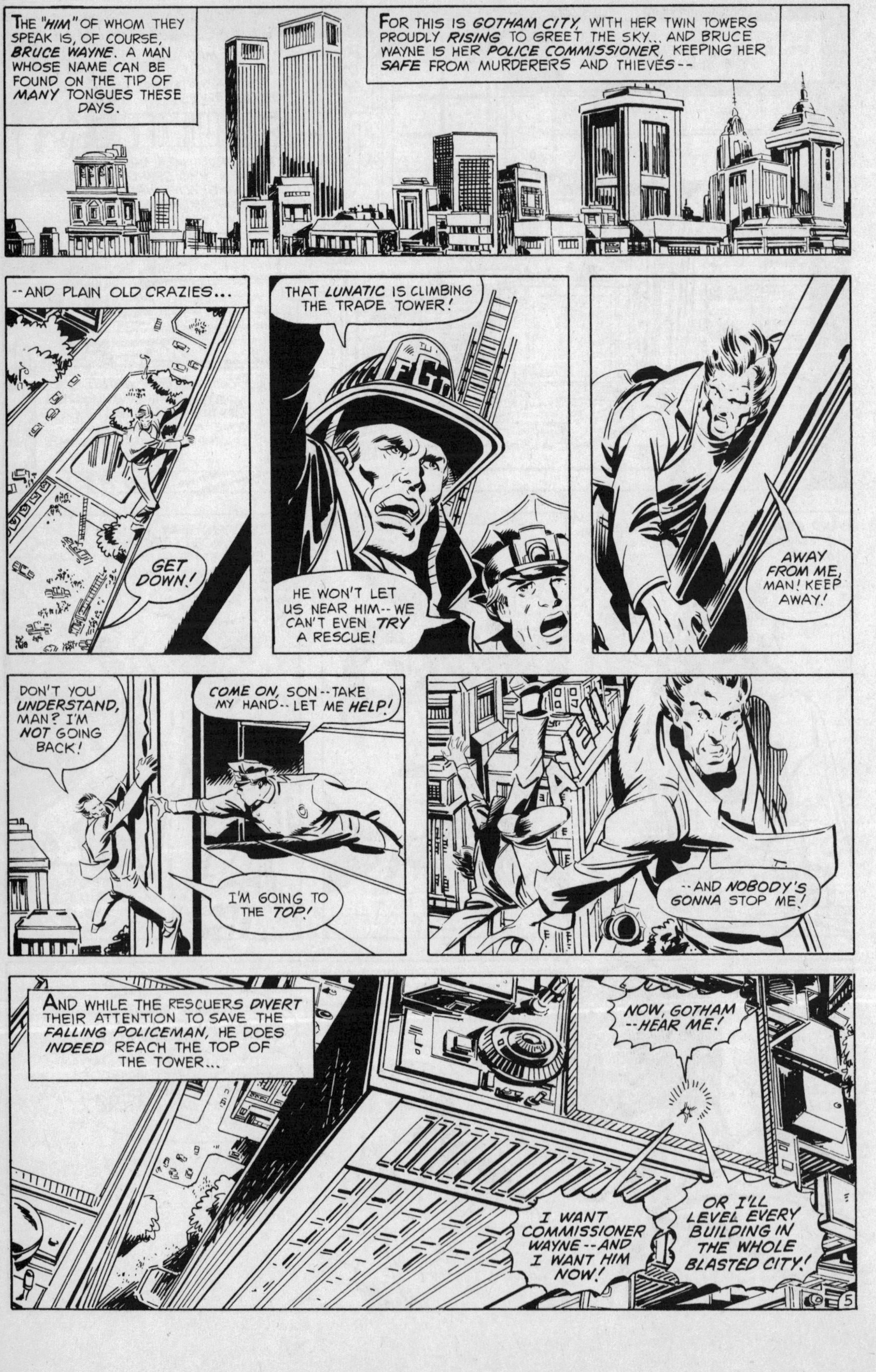
THE "HIM" OF WHOM THEY SPEAK IS, OF COURSE, BRUCE WAYNE. A MAN WHOSE NAME CAN BE FOUND ON THE TIP OF MANY TONGUES THESE DAYS.
FOR THIS IS GOTHAM CITY, WITH HER TWIN TOWERS PROUDLY RISING TO GREET THE SKY... AND BRUCE WAYNE IS HER POLICE COMMISSIONER, KEEPING HER SAFE FROM MURDERERS AND THIEVES--
--AND PLAIN OLD CRAZIES...
GET DOWN!
THAT LUNATIC IS CLIMBING THE TRADE TOWER!
HE WON'T LET US NEAR HIM--WE CAN'T EVEN TRY A RESCUE!
AWAY FROM ME, MAN! KEEP AWAY!
DON'T YOU UNDERSTAND, MAN? I'M NOT GOING BACK!
COME ON, SON--TAKE MY HAND--LET ME HELP!
I'M GOING TO THE TOP!
--AND NOBODY'S GONNA STOP ME!
AND WHILE THE RESCUERS DIVERT THEIR ATTENTION TO SAVE THE FALLING POLICEMAN, HE DOES INDEED REACH THE TOP OF THE TOWER...
NOW, GOTHAM --HEAR ME!
I WANT COMMISSIONER WAYNE--AND I WANT HIM NOW!
OR I'LL LEVEL EVERY BUILDING IN THE WHOLE BLASTED CITY!
5

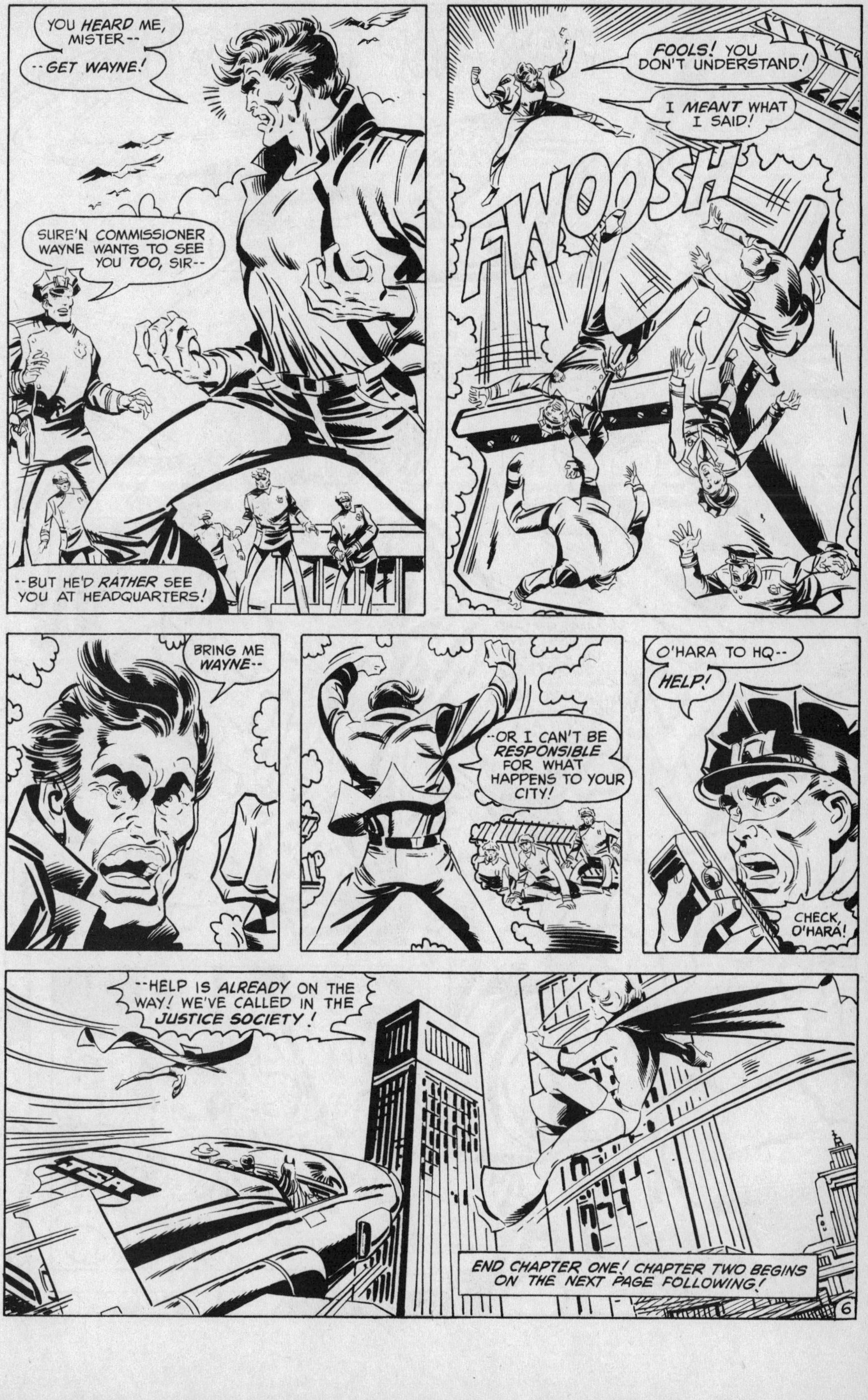
YOU HEARD ME, MISTER--
--GET WAYNE!
SURE'N COMMISSIONER WAYNE WANTS TO SEE YOU TOO, SIR--
--BUT HE'D RATHER SEE YOU AT HEADQUARTERS!
FOOLS! YOU DON'T UNDERSTAND!
I MEANT WHAT I SAID!
FWOOSH
BRING ME WAYNE--
--OR I CAN'T BE RESPONSIBLE FOR WHAT HAPPENS TO YOUR CITY!
O'HARA TO HQ--
HELP!
CHECK, O'HARA!
--HELP IS ALREADY ON THE WAY! WE'VE CALLED IN THE JUSTICE SOCIETY!
END CHAPTER ONE! CHAPTER TWO BEGINS ON THE NEXT PAGE FOLLOWING!
6

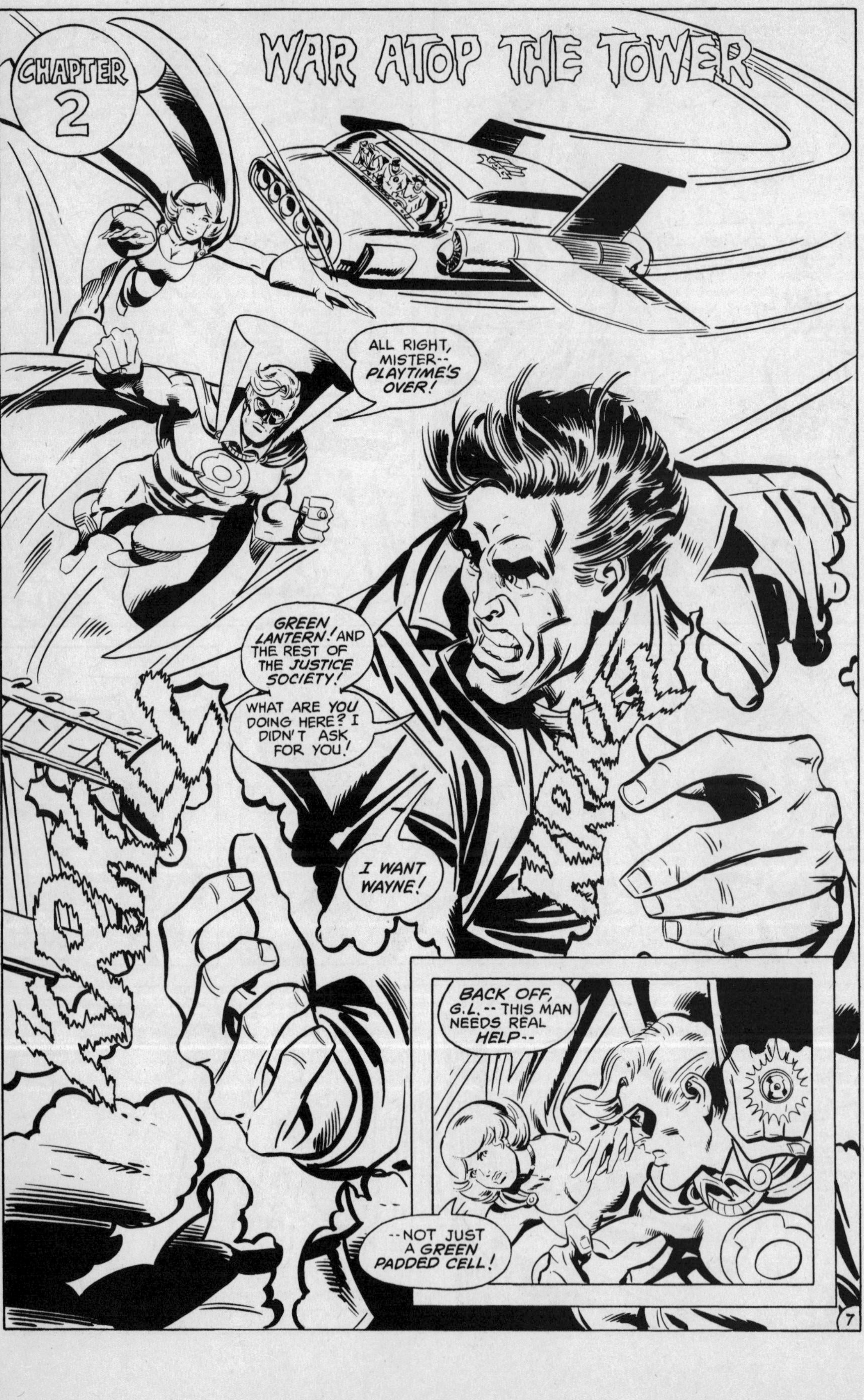
CHAPTER 2
WAR ATOP THE TOWER
ALL RIGHT, MISTER-- PLAYTIME'S OVER!
GREEN LANTERN! AND THE REST OF THE JUSTICE SOCIETY!
WHAT ARE YOU DOING HERE? I DIDN'T ASK FOR YOU!
I WANT WAYNE!
BACK OFF, G.L. -- THIS MAN NEEDS REAL HELP--
--NOT JUST A GREEN PADDED CELL!
7

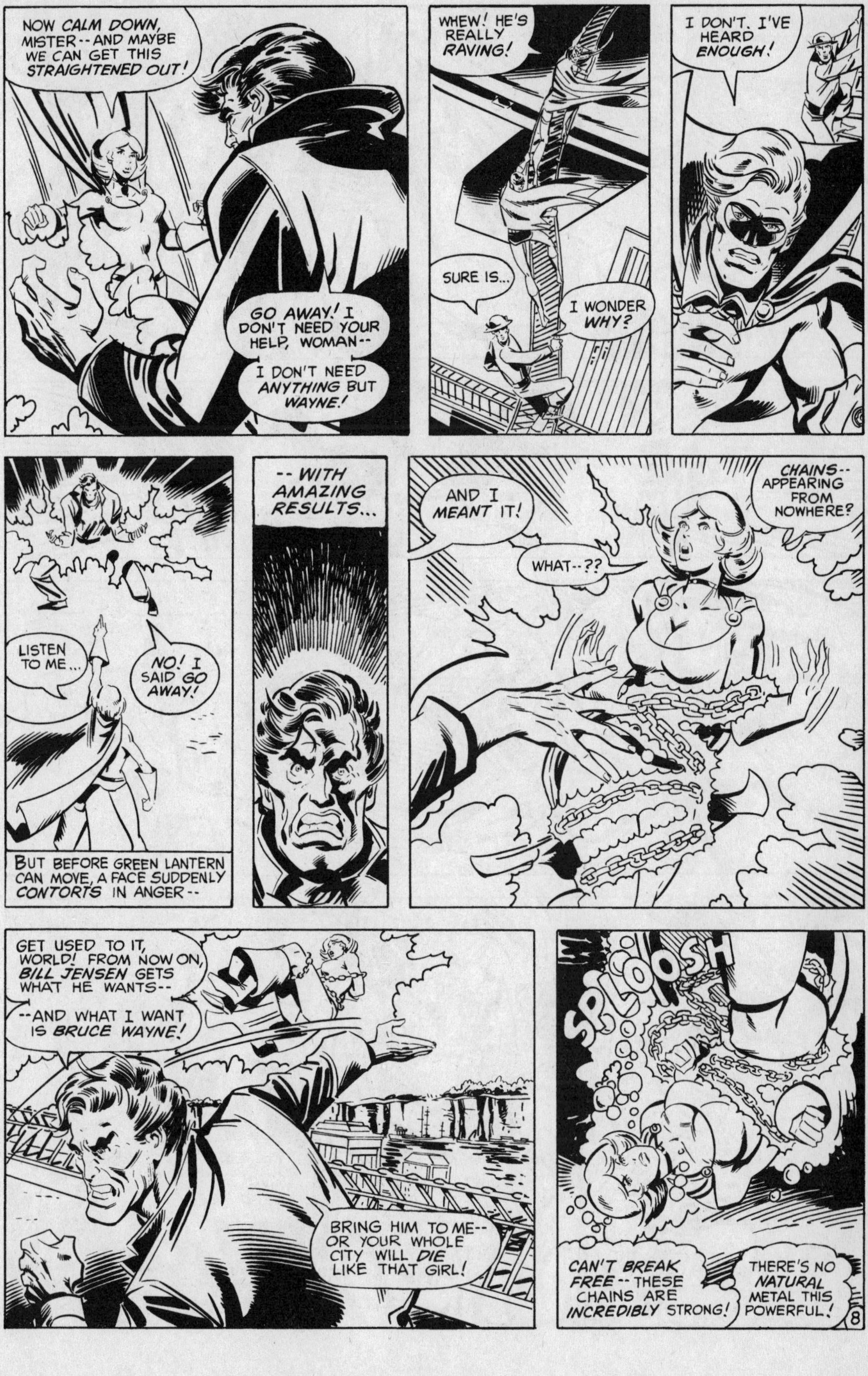
NOW CALM DOWN, MISTER -- AND MAYBE WE CAN GET THIS STRAIGHTENED OUT!
GO AWAY! I DON'T NEED YOUR HELP, WOMAN--
I DON'T NEED ANYTHING BUT WAYNE!
WHEW! HE'S REALLY RAVING!
SURE IS...
I WONDER WHY?
I DON'T. I'VE HEARD ENOUGH!
LISTEN TO ME...
NO! I SAID GO AWAY!
BUT BEFORE GREEN LANTERN CAN MOVE, A FACE SUDDENLY CONTORTS IN ANGER--
-- WITH AMAZING RESULTS...
AND I MEANT IT!
WHAT--??
CHAINS-- APPEARING FROM NOWHERE?
GET USED TO IT, WORLD! FROM NOW ON, BILL JENSEN GETS WHAT HE WANTS--
--AND WHAT I WANT IS BRUCE WAYNE!
BRING HIM TO ME-- OR YOUR WHOLE CITY WILL DIE LIKE THAT GIRL!
SPLOOSH
CAN'T BREAK FREE -- THESE CHAINS ARE INCREDIBLY STRONG!
THERE'S NO NATURAL METAL THIS POWERFUL!
8

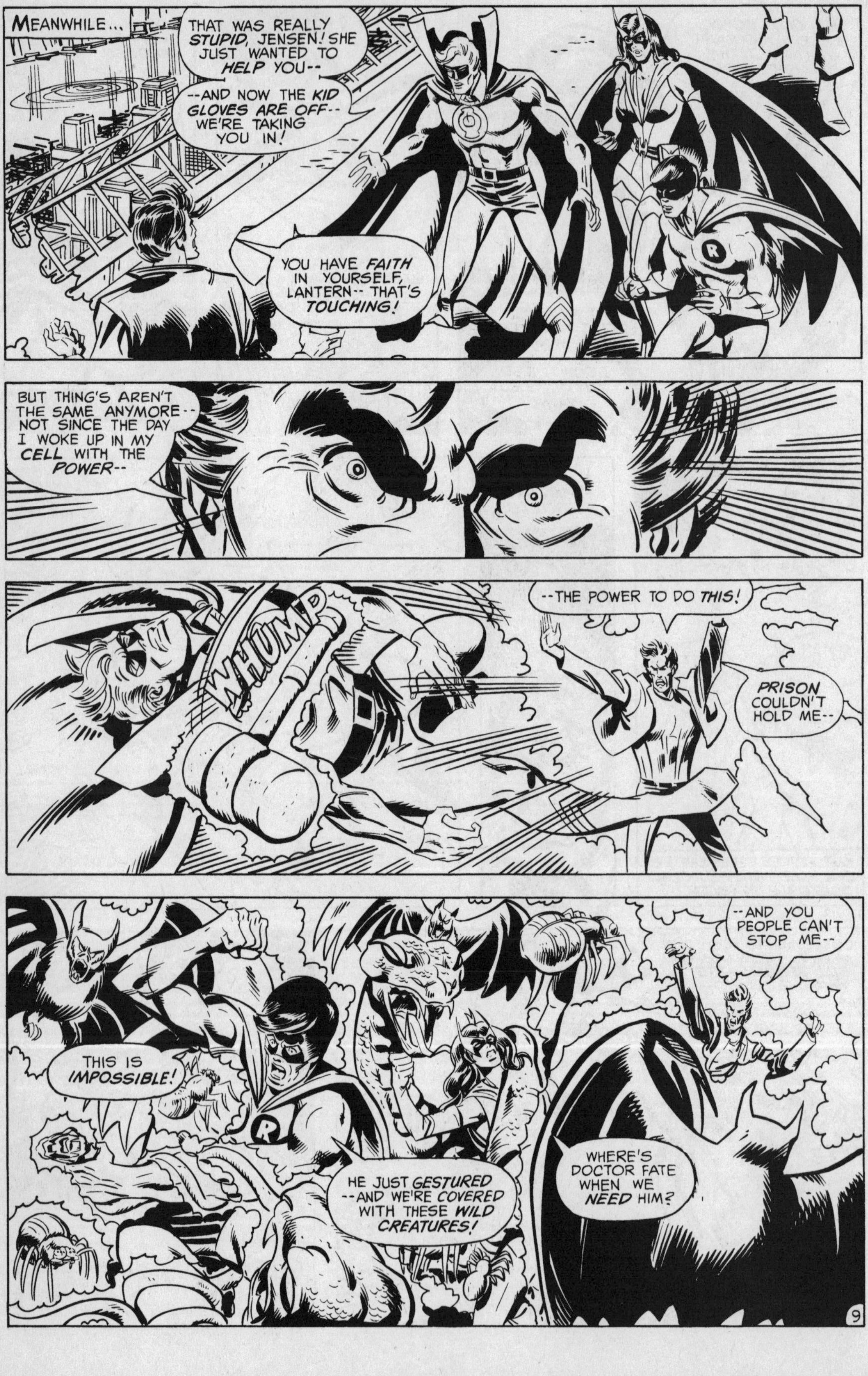
MEANWHILE...
THAT WAS REALLY STUPID, JENSEN! SHE JUST WANTED TO HELP YOU--
--AND NOW THE KID GLOVES ARE OFF--WE'RE TAKING YOU IN!
YOU HAVE FAITH IN YOURSELF, LANTERN-- THAT'S TOUCHING!
BUT THING'S AREN'T THE SAME ANYMORE-- NOT SINCE THE DAY I WOKE UP IN MY CELL WITH THE POWER--
--THE POWER TO DO THIS!
WHUMP
PRISON COULDN'T HOLD ME--
--AND YOU PEOPLE CAN'T STOP ME--
THIS IS IMPOSSIBLE!
HE JUST GESTURED --AND WE'RE COVERED WITH THESE WILD CREATURES!
WHERE'S DOCTOR FATE WHEN WE NEED HIM?
9

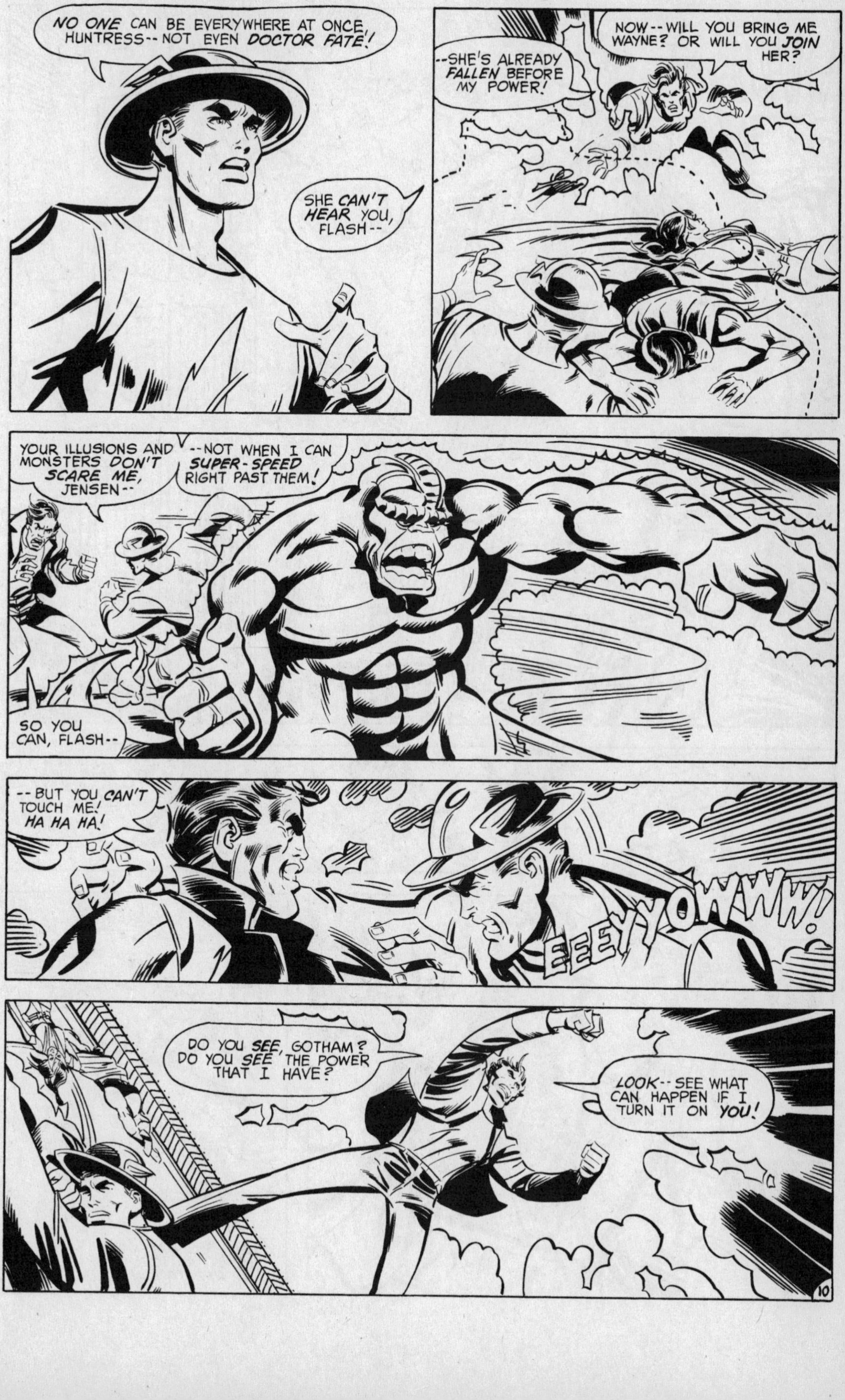
NO ONE CAN BE EVERYWHERE AT ONCE, HUNTRESS-- NOT EVEN DOCTOR FATE!
SHE CAN'T HEAR YOU, FLASH--
--SHE'S ALREADY FALLEN BEFORE MY POWER!
NOW--WILL YOU BRING ME WAYNE? OR WILL YOU JOIN HER?
YOUR ILLUSIONS AND MONSTERS DON'T SCARE ME, JENSEN--
--NOT WHEN I CAN SUPER-SPEED RIGHT PAST THEM!
SO YOU CAN, FLASH--
--BUT YOU CAN'T TOUCH ME! HA HA HA!
EEEYYYOWWWW!
DO YOU SEE, GOTHAM? DO YOU SEE THE POWER THAT I HAVE?
LOOK--SEE WHAT CAN HAPPEN IF I TURN IT ON YOU!
10

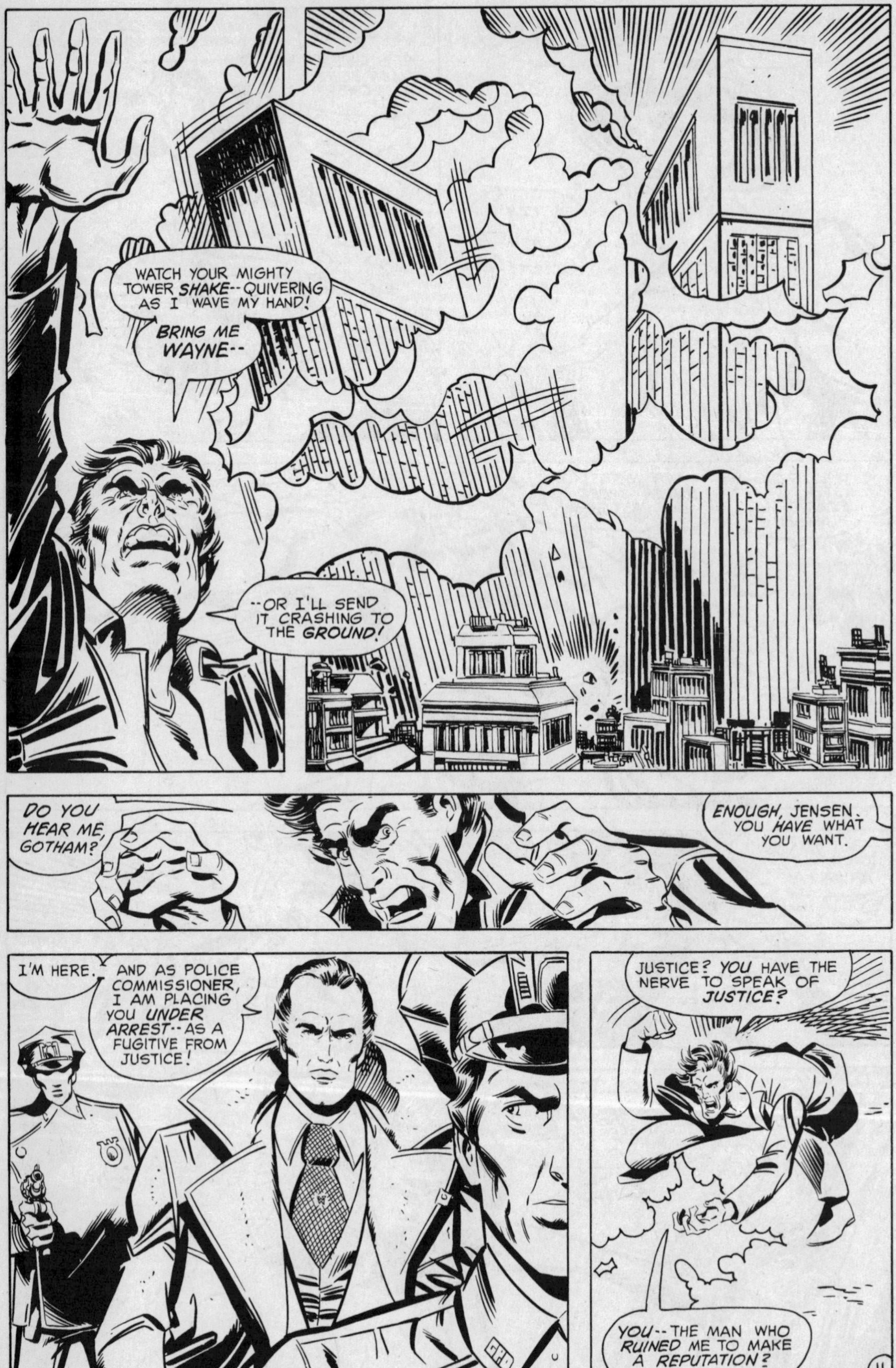
WATCH YOUR MIGHTY TOWER SHAKE-- QUIVERING AS I WAVE MY HAND!
BRING ME WAYNE--
--OR I'LL SEND IT CRASHING TO THE GROUND!
DO YOU HEAR ME, GOTHAM?
ENOUGH, JENSEN. YOU HAVE WHAT YOU WANT.
I'M HERE.
AND AS POLICE COMMISSIONER, I AM PLACING YOU UNDER ARREST-- AS A FUGITIVE FROM JUSTICE!
JUSTICE? YOU HAVE THE NERVE TO SPEAK OF JUSTICE?
YOU-- THE MAN WHO RUINED ME TO MAKE A REPUTATION?
11

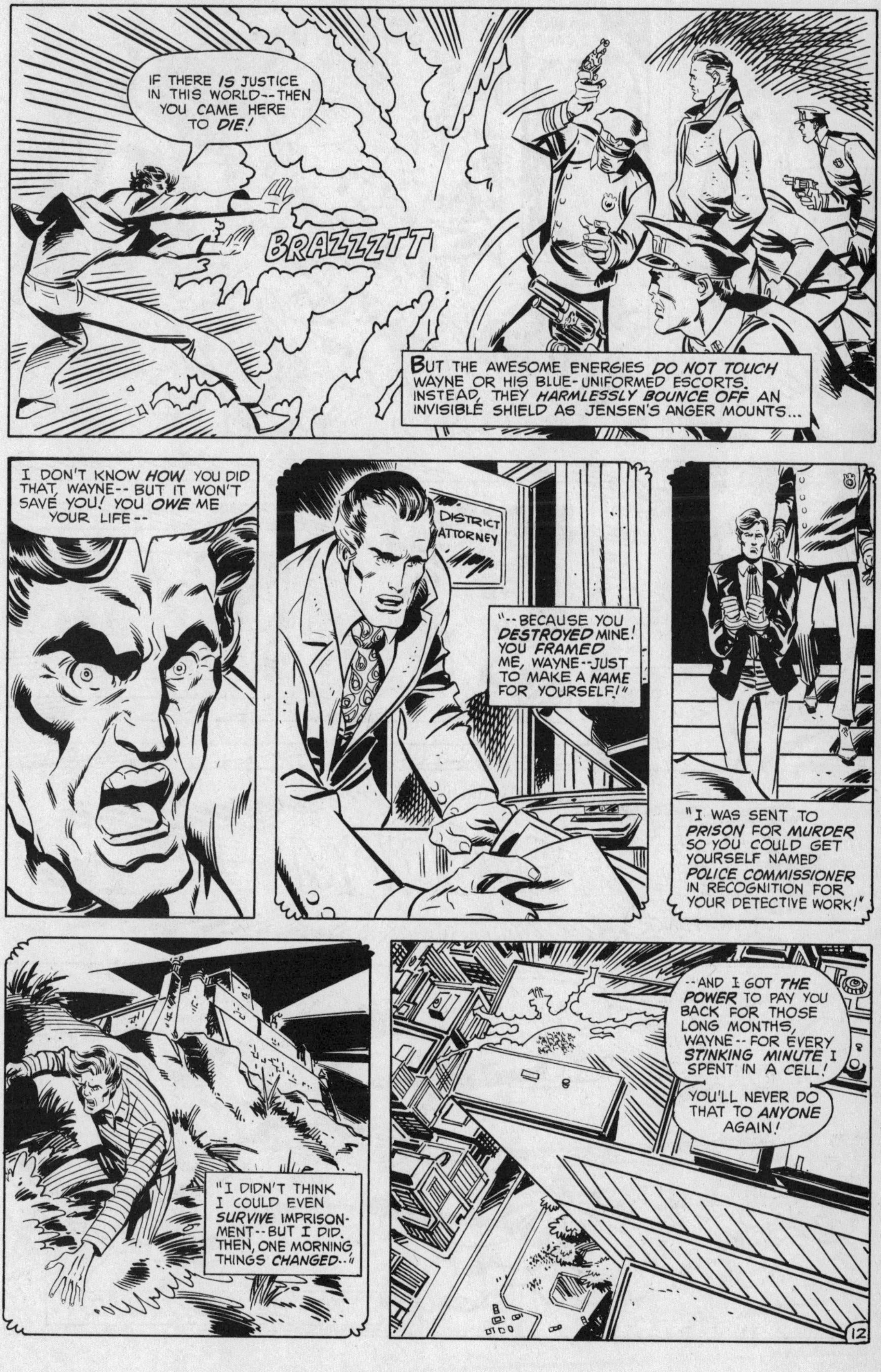
IF THERE IS JUSTICE IN THIS WORLD--THEN YOU CAME HERE TO DIE!
BRAZZZZTT
BUT THE AWESOME ENERGIES DO NOT TOUCH WAYNE OR HIS BLUE-UNIFORMED ESCORTS. INSTEAD, THEY HARMLESSLY BOUNCE OFF AN INVISIBLE SHIELD AS JENSEN'S ANGER MOUNTS...
I DON'T KNOW HOW YOU DID THAT, WAYNE-- BUT IT WON'T SAVE YOU! YOU OWE ME YOUR LIFE--
DISTRICT ATTORNEY
"--BECAUSE YOU DESTROYED MINE! YOU FRAMED ME, WAYNE--JUST TO MAKE A NAME FOR YOURSELF!"
"I WAS SENT TO PRISON FOR MURDER SO YOU COULD GET YOURSELF NAMED POLICE COMMISSIONER IN RECOGNITION FOR YOUR DETECTIVE WORK!"
"I DIDN'T THINK I COULD EVEN SURVIVE IMPRISONMENT--BUT I DID. THEN, ONE MORNING THINGS CHANGED--"
--AND I GOT THE POWER TO PAY YOU BACK FOR THOSE LONG MONTHS, WAYNE--FOR EVERY STINKING MINUTE I SPENT IN A CELL!
YOU'LL NEVER DO THAT TO ANYONE AGAIN!
12

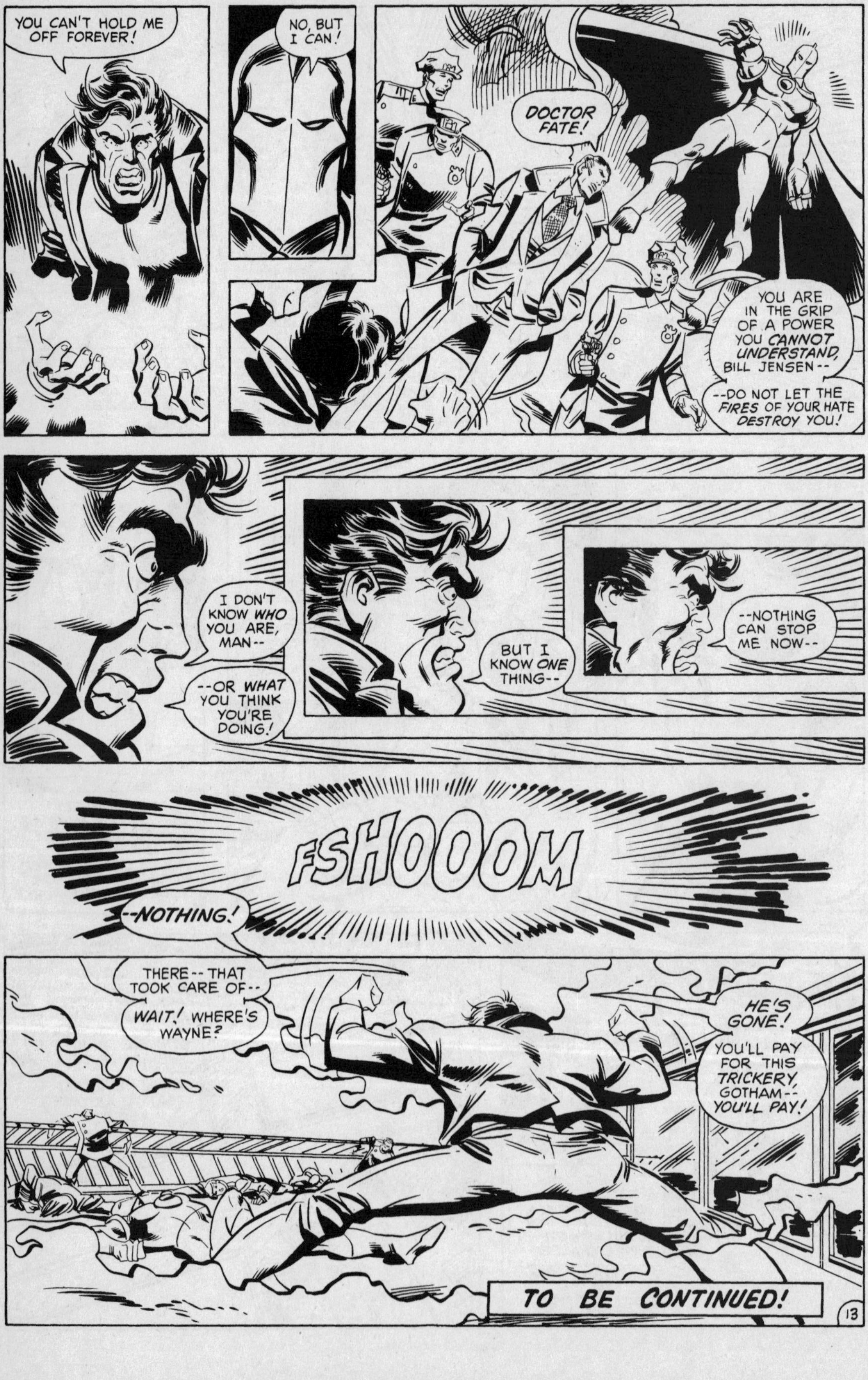
YOU CAN'T HOLD ME OFF FOREVER!
NO, BUT I CAN!
DOCTOR FATE!
YOU ARE IN THE GRIP OF A POWER YOU CANNOT UNDERSTAND, BILL JENSEN--
--DO NOT LET THE FIRES OF YOUR HATE DESTROY YOU!
I DON'T KNOW WHO YOU ARE, MAN--
--OR WHAT YOU THINK YOU'RE DOING!
BUT I KNOW ONE THING--
--NOTHING CAN STOP ME NOW--
FSHOOOM
--NOTHING!
THERE-- THAT TOOK CARE OF--
WAIT! WHERE'S WAYNE?
HE'S GONE!
YOU'LL PAY FOR THIS TRICKERY, GOTHAM-- YOU'LL PAY!
TO BE CONTINUED!
13

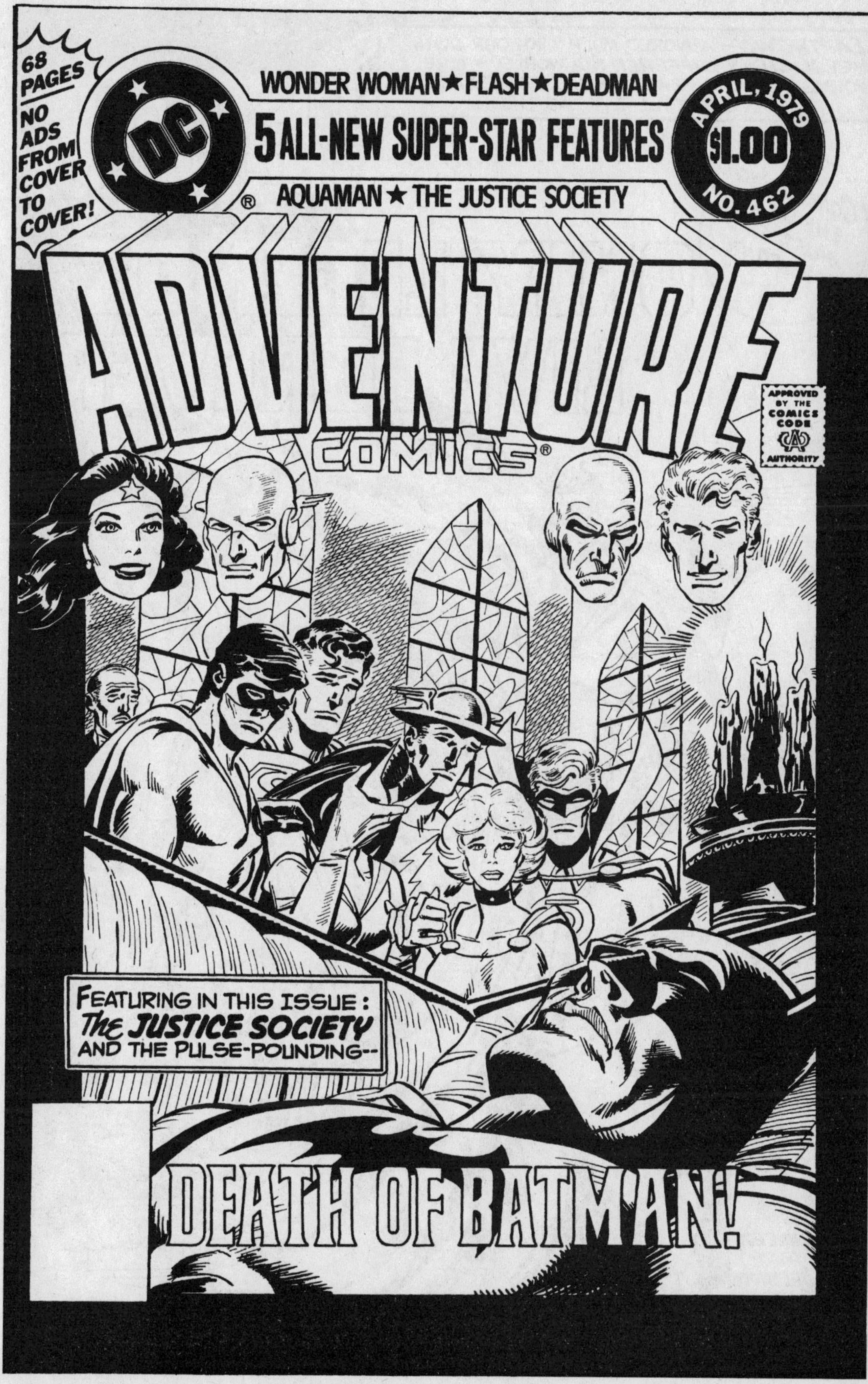
68 PAGES
NO ADS FROM COVER TO COVER!
DC
WONDER WOMAN★FLASH★DEADMAN
5 ALL-NEW SUPER-STAR FEATURES
AQUAMAN★THE JUSTICE SOCIETY
APRIL, 1979
$1.00
NO. 462
ADVENTURE COMICS
APPROVED BY THE COMICS CODE AUTHORITY
FEATURING IN THIS ISSUE: The JUSTICE SOCIETY AND THE PULSE-POUNDING--
DEATH OF BATMAN!

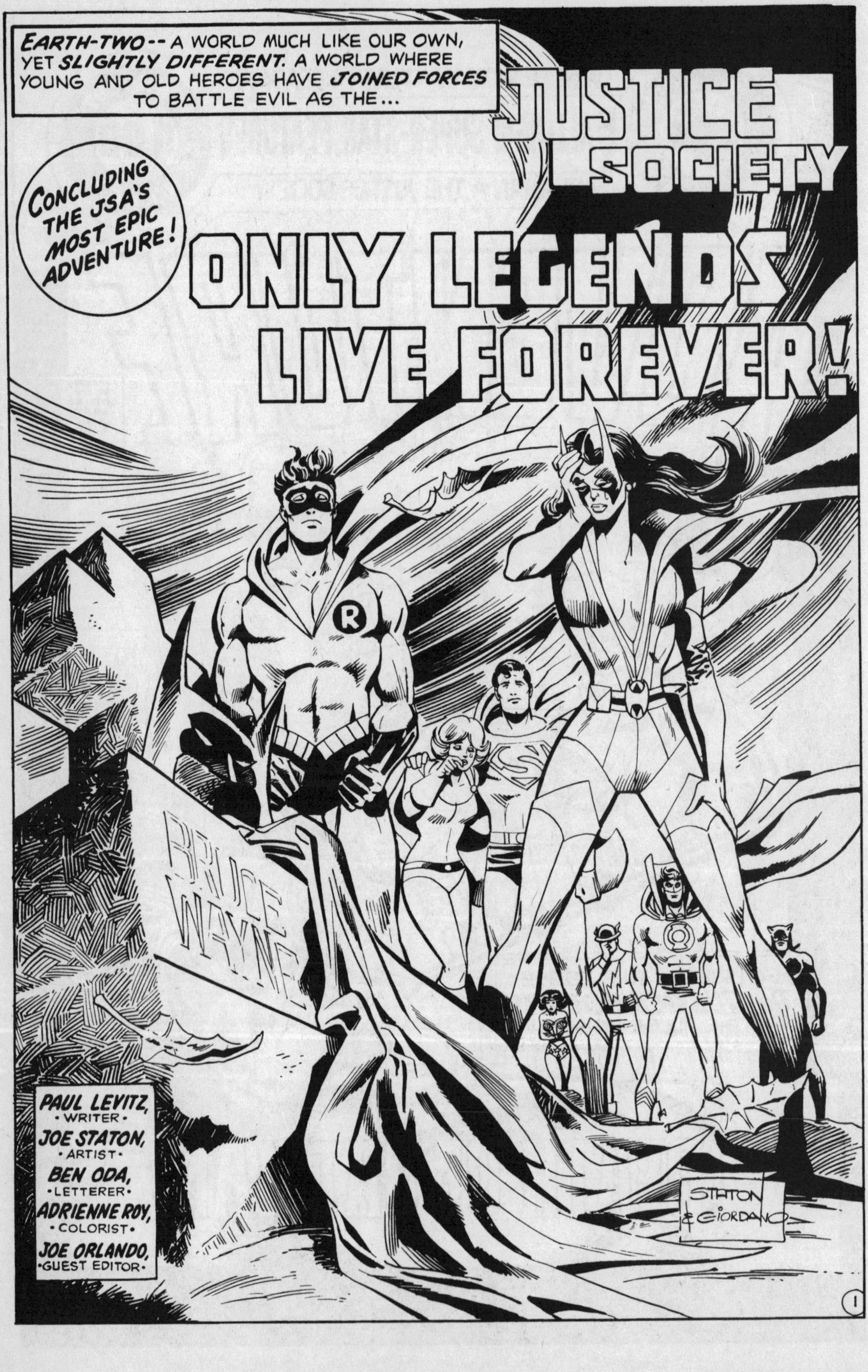
EARTH-TWO-- A WORLD MUCH LIKE OUR OWN, YET SLIGHTLY DIFFERENT. A WORLD WHERE YOUNG AND OLD HEROES HAVE JOINED FORCES TO BATTLE EVIL AS THE...
JUSTICE SOCIETY
CONCLUDING THE JSA'S MOST EPIC ADVENTURE!
ONLY LEGENDS LIVE FOREVER!
R
BRUCE WAYNE
PAUL LEVITZ, WRITER
JOE STATON, ARTIST
BEN ODA, LETTERER
ADRIENNE ROY, COLORIST
JOE ORLANDO, GUEST EDITOR
STATON & GIORDANO
1

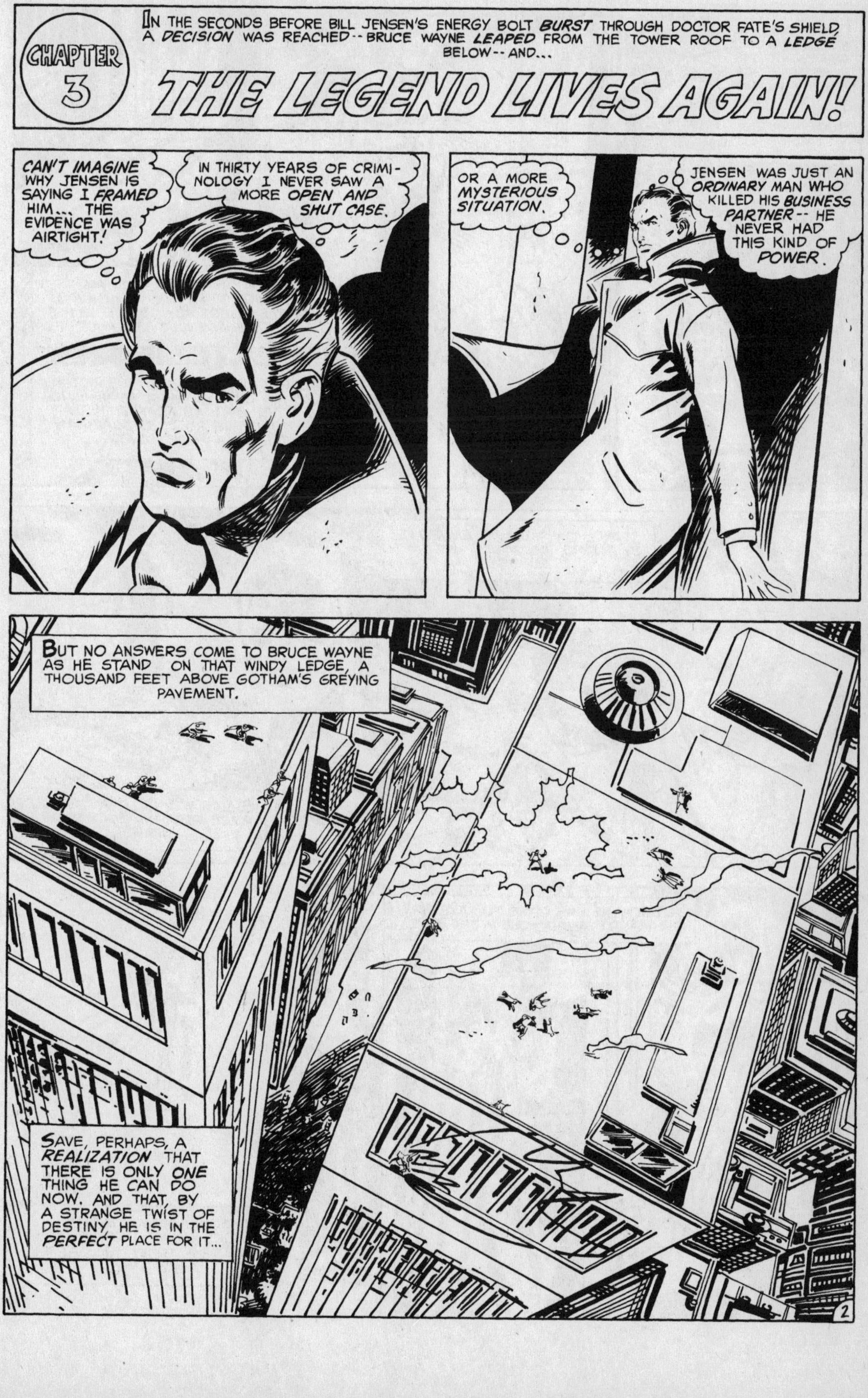
CHAPTER 3
IN THE SECONDS BEFORE BILL JENSEN'S ENERGY BOLT BURST THROUGH DOCTOR FATE'S SHIELD, A DECISION WAS REACHED -- BRUCE WAYNE LEAPED FROM THE TOWER ROOF TO A LEDGE BELOW -- AND...
THE LEGEND LIVES AGAIN!
CAN'T IMAGINE WHY JENSEN IS SAYING I FRAMED HIM... THE EVIDENCE WAS AIRTIGHT!
IN THIRTY YEARS OF CRIMINOLOGY I NEVER SAW A MORE OPEN AND SHUT CASE.
OR A MORE MYSTERIOUS SITUATION.
JENSEN WAS JUST AN ORDINARY MAN WHO KILLED HIS BUSINESS PARTNER -- HE NEVER HAD THIS KIND OF POWER.
BUT NO ANSWERS COME TO BRUCE WAYNE AS HE STAND ON THAT WINDY LEDGE, A THOUSAND FEET ABOVE GOTHAM'S GREYING PAVEMENT.
SAVE, PERHAPS, A REALIZATION THAT THERE IS ONLY ONE THING HE CAN DO NOW. AND THAT, BY A STRANGE TWIST OF DESTINY, HE IS IN THE PERFECT PLACE FOR IT...
2

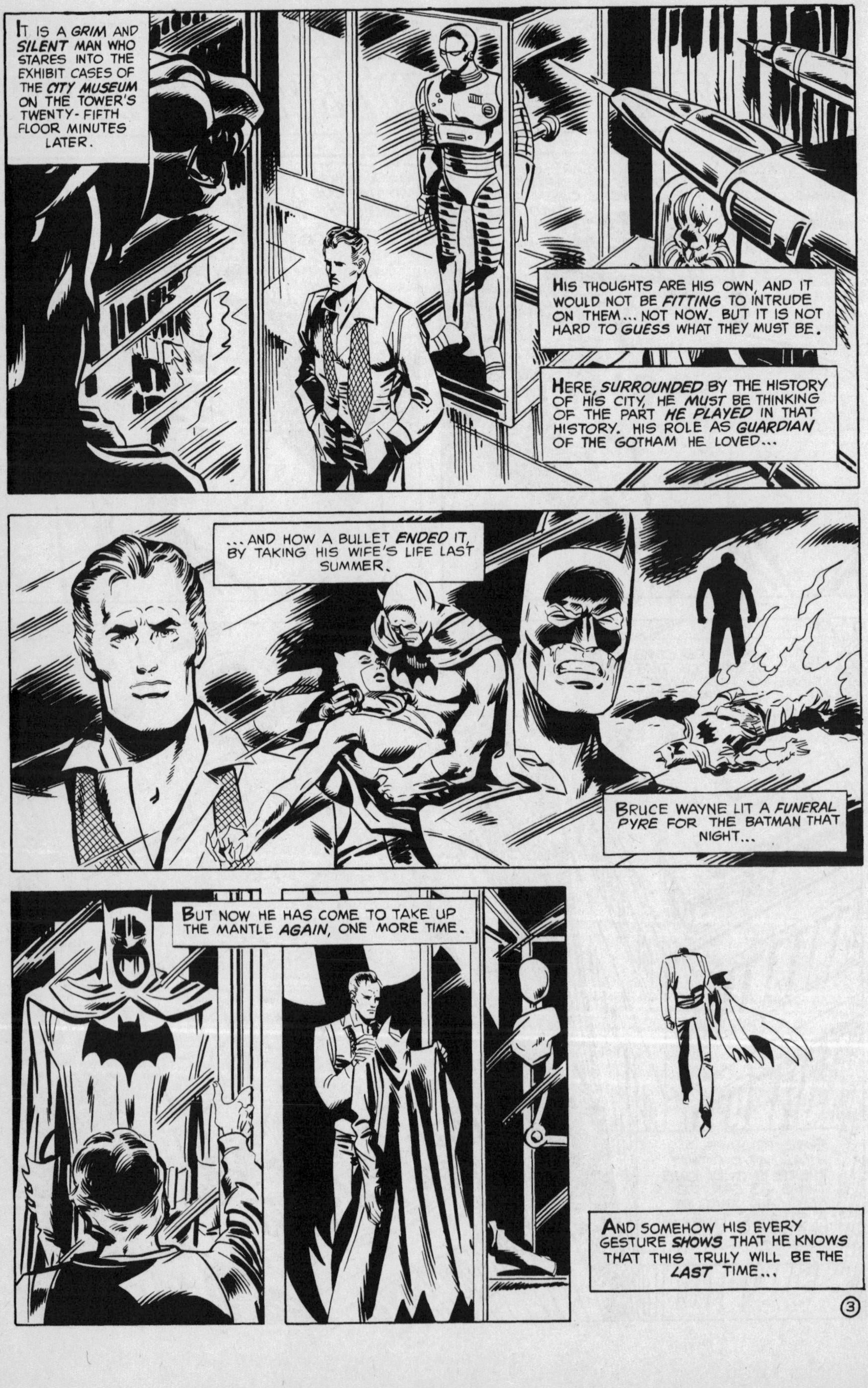
IT IS A GRIM AND SILENT MAN WHO STARES INTO THE EXHIBIT CASES OF THE CITY MUSEUM ON THE TOWER'S TWENTY-FIFTH FLOOR MINUTES LATER.
HIS THOUGHTS ARE HIS OWN, AND IT WOULD NOT BE FITTING TO INTRUDE ON THEM... NOT NOW. BUT IT IS NOT HARD TO GUESS WHAT THEY MUST BE.
HERE, SURROUNDED BY THE HISTORY OF HIS CITY, HE MUST BE THINKING OF THE PART HE PLAYED IN THAT HISTORY. HIS ROLE AS GUARDIAN OF THE GOTHAM HE LOVED...
...AND HOW A BULLET ENDED IT, BY TAKING HIS WIFE'S LIFE LAST SUMMER.
BRUCE WAYNE LIT A FUNERAL PYRE FOR THE BATMAN THAT NIGHT...
BUT NOW HE HAS COME TO TAKE UP THE MANTLE AGAIN, ONE MORE TIME.
AND SOMEHOW HIS EVERY GESTURE SHOWS THAT HE KNOWS THAT THIS TRULY WILL BE THE LAST TIME...
3

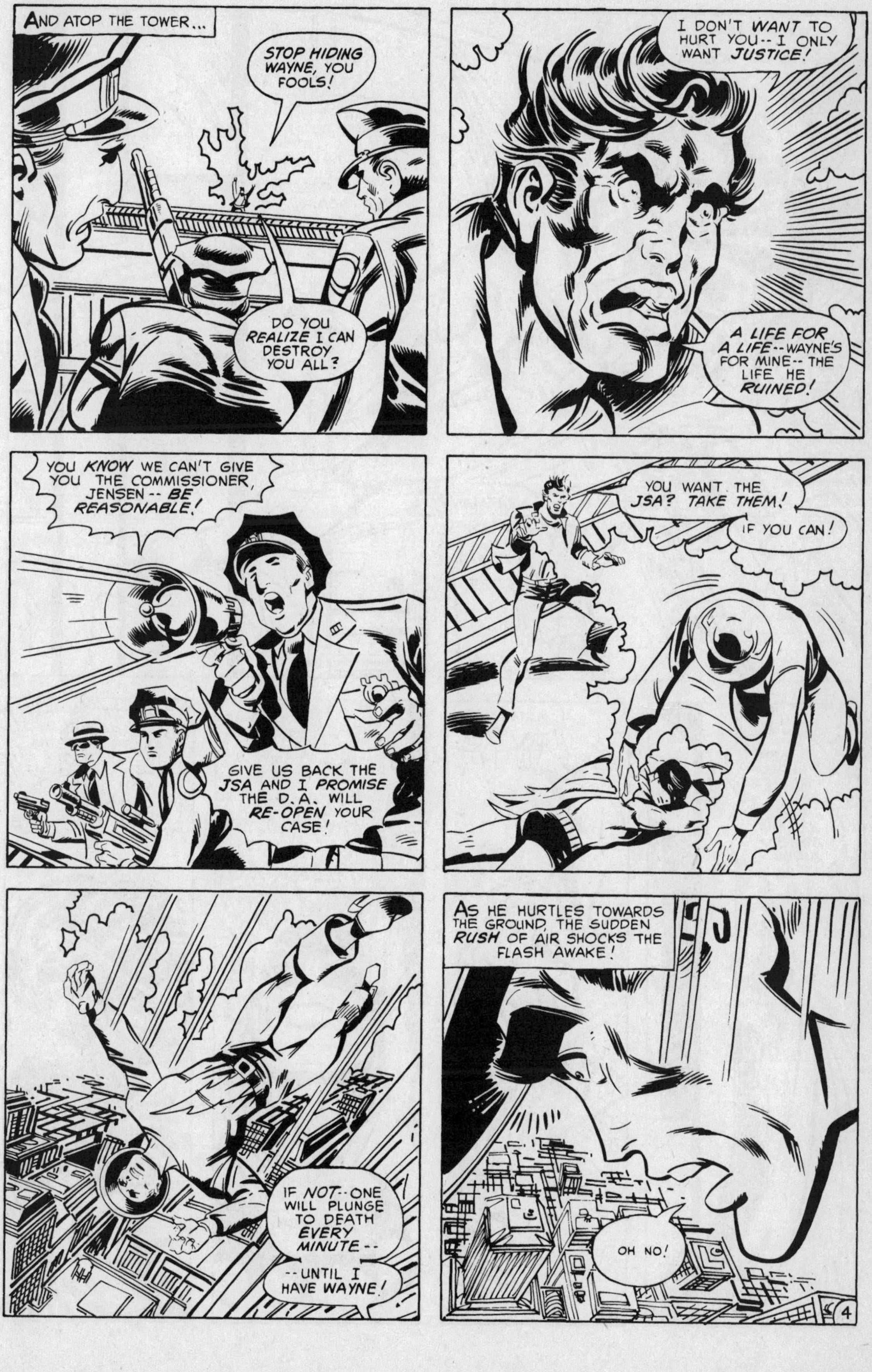
AND ATOP THE TOWER...
STOP HIDING WAYNE, YOU FOOLS!
DO YOU REALIZE I CAN DESTROY YOU ALL?
I DON'T WANT TO HURT YOU-- I ONLY WANT JUSTICE!
A LIFE FOR A LIFE-- WAYNE'S FOR MINE-- THE LIFE HE RUINED!
YOU KNOW WE CAN'T GIVE YOU THE COMMISSIONER, JENSEN-- BE REASONABLE!
GIVE US BACK THE JSA AND I PROMISE THE D.A. WILL RE-OPEN YOUR CASE!
YOU WANT THE JSA? TAKE THEM!
IF YOU CAN!
IF NOT-- ONE WILL PLUNGE TO DEATH EVERY MINUTE--
--UNTIL I HAVE WAYNE!
AS HE HURTLES TOWARDS THE GROUND, THE SUDDEN RUSH OF AIR SHOCKS THE FLASH AWAKE!
OH NO!
4

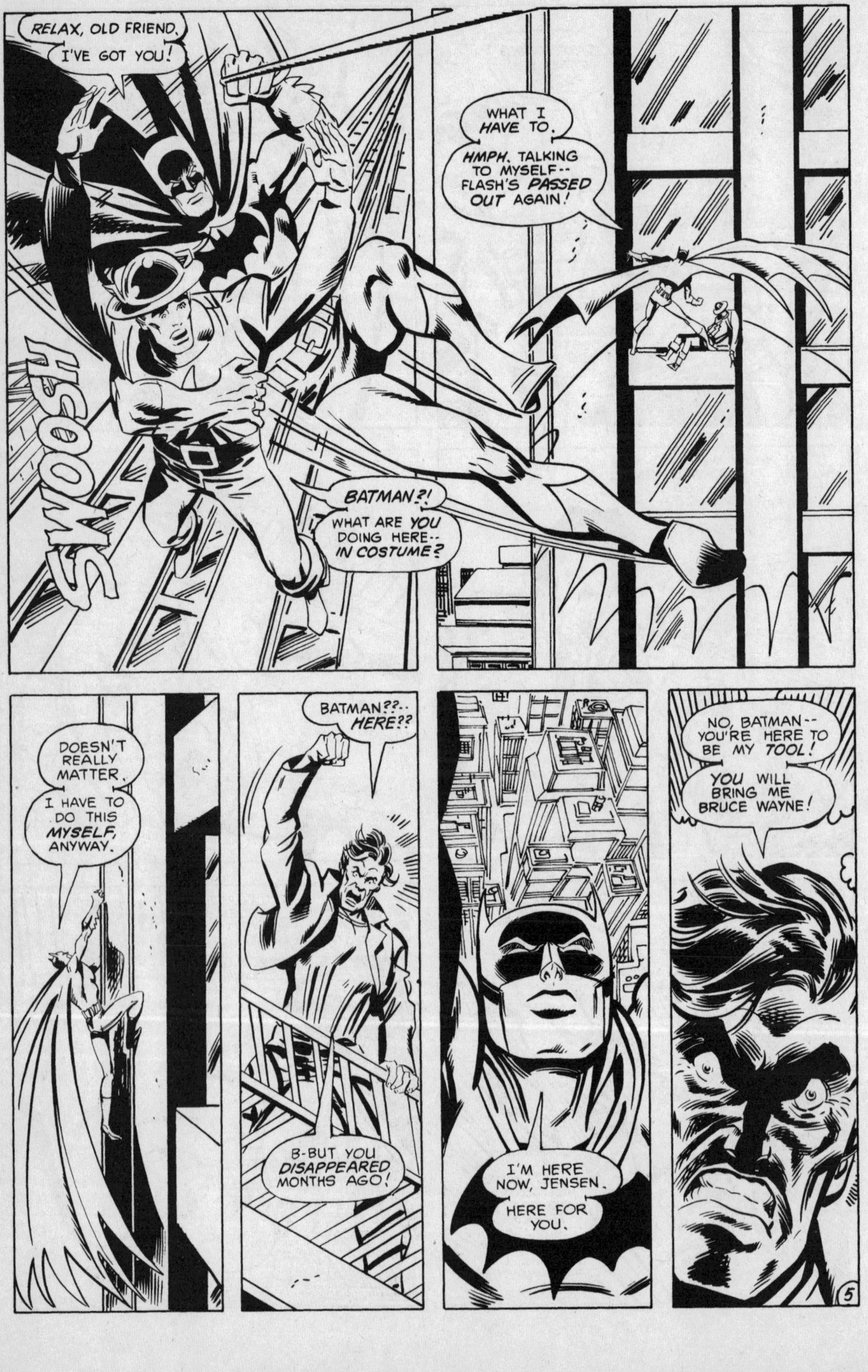
RELAX, OLD FRIEND.
I'VE GOT YOU!
SWOOSH
BATMAN?!
WHAT ARE YOU DOING HERE-- IN COSTUME?
WHAT I HAVE TO.
HMPH. TALKING TO MYSELF-- FLASH'S PASSED OUT AGAIN!
DOESN'T REALLY MATTER.
I HAVE TO DO THIS MYSELF, ANYWAY.
BATMAN??.. HERE??
B-BUT YOU DISAPPEARED MONTHS AGO!
I'M HERE NOW, JENSEN.
HERE FOR YOU.
NO, BATMAN-- YOU'RE HERE TO BE MY TOOL!
YOU WILL BRING ME BRUCE WAYNE!
5

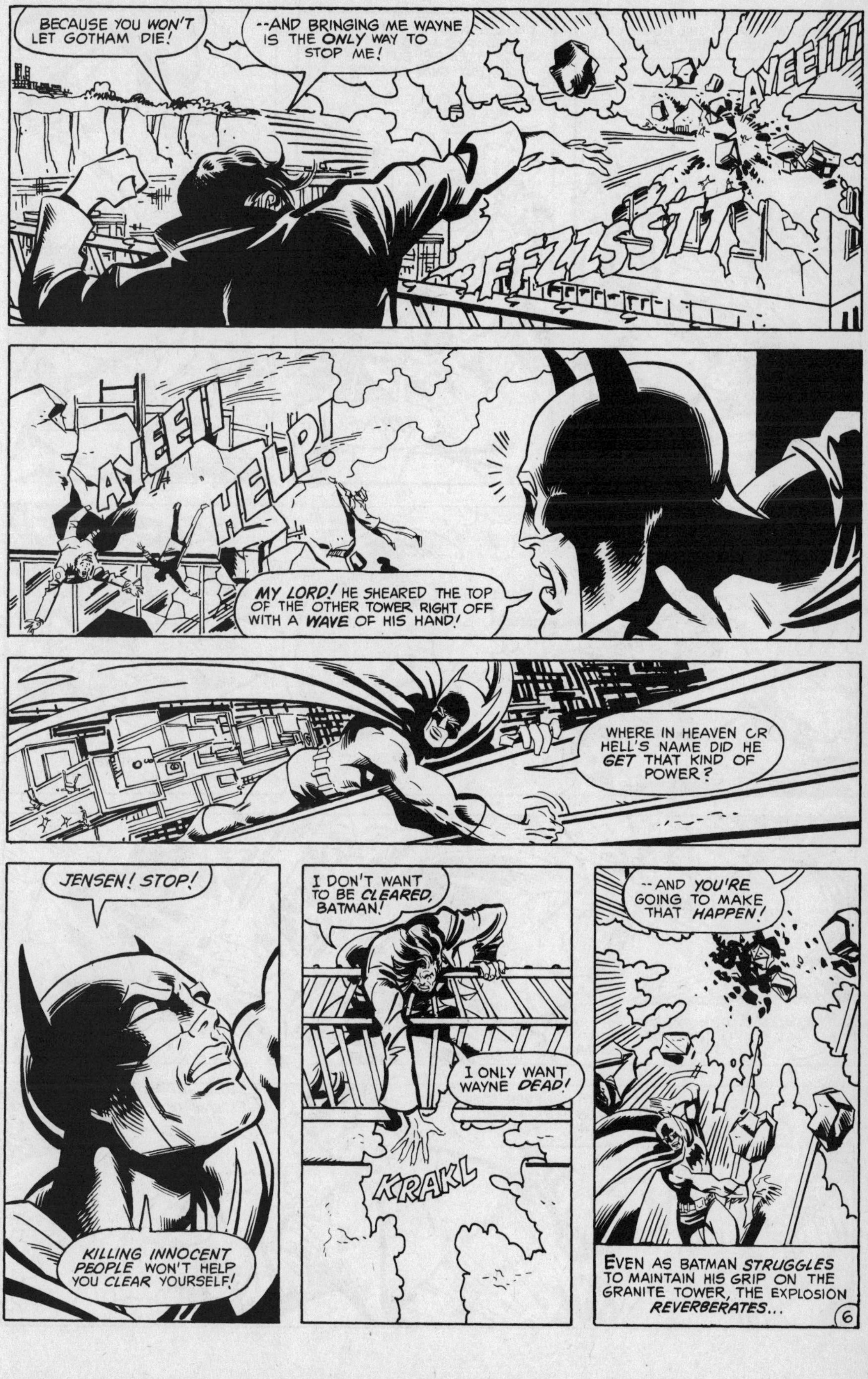
BECAUSE YOU WON'T LET GOTHAM DIE!
--AND BRINGING ME WAYNE IS THE ONLY WAY TO STOP ME!
AYEEIII!
FFZZZSSTT
AYEEII
HELP!
MY LORD! HE SHEARED THE TOP OF THE OTHER TOWER RIGHT OFF WITH A WAVE OF HIS HAND!
WHERE IN HEAVEN OR HELL'S NAME DID HE GET THAT KIND OF POWER?
JENSEN! STOP!
KILLING INNOCENT PEOPLE WON'T HELP YOU CLEAR YOURSELF!
I DON'T WANT TO BE CLEARED, BATMAN!
I ONLY WANT WAYNE DEAD!
KRAKL
--AND YOU'RE GOING TO MAKE THAT HAPPEN!
EVEN AS BATMAN STRUGGLES TO MAINTAIN HIS GRIP ON THE GRANITE TOWER, THE EXPLOSION REVERBERATES...
6

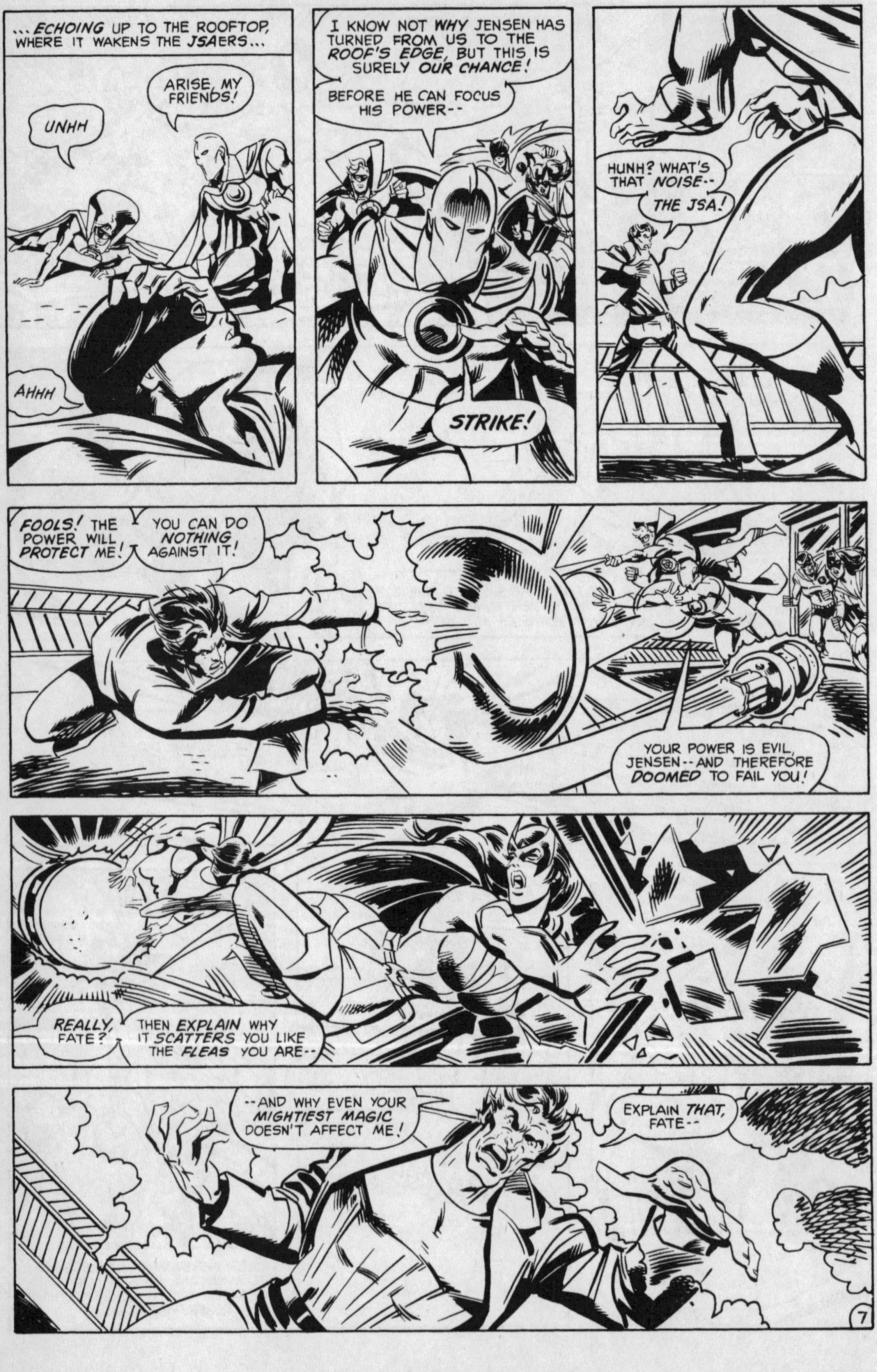
...ECHOING UP TO THE ROOFTOP, WHERE IT WAKENS THE JSAERS...
ARISE, MY FRIENDS!
UNHH
AHHH
I KNOW NOT WHY JENSEN HAS TURNED FROM US TO THE ROOF'S EDGE, BUT THIS IS SURELY OUR CHANCE!
BEFORE HE CAN FOCUS HIS POWER--
STRIKE!
HUNH? WHAT'S THAT NOISE--
THE JSA!
FOOLS! THE POWER WILL PROTECT ME!
YOU CAN DO NOTHING AGAINST IT!
YOUR POWER IS EVIL, JENSEN--AND THEREFORE DOOMED TO FAIL YOU!
REALLY, FATE?
THEN EXPLAIN WHY IT SCATTERS YOU LIKE THE FLEAS YOU ARE--
--AND WHY EVEN YOUR MIGHTIEST MAGIC DOESN'T AFFECT ME!
EXPLAIN THAT, FATE--
7

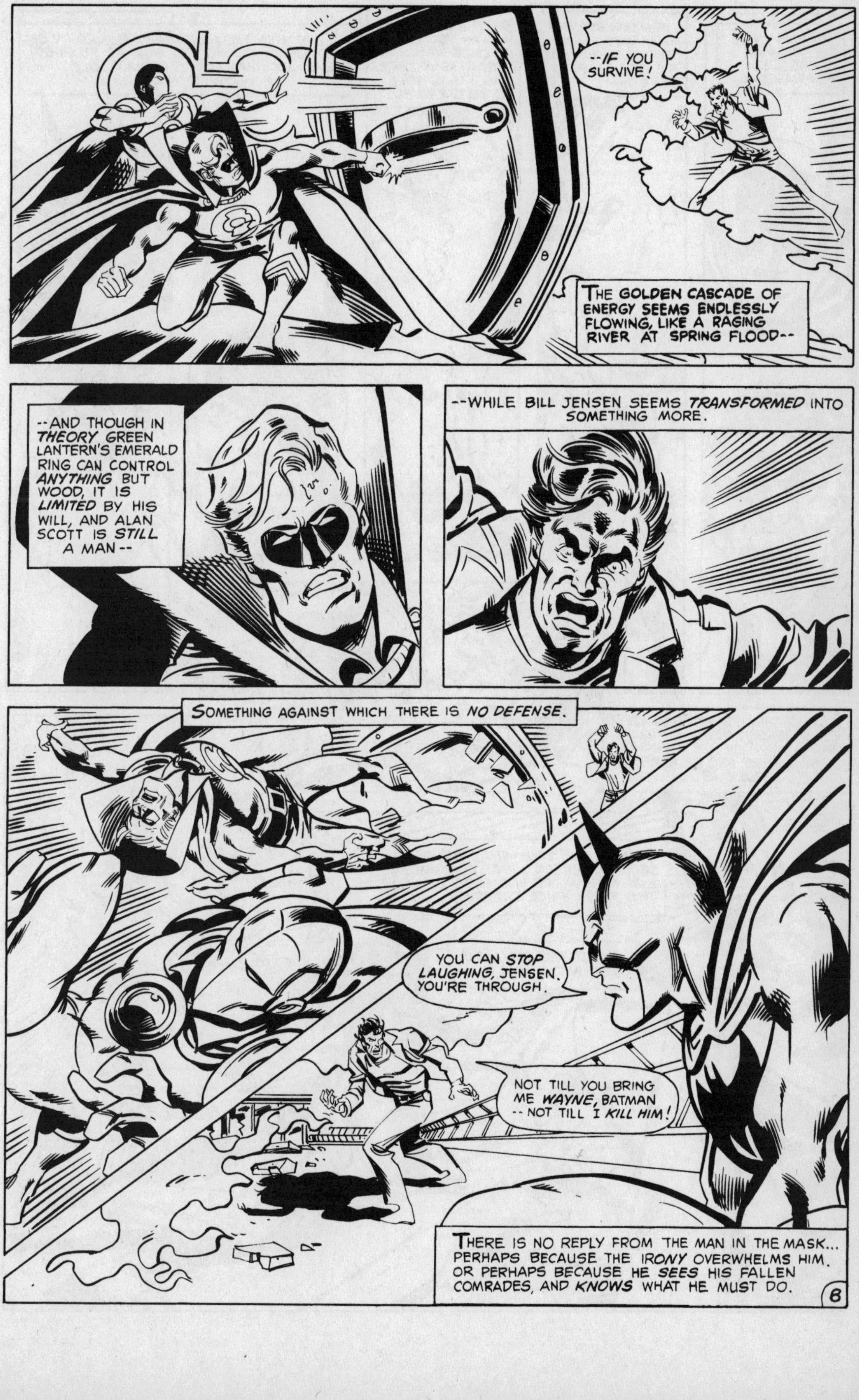
--IF YOU SURVIVE!
THE GOLDEN CASCADE OF ENERGY SEEMS ENDLESSLY FLOWING, LIKE A RAGING RIVER AT SPRING FLOOD--
--AND THOUGH IN THEORY GREEN LANTERN'S EMERALD RING CAN CONTROL ANYTHING BUT WOOD, IT IS LIMITED BY HIS WILL, AND ALAN SCOTT IS STILL A MAN--
--WHILE BILL JENSEN SEEMS TRANSFORMED INTO SOMETHING MORE.
SOMETHING AGAINST WHICH THERE IS NO DEFENSE.
YOU CAN STOP LAUGHING, JENSEN. YOU'RE THROUGH.
NOT TILL YOU BRING ME WAYNE, BATMAN --NOT TILL I KILL HIM!
THERE IS NO REPLY FROM THE MAN IN THE MASK... PERHAPS BECAUSE THE IRONY OVERWHELMS HIM. OR PERHAPS BECAUSE HE SEES HIS FALLEN COMRADES, AND KNOWS WHAT HE MUST DO.
8

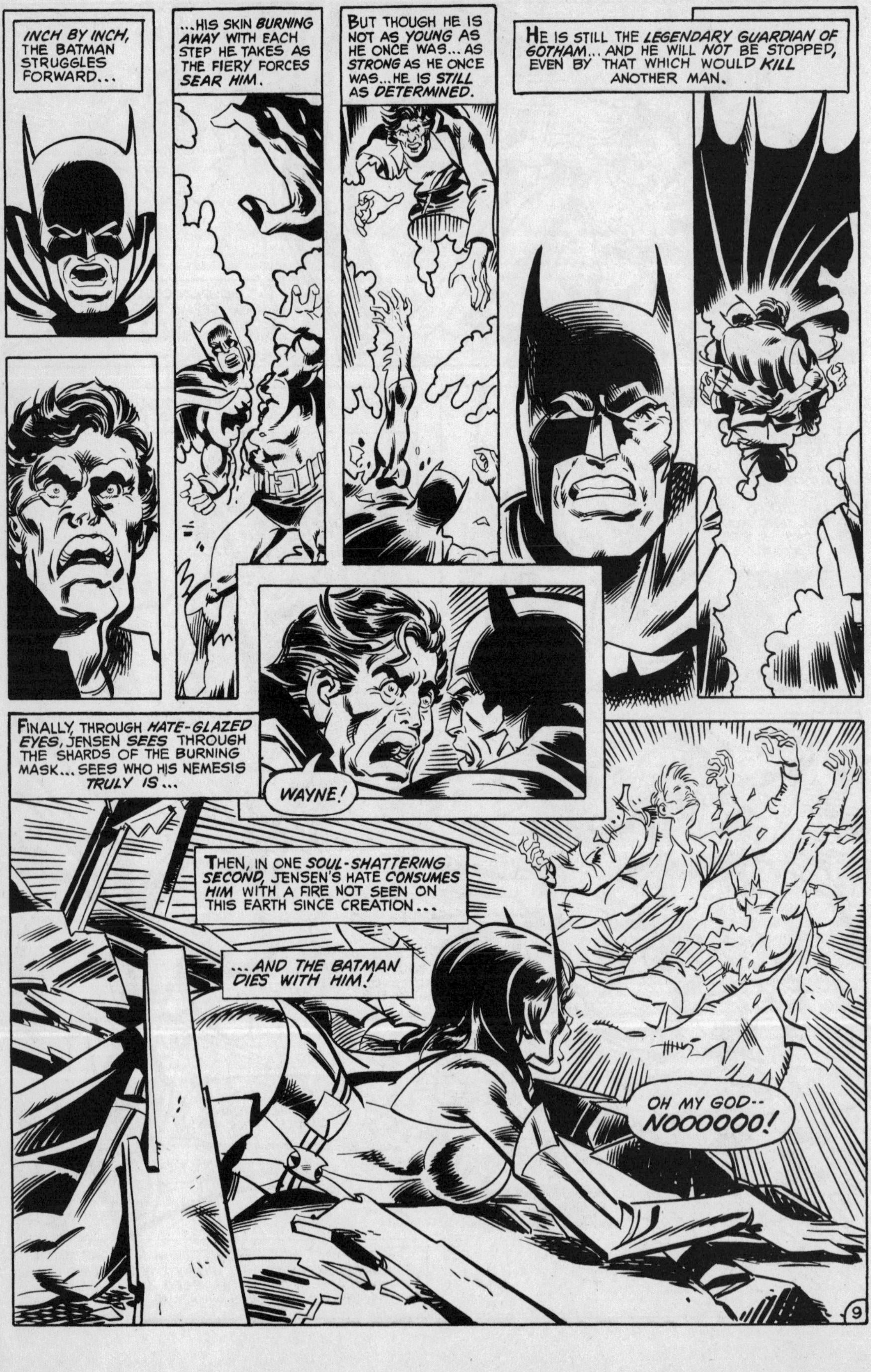
INCH BY INCH, THE BATMAN STRUGGLES FORWARD...
...HIS SKIN BURNING AWAY WITH EACH STEP HE TAKES AS THE FIERY FORCES SEAR HIM.
BUT THOUGH HE IS NOT AS YOUNG AS HE ONCE WAS... AS STRONG AS HE ONCE WAS... HE IS STILL AS DETERMINED.
HE IS STILL THE LEGENDARY GUARDIAN OF GOTHAM... AND HE WILL NOT BE STOPPED, EVEN BY THAT WHICH WOULD KILL ANOTHER MAN.
FINALLY, THROUGH HATE-GLAZED EYES, JENSEN SEES THROUGH THE SHARDS OF THE BURNING MASK... SEES WHO HIS NEMESIS TRULY IS...
WAYNE!
THEN, IN ONE SOUL-SHATTERING SECOND, JENSEN'S HATE CONSUMES HIM WITH A FIRE NOT SEEN ON THIS EARTH SINCE CREATION...
...AND THE BATMAN DIES WITH HIM!
OH MY GOD-- NOOOOOO!
9

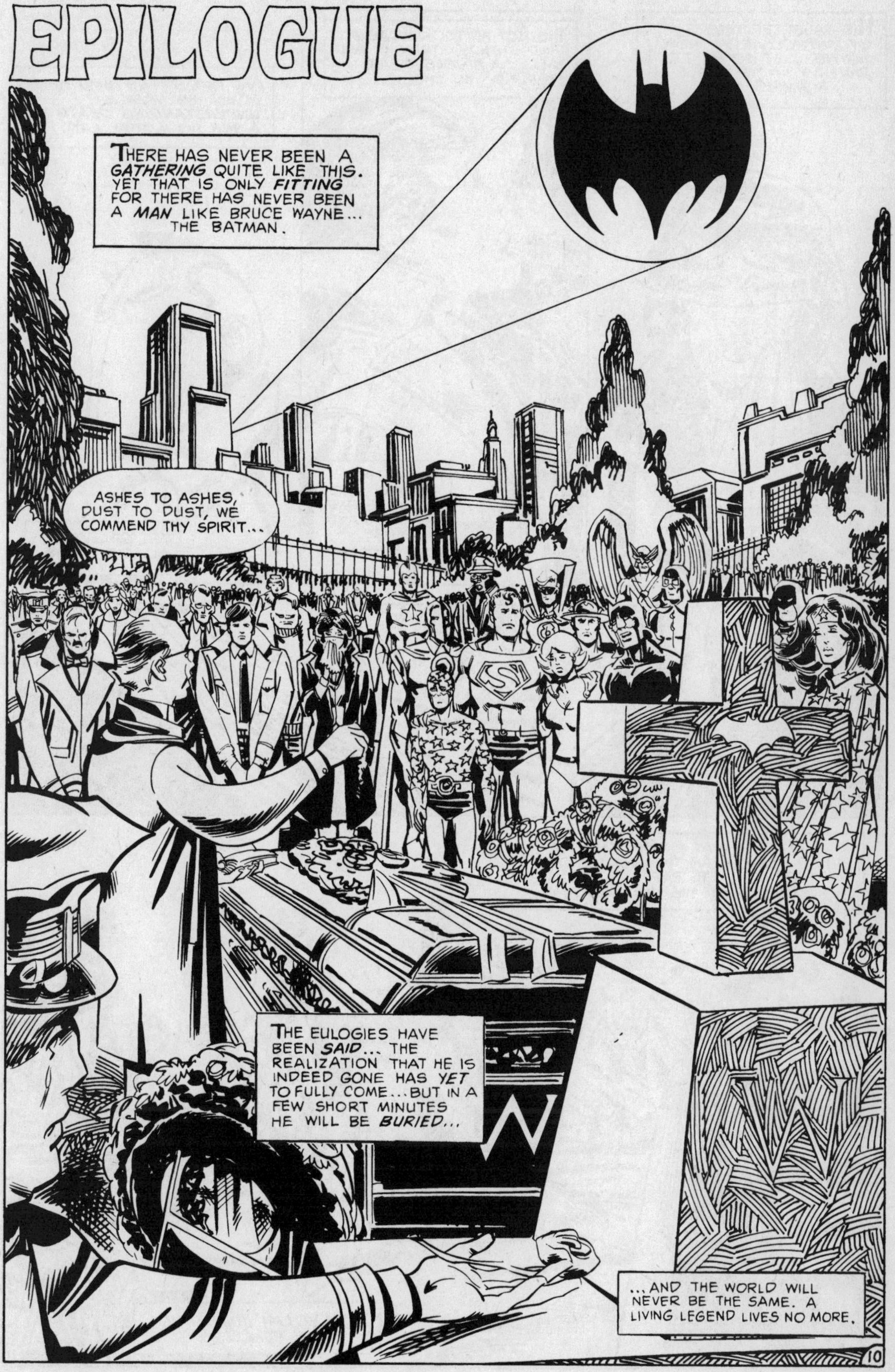
EPILOGUE
THERE HAS NEVER BEEN A GATHERING QUITE LIKE THIS. YET THAT IS ONLY FITTING FOR THERE HAS NEVER BEEN A MAN LIKE BRUCE WAYNE... THE BATMAN.
ASHES TO ASHES, DUST TO DUST, WE COMMEND THY SPIRIT...
THE EULOGIES HAVE BEEN SAID... THE REALIZATION THAT HE IS INDEED GONE HAS YET TO FULLY COME... BUT IN A FEW SHORT MINUTES HE WILL BE BURIED...
...AND THE WORLD WILL NEVER BE THE SAME. A LIVING LEGEND LIVES NO MORE.
10

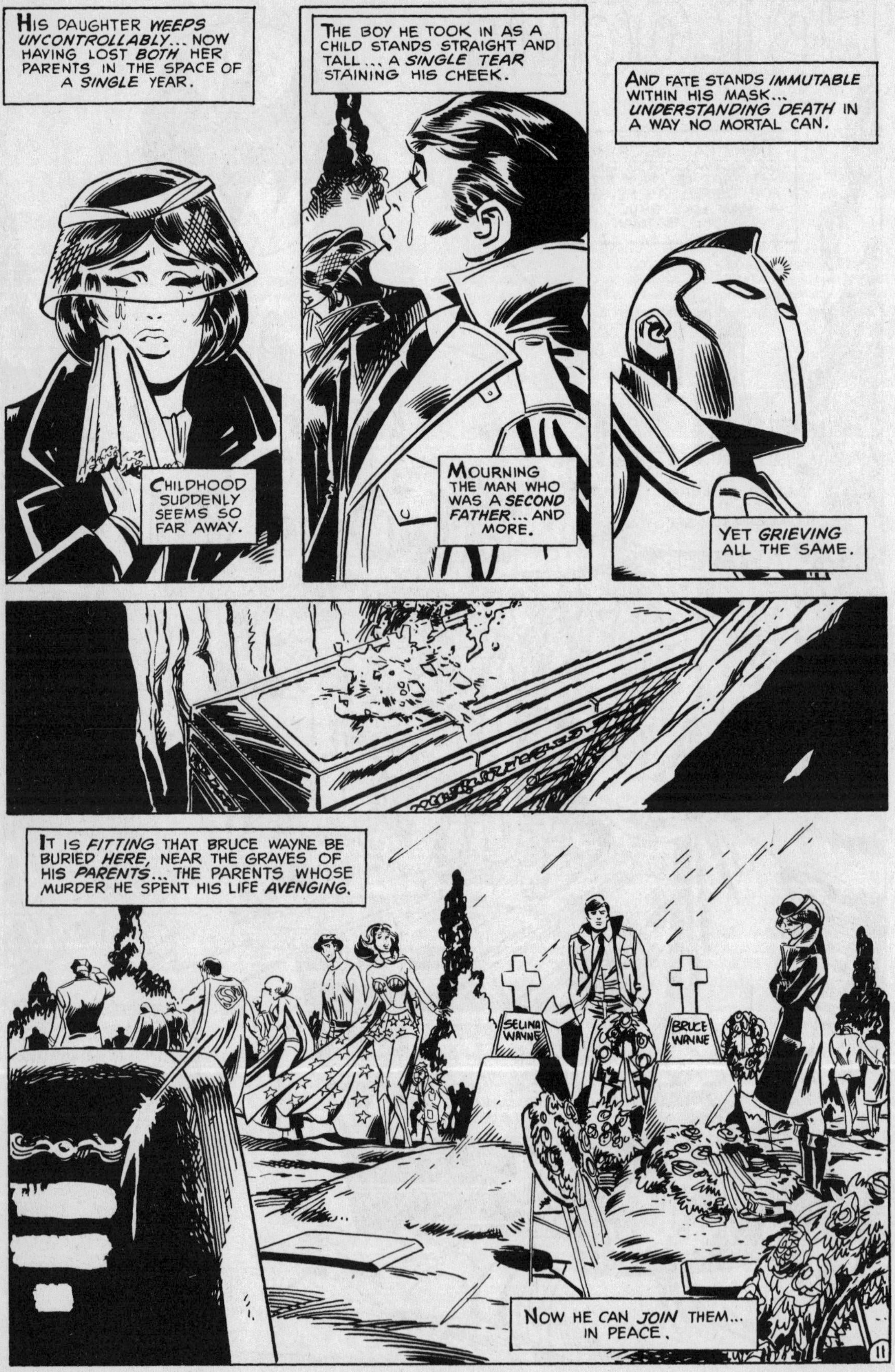
HIS DAUGHTER WEEPS UNCONTROLLABLY... NOW HAVING LOST BOTH HER PARENTS IN THE SPACE OF A SINGLE YEAR.
CHILDHOOD SUDDENLY SEEMS SO FAR AWAY.
THE BOY HE TOOK IN AS A CHILD STANDS STRAIGHT AND TALL... A SINGLE TEAR STAINING HIS CHEEK.
MOURNING THE MAN WHO WAS A SECOND FATHER... AND MORE.
AND FATE STANDS IMMUTABLE WITHIN HIS MASK... UNDERSTANDING DEATH IN A WAY NO MORTAL CAN.
YET GRIEVING ALL THE SAME.
IT IS FITTING THAT BRUCE WAYNE BE BURIED HERE, NEAR THE GRAVES OF HIS PARENTS... THE PARENTS WHOSE MURDER HE SPENT HIS LIFE AVENGING.
SELINA WAYNE
BRUCE WAYNE
NOW HE CAN JOIN THEM... IN PEACE.
11

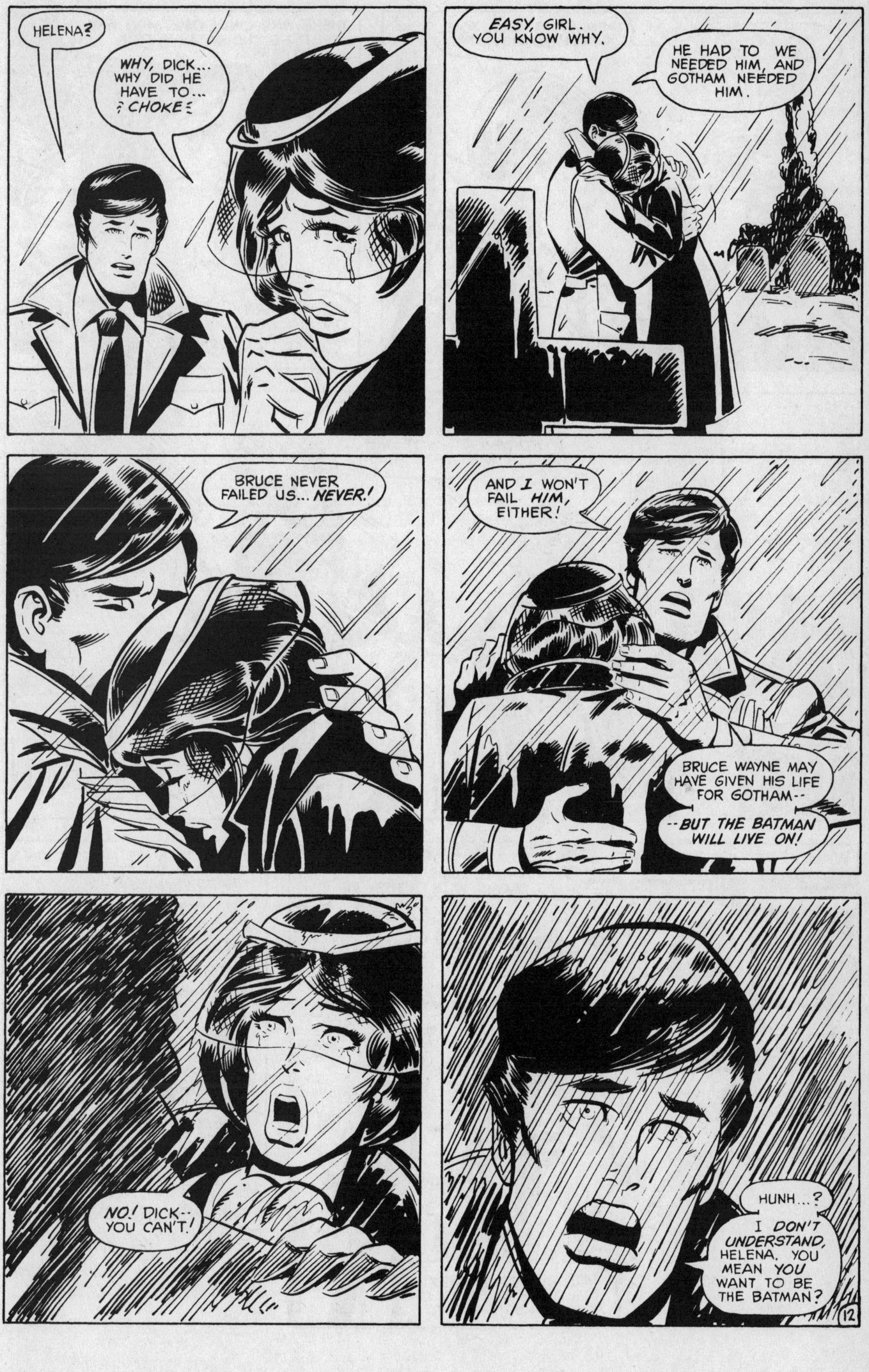
HELENA?
WHY, DICK... WHY DID HE HAVE TO... CHOKE
EASY, GIRL. YOU KNOW WHY.
HE HAD TO WE NEEDED HIM, AND GOTHAM NEEDED HIM.
BRUCE NEVER FAILED US... NEVER!
AND I WON'T FAIL HIM, EITHER!
BRUCE WAYNE MAY HAVE GIVEN HIS LIFE FOR GOTHAM--
--BUT THE BATMAN WILL LIVE ON!
NO! DICK-- YOU CAN'T!
HUNH...?
I DON'T UNDERSTAND, HELENA. YOU MEAN YOU WANT TO BE THE BATMAN?
12

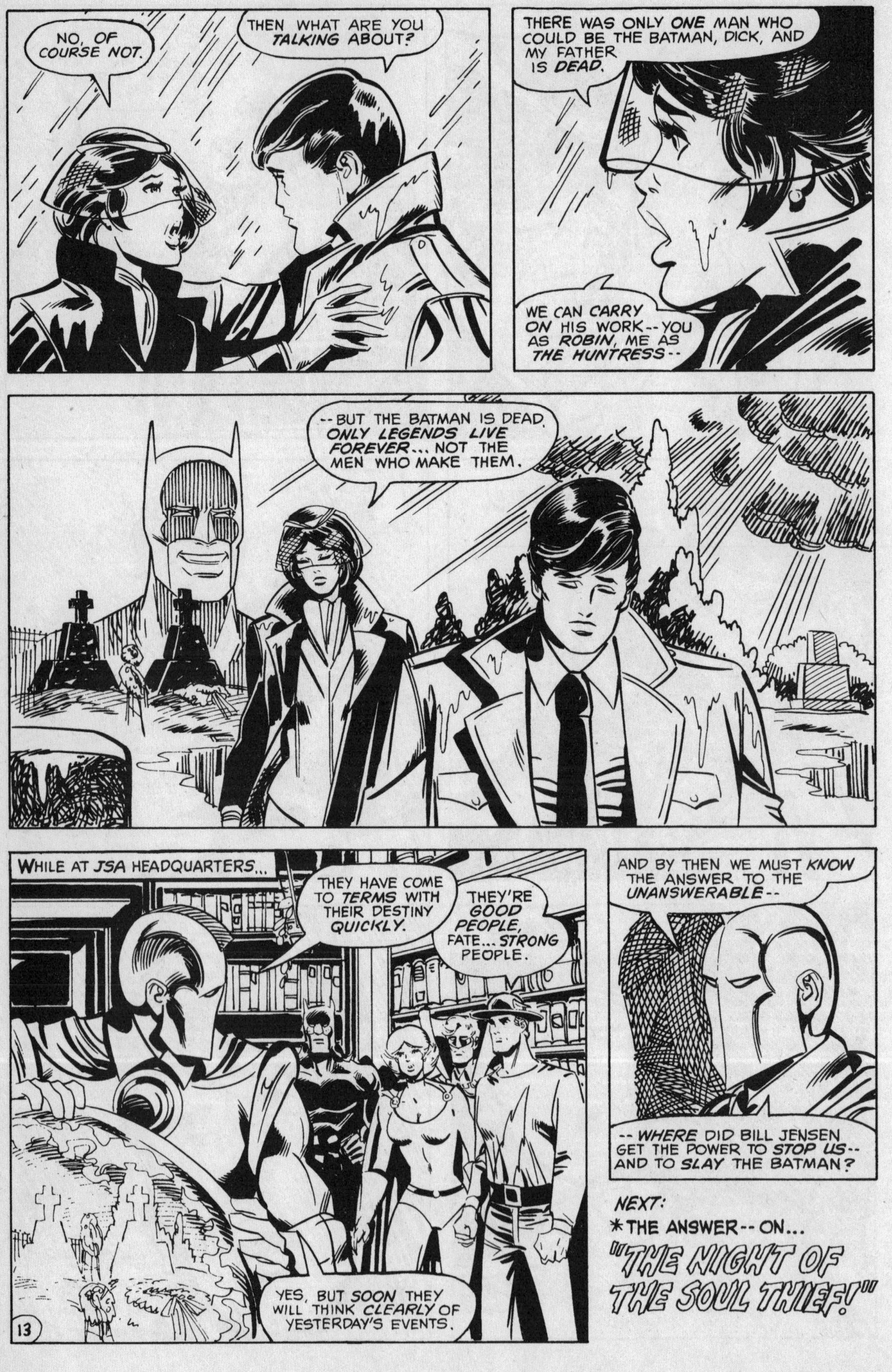
NO, OF COURSE NOT.
THEN WHAT ARE YOU TALKING ABOUT?
THERE WAS ONLY ONE MAN WHO COULD BE THE BATMAN, DICK, AND MY FATHER IS DEAD.
WE CAN CARRY ON HIS WORK--YOU AS ROBIN, ME AS THE HUNTRESS--
--BUT THE BATMAN IS DEAD. ONLY LEGENDS LIVE FOREVER... NOT THE MEN WHO MAKE THEM.
WHILE AT JSA HEADQUARTERS...
THEY HAVE COME TO TERMS WITH THEIR DESTINY QUICKLY.
THEY'RE GOOD PEOPLE, FATE... STRONG PEOPLE.
YES, BUT SOON THEY WILL THINK CLEARLY OF YESTERDAY'S EVENTS.
13
AND BY THEN WE MUST KNOW THE ANSWER TO THE UNANSWERABLE--
--WHERE DID BILL JENSEN GET THE POWER TO STOP US--AND TO SLAY THE BATMAN?
NEXT:
* THE ANSWER--ON...
"THE NIGHT OF THE SOUL THIEF!"

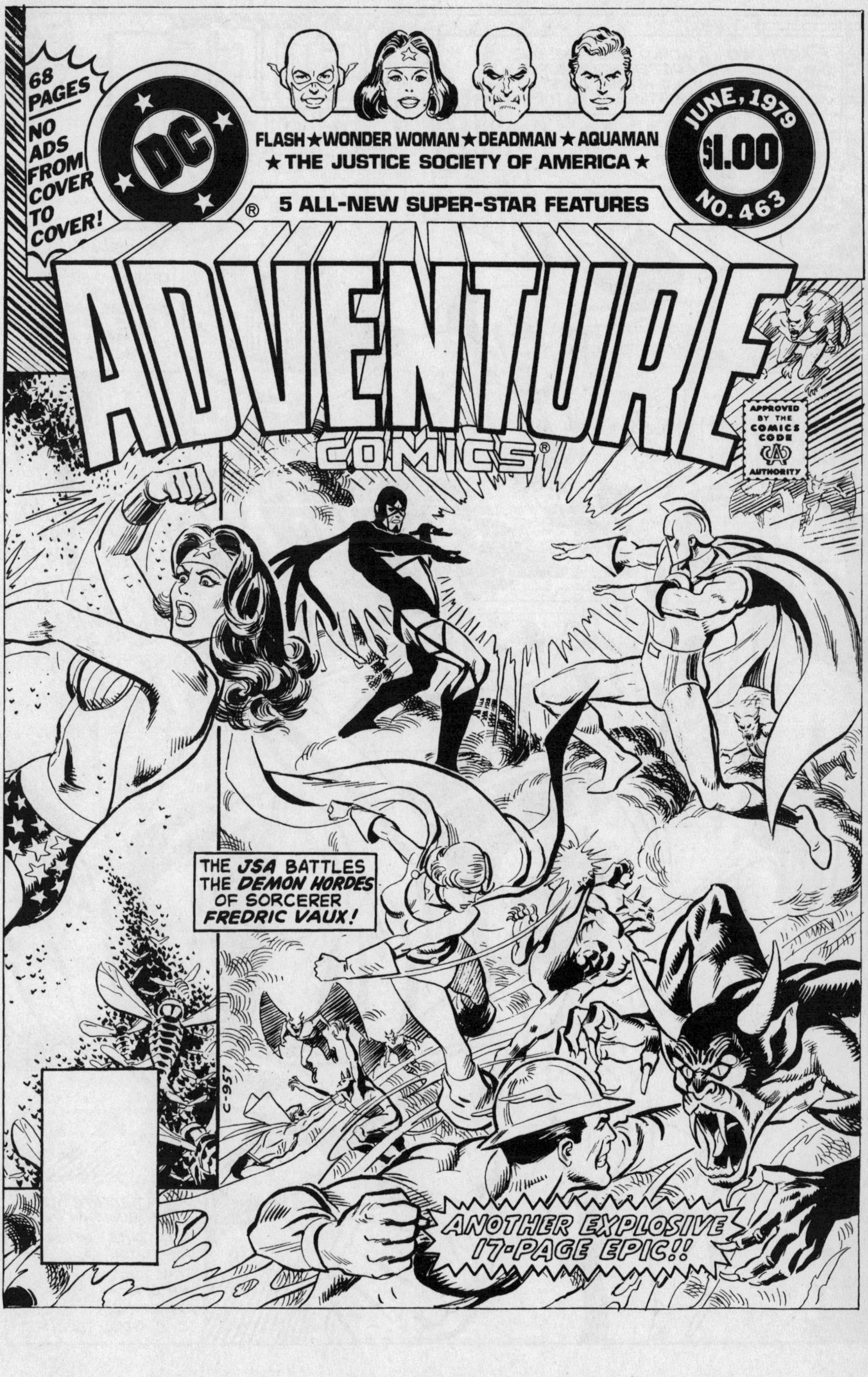
68 PAGES
NO ADS FROM COVER TO COVER!
DC
FLASH ★ WONDER WOMAN ★ DEADMAN ★ AQUAMAN
★ THE JUSTICE SOCIETY OF AMERICA ★
5 ALL-NEW SUPER-STAR FEATURES
JUNE, 1979
$1.00
NO. 463
ADVENTURE
COMICS
APPROVED BY THE COMICS CODE AUTHORITY
THE JSA BATTLES THE DEMON HORDES OF SORCERER FREDRIC VAUX!
C-957
ANOTHER EXPLOSIVE 17-PAGE EPIC!!

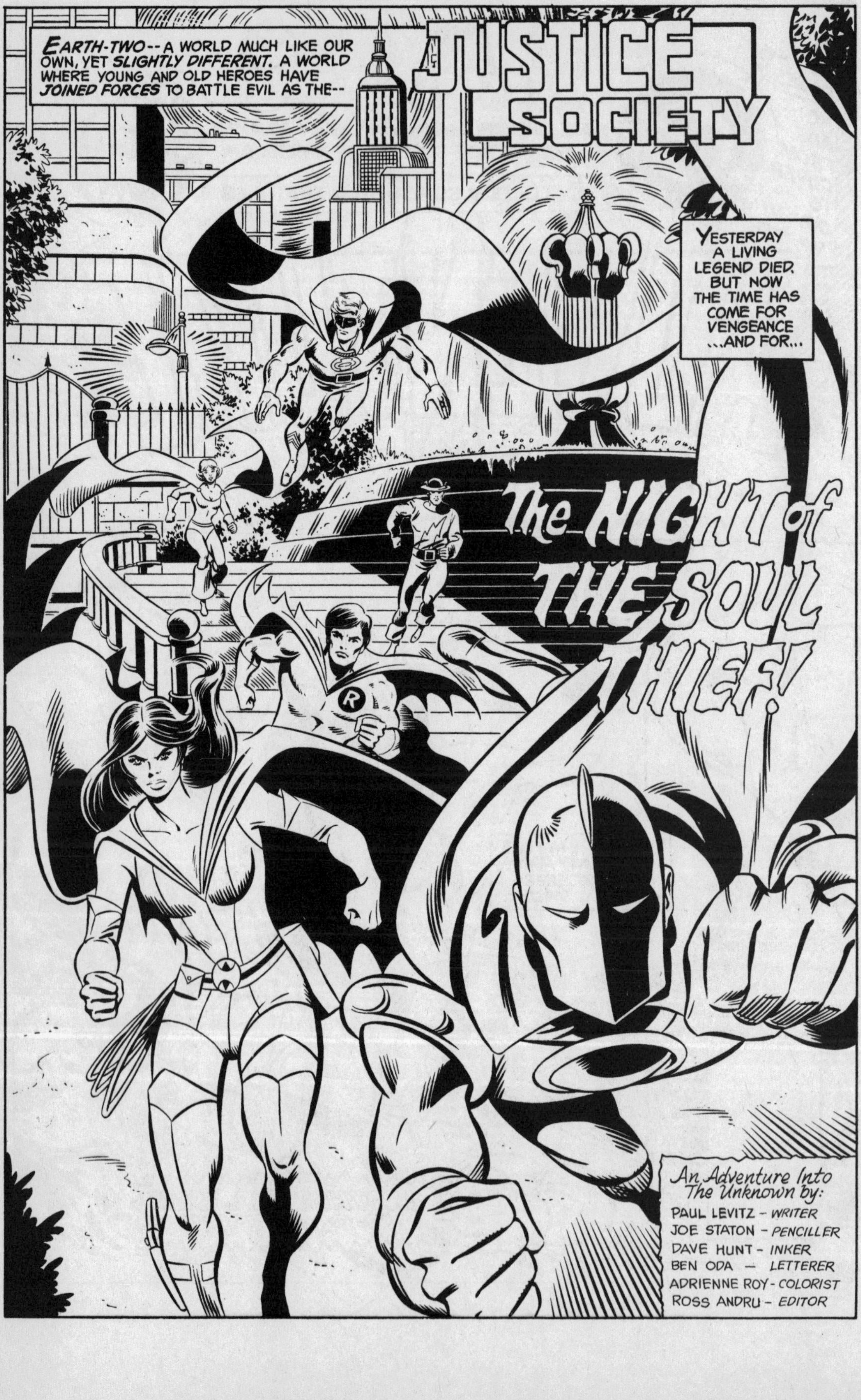
EARTH-TWO-- A WORLD MUCH LIKE OUR OWN, YET SLIGHTLY DIFFERENT. A WORLD WHERE YOUNG AND OLD HEROES HAVE JOINED FORCES TO BATTLE EVIL AS THE--
JUSTICE SOCIETY
YESTERDAY A LIVING LEGEND DIED. BUT NOW THE TIME HAS COME FOR VENGEANCE ...AND FOR...
The NIGHT of THE SOUL THIEF!
An Adventure Into The Unknown by:
PAUL LEVITZ - WRITER
JOE STATON - PENCILLER
DAVE HUNT - INKER
BEN ODA - LETTERER
ADRIENNE ROY - COLORIST
ROSS ANDRU - EDITOR

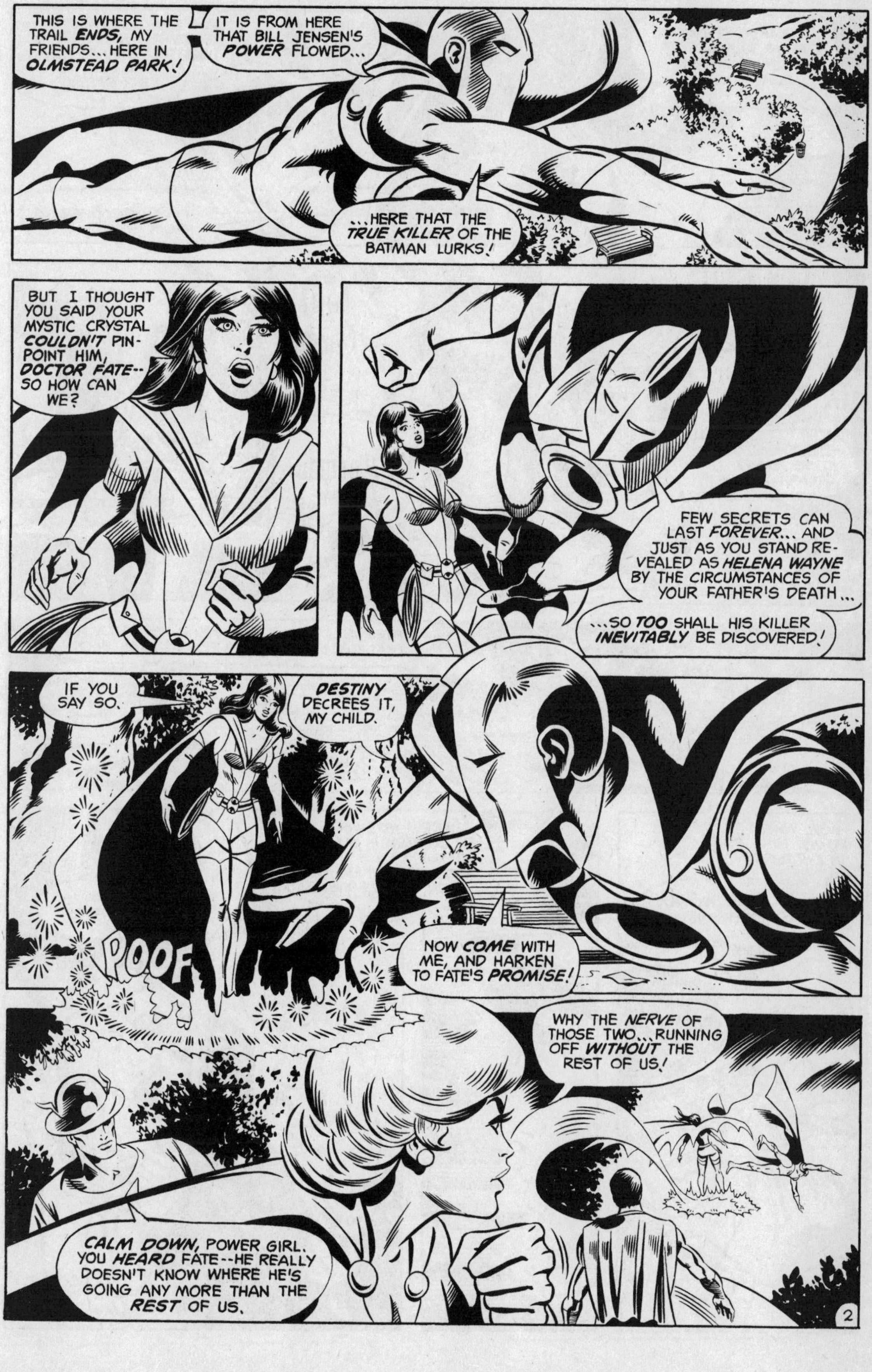
THIS IS WHERE THE TRAIL ENDS, MY FRIENDS... HERE IN OLMSTEAD PARK!
IT IS FROM HERE THAT BILL JENSEN'S POWER FLOWED...
...HERE THAT THE TRUE KILLER OF THE BATMAN LURKS!
BUT I THOUGHT YOU SAID YOUR MYSTIC CRYSTAL COULDN'T PIN-POINT HIM, DOCTOR FATE-- SO HOW CAN WE?
FEW SECRETS CAN LAST FOREVER... AND JUST AS YOU STAND RE-VEALED AS HELENA WAYNE BY THE CIRCUMSTANCES OF YOUR FATHER'S DEATH...
...SO TOO SHALL HIS KILLER INEVITABLY BE DISCOVERED!
IF YOU SAY SO.
DESTINY DECREES IT, MY CHILD.
NOW COME WITH ME, AND HARKEN TO FATE'S PROMISE!
POOF
WHY THE NERVE OF THOSE TWO... RUNNING OFF WITHOUT THE REST OF US!
CALM DOWN, POWER GIRL. YOU HEARD FATE--HE REALLY DOESN'T KNOW WHERE HE'S GOING ANY MORE THAN THE REST OF US.
2

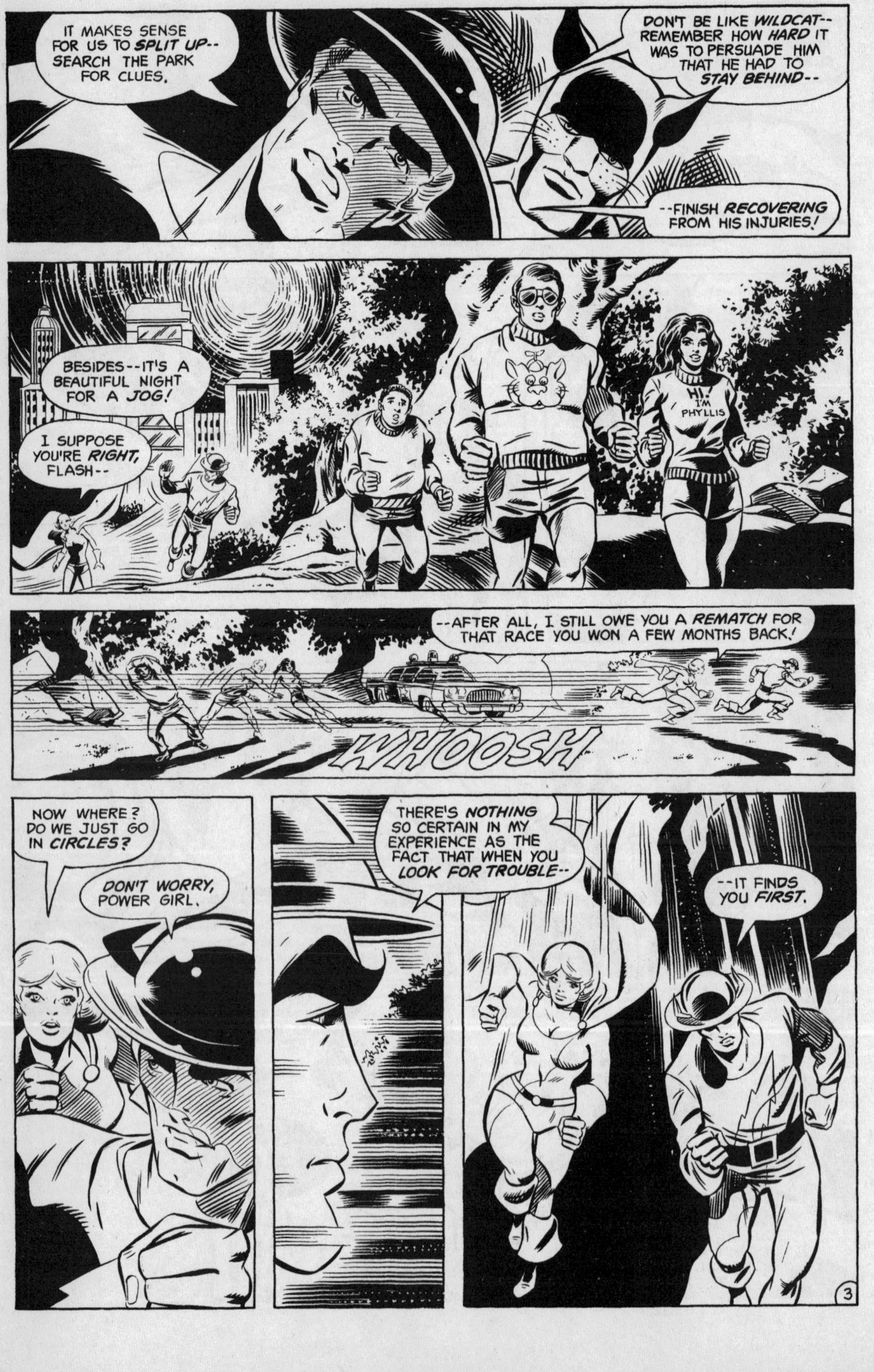
IT MAKES SENSE FOR US TO SPLIT UP-- SEARCH THE PARK FOR CLUES.
DON'T BE LIKE WILDCAT-- REMEMBER HOW HARD IT WAS TO PERSUADE HIM THAT HE HAD TO STAY BEHIND--
--FINISH RECOVERING FROM HIS INJURIES!
BESIDES--IT'S A BEAUTIFUL NIGHT FOR A JOG!
I SUPPOSE YOU'RE RIGHT, FLASH--
HI. I'M PHYLLIS
--AFTER ALL, I STILL OWE YOU A REMATCH FOR THAT RACE YOU WON A FEW MONTHS BACK!
WHOOSH
NOW WHERE? DO WE JUST GO IN CIRCLES?
DON'T WORRY, POWER GIRL.
THERE'S NOTHING SO CERTAIN IN MY EXPERIENCE AS THE FACT THAT WHEN YOU LOOK FOR TROUBLE--
--IT FINDS YOU FIRST.
3

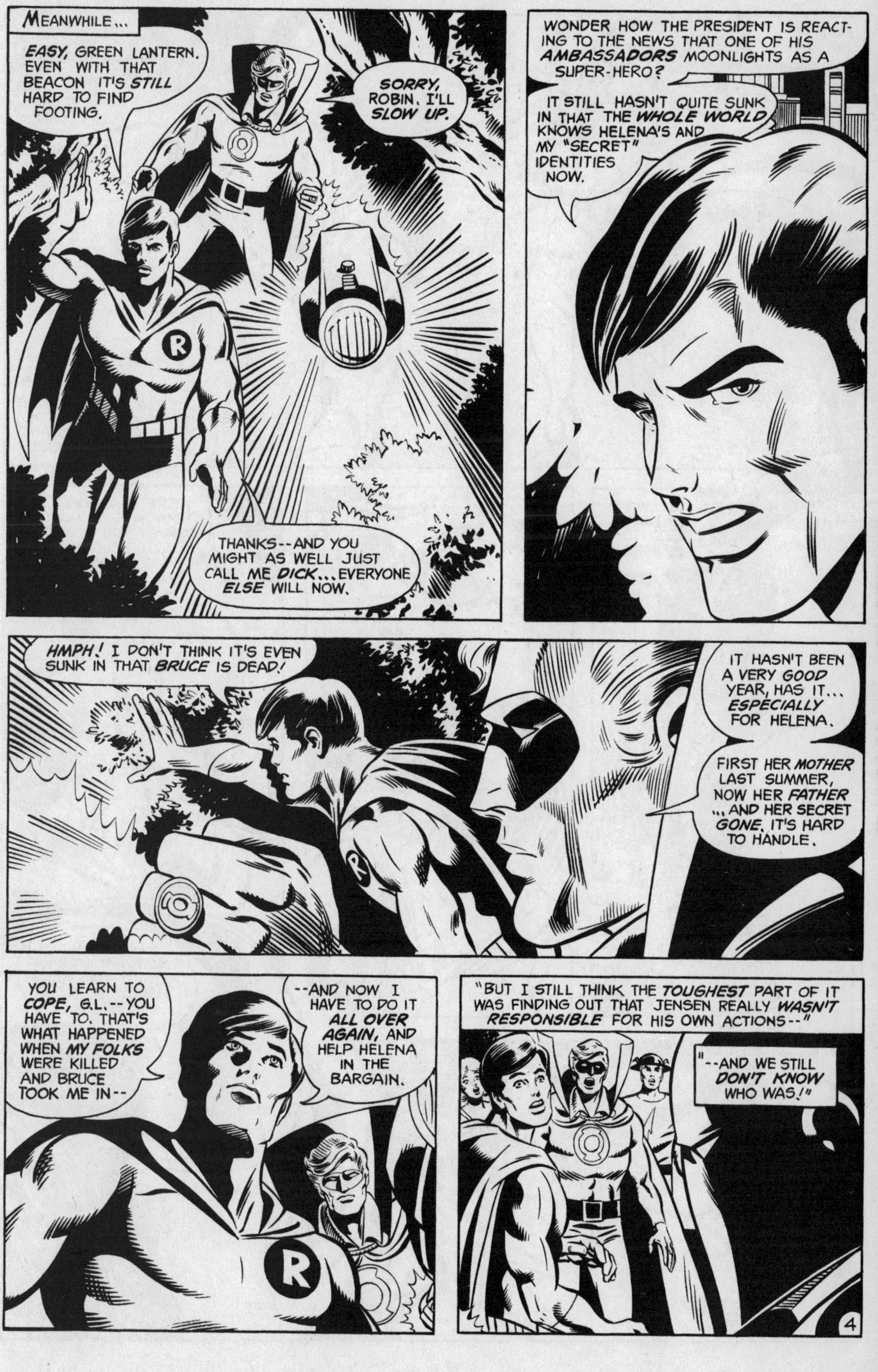
MEANWHILE...
EASY, GREEN LANTERN. EVEN WITH THAT BEACON IT'S STILL HARD TO FIND FOOTING.
SORRY, ROBIN. I'LL SLOW UP.
THANKS--AND YOU MIGHT AS WELL JUST CALL ME DICK... EVERYONE ELSE WILL NOW.
WONDER HOW THE PRESIDENT IS REACTING TO THE NEWS THAT ONE OF HIS AMBASSADORS MOONLIGHTS AS A SUPER-HERO?
IT STILL HASN'T QUITE SUNK IN THAT THE WHOLE WORLD KNOWS HELENA'S AND MY "SECRET" IDENTITIES NOW.
HMPH! I DON'T THINK IT'S EVEN SUNK IN THAT BRUCE IS DEAD!
IT HASN'T BEEN A VERY GOOD YEAR, HAS IT... ESPECIALLY FOR HELENA.
FIRST HER MOTHER LAST SUMMER, NOW HER FATHER ... AND HER SECRET GONE. IT'S HARD TO HANDLE.
YOU LEARN TO COPE, G.L.--YOU HAVE TO. THAT'S WHAT HAPPENED WHEN MY FOLKS WERE KILLED AND BRUCE TOOK ME IN--
--AND NOW I HAVE TO DO IT ALL OVER AGAIN, AND HELP HELENA IN THE BARGAIN.
"BUT I STILL THINK THE TOUGHEST PART OF IT WAS FINDING OUT THAT JENSEN REALLY WASN'T RESPONSIBLE FOR HIS OWN ACTIONS--"
"--AND WE STILL DON'T KNOW WHO WAS!"
4

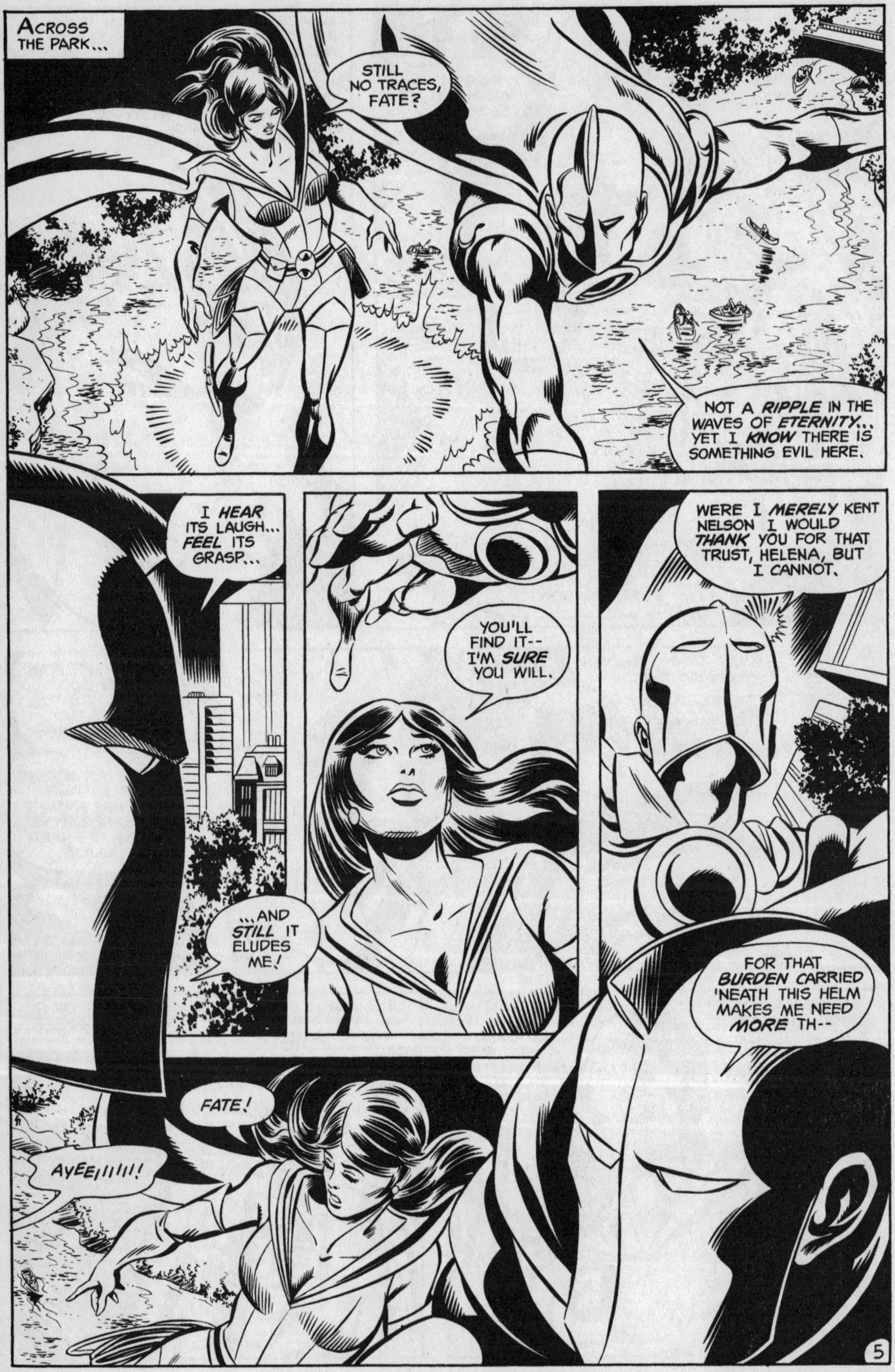

ACROSS THE PARK...
STILL NO TRACES, FATE?
NOT A RIPPLE IN THE WAVES OF ETERNITY... YET I KNOW THERE IS SOMETHING EVIL HERE.
I HEAR ITS LAUGH... FEEL ITS GRASP...
...AND STILL IT ELUDES ME!
YOU'LL FIND IT-- I'M SURE YOU WILL.
WERE I MERELY KENT NELSON I WOULD THANK YOU FOR THAT TRUST, HELENA, BUT I CANNOT.
FOR THAT BURDEN CARRIED 'NEATH THIS HELM MAKES ME NEED MORE TH--
FATE!
AYEEIIIII!
5

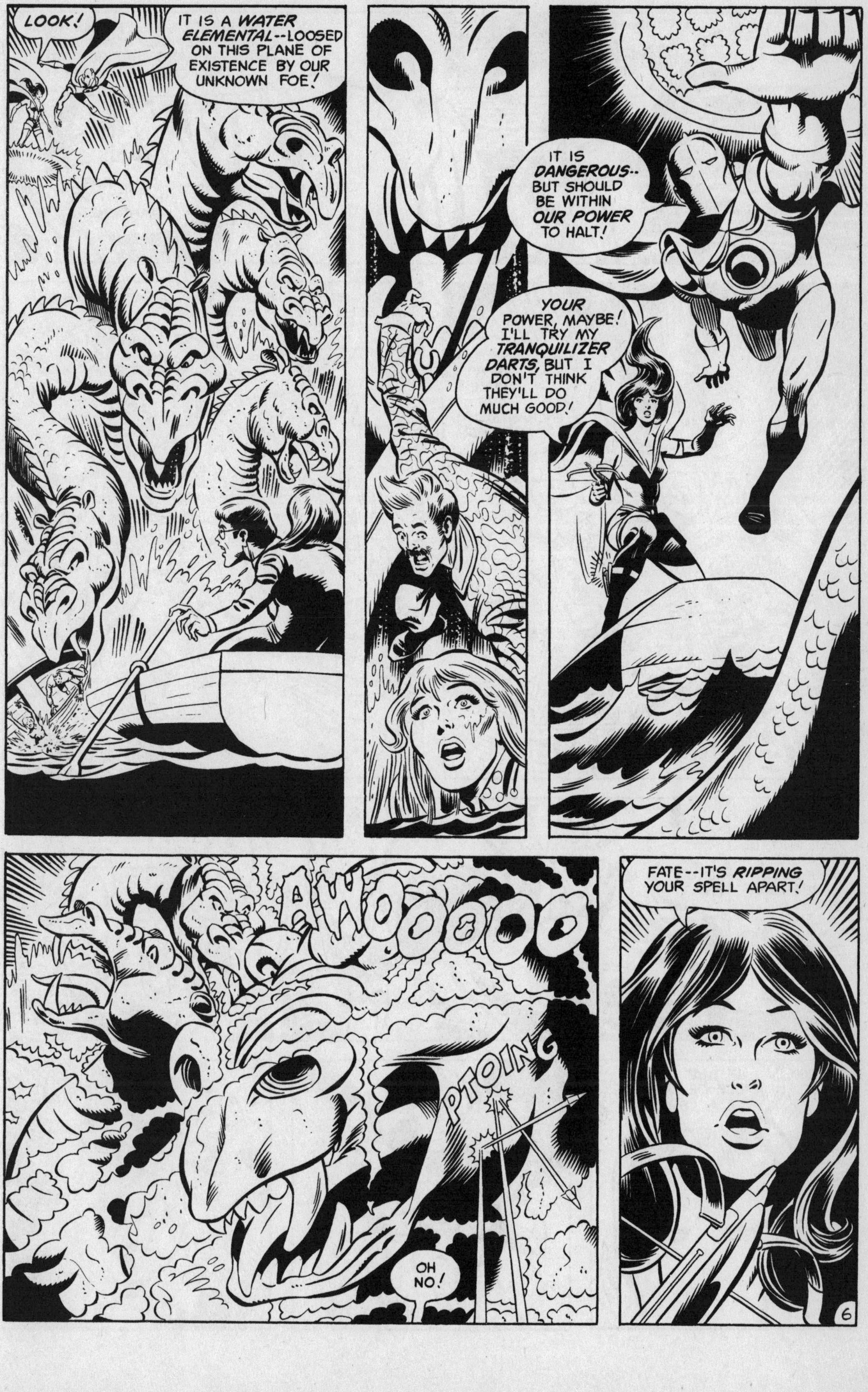
LOOK!
IT IS A WATER ELEMENTAL--LOOSED ON THIS PLANE OF EXISTENCE BY OUR UNKNOWN FOE!
IT IS DANGEROUS-- BUT SHOULD BE WITHIN OUR POWER TO HALT!
YOUR POWER, MAYBE! I'LL TRY MY TRANQUILIZER DARTS, BUT I DON'T THINK THEY'LL DO MUCH GOOD!
AWOOOOOO
PTOING
OH NO!
FATE--IT'S RIPPING YOUR SPELL APART!
6

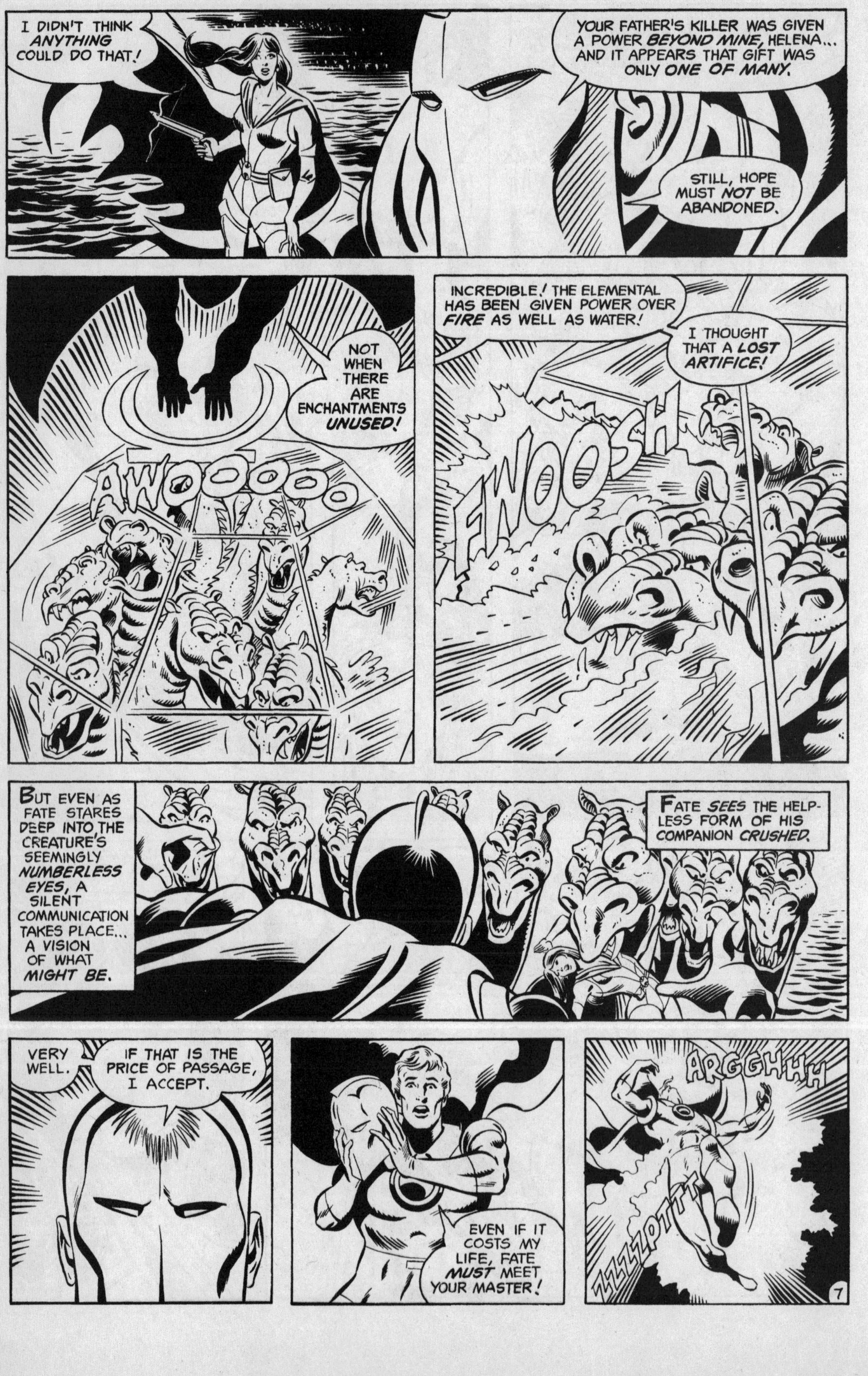
I DIDN'T THINK ANYTHING COULD DO THAT!
YOUR FATHER'S KILLER WAS GIVEN A POWER BEYOND MINE, HELENA... AND IT APPEARS THAT GIFT WAS ONLY ONE OF MANY.
STILL, HOPE MUST NOT BE ABANDONED.
NOT WHEN THERE ARE ENCHANTMENTS UNUSED!
AWOOOOOO
INCREDIBLE! THE ELEMENTAL HAS BEEN GIVEN POWER OVER FIRE AS WELL AS WATER!
I THOUGHT THAT A LOST ARTIFICE!
FWOOSH
BUT EVEN AS FATE STARES DEEP INTO THE CREATURE'S SEEMINGLY NUMBERLESS EYES, A SILENT COMMUNICATION TAKES PLACE... A VISION OF WHAT MIGHT BE.
FATE SEES THE HELPLESS FORM OF HIS COMPANION CRUSHED.
VERY WELL.
IF THAT IS THE PRICE OF PASSAGE, I ACCEPT.
EVEN IF IT COSTS MY LIFE, FATE MUST MEET YOUR MASTER!
ARGGHHH
ZZZZPTTT
7

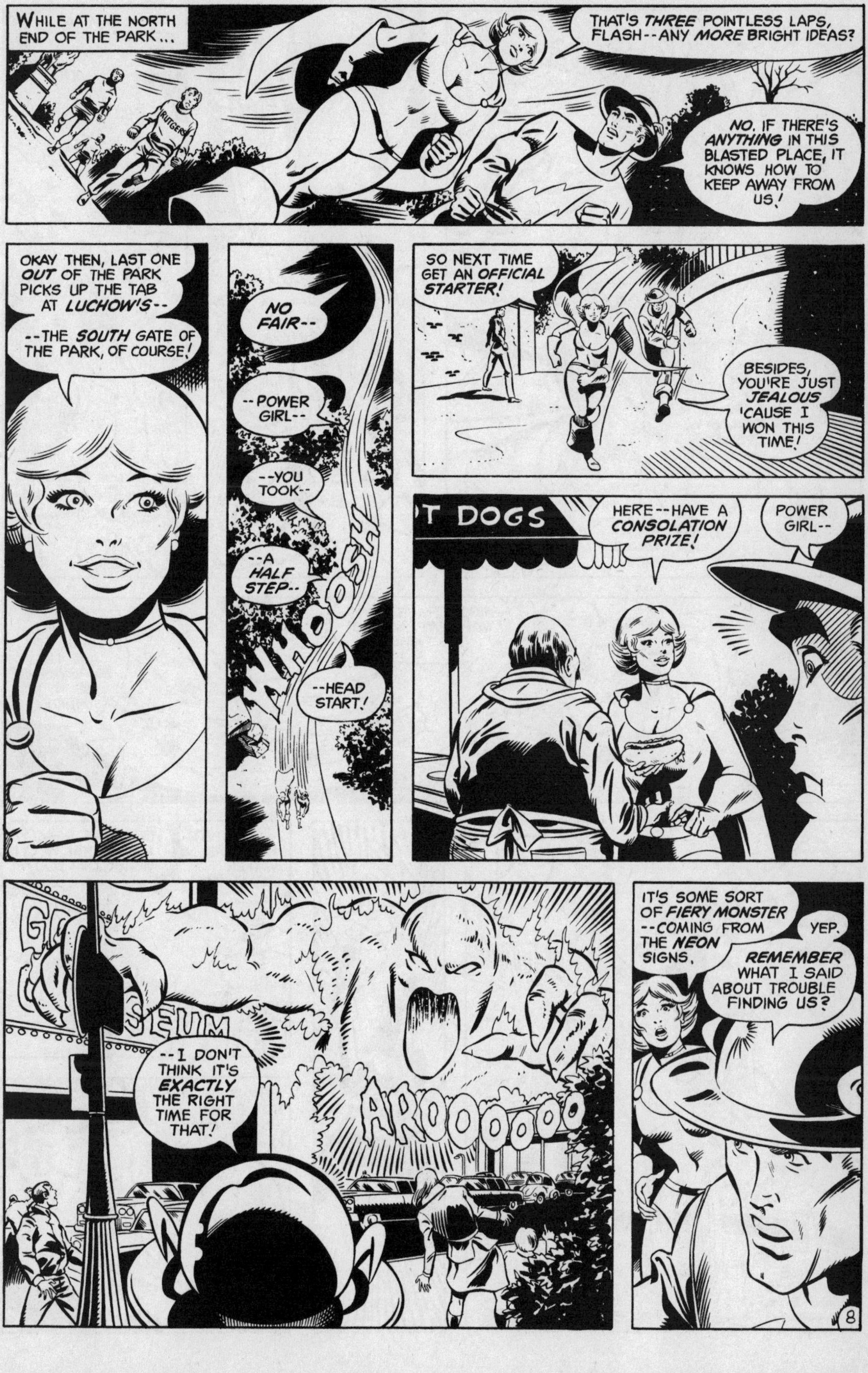
WHILE AT THE NORTH END OF THE PARK...
THAT'S THREE POINTLESS LAPS, FLASH--ANY MORE BRIGHT IDEAS?
RUTGERS
NO. IF THERE'S ANYTHING IN THIS BLASTED PLACE, IT KNOWS HOW TO KEEP AWAY FROM US!
OKAY THEN, LAST ONE OUT OF THE PARK PICKS UP THE TAB AT LUCHOW'S--
--THE SOUTH GATE OF THE PARK, OF COURSE!
NO FAIR--
--POWER GIRL--
--YOU TOOK--
--A HALF STEP--
--HEAD START!
WHOOSH
SO NEXT TIME GET AN OFFICIAL STARTER!
BESIDES, YOU'RE JUST JEALOUS 'CAUSE I WON THIS TIME!
T DOGS
HERE--HAVE A CONSOLATION PRIZE!
POWER GIRL--
--I DON'T THINK IT'S EXACTLY THE RIGHT TIME FOR THAT!
AROOOOOOO
IT'S SOME SORT OF FIERY MONSTER--COMING FROM THE NEON SIGNS.
YEP. REMEMBER WHAT I SAID ABOUT TROUBLE FINDING US?
8

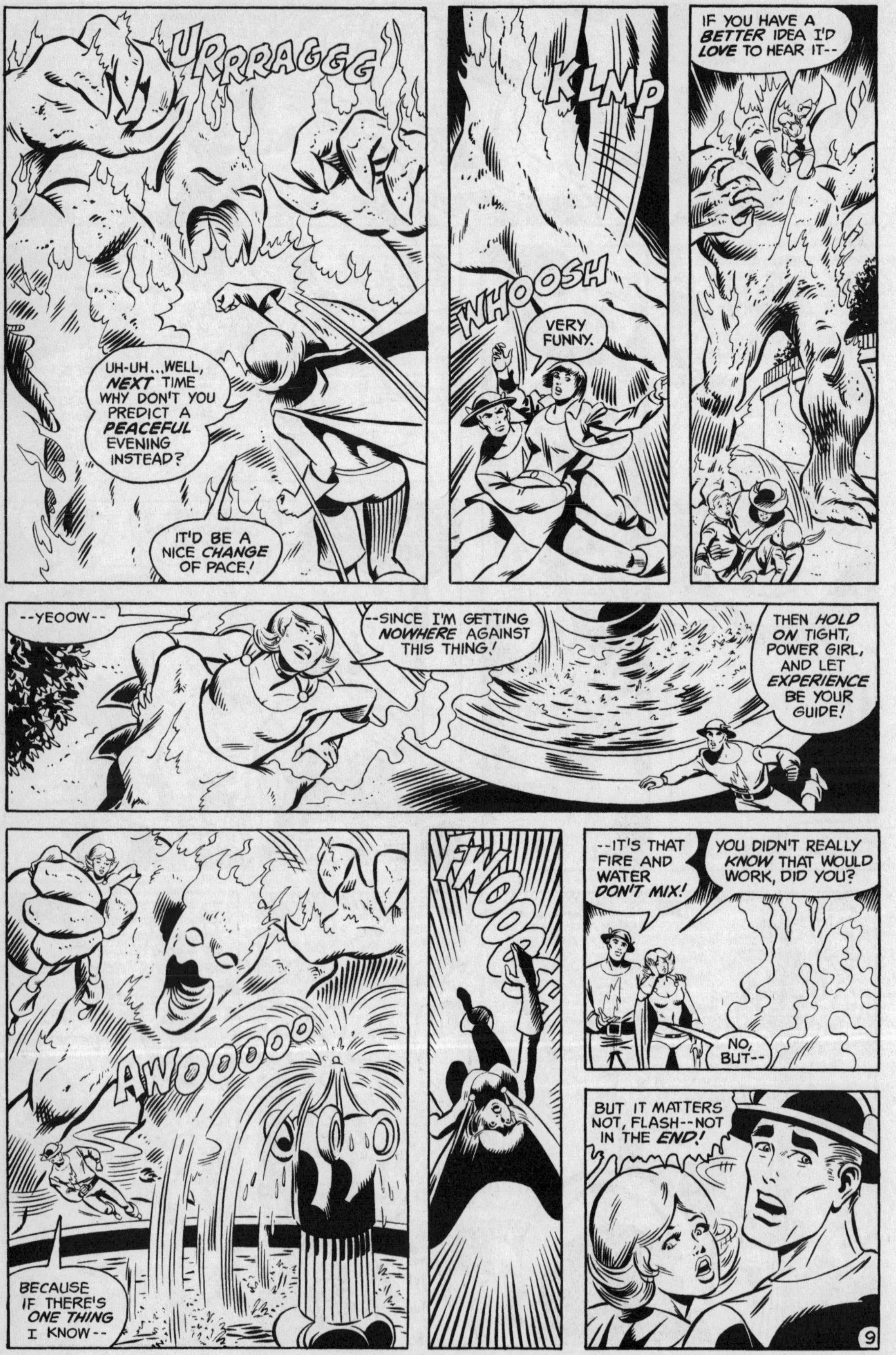
URRRAGGG
UH-UH...WELL, NEXT TIME WHY DON'T YOU PREDICT A PEACEFUL EVENING INSTEAD?
IT'D BE A NICE CHANGE OF PACE!
KLMP
WHOOSH
VERY FUNNY.
IF YOU HAVE A BETTER IDEA I'D LOVE TO HEAR IT--
--YEOOW--
--SINCE I'M GETTING NOWHERE AGAINST THIS THING!
THEN HOLD ON TIGHT, POWER GIRL, AND LET EXPERIENCE BE YOUR GUIDE!
AWOOOOO
BECAUSE IF THERE'S ONE THING I KNOW--
FWOOOSH
--IT'S THAT FIRE AND WATER DON'T MIX!
YOU DIDN'T REALLY KNOW THAT WOULD WORK, DID YOU?
NO, BUT--
BUT IT MATTERS NOT, FLASH--NOT IN THE END!

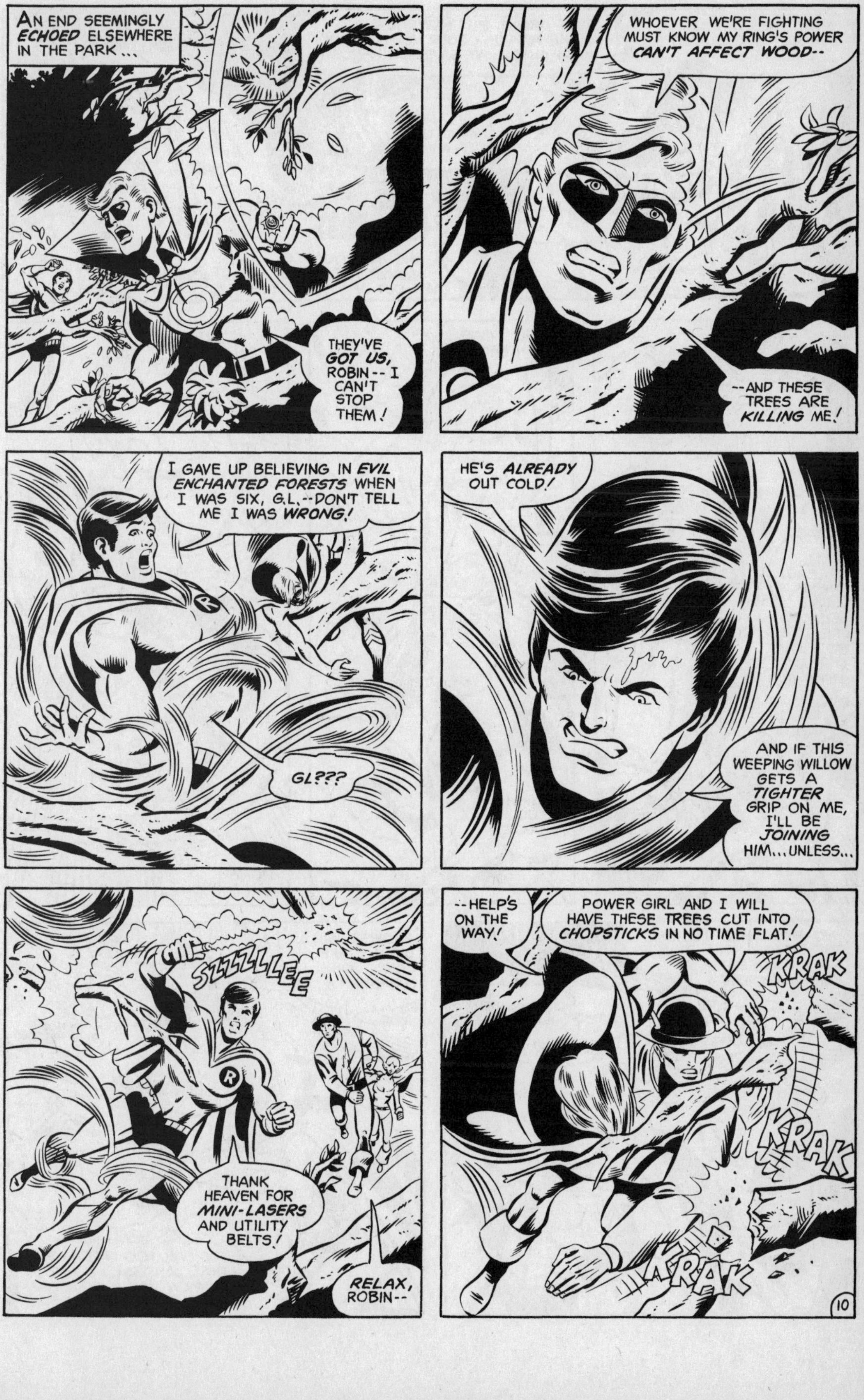
AN END SEEMINGLY ECHOED ELSEWHERE IN THE PARK...
THEY'VE GOT US, ROBIN-- I CAN'T STOP THEM!
WHOEVER WE'RE FIGHTING MUST KNOW MY RING'S POWER CAN'T AFFECT WOOD--
--AND THESE TREES ARE KILLING ME!
I GAVE UP BELIEVING IN EVIL ENCHANTED FORESTS WHEN I WAS SIX, G.L.--DON'T TELL ME I WAS WRONG!
GL???
HE'S ALREADY OUT COLD!
AND IF THIS WEEPING WILLOW GETS A TIGHTER GRIP ON ME, I'LL BE JOINING HIM...UNLESS...
SZZZLLEEE
THANK HEAVEN FOR MINI-LASERS AND UTILITY BELTS!
RELAX, ROBIN--
--HELP'S ON THE WAY!
POWER GIRL AND I WILL HAVE THESE TREES CUT INTO CHOPSTICKS IN NO TIME FLAT!
KRAK
KRAK
KRAK
10

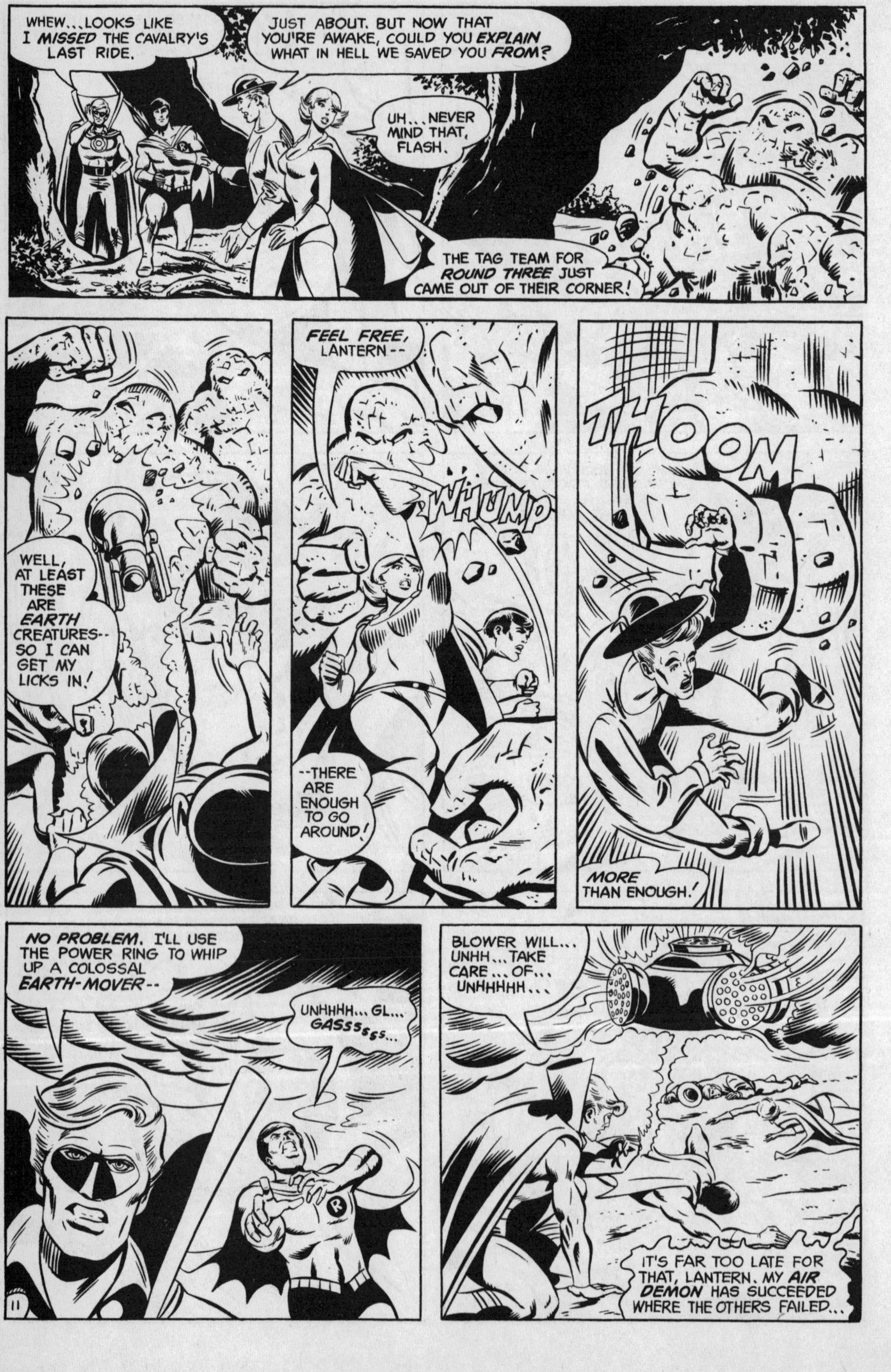
WHEW...LOOKS LIKE I MISSED THE CAVALRY'S LAST RIDE.
JUST ABOUT. BUT NOW THAT YOU'RE AWAKE, COULD YOU EXPLAIN WHAT IN HELL WE SAVED YOU FROM?
UH...NEVER MIND THAT, FLASH.
THE TAG TEAM FOR ROUND THREE JUST CAME OUT OF THEIR CORNER!
WELL, AT LEAST THESE ARE EARTH CREATURES-- SO I CAN GET MY LICKS IN!
FEEL FREE, LANTERN--
WHUMP
--THERE ARE ENOUGH TO GO AROUND!
THOOM
MORE THAN ENOUGH!
NO PROBLEM. I'LL USE THE POWER RING TO WHIP UP A COLOSSAL EARTH-MOVER--
UNHHHH...GL... GASSSsss...
BLOWER WILL... UNHH...TAKE CARE...OF... UNHHHHH...
IT'S FAR TOO LATE FOR THAT, LANTERN. MY AIR DEMON HAS SUCCEEDED WHERE THE OTHERS FAILED...
11

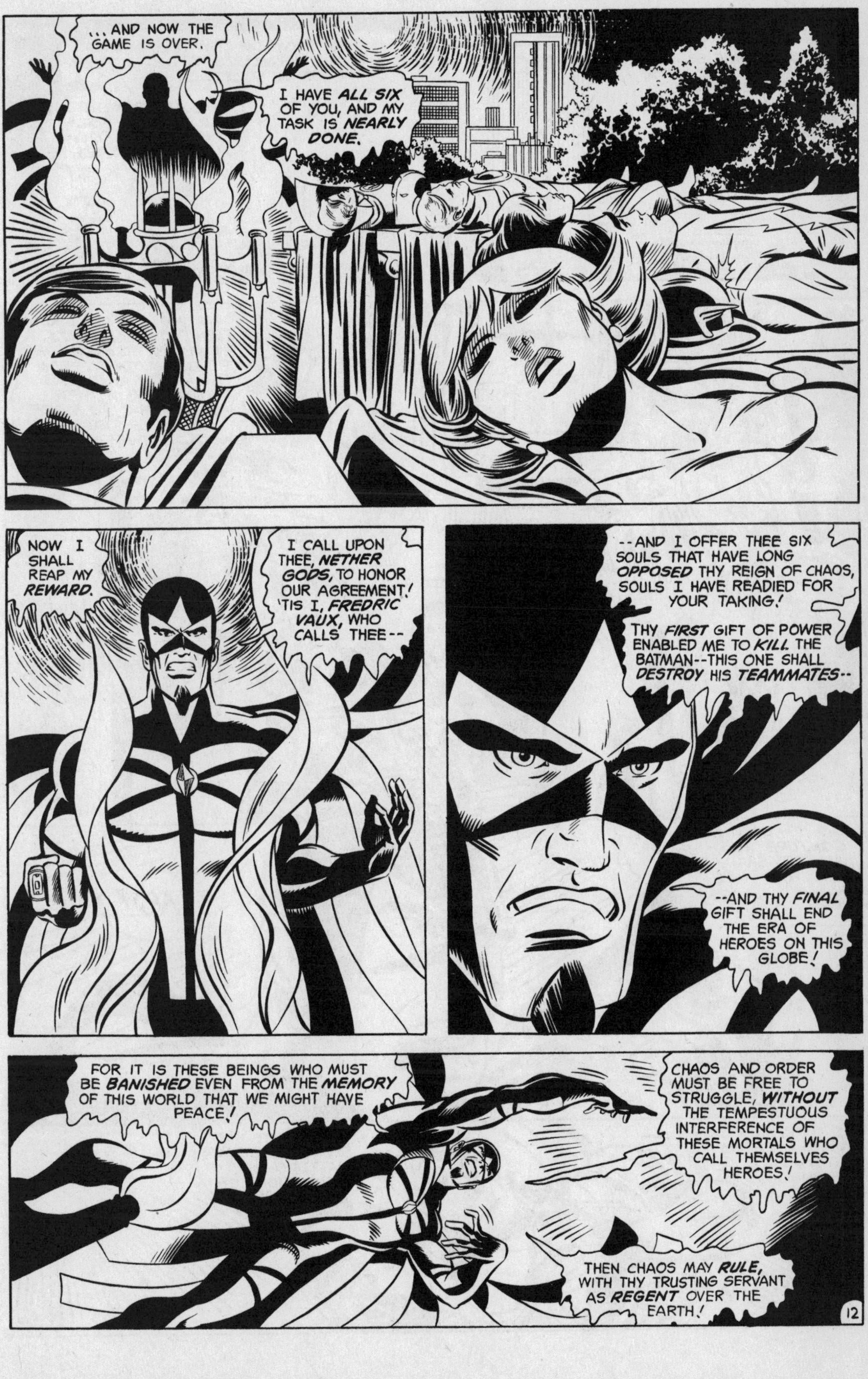
...AND NOW THE GAME IS OVER.
I HAVE ALL SIX OF YOU, AND MY TASK IS NEARLY DONE.
NOW I SHALL REAP MY REWARD.
I CALL UPON THEE, NETHER GODS, TO HONOR OUR AGREEMENT! 'TIS I, FREDRIC VAUX, WHO CALLS THEE--
--AND I OFFER THEE SIX SOULS THAT HAVE LONG OPPOSED THY REIGN OF CHAOS, SOULS I HAVE READIED FOR YOUR TAKING!
THY FIRST GIFT OF POWER ENABLED ME TO KILL THE BATMAN--THIS ONE SHALL DESTROY HIS TEAMMATES--
--AND THY FINAL GIFT SHALL END THE ERA OF HEROES ON THIS GLOBE!
FOR IT IS THESE BEINGS WHO MUST BE BANISHED EVEN FROM THE MEMORY OF THIS WORLD THAT WE MIGHT HAVE PEACE!
CHAOS AND ORDER MUST BE FREE TO STRUGGLE, WITHOUT THE TEMPESTUOUS INTERFERENCE OF THESE MORTALS WHO CALL THEMSELVES HEROES!
THEN CHAOS MAY RULE, WITH THY TRUSTING SERVANT AS REGENT OVER THE EARTH!
12

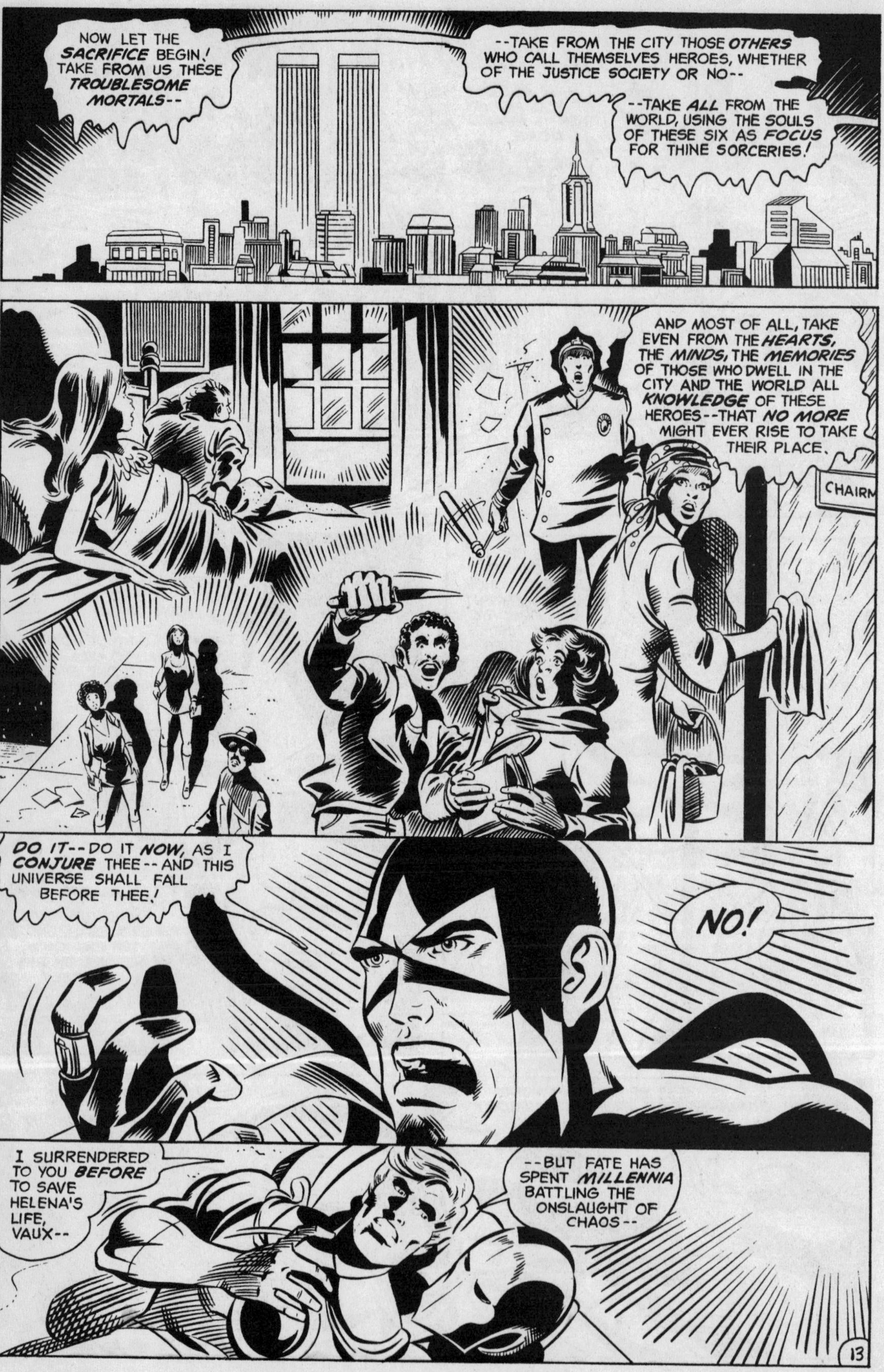
NOW LET THE SACRIFICE BEGIN! TAKE FROM US THESE TROUBLESOME MORTALS--
--TAKE FROM THE CITY THOSE OTHERS WHO CALL THEMSELVES HEROES, WHETHER OF THE JUSTICE SOCIETY OR NO--
--TAKE ALL FROM THE WORLD, USING THE SOULS OF THESE SIX AS FOCUS FOR THINE SORCERIES!
AND MOST OF ALL, TAKE EVEN FROM THE HEARTS, THE MINDS, THE MEMORIES OF THOSE WHO DWELL IN THE CITY AND THE WORLD ALL KNOWLEDGE OF THESE HEROES--THAT NO MORE MIGHT EVER RISE TO TAKE THEIR PLACE.
CHAIRM
DO IT--DO IT NOW, AS I CONJURE THEE--AND THIS UNIVERSE SHALL FALL BEFORE THEE!
NO!
I SURRENDERED TO YOU BEFORE TO SAVE HELENA'S LIFE, VAUX--
--BUT FATE HAS SPENT MILLENNIA BATTLING THE ONSLAUGHT OF CHAOS--
13

--AND *NO MORTAL'S* LIFE IS AS *IMPORTANT* AS THAT *BATTLE!*

KRASH

I AM ALREADY *PROVEN* YOUR MASTER, FATE-- BUT I SHALL *REPEAT* THE LESSON IF I *MUST!*

THOUGH YOU SHOULD *KNOW* YOU CANNOT STAND ALONE AGAINST MY *ELEMENTALS!*

I DO *NOT* STAND ALONE-- *NOW OR EVER,* VAUX!

*B*UT AS WITH ALL MAGIC THERE IS *MORE* TO THIS BATTLE THAN MEETS THE EYE. FOR EVEN AS THE STRUGGLE IN THE PARK BEGINS--

--VAUX'S ENCHANTMENT TAKES HOLD IN THE CITY!

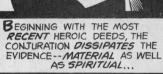

GOTHAM GLOBE

BATMAN DEAD!

*B*EGINNING WITH THE MOST *RECENT* HEROIC DEEDS, THE CONJURATION *DISSIPATES* THE EVIDENCE--*MATERIAL* AS WELL AS *SPIRITUAL...*

GOTI...

BATMAN DEAD!

14

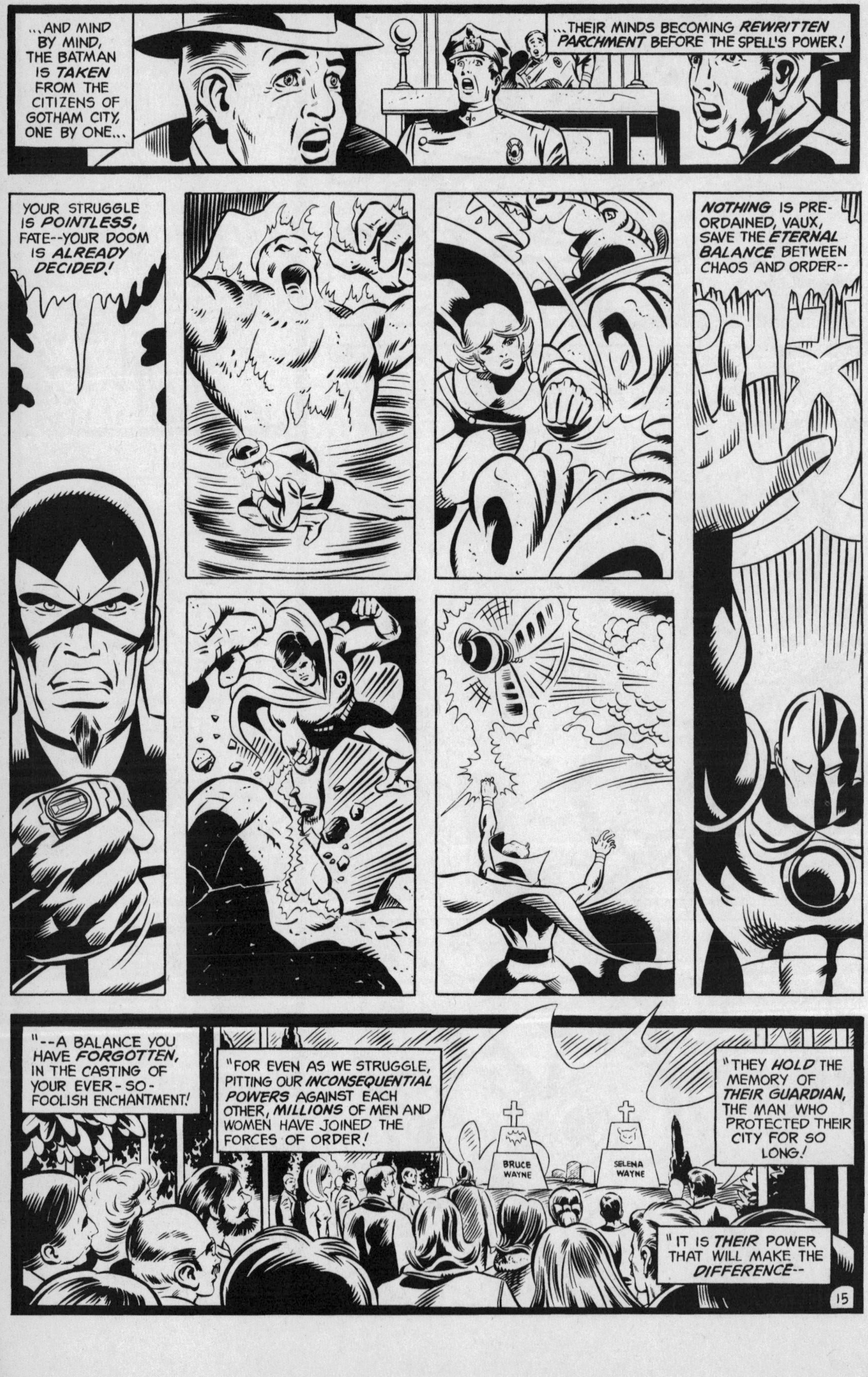
...AND MIND BY MIND, THE BATMAN IS TAKEN FROM THE CITIZENS OF GOTHAM CITY, ONE BY ONE...
...THEIR MINDS BECOMING REWRITTEN PARCHMENT BEFORE THE SPELL'S POWER!
YOUR STRUGGLE IS POINTLESS, FATE--YOUR DOOM IS ALREADY DECIDED!
NOTHING IS PRE-ORDAINED, VAUX, SAVE THE ETERNAL BALANCE BETWEEN CHAOS AND ORDER--
"--A BALANCE YOU HAVE FORGOTTEN, IN THE CASTING OF YOUR EVER-SO-FOOLISH ENCHANTMENT!
"FOR EVEN AS WE STRUGGLE, PITTING OUR INCONSEQUENTIAL POWERS AGAINST EACH OTHER, MILLIONS OF MEN AND WOMEN HAVE JOINED THE FORCES OF ORDER!
BRUCE WAYNE
SELENA WAYNE
"THEY HOLD THE MEMORY OF THEIR GUARDIAN, THE MAN WHO PROTECTED THEIR CITY FOR SO LONG!
"IT IS THEIR POWER THAT WILL MAKE THE DIFFERENCE--
15

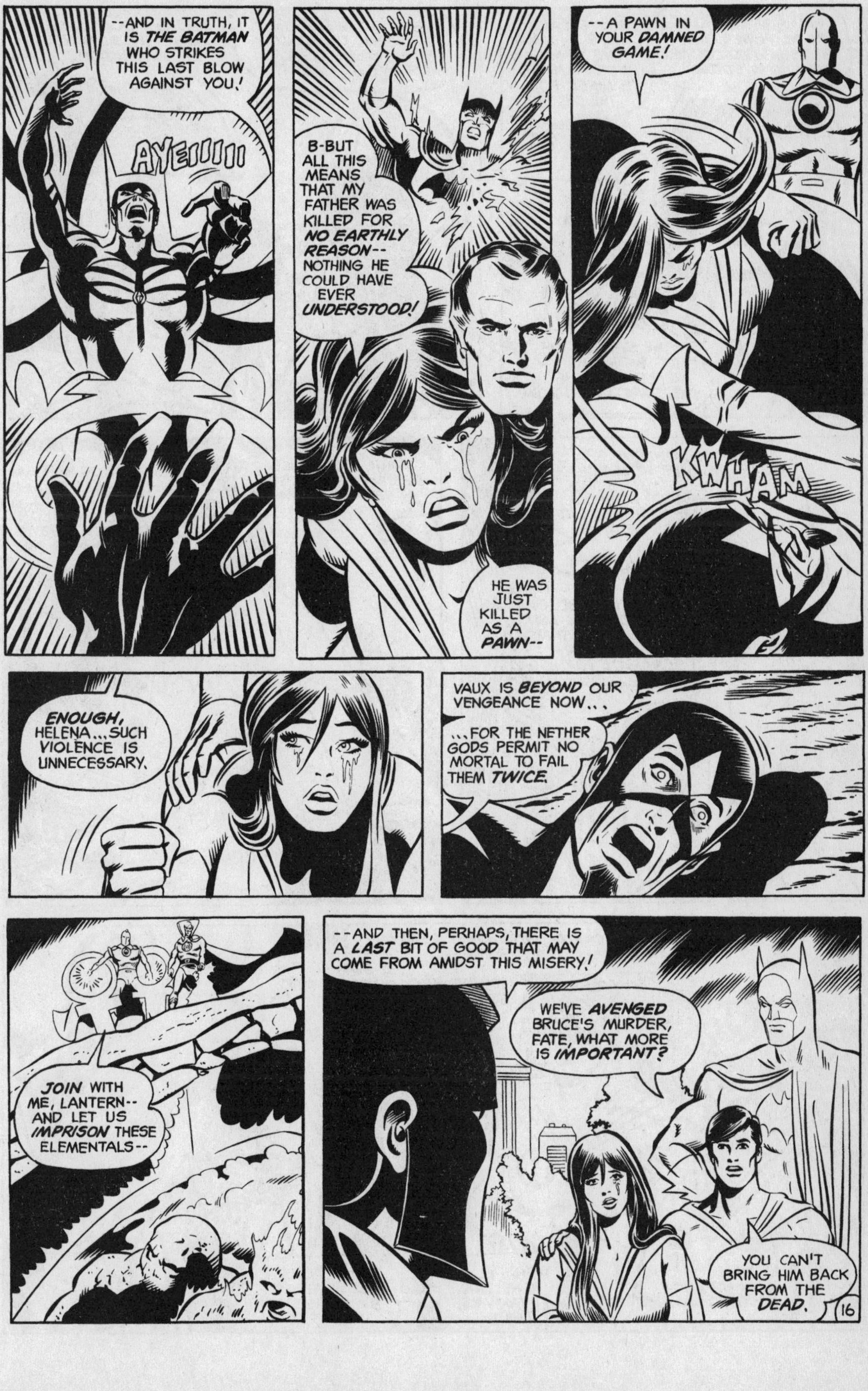
--AND IN TRUTH, IT IS THE BATMAN WHO STRIKES THIS LAST BLOW AGAINST YOU!
AYEIIIII
B-BUT ALL THIS MEANS THAT MY FATHER WAS KILLED FOR NO EARTHLY REASON-- NOTHING HE COULD HAVE EVER UNDERSTOOD!
HE WAS JUST KILLED AS A PAWN--
--A PAWN IN YOUR DAMNED GAME!
KWHAM
ENOUGH, HELENA...SUCH VIOLENCE IS UNNECESSARY.
VAUX IS BEYOND OUR VENGEANCE NOW...
...FOR THE NETHER GODS PERMIT NO MORTAL TO FAIL THEM TWICE.
JOIN WITH ME, LANTERN-- AND LET US IMPRISON THESE ELEMENTALS--
--AND THEN, PERHAPS, THERE IS A LAST BIT OF GOOD THAT MAY COME FROM AMIDST THIS MISERY!
WE'VE AVENGED BRUCE'S MURDER, FATE, WHAT MORE IS IMPORTANT?
YOU CAN'T BRING HIM BACK FROM THE DEAD.
16

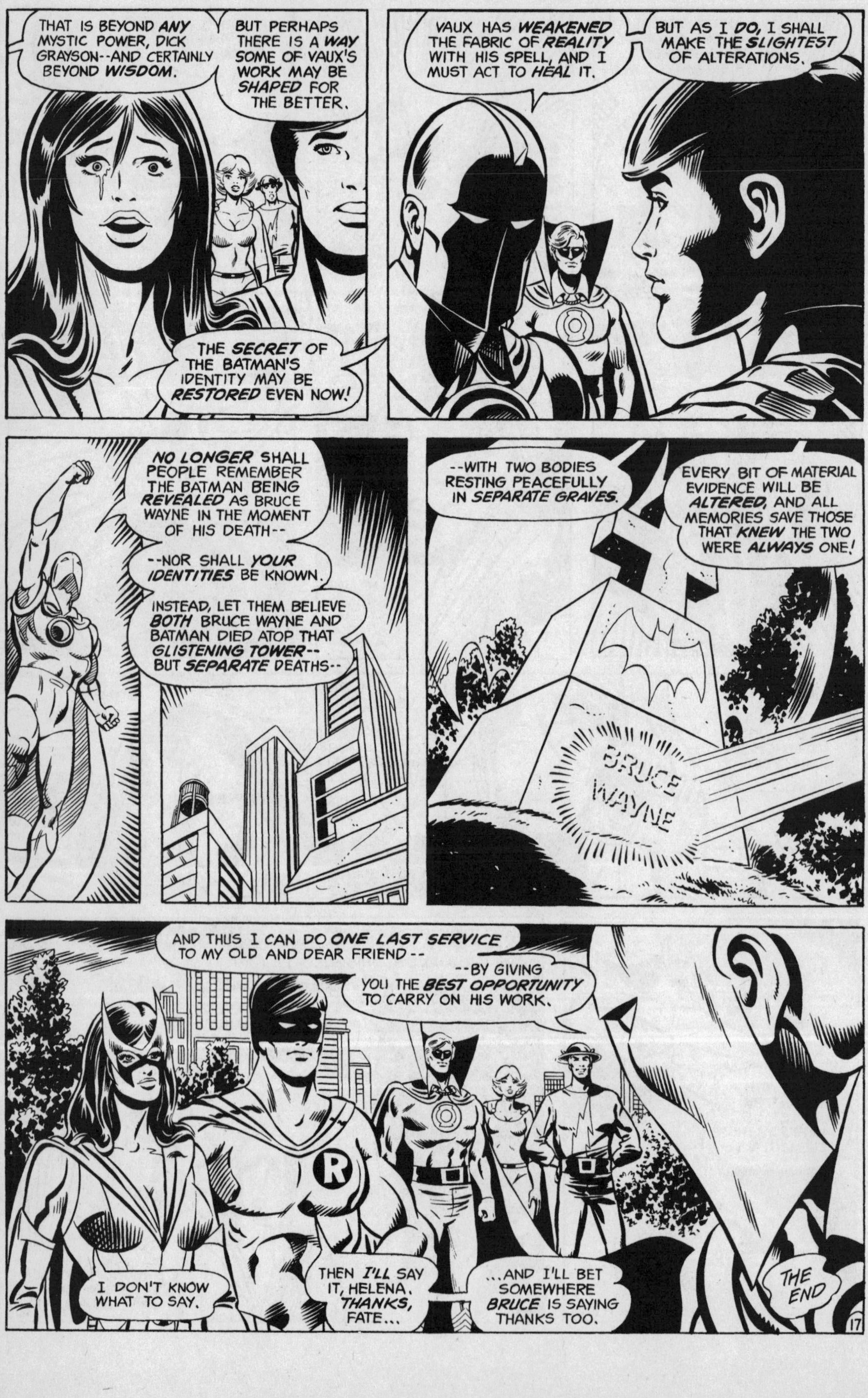
THAT IS BEYOND ANY MYSTIC POWER, DICK GRAYSON--AND CERTAINLY BEYOND WISDOM.
BUT PERHAPS THERE IS A WAY SOME OF VAUX'S WORK MAY BE SHAPED FOR THE BETTER.
THE SECRET OF THE BATMAN'S IDENTITY MAY BE RESTORED EVEN NOW!
VAUX HAS WEAKENED THE FABRIC OF REALITY WITH HIS SPELL, AND I MUST ACT TO HEAL IT.
BUT AS I DO, I SHALL MAKE THE SLIGHTEST OF ALTERATIONS.
NO LONGER SHALL PEOPLE REMEMBER THE BATMAN BEING REVEALED AS BRUCE WAYNE IN THE MOMENT OF HIS DEATH--
--NOR SHALL YOUR IDENTITIES BE KNOWN.
INSTEAD, LET THEM BELIEVE BOTH BRUCE WAYNE AND BATMAN DIED ATOP THAT GLISTENING TOWER-- BUT SEPARATE DEATHS--
--WITH TWO BODIES RESTING PEACEFULLY IN SEPARATE GRAVES.
EVERY BIT OF MATERIAL EVIDENCE WILL BE ALTERED, AND ALL MEMORIES SAVE THOSE THAT KNEW THE TWO WERE ALWAYS ONE!
BRUCE WAYNE
AND THUS I CAN DO ONE LAST SERVICE TO MY OLD AND DEAR FRIEND--
--BY GIVING YOU THE BEST OPPORTUNITY TO CARRY ON HIS WORK.
I DON'T KNOW WHAT TO SAY.
THEN I'LL SAY IT, HELENA. THANKS, FATE...
...AND I'LL BET SOMEWHERE BRUCE IS SAYING THANKS TOO.
THE END
17

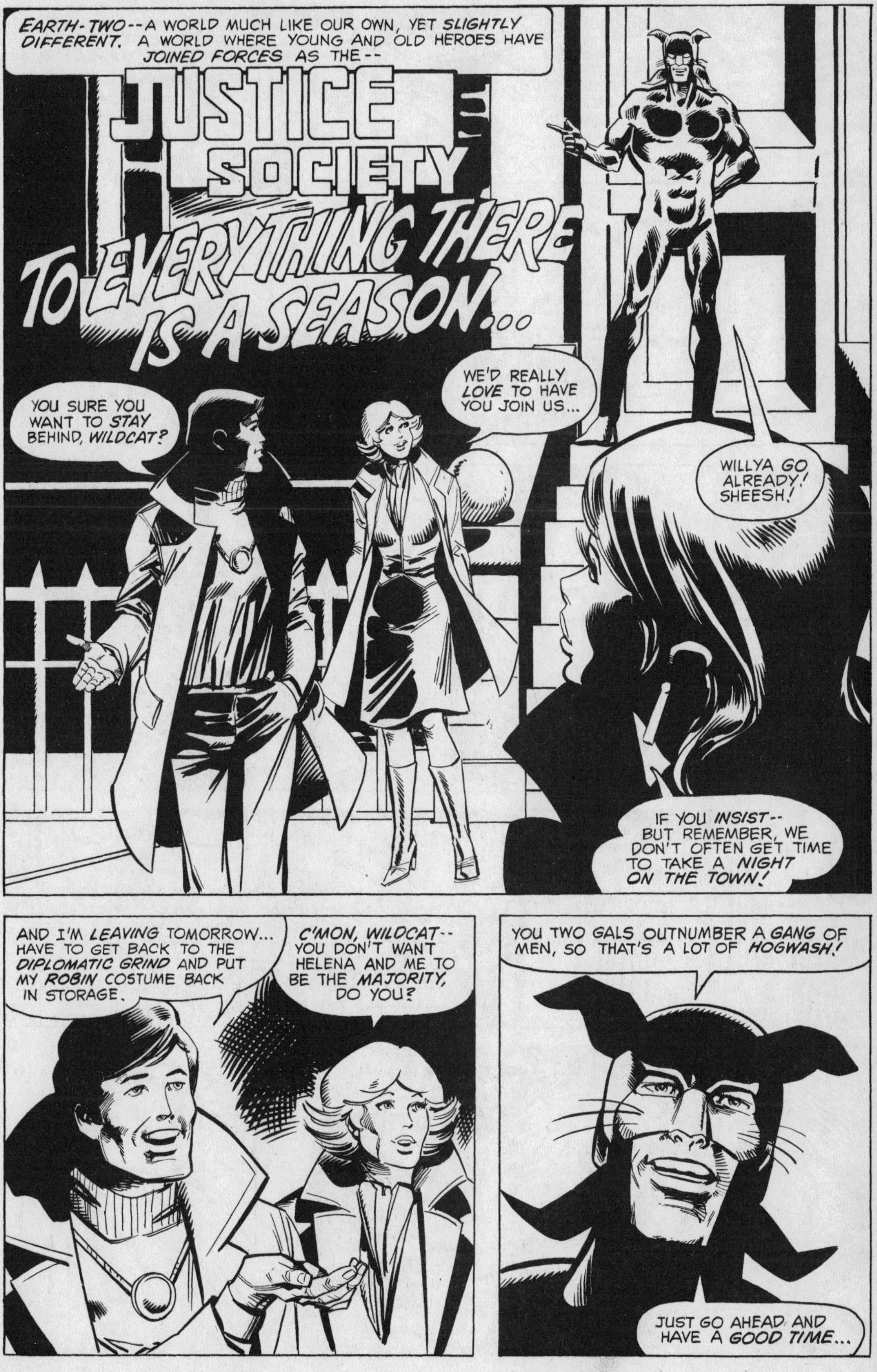
EARTH-TWO--A WORLD MUCH LIKE OUR OWN, YET SLIGHTLY DIFFERENT. A WORLD WHERE YOUNG AND OLD HEROES HAVE JOINED FORCES AS THE--
JUSTICE SOCIETY
TO EVERYTHING THERE IS A SEASON...
YOU SURE YOU WANT TO STAY BEHIND, WILDCAT?
WE'D REALLY LOVE TO HAVE YOU JOIN US...
WILLYA GO ALREADY! SHEESH!
IF YOU INSIST-- BUT REMEMBER, WE DON'T OFTEN GET TIME TO TAKE A NIGHT ON THE TOWN!
AND I'M LEAVING TOMORROW... HAVE TO GET BACK TO THE DIPLOMATIC GRIND AND PUT MY ROBIN COSTUME BACK IN STORAGE.
C'MON, WILDCAT-- YOU DON'T WANT HELENA AND ME TO BE THE MAJORITY, DO YOU?
YOU TWO GALS OUTNUMBER A GANG OF MEN, SO THAT'S A LOT OF HOGWASH!
JUST GO AHEAD AND HAVE A GOOD TIME...

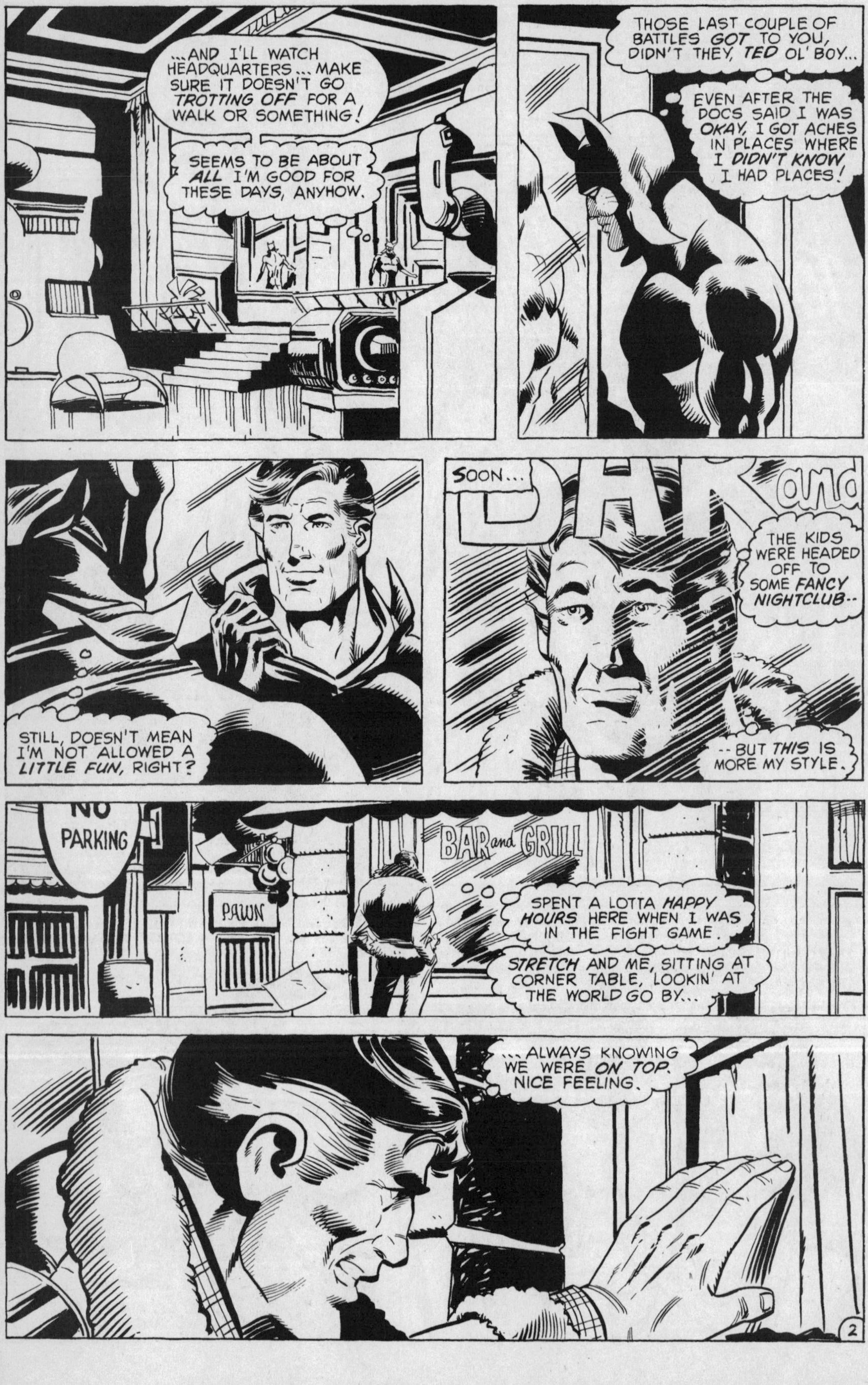
...AND I'LL WATCH HEADQUARTERS... MAKE SURE IT DOESN'T GO TROTTING OFF FOR A WALK OR SOMETHING!
SEEMS TO BE ABOUT ALL I'M GOOD FOR THESE DAYS, ANYHOW.
THOSE LAST COUPLE OF BATTLES GOT TO YOU, DIDN'T THEY, TED OL' BOY...
EVEN AFTER THE DOCS SAID I WAS OKAY, I GOT ACHES IN PLACES WHERE I DIDN'T KNOW I HAD PLACES!
STILL, DOESN'T MEAN I'M NOT ALLOWED A LITTLE FUN, RIGHT?
SOON...
THE KIDS WERE HEADED OFF TO SOME FANCY NIGHTCLUB--
--BUT THIS IS MORE MY STYLE.
NO PARKING
BAR and GRILL
PAWN
SPENT A LOTTA HAPPY HOURS HERE WHEN I WAS IN THE FIGHT GAME.
STRETCH AND ME, SITTING AT CORNER TABLE, LOOKIN' AT THE WORLD GO BY...
...ALWAYS KNOWING WE WERE ON TOP. NICE FEELING.
2

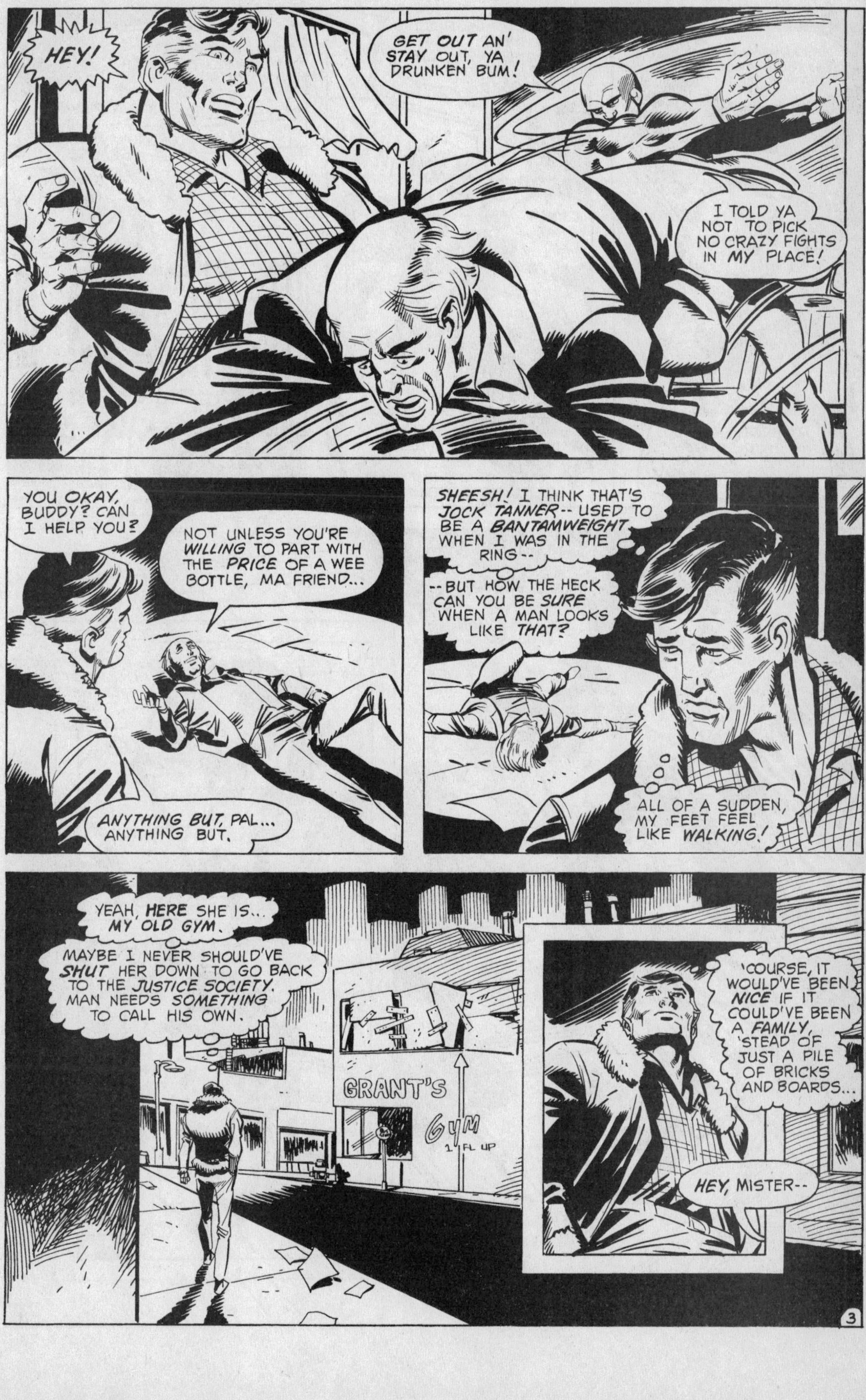
HEY!
GET OUT AN' STAY OUT, YA DRUNKEN BUM!
I TOLD YA NOT TO PICK NO CRAZY FIGHTS IN MY PLACE!
YOU OKAY, BUDDY? CAN I HELP YOU?
NOT UNLESS YOU'RE WILLING TO PART WITH THE PRICE OF A WEE BOTTLE, MA FRIEND...
ANYTHING BUT, PAL... ANYTHING BUT.
SHEESH! I THINK THAT'S JOCK TANNER-- USED TO BE A BANTAMWEIGHT WHEN I WAS IN THE RING--
--BUT HOW THE HECK CAN YOU BE SURE WHEN A MAN LOOKS LIKE THAT?
ALL OF A SUDDEN, MY FEET FEEL LIKE WALKING!
YEAH, HERE SHE IS... MY OLD GYM.
MAYBE I NEVER SHOULD'VE SHUT HER DOWN TO GO BACK TO THE JUSTICE SOCIETY. MAN NEEDS SOMETHING TO CALL HIS OWN.
GRANT'S
GYM
1 FL UP
'COURSE, IT WOULD'VE BEEN NICE IF IT COULD'VE BEEN A FAMILY, 'STEAD OF JUST A PILE OF BRICKS AND BOARDS...
HEY, MISTER--
3

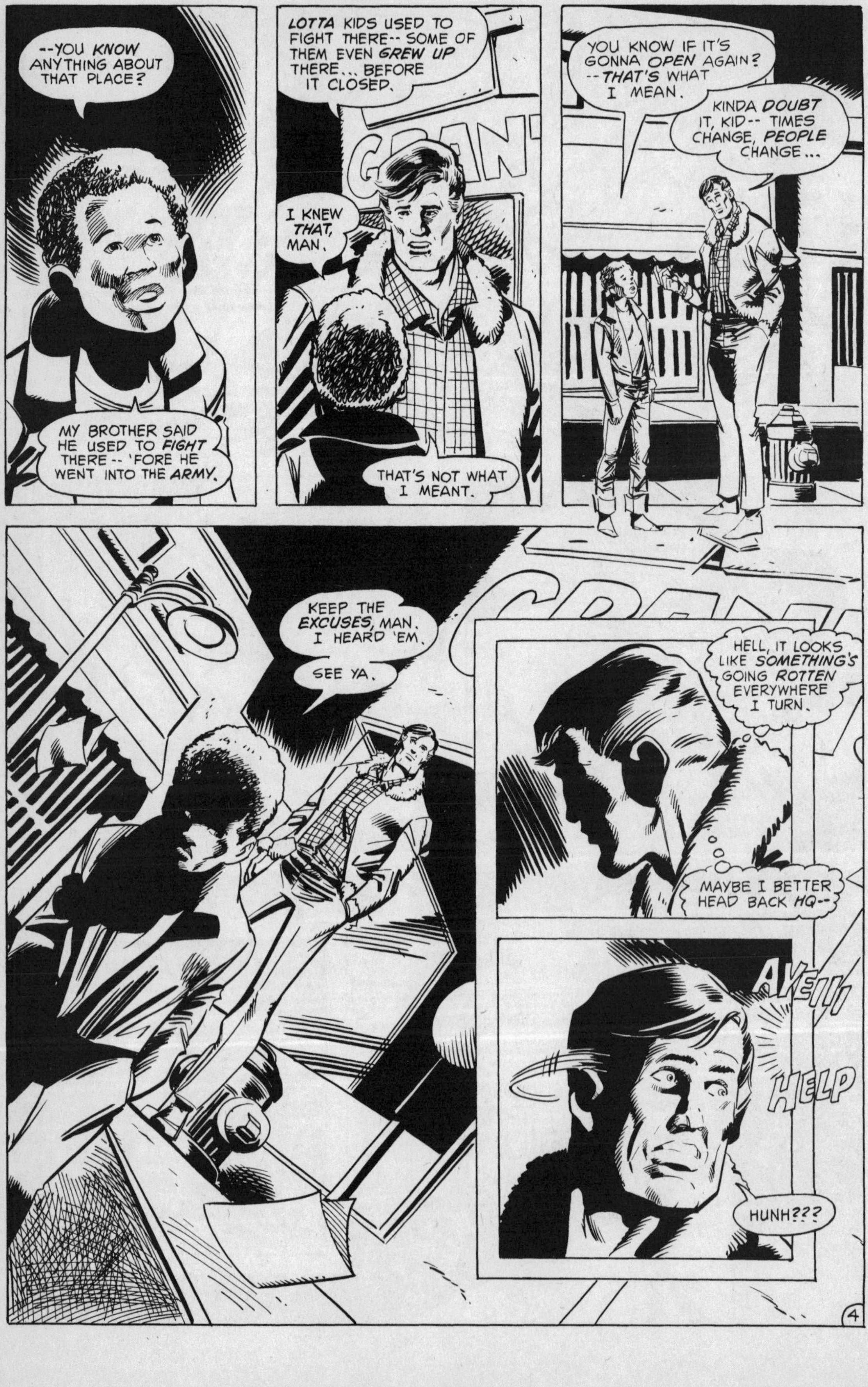
--YOU KNOW ANYTHING ABOUT THAT PLACE?
MY BROTHER SAID HE USED TO FIGHT THERE -- 'FORE HE WENT INTO THE ARMY.
LOTTA KIDS USED TO FIGHT THERE-- SOME OF THEM EVEN GREW UP THERE... BEFORE IT CLOSED.
I KNEW THAT, MAN.
THAT'S NOT WHAT I MEANT.
YOU KNOW IF IT'S GONNA OPEN AGAIN? --THAT'S WHAT I MEAN.
KINDA DOUBT IT, KID-- TIMES CHANGE, PEOPLE CHANGE...
KEEP THE EXCUSES, MAN. I HEARD 'EM.
SEE YA.
HELL, IT LOOKS LIKE SOMETHING'S GOING ROTTEN EVERYWHERE I TURN.
MAYBE I BETTER HEAD BACK HQ--
AYEIII
HELP
HUNH???
4

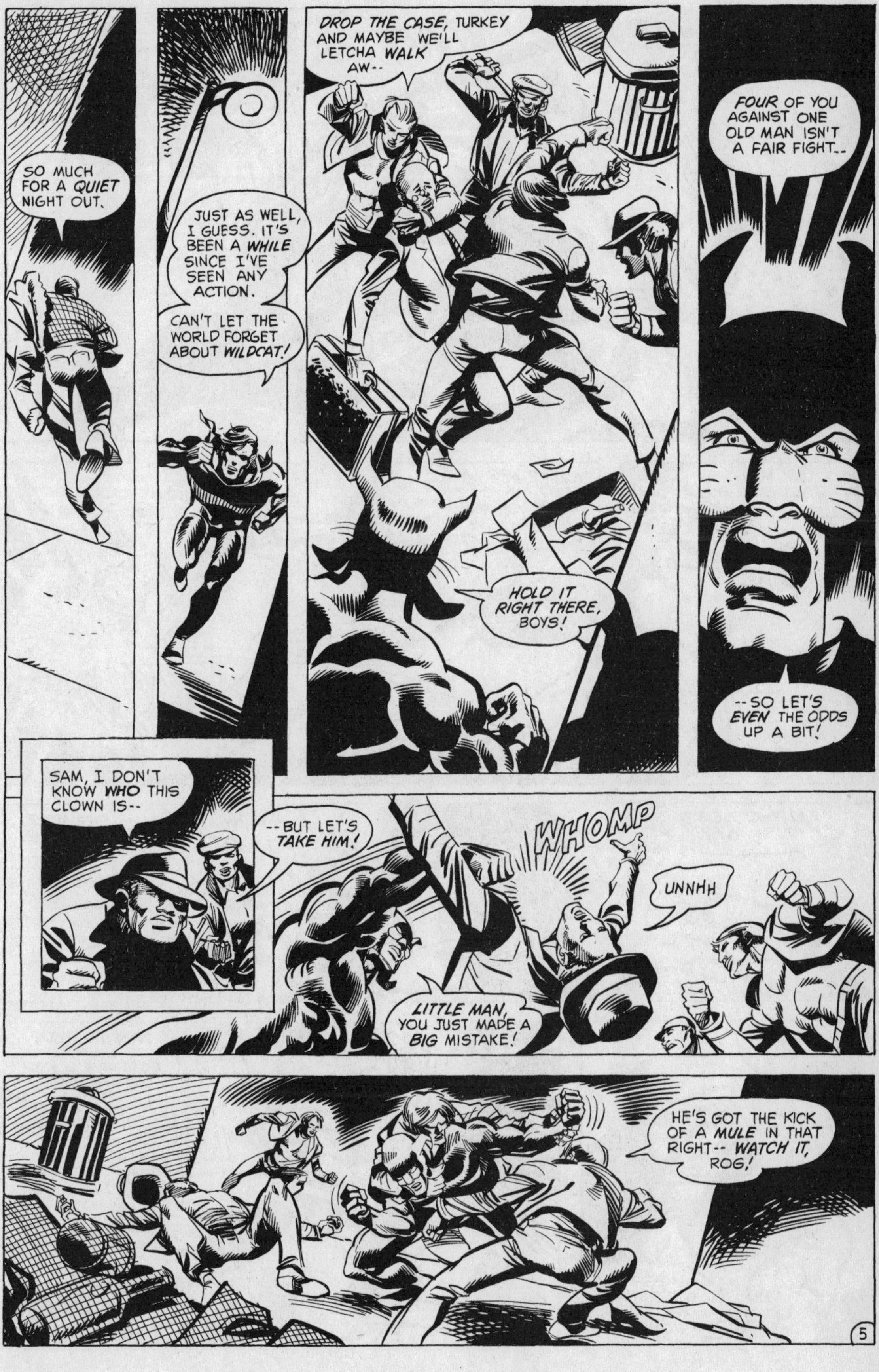
SO MUCH FOR A QUIET NIGHT OUT.
JUST AS WELL, I GUESS. IT'S BEEN A WHILE SINCE I'VE SEEN ANY ACTION.
CAN'T LET THE WORLD FORGET ABOUT WILDCAT!
DROP THE CASE, TURKEY AND MAYBE WE'LL LETCHA WALK AW--
HOLD IT RIGHT THERE, BOYS!
FOUR OF YOU AGAINST ONE OLD MAN ISN'T A FAIR FIGHT..
--SO LET'S EVEN THE ODDS UP A BIT!
SAM, I DON'T KNOW WHO THIS CLOWN IS--
--BUT LET'S TAKE HIM!
WHOMP
UNNHH
LITTLE MAN, YOU JUST MADE A BIG MISTAKE!
HE'S GOT THE KICK OF A MULE IN THAT RIGHT-- WATCH IT, ROG!
5

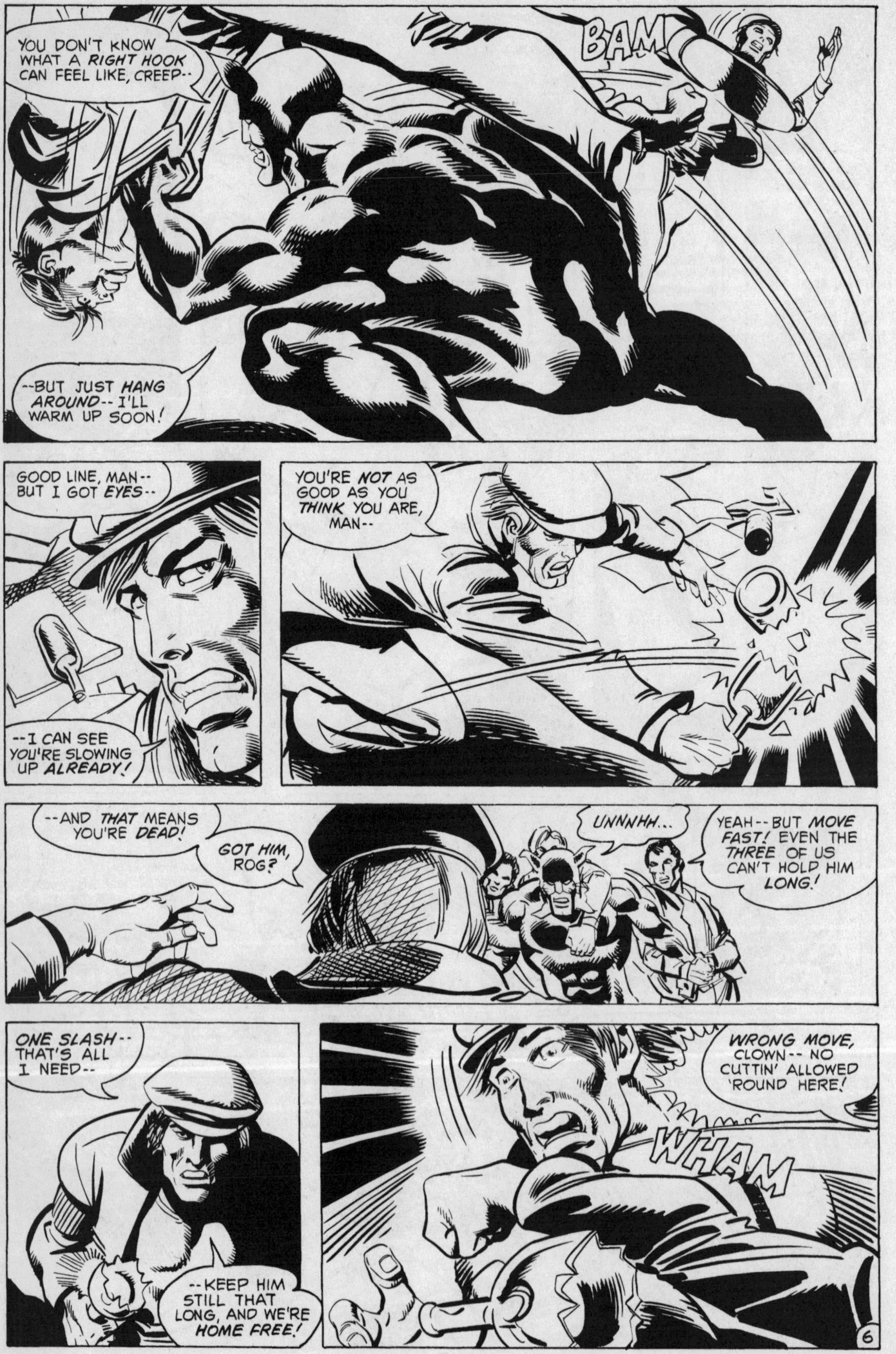
YOU DON'T KNOW WHAT A RIGHT HOOK CAN FEEL LIKE, CREEP--
BAM
--BUT JUST HANG AROUND--I'LL WARM UP SOON!
GOOD LINE, MAN-- BUT I GOT EYES--
--I CAN SEE YOU'RE SLOWING UP ALREADY!
YOU'RE NOT AS GOOD AS YOU THINK YOU ARE, MAN--
--AND THAT MEANS YOU'RE DEAD!
GOT HIM, ROG?
UNNNHH...
YEAH--BUT MOVE FAST! EVEN THE THREE OF US CAN'T HOLD HIM LONG!
ONE SLASH-- THAT'S ALL I NEED--
--KEEP HIM STILL THAT LONG, AND WE'RE HOME FREE!
WRONG MOVE, CLOWN--NO CUTTIN' ALLOWED 'ROUND HERE!
WHAM
6

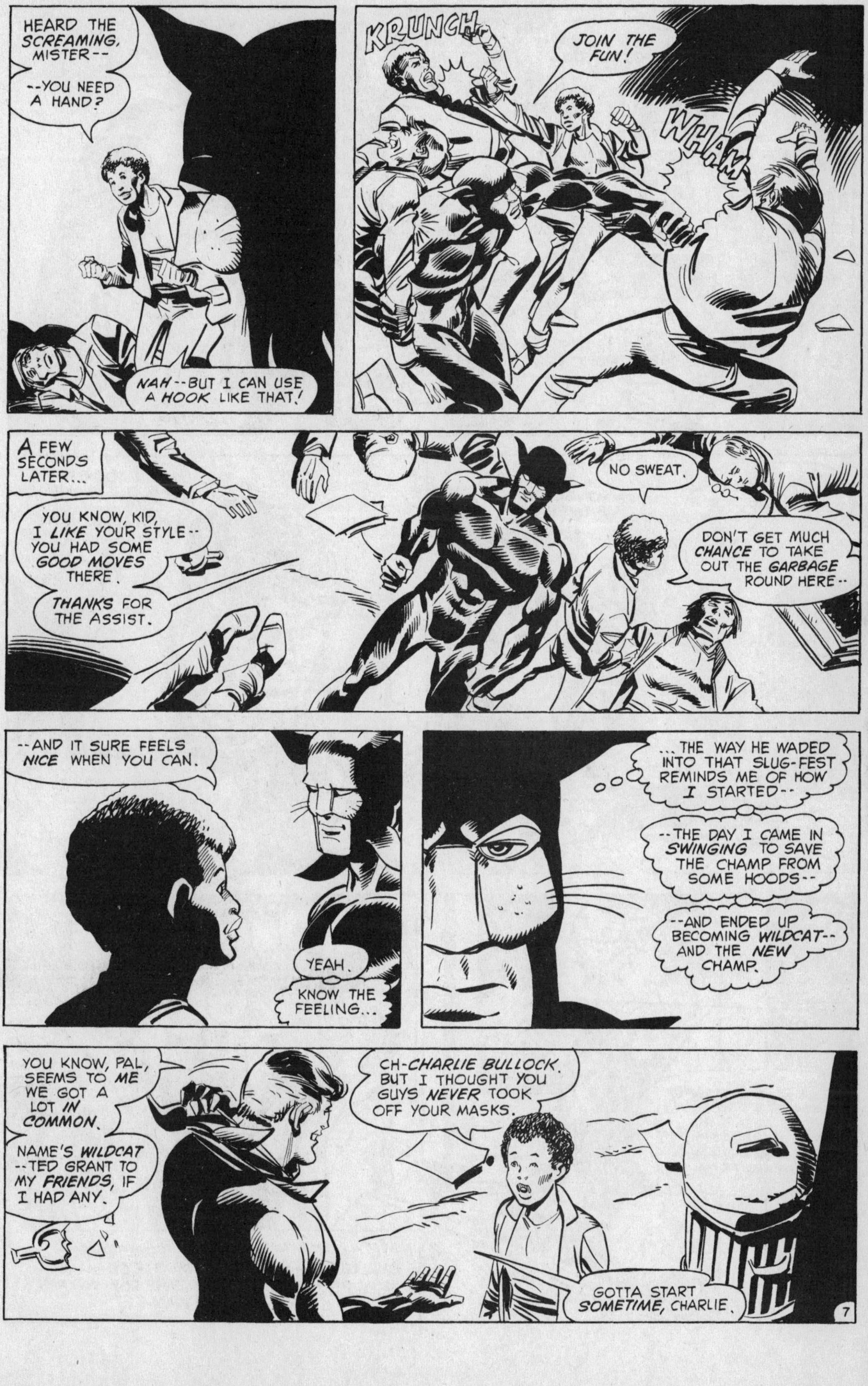
HEARD THE SCREAMING, MISTER--
--YOU NEED A HAND?
NAH--BUT I CAN USE A HOOK LIKE THAT!
KRUNCH
JOIN THE FUN!
WHAM
A FEW SECONDS LATER...
YOU KNOW, KID, I LIKE YOUR STYLE--YOU HAD SOME GOOD MOVES THERE.
THANKS FOR THE ASSIST.
NO SWEAT.
DON'T GET MUCH CHANCE TO TAKE OUT THE GARBAGE ROUND HERE--
--AND IT SURE FEELS NICE WHEN YOU CAN.
YEAH.
KNOW THE FEELING...
...THE WAY HE WADED INTO THAT SLUG-FEST REMINDS ME OF HOW I STARTED--
--THE DAY I CAME IN SWINGING TO SAVE THE CHAMP FROM SOME HOODS--
--AND ENDED UP BECOMING WILDCAT--AND THE NEW CHAMP.
YOU KNOW, PAL, SEEMS TO ME WE GOT A LOT IN COMMON.
NAME'S WILDCAT--TED GRANT TO MY FRIENDS, IF I HAD ANY.
CH-CHARLIE BULLOCK. BUT I THOUGHT YOU GUYS NEVER TOOK OFF YOUR MASKS.
GOTTA START SOMETIME, CHARLIE.
7

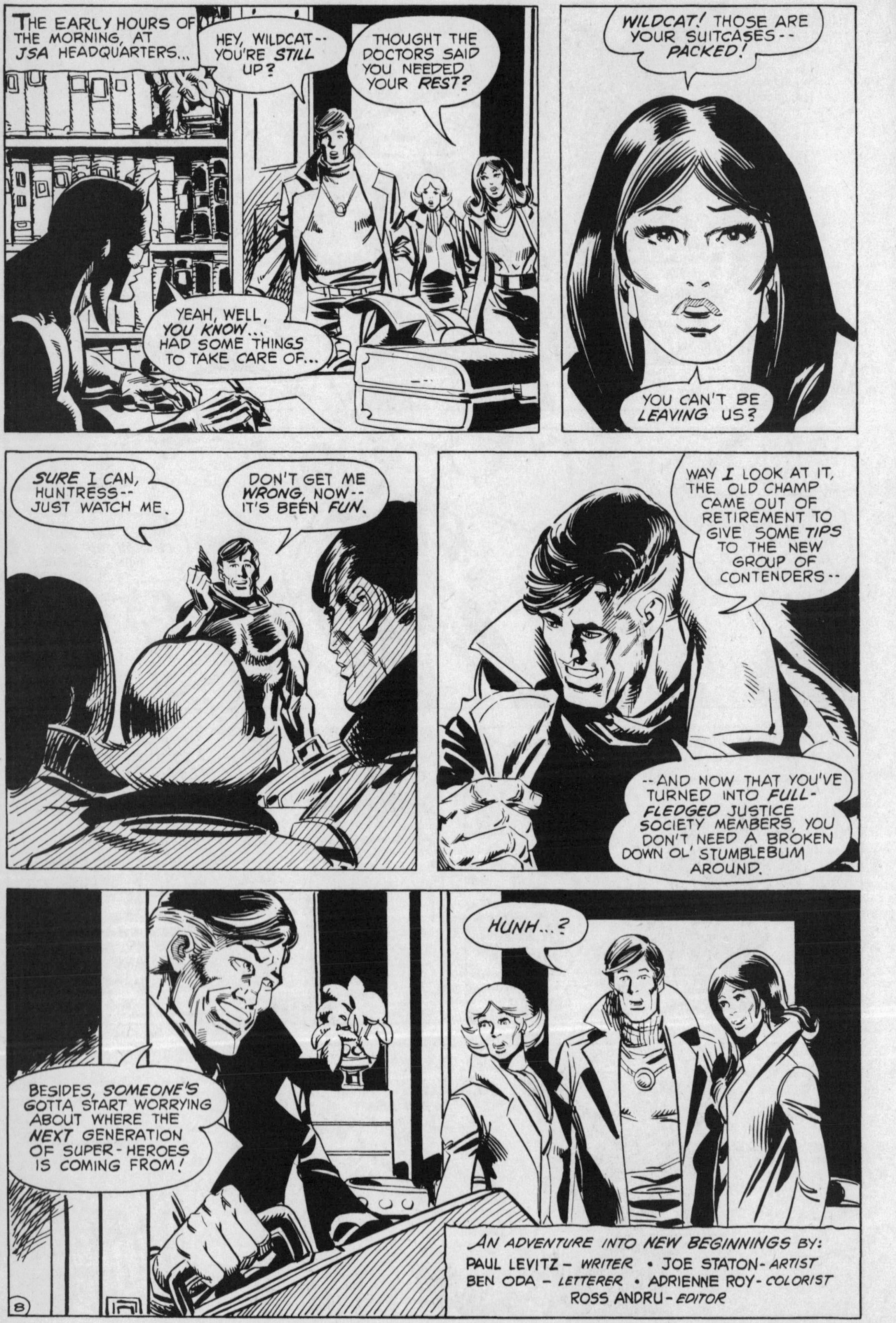
THE EARLY HOURS OF THE MORNING, AT JSA HEADQUARTERS...
HEY, WILDCAT-- YOU'RE STILL UP?
THOUGHT THE DOCTORS SAID YOU NEEDED YOUR REST?
YEAH, WELL, YOU KNOW... HAD SOME THINGS TO TAKE CARE OF...
WILDCAT! THOSE ARE YOUR SUITCASES-- PACKED!
YOU CAN'T BE LEAVING US?
SURE I CAN, HUNTRESS-- JUST WATCH ME.
DON'T GET ME WRONG, NOW-- IT'S BEEN FUN.
WAY I LOOK AT IT, THE OLD CHAMP CAME OUT OF RETIREMENT TO GIVE SOME TIPS TO THE NEW GROUP OF CONTENDERS--
--AND NOW THAT YOU'VE TURNED INTO FULL-FLEDGED JUSTICE SOCIETY MEMBERS, YOU DON'T NEED A BROKEN DOWN OL' STUMBLEBUM AROUND.
BESIDES, SOMEONE'S GOTTA START WORRYING ABOUT WHERE THE NEXT GENERATION OF SUPER-HEROES IS COMING FROM!
HUNH...?
AN ADVENTURE INTO NEW BEGINNINGS BY:
PAUL LEVITZ - WRITER • JOE STATON - ARTIST
BEN ODA - LETTERER • ADRIENNE ROY - COLORIST
ROSS ANDRU - EDITOR
8

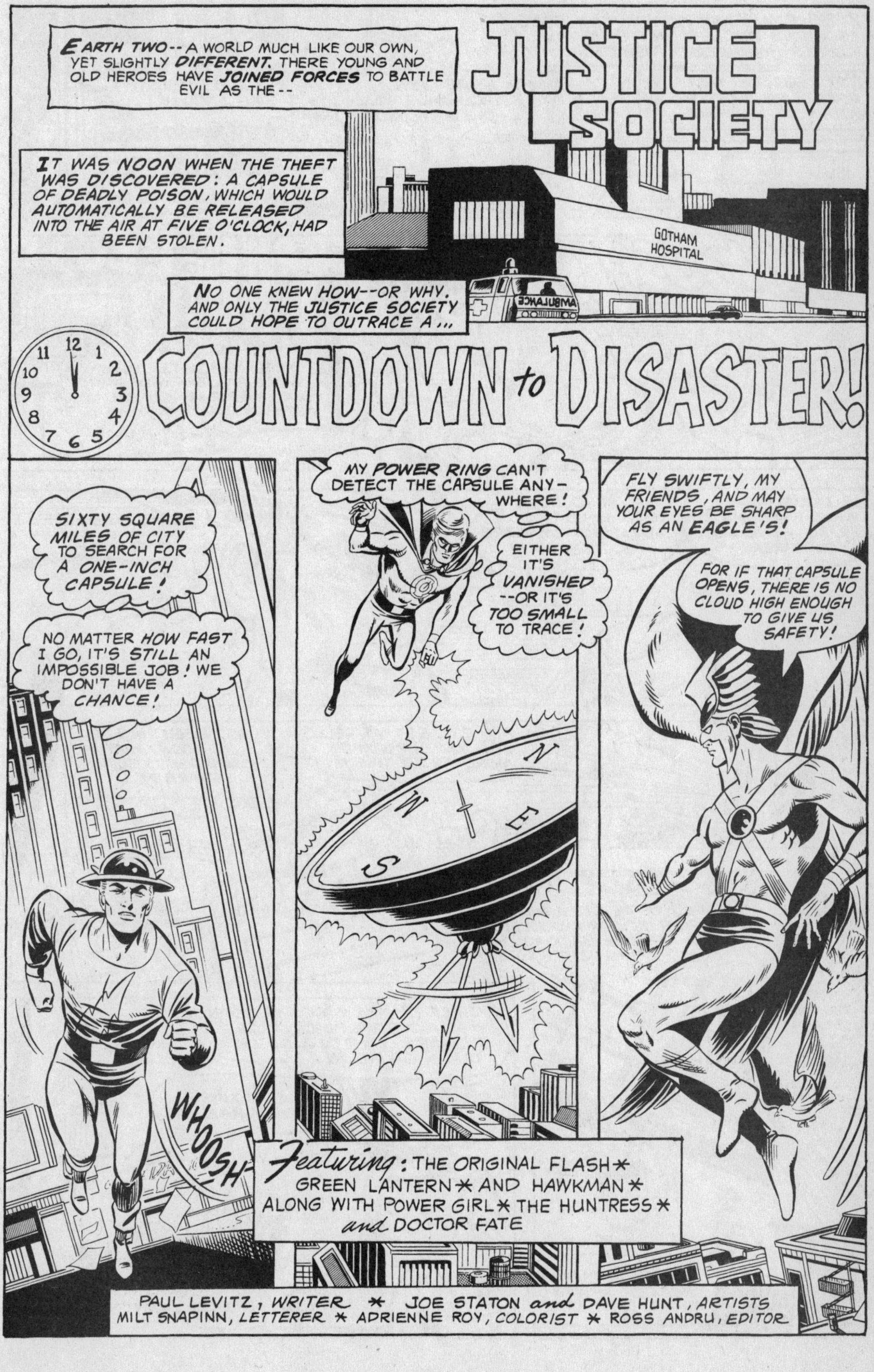
EARTH TWO-- A WORLD MUCH LIKE OUR OWN, YET SLIGHTLY DIFFERENT. THERE YOUNG AND OLD HEROES HAVE JOINED FORCES TO BATTLE EVIL AS THE--
JUSTICE SOCIETY
IT WAS NOON WHEN THE THEFT WAS DISCOVERED: A CAPSULE OF DEADLY POISON, WHICH WOULD AUTOMATICALLY BE RELEASED INTO THE AIR AT FIVE O'CLOCK, HAD BEEN STOLEN.
GOTHAM HOSPITAL
NO ONE KNEW HOW--OR WHY. AND ONLY THE JUSTICE SOCIETY COULD HOPE TO OUTRACE A...
COUNTDOWN to DISASTER!
SIXTY SQUARE MILES OF CITY TO SEARCH FOR A ONE-INCH CAPSULE!
NO MATTER HOW FAST I GO, IT'S STILL AN IMPOSSIBLE JOB! WE DON'T HAVE A CHANCE!
WHOOSH
MY POWER RING CAN'T DETECT THE CAPSULE ANYWHERE!
EITHER IT'S VANISHED --OR IT'S TOO SMALL TO TRACE!
FLY SWIFTLY, MY FRIENDS, AND MAY YOUR EYES BE SHARP AS AN EAGLE'S!
FOR IF THAT CAPSULE OPENS, THERE IS NO CLOUD HIGH ENOUGH TO GIVE US SAFETY!
Featuring: THE ORIGINAL FLASH * GREEN LANTERN * AND HAWKMAN * ALONG WITH POWER GIRL * THE HUNTRESS * and DOCTOR FATE
PAUL LEVITZ, WRITER * JOE STATON and DAVE HUNT, ARTISTS
MILT SNAPINN, LETTERER * ADRIENNE ROY, COLORIST * ROSS ANDRU, EDITOR

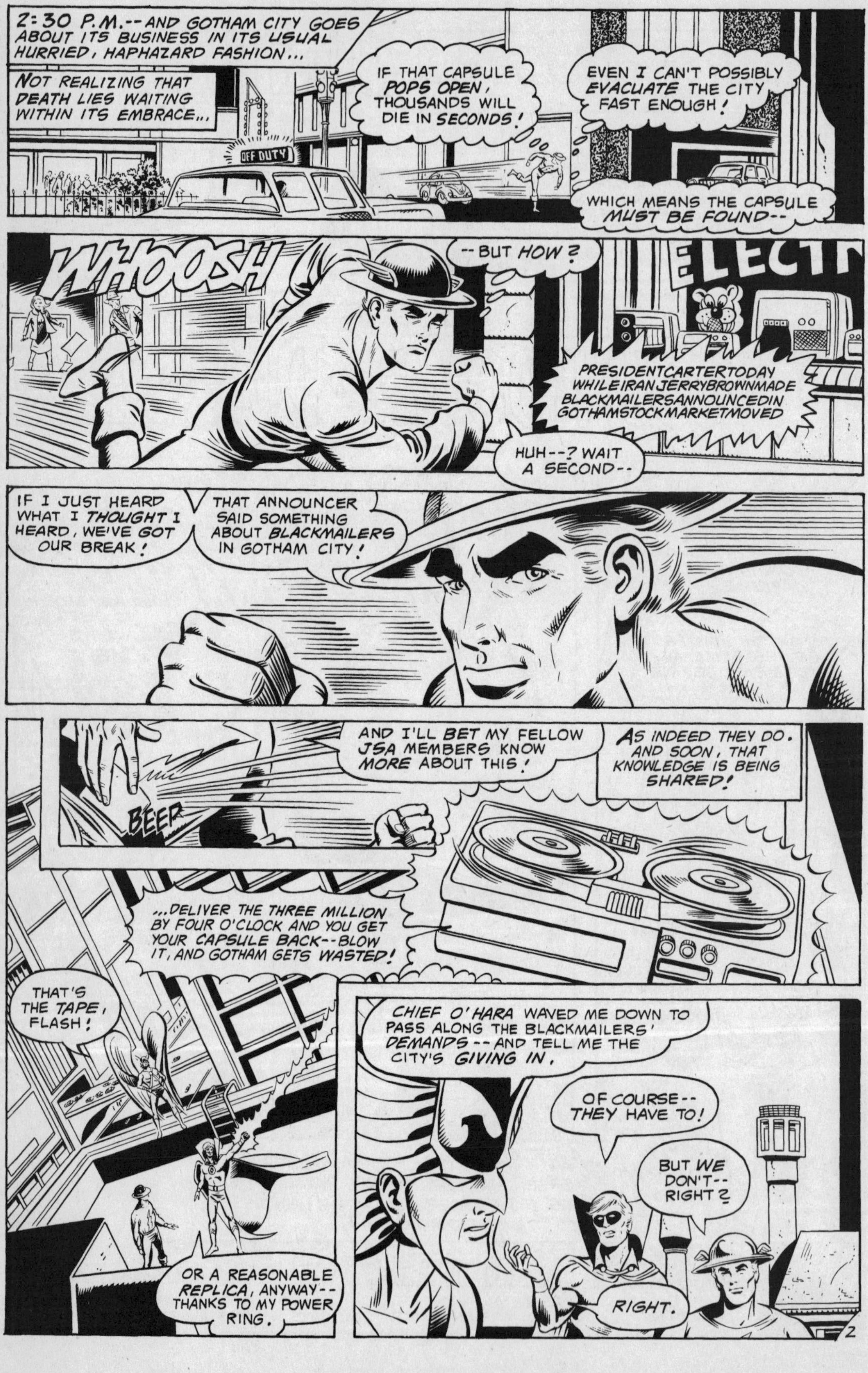
2:30 P.M.-- AND GOTHAM CITY GOES ABOUT ITS BUSINESS IN ITS USUAL HURRIED, HAPHAZARD FASHION...
NOT REALIZING THAT DEATH LIES WAITING WITHIN ITS EMBRACE...
OFF DUTY
IF THAT CAPSULE POPS OPEN, THOUSANDS WILL DIE IN SECONDS!
EVEN I CAN'T POSSIBLY EVACUATE THE CITY FAST ENOUGH!
WHICH MEANS THE CAPSULE MUST BE FOUND--
WHOOSH
--BUT HOW?
ELECT
PRESIDENTCARTERTODAY WHILEIRANJERRYBROWNMADE BLACKMAILERSANNOUNCEDIN GOTHAMSTOCKMARKETMOVED
HUH--? WAIT A SECOND--
IF I JUST HEARD WHAT I THOUGHT I HEARD, WE'VE GOT OUR BREAK!
THAT ANNOUNCER SAID SOMETHING ABOUT BLACKMAILERS IN GOTHAM CITY!
AND I'LL BET MY FELLOW JSA MEMBERS KNOW MORE ABOUT THIS!
AS INDEED THEY DO. AND SOON, THAT KNOWLEDGE IS BEING SHARED!
BEEP
...DELIVER THE THREE MILLION BY FOUR O'CLOCK AND YOU GET YOUR CAPSULE BACK--BLOW IT, AND GOTHAM GETS WASTED!
THAT'S THE TAPE, FLASH!
OR A REASONABLE REPLICA, ANYWAY-- THANKS TO MY POWER RING.
CHIEF O'HARA WAVED ME DOWN TO PASS ALONG THE BLACKMAILERS' DEMANDS--AND TELL ME THE CITY'S GIVING IN.
OF COURSE-- THEY HAVE TO!
BUT WE DON'T-- RIGHT?
RIGHT.
2

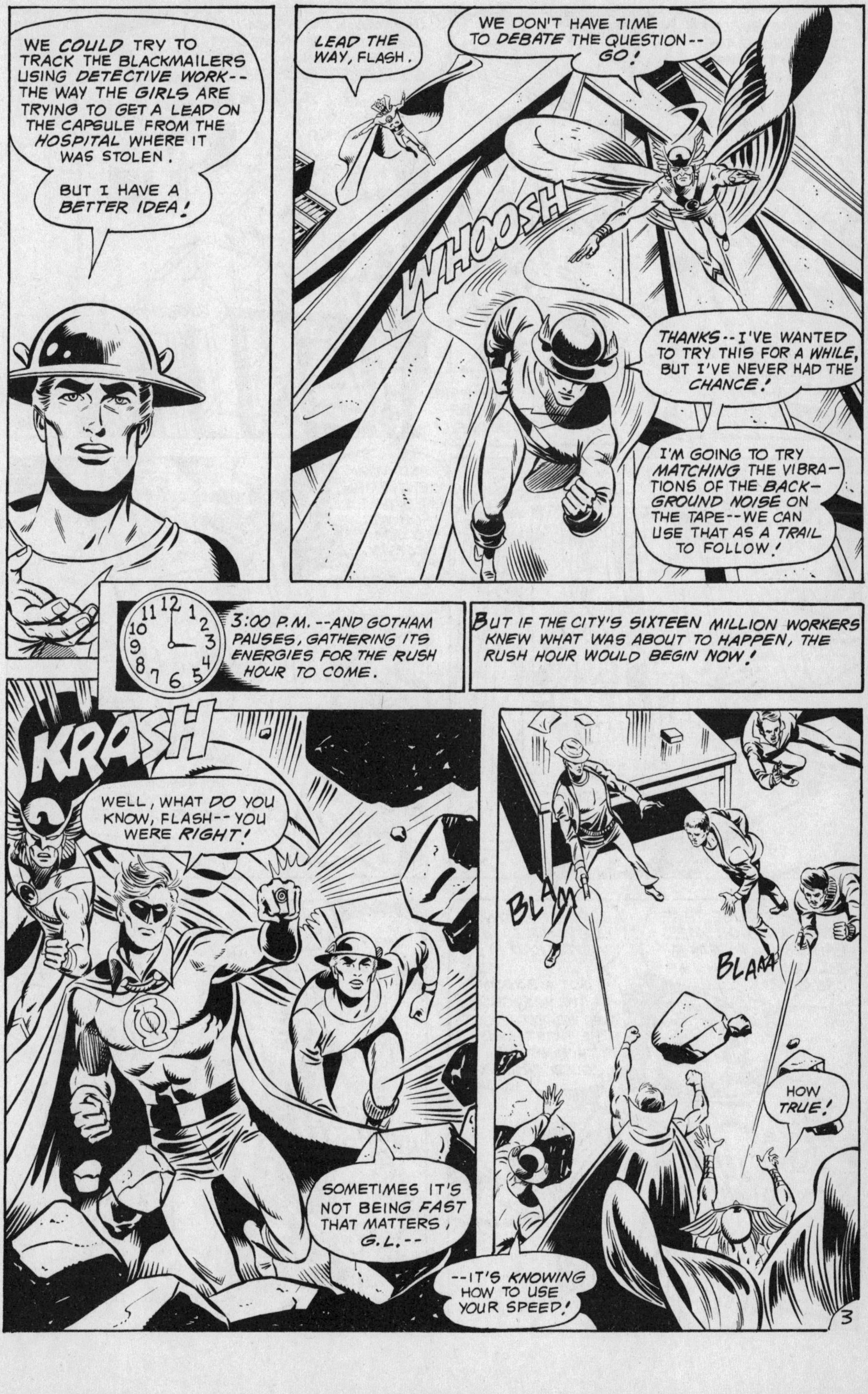
WE COULD TRY TO TRACK THE BLACKMAILERS USING DETECTIVE WORK-- THE WAY THE GIRLS ARE TRYING TO GET A LEAD ON THE CAPSULE FROM THE HOSPITAL WHERE IT WAS STOLEN.
BUT I HAVE A BETTER IDEA!
LEAD THE WAY, FLASH.
WE DON'T HAVE TIME TO DEBATE THE QUESTION-- GO!
WHOOSH
THANKS--I'VE WANTED TO TRY THIS FOR A WHILE, BUT I'VE NEVER HAD THE CHANCE!
I'M GOING TO TRY MATCHING THE VIBRATIONS OF THE BACKGROUND NOISE ON THE TAPE--WE CAN USE THAT AS A TRAIL TO FOLLOW!
3:00 P.M.--AND GOTHAM PAUSES, GATHERING ITS ENERGIES FOR THE RUSH HOUR TO COME.
BUT IF THE CITY'S SIXTEEN MILLION WORKERS KNEW WHAT WAS ABOUT TO HAPPEN, THE RUSH HOUR WOULD BEGIN NOW!
KRASH
WELL, WHAT DO YOU KNOW, FLASH--YOU WERE RIGHT!
SOMETIMES IT'S NOT BEING FAST THAT MATTERS, G.L.--
--IT'S KNOWING HOW TO USE YOUR SPEED!
BLAM
BLAAA
HOW TRUE!
3

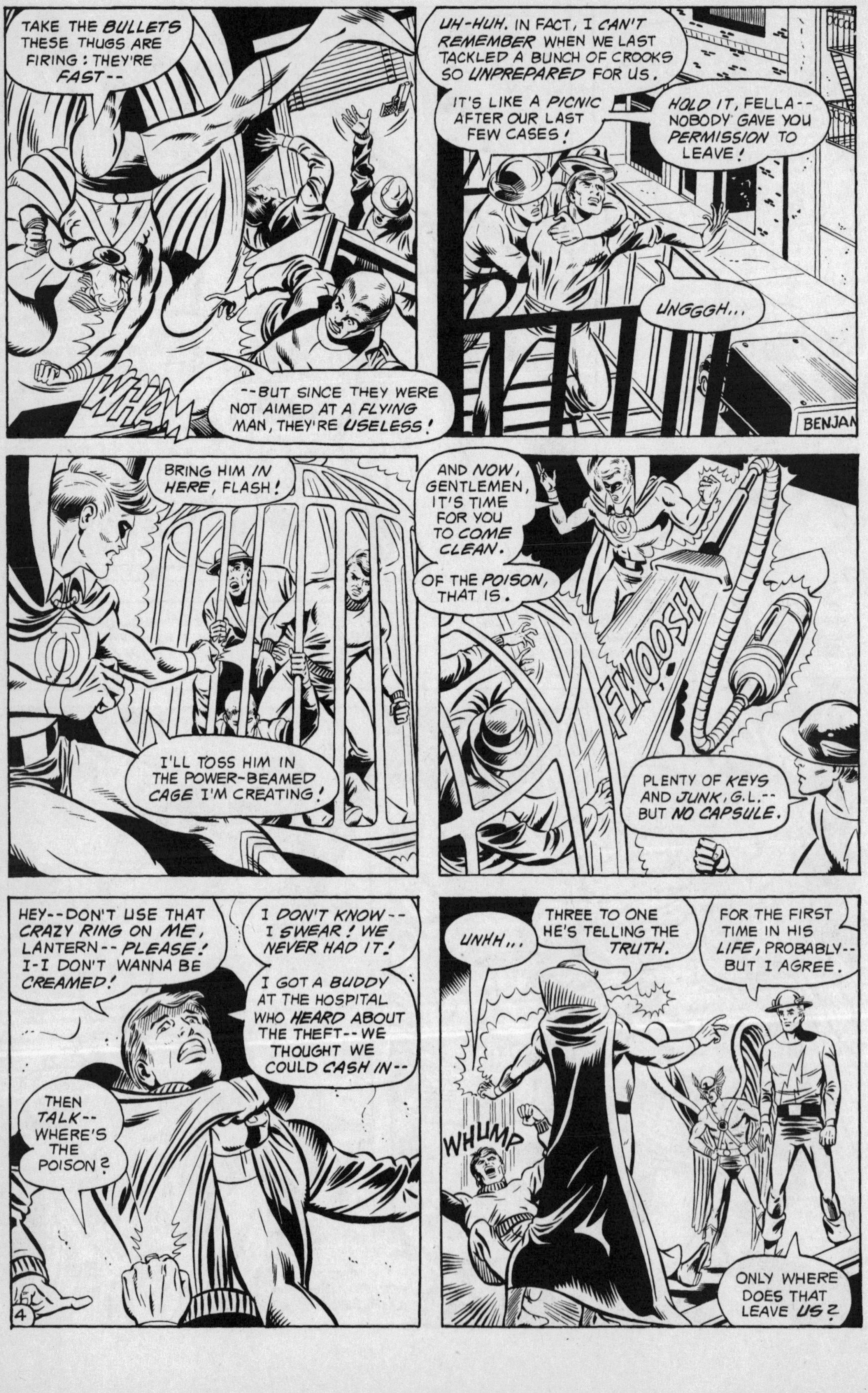
TAKE THE BULLETS THESE THUGS ARE FIRING: THEY'RE FAST--
WHAM
--BUT SINCE THEY WERE NOT AIMED AT A FLYING MAN, THEY'RE USELESS!
UH-HUH. IN FACT, I CAN'T REMEMBER WHEN WE LAST TACKLED A BUNCH OF CROOKS SO UNPREPARED FOR US.
IT'S LIKE A PICNIC AFTER OUR LAST FEW CASES!
HOLD IT, FELLA--NOBODY GAVE YOU PERMISSION TO LEAVE!
UNGGGH...
BRING HIM IN HERE, FLASH!
I'LL TOSS HIM IN THE POWER-BEAMED CAGE I'M CREATING!
AND NOW, GENTLEMEN, IT'S TIME FOR YOU TO COME CLEAN.
OF THE POISON, THAT IS.
FWOOSH
PLENTY OF KEYS AND JUNK, G.L.--BUT NO CAPSULE.
HEY--DON'T USE THAT CRAZY RING ON ME, LANTERN--PLEASE! I-I DON'T WANNA BE CREAMED!
I DON'T KNOW--I SWEAR! WE NEVER HAD IT!
I GOT A BUDDY AT THE HOSPITAL WHO HEARD ABOUT THE THEFT--WE THOUGHT WE COULD CASH IN--
THEN TALK--WHERE'S THE POISON?
4
UNHH...
THREE TO ONE HE'S TELLING THE TRUTH.
FOR THE FIRST TIME IN HIS LIFE, PROBABLY--BUT I AGREE.
WHUMP
ONLY WHERE DOES THAT LEAVE US?

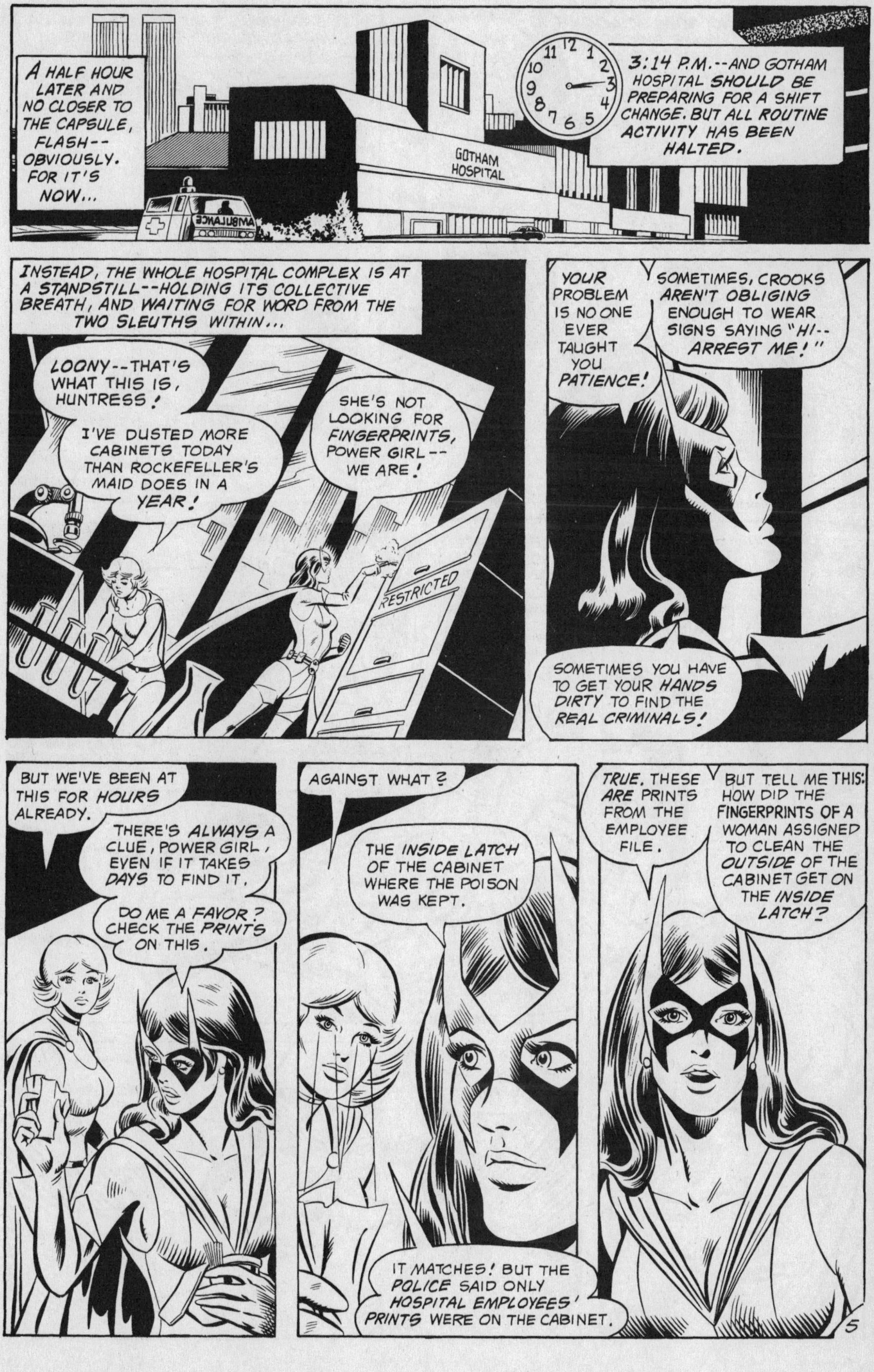
A HALF HOUR LATER AND NO CLOSER TO THE CAPSULE, FLASH--OBVIOUSLY. FOR IT'S NOW...
3:14 P.M.--AND GOTHAM HOSPITAL SHOULD BE PREPARING FOR A SHIFT CHANGE. BUT ALL ROUTINE ACTIVITY HAS BEEN HALTED.
GOTHAM HOSPITAL
AMBULANCE
INSTEAD, THE WHOLE HOSPITAL COMPLEX IS AT A STANDSTILL--HOLDING ITS COLLECTIVE BREATH, AND WAITING FOR WORD FROM THE TWO SLEUTHS WITHIN...
LOONY--THAT'S WHAT THIS IS, HUNTRESS!
I'VE DUSTED MORE CABINETS TODAY THAN ROCKEFELLER'S MAID DOES IN A YEAR!
SHE'S NOT LOOKING FOR FINGERPRINTS, POWER GIRL--WE ARE!
RESTRICTED
YOUR PROBLEM IS NO ONE EVER TAUGHT YOU PATIENCE!
SOMETIMES, CROOKS AREN'T OBLIGING ENOUGH TO WEAR SIGNS SAYING "HI--ARREST ME!"
SOMETIMES YOU HAVE TO GET YOUR HANDS DIRTY TO FIND THE REAL CRIMINALS!
BUT WE'VE BEEN AT THIS FOR HOURS ALREADY.
THERE'S ALWAYS A CLUE, POWER GIRL, EVEN IF IT TAKES DAYS TO FIND IT.
DO ME A FAVOR? CHECK THE PRINTS ON THIS.
AGAINST WHAT?
THE INSIDE LATCH OF THE CABINET WHERE THE POISON WAS KEPT.
IT MATCHES! BUT THE POLICE SAID ONLY HOSPITAL EMPLOYEES' PRINTS WERE ON THE CABINET.
TRUE. THESE ARE PRINTS FROM THE EMPLOYEE FILE.
BUT TELL ME THIS: HOW DID THE FINGERPRINTS OF A WOMAN ASSIGNED TO CLEAN THE OUTSIDE OF THE CABINET GET ON THE INSIDE LATCH?
5

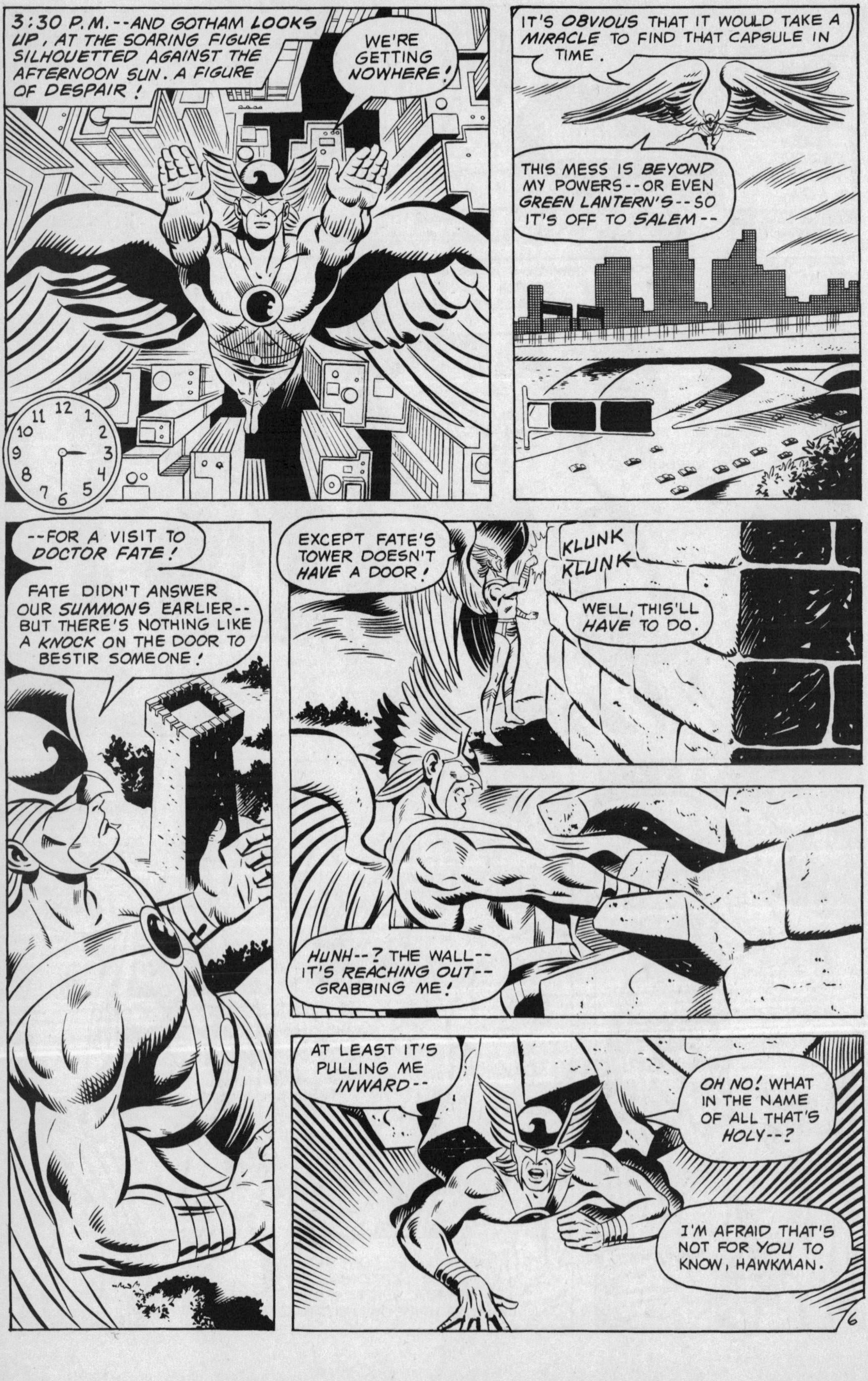
3:30 P.M.--AND GOTHAM LOOKS UP, AT THE SOARING FIGURE SILHOUETTED AGAINST THE AFTERNOON SUN. A FIGURE OF DESPAIR!
WE'RE GETTING NOWHERE!
12 1 2 3 4 5 6 7 8 9 10 11
IT'S OBVIOUS THAT IT WOULD TAKE A MIRACLE TO FIND THAT CAPSULE IN TIME.
THIS MESS IS BEYOND MY POWERS--OR EVEN GREEN LANTERN'S--SO IT'S OFF TO SALEM--
--FOR A VISIT TO DOCTOR FATE!
FATE DIDN'T ANSWER OUR SUMMONS EARLIER--BUT THERE'S NOTHING LIKE A KNOCK ON THE DOOR TO BESTIR SOMEONE!
EXCEPT FATE'S TOWER DOESN'T HAVE A DOOR!
KLUNK
KLUNK
WELL, THIS'LL HAVE TO DO.
HUNH--? THE WALL--IT'S REACHING OUT--GRABBING ME!
AT LEAST IT'S PULLING ME INWARD--
OH NO! WHAT IN THE NAME OF ALL THAT'S HOLY--?
I'M AFRAID THAT'S NOT FOR YOU TO KNOW, HAWKMAN.
6

3:45 P.M.--AND GOTHAM OFFICE-WORKERS STARE OUT THEIR WINDOWS ONCE AGAIN, AS TWO WOMEN FLASH BY, IN A RACE AGAINST TIME.

SORRY ABOUT THE *SUDDEN LEAP,* BUT IT'S HARD TO MANEUVER UP HERE--

--I HAVE TO TAKE THE *BOUNCES* WHEN I CAN.

NO SWEAT, POWER GIRL-- IT'S NOT THE *JUMP* THAT KNOCKED THE WIND OUT OF ME, ANYWAY.

REMEMBER, SUPERMAN STARTED TAKING ME FOR *PIGGY-BACK* RIDES BEFORE I COULD WALK!

I DON'T GET IT, THEN--*WHY?*

OH, I WAS THINKING OF THE *CLEANING WOMAN* WE'RE HERE TO SEE--

--AND *REALIZING* WHAT SOME PEOPLE WILL DO TO GET *MONEY!*

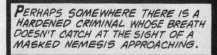

P̲ERHAPS SOMEWHERE THERE IS A HARDENED CRIMINAL WHOSE BREATH DOESN'T CATCH AT THE SIGHT OF A MASKED NEMESIS APPROACHING.

B̲UT THOSE WHO DRIFT INTO CRIME HAVE NO SUCH PROTECTIVE REFLEXES. FOR THEM, THE ARRIVAL OF A SUPER-HERO MEANS DISCOVERY--AND NO MORE PURPOSE IN HIDING.

YOU STOLE THE POISON CAPSULE FOR YOUR SON?

I DON'T UNDERSTAND.

WERE YOU TRYING TO *KILL HIM?*

NO! I WAS TRYIN' TO KEEP MICHAEL *ALIVE!*

I *DIDN'T CARE* WHAT IT WAS--POISON WAS GOOD AS *ANYTHIN'*--HE JUST *HADDA* HAVE SOMETHIN' TO TRADE!

THE BOY'S AN *ADDICT*--I FOUND HIS *WORKS* IN HIS ROOM.

HE MUST BE *TRADING* THE PUSHER'S HOSPITAL DRUGS FOR HIS FIXES!

OH--THEN SHE *WAS* TRYING TO KEEP HIM ALIVE.

7

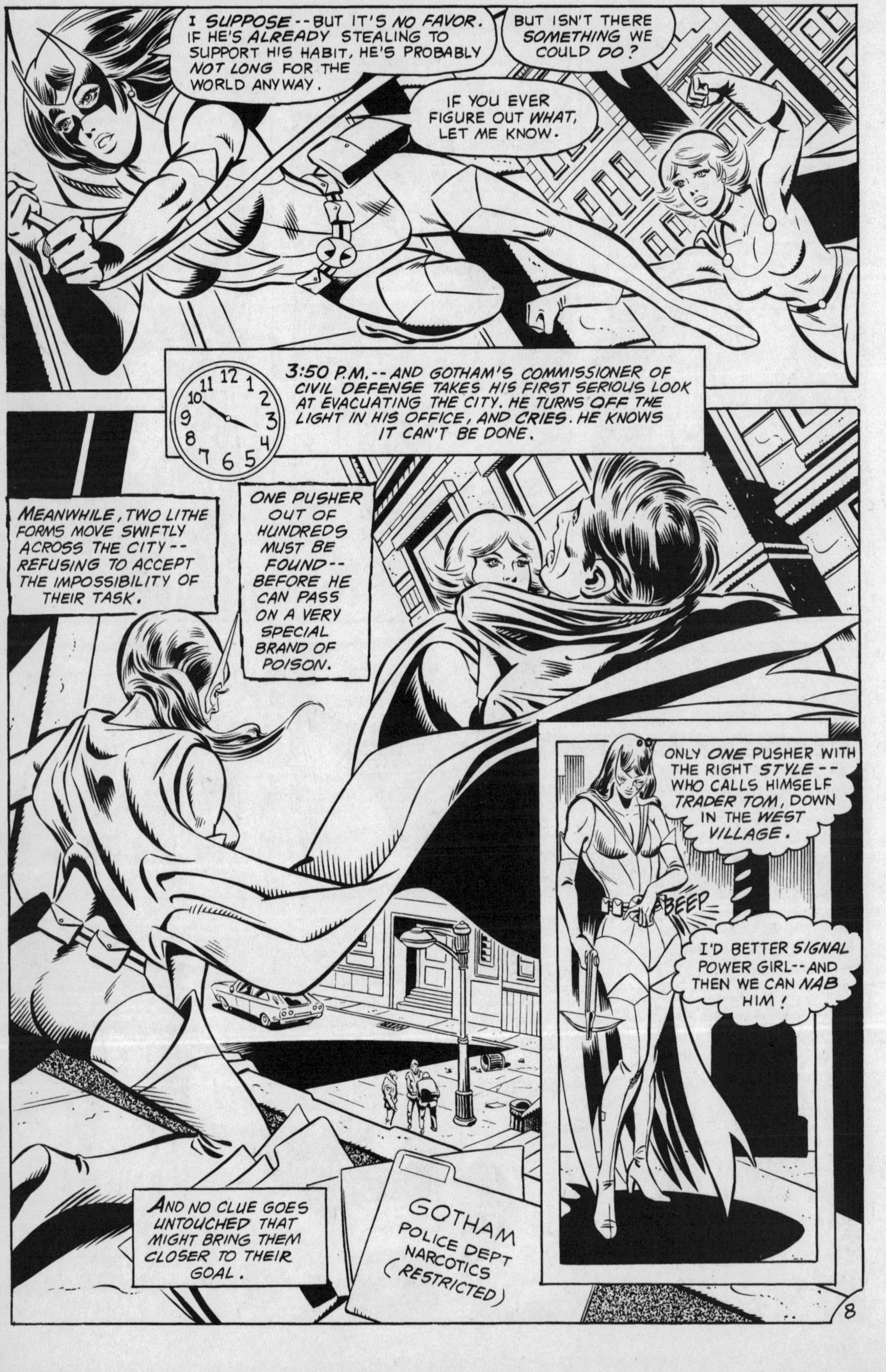

I SUPPOSE--BUT IT'S NO FAVOR. IF HE'S ALREADY STEALING TO SUPPORT HIS HABIT, HE'S PROBABLY NOT LONG FOR THE WORLD ANYWAY.
BUT ISN'T THERE SOMETHING WE COULD DO?
IF YOU EVER FIGURE OUT WHAT, LET ME KNOW.
3:50 P.M.--AND GOTHAM'S COMMISSIONER OF CIVIL DEFENSE TAKES HIS FIRST SERIOUS LOOK AT EVACUATING THE CITY. HE TURNS OFF THE LIGHT IN HIS OFFICE, AND CRIES. HE KNOWS IT CAN'T BE DONE.
MEANWHILE, TWO LITHE FORMS MOVE SWIFTLY ACROSS THE CITY--REFUSING TO ACCEPT THE IMPOSSIBILITY OF THEIR TASK.
ONE PUSHER OUT OF HUNDREDS MUST BE FOUND--BEFORE HE CAN PASS ON A VERY SPECIAL BRAND OF POISON.
AND NO CLUE GOES UNTOUCHED THAT MIGHT BRING THEM CLOSER TO THEIR GOAL.
GOTHAM POLICE DEPT NARCOTICS (RESTRICTED)
ONLY ONE PUSHER WITH THE RIGHT STYLE--WHO CALLS HIMSELF TRADER TOM, DOWN IN THE WEST VILLAGE.
BEEP
I'D BETTER SIGNAL POWER GIRL--AND THEN WE CAN NAB HIM!
8

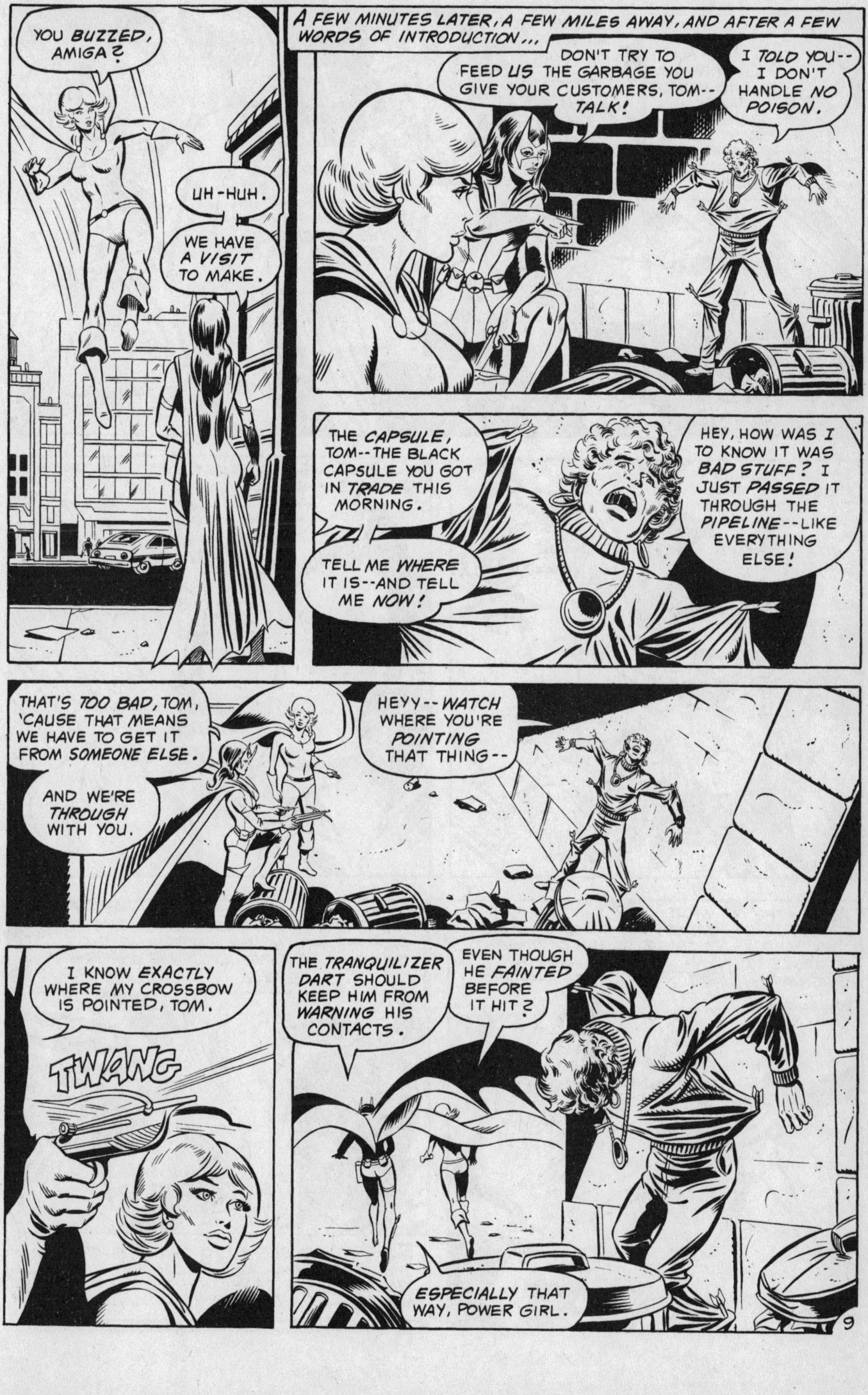
YOU BUZZED, AMIGA?
UH-HUH.
WE HAVE A VISIT TO MAKE.
A FEW MINUTES LATER, A FEW MILES AWAY, AND AFTER A FEW WORDS OF INTRODUCTION...
DON'T TRY TO FEED US THE GARBAGE YOU GIVE YOUR CUSTOMERS, TOM--TALK!
I TOLD YOU--I DON'T HANDLE NO POISON.
THE CAPSULE, TOM--THE BLACK CAPSULE YOU GOT IN TRADE THIS MORNING.
TELL ME WHERE IT IS--AND TELL ME NOW!
HEY, HOW WAS I TO KNOW IT WAS BAD STUFF? I JUST PASSED IT THROUGH THE PIPELINE--LIKE EVERYTHING ELSE!
THAT'S TOO BAD, TOM, 'CAUSE THAT MEANS WE HAVE TO GET IT FROM SOMEONE ELSE.
AND WE'RE THROUGH WITH YOU.
HEYY--WATCH WHERE YOU'RE POINTING THAT THING--
I KNOW EXACTLY WHERE MY CROSSBOW IS POINTED, TOM.
TWANG
THE TRANQUILIZER DART SHOULD KEEP HIM FROM WARNING HIS CONTACTS.
EVEN THOUGH HE FAINTED BEFORE IT HIT?
ESPECIALLY THAT WAY, POWER GIRL.
9

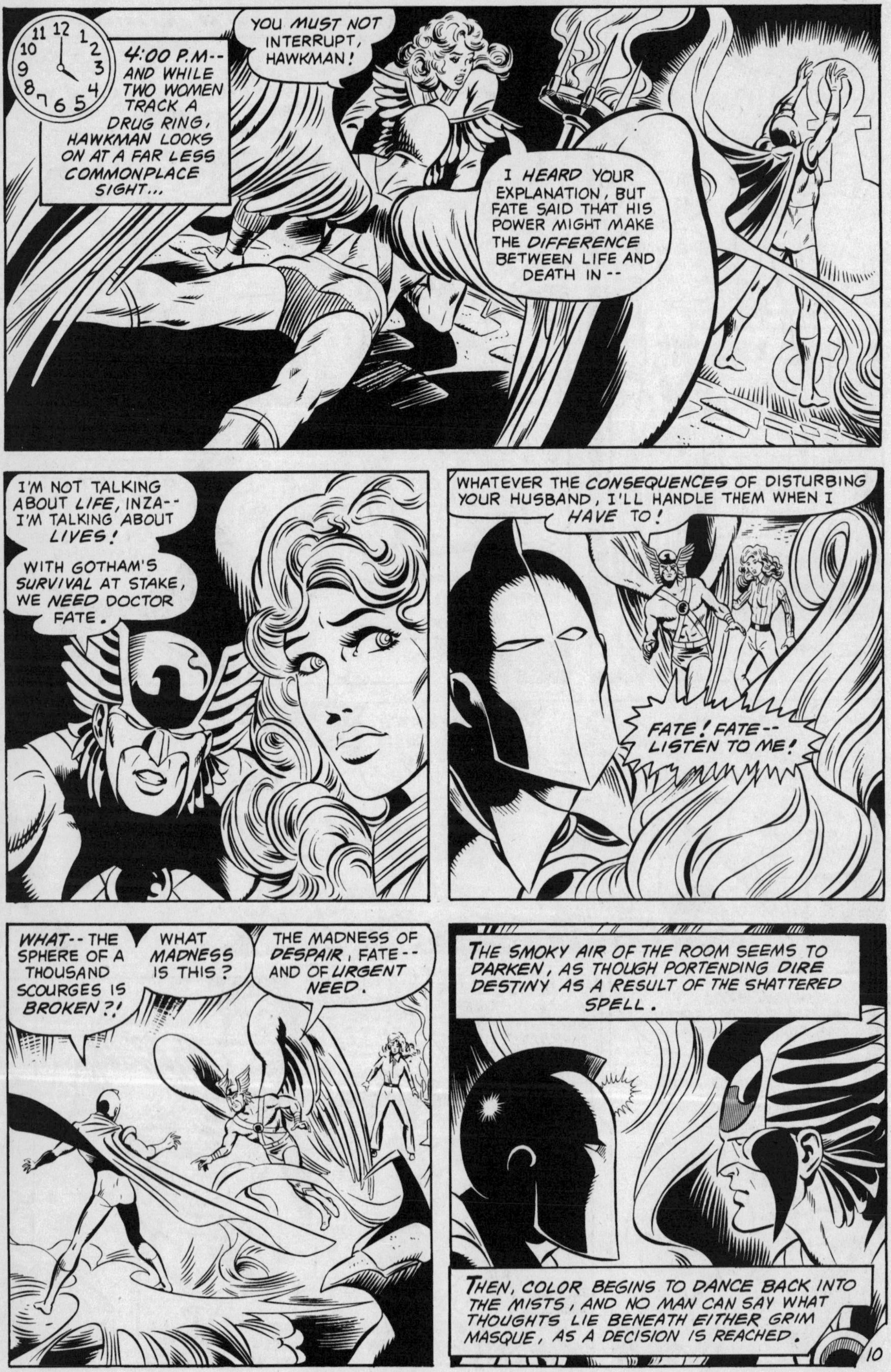
4:00 P.M.-- AND WHILE TWO WOMEN TRACK A DRUG RING, HAWKMAN LOOKS ON AT A FAR LESS COMMONPLACE SIGHT...
YOU MUST NOT INTERRUPT, HAWKMAN!
I HEARD YOUR EXPLANATION, BUT FATE SAID THAT HIS POWER MIGHT MAKE THE DIFFERENCE BETWEEN LIFE AND DEATH IN --
I'M NOT TALKING ABOUT LIFE, INZA-- I'M TALKING ABOUT LIVES!
WITH GOTHAM'S SURVIVAL AT STAKE, WE NEED DOCTOR FATE.
WHATEVER THE CONSEQUENCES OF DISTURBING YOUR HUSBAND, I'LL HANDLE THEM WHEN I HAVE TO!
FATE! FATE-- LISTEN TO ME!
WHAT-- THE SPHERE OF A THOUSAND SCOURGES IS BROKEN?!
WHAT MADNESS IS THIS?
THE MADNESS OF DESPAIR, FATE-- AND OF URGENT NEED.
THE SMOKY AIR OF THE ROOM SEEMS TO DARKEN, AS THOUGH PORTENDING DIRE DESTINY AS A RESULT OF THE SHATTERED SPELL.
THEN, COLOR BEGINS TO DANCE BACK INTO THE MISTS, AND NO MAN CAN SAY WHAT THOUGHTS LIE BENEATH EITHER GRIM MASQUE, AS A DECISION IS REACHED.
10

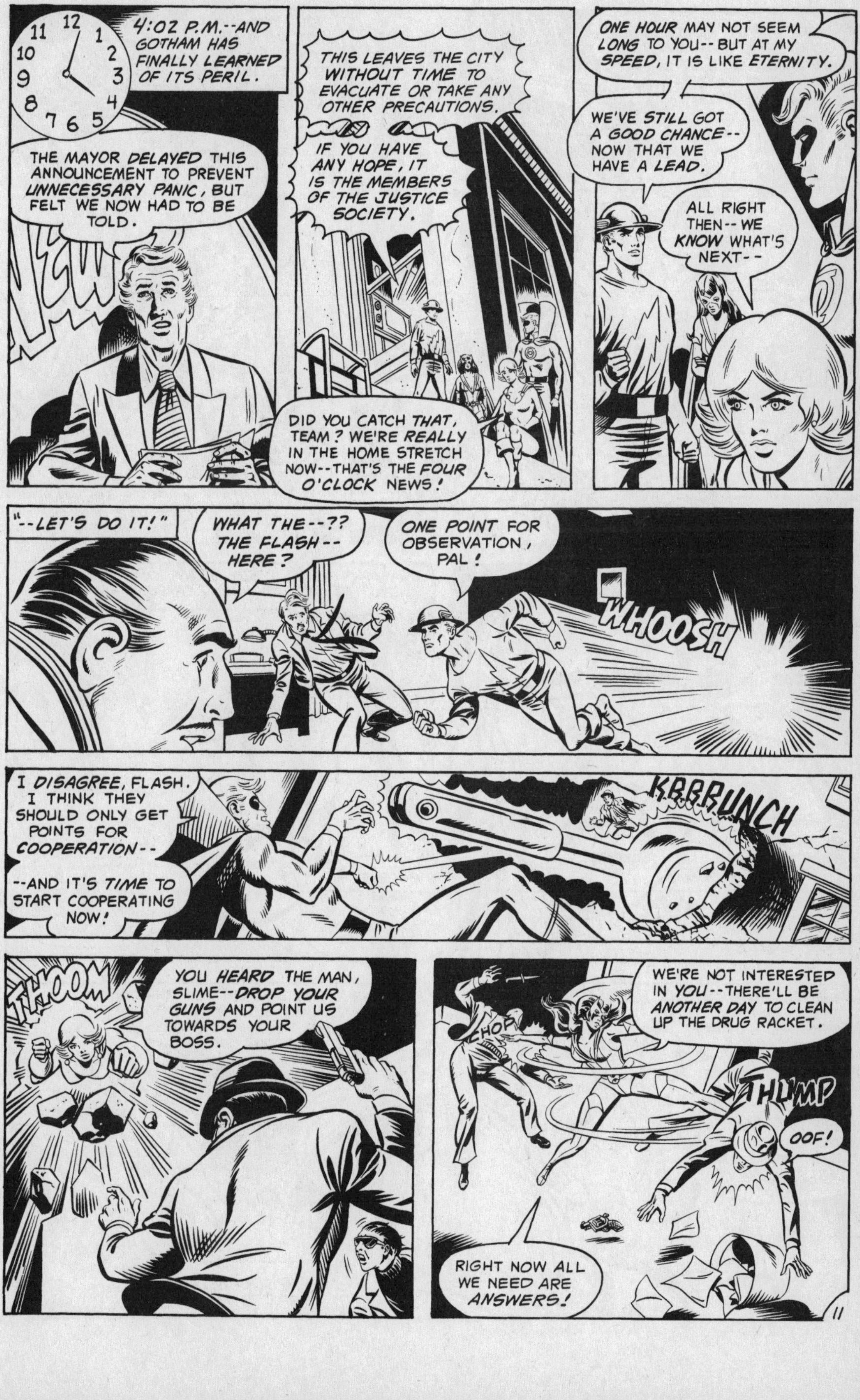
4:02 P.M.--AND GOTHAM HAS FINALLY LEARNED OF ITS PERIL.
THE MAYOR DELAYED THIS ANNOUNCEMENT TO PREVENT UNNECESSARY PANIC, BUT FELT WE NOW HAD TO BE TOLD.
THIS LEAVES THE CITY WITHOUT TIME TO EVACUATE OR TAKE ANY OTHER PRECAUTIONS.
IF YOU HAVE ANY HOPE, IT IS THE MEMBERS OF THE JUSTICE SOCIETY.
DID YOU CATCH THAT, TEAM? WE'RE REALLY IN THE HOME STRETCH NOW--THAT'S THE FOUR O'CLOCK NEWS!
ONE HOUR MAY NOT SEEM LONG TO YOU--BUT AT MY SPEED, IT IS LIKE ETERNITY.
WE'VE STILL GOT A GOOD CHANCE--NOW THAT WE HAVE A LEAD.
ALL RIGHT THEN--WE KNOW WHAT'S NEXT--
"--LET'S DO IT!"
WHAT THE--?? THE FLASH--HERE?
ONE POINT FOR OBSERVATION, PAL!
WHOOSH
I DISAGREE, FLASH. I THINK THEY SHOULD ONLY GET POINTS FOR COOPERATION--
--AND IT'S TIME TO START COOPERATING NOW!
KRRRUNCH
THOOM
YOU HEARD THE MAN, SLIME--DROP YOUR GUNS AND POINT US TOWARDS YOUR BOSS.
CHOP
WE'RE NOT INTERESTED IN YOU--THERE'LL BE ANOTHER DAY TO CLEAN UP THE DRUG RACKET.
THUMP
OOF!
RIGHT NOW ALL WE NEED ARE ANSWERS!
11

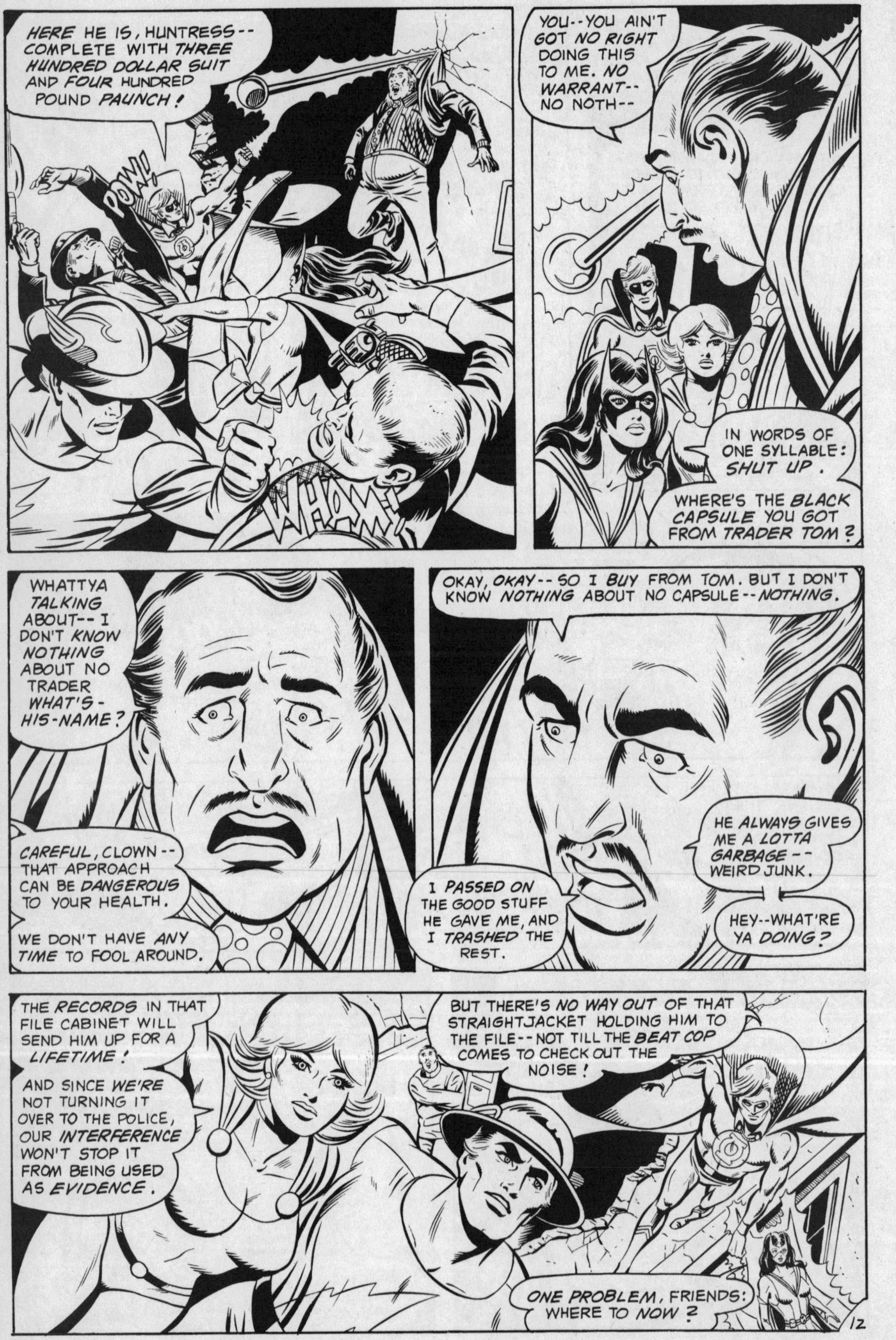
HERE HE IS, HUNTRESS-- COMPLETE WITH THREE HUNDRED DOLLAR SUIT AND FOUR HUNDRED POUND PAUNCH!
POW!
WHAM!
YOU--YOU AIN'T GOT NO RIGHT DOING THIS TO ME. NO WARRANT-- NO NOTH--
IN WORDS OF ONE SYLLABLE: SHUT UP.
WHERE'S THE BLACK CAPSULE YOU GOT FROM TRADER TOM?
WHATTYA TALKING ABOUT-- I DON'T KNOW NOTHING ABOUT NO TRADER WHAT'S-HIS-NAME?
CAREFUL, CLOWN-- THAT APPROACH CAN BE DANGEROUS TO YOUR HEALTH.
WE DON'T HAVE ANY TIME TO FOOL AROUND.
OKAY, OKAY-- SO I BUY FROM TOM. BUT I DON'T KNOW NOTHING ABOUT NO CAPSULE--NOTHING.
HE ALWAYS GIVES ME A LOTTA GARBAGE-- WEIRD JUNK.
I PASSED ON THE GOOD STUFF HE GAVE ME, AND I TRASHED THE REST.
HEY--WHAT'RE YA DOING?
THE RECORDS IN THAT FILE CABINET WILL SEND HIM UP FOR A LIFETIME!
AND SINCE WE'RE NOT TURNING IT OVER TO THE POLICE, OUR INTERFERENCE WON'T STOP IT FROM BEING USED AS EVIDENCE.
BUT THERE'S NO WAY OUT OF THAT STRAIGHTJACKET HOLDING HIM TO THE FILE--NOT TILL THE BEAT COP COMES TO CHECK OUT THE NOISE!
ONE PROBLEM, FRIENDS: WHERE TO NOW?
12

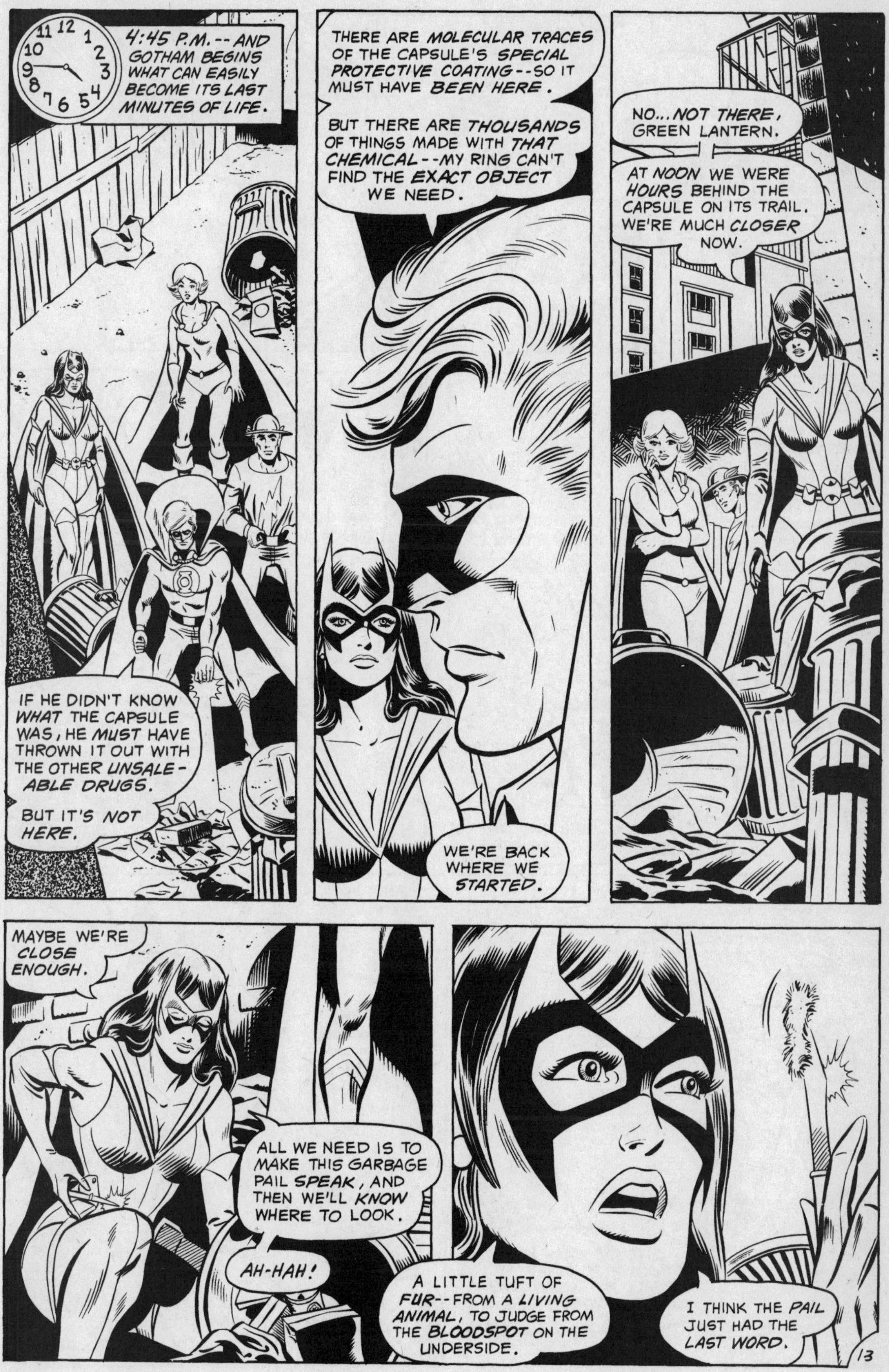
4:45 P.M.-- AND GOTHAM BEGINS WHAT CAN EASILY BECOME ITS LAST MINUTES OF LIFE.
IF HE DIDN'T KNOW WHAT THE CAPSULE WAS, HE MUST HAVE THROWN IT OUT WITH THE OTHER UNSALE-ABLE DRUGS.
BUT IT'S NOT HERE.
THERE ARE MOLECULAR TRACES OF THE CAPSULE'S SPECIAL PROTECTIVE COATING--SO IT MUST HAVE BEEN HERE.
BUT THERE ARE THOUSANDS OF THINGS MADE WITH THAT CHEMICAL--MY RING CAN'T FIND THE EXACT OBJECT WE NEED.
WE'RE BACK WHERE WE STARTED.
NO...NOT THERE, GREEN LANTERN.
AT NOON WE WERE HOURS BEHIND THE CAPSULE ON ITS TRAIL. WE'RE MUCH CLOSER NOW.
MAYBE WE'RE CLOSE ENOUGH.
ALL WE NEED IS TO MAKE THIS GARBAGE PAIL SPEAK, AND THEN WE'LL KNOW WHERE TO LOOK.
AH-HAH!
A LITTLE TUFT OF FUR--FROM A LIVING ANIMAL, TO JUDGE FROM THE BLOODSPOT ON THE UNDERSIDE.
I THINK THE PAIL JUST HAD THE LAST WORD.
13

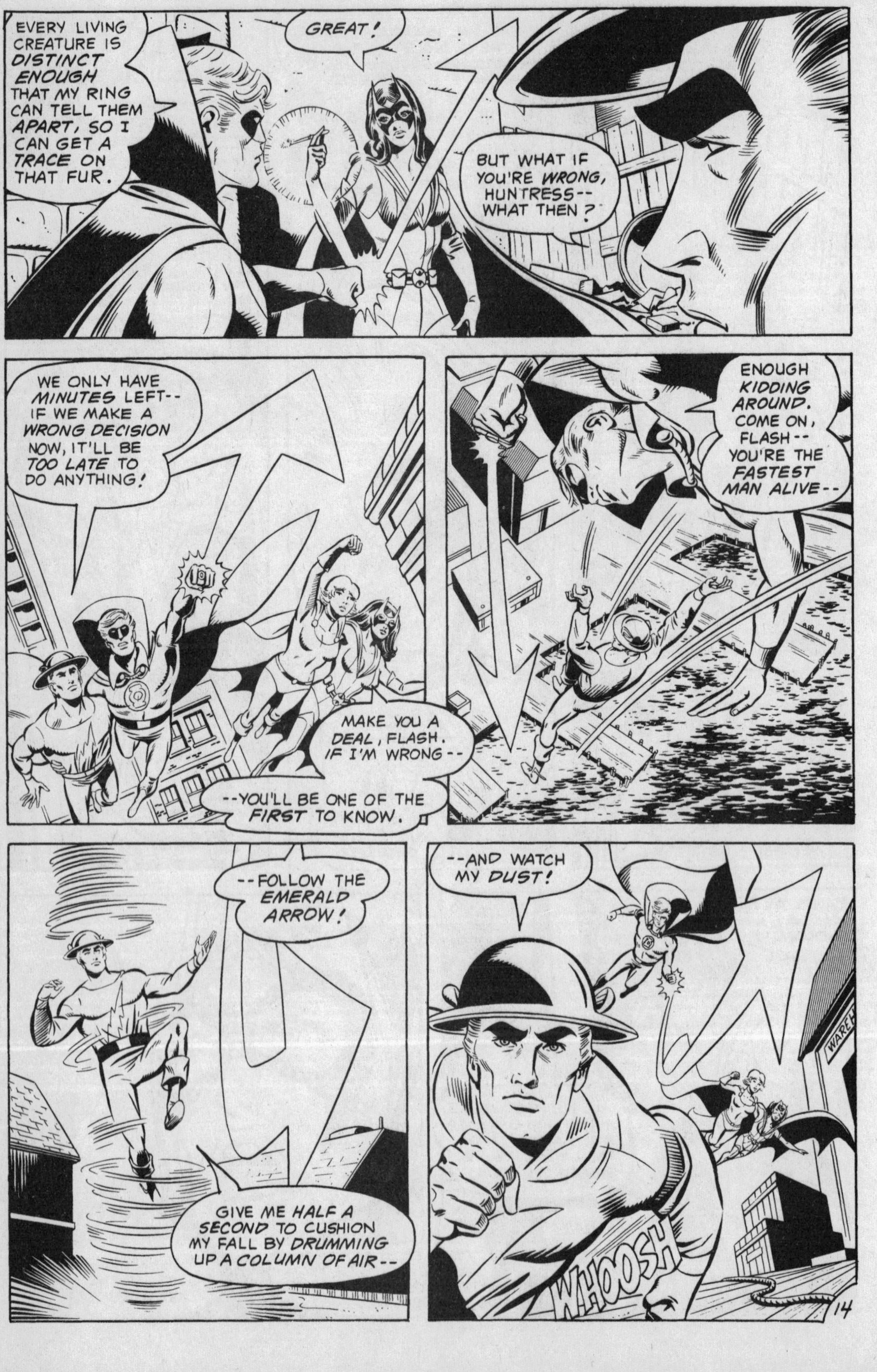
EVERY LIVING CREATURE IS DISTINCT ENOUGH THAT MY RING CAN TELL THEM APART, SO I CAN GET A TRACE ON THAT FUR.
GREAT!
BUT WHAT IF YOU'RE WRONG, HUNTRESS-- WHAT THEN?
WE ONLY HAVE MINUTES LEFT-- IF WE MAKE A WRONG DECISION NOW, IT'LL BE TOO LATE TO DO ANYTHING!
MAKE YOU A DEAL, FLASH. IF I'M WRONG--
--YOU'LL BE ONE OF THE FIRST TO KNOW.
ENOUGH KIDDING AROUND. COME ON, FLASH-- YOU'RE THE FASTEST MAN ALIVE--
--FOLLOW THE EMERALD ARROW!
GIVE ME HALF A SECOND TO CUSHION MY FALL BY DRUMMING UP A COLUMN OF AIR--
--AND WATCH MY DUST!
WHOOSH
14

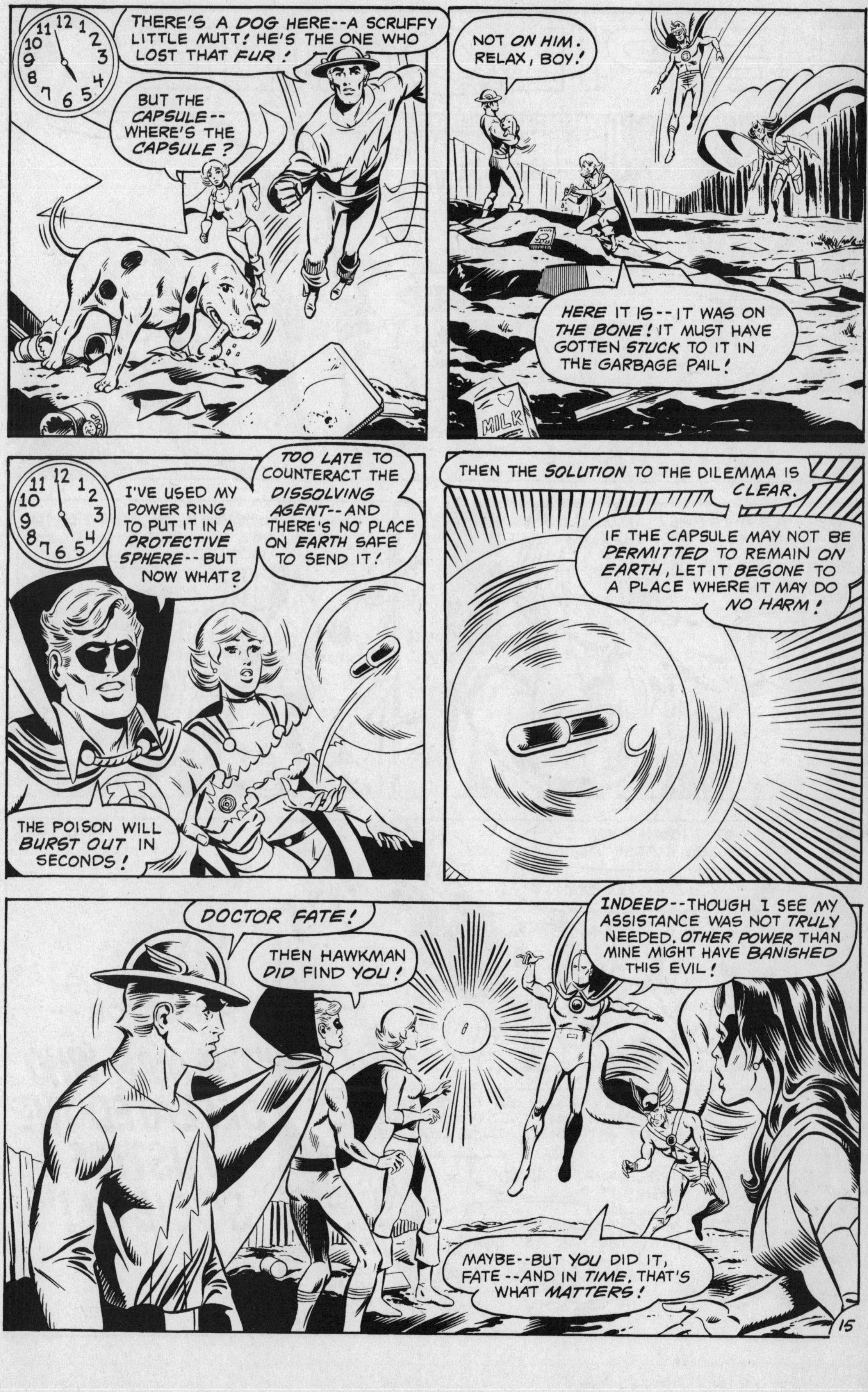
THERE'S A DOG HERE--A SCRUFFY LITTLE MUTT! HE'S THE ONE WHO LOST THAT FUR!
BUT THE CAPSULE--WHERE'S THE CAPSULE?
NOT ON HIM. RELAX, BOY!
HERE IT IS--IT WAS ON THE BONE! IT MUST HAVE GOTTEN STUCK TO IT IN THE GARBAGE PAIL!
MILK
I'VE USED MY POWER RING TO PUT IT IN A PROTECTIVE SPHERE--BUT NOW WHAT?
TOO LATE TO COUNTERACT THE DISSOLVING AGENT--AND THERE'S NO PLACE ON EARTH SAFE TO SEND IT!
THE POISON WILL BURST OUT IN SECONDS!
THEN THE SOLUTION TO THE DILEMMA IS CLEAR.
IF THE CAPSULE MAY NOT BE PERMITTED TO REMAIN ON EARTH, LET IT BEGONE TO A PLACE WHERE IT MAY DO NO HARM!
DOCTOR FATE!
THEN HAWKMAN DID FIND YOU!
INDEED--THOUGH I SEE MY ASSISTANCE WAS NOT TRULY NEEDED. OTHER POWER THAN MINE MIGHT HAVE BANISHED THIS EVIL!
MAYBE--BUT YOU DID IT, FATE--AND IN TIME. THAT'S WHAT MATTERS!
15

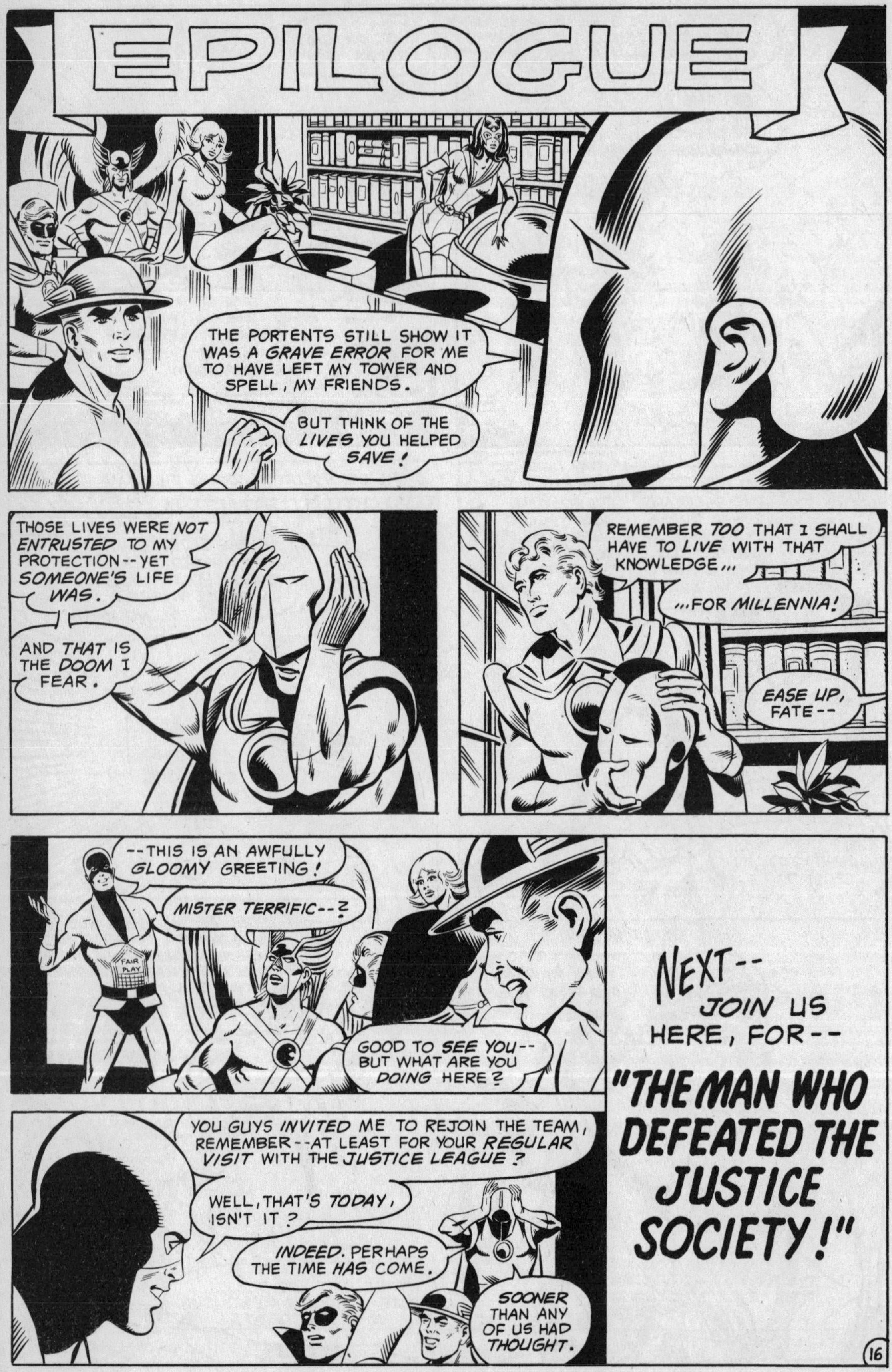
EPILOGUE
THE PORTENTS STILL SHOW IT WAS A GRAVE ERROR FOR ME TO HAVE LEFT MY TOWER AND SPELL, MY FRIENDS.
BUT THINK OF THE LIVES YOU HELPED SAVE!
THOSE LIVES WERE NOT ENTRUSTED TO MY PROTECTION--YET SOMEONE'S LIFE WAS.
AND THAT IS THE DOOM I FEAR.
REMEMBER TOO THAT I SHALL HAVE TO LIVE WITH THAT KNOWLEDGE...
...FOR MILLENNIA!
EASE UP, FATE--
--THIS IS AN AWFULLY GLOOMY GREETING!
MISTER TERRIFIC--?
FAIR PLAY
GOOD TO SEE YOU--BUT WHAT ARE YOU DOING HERE?
YOU GUYS INVITED ME TO REJOIN THE TEAM, REMEMBER--AT LEAST FOR YOUR REGULAR VISIT WITH THE JUSTICE LEAGUE?
WELL, THAT'S TODAY, ISN'T IT?
INDEED. PERHAPS THE TIME HAS COME.
SOONER THAN ANY OF US HAD THOUGHT.
NEXT-- JOIN US HERE, FOR--
"THE MAN WHO DEFEATED THE JUSTICE SOCIETY!"
16

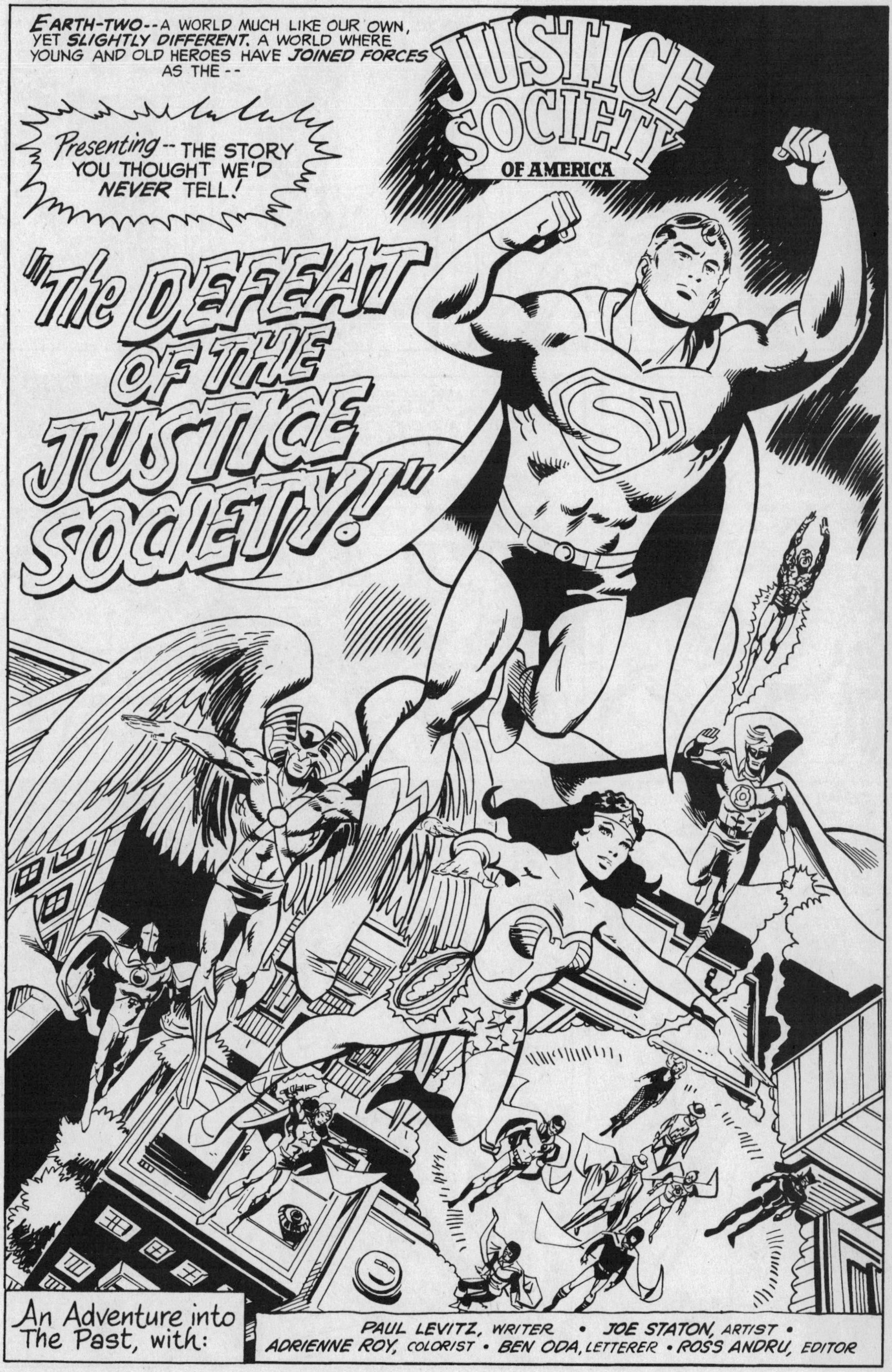
EARTH-TWO--A WORLD MUCH LIKE OUR OWN, YET SLIGHTLY DIFFERENT. A WORLD WHERE YOUNG AND OLD HEROES HAVE JOINED FORCES AS THE --
JUSTICE SOCIETY OF AMERICA
Presenting -- THE STORY YOU THOUGHT WE'D NEVER TELL!
"The DEFEAT OF THE JUSTICE SOCIETY!"
An Adventure into The Past, with:
PAUL LEVITZ, WRITER • JOE STATON, ARTIST • ADRIENNE ROY, COLORIST • BEN ODA, LETTERER • ROSS ANDRU, EDITOR

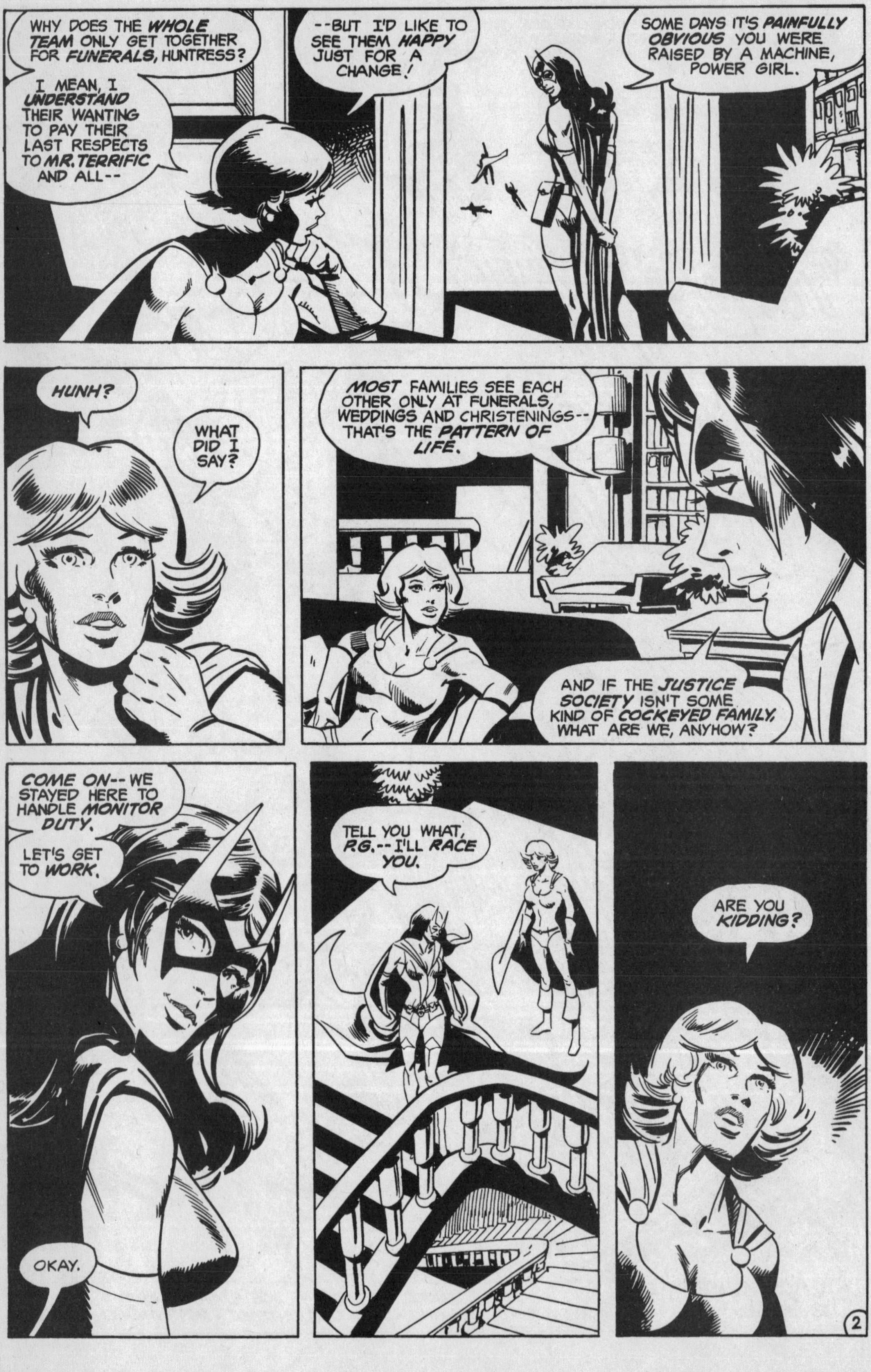
WHY DOES THE *WHOLE TEAM* ONLY GET TOGETHER FOR *FUNERALS*, HUNTRESS?
I MEAN, I *UNDERSTAND* THEIR WANTING TO PAY THEIR LAST RESPECTS TO *MR. TERRIFIC* AND ALL--
--BUT I'D LIKE TO SEE THEM *HAPPY* JUST FOR A CHANGE!
SOME DAYS IT'S *PAINFULLY OBVIOUS* YOU WERE RAISED BY A MACHINE, POWER GIRL.
HUNH?
WHAT DID I SAY?
MOST FAMILIES SEE EACH OTHER ONLY AT FUNERALS, WEDDINGS AND CHRISTENINGS-- THAT'S THE *PATTERN OF LIFE*.
AND IF THE *JUSTICE SOCIETY* ISN'T SOME KIND OF *COCKEYED FAMILY*, WHAT ARE WE, ANYHOW?
COME ON-- WE STAYED HERE TO HANDLE *MONITOR DUTY*.
LET'S GET TO *WORK*.
OKAY.
TELL YOU WHAT, *P.G.*-- I'LL *RACE YOU*.
ARE YOU *KIDDING?*
2

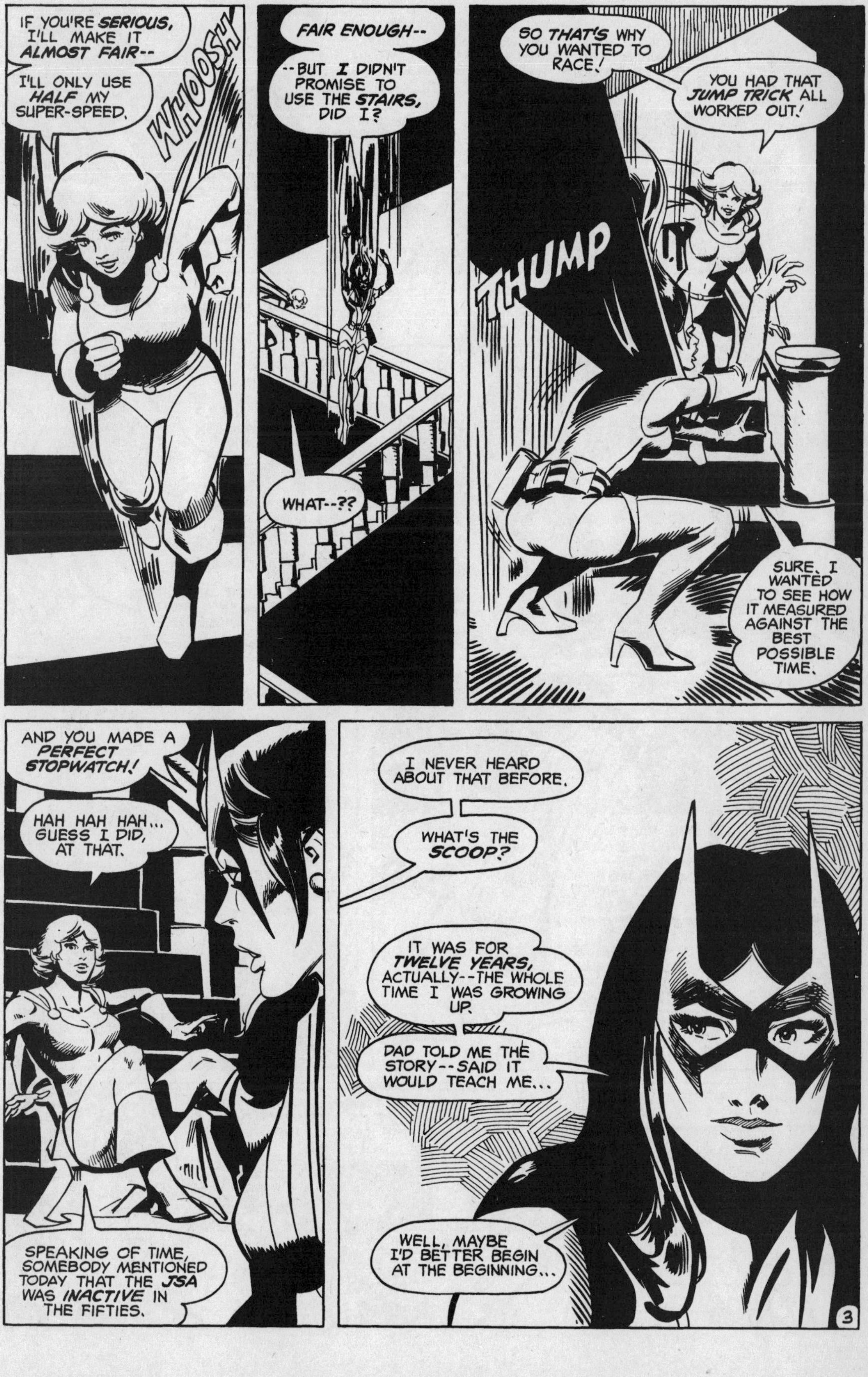
IF YOU'RE SERIOUS, I'LL MAKE IT ALMOST FAIR--
I'LL ONLY USE HALF MY SUPER-SPEED.
WHOOSH
FAIR ENOUGH--
--BUT I DIDN'T PROMISE TO USE THE STAIRS, DID I?
WHAT--??
SO THAT'S WHY YOU WANTED TO RACE!
YOU HAD THAT JUMP TRICK ALL WORKED OUT!
THUMP
SURE. I WANTED TO SEE HOW IT MEASURED AGAINST THE BEST POSSIBLE TIME.
AND YOU MADE A PERFECT STOPWATCH!
HAH HAH HAH... GUESS I DID, AT THAT.
SPEAKING OF TIME, SOMEBODY MENTIONED TODAY THAT THE JSA WAS INACTIVE IN THE FIFTIES.
I NEVER HEARD ABOUT THAT BEFORE.
WHAT'S THE SCOOP?
IT WAS FOR TWELVE YEARS, ACTUALLY--THE WHOLE TIME I WAS GROWING UP.
DAD TOLD ME THE STORY--SAID IT WOULD TEACH ME...
WELL, MAYBE I'D BETTER BEGIN AT THE BEGINNING...
3

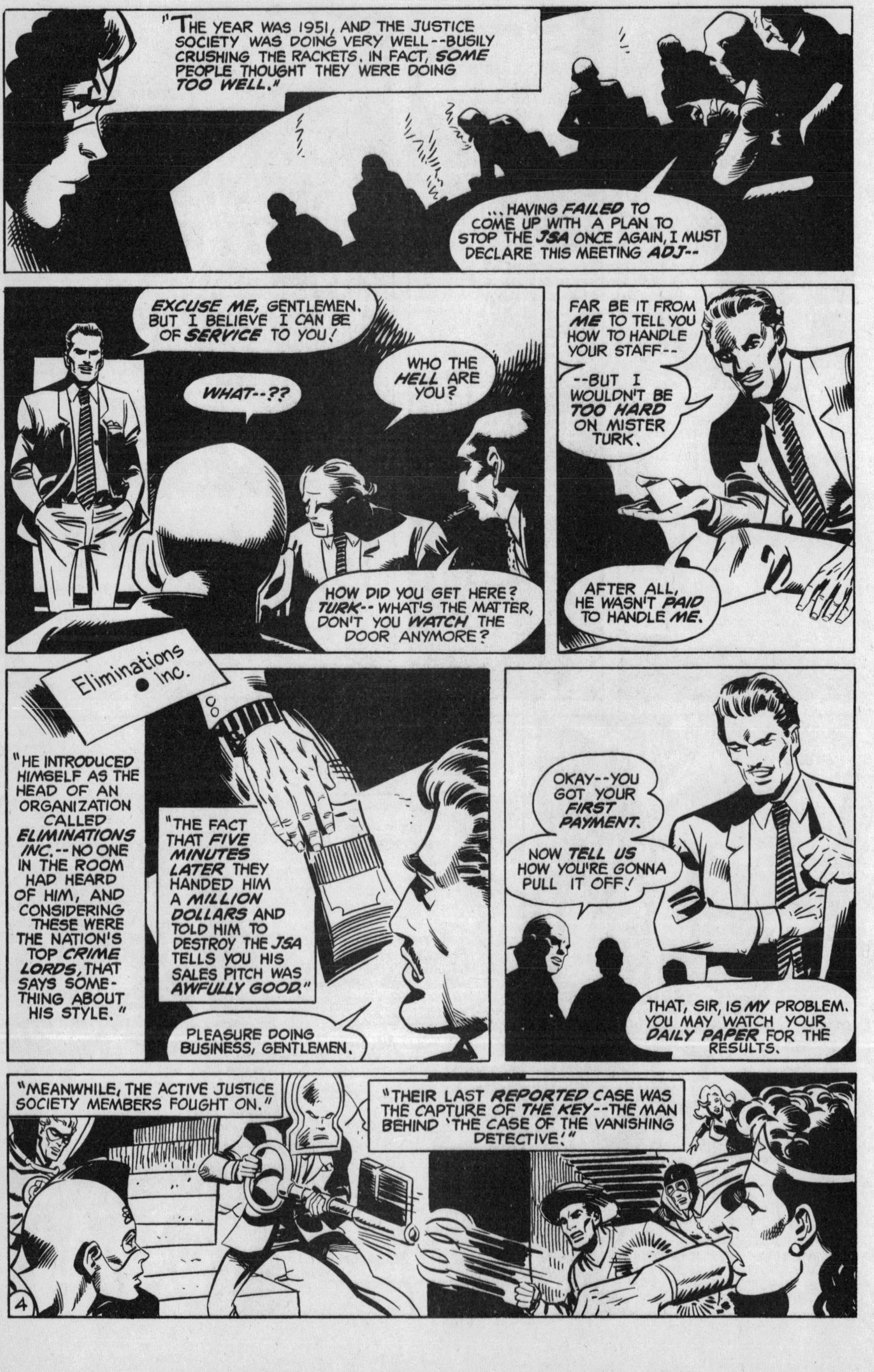
"THE YEAR WAS 1951, AND THE JUSTICE SOCIETY WAS DOING VERY WELL--BUSILY CRUSHING THE RACKETS. IN FACT, SOME PEOPLE THOUGHT THEY WERE DOING TOO WELL."
...HAVING FAILED TO COME UP WITH A PLAN TO STOP THE JSA ONCE AGAIN, I MUST DECLARE THIS MEETING ADJ--
EXCUSE ME, GENTLEMEN. BUT I BELIEVE I CAN BE OF SERVICE TO YOU!
WHAT--??
WHO THE HELL ARE YOU?
HOW DID YOU GET HERE? TURK--WHAT'S THE MATTER, DON'T YOU WATCH THE DOOR ANYMORE?
FAR BE IT FROM ME TO TELL YOU HOW TO HANDLE YOUR STAFF--
--BUT I WOULDN'T BE TOO HARD ON MISTER TURK.
AFTER ALL, HE WASN'T PAID TO HANDLE ME.
Eliminations Inc.
"HE INTRODUCED HIMSELF AS THE HEAD OF AN ORGANIZATION CALLED ELIMINATIONS INC.--NO ONE IN THE ROOM HAD HEARD OF HIM, AND CONSIDERING THESE WERE THE NATION'S TOP CRIME LORDS, THAT SAYS SOME-THING ABOUT HIS STYLE."
"THE FACT THAT FIVE MINUTES LATER THEY HANDED HIM A MILLION DOLLARS AND TOLD HIM TO DESTROY THE JSA TELLS YOU HIS SALES PITCH WAS AWFULLY GOOD."
PLEASURE DOING BUSINESS, GENTLEMEN.
OKAY--YOU GOT YOUR FIRST PAYMENT.
NOW TELL US HOW YOU'RE GONNA PULL IT OFF!
THAT, SIR, IS MY PROBLEM. YOU MAY WATCH YOUR DAILY PAPER FOR THE RESULTS.
"MEANWHILE, THE ACTIVE JUSTICE SOCIETY MEMBERS FOUGHT ON."
"THEIR LAST REPORTED CASE WAS THE CAPTURE OF THE KEY--THE MAN BEHIND 'THE CASE OF THE VANISHING DETECTIVE!'"
4

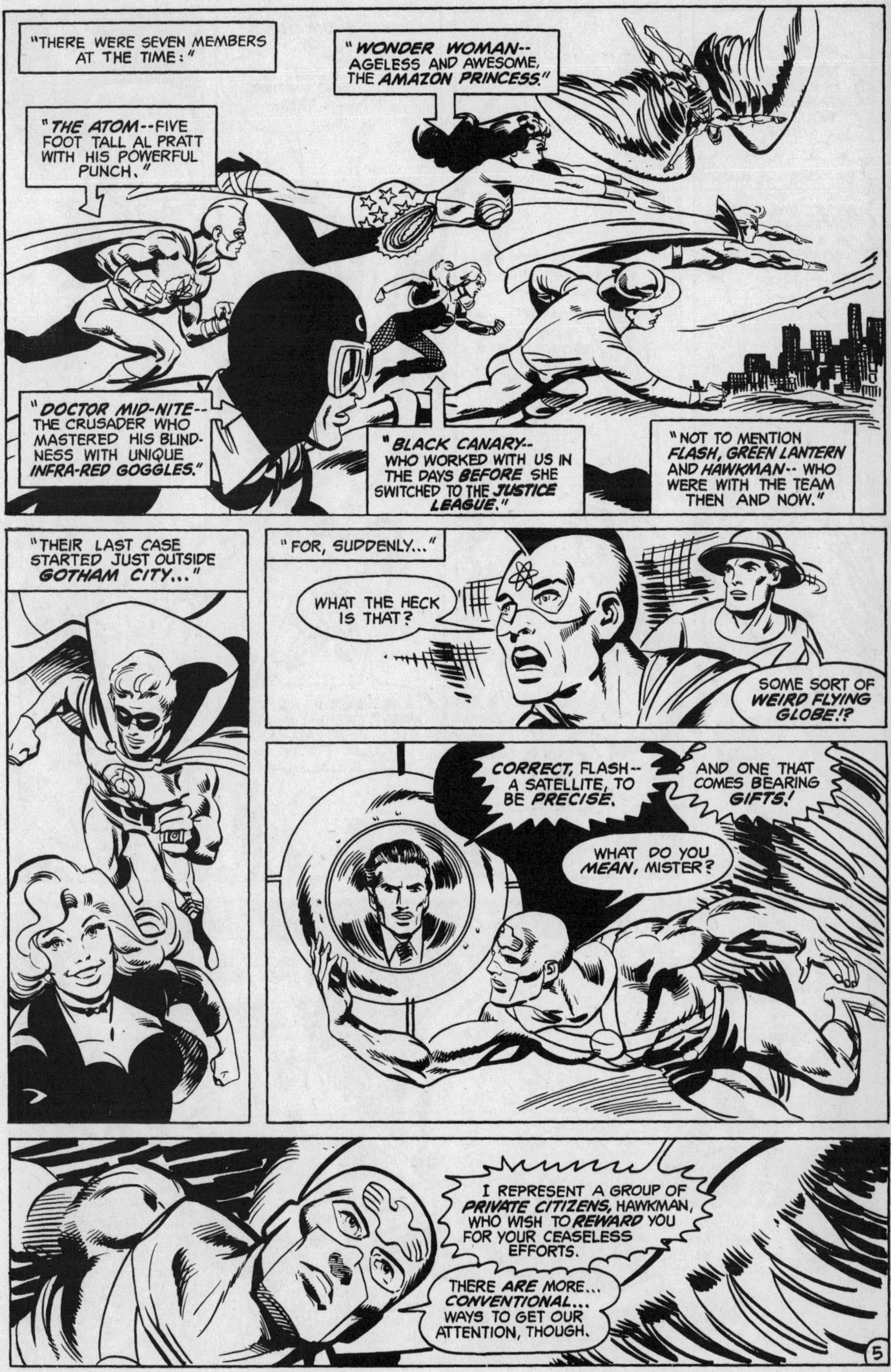
"THERE WERE SEVEN MEMBERS AT THE TIME:"
"WONDER WOMAN-- AGELESS AND AWESOME, THE AMAZON PRINCESS."
"THE ATOM--FIVE FOOT TALL AL PRATT WITH HIS POWERFUL PUNCH."
"DOCTOR MID-NITE-- THE CRUSADER WHO MASTERED HIS BLINDNESS WITH UNIQUE INFRA-RED GOGGLES."
"BLACK CANARY-- WHO WORKED WITH US IN THE DAYS BEFORE SHE SWITCHED TO THE JUSTICE LEAGUE."
"NOT TO MENTION FLASH, GREEN LANTERN AND HAWKMAN-- WHO WERE WITH THE TEAM THEN AND NOW."
"THEIR LAST CASE STARTED JUST OUTSIDE GOTHAM CITY..."
"FOR, SUDDENLY..."
WHAT THE HECK IS THAT?
SOME SORT OF WEIRD FLYING GLOBE!?
CORRECT, FLASH-- A SATELLITE, TO BE PRECISE.
AND ONE THAT COMES BEARING GIFTS!
WHAT DO YOU MEAN, MISTER?
I REPRESENT A GROUP OF PRIVATE CITIZENS, HAWKMAN, WHO WISH TO REWARD YOU FOR YOUR CEASELESS EFFORTS.
THERE ARE MORE... CONVENTIONAL... WAYS TO GET OUR ATTENTION, THOUGH.
5

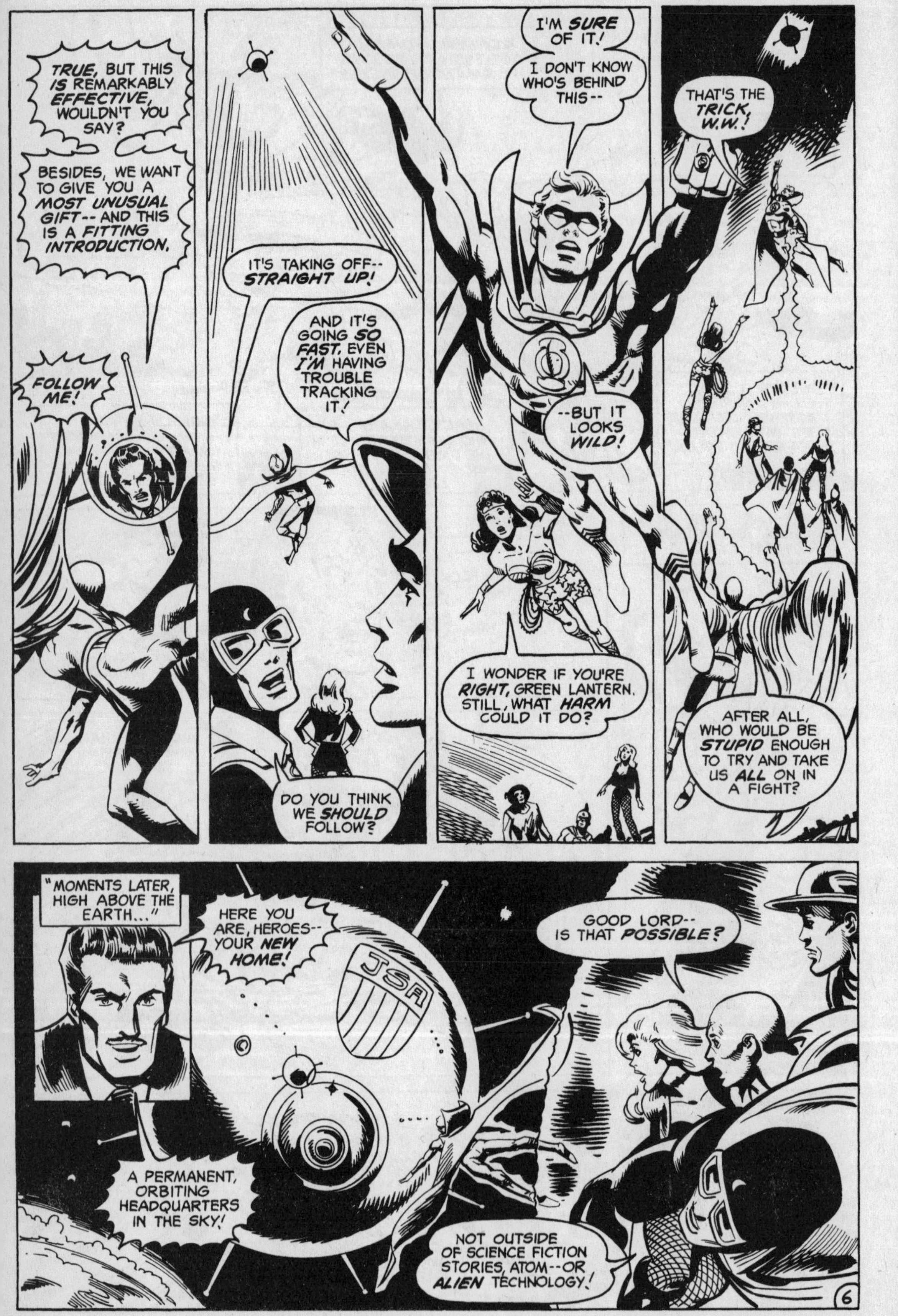
TRUE, BUT THIS IS REMARKABLY EFFECTIVE, WOULDN'T YOU SAY?
BESIDES, WE WANT TO GIVE YOU A MOST UNUSUAL GIFT-- AND THIS IS A FITTING INTRODUCTION.
FOLLOW ME!
IT'S TAKING OFF-- STRAIGHT UP!
AND IT'S GOING SO FAST, EVEN I'M HAVING TROUBLE TRACKING IT!
DO YOU THINK WE SHOULD FOLLOW?
I'M SURE OF IT!
I DON'T KNOW WHO'S BEHIND THIS--
--BUT IT LOOKS WILD!
I WONDER IF YOU'RE RIGHT, GREEN LANTERN. STILL, WHAT HARM COULD IT DO?
THAT'S THE TRICK, W.W.!
AFTER ALL, WHO WOULD BE STUPID ENOUGH TO TRY AND TAKE US ALL ON IN A FIGHT?
"MOMENTS LATER, HIGH ABOVE THE EARTH..."
HERE YOU ARE, HEROES-- YOUR NEW HOME!
JSA
A PERMANENT, ORBITING HEADQUARTERS IN THE SKY!
GOOD LORD-- IS THAT POSSIBLE?
NOT OUTSIDE OF SCIENCE FICTION STORIES, ATOM--OR ALIEN TECHNOLOGY!
6

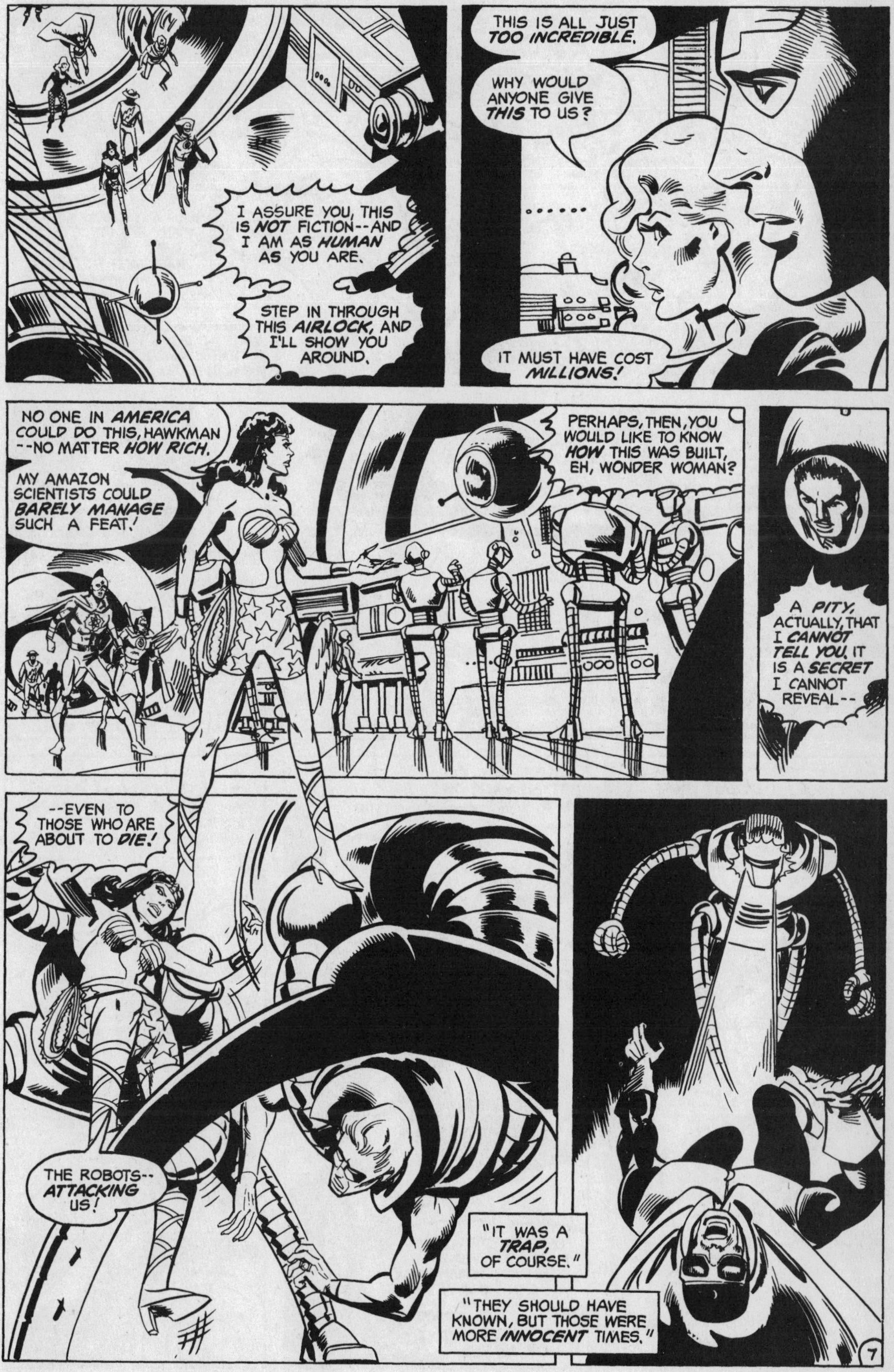
I ASSURE YOU, THIS IS NOT FICTION--AND I AM AS HUMAN AS YOU ARE.
STEP IN THROUGH THIS AIRLOCK, AND I'LL SHOW YOU AROUND.
THIS IS ALL JUST TOO INCREDIBLE.
WHY WOULD ANYONE GIVE THIS TO US?
......
IT MUST HAVE COST MILLIONS!
NO ONE IN AMERICA COULD DO THIS, HAWKMAN--NO MATTER HOW RICH.
MY AMAZON SCIENTISTS COULD BARELY MANAGE SUCH A FEAT!
PERHAPS, THEN, YOU WOULD LIKE TO KNOW HOW THIS WAS BUILT, EH, WONDER WOMAN?
A PITY, ACTUALLY, THAT I CANNOT TELL YOU. IT IS A SECRET I CANNOT REVEAL--
--EVEN TO THOSE WHO ARE ABOUT TO DIE!
THE ROBOTS--ATTACKING US!
"IT WAS A TRAP, OF COURSE."
"THEY SHOULD HAVE KNOWN, BUT THOSE WERE MORE INNOCENT TIMES."
7

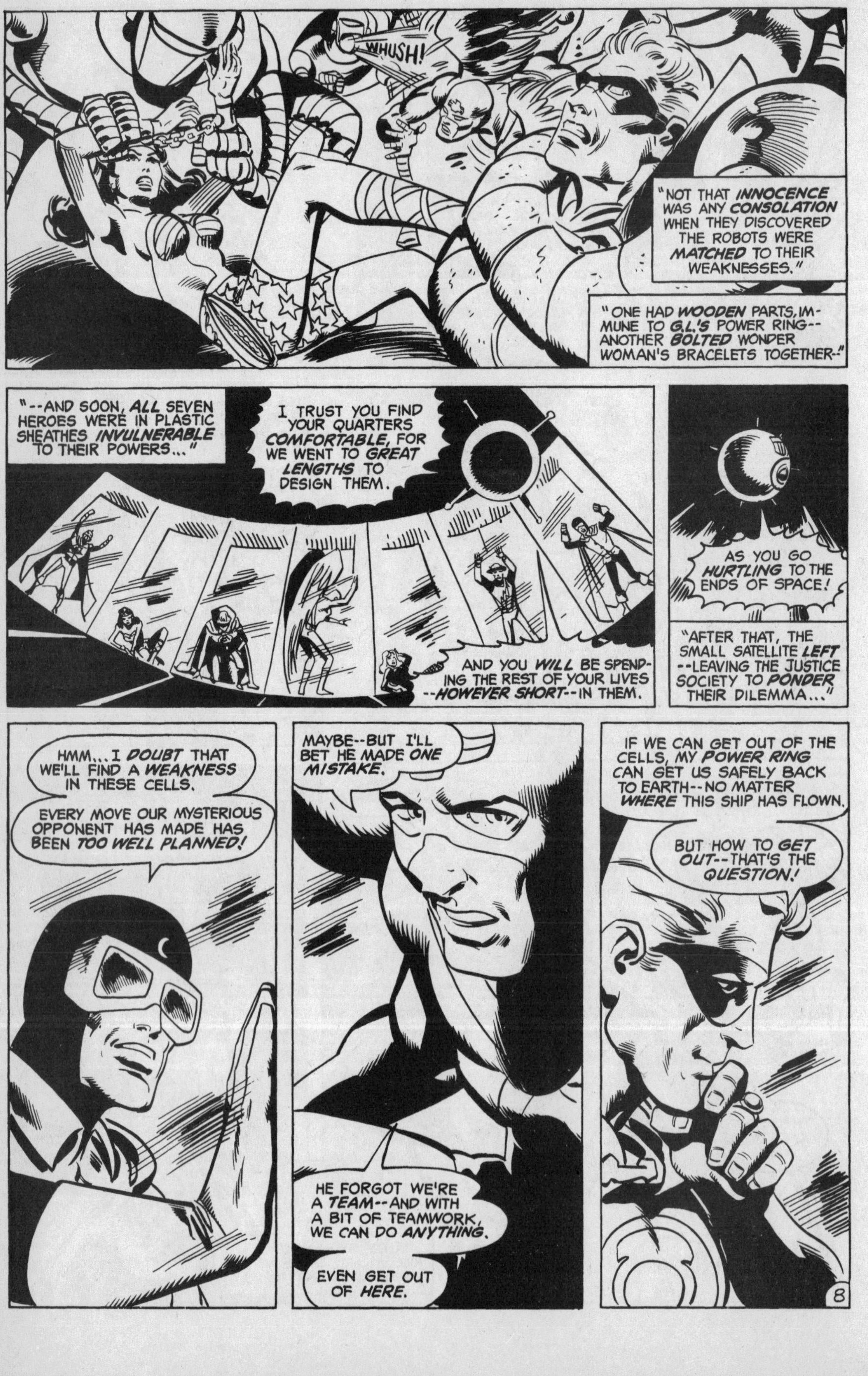
WHUSH!
"NOT THAT INNOCENCE WAS ANY CONSOLATION WHEN THEY DISCOVERED THE ROBOTS WERE MATCHED TO THEIR WEAKNESSES."
"ONE HAD WOODEN PARTS, IM-MUNE TO G.L.'S POWER RING--ANOTHER BOLTED WONDER WOMAN'S BRACELETS TOGETHER--"
"--AND SOON, ALL SEVEN HEROES WERE IN PLASTIC SHEATHES INVULNERABLE TO THEIR POWERS..."
I TRUST YOU FIND YOUR QUARTERS COMFORTABLE, FOR WE WENT TO GREAT LENGTHS TO DESIGN THEM.
AND YOU WILL BE SPEND-ING THE REST OF YOUR LIVES --HOWEVER SHORT--IN THEM.
AS YOU GO HURTLING TO THE ENDS OF SPACE!
"AFTER THAT, THE SMALL SATELLITE LEFT --LEAVING THE JUSTICE SOCIETY TO PONDER THEIR DILEMMA..."
HMM... I DOUBT THAT WE'LL FIND A WEAKNESS IN THESE CELLS.
EVERY MOVE OUR MYSTERIOUS OPPONENT HAS MADE HAS BEEN TOO WELL PLANNED!
MAYBE--BUT I'LL BET HE MADE ONE MISTAKE.
HE FORGOT WE'RE A TEAM--AND WITH A BIT OF TEAMWORK, WE CAN DO ANYTHING.
EVEN GET OUT OF HERE.
IF WE CAN GET OUT OF THE CELLS, MY POWER RING CAN GET US SAFELY BACK TO EARTH--NO MATTER WHERE THIS SHIP HAS FLOWN.
BUT HOW TO GET OUT--THAT'S THE QUESTION!
8

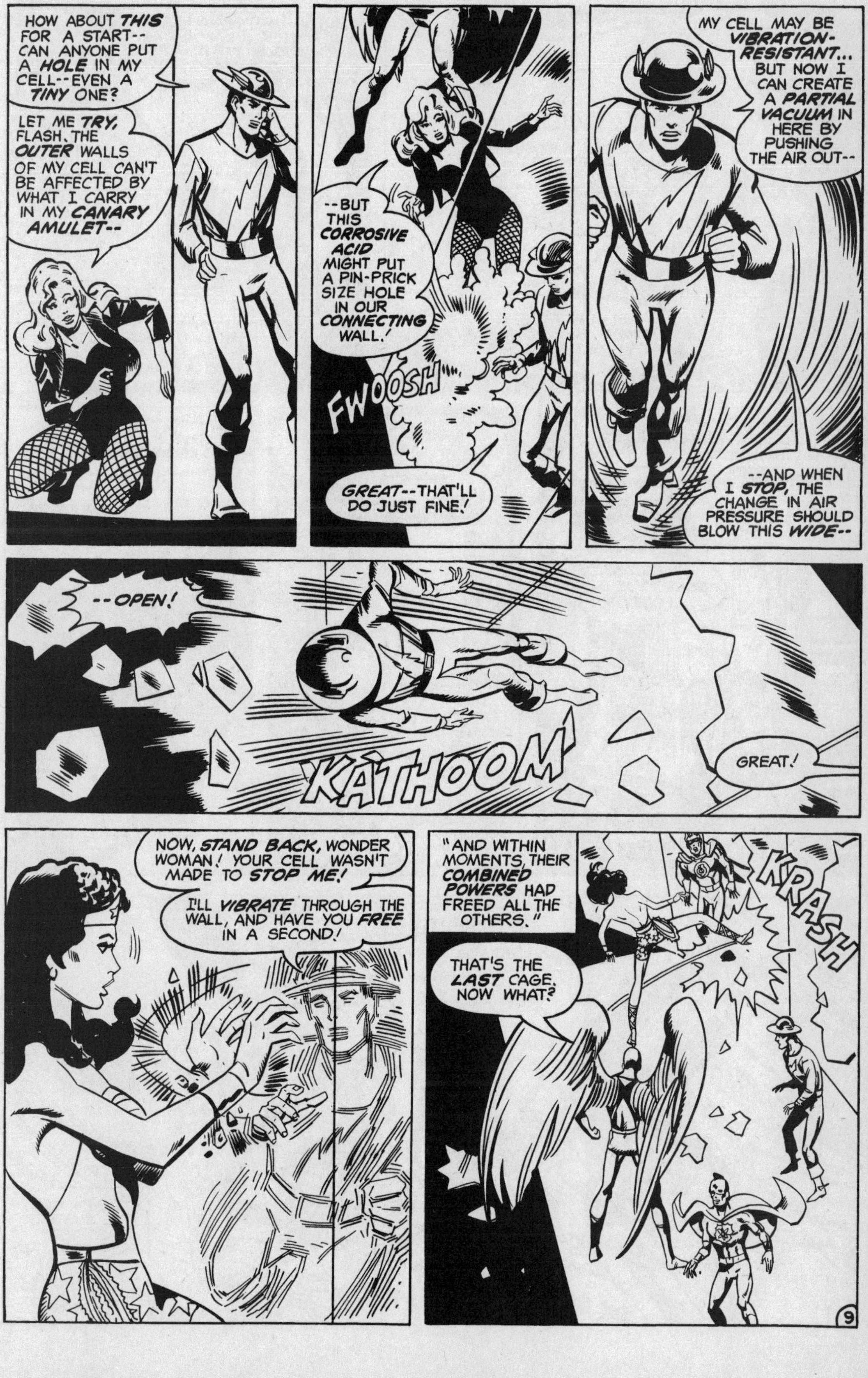
HOW ABOUT THIS FOR A START--CAN ANYONE PUT A HOLE IN MY CELL--EVEN A TINY ONE?
LET ME TRY, FLASH. THE OUTER WALLS OF MY CELL CAN'T BE AFFECTED BY WHAT I CARRY IN MY CANARY AMULET--
--BUT THIS CORROSIVE ACID MIGHT PUT A PIN-PRICK SIZE HOLE IN OUR CONNECTING WALL!
FWOOSH
GREAT--THAT'LL DO JUST FINE!
MY CELL MAY BE VIBRATION-RESISTANT... BUT NOW I CAN CREATE A PARTIAL VACUUM IN HERE BY PUSHING THE AIR OUT--
--AND WHEN I STOP, THE CHANGE IN AIR PRESSURE SHOULD BLOW THIS WIDE--
--OPEN!
KATHOOM
GREAT!
NOW, STAND BACK, WONDER WOMAN! YOUR CELL WASN'T MADE TO STOP ME!
I'LL VIBRATE THROUGH THE WALL, AND HAVE YOU FREE IN A SECOND!
"AND WITHIN MOMENTS, THEIR COMBINED POWERS HAD FREED ALL THE OTHERS."
KRASH
THAT'S THE LAST CAGE. NOW WHAT?
9

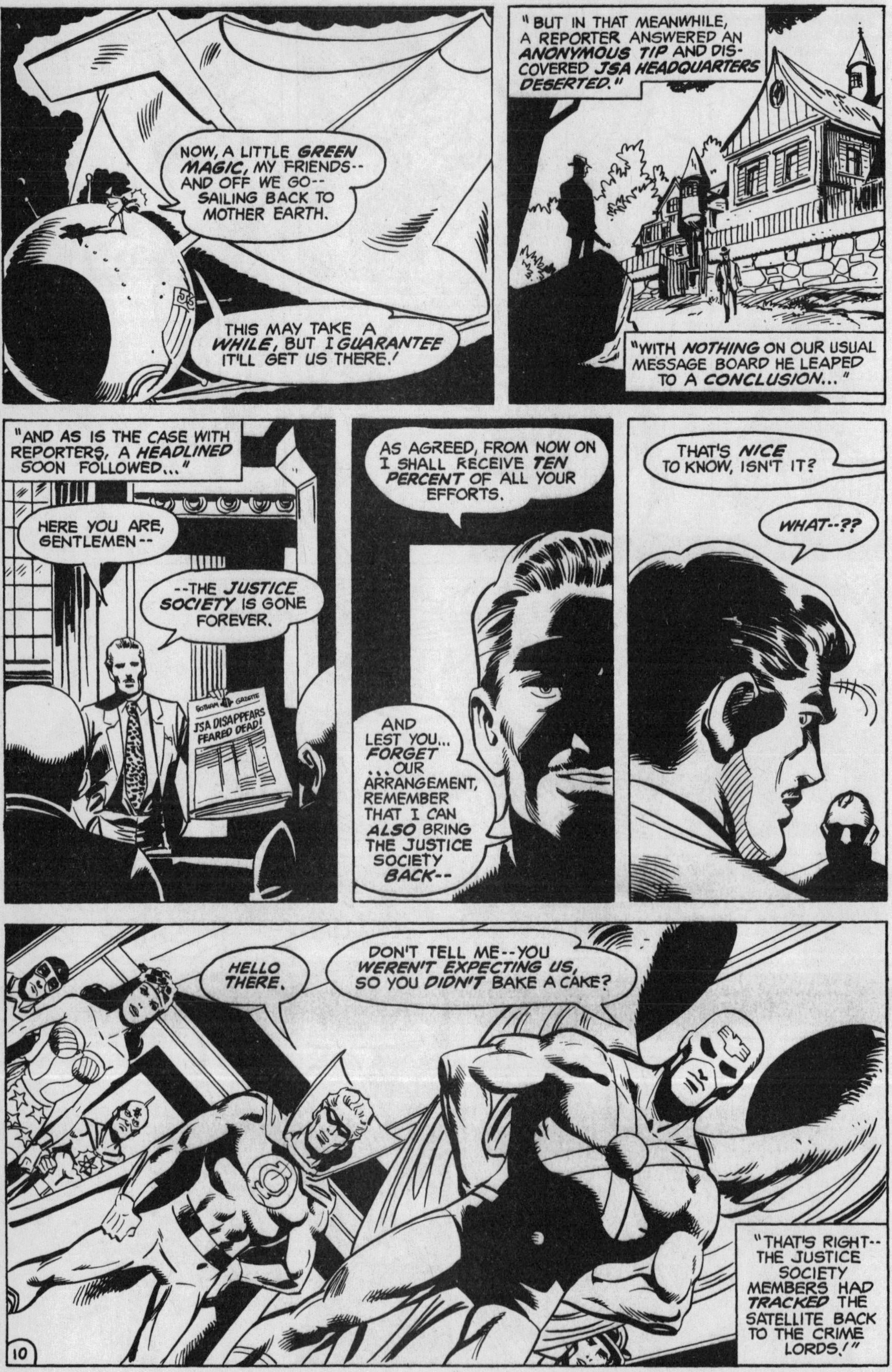
NOW, A LITTLE GREEN MAGIC, MY FRIENDS-- AND OFF WE GO-- SAILING BACK TO MOTHER EARTH.
THIS MAY TAKE A WHILE, BUT I GUARANTEE IT'LL GET US THERE!
"BUT IN THAT MEANWHILE, A REPORTER ANSWERED AN ANONYMOUS TIP AND DISCOVERED JSA HEADQUARTERS DESERTED."
"WITH NOTHING ON OUR USUAL MESSAGE BOARD HE LEAPED TO A CONCLUSION..."
"AND AS IS THE CASE WITH REPORTERS, A HEADLINED SOON FOLLOWED..."
HERE YOU ARE, GENTLEMEN--
--THE JUSTICE SOCIETY IS GONE FOREVER.
JSA DISAPPEARS FEARED DEAD!
AS AGREED, FROM NOW ON I SHALL RECEIVE TEN PERCENT OF ALL YOUR EFFORTS.
AND LEST YOU... FORGET ...OUR ARRANGEMENT, REMEMBER THAT I CAN ALSO BRING THE JUSTICE SOCIETY BACK--
THAT'S NICE TO KNOW, ISN'T IT?
WHAT--??
HELLO THERE.
DON'T TELL ME--YOU WEREN'T EXPECTING US, SO YOU DIDN'T BAKE A CAKE?
"THAT'S RIGHT-- THE JUSTICE SOCIETY MEMBERS HAD TRACKED THE SATELLITE BACK TO THE CRIME LORDS!"
10

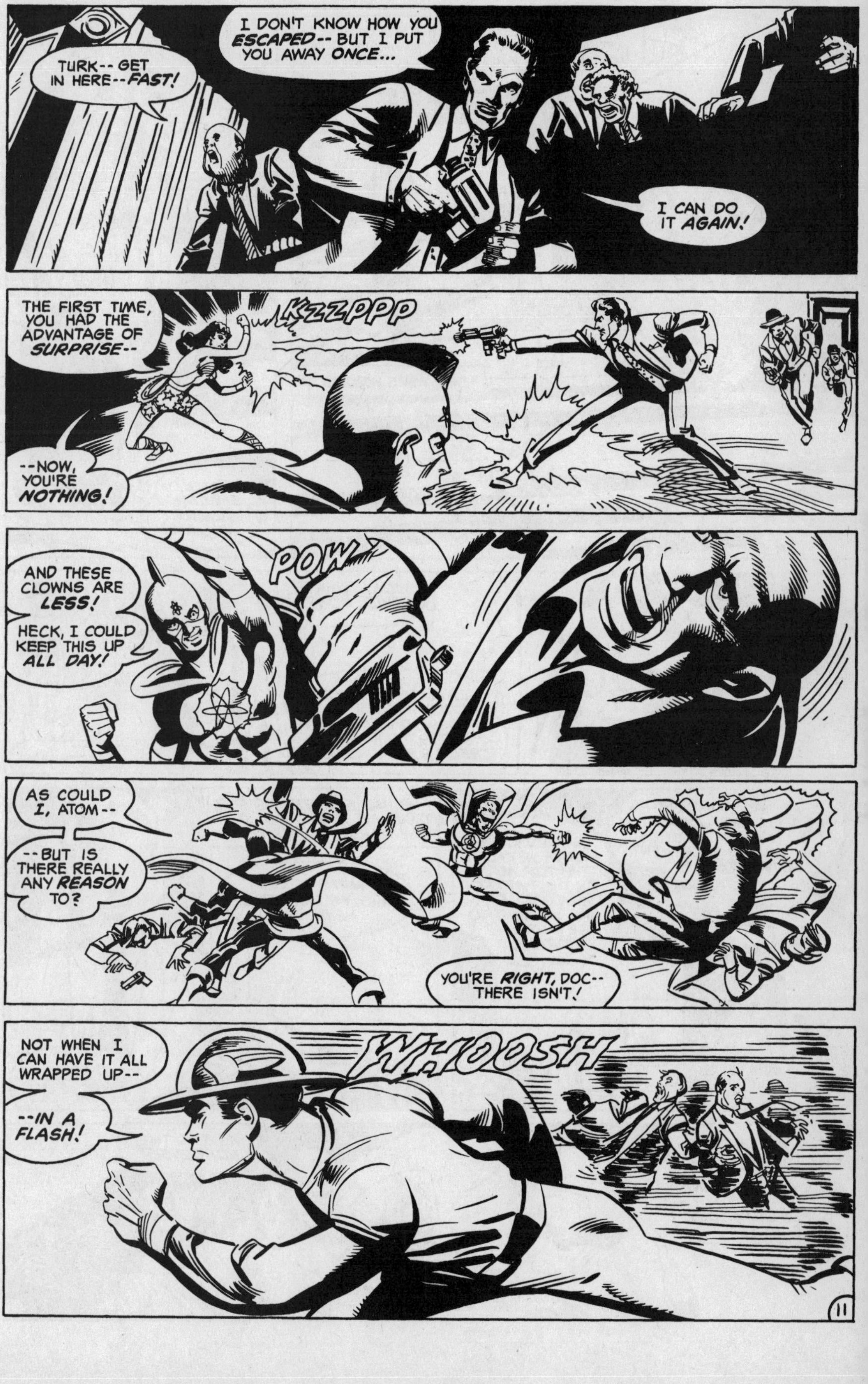
TURK-- GET IN HERE--FAST!
I DON'T KNOW HOW YOU ESCAPED-- BUT I PUT YOU AWAY ONCE...
I CAN DO IT AGAIN!
THE FIRST TIME, YOU HAD THE ADVANTAGE OF SURPRISE--
KZZPPP
--NOW, YOU'RE NOTHING!
POW
AND THESE CLOWNS ARE LESS!
HECK, I COULD KEEP THIS UP ALL DAY!
AS COULD I, ATOM--
--BUT IS THERE REALLY ANY REASON TO?
YOU'RE RIGHT, DOC-- THERE ISN'T!
NOT WHEN I CAN HAVE IT ALL WRAPPED UP--
--IN A FLASH!
WHOOSH
11

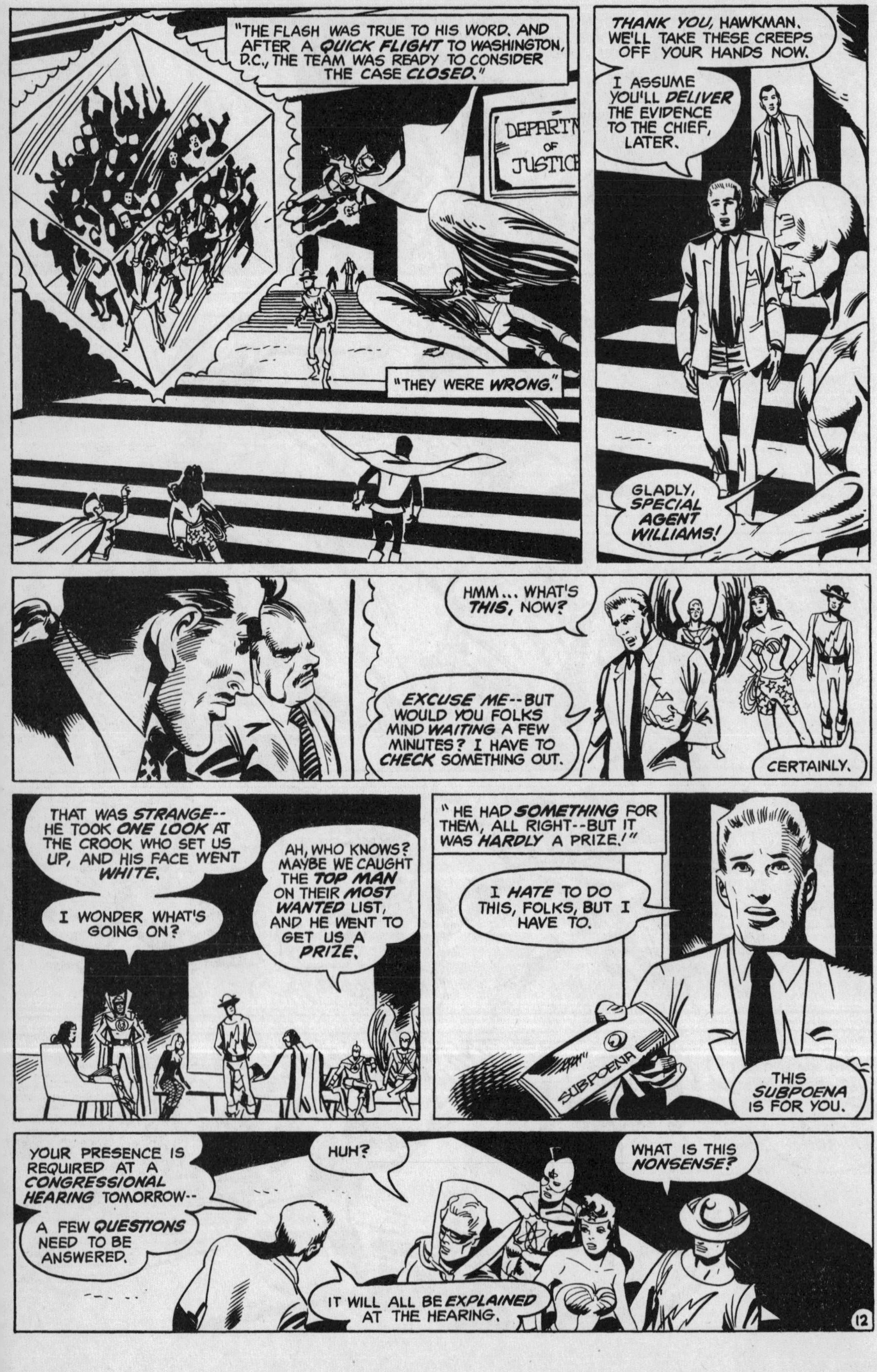
"THE FLASH WAS TRUE TO HIS WORD. AND AFTER A QUICK FLIGHT TO WASHINGTON, D.C., THE TEAM WAS READY TO CONSIDER THE CASE CLOSED."
DEPARTM OF JUSTICE
"THEY WERE WRONG."
THANK YOU, HAWKMAN. WE'LL TAKE THESE CREEPS OFF YOUR HANDS NOW.
I ASSUME YOU'LL DELIVER THE EVIDENCE TO THE CHIEF, LATER.
GLADLY, SPECIAL AGENT WILLIAMS!
HMM... WHAT'S THIS, NOW?
EXCUSE ME--BUT WOULD YOU FOLKS MIND WAITING A FEW MINUTES? I HAVE TO CHECK SOMETHING OUT.
CERTAINLY.
THAT WAS STRANGE-- HE TOOK ONE LOOK AT THE CROOK WHO SET US UP, AND HIS FACE WENT WHITE.
I WONDER WHAT'S GOING ON?
AH, WHO KNOWS? MAYBE WE CAUGHT THE TOP MAN ON THEIR MOST WANTED LIST, AND HE WENT TO GET US A PRIZE.
"HE HAD SOMETHING FOR THEM, ALL RIGHT--BUT IT WAS HARDLY A PRIZE!"
I HATE TO DO THIS, FOLKS, BUT I HAVE TO.
SUBPOENA
THIS SUBPOENA IS FOR YOU.
YOUR PRESENCE IS REQUIRED AT A CONGRESSIONAL HEARING TOMORROW--
A FEW QUESTIONS NEED TO BE ANSWERED.
HUH?
WHAT IS THIS NONSENSE?
IT WILL ALL BE EXPLAINED AT THE HEARING.
12

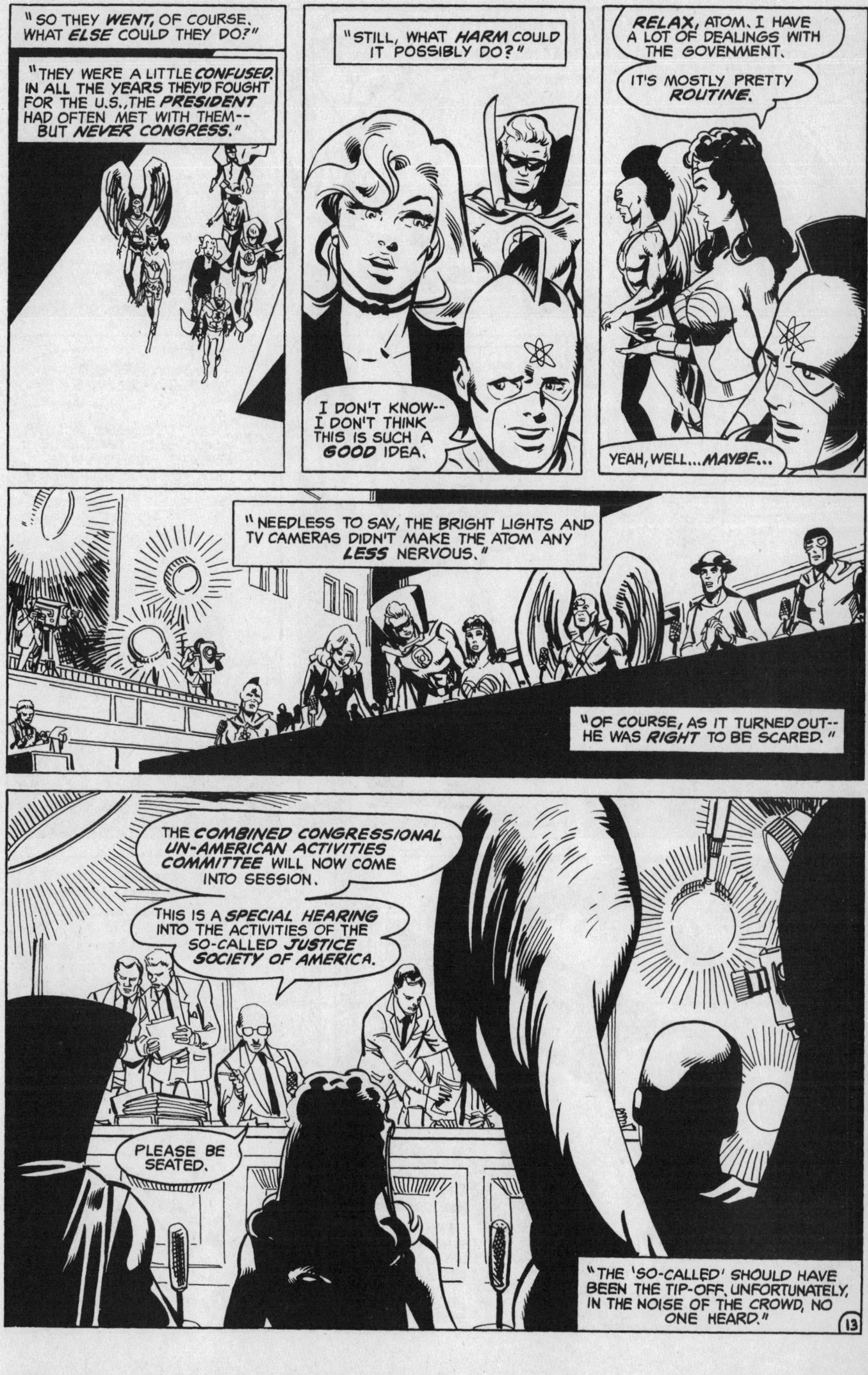
"SO THEY WENT, OF COURSE. WHAT ELSE COULD THEY DO?"
"THEY WERE A LITTLE CONFUSED. IN ALL THE YEARS THEY'D FOUGHT FOR THE U.S., THE PRESIDENT HAD OFTEN MET WITH THEM-- BUT NEVER CONGRESS."
"STILL, WHAT HARM COULD IT POSSIBLY DO?"
I DON'T KNOW-- I DON'T THINK THIS IS SUCH A GOOD IDEA.
RELAX, ATOM. I HAVE A LOT OF DEALINGS WITH THE GOVENMENT.
IT'S MOSTLY PRETTY ROUTINE.
YEAH, WELL...MAYBE...
"NEEDLESS TO SAY, THE BRIGHT LIGHTS AND TV CAMERAS DIDN'T MAKE THE ATOM ANY LESS NERVOUS."
"OF COURSE, AS IT TURNED OUT-- HE WAS RIGHT TO BE SCARED."
THE COMBINED CONGRESSIONAL UN-AMERICAN ACTIVITIES COMMITTEE WILL NOW COME INTO SESSION.
THIS IS A SPECIAL HEARING INTO THE ACTIVITIES OF THE SO-CALLED JUSTICE SOCIETY OF AMERICA.
PLEASE BE SEATED.
"THE 'SO-CALLED' SHOULD HAVE BEEN THE TIP-OFF. UNFORTUNATELY, IN THE NOISE OF THE CROWD, NO ONE HEARD."
13

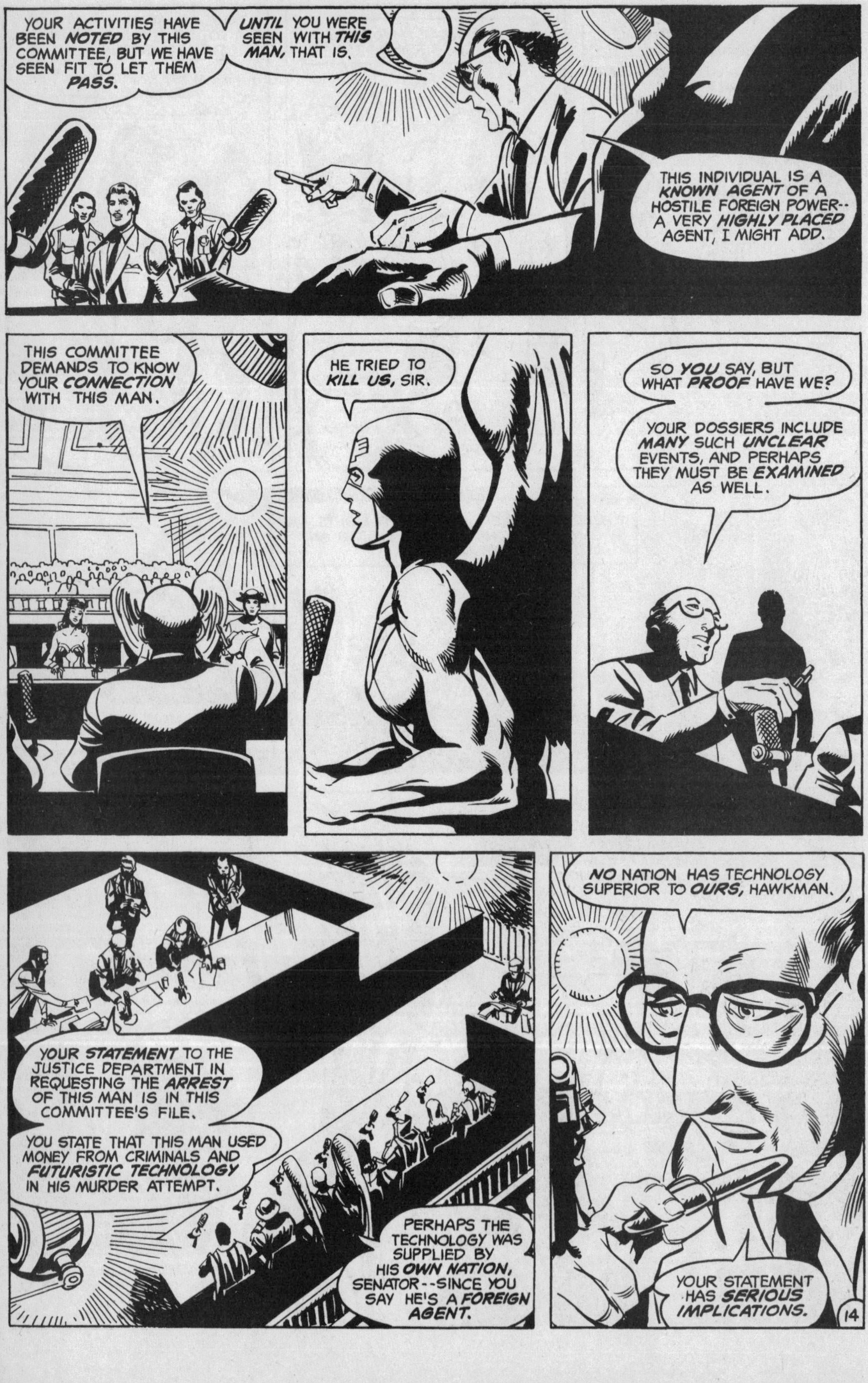
YOUR ACTIVITIES HAVE BEEN NOTED BY THIS COMMITTEE, BUT WE HAVE SEEN FIT TO LET THEM PASS.
UNTIL YOU WERE SEEN WITH THIS MAN, THAT IS.
THIS INDIVIDUAL IS A KNOWN AGENT OF A HOSTILE FOREIGN POWER-- A VERY HIGHLY PLACED AGENT, I MIGHT ADD.
THIS COMMITTEE DEMANDS TO KNOW YOUR CONNECTION WITH THIS MAN.
HE TRIED TO KILL US, SIR.
SO YOU SAY, BUT WHAT PROOF HAVE WE?
YOUR DOSSIERS INCLUDE MANY SUCH UNCLEAR EVENTS, AND PERHAPS THEY MUST BE EXAMINED AS WELL.
YOUR STATEMENT TO THE JUSTICE DEPARTMENT IN REQUESTING THE ARREST OF THIS MAN IS IN THIS COMMITTEE'S FILE.
YOU STATE THAT THIS MAN USED MONEY FROM CRIMINALS AND FUTURISTIC TECHNOLOGY IN HIS MURDER ATTEMPT.
PERHAPS THE TECHNOLOGY WAS SUPPLIED BY HIS OWN NATION, SENATOR--SINCE YOU SAY HE'S A FOREIGN AGENT.
NO NATION HAS TECHNOLOGY SUPERIOR TO OURS, HAWKMAN.
YOUR STATEMENT HAS SERIOUS IMPLICATIONS.
14

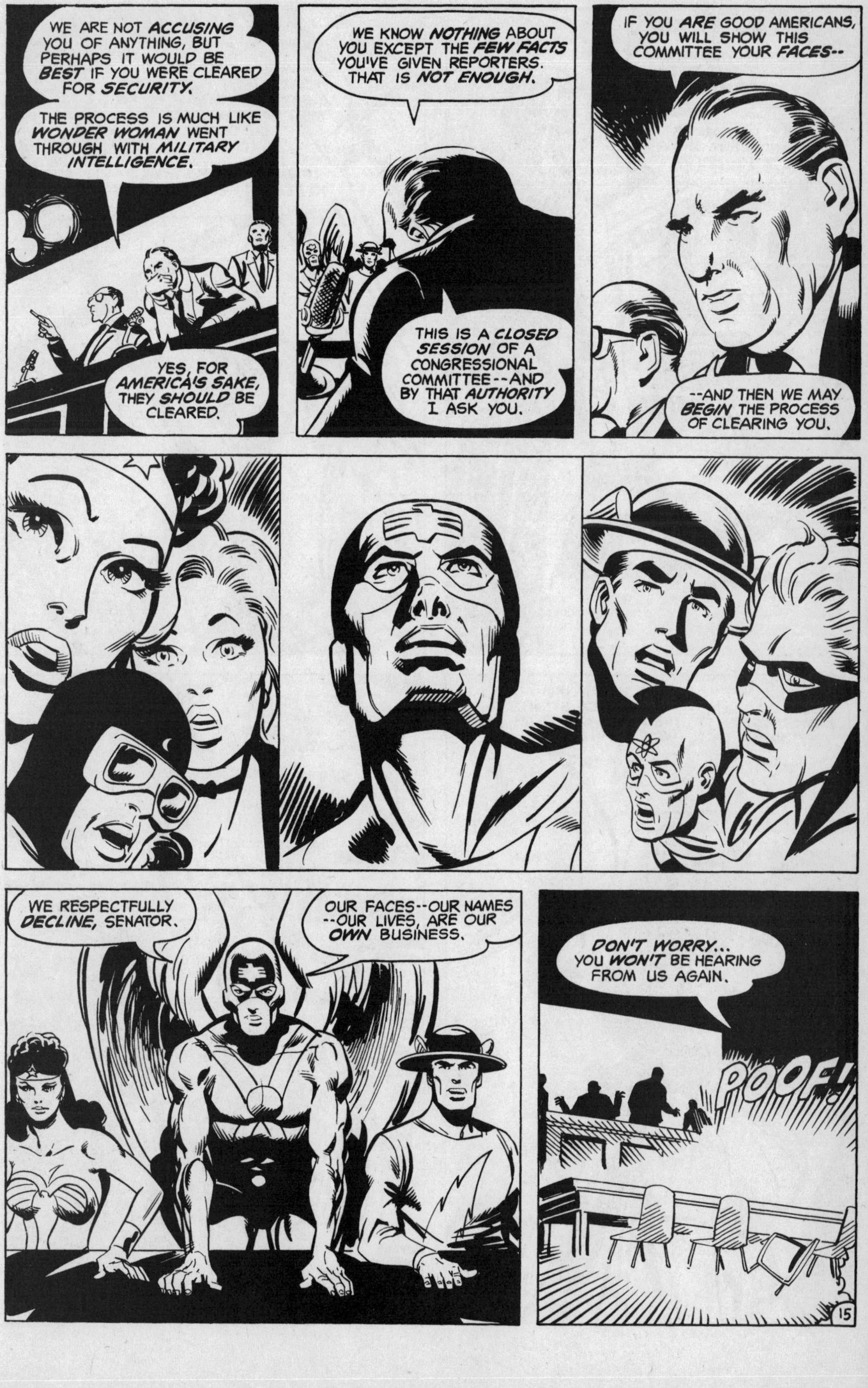
WE ARE NOT ACCUSING YOU OF ANYTHING, BUT PERHAPS IT WOULD BE BEST IF YOU WERE CLEARED FOR SECURITY.
THE PROCESS IS MUCH LIKE WONDER WOMAN WENT THROUGH WITH MILITARY INTELLIGENCE.
YES, FOR AMERICA'S SAKE, THEY SHOULD BE CLEARED.
WE KNOW NOTHING ABOUT YOU EXCEPT THE FEW FACTS YOU'VE GIVEN REPORTERS. THAT IS NOT ENOUGH.
THIS IS A CLOSED SESSION OF A CONGRESSIONAL COMMITTEE--AND BY THAT AUTHORITY I ASK YOU.
IF YOU ARE GOOD AMERICANS, YOU WILL SHOW THIS COMMITTEE YOUR FACES--
--AND THEN WE MAY BEGIN THE PROCESS OF CLEARING YOU.
WE RESPECTFULLY DECLINE, SENATOR.
OUR FACES--OUR NAMES --OUR LIVES, ARE OUR OWN BUSINESS.
DON'T WORRY... YOU WON'T BE HEARING FROM US AGAIN.
POOF!
15

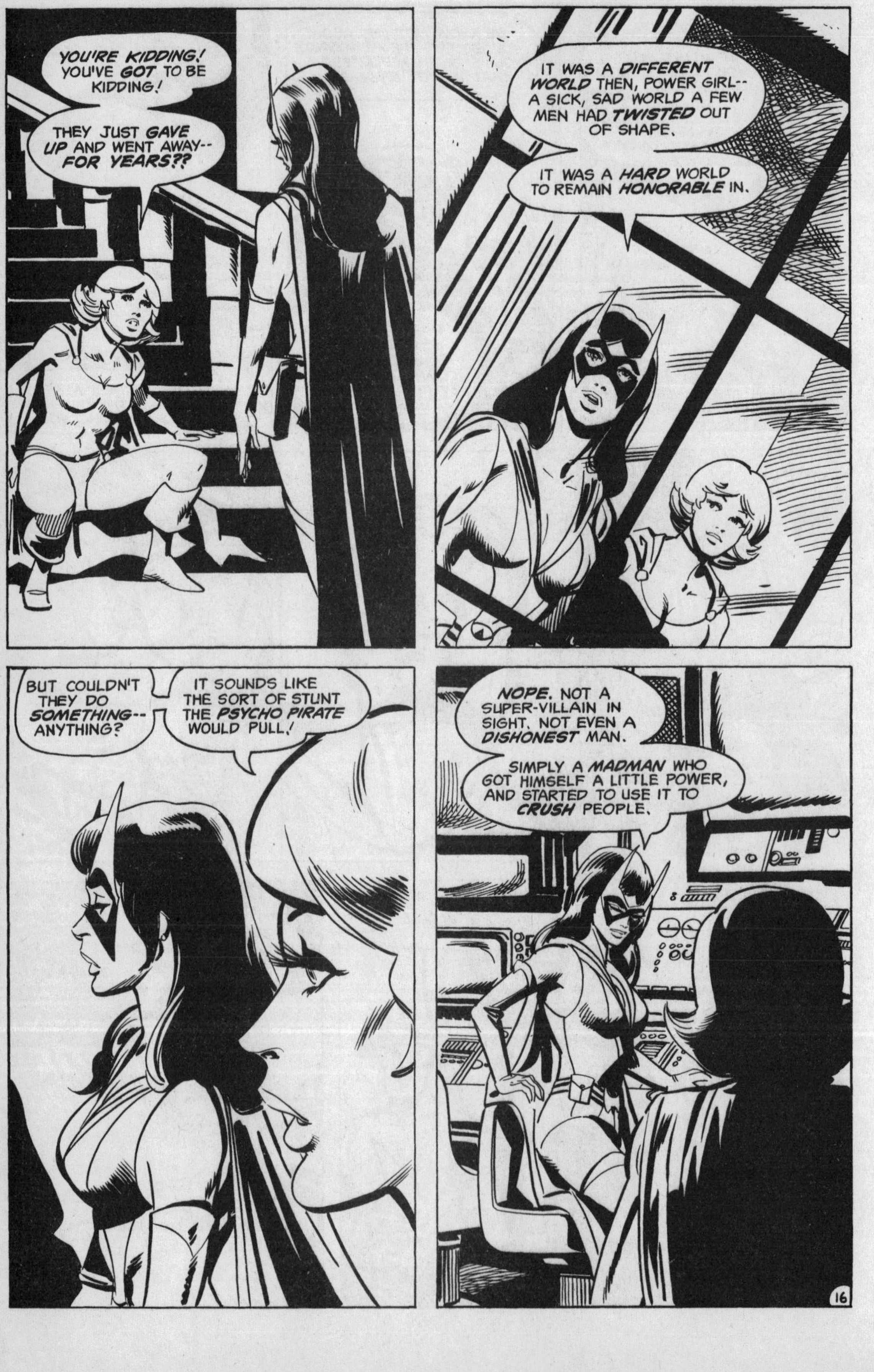
YOU'RE KIDDING! YOU'VE GOT TO BE KIDDING!
THEY JUST GAVE UP AND WENT AWAY-- FOR YEARS??
IT WAS A DIFFERENT WORLD THEN, POWER GIRL-- A SICK, SAD WORLD A FEW MEN HAD TWISTED OUT OF SHAPE.
IT WAS A HARD WORLD TO REMAIN HONORABLE IN.
BUT COULDN'T THEY DO SOMETHING-- ANYTHING?
IT SOUNDS LIKE THE SORT OF STUNT THE PSYCHO PIRATE WOULD PULL!
NOPE. NOT A SUPER-VILLAIN IN SIGHT. NOT EVEN A DISHONEST MAN.
SIMPLY A MADMAN WHO GOT HIMSELF A LITTLE POWER, AND STARTED TO USE IT TO CRUSH PEOPLE.
16

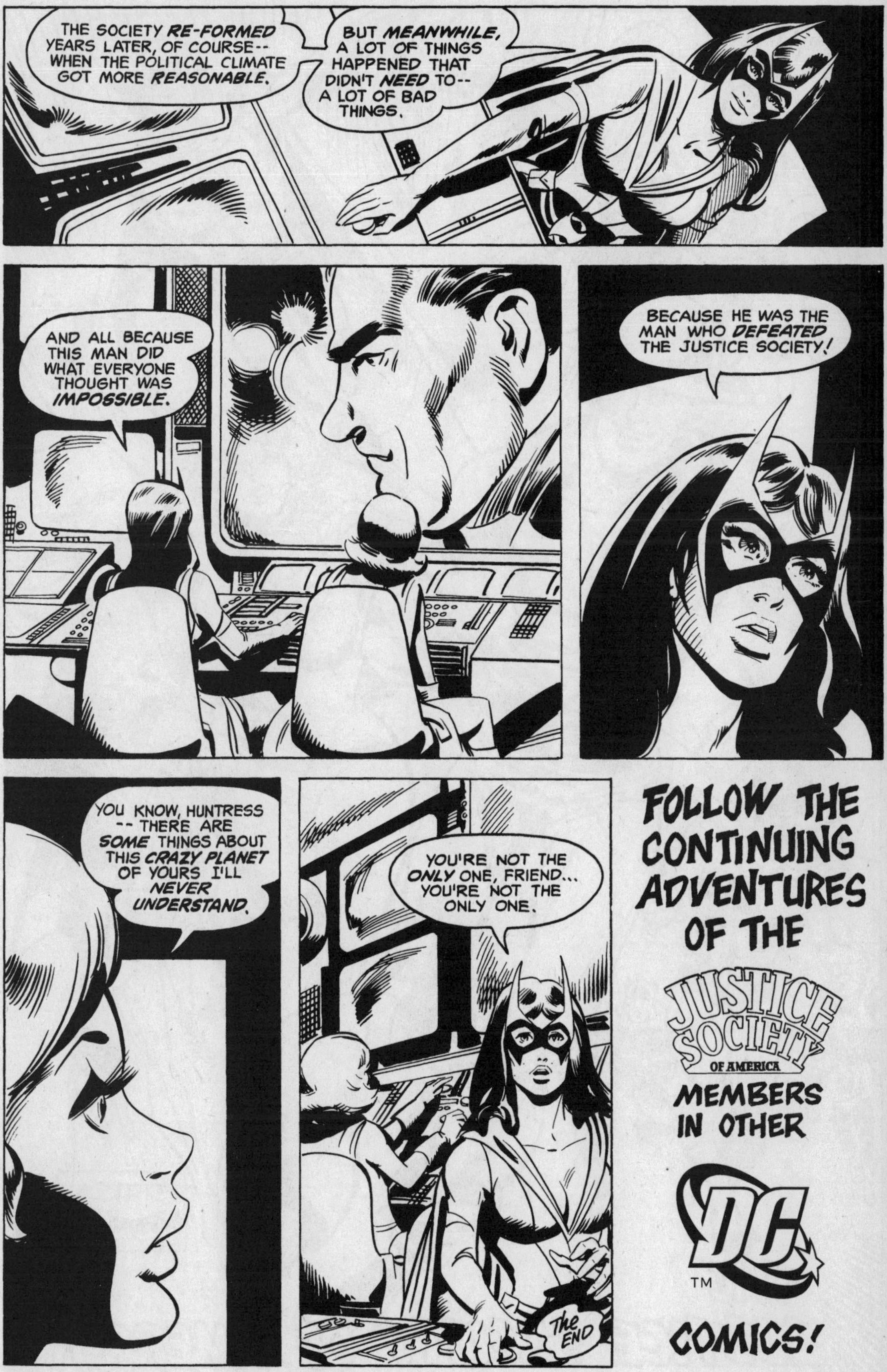
THE SOCIETY RE-FORMED YEARS LATER, OF COURSE-- WHEN THE POLITICAL CLIMATE GOT MORE REASONABLE.
BUT MEANWHILE, A LOT OF THINGS HAPPENED THAT DIDN'T NEED TO-- A LOT OF BAD THINGS.
AND ALL BECAUSE THIS MAN DID WHAT EVERYONE THOUGHT WAS IMPOSSIBLE.
BECAUSE HE WAS THE MAN WHO DEFEATED THE JUSTICE SOCIETY!
YOU KNOW, HUNTRESS -- THERE ARE SOME THINGS ABOUT THIS CRAZY PLANET OF YOURS I'LL NEVER UNDERSTAND.
YOU'RE NOT THE ONLY ONE, FRIEND... YOU'RE NOT THE ONLY ONE.
The END
FOLLOW THE CONTINUING ADVENTURES OF THE
JUSTICE SOCIETY OF AMERICA
MEMBERS IN OTHER
DC TM
COMICS!

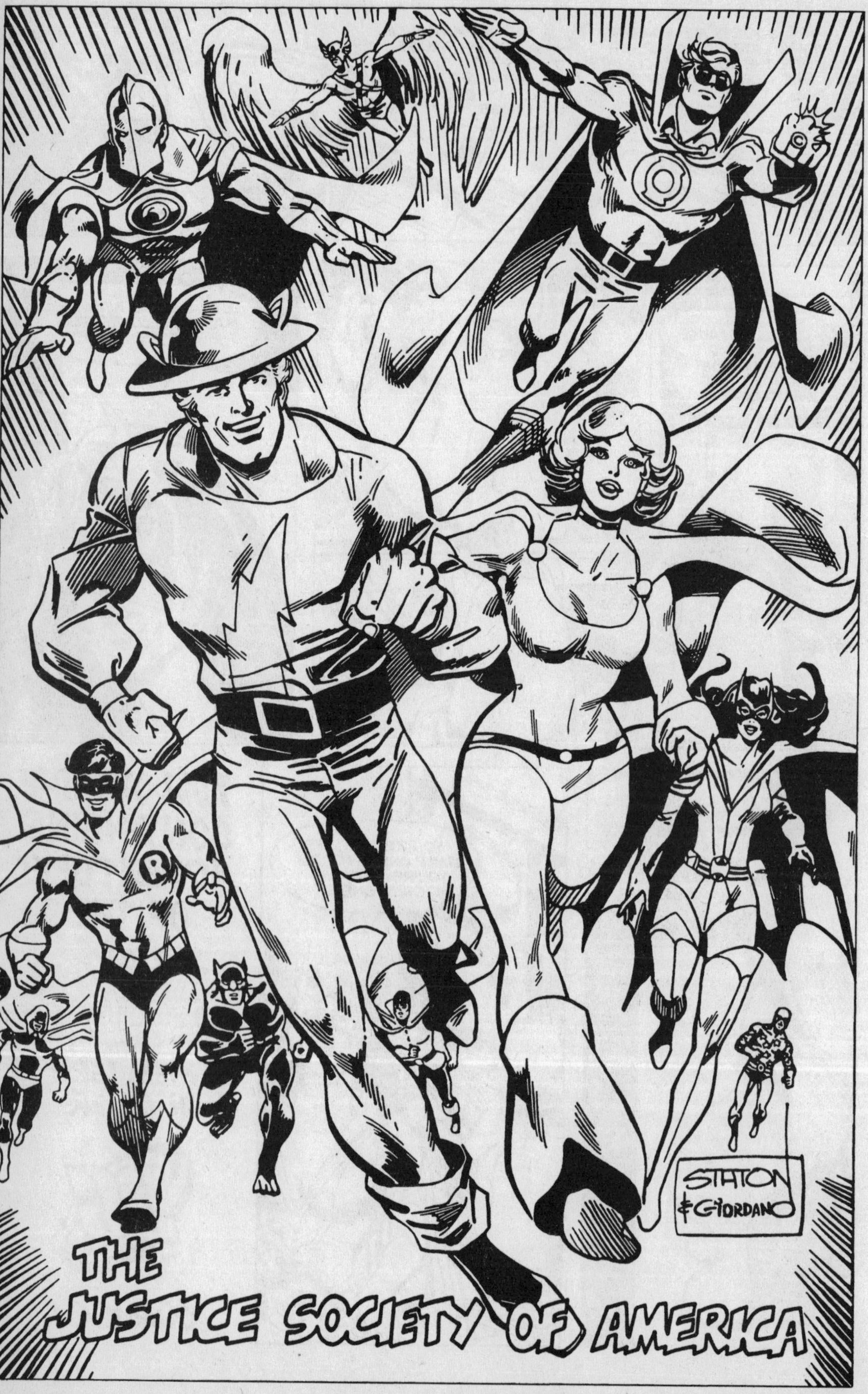
STATON & GIORDANO
THE
JUSTICE SOCIETY OF AMERICA

SHOWCASE
PRESENTS

LOOK FOR THESE OTHER TITLES FEATURING CLASSIC TALES OF THE MAN OF STEEL!

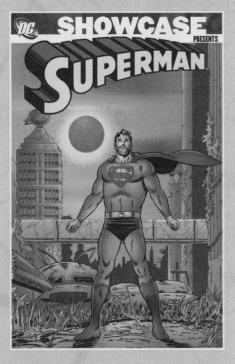

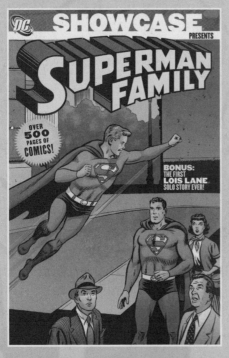

SEARCH THE GRAPHIC NOVELS SECTION OF **DCCOMICS.COM**
FOR INFORMATION ON EVERY VOLUME IN THE **SHOWCASE** SERIES!

SHOWCASE

PRESENTS

LOOK FOR THESE OTHER TITLES FEATURING CLASSIC TALES OF THE MEMBERS OF THE JUSTICE LEAGUE OF AMERICA!

SEARCH THE GRAPHIC NOVELS SECTION OF **DCCOMICS.COM** FOR INFORMATION ON EVERY VOLUME IN THE SHOWCASE SERIES!